THE
WRITER'S
HANDBOOK
2007

Barry Turner has worked on both sides of publishing, as an editor and marketing director and as an author. He started his career as a journalist with *The Observer* before moving on to television and radio. He has written over twenty books including *A Place in the Country*, which inspired a television series, and a best-selling biography of the actor Richard Burton.

His recent work includes *Suez 1956: The Forgotten War, Countdown to Victory*, a book about the last months of World War II, a radio play, travel articles, serialising books for *The Times*, editing the magazine *Country* and writing a one-man show based on the life of the legendary theatre critic James Agate. Barry has been editor of *The Writer's Handbook* for twenty years and editor of *The Statesman's Yearbook* for nine.

THE
WRITER'S
HANDBOOK
2007

EDITOR
BARRY TURNER

MACMILLAN

First published 2006 by Macmillan
an imprint of Pan Macmillan Ltd
Pan Macmillan, 20 New Wharf Road,
London N1 9RR
Basingstoke and Oxford
Associated companies throughout the world
www.panmacmillan.com

ISBN-13: 978-1-4050-4937-5
ISBN-10: 1-4050-4937-5

9 8 7 6 5 4 3 2 1

The listings information contained in this Handbook is available on disk as mailing labels.
For further information, please email writersmailing@macmillan.co.uk

Inclusion in *The Writer's Handbook* is entirely at the editor's discretion. Macmillan Publishers
Ltd makes no recommendation whatsoever by the inclusion or omission of any agency,
publisher or organisation.
    While every effort has been made to ensure all of the information contained in this
publication is correct and accurate, the publisher cannot accept any responsibility for any
omission or errors that may occur or for any consequences arising therefrom.

A CIP catalogue record for this book is available from
the British Library

Credits
Editor *Barry Turner*
Assistant Editor *Jill Fenner*
Editorial Assistants *Kenneth Hadley, Kyra Williams*
Poetry Editor *Peter Finch*
Contributors *David Hooper*
          Ann Lingard
          Brian MacArthur
          Simon Tait
Tax and Finance Adviser *Ian Spring*

Typeset by Heronwood Press, Medstead, Hants
Printed and bound in Great Britain by Mackays of Chatham plc, Kent

Contents

What's Next? Who Knows?

Barry Turner looks to the future of books

It was the best of times, it was the worst of times. Dickens' verdict on the French Revolution carries over neatly to the current state of the writing trade. The communications revolution of which we are part is every bit as radical and far reaching as the first leap into modern democracy. The guillotine may be missing but, commercially, there is plenty of bloodletting with more to come. And nowhere is the upheaval more severe than in book publishing.

The great destroyer of convention or, to put it another way, the great energiser of new thinking is, of course, the Internet with its capacity for taking anything the creative mind can throw at it. Publishers have been slow to adapt. After the early shock of discovering that the future was on-screen, there was consolation to be found in the disappointing response to those writers who were among the first to open websites. Browsers who clicked on to an author, even one with an established name, were disinclined to stay tuned long enough to absorb the contents of a full-length volume. And they were certainly not prepared to pay for the privilege. It seemed that while the desk or laptop screen could hold its fascination for rapidly changing images, the rolling on of words, words, words numbed the senses. A printed book did not have the same effect. Therefore, the book was king.

The conclusion was premature. Lately, the realisation has dawned that while the book does have great virtues as a convenience item, it is only a matter of time before the backroom geeks come up with a cheap handy-sized electronic reader which is like a book in every respect except for the business of page turning.

The prototype is already with us. The Sony Reader, set to be launched in the US this year, can store a hundred books on a £30 memory chip. Random House and HarperCollins are among the publishers who have signed up to put lead titles online. It will take a few more years to attract a mass readership but when there is an e-reader that can accommodate a thousand books or a hundred thousand, even the most ardent of traditional bibliophiles will begin to doubt the virtues of hard print.

The first impact is likely to be on the reproduction of the classics and other works that are out of copyright. Google has already launched an ambitious scheme to put the whole canon online. It should be a relatively simple matter to download these books from a computer on to an e-reader. Meanwhile, the Google service will have its strongest appeal for students and for those in pursuit of a particular reference. Thinking ahead, publishers would be wise to discount continuing profits from their far back lists. Few people will be ready to pay for a Dickens novel or a Shakespeare play in hard print when such can be provided by Google – and for free.

The impact will soon spread – is already spreading – to academic, reference and school material. Popular fiction and non-fiction are bound to follow, though here Google will have a fight on its hands. A first bid to add extracts from copyright publications to its portfolio has met with the predictable squeal of protest from publishers and writers. But however that particular issue is resolved, it has removed any remaining vestiges of complacency in publishing that nothing can touch the printed book.

Writers are taking longer to catch up with reality. It is one of the great ironies that while literary types are supposed to be the wellspring of radical ideas and new ways of looking at life, when it comes to distributing their own product they are positively Neanderthal. Think only of the opposition of writers' organisations to changes in the pattern of library provision to take in services other than books, or the outcry that followed the ending of price fixing, otherwise known as the net book agreement, which for years inhibited initiatives to sell books more competitively. Now we have the siren voices raised against any proposal to vary the standard formula for linking royalties on a book to a recommended retail price.

One might think that bookshop promotions, such as three for the price of two, have put paid to inflexible percentage deals but what is left of the old system will go when Internet publishing catches on. The IT revolution demands changes all along the production line. We may not like it but that's the way it is.

The comfort for writers is in knowing that whatever changes shock the system, the demands on them to deliver the goods will remain as keen as ever. Moreover, the printed book does have a future. As it has been so often pointed out, the cinema did not destroy the theatre and, later, movies overcame the competition from television. Survival was conditional. The medium under threat had to adapt to prosper. So it will be with books.

Some of the trends can be spotted by a tour of any high-street bookshop. The days when one title was presented much like another are long gone. Tantalising counter displays and special offers backed by advertising inevitably focus on prospective bestsellers, books with mass appeal (cookery, gardening, pets) or those by authors well known for past literary triumphs or other achievements which bestow instant recognition.

But the customer engaging razzmatazz accounts for no more than fifty to a hundred titles at any one time. In a decent-sized shop – and there are more of these today than there were, say, twenty years ago – thousands of other books are sectioned off into niche markets from crime fiction and children's stories to self-improvement and military history. But this does not mean that any book that makes it into print will automatically be given shelf space.

With printing and other features of production reduced to a simple and, for minimum standards, a cheap process, titles are appearing at an ever accelerating rate. The total last year was 161,000, up by about two-thirds over fifteen years. Many of these are so esoteric as to fail any assessment, however modest, of general demand. It is not just the mass of academic tomes that bypasses public display on the way to specialist libraries, there are also those truckloads of vanity or near vanity publications (*Memoirs of a Quantity Surveyor*) that have limited appeal, to put it mildly.

Local and regional books (*Timber Framed Buildings in Watford* – I am not making this up) may get one or two bookshop appearances but are unlikely to travel. Further on in this edition of *Writer's Handbook*, Peter Finch reveals that the poetry output now adds up to 30,000 volumes a year. You won't find many of those in Waterstone's and for the very good reason that the profit motive does not allow for charitable sentiments.

Booksellers and publishers should be given credit for having a fair idea of customer demand. It is up to the writer to study the market. The authors who complain most are in two categories: those who cannot bring themselves to believe that what sold ten years ago does not necessarily sell now and those who slavishly follow a current fashion only to find that by the time they get in on the act, the market has moved on.

The secret is to find an original idea which fits into one of the identifiable market sectors. As a formula for literary success this may be irritatingly vague but no one ever said it was easy and if it was, the market would be swamped and we would be back at square one trying to find an identifiable voice that somehow could be heard above all others.

But for what they are worth, here are two pointers to consider. While travel guides may lose out to the Net, books for travellers, fiction and non-fiction, have a big future. Airport and rail-station bookstores are among the most profitable of trade outlets. It is easy to see why. There is nothing quite like being encased in a metal tube for a few hours to encourage the reading habit. Study the sorts of books travellers like to buy. You could spot a gap in the market.

Think in terms of a book as a gift. Up to 50 per cent of hardbacks are bought to give to someone else. If this sounds unlikely just contrast bookshop activity in the month up to Christmas with the feeling of space during the rest of the year. Books linked to anniversaries or matched to birthdays are likely to do well. Having suggested earlier that poetry is a non-starter in the sales league, I can make amends by revealing that two collections of poems, spin-offs from A.A. Milne, called *Now We Are Sixty* and *Now We Are Sixty and a Bit* by Christopher Matthew, have shifted over 500,000 copies. For those of a certain age, they are the perfect bedside companion.

Whatever niche you choose to occupy, there can be no guarantee that success will last. Never forget the IT revolution. The cultural flow is faster now than at any time in history. The e-reader, when it does get a commercial grip, may change not only the way we think about books but also our expectations of what we get from them. A new generation of readers will set up their own demands which may, or more likely, may not be satisfied by established writers. The call will be heard throughout the land: it is all so desperately unfair. Perhaps, but the fact remains that those of us who aim to make a living from words must adapt to the market or find another occupation.

UK Publishers

AA Publishing

The Automobile Association, Fanum House, Basingstoke RG21 4EA
☎01256 491524 Fax 01256 491974
✉ AAPublish@TheAA.com
www.theAA.com

Managing Director *Simon Davies*
Acting Manager, Publishing *David Watchus*

Publishes maps, atlases and guidebooks, motoring, travel and leisure; also children's books. About 100 titles a year.

Abacus

See **Little, Brown Book Group UK**

ABC–Clio

PO Box 1437, Oxford OX4 9AZ
☎01865 481403 Fax 01865 481482
✉ salesuk@abc-clio.com
www.abc-clio.com

Formerly Clio Press Ltd. Publishes academic and general reference works, social sciences and humanities. Markets, outside North America, the Web and reference books of the American parent company.
    ROYALTIES twice-yearly.

Absolute Press

Scarborough House, 29 James Street West, Bath BA1 2BT
☎01225 316013 Fax 01225 445836
✉ info@absolutepress.co.uk
www.absolutepress.co.uk

Managing Director *Jon Croft*

Founded 1979. Publishes food and wine-related subjects. About 15 titles a year. No unsolicited mss. Synopses and ideas for books welcome.
    ROYALTIES twice-yearly.

Abson Books London

5 Sidney Square, London E1 2EY
☎020 7790 4737 Fax 020 7790 7346
✉ absonbooks@aol.com
www.absonbooks.co.uk

Publisher *M.J. Ellison*
Manager *Sharon Wright*

Founded 1971 in Bristol. Publishes language and dialect glossaries and curiosities. No unso-licited mss; synopses and ideas for books welcome.
    ROYALTIES twice-yearly.

Academic Press

See **Elsevier Ltd**

Acair Ltd

Unit 7, 7 James Street, Stornoway, Isle of Lewis HS1 2QN
☎01851 703020 Fax 01851 703294
✉ info@acairbooks.com
www.acairbooks.com

Specialising in matters pertaining to the Gaidhealtachd, Acair publishes books in Gaelic and English on Scottish history, culture and the Gaelic language. 75% of their children's books are targeted at primary school usage and are published exclusively in Gaelic.
    ROYALTIES twice-yearly.

Acumen Publishing Limited

15A Lewins Yard, East Street, Chesham HP5 1HQ
☎01494 794398 Fax 01494 784850
✉ steven.gerrard@acumenpublishing.co.uk
www.acumenpublishing.co.uk

Managing Director *Steven Gerrard*

Founded in 1998 as an independent publisher for the higher education market. Publishes academic books on philosophy, classics and history of ideas. 15 titles in 2005 No unsolicited mss. Synopses and ideas for books welcome; send written proposal as per Acumen guidelines.
    ROYALTIES annually.

Addison Wesley

See **Pearson Education**

Adlard Coles Nautical

See **A.&C. Black Publishers Ltd**

African Books Collective

Unit 13, Kings Meadow, Ferry Hinksey Road, Oxford OX2 0DP
☎01865 726686 Fax 01865 793298
✉ abc@africanbookscollective.com
www.africanbookscollective.com

Founded 1990. Collectively owned by its 17 founder publishers. Exclusive distribution in North America, UK, Europe and Commonwealth countries outside Africa for 109 African participating publishers. Concentration is on scholarly/academic, literature and children's books. Mainly concerned with the promotion and dissemination of African-published material outside Africa. Supplies African-published books to African libraries and organisations, and publishes resource books on the African publishing industry. TITLES *The African Writers' Handbook*; *African Publishers Networking Directory*; *The Electronic African Bookworm: A Web Navigator*; *Courage and Consequence: Women Publishing in Africa*.

Age Concern Books

1268 London Road, London SW16 4ER
☎020 8765 7200 Fax 020 8765 7211
✉ books@ace.org.uk
www.ageconcern.org.uk/bookshop
Approx. Annual Turnover £400,000+

Publishing arm of Age Concern England. Publishes related non-fiction only. No fiction. About 18 titles a year. Synopses and ideas welcome.

Airlife Publishing

See **The Crowood Press Ltd**

Akros Publications

33 Lady Nairn Avenue, Kirkcaldy KY1 2AW
☎01592 651522
Publisher *Duncan Glen*

Founded 1965. Publishes poetry collections, pamphlets and anthologies; literary essays and studies; local histories. Also *Z2O* poetry magazine. No fiction. About 10 titles a year. No unsolicited mss.
ROYALTIES twice-yearly.

Ian Allan Publishing Ltd

Riverdene Business Park, Molesey Road, Hersham KT12 4RG
☎01932 266600 Fax 01932 266601
✉ info@ianallanpublishing.co.uk
www.ianallanpublishing.com
Chairman *David Allan*
Managing Director *Tristan Hilderley*

Specialist transport publisher – atlases, maps, railway, aviation, road transport, military, maritime, reference. Manages distribution and sales for third party publishers. IMPRINTS **Midland**

Publishing (see entry); **Classic Publications**; **OPC** Railway titles; **Lewis Masonic**. About 120 titles a year. Send sample chapter and synopsis with s.a.e

J.A. Allen & Co.

An imprint of Robert Hale Ltd, Clerkenwell House, 45–47 Clerkenwell Green, London EC1R 0HT
☎020 7251 2661 Fax 020 7490 4958
✉ allen@halebooks.com
Commissioning Editor *Cassandra Campbell*
Approx. Annual Turnover £1 million

Founded 1926 as part of J.A. Allen & Co. (The Horseman's Bookshop) Ltd. Bought by **Robert Hale Ltd** in 1999. Publishes equine and equestrian non-fiction. About 20 titles a year. Mostly commissioned but willing to consider unsolicited mss of technical/instructional material related to all aspects of horses and horsemanship.
ROYALTIES twice-yearly.

Allen Lane

See **Penguin Group (UK)**

Allison & Busby

13 Charlotte Mews, London W1T 4EJ
☎020 7580 1080 Fax 020 7580 1180
✉ susie@allisonandbusby.com
www.allisonandbusby.com
Publishing Director *Susie Dunlop*
Approx. Annual Turnover £1 million

Founded 1967. Publishes literary fiction, fiction, crime fiction, true crime, pop culture, biography and writers' guides. TITLES *Little Children* Tom Perrotta; *Best British Mysteries* ed. Maxim Jacubowski; *The Ultimate Book of British Comics* Graham Kibble-White; *Guns & Gangs* Graeme McLagan. About 90 titles a year. No unsolicited mss.

Authors' Rating 'A testament to the ability of smaller publishers to survive in the retail jungle' (*Publishing News*), A&B is putting its effort into promoting lead titles with crime at the top of the list.

Alma Books Ltd

London House, 243–253 Lower Mortlake Road, Richmond TW9 2LL
☎020 8948 9550 Fax 020 8948 5599
✉ info@almabooks.com
www.almabooks.com
Chairman *Elisabetta Minervini*
Managing Director *Alessandro Gallenzi*

Approx. Annual Turnover £350,000

Established in 2005 by founders of **Hesperus Press**. Publishes general fiction, biography, history. 20 titles in 2005. No unsolicited material. Approach through agents only.
ROYALTIES annually.

Authors' Rating Alma is Spanish for 'soul', an apt name say the company founders for a publisher that 'regards a book as an aesthetic artefact rather than a mass produced commodity'.

Alpha Press
See **Sussex Academic Press**

Alphabet & Image Ltd
77 High Street, Totnes TQ9 5PB
☎01803 866946/868861
✉ miranda@alphabetandimage.com
www.alphabetandimage.com

Publisher/Managing Director *Miranda Spicer*

Founded 1989. Publishes horticulture, beekeeping, architecture, ceramics and crafts. IMPRINTS include **Marston House**. Unsolicited mss accepted with s.a.e.
ROYALTIES twice-yearly, or flat fee.

Alton Douglas Books
See **Brewin Books Ltd**

Amber Lane Press Ltd
Cheorl House, Church Street, Charlbury OX7 3PR
☎01608 810024   Fax 01608 810024
✉ info@amberlanepress.co.uk
www.amberlanepress.co.uk

Chairman *Brian Clark*
Managing Director/Editorial Head *Judith Scott*

Founded 1979 to publish modern play texts. Publishes plays and books on the theatre. TITLES *Whose Life is it Anyway?* Brian Clark; *The Dresser* Ronald Harwood; *Once a Catholic* Mary O'Malley (play texts); *Strindberg and Love* Eivor Martinus. About 4 titles a year. 'Expressly *not* interested in poetry.' No unsolicited mss.
ROYALTIES twice-yearly.

Amsco
See **Omnibus Press**

Andersen Press Ltd
20 Vauxhall Bridge Road, London SW1V 2SA
☎020 7840 8703/8700   Fax 020 7233 6263
✉ andersenpress@randomhouse.co.uk

www.andersenpress.co.uk

Managing Director/Publisher *Klaus Flugge*
Editorial Director *Rona Selby*
Editor, Fiction *Elizabeth Maude*

Founded 1976 by Klaus Flugge and named after Hans Christian Andersen. Publishes children's high-quality picture books and fiction sold in association with Random House Children's Books. Seventy per cent of the books are sold as co-productions abroad. TITLES *Elmer* David McKee; *I Want My Potty* Tony Ross; *little.com* Ralph Steadman; *Cat in the Manger* Michael Foreman; *Preston Pig Books* Colin McNaughton; *Junk* Melvin Burgess; *You* Sandra Glover; *I Love You, Blue Kangaroo* Emma Chichester Clark. Unsolicited mss welcome for picture books; synopsis in the first instance for books for young readers up to age 12. No poetry or short stories.
ROYALTIES twice-yearly.

Authors' Rating The secret of Andersen's success is publishing children's books that are loved by adults. That and a wicked sense of fun that has been known to upset the education establishment – and hooray for that.

Chris Andrews Publications
15 Curtis Yard, North Hinksey Lane, Oxford OX2 0LX
☎01865 723404   Fax 01865 725294
✉ chris.andrews1@btclick.com
www.cap-ox.co.uk

Partner *Chris Andrews*

Founded 1982. Publishes coffee-table, scenic travel guides. Also calendars, diaries, cards and posters. TITLES *Romance of Oxford*; *Romance of the Cotswolds*; *Romance of the Thames & Chilterns*. Also owns the **Oxford Picture Library** (see entry under *Picture Libraries*). Unsolicited synopses and ideas for travel/guide books in the areas listed above will be considered; phone in the first instance.

Andromeda Children's Books
See **Pinwheel Limited**

The Angels' Share
See **Neil Wilson Publishing Ltd**

Anness Publishing Ltd
Hermes House, 88–89 Blackfriars Road, London SE1 8HA
☎020 7401 2077   Fax 020 7633 9499
✉ info@anness.com

www.aquamarinebooks.com
www.lorenzbooks.com
www.southwaterbooks.com
Chairman/Managing Director *Paul Anness*
Publisher/Partner *Joanna Lorenz*
Approx. Annual Turnover £15.7 million
Founded 1989. Publishes highly illustrated co-edition titles: general non-fiction – cookery, crafts, interior design, gardening, photography, decorating, lifestyle, health, refererence, military, transport and children's. IMPRINTS **Lorenz Books**; **Aquamarine**; **Hermes House**; **Southwater**. About 200 titles a year.

Anova Books
151 Freston Road, London W10 6TH
☎020 7314 1400
✉ firstinitialsurname@anovabooks.com
www.anovabooks.com
CEO *Robin Wood*
Publishing Director *Polly Powell*
Approx. Annual Turnover £33.9 million

Anova Books, formerly Chrysalis Books Group, specialises in illustrated non-fiction, publishing under the IMPRINTS **B.T. Batsford**; **Brassey's**; **Collins & Brown**; **Conway Maritime Press**; **National Trust Books**; **Paper Tiger**; **Pavilion**; **Putnam Aeronautical Books**; **Robson Books**; **Salamander**.
IMPRINTS **B.T. Batsford** Associate Publisher *Tina Persaud* Founded in 1843 as a bookseller, and began publishing in 1874. A world leader in books on chess, arts and craft. Publishes non-fiction, architecture, heritage, bridge and chess, film and entertainment, fashion, crafts and hobbies. About 100 titles a year. ROYALTIES twice in the first year, annually thereafter.
Brassey's Associate Publisher *John Lee* Publishes military history and technology. ROYALTIES annually.
Collins & Brown Associate Publisher *Katie Cowan* Publishes a range of lifestyle categories especially in the areas of practical art, photography and needlecrafts.
Conway Maritime Press Associate Publisher *John Lee* Publishes naval history, maritime culture and ship modelling. ROYALTIES annually.
National Trust Books Associate Publisher *Tina Persaud* Imprint of Anova Books since 2005. Publishes heritage, gardening, architecture, gift and cookery-based titles. Unsolicited mss not welcome.
Paper Tiger Associate Publisher *Katie Cowan* (Part of Collins & Brown) Publishes science fiction and fantasy art.

Pavilion Associate Publisher *Kate Oldfield* Publishes illustrated books in biography, cookery, gardening, humour, art, interiors, music, sport and travel. Ideas and synopses for non-fiction titles considered. ROYALTIES twice-yearly.
Putnam Aeronautical Books Associate Publisher *John Lee* Publishes classic aeronautical histories, technical and reference.
Robson Books Associate Publisher *Jeremy Robson* Founded 1973. Publishes general non-fiction including biography, cookery, gardening, sport and travel. About 60 titles a year. Unsolicited synopses and ideas for books welcome (s.a.e. essential for reply). ROYALTIES twice-yearly.
Salamander Publisher *Polly Powell* Founded 1973. Publishes colour illustrated books on collecting, cookery, interiors, gardening, music, crafts, military, aviation, sport and transport. Also a wide range of books on American interest subjects. No unsolicited mss but synopses and ideas for the above subjects welcome. ROYALTIES Outright fee paid instead of royalties.
DIVISION **Anova Children's Books** IMPRINTS **Pavilion Children's Books**; **David Bennett Books**; **Belitha Press**; **Big Fish**; **Zigzag**. No unsolicited mss.

Authors' Rating Growth by acquisition has brought problems of over production and over manning. The publishing list is to be cut from 250 to 150 titles over two years. The cutback has been hastened by a management buyout which should help the company re-establish a firm base.

Anthem Press
See **Wimbledon Publishing Company**

Antique Collectors' Club
Sandy Lane, Old Martlesham, Woodbridge IP12 4SD
☎01394 389950 Fax 01394 389999
✉ sales@antique-acc.com
www.antiquecollectorsclub.com
Managing Director *Diana Steel*
Sales Director *Mark Eastment*

Founded 1966. Publishes specialist books on antiques and collecting, the decorative arts, architecture and gardening. The price guide series was introduced in 1968 with the first edition of *The Price Guide to Antique Furniture*. Subject areas include furniture, silver and gold, metalwork, jewellery, glass, textiles, art reference, ceramics, horology. TITLES *Biba. The Biba Experience* Alwyn Turner; *Understanding Jewellery* David Bennett and Daniela Mascetti; *Margaret*

Mee's Amazon. Diaries of an Artist Explorer; British Antique Furniture John Andrews. Also publishes subscription-only magazine, *Antique Collecting*, published 10 times a year. Unsolicited synopses and ideas for books welcome; no mss.

ROYALTIES twice-yearly as a rule, but can vary.

Anvil Press Poetry Ltd

Neptune House, 70 Royal Hill, London SE10 8RF
☎020 8469 3033   Fax 020 8469 3363
✉ anvil@anvilpresspoetry.com
www.anvilpresspoetry.com

Managing Director *Peter Jay*

Founded 1968. England's oldest independent publishing house dedicated to poetry. Publishes new poets and translated classics. Contemporary list includes Ros Barber, Martina Evans, Michael Hamburger, Dennis O'Driscoll, A.B. Jackson, Stanley Moss and Greta Stoddart. The backlist includes translations of Apollinaire, Baudelaire, Celan, Dante, Hikmet, Neuda, Tagore and Verlaine. Preliminary enquiry required for translations. Unsolicited book-length collections of poems are welcome from writers whose work has appeared in poetry magazines or literary journals. Please enclose adequate return postage.

Authors' Rating With a little help from the Arts Council, Anvil has become one of the foremost publishers of living poets.

Apollos
See **Inter-Varsity Press**

Apple
See **Quarto Publishing** under *UK Packagers*

Appletree Press Ltd

The Old Potato Station, 14 Howard Street South, Belfast BT7 1AP
☎028 9024 3074   Fax 028 9024 6756
✉ reception@appletree.ie
www.appletree.ie

Managing Director *John Murphy*

Founded 1974. Publishes cookery and other small-format gift books, plus general non-fiction of Irish and Scottish interest. TITLES *Little Cookbook* series (about 40 titles); *Ireland: The Complete Guide*. No unsolicited mss; send initial letter or synopsis.

ROYALTIES twice-yearly in the first year, annually thereafter.

Aquamarine
See **Anness Publishing Ltd**

Arc Publications

Nanholme Mill, Shaw Wood Road, Todmorden OL14 6DA
☎01706 812338   Fax 01706 818948
✉ arc.publications@btconnect.com
www.arcpublications.co.uk

Editorial Director *Tony Ward*
Associate Editors *John Kinsella* (international), *Jo Shapcott* (UK), *Jean Boase-Beier* (translations), *Angela Jarman* (music)

Founded in 1969 to specialise in the publication of contemporary poetry from new and established writers both in the UK and abroad. AUTHORS John Kinsella, Anthony Lawrence and Katherine Gallagher (Australia), Juris Kronbergs (Latvia), Larissa Miller (Russia), Tony Curtis (Ireland), Mutsuo Takahashi (Japan), Remco Campert (Netherlands), David Baker and Terry Hummer (USA), Patrick Lane (Canada), Tomas Salamun (Slovenia), Joanna Boulter, Lorna Thorpe and Tariq Latif (UK). IMPRINT **Arc Music** specialises in profiles of contemporary composers (particularly where none have existed hitherto) and symposia which take a 'new approach' to well-visited territory. Commissioned work only. About 25 titles a year. Unable to accept unsolicited material for the foreseeable future. 'However, if authors feel impelled to submit material they should ensure that it is fully compatible with the current list, include a history of published works and enclose an s.a.e. if they wish mss to be returned.' Electronic submissions are not accepted.

ROYALTIES as per contracts.

Arcadia Books

15–16 Nassau Street, London W1W 7AB
☎020 7436 9898   Fax 020 7436 9898
✉ info@arcadiabooks.co.uk
www.arcadiabooks.co.uk

Managing Director *Gary Pulsifer*
Publishing Director *Daniela de Groote*
Commissioning Editor (BlackAmber) *Rosemarie Hudson*

Independent publishing house now celebrating its tenth anniversary. IMPRINTS **Arcadia**; **BlackAmber; Bliss; EuroCrime**. TITLES Mass-market edition of Corinne Hofmann's four-million-copy bestseller *The White Masai* plus her latest, *Reunion in Barsaloi*, as well as the 500th Lisbon Massacre Anniversary edition of Richard Zimler's *The Last Kabbalist of Lisbon*. 'We specialise

in quality translated fiction from around the world.'
Does not welcome unsolicited material.
ROYALTIES twice-yearly.

Authors' Rating A quality publisher that has great success with translated fiction.

Architectural Press
See **Elsevier Ltd**

Ardis
See **Gerald Duckworth & Co. Ltd**

Argentum
See **Aurum Press Ltd**

Aris & Phillips
See **Oxbow Books**

The Armchair Traveller
See **Haus Publishing**

Arnefold Publishing
PO Box 22, Maidstone ME14 1AH
☎01622 759591 Fax 01622 209193
Chairman/Managing Director *I.G. Mann*

Publishes original non-fiction and selected fiction, and non-fiction reprints. No new fiction. IMPRINTS **Arnefold**; **George Mann Books**; **Recollections**. 'Will consider non-fiction titles (which authors find hard to place) on a joint venture/shared profit basis if they are worthy of publication or can be made so. Unsolicited material not accompanied by return postage will neither be read nor returned.'
ROYALTIES annually.

Arris Publishing Ltd
12 Main Street, Adlestrop, Moreton in Marsh GL56 0YN
☎01608 658758 Fax 01608 659328
✉ gcs@arrisbooks.com
www.arrisbooks.com
Joint Managing Directors *Geoffrey Smith, Michel Moushabeck*

Founded in 2001. Publishes politics, history, biography, travel, art and culture. IMPRINTS **Arris Books** *Geoffrey Smith* TITLES *9/11: The New Pearl Harbour*; *Hitler's British Slaves*; **Chastleton Travel** *Victoria Huxley* TITLES *Palestine: An Illustrated Guide*; *A Traveller's History of Cyprus*. 25 titles in 2005. No unsolicited mss; synopses and ideas for books welcome. Send introductory letter, synopsis and specimen

chapter by post; no e-mail submissions or CDs.
No poetry or fiction.
ROYALTIES annually.

Arrow
See **The Random House Group Ltd**

Artech House
46 Gillingham Street, London SW1V 1AH
☎020 7596 8750 Fax 020 7630 0166
✉ truonamaa@artechhouse.co.uk
www.artech-uk@artechhouse.com
Managing Director (USA) *William M. Bazzy*
Commissioning Editor *Tiina Ruonamaa*

Founded 1969. European office of Artech House Inc., Boston. Publishes books for practising professionals in biomedical engineering, bioinformatics, MEMS, nanotechnology, microwaves, radar, antennas and propagation, electro-magnetic analysis, wireless communications, telecommunications, space applications, remote sensing, solid state technology and devices, technology management. 60–70 titles a year. Unsolicited mss and synopses in the specialised areas listed are considered.
ROYALTIES twice-yearly

Ashgate Publishing Ltd
Gower House, Croft Road, Aldershot GU11 3HR
☎01252 331551 Fax 01252 344405 (Ashgate and Gower)/020 7837 6322 (Lund Humphries)
✉ info@ashgatepublishing.com
www.ashgate.com
www.gowerpub.com
www.lundhumphries.com
Chairman *Nigel Farrow*

Founded 1967. Publishes business and professional titles under the Gower imprint, humanities, social sciences, law and legal studies under the Ashgate imprint and art and art history under the Lund Humphries imprint. Acquired Lund Humphries, publisher of art books and exhibition catalogues in 1999. DIVISIONS **Ashgate** *Rachel Lynch* Social sciences; *John Smedley* History/Variorum collected studies; *Heidi May* Music; *Erika Gaffney* Literary studies; *Tom Gray* History; *Sarah Lloyd* Theology and religious studies; *Paul Coulam* Philosophy; *John Hindley* Aviation studies. **Gower** *Jo Burges, Jonathan Norman* Business, management and training; *John Irwin* Law and legal studies. **Lund Humphries** *Lucy Myers*. Access the websites for information on submission of material.

Ashgrove Publishing
27 John Street, London WC1N 2BX
☎020 7831 5013   Fax 020 7831 5011
✉ gmo73@dial.pipex.com
www.ashgrovepublishing.com

Chairman/Managing Director *Brad Thompson*

Acquired by Hollydata Publishers in 1999, Ashgrove has been publishing for over 20 years. Publishes mind, body, spirit, health, cookery, sports. 3 titles in 2005. No unsolicited mss; approach with letter and outline in the first instance.

Royalties twice-yearly.

Ashmolean Museum Publications
Ashmolean Museum, Beaumont Street, Oxford OX1 2PH
☎01865 278010   Fax 01865 278106
✉ publications@ashmus.ox.ac.uk
www.ashmol.ox.ac.uk

Contact *Declan McCarthy*

The Ashmolean Museum, which is wholly owned by Oxford University, was founded in 1683. The first publication appeared in 1890 but publishing did not really start in earnest until the 1960s. Publishes European and Oriental fine and applied arts, European archaeology and ancient history, Egyptology and numismatics, for both adult and children's markets. No fiction, American/African art, ethnography or post-medieval history. Most publications are based on and illustrated from the Museum's collections. About 8 titles a year. No unsolicited mss.

Royalties annually.

Atlantic Books
26–27 Boswell Street, London WC1N 3JZ
☎020 7269 1610   Fax 020 7430 0916
✉ enquiries@groveatlantic.co.uk
www.groveatlantic.co.uk

Chairman *Morgan Entrekin*
Managing Director/Publisher *Toby Mundy*

Founded 2000. A subsidiary of **Grove/Atlantic Inc.** (see entry under *US Publishers*), New York. Publishes literary fiction, history, current affairs, autobiography, biography, memoir, politics and reference books. IMPRINT **Guardian/Observer Books** Editorial Head *Louisa Joyner* TITLES *Guardian Media Directory; Guardian University Guide* (both annual). 70 titles a year No unsolicited material

Royalties twice-yearly

Authors' Rating The offshoot of US Grove/Atlantic has a reputation for punching above its weight. Clever marketing has a lot to do with it but it is marketing based on an instinct for what sells - still not the most common attribute in trade publishing.

Atlantic Europe Publishing Co. Ltd
Greys Court Farm, Greys Court, Nr Henley on Thames RG9 4PG
☎01491 628188   Fax 01491 628189
✉ writers@atlanticeurope.com
www.AtlanticEurope.com
www.curriculumVisions.com

Director *Dr B.J. Knapp*

Publishes full-colour, highly illustrated children's non-fiction in hardback for international co-editions and text books. Not interested in any other material. Main focus is on National Curriculum titles, especially in the fields of mathematics, science, technology, social history and geography. About 50 titles a year. Unsolicited synopses and ideas for non-fiction curriculum-based books welcome by e-mail only – does not accept material sent by post.

Fees paid.

Atom
See **Little, Brown Book Group UK**

Aurora Metro
2 Oriel Court, The Green, Twickenham TW2 5AG
☎020 8898 4488   Fax 020 8898 0735
✉ info@aurorametro.com
www.aurorametro.com

Managing Director *Cheryl Robson*

Founded in 1989 by writers with the aim of publishing new writing by women. Now publishes writing by both new and established authors as well as international work in translation – fiction, children's, drama, biography, cookery, non-fiction. 7 titles in 2005. No unsolicited mss; send synopses and ideas by e-mail.

Royalties annually.

Aurum Press Ltd
25 Bedford Avenue, London WC1B 3AT
☎020 7637 3225   Fax 020 7580 2469
✉ editorial@aurumpress.co.uk
www.aurumpress.co.uk
www.jacquismallpub.com

Managing Director *Bill McCreadie*
Editorial Director *Graham Coster*
Approx. Annual Turnover £4 million
Founded 1976. Acquired by the Quarto Group

in August 2004. High-quality, illustrated/non-illustrated adult non-fiction in the areas of biography, sport, current affairs, military history, travel, music and film. IMPRINTS **Argentum** Practical photography books; **Jacqui Small** High-quality lifestyle books. About 70 titles a year.
ROYALTIES twice-yearly.

Authors' Rating With an ever strengthening list, Aurum has thrived on the ambitions of parent company Quarto to expand from packaging into trade publishing.

Austin & Macauley Publishers
25 Canada Square, Canary Wharf, London E14 5LB
☎020 7038 8212 Fax 020 7038 8312
✉ editors@austinmacauley.com
www.austinmacauley.com

General Manager *Alan Forster*
Managing Editor *Annette Longman*

Founded 2005. Publishes fiction and non-fiction, autobiography, biography, memoirs, post-1945 fiction, true life experiences. Expanding educational list, IT, business studies, mathematics, English, world religions, sociology, mythology, politics, human interest, war, crime, horror thrillers, current affairs, romance, women's issues, humour, music, sport, cinema and TV. Unsolicited synopsis and ideas considered. Postal submissions must include return postage. No short stories or poetry.
ROYALTIES annually.

Authentic Media
9 Holdom Avenue, Bletchley, Milton Keynes MK1 1QR
☎01908 364200 Fax 01908 277169
www.authenticmedia.co.uk

Publishing Director *Mark Finnie*
Approx. Annual Turnover £2 million

A division of STL Ltd. IMPRINTS **Paternoster Press** Founded 1935. Editorial Coordinator *Charlotte Hubback* Publishes academic, religion and learned/church/life-related books and journals. TITLES *Relational Leadership*; *After Christendom*. **Authentic Lifestyle**. Editorial Coordinator *Charlotte Hubback* Publishes Christian books on evangelism, discipleship and mission for Evangelical Alliance, Keswick Ministries, Icthus, Youth Work. Over 50 titles a year. Unsolicited mss, synopses and ideas for books welcome. No poetry.
ROYALTIES twice-yearly.

AuthorHouse UK
500 Avebury Boulevard, Milton Keynes MK9 2BE
☎0800 197 4150 Fax 0800 197 4151
✉ info@authorhouse.co.uk
www.authorhouse.co.uk

President & CEO *Bryan S. Smith*
Vice President *W. Herbert Senft II*

Founded 1997. Publishes fiction, biography and memoirs, current affairs, history, politics, humour, travel, health, spirituality, sports and academic. Provides a comprehensive range of publishing and promotional services including editorial, design, production, distribution and marketing paid for by the author who retains editorial and creative control.

Authors OnLine
19 The Cinques, Gamlingay, Sandy SG19 3NU
☎01767 652005 Fax 01767 652005
✉ theeditor@authorsonline.co.uk
www.authorsonline.co.uk

Submissions: Freephone 0800 107 2423
Managing Director *Richard Ovenden*
Editor *Richard Fitt*
Submissions Editor *Mrs Gaynor Johnson*
Approx. Annual Turnover £250,000

Founded 1998. A service for authors wishing to self-publish. Publishes new and reverted rights work in both electronic format via their website and traditional hard-copy mainly using digital Print On Demand technology All genres welcome. Submit mss by e-mail or post (disk or CD-ROM) to the Submissions Editor.
PAYMENT 60% net paid quarterly.

Autumn Publishing Ltd
Appledram Barns, Birdham Road, Chichester PO20 7EQ
☎01243 531660 Fax 01243 774433
✉ autumn@autumnpublishing.co.uk
www.autumnpublishing.co.uk

Managing Director *Michael Herridge*
Editorial Director *Lyn Coutts*

Founded 1976. Part of the Bonnier Group. Publishes baby and toddler books, children's activity, sticker and early learning books. About 200 titles a year. No responsibility accepted for the return of unsolicited mss.

Award Publications Limited
The Old Riding School, The Welbeck Estate, Worksop S80 3LR
☎01909 478170 Fax 01909 484632

✉ info@awardpublications.co.uk
www.awardpublications.co.uk

Founded 1958. Publishes children's books, both fiction and reference. IMPRINT **Horus Editions**. No unsolicited mss, synopses or ideas.

Azure
See **Society for Promoting Christian Knowledge**

Baillière Tindall
See **Elsevier Ltd**

Duncan Baird Publishers
Castle House, 75–76 Wells Street, London W1T 3QH
☎020 7323 2229 Fax 020 7580 5692
✉ info@dbairdpub.co.uk
Managing Director *Duncan Baird*
Editorial Director *Bob Saxton*
Approx. Annual Turnover £7.5 million

Founded in 1992 to publish and package co-editions overseas and went on to launch its own publishing operation in 1998. Publishes illustrated cultural reference, world religions, health, mind, body and spirit, lifestyle, graphic design. 60 titles in 2006. No unsolicited mss. Synopses and ideas welcome; approach in writing in the first instance with s.a.e. No fiction or UK-only subjects.
ROYALTIES twice-yearly.

Bantam/Bantam Press
See **Transworld Publishers**

Barefoot Books Ltd
124 Walcot Street, Bath BA1 5BG
☎01225 322400 Fax 01225 322499
✉ sales@barefootbooks.co.uk
www.barefootbooks.com
Publisher *Tessa Strickland*

Founded 1993. Publishes high-quality children's picture books, particularly new and traditional stories from a wide range of cultures. No unsolicited mss. See website for submission guidelines.
ROYALTIES twice-yearly.

Authors' Rating Writers of children's books would do well to keep track of Barefoot which, from small beginnings, is building a quality list that must be the envy of bigger publishers.

Barrington Stoke
Sandeman House, Trunk's Close, 55 High Street, Edinburgh EH1 1SR
☎0131 557 2020 Fax 0131 557 6060
✉ info@barringtonstoke.co.uk

www.barringtonstoke.co.uk
Chairman *David Croom*
Managing Director *Sonia Raphael*
Editorial Head *Kate Paice*
Approx. Annual Turnover £600,000

Founded in 1998 to publish books for 'reluctant, disenchanted and under-confident' young readers. Produces a series of audio books and issues teachers' notes to acccompany teenage fiction titles. DIVISIONS **4u2read.OK** for children aged 8–13 with a reading age below 8; **Fiction** for 8–13-year olds TITLES *Living With Vampires; Tod in Biker City*. **Teenage Fiction** TITLES *Runaway Teacher; No Stone Unturned*. Books commissioned via literary agents only. *No* unsolicited material.
ROYALTIES twice-yearly.

B.T. Batsford
See **Anova Books**

BBC Books
Room A3100, BBC Worldwide Ltd, 80 Wood Lane, London W12 0TT
☎020 8433 2000 Fax 020 8749 0538
www.bbcworldwide.com
Director *Stuart Biles*

Publishes TV and radio tie-in titles including books which, though linked with BBC television or radio, may not simply be the 'book of the series'. TITLES *Delia's Vegetarian Collection*; *Rick Stein's Food Heroes*; *A History of Britain* Simon Schama; *Grumpy Old Men The Official Handbook*; *British Isles A Natural History* as well as TV personality autobiographies such as Terry Wogan and David Attenborough. 50 titles a year. Unsolicited mss are not accepted. However, strong ideas well expressed will always be considered, and promising letters stand a chance of further scrutiny.
ROYALTIES twice-yearly.

Authors' Rating With an increasing share of BBC output going to independent companies, the hold over programme spinoffs is getting weaker. BBC Books remains the leader in gardening, food and drink with BBC Audio Books having the lion's share of that business.

BBC Children's Books
See **Penguin Group (UK)**

Beautiful Books Ltd
117 Sugden Road, London SW11 5ED
☎020 7738 2428 Fax 020 7223 4841
✉ office@beautiful-books.co.uk
www.beautiful-books.co.uk

Managing Director *Simon Petherick*
Approx. Annual Turnover £500,000
Founded 2004. Publishes adult and children's fiction and non-fiction. DIVISION **The Young Travellers Club** Title *Bonjour France!* IMPRINT **Bloody Books** Horror fiction. Unsolicited mss, synopses and ideas welcome. Approach by letter in the first instance with outline and synopsis plus biographical information. Include s.a.e.

Belair
See **Folens Limited**

Belitha Press
See **Anova Books**

David Bennett Books
See **Anova Books**

Berg Publishers
1st Floor, Angel Court, 81 St Clements Street, Oxford OX4 1AW
☎01865 245104   Fax 01865 791165
✉ enquiry@bergpublishers.com
www.bergpublishers.com
Managing Director *Kathryn Earle*
Editorial Director *Tristan Palmer*
Publishes scholarly books in the fields of fashion, cultural studies, social sciences, history and humanities. TITLES *Shoes* eds. Giorgio Riello and Peter McNeil; *Fashion* Rolan Barthes; *The Hollywood Interviews* Cahiers du Cinema; *Sobibor: A History of a Nazi Death Camp* Jules Schelvis; *The World of the Anthropologist* Marc Auge. IMPRINT **Oswald Wolff Books**. About 65 titles a year plus six journals, *Fashion Theory, Home Cultures, Textile: The Journal of Cloth and Culture, Cultural Politics, The Senses and Society* and *Material Religion*. No unsolicited mss. Synopses and ideas for books welcome.
ROYALTIES annually.

Berghahn Books
3 Newtec Place, Magdalen Road, Oxford OX4 1RE
☎01865 250011   Fax 01865 250056
✉ publisher@berghahnbooks.com
www.berghahnbooks.com
Chairman/Managing Director *Marion Berghahn*
Approx. Annual Turnover £700,000
Founded 1994. Academic publisher of books and journals. TITLES *Imperial Germany, 1871–1918; Children of Palestine; Critical Interventions*. OVERSEAS ASSOCIATE Berghahn Books Inc., New York. About 90 titles a year. No unsolicited mss; will consider synopses and ideas for books.

Approach by e-mail in the first instance. No fiction or trade books.
ROYALTIES annually.

Berlitz Publishing
58 Borough High Stret, London SE1 1XF
☎020 7403 0284   Fax 020 7403 0290
✉ berlitz@apaguide.co.uk
www.berlitzpublishing.com
Managing Director *Jeremy Westwood*
Founded 1970. Acquired by the Langenscheidt Publishing Group in February 2002. Publishes travel and language-learning products only: visual travel guides, phrasebooks and language courses. SERIES *Pocket Guides; Berlitz Complete Guide to Cruising and Cruise Ships; Phrase Books; Pocket Dictionaries; Business Phrase Books; Self-teach: Rush Hour Commuter Cassettes; Think & Talk; Berlitz Kids*. No unsolicited mss.

BeWrite Books
See entry under *Electronic Publishing and Other Services*

BFI Publishing
British Film Institute, 21 Stephen Street, London W1T 1LN
☎020 7255 1444   Fax 020 7636 2516
www.bfi.org.uk
Approx. Annual Turnover £600,000
Founded 1980. Part of the **British Film Institute**. Publishes academic, schools and general film/television-related books and resources. TITLE *The Cinema Book*, revised edition, eds. Pam Cook and Mieke Bernink. SERIES *Film Classics; BFI Screen Guides; Modern Classics; World Directors*. About 30 titles a year. E-mail submissions preferred.
ROYALTIES annually.

BFP Books
Focus House, 497 Green Lanes, London N13 4BP
☎020 8882 3315   Fax 020 8886 5174
✉ mail@thebfp.com
Chief Executive *John Tracy*
Commissioning Editor *Stewart Gibson*
Founded 1982. The publishing arm of the Bureau of Freelance Photographers. Publishes illustrated books on photography, mainly aspects of freelancing and marketing pictures. No unsolicited mss but ideas welcome.

Big Fish
See **Anova Books**

Clive Bingley Books
See **Facet Publishing**

Birlinn Ltd
West Newington House, 10 Newington
Road, Edinburgh EH9 1QS
☎0131 668 4371 Fax 0131 668 4466
✉ info@birlinn.co.uk
www.birlinn.co.uk
Managing Director *Hugh Andrew*

Founded 1992. Publishes local and military history, adventure, Gaelic, humour, Scottish history, Scottish reference, guidebooks and folklore. IMPRINT **John Donald Publishers** (see entry). Acquired **Polygon** in 2002 (see entry) and Tuckwell Press in 2005. 170 titles in 2005 across all imprints. No unsolicited mss; synopses and ideas welcome.

ROYALTIES paid.

Authors' Rating One of the fastest growing regional publishers.

Bitter Lemon Press
37 Arundel Gardens, London W11 2LW
☎020 7221 2829 Fax 020 7460 2164
✉ lcolchester@bitterlemonpress.com
www.bitterlemonpress.com
Directors *Laurence Colchester, François von Hurter*

Founded 2003. Specialises in thrillers, *romans noir* and other contemporary fiction from abroad. 7 titles in 2005. Will consider thriller mss; no unsolicited synopses or ideas. No non-fiction.

ROYALTIES annually.

Black & White Publishing Ltd
99 Giles Street, Edinburgh EH6 6BZ
☎0131 625 4500 Fax 0131 625 4501
✉ mail@blackandwhitepublishing.com
www.blackandwhitepublishing.com
Director *Campbell Brown*

Founded 1990. Publishes general fiction and non-fiction, including memoirs, sport, cookery, humour and guidebooks. IMPRINTS **Itchy Coo** Scots language resources for use in schools; **Chroma** Literary fiction. Text only submissions via website, or synopsis and sample chapter by post with s.a.e. or return postage.

ROYALTIES twice-yearly.

A.&C. Black Publishers Ltd
Alderman House, 38 Soho Square, London
W1D 3HB
☎020 7758 0200 Fax 020 7758 0222
✉ enquiries@acblack.com
www.acblack.com
Chairman *Nigel Newton*
Managing Director *Jill Coleman*
Deputy Managing Director *Jonathan Glasspool*

Publishes children's and educational books, including music, for 0–15 year-olds, arts, crafts, ceramics, natural history, ornithology, nautical, reference, fitness, sport, theatre and writing books. Acquisitions brought the Herbert Press' art, design and general books, Adlard Coles' and Thomas Reed's sailing lists, plus *Reeds Nautical Almanac*, Christopher Helm, Pica Press and T&AD Poyser's natural history and ornithology lists, children's educational publisher Andrew Brodie and Whitakers Almanack into A.&C. Black's stable. Bought by **Bloomsbury Publishing** in May 2000. Acquired **Methuen**'s drama list in 2006. IMPRINTS **Adlard Coles Nautical**; **Thomas Reed**; **Christopher Helm**; **T&AD Poyser**; **The Herbert Press**; **Andrew Brodie**. TITLES *New Mermaid* drama series; *Who's Who*; *Writers' & Artists' Yearbook*; *Know the Game* sports series; *White Wolves* fiction series.

Initial enquiry appreciated before submission of mss.

ROYALTIES vary according to contract.

Black Ace Books
PO Box 6557, Forfar DD8 2YS
☎01307 465096 Fax 01307 465494
www.blackacebooks.com
Managing Director *Hunter Steele*

Founded 1991. Publishes new fiction, Scottish and general; some non-fiction including biography, history, philosophy and psychology. IMPRINTS **Black Ace Books**; **Black Ace Paperbacks** TITLES *Succeeding at Sex and Scotland, Or the Case of Louis Morel* Hunter Steele; *La Tendresse* Ken Strauss MD; *Count Dracula (The Authorized Version)* Hagen Slawkberg; *Caryddwen's Cauldron* Paul Hilton; *The Sinister Cabaret* John Herdman. No children's, poetry, cookery, DIY, religion. 36 titles in print. 'No submissions at all, please, without first checking our website for details of current requirements and submission guidelines.'

ROYALTIES twice-yearly.

Black Lace
See **Virgin Books Ltd**

Black Spring Press Ltd
Curtain House, 134–146 Curtain Road,
London EC2A 3AR
☎020 7613 3066 Fax 020 7613 0028
✉ general@blackspringpress.co.uk

Directors *Robert Hastings, Alexander Hastings*

Founded 1986. Publishes fiction and non-fiction, literary criticism, biography. TITLES *The Lost Weekend* Charles Jackson; *The Big Brass Ring* Orson Welles; *The Tenant* Roland Topor; *Julian Maclaren-Ross Collected Memoirs.* About 5 titles a year. No unsolicited mss.

ROYALTIES annually.

Black Swan
See **Transworld Publishers**

BlackAmber
See **Arcadia Books**

Blackstaff Press Ltd
4C Heron Wharf, Sydenham Business Park, Belfast BT3 9LE

☎028 9045 5006 Fax 028 9046 6237

✉ info@blackstaffpress.com

www.blackstaffpress.com

Managing Editor *Patsy Horton*

Founded 1971. Publishes mainly, but not exclusively, Irish interest books, fiction, poetry, history, sport, cookery, politics, illustrated editions, natural history and humour. About 20 titles a year. Unsolicited mss considered, but preliminary submission of synopsis plus short sample of writing preferred. Return postage *must* be enclosed.

ROYALTIES twice-yearly.

Authors' Rating Regional and proud of it, this Belfast publisher is noted for bringing on young talent and for 'wonderfully well-presented catalogues and promotional material'.

Blackwell Publishing
9600 Garsington Road, Oxford OX4 2DQ

☎01865 776868 Fax 01865 714591

www.blackwellpublishing.com

Chief Executive *René Olivieri*

President *Robert Campbell*

Chairman *Nigel Blackwell*

Blackwell Publishing was formed by merging Blackwell Science (founded 1939) and Blackwell Publishers (founded 1926). Publishes around 700 new books a year and 800 journals in medicine, veterinary medicine, dentistry, nursing and allied health, science (particularly biology, chemistry and geology), social sciences, business and humanities. Journals are delivered online through Blackwell Synergy. Acquired BMJ Books in 2004.

ROYALTIES annually.

John Blake Publishing Ltd
3 Bramber Court, 2 Bramber Road, London W14 9PB

☎020 7381 0666 Fax 020 7381 6868

✉ words@blake.co.uk

Managing Director *John Blake*

Deputy Managing Director *Rosie Ries*

Founded 1991 and expanding rapidly. Bought the assets of Smith Gryphon Ltd in 1997 and acquired Metro Publishing in 2001. Publishes mass-market non-fiction. No fiction, children's, specialist or non-commercial. About 100 titles a year. No unsolicited mss; synopses and ideas welcome. Please enclose s.a.e.

ROYALTIES twice-yearly.

Authors' Rating One of the few publishers able to crack the market for celebrity memoirs, John Blake brings the tabloid touch to books.

Blandford Press
See **Octopus Publishing Group**

Bliss
See **Arcadia Books**

Bloodaxe Books Ltd
Highgreen, Tarset NE48 1RP

☎01434 240500 Fax 01434 240505

✉ editor@bloodaxebooks.com

www.bloodaxebooks.com

Managing/Editorial Director *Neil Astley*

Publishes poetry, literature and criticism, and related titles by British, Irish, European, Commonwealth and American writers. Ninety-five per cent of the list is poetry. TITLES include six major anthologies, *Staying Alive; real poems for unreal times* and *Being Alive*, both edited by Neil Astley; *The Bloodaxe Book of 20th Century Poetry* ed. Edna Longley; *The New Poetry* eds. Hulse, Kennedy and Morley; *Modern Women Poets* ed. Deryn Rees-Jones; collected editions of Fleur Adcock, David Constantine, Helen Dunmore, Roy Fisher, Brendan Kennelly, J.H. Prynne, Peter Reading, Carol Rumens, Ken Smith, Anne Stevenson and C.K. Williams. About 30–40 titles a year. Unsolicited poetry mss welcome; send a sample of no more than 10 poems with s.a.e., 'but if you don't read contemporary poetry, don't bother'. No e-mail submissions of any kind.

ROYALTIES annually.

Authors' Rating Assisted by regional Arts Council funding, Bloodaxe is one of the liveliest and most innovative of poetry publishers with a list that takes in some of the best of the younger poets.

Bloody Books
See **Beautiful Books Ltd**

Bloomsbury Publishing Plc
36 Soho Square, London W1D 3QY
☎020 7494 2111   Fax 020 7434 0151
www.bloomsburymagazine.com
Chairman/Chief Executive *Nigel Newton*
Publishing Directors *Alexandra Pringle, Liz Calder, Kathy Rooney, Sarah Odedina, Arzu Tahsin, Michael Fishwick*
Approx. Annual Turnover £109 million
Founded in 1986 by Nigel Newton, David Reynolds, Alan Wherry and Liz Calder. Many of its authors have gone on to win prestigious literary prizes, most recently J.K. Rowling's *Harry Potter and the Philosopher's Stone, Harry Potter and the Chamber of Secrets* and *Harry Potter and the Prisoner of Azkaban* won the **Nestlé Smarties Book Prize** in 1997, 1998 and 1999 respectively. Margaret Atwood's *The Blind Assassin* won the **Booker Prize** in 2000.
Started Bloomsbury USA in 1998. Acquired **A.&C. Black Publishers Ltd** in May 2000 (see entry), Peter Collin Publishing Ltd in September 2002, Berlin Verlag in 2003 and Walker Publishing Inc in New York in 2004. Publishes literary fiction and non-fiction, including general reference; also audiobooks. AUTHORS include Margaret Atwood, T.C. Boyle, Sophie Dahl, Jeffrey Eugenides, Neil Gaiman, Daniel Goleman, David Guterson, Sheila Hancock, Ethan Hawke, John Irving, Jay McInerney, Tim Pears, Celia Rees, J.K. Rowling, Ben Schott, Will Self, Donna Tartt, Rupert Thomson, Barbara Trapido, Joanna Trollope, Benjamin Zephaniah. Unsolicited mss and synopses for adult titles only; no poetry.
ROYALTIES twice-yearly.

Authors' Rating Liz Calder has called it 'the greatest phenomenon in publishing history'. She had in mind, of course, the Harry Potter success story which probably accounts for around half of Bloomsbury's turnover. The challenge now for the 20-year-old publisher is to find other mega sellers to keep the company moving onwards and upwards. Handsome advances are being handed out to attract big names and hot topics. All divisions, fiction and non-fiction, are open for talent including a new music, film, TV and sport list.

BMJ Books
See **Blackwell Publishing**

BMM
See **SportsBooks Limited**

Boatswain Press
See **Kenneth Mason Publications Ltd**

Bobcat
See **Omnibus Press**

Bodley Head Children's Books
See **The Random House Group Ltd**

Book Blocks
See **CRW Publishing Ltd**

The Book Guild Ltd
Temple House, 25 High Street, Lewes BN7 2LU
☎01273 472534   Fax 01273 476472
✉ info@bookguild.co.uk
www.bookguild.co.uk
Chairman *George M. Nissen, CBE*
Managing Director *Carol Biss*
Founded 1982. Publishes fiction, human interest, media, children's fiction, academic, natural history, naval and military, biography, art. Expanding mainstream list plus developing the human interest/media genre. DIVISIONS **Current Affairs** TITLE *A Land Fit for Criminals*. **Human Interest** TITLES *Before the Last All Clear, Out of Time*. **Biography** TITLE *Headlong Through Life: The Story of Isadora Duncan*. **Sport** TITLE *Under Auntie's Skirts: The Life and Times of a BBC Sports Producer*. **Fiction** TITLES *The Network; According to Robin*. **Children's** TITLE *Easy Reading Shakespeare: The Bard in Bite-Size Verse*. About 80 titles a year. Unsolicited mss, ideas and synopses welcome.
ROYALTIES twice-yearly.

Authors' Rating Keen to firm up its reputation as a conventional publisher with a strong list of general titles, The Book Guild also offers a shared cost service to authors. A readily accessible and comprehensive code of practice sets out the terms of engagement well before a signature is inscribed on the dotted line.

Book House
See **Salariya Book Company Ltd** under *UK Packagers*

Border Lines Biographies
See **Seren**

Boulevard Books & The Babel Guides
71 Lytton Road, Oxford OX4 3NY
☎01865 712931
✉ ray.keenoy@gmail.com

www.babelguides.com

Managing Director *Ray Keenoy*

Specialises in contemporary world fiction by young writers in English translation. Existing or forthcoming series of fiction from Brazil, Italy, Latin America, Low Countries, Greece, and elsewhere. The Babel Guides series of popular guides to fiction in translation started in 1995. DIVISONS **Latin American** *Ray Keenoy* TITLE *Hotel Atlantico* J.G. Noll. **Italian** *Fiorenza Conte* TITLE *The Toy Catalogue* Sandra Petrignani. **Brazil** *Dr David Treece* TITLE *The Jaguar.* **Babel Guides to Fiction in Translation** Series Editor *Ray Keenoy* TITLES *Babel Guide to Italian Fiction in Translation; Babel Guide to the Fiction of Portugal, Brazil & Africa in Translation; Babel Guide to French Fiction in English Translation; Babel Guide to Jewish Fiction; Babel Guide to Brazilian Fiction.* Suggestions and proposals for translations of contemporary fiction welcome. Also seeking contributors to forthcoming Babel Guides (all literatures).

ROYALTIES annually.

Bound Biographies Limited

Heyford Park House, Heyford Park, Bicester OX25 5HD
☎01869 232911 Fax 01869 232698
✉ office@boundbiographies.com
www.boundbiographies.com

Managing Director *Michael Oke*
Editorial Head *Dr A.J. Gray*
Approx. Annual Turnover £150,000

Founded in 1992 to assist in the writing and production of low numbers of private life stories. Print-on-demand facilities to provide short runs of paper or hardback books to complement the Bound Biographies leather-bound range. Publishes autobiographies predominantly although novels, poetry and special interest books are considered. TITLES *Jungle Juice* E. Goodger; *Doctor at the Cutting Edge* D.H. Wilson.

35 titles in 2005. Unsolicited material welcome; approach by post, telephone or e-mail.

ROYALTIES annually.

Bounty

See **Octopus Publishing Group**

Bowker (UK) Ltd

3rd Floor, Farringdon House, Wood Street, East Grinstead RH19 1UZ
☎01342 310450 Fax 01342 310486
✉ sales@bowker.co.uk
www.bowker.co.uk

Managing Director *Doug McMillan*

Publisher *Michael Cairns*

Part of the Cambridge Information Group (CIG), based in Maryland in the USA. Publishes library reference, bibliography, biography, business and professional directories. TITLES *Books In Print; Ulrich's Periodicals Directory; Children's Books in Print; Ulrich's Serials Analysis System.* Unsolicited material will not be read.

ROYALTIES annually.

Boxtree

See **Macmillan Publishers Ltd**

Marion Boyars Publishers Ltd

24 Lacy Road, London SW15 1NL
☎020 8788 9522 Fax 020 8789 8122
✉ rebecca@marionboyars.com
www.marionboyars.co.uk

Editor *Rebecca Gillieron*
Editor, Non-fiction *Amy Christian*

Founded 1975, formerly Calder and Boyars. Publishes biography and autobiography, fiction, literature and criticism, music, philosophy, psychology, sociology and anthropology, theatre and drama, film and cinema, women's studies. AUTHORS include Georges Bataille, Ingmar Bergman, Heinrich Böll, Hortense Calisher, Jean Cocteau, Carlo Gébler, Julian Green, Ivan Illich, Pauline Kael, Ken Kesey, Toby Litt, Kenzaburo Oe, Hubert Selby, Igor Stravinsky, Frederic Tuten, Eudora Welty, Judith Williamson, Tom Wiseman, Hong Ying. About 30 titles a year. Unsolicited mss not welcome for fiction or poetry; submissions from agents only. Unsolicited synopses and ideas welcome for non-fiction. OVERSEAS ASSOCIATES Marion Boyars Publishers Inc.

ROYALTIES annually.

Bradt Travel Guides

23 High Street, Chalfont St Peter SL9 9QE
☎01753 893444 Fax 01753 892333
✉ info@bradtguides.com
www.bradtguides.com

Managing Director *Hilary Bradt*
Editorial Director *Tricia Hayne*
Approx. Annual Turnover £800,000

Founded in 1974 by Hilary Bradt. Specialises in travel guides to off-beat places. SERIES Country guides and island guides (Azores, Falklands, St Helena); wildlife guides (Madagascar, Galapagos, Arctic, Antarctica, Southern Africa); mini guides to cities (Lille, Budapest, Bratislava, Tallinn, Riga) and the 'Eccentric' series (Britain, London, France, America, Oxford, Cambridge, Edinburgh). 30 titles in 2005. No

unsolicited mss; synopses and ideas for travel guidebooks (not travelogues) welcome.
ROYALTIES twice-yearly.

Brassey's
See **Anova Books**

Nicholas Brealey Publishing
3–5 Spafield Street, London EC1R 4QB
☎020 7239 0360 Fax 020 7239 0370
✉ rights@nbrealey-books.com
www.nbrealey-books.com
Managing Director *Nicholas Brealey*

Founded 1992. Independent publishing group focusing on innovative trade/professional books covering business and finance, intelligent self-help, popular psychology and the increasingly active fields of crossing cultures and travel writing. The group has offices in Boston and includes Intercultural Press Inc. TITLES *It's All Greek to Me!*; *Almost French*; *Money for Nothing*; *Authentic Happiness*; *50 Self-Help Classics*. No fiction, poetry or leisure titles. 30 titles a year. No unsolicited mss; synopses and ideas welcome.
ROYALTIES twice-yearly.

Authors' Rating Looks to be succeeding in breaking away from the usual computer-speak business manuals to publish information and literate texts. Lead titles have a distinct trans-Atlantic feel.

The Breedon Books Publishing Co. Ltd
Breedon House, 3 Parker Centre, Derby DE21 4SZ
☎01332 384235 Fax 01332 292755
✉ susan.last@breedonpublishing.co.uk
www.breedonbooks.co.uk
Owner *Steve Caron*
Commissioning Editor *Susan Last*
Approx. Annual Turnover £1 million

Founded 1983. Publishes football and sport, local history, old photographs, heritage. About 45 titles a year. Unsolicited mss, synopses and ideas welcome if accompanied by s.a.e. No poetry or fiction.
ROYALTIES annually.

Breese Books Ltd
10 Hanover Crescent, Brighton BN2 9SB
☎01273 687555
✉ MBreese999@aol.com
www.abracadabra.co.uk
Chairman/Managing Director *Martin Ranicar-Breese*

Founded in 1975 to produce specialist conjuring books. No unsolicited submissions.

Brewin Books Ltd
Doric House, 56 Alcester Road, Studley B80 7LG
☎01527 854228 Fax 01527 852746
✉ admin@brewinbooks.com
www.brewinbooks.com
Chairman/Managing Director *Alan Brewin*
Company Secretary *Julie Brewin*

Founded 1976. Publishes books on all aspects of Midland life and history including social, hospital, police, military, transport and family histories as well as biographies and contemporary fiction. TITLES *The Worcester and Birmingham Canal* Rev. Alan White; *Travel Allenways Always* Andrew Roberts; *Bow and Arrow War* Marjorie Inkster; *Life and Tales of a Locksmith* K.E. 'Bob' Sidbotham. IMPRINTS **Alton Douglas Books**; **History Into Print**; **Brewin Books**. About 25 titles a year. Not interested in children's, poetry, short stories or novels. Approach by letter, but do not send full mss. Unsolicited synopses and ideas welcome with s.a.e.
ROYALTIES twice-yearly.

Bristol Classical Press
See **Gerald Duckworth & Co. Ltd**

Bristol Phoenix Press
See **University of Exeter Press**

British Academic Press
See **I.B. Tauris & Co. Ltd**

The British Academy
10 Carlton House Terrace, London SW1Y 5AH
☎020 7969 5200 Fax 020 7969 5300
✉ secretary@britac.ac.uk
www.britac.ac.uk
Publications Officer *James Rivington*
Assistant Publications Officer *Janet English*
Publications Assistant *Amrit Bangard*

Founded 1902. The primary body for promoting scholarship in the humanities and social sciences, the Academy publishes many series stemming from its own long-standing research projects, or series of lectures and conference proceedings. Main subjects include history, philosophy and archaeology. SERIES *Auctores Britannici Medii Aevi*; *Early English Church Music*; *Fontes Historiae Africanae*; *Records of Social and Economic History*. About 20 titles a year. Proposals for these series are welcome and are forwarded to the relevant project committees. The British Academy is a registered charity and does not publish for profit. ROYALTIES only when titles have covered their costs.

The British Computer Society
First Floor, Block D, North Star House, North Star Avenue, Swindon SN2 1FA
☎0845 300 4417 Fax 01793 480270
✉ publishing@hq.bcs.org.uk
www.bcs.org/books
Chief Executive *David Clarke*
Head of Publishing & Information Products *Elaine Boyes*
Approx. Annual Turnover £15 million (Society)

Founded 1957. BCS is the leading professional and learned society in the field of computers and information systems. Publishes books which support the professional, academic and practical needs of the IT community. TITLES *A Guide to Global Sourcing*; *A Manager's Guide to IT Law*; *Project Management for IT-Related Projects*; *Business Process Management*; *Professional Issues in Information Technology*; *A Pragmatic Guide to Business Process Modelling*. 5 titles in 2005. Unsolicited material welcome; submissions form and guide on website page: www.bcs.org/books/ writer ROYALTIES annually.

The British Library
96 Euston Road, London NW1 2DB
☎020 7412 7469 Fax 020 7412 7768
✉ blpublications@bl.uk
www.bl.uk
Head of Publishing *David Way*
Approx. Annual Turnover £950,000

Founded 1979 as the publishing arm of The British Library to publish works based on the historic collections and related subjects. Publishes bibliographical reference, manuscript studies, illustrated books based on the Library's collections, and book arts. TITLES *1000 Years of English Literature*; *The Books of Henry VIII and His Wives*; *Futurist Typography*. About 50 titles a year. Unsolicited mss, synopses and ideas welcome if related to the history of the book, book arts or bibliography. No fiction or general non-fiction. ROYALTIES annually.

The British Museum Press
33 Russell Square, London WC1B 3QQ
☎020 7323 1234 Fax 020 7436 7315
www.britishmuseum.co.uk

Managing Director *Andrew Thatcher*
Director of Publishing *Rosemary Bradley*
The book publishing division of The British Museum Company Ltd. Founded 1973 as British Museum Publications Ltd; relaunched 1991 as British Museum Press. Publishes ancient history, archaeology, ethnography, art history, exhibition catalogues, guides, children's books and all official publications of the British Museum. TITLES *Michelangelo Drawings: Closer to the Master*; *The British Museum Concise Introduction to Ancient Egypt*; *Japanese Art in Detail*; *The Persian Empire: A History*. About 50 titles a year. Synopses and ideas for books welcome. ROYALTIES twice-yearly.

Brockhampton Press Ltd
See **Caxton Publishing Group**

Andrew Brodie
See **A.&C. Black Publishers Ltd**

John Brown Citrus Publishing
The New Boathouse, 136–142 Bramley Road, London W10 6SR
☎020 7565 3000 Fax 020 7565 3060
✉ info@jbcp.co.uk
www.jbcp.co.uk
Chief Executive *Andrew Hirsch*
Managing Director *Dean Fitzpatrick*
Operations Director *Andrew Jarvis*

Founded 1987. Contract magazine publisher. TITLES include *Sky Magazine* and *Waitrose Food Illustrated*.

Brown Skin Books
PO Box 46504, London N1 3YA
☎020 7226 4789
✉ info@brownskinbooks.co.uk
www.brownskinbooks.co.uk
Chairman *Dr John Lake*
Managing Director *Vastiana Belfon*

Founded 2002. Publishes 'quality, intelligent erotic fiction by black women around the world' and a new series of erotic crime thrillers. TITLES *Body and Soul* Jade Williams; *Personal Business* Isabel Baptiste; *Scandalous* Angela Campion; *Playthings* Faith Graham; *Online Wildfire* Crystal Humphries; *Strip Poker* Lisa Lawrence; *The Singer* Aisha DuQuesne. 4 titles in 2005. No unsolicited mss; synopses and sample chapters welcome. Send by e-mail or post. No poetry. ROYALTIES annually.

Brown, Son & Ferguson, Ltd
4–10 Darnley Street, Glasgow G41 2SD
☎0141 429 1234 Fax 0141 420 1694
✉ info@skipper.co.uk
www.skipper.co.uk

Chairman/Joint Managing Director *T. Nigel Brown*

Founded 1850. Specialises in nautical textbooks, both technical and non-technical. Also Scottish one-act/three-act plays. Unsolicited mss, synopses and ideas for books welcome.
ROYALTIES annually.

Bryntirion Press
Bryntirion, Bridgend CF31 4DX
☎01656 655886 Fax 01656 665919
✉ office@emw.org.uk
www.emw.org.uk

Press Manager *Huw Kinsey*

Owned by the Evangelical Movement of Wales. Publishes Christian books in English and Welsh. No unsolicited mss; synopses and ideas welcome.
ROYALTIES annually.

Burns & Oates
See **The Continuum International Publishing Group Limited**

Business Education Publishers Ltd
The Teleport Doxford International, Sunderland SR3 3XD
☎0191 525 2410
✉ info@bepl.com
www.bepl.com

Managing Director *Mrs A. Murphy*
Approx. Annual Turnover £400,000

Founded 1981. Publishes business education, economics and law for BTEC and GNVQ reading. Currently expanding into further and higher education, computing, IT, business, travel and tourism, occasional papers for institutions and local government administration. Unsolicited mss and synopses welcome.
ROYALTIES annually.

Buster Books
See **Michael O'Mara Books Ltd**

Butterworth Heinemann
See **Elsevier Ltd**

Cadogan Guides
2nd Floor, 233 High Holborn, London WC1V 7DN
☎020 7611 4660 Fax 020 7611 4665
✉ info@cadoganguides.co.uk
www.cadoganguides.com

Managing Director *Jenny Calcutt*
Managing Editor *Natalie Pomier*

Founded 1982. Travel guide publisher: country, regional and city guides; parent travel guides (*Take the Kids*); guides to living, working and buying property abroad. Also publishes some travel literature. Most titles are commissioned. No unsolicited material.

Calder Publications Ltd
51 The Cut, London SE1 8LF
☎020 7633 0599 Fax 020 7928 5930
✉ info@calderpublications.com
www.calderpublications.com

Chairman/Managing Director/Editorial Head *John Calder*

Formerly John Calder (Publishers) Ltd. A publishing company which has grown around the tastes and contacts of John Calder, the iconoclast of the literary establishment. The list has a reputation for controversial and opinion-forming publications; Samuel Beckett is perhaps the most prestigious name. The list includes all of Beckett's prose and poetry. Publishes autobiography, biography, drama, literary fiction, literary criticism, music, opera, poetry, politics, sociology, ENO opera guides. AUTHORS Antonin Artaud, Marguerite Duras, Martin Esslin, Erich Fried, P.J. Kavanagh, Robert Menasse, Robert Pinget, Luigi Pirandello, Alain Robbe-Grillet, Nathalie Sarraute, L.F. Celine, Eva Figes, Claude Simon, Howard Barker (plays). No new material accepted.
ROYALTIES annually.

Authors' Rating Known for his patronage of eccentric talents, John Calder is one of the few publishers to carry the flag for the English language '... which is in great danger of disappearing under the American vernacular'.

California University Press
See **University Presses of California, Columbia & Princeton Ltd**

Cambridge University Press
The Edinburgh Building, Shaftesbury Road, Cambridge CB2 2RU
☎01223 312393 Fax 01223 315052
www.cambridge.org

Chief Executive *Stephen R.R. Bourne*

The oldest printer and publisher in the world, now a global company with a regional structure operating in the UK, Europe, the Middle East,

Africa, in the Americas and in Asia-Pacific. Has warehousing centres in Cambridge, New York, Melbourne, Madrid, Cape Town, São Paulo and Singapore, with offices and agents in many other countries. Publishing includes major ELT courses; tertiary textbooks and monographs; scientific and medical reference; professional lists in law, management and engineering; educational coursebooks for the National Curriculum; and e-learning materials for schools via the Cambridge-Hitachi joint venture. Publishes academic/educational, ELT and reference books for markets worldwide, at all levels from primary school to postgraduate and professional. Also Bibles and some 200 academic journals. Around 25,000 authors in 116 countries and between 1500 and 2000 new titles a year.

PUBLISHING GROUPS
Bibles *C.J. Wright*; **ELT** *A.C. Gilfillan*; **Humanities and Social Sciences** *R.K. Fisher*; **STM** *R.W.A. Barling*; **Education** *J.G. Tuttle*; **Journals** *G.L. Nuttall*. Synopses and ideas for books are welcome (and preferable to the submission of unsolicited mss). No fiction or poetry.
ROYALTIES twice-yearly.

Authors' Rating With its traditional strength in the academic market CUP is well placed to create such intellectual blockbusters as the three volume *Economic History of Modern Britain*. An increasing number of titles reach out to the general reader.

Camden Press Ltd
43 Camden Passage, London N1 8EA
☎020 7226 4673
Chairman *Bob Borzello*

Founded 1985. Publishes social issues; all books are launched in connection with major national conferences. DIVISION **Publishing for Change** *Bob Borzello* TITLE *Living with the Legacy of Abuse*. IMPRINT **Mindfield** TITLES *Hate Thy Neighbour: The Race Issue*; *Therapy on the Couch*. No unsolicited material. Approach by telephone in the first instance.
ROYALTIES annually.

Campbell Books
See **Macmillan Publishers Ltd**

Candle
See **Lion Hudson plc**

Canongate Books Ltd
14 High Street, Edinburgh EH1 1TE
☎0131 557 5111 Fax 0131 557 5211
✉ info@canongate.co.uk
www.canongate.net
Also at: Lower Basement, 151 Chesterton Road, London W10 6ET
Publisher *Jamie Byng*
Approx. Annual Turnover £6 million

Founded 1973. Won 'Publisher of the Year' (2002) at the British Book Awards. Publishes a wide range of literary fiction and non-fiction. Historically there is a strong Scottish slant to the list but its output is increasingly international, especially now with its joint venture with Grove Atlantic in the US and co-publishing agreement with Text Publishing in Australia. Canongate also has a growing reputation for originating unusual projects (typified by *The Pocket Canons* and more recently by *The Myths* series launched in 2005). Key AUTHORS include Michel Faber, Yann Martel, Alasdair Gray, John Fante, James Meek and Louise Welsh. IMPRINTS **Canongate Classics** Adult paperback series dedicated solely to important works of Scottish literature; **Canongate International** Fiction in translation.
ROYALTIES twice-yearly.

Authors' Rating *Esquire* magazine has named publisher Jamie Byng as the most influential man under 40 in UK literature, quite a compliment in what is increasingly a youth driven industry. Canongate's steady growth based on an imaginative list would seem to support the *Esquire* verdict.

Canterbury Press
See **SCM – Canterbury Press Ltd**

Capall Bann Publishing
Auton Farm, Milverton TA4 1NE
☎01823 401528 Fax 01823 401529
✉ enquiries@capallbann.co.uk
www.capallbann.co.uk
Chairman *Julia Day*
Editorial Head *Jon Day*

Founded in 1993, Capall Bann now has well over 300 titles in print. Family-owned and run company, 'operated by people with real experience in the topics we publish' which include British traditions, folklore, animals, alternative healing, environmental, Celtic lore, mind, body and spirit. TITLES *Tarot Therapy*; *How to Talk with Fairies*; *Mary Magdalene, Lost Goddess, Lost Gospels*; *Crystals Folklore & Healing*; *Understanding Star Children*. About 40 titles a year. Unsolicited proposals for books welcome. No fiction or poetry.
ROYALTIES twice-yearly.

Jonathan Cape/Jonathan Cape Children's Books
See **The Random House Group Ltd**

Capstone Publishing
John Wiley & Sons Ltd, The Atrium, Southern Gate, Chichester PO19 8SQ
☎01243 779777   Fax 01243 775878
✉ info@wiley-capstone.co.uk
www.wiley.com

Founded 1997. Part of **John Wiley & Sons Inc**. Publishes business, personal development, lifestyle and humour books.

Carcanet Press Ltd
4th Floor, Alliance House, 30 Cross Street, Manchester M2 7AQ
☎0161 834 8730   Fax 0161 832 0084
✉ pnr@carcanet..co.uk
www.carcanet.co.uk

Owner *Folio Holdings*
Chairman *Kate Gavron*
Managing Director/Editorial Director *Michael Schmidt, FRSL*

In the last 30 years Carcanet has grown from an undergraduate hobby into a substantial venture. Robert Gavron bought the company in 1983 and it has established strong European, Commonwealth and American links. Winner of the **Sunday Times Small Publisher of the Year** award in 2000, it took over the Oxford Poets list from **Oxford University Press** in 1999, which it now publishes as a distinct imprint. Primarily a poetry publisher but also publishes academic, literary biography, fiction in translation and translations. AUTHORS John Ashbery, Eavan Boland, Donald Davie, Natalia Ginzburg, Robert Graves, Elizabeth Jennings, Hugh MacDiarmid, Edwin Morgan, Sinead Morrissey, Les Murray, Frank O'Hara, Richard Price, Frederic Raphael, C.H. Sisson, Charles Tomlinson, Jane Yeh. About 40 titles a year, including the *PN Review* (six issues yearly). Poetry submissions (hard copy only): 6–10 poems with covering letter and return postage. Prospective writers should familiarise themselves with the Carcanet list before submitting work.
ROYALTIES annually.

Authors' Rating Ever in the forefront of imaginative publishing, Carcanet has taken a step closer to the source of its literary creativity by setting up a postgraduate Writing School at Manchester Metropolitan University. (See entry under *Writers' Courses*.)

Cardiff Academic Press
St Fagans Road, Fairwater, Cardiff CF5 3AE
☎029 2056 0333   Fax 029 2055 4909
✉ drakegroup@btinternet.co.uk
www.drakegroup.co.uk

Managing Director *R.G. Drake*
Academic publishers and Drake Audio Visual.

Carlton Publishing Group
20 Mortimer Street, London W1T 3JW
☎020 7612 0400   Fax 020 7612 0401
✉ enquiries@carltonbooks.co.uk

Managing Director *Jonathan Goodman*
Editorial Director *Piers Murray Hill*

Founded 1992. Carlton Publishing Group is an independent publishing house. It has three main divisions: **Carlton Books** Illustrated leisure and entertainment books aimed at the mass market. Subjects include history, sport, puzzles, health, popular science, music and design. **André Deutsch** Autobiography, biography, history, current affairs and the arts. **Prion Books** Humour, drink and classic literature. No unsolicited mss; synopses and ideas welcome. No novels, science fiction, poetry or children's fiction.

Carroll & Brown Publishers Limited
20 Lonsdale Road, London NW6 6RD
☎020 7372 0900   Fax 020 7372 0460
✉ mail@carrollandbrown.co.uk
www.carrollandbrown.co.uk

Editorial Director *Louise Dixon*
Approx. Annual Turnover £4 million

Publishes practical parenting, health, fitness, lifestyle, mind, body and spirit. TITLES *3 Steps to Fertility*; *Your Child's Hand*; *Pregnancy Day by Day*; *Your Pregnancy Bible*. Synopses and ideas for illustrated books welcome; approach in writing in the first instance. No fiction
PAYMENT Fees or royalties paid.

Cassell Illustrated
See **Octopus Publishing Group**

Cassell Reference
See **The Orion Publishing Group Limited**

Castle Publications
See **Nottingham University Press**

Kyle Cathie Ltd
122 Arlington Road, London NW1 7HP
☎020 7692 7215   Fax 020 7692 7260

✉ general.enquiries@kyle-cathie.com
www.kylecathie.co.uk

Founded 1990 to publish and promote 'books we have personal enthusiasm for'. Publishes non-fiction: cookery, food and drink, health and beauty, mind, body & spirit, gardening, homes and interiors, reference and occasional books of classic poetry. TITLES *The GI Diet* Antony Worrall Thompson; *Easy Entertaining* Darina Allen; *The Handbag Beauty Bible* Sarah Stacey and Josephine Fairley; *Free Yourself From Smoking* Christina Irvings; *The Gourmet Gardener* Bob Flowerdew. About 25 titles a year. No unsolicited mss. 'Synopses and ideas are considered in the fields in which we publish.'
ROYALTIES twice-yearly.

Catholic Truth Society (CTS)
40–46 Harleyford Road, London SE11 5AY
☎020 7640 0042 Fax 020 7640 0046
✉ f.martin@cts-online.org.uk
www.cts-online.org.uk

Chairman *Most Rev. Peter Smith*
General Secretary *Fergal Martin*

Founded originally in 1868 and re-founded in 1884. Publishes religious books – Roman Catholic; a variety of doctrinal, moral, biographical, devotional and liturgical publications, including a large body of Vatican documents and sources. Unsolicited mss, synopses and ideas welcome if appropriate to their list.
ROYALTIES annually.

Causeway Press
See **Pearson Education**

Caxton Publishing Group
20 Bloomsbury Street, London WC1B 3JH
☎020 7636 7171 Fax 020 7636 1922
✉ office@caxtonpublishing.com
www.caxtonpublishing.com

Managing Director *John Maxwell*
Approx. Annual Turnover £4 million

Founded 1999. Specialises in reprinting out-of-print works for the 'value' market worldwide and commissioning new general non-fiction publications in reference, cookery, gardening and children's. DIVISIONS/IMPRINTS **Brockhampton Press Ltd** Children's fiction and non-fiction. **Caxton Editions Ltd** General non-fiction, reference and military. **Knight Paperbacks Ltd** Fiction. **Chaucer Press** Art, architecture and literature. **Mercury Books** Illustrated non-fiction. **Mercury Junior** Children's books, illustrated, educational, novelty. 200 titles a year. No unso-

licited mss; synopses and ideas welcome; send letter in the first instance.
ROYALTIES twice-yearly.

CBA Publishing
St Mary's House, 66 Bootham, York YO30 7BZ
☎01904 671417 Fax 01904 671384
www.britarch.ac.uk

Publications Officer *Jane Thorniley-Walker*
British Archaeology Editor *Mike Pitts*
Young Archaeologists' Club Coordinator *Wendi Terry*
Approx. Annual Turnover £110,000

Publishing arm of the **Council for British Archaeology**. Publishes academic archaeology reports, practical handbooks, yearbook, *British Archaeology* (bi-monthly magazine), *Young Archaeologist* (Young Archaeologists' Club magazine), monographs, archaeology and education. TITLES *Garden Archaeology: a Handbook*; *Approaches to Archaeological Illustration: a Handbook*; *Women in Roman Britain*. Please contact by telephone before submitting mss and proposals.
ROYALTIES paid for hardback and commercial publications.

CBD Research Ltd
Chancery House, 15 Wickham Road, Beckenham BR3 5JS
☎020 8650 7745 Fax 020 8650 0768
✉ cbd@cbdresearch.com
www.cbdresearch.com

Managing Director *S.P.A. Henderson*
Approx. Annual Turnover £500,000

Founded 1961. Publishes directories and other reference guides to sources of information. No fiction. IMPRINT **Chancery House Press** Non-fiction of an esoteric/specialist nature for 'serious researchers and the dedicated hobbyist'. About 6 titles a year.
ROYALTIES quarterly.

Centaur Press
See **Open Gate Press**

Century
See **The Random House Group Ltd**

CF4K
See **Christian Focus Publications**

Chambers Harrap Publishers Ltd
7 Hopetoun Crescent, Edinburgh EH7 4AY
☎0131 556 5929 Fax 0131 556 5313
✉ admin@chambersharrap.co.uk

www.chambersharrap.co.uk
Managing Director *Patrick White*
Administrator *Esther Fulton*
Part of Hachette-Livre (UK). Publishes diction-aries and reference. The Chambers imprint was founded in the early 1800s to publish self-edu-cation books but soon diversified into diction-aries and other reference works. The current list covers a broad range of subject areas and includes crossword titles. The Harrap imprint dates from 1901 and is used for bilingual dic-tionaries and study aids. About 75 titles a year. Send synopsis with accompanying letter rather than completed mss.

Chancery House Press
See **CBD Research Ltd**

Channel 4 Books
See **Transworld Publishers**

Paul Chapman Publishing Ltd
See **Sage Publications**

Chapman Publishing
4 Broughton Place, Edinburgh EH1 3RX
☎0131 557 2207
✉ chapman-pub@blueyonder.co.uk
www.chapman-pub.co.uk
Managing Editor *Joy Hendry*
Assistant Editor *Edmund O'Connor*

A venture devoted to publishing works by the best of Scottish writers, both up-and-coming and established, published in *Chapman*, Scotland's leading literary magazine. Has expanded publish-ing activities considerably over the last three years and is now publishing a wider range of works though the broad policy stands. Publishes poetry, drama, short stories, books of contemporary importance in 20th-century Scotland. TITLES *Winter Barley* George Gunn; *Lure* Dilys Rose; *Wild Women Series – Wild Women of a Certain Age* Magi Gibson; *Ye Cannae Win* Janet Paisley. About 4 titles a year. No unsolicited mss; synopses and ideas for books welcome.
ROYALTIES annually.

Charnwood
See **F.A. Thorpe (Publishing)**

Chartered Institute of Personnel and Development (CIPD)
151 The Broadway, London SW19 1JQ
☎020 8612 6200   Fax 020 8612 6201
✉ publish@cipd.co.uk
www.cipd.co.uk/bookstore

Publishing Manager *Sarah Brown*
Approx. Annual Turnover £2.3 million
Part of CIPD Enterprises Limited. Publishes on personnel, training and management. A list of around 160 titles including looseleaf and online subscription products, student textbooks and professional information resources. New prod-uct proposals welcome.
ROYALTIES annually or flat fees paid.

Chastleton Travel
See **Arris Publishing Ltd**

Chatto & Windus
See **The Random House Group Ltd**

Chaucer Press
See **Caxton Publishing Group**

Cheek
See **Virgin Books Ltd**

Cherrytree Books
See **Evans Brothers Ltd**

Chicken House Publishing
2 Palmer Street, Frome BA11 1DS
☎01373 454488   Fax 01373 454499
✉ chickenhouse@doublecluck.com
Chairman/Managing Director *Barry Cunningham*

Children's publishing house founded in 2000. Acquired by Scholastic Inc. in May 2005. Publishes books 'that are aimed at real children' – fiction, original picture books, gift books and fun non-fiction. Aiming to publish about 25 titles a year. 'We are always on the lookout for new talent.' Unsolicited fiction and picture book material welcome; send letter with syn-opsis, three sample chapters and s.a.e.
ROYALTIES twice-yearly.

Authors' Rating Set up as a 'small, creative com-pany', Chicken House has made such rapid progress as to attract a successful bid from Scholastic. Editorial freedom is part of the deal 'with no rules about what to publish as long as it's good'.

Child's Play (International) Ltd
Ashworth Road, Bridgemead, Swindon SN5 7YD
☎01793 616286   Fax 01793 512795
✉ allday@childs-play.com
www.childs-play.com
Chief Executive *Neil Burden*

Founded in 1972, Child's Play is an independent publisher specialising in learning through play, whole child development, life-skills and values. Publishes books, games and A-V materials. TITLES *Big Hungry Bear; There Was an Old Lady; Our Cat Cuddles; Royston Knapper; Children of the Sun; Ten Beads Tall; Pocket Pals; Sliders; Roly Poly Books; Animal Lullabies; Monkey's Clever Tale; What's the Time, Mr Wolf?; Sign and Sing-Along; Arithmetic Lotto*. Unsolicited mss welcome. Send s.a.e. for return or response. Expect to wait two months for a reply.

ROYALTIES Outright or royalty payments are subject to negotiation.

Chimera
See **Pegasus Elliot Mackenzie Publishers Ltd**

Christian Focus Publications
Geanies House, Fearn, Tain IV20 1TW
☎01862 871011 Fax 01862 871699
✉ info@christianfocus.com
www.christianfocus.com
Owner *Balintore Holdings plc*
Chairman *R.W.M. Mackenzie*
Managing Director *William Mackenzie*
Editorial Manager *Willie Mackenzie*
Children's Editor *Catherine Mackenzie*
Approx. Annual Turnover £1.5 million

Founded 1979 to produce children's books for the co-edition market. Now a major producer of Christian books. Publishes adult and children's books, including some fiction for children but not adults. No poetry. Publishes for all English-speaking markets, as well as the UK. IMPRINTS **CF4K** Children's books; **Christian Focus** General books; **Mentor** Study books; **Christian Heritage** Classic reprints. About 90 titles a year. Unsolicited mss, synopses and ideas welcome from Christian writers. See website for submission criteria.
ROYALTIES annually.

Christian Heritage
See **Christian Focus Publications**

Chroma
See **Black & White Publishing Ltd**

Chrome Dreams
See entry under *Audio Books*

Chrysalis Books Group
See **Anova Books**

Churchill Livingstone
See **Elsevier Ltd**

Churchwarden Publications Ltd
PO Box 420, Warminster BA12 9XB
☎01985 840189 Fax 01985 840243
Managing Director *John Stidolph*
Founded 1974. Publishes books and stationery for churchwardens and church administrators including *The Churchwarden's Yearbook*. About 2 titles a year. Unsolicited mss, synopses and ideas for books welcome.
ROYALTIES paid according to contract.

Cicerone Press
2 Police Square, Milnthorpe LA7 7PY
☎01539 562069 Fax 01539 563417
✉ info@cicerone.co.uk
www.cicerone.co.uk
Managing/Editorial Director *Jonathan Williams*
Founded 1969. Guidebook publisher for outdoor enthusiasts. No fiction or poetry. TITLES *Hillwalker's Guide to Mountaineering; Tour of Mont Blanc; Coast to Coast Trail*. SERIES include *Alpine Walking; International Walking; British Long-Distance Trails, Cycling* and *Winter Activities*. About 30 titles a year. No unsolicited mss; synopses and ideas considered.
ROYALTIES twice-yearly.

Cico Books
20–21 Jockey Fields, London WC1R 4BW
☎020 7025 2289 Fax 020 7025 2281
✉ mail@cicobooks.co.uk
Managing Director *Mark Collins*
Publisher *Cindy Richards*
Founded in 1999 by Mark Collins and Cindy Richards (both formerly with **Collins & Brown**) 'to offer flexibility by being small, selling co-edition rights to overseas publishers'. Acquired by **Ryland, Peters & Small Limited** in 2006. Publishes lifestyle and interiors, mind, body and spirit. About 15 titles a year. No unsolicited mss, synopses or ideas.
ROYALTIES twice-yearly.

Clairview Books Ltd
Hillside House, The Square, Forest Row RH18 5ES
☎0870 486 3526
✉ office@clairviewbooks.com
www.clairviewbooks.com
Managing Director *Mr S. Gulbekian*
Approx. Annual Turnover £75,000
Founded 2000. Publishes non-fiction. General

books challenging conventional thinking: mind, body & spirit, current affairs, the arts, health and therapy. TITLES *Imperial America* Gore Vidal; *The Biodynamic Food and Cookbook* Wendy Cook; *My Descent Into Death* Howard Storm.

No unsolicited material; send initial letter of enquiry. No poetry or fiction.

ROYALTIES annually.

Clarion
See **Elliot Right Way Books**

T&T Clark
See **The Continuum International Publishing Group Ltd**

James Clarke & Co.
PO Box 60, Cambridge CB1 2NT
☎01223 350865   Fax 01223 366951
✉ publishing@jamesclarke.co.uk
www.jamesclarke.co.uk
Managing Director *Adrian Brink*

Parent company of **The Lutterworth Press** (see entry). Publishes scholarly and academic works, mainly theological, directory and reference titles. TITLES *Libraries Directory* (book and CD-ROM); *Encyclopedia of the Middle Ages*; *Henry VIII's Bishops*; *The Theology of Tyndale*; *Patrology*. Approach in writing with ideas in the first instance.

Classic Publications
See **Ian Allan Publishing Ltd**

Collector's Library
See **CRW Publishing Ltd**

Peter Collin Publishing Ltd
See **Bloomsbury Publishing Plc**

Collins
See **HarperCollins Publishers Ltd**

Collins & Brown
See **Anova Books**

Colourpoint Books
Colourpoint House, Jubilee Business Park, 21 Jubilee Road, Newtownards BT23 4YH
☎028 9182 0505   Fax 028 9182 1900
✉ info@colourpoint.co.uk
www.colourpoint.co.uk
Partners *Wesley Johnston, Malcolm Johnston, Norman Johnston* (transport editor), *Sheila M. Johnston* (commissioning editor)

Founded 1993. Publishes school textbooks and transport (covering the whole of the British Isles), plus books of Irish and general interest. No fiction. About 25 titles a year. Unsolicited material accepted but approach in writing in the first instance; include return postage, please.

ROYALTIES twice-yearly.

Columbia University Press
See **University Presses of California, Columbia & Princeton Ltd**

Compendium Publishing Ltd
43 Frith Street, London W1D 4SA
☎020 7287 4570   Fax 020 7494 0583
✉ alan.greene@compendiumpublishing.com
Managing Director *Alan Greene*
Editorial Director *Simon Forty*

Founded 2000. Publishes and packages for international publishing companies, general illustrated non-fiction: history, reference, hobbies, children's and educational transport and militaria. No unsolicited mss; synopses and ideas preferred.

ROYALTIES twice-yearly.

Condor
See **Souvenir Press Ltd**

Conran Octopus
See **Octopus Publishing Group**

Constable & Robinson Ltd
3 The Lanchesters, 162 Fulham Palace Road, London W6 9ER
☎020 8741 3663   Fax 020 8748 7562
✉ enquiries@constablerobinson.com
www.constablerobinson.com
Chairman *Nick Robinson*
Joint Managing Directors *Jan Chamier, Nova Jayne Heath*
Editorial Director, Crime List *Krystyna Green*
Editorial Director, Mammoth series *Pete Duncan*
Manager, Overcoming series *Fritha Saunders*

Archibald Constable, Walter Scott's publisher and the originator of the '3 decker novel', published his first titles in Edinburgh in 1795. Constable & Robinson Ltd are now in the third century of publishing under the Constable imprint, still independent, with shareholders who work or have worked in the business running the company. IMPRINTS **Constable** Commissioning Editors *Becky Hardie, Leo Hollis* Current affairs, biography, general and military history, psychology, travel, photography and crime fiction mainly in hardback. **Robinson** Crime fiction in paperback. SERIES **Mammoth**; **Overcoming** Psychology, popular health, self help, military history and true crime. Unsolicited sample chapters, synopses and ideas for books welcome. No mss; no e-mail submissions. Enclose return postage.

The Continuum International Publishing Group Limited

The Tower Building, 11 York Road, London SE1 7NX
☎020 7922 0880 Fax 020 7922 0881
www.continuumbooks.com

Chairman & Chief Executive *Philip Sturrock*
Approx. Annual Turnover £16 million

Founded in 1999 by a buy-out of the academic and religious publishing of Cassell and the acquisition of Continuum New York. Publishes academic, religious and general books.

DIVISIONS **Academic Humanities** Publishing Director *Alexandra Webster* Education, social sciences, literature, film and music, philosophy (including the **Thoemmes** imprint), linguistics, biblical studies and theology printed under the **T&T Clark** imprint. TITLES *Getting the Buggers to Behave*; *Teaching in Further Education*; *What Philosophy Is*; *The Guerrilla Film Makers Handbook*. **General Trade & Continuum Religion** Publishing Director *Robin Baird-Smith* Publishes under **Continuum Burns & Oates** (RC books) TITLES *Seven Basic Plots*; *Seven Last Words*. IMPRINTS **Continuum**; **T&T Clark Intl**; **Thoemmes**; **Burns & Oates**; **Hambledon Continuum**. 550 titles in 2005. Unsolicited synopses and ideas within the subject areas listed above are welcome; approach in writing in the first instance. OVERSEAS SUBSIDIARIES The Continuum International Publishing Group Inc., New York and Harrisburg.
ROYALTIES twice-yearly.

Authors' Rating Now embracing the University of Birmingham Press, Continuum continues to make an impact with readable, often controversial, religious and academic titles.

Conway Maritime Press

See **Anova Books**

Thomas Cook Publishing

PO Box 227, Peterborough PE3 8SB
☎01733 416477 Fax 01733 416688
Head of Publishing *Chris Young*

Part of the Thomas Cook Group Ltd, publishing commenced in 1873 with the first issue of *Cook's Continental Timetable*. Publishes guidebooks, maps and timetables. About 20 titles a year. No unsolicited mss; synopses and ideas welcome as long as they are travel-related.
ROYALTIES annually.

Authors' Rating Selling largely through Thomas Cook outlets (there are 600 branches in the UK) the travel list is doing so well it is being expanded by nearly half over two years with more titles being sold from high street bookshops.

Leo Cooper

See **Pen & Sword Books Ltd**

Corgi

See **Transworld Publishers**

Corgi Children's Books

See **The Random House Group Ltd**

Country Publications Ltd

The Water Mill, Broughton Hall, Skipton BD23 3AG
☎01756 701381 Fax 01756 701326
✉ editorial@dalesman.co.uk
www.dalesman.co.uk

Book Editor *Mark Whitley*

Publishers of *Countryman*, *Dalesman*, *Cumbria* and *Down Your Way* magazines, and regional books covering the North of England. Subjects include walking, guidebooks, history, humour and folklore. About 10 titles a year. Will consider mss on subjects listed above, relating to the North.
ROYALTIES annually.

Countryside Books

2 Highfield Avenue, Newbury RG14 5DS
☎01635 43816 Fax 01635 551004
✉ info@countrysidebooks.co.uk
www.countrysidebooks.co.uk

Publisher *Nicholas Battle*

Founded 1976. Publishes local interest paperbacks on regional subjects, generally by English county. Local history, dialects, genealogy, walking and photographic, aviation and military, some transport. Over 400 titles available. Unsolicited mss and synopses welcome but no fiction, poetry, natural history or personal memories.
ROYALTIES twice-yearly.

Crème de la Crime Ltd

PO Box 523, Chesterfield S40 9AT
☎01246 520835 Fax 01246 520835
✉ info@cremedelacrime.com
www.cremedelacrime.com

Managing Director *Lynne Patrick*

Approx. Annual Turnover £60,000

Founded in 2003 to discover and publish crime fiction by new authors. 6 titles in 2005. Welcomes enquiries and unsolicited submissions, 'especially from talented but unpublished authors who are urged to read the detailed guidelines on the website; or send £2.50 with A4 s.a.e. and two first-class stamps for hard copy'.

ROYALTIES annually.

Crescent Books
See **Mercat Press Ltd**

Cressrelles Publishing Co. Ltd
10 Station Road Industrial Estate, Colwall, Malvern WR13 6RN
☎01684 540154   Fax 01684 540154
✉ simonsmith@cressrelles4drama.
fsbusiness.co.uk

Managing Director *Leslie Smith*

Publishes a range of local interest books and drama titles. IMPRINTS **J. Garnet Miller** Plays and theatre texts; **Kenyon–Deane** Plays and drama textbooks. Submissions welcome.

Crombie Jardine Publishing Limited
13 Nonsuch Walk, Cheam SM2 7LG
☎020 8393 5454
✉ catriona@crombiejardine.com
www.crombiejardine.com

Sales & Publishing Director *David Crombie*
Publishing Director *Catriona Jardine*

Founded in 2004. Specialises in fun, quirky and topical humour books only. TITLES *The Little Book of Chavs*; *The World's Funniest Proverbs*; *Shag Yourself Slim*; *The Sudoku & Kakuro Challenge*; *Britain's Rudest Place Names*. 34 titles in 2005

Authors' Rating Having cut their teeth with **Michael O'Mara Books**, the co-founders of Crombie Jardine are out to grab a share of the young adult humour market.

Crossway
See **Inter-Varsity Press**

The Crowood Press Ltd
The Stable Block, Crowood Lane, Ramsbury, Marlborough SN8 2HR
☎01672 520320   Fax 01672 520280
✉ enquiries@crowood.com
www.crowood.com

Chairman *John Dennis*
Managing Director *Ken Hathaway*

Publishes sport and leisure titles, including ani-mal and land husbandry, climbing and walking, maritime, country sports, equestrian, fishing and shooting; also crafts, dogs, gardening, DIY, theatre, natural history, aviation, military history and motoring. IMPRINT **Airlife Publishing** Specialist aviation titles for pilots, historians and enthusiasts. About 70 titles a year. Preliminary letter preferred in all cases.

ROYALTIES annually.

CRW Publishing Ltd
69 Gloucester Crescent, London NW1 7EG
☎020 7485 5764   Fax 0870 751 7254
✉ marcus.clapham@crw-publishing.co.uk
www.collectors-library.com

Also at: 6 Turville Barns, Eastleach, Cirencester GL7 3QB

Chairman *Ken Webb*
Editorial Director *Marcus Clapham*
Approx. Annual Turnover £2 million

Founded 2003. Publishes literary classics, gift, children's, philosophy, myth and legend, reference, boxed sets. IMPRINTS **Collector's Library**; **Book Blocks**; **Essential Thinkers**; **Poetry Library**; **Myth & Legend**; **Reference Library**. 130 titles in 2006. No unsolicited mss. Synopses and ideas are welcome; send by post to the editorial director.

ROYALTIES annually.

James Currey Publishers
73 Botley Road, Oxford OX2 0BS
☎01865 244111   Fax 01865 246454
✉ editorial@jamescurrey.co.uk
www.jamescurrey.co.uk

Chairman *James Currey*
Managing Director/Editorial Director *Douglas H. Johnson*

Founded 1985. A specialist publisher of academic paperback books on Africa and the Third World: history, anthropology, economics, sociology, politics and literary criticism. Approach in writing by post with synopsis if material is 'relevant to our needs'.

ROYALTIES annually.

Custom Publishing
See **The Orion Publishing Group Limited**

D&B Publishing
PO Box 18, Hassocks BN6 9WR
☎01273 834680   Fax 01273 831629
✉ info@dandbpublishing.com
www.dandbpublishing.com

Joint Managing Directors *Dan Addelman, Byron Jacobs*

Founded 2002. Publishes games books, specialising in gambling, primarily. 6 titles in 2005. Unsolicited mss, synopses and ideas welcome; approach by e-mail in the first instance.
ROYALTIES annually.

Terence Dalton Ltd
Water Street, Lavenham, Sudbury CO10 9RN
☎01787 249291   Fax 01787 248267
www.terencedalton.com
Director/Editorial Head *Elisabeth Whitehair*
Founded 1967. Part of the Lavenham Group Plc, a family company. No unsolicited mss. Ideas welcome; telephone in the first instance. Non-fiction only.
ROYALTIES annually.

Darton, Longman & Todd Ltd
1 Spencer Court, 140–142 Wandsworth High Street, London SW18 4JJ
☎020 8875 0155   Fax 020 8875 0133
✉ tradesales@darton-longman-todd.co.uk
www.darton-longman-todd.co.uk
Editorial Director *Brendan Walsh*
Editor/Rights Officer *Elizabeth Piercy*
Approx. Annual Turnover £1 million
Founded 1959. In July 1990 DLT became a common ownership company, owned and run by staff members. A leading ecumenical, predominantly Christian, publisher, with a strong emphasis on spirituality, theology and the ministry and mission of the Church. TITLES *Jerusalem Bible*; *New Jerusalem Bible*; *The Return of the Prodigal Son*; *Resurrection*. About 50 titles a year. Sample material for books on theological or spiritual subjects considered.
ROYALTIES twice-yearly.

David & Charles Publishers
Brunel House, Forde Close, Newton Abbot TQ12 4PU
☎01626 323200   Fax 01626 323317
✉ mail@davidandcharles.co.uk
www.davidandcharles.co.uk
Managing Director & Publisher *Sara Domville*
Head of Publishing *Alison Myer*
Founded 1960, owned by F+W. Publications. Publishes illustrated non-fiction for international markets, specialising in needlecraft, crafts, art techniques, practical photography, military history, equestrian and gardening. No fiction, poetry or memoirs. TITLES *Voices from the Battle of Trafalgar*; *Branchline Britain*; *Shoes*; *The Knitter's Bible*; *100 Ways to Improve Your Riding*. About 200 titles a year. Unsolicited mss will be considered if return postage is included; synopses and ideas welcome for the subjects listed above.
ROYALTIES twice-yearly or flat fees.

Christopher Davies Publishers Ltd
PO Box 403, Swansea SA1 4YF
☎01792 648825   Fax 01792 648825
✉ chris@cdaviesbookswales.com
Managing Director/Editorial Head *Christopher T. Davies*
Approx. Annual Turnover £20,000
Founded 1949 to promote and expand Welsh-language publications. Publishes biography, cookery, history, sport and literature of Welsh interest. TITLES *An A–Z of Wales and the Welsh*; *Welsh Birthplaces*; *Carwyn: A Personal Memoir*; *Who's Who in Welsh History*. About 2 titles a year. No unsolicited mss. Synopses and ideas for books welcome.
ROYALTIES twice-yearly.

Authors' Rating A favourite for Celtic readers and writers.

Giles de la Mare Publishers Ltd
PO Box 25351, London NW5 1ZT
☎020 7485 2533   Fax 020 7485 2534
✉ gilesdelamare@dial.pipex.com
www.gilesdelamare.co.uk
Chairman/Managing Director *Giles de la Mare*
Approx. Annual Turnover £30,000
Founded 1995 and commenced publishing in April 1996. Publishes mainly non-fiction, especially art and architecture, biography, history, music. TITLES *Flint Architecture of East Anglia* Stephen Hart; *19th Century British Painting* Luke Herrmann; *Short Stories, Vols I, II & III* Walter de la Mare; *Handsworth Revolution* David Winkley; *The Life of Henry Moore* Roger Berthoud; *Becoming an Orchestral Musician* Richard Davis; *Romanesque Churches of France: A Traveller's Guide* Peter Strafford; *Blindness and the Visionary* John Coles. Unsolicited mss, synopses and ideas welcome after initial telephone call.
ROYALTIES twice-yearly.

Debrett's Ltd
1 Whittaker House, 2 Whittaker Avenue, Richmond TW9 1EH
☎020 8213 5263   Fax 020 8213 5261
✉ people@debretts.co.uk
www.debretts.co.uk
Publishing Director *Ian Castello-Cortes*
Chairman *Conrad Free*
Biographical reference plus etiquette, correct form and other social guides; also magazines.

Book TITLES include triennial *Debrett's Peerage & Baronetage* and annual *People of Today* (as book, CD-ROM and online). *Debrett's Review* is now main periodical. Book and article proposals welcome.

Dedalus Ltd

Langford Lodge, St Judith's Lane, Sawtry PE28 5XE
☎01487 832382
✉ info@dedalusbooks.com
www.dedalusbooks.com

Chairman *Juri Gabriel*
Managing Director *Eric Lane*
Approx. Annual Turnover £200,000

Founded 1983. Publishes contemporary European fiction and classics and original literary fiction. TITLES *The Dedalus Book of the Occult*; *The Arabian Nightmare* Robert Irwin; *Memoirs of a Gnostic Dwarf* David Madsen; *The Double Life of Daniel Glick* Maurice Caldera; *Music in a Foreign Language* Andrew Crumey (winner of the Saltire Best First Book Award in 1994).

DIVISIONS/IMPRINTS **Original Fiction in Paperback**; **Contemporary European Fiction 1992–2004**; **Dedalus European Classics**; **Literary Concept Books**. Welcomes submissions for original fiction and books suitable for its list but 'most people sending work in have no idea what kind of books Dedalus publishes and merely waste their efforts'. Author guidelines on website. Particularly interested in intellectually clever and unusual fiction. A letter about the author should always accompany any submission. No replies without s.a.e.
ROYALTIES annually.

Authors' Rating A small, quality publisher which actually recognises that good books can come from foreign language writers.

JM Dent
See **The Orion Publishing Group Ltd**

André Deutsch Ltd
See **Carlton Publishing Group**

Digital Press
See **Elsevier Ltd**

Dinas
See **Y Lolfa Cyf**

John Donald Publishers Ltd

West Newington House, 10 Newington Road, Edinburgh EH9 1QS
☎0131 668 4371 Fax 0131 668 4466
✉ info@birlinn.co.uk
www.birlinn.co.uk

Managing Director *Hugh Andrew*
Commissioning Editor *John Tuckwell*

Bought by **Birlinn Ltd** in 1999. Publishes academic and scholarly, archaeology, architecture, textbooks, guidebooks, local, and social history. New books are published as an imprint of Birlinn Ltd. About 30 titles a year.

Donhead Publishing Ltd

Lower Coombe, Donhead St Mary, Shaftesbury SP7 9LY
☎01747 828422 Fax 01747 828522
✉ jillpearce@donhead.com
www.donhead.com

Contact *Jill Pearce*

Founded 1990 to specialise in publishing how-to books for building practitioners; particularly interested in architectural conservation material. Publishes building, architecture and heritage only. TITLES *Preserving Post-War Heritage*; *Stone Cleaning*; *Architecture 1900*; *Encyclopaedia of Architectural Terms*; *Cleaning Historic Buildings*; *Brickwork*; *Practical Stone Masonry*; *Conservation of Timber Buildings*; *Surveying Historic Buildings*; *English Heritage Directory of Building Limes*; *Heritage, Sands and Aggregates*; *Journal of Architectural Conservation* (3 issues yearly). 6 titles a year. Unsolicited mss, synopses and ideas welcome.

Dorling Kindersley Ltd

Part of the Penguin Group, 80 Strand, London WC2R 0RL
☎020 7010 3000 Fax 020 7010 6060
www.dk.com

Chief Executive *Anthony Forbes Watson*
Managing Director *Andrew Welham*
Publisher *Christopher Davis*

Founded 1974. Packager and publisher of illustrated non-fiction: cookery, crafts, gardening, health, travel guides, atlases, natural history and children's information and fiction. Launched a US imprint in 1991 and an Australian imprint in 1997. Acquired Henderson Publishing in 1995 and was purchased by Pearson plc for £311 million in 2000.

DIVISIONS Adult: **Travel/Reference** Publisher *Douglas Amrine*; **General/Lifestyle** Publisher *John Roberts*. Children's: **Reference** Publisher *Miriam Farby*; **PreSchool/Primary** Publisher *Sophie Mitchell*. IMPRINTS **Ladybird**; **Ladybird Audio**; **Funfax**; **Eyewitness Guides**; **Eyewitness Travel Guides**. TITLES *BMA*

Complete Family Health Encyclopedia; RHS A–Z Encyclopedia of Garden Plants; Children's Illustrated Encyclopedia; The Way Things Work. Unsolicited synopses/ideas for books welcome.

Authors' Rating A much slimmed version of the old DK is heavily dependent on 'soft learning' products for education markets. The aim is to make Dorling Kindersley products distinctive against low priced rivals and retailers' own brand product, not to mention the Internet. Most titles are team efforts with writers and illustrators working closely with an in-house editor.

Doubleday
See **Transworld Publishers**

Doubleday Children's Books
See **The Random House Group Ltd**

Drake Educational Associates
St Fagans Road, Fairwater, Cardiff CF5 3AE
☎029 2056 0333 Fax 029 2956 0313
✉ info@drakeed.com
www.drakeed.com

Managing Director *R.G. Drake*

Literacy, phonics and language development games and activities. Ideas and scripts in these fields welcome. Also resources for subject areas in the primary school and modern languages at KS2.

Dref Wen
28 Church Road, Whitchurch, Cardiff
CF14 2EA
☎029 2061 7860 Fax 029 2061 0507
✉ gwilym@drefwen.com

Chairman *R. Boore*
Managing Director *G. Boore*

Founded 1970. Publishes Welsh language and bilingual children's books, Welsh and English educational books for Welsh learners.
ROYALTIES annually.

Gerald Duckworth & Co. Ltd
First Floor, 90–93 Cowcross Street, London
EC1M 6BF
☎020 7490 7300 Fax 020 7490 0080
✉ info@duckworth-publishers.co.uk
www.ducknet.co.uk

Managing Director *Peter Mayer*
Editorial Director (General) *Dan Hind*
Editorial Director (Academic) *Deborah Blake*
Approx. Annual Turnover £2 million

Founded 1898 by Gerald Duckworth. Original publishers of Virginia Woolf. Other early authors include Hilaire Belloc, John Galsworthy, D.H. Lawrence and George Orwell. Duckworth is a general trade publisher whose authors include John Bayley, Mary Warnock, Joan Bakewell and J.J. Connolly. In addition to its trade list, Duckworth has a strong academic division. Acquired by Peter Mayer in 2003.

IMPRINTS/DIVISIONS **Bristol Classical Press** Classical texts and modern languages; **Ardis** Russian literature; **Duckworth Academic**; **Duckworth General**. No unsolicited mss; synopses and sample chapters only. Enclose s.a.e. or return postage for response/return.

ROYALTIES twice-yearly at first, annually thereafter.

Dunedin Academic Press Ltd
Hudson House, 8 Albany Street, Edinburgh
EH1 3QB
☎0131 473 2397 Fax 01250 870920
✉ mail@dunedinacademicpress.co.uk
www.dunedinacademicpress.co.uk

Managing Director *Anthony Kinahan*

Founded 2001. Publishes academic and serious general non-fiction. Considerable experience in academic and professional publishing. 8 titles in 2005. Not interested in science (other than earth sciences), fiction or children's. Check website for active subject areas. No unsolicited mss. Synopses and ideas welcome. Approach first in writing outlining proposal and identifying market.

ROYALTIES annually.

Ebury Press/Ebury Publishing
See **The Random House Group Ltd**

Economist Books
See **Profile Books**

Eden
See **Transworld Publishers**

Edinburgh University Press
22 George Square, Edinburgh EH8 9LF
☎0131 650 4218 Fax 0131 662 0053
www.eup.ed.ac.uk

Chairman *Timothy Rix*
Chief Executive *Timothy Wright*
Deputy Chief Executive/Head of Book
   Publishing *Jackie Jones*
Senior Editor *Nicola Carr*

Publishes academic and scholarly books (and journals): film and media studies, gender studies, geography, history – ancient, classical, medieval and modern – Islamic studies, linguistics, literary

criticism, sociology and social theory, philosophy, politics, Scottish studies, theology and religious studies. About 100 titles a year.
ROYALTIES annually.

Egmont UK Limited
239 Kensington High Street, London W8 6SA
☎020 7761 3500 Fax 020 7761 3510
www.egmont.co.uk
Vice President/UK General Manager *Robert McMenemy*
Director of Egmont Press *Cally Poplak*
Director of Egmont Publishing *David Riley*
Approx. Annual Turnover £39 million

Part of the Egmont Group (Copenhagen), Egmont Press publishes children's fiction and picture books, while Egmont Publishing publishes classic and contemporary characters, learning and colour & activity. TITLES *Thomas the Tank Engine; Winnie the Pooh; A Series of Unfortunate Events; The Wind on Fire* trilogy. About 500 titles a year. Synopses and sample chapters welcome; approach in writing with s.a.e. marked for the attention of 'The Reader'. 'We regret that we are unable to return unsolicited material without s.a.e.'

Authors' Rating The fourth largest children's book publishing group in the UK, Egmont plans to move into animated books.

Eland Publishing Ltd
Third Floor, 61 Exmouth Market, London EC1R 4QL
☎020 7833 0762 Fax 020 7833 4434
✉ info@travelbooks.co.uk
www.travelbooks.co.uk
Directors *Rose Baring, John Hatt, Barnaby Rogerson*
Approx. Annual Turnover £250,000

Eland reprints classics of travel literature with a backlist of 60 titles, including *Naples '44* Norman Lewis; *Travels with Myself and Another* Martha Gelhorn; *Portrait of a Turkish Family* Irfan Orga; *Jigsaw* Sybille Bedford. No unsolicited mss. Postcards and e-mails welcome.
ROYALTIES annually.

Element
See **HarperCollins Publishers Ltd**

11:9
See **Neil Wilson Publishing Ltd**

Edward Elgar Publishing Ltd
Glensanda House, Montpellier Parade, Cheltenham GL50 1UA
☎01242 226934 Fax 01242 262111
✉ info@e-elgar.co.uk
www.e-elgar.com
Managing Director *Edward Elgar*

Founded 1986. International publisher in economics, the environment, public policy, business and management and law. TITLES *Who's Who in Economics* (3rd ed.); *Handbook of Environmental and Resource Economics; Who's Who in the Management Sciences.* 272 titles in 2005. No unsolicited mss; synopses and ideas in the subject areas listed above welcome. Approach by letter or e-mail; no telephone inquiries.

Elliot Right Way Books
Kingswood Buildings, Lower Kingswood, Tadworth KT20 6TD
☎01737 832202 Fax 01737 830311
✉ info@right-way.co.uk
www.right-way.co.uk
Managing Directors *A. Clive Elliot, Malcolm G. Elliot*

Founded 1946 by Andrew G. Elliot. Publishes paperback how-to and educative titles on an unlimited variety of home reference, indoor and outdoor leisure hobbies and pursuits, careers and business. Subjects include cookery, wine, family financial and legal matters, public speaking, weddings, jokes, parenting, etiquette, English skills, driving, fishing, horse riding, drawing, music, puzzles, crosswords and quizzes, job seeking, running your own company.
IMPRINTS **Right Way** Instructional paperbacks in B format for the most popular subjects; **Right Way Plus** Larger C format for more specialised subjects; **Clarion** B format for promotional/ultra low-price range. Unsolicited mss, synopses and ideas for books welcome.
ROYALTIES annually.

Elliott & Thompson
27 John Street, London WC1N 2BX
☎020 7831 5013 Fax 020 7831 5011
www.elliottthompson.com
Publishers *David Elliott, Brad Thompson*
Approx. Annual Turnover £92,000

Founded 2001. Publishes literary fiction, biography, belles lettres, reprints of classic male writers. 15 titles in 2005. New proposals welcome (send synopsis and sample pages initially) but s.a.e. essential.

Aidan Ellis Publishing
Whinfield, Herbert Road, Salcombe TQ8 8HN
☎01548 842755

✉ mail@aidanellispublishing.co.uk
www.aepub.demon.co.uk

Partners/Editorial Heads *Lucinda Ellis, Aidan Ellis*

Founded in 1971. Specialises in general trade books and non-fiction. TITLES *The Royal Gardens in Windsor Great Park* Charles Lyte; *Trees For Your Garden* Roy Lancaster; *Pesca* Ian B. Hart; *The Bird Table Book* Tony Soper; *Seahorses* Plymouth Marine Aquarium. Ideas and synopses welcome (return postage, please).

ROYALTIES twice-yearly.

Elm Publications/Training
(wholly owned subsidiary of **Elm Consulting Ltd**)

Seaton House, Kings Ripton, Huntingdon PE28 2NJ

☎01487 773254

✉ sritchie@elm-training.co.uk
www.elm-training.co.uk

Managing Director *Sheila Ritchie*

Founded 1977. Publishes textbooks, teaching aids, educational resources and educational software in the fields of business and management for adult learners. Books and teaching/training resources are generally commissioned to meet specific business, management and other syllabuses. 'We seek good training materials for business/management, especially tested and proven.' About 30 titles a year. Ideas are welcome; initial approach by post or e-mail with outline, or by a brief telephone call.

ROYALTIES annually.

Elsevier Ltd

The Boulevard, Langford Lane, Kidlington, Oxford OX5 1GB

☎01865 843000 Fax 01865 843010
www.elsevier.com

Managing Director *Anna Moon* (Oxford)
CEO, Science & Technology (books & journals) *Herman van Campenhout*

Parent company Reed Elsevier, Amsterdam. Now incorporates Pergamon Press and Harcourt Publishers International. Publishes academic and professional reference books, scientific, technical and medical books, journals, CD-ROMs and magazines. IMPRINTS **Academic Press; Architectural Press; Butterworth Heinemann; Digital Press; Elsevier; Elsevier Advanced Technology; Focal Press; Gulf Professional Press; JAI; Made Simple Books; Morgan Kauffman; Newnes; North-Holland.**

DIVISION **Elsevier (Health Sciences)** 32 Jamestown Road, London NW1 7BY ☎020 7424 4200 Fax 020 7483 2293 www.elsevier-health.com CEO Health Sciences (Books & Journals) *Brian Nairn*, Managing Director (UK & Netherlands) *Mary Ging* Publishes scientific, technical, medical books and journals. IMPRINTS **Baillière Tindall; Churchill Livingstone; Mosby; Pergamon; Saunders.** No unsolicited mss, but synopses and project proposals welcome.

ROYALTIES annually.

Emissary Publishing

PO Box 33, Bicester OX26 4ZZ
☎01869 323447

Editorial Director *Val Miller*

Founded 1992. Publishes mainly humorous paperback books including the complete set of Peter Pook novels; no poetry or children's. No unsolicited mss or synopses.

ROYALTIES twice-yearly.

Emma Treehouse Ltd

2nd Floor, The Old Brewhouse, Lower Charlton Trading Estate, Shepton Mallet BA4 5QE
☎01749 330529 Fax 01749 330544
✉ richard.powell4@virgin.net
www.emmatreehouse.com

Co-Directors *Richard Powell, David Bailey*
Approx. Annual Turnover £1 million

Founded 1992. Publishes children's pre-school novelty books. No mss. Illustrations, synopses and ideas for books welcome; write in the first instance.

FEES paid; no royalties.

Empiricus Books
See **Janus Publishing Company Ltd**

English Heritage (Publishing)

Kemble Drive, Swindon SN2 2GZ
☎01793 414497 Fax 01793 414769
www.english-heritage.org.uk

Head of Publishing *Rob Richardson*
Commercial Publishing Manager *Adèle Campbell*
Publishing Manager *Robin Taylor*

English Heritage's publishing programme is divided into two streams: commercial (titles commissioned to generate revenue) and not-for-profit, reflecting the organisation's academic and specialist publishing. 30 titles a year. 'All titles relate directly to the work of the organisation, so we do not accept unsolicited material.'

Enitharmon Press

26B Caversham Road, London NW5 2DU
☎020 7482 5967 Fax 020 7284 1787
✉ books@enitharmon.co.uk
www.enitharmon.co.uk

Director *Stephen Stuart-Smith*

Founded 1967. An independent company with an enterprising editorial policy, Enitharmon has established itself as one of Britain's leading literary presses. Patron of 'the new and the neglected', Enitharmon also prides itself on the success of its collaborations between writers and artists, now published by its associate company, **Enitharmon Editions**. Publishes poetry, literary criticism, fiction, art and photography. TITLES *Collected Poems* Alan Brownjohn; *The Apple That Astonished Paris* Billy Collins; *The Cut of the Light* Jeremy Hooker; *A Cypress Walk* Alun Lewis; *Thirteen Ways of Looking at Rillie* Edwin Morgan. No unsolicited mss.

ROYALTIES according to contract.

Epworth

c/o Methodist Publishing House, 4 John Wesley Road, Werrington, Peterborough PE4 6ZP
☎01733 325002 Fax 01733 384180
✉ comm.editor@mph.org.uk
www.mph.org.uk
www.scm-canterburypress.co.uk

Chairman *The Revd. Michael Townsend*
Head of Publishing *Dr Natalie K. Watson*

Publishes Christian books only: philosophy, theology, biblical studies, pastoralia, social concern and Methodist studies. No fiction, poetry or children's. About 12 titles a year. Unsolicited mss, synopses and ideas welcome; send sample chapter and contents with covering letter and s.a.e.

ROYALTIES annually.

The Erotic Print Society

17 Harwood Road, London SW6 4QP
☎020 7736 5800 Fax 020 7736 6330
✉ eros@eroticprints.org
www.eroticprints.org

Managing Director *Mr J. Maclean*

Publishes books of erotic art and photography and erotic literature. Unsolicited material accepted but approach in writing in the first instance with a summary or first chapter.

Essential Thinkers

See **CRW Publishing Ltd**

EuroCrime

See **Arcadia Books**

Euromonitor International

60–61 Britton Street, London EC1M 5UX
☎020 7251 8024 Fax 020 7608 3149
www.euromonitor.com

Chairman *R.N. Senior*
Managing Director *T.J. Fenwick*
Approx. Annual Turnover £20 million

Founded 1972. International business information publisher specialising in library and professional reference books, market reports, electronic databases. Publishes business reference, market analysis and information directories only. DIVISIONS **Market Analysis** *A. Irwin*; **Reference Books & Directories** *S. Holmes*. About 1000 titles a year.

PAYMENT is generally by flat fee.

Evans Brothers Ltd

2A Portman Mansions, Chiltern Street, London W1U 6NR
☎020 7487 0920 Fax 020 7487 0921
✉ sales@evansbrothers.co.uk
www.evansbooks.co.uk

Managing Director *Stephen Pawley*
International Publishing Director *Brian Jones*
UK Publisher *Su Swallow*
Approx. Annual Turnover £4.5 million

Founded 1908 by Robert and Edward Evans. Publishes UK children's and educational books, and educational books for Africa, the Caribbean and Latin America. IMPRINTS **Cherrytree Books**; **Zero to Ten**. OVERSEAS ASSOCIATES in Kenya, Cameroon, Sierra Leone; Evans Bros (Nigeria Publishers) Ltd. About 160 titles a year.

ROYALTIES annually.

Everyman

See **The Orion Publishing Group Ltd**

Everyman Chess

See **Gloucester Publishers Plc**

Everyman's Library

Northburgh House, 10 Northburgh Street, London EC1V 0AT
☎020 7566 6350 Fax 020 7490 3708
✉ books@everyman.uk.com

Publisher *David Campbell*
Approx. Annual Turnover £3.5 million

Founded 1906. Publishes hardback classics of world literature, pocket poetry anthologies, children's books and travel guides. Publishes no new titles apart from poetry anthologies; only classics (no new authors). AUTHORS include Bulgakov, Bellow, Borges, Heller, Marquez,

Nabokov, Naipaul, Orwell, Rushdie, Updike, Waugh and Wodehouse. No unsolicited mss. ROYALTIES annually.

University of Exeter Press

Reed Hall, Streatham Drive, Exeter EX4 4QR
☎01392 263066 Fax 01392 263064
✉ uep@exeterpress.co.uk
www.exeterpress.co.uk

Publisher *Simon Baker*

Founded 1956. Publishes academic books: archaeology, classical studies and ancient history, history, maritime studies, English literature (especially medieval), European studies, modern languages and literature, film history, performance studies, Arabic studies and books on Exeter and the South West. IMPRINT **Bristol Phoenix Press** Commissioning Editor *John Betts* Classics and ancient history. About 30 titles a year. Proposals welcomed in the above subject areas.
ROYALTIES annually.

Exley Publications Ltd

16 Chalk Hill, Watford WD19 4BG
☎01923 248328 Fax 01923 800440
✉ editorial@exleypublications.co.uk
www.helenexleygiftbooks.com

Editorial Director *Helen Exley*

Founded 1976. Independent family company. Publishes giftbooks, quotation anthologies and humour. No submissions, please.

Expert Books

See **Transworld Publishers**

Eyewitness Guides/ Eyewitness Travel Guides

See **Dorling Kindersley Ltd**

Faber & Faber Ltd

3 Queen Square, London WC1N 3AU
☎020 7465 0045 Fax 020 7465 0034
www.faber.co.uk

Chief Executive *Stephen Page*
Approx. Annual Turnover £12.97 million

Geoffrey Faber founded the company in the 1920s, with T.S. Eliot as an early recruit to the board. The original list was based on contemporary poetry and plays (the distinguished backlist includes Eliot, Auden and MacNeice). Publishes poetry and drama, children's, fiction, film, music, politics, biography. DIVISIONS **Fiction** *Lee Brackstone, Hannah Griffiths, Angus Cargill* AUTHORS P.D. James, Peter Carey, Rachel Cusk, Giles Foden, Michael Frayn, Tobias Hill, Kazuo Ishiguro, Barbara Kingsolver, Milan Kundera, Hanif Kureishi, John Lanchester, John McGahern, Rohinton Mistry, Lorrie Moore, Andrew O'Hagan, DBC Pierre, Jane Smiley; **Children's** *Suzy Jenvey, Julia Wells* AUTHORS Philip Ardagh, Terry Deary, Ricky Gervais, Russell Stannard, G.P. Taylor; **Film** *Walter Donohue* and **Plays** *Dinah Wood* AUTHORS Samuel Beckett, Alan Bennett, David Hare, Brian Friel, Patrick Marber, Harold Pinter, Tom Stoppard, Woody Allen, John Boorman, Joel and Ethan Coen, John Hodge, Martin Scorsese, Quentin Tarantino; **Music** *Belinda Matthews* AUTHORS Alfred Brendel, Humphrey Burton, Rupert Christiansen, Nicholas Kenyon, Richard Morrison, Susan Tomes, John Tyrrell, Elizabeth Wilson; **Poetry** *Paul Keegan* AUTHORS Simon Armitage, Douglas Dunn, Seamus Heaney, Ted Hughes, Paul Muldoon, Tom Paulin; **Non-fiction** *Neil Belton, Julian Loose* AUTHORS John Carey, Simon Garfield, John Gray, Jan Morris, Francis Spufford, Frances Stonor Saunders, Jenny Uglow.
ROYALTIES twice-yearly.

Authors' Rating Recording its best ever year, Faber has experienced something of a rebirth with authors benefiting from more energetic and imaginative marketing.

Facet Publishing

7 Ridgmount Street, London WC1E 7AE
☎020 7255 0590/0505 (text phone)
Fax 020 7255 0591
✉ info@facetpublishing.co.uk
www.facetpublishing.co.uk

Managing Director *John Woolley*

Publishing arm of **CILIP: The Chartered Institute of Library and Information Professionals** (formerly the Library Association). Publishes library and information science, monographs, reference, IT training materials and bibliography aimed at library and information professionals. IMPRINTS **Library Association Publishing; Clive Bingley Books; Facet Publishing**. Over 200 titles in print, including *The New Walford* and *AACR2*. 25–30 titles a year. Unsolicited mss, synopses and ideas welcome provided material falls firmly within the company's specialist subject areas.
ROYALTIES annually.

Fernhurst Books

Duke's Path, High Street, Arundel BN18 9AJ
☎01903 882277 Fax 01903 882715
✉ sales@fernhurstbooks.co.uk
www.fernhurstbooks.co.uk

Chairman/Managing Director *Tim Davison*

Founded 1979. Books for people who love

watersports. Publishes practical, highly-illustrated handbooks on sailing and watersports. TITLES *Laser Book; Rules in Practice; Wind Strategy; Weather at Sea; Simple Boat Maintenance; Electrics Afloat.* No unsolicited mss; synopses and ideas welcome. ROYALTIES twice-yearly.

David Fickling Books
See **The Random House Group Ltd**

Findhorn Press Ltd
305A The Park, Findhorn IV36 3TE
☎01309 690582   Fax 01309 690036
✉ info@findhornpress.com
www.findhornpress.com
Directors *Karin Bogliolo, Thierry Bogliolo*
Founded 1971. Publishes mind, body, spirit, New Age and healing. 24 titles in 2005. Unsolicited synopses and ideas via e-mail only if they come within Findhorn's subject areas. No children's books, fiction or poetry. ROYALTIES twice-yearly.

Firefly Publishing
See **Helter Skelter Publishing**

First & Best in Education Ltd
Unit K, Earlstrees Court, Earlstrees Road, Corby NN17 4HH
☎01536 399005   Fax 01536 399012
✉ editorial@firstandbest.co.uk
www.firstandbest.co.uk
www.shop.firstandbest.co.uk
Publisher *Tony Attwood*
Editor *Anne Cockburn*
Publishers of over 1000 educational books of all types for all ages of children and for parents and teachers. All books are published as being suitable for photocopying and/or as electronic books. 'Looking for new authors of educational books all the time. No fiction, please.' TITLES *Raising Grades Through Study Skills; Business Sponsorship of Secondary Schools; Policy Documents for Day Nurseries and Nursery Units.* IMPRINT **School Improvement Reports.** In the first instance check the website or send s.a.e. for details of requirements and current projects to *Anne Cockburn*, Editorial Dept. at the address above. ROYALTIES twice-yearly.

Fitzgerald Publishing
89 Ermine Road, Ladywell, London SE13 7JJ
☎020 8690 0597
✉ fitzgeraldbooks@yahoo.co.uk
Managing Editors *Tim Fitzgerald, Michael Fitzgerald*

General Editor *Andrew Smith*
Founded 1974. Specialises in scientific studies of insects and spiders. TITLES *The Tarantula; Keeping Spiders and Insects in Captivity; Tarantulas of the USA; Scorpions of Medical Importance* (books) and *Earth Tigers – Tarantulas of Borneo; Desert Tarantulas* (TV/video documentaries). 1–2 titles a year. Unsolicited mss, synopses and ideas for books welcome. Also considers video scripts for video documentaries.

Fitzjames Press
See **Motor Racing Publications**

Fitzwarren Publishing
51 Nicolson Drive, Leighton Buzzard LU7 4HQ
☎01525 384433
✉ pen2paper@btopenworld.com
Contact *Julie Stretton*
Publishes two or three books a year, mainly layman's handbooks on legal matters. All books follow a rigid 128-page format. TITLES *The E-Commerce Handbook; Landlord & Tenants Handbook; The Election Handbook; Licensing Handbook; Employment Handbook.* Welcomes written approaches and synopses from prospective authors who, though not necessarily legally qualified, are expected to know their subject as well as a lawyer would. No unsolicited mss. ROYALTIES twice-yearly.

Five Star
See **Serpent's Tail**

Floris Books
15 Harrison Gardens, Edinburgh EH11 1SH
☎0131 337 2372   Fax 0131 347 9919
✉ floris@florisbooks.co.uk
www.florisbooks.co.uk
Managing Director *Christian Maclean*
Editors *Christopher Moore, Gale Winskill*
Approx. Annual Turnover £350,000
Founded 1977. Publishes books related to the Steiner movement, including The Christian Community, as well as arts & crafts, children's (including fiction with a Scottish theme), history, religious, science, social questions and Celtic studies. No unsolicited mss. Synopses and ideas for books welcome, except for children's picture books (not accepted). ROYALTIES annually.

Focal Press
See **Elsevier Ltd**

Folens Limited

Apex Business Centre, Boscombe Road,
Dunstable LU5 4RL
☎0870 609 1237 Fax 0870 609 1236
✉ folens@folens.com
www.folens.com

Chairman *Dirk Folens*
Managing Director *Malcolm Watson*

Founded 1987. A leading educational publisher.
IMPRINTS **Folens**; **Belair**. About 150 titles a
year. Unsolicited mss, synopses and ideas for
educational books welcome.
ROYALTIES annually.

Fort Publishing Ltd

Old Belmont House, 12 Robsland Avenue, Ayr
KA7 2RW
☎01292 880693 Fax 01292 270134
✉ fortpublishing@aol.com
www.fortpublishing.co.uk

Chairman *Agnes Jane McCarroll*
Managing Director *James McCarroll*
Approx. Annual Turnover £95,000

Founded 1999. Publishes general non-fiction,
history, sport, crime and local interest. TITLES
Glasgow Then and Now; *Great Hull Stories*; *Evil
Scotland*; *Ten Days That Shook Rangers*. 9 titles in
2005. No unsolicited mss; send synopses and
ideas for books by post or e-mail.
ROYALTIES twice-yearly.

Foulsham Publishers

The Publishing House, Bennetts Close, Slough
SL1 5AP
☎01753 526769 Fax 01753 535003
✉ reception@foulsham.com
www.foulsham.com

Chairman/Managing Director *B.A.R. Belasco*
Approx. Annual Turnover £2.5 million

Founded 1819 and now one of the few remaining independent family companies to survive
takeover. Publishes non-fiction on most subjects including lifestyle, travel guides, family reference, cookery, diet, health, DIY, business, self
improvement, self development, astrology,
dreams, MBS. No fiction. IMPRINT **Quantum**
Mind, body and spirit titles. TITLES *Classic 1000
Cocktails*; *A Brit's Guide to Orlando and Walt
Disney World 2006*; *Old Moore's Almanack*;
Raphael's Astrological Ephemeris. Around 60 titles
a year. Unsolicited mss, synopses and ideas welcome – in hard copy.
ROYALTIES twice-yearly.

Fountain Press

Newpro UK Ltd., Old Sawmills Road,
Faringdon SN7 7DS
☎01367 242411 Fax 01367 241124
✉ sales@newprouk.co.uk
www.newprouk.co.uk

Publisher *C.J. Coleman*
Approx. Annual Turnover £800,000

Founded 1923 when it was part of the
Rowntree Trust Social Service. Owned by the
British Electric Traction Group until 1982
when it was bought out by H.M. Ricketts.
Acquired by Newpro UK Ltd in July 2000.
Publishes mainly photography and natural his-
tory. TITLES *Photography and Digital 'Workshop'*;
Antique and Collectable Cameras; *Camera Manual*
(series). About 2 titles a year. Unsolicited mss
and synopses welcome.
ROYALTIES twice-yearly.

Authors' Rating Highly regarded for production values, Fountain has the reputation for
involving authors in every stage of the publishing process.

Fourth Estate
See **HarperCollins Publishers Ltd**

Free Association Books Ltd

PO Box 37664, London NW7 2XU
☎020 8906 0396 Fax 020 8906 0006
✉ info@fabooks.com
www.fabooks.com

Managing Director/Publisher *T.E. Brown*

Publishes psychoanalysis and psychotherapy,
psychology, cultural studies, sexuality and gen-
der, women's studies, applied social sciences.
TITLES *Drug Use and Cultural Context* eds. Ross
Coomber and Nigel South; *Skin Disease* Ann
Maguire; *Caring for the Dying at Home* Gill
Pharoah; *A History of Group Study and
Psychodynamic Organizations* Amy L. Fraher.
Always send a letter in the first instance accom-
panied by a book outline. OVERSEAS ASSOCI-
ATES ISBS, USA; Astam, Australia.
ROYALTIES twice-yearly.

The Free Press
See **Simon & Schuster UK Ltd**

W.H. Freeman

Palgrave, Houndsmill, Basingstoke RG21 6XS
☎01256 329242 Fax 01256 330688
www.palgrave.com

President *Elizabeth Widdicombe* (New York)
Editorial Director *Margaret Hewinson*

Following integration into the BFW (Bedford, Freeman, Worth) College Group, USA, W.H. Freeman now publishes academic educational and textbooks in biochemistry, biology and zoology, chemistry, economics, mathematics and statistics, natural history, neuroscience, palaeontology, physics. W.H. Freeman's editorial office is in New York (Basingstoke is a sales and marketing office only) but unsolicited mss can go through Basingstoke. Those which are obviously unsuitable will be sifted out; the rest will be forwarded to New York.
ROYALTIES annually.

Samuel French Ltd
52 Fitzroy Street, London W1T 5JR
☎020 7387 9373 Fax 020 7387 2161
✉ theatre@samuelfrench-london.co.uk
www.samuelfrench-london.co.uk

Chairman *Charles R. Van Nostrand*
Managing Director *Vivien Goodwin*

Founded 1830 with the object of acquiring acting rights and publishing plays. Publishes plays only. About 50 titles a year. Unsolicited mss considered only after initial submission of synopsis and specimen scene. Such material should be addressed to the Performing Rights Department.
ROYALTIES twice-yearly for books; performing royalties monthly, subject to a minimum amount.

Authors' Rating Thrives on the amateur dramatic societies who are forever in need of play texts. Editorial advisers give serious attention to new material but a high proportion of the list is staged before it goes into print. New writers are advised to try one-act plays, much in demand by the amateur dramatic societies but rarely turned out by established playwrights.

Friday Books
See **The Friday Project Ltd**

The Friday Project Ltd
83 Victoria Street, London SW1H 0HW
☎020 7078 6456 Fax 020 7078 6030
✉ mail@thefridayproject.co.uk
www.thefridayproject.co.uk

Chairman *Anthony Cheetham*
Joint Managing Directors *Paul Carr, Clare Christian*
Approx. Annual Turnover £1.8 million

Founded in 2005, The Friday Project specialises in 'turning the best of the Web into the finest of books'. Publishes fiction and non-fiction.

IMPRINT **Friday Books** Publishing Director *Clare Christian* TITLES *London by London: The Insiders' Guide; The Holy Moly! Rules of Modern Life; 2005 Blogged: Dispatches from the Blogosphere* ed. Tim Worstall. 30 titles in 2006. Unsolicited mss, synopses and ideas for books welcome; approach by e-mail. No academic books.
ROYALTIES twice-yearly.

David Fulton Publishers Ltd
The Chiswick Centre, 414 Chiswick High Road, London W4 5TF
☎020 8996 3610 Fax 020 8996 3622
✉ mail@fultonpublishers.co.uk
www.fultonpublishers.co.uk

Owner *Granada Learning*
Senior Publisher *Tracey Alcock*
Approx. Annual Turnover £2.4 million

Founded 1987. Publishes books for trainee and working teachers at all levels of the curriculum (foundation stage to post compulsory), with particular emphasis on special educational needs (SEN) and inclusion. Special educational needs books also published in collaboration with the National Association for Special Educational Needs (NASEN); some overlap into other areas of health and social care, therapy, educational psychology, and speech and language therapy. A growing list of early years books for pre-school and nursery staff. About 100 titles a year. No unsolicited mss; synopses and ideas for books welcome.
ROYALTIES twice-yearly.

Funfax
See **Dorling Kindersley Ltd**

Gaia Books
See **Octopus Publishing Group**

J. Garnet Miller
See **Cressrelles Publishing Co. Ltd**

Garnet Publishing Ltd
8 Southern Court, South Street, Reading RG1 4QS
☎0118 959 7847 Fax 0118 959 7356
✉ enquiries@garnetpublishing.co.uk
www.garnetpublishing.co.uk

Editorial Manager *Emma G. Hawker*

Founded 1992 and purchased Ithaca Press in the same year. Publishes art, architecture, photography, archive photography, cookery, travel classics, comparative religion, Islamic culture and history, foreign fiction in translation. Core subjects are Middle Eastern but list is rapidly expanding to be more general.

IMPRINTS **Garnet Publishing** TITLES *Simply Lebanese*; *The Art and Architecture of Islamic Cairo*. **Ithaca Press** Specialises in post-graduate academic works on the Middle East, political science and international relations TITLES *The Making of the Modern Gulf States*; *The Palestinian Exodus*; *French Imperialism in Syria*; *Philby of Arabia*. About 20 titles a year. Unsolicited mss not welcome; write with outline and ideas first plus current c.v.

ROYALTIES twice-yearly.

Geddes & Grosset
David Dale House, New Lanark ML11 9DJ
☎01555 665000 Fax 01555 665694

Publishers *Ron Grosset, R. Michael Miller*
Approx. Annual Turnover £3 million

Founded 1989. Publisher of children's and reference books. Unsolicited mss, synopses and ideas welcome. No adult fiction.

GEE
See **Sweet & Maxwell Group**

The Geological Society Publishing House
Unit 7, Brassmill Enterprise Centre, Brassmill Lane, Bath BA1 3JN
☎01225 445046 Fax 01225 442836
✉ sales@geolsoc.org.uk or enquiries@geolsoc.org.uk
www.geolsoc.org.uk

Commissioning Editor *Angharad Hills*

Publishing arm of the Geological Society which was founded in 1807. Publishes postgraduate texts in the earth sciences. 30 titles a year. Unsolicited synopses and ideas welcome.

Stanley Gibbons Publications
7 Parkside, Christchurch Road, Ringwood BH24 3SH
☎01425 472363 Fax 01425 470247
www.stanleygibbons.com

Chairman *P. Fraser*
Editorial Head *H. Jefferies*

Long-established force in the philatelic world with 150 years in the business. Publishes philatelic reference catalogues and handbooks. Reference works relating to other areas of collecting may be considered. TITLES *Stanley Gibbons British Commonwealth Stamp Catalogue*; *Stamps of the World*. Foreign catalogues include

Japan and Korea, Portugal and Spain, Germany, Middle East, Balkans, China. Monthly publication: *Gibbons Stamp Monthly* (see entry under *Magazines*). www.collectorcafe.com – Internet site covering full range of collectables – editorial input always considered. About 20 titles a year. Unsolicited mss, synopses and ideas welcome.

ROYALTIES by negotiation.

Robert Gibson and Sons (Glasgow)
See **Hodder Gibson**

Gibson Square
47 Lonsdale Square, London N1 1EW
☎020 7096 1100 Fax 020 7993 2214
✉ info@gibsonsquare.com
www.gibsonsquare.com

Chairman *Martin Rynja*

Founded 2001. Publishes exclusively non-fiction: biography, current affairs, politics, cultural criticism, psychology, history, travel, art history, philosophy. Books must have high publicity profile. IMPRINTS **Gibson Square** TITLES *Londonistan* Melanie Phillips; *House of Bush House of Saud* Craig Unger; *A Dictionary of Idiocy* Stephen Bayley; *More France Please* Helena Frith Powell. **New Editions** Reprints TITLES *The Art of Always Being Right* Schopenhauer; *Nancy Mitford* Harold Acton. Welcomes unsolicited mss, synopses and ideas. Send self-addressed, franked, return envelope. No fiction.

ROYALTIES twice-yearly.

Ginn & Co
See **Harcourt Education**

Gloucester Publishers Plc
10 Northburgh Street, London EC1V 0AT
☎020 7253 7887 Fax 020 7490 3708
✉ markbicknell@everyman.uk.com
www.everymanchess.com

Managing Director *Mark Bicknell*
Approx. Annual Turnover £1 million

Publishes exclusively academic and leisure books relating to chess. IMPRINT **Everyman Chess** TITLES *Garry Kasparov: My Great Predecessors, Vols 1–4*; *Play Winning Chess* Yasser Seirawan; *Art of Attack in Chess* Vladimir Vukovich. 31 titles in 2005. No unsolicited material.

ROYALTIES annually.

Godsfield Press
See **Octopus Publishing Group**

Gollancz
See **The Orion Publishing Group Limited**

Gomer Press/Gwasg Gomer
Llandysul Enterprise Park, Llandysul SA44 4JL
☎01559 363090   Fax 01559 363758
✉ gwasg@gomer.co.uk
www.gomer.co.uk

Chairman/Managing Director *J.E. Lewis*
Publishing Director *Mairwen Prys Jones*

Founded 1892. Publishes adult fiction and non-fiction, children's fiction and educational material in English and Welsh.

IMPRINTS **Gomer** *Bethan Mair, Bryan James* (adult books – Welsh), *Ceri Wyn Jones* (adult books – English), *Sioned Lleinau, Helen Evans, Rhiannon Davies* (children's books – Welsh). **Pont Books** *Viv Sayer* (children's books – English). 125 titles a year. Unsolicited mss welcome.
ROYALTIES twice-yearly.

Gower
See **Ashgate Publishing Ltd**

Graham-Cameron Publishing & Illustration
The Studio, 23 Holt Road, Sheringham NR26 8NB
☎01263 821333   Fax 01263 821334
✉ enquiry@graham-cameron-illustration.com
www.graham-cameron-illustration.com

Also at: 59 Redvers Road, Brighton BN2 4BF
☎01273 385890

Editorial Director *Mike Graham-Cameron*
Art Director *Helen Graham-Cameron*

Founded 1984 as a packaging operation. Publishes illustrated books for children and adults for institutions and business. TITLES *Up From the Country; In All Directions; The Holywell Story; Flashbacks; Let's Look at Dairying.* Has 37 contracted book illustrators concentrating on educational and children's books. *Absolutely no unsolicited mss.*
ROYALTIES annually.

Granta Books
2–3 Hanover Yard, Noel Road, London N1 8BE
☎020 7704 9776   Fax 020 7354 3469
www.granta.com

Editorial Director *George Miller*

Founded 1979. Acquired by **Portobello Books** in 2005. Publishes general non-fiction and some literary fiction. About 35 titles a year.

No unsolicited mss; synopses and sample chapters welcome.
ROYALTIES twice-yearly.

W. Green (Scotland)
See **Sweet & Maxwell Group**

Green Books
Foxhole, Dartington, Totnes TQ9 6EB
☎01803 863260   Fax 01803 863843
✉ edit@greenbooks.co.uk
www.greenbooks.co.uk

Chairman *Satish Kumar*
Publisher *John Elford*
Approx. Annual Turnover £500,000

Founded in 1987 with the support of a number of Green organisations. Closely associated with *Resurgence* magazine. Publishes high-quality books on a wide range of Green issues, including economics, politics and the practical application of Green thinking. No fiction or books for children. TITLES *The Organic Directory* ed. Clive Litchfield; *Timeless Simplicity* John Lane; *Allotment Gardening* Susan Berger. No unsolicited mss. Synopses and ideas welcome but check guidelines on the website in the first instance.
ROYALTIES twice-yearly.

Green Print
See **The Merlin Press Ltd**

Greenhill Books/ Lionel Leventhal Ltd
Park House, 1 Russell Gardens, London NW11 9NN
☎020 8458 6314   Fax 020 8905 5245
✉ L.Leventhal@greenhillbooks.com
www.greenhillbooks.com

Director *Michael Leventhal*

Founded 1984 by Lionel Leventhal (ex-Arms & Armour Press). Publishes aviation, military and naval books. Synopses and ideas for books welcome. No unsolicited mss.
ROYALTIES twice-yearly.

Gresham Books Ltd
46 Victoria Road, Summertown, Oxford OX2 7QD
☎01865 513582   Fax 01865 512718
✉ info@gresham-books.co.uk
www.gresham-books.co.uk

Managing Director *Paul Lewis*
Approx. Annual Turnover £350,000

A small specialist publishing house. Publishes hymn and service books for schools and churches, school histories, also craft-bound choir and orchestral folders and Records of Achievement. No unsolicited material but ideas welcome.

Grisewood & Dempsey
See **Kingfisher Publications Plc**

Grub Street
4 Rainham Close, London SW11 6SS
☎020 7924 3966/7738 1008
Fax 020 7738 1009
✉ post@grubstreet.co.uk
www.grubstreet.co.uk
Managing Director *John Davies*

Founded 1982. Publishes cookery, food and wine, military and aviation history books. About 20 titles a year. Unsolicited mss and synopses welcome in the above categories but please enclose return postage.
ROYALTIES twice-yearly.

Guardian/Observer Books
See **Atlantic Books**

Guild of Master Craftsman Publications Ltd
166 High Street, Lewes BN7 1XU
☎01273 477374 Fax 01273 402866
✉ pubs@thegmcgroup.com
www.thegmcgroup.com
Joint Managing Directors *J.A.J. Phillips, J.A.B. Phillips*
Managing Editor *Gerrie Purcell*

Founded 1974. Publishes woodworking, craft, photography and gardening books, magazines and videos; also books on dolls' houses and miniatures. IMPRINT **Photographers' Institute Press (PIP)** Launched in 2004. 39 titles in 2005 Unsolicited mss, synopses and ideas for books welcome. No fiction.
ROYALTIES twice-yearly.

Guinness World Records Ltd
338 Euston Road, London NW1 3BD
☎020 7891 4567 Fax 020 7891 4501
✉ info@guinnessrecords.com
www.guinnessworldrecords.com
Chief Operations Officer *Alistair Richards*

First published in 1955, the annual Guinness World Records book is published in more than 100 countries and 20 languages and is the highest-selling copyright book of all time, with more than 3 million copies sold annually across the globe. In addition to *Guinness World Records*

the company publishes the annual industry-standard volume *British Hit Singles & Albums*. Guinness World Records is part of HIT EntertainmentLtd. Contact from prospective researchers, editors and designers welcome.

Gulf Professional Press
See **Elsevier Ltd**

Gullane Children's Books
See **Pinwheel Limited**

Gwasg Carreg Gwalch
12 Iard yr Orsaf, Llanrwst LL26 0EH
☎01492 642031 Fax 01492 641502
✉ books@carreg-gwalch.co.uk
www.carreg-gwalch.co.uk
Managing Editor *Myrddin ap Dafydd*

Founded in 1980. Publishes Welsh language; English books of Welsh interest – history, folklore, guides and walks. About 90 titles a year. Unsolicited mss, synopses and ideas welcome if of Welsh interest.
ROYALTIES paid.

Hachette Children's Books
338 Euston Road, London NW1 3BH
☎020 7873 6000
Managing Director *Marlene Johnson*

Formed by the combining of Watts Publishing Group with Hodder Children's Books in April 2005. Publishes children's non-fiction, reference, information, gift, fiction, picture and novelty books and audio books. IMPRINTS **Hodder Children's Books** *Anne McNeil* Fiction, picture books, novelty, general non-fiction and audio. **Orchard Books** *Ann-Janine Murtagh* Fiction, picture and novelty books. **Franklin Watts** *Rachel Cooke* Non-fiction and information books. **Wayland** *Joyce Bentley* Non-fiction and information books.

Unsolicited material is not considered other than by referral or recommendation.
ROYALTIES twice-yearly.

Hachette-Livre
French publishing conglomerate which embraces **Chambers Harrap Publishers**, **Hodder Headline**, **Orion Publishing Group**, **Octopus Publishing Group**, **Little, Brown Book Group**. For further information, see entry under *European Publishers*.

Halban Publishers
22 Golden Square, London W1F 9JW
☎020 7437 9300 Fax 020 7437 9512

✉ books@halbanpublishers.com
www.halbanpublishers.com

Directors *Peter Halban, Martine Halban*

Founded 1986. Independent publisher. Publishes biography, autobiography and memoirs, history, literature and Judaica. 8–10 titles a year. No unsolicited material. Approach by letter in first instance.

ROYALTIES twice-yearly for first two years, thereafter annually in December.

Robert Hale Ltd

Clerkenwell House, 45–47 Clerkenwell Green, London EC1R 0HT
☎020 7251 2661   Fax 020 7490 4958
✉ enquire@halebooks.com

Chairman/Managing Director *John Hale*

Founded 1936. Family-owned company. Publishes adult fiction (but not interested in category romance or science fiction) and nonfiction. No specialist material (education, law, medical or scientific). Acquired **NAG Press Ltd** in 1993 with its list of horological, gemmological, jewellery and metalwork titles, and **J.A. Allen & Co.** in 1999 with its extensive list of horse and dog books (see entry). TITLES Non-fiction: *Artificial Gemstones* Michael O'Donoghue; *The DNA Detectives* W.J. Wall; *The Salmon Rivers of the North Highlands and Outer Hebrides* Andrew Graham-Stewart; *The Hidden Houses of Virginia Woolf and Vanessa Bell* Vanessa Curtis; *Samuel Beckett* John Minihan. Fiction: *The Tower* Simon Clark; *The Bonaparte Plot* Hugh McLeave; *The Longest Winter* Julie Harris; *Clemmie* John D. MacDonald. Over 250 titles a year. Unsolicited mss, synopses and ideas for books welcome.

ROYALTIES twice-yearly.

Authors' Rating Smiled upon in a Society of Authors survey on author relations, Robert Hale has carved out a profitable niche for popular non-fiction.

Halsgrove

Halsgrove House, Tiverton Business Park, Lower Moor Way, Tiverton EX16 6SS
☎01884 243242   Fax 01884 243325
✉ sales@halsgrove.com
www.halsgrove.com

Publisher *Simon Butler*

Founded in 1990 and now a leading publisher and distributor of regional books, DVDs and magazines. Publishes books of regional interest throughout the UK: local history (including the *Community History* series), biography, photography and art, mainly in hardback. Also a series of local interest magazines in southern England. No fiction or poetry. 150 titles in 2005. Unsolicited mss, synopses and ideas for books of regional interest welcome.

ROYALTIES annually.

Hambledon Continuum

See **The Continuum International Publishing Group Limited**

Hamish Hamilton

See **Penguin Group (UK)**

Hamlyn Octopus

See **Octopus Publishing Group**

Hammersmith Press Ltd

496 Fulham Palace Road, London SW6 6JD
☎020 7736 9132   Fax 020 7348 7521
✉ gmb@hammersmithpress.co.uk
www.hammersmithpress.co.uk

Managing Director *Georgina Bentliff*

Founded 2004. Publishes health, nutrition, diet, academic medicine, and memoirs related to medicine and health. TITLES *Chronic Fatigue Syndrome: A Natural Way to Treat ME* Prof. Basant K. Puri; *Suburban Shaman: Tales From Medicine's Front Line* Cecil Helman. 3 titles in 2005. No unsolicited mss; synopses and ideas for books welcome; approach by e-mail. No fiction or children's material.

ROYALTIES twice-yearly.

Harcourt Education

Halley Court, Jordan Hill, Oxford OX2 8EJ
☎01865 311366   Fax 01865 314641
www.harcourteducation.co.uk

CEO *Christopher Jones*

A member of the **Reed Elsevier Group plc**, Harcourt Education incorporates Heinemann Educational and Ginn in the UK; Greenwood Heinemann in the USA; Rigby Heinemann in Australia.

Heinemann Educational Fax 01865 314140 Textbooks, literature and other educational resources for primary and secondary school and further education. Mss, synopses and ideas welcome.

Ginn & Co Fax 01865 314189 Textbooks and other educational resources for primary and secondary schools. Managing Director *Stephen Fahey*.

ROYALTIES twice-yearly/annually, according to contract in all divisions.

Harlequin Mills & Boon Limited

Eton House, 18–24 Paradise Road, Richmond TW9 1SR
☎020 8288 2800 Fax 020 8288 2898
www.eharlequin.com
www.millsandboon.co.uk

Managing Director *Guy Hallowes*
Editorial Director *Karin Stoecker*
Approx. Annual Turnover £18.97 million

Founded 1908. Owned by the Canadian-based Torstar Group. Publishes a wide range of women's fiction including romantic novels.

IMPRINTS **Mills & Boon Modern Romance** *Tessa Shapcott* (50–55,000 words) Alpha males and attractive women swept up in intense emotions set against a backdrop of international locations, luxury and wealth; passion is guaranteed. **Mills & Boon Modern Extra** *Tessa Shapcott* (60,000 words) Delivers a feel-good experience, focusing on the kind of relationship that women aged 18 to 35 aspire to. Young characters in urban settings meet, flirt, share experiences, have great sex and fall in love, finally making a commitment that will bind them forever. Based around emotional issues, other concerns – e.g. jobs and friendships – are also touched upon and resolved in upbeat way. **Mills & Boon Tender Romance** *Bryony Green* (50–55,000 words) Contemporary upbeat and heroine-focused romance, driven by strongly emotional conflicts which are believable and relevant to today's women. Capturing the depth of emotion and sheer excitement of falling in love in a variety of international settings. **Mills & Boon Medical Romance** *Sheila Hodgson* (50–55,000 words) Modern medical practice provides a unique background to highly emotional contemporary romances. **Mills & Boon Historical Romance** *Linda Fildew* (80–95,000 words) Richly textured, emotionally intense historical novels covering a wide range of settings and periods from ancient civilisations up to and including the Second World War.

Over 600 titles a year. Other submissions: also accepting submissions in all general women's fiction genres (contemporary and historical) for longer series and single title imprints. Tip sheets and guidelines are available from the Mills & Boon or eHarlequin websites (see above) or Harlequin Mills & Boon Editorial Dept. (telephone or write sending s.a.e.). Agented and unagented submissions accepted. Send query letter, synopsis and first three chapters in the first instance.

Authors' Rating Sex has overtaken romance at M&B where the latest imprints allow writers' erotic imagination to run riot. But the staple M&B romance is still going strong providing a good income for writers who can adapt to the clearly defined M&B formula. Just think, M&B has a network of 12,000 authors worldwide and every title scores six-figure sales. But be warned. M&B gets 2000 unsolicited manuscripts a year. The latest initiative is an audio list growing at a rate of four new titles a month.

Harley Books

Martins, Great Horkesley, Colchester CO6 4AH
☎01206 271216 Fax 01206 271182
✉ harley@harleybooks.co.uk
www.harleybooks.com

Managing Director *Basil Harley*
Owners *B.H. & A. Harley*

Founded 1983. Natural history publishers specialising in entomological and botanical books. Mostly definitive, high-quality illustrated reference works. TITLES *The Moths and Butterflies of Great Britain and Ireland; Dragonflies of Europe; The Aurelian Legacy: British Butterflies and their Collectors; The Liverwort Flora of the British Isles; Maggots, Murder and Men: Memories and Reflections of a Forensic Entomologist; Freshwater Fishes in Britain. 58 titles.* No unsolicited material (no longer publishing new titles).

ROYALTIES twice-yearly in the first year, annually thereafter.

HarperCollins Publishers Ltd

77–85 Fulham Palace Road, London W6 8JB
☎020 8741 7070 Fax 020 8307 4440
www.harpercollins.co.uk

Also at: Westerhill Road, Bishopbriggs, Glasgow G64 2QT
☎0141 772 3200 Fax 0141 306 3119

Owner *News Corporation*
CEO/Publisher *Victoria Barnsley*
Approx. Annual Turnover £165.56 million (UK)

HarperCollins is one of the leading book publishers in the UK, with a wider range of books than any other publisher; from cutting-edge contemporary fiction to block-busting thrillers, from fantasy literature and children's stories to enduring classics. The wholly-owned division of News Corporation also publishes a wide selection of non-fiction including history, celebrity memoirs, biography, popular science, mind, body and spirit, dictionaries, maps and reference books. HarperCollins is also one of the largest education publishers in the UK. Authors include many award-winning and international bestsellers such as Isabel Allende, Paulo Coelho, Josephine Cox, Michael Crichton, Cathy Kelly, Judith Kerr, Doris Lessing, Frank McCourt, Tony Parsons, Nigel Slater and Diana Wynne Jones. Bestselling licensed properties include Dr Seuss and Noddy. About 1500 titles a year.

GENERAL BOOKS DIVISION
Managing Director *Amanda Ridout*

Harper Fiction Publisher *Lynne Drew* IMPRINTS **HarperCollins** Publishing Directors *Susan Watt, Julia Wisdom*; **Voyager** Fantasy/science fiction Publishing Director *Jane Johnson* General, historical fiction, crime and thrillers and women's fiction.

HarperEntertainment Managing Director/Publisher *Trevor Dolby* IMPRINTS **HarperCollins** Publishing Director *Ben Dunn*; Publishing Director *David Brawn* (Agatha Christie, J.R.R. Tolkien, C.S. Lewis) Media-related books from film companions to celebrity autobiographies and TV tie-ins; **HarperSport** Publishing Director *Michael Doggart* Sporting biographies, guides and histories; **HarperCollins Audio** Managing Director *Trevor Dolby* (see entry under *Audio Books*).

HarperThorsons/Element (division & imprint) Managing Director *Belinda Budge*, Publishing Directors *Wanda Whiteley* (health), *Carole Tonkinson* (mind, body & spirit), *Sally Potter* (media tie-ins).

HarperCollins Children's Books Managing Director *Sally Gritten* Quality picture books for under-7s; fiction for age 6 up to young adult; TV and film tie-ins and properties Publishing Directors *Gillie Russell* (fiction), *Sue Buswell* (picture books)

PRESS BOOKS DIVISION
Managing Director *John Bond*

IMPRINTS **Fourth Estate** Publishing Director/Publisher *Nick Pearson* Fiction, literary fiction, current affairs, popular science, biography, humour, travel; **HarperPress** General trade non-fiction and fiction Publishing Directors *Arabella Pike* (non-fiction), *Clare Smith* (fiction); **HarperPerennial** Paperback imprint. Publishing Director *Paul Baggaley*

COLLINS DIVISION
Managing Director *Thomas Webster*

Collins Reference Managing Director *Sarah Bailey* Guides and handbooks, Times World Atlases, Collins World Atlases, phrase books and manuals on popular reference, art instruction, illustrated, cookery and wine, crafts, DIY, gardening, military, natural history, pet care,

pastimes Publishing Directors *Denise Bates* (illustrated reference), *Martin Toseland* (text reference), *Sheena Barclay* (world atlases), Associate Publisher *Myles Archibald* (natural history) IMPRINTS **Collins**; **Collins Gem**; **Times Books**; **Jane's**.

Collins Dictionaries/COBUILD (division & imprint) Managing Director *Lorna Knight* Bilingual and English dictionaries, English dictionaries for foreign learners. Publishing Directors *Helen Newstead* (digital development), *Michela Clari* (editorial), *Elaine Higgleton* (editorial).

Collins Education Managing Director *Jim Green* Books, CD-ROMs and online material for UK primary and secondary schools and colleges. Publishing Director *Paul Cherry* (educational).

Collins Maps and Road Atlases (division & imprint) General Manager/Publisher *Mike Cottingham*, Publishing Director *Helen Gordon* Maps, atlases, street plans and leisure guides.

Authors' Rating In these uncertain times the new titles favoured by the big name publishers are the likeliest indicator of market trends. So, for what it is worth, having had a good year with half the number of books it published in 2000, HarperCollins is developing home grown fiction under its Fourth Estate imprint while Thorsons/Element is moving on from 'mind body and spirit' to more serious non-fiction including 'nursery memoirs'. Children's books are doing well. Oh yes, and the US imprint Avon Books is launching a paperback list that takes in 'historical, paranormal and ethnic erotic fiction'. The next big expansion is into graphic novels.

Harrap
See **Chambers Harrap Publishers Ltd**

Harvard University Press
Fitzroy House, 11 Chenies Street, London WC1E 7EY
☎020 7306 0603 Fax 020 7306 0604
✉ info@HUP-MITpress.co.uk
www.hup.harvard.edu

Director *William Sisler*
General Manager *Ann Sexsmith*

European office of **Harvard University Press**, USA. Publishes academic and scholarly works in history, politics, philosophy, economics, literary criticism, psychology, sociology, anthropology, women's studies, biological sciences, classics, history of science, art, music, film, reference. All mss go to the American office: 79 Garden Street, Cambridge, MA 02138 (see entry under *US Publishers*).

Harvill Secker
See **The Random House Group Ltd**

Haus Publishing
26 Cadogan Court, Draycott Avenue, London
SW3 3BX
☎020 7584 6738 Fax 020 7584 9501
✉ haus@hauspublishing.com
www.hauspublishing.co.uk

Managing Director *Barbara Schwepcke*

Founded 2002. Publishes biographies and literary travel books. DIVISIONS/IMPRINTS **Life&Times** Non-academic biographies of well-known and lesser-known personalities TITLES *Mary Seacole*; *Moreschi*; *Einstein*. **The Armchair Traveller** Literary travel series TITLES *Along the Ganges*; *Venice for Lovers*. **HausBooks** Hardcover biographies TITLES *Rommel*; *Kipling*. 26 titles in 2005. Unsolicited mss, synopses and ideas within the subject areas above are welcome; approach by e-mail or post. No children's, fiction or poetry.
ROYALTIES twice-yearly.

Haynes Publishing
Sparkford, Near Yeovil BA22 7JJ
☎01963 440635 Fax 01963 440825
✉ info@haynes.co.uk
www.haynes.co.uk

Chairman *John H. Haynes, OBE*
Approx. Annual Turnover £36 million

Founded in 1960 by John H. Haynes. Listed public company with majority family ownership. The mainstay of its programme has been the *Owners' Workshop Manual*, first published in the mid 1960s and still running off the presses today. Acquired Sutton Publishing Ltd in March 2000. Publishes DIY service and repair manuals for cars, motorbikes and leisure plus other related topics under the Haynes imprint and a broad range of general non-fiction under the Sutton imprint.
AUTOMOTIVE DIVISION IMPRINT **Haynes** Editorial Director *Matthew Minter* Service and repair manuals; Editorial Director *Mark Hughes* Motoring, motor sport, cars, motorcycles, home, DIY and leisure titles.
GENERAL PUBLISHING DIVISION IMPRINT **Sutton Publishing Ltd** (see entry). Unsolicited submissions welcome if they come within the subject areas covered. OVERSEAS SUBSIDIARIES Haynes Manuals Inc., California, USA, Editions Haynes S.A., France, Haynes Publishing Nordiska AB, Sweden.
ROYALTIES twice-yearly.

Headline
See **Hodder Headline Ltd**

William Heinemann
See **The Random House Group Ltd**

Heinemann Educational
See **Harcourt Education**

Helicon Publishing
RM plc, New Mill House, 183 Milton Park, Abingdon OX14 4SE
☎01235 823816 Fax 01235 823222
✉ helicon@rm.com
www.helicon.co.uk

Business Manager *Caroline Dodds*

A division of Research Machines plc. Helicon is a general reference database publisher for the UK, US and Australian markets. Licenses quality reference content for online, print, and CD-ROM publications. TITLES include the flagship single-volume *Hutchinson 2005 Encyclopedia* published under licence from **Hodder Headline**. CD-ROM TITLES include *The Hutchinson Encyclopedia*; *The Hutchinson Science Reference Suite*; *The Hutchinson History Reference Suite*; *The Hutchinson Music Reference Suite*.

Christopher Helm
See **A.&C. Black Publishers Ltd**

Helm Information Ltd
The Banks, Mountfield, Nr Robertsbridge TN32 5JY
☎01580 880561 Fax 01580 880541
✉ amandahelm@helm-information.co.uk
www.helm-information.co.uk

Directors *Amanda Helm, Christopher Helm*

Founded 1990. Publishes academic books for students and university libraries. SERIES *The Critical Assessments of Writers in English* (collected criticism); *Literary Sources & Documents* (primary source material on various themes/events/cultural/aesthetic movements ranging from the American Civil War to the Gothic Revival); *The Dickens Companions*; and a new series, *Icons*, which exposes the processes by which a figure, historical or fictional, achieves iconic status, e.g. Faust, Robin Hood. Will consider ideas and proposals provided they are relevant to the series listed above.
ROYALTIES annually.

Helter Skelter Publishing
South Bank House, Black Prince Road, London SE1 7SJ

☎020 7463 2204 Fax 020 7463 2295
✉ info@helterskelterbooks.com
www.helterskelterbooks.com
Editorial *Sean Body*

Founded 1995. Publishes music and film books only. IMPRINTS **Helter Skelter Publishing**; **Firefly Publishing**. 15 titles a year. Unsolicited mss, synopses and ideas welcome.

Ian Henry Publications Ltd

20 Park Drive, Romford RM1 4LH
☎01708 749119 Fax 01708 736213
✉ info@ian-henry.com
www.ian-henry.com
Managing Director *Ian Wilkes*

Founded 1976. Publishes local history, humour, transport history and Sherlockian pastiches. TITLES *Ordeal in Romford*; *How to Support a Crap Football Team*. 6–8 titles a year. No unsolicited mss. Synopses and ideas for books welcome.
ROYALTIES twice-yearly.

The Herbert Press

See **A.&C. Black Publishers Ltd**

Hermes House

See **Anness Publishing Ltd**

Nick Hern Books

The Glasshouse, 49a Goldhawk Road, London W12 8QP
☎020 8749 4953 Fax 020 8735 0250
✉ info@nickhernbooks.demon.co.uk
www.nickhernbooks.co.uk
Chairman/Managing Director *Nick Hern*

Founded 1988. Fully independent since 1992. Publishes books on theatre and film: from how-to and biography to plays and screenplays. About 40 titles a year. No unsolicited playscripts. Synopses, ideas and proposals for other theatre material welcome. Not interested in material unrelated to the theatre or cinema.

University of Hertfordshire Press

Learning and Information Services, Learning Resources Centre, College Lane, Hatfield AL10 9AB
☎01707 284681 Fax 01707 284666
✉ UHPress@herts.ac.uk
www.herts.ac.uk/UHPress
Contact *Jane Housham*

Founded 1992. Publishes academic books on Gypsies, literature, regional and local history, parapsychology. IMPRINTS **University of Hertfordshire Press; Interface Collection; Hertfordshire Publications**. TITLES *Here to Stay: The Gypsies and Travellers of Britain* Colin Clark and Margaret Greenfields; *Selling Shakespeare to Hollywood: The marketing of filmed Shakespeare adaptations from 1989 into the new millennium* Emma French; *An Historical Atlas of Hertfordshire* ed. David Short. 15 titles a year

Hesperus Press Limited

4 Rickett Street, London SW6 1RU
☎020 7610 3331 Fax 020 7610 3217
www.hesperuspress.com
Managing Editor *Katherine Venn*

Founded 2001. Publishes lesser-known works by classical authors, both in English and in translation. TITLES *Carlyle's House* Virginia Woolf; *The Rich Boy* Francis Scott Fitzgerald; *Arctic Summer* E.M. Forster; *Hadji Murat* Lev Tolstoy. *Modern Classics* series launched in 2005; literary fiction list in 2006. 40 titles in 2004, including 5 poetry titles. Does not accept unsolicited mss.
ROYALTIES annually.

Authors' Rating Much praised for matching book design with quality content.

High Stakes

See **Oldcastle Books Ltd**

History Into Print

See **Brewin Books Ltd**

HMSO

See **TSO**

Hobsons Plc

Challenger House, 42 Adler Street, London E1 1EE
☎020 7958 5000 Fax 020 7958 5001
www.hobsons.com
Chairman *Martin Morgan*
Group Managing Director *Christopher Letcher*

Founded 1974. Part of the Daily Mail & General Trust. Publishes course and career guides, under exclusive licence and royalty agreements for CRAC (Careers Research and Advisory Centre), directories and specialist titles for students and young professionals. TITLES *The Hobson's Study Netherlands Guide 2006*; *The Hobsons Postgrad Guide – May 2006*; *The Hobsons Boarding UK Magazine*; *GET Guide for Ethnic Minorities 2007*; *The Hobsons Study Europe Guide 2007*; *GET Engineering 2007*; *GET Guide for Students with Disabilities 2007*.

Hodder & Stoughton

See **Hodder Headline Ltd**

Hodder Gibson

2a Christie Street, Paisley PA1 1NB
☎0141 848 1609 Fax 0141 889 6315
✉ hoddergibson@hodder.co.uk
www.hoddereducation.co.uk

Managing Director *John Mitchell*

Part of the **Hodder Headline Group**. Publishes educational books specifically for Scotland. Combines the former Robert Gibson and Sons (Glasgow) with the Scottish branch of Hodder Murray (a merger of **John Murray** and **Hodder Stoughton Educational**). About 50 titles a year. Synopses/ideas preferred to unsolicited mss.

ROYALTIES annually.

Hodder Headline Ltd

338 Euston Road, London NW1 3BH
☎020 7873 6000 Fax 020 7873 6024
www.hodderheadline.co.uk

Group Chief Executive *Tim Hely Hutchinson*
Approx. Annual Turnover £130 million

Formed in June 1993 through the merger of Headline Book Publishing and Hodder & Stoughton. Headline was founded in 1986 and had grown dramatically, whereas Hodder & Stoughton was 125 years old with a diverse range of publishing. The company was acquired by WHSmith plc in 1999 and subsequently by Hachette Livre S.A. in October 2004. Purchased **John Murray (Publishers) Ltd** in 2002. About 2000 titles a year.

DIVISIONS

Headline Book Publishing Managing Director *Martin Neild*, Deputy Managing Director *Kerr MacRae*, Director of Non-fiction *Val Hudson*, Director of Fiction *Jane Morpeth* Publishes commercial and literary fiction (hardback and paperback) and popular non-fiction including autobiography, biography, food and wine, history, humour, popular science, sport and TV tie-ins. IMPRINTS **Headline; Headline Review; Little Black Dress**. AUTHORS Kate Adie, Catherine Alliott, Lyn Andrews, Emily Barr, Louise Bagshaw, Colin Bateman, Martina Cole, Janet Evanovich, Sophie Grigson, Wendy Holden, Matthew Jukes, Faye and Jonathan Kellerman, Jill Mansell, Maggie O'Farrell, Sheila O'Flanagan, James Patterson, Pamela Stephenson, Penny Vincenzi.
Hodder & Stoughton General Managing Director *Jamie Hodder-Williams*, Deputy Managing Director *Lisa Highton*; **Non-fiction** *Rowena Webb*; **Sceptre** *Carole Welch*; **Fiction** *Carolyn Mays*; **Audio** (see entry under *Audio Books*). Publishes commercial and literary fiction; biography, autobiography, history, self-help, humour, travel and other general interest non-fiction; audio. IMPRINTS **Hodder & Stoughton; Hodder Paperbacks; Sceptre; Mobius**. AUTHORS Melvyn Bragg, Bill Cullen, Jeffrey Deaver, Charles Frazier, Elizabeth George, Thomas Keneally, Stephen King, John le Carré, Andrew Miller, David Mitchell, Elizabeth Noble, Rosamunde Pilcher, Mary Stewart, Fiona Walker.
Hodder Children's Books (See **Hachette Children's Books**)
Hodder & Stoughton Religious Managing Director *Martin Mullin*, Publishing Director *Judith Longman*, Bibles & Hodder Christian Books *David Moloney*. Publishes TNIV, NIV and NIrV Bibles, Christian books, autobiography, biography, TV-tie-ins, gift/humour books, self-help. IMPRINTS **Hodder & Stoughton; Hodder Paperbacks; TNIV; NIV; NIrV**.
Hodder Education Managing Director *Philip Walters* Publishes in the following areas: **Schoolbooks** *Lis Tribe*; **Consumer Education** *Katie Roden*; **Further Education/Higher Education Textbooks**; **Health Sciences**; **Journals/Reference Books** *Mary Attree*. IMPRINTS **Hodder Murray; Teach Yourself; Hodder Arnold; Hodder Gibson** (see entry). **John Murray (Publishers) Ltd** (see entry).

Authors' Rating Into its twentieth year, Hodder Headline is holding its reputation for publishing what Tim Hely Hutchinson describes as 'a broad range of stylish bestsellers'. That it will continue to do so and more seems certain now that Hodder Headline, Orion and Little, Brown are all under the Hachette Livre umbrella. While each company will maintain its editorial independence, the joint strength of marketing muscle, at a time when bookselling is increasingly dominated by the high street chains and Amazon, will benefit authors across the popularity range.

Honeyglen Publishing Ltd

56 Durrels House, Warwick Gardens, London W14 8QB
☎020 7602 2876 Fax 020 7602 2876

Directors *N.S. Poderegin, J. Poderegin*

Founded 1983. A small publishing house whose output is 'extremely limited'. Publishes history, philosophy of history, biography and selective fiction. No children's or science fiction. TITLES *The Soul of China; The Soul of India; Woman and Power in History; Lost World – Tibet; A Child of the Century* all by Amaury de Riencourt; *With Duncan Grant in South Turkey* Paul Roche; *Vladimir, The Russian Viking* Vladimir Volkoff; *The Dawning* Milka Bajic-Poderegin; *Quicksand* Louise Hide. Unsolicited mss welcome.

Honno Welsh Women's Press
c/o Canolfan Merched y Wawr, Vulcan Street, Aberystwyth SY23 1JH
☎01970 623150   Fax 01970 623150
✉ post@honno.co.uk
www.honno.co.uk

Editor *Caroline Oakley*

Founded in 1986 by a group of women who wanted to create more opportunities for women in publishing. A co-operative operation which publishes mainly fiction and autobiography. 'Contact us for current calls for short story submissions.' 7 titles a year. Welcomes mss and ideas for books from women who are Welsh or have a significant Welsh connection only Send as hard copy, not by e-mail.
ROYALTIES annually.

Horus Editions
See **Award Publications Limited**

How To Books Ltd
3 Newtec Place, Magdalen Road, Oxford OX4 1RE
☎01865 793806   Fax 01865 248780
✉ info@howtobooks.co.uk
www.howtobooks.co.uk

Managing Director *Giles Lewis*
Editorial Director *Nikki Read*

An independent publishing house, founded in 1991. Publishes non-fiction, self-help reference books. How To titles are practical, accessible books that enable their readers to achieve their goals in life and work. How To authors must have first-hand experience of the subject about which they are writing. Subjects covered include management, leisure learning, career choices and career development, living and working abroad, small business and self employment, study skills & student guides, creative writing and property. 250 titles a year. Submit outline followed by sample chapter.

Human Horizons
See **Souvenir Press Ltd**

John Hunt Publishing Ltd
The Bothy, Deershot Lodge, Park Lane, Ropley SO24 0BE
☎01962 773768   Fax 01962 773769
✉ office@johnhunt-publishing.com
www.o-books.net
Approx. Annual Turnover £1.5 million

Publishes children's and world religions as well as mind, body & spirit titles. IMPRINT **John Hunt Publishing**. About 50 titles a year. Unsolicited material welcome.

C. Hurst & Co. Publishers
41 Great Russell Street, London WC1B 3PL
☎020 7255 2201   Fax 020 7255 2204
✉ hurst@atlas.co.uk
www.hurstpub.co.uk

Chairman/Managing Director *Christopher Hurst*
Editorial Heads *Christopher Hurst, Michael Dwyer*

Founded 1967. An independent company publishing contemporary history, politics, religion (not theology) and sociology. TITLES *Sarajevo: A Biography* Robert J. Donia; *The Barbarisation of Warfare* ed. George Kassimeris; *Losing Arab Hearts and Minds* Steve Tatham. About 25 titles a year. No unsolicited mss. Synopses and ideas welcome.
ROYALTIES annually.

Hutchinson/Hutchinson Children's Books
See **The Random House Group Ltd**

Hymns Ancient & Modern Ltd
St Mary's Works, St Mary's Plain, Norwich NR3 3BH
☎01603 612914   Fax 01603 624483
✉ admin@scm-canterburypress.co.uk
www.scm-canterburypress.co.uk

Also at: 9–17 St Albans Place, London N1 0NX

Chairman *Patrick Coldstream, CBE*
Chief Executive *Andrew Moore*
Publisher, SCM Press and Canterbury Press *Christine Smith*
Publisher, RMEP *Mary Mears*
Approx. Annual Turnover £4.4 million

Publishing subsidiary **SCM-Canterbury Press Ltd** (see entry) controls **SCM Press**, **Canterbury Press** and **RMEP** IMPRINTS which cover hymn books, liturgical material, academic and general religious books, and multi-faith religious and social education resources for pupils and teachers. Media subsidiary **G.J. Palmer & Sons Ltd** includes *Church Times* (see entry under *Magazines*); monthly magazine inserts *The Sign* and *Home Words* and *Crucible*, a quarterly magazine. About 100 titles a year. Ideas for new titles welcome but no unsolicited mss.

ROYALTIES annually.

Icon Books Ltd

The Old Dairy, Brook Road, Thriplow, Cambridge SG8 7RG

☎01763 208008 Fax 01763 208080

✉ info@iconbooks.co.uk

www.iconbooks.co.uk

Managing Director *Peter Pugh*
Publishing Director *Simon Flynn*

Founded 1992. SERIES *Introducing* Graphic introductions to key figures and ideas in the history of science, philosophy, psychology, religion and the arts. TITLE *Introducing Quantum Theory*. Publishes 'provocative and intelligent' non-fiction in science, politics and philosophy. TITLE *Why do People Hate America?* IMPRINT **Wizard Books** Children's fiction and non-fiction including SERIES *Fighting Fantasy* (adventure gamebooks). Submit synopsis only. OVERSEAS ASSOCIATE Totem Books, USA, distributed by National Book Network.

ROYALTIES twice yearly.

I.M.P. Fiction Ltd

PO Box 69, Church Stretton SY6 6WZ

☎01694 720049 Fax 01694 720049

✉ info@impbooks.com

www.impbooks.com

Managing Director *Kaye Roach*

Founded 1998. Publishes 'quality new fiction'. No crime, science fiction, horror or fantasy. 2 titles in 2005. Mss only accepted from recognised agents; no unsolicited mss.

ROYALTIES twice-yearly.

Imprint Academic

PO Box 200, Exeter EX5 5YX

☎01392 841600 Fax 01392 841478

✉ keith@imprint.co.uk

www.imprint-academic.com

Publisher *Keith Sutherland*

Founded 1980. Publishes books and journals in politics, philosophy and psychology for both academic and general readers. Book series include *St. Andrews Studies in Philosophy and Public Affairs* and *Societas: Essays in political and cultural criticism*. Unsolicited mss, synopses and ideas welcome with return postage only.

The In Pinn

See **Neil Wilson Publishing Ltd**

Incomes Data Services

See **Sweet & Maxwell Group**

Independent Music Press

PO Box 69, Church Stretton SY6 6WZ

☎01694 720049 Fax 01694 720049

✉ info@impbooks.com

www.impbooks.com

Managing Director *Martin Roach*

Founded 1992. Publishes music biography and youth culture. No jazz or classical. TITLES include biographies of Green Day, Muse, The Killers, The Cure, Dave Grohl, The Streets, Oasis, Prodigy as well as subculture classics such as *Scooter Boys* and Ian Hunter's *Diary of a Rock 'n' Roll Star*. Approach by e-mail, enclosing biography and synopsis only.

ROYALTIES twice-yearly.

Independent Voices

See **Souvenir Press Ltd**

Infinite Ideas

36 St Giles, Oxford OX1 3LD

☎01865 514888 Fax 01865 514777

✉ info@infideas.com

www.infideas.com

Chairman *Jesse Norman*
Joint Managing Directors *David Grant, Richard Burton*

Approx. Annual Turnover £1 million

Founded 2004. Publishes inspirational self-help. SERIES **52 Brilliant Ideas** Subject areas cover health and relationships; careers, finance and personal development; sports, hobbies and games; leisure and lifestyle; art, literature and music. No fiction, illustrated or children's books.

40 titles a year. No unsolicited mss. Synopses and ideas welcome; initial contact by e-mail or letter.

Flat FEES paid.

Informa Law

Informa House, 30–32 Mortimer Street, London W1W 7RE

☎020 7017 4600

Managing Director *Fotini Liontou*
Publishing Director *Wendy Gill*

Part of LLP Professional Publishing, a trading division of Informa Publishing Group Ltd. Publishes a range of maritime law, commercial law, insurance law, banking law, intellectual property law publications including newsletters, law reports, books, journals and magazines aimed at senior management and professional practices.

Inspire

c/o mph, 4 John Wesley Road, Werrington, Peterborough PE4 6ZP
☎01733 325002   Fax 01733 384180
✉ comm.editor@mph.org.uk
www.mph.org.uk

Head of Publishing *Dr Natalie K. Watson*

Publishes accessible Christian books for the wider ecumenical market. Spirituality, social concern, worship resources, mission and evangelism, discipleship, prayer. No fiction or children's. 12 titles a year. Unsolicited mss, synopses and ideas welcome; send two sample chapters and proposal with covering letter and s.a.e. for return of mss.
ROYALTIES annually.

Inter-Varsity Press

38 De Montfort Street, Leicester LE1 7GP
☎0116 255 1754   Fax 0116 254 2044
✉ ivp@uccf.org.uk
www.ivpbooks.com

Chairman *Ralph Evershed*
Chief Executive *Brian Wilson*

Founded mid-1930s as the publishing arm of Universities and Colleges Christian Fellowship, it has expanded to wider Christian markets worldwide. Publishes Christian belief and lifestyle, reference and bible commentaries. No secular material or anything which fails to empathise with orthodox Protestant Christianity. IMPRINTS **IVP**; **Apollos**; **Crossway** TITLES *The Bible Speaks Today*; *I'd like to believe, but ...* Michael Green; *Jubilee Manifesto* eds. Michael Schluter and John Ashcroft. About 50 titles a year. Synopses and ideas welcome.
ROYALTIES twice-yearly.

Interface Collection

See **University of Hertfordshire Press**

Isis Publishing

7 Centremead, Osney Mead, Oxford OX2 0ES
☎01865 250333   Fax 01865 790358
✉ sales@isis-publishing.co.uk
www.isis-publishing.co.uk

Part of the Ulverscroft Group Ltd. Publishes large-print books – fiction and non-fiction – and unabridged audio books. Together with **Soundings** (see entry under *Audio Books*) produces around 4000 titles on audio tape and CD. AUTHORS Lee Child, Martina Cole, Terry Pratchett, Susan Sallis. No unsolicited mss as Isis undertakes no original publishing.
ROYALTIES twice-yearly.

Itchy Coo

See **Black & White Publishing Ltd**

Ithaca Press

See **Garnet Publishing Ltd**

IVP

See **Inter-Varsity Press**

Jacqui Small

See **Aurum Press Ltd**

JAI

See **Elsevier Ltd**

Jane's Information Group

Sentinel House, 163 Brighton Road, Coulsdon CR5 2YH
☎020 8700 3700   Fax 020 8763 1006
✉ info.uk@janes.com
www.janes.com

Owner *The Woodbridge Company*
Managing Director *Alfred Rolington*

Founded 1898 by Fred T. Jane with the publication of *All The World's Fighting Ships*. Now part of the Woodbridge Company Limited. In recent years management has been focusing on growth opportunities in its core business and in enhancing the performance of initiatives like Jane's information available online and on in-depth intelligence centres. Publishes Web journals, magazines and yearbooks on defence, aerospace, security and transport topics, with details of equipment and systems; plus directories and strategic studies. Also *Jane's Defence Weekly* (see entry under *Magazines*). DIVISIONS **Magazines** *Sean Howe* TITLES *Jane's Defence Weekly*; *Jane's International Defence Review*; *Jane's Airport Review*, *Jane's Navy International*; *Jane's Islamic Affairs Analyst*; *Jane's Missiles and Rockets*. **Publishing for Defence, Aerospace, Transport** *Ian Kay* TITLES *Defence, Aerospace Yearbooks*. **Transport** TITLE *Transportation Yearbooks*. **Security** *Sean Howe* TITLES *Jane's Intelligence Review*; *Foreign Report*; *Jane's Sentinel* (regional security assessment); *Jane's Police Review*. CD-ROM and electronic development and publication. Over 100 titles a year. Unsolicited mss, synopses and ideas for reference/yearbooks welcome. OVERSEAS ASSOCIATES Jane's Information Group Inc., USA.
ROYALTIES twice-yearly.

Janus Publishing Company Ltd

105–107 Gloucester Place, London W1U 6BY
☎020 7580 7664   Fax 020 7636 5756
✉ publisher@januspublishing.co.uk

www.januspublishing.co.uk

Managing Director *Sandy Leung*

Publishes fiction, human interest, memoirs, philosophy, mind, body and spirit, religion and theology, social questions, popular science, history, spiritualism and the paranormal, poetry and young adults. IMPRINTS **Janus Books** Subsidy publishing; **Empiricus Books** Non-subsidy publishing. TITLES *The Anarchists in the Spanish Civil War; Nature of the Self; Politics and Human Nature; Napoleon 1813; King David; Chameleon Candidate; Love Emporium; Digby.* 'Two of our authors won the European Literary Award in 2002.' About 400 titles in print. Unsolicited mss welcome. Agents in the USA, Europe and Asia.
ROYALTIES twice-yearly.

Authors' Rating Authors may be asked to cover their own productions costs but Janus has moved into conventional publishing with its Empiricus imprint.

Jarrold Publishing

Whitefriars, Norwich NR3 1JR
☎01603 763300 Fax 01603 662748
✉ info@jarrold-publishing.co.uk
www.jarrold-publishing.co.uk

Managing Director *Margot Russell-King*

Part of Jarrold & Sons Ltd, the printing and publishing company founded in 1770. Publishes UK tourism, travel, leisure, history and calendars. Material tends to be of a high pictorial content. IMPRINTS **Pitkin**; **Unichrome**. About 30 titles a year. Unsolicited mss, synopses and ideas welcome but before submitting anything, approach in writing to the editorial department.

Michael Joseph

See **Penguin Group (UK)**

Kahn & Averill

9 Harrington Road, London SW7 3ES
☎020 8743 3278 Fax 020 8743 3278
✉ kahn@averill23.freeserve.co.uk

Managing Director *Mr M. Kahn*

Founded 1967 to publish children's titles but now specialises in music titles. A small independent publishing house. No unsolicited mss; synopses and ideas for books considered.
ROYALTIES twice-yearly.

Karnak House

157 Dudden Hill Lane, London NW10 1AU
☎020 8830 8301 Fax 020 8830 8301
✉ karnakhouse@aol.com
www.karnakhouse.co.uk

Publisher/Commissioning Editor *Amon Saba Saakana*

Founded 1979. Specialises in African and Caribbean studies. Publishes anthropology, education, Egyptology, history, language and linguistics, literary criticism, music, prehistory. No poetry, humour or sport. About 7 titles a year. No unsolicited mss; send introduction or synopsis with one sample chapter. Synopses and ideas welcome. OVERSEAS SUBSIDIARIES The Intef Institute, and Karnak House, Illinois, USA.
ROYALTIES annually.

Kenilworth Press Ltd

See **Quiller Press**

Kenyon-Deane

See **Cressrelles Publishing Co. Ltd**

Laurence King Publishing Ltd

71 Great Russell Street, London WC1B 3BP
☎020 7430 8850 Fax 020 7430 8880
✉ enquiries@laurenceking.co.uk
www.laurenceking.co.uk

Chairman *Nick Perren*
Managing Director *Laurence King*
Approx. Annual Turnover £6 million

Founded in 1976 as a book packager under the name Calmann & King Ltd, the Laurence King publishing division commenced operations in 1991. College and trade divisions were united in 2002 under Laurence King Publishing Ltd. Publishes illustrated books on graphic design, contemporary architecture, fashion, interiors, product design, art history and religion. TITLES *Atlas of World Art; A World History of Art; History of Modern Design; The Design Encyclopedia; A History of Western Architecture; A History of Interior Design.* About 50 titles a year. Unsolicited material welcome; send synopsis by post or e-mail.
ROYALTIES twice-yearly.

Kingfisher Publications Plc

New Penderel House, 283–288 High Holborn, London WC1V 7HZ
☎020 7903 9999 Fax 020 7242 4979
✉ sales@kingfisherpub.com

Managing Director *John Richards*

Formerly Larousse plc until 1997 when the company name changed to Kingfisher Publications Plc. Founded 1994 when owners, Groupe de la Cité (also publishers of the Larousse dictionaries in France), merged their UK operations of Grisewood & Dempsey and **Chambers Harrap Publishers Ltd** (see entry). In 2002, Kingfisher officially became an imprint of **Houghton Mifflin Company** (see entry under *US Publishers*).

DIVISION **Kingfisher** Non-fiction Publishing Director *Melissa Fairley*, Fiction Publishing Director *Anne Marie Ryan*. Founded in 1973 by Grisewood & Dempsey Ltd. Publishes children's fiction and non-fiction in hardback and paperback: story books, rhymes and picture books, fiction and poetry anthologies, young non-fiction, activity books, general series and reference. No unsolicited mss accepted.

ROYALTIES twice-yearly where applicable.

Jessica Kingsley Publishers Ltd
116 Pentonville Road, London N1 9JB
☎020 7833 2307   Fax 020 7837 2917
✉ post@jkp.com
www.jkp.com

Managing Director and Publisher *Jessica Kingsley*
Senior Acquisitions Editor *Stephen Jones*

Founded 1987. Independent, international publisher of books for professionals, academics and the general reader on autism, disability, special education, arts therapies, child psychology, mental health, practical theology and social work. Over 100 titles a year. 'We are actively publishing and commissioning in all these areas. We welcome suggestions for books and proposals from prospective authors. Proposals should consist of an outline of the book, a contents list, assessment of the market and author's c.v., and should be addressed to *Jessica Kingsley* or *Stephen Jones*. Complete manuscript should not be sent.' OVERSEAS SUBSIDIARY in Philadelphia, USA.

ROYALTIES twice-yearly.

Kluwer Law International
Prospero House, Lower Ground Floor, 24A Borough High Street, London SE1 1GA
Publisher *Sasha Radoja*

Founded 1995. Parent company: Wolters Kluwer Group. Publishes international law. About 200 titles a year, including online, CD-ROM, loose-leaf journals and monographs. Unsolicited synopses and ideas for books on law at an international level welcome.

ROYALTIES annually.

Knight Paperbacks Ltd
See **Caxton Publishing Group**

Kogan Page Ltd
120 Pentonville Road, London N1 9JN
☎020 7278 0433   Fax 020 7837 3768/6348
✉ kpinfo@kogan-page.co.uk
www.kogan-page.co.uk

Managing Director *Philip Kogan*
Approx. Annual Turnover £6 million

Founded 1967 by Philip Kogan to publish *The Industrial Training Yearbook*. Publishes business and management reference books and monographs, careers, marketing, personal finance, personnel, small business, training and industrial relations, transport. Further expansion is planned, particularly in the finance and high-tech, EC publications areas, yearbooks and directories. Has initiated a number of electronic publishing projects and provision of EP content. DIVISION **Kogan Page** *Pauline Goodwin, Helen Kogan, Jon Finch, Ian Hawsworth*. About 150 titles a year.

ROYALTIES twice-yearly.

Authors' Rating Kogan Page is one of the few, an independent publisher of nearly forty years' standing, dedicated to books about and for business. After a difficult couple of years, company founder and soon to be chairman Philip Kogan promises 'new product and publishing initiatives'.

Ladybird
See **Dorling Kindersley Ltd**

Landmark Publishing Ltd
Ashbourne Hall, Cokayne Avenue, Ashbourne DE6 1EJ
☎01335 347349   Fax 01335 347303
✉ landmark@clara.net
www.landmarkpublishing.co.uk

Chairman *Mr R. Cork*
Managing Director *Mr C.L.M. Porter*
Approx. Annual Turnover £450,000

Founded in 1996. Publishes itinerary-based travel guides, regional, industrial countryside and local history. About 50 titles in 2005. No unsolicited mss; telephone in the first instance.

ROYALTIES annually.

Lawrence & Wishart Ltd
99A Wallis Road, London E9 5LN
☎020 8533 2506   Fax 020 8533 7369
✉ lw@lwbooks.co.uk
www.lwbooks.co.uk

Managing Director/Editor *Sally Davison*

Founded 1936. An independent publisher with a substantial backlist. Publishes current affairs, cultural politics, economics, history, politics and education. TITLES *A New Modernity; Liberty or Death; The Struggle for Democracy in Britain 1780–1830; Rosa Luxemburg: An Intimate Portrait.* 10 titles a year.

ROYALTIES annually, unless by arrangement.

The Learning Institute
Overbrook Business Centre, Blackford,
Wedmore BS28 4PA
☎01934 713563 Fax 01934 713492
✉ courses@inst.org
www.inst.org

Managing Director *Kit Sadgrove*

Founded 1994 to publish home-study courses in vocational subjects such as garden design, writing and computing. Publishes subjects that show the reader how to work from home, gain a new skill or enter a new career. Interests include home working and self employment, especially in 21st century jobs. TITLES *Diploma in Interior Design*; *Become a Garden Designer*. Author's guidelines sent on receipt of s.a.e. No unsolicited mss; send synopses and ideas only.
ROYALTIES quarterly.

Lennard Associates Ltd
Windmill Cottage, Mackerye End, Harpenden AL5 5DR
☎01582 715866 Fax 01582 715866
✉ stephenson@lennardqap.co.uk

Chairman/Managing Director *Adrian Stephenson*

Founded 1979. Sponsored and commissioned projects only. IMPRINTS **Lennard Publishing**; **Queen Anne Press**. Acquired the latter and most of its assets in 1992. No unsolicited mss.
PAYMENT Both fees and royalties by arrangement.

Lionel Leventhal Ltd
See **Greenhill Books**

Dewi Lewis Publishing
8 Broomfield Road, Heaton Moor, Stockport SK4 4ND
☎0161 442 9450 Fax 0161 442 9450
✉ mail@dewilewispublishing.com
www.dewilewispublishing.com

Contacts *Dewi Lewis, Caroline Warhurst*

Approx. Annual Turnover £250,000

Founded 1994. Publishes fiction, photography and visual arts. TITLES *Industry of Souls* Martin Booth (Booker Prize shortlist, 1998); *Wolfy and the Strudelbakers* Zvi Jagendorf (Booker Prize longlist, 2001; Sagittarius Prize, 2002); *Common Sense* Martin Parr; *New York 1954–5* William Klein. IMPRINT **Dewi Lewis Media** Publishes non-fiction, biography, sports and celebrity books. TITLES *David Beckham: Made in Manchester* Eamonn and James Clarke; *500 Flowers* Roger Camp. 16 titles in 2005.

Submissions: 'essential to check website before submitting'.
ROYALTIES annually.

Lewis Masonic
See **Ian Allan Publishing Ltd**

LexisNexis
See **Reed Elsevier Group plc**

John Libbey Publishing
PO Box 276, Eastleigh SO50 5YS
☎01342 315440 Fax 023 8065 0259
✉ johnlibbey@aol.com
www.johnlibbey.com

Publisher *John Libbey*

Founded 1979. Publishes books and journals on cinema, animation and media. Now the publisher of the media series from University of Luton Press. Synopses and ideas welcome. OVERSEAS SUBSIDIARY John Libbey Eurotext Ltd, France (medical publishers).

Librapharm Ltd
29 Venture West, New Greenham Park, Newbury RG19 6HX
☎01635 522651 Fax 01635 36294
www.librapharm.com

Chairman *Mr M.W. Frost*
Managing Director *Dr P.L. Clarke*
Approx. Annual Turnover £4 million

Founded 1995 as a partial buyout from Kluwer Academic Publishers (UK) academic list. Publishes medical and scientific periodicals. No book publishing.

Library Association Publishing
See **Facet Publishing**

Library of Wales
See **Parthian**

Life&Times
See **Haus Publishing**

Frances Lincoln Ltd
4 Torriano Mews, Torriano Avenue, London NW5 2RZ
☎020 7284 4009 Fax 020 7485 0490
✉ firstname and initial of surname@ frances-lincoln.com
www.franceslincoln.com

Managing Director *John Nicoll*
Approx. Annual Turnover £5 million

Founded 1977. Publishes highly illustrated

non-fiction: gardening, art and interiors, architecture, parenting, walking and climbing, children's picture and information books; and stationery. DIVISIONS **Adult Non-fiction** *Jo Christian* TITLES *Chatsworth* Duchess of Devonshire; *Grow Your Own Vegetables* Joy Larkcom; *Pictorial Guides to the Lakeland Fells* A. Wainwright; **Children's General Fiction and Non-fiction** *Janetta Otter-Barry* TITLE *The Wanderings of Odysseus* Rosemary Sutcliffe, illus. Alan Lee; **Stationery** *Anne Fraser* TITLES *RHS Diary and Address Book*; *British Library Diary*. About 100 titles a year. Synopses and ideas for books considered.

ROYALTIES twice-yearly.

Linden Press
See **Open Gate Press**

Linford Romance/Linford Mystery/Linford Western
See **F.A. Thorpe (Publishing)**

Lion Hudson plc
Mayfield House, 256 Banbury Road, Oxford OX2 7DH
☎01865 302750 Fax 01865 302757
✉ enquiries@lionhudson.com
www.lionhudson.com

Managing Director *Paul Clifford*
Approx. Annual Turnover £8.5 million

Founded 1971. A Christian book publisher, strong on illustrated books for a popular international readership, with rights sold in over 150 languages worldwide. Publishes a diverse list with Christian viewpoint the common denominator. All ages, from board books for children to multi-contributor adult reference, educational, paperbacks and colour co-editions and gift books. IMPRINTS **Lion** and **Lion Children's** *Kate Leech*; **Candle** and **Monarch** *Caroline Nicholls* (see entry). About 175 titles a year. Unsolicited mss accepted provided they have a positive Christian viewpoint intended for a Christian or wide general and international readership.

ROYALTIES twice-yearly.

Little Black Dress
See **Hodder Headline Ltd**

Little Books Ltd
48 Catherine Place, London SW1E 6HL
☎020 7828 4422
www.littlebooks.net

Managing Director *Max Hamilton-Little*
Founded 2001. Publishes general trade books,

history, biography, health, natural history. IMPRINT **Max** TITLES *Freud: A Life in Our Time* Peter Gay; *Watching* Desmond Morris; *Lawrence of Arabia Letters* ed. Malcolm Brown. 16 titles in 2005. No unsolicited material.

ROYALTIES annually.

Little, Brown Book Group UK
Brettenham House, Lancaster Place, London WC2E 7EN
☎020 7911 8000 Fax 020 7911 8100
✉ uk@twbg.co.uk
www.littlebrown.co.uk

CEO/Publisher *Ursula Mackenzie*
Approx. Annual Turnover £50 million

Founded 1988 as Little, Brown & Co. (UK) and became Time Warner Book Group UK in 2002. Purchased by Hachette in March 2006 and renamed Little, Brown Book Group UK. Began by importing its US parent company's titles and in 1990 launched its own illustrated non-fiction list. Two years later the company took over former Macdonald & Co. Publishes hardback and paperback fiction, literary fiction, crime, science fiction and fantasy; and general non-fiction including true crime, biography and autobiography, cinema, history, humour, popular science, travel, reference, sport. IMPRINTS **Little, Brown** *Ursula Mackenzie, Richard Beswick, Stephen Guise, David Shelley, Hilary Hale* Hardback fiction and general non-fiction; **Abacus** *Richard Beswick, Stephen Guise* Literary fiction and non-fiction paperbacks; **Atom** *Tim Holman* Young adult/teen paperbacks; **Time Warner Audio Books** *Sarah Shrubb* (see entry under **Audio Books**); **Orbit** *Tim Holman, Darren Nash* Science fiction and fantasy; **Time Warner** *Antonia Hodgson, Joanne Dickinson, Hilary Hale, David Shelley, Rosie deCourcy, Tom Bromley* Mass-market fiction and non-fiction hardbacks and paperbacks; **Virago Press** *Lennie Goodings* (see entry). Approach in writing in the first instance. 350 titles in 2006. No unsolicited mss.

ROYALTIES twice-yearly.

Authors' Rating The change of name can be confusing (it was Time Warner) but authors continue to speak highly of a quality list strongly marketed.

Little Tiger Press
An imprint of Magi Publications, 1 The Coda Centre, 189 Munster Road, London SW6 6AW
☎020 7385 6333 Fax 020 7385 7333
✉ info@littletiger.co.uk

www.littletigerpress.com
Publisher *Monty Bhatia*
Editors *Jude Evans, Laura Workman*
Approx. Annual Turnover £5 million

Little Tiger Press imprint publishes children's picture and novelty books for ages 0–7. No texts over 750 words. IMPRINT **Stripes** Fiction for the 6–12 age range. About 30 titles a year. Unsolicited mss, synopses and new ideas welcome. See website for submission guidelines.
ROYALTIES annually.

Authors' Rating A thriving small publisher with imaginative output.

Liverpool University Press
4 Cambridge Street, Liverpool L69 7ZU
☎0151 794 2233   Fax 0151 794 2235
✉ robblo@liv.ac.uk
www.liverpool-unipress.co.uk
Managing Director/Editorial Head *Robin Bloxsidge*

LUP's primary activity is the publication of academic and scholarly books and journals but it also has a limited number of trade titles. Its principal focus is on the arts and social sciences, in which it is active in a variety of disciplines. TITLES *The Leaguers: The Making of Professional Football in England 1900–1939; Martin Mere: Lancashire's Lost Lake; Henry James: A Bibliographical Catalogue of a Collection of Editions to 1921; Transformations: The History of the Science Fiction Magazine from 1950 to 1970; Georges Brassens and Jacques Brel: Personal and Social Narratives in Post-War Chanson; Travellers' Visions: French Literary Encounters with Japan 1897–2004; Summer of Love: Psychedelic Art, Social Crisis and Counterculture in the 1960s; Faith, Fraternity and Fighting: The Orange Order and Irish Migrants in Northern England c.1850–1920.* 30–40 titles a year.
ROYALTIES annually.

Livewire Books for Teenagers
See **The Women's Press**

Lonely Planet Publications Ltd
72–82 Rosebery Avenue, London
EC1R 4RW
☎020 7841 9000   Fax 020 7841 9001
✉ go@lonelyplanet.co.uk
www.lonelyplanet.com
Owner *Lonely Planet (Australia)*
Editorial Head *Imogen Hall*
Approx. Annual Turnover £40 million

Lonely Planet, 'the world's largest independent guidebook publisher', has been producing award-winning guidebooks for independent travellers for over 30 years. With over 500 titles in print, publications include travel guidebooks, phrasebooks, travel literature, pictorial books, city maps, diving and snorkelling, walking, cycling, wildlife, health and How To guides. No unsolicited mss; synopses and ideas welcome. Author guidelines available at www.lonelyplanet.com/help/guide

Longman
See **Pearson Education**

Lorenz Books
See **Anness Publishing Ltd**

Lucky Duck Publishing
See **Sage Publications**

Lulu.com
www.lulu.com

A self publishing, print on demand service for individuals and companies. Produces a variety of digital content including books, music, video, software, calendars, photos and artwork with no set-up fee and no requirement to buy copies. Authors supply a digital file of their book and a print-ready version of the file is created by the company. Lulu handles sales and pays the royalty specified by the client with a small mark-up as commission. Offers two retail distribution services for a fee. Full details available on the website. Runs the **The Lulu Blooker Prize** (see entry under *Prizes*).

Authors' Rating Authors who find it hard to get into print now have recourse to an option that is not vanity publishing, at least not in the strict sense of the word. Launched in the US in 2002, Lulu is a website designed to carry anything that writers can throw at it, and for free. If browsers show an interest in a particular title, the book can be produced to order and shipped direct. To stay in business and, by all accounts, thrive Lulu takes a twenty per cent share of any royalties to which an author is entitled. Publishing services such as editing, proofing and marketing must be contracted separately. Anyone joining the game should not expect too much – as in all publishing luck plays a big part - but as an economic proposition Lulu has the edge on conventional vanity and self publishing operations.

Lund Humphries
See **Ashgate Publishing Ltd**

The Lutterworth Press

PO Box 60, Cambridge CB1 2NT
☎01223 350865 Fax 01223 366951
✉ publishing@jamesclarke.co.uk
www.lutterworth.com

Managing Director *Adrian Brink*

The Lutterworth Press dates back to the 18th century when it was founded as the Religious Tract Society. In the 19th century it was best known for its children's books and magazines, both religious and secular, including *The Boys' Own Paper* . Since 1984 it has been an imprint of **James Clarke & Co** (see entry). Publishes religious books for adults and children, adult non-fiction, children's fiction and non-fiction. TITLES *Artist of Wonderland* Frankie Morris; *A Spiritual Guide* Miguel de Molinos; *The Lost People of Malplaquet* Andrew Dalton; *From the Dairyman's Daughter to Worrals of the WAAF* ed. Dennis Butts. Approach in writing with ideas in the first instance.

ROYALTIES annually.

Macdonald & Co.

See **Little, Brown Book Group UK**

McGraw Hill Education

McGraw-Hill House, Shoppenhangers Road, Maidenhead SL6 2QL
☎01628 502500 Fax 01628 770224
www.mcgraw-hill.co.uk

General Manager *Shona Mullen*

Owned by US parent company, founded in 1888. Began publishing in Maidenhead in 1965, having had an office in the UK since 1899. Publishes business, economics, finance, accounting, computing science, social sciences and engineering for the academic, student and professional markets. Acquired **Open University Press** in 2002 (see entry). Around 200 titles a year. See website for author guidelines. Unsolicited proposals via website only.

ROYALTIES twice-yearly.

Macmillan Publishers Ltd

The Macmillan Building, 4 Crinan Street, London N1 9XW
☎020 7833 4000 Fax 020 7843 4640
www.macmillan.com

Owner *Verlagsgruppe Georg von Holtzbrinck*
Chief Executive *Richard Charkin*
Approx. Annual Turnover £300 million (Book Publishing Group)

Founded 1843. Macmillan is one of the largest publishing houses in Britain, publishing approximately 1400 titles a year. In 1995, Verlagsgruppe Georg von Holtzbrinck, a major German publisher, acquired a majority stake in the Macmillan Group and in 1999 purchased the remaining shares. In 1996, Macmillan bought Boxtree, the successful media tie-in publisher and, in 1997, it purchased the Heinemann English language teaching list from Reed Elsevier. The educational publishing division was strengthened by the acquisitions of the Mexican list, Ediciones Castillo and the Argentine company Puerto de Palos. No unsolicited material, except for the **Macmillan New Writing** list (see Authors' Rating).

DIVISIONS

Palgrave Macmillan Brunel Road, Houndmills, Basingstoke, Hampshire RG21 6XS ☎01256 329242 Fax 01256 479476 Managing Director *Dominic Knight*; **College** *Frances Arnold*; **Scholarly & Reference** *Sam Burridge*; **Journals** *David Bull*. Publishes textbooks, monographs and journals in academic and professional subjects. Publications in both hard copy and electronic format.

Macmillan Education Macmillan Oxford, 4 Between Towns Road, Oxford OX4 3PP ☎01865 405700 Fax 01865 405701 ✉ info@ macmillan.com www.macmillaneducation.com Executive Director *Christopher Paterson*, Managing Director *Chris Harrison*, Publishing Directors *Sue Bale* (ELT), *Alison Hubert* (education) Publishes a wide range of ELT titles and educational materials for the international education market from Oxford and through 30 subsidiaries worldwide.

Pan Macmillan 20 New Wharf Road, London N1 9RR ☎020 7014 6000 Fax 020 7014 6001 www.panmacmillan.com Managing Director *David North* Publishes under **Macmillan, Pan, Picador, Sidgwick & Jackson, Boxtree, Macmillan Children's Books, Campbell Books**.

IMPRINTS

Macmillan (founded 1843) Fiction: Publisher *Andrew Kidd*, Editorial Director *Imogen Taylor* Publishes hardback commercial fiction including genre fiction, romantic, crime and thrillers. IMPRINT **Tor** (founded 2003) Editorial Director *Peter Lavery* Publishes science fiction, fantasy and thrillers. Non-Fiction: Publisher *Richard Milner*, Editorial Director *Georgina Morley* Publishes serious and general non-fiction: autobiography, biography, economics, history, philosophy, politics and world affairs, psychology, popular science, trade reference titles.

Pan (founded 1947) Paperback imprint for Pan Macmillan.

Picador (founded 1972) Publisher *Andrew Kidd*, Deputy Publisher *Maria Rejt*, Senior Editorial Director *Ursula Doyle* Publishes literary international fiction, non-fiction and poetry.

Sidgwick & Jackson (founded 1908) Editorial Director *Ingrid Connell* Publishes popular non-fiction in hardback and trade paperback with strong personality or marketable identity, from celebrity and showbusiness to music and sport. Also military history list.

Boxtree (founded 1986) Publisher *Richard Milner* Publishes brand and media tie-in titles, including TV, film, music and Internet, plus entertainment licences, pop culture, humour and event-related books. TITLES *Dilbert*; *James Bond*; *Purple Ronnie*; *Wallace & Gromit*; *The Onion*.

Macmillan Children's Books (New Wharf Road address) Managing Director *Emma Hopkin*, Publishing Director *Sarah Davies*; Fiction: Editorial Director *Sarah Dudman*; Non-Fiction and Poetry: Editorial Director *Gaby Morgan*; Picture Books & Gift Books: Editorial Director *Suzanne Carnell*. **Campbell Books** Editorial Director *Sarah Fabiny*; **Young Picador** Editorial Director *Sarah Dudman* Publishes fiction, non-fiction and poetry in paperback and hardback.

ROYALTIES annually or twice-yearly depending on contract.

Authors' Rating Confounding the literary purists who are disposed to object to anything that might actually encourage fresh talent, the Macmillan New Writing project got off to a splendid start with eight titles chosen from nearly 3,000 submissions. The deal for first-time authors is a fixed contract with no advance but with a twenty per cent royalty. A new title appears each month. On the academic side, Palgrave is thriving on technological innovation ranging from hard print links to websites to print-on-demand. Macmillan CEO Richard Charkin looks to the day when every library and bookshop will be able to offer print-on-demand, a service that will offer speedier delivery at lower cost.

Made Simple Books

See **Elsevier Ltd**

Mainstream Publishing Co. (Edinburgh) Ltd

7 Albany Street, Edinburgh EH1 3UG
☎0131 557 2959 Fax 0131 556 8720
✉ editorial@mainstreampublishing.com
www.mainstreampublishing.com

Directors *Bill Campbell, Peter MacKenzie*
Approx. Annual Turnover £3 million

Publishes art, autobiography/biography, current affairs, health, sport, history, illustrated and fine editions, photography, politics and world affairs, popular paperbacks. TITLES *Soldier Five* Mike Coburn; *The Real Nureyev* Carolyn Soutar; *Woodward's England* Mick Collins. Over 80 titles a year. Ideas for books considered, but they should be preceded by a letter, synopsis and s.a.e. or return postage.

ROYALTIES twice-yearly.

Authors' Rating Financial backing from Random House has strengthened marketing and editorial reach.

Management Books 2000 Ltd

Forge House, Limes Road, Kemble,
Cirencester GL7 6AD
☎01285 771441 Fax 01285 771055
✉ info@mb2000.com
www.mb2000.com

Publisher *James Alexander*
Approx. Annual Turnover £500,000

Founded 1993 to develop a range of books for executives and managers working in the modern world of business. 'Essentially, the books are working books for working managers, practical and effective.' Publishes business, management, self-development and allied topics as well as sponsored titles. Launched the *In Ninety Minutes* series of compact guide books for managers in 2004, offering advice, ideas and practical help across a range of highly relevant business topics in an hour and a half of study. New ideas for this series are welcome. About 30 titles a year. Unsolicited mss, synopses and ideas for books welcome.

Manchester University Press

Oxford Road, Manchester M13 9NR
☎0161 275 2310 Fax 0161 274 3346
✉ mup@manchester.ac.uk
www.manchesteruniversitypress.co.uk

Publisher/Chief Executive *David Rodgers*
Head of Editorial *Matthew Frost*
Approx. Annual Turnover £2 million

Founded 1904. MUP is Britain's third largest university press, with a list marketed and sold worldwide. Remit consists of occasional trade publications but mainly A-level and undergraduate textbooks and research monographs. Publishes in the areas of: literature, TV, film, theatre and media, history and history of art, design, politics, economics and international

law. DIVISIONS **Humanities** *Matthew Frost*; **History/Art History** *Alison Welsby*; **Politics and Law** *Tony Mason*. About 120 titles a year. Unsolicited mss welcome.
ROYALTIES annually.

George Mann Books
See **Arnefold Publishing**

Manson Publishing Ltd
73 Corringham Road, London NW11 7DL
☎020 8905 5150   Fax 020 8201 9233
✉ manson@mansonpublishing.com
www.mansonpublishing.com
Chairman/Managing Director *Michael Manson*
Founded 1992. Publishes highly illustrated book for study and reference. Subject areas covered include medicine, veterinary medicine, earth science, plant science, agriculture and microbiology. About 10 titles a year. No unsolicited mss; synopses and ideas will be considered.
ROYALTIES twice-yearly.

Marston House
See **Alphabet & Image Ltd**

Martin Books
See **Simon & Schuster UK Ltd**

Kenneth Mason Publications Ltd
The Book Barn, Westbourne, Emsworth PO10 8RS
☎01243 377977   Fax 01243 379136
✉ info@whitechimney.com
www.researchdisclosure.com
Chairman *Kenneth Mason*
Managing Director *Piers Mason*
Founded 1958. Publishes diet, health, fitness, nutrition and nautical. No fiction. IMPRINTS **Boatswain Press**; **Research Disclosure**. Initial approach by letter with synopsis only.
ROYALTIES twice-yearly in first year, annually thereafter.

Matador
See **Troubador Publishing Ltd**

Max
See **Little Books Ltd**

Kevin Mayhew Publishers
Buxhall, Stowmarket IP14 3BW
☎01449 737978   Fax 01449 737834
✉ info@kevinmayhewltd.com
www.kevinmayhewltd.com
Chairman/Commissioning Editor *Kevin Mayhew*

Founded in 1976. One of the leading sacred music and Christian book publishers in the UK. Publishes religious titles – liturgy, sacramental, devotional, also children's books and school resources. IMPRINT **Palm Tree Press** Worldwide worship. Unsolicited synopses and mss welcome; telephone prior to sending material, please.
ROYALTIES annually.

Meadowside Children's Books
185 Fleet Street, London EC4A 2HS
☎020 7400 1092   Fax 020 7400 1037
✉ info@meadowsidebooks.com
www.meadowsidebooks.com
Owner *D.C. Thomson*
Publisher *Simon Rosenheim*
Art Director *Mark Mills*
Founded in September 2003. Publishes pre-school picture books, novelty books and junior fiction. Over 100 titles a year. Unsolicited mss, synopses and ideas accepted. Send to the Editorial Department by mail or e-mail. Only successful submissions will be answered.

Melrose Books
St Thomas Place, Ely CB7 4GG
☎01353 646608   Fax 01353 646602
✉ info@melrosebooks.co.uk
www.melrosebooks.com
Chairman *Richard A. Kay*
Managing Director *Nicholas S. Law*
Approx. Annual Turnover £100,000
Independent subsidy publisher established by **Melrose Press** in 2004. To-date has published general and children's fiction, literature, fantasy, biography, travel, religion and science reference. Welcomes submissions by e-mail or post
ROYALTIES 50%.

Melrose Press Ltd
St Thomas Place, Ely CB7 4GG
☎01353 646600   Fax 01353 646601
✉ tradesales@melrosepress.co.uk
www.melrosepress.co.uk
Chairman *Richard A. Kay*
Managing Director *Nicholas S. Law*
Approx. Annual Turnover £2 million
Founded 1960. Took on its present name in 1969. Publishes biographical who's who reference only (not including *Who's Who*, which is published by **A.&C. Black**). About 10 titles a year.

Mentor
See **Christian Focus Publications**

Mercat Press Ltd

10 Coates Crescent, Edinburgh EH3 7AL
☎0131 225 5324 Fax 0131 226 6632
✉ enquiries@mercatpress.com
www.mercatpress.com

Directors *Seán Costello, Tom Johnstone*

Founded 1971. Publishes fiction and non-fiction, mainly of Scottish interest. The Press was established as a stand-alone company in 2002 in a management buy-out following the collapse of parent firm James Thin Booksellers. It began by publishing reprints of classic Scottish literature but now produces a wide range of new titles. Subject areas include biography, photography and walking guides. IMPRINT **Crescent Books** Adult fiction. TITLES *Wild Land: Images of Nature from the Cairngorms* Mark Hamblin and Peter Cairns; *Nova Scotia: New Scottish Speculative Fiction* eds. Neil Williamson and Andrew J. Wilson; *West Highland Way, Official Guide* Bob Aitken and Roger Smith; *25 Walks* series; *Tears for a Tinker* Jess Smith; *The Glasgow Detective* J.E. Preston Muddock. Unsolicited synopses, preferably with sample chapters, are welcome. No new poetry.
ROYALTIES annually.

Mercury Books/Mercury Junior

See **Caxton Publishing Group**

The Merlin Press Ltd

Suite 4, 96 Monnow Street, Monmouth NP25 3EQ
☎01600 775663 Fax 01600 775663
✉ info@merlinpress.co.uk
www.merlinpress.co.uk

Managing Director *Anthony W. Zurbrugg*
Director *Adrian Howe*

Founded 1956. Publishes economics, history, philosophy, left-wing politics. No fiction. IMPRINTS **Merlin Press**; **Green Print**. TITLES *Socialist Register* (annual); *Ralph Miliband and the Politics of the New Left*; *Pit Women*. About 10 titles a year.
ROYALTIES twice-yearly.

Merrell Publishers Ltd

Head office: 81 Southwark Street, London SE1 0HX
☎020 7928 8880 Fax 020 7928 1199
✉ mail@merrellpublishers.com
www.merrellpublishers.com

US office: 49 West 24th Street, 8th Floor, New York, NY 10010
☎001 212 929 8344 Fax 001 212 929 8346
✉ info@merrellpublishersusa.com

Managing Director *Hugh Merrell*
Editorial Director *Julian Honer*
US Director *Joan Brookbank*
Approx. Annual Turnover £2.6 million

Founded 1993. Publishes art, architecture, design and photography. 32 titles in 2005. Unsolicited synopses and ideas for books welcome. Send c.v. and synopsis giving details of the book's target markets and funding of illustrations.
ROYALTIES annually.

Methodist Publishing House

See **mph**

Methuen Publishing Ltd

11–12 Buckingham Gate, London SW1E 6LB
☎020 7798 1600 Fax 020 7828 2098
✉ name@methuen.co.uk
www.methuen.co.uk

Managing Director *Peter Tummons*
Publishing Consultant (Methuen) *Max Eilenberg*
Publishing Consultant (Politico's) *Alan Gordon Walker*

Founded 1889. Methuen was owned by Reed International until it was bought by Random House in 1997. Purchased by a management buy-out team in 1998. Acquired **Politico's Publishing** in 2003 (see entry). Publishes fiction and non-fiction; travel, sport, film, performing arts, humour.
DIVISIONS **General**; **Film**; **Theatre**; **Politics**; **Current Affairs**. No unsolicited mss; synopses and ideas welcome. Prefers to be approached via agents or a letter of inquiry. No first novels, cookery books, personal memoirs.
ROYALTIES twice-yearly.

Metro Publishing

See **John Blake Publishing Ltd**

Michelin Travel Publications

Hannay House, 39 Clarendon Road, Watford WD17 1JA
☎01923 205240 Fax 01923 205241
www.Viamichelin.co.uk

Founded 1900 as a travel publisher. Publishes travel guides, maps and atlases. Travel-related synopses and ideas welcome; no mss.

Midland Publishing

An imprint of Ian Allan Publishing Ltd, 4 Watling Drive, Hinckley LE10 3EY
☎01455 255490 Fax 01455 255495
✉ midlandbooks@compuserve.com

Publisher *Peter Waller*

Publishes aviation, military and railways. No wartime memoirs. No unsolicited mss; synopses and ideas welcome.
ROYALTIES quarterly.

Milet Publishing Limited
See entry under **US Publishers**

Miller's
See **Octopus Publishing Group**

Millivres Prowler Limited
Unit M, Spectrum House, 32–34 Gordon House Road, London NW5 1LP
☎020 7424 7400 Fax 020 7424 7401
www.millivres.co.uk

Publishes *Gay Times, Diva Magazine, The Pink Paper*, the national free gay newspaper.
Authors' Rating No longer interested in books; the focus is entirely on journals.

Mills & Boon
See **Harlequin Mills & Boon Ltd**

Mindfield
See **Camden Press Ltd**

Mitchell Beazley
See **Octopus Publishing Group**

Mobius
See **Hodder Headline Ltd**

Monarch Books
Lion Hudson plc, Mayfield House, 256 Banbury Road, Oxford OX2 7DH
☎01865 302750 Fax 01865 302757
✉ monarch@lionhudson.com
Editorial Director *Tony Collins*

An imprint of **Lion Hudson plc**. Publishes an independent list of Christian books across a wide range of concerns. IMPRINT **Monarch** Upmarket paperback list with Christian basis and strong social concern agenda including psychology, future studies, politics, mission, theology, leadership and spirituality. About 35 titles a year. Unsolicited mss, synopses and ideas welcome.

Morgan Kauffman
See **Elsevier Ltd**

Mosby
See **Elsevier Ltd**

Motor Racing Publications
PO Box 1318, Croydon CR9 5YP
☎020 8654 2711 Fax 020 8407 0339
✉ mrp.books@virgin.net
www.mrpbooks.co.uk
Chairman/Editorial Head *John Blunsden*

Founded soon after the end of World War II to concentrate on motor-racing titles. Fairly dormant in the mid 1960s but was reactivated in 1968 by a new shareholding structure. John Blunsden later acquired a majority share and major expansion followed in the 1970s. Publishes motor-sport history, classic and performance car collection and restoration, race track and off-road driving and related subjects. IMPRINTS **Fitzjames Press; Motor Racing Publications**. About 4–6 titles a year. No unsolicited mss. Send synopses and ideas in specified subject areas in the first instance.
ROYALTIES twice-yearly.

mph
4 John Wesley Road, Werrington, Peterborough PE4 6ZP
☎01733 325002 Fax 01733 384180
www.mph.org.uk
Chair *Eric Jarvis*
Chief Executive *Martin Stone*
Head of Publishing *Dr Natalie K. Watson*
Approx. Annual Turnover £2 million

Founded 1800. Owned by the Methodist Church. Publishes a wide range of books, magazines and resources which are sold in the UK and overseas. Also *Epworth Review* quarterly magazine. IMPRINTS **Epworth** (see entry); **Inspire** (see entry); **Methodist Publishing House**. Approx 30 titles a year. Unsolicited mss, synopses and ideas welcome; send sample chapter and contents with covering letter and s.a.e. for return of mss.
ROYALTIES annually.

Murdoch Books UK Ltd
Erico House, 6th Floor North, 93–99 Upper Richmond Road, London SW15 2TG
☎020 8785 5995 Fax 020 8785 5985
Managing Director *Tim Whale*
Publisher *Kay Scarlett*

Owned by Australian media group Murdoch Books Pty Ltd. Publishes full-colour non-fiction: homes and interiors, gardening, cookery, craft, DIY and narrative non-fiction. About 80 titles a year.

John Murray (Publishers) Ltd
338 Euston Road, London NW1 3BH
☎020 7873 6000 Fax 020 7873 6446
✉ firstname.lastname@johnmurrays.co.uk
www.madaboutbooks.com

Owner *Hodder Headline*
Managing Director *Roland Philipps*

Founded 1768. Acquired by **Hodder Headline** in May 2002. Publishes general trade books. **Non-fiction** *Eleanor Birne*; **Fiction** *Anya Serota, Kate Parkin*.
No unsolicited material; send preliminary letter.
ROYALTIES twice-yearly.

Authors' Rating Benefiting from the administrative and marketing backup from its new owners, Murray remains loyal to the editorial policy of turning out quality general non-fiction.

Myth & Legend
See **CRW Publishing Ltd**

NAG Press Ltd
See **Robert Hale Ltd**

The National Archives
Kew TW9 4DU
☎020 8392 5289 Fax 020 8487 1974
✉ catherine.bradley@nationalarchives.gov.uk
www.nationalarchives.gov.uk

Publisher *Catherine Bradley*

Publishes non-fiction books, guides relating to the thousand years of historical records held in The National Archives. Specialist areas: general history, family history, military history and intelligence history. TITLES *Gunpowder: The Players Behind the Plot* James Travers; *All for Love: a history of illicit liaison* Val Horsler; *The Scotland Yard Files* Alan Moss and Keith Skinner; *Germany: A British Soldier's Pocketbook*; *The Genealogist's Internet* Pete Christian; *Easy Family History* David Annal. Also publishes *Ancestors*, a full-colour family history magazine.

National Trust Books
See **Anova Books**

Nautical Data Ltd
The Book Barn, Westbourne, Emsworth PO10 8RS
☎01243 389352 Fax 01243 379136
✉ info@nauticaldata.com
www.nauticaldata.com

Managing Director *Piers Mason*

Founded 1999. Publishes pilots and nautical reference. No unsolicited mss; synopses and ideas welcome. No fiction or non-nautical themes.
ROYALTIES twice-yearly.

NCVO Publications
Regent's Wharf, 8 All Saints Street, London N1 9RL
☎020 7713 6161/HelpDesk: 0800 2798 798
Fax 020 7713 6300
www.ncvo-vol.org.uk/publications

Publications and Promotions Coordinator *Daniel Fluskey*
Approx. Annual Turnover £140,000

Founded 1928. Publishing imprint of the National Council for Voluntary Organisations, embracing former Bedford Square Press titles and NCVO's many other publications. The list reflects NCVO's role as the representative body for the voluntary sector. Publishes directories, good practice information on management and trustee development, finance and employment titles and information of primary interest to the voluntary sector. TITLES *The Voluntary Agencies Directory*; *The Good Trustee Guide*; *The Good Campaigns Guide*; *The Good Financial Management Guide*; *The Good Employment Guide*; *The Good Management Guide*; *The Good Membership Guide*; *The UK Voluntary Sector Almanac*. No unsolicited mss as all projects are commissioned in-house.

Thomas Nelson & Sons Ltd
See **Nelson Thornes Limited**

Nelson Thornes Limited
Delta Place, 27 Bath Road, Cheltenham GL53 7TH
☎01242 267100 Fax 01242 221914
✉ info@nelsonthornes.com
www.nelsonthornes.com

Owner *Wolters Kluwer*
Managing Director *Mary O'Connor*

Based in Cheltenham and a division of Wolters Kluwer, the Amsterdam based global publishing and services business, Nelson Thornes was formed by the merger of Thomas Nelson and Stanley Thornes publishing companies in 2000. Educational publisher of printed and electronic product, from pre-school to Higher Education. Unsolicited mss, synopses and ideas for books welcome if appropriate to specialised lists.
ROYALTIES annually.

New Beacon Books Ltd

76 Stroud Green Road, London N4 3EN
☎020 7272 4889   Fax 020 7281 4662
✉ newbeaconbooks@btconnect.com
Chairman *John La Rose*
Managing Director *Sarah White*
Approx. Annual Turnover £120,000

Founded 1966. Publishes fiction, history, politics, poetry and language, all concerning black people. No unsolicited material.
ROYALTIES annually.

New Editions

See **Gibson Square**

New Holland Publishers (UK) Ltd

Garfield House, 86–88 Edgware Road,
London W2 2EA
☎020 7724 7773   Fax 020 7258 1293
(editorial)
✉ postmaster@nhpub.co.uk
www.newhollandpublishers.com
Managing Director *John Beaufoy*
Publishing Managers *Rosemary Wilkinson,
   Jo Hemmings*
Approx. Annual Turnover £6 million

With its headquarters in London, New Holland Publishers (UK) Ltd is the International Publishing Division of Johnnic Communications, one of Africa's leading publishing groups, with offices in Australia and New Zealand. Publishes non-fiction, practical and inspirational books across a range of categories, including food and drink, DIY, practical art, crafts, interiors, health and fitness, gardening, pets, humour and gift, reference, history, sports and outdoor pursuits, natural history, general travel books and Globetrotter travel guides. TITLES *Men and Sheds*; *The Allotment Handbook*; *The Big Book of Handmade Cards*; *The Garden Bird Handbook*; *Diving the World's Coral Reefs*; *Worst Album Covers in the World*.
   No unsolicited mss; synopses and ideas welcome.

Newnes

See **Elsevier Ltd**

Nexus

See **Virgin Books Ltd**

nferNELSON

The Chiswick Centre, 414 Chiswick High Road, London W4 5TF
☎020 8996 3333   Fax 020 8742 8390
www.nfer-nelson.co.uk

Founded 1981. A division of Granada Learning Ltd. Publishes educational and psychological tests and training materials. Main interest is in educational, clinical and occupational assessment and training material.

Nia

See **The X Press**

Nielsen BookData

3rd Floor, Midas House, 62 Goldsworth Road,
Woking GU21 6LQ
☎0870 777 8710   Fax 0870 777 8711
✉ info@nielsenbookdata.co.uk
www.nielsenbookdata.co.uk

Creates and maintains a unique database of timely, accurate and content rich records for English-language books and other published media, collected from publishers in over 70 countries. The enriched data includes: price, availability, table of contents (where applicable), subject classifications, market rights, publisher and distributor details, cover/jacket images and book descriptions. The data is disseminated worldwide in a variety of formats: data feed, dynamic XML, CD-ROMs and online services.

Nightingale Books

See **Pegasus Elliot Mackenzie Publishers Ltd**

NMS Enterprises Limited – Publishing

National Museums of Scotland, Chambers Street, Edinburgh EH1 1JF
☎0131 247 4026   Fax 0131 247 4012
✉ publishing@nms.ac.uk
www.nms.ac.uk
Director *Lesley A. Taylor*
Approx. Annual Turnover £150,000

Publishes non-fiction related to the National Museums of Scotland collections: academic and general; children's; archaeology, history, decorative arts worldwide, history of science, technology, natural history and geology, poetry. TITLES *Nicholas and Alexandra: The Last Tsar and Tsarina*; *Renaissance Decorative Painting in Scotland*; *Minerals of Scotland*; *Audubon in Edinburgh*; *The Thin Red Line: War, Empire and Visions of Scotland*; *Weights and Measures in Scotland: a European Perspective* (2005 Saltire Society/National Library of Scotland Research Book of the Year). No unsolicited mss; only interested in synopses and ideas for books which are genuinely related to NMS collections and to Scotland in general.
ROYALTIES twice-yearly.

No Exit Press
See **Oldcastle Books Ltd**

North–Holland
See **Elsevier Ltd**

Northcote House Publishers Ltd
Horndon House, Horndon, Tavistock
PL19 9NQ
☎01822 810066 Fax 01822 810034
✉ northcote.house@virgin.net
www.northcotehouse.co.uk
Managing Director *Brian Hulme*

Founded 1985. Publishes a series of literary critical studies, in association with the British Council, *Writers and their Work*; education management, literary criticism, educational dance and drama. 30 titles in 2006. 'Well–thought–out proposals, including contents and sample chapter(s), with strong marketing arguments welcome.'
ROYALTIES annually.

W.W. Norton & Company Ltd
Castle House, 75–76 Wells Street, London
W1T 3QT
☎020 7323 1579 Fax 020 7436 4553
✉ office@wwnorton.co.uk
Managing Director *Alan Cameron*

Subsidiary of the US parent company founded in 1923. Publishes non-fiction and academic books.

Nottingham University Press
Manor Farm, Church Lane, Thrumpton
NG11 0AX
☎0115 983 1011 Fax 0115 983 1003
✉ editor@nup.com
www.nup.com
Managing Editor *Dr D.J.A. Cole*

Initially concentrated on agricultural and food sciences titles but has now branched into new areas including engineering, lifesciences, medicine and law. TITLES *The Alcohol Textbooks*; *The Mycotoxin Handbook*; *Emerging Equine Science*; *Writing and Presenting Scientific Papers*. **Castle Publications** TITLES *The Cricket Coach's Guide to Man Management*; *The Games Guide*.
ROYALTIES twice-yearly.

NWP
See **Neil Wilson Publishing Ltd**

Oak
See **Omnibus Press**

Oberon Books
521 Caledonian Road, London N7 9RH
☎020 7607 3637 Fax 020 7607 3629
✉ info@oberonbooks.com
www.oberonbooks.com
Publishing Director *James Hogan*
Managing Director *Charles D. Glanville*
Editor *Dan Steward*

A leading theatre publisher, Oberon publishes play texts (usually in conjunction with a production), and books on theatre and dance. Specialises in contemporary plays and translations of European classics. IMPRINTS **Oberon Modern Plays**; **Oberon Classics**. Publishes for the National Theatre, Royal Opera House, Royal Court, English Touring Theatre, LAMDA, Gate Theatre, Bush Theatre, West Yorkshire Playhouse, Chichester Festival Theatre, Salisbury Playhouse and many other London and regional theatre companies. Publishes over 300 writers and translators including Rodney Ackland, Tariq Ali, Howard Barker, John Barton, Ranjit Bolt, Howard Brenton, Ken Campbell, Pam Gems, Sir Peter Hall, Christopher Hampton, Bernard Kops, Adrian Mitchell, Sir John Mortimer. An extensive classics list includes performance (edited) versions of Shakespeare including *King Lear*, *A Midsummer Night's Dream*; *Romeo and Juliet* and *Twelfth Night*, as well as new translations of plays by Chekhov, Molière, Strindberg and others. About 80 titles a year.

Octagon Press Ltd
78 York Road, London W1H 1DP
☎020 7168 5308 Fax 020 7168 5308
✉ info@octagonpress.com
www.octagonpress.com
Managing Director *George R. Schrager*
Approx. Annual Turnover £100,000

Founded 1960. Publishes travel, biography, literature, folklore, psychology, philosophy with the focus on East–West studies. Also distributes research monographs published by The Institute for Cultural Research. 4–5 titles a year. Unsolicited mss not accepted. Enquiries in writing only. Welcomes book proposals of no more than a single page; e-mail to editor@octagonpress.com
ROYALTIES annually.

Octopus Publishing Group
2–4 Heron Quays, London E14 4JP
☎020 7531 8400 Fax 020 7531 8650
www.octopus-publishing.co.uk
Chief Executive *Alison Goff*
Approx. Annual Turnover £45 million (Group)

Formed following a management buyout of Reed Consumer Books from Reed Elsevier plc in 1998. Bought by French publishers Hachette-Livre in 2001 and acquired Cassell Illustrated and the lists of Ward Lock and Blandford Press; also, Gaia Books acquired in 2004.

Conran Octopus Fax 020 7531 8627 ✉ info-co@conran-octopus.co.uk   www. conran-octopus.co.uk Publishing Director *Lorraine Dickey* Quality illustrated lifestyle books, particularly interiors, design, cookery, gardening and crafts TITLES *The Essential House Book* Terence Conran; *Fork to Fork* Monty Don; *Passion for Seafood* Gordon Ramsay; *New Retail* Rasshied Din.

Hamlyn Octopus Fax 020 7531 8562 ✉ info-ho@hamlyn.co.uk   www.hamlyn.co.uk Publisher *Jane Birch* Popular non-fiction, particularly cookery, gardening, craft, sport, health, film and music TITLES *Larousse Gastronomique*; *Hamlyn All Colour Cookbook*; *Hamlyn Book of Gardening*; *Hamlyn Book of DIY & Decorating*.

Mitchell Beazley/Miller's Fax 020 7537 0773   ✉ info-mb@mitchell-beazley.co.uk www.mitchell-beazley.co.uk Publisher *David Lamb* Quality illustrated reference books, particularly food and wine, gardening, interior design and architecture, antiques, general reference TITLES *Hugh Johnson's Pocket Wine Book*; *The New Joy of Sex*; *Miller's Antiques and Collectibles Price Guides*.

Philip's Fax   020   7531   8460   ✉ george. philip@philips-maps.co.uk www. philips-maps.co.uk Managing Director *John Gaisford* World atlases, globes, astronomy, road atlases, encyclopaedias, thematic reference TITLES *Philip's Atlas of the World*; *Philip's Modern School Atlas*; *Philip's Guide to the Stars and Planets*; *Ordnance Survey Street Atlas*; *Philip's Millennium Encyclopaedia*; *Philip's Atlas of World History*.

Bounty Fax   020   7531   8607   ✉ bountybooksinfo-bp@bountybooks.co.uk Publishing and International Sales Director *Polly Manguel* Bargain and promotional books. New, repackaged and reissued titles.

Cassell Illustrated Fax 020 731 8624 Publishing Director *Iain MacGregor* Serious non-fiction covering a wide range of topics from history and cookery to fitness and art.

Godsfield Press Fax 020 7531 8562 ✉ enquiries@godsfieldpress.com Publisher *Jane Birch* Mind, body and spirit encompassing original psychology, health and gift books.

Gaia Books Publisher *Jane Birch* Mind, body and spirit and natural/eco titles.

ROYALTIES twice-yearly/annually, according to contract in all divisions.

Oldcastle Books Ltd

PO Box 394, Harpenden AL5 1XJ
☎01582 761264 Fax 01582 761264
www.noexit.co.uk
www.pocketessentials.com
www.highstakespublishing.com
Managing Director *Ion Mills*

Founded 1985. Publishes crime/noir fiction, gambling non-fiction and 160pp mini-reference titles on film, ideas, history, music, etc. IMPRINTS **No Exit Press**; **High Stakes**; **Pocketessentials**.

Olympia Publishers

78 Cannon Street, London EC4N 6NQ
☎020 7618 6424 Fax 020 7618 8001
✉ info@olympiapublishers.com
www.olympiapublishers.com
Managing Editor *G. Bartlett*
Assistant Editor *M. Marlowe*

Founded 2004. Publishes a wide range of non-fiction and some fiction. Educational books include English language textbooks and TEFL. General interest titles cover autobiography, biography, crime, history, travel, mind body and soul, gardening, cookery and humour. Specialises in books for international markets by Far Eastern authors and Europeans. TITLES *The A-Z of Practical Wisdom*; *Essay Writing for TEFL*. 40–50 titles a year. See website for submissions form and author guidelines; unsolicited synopses and ideas will be considered (as will poetry and short stories). Postal submissions must be accompanied by s.a.e.

ROYALTIES twice-yearly.

Michael O'Mara Books Ltd

9 Lion Yard, Tremadoc Road, London SW4 7NQ
☎020 7720 8643 Fax 020 7627 8953
✉ firstname.lastname@
    michaelomarabooks.com
www.mombooks.com
www.busterpreviews.com
Chairman *Michael O'Mara*
Managing Director *Lesley O'Mara*
Editorial Director (Commissioning) *Lindsay Davies*
Approx. Annual Turnover £7 million

Founded 1985. Independent publisher. Publishes general non-fiction, humour, anthologies, history, royalty and celebrity biographies. TITLES *The Timewaster Letters* Robin Cooper; *The Little Book of Sudoku*; *The Pedant's Revolt* Andrea Barham. IMPRINT **Buster Books**

Children's titles: board books, picture books, novelty books, humour and quirky non-fiction. Unsolicited mss, synopses and ideas for books welcome.
ROYALTIES twice-yearly.

Authors' Rating Most of the creative work for bestselling humour titles is done in-house but strong ideas for the gift market may well attract interest.

Omnibus Press
Music Sales Ltd, 8–9 Frith Street, London W1D 3JB
☎020 7434 0066 Fax 020 7734 2246
✉ chris.charlesworth@musicsales.co.uk
www.omnibuspress.com
Editorial Head *Chris Charlesworth*

Founded 1971. Independent publisher of music books, rock and pop biographies, song sheets, educational tutors, cassettes, videos and software. A Division of the Music Sales Group of Companies. IMPRINTS **Amsco**; **Bobcat**; **Oak**; **Omnibus**; **Vision On**; **Wise Publications**. About 25 titles a year. Unsolicited mss, synopses and ideas for music-related titles welcome.
ROYALTIES twice-yearly.

Oneworld Publications
185 Banbury Road, Oxford OX2 7AR
☎01865 310597 Fax 01865 310598
✉ info@oneworld-publications.com
www.oneworld-publications.com
Editorial Director *Juliet Mabey*

Founded 1986. Publishes adult non-fiction across a range of subjects from world religions to psychology and philosophy, history, politics, and popular science. SERIES include short histories of countries and one on world religions (with authors such as Geoffrey Parrinder, Keith Ward, Klaus Klostermaier and John Hick); also concise encyclopedias on world religions. **Oneworld Philosophers** series was launched in 2001 and **Oneworld Beginners' Guides** in 2002. **Coping With** is a new series aimed at the self-help and counselling market; **Makers of the Muslim World** introduces key people from Muslim history, politics and religion to a broad audience, while a new popular science list explores scientific discoveries and ideas for the specialist and lay reader. TITLES *Pascal's Fire*; *Bioterror & Biowarfare: A Beginner's Guide*; *The New Imperialists*; *25 Big Ideas: The Science that Changed our World*. About 45 titles a year. No unsolicited mss; synopses and ideas welcome, but should be accompanied by s.a.e. for return

of material and/or notification of receipt. No autobiographies, fiction, poetry or children's.
ROYALTIES annually.

Onlywomen Press Ltd
40 St Lawrence Terrace, London W10 5ST
☎020 8354 0796 Fax 020 8960 2817
✉ onlywomenpress@btconnect.com
www.onlywomenpress.com
Editorial Director *Lilian Mohin*

Founded 1974. Publishes feminist lesbian literature: fiction, poetry, literary criticism and political theory. Unsolicited mss and proposals welcome. Submissions details on the website.

OPC
See **Ian Allan Publishing Ltd**

Open Gate Press (incorporating Centaur Press 1954)
51 Achilles Road, London NW6 1DZ
☎020 7431 4391 Fax 020 7431 5129
✉ books@opengatepress.co.uk
Managing Directors *Jeannie Cohen, Elisabeth Petersdorff*

Founded in 1989 to provide a forum for psychoanalytic social and cultural studies. Publishes psychoanalysis, philosophy, social sciences, politics, literature, religion, animal rights, environment. SERIES *Psychoanalysis and Society*. Also publishes a journal of psychoanalytic social studies, *New Analysis*. IMPRINTS **Open Gate Press**; **Centaur Press**; **Linden Press**. Since the acquisition of Centaur Press, Open Gate Press is continuing its work, in particular the *Kinship Library* – a series on the philosophy, politics and application of humane education. No unsolicited mss.
ROYALTIES twice-yearly.

Open University Press
McGraw-Hill House, Shoppenhangers Road, Maidenhead SL6 2QL
☎01628 502500 Fax 01628 770224
✉ enquiries@openup.co.uk
www.openup.co.uk
Managing Director *Paul Maraviglia*

Founded 1977 as an imprint independent of the Open University's course materials. Acquired by **McGraw Hill Education** in 2002. Publishes academic and professional books in the fields of education, sociology, health, psychology, psychotheraphy and counselling, education and study skills materials. No economics or anthropology. Not interested in anything outside the social sciences. About 100 titles a year. No unsolicited mss; enquiries/proposals only.

ROYALTIES annually.

Orbit
See **Little, Brown Book Group UK**

Orchard Books
See **Hachette Children's Books**

The Orion Publishing Group Limited
Orion House, 5 Upper St Martin's Lane, London WC2H 9EA
☎020 7240 3444 Fax 020 7240 4822
www.orionbooks.co.uk/pub/index.htm

Chairman *Arnaud Nourry*
Chief Executive *Peter Roche*
Deputy Chief Executive *Malcolm Edwards*
Approx. Annual Turnover £70 million

Founded 1992. Incorporates Weidenfeld & Nicolson, JM Dent, Gollancz and Cassell.

DIVISIONS **Orion** Managing Director *Lisa Milton* IMPRINTS **Orion Fiction** Publishing Director *Jon Wood* Hardcover fiction; **Orion Media** Publishing Director *Ian Marshall* Hardcover non-fiction; **Orion Children's** Publisher *Fiona Kennedy* Children's fiction/non-fiction; **Gollancz** Editorial Directors *Simon Spanton, Jo Fletcher* Science fiction and fantasy.
Weidenfeld & Nicolson Managing Director *Malcolm Edwards*, Publisher *Alan Samson* IMPRINTS **Weidenfeld Illustrated** Editor-in-Chief *Michael Dover* Illustrated non-fiction; **Weidenfeld General** Publishing Director *Ian Drury* General non-fiction, history and military; **Weidenfeld Fiction** Editorial Director *Helen Garnons Williams* History; **Cassell Reference** General reference; **Custom Publishing** Managing Director *Alasdair MacLeod*.
Paperback Division Managing Director *Susan Lamb* IMPRINTS **Orion**; **Phoenix**; **Everyman**.

Authors' Rating Ever in pursuit of the big titles, Orion backs talent with energetic marketing.

Osprey Publishing Ltd
Midland House, West Way, Botley, Oxford OX2 0PH
☎01865 727022 Fax 01865 727017/727019
✉ info@ospreypublishing.com
www.ospreypublishing.com

Also at: 443 Park Avenue, Suite 806, New York, NY 10016, USA

Managing Director *William Shepherd*
Business Development Manager *Simone Drinkwater*
Editorial Development Manager *Anita Baker*

Publishes military history and aviation from around the world. Founded 1969, Osprey became independent from **Reed Elsevier** in February 1998 and launched Osprey Publishing Inc. as a wholly owned subsidiary in North America in 2004. Major illustrated SERIES include *Men-at-Arms*; *Fortress*; *Campaign*; *Essential Histories*; *Warrior*; *Elite*; *New Vanguard*; *Osprey Modelling*; *Osprey Duel*; *Aircraft of the Aces*; *Aviation Elite Units*; *Combat Aircraft*. Non-series books are also considered. About 130 titles a year. No unsolicited mss; ideas and synopses welcome.

ROYALTIES twice-yearly.

Peter Owen Publishers
73 Kenway Road, London SW5 0RE
☎020 7373 5628/7370 6093
Fax 020 7373 6760
✉ admin@peterowen.com
www.peterowen.com

Chairman *Peter Owen*
Editorial Director *Antonia Owen*

Founded 1951. Publishes biography, general non-fiction, English-language literary fiction and translations, history, literary criticism, the arts and entertainment. 'No genre or children's fiction; the company is taking on no first novels or short stories at present.' AUTHORS Jane Bowles, Paul Bowles, Yuri Druzhnikov, Shusaku Endo, Philip Freund, Anna Kavan, Jean Giono, Anaïs Nin, Jeremy Reed, Peter Vansittart. 30–40 titles a year. Unsolicited synopses welcome for non-fiction material. Please call in advance to submit fiction. Mss should be preceded by a descriptive letter and synopsis with s.a.e. OVERSEAS ASSOCIATES worldwide.

ROYALTIES twice-yearly.

Authors' Rating Peter Owen has been described as 'a publisher of the old and idiosyncratic school'. He has seven Nobel prizewinners on his list to prove it.

Oxbow Books
Park End Place, Oxford OX1 1HN
☎01865 241249 Fax 01865 794449
✉ oxbow@oxbowbooks.com
www.oxbowbooks.com

Editorial *Clare Litt*

Founded 1983. Publishes academic archaeology, Egyptology, ancient and medieval history.

IMPRINT **Aris & Phillips** Greek, Latin and Hispanic texts and translations. About 60 titles a year.

Oxford University Press

Great Clarendon Street, Oxford OX2 6DP
☎01865 556767 Fax 01865 556646
✉ enquiry@oup.com
www.oup.com
Chief Executive *Henry Reece*
Approx. Annual Turnover £389 million

A department of Oxford University, OUP started as the university's printing business and developed into a major publishing operation in the 19th century. Publishes academic works in all formats (print and online): dictionaries, lexical and non-lexical reference, scholarly journals, student texts, schoolbooks, ELT materials, music, bibles, paperbacks, and children's books. Around 6000 titles a year.

DIVISIONS **Academic** *T.M. Barton* Academic and higher education titles in major disciplines, dictionaries, non-lexical reference and trade books. OUP welcomes first-class academic material in the form of proposals or accepted theses. **Journals** *M. Richardson* Academic and research journals. **Education** *K. Harris* National Curriculum courses and support materials as well as children's literature. **ELT** *P.R.C. Marshall* ELT courses and dictionaries for all levels. OVERSEAS BRANCHES/SUBSIDIARIES Sister company in USA with branches or subsidiaries in Argentina, Australia, Brazil, Canada, China, East Africa, India, Japan, Malaysia, Mexico, Pakistan, Southern Africa, Spain and Turkey. Offices in France, Greece, Italy, Poland, Taiwan, Thailand. ROYALTIES twice-yearly.

Authors' Rating There are so many facets to OUP it might almost be described as a general publisher. But academic books and reference are the bedrock. Increased investment in new publishing includes the *New Dictionary of National Biography*, one of the biggest projects of its kind in contemporary publishing, the *Grove Dictionary of Music* and the *Grove Dictionary of Art*.

Palgrave Macmillan

See **Macmillan Publishers Ltd**

Palm Tree Press

See **Kevin Mayhew Publishers**

G.J. Palmer & Sons Ltd

See **Hymns Ancient & Modern Ltd**

Pan

See **Macmillan Publishers Ltd**

Paper Tiger

See **Anova Books**

Parthian

The Old Surgery, Napier Street, Aberteifi (Cardigan) SA43 1ED
☎01239 612059
✉ parthianbooks@yahoo.co.uk
www.parthianbooks.co.uk

Also: **Library of Wales**
Trinity College, Carmarthen SA31 3EP
Fax 01239 612059
www.libraryofwales.org
Publisher *Richard Davies*
Fiction Editor *Gwen Davies*
Poetry Editor *Jasmine Donahaye*
Editor, Library of Wales *Professor Dai Smith*

Founded 1993. Publishes contemporary Welsh writing in English including novels, poetry and drama, also translations from Welsh. A keen interest in short stories. Its list includes many young writers. TITLES *Fresh Apples* Rachel Trezise; *Circle Games* Jo Mazelis; *Nightsounds* Karen Gettert Shoemaker. A new non-fiction list is planned for 2007. Increasing interest in translation with new titles planned from Catalan an Basque. Also publishes **Library of Wales** classic series including Raymond Williams' *Border Country*, ed. Prof. Dai Smith. 12–15 titles a year. 12–15 titles a year. Synopsis with first three sample chapters welcome. 'An idea of what we do is always an advantage.' ROYALTIES twice-yearly.

Paternoster Press

See **Authentic Media**

Pavilion/Pavilion Children's Books

See **Anova Books**

Pearson Education

Edinburgh Gate, Harlow CM20 2JE
☎01279 623623 Fax 01279 431059
www.pearsoned.com

The world's largest educational publisher was created by the merger of Addison Wesley Longman, Financial Times Management and **Simon & Schuster**'s educational list. Publishes across a wide range of curriculum subjects from primary students to professional practictioners. IMPRINTS **Longman**; **Causeway Press**; **Prentice Hall**; **Addison Wesley**. OVERSEAS

ASSOCIATES worldwide. Unsolicited mss should be addressed to the appropriate department: **ELT** *Lyn Kitteridge*; **Schools** *Carol Hayward*; **University & Professional Level** *Anna Campling*.
ROYALTIES twice-yearly.

Authors' Rating A fabulous year for school books was led by ELT including a new primary level English language course. And this at a time when overall education publishing has been going through a rough patch.

Pegasus Elliot Mackenzie Publishers Ltd

Sheraton House, Castle Park, Cambridge CB3 0AX
☎01223 370012   Fax 01223 370040
✉ editors@pegasuspublishers.com
www.pegasuspublishers.com
Senior Editor *D. W. Stern*
Editor *R. Sabir*

Publishes fiction and non-fiction, general interest, biography, autobiography, children's, history, humour, fantasy, self-help, educational, science fiction, poetry, travel, war, memoirs, crime and eroticism, also Internet and e-books. IMPRINTS **Vanguard Press**; **Nightingale Books**; **Chimera** Titles *Friendly Fire* Mike Edwards; *The Fourth Movement* Daniel Kane; *The Widow Makers* Jean Mead; *Exile Child* Suzanne Franco; *The Maltese House with the Bright Yellow Door* Connie Anderson. Unsolicited mss, synopses and ideas considered if accompanied by return postage.
ROYALTIES twice-yearly.

Authors' Rating Liable to ask authors to contribute to production costs.

Pen & Sword Books Ltd

47 Church Street, Barnsley S70 2AS
☎01226 734222   Fax 01226 734438
✉ editorial@pen-and-sword.co.uk
www.pen-and-sword.co.uk
Commissioning Editor, Aviation *Peter Coles*
Commissioning Editor, Military & Maritime *Henry Wilson*
Commissioning Editor, History, Local History & Family History *Rupert Harding*

One of the leading military history publishers in the UK. Publishes non-fiction only, specialising in naval and aviation history, WW1, WW2, Napoleonic, autobiography and biography. Also publishes *Battleground* series for battlefield tourists. IMPRINTS **Leo Cooper**; **Pen &** **Sword Aviation**; **Pen & Sword Family History**; **Pen & Sword Maritime**; **Pen & Sword Military**; **Wharncliffe Books** (see entry). About 200 titles a year. Unsolicited synopses and ideas welcome; no unsolicited mss.
ROYALTIES twice-yearly.

Penguin Group (UK)

A Pearson Company, 80 Strand, London WC2R 0RL
☎020 7010 3000   Fax 020 7010 6060
www.penguin.co.uk

Group Chairman & Chief Executive *John Makinson*
Managing Director: Penguin *Helen Fraser*
Approx. Annual Turnover £121 million

Owned by Pearson plc. The world's best known book brand and for more than 70 years a leading publisher whose adult and children's lists include fiction, non-fiction, poetry, drama, classics, reference and special interest areas. Reprints and new work.

DIVISIONS
Penguin General Books Managing Director *Tom Weldon* Adult fiction and non-fiction is published in hardback under Michael Joseph, Viking and Hamish Hamilton imprints. Paperbacks come under the Penguin imprint. IMPRINTS **Viking/Penguin** Publisher *Venetia Butterfield* Publishing Director *Tony Lacey*; **Hamish Hamilton** Publishing Director *Simon Prosser*; **Michael Joseph/Penguin** Managing Director *Louise Moore* Does not accept unsolicited mss.
Penguin Press Managing Director *Stefan McGrath* Publishing Directors *Stuart Proffitt, Simon Winder* Academic adult non-fiction, reference, specialist and classics. IMPRINTS **Allen Lane**; **Penguin Reference** Publishing Director *Georgina Laycock* No unsolicited mss.
Dorling Kindersley Ltd (see entry).
Frederick Warne Managing Director *Sally Floyer* Classic children's publishing and merchandising including *Beatrix Potter*™; *Flower Fairies*; *Orlando*. **Ventura** Publisher *Sally Floyer* Producer and packager of *Spot* titles by Eric Hill.
Ladybird (see **Dorling Kindersley Ltd**).
BBC Children's Books *Sally Floyer* Children's imprint launched in 2004.
Puffin Managing Director *Francesca Dow* (poetry and picture books) Publisher *Rebecca McNally* (fiction), Senior Editor *Fran Hammond* (media and popular non-fiction) Leading children's paperback list, publishing in virtually all fields including fiction, non-fiction, poetry, pic-

ture books, media-related titles. No unsolicited mss; synopses and ideas welcome.

Penguin Audiobooks (see entry under *Audio Books*).

ePenguin Commissioning Editor *Jeremy Ettinghausen* e-books list launched in 2001. OVERSEAS ASSOCIATES worldwide.

ROYALTIES twice-yearly.

Authors' Rating One of the best known names in publishing, now into its seventy-first year, Penguin has come through a rough passage to achieve a 'good all-round performance', according to CEO John Makinson. In third place behind Random House and Hachette in terms of UK market share, Penguin holds the number one position for non-fiction. The emphasis now is on strengthening the paperback fiction list. Looking to extend its reach to the great unread, Penguin has acquired direct sales operation Index Books. This follows a move into packaging with products designed specifically for high-street outlets such as Marks & Spencer and Wal-Mart.

Pergamon
See **Elsevier Ltd**

Persephone Books
59 Lamb's Conduit Street, London WC1N 3NB
☎020 7242 9292 Fax 020 7242 9272
✉ sales@persephonebooks.co.uk
www.persephonebooks.co.uk

Managing Director *Nicola Beauman*

Founded 1999. Publishes reprint fiction and non-fiction, mostly 'by women, for women and about women'. TITLES *Miss Pettigrew Lives for a Day* Winifred Watson; *Kitchen Essays* Agnes Jekyll; *The Far Cry* Emma Smith; *The Priory* Dorothy Whipple. 8 titles a year. No unsolicited material.

ROYALTIES twice-yearly.

Phaidon Press Limited
Regent's Wharf, All Saints Street, London N1 9PA
☎020 7843 1000 Fax 020 7843 1010
✉ name@phaidon.com
www.phaidon.com

Group Chairman & Publisher *Richard Schlagman*
Chairman *Andrew Price*
Managing Director *Christopher North*
Deputy Publisher *Amanda Renshaw*
Approx. Annual Turnover £18.8 million

Publishes quality books on the visual arts, including fine art, art history, architecture, design, photography, decorative arts, music and performing arts, cookery and children's books. Also produces videos. DIVISIONS/SERIES (with Editorial Heads) **Architecture and Design** *Emilia Terragni*; **Contemporary Art** *Kathleen Madden*; **Photography** *Amanda Renshaw*; **Art & Academic** *David Anfan*. About 100 titles a year. Unsolicited mss welcome but 'only a small amount of unsolicited material gets published'.

ROYALTIES twice-yearly.

Authors' Rating A move into the children's market will focus on art and design. With French and German subsidiaries, Phaidon's European scope gives it added appeal here and in the US for titles that might not otherwise enter the English language market.

Philip's
See **Octopus Publishing Group**

Phillimore & Co. Ltd
Shopwyke Manor Barn, Chichester PO20 2BG
☎01243 787636 Fax 01243 787639
✉ bookshop@phillimore.co.uk
www.phillimore.co.uk

Chairman *Louise Harris*
Managing Director *Noel Osborne*
Approx. Annual Turnover £1.3 million

Founded in 1897 by W.P.W. Phillimore, Victorian campaigner for local archive conservation in Chancery Lane, London. Became the country's leading publisher of historical source material and local histories. Somewhat dormant in the 1960s, it was revived by Philip Harris in 1968. Publishes British local and family history, including histories of institutions, buildings, villages, towns and counties, plus guides to research and writing in these fields. IMPRINT **Phillimore** *Noel Osborne* TITLES *Domesday Book*; *A History of Essex*; *Newcastle upon Tyne: A Modern History*; *The Haberdashers' Company*; *The North Downs*; *A History of Manchester*; *Warwickshire Country Houses*. About 50 titles a year. No unsolicited mss; synopses/ideas welcome for local or family histories.

ROYALTIES annually.

Phoenix
See **The Orion Publishing Group Limited**

Photographers' Institute Press (PIP)
See **Guild of Master Craftsman Publications Ltd**

Piatkus Books
5 Windmill Street, London W1T 2JA
☎020 7631 0710   Fax 020 7436 7137
✉ info@piatkus.co.uk
www.piatkus.co.uk
Managing Director *Judy Piatkus*
Approx. Annual Turnover £8.5 million

Founded 1979 by Judy Piatkus, the company continues to be one of the UK's leading independent publishing houses. The Piatkus imprint specialises in lifestyle, health, self-help, mind, body and spirit, popular psychology and business titles. Piatkus fiction includes new novels from many of the world's bestselling international authors. Portrait imprint publishes biography, autobiography, history, popular culture, humour and serious non-fiction in both hardback and paperback. DIVISIONS **Non-fiction** Publisher *Judy Piatkus*, Editorial Director *Gill Bailey* IMPRINTS **Portrait** TITLES *The Gripes of Wrath* Simon Carr; *Yob Nation* Francis Gilbert; *Katherine Howard* Joanna Denny; *Girl Next Door* Anne Diamond. **Piatkus** TITLES *The Holford Low GL Diet* Patrick Holford; *Women Who Think Too Much* Susan Nolan-Hoeksema. **Fiction** Publisher *Judy Piatkus*, Senior Commissioning Editor *Gillian Green* TITLES *Blue Smoke* Nora Roberts; *Seeing Stars* Christina Jones; *Sex Wars* Marge Piercy. About 150 titles a year (70 of which are fiction). Piatkus is expanding its range of books and welcomes synopses together with first three chapters.
ROYALTIES twice-yearly.

Authors' Rating A thriving independent publisher, Piatkus is on the lookout for bright ideas. 'Company policy is to work closely with authors and to give every title time and attention and its own marketing budget. We feel if we are not going to do this for each book then there is no point in our publishing it,' says Judy Piatkus.

Pica Press
See **A.&C. Black Publishers Ltd**

Picador/Young Picador
See **Macmillan Publishers Ltd**

Piccadilly Press
5 Castle Road, London NW1 8PR
☎020 7267 4492   Fax 020 7267 4493
✉ books@piccadillypress.co.uk
www.piccadillypress.co.uk
Publisher/Managing Director *Brenda Gardner*
Approx. Annual Turnover £1.4 million

Founded 1983. Independent publisher of children's and parental books. 28 titles in 2005. Welcomes approaches from authors 'but we would like them to know the sort of books we do. It is frustrating to get inappropriate material. They should check in their local libraries, bookshops or look at our website. We will send a catalogue (please enclose s.a.e.).' No adult or cartoon-type material.
ROYALTIES twice-yearly.

Pictorial Presentations
See **Souvenir Press Ltd**

Pimlico
See **The Random House Group Ltd**

Pinwheel Limited
Winchester House, 259–269 Old Marylebone Road, London NW1 5XJ
☎020 7616 7200   Fax 020 7616 7201
Managing Director *Andrew Flatt*

Children's non-fiction, picture books and novelty titles. IMPRINTS **Andromeda Children's Books** Publishing/Creative Director *Linda Cole* Illustrated non-fiction for children from 3–12 years; **Gullane Children's Books** Creative Director *Paula Burgess* Picture books for children from 0–8 years; **Pinwheel Children's Books** Publishing/Creative Director *Linda Cole* Cloth and novelty books for children from 0–5 years. Unsolicited mss will not be returned.

Pitkin
See **Jarrold Publishing**

Pluto Press Ltd
345 Archway Road, London N6 5AA
☎020 8348 2724   Fax 020 8348 9133
✉ pluto@plutobooks.com
www.plutobooks.com
Chair *Roger Van Zwanenberg*
Managing Director/Publisher *Anne Beech*

Founded 1970. Has developed a reputation for innovatory publishing in the field of non-fiction. Publishes academic and scholarly books across a range of subjects including cultural studies, politics and world affairs and more general titles on key aspects of currrent affairs. About 70 titles a year. Prospective authors are encouraged to consult the website for guidelines on submitting proposals.

Pocket Books
See **Simon & Schuster UK Limited**

Pocket Mountains Ltd
6 Church Wynd, Bo'ness EH51 0AN
Fax 01506 500405
✉ info@pocketmountains.com
www.pocketmountains.com
Managing Directors *Robbie Porteous, April Simmons*
Approx. Annual Turnover £100,000

Founded in 2003 to publish a series of guidebooks to the Scottish hills and now publishing other guides covering Europe: mountaineering, walking, cycling and wildlife books. 3 titles in 2005. Unsolicited mss, synopses and ideas welcome; approach by e-mail or letter. No fiction, children's or cookery.
ROYALTIES quarterly.

Pocketessentials
See **Oldcastle Books Ltd**

Poetry Library
See **CRW Publishing Ltd**

Poisoned Pen Press
6 Rodney Place, Clifton, Bristol BS8 4HY
☎0117 907 5949
✉ info@poisonedpenpress.com
www.poisonedpenpress.com
Managing Director *Jennifer Muller*
Editorial Head *Barbara Peters*

UK subsidiary of Poisoned Pen Press US, founded in 1996. Publishes adult crime fiction and mystery books. TITLES *Get Out or Die*; *Scare the Light Away*; *Beware the Solitary Drinker*. Unsolicited mss welcome; electronic submissions only.
ROYALTIES annually.

The Policy Press
Fourth Floor, Beacon House, Queen's Road, Bristol BS8 1QU
☎0117 331 4054 Fax 0117 331 4093
✉ tpp-info@bristol.ac.uk
www.policypress.org.uk
Managing Director *Alison Shaw*

Publishes social welfare and policy work for students, academics, practitioners, professionals and policy-makers.

Politico's Publishing Ltd
11–12 Buckingham Gate, London SW1E 6LB
☎020 7798 1600 Fax 020 7828 2098
✉ sales@methuen.co.uk
Chairman/Managing Director *Peter Tummons*
Publishing Consultant *Alan Gordon Walker*

Founded 1998. Acquired by **Methuen Publishing Ltd** in April 2003. Publishes political books. 30 titles in 2005. Unsolicited mss, synopses and ideas welcome; telephone in the first instance.
ROYALTIES twice-yearly.

Polity Press
65 Bridge Street, Cambridge CB2 1UR
☎01223 324315 Fax 01223 461385
www.polity.co.uk

Founded 1984. Publishes archaeology and anthropology, criminology, economics, feminism, general interest, history, human geography, literature, media and cultural studies, medicine and society, philosophy, politics, psychology, religion and theology, social and political theory, sociology. Unsolicited synopses and ideas for books welcome.
ROYALTIES annually.

Polygon
West Newington House, 10 Newington Road, Edinburgh EH9 1QS
☎0131 668 4371 Fax 0131 668 4466
✉ info@birlinn.co.uk
www.birlinn.co.uk
Publishing Director *Neville Moir*
Managing Editor *Alison Rae*

Bought by **Birlinn Ltd** in 2002. Publishes literary fiction and poetry. About 30 titles a year. Unsolicited mss, synopses and ideas welcome.
ROYALTIES twice-yearly.

Pont Books
See **Gomer Press**

Pop Universal
See **Souvenir Press Ltd**

Portland Press Ltd
3rd Floor, Eagle House, 16 Procter Street, London WC1V 6NX
☎020 7280 4110 Fax 020 7280 4169
✉ editorial@portlandpress.com
www.portlandpress.com
Chairman *Professor A.J. Turner*
Managing Director *Rhonda Oliver*
Managing Editor *Pauline Starley*
Approx. Annual Turnover £2.5 million

Founded 1990 to expand the publishing activities of the Biochemical Society (1911). Publishes biochemisty and medicine for graduate, postgraduate and research students. Expanding the list to include schools and general readership. TITLES

The Ubiquitin-Proteasome System; Transcription; Fundamentals of Enzyme Kinetics. 3 titles in 2005. Unsolicited mss, synopses and ideas welcome. No fiction.
ROYALTIES twice-yearly.

Portobello Books
Eardley House, 4 Uxbridge Street, Notting Hill Gate, London W8 7SY
☎020 7908 9892 Fax 020 7908 9899
✉ mail@portobellobooks.com
www.portobellobooks.com
Owners *Sigrid Rausin, Eric Abraham, Philip Gwyn Jones*
Managing Director *David Graham*
Publishing Assistant *Sophie Garland*

Founded in 2005 by Philip Gwyn Jones, formerly publishing director of HarperCollins' literary imprint Flamingo. Acquired **Granta Books** in 2005. Publishes international literature and activist non-fiction. About 15 titles a year. No unsolicited mss; synopses and ideas for books welcome. Approach by post in the first instance. No science fiction, romance or genre fiction of any kind, no gardening, cookery, mind, body & spirit or reference.

Portrait
See **Piatkus Books**

T&AD Poyser
See **A.&C. Black Publishers Ltd**

Prentice Hall
See **Pearson Education**

Prestel Publishing Limited
4 Bloomsbury Place, London WC1A 2QA
☎020 7323 5004 Fax 020 7636 8004
✉ sales@prestel-uk.co.uk
www.prestel.com
UK Editor *Philippa Hurd*
Editor-in-Chief (Germany) *Curt Holtz*

Founded 1924. Publishes art, architecture, photography, design, fashion, children's and general illustrated books. No fiction. Unsolicited mss, synopses and ideas welcome. Approach by post or e-mail.

Princeton University Press
See **University Presses of California, Columbia & Princeton Ltd**

Prion Books
See **Carlton Publishing Group**

Profile Books
3A Exmouth House, Pine Street, Exmouth Market, London EC1R 0JH
☎020 7841 6300 Fax 020 7833 3969
✉ info@profilebooks.com
www.profilebooks.com
Managing Director *Andrew Franklin*
Approx. Annual Turnover £6.67 million

Founded 1996. Publishes interesting non-fiction including current affairs, history, politics, psychology, cultural criticism, business management and economics. Named Small Publisher of the Year in 2004 and published the No.1 Christmas 2003 bestseller, *Eats, Shoots and Leaves* by Lynne Truss. AUTHORS include Alan Bennett, J.M. Coetzee, Francis Fukuyama and Peter Nichols. IMPRINTS **Profile Books** *Andrew Franklin*; **Economist Books** *Stephen Brough*. No unsolicited mss.
ROYALTIES twice-yearly.

Authors' Rating Like any successful publisher, Profile does well by and for its top author; in this case Lynne Truss with her books on grammar and manners. But the full list has quality stamped all over it. That the titles also sell suggests that crediting readers' intelligence can be good business.

ProQuest Information and Learning Ltd
The Quorum, Barnwell Road, Cambridge CB5 8SW
☎01223 215512 Fax 01223 215514
www.proquest.co.uk
Vice President, Technology/General Manager *John Taylor*
Vice President, International Sales, Marketing & Business Development *Simon Beale*

Collects, organises and publishes information for researchers, faculty and students, and general users in higher education, schools, public, government and workplace libraries. Users access information through the ProQuest online information system, Chadwyck-Healey™ electronic and microform resources, UMI microform and print reference products, eLibrary and SIRS educational resources and XanEdu resources.

Psychology Press (An imprint of Taylor & Francis Group, an Informa plc business)
27 Church Road, Hove BN3 2FA
☎01273 207411 Fax 01273 205612
www.psypress.co.uk
Managing Director *Mike Forster*

Deputy Managing Director *Rohays Perry*

Publishes psychology textbooks, monographs, professional books, tests and numerous journals which are available in both printed and online formats. Send detailed proposal plus c.v. and sample chapters. Proposal requirements and submission procedures available on the website. No poetry, fiction, travel or astrology.

ROYALTIES according to contract.

Publishing House

Trinity Place, Barnstaple EX32 9HG
☎01271 328892 Fax 01271 328768
✉ info@vernoncoleman.com
www.vernoncoleman.com

Managing Director *Vernon Coleman*
Publishing Director *Sue Ward*
Approx. Annual Turnover £750,000

Founded 1989. Self-publisher of fiction, health, humour, animals, politics. Over 90 books published. TITLES *Mrs Caldicot's Cabbage War*; *England our England*; *Bodypower*; *Bilbury Chronicles*; *Second Innings*; *It's Never Too Late*; *How to Publish Your Own Book*; *Alice's Diary*; *Rogue Nation*; *Food for Thought*, all by Vernon Coleman. No submissions.

Puffin

See **Penguin Group (UK)**

Pushkin Press Ltd

12 Chester Terrace, London NW1 4ND
☎01362 861089 Fax 0870 051 2701
✉ books@pushkinpress.com
www.pushkinpress.com

Chairman *Melissa Ulfane*
Editorial Head *Christopher Scott Vann*
Approx. Annual Turnover £250,000

Publishes novels and essays in translation drawn from the best of classic and contemporary European literature.

ROYALTIES annually.

Authors' Rating English language writers who are short on ideas might do worse than raid this select list of translated European works for something fresh to say. A bold and imaginative venture.

Putnam Aeronautical Books

See **Anova Books**

QED Publishing

226 City Road, London EC1V 2TT
☎020 7812 8600 Fax 020 7253 4370
✉ stevee@quarto.com
www.qed-publishing.co.uk
www.qeb-publishing.com

Owner *Quarto Publishing plc*
Chairman, Quarto Group *Laurence Orbach*
Director of Co-edition Publishing, Quarto Group *Piers Spence*
Publisher *Steve Evans*
Editorial Head *Jean Coppendale*
Approx. Annual Turnover £2 million

Founded in 2003 by the Quarto Group. Publishes children's: education, reference, literacy, numeracy, fiction, geography, history, picture books, non-fiction. TITLES *QED Start Series*; *QED Learn Computing*; *QED Learn Art*; *QED You and Your Pet*; *QED Maths Club*. 50 titles in 2006. No unsolicited material; initial approach by e-mail. No adult books. OVERSEAS SUBSIDIARY QEB Publishing Inc., USA.

FEES paid.

Quadrille Publishing Ltd

Alhambra House, 27–31 Charing Cross Road, London WC2H 0LS
☎020 7839 7117 Fax 020 7839 7118
www.quadrille.co.uk

Chairman *Sir David Cooksey*
Managing Director *Alison Cathie*
Editorial Director *Jane O'Shea*
Approx. Annual Turnover £6 million

Founded in 1994 with a view to producing a small list of top-quality illustrated books. Publishes non-fiction, including cookery, gardening, interior design and decoration, craft, health. TITLES *F-word Cookbook* Gordon Ramsay; *Home* Stafford Cliff; *Collectable Knits* Erika Knight; *The Bentley Era* Nicholas Foulkes; *Angel Heart and Soul Cards* Angela McGerr. 58 titles in 2005. Synopses and ideas for books welcome. No fiction or children's books.

ROYALTIES twice-yearly.

Authors' Rating The top publisher for cookbooks, Quadrille has achieved an enviable reputation for high production values. Alison Cathie has been dubbed 'the best illustrated publisher of her generation'. The latest progress for Quadrille is into humorous travel guides and book spinoffs from popular newspaper columns.

Quantum

See **Foulsham Publishers**

Quartet Books

27 Goodge Street, London W1T 2LD
☎020 7636 3992 Fax 020 7637 1866

Chairman *Naim Attallah*
Managing Director *Jeremy Beale*
Publishing Director *Stella Kane*

Founded 1972. Independent publisher. Publishes contemporary literary fiction including translations, popular culture, biography, music, history, politics and some photographic books. Unsolicited sample chapters with return postage welcome; no poetry, romance or science fiction. Submissions by disk or e-mail are not accepted.
ROYALTIES twice-yearly.

Queen Anne Press
See **Lennard Associates Ltd**

Quercus Publishing
46 Dorset Street, London W1U 7NB
☎020 7486 2012   Fax 0870 730 1482
✉ mail@quercusbooks.co.uk
Chairman *Anthony Cheetham*
Managing Director *Mark Smith*
Approx. Annual Turnover £3 million

Founded in 2005 as a commercial publisher of quality fiction and non-fiction. DIVISIONS **Trade Publishing** Editorial Head *Nicolas Cheetham* TITLE *The Broken Shore*; **Contract Publishing** Editorial Head *Wayne Davies* TITLE *Speeches That Changed the World*. 8 titles in 2005. No unsolicited material.
ROYALTIES annually.

Authors' Rating A new name on the block, Quercus launched off with strong contract sales for two non-fiction titles and is now on the lookout for 'smart but approachable illustrated reference books'. A fiction list will be led by crime titles. Quercus plans 60 titles for its second year.

Quiller Press
(An imprint of Quiller Publishing Ltd), Wykey House, Wykey, Shrewsbury SY4 1JA
☎01939 261616   Fax 01939 261606
✉ info@quillerbooks.com

Managing Director *Andrew Johnston*

Specialises in sponsored books and publications sold through non-book trade channels as well as bookshops. Publishes architecture, biography, business and industry, collecting, cookery, DIY, gardening, guidebooks, humour, reference, sports, travel, wine and spirits. IMPRINTS **Kenilworth Press**; **The Sportsman's Press** (see entry); **Swan Hill Press** (see entry). About 10 titles a year. Unsolicited mss only if the author sees some potential for sponsorship or guaranteed sales.
ROYALTIES twice-yearly.

Quince Books
209 Hackney Road, London E2 8JL
☎020 7033 4265
✉ quincebooks@hotmail.com

www.quince.webeden.co.uk
Proprietor *Simon Mitchell*
Founded 2005. Publishes commercial ficton. About 15 books a year. Welcomes submissions; send synopsis and three chapters, ideally by e-mail.
ROYALTIES annually.

Radcliffe Press
See **I.B. Tauris & Co. Ltd**

Radcliffe Publishing Ltd
18 Marcham Road, Abingdon OX14 1AA
☎01235 528820   Fax 01235 528830
✉ contact.us@radcliffemed.com
www.radcliffe-oxford.com
Managing Director *Andrew Bax*
Editorial Director *Gillian Nineham*
Approx. Annual Turnover £2 million

Founded 1987. Medical publishers which began by specialising in books for general practice and health service management. Publishes clinical, management, health policy books, training materials and CD-ROMs. 100 titles in 2005. Unsolicited mss, synopses and ideas welcome. No non-medical books.
ROYALTIES twice-yearly.

The Random House Group Ltd
Random House, 20 Vauxhall Bridge Road, London SW1V 2SA
☎020 7840 8400   Fax 020 7233 6058
✉ enquiries@randomhouse.co.uk
www.randomhouse.co.uk
Chief Executive/Chairman *Gail Rebuck*
Deputy CEO *Ian Hudson*
Group Managing Director *Peter Bowron*

The Random House Group is the UK's leading trade publisher comprising 32 diverse imprints in four separate substantially autonomous divisions: the Random House Division, Ebury Publishing, Transworld (see entry) and Random House Children's Books.

RANDOM HOUSE DIVISION
Managing Director *Richard Cable*

CCV DIVISION (Publisher *Dan Franklin*):
IMPRINTS **Jonathan Cape** ☎020 7840 8576 Fax 020 7233 6117 Publishing Director *Dan Franklin* Biography and memoirs, current affairs, fiction, history, photography, poetry, politics and travel.
    Yellow Jersey Press ☎020 7840 8637 Fax 020 7223 6117 Editorial Director *Tristan Jones* Narrative sports books.
    Harvill Secker ☎020 7840 8649 Fax 020

7233 6117 Publishing Director *Geoff Mulligan* Principally literary fiction with some non-fiction. Literature in translation, English literature, quality thrillers.

Chatto & Windus ☎020 7840 8522 Fax 020 7233 6117 Publishing Director *Alison Samuel* Memoirs, current affairs, essays, literary fiction, history, poetry, politics, philosophy and translations.

Pimlico ☎020 7840 8784 Fax 020 7233 6117 Publisher *Will Sulkin* Quality non-fiction paperbacks, specialising in history, biography, popular culture and the arts.

Vintage ☎020 7840 8573 Fax 020 7233 6117 Publisher *Rachel Cugnoni* Quality paperback fiction and non-fiction. Vintage (founded in 1990) has been described as one of the 'greatest literary success stories in recent British publishing'.

CHA DIVISION (Publisher *Susan Sandon*): IMPRINTS **Century** ☎020 7840 8554 Fax 020 7233 6127 Publishing Director *Mark Booth* General fiction and non-fiction including commercial fiction, autobiography, biography, history and self-help.

William Heinemann ☎020 7840 8400 Fax 020 7233 6127 Publishing Director *Ravi Mirchandani* General non-fiction and fiction, especially history, literary fiction, crime, science, thrillers and women's fiction.

Hutchinson ☎020 7840 8564 Fax 020 7233 7870 Publishing Director *Sue Freestone* General fiction and non-fiction including notably belles-lettres, current affairs, politics, travel and history.

Random House Books (incorporating **Random House Business Books**) ☎020 7840 8666 Fax 020 7233 6127 Publisher *Nigel Wilcockson.* **Arrow** ☎020 7840 8557 Fax 020 7840 6127 Publishing Director *Kate Elton* Mass-market paperback fiction and non-fiction.

EBURY PUBLISHING DIVISION (☎020 7840 8400 Fax 020 7840 8406) Publisher *Fiona MacIntyre,* Deputy Publisher *Jake Lingwood* IMPRINTS **Ebury Press** Publishing Director (non-fiction) *Hannah MacDonald,* Publishing Director (illustrated) *Carey Smith* Popular non-fiction, including memoir and popular history, humour, cookery, travel-writing, sport, music, TV tie-ins and reference. **Vermilion** Publishing Director *Clare Hulton* Personal development, health, diet, relationships and parenting. **Rider** Publishing Director *Judith Kendra* Psychology, philosophy, spirituality and personal development, travel, history, inspirational memoir, paranormal, divination. **Time Out Guides** Brand Manager *Luthfa Begum* Travel

guides published in a unique partnership with *Time Out* magazine.

RANDOM HOUSE CHILDREN'S BOOKS DIVISION (at Transworld Publishers, 61–63 Uxbridge Road, London W5 5SA ☎020 8579 2652 Fax 020 8231 6737) Managing Director *Philippa Dickinson,* Publisher (fiction) *Annie Eaton,* Editorial Director (fiction) *Charlie Sheppard,* Senior Commissioning Editor (fiction) *Alex Antscherl,* Senior Commissioning Editor (picture books) *Natascha Biebow,* Senior Commissioning Editor (Jonathan Cape Picture Books) *Helen Mackenzie-Smith,* Publisher (Colour and Custom Publishing) *Fiona Macmillan* Picture books, fiction, poetry, non-fiction and audio cassettes under IMPRINTS **Bodley Head Children's Books**; **Corgi Children's Books**; **Jonathan Cape Children's Books**; **Doubleday Children's Books**; **Hutchinson Children's Books**; **Red Fox Children's Books**; and **David Fickling Books** (31 Beaumont Street, Oxford OX1 2NP ☎01865 339000 Fax 01865 339009 ✉ dfickling @randomhouse.co.uk www.davidficklingbooks. co.uk) Publisher *David Fickling,* Senior Editor *Bella Pearson* Children's fiction and picture books. Unsolicited mss, synopses and ideas for books welcome.

ROYALTIES twice-yearly for the most part.

Authors' Rating It used to be agents who chased after the subsidiary markets for books but now the publishers are getting into the game. The latest ruse from Random House is a BMW-sponsored set of short stories, each featuring one of its latest models. More significantly, perhaps, Random is investing heavily in a digital archive and exploring ways to exploit the Internet. But it is conventional trade publishing that brings in the money. Last year Random scored 103 number one bestsellers with Transworld turning in the best performance.

Ransom Publishing Ltd
Rose Cottage, Howe Hill, Watlington OX49 5HB
☎01491 613711 Fax 01491 613733
✉ jenny@ransom.co.uk
www.ransom.co.uk
Managing Director *Jenny Ertle*

Ransom Publishing was founded as an educational publisher specialising in software but their growth in children's literacy has lead to the launch of a wide children's list. The new publishing programme includes fiction for older children and teenagers, high interest low reading level fiction and non-fiction for older children and teenagers, early readers and phonics. 'Actively looking for new children's writers, particularly for ages 8 to young adult.' Initial enquiries by e-mail with details on the submission and three sample chapters. 'A response cannot be guaranteed but we try to respond to all submissions within a month.' Materials returned if supplied with s.a.e.

Reader's Digest Association Ltd

11 Westferry Circus, Canary Wharf, London E14 4HE
☎020 7715 8000 Fax 020 7715 8181
✉ gbeditorial@readersdigest.co.uk
www.readersdigest.co.uk
Managing Director *Andrew Lynam-Smith*
Editorial Director, Books *Julian Browne*

Editorial office in the USA (see entry under *US Publishers*). Publishes gardening, natural history, cookery, history, DIY, travel and word books. About 20 titles a year.

Reaktion Books

33 Great Sutton Street, London EC1V 0DX
☎020 7253 1071 Fax 020 7253 1208
✉ info@reaktionbooks.co.uk
www.reaktionbooks.co.uk
Managing Director *Michael R. Leaman*

Founded 1985. Publishes art history, architecture, animal studies, Asian studies, cultural studies, design, film, geography, history, natural history, photography and travel literature (*not* travel guides or journals). TITLES *Mad, Bad and Dangerous: The Scientist and the Cinema* Christopher Frayling; SERIES **Critical Lives** TITLES *Franz Kafka* Sander L. Gilman; *Marcel Duchamp* Caroline Cros; **Animal** TITLE *Bee* Claire Preston. About 44 titles a year.
ROYALTIES twice-yearly.

Reardon Publishing

PO Box 919, Cheltenham GL50 8AN
☎01242 231800
✉ reardon@bigfoot.com
www.reardon.co.uk
www.cotswoldbookshop.com
www.antarcticbookshop.com
Managing Editor *Nicholas Reardon*

Founded in the mid-1970s. Family-run publishing house specialising in local interest and tourism in the Cotswold area and books on Antarctica. Member of the **Outdoor Writers Guild**. Publishes walking and driving guides, and family history for societies. TITLES *The Cotswold Way* (video); *The Cotswold Way Map*; *Cotswold Walkabout*; *Cotswold Driveabout*; *The Donnington Way*; *The Haunted Cotswolds*. Also distributes for other publishers such as Ordnance Survey. 10 titles a year. Unsolicited mss, synopses and ideas welcome with return postage only.
ROYALTIES twice-yearly.

Recollections

See **Arnefold Publishing**

Red Fox Children's Books

See **The Random House Group Ltd**

Thomas Reed

See **A.&C. Black Publishers Ltd**

William Reed Directories

Broadfield Park, Crawley RH11 9RT
☎01293 613400 Fax 01293 610322
✉ directories@william-reed.co.uk
www.grocerdirectories.co.uk
Head of Content *Daniel Verrells*

William Reed Directories, a division of William Reed Publishing, was established in 1990. Its portfolio includes 13 titles covering the food, drink, non-food, catering, retail and export industries, including European versions. The titles are produced as directories, market research reports, exhibition catalogues and electronic publishing.

Reed Elsevier Group plc

1–3 Strand, London WC2N 5JR
☎020 7930 7077
www.reedelsevier.com
Also at: 125 Park Avenue, 23rd Floor, New York, NY 10017, USA
☎001 212 309 5498 Fax 001 212 309 5480
And: Raderweg 29, 1043 NX Amsterdam, The Netherlands
☎00 31 20 485 2434
Chief Executive Officer (UK) *Sir Crispin Davis*

Reed Elsevier Group plc is a world-leading publisher and information provider, operating in four core segments: science and medical, legal, education, business.

DIVISIONS **Harcourt Education** (see entry); **Elsevier** (see entry); **LexisNexis** (formerly Butterworths) Halsbury House, 35 Chancery Lane, London WC2A 1EL ☎020 7400 2500 Fax 020 7400 2842 Publishes legal and accountancy textbooks, journals, law reports, CD-ROMs and online services; **Harcourt School**

Publishers (see entry under *US Publishers*); **Reed Business** Quadrant House, The Quadrant, Sutton SM2 5AS ☎020 8652 3500. No unsolicited material.

Reference Library
See **CRW Publishing Ltd**

Regency House Publishing Limited
Niall House, 24–26 Boulton Road, Stevenage SG1 4QX
☎01438 314488 Fax 01438 311303
✉ regency-house@btconnect.com

Chairman *Brian Trodd*
Managing Director *Nicolette Trodd*

Founded 1991. Publisher and packager of mass-market non-fiction. No fiction. No unsolicited material.

Research Disclosure
See **Kenneth Mason Publications Ltd**

Reverb
Osiris Press Ltd, PO Box 615, Oxford OX1 9AL
✉ mail@readreverb.com
www.readreverb.com
Directors *Andrew Chapman, Paul Lenz*

Founded 2004. 'Reverb has become known for innovation, being the first UK publisher to offer a novel as a free download and working with www.whatshouldireadnext.com' Publishes contemporary literary fiction, showing an awareness of popular culture, and occasional non-fiction in the same culturally literate spirit. TITLES *Light* C.M. Taylor; *The Group* Ravinder Chahal. 7 titles in 2005. Unsolicited mss, synopses and ideas welcome but only in strict accordance with author guidelines on the website. Always approach by e-mail. No poetry, children's fiction, romance, downmarket thrillers or short stories.
ROYALTIES quarterly.

Richmond House Publishing Company Ltd
70–76 Bell Street, Marylebone, London NW1 6SP
☎020 7224 9666 Fax 020 7224 9688
✉ sales@rhpco.co.uk
www.rhpco.co.uk

Managing Directors *Gloria Gordon, Spencer Block*

Publishes directories for the theatre and entertainment industries. TITLES *British Theatre Directory*; *Artistes and Agents*; *London Seating Plan Guide*. Synopses and ideas welcome.

Rider
See **The Random House Group Ltd**

Right Way/Right Way Plus
See **Elliot Right Way Books**

RMEP
See **Hymns Ancient & Modern Ltd**

Robinson
See **Constable & Robinson Ltd**

Robson Books
See **Anova Books**

RotoVision
Sheridan House, 114 Western Road, Hove BN3 1DD
☎01273 727268 Fax 01273 727269
www.rotovision.com

Managing Director *Piers Spence*
Publisher *April Sankey*

Founded 1996. Rapidly-expanding visual arts publishers with a strong emphasis on education and inspiration. Publishes graphic design, photography, digital design, advertising, film, architecture, lighting design, interiors, product design, packaging design. TITLES *World's Top Photographers: Nudes*; *What Is Graphic Design For?*; *Designs of the Times*; *First Steps in Digital Design*; *500 Digital Photography Hints, Tips and Techniques*; *Print and Production Techniques for Brochures and Catalogues*. No unsolicited mss; written synopses and ideas welcome. No phone calls, please. No academic or fiction.
Flat FEE paid.

Roundhouse Group
Millstone, Limers Lane, Northam EX39 2RG
☎01237 474474 Fax 01237 474774
✉ roundhouse.group@ukgateway.net
Editorial Head *Alan Goodworth*

Founded 1991. Publishes cinema and media-related titles. TITLES *The Bent Lens: A World Guide to Gay & Lesbian Films*; *Cinema of Oliver Stone*; *Cinema of Martin Scorsese*. Represents and distributes (via Orca Books Services) a broad range of non-fiction publishing houses throughout the UK and Europe. No unsolicited mss.
ROYALTIES twice-yearly.

Routledge (An imprint of Taylor & Francis Group, an Informa plc business)

2 Park Square, Milton Park, Abingdon OX14 4RN

☎020 7017 6000 Fax 020 7017 6699

www.routledge.com

CEO *Roger Horton*
Managing Director *Roger Horton*
Publishing Directors *Claire L'Enfant, Alan Jarvis*
Approx. Annual Turnover £40 million (Group)

Routledge is an international academic imprint publishing books primarily for university students, researchers, academics and professionals. Most Routledge authors are academics with specialist knowledge of their subject. Publishes everything from core text books to research monographs and journals in the following subject areas: humanities, including anthropology, archaeology, classical studies, communications and media studies, cultural studies, history, language and literature, music, philosophy, religious studies, theatre studies and sports studies; social sciences, including geography, politics, military and strategic studies, sociology and urban studies; business, management, law and economics; education; Asian and Middle Eastern studies. Over 1000 titles a year. Send a detailed proposal plus c.v. and sample chapters. Proposal requirements and submission procedures can be found on the website. No poetry, fiction, travel or astrology. ROYALTIES annually or twice-yearly, according to contract.

RYA (Royal Yachting Association)

RYA House, Ensign Way, Hamble, Southampton SO31 4YA

☎023 8060 4100 Fax 023 8060 4299

✉ phil.williamsellis@rya.org.uk

www.rya.org.uk

Chief Executive *Rod Carr*
Publishing Editor/Publications Manager *Phil Williams-Ellis*
Approx. Annual Turnover £10 million+

The Royal Yachting Association, the UK governing body representing sailing, windsurfing, motorboating, powerboat racing both at sea and on inland waters, was founded in 1875. Publishes sports instruction books relating to specific training courses, technical, legal and boating advice, all written by experts in their field. TITLES *RYA Weather Handbook; RYA Navigation Exercises; RYA Powerboat Handbook; RYA Go Sailing!.* 8 titles a year. No unsolicited mss; synopses and ideas for books welcome.

Approach by e-mail or post in the first instance. ROYALTIES annually.

Ryland Peters and Small Limited

20–21 Jockey's Fields, London WC1R 5BN

☎020 7025 2200 Fax 020 7025 2201

✉ info@rps.co.uk

www.rylandpeters.com

Managing Director *David Peters*
Publishing Director *Alison Starling*

Founded 1996. Publishes highly illustrated lifestyle books aimed at an international market, covering gardening, cookery, interior design and mind, body, spirit. No fiction. Acquired **Cico Books** in 2006. No unsolicited mss; synopses and ideas welcome. ROYALTIES twice-yearly.

Sage Publications

1 Oliver's Yard, 55 City Road, London EC1Y 1SP

☎020 7324 8500 Fax 020 7324 8600

✉ info@sagepub.co.uk

www.sagepub.co.uk

Managing Director *Stephen Barr*
Editorial Director *Ziyad Marar*

Founded 1971. Publishes academic books and journals in humanities and the social sciences, education and science, technology and medicine. Bought academic and professional books publisher Paul Chapman Publishing Ltd in 1998 and Lucky Duck Publishing in 2004. ROYALTIES twice-yearly.

Saint Andrew Press

Church of Scotland, 121 George Street, Edinburgh EH2 4YN

☎0131 240 2236 Fax 0131 220 3113

✉ standrewpress@cofscotland.org.uk

www.standrewpress.com

www.williambarclay.org

Head of Publishing *Ann Crawford*
Approx. Annual Turnover £225,000

Founded in 1954. Owned by the Church of Scotland. Publishes religious, general reference and children's books aimed at the Christian trade and retail market in the UK and internationally. TITLES BBC Scotland's *The Scots at Sea; Silent Heroes* John D. Mills; *Jesus and People Like Us* Nick Baines. About 20 titles a year. 'Saint Andrew Press is expanding and is actively seeking high-quality writing that is thought-provoking and, above all, helps readers to wrestle with the complexities of life today.' No unsolicited mss but proposals very welcome in synopsis form; approach in writing. ROYALTIES annually.

St Pauls Publishing
187 Battersea Bridge Road, London
SW11 3AS
☎020 7978 4300 Fax 020 7978 4370
✉ editions@stpauls.org.uk
www.stpauls.ie

Publisher *Andrew Pudussery*

Publishing division of the Society of St Paul. Began publishing in 1914 but activities were fairly limited until around 1948. Publishes religious material mainly: theology, scripture, catechetics, prayer books and biography. About 25 titles a year. Unsolicited mss, synopses and ideas welcome with s.a.e.

Salamander
See **Anova Books**

Sangam Books Ltd
57 London Fruit Exchange, Brushfield Street, London E1 6EP
☎020 7377 6399 Fax 020 7375 1230
✉ sangambks@aol.com

Executive Director *Anthony de Souza*

Traditionally an educational publisher of school and college level textbooks. Also publishes art, India, medicine, science, technology, social sciences, religion, plus some fiction in paperback.

Saqi Books
26 Westbourne Grove, London W2 5RH
☎020 7221 9347 Fax 020 7229 7492
✉ enquiries@saqibooks.com
www.saqibooks.com

Chairman/Managing Director *André Gaspard*
Commissioning Editor *Mitch Albert*

Founded 1981, initially as a specialist publisher of books on the Middle East and Arab world but now includes Central Asia, South Asia and European fiction. Publishes fiction and non-fiction – academic and illustrated. About 20 titles a year. Welcomes unsolicited material; approach by post or e-mail.
ROYALTIES annually.

Authors' Rating A blunt warning from the managing editor that unsolicited manuscripts are not returned. Saqi is not alone in this. Authors should retain copies of everything they send out.

Saunders
See **Elsevier Ltd**

Savitri Books Ltd
See entry under *UK Packagers*

SB Publications
14 Bishopstone Road, Seaford BN25 2UB
☎01323 893498 Fax 01323 893860
✉ sbpublications@tiscali.co.uk
www.sbpublications.co.uk

Owner *Mrs Lindsay Woods*

Founded 1987. Specialises in local history, including themes illustrated by old picture postcards and photographs; also travel, guides (town, walking) and railways. TITLES *Dorset As She Wus Spoke*; *The Neat and Nippy Guide to Brighton*; *Pre-Raphaelite Trail in Sussex*. Also provides marketing and distribution services for local authors. 20 titles a year.
ROYALTIES annually.

Sceptre
See **Hodder Headline Ltd**

Scholastic Ltd
Villiers House, Clarendon Avenue, Leamington Spa CV32 5PR
☎01926 887799 Fax 01926 883331
www.scholastic.co.uk

Chairman *M.R. Robinson*
Managing Director *Kate Wilson*
Approx. Annual Turnover £32.9 million

Founded 1964. Owned by US parent company, Scholastic Inc. who acquired **Chicken House Publishing** in May 2005. Publishes children's fiction and non-fiction and education for primary schools.
DIVISIONS **Scholastic Children's Books** *Elaine McQuade* Euston House, 24 Eversholt Street, London NW1 1DB ☎020 7756 7756 Fax 020 7756 7795 IMPRINT **Scholastic** TITLES *Horrible Histories* Terry Deary, illus. Martin Brown; *His Dark Materials Trilogy* Philip Pullman; *Mortal Engines* Philip Reeve.
Educational Publishing (Villiers House address) Professional books and classroom materials for primary teachers, plus magazines such as *Child Education, Junior Education, Junior Focus, Infant Projects, Nursery Education, Literacy Time*.
Scholastic Book Clubs, Getting Children Reading, Giving Books to Schools *Miles Stevens-Hoare* Windrush Park, Witney, Oxford OX29 0YT ☎01993 893456 Fax 01993 776813 SBC is the UK's number one Schools Book Club. Offering five age specific clubs, it provides 'the best books at great prices and supports teachers in the process'.
School Book Fairs, Getting Children Reading, Giving Books to Schools *Miles Stevens-Hoare* The Book Fair Division sells directly to children, parents and teachers in

schools through 25,000 week-long book events held in schools throughout the UK.
ROYALTIES twice-yearly.

Authors' Rating Big changes all round with new people in most of the top jobs. The aim is to expand the clubs and fairs business to raise the Scholastic profile.

SCM – Canterbury Press Ltd
9–17 St Albans Place, London N1 0NX
☎020 7359 8033   Fax 020 7359 0049
✉ admin@scm-canterburypress.co.uk
www.scm-canterburypress.co.uk
Publishing Director *Christine Smith*
Commissioning Editor *Barbara Laing*
Approx. Annual Turnover £2.3 million

Part of **Hymns Ancient & Modern Ltd** (see entry). Has two publishing imprints: **SCM Press** Text and reference books for the study of theology, philosophy of religion, ethics and religious studies; **Canterbury Press** Religious titles for the general market, liturgy, spirituality and church resources. AUTHORS include Rowan Williams, Ronald Blythe, Libby Purves. 80 titles a year. Refer to website for guidelines on submitting proposals.
ROYALTIES annually.

Authors' Rating Leading publisher of religious ideas with well-deserved reputation for fresh thinking. At SCM, 'questioning theology is the norm'.

Scottish Cultural Press/ Scottish Children's Press
Unit 6, Newbattle Abbey Business Park, Newbattle Road, Dalkeith EH22 3LJ
☎0131 660 6366   Fax 0131 660 4666
✉ info@scottishbooks.com
www.scottishbooks.com
Directors *Avril Gray, Brian Pugh*

Founded 1992. Publishes Scottish interest titles, including cultural literature, poetry, archaeology, local history. DIVISION **S.C.P. Children's Ltd** (trading as **Scottish Children's Press**) Children's fiction and non-fiction. Unsolicited mss, synopses and ideas accepted provided return postage is included, but *always* telephone before sending material, please. 'Mss sent without advance telephone call and return postage will be destroyed.'
ROYALTIES paid.

Scribner
See **Simon & Schuster UK Limited**

Seafarer Books
102 Redwald Road, Rendlesham, Woodbridge IP12 2TE
☎01394 420789   Fax 01394 461314
✉ info@seafarerbooks.com
www.seafarerbooks.com
Managing Director *Patricia M. Eve*

Founded 1968. Publishes sailing titles, with an emphasis on the traditional. AUTHORS Erskine Childers, Cecily Gould, Bjorn Larsson, John Leather, Jack London, Frank Mulville, Bob Roberts, Adrian Seligman. About 6 titles a year. No unsolicited mss; preliminary letter essential before making any type of submission.
ROYALTIES twice-yearly.

SeaNeverDry Publishing
6 Alexandra Road, East Twickenham TW1 2HE
☎020 8892 2855
✉ orders@seaneverdrypub.com
www.seaneverdrypub.com
Chairman *B. de Vaatt*
Managing Director *D.R. Abbott*
Approx. Annual Turnover £300,000

Founded 2003. Publishes general fiction, erotica and humour. DIVISIONS **General Fiction** *S. Hytte* TITLES *The Book*; *Empire*; **Humour** *D.R. Abbott* TITLES *Fake Honesty*; *His/Her Words of Love*. Unsolicited mss, synopses and ideas for books welcome; approach by e-mail. No academic texts or science fiction.
ROYALTIES quarterly.

Authors' Rating Not to be confused with vanity publishing, SeaNeverDry Publishing offers advanced technology to produce a low cost, low volume print run to test the market. If the book takes off well, good luck; the author gets a higher than average royalty of 15%. But there may be a long stretch between hope and realisation.

Search Press Ltd
Wellwood, North Farm Road, Tunbridge Wells TN2 3DR
☎01892 510850   Fax 01892 515903
✉ searchpress@searchpress.com
www.searchpress.com
Managing Director *Martin de la Bédoyère*
Commissioning Editor *Rosalind Dace*

Founded 1970. Publishes full-colour art, craft, needlecrafts – papermaking and papercrafts, painting on silk, art techniques and embroidery. No unsolicited mss; synopsis with sample chapter welcome.
ROYALTIES annually.

Seren

57 Nolton Street, Bridgend CF31 3AE
☎01656 663018   Fax 01656 649226
✉ general@seren-books.com
www.seren-books.com

Chairman *Cary Archard*
Publisher *Mick Felton*
Approx. Annual Turnover £150,000

Founded 1981 as a specialist poetry publisher but has now moved into general literary publishing with an emphasis on Wales. Publishes poetry, fiction, literary criticism, drama, biography, art, history and translations of fiction. DIVISIONS **Poetry** *Amy Wack* AUTHORS Owen Sheers, Pascale Petit, Sheenagh Pugh, Kathryn Gray, Deryn Rees-Jones. **Drama** *Amy Wack* AUTHORS Edward Thomas, Charles Way, Lucinda Coxon. **Fiction** *Cary Archard* Authors Leonora Brito, Richard Collins, Lloyd Jones, Richard John Evans. **Art, Literary Criticism, History, Translations** *Mick Felton* IMPRINT **Border Lines Biographies** TITLES *Bruce Chatwin; Dennis Potter; Mary Webb; Wilfred Owen; Raymond Williams*. About 25 titles a year. Unsolicited mss, synopses and ideas for books welcome.
ROYALTIES twice-yearly or annually.

Serpent's Tail

4 Blackstock Mews, London N4 2BT
☎020 7354 1949   Fax 020 7704 6467
✉ info@serpentstail.com
www.serpentstail.com

Contact *Martin Worthington*
Approx. Annual Turnover £650,000

Founded 1986. Winner of the Sunday Times Small Publisher of the Year Award (1989) and the Ralph Lewis Award for new fiction (1992). Serpent's Tail has introduced to British audiences a number of major internationally known writers. Noted for its strong emphasis on design and an eye for the unusual. Publishes contemporary fiction, contemporary gay fiction and non-fiction, including works in translation, crime, popular culture and biography. No poetry, romance or fantasy.
IMPRINTS **Serpent's Tail** TITLES *Fearless Jones* Walter Mosley; *Whatever* Michel Houellebecq; *This is Serbia Calling* Matthew Collin; *Pornocopia* Laurence O'Toole. **Five Star** TITLES *Nineteen Seventy Four* David Peace; *Always Outnumbered, Always Outgunned* Walter Mosley; *Beneath the Blonde* Stella Duffy. About 40 titles a year. Send preliminary letter outlining proposal with a sample chapter and s.a.e.

No unsolicited mss. Prospective authors unfamiliar with Serpent's Tail are advised to study the list before submitting anything.
ROYALTIES annually.

Authors' Rating A publisher noted for originality which means doing what the conglomerates are unwilling or unable to do. An exciting fiction list much praised by its own and other publishers' authors.

Severn House Publishers

9–15 High Street, Sutton SM1 1DF
☎020 8770 3930   Fax 020 8770 3850
✉ info@severnhouse.com
www.severnhouse.com

Chairman *Edwin Buckhalter*
Editorial *Amanda Stewart*

Founded 1974. A leader in library fiction publishing. Publishes hardback fiction: romance, science fiction, horror, fantasy, crime. Also large print and trade paperback editions of their fiction titles. About 140 titles a year. No unsolicited material. Synopses/proposals preferred through *bona fide* literary agents only. OVERSEAS ASSOCIATE Severn House Publishers Inc., New York.
ROYALTIES twice-yearly.

Authors' Rating Having established a strong hardback list, Severn has now entered the paperback market with its crime and romance titles.

Sheldon Press

See **Society for Promoting Christian Knowledge**

Sheldrake Press

188 Cavendish Road, London SW12 0DA
☎020 8675 1767   Fax 020 8675 7736
✉ enquiries@sheldrakepress.co.uk
www.sheldrakepress..co.uk

Publisher *Simon Rigge*

Founded in 1979 as a book packager and commenced publishing under its own imprint in 1991. Publishes illustrated non-fiction: history, travel, style, cookery and stationery. TITLES *The Victorian House Book; The Shorter Mrs Beeton; The Power of Steam; The Railway Heritage of Britain; Wild Britain; Wild France; Wild Spain; Wild Italy; Wild Ireland; Amsterdam: Portrait of a City* and Kate Greenaway stationery books. Synopses and ideas for books welcome, but not interested in fiction.

Shepheard-Walwyn (Publishers) Ltd
Suite 604, The Chandlery, 50 Westminster
Bridge Road, London SE1 7QY
☎020 7721 7666 Fax 020 7721 7667
✉ books@shepheard-walwyn.co.uk
www.shepheard-walwyn.co.uk
Managing Director *Anthony Werner*
Approx. Annual Turnover £150,000

Founded 1972. 'We regard books as food for the
mind and want to offer a wholesome diet of
original ideas and fresh approaches to old subjects.' Publishes general non-fiction in three
main areas: Scottish interest; gift books in calligraphy and/or illustrated; biography, history,
political economy, perennial philosophy. About
6–7 titles a year. Synopses and ideas for books
welcome.
ROYALTIES twice-yearly.

The Shetland Times Ltd
Gremista, Lerwick ZE1 0PX
☎01595 693622 Fax 01595 694637
✉ publishing@shetland-times.co.uk
www.shetland-books.co.uk
Managing Director *Brian Johnston*
Publications Manager *Charlotte Black*

Founded 1872 as publishers of the local newspaper. Book publishing followed thereafter plus
publication of monthly magazine, *Shetland Life*.
Publishes anything with Shetland connections
– local and natural history, music, crafts, maritime. Prefers material with a Shetland
theme/connection.
ROYALTIES annually.

Shire Publications Ltd
Cromwell House, Church Street, Princes
Risborough HP27 9AA
☎01844 344301 Fax 01844 347080
✉ shire@shirebooks.co.uk
www.shirebooks.co.uk
General Manager *Sue Ross*

Founded 1962. Publishes original non-fiction
paperbacks. About 25 titles a year. No unsolicited material; send introductory letter with
detailed outline of idea.
ROYALTIES annually.

Authors' Rating You don't have to live in the
country to write books for Shire but it helps.
With titles like *Church Fonts, Haunted Inns* and
Discovering Preserved Railways there is a distinct
rural feel to the list. Another way of putting it,
to quote owner John Rotheroe, Shire specialises in 'small books on all manner of obscure
subjects'.

Short Books
3A Exmouth House, Pine Street, Exmouth
Market, London EC1R 0JH
☎020 7833 9429 Fax 020 7833 9500
✉ emily@shortbooks.biz
www.shortbooks.co.uk
Editorial Directors *Rebecca Nicolson, Aurea
Carpenter*

Founded 2001. Publishes general adult and
children's non-fiction and fiction; biography,
history and politics, humour and children's narrative history. No unsolicited mss.

Sidgwick & Jackson
See **Macmillan Publishers Ltd**

Sigma Press
5 Alton Road, Wilmslow SK9 5DY
☎01625 531035 Fax 01625 531035
✉ info@sigmapress.co.uk
www.sigmapress.co.uk
Chairman/Managing Director *Graham Beech*

Founded in 1980 as a publisher of technical
books, Sigma Press now publishes mainly in the
leisure area. Publishes outdoor, local heritage,
adventure and biography. DIVISION **Sigma
Leisure** TITLES *Holiday Walks in the Loire Valley*;
Leap into Legend (biography); *Walks in Ancient
Wales*; *All-Terrain Pushchair Walks*; *Discovering
Manchester*. About 10 titles a year. No unsolicited mss; synopses and ideas welcome. No
poetry or novels required.
ROYALTIES twice-yearly.

Simon & Schuster UK Limited
Africa House, 64–78 Kingsway, London
WC2B 6AH
☎020 7316 1900 Fax 020 7316 0331
www.simonsays.co.uk
CEO/Managing Director *Ian S. Chapman*
Publishing Director *Suzanne Baboneau*
Publishers, Non-fiction *Andrew Gordon* (also
The Free Press), *Angela Herlihy*
Publishers, Fiction *Suzanne Baboneau, Kate
Lyall-Grant*
Approx. Annual Turnover £27.2 million

Founded 1986. Sister company of the leading
American company. Publishes hardback (**Simon
& Schuster**) and paperback (**Pocket Books**)
commercial and literary fiction and non-fiction,
including autobiography, biography, sport, mind,
body & spirit, humour, travel and other general
interest non-fiction. **The Free Press** publishes
serious non-fiction, including popular science,
politics, history and current business. Literary

international fiction and non-fiction is published under the **Scribner** imprint.

DIVISIONS **Martin Books** Director *Janet Copleston* Specialises in bespoke publishing and branded editions, and the Simon & Schuster UK cookery list.

Simon & Schuster Children's Books Publishing Director *Ingrid Selberg*, Editor (fiction) *Venetia Gosling*, Editor (picture books) *Katherine Halligan* Media tie-ins, picture books and fiction titles.

ROYALTIES twice-yearly.

Authors' Rating Setbacks last year following staff changes should not detract from the achievements of a medium-sized publisher with a talent for spotting quality titles. The latest initiative is a new fiction list for young people who are not yet ready for the 'marathon reads'. At the same time, the adult publishing programme is being cut from 350 to 250 titles a year.

Smith Gryphon Ltd
See **John Blake Publishing Ltd**

Colin Smythe Ltd
38 Mill Lane, Gerrards Cross SL9 8BA
☎01753 886000 Fax 01753 886469
✉ cs@colinsmythe.co.uk
www.colinsmythe.co.uk
Managing Director *Colin Smythe*
Approx. Annual Turnover £3.45 million

Founded 1966. Publishes Anglo-Irish literature, drama; criticism and Irish history. Also acts as agent for Terry Pratchett. About 5 titles a year. No unsolicited mss.

ROYALTIES annually/twice-yearly.

Snowbooks Ltd
120 Pentonville Road, London N1 9JN
☎020 7837 6482 Fax 020 7837 6348
✉ submissions@snowbooks.com
www.snowbooks.com
Managing Director *Emma Barnes*
Approx. Annual Turnover £250,000

Founded 2003. Publishes mainly fiction and some non-fiction. 'Keen on promoting open, friendly, productive relationships with authors and retailers.' TITLES *Adept* Robert Finn; *Paradise Jazz* Kat Pomfret; *The Idle Thoughts of an Idle Fellow* J.K. Jerome; *The London Scene* Virginia Woolf; *Boxing Fitness* Ian Oliver; *The Romanian* Bruce Benderson; *Plotting for Beginners* Sue Hepworth and Jane Linfoot; *The Other Eden* Sarah Bryant. 10–15 titles a year. Unsolicited mss 'very welcome', by e-mail only. Read the submis-

sion guidelines in the authors' section of the website first: www.snowbooks.com/authors.html

ROYALTIES vary according to contract 'but tend to be higher than the industry average'.

Society for Promoting Christian Knowledge (SPCK)
36 Causton Street, London SW1P 4ST
☎020 7592 3900 Fax 020 7592 3939
www.spck.org.uk
www.sheldonpress.co.uk
Director of Publishing *Simon Kingston*

Founded 1698, SPCK is the third oldest publisher in the country. IMPRINTS **SPCK** Editorial Director *Joanna Moriarty* Theology, academic, liturgy, prayer, spirituality, biblical studies, educational resources, mission, pastoral care, gospel and culture, worldwide. **Sheldon Press** Editor *Fiona Marshall* Popular medicine, health, self-help, psychology. **Azure** Senior Editor *Alison Barr* General spirituality.

ROYALTIES annually.

Authors' Rating Religion with a strong social edge.

Sophia Books
See **Rudolf Steiner Press**

Southwater
See **Anness Publishing Ltd**

Souvenir Press Ltd
43 Great Russell Street, London WC1B 3PA
☎020 7580 9307/8 & 7637 5711/2/3
Fax 020 7580 5064
✉ souvenirpress@ukonline.co.uk
Chairman/Managing Director *Ernest Hecht*

Independent publishing house. Founded 1951. Publishes academic and scholarly, animal care and breeding, antiques and collecting, archaeology, autobiography and biography, business and industry, children's, cookery, crafts and hobbies, crime, educational, fiction, gardening, health and beauty, history and antiquarian, humour, illustrated and fine editions, magic and the occult, medical, military, music, natural history, philosophy, poetry, psychology, religious, sociology, sports, theatre and women's studies. Souvenir's Human Horizons series for the disabled and their carers is one of the most preeminent in its field and recently celebrated 31 years of publishing for the disabled.

IMPRINTS/SERIES **Condor; Human Horizons; Independent Voices; Pictorial Presentations; Pop Universal; The Story-**

Tellers. TITLES *To the Kwai – and Back, War Drawings 1939–1945* Ronald Searle; *If I Should Die Before I Wake* Michelle Morris; *Down Syndrome* Cliff Cunningham; *The Hibernation Diet* Mike and Stuart McInnes; *The Tricky Part* Martin Moran; *Mysteries* Knut Hamsun. About 55 titles a year. Unsolicited mss considered but initial letter of enquiry and outline always required in the first instance.
ROYALTIES twice-yearly.

Authors' Rating Ever ready for a party, Ernest Hecht celebrated Souvenir's 55th anniversary with a week of theatrical and musical performances. The same showbusiness talent characterises the publishing list with the *Playboy Reader* nudging *Zen Buddhism*.

SPCK
See **Society for Promoting Christian Knowledge**

Special Interest Model Books Ltd
Stanley House, 3 Fleets Lane, Poole BH15 3AJ
☎01202 649930 Fax 01202 649950
✉ chrlloyd@globalnet.co.uk
www.specialinterestmodelbooks.co.uk
Contact *Chris Lloyd*
Commissioning Editor *Bill Burkinshaw*

Publishes aviation, engineering, leisure and hobbies, modelling, electronics, wine and beer making. Send synopses rather than completed mss.
ROYALTIES twice-yearly.

Speechmark Publishing Ltd
Telford Road, Bicester OX26 4LQ
☎01869 244644 Fax 01869 320040
✉ info@speechmark.net
www.speechmark.net
Chairman and Managing Director *Ian Franklin*
Publishing Director *Sarah Miles*
Approx. Annual Turnover £1.58 million

Founded 1979. Formerly known as Winslow Publishing, Speechmark publishes practical books and *ColorCards* for health, education and special needs practitioners and students. Unsolicited mss, synopses and ideas welcome. Approach by letter or e-mail.
ROYALTIES twice-yearly.

Spellmount Ltd
The Village Centre, Staplehurst TN12 0BJ
☎01580 893730 Fax 01580 893731
✉ enquiries@spellmount.com
www.spellmount.com

Managing Director *Jamie Wilson*
Approx. Annual Turnover £500,000

Founded 1983. Publishes history and military history. About 40 titles a year. Synopses/ideas for books in these specialist fields welcome but no personal memoirs. Enclose return postage.
ROYALTIES biannually for two years, then annually.

Spiro Press
17–19 Rochester Row, London SW1P 1LA
☎0870 165 8968 Fax 0870 165 8989
www.spiropress.com
Publisher *Susannah Lear*
Approx. Annual Turnover (Publishing Division) £1 million

Spiro Press, formerly The Industrial Society Publishing, is part of the Capita Group and has been publishing for over 20 years. Specialises in business, management and self-development – books, manuals and special reports. TITLES *The Heart Aroused*; *Business 2010*; *Why Innovation Fails*. SERIES *Your Personal Trainer*. Unsolicited mss, synopses and ideas welcome. No fiction or illustrated non-fiction.
ROYALTIES twice-yearly.

SportsBooks Limited
PO Box 422, Cheltenham GL50 2YN
☎01242 256755 Fax 01242 254694
✉ randall@sportsbooks.ltd.uk
www.sportsbooks.ltd.uk
Chairman & Managing Director *Randall Northam*
Approx. Annual Turnover £150,000

Founded 1995. Publishes sports books including biographies, statistical and practical. TITLES *Twickenham, the History of the Cathedral of Rugby*; *Test Cricket Grounds*; *The Complete Record of the FA Cup*. IMPRINT **BMM** Editorial Head *Mark Jones*. 10 titles in 2006. No unsolicited mss. Synopses and ideas welcome. Approach by letter or e-mail.

The Sportsman's Press
(An imprint of Quiller Publishing Ltd), Wykey House, Wykey, Shrewsbury SY4 1JA
☎01939 261616 Fax 01939 261606
✉ info@quillerbooks.com
www.countrybooksdirect.com
Managing Director *Andrew Johnston*

Specialises in books on all country subjects and general sports including fishing, fencing, shooting, equestrian, cookery, gunmaking and wildlife art. About 10 titles a year.
ROYALTIES twice-yearly.

Springer-Verlag London Ltd
Ashbourne House, The Guildway, Old
Portsmouth Road, Guildford GU3 1LP
☎01483 734433   Fax 01483 734411
www.springer.com

General Manager *Beverley Ford*
Approx. Annual Turnover £5 million

The UK subsidiary of Springer Science &
Business Media. Publishes science, technical and
medical books and journals. Specialises in computing, engineering, medicine, mathematics,
chemistry, biosciences, astronomy. All UK published books are sold through Springer's German
and US companies as well as in the UK. Globally:
4000 books and 1250 journals; UK: 150 titles plus
27 journals. Not interested in social sciences, fiction or school books but academic and professional science mss or synopses welcome.
    ROYALTIES annually.

Stainer & Bell Ltd
PO Box 110, 23 Gruneisen Road, London
N3 1DZ
☎020 8343 3303   Fax 020 8343 3024
✉ post@stainer.co.uk
www.stainer.co.uk

Managing Directors *Carol Y. Wakefield, Keith
    M. Wakefield*
Publishing Director *Nicholas Williams*
Approx. Annual Turnover £830,000

Founded 1907 to publish sheet music. Publishes
music and religious subjects related to
hymnody. Unsolicited synopses/ideas for books
welcome. Send letter enclosing brief précis.
    ROYALTIES annually.

The Stationery Office
See **TSO**

Rudolf Steiner Press
Hillside House, The Square, Forest Row
RH18 5ES
☎01342 824433   Fax 01342 826437
✉ office@rudolfsteinerpress.com
www.rudolfsteinerpress.com

Chairman *Mr P. Martyn*
Manager *Mr S. Gulbekian*
Approx. Annual Turnover £170,000

Founded in 1925 to publish the work of Rudolf
Steiner and related materials. Publishes non-fic-
tion: spirituality and philosophy. IMPRINT **Sophia
Books** *S. Gulbekian* TITLES *From Stress to Serenity*;
Homemaking as a Social Art. 15 titles in 2005. No
unsolicited material.
    ROYALTIES annually.

The Story-Tellers
See **Souvenir Press Ltd**

Straightline Publishing Ltd
29 Main Street, Bothwell G71 8RD
☎01698 853000   Fax 01698 854208

Director *Patrick Bellew*
Editor *Colin Calder*

Founded 1989. Publishes magazines and directories – trade and technical – books of local
interest. TITLES *Wired In*; *enterprisingglasgow*;
enterprisinglanarkshire. No unsolicited material.
    ROYALTIES annually.

Stripes
See **Little Tiger Press**

Studymates Limited
PO Box 225, Abergele, Conwy LL18 9AY
☎01745 832863   Fax 01745 826606
✉ info@studymates.co.uk
www.studymates.co.uk

Managing Editor *Graham Lawler, MA*

Publishes **Studymates** Academic books for the
16 to 21 age group, covering A Levels and
undergraduate studies and writers' guides for
aspiring writers. Authors need to be practising or
recently-retired teachers/lecturers, or published
authors for the writers' guides. Ideas in writing
first; unsolicited mss will not be considered.

Summersdale Publishers Ltd
46 West Street, Chichester PO19 1RP
☎01243 771107   Fax 01243 786300
✉ submissions@summersdale.com
www.summersdale.com

Directors *Stewart Ferris, Alastair Williams*
Commissioning Editor *Jennifer Barclay*
Approx. Annual Turnover £1.2 million

Founded 1990. Publishes travel literature, mar-
tial arts, self-help, cookery, humour and gift
books. TITLES *How to be a Writer*; *How to Get
Published*; *Pint-Sized Ireland*; *Shape Shifter*; *Exam-
Busting Tips*; *From Paella to Porridge*. 50–60 titles
a year. No unsolicited mss; synopses and ideas
welcome by e-mail.
    ROYALTIES paid.

Sussex Academic Press
PO Box 139, Eastbourne BN24 9BP
☎01323 479220   Fax 01323 478185
✉ edit@sussex-academic.co.uk
www.sussex-academic.co.uk

Managing Director *Anthony Grahame*
Approx. Annual Turnover £250,000

Founded 1994. Academic publisher. DIVISION/ IMPRINT **Sussex Academic** TITLES *Nazis in Pre-War London, 1930–1939*; *Cunning Folk and Familiar Spirits: Shamanistic Visionary Traditions in Early Modern British Witchcraft and Magic.* **Alpha Press** TITLE *The Financial Universe: Planning Your Investments Using Astrological Forecasting.* 45 titles in 2005 No unsolicited material; send letter of inquiry in the first instance.

ROYALTIES annually.

Sutton Publishing Ltd

Phoenix Mill, Thrupp, Stroud GL5 2BU
☎01453 731114 Fax 01453 731117
✉ publishing@sutton-publishing.co.uk

Managing Director *Jeremy Yates-Round*
Senior Commissioning Editors *Jaqueline Mitchell* (biography), *Christopher Feeney* (general history), *Jonathan Falconer* (military), *Simon Fletcher* (local history)

Founded 1978. Acquired by **Haynes Publishing** in March 2000. Publishes academic, archaeology, biography, countryside, history, military, aviation, regional interest, local history. About 200 titles a year. Send synopses rather than complete mss.

ROYALTIES twice-yearly.

Authors' Rating Having started as a regional publisher, Sutton has branched out into general non-fiction. Strong on popular history.

Swan Hill Press (An imprint of Quiller Publishing Ltd)

Wykey House, Wykey, Shrewsbury SY4 1JA
☎01939 261616 Fax 01939 261606
✉ info@quillerbooks.com
www.countrybooksdirect.com

Managing Director *Andrew Johnston*

Specialises in practical books on all country and field sports activities. Publishes books on fishing, shooting, gundog training, falconry, equestrian, deer, cookery, wildlife. About 20 titles a year. Unsolicited mss must include s.a.e.

ROYALTIES twice-yearly.

Sweet & Maxwell Group

100 Avenue Road, London NW3 3PF
☎020 7393 7000 Fax 020 7393 7010
✉ sweetandmaxwellcustomerservices@ thomson.com
www.sweetandmaxwell.thomson.com

Managing Director *Peter Lake*

Founded 1799. Part of the Thomson Corporation. Publishes materials in all media; looseleaf works, journals, law reports, CD-ROMs and online. The legal and professional list is varied and contains academic titles as well as treatises and reference works in the legal and related professional fields.

IMPRINTS **Sweet & Maxwell**; **GEE**; **W. Green (Scotland)**; **Incomes Data Services**; **Thomson Round Hall (Ireland)**. Over 1100 products, including 180 looseleafs, 80 periodicals, more than 40 digital products and online information services and 200 new titles each year. Ideas welcome. Writers with legal/professional projects in mind are advised to contact the Legal Business Unit at the earliest possible stage in order to lay the groundwork for best design, production and marketing of a project.

ROYALTIES and fees according to contract.

Tango Books Ltd

PO Box 32595, London W4 5YD
☎020 8996 9970 Fax 020 8996 9977
✉ sales@tangobooks.co.uk
www.tangobooks.co.uk

Directors *David Fielder, Sheri Safran*
Approx. Annual Turnover £1 million

Founded 1981. Children's books publisher with international co-edition potential: pop-ups, three-dimensional, novelty, picture and board books, 1000 words maximum. About 30 titles a year. Approach with preliminary letter, sample material and s.a.e. in the first instance.

Primarily, FEES paid.

Taschen UK

1 Heathcock Court, 415 Strand, London WC2R 0NS
☎020 7845 8585 Fax 020 7836 3696
www.taschen.com

UK office of the German photographic, art and architecture publisher. Editorial office in Cologne (see entry under *European Publishers*).

I.B. Tauris & Co. Ltd

6 Salem Road, London W2 4BU
☎020 7243 1225 Fax 020 7243 1226
✉ mail@ibtauris.com
www.ibtauris.com

Chairman/Publisher *Iradj Bagherzade*
Managing Director *Jonathan McDonnell*

Founded 1984. Independent publisher. Publishes general non-fiction and academic in the fields of international relations, religion, current affairs, history, politics, cultural, media and film studies, Middle East studies. Distributes Philip Wilson Publishers, The Federal Trust and the Khalili Collections worldwide. IMPRINTS **Tauris   Parke   Books**

Illustrated books on architecture, travel, design and culture. **Tauris Parke Paperbacks** Trade titles, including art, travel and biography. **British Academic Press** and **Tauris Academic Studies** Academic monographs. **Radcliffe Press** Colonial history and biography. Unsolicited synopses and book proposals welcome.
ROYALTIES twice-yearly.

Authors' Rating Imprint Radcliffe Press may require authors to contribute towards costs of publication.

Taylor & Francis (An imprint of Taylor & Francis Group, an Informa plc business)
2 Park Square, Milton Park, Abingdon OX14 4RN
☎020 7017 6000 Fax 020 7017 6699
www.tandf.co.uk
CEO *Roger Horton*
Managing Director *Emmett Dages* (US)
Publishing Director (US) *John Lavender*
Approx. Annual Turnover £200 million

Specialises in scientific and technical books for university students and academics in the following subjects: built environment, architecture, planning and civil engineering; biology, including genetics, plant architecture, molecular biology and biotechnology. About 1100 titles a year. Send detailed proposal plus c.v. and sample chapters. Proposal requirements and submission procedures can be found on the website. No poetry, fiction, travel or astrology.
ROYALTIES annually.

Authors' Rating One of those companies that barely registers with authors until they look at some of the famous imprints that are gathered under the corporate umbrella. Very much into higher education and reference, further expansion is predicted. Recent restructuring reflects the growing importance of the US market.

Teach Yourself
See **Hodder Headline Ltd**

Telegram Books
26 Westbourne Grove, London W2 5RH
☎020 7221 9347 Fax 020 7229 7492
✉ info@telegrambooks.com
www.telegrambooks.com
Chairman/Managing Director *André Gaspard*
Commissioning Editor *Rebecca O'Connor*

New independent publisher of literary fiction from around the world. 15 titles a year.

Welcomes unsolicited material; approach by post or e-mail.
ROYALTIES annually.

Telegraph Books
1 Canada Square, Canary Wharf, London E14 5DT
☎020 7538 6826 Fax 020 7538 6064
www.books.telegraph.co.uk
Owner *Telegraph Group Ltd*
Publisher *Morven Knowles*
Approx. Annual Turnover £3 million

Concentrates on Telegraph branded books in association/collaboration with other publishers. Also runs Telegraph Books Direct, a direct mail, phone-line bookselling service and off-the-page sales for other publishers' books. Publishes general non-fiction: reference, personal finance, health, gardening, guides, sport, humour, puzzles and games. Mainly interested in books if a Telegraph link exists. About 50 titles a year. No unsolicited material.
ROYALTIES twice-yearly.

Temple Lodge Publishing Ltd
Hillside House, The Square, Forest Row RH18 5ES
☎01342 824000
✉ office@templelodge.com
www.templelodge.com
Chairman *Mr R. Pauli*
Chief Editor *Mr S. Gulbekian*
Approx. Annual Turnover £65,000

Founded in 1990 to develop the work of Rudolf Steiner (see also **Rudolf Steiner Press**). Publishes non-fiction: mind, body & spirit, current affairs, health and therapy. IMPRINT **Clairview Books** (see entry). 12 titles in 2005. No unsolicited material; send initial letter of enquiry. No poetry or fiction.
ROYALTIES annually.

Texere
See **Thomson Learning**

Thames and Hudson Ltd
181A High Holborn, London WC1V 7QX
☎020 7845 5000 Fax 020 7845 5050
✉ mail@thameshudson.co.uk
www.thamesandhudson.com
Chairman *Thomas Neurath*
Managing Director *Jamie Camplin*
Approx. Annual Turnover £30 million

Publishes art, archaeology, architecture and design, biography, fashion, garden and landscape

design, graphics, history, illustrated and fine editions, mythology, photography, popular culture, style, travel and topography. SERIES *World of Art*; *Hip Hotels*; *StyleCity*; *New Horizons*; *Most Beautiful Villages*; *Earth From the Air*. TITLES *Fashion Illustration Next*; *Art Since 1900*; *The Artist's Yearbook*; *Art Photography Now*; *Architecture in Wood*; *Hockney's Pictures*; *Sensation*; *The Shock of the New*; *Germaine Greer's The Boy*; *Graffiti World*; *Blahnik by Boman*; *Sneakers*; *The Way We Live*; *The Eco-Design Handbook*; *The Seventy Battles of All Time*; *The Complete World of Human Evolution*; *Lawrence of Arabia*. 200 titles a year. Send preliminary letter and outline before mss.
ROYALTIES twice-yearly.

Authors' Rating Once dedicated exclusively to smart art books, Thames and Hudson is showing distinct signs of branching out into reference with the acclaimed *Artist's Yearbook* and travel with the Hip Hotel city guides.

Third Millennium Publishing
Third Millennium Information Ltd, 2–5 Benjamin Street, London EC1M 5QL
☎020 7336 0144 Fax 020 7608 1188
✉ info@tmiltd.com
www.tmiltd.com

Managing Director *Julian Tunstall*
Approx. Annual Turnover £750,000

Founded 1999 as a highly illustrated book publisher in the international museum, heritage and art gallery markets. Also some 'coffee-table' titles in association with various universities, Oxbridge colleges, independent schools and military organisations. 10–15 titles annually. Unsolicited material welcome; approach in writing with c.v., book synopsis, target market and any supporting information. No fiction.
ROYALTIES annually.

Thoemmes
See **The Continuum International Publishing Group Limited**

Thomson Learning
High Holborn House, 50–51 Bedford Row, London WC1R 4LR
☎020 7067 2500 Fax 020 7067 2600
www.thomson.com

CEO (Worldwide) *Ron Schlosser*
CEO/MD (Thomson Learning EMEA) *Tom Davy*
Publishing Director (Thomson Learning EMEA) *John Yates*

Founded 1993. Formerly International Thomson Publishing, part of the Thomson Corporation

and as such has offices worldwide with the UK office being reported to by Copenhagen (for Europe), Turkey (Middle East) and South Africa. Acquired Texere in 2003. Publishes education. TITLES *Management and Cost Accounting* Drury; *Strategy – Process, Content, Contact* DeWit and Meyer. Unsolicited material aimed at students is welcome but telephone in the first instance to check out the idea.
ROYALTIES vary according to contract.

Thomson Round Hall (Ireland)
See **Sweet & Maxwell Group**

Stanley Thornes (Publishers) Ltd
See **Nelson Thornes Ltd**

F.A. Thorpe (Publishing)
The Green, Bradgate Road, Anstey LE7 7FU
☎0116 236 4325 Fax 0116 234 0205

Group Chief Executive *Robert Thirlby*
Approx. Annual Turnover £6 million

Founded in 1964 to supply large print books to libraries. Part of the Ulverscroft Group Ltd. Publishes fiction and non-fiction large print books. No educational, gardening or books that would not be suitable for large print. IMPRINTS **Charnwood**; **Ulverscroft**; **Linford Romance**; **Linford Mystery**; **Linford Western**. 456 titles in 2004. No unsolicited material.

Thorsons
See **HarperCollins Publishers Ltd**

Time Out Guides
See **The Random House Group Ltd**

Time Warner
See **Little, Brown Book Group UK**

Times Books
See **HarperCollins Publishers Ltd**

Timewell Press
10 Porchester Terrace, London W2 3TL
☎0870 760 5250 Fax 0870 760 5250
✉ info@timewellpress.com
www.timewellpress.com

Chairman *Gerard Noel*
Managing Director *Andreas Campomar*

Founded 1997. Publishes literary international fiction and non-fiction. AUTHORS include Anthony Blond, Francis Fulford, Ralph Lownie, C.S. Nicholls, M-J. Lancaster, Jonathan Gathorne-Hardy (J.R. Ackerley Prize, 2005), Charles Campion (Gourmand World Cookbook

Awards, 2004), Anthony Powell, George Orwell. 6 titles in 2005. No unsolicited mss; send synopses and ideas with letter and s.a.e.

ROYALTIES twice-yearly.

Titan Books

144 Southwark Street, London SE1 0UP
☎020 7620 0200 Fax 020 7620 0032
✉ editorial@titanemail.com
www.titanbooks.com

Managing Director *Nick Landau*
Editorial Director *Katy Wild*

Founded 1981. Now a leader in the publication of graphic novels and film and television tie-ins. Publishes comic books/graphic novels, film and television titles. IMPRINT **Titan Books** TITLES *Batman; The Battlestar Galactica Companion: Season 2; The Official Companion Seasons 1&2; Scooby-Doo; The Simpsons; Star Wars; Superman; Transformers; Wallace & Gromit.* About 200 titles a year. No unsolicited fiction or children's books. Ideas for film and TV titles considered; send synopsis/outline with sample chapter. No e-mail submissions. Author guidelines available.

ROYALTIES twice-yearly.

Tor

See **Macmillan Publishers Ltd**

Transita Ltd

3 Newtec Place, Magdalen Road, Oxford OX4 1RE
☎01865 204393 Fax 01862 248780
✉ info@transita.co.uk
www.transita.co.uk

Managing Director *Giles Lewis*
Editorial Director *Nikki Read*

Independent publisher specialising in publishing contemporary fiction for women over 45. Synopsis and three chapters required.

Transworld Publishers, A division of the Random House Group Ltd

61–63 Uxbridge Road, London W5 5SA
☎020 8579 2652 Fax 020 8579 5479
✉ info@transworld-publishers.co.uk
www.booksattransworld.co.uk

Managing Director *Larry Finlay*
Publisher *Bill Scott-Kerr*
Senior Publishing Director *Francesca Liversidge*
Approx. Annual Turnover £72 million

Founded 1950. A subsidiary of **Random House, Inc.**, New York, which in turn is a wholly-owned subsidiary of **Bertelsmann AG**, Germany. Publishes general fiction and non-fiction, gardening, sports and leisure. IMPRINTS **Bantam** *Francesca Liversidge*; **Bantam Press** *Sally Gaminara*; **Corgi** & **Black Swan** *Bill Scott-Kerr*; **Doubleday** *Marianne Velmans*; **Channel 4 Books** *Doug Young*; **Eden** *Susanna Wadeson*; **Expert Books** *Gareth Pottle.* AUTHORS Monica Ali, Kate Atkinson, Charlotte Bingham, Dan Brown, Bill Bryson, Lee Child, Jilly Cooper, Ben Elton, Frederick Forsyth, David Gemmell, Tess Gerritsen, Robert Goddard, Joanne Harris, Stephen Hawking, D.G. Hessayon, John Irving, Sophie Kinsella, Anne McCaffrey, Paul McKenna, Andy McNab, John O'Farrell, Terry Pratchett, Patricia Scanlan, Gerald Seymour, Danielle Steel, Joanna Trollope. No unsolicited mss. OVERSEAS ASSOCIATES Random House Australia Pty Ltd; Random House New Zealand; Random House (Pty) Ltd (South Africa).

ROYALTIES twice-yearly.

Travel Publishing Ltd

7A Apollo House, Calleva Park, Aldermaston RG7 8TN
☎0118 981 7777 Fax 0118 940 8428
✉ info@travelpublishing.co.uk
www.travelpublishing.co.uk

Directors *Peter Robinson, Chris Day*

Founded in 1997 by two former directors of Reed Elsevier plc. Publishes travel guides covering places of interest, accommodation, food, drink and specialist shops in Britain and Ireland. SERIES *Hidden Places; Hidden Inns; Country Pubs; Country Living Rural Guides* (in conjunction with *Country Living* magazine); *Off the Motorway.* Over 40 titles in print. Welcomes unsolicited material; send letter in the first instance.

ROYALTIES twice-yearly.

Trentham Books Ltd

Westview House, 734 London Road, Stoke-on-Trent ST4 5NP
☎01782 745567/844699 Fax 01782 745553
www.trentham-books.co.uk

Directors *Dr Gillian Klein, Barbara Wiggins*
Approx. Annual Turnover £1 million

Publishes education (nursery, school to higher), social sciences, intercultural studies, gender studies and law for professional readers *not* for children and parents. Also academic and professional journals. No fiction, biography or poetry. Over 30 titles a year. Unsolicited mss, synopses and ideas welcome if relevant to their interests. Material only returned if adequate s.a.e. sent.

ROYALTIES annually.

Trident Press Ltd

Empire House, 175 Piccadilly, London
W1J 9TB
☎020 7491 8770 Fax 020 7491 8664
✉ admin@tridentpress.com
www.tridentpress.com
Managing Director *Peter Vine*
Approx. Annual Turnover £550,000

Founded 1997. Publishes TV tie-ins, natural history, travel, geography, underwater/marine life, history, archaeology, culture and fiction. DIVISIONS **Fiction/General Publishing** *Paula Vine*, **Natural History** *Peter Vine*. TITLES *Red Sea Sharks; The Elysium Testament; BBC Wildlife Specials; UAE in Focus*. No unsolicited mss; synopses and ideas welcome, particularly TV tie-ins. Approach in writing or *brief* communications by e-mail, fax or telephone.

ROYALTIES annually.

Trotman & Co. Ltd

2 The Green, Richmond TW9 1PL
☎020 8486 1150 Fax 020 8486 1161
www.trotman.co.uk
Editorial Director *Mina Patria*
Approx. Annual Turnover £3 million

Publishes general careers books, higher education guides, teaching support material, employment and training resources. TITLES *Degree Course Offers; The Student Book; Trotman Green Guides; Students' Money Matters; CRAC Degree Course Guides; Real Life Guides; Real Life Issues; Newscheck* (journal for careers professionals); *Careers 2006*. About 60 titles a year. Unsolicited material welcome.

ROYALTIES twice-yearly.

Troubador Publishing Ltd

9 De Montfort Mews, Leicester LE1 7FW
☎0116 255 9311 Fax 0116 244 9323
✉ books@troubador.co.uk
www.troubador.co.uk
Chairman *Jane Rowland*
Managing Director *Jeremy Thompson*
Approx. Annual Turnover £300,000

Founded 1998. Publishes fiction, children's, academic, non-fiction, translation and poetry. Offers self-publishing agreement for fiction and non-fiction under its Matador imprint. DIVISIONS **Academic** *Jane Rowland*; **Fiction/Non-Fiction** *Jeremy Thompson*. IMPRINTS **Matador**; **Troubador Italian Studies** TITLES *Energy Beyond Oil; Grazia Deledda: A Biography; The Ethics of Teaching Practice*. 55 titles in 2005. Unsolicited mss welcome, by e-mail only. No synopses or ideas for books.

ROYALTIES quarterly.

TSO (The Stationery Office)

St Crispins, Duke Street, Norwich NR3 1PD
☎01603 622211 Fax 01603 694313
(Editorial)
www.tso.co.uk
Chairman *Richard Dell*
Approx. Annual Turnover £250 million

Formerly HMSO, which was founded in 1786. Became part of the private sector in October 1996. Publisher of material sponsored by Parliament, government departments and other official bodies. Also commercial publishing in the following broad categories: business and professional, environment, transport, education and law. 11,000 new titles each year with 50,000 titles in print.

Tuckwell Press

See **Birlinn Ltd**

Twenty First Century Publishers Ltd

Braunton Barn, Kiln Lane, Isfield TN22 5UE
☎01892 522802
✉ TFCP@btinternet.com
www.twentyfirstcenturypublishers.com
Chairman *Fred Piechoczek*

Founded 2002. Publishes general fiction, financial thrillers and crime. Welcomes submissions by e-mail: manuscripts@connectfree.co.uk (contact *Fred Piechoczek*). Send brief synopsis in the body of the e-mail with extracts from the book in a file attachment (two to three chapters from anywhere in the book). No non-fiction or children's.

ROYALTIES twice-yearly.

20/20

See **The X Press**

Ulverscroft

See **F.A. Thorpe (Publishing)**

Unichrome

See **Jarrold Publishing**

University Presses of California, Columbia & Princeton Ltd

1 Oldlands Way, Bognor Regis PO22 9SA
☎01243 842165 Fax 01243 842167
✉ lois@upccp.demon.co.uk

Publishes academic titles only. US-based editorial offices. Enquiries only. Over 200 titles a year.

Usborne Publishing Ltd
83–85 Saffron Hill, London EC1N 8RT
☎020 7430 2800   Fax 020 7430 1562
✉ mail@usborne.co.uk
www.usborne.com

Managing Director *Peter Usborne*
Publishing Director *Jenny Tyler*
Approx. Annual Turnover £26 million

Founded 1973. Publishes non-fiction, fiction, art and activity books, puzzle books and music for children, young adults and pre-school. Some titles for parents. Up to 250 titles a year. Non-fiction books are written in-house to a specific format and therefore unsolicited mss are not normally welcome. Ideas which may be developed in-house are sometimes considered. Fiction for children will be considered. Keen to hear from new illustrators and designers.

ROYALTIES twice-yearly.

Authors' Rating A children's publisher that finds favour with parents who can learn a thing or two from an imaginative non-fiction list. But fiction too is growing – up to 30 titles a year.

Vanguard Press
See **Pegasus Elliot Mackenzie Publishers Ltd**

Ventura
See **Penguin Group (UK)**

Vermilion
See **The Random House Group Ltd**

Verso
6 Meard Street, London W1F 0EG
☎020 7437 3546   Fax 020 7734 0059
✉ info@verso.co.uk
www.versobooks.com

Managing Director *Giles O'Bryen*
Approx. Annual Turnover £2 million

Formerly New Left Books which grew out of the *New Left Review*. Publishes politics, history, sociology, economics, philosophy, cultural studies, feminism. TITLES *Wobblies! A Graphic History* eds. Paul Buhle and Nicole Schulman; *The Soviet Century* Moshe Lewin; *NHS plc: The Privatisation of our Health Care* Allyson M. Pollock; *Street-Fighting Years* Tariq Ali; *Planet of Slums* Mike Davis. No unsolicited mss; synopses and ideas for books welcome. OVERSEAS OFFICE in New York.

ROYALTIES annually.

Authors' Rating Dubbed by the *Bookseller* as 'one of the most successful small independent publishers'. The aim is to double the publishing programme over three years with the backlist supported by print-on-demand.

Viking
See **Penguin Group (UK)**

Vintage
See **The Random House Group Ltd**

Virago Press
Little, Brown Book Group UK, Brettenham House, Lancaster Place, London WC2E 7EN
☎020 7911 8000   Fax 020 7911 8100
www.virago.co.uk

Publisher *Lennie Goodings*
Editorial Director *Antonia Hodgson*
Editor, Virago Modern Classics *Donna Coonan*

An imprint of **Little, Brown Book Group UK**. Founded in 1973 by Carmen Callil, Virago publishes women's literature, both fiction and non-fiction. IMPRINT **Virago Modern Classics** 19th and 20th-century fiction reprints by writers such as Daphne du Maurier, Angela Carter and Edith Wharton. Virago AUTHORS include Margaret Atwood, Maya Angelou, Jennifer Belle, Waris Dirie, Sarah Dunant, Germaine Greer, Michèle Roberts, Gillian Slovo, Talitha Stevenson, Natasha Walter, Sarah Waters. 50 titles a year. 'We do not currently accept unsolicited fiction.'

ROYALTIES twice-yearly.

Authors' Rating The first name in women's publishing has gained marketing strength from its association with Time Warner. A team of young editors favours writers with something new to say.

Virgin Books Ltd
Thames Wharf Studios, Rainville Road, London W6 9HT
☎020 7386 3300   Fax 020 7386 3360
✉ info@virgin-books.co.uk
www.virgin.com/books

Managing Director *KT Forster*
Approx. Annual Turnover £10 million

The Virgin Group's book publishing company. Publishes non-fiction, reference and large-format illustrated books on lifestyle, health, music, sport, biography, crime, film, TV and current affairs. No poetry, short stories, individual novels, children's books.

DIVISIONS **Non-fiction** IMPRINT **Virgin** Editorial Directors *Carolyn Thorne, Natalie*

Jerome. **Fiction** IMPRINTS **Virgin**; **Black Lace**; **Nexus**; **Cheek** Editor *Adam Nevill* Erotic fiction 'written by women for women'.
ROYALTIES twice-yearly.

Vision On
See **Omnibus Press**

The Vital Spark
See **Neil Wilson Publishing Ltd**

Voyager
See **HarperCollins Publishers Ltd**

University of Wales Press
10 Columbus Walk, Brigantine Place, Cardiff CF10 4UP
☎029 2049 6899   Fax 029 2049 6108
✉ press@press.wales.ac.uk
www.wales.ac.uk/press
Director *Ashley Drake*
Commissioning Editor *Sarah Lewis*
Approx. Annual Turnover £500,000

Founded 1922. Publishes academic and scholarly books in English and Welsh in six main subject areas: History, Political Philosophy and Religious Studies, Welsh and Celtic Studies, Literary Studies, European Studies and Medieval Studies. SERIES include *Iberian and Latin American Studies*; *Gender Studies in Wales*; *Gothic Literary Studies*; *Kantian Studies*; *Television and Genre*. 55 titles a year. Unsolicited mss considered but see website for further guidance.
ROYALTIES annually.

Walker Books Ltd
87 Vauxhall Walk, London SE11 5HJ
☎020 7793 0909   Fax 020 7587 1123
✉ editorial@walker.co.uk
www.walkerbooks.co.uk
Publisher *Jane Winterbotham*
Editors *Gill Evans* (fiction & paperbacks), *Deirdre McDermott* (picture books), *Caroline Royds* (early learning, non-fiction & gift books), *Denise Johnstone-Burt* (picture books, board & novelty), *Loraine Taylor* (audio and books plus)
Approx. Annual Turnover £34.6 million

Founded 1979. Publishes illustrated children's books, children's fiction and non-fiction. TITLES *Maisy* Lucy Cousins; *Where's Wally?* Martin Handford; *Five Minutes' Peace* Jill Murphy; *Can't You Sleep, Little Bear?* Martin Waddell and Barbara Firth; *Guess How Much I Love You* Sam McBratney and Anita Jeram; *Alex*

Rider series Anthony Horowitz. About 300 titles a year.
ROYALTIES twice-yearly.

Authors' Rating Much loved by its authors, Walker Books is enlivening its backlist with animated films of classic titles.

Wallflower Press
6a Middleton Place, Langham Street, London W1W 7TE
☎020 7436 9494
✉ info@wallflowerpress.co.uk
www.wallflowerpress.co.uk
Editorial Director *Yoram Allon*
Chief Editor *Del Cullen*
Approx. Annual Turnover £200,000

Founded 1999. Publishes academic and popular film studies and related media and cultural studies. SERIES *Short Cuts* Introductory undergraduate books; *Director's Cuts* Studies on significant international film-makers; *24 Frames* Anthologies focusing on national and regional cinemas. Over 25 titles a year. Unsolicited mss, synopses and proposals welcome. No fiction or academic material not related to the moving image.
ROYALTIES annually.

Ward Lock
See **Octopus Publishing Group**

Ward Lock Educational Co. Ltd
BIC Ling Kee House, 1 Christopher Road, East Grinstead RH19 3BT
☎01342 318980   Fax 01342 410980
✉ wle@lingkee.com
www.wardlockeducational.com
Owner *Ling Kee (UK) Ltd*

Founded 1952. Publishes educational books (primary, middle, secondary, teaching manuals) for all subjects, specialising in maths, science, geography, reading and English and currently focusing on Key Stages 1 and 2.

Frederick Warne
See **Penguin Group (UK)**

Franklin Watts
See **Hachette Children's Books**

Wayland
See **Hachette Children's Books**

Weidenfeld & Nicolson
See **The Orion Publishing Group Ltd**

Wharncliffe Books

47 Church Street, Barnsley S70 2AS
☎01226 734222 Fax 01226 734438
✉ enquiries@wharncliffebooks.co.uk
www.wharncliffebooks.co.uk

Commissioning Editor *Rupert Harding*

An imprint of **Pen & Sword Books Ltd**. Wharncliffe is the book and magazine publishing arm of an old-established, independently owned newspaper publishing and printing house. Publishes local history throughout the UK, focusing on nostalgia and old photographs. SERIES *Foul Deeds*; *Local History Companions*; *Pals*; *Aspects*. No unsolicited mss; synopses and ideas welcome.

ROYALTIES twice-yearly.

Which? Books

2 Marylebone Road, London NW1 4DF
☎020 7770 7000 Fax 020 7770 7660
www.which.net

Editorial Director *Helen Parker*

Founded 1957. Publishing arm of Which? Publishes non-fiction: information and reference on personal finance, property, divorce, consumer law. All titles offer direct value to the consumer. IMPRINT **Which? Books** TITLES *The Good Food Guide*; *Wills and Probate*; *Be Your Own Financial Adviser*. 10–12 titles a year. No unsolicited mss; send synopses and ideas only.

ROYALTIES, if applicable, twice-yearly.

Whittet Books Ltd

Hill Farm, Stonham Road, Cotton, Stowmarket IP14 4RQ
☎01449 781877 Fax 01449 781898
✉ annabel@whittet.dircon.co.uk
www.whittetbooks.com

Owner *A. Whittet & Co.*
Managing Director *Annabel Whittet*

Publishes natural history, pets, poultry, horses, domestic livestock, horticulture, rural interest. 6 titles in 2005. Synopses and ideas for books on the subjects listed are welcome.

ROYALTIES twice-yearly.

Whydown Books Limited,

Sedlescombe TN33 0RN
☎01424 870875 Fax 01424 870083
✉ readerspost@whydownbooks.com
www.whydownbooks.com

Chairman *Dick Nesbitt-Dufort*
Managing & Finance Director *Chris Martin*
Editorial Head *Pamela Richards*

Founded 2002. Publishes biography, fiction, general interest with a slant towards writers with first-hand experience of distant places and profound events. TITLES *Spies and Lovers* Adrian Hill; *Black Lysander* John Nesbitt-Dufort; *The Apothecary's Gift* Bradley Bernarde; *Chinnery's Hotel* Jaysinh Birje; *A Sussex Highlander Memoirs 1790–1815* Sergeant William Kenward. No children's or poetry at present. Developing their non-fiction list and film/television projects from fiction list. No unsolicited mss. Synopses and ideas welcome; even better a few chapters. Approach by letter or e-mail with idea and writing history.

ROYALTIES twice-yearly.

Wild Goose Publications

Iona Community, 4th Floor, The Savoy Centre, 140 Sauchiehall Street, Glasgow G2 3DH
☎0141 332 6292 Fax 0141 332 1090
✉ admin@ionabooks.com
www.ionabooks.com

Editorial Head *Sandra Kramer*

The publishing house of the Iona Community, established in the Celtic Christian tradition of St Columba, publishes books, tapes and CDs on holistic spirituality, social justice, political and peace issues, healing, innovative approaches to worship, song and material for meditation and reflection.

Wiley Europe Ltd

The Atrium, Southern Gate, Chichester PO19 8SQ
☎01243 779777 Fax 01243 775878
✉ europe@wiley.co.uk
www.wiley.com

Managing Director *Dr John Jarvis*
Publishing Directors *Mike Davis, Stephen Smith*
Approx. Annual Turnover £91 million

Founded 1807. US parent company. Publishes professional, reference trade and text books, scientific, technical and biomedical. DIVISIONS **Architecture, Higher Education Group** *Vivien Ward*; **Business, Computing, Finance, General Interest** *Sarah Stevens*; **Communications, Engineering, Statistics** *Ann-Marie Halligan*; **Health Sciences** *Deborah Dixon*; **Physical Sciences & Reference Publishing Group** *Ernest Kirkwood*.

ROYALTIES annually.

Authors' Rating With an ever growing list of scientific, technical and medical books, Wiley is among the top educational and professional publishers. Academic authors are attracted by the American connection. Online publishing is set to increase.

Wiley–Academy

John Wiley & Sons, 3rd Floor, International House, 7 High Street, Ealing Broadway, London W5 5DB
☎020 8326 3800 Fax 020 8326 3801
Chairman *Dr John Jarvis*
Commissioning Editor *Helen Castle*

Founded 1969. Became part of the **John Wiley & Sons, Inc.** group in 1997. Publishes architectural design. No unsolicited mss; synopses and ideas only.
ROYALTIES annually.

Neil Wilson Publishing Ltd

Suite 303, The Pentagon Centre, 36 Washington Street, Glasgow G3 8AZ
☎0141 221 1117 Fax 0141 221 5363
✉ info@nwp.co.uk
www.nwp.co.uk
www.11-9.co.uk
Managing Director/Editorial Director *Neil Wilson*
Editorial Administrator *Doug Zabel*
Approx. Annual Turnover £250,000

Founded 1992. Publishes Scottish interest and history, biography, humour and hillwalking, whisky; also Scottish cookery and travel. IMPRINTS **The In Pinn** Outdoor pursuits; **The Angels' Share** Whisky, drink and food-related subjects; **The Vital Spark** Humour; **NWP** History, biography, reference, true crime; **11:9** Scottish fiction. About 10–15 titles a year. Unsolicited mss, synopses and ideas welcome. No politics, academic or technical.
ROYALTIES twice-yearly.

Philip Wilson Publishers Ltd

109 Drysdale Street, The Timber Yard, London N1 6ND
☎020 7033 9900 Fax 020 7033 9922
✉ pwilson@philip-wilson.co.uk
www.philip-wilson.co.uk
Chairman *Philip Wilson*

Founded 1976. Publishes art, art history, antiques and collectibles. About 14 titles a year.

Wimbledon Publishing Company

75–76 Blackfriars Road, London SE1 8HA
☎020 7401 4200 Fax 020 7401 4201
✉ info@wpcpress.com
www.wpcpress.com
Managing Director *Kamaljit Sood*

General Manager *Renu Sood*

Founded in 1992 as a publisher of school texts, going on to launch Anthem Press, an academic and trade imprint focusing on world history, politics, economics, international affairs, literature and culture. IMPRINTS **Anthem Press** *Tej Sood*; **WPC Education** *K. Sood*. Welcomes mss, synopses and ideas for books. PARTNER ORGANISATION Stylus Publishing LLC, Sterling, VA, US.
ROYALTIES annually.

Windhorse Publications

11 Park Road, Moseley B13 8AB
☎0121 449 9191 Fax 0121 449 9191
✉ jnanasiddhi@windhorsepublications.com
www.windhorsepublications.com
Chairman/Editorial Head *Jnanasiddhi*
Approx. Annual Turnover £250,000

Founded 1977. Publishes meditation and Buddhism. Associated with the FWBO, a worldwide Buddhist movement. Publishes across the Buddhist traditions. Unsolicited mss, synopses and ideas welcome; approach by letter or e-mail in the first instance.
ROYALTIES quarterly.

Wise Publications

See **Omnibus Press**

WIT Press

Ashurst Lodge, Ashurst, Southampton SO40 7AA
☎023 8029 3223 Fax 023 8029 2853
✉ marketing@witpress.com
www.witpress.com
Owner *Computational Mechanics International Ltd, Southampton*
Chairman/Managing Director/Editorial Head *Professor C.A. Brebbia*

Founded in 1980 as Computational Mechanics Publications to publish engineering analysis titles. Changed to WIT Press to reflect the increased range of publications. Publishes scientific and technical, mainly at postgraduate level and above, including architecture, environmental engineering, bioengineering. TITLES *The Sustainable City*; *Handling Missing Data*; *Human Exposure to Electromagnetic Fields*; *Computational Ballistics*. 50 titles in 2005. Unsolicited mss, synopses and ideas welcome; approach by post or e-mail. No non-scientific or technical material or lower level (school and college-level texts). OVERSEAS SUBSIDIARY Computational Mechanics, Inc., Billerica, USA.
ROYALTIES annually.

Wizard Books
See **Icon Books Ltd**

Oswald Wolff Books
See **Berg Publishers**

The Women's Press
27 Goodge Street, London W1T 2LD
☎020 7636 3992 Fax 020 7637 1866
www.the-womens-press.com
Managing Director *Stella Kane*
Approx. Annual Turnover £1 million

Part of the Namara Group. First title published in 1978. Publishes women only: quality fiction and non-fiction. Fiction usually has a female protagonist and a woman-centred theme. International writers and subject matter encouraged. Non-fiction: books for and about women generally; gender politics, race politics, disability, feminist theory, health and psychology, literary criticism. IMPRINTS **Women's Press Classics**; **Livewire Books for Teenagers** Fiction and non-fiction series for young adults. No mss without previous letter, synopsis and sample material.
ROYALTIES twice-yearly.

Woodhead Publishing Ltd
Abington Hall, Abington, Cambridge CB1 6AH
☎01223 891358 Fax 01223 893694
✉ wp@woodhead-publishing.com
www.woodheadpublishing.com
Chairman *Alan Jessup*
Managing Director *Martin Woodhead*
Approx. Annual Turnover £1.8 million

Founded 1989. Publishes engineering, materials technology, textile technology, finance and investment, food technology, environmental science. TITLES *Welding International* (journal); *Reinforced Plastics Durability*; *Meat Science 6e*; *Base Metals Handbook*; *Foreign Exchange Options*. DIVISION **Woodhead Publishing** *Martin Woodhead*. About 60 titles a year. Unsolicited material welcome.
ROYALTIES annually.

Wordsworth Editions Ltd
8B East Street, Ware SG12 9HJ
☎01920 465167 Fax 01920 462267
✉ enquiries@wordsworth-editions.com *or* dennis.hart@wordsworth-editions.com (editorial)
www.wordsworth-editions.co.uk
Directors *E.G. Trayler, D.R. Hart*
Approx. Annual Turnover £4 million

Founded 1987. Publishes classics of English and world literature, reference books, poetry, children's classics, mystery and the supernatural, military history and special editions. About 75 titles a year. No unsolicited mss.

WPC Education
See **Wimbledon Publishing Company**

The X Press
PO Box 25694, London N17 6FP
☎020 8801 2100 Fax 020 8885 1322
✉ vibes@xpress.co.uk
www.xpress.co.uk
Editorial Director *Dotun Adebayo*
Publisher *Steve Pope*

Launched in 1992 with the cult bestseller *Yardie*, The X Press is the leading publisher of Black-interest fiction in the UK. Also publishes general fiction and children's fiction. IMPRINTS **The X Press**; **Nia**; **20/20**. About 26 titles a year. Send mss rather than synopses or ideas (enclose s.a.e.). No poetry.

Authors' Rating A small company that has done an inestimable service by introducing Black writers to the publishing mainstream. Popular fiction is the mainstay but the list also covers reprints of classic Black fiction.

Y Lolfa Cyf
Talybont, Ceredigion SY24 5AP
☎01970 832304 Fax 01970 832782
✉ ylolfa@ylolfa.com
www.ylolfa.com/
Managing Director *Garmon Gruffudd*
General Editor *Lefi Gruffudd*
Approx. Annual Turnover £800,000

Founded 1967. Small company which publishes mainly in Welsh; has its own four-colour printing and binding facilities. Publishes Welsh language publications; Celtic language tutors; English language books for the Welsh and Celtic tourist trade. Expanding slowly. TITLES *My Kingdom of Books* Richard Booth; *The Welsh Learner's Dictionary* Heini Gruffudd; *The Fight for Welsh Freedom* Gwynfor Evans; *Celtic Vision* John Merion Morris. IMPRINT **Dinas** Part-author-subsidised imprint for non-mainstream books of Welsh interest in English and Welsh. About 50 titles a year. Write first with synopses or ideas.
ROYALTIES twice-yearly.

Yale University Press (London)
47 Bedford Square, London WC1B 3DP
☎020 7079 4900 Fax 020 7079 4901
✉ sales@yaleup.co.uk
www.yalebooks.co.uk

Founded 1961. Owned by US parent company. Publishes academic and humanities. About 200 titles (worldwide) a year. Unsolicited mss and synopses welcome if within specialised subject areas.

ROYALTIES annually.

Authors' Rating A publisher with a marvellous talent for turning out scholarly books which appeal to the general reader. Academic writers who want to reach a wider audience take note.

Yellow Jersey Press
See **The Random House Group Ltd**

The Young Travellers Club
See **Beautiful Books Ltd**

Zambezi Publishing Ltd
PO Box 221, Plymouth PL2 2YJ
☎01752 367300 Fax 01752 350453
✉ info@zampub.com
www.zampub.com

Chair *Sasha Fenton*
Managing Director *Jan Budkowski*

Founded 1999. Publishes non-fiction: mind, body and spirit, self-help, finance and business. IMPRINT **Zambezi Publishing** TITLES *Sun Signs Made Simple; The Last Bastion; Develop Your ESP; Fortune Telling With Playing Cards.* About 12 titles a year.

Send synopsis and sample chapter by mail. Brief e-mail communication acceptable but *no* attachments, please.

ROYALTIES twice-yearly.

Zed Books Ltd
7 Cynthia Street, London N1 9JF
☎020 7837 4014 Fax 020 7833 3960
✉ sales@zedbooks.net
www.zedbooks.co.uk

Approx. Annual Turnover £1.4 million

Founded 1976. Publishes international and Third World affairs, development studies, women's studies, environmental studies, human rights and specific area studies. No fiction, children's or poetry. DIVISIONS **Development & Environment** *Dr Anna Hardman, Ellen Mackinlay;* **Women's Studies**. TITLES *Rogue State: A Guide to the World's Only Superpower* William Blum; *Staying Alive* Vandana Shiva; *The Autobiography of Nawal* Nawal El Saadawi. About 60 titles a year. No unsolicited mss; synopses and ideas welcome though.

ROYALTIES annually.

Zero to Ten
See **Evans Brothers Ltd**

Zigzag
See **Anova Books**

Irish Publishers

International Reply Coupons (IRCs) For return postage, IRCs are required (*not* UK postage stamps). These are available from post offices: letters, 60 pence; mss, according to weight. For current postal rates from the Republic of Ireland to the UK go to www.letterpost.ie and click on 'Letterpost Services'.

An Gúm
27 Sr. Fhreidric Thuaidh, Baile Átha Cliath 1
☎00 353 1 889 2800 Fax 00 353 1 873 1140
✉ angum@forasnagaeilge.ie
www.gaeilge.ie
Senior Editor *Seosamh Ó Murchú*
Editors *Máire Nic Mheanman*

Founded 1926. Formerly the Irish language publications branch of the Department of Education and Science. Has now become part of the North/South Language Body, Foras na Gaeilge. Publishes educational, children's, young adult, music, lexicography and general. Little adult fiction or poetry. About 50 titles a year. Unsolicited mss, synopses and ideas for books welcome. Also welcomes reading copies of first and second level school textbooks with a view to translating them into the Irish language.
ROYALTIES annually.

Anvil Books
45 Palmerston Road, Dublin 6
☎00 353 1 497 3628 Fax 00 353 1 496 8263
Managing Director *Rena Dardis*
Founded 1964 with emphasis on Irish history and biography. IMPRINT **The Children's Press**. Publishes Irish history, biography (particularly 1916–22), folklore and children's fiction. No adult fiction, poetry, fantasy, short stories or full-colour books for children. About 7 titles a year. 'Because of promotional requirements, only books by Irish-based authors considered and only books of Irish interest.' Send synopsis only with IRCs (no UK stamps); unsolicited mss not returned.
ROYALTIES annually.

Ashfield Press
30 Linden Grove, Blackrock, Co. Dublin
☎00 353 1 288 9808
✉ susanwaine@ashfieldpress.com
Directors *Susan Waine, John Davey, Gerry O'Connor*
Publishes Irish-interest non-fiction books.

TITLES *Lady Icarus; The Weather is a Good Storyteller; Secret Sights II*. Unsolicited mss and synopses welcome. ASSOCIATE COMPANY Ashfield Press Publishing Services.
ROYALTIES twice-yearly.

Atrium
See **Cork University Press**

Attic Press
See **Cork University Press**

Blackhall Publishing Ltd
33 Carysfort Avenue, Blackrock, Co. Dublin
☎00 353 1 278 5090 Fax 00 353 1 278 4446
✉ info@blackhallpublishing.com
www.blackhallpublishing.com
Managing Director *Gerard O'Connor*
Commissioning Editor *Mariel Deegan*

Publishes business, management, law and living books. Main subject areas include accounting, finance, management, HRM and law books aimed at both students and professionals in the industry. Also provides legal publishing sevices including Statute Law Revision, Law Reporting, Legislative Drafting and Subscription Services. 15 titles a year. Unsolicited mss and synopses welcome.
ROYALTIES annually.

Bradshaw Books
Tigh Filí, Thompson House, MacCurtain Street, Cork
☎00 353 21 450 9274
Fax 00 353 21 455 1617
✉ admin@cwpc.ie
www.tighfili.com
Managing Director *Maire Bradshaw*
Founded 1985. Publishes poetry, women's issues, spiritual, children's books. Organisers of the annual Cork Literary Review poetry manuscript competition. SERIES *Cork Literary Review*.
ROYALTIES not generally paid.

Brandon/Mount Eagle
Dingle, Co. Kerry
☎00 353 66 915 1463
Fax 00 353 66 915 1234
www.brandonbooks.com
Publisher *Steve MacDonogh*
Approx. Annual Turnover €500,000
Founded in 1997. Publishes Irish fiction, biography, memoirs and other non-fiction. About 15 titles a year. Not seeking unsolicited mss.

Brookside
See **New Island**

Edmund Burke Publisher
Cloonagashel, 27 Priory Drive, Blackrock, Co. Dublin
☎00 353 1 288 2159   Fax 00 353 1 283 4080
✉ deburca@indigo.ie
www.deburcararebooks.com
Managing Director *Eamonn De Búrca*
Publications Manager *Regina De Búrca-McAuley*
Approx. Annual Turnover €320,000
Small family-run business publishing historical and topographical and fine limited-edition books relating to Ireland. TITLES *The Great Book of Irish Genealogies*, 5 vols.; *The Annals of the Four Masters*, 7 vols; *Flowers of Mayo* (illus. Wendy Walsh); *O'Curry's Manners and Customs of the Ancient Irish; Joyce's Irish Names of Places.* Unsolicited mss welcome. No synopses or ideas.
ROYALTIES annually.

The Children's Press
See **Anvil Books**

Church of Ireland Publishing
Church of Ireland House, Church Avenue, Rathmines, Dublin 6
☎00 353 1 492 3979   Fax 00 353 1 492 4770
✉ susan.hood@rcbdub.org
www.cip.ireland.anglican.org
Chairman *Dr Kenneth Milne*
Publications Officer *Dr Susan Hood*
Founded 2004. Publishes official publications of the Church of Ireland: theological, historical and administrative, and facilitates publication for other church-related bodies. 3 titles in 2005. No unsolicited material.

Cló Iar-Chonnachta
Indreabhán, Connemara, Galway
☎00 353 91 593307   Fax 00 353 91 593362
✉ cic@iol.ie
www.cic.ie

Chairman/Director *Micheál Ó Conghaile*
Approx. Annual Turnover €400,000
Founded 1985. Publishes fiction, poetry, plays, teenage fiction and children's, mostly in Irish, including translations. Also publishes cassettes of writers reading from their own works. TITLES *Ag Greadadh Bas sa Reilig/Clapping in the Cemetery* Louis de Paorp; *Keening and Other Old Irish Musics* Breandán Ó Madagáin; *Máire Mhic Ghiolla Íosa: Beathaisnéis* Ray Mac Mánais; *Fardoras* Michael Daviett. 11 titles in 2005.
ROYALTIES annually.

The Collins Press
West Link Park, Doughcloyne, Wilton, Cork
☎00 353 21 434 7717
Fax 00 353 21 434 7720
✉ enquiries@collinspress.ie
www.collinspress.ie
Managing Director *Con Collins*
Approx. Annual Turnover €750,000
Founded 1989. Publishes general non-fiction, Irish interest and children's books. TITLES *An Unsung Hero; British Voices; Travelling with Lions; Ireland's Coastline.* 24 titles in 2005. No unsolicited mss; synopses and ideas welcome; approach by e-mail. See website for submission information. No academic, technical, professional or poetry.

The Columba Press
55A Spruce Avenue, Stillorgan Industrial Park, Blackrock, Co. Dublin
☎00 353 1 294 2556   Fax 00 353 1 294 2564
✉ sean@columba.ie (editorial) *or* info@columba.ie (general)
www.columba.ie
Chairman *Neil Kluepfel*
Managing Director *Seán O'Boyle*
Approx. Annual Turnover €1.02 million
Founded 1985. Small company committed to growth. Publishes religious and counselling titles. TITLES *Prism of Love* Donal O'Leary; *That Could Never Be* Kevin Dalton. IMPRINT **Currach Press** (see entry). 35 titles in 2004. Backlist of 250 titles. Unsolicited ideas and synopses rather than full mss preferred.
ROYALTIES twice-yearly.

Cork University Press
Youngline Industrial Estate, Pouladuff Road, Togher, Cork
☎00 353 21 490 2980
Fax 00 353 21 431 5329
✉ corkuniversitypress@ucc.ie
www.corkuniversitypress.com

Publications Director *Mike Collins*
Editorial Manager *Tom Dunne*

Founded 1925. Relaunched in 1992, the Press publishes academic and some trade titles. TITLES *Staging the Easter Rising: 1916 as Theatre*; *Foreign Affections: Ireland and the Global Question*; *The Irish Red Setter*, *The Barrytown Trilogy*. Also a biannual journal, *The Irish Review*, an interdisciplinary cultural review. No fiction. IMPRINTS **Attic Press**; **Atrium**. 10 titles in 2006 Unsolicited synopses and ideas welcome for textbooks, academic monographs, belles lettres, illustrated histories and journals.

ROYALTIES annually.

Currach Press

55A Spruce Avenue, Stillorgan Industrial Park, Blackrock, Co. Dublin
☎00 353 1 294 2556 Fax 00 353 1 294 2564
✉ jo@currach.ie
www.currach.ie

Publisher *Jo O'Donoghue*

Founded 2002. An imprint of **The Columba Press**. Publishes non-fiction titles of Irish interest, including politics, history, biography, sport, music and criticism. TITLES *A Memoir* Terry de Valera; *The Harcourt Street Line* Brian Mac Aongusa; *Short Hands, Long Pockets* Eddie Hobbs. Unsolicited ideas welcome; synopses rather than full mss preferred.

A.&A. Farmar Ltd

78 Ranelagh Village, Dublin 6
☎00 353 1 496 3625 Fax 00 353 1 497 0107
✉ afarmar@iol.ie
www.aafarmar.ie

Managing Director *Anna Farmar*
Production Director *Tony Farmar*

Founded 1992. Publishes Irish social history, business, food and wine. 10 titles in 2005. No unsolicited mss. Synopses and ideas welcome; approach by letter or e-mail in the first instance.

Flyleaf Press

4 Spencer Villas, Glenageary, Co. Dublin
☎00 353 1 284 5906
✉ books@flyleaf.ie
www.flyleaf.ie

Managing Director *Dr James Ryan*
Sales & Administration *Brian Smith*

Founded 1981. Concentrates on family history and Irish history as a background to family history. No fiction. TITLES *Irish Records*; *Longford and its People*; *Tracing Your Kerry Ancestors*; *Tracing*

Your Limerick Ancestors. Unsolicited mss, synopses and ideas for books welcome.

ROYALTIES twice-yearly.

Four Courts Press Ltd

7 Malpas Street, Dublin 8
☎00 353 1 453 4668 Fax 00 353 1 453 4672
✉ info@four-courts-press.ie
www.four-courts-press.ie

Chairman/Managing Director *Michael Adams*
Director *Martin Healy*

Founded 1972. Publishes mainly scholarly books in the humanities. About 65 titles a year. Synopses and ideas for books welcome.

ROYALTIES annually.

Gill & Macmillan

10 Hume Avenue, Park West, Dublin 12
☎00 353 1 500 9500 Fax 00 353 1 500 9599
www.gillmacmillan.ie

Chairman *M.H. Gill*
Managing Director *Dermot O'Dwyer*
Approx. Annual Turnover €12 million

Founded 1968 when M.H. Gill & Son Ltd and Macmillan Ltd formed a jointly owned publishing company. Publishes biography/autobiography, history, current affairs, literary criticism (all mainly of Irish interest), guidebooks and cookery. Also educational textbooks for secondary and tertiary levels. Contacts: *Hubert Mahony* (educational), *Marion O'Brien* (college), *Fergal Tobin* (general). About 80 titles a year. Unsolicited synopses and ideas welcome.

ROYALTIES subject to contract.

Hodder Headline Ireland

8 Castlecourt Centre, Castleknock, Dublin 15
☎00 353 1 824 6288 Fax 00 353 1 824 6289
✉ info@hhireland.ie
www.hhireland.ie

Managing Director *Breda Purdue*
Publisher *Ciara Considine*
Senior Editor *Claire Rourke*
Approx. Annual Turnover €1 million

Founded 2002. Irish division of **Hodder Headline Ltd**. Publishes general fiction and non-fiction: memoirs, biography, sport, politics, current affairs, humour, food and drink. TITLES *Don't Wake Me at Doyles* Maura Murphy; *Straight Left* Ruairi Quinn; *Connections* Sheila S. Flanagan. 20 titles in 2005. Unsolicited mss, synopses and ideas welcome. No e-mail submission. For fiction send first three chapters, short synopsis/blurb with covering letter; non-fiction: proposal, sample chapter and layout

with covering letter. No children's, science fiction or poetry.
ROYALTIES twice-yearly.

Institute of Public Administration
57–61 Lansdowne Road, Dublin 4
☎00 353 1 240 3600 Fax 00 353 1 269 8644
✉ Sales@ipa.ie
www.ipa.ie
Director-General *John Cullen*
Publisher *Declan McDonagh*
Approx. Annual Turnover €1.3 million

Founded 1957 by a group of public servants, the Institute of Public Administration is the Irish public sector management development agency. The publishing arm of the organisation is one of its major activities. Publishes academic and professional books and periodicals: history, law, politics, economics and Irish public administration for students and practitioners. TITLES *Local Government in Ireland*; *E-Government and the Decentralisation of Service Delivery*; *Governance and Policy in Ireland*; *Crime, Punishment and the Search for Order in Ireland*; *Accountability in Irish Politics*. About 15 titles a year. No unsolicited mss; synopses and ideas welcome. No fiction or children's publishing.
ROYALTIES annually.

Irish Academic Press Ltd
44 Northumberland Road, Ballsbridge, Dublin 4
☎00 353 1 668 8244 Fax 00 353 1 660 1610
✉ info@iap.ie
www.iap.ie
Chairman *Frank Cass* (London)
Dublin Office *Rachel Milotte*

Founded 1974. Publishes academic monographs and humanities. 24 titles in 2005. Unsolicited mss, synopses and ideas welcome.
ROYALTIES annually.

Irish Management Institute (IMI)
Sandyford Road, Dublin 16
☎00 353 1 207 8400 Fax 00 353 1 295 5150
✉ reception@imi.ie
www.imi.ie
Chief Executive *Dr Tom McCarthy*
Approx. Annual Turnover €14 million

Founded 1952. The IMI, owned by its members, both corporate and individual, works to improve the practice of management. Offers managers a wide range of management development services. Publishes a quarterly newsletter, *Management Focus*, distributed to members,

featuring latest IMI research, case studies and management theory. Other publications include *Executive Salaries in Ireland* – annual publication that reviews managerial salaries and fringe benefits. Mss, synopses and ideas relevant to Irish management practice welcome.
ROYALTIES annually.

The Liffey Press Ltd
Ashbrook House, 10 Main Street, Raheny, Dublin 5
☎00 353 1 851 1458 Fax 00 353 1 851 1459
✉ info@theliffeypress.com
www.theliffeypress.com
Managing Director/Publisher *David Givens*
Editor *Brian Langan*

Founded 2001. Publishes general interest, Irish-focused non-fiction. 15 titles in 2005. Synopses, ideas and proposals with sample chapters welcome; approach by letter or e-mail in the first instance. No fiction, children's or books not of interest to Irish readers.
ROYALTIES twice-yearly.

The Lilliput Press
62–63 Sitric Road, Arbour Hill, Dublin 7
☎00 353 1 671 1647 Fax 00 353 1 671 1233
✉ info@lilliputpress.ie
www.lilliputpress.ie
Chair *Vivienne Guinness*
Managing Director *Antony Farrell*
Approx. Annual Turnover €255,000

Founded 1984. Publishes non-fiction: literature, history, autobiography and biography, ecology, essays; criticism; fiction and poetry. TITLES *Lark's Eggs*; *Vintage Nell*; *Wordgloss*; *The Bible War in Ireland*; *The Songman*; *Belios*. DIVISION **Sitric Books**. About 20 titles a year. Unsolicited mss, synopses and ideas welcome. No children's or sport titles.
ROYALTIES annually.

Marino Books
See **Mercier Press Ltd**

Maverick House Publishers
Main Street, Dunshaughlin, Co. Meath
☎00 353 1 824 0077 Fax 00 353 1 824 1746
✉ info@maverickhouse.com
www.maverickhouse.com
Managing Director *Jean Harrington*

Founded 2001. Publishes biography and autobiography, current affairs, non-fiction (mainly of Irish interest), politics. TITLES *Welcome to Hell* Colin Martin; *Black Operations: A Secret History of* the Real IRA John Mooney; *Surprised Joy* Michael Meegan. Unsolicited material welcome; send by post. No fiction, children's books or poetry. ROYALTIES twice-yearly.

Mercier Press Ltd
Douglas Village, Cork
☎00 353 21 489 9858
Fax 00 353 21 489 9887
✉ books@mercierpress.ie
www.mercierpress.ie

Chairman *John Spillaner*
Managing Director *Clodagh Feehan*

Founded 1944. One of Ireland's largest publishers with a list of approx 250 Irish interest titles. IMPRINTS **Mercier Press**; **Marino Books** Editorial Director *Mary Feehan* Children's, politics, history, folklore, biography, mind, body and spirit, current affairs, women's interest. TITLES *The Course of Irish History*; all of John B. Keane's works; *Beyond Prozac*; *It's a Long Way from Penny Apples*; *Ireland's Master Storyteller.* Unsolicited synopses and ideas welcome. ROYALTIES annually.

Merlin Publishing
16 Upper Pembroke Street, Dublin 2
☎00 353 1 676 4373   Fax 00 353 1 676 4368
www.merlinwolfhound.com

Managing Director *Chenile Keogh*
Managing Editor *Aoife Barrett*

Founded 2000. Member of **Clé**. Publishes film, music, art, biography, general non-fiction, history, photography and gift books. IMPRINT **Wolfhound Press** Founded 1974. Non-fiction. TITLES *Famine*; *Eyewitness Bloody Sunday*; *Father Browne's Titanic Album*. About 20 titles a year (mainly Irish interest). Sample chapters of unsolicited mss (with synopses and s.a.e.) welcome by e-mail (aoife@merlin.ie). See Merlin website for submission guidelines and proposal form.

Mount Eagle
See **Brandon/Mount Eagle**

National Library of Ireland
Kildare Street, Dublin 2
☎00 353 1 603 0200   Fax 00 353 1 676 6690
✉ info@nli.ie
www.nli.ie

Founded 1877. Publishes books and booklets based on the library's collections; folders of historical documents; academic and specialist books; reproduction folders and CD-ROMs.

TITLES *Ulysses Unbound: A Reader's Companion to James Joyce's Ulysses* Terence Killeen; *Cooper's Ireland: Drawings and Notes from an Eighteenth Century Gentleman* Peter Harbison; *Into the Light: An Illustrated Guide to the Photographic Collections in the National Library of Ireland* Sarah Rouse; *Treasures from the National Library of Ireland* ed. Dr Noel Kissane. 7 titles in 2005.

New Island
2 Brookside, Dundrum Road, Dundrum, Dublin 14
☎00 353 1 298 9937/298 3411
Fax 00 353 1 298 7912
✉ fidelma.slattery@newisland.ie
www.newisland.ie

Managing Director/Editorial Head *Edwin Higel*
Editorial Manager *Deirdre Nolan*

Founded 1990. Publishes fiction, Irish non-fiction, poetry and drama. Branching out into popular fiction and memoirs. IMPRINT **Brookside**. About 25 titles a year. Unsolicited mss, synopses and ideas welcome. Send three chapters and synopsis by post. ROYALTIES twice-yearly

The O'Brien Press Ltd
20 Victoria Road, Rathgar, Dublin 6
☎00 353 1 492 3333   Fax 00 353 1 492 2777
✉ books@obrien.ie
www.obrien.ie

Managing Director *Ivan O'Brien*
Publisher *Michael O'Brien*
Editorial Director *Íde Ní Laoghaire*

Founded 1974. Publishes business, true crime, biography, music, travel, sport, Celtic subjects, food and drink, history, humour, politics, reference. Children's publishing – mainly fiction for every age from tiny tots to teenage. Illustrated fiction SERIES *Solos* (3 years+); *Pandas* (5 years+); *Flyers* (6 years+); *Red Flag* (8 years+). Novels (10 years+) – contemporary, historical, fantasy. Some non-fiction – mainly historical, and art and craft, resource books for teachers. No poetry, adult fiction or academic. Unsolicited mss (sample chapters only), synopses and ideas for books welcome. No e-mail submissions. Submissions will not be returned. ROYALTIES annually.

Oak Tree Press
19 Rutland Street, Cork
☎00 353 21 431 3855
Fax 00 353 21 431 3496
✉ info@oaktreepress.com
www.oaktreepress.com

Owners *Brian O'Kane, Rita O'Kane*
Managing Director *Brian O'Kane*

Founded 1992. Specialist publisher of business and professional books with a focus on small business start-up and development. Unsolicited mss and synopses welcome; send to the managing director, at the address above.
ROYALTIES annually.

On Stream Publications Ltd

Currabaha, Cloghroe, Co. Cork
☎00 353 21 438 5798
✉ info@onstream.ie
www.onstream.ie

Chairman/Managing Director *Roz Crowley*

Founded 1992. Formerly Forum Publications. Publishes academic, cookery, wine, general health and fitness, local history, railways, photography and practical guides. TITLES *The Health Squad Guide to Health and Fitness*; *A Kingdom of Wine: A Celebration of Ireland's Winegeese*; *At Home in Renvyle*. About 3 titles a year. Synopses and ideas welcome. No children's books.
ROYALTIES annually.

Penguin Ireland

25 St Stephen's Green, Dublin 2
☎00 353 1 661 7695   Fax 00 353 1 661 7696
✉ info@penguin.ie
www.penguin.ie

Managing Director *Michael McLoughlin*

Founded 2002. Part of the **Penguin Group UK**. DIVISIONS **Commercial fiction/non-fiction** Senior Editor *Patricia Deevy* TITLES *The Baby Trail* Sinéad Moriaty; *Nell* Nell McCafferty. **Literary fiction/non-fiction** *Brendan Barrington* TITLES *Sailing for Home* Theo Dorgan; *In the Dark Room* Brian Dillon 15 titles in 2005. Unsolicited mss, synopses and ideas for books welcome; send by post.
ROYALTIES twice-yearly.

Poolbeg Press Ltd

123 Grange Hill, Baldoyle, Dublin 13
☎00 353 1 832 1477   Fax 00 353 1 832 1430
✉ poolbeg@poolbeg.com
www.poolbeg.com

Managing Director *Kieran Devlin*
Publisher *Paula Campbell*

Founded 1976 to publish the Irish short story and has since diversified to include all areas of fiction (literary and popular), children's fiction and non-fiction, and adult non-fiction: history, biography and topics of public interest. AUTHORS discovered and first published by Poolbeg include Maeve Binchy, Marian Keyes, Sheila O'Flanagan, Cathy Kelly and Patricia Scanlan. 'Our slogan is Poolbeg.com – The *Irish* for Bestsellers!' IMPRINTS **Poolbeg** (paperback and hardback); **Poolbeg For Children**. About 40 titles a year. Unsolicited mss, synopses and ideas welcome (mss preferred). No drama.
ROYALTIES twice-yearly.

Royal Dublin Society

Science Section, Ballsbridge, Dublin 4
☎00 353 1 668 0866   Fax 00 353 1 660 4014
✉ science@rds.ie
www.rds.ie

President *Dr Austin Mescal*

Founded 1731 for the promotion of agriculture, science and the arts, and throughout its history has published books and journals towards this end. Publishes conference proceedings, biology and the history of Irish science. TITLES *Agricultural Development for the 21st Century*; *The Right Trees in the Right Places*; *Agriculture & the Environment*; *Water of Life*; *Science, Technology & Realism*; *Science Centres for Ireland*; *Blueprint for a National Irish Science Centre*; *Science Education in Crisis*; *Science in the Service of the Fishing Industry*; occasional papers in *Irish Science & Technology* series.
ROYALTIES not generally paid.

Royal Irish Academy

19 Dawson Street, Dublin 2
☎00 353 1 676 2570   Fax 00 353 1 676 2346
✉ publications@ria.ie
www.ria.ie/publications

Executive Secretary *Patrick Buckley*
Managing Editor *Ruth Hegarty*

Founded in 1785, the Academy has been publishing since 1787. Core publications are journals but more books published in last 15 years. Publishes academic, Irish interest and Irish language. About 7 titles a year. Welcomes mss, synopses and ideas of an academic standard. Address correspondence to the managing editor of publications.

Sitric Books
See **The Lilliput Press**

Swordpoint Intercontinental Limited

'Solas Tobann', Ballyhillion, Malin Head, Co. Donegal
☎00 353 74 937 0278
Fax 00 353 74 937 0279
✉ jgreenleaf@swordpoint.com

www.swordpoint.com
Chairman/Managing Director *Joseph A. Greenleaf*
Swordpoint was established in 1995 as a media company and branched out into books in 2003. Publishes fiction, children's, non-fiction, historical, travel, technical, Irish, poetry, plays, business, management, law, biography, fantasy, teenage fiction. Publication on cassettes and CDs as well as e-books. 15 titles in 2006. Unsolicited mss, synopses and ideas welcome by post with return postage. Enclosure of Microsoft Word CD in addition to mss is encouraged, but not required.
ROYALTIES twice-yearly.

Tír Eolas
Newtownlynch, Doorus, Kinvara, Co. Galway
☎00 353 91 637452 Fax 00 353 91 637452
✉ info@tireolas.com
www.tireolas.com
Publisher/Managing Director *Anne Korff*

Founded 1987. Publishes books and guides on ecology, archaeology, folklore and culture. TITLES *The Book of the Burren*; *The Shores of Connemara*; *Not a Word of a Lie*; *The Book of Aran*; *Women of Ireland, A Biographic Dictionary*; *Kinvara, A Seaport Town on Galway Bay*; *A Burren Journal*; *Alive, Alive-O, The Shellfish and Shellfisheries of Ireland*. Unsolicited mss, synopses and ideas for books welcome. No specialist scientific and technical, fiction, plays, school textbooks or philosophy.
ROYALTIES annually.

Town House Dublin
Mountpleasant Business Centre, Mountpleasant Avenue, Ranelagh, Dublin 6
☎00 353 1 497 2399 Fax 00 353 1 497 0927
✉ books@townhouse.ie
www.townhouse.ie

Managing Director *Treasa Coady*

Irish interest trade non-fiction including, art, archaeology, biography, spirituality, sport, environment, human interest, anthologies etc. About 5 titles a year. Unsolicited mss, synopses and ideas welcome. No children's books.
ROYALTIES twice-yearly.

University College Dublin Press
Newman House, 86 St Stephen's Green, Dublin 2
☎00 353 1 716 7397 Fax 00 353 1 716 7211
✉ ucdpress@ucd.ie
www.ucdpress.ie
Executive Editor *Barbara Mennell*

Founded 1995. Academic publisher. 16 titles in 2005. Unsolicited mss, synopses and ideas welcome by post. No non-academic, journals, poetry, novels or books based on academic conferences.
ROYALTIES annually.

Veritas Publications
7–8 Lower Abbey Street, Dublin 1
☎00 353 1 878 8177 Fax 00 353 1 878 6507
✉ publications@veritas.ie
www.veritas.ie
Director *Maura Hyland*
Managing Editor *Ruth Garvey*

Founded 1969 to supply religious textbooks to schools and later introduced a wide-ranging general list. Part of the Catholic Communications Institute. Publishes books on religious, ethical, moral, societal and social issues. 30 titles a year. Unsolicited mss, synopses and ideas for books welcome.
ROYALTIES annually.

Wolfhound Press
See **Merlin Publishing**

Irish Literary Agents

The Book Bureau Literary Agency
7 Duncairn Avenue, Bray, Co. Wicklow
☎00 353 1 276 4996 Fax 00 353 1 276 4834
✉ thebookbureau@oceanfree.net

Contact *Ger Nichol*

Handles general and literary fiction. Special interest in women's fiction, crime and thrillers. Will suggest revision. Send preliminary letter, synopsis and first three chapters; return postage essential (IRCs only from UK and abroad). No reading fee. COMMISSION Home 10%; Overseas 20%. Works with foreign associates.

Font International Literary Agency
45 Victoria Road, Clontarf, Dublin 3
☎00 353 1 853 2356
✉ info@fontwriters.com

Contacts *Aine McCarthy, Ita O'Driscoll*

Founded 2003. Handles book-length adult fiction and non-fiction from previously published writers (no children's, drama, sci-fi, erotic, technical or poetry). No unsolicited mss. 'As an initial contact, please query our interest in your property either by e-mail or post.' Include details of writing and other media experience. S.a.e. required. 'We regret that we cannot discuss queries over the phone.' No reading fee. COMMISSION 15–20%; Translation 20–25%. ASSOCIATE The Marsh Agency, London for translation rights.

Marianne Gunn O'Connor Literary Agency
Morrison Chambers, Suite 17, 32 Nassau Street, Dublin 2
✉ mgoclitagency@eircom.net

Contact *Marianne Gunn O'Connor*

Founded 1996. Handles commercial and literary fiction, non-fiction: biography, health and children's fiction. CLIENTS include Patrick McCabe, Morag Prunty, Claire Kilroy, Julie Dam, Cecelia Ahern, Paddy McMahon, Chris Binchy, Anita Notaro, Mike McCormack, Noelle Harrison, Claudia Carroll, Ken Bruen, John Lynch. No unsolicited mss; send preliminary enquiry letter plus half-page synopsis per e-mail. COMMISSION UK 15%; Overseas 20%;

Film & TV 20%. Translation rights handled by Vicki Satlow Literary Agency, Milan.

The Lisa Richards Agency
46 Upper Baggot Street, Dublin 4
☎00 353 1 660 3534 Fax 00 353 1 660 3545
✉ faith@lisarichards.ie

Contact *Faith O'Grady*

Founded 1998. Handles fiction and general non-fiction. Approach with proposal and sample chapter for non-fiction, and 3–4 chapters and synopsis for fiction (s.a.e. essential). No reading fee. AUTHORS include June Considine, Judi Curtin, Denise Deegan, Christine Dwyer Hickey, Karen Gillece, Tara Heavey, Paul Howard (Ross O'Carroll-Kelly), Arlene Hunt, Roisin Ingle, Alison Jameson, Declan Lynch, Martin Malone, Roisin Meaney, Pauline McLynn, Sarah O'Brien (Helena Close and Trisha Rainsford), Hector O'hEochagàin, Damien Owens, Kevin Rafter. COMMISSION Home 10%; UK 15%; US & Translation 20%; Film & TV 15%. OVERSEAS ASSOCIATE The Marsh Agency for translation rights.

Jonathan Williams Literary Agency
Rosney Mews, Upper Glenageary Road, Glenageary, Co. Dublin
☎00 353 1 280 3482 Fax 00 353 1 280 3482

Contact *Jonathan Williams*

Founded 1980. Handles general trade books: fiction, auto/biography, travel, politics, history, music, literature and criticism, gardening, cookery, sport and leisure, humour, reference, social questions, photography. Some poetry, business and children's, but less of a speciality. No plays, science fiction, mind, body and spirit, computer books, theology, multimedia, motoring, aviation. No reading fee 'unless the author wants a very fast opinion'. Initial approach by phone or letter. COMMISSION Home 10%; US 20%; Translation 20%. OVERSEAS ASSOCIATES Lora Fountain & Associates Agency, France; Piergiorgio Nicolazzini Literary Agency, Italy; Linda Kohn, International Literature Bureau, Holland; Antonia Kerrigan Literary Agency, Spain; Tuttle-Mori Agency Inc., Japan.

Audio Books

AudioBooksForFree.Com Limited

25 Green Lane, Amersham HP6 6AS
☎01494 431119
✉ ToUs@AudioBooksForFree.Com
www.AudioBooksForFree.Com
www.DVDAudioBooks.com
www.MobileAudioBooks.com

Managing Director *Ruslan G. Fedorovsky*
CTO *Peter Morris*

Founded 2000. Publishes and sells MP3 and DVD audiobooks on and offline. Genres: fiction, adventure, thrillers, crime, science fiction, children's, non-fiction, etc. AUTHORS include Michael Hartland, James Herlihy, Jon Schiller, Patrick Walsh, Jules Verne, Dumas. 100 titles in 2005.

Pays 100% royalties to 'contributors' (audiobook publishers, famous narrators or famous authors) for individual audiobook downloads.

BBC Audiobooks Ltd

St James House, The Square, Lower Bristol Road, Bath BA2 3BH
☎01225 335336 Fax 01225 310771
✉ bbcaudiobooks@bbc.co.uk
www.bbcworldwide.com

Managing Director *Paul Dempsey*
Publishing Director *Jan Paterson*

BBC Audiobooks Ltd was established in 2003 with the integration of BBC Radio Collection, Cover to Cover and Chivers Audio Books. Since then it has become a leading trade and library publisher in the UK, publishing a wide range of entertainment on a variety of formats including CD, cassette and MP3-CD.

DIVISIONS
Trade Titles range from original books and full-cast radio dramas through to abridged readings and full, unabridged recordings. TITLES *War and Peace*; *The Odyssey*; *Captain Corelli's Mandolin*; the complete Sherlock Holmes canon. IMPRINTS **BBC Audio – Children's** From pre-school nursery rhymes to modern classics. TITLES *The Chronicles of Narnia*; *His Dark Materials* trilogy. **BBC Audio – Radio Collection** Comedy classics from TV and radio. TITLES *The Goons*; *Hancock's Half Hour*; *Fawlty Towers*; *The News Quiz*; *Just a Minute*. **BBC Audio** Contemporary comedy. TITLES *Little Britain*; *Have I Got News For You*; *The League of Gentlemen*. **BBC Audio – Lifestyle** A range of titles to help the listener improve or learn. TITLES include the *Glenn Harrold's Ultimate Guide to ...* series. **BBC Audio – Radio 4** TITLES *This Sceptred Isle*; *Letter from America*; *A Suitable Boy*. **Science Fiction & Fantasy** TITLES *The Hitchhiker's Guide to the Galaxy*; *Doctor Who*; *Journey into Space*; *The Lord of the Rings*.

Library IMPRINTS **Chivers Audio Books**; **Chivers Children's Audio Books** Founded 1980. Publishes over 500 titles annually. Complete and unabridged books for adults and children are sold to libraries and to the public by direct mail through **The Audiobook Collection**. CDs and cassettes covering best-selling fiction and popular non-fiction.

Bloomsbury Publishing

See entry under *UK Publishers*

Chivers Audio Books/Chivers Children's Audio Books

See **BBC Audiobooks Ltd**

Chrome Dreams

12 Seaforth Avenue, New Malden KT3 6JP
☎020 8715 9781 Fax 020 8241 1426
✉ mail@chromedreams.co.uk
www.chromedreams.co.uk

Managing Director *Rob Johnstone*

A small record company and publisher founded 1998 to produce audio-biographies of current rock and pop artists and legendary performers on CD and, more recently, books on the same subjects. Ideas for biographies welcome.

Corgi Audio

Transworld Publishers, A division of the Random House Group Ltd, 61–63 Uxbridge Road, London W5 5SA
☎020 8579 2652

Managing Director *Larry Finlay*

Publishes fiction, autobiography and humour. TITLES *Discworld Series* Terry Pratchett; *Down Under* Bill Bryson and other travel writing; *High Society* and *Past Mortem* Ben Elton.

Cover to Cover
See **BBC Audiobooks Ltd**

CSA Word
6a Archway Mews, 241a Putney Bridge Road, London SW15 2PE
☎020 8871 0220 Fax 020 8877 0712
✉ info@csaword.co.uk
www.csaword.co.uk
Managing Director *Clive Stanhope*
Audio Director *Victoria Williams*

Founded 1989. Publishes fiction, children's, short stories, poetry, travel, biographies, classics. Over 100 titles to-date on cassette and CD. Tends to favour quality/classic/nostalgic/timeless literature. TITLES *Carry on Jeeves* P.G. Wodehouse; *Alfie* Bill Naughton; *Decline and Fall* and *Brideshead Revisited* Evelyn Waugh; *Just William – Home for the Holidays* Richmal Crompton; *Classic Detective Stories* various authors; *Lady Chatterley's Lover* D.H. Lawrence; *The Statement* Brian Moore; *Billy Bunter's Banknote* Frank Richards; *The Ragged Trousered Philanthropists* Robert Tressell; *Cautionary Verses* Hilaire Belloc.

CYP Children's Audio & Video
The Fairway, Bush Fair, Harlow CM18 6LY
☎01279 444707 Fax 01279 445570
✉ enquiries@cypmusic.co.uk
www.cyp.co.uk
Operations Director *Mike Kitson*

Founded 1978. Publishes music video and audiobooks for young children; educational, entertainment, licensed characters (*Mr Men*; *Little Miss*; *Wheels On the Bus*). TV music and soundtrack production.

Faber.Penguin Audiobooks
80 Strand, London WC2R 0RL
☎020 7010 3000 Fax 020 7010 6060
✉ audio@penguin.co.uk
www.penguin.co.uk

Also at: 3 Queen Square, London WC1N 3AU
☎020 7465 0045 Fax 020 7465 0108
Head of Audio Publishing *Jeremy Ettinghausen*

A joint venture between **Penguin Books** and **Faber & Faber**. AUTHORS include Peter Carey, Alex Garland, D.B.C. Pierre, Philip Ardagh. Publishes up to 5 titles per year, drawing on the strength of Faber's authors.

57 Productions
See entry under *Organisations of Interest to Poets*

Hachette Children's Books
See entry under *UK Publishers*

HarperCollins AudioBooks
77–85 Fulham Palace Road, London W6 8JB
☎020 8741 7070 Fax 020 8307 4517
www.harpercollins.co.uk
Managing Director *Trevor Dolby*

The HarperCollins audio list was launched in 1990. ADULT Senior Editor *Nicky Townsend*. Publishes a wide range including popular and classic fiction, non-fiction, Shakespeare, poetry and self help (Thorsons' imprint) on cassette and CD. 50 titles in 2005. CHILDREN'S DIVISION Divisional Publishing Director *Sally Gritten*. Publishes picture books/cassettes and story books/cassettes as well as single and double tapes and CDs for children aged 2–13 years. Fiction, songs, early learning, poetry, etc. 20 titles in 2005. AUTHORS C.S. Lewis, Roald Dahl, Dr Seuss, Lemony Snicket, J.R.R. Tolkien, Enid Blyton, Robin Jarvis, Ian Whybrow, Nick Butterworth, Judith Kerr.

Hodder & Stoughton Audiobooks
338 Euston Road, London NW1 3BH
☎020 7873 6000 Fax 020 7873 6194
www.madaboutbooks.co.uk
Publisher *Rupert Lancaster*

Launched 1994. Publishes fiction and non-fiction. AUTHORS Pam Ayres, Tony Benn, Dickie Bird, Mevyn Bragg, John LeCarré, Ranulph Fiennes, Andrew Flintoff, Elizabeth George, Joanne Harris, John Humphries, Stephen King, David Mitchell, Ellis Peters, Jodi Picoult, Rosamunde Pilcher, Peter Robinson. About 30 titles a year.

Ladybird Audio
See **Dorling Kindersley Ltd** under *UK Publishers*

Laughing Stock Productions
81 Charlotte Street, London W1T 4PP
☎020 7637 7943 Fax 020 7436 1666
Managing Director *Michael O'Brien*

Founded 1991. Issues a wide range of comedy cassettes/CDs from family humour to alternative comedy. TITLES *Red Dwarf*; *Shirley Valentine* (read by Willy Russell); *Rory Bremner*; *Peter Cook Anthology*; *Sean Hughes*; *John Bird and John Fortune*; *Eddie Izzard*. 12–16 titles a year.

Macmillan Audio Books
20 New Wharf Road, London N1 9RR
☎020 7014 6040 Fax 020 7014 6141

✉ a.muirden@macmillan.co.uk
www.panmacmillan.co.uk

Owner *Macmillan Publishers Ltd*
Audio Publisher *Alison Muirden*

Founded 1995. Publishes adult fiction, non-fiction and autobiography, focusing mainly on lead book titles and releasing audio simultaneously with hard or paperback publication. Also publishes children's audio titles. Won Audio Publisher of the Year at the 2003 Spoken Word Awards and has won many other Spoken Word Awards for individual audio titles in previous years About 40–60 titles a year. Submissions not accepted.

Naxos AudioBooks
18 High Street, Welwyn AL6 9EQ
☎01438 717808   Fax 01438 717809
✉ naxos_audiobooks@compuserve.com
www.naxosaudiobooks.com

Owner *HNH International, Hong Kong/Nicolas Soames*
Managing Director *Nicolas Soames*

Founded 1994. Part of Naxos, the classical budget CD company. Publisher of the Year in the 2001 Spoken Word Awards. Publishes classic and modern fiction, non-fiction, children's and junior classics, drama and poetry. TITLES *Ulysses* Joyce; *King Lear* Shakespeare; *History of the Musical* Fawkes; *Just So Stories* Kipling.

Orion Audio Books (Division of the Orion Publishing Group Ltd)
Orion House, 5 Upper St Martin's Lane, London WC2H 9EA
☎020 7520 4425   Fax 020 7379 6518
✉ pandora.white@orionbooks.co.uk
www.orionbooks.co.uk

Publisher *Pandora White*

Orion Audio has released over 300 titles since it was founded in 1998. Publishes fiction, non-fiction, humour, autobiographies, children's, poetry, science, crime and thrillers. AUTHORS Maeve Binchy, Ian Rankin, Robert Crais, Michael Connelly, Francesca Simon (*Horrid Henry* series), Harlan Coben, Dan Brown, Sally Gardner, Michelle Paver and Erica James. In 2006 all Orion audio titles will be available for digital download on www.audible.co.uk
   Ideas for cassettes/CDs welcome.

Penguin Audiobooks
80 Strand, London WC2R 0RL
☎020 7010 3000   Fax 020 7010 6695
✉ audio@penguin.co.uk

www.penguin.co.uk

Head of Audio Publishing *Jeremy Ettinghausen*

Launched in November 1993 and has rapidly expanded since then to reflect the diversity of Penguin Books' list. Publishes mostly fiction, both classical and contemporary, non-fiction, autobiography and an increasing range of digital audiobooks as well as children's titles under the **Puffin Audiobooks** imprint. Contemporary AUTHORS include: Zadie Smith, Anne Fine, Eoin Colfer, John Mortimer, Roald Dahl, Sue Townsend, Nicci French, Gervase Phinn, Michael Moore, Jonathan Coe. About 50 titles a year.

Puffin Audiobooks
See **Penguin Audiobooks**

Random House Audiobooks
20 Vauxhall Bridge Road, London SW1V 2SA
☎020 7840 8400   Fax 020 7233 6127

Owner *The Random House Group Ltd.*
Commissioning Editor *Zoe Howes*

The audiobooks division of Random House started early in 1991. Acquired the Reed Audio list in 1997. Publishes fiction, non-fiction and self help. AUTHORS include Sebastian Faulks, John Grisham, Mark Haddon, Robert Harris, Thomas Harris, Tony Hawks, Andy McNab, Alison Pearson, Ruth Rendell, Kathy Reichs, Chris Ryan.

Rickshaw Productions
Suite 125, 99 Warwick Street, Leamington Spa CV32 4RB
☎0780 3553214   Fax 01926 402490
✉ rickprod@aol.com
www.rickshawaudiobooks.co.uk

Contact *Commissioning Editor*

Publishes adult fiction and non-fiction. Founded 1998, Rickshaw Productions' first audiobooks were English translations of Chinese stories. Other titles include a gothic fictional novella, four short stories and an anthology of music and poetry by Mark Yakes. TITLES *Chinese Classic Stories; Chinese Women's Stories; The Carved Pipe/The Tall Woman and Her Short Husband; The Halfway-House Hotel; Wednesdays and Other Stories; The Tailor of Salisbury; Poems and Music Vol I; The First Line of Defence – The Kent Castles; The Churchills and their Palace.* Paperback titles: *Mary, A Nonagenarian's Story; The Tailor of Salisbury.* 6 audiobooks and 2 paperbacks; first hardback released Spring 2006. Submissions by snail-mail *only*; salacious material will not be accepted.

Two sample chapters, one-page synopsis and s.a.e. to cover return by Recorded Delivery.

Simon & Schuster Audio

Africa House, 64–78 Kingsway, London WC2B 6AH
☎020 7316 1900   Fax 020 7316 0332
✉ info@simonandschuster.co.uk
www.simonsays.co.uk

Audio Manager *Rumana Haider*

Simon & Schuster Audio began by distributing their American parent company's audio products. Moved on to repackaging products specifically for the UK market and in 1994 became more firmly established in this market with a huge rise in turnover. Publishes adult fiction, self help and business titles. TITLES *Above Suspicion* Lynda la Plante; *Rosie* Alan Titchmarsh; *The 7 Habits of Highly Effective People* Stephen R. Covey; *Chronicles* Bob Dylan; *Angels and Demons* and *Deception Point* Dan Brown; *Kate Remembered* A. Scott Berg.

SmartPass Ltd

15 Park Road, Rottingdean, Brighton BN2 7HL
☎01273 300742
✉ info@smartpass.co.uk
www.smartpass.co.uk

Managing Director *Phil Viner*
Creative Director *Jools Viner*

Founded 1999. Triple Spoken Word Award-winning publisher produces audio education study guides, full-cast drama with commentary analysis and study strategies for English Literature set texts – novels, plays and poetry. Available in student and teacher formats, including audio linked study materials. TITLES include *A Kestrel for a Knave* Barry Hines; *Animal Farm* George Orwell; *Pride and Prejudice* Jane Austen; *Great Expectations* Charles Dickens; *The Mayor of Casterbridge* Thomas Hardy; *Romeo and Juliet*; *Twelfth Night*; *Henry V*; Shakespeare: the

works; *War Poetry*; *Classical Poetry*. IMPRINT **SPAudiobooks** Full-cast unabridged dramas. TITLE *The Antipope* Robert Rankin. Welcomes ideas from authors who are teachers and from agents who represent the authors of studied texts.

Soundings Audio Books

Isis House, Kings Drive, Whitley Bay NE26 2JT
☎0191 253 4155   Fax 0191 251 0662
www.isis-publishing.co.uk

Founded in 1982. Part of the Ulverscroft Group Ltd. Together with Isis Publishing publishes fiction and non-fiction; crime, romance. AUTHORS include Lyn Andrews, Rita Bradshaw, Lee Child, Catherine Cookson, Alexander Fullerton, Joanne Harris, Anna Jacobs, Robert Ludlum, Patrick O'Brian, Pamela Oldfield, Susan Sallis, Judith Saxton, Mary Jane Staples, Sally Worboyes. About 190 titles a year. Many also available on CD.

SPAudiobooks

See **SmartPass Ltd**

Time Warner Audiobooks

Brettenham House, Lancaster Place, London WC2E 7EN
☎020 7911 8044   Fax 020 7911 8100
✉ sarah.shrub@twbg.co.uk
www.littlebrown.co.uk

Publisher *Ursula Mackenzie*
Editor *Sarah Shrub*

Launched in 2003 with titles from Time Warner Books' bestselling authors Alexander McCall Smith, Mitch Albom and David Sedaris. Publishes fiction, humour, poetry and non-fiction. TITLES include new fiction from Patricia Cornwell and Anita Shreve, Mark Billingham's detective series featuring D.I. Tom Thorne and Sharon Osbourne's bestselling autobiography *Extreme*. 42 titles in 2005.

Poetry – No Longer a Rare Commodity

Peter Finch

Poetry has not turned out to be the new rock and roll that many thought it would be some ten years back. Instead, dropping its image as fey art of the lost, it has gone thoroughly mainstream. Poetry is easy and everywhere, anyone can do it, thousands do. In our multicultural, politically correct society my poem is just as good as your poem. Always. Which of course might now be one of poetry's problems. The irony is that ten years ago poetry was a rare commodity, under-valued, elusive, hard to find. Today it is over-produced, ever present and, with the aid of ever cheaper print-on-demand technology, clogging the shelves and ware-houses of the book world in ever increasing number. Slim volumes are vanish-ing, to be replaced by all-inclusive tomes. Write it and, if you've a modicum of talent, it will end up out there. Slick, shiny and published, although maybe not all that often *read*. But that's another matter. Nearly 200,000 new books were published in the UK last year, many of them poetry. The figure was nearer 30,000 fifty years ago. Where are they coming from?

Stephen Fry has attacked much of contemporary poetry as being 'listless and utterly drained of energy and drive'. 'We have been encouraged to believe,' he writes, 'that form is a kind of fascism.' His *The Ode Less Travelled* (Hutchinson) is both handbook to the forms of rhyme and rhythm he imagines we have lost and virulent attack on what, by common consent, we use instead. *Vers libre*, free verse – you hear that descriptor little these days – but Fry and his supporters reckon it to be at the core of the signal failure of poetry in the twenty-first century to take over anything, let alone the world.

We've been here before, of course. It was American Dan Gioia, a couple of years ago who promised a poetry revolution in which only rhyme survived. Didn't happen. Poetry is such a broad church, thank the Lord.

In his poem *In Memory of W.B. Yeats*, written in 1939, W.H. Auden suggested that 'poetry makes nothing happen'. For most of the sixty-five years since, poetry creators have wallowed in that suggestion. Poetry just is. 'A way of happening, a mouth.' In recent years, however, we've seen a significant move away from this position of glorious isolation. In 2005 a poet was appointed in the Highlands of Scotland to help reduce their burgeoning suicide rate. New poetry has been in action as soccer chants and as hakas on the rugby field. The Health Service engages poets to work with the declining and the mentally uncertain. Poetry increases feelings of self worth. It can also be a real entertainment. Check your local poetry slam for streetwise proof. Amid the flurry of recent generic anthologies of verse it has become obvious that poetry is always the best tool when it comes to saying things of significance at christenings, at weddings, in dealing with love and death and success. *Poems to Get you Through your Interview. Poems for Times of Indecision in the Supermarket. Poetry to Make the Trains Run on Time.* There is even a compilation of business haiku appropriate for that moment of decision in the board room. And then there's hip hop. That's where your rhyme has gone, S. Fry, MCs use it every day, they just rarely write it down.

The message to new poets (as well as to some old ones, come to that) wishing to engage with this world of increasing and apparently bottomless opportunity is to make sure that what you write is *really* worth keeping. Spell-checkers, mobile notebooks and the industrial vastness of our hard disks make it too easy to be garrulous and over productive. The poems stack far too readily. Leave the things on the drive for a while after you've written them. Do not rush. Come back a few weeks later when the weather is different and see if they still seem worthwhile. If they don't then delete them. The world out there is creaking under the weight of our output.

What's new in the poetry world?

Nursery rhymes are back. Competitions run by Nickelodeon TV and the publication of Amy Allen's *This Little Piggy Went to Prada* have seen poetry reaching right down to the pre-schools. Sample: 'Hey diddle, diddle . . . the skirt fits my middle'. In Scotland, Starbucks have opened the first poetry-themed coffee shop on Edinburgh's Canongate. Poetry distributors recycle. Once we had Password, the subsidised poetry reseller. Now we have Inpress (www.inpressbooks.co.uk) tackling the unsolvable problem of making poetry sell once again. Poetry magazines proliferate on the Web. More than ever this year. The Poetry Library continues its admirable programme of digitising as much of the present and the past that it can gain access to. The ALP, the Association of Little Presses, home of the poetry alternative, faded back in the early nineties. Now we have RGAP, the Research Group for Artists Publications (www.rgap.co.uk) filling the gulf. North of the border the unexpected rise of interest in the poetry chapbook has seen the establishment of Scottish Pamphlet Poetry with an attendant flurry of websites, awards and reading tours. Faber has been promoting poetry among reading groups. No surprises – Sassoon, Heaney and Hughes came out tops. Translated verse is on the rise. There's world poetry to go with world music – and about time too. Check the work of the Poetry Translation Centre at www.poetrytranslation.soas.ac.uk Mike Horovitz, OBE, and over seventy has been rerunning the sixties with his Albert Hall Poetry Olympics. Bards on sticks. Singer Jarvis Cocker's first poem appeared in giant brushed-steel letters as part of Sheffield's Off the Shelf literary festival. The National Poet of Wales, Gwyneth Lewis, beat this with her twelve-word inscription build into the fabric of the new Wales Millennium Centre in Cardiff Bay. In Perthshire, the poet Robin Bell won himself £30,000 to write up the G8 summit in verse. Poetry can earn a decent wage if you know where to look. National Poetry Day, annually at the start of October, the Forward Prize and the whole media razzamatazz that is supposed to set the world alight with rhyming couplets has been less of a success than it once was. Overproduction is the culprit blamed. More support for keeping your poems locked up until they come of age. Access and engagement for everyone is all very well but if the product ends up feeling like processed Cheddar then clearly we are all working too hard. There's much more to good verse than reading an example by someone else and then having a go yourself. What's new in the poetry world ought to be a big rise in sales and a tenfold increase in the number of poetry books read *before* putting hand to keyboard. For those of you proceeding through the rest of this article let's assume that has already happened.

What should you be reading?

The way in, as we've seen, is first to discover what poetry actually is. To do this means putting some time in. Be as open and catholic as you can in your selection. Ensure you check out the whole scene – the past, the present, mainstream English literature along with work in translation, the obvious poets you find you like as well as those you find difficult. Appreciation will not come without effort. Stay the course.

Start with a recent anthology of contemporary verse. You'll be spoilt for choice here, there are a whole new crop of century-definers in print. To get a broad view of what's going on, not only should you read Simon Armitage and Robert Crawford's *British and Irish Poetry Since the War* (Penguin); Michael Schmidt's *The Harvill Book of Twentieth-Century Poetry in English* (Harvill); Andy Croft and Adrian Mitchell's *Red Sky at Night – Socialist Poetry* (Five Leaves); the latest annual *Forward Book of Poetry* (Faber) and Richard Caddel and Peter Quartermain's *Other: British and Irish Poetry since 1970* (Wesleyan); but also Keith Tuma's *Anthology of Twentieth-Century British and Irish Poetry* (OUP); Rod Mengham and John Kinsella's *Vanishing Points – New Modernist Poems* (Salt); Neil Astley's *Staying Alive* and *Being Alive* (Bloodaxe), Jeni Couzyn's *The Bloodaxe Book of Contemporary Women Poets*; Jerome Rothenberg and Pierre Joris's two-volume *Poems for the Millennium* (California) and Paul Hoover's *Postmodern American Poetry* (Norton). This last title might be harder to find but will be worth the effort. Fill in with a standard overview of poetry in English since Chaucer. John Gallas's *The Song Atlas: A Book of World Poetry* (Carcanet) is a good scattergun.

Progress to the literary magazine. Read the online journals. The Poetry Library offer a good list of e-magazines at www.poetrylibrary.org.uk/magazines/emagazines For traditional print write off to a number of the magazine addresses which follow this article and ask the price of sample copies. As you know, it is more important than ever today that poets read not only to familiarise themselves with what is currently fashionable and to increase their own facility for self-criticism, but to help support the activity in which they wish to participate. Buy

– this is vital for little magazines; it is the only way in which they are going to survive.

OK, I've read until my eyes don't work anymore. What next?

Take a long look at your own material. Are you convinced that it's ready? If you are uncertain, then most likely that will be the view of everyone else. Check your text for glips and blips. Rework it. Root out any clichés or archaic poetry expressions such as O, doeth, bewilld'd and the like. Drop any of what Peter Sansom calls 'spirit of the age' poetry words. Do without shards and sherds, lozenges, lambent patina and stippled seagulls. Try to avoid shopping trolleys or tramps. If you work with rhyme avoid the obvious. Check that any meter you may be using actually works. Do not clank. If by this time your writing still sounds OK, then go ahead.

Internet

With the advent of cheap access, always-on, lightning-fast Broadband and complimentary Web space a huge number of poetry enthusiasts, organisations and publishers have now established themselves on the Internet. The drift has been inexorable. Some have abandoned conventional print to operate solely online; others have launched without ever having known ink and paper. Cyberspace – the place where it all happens – is a mirror of the conventional world. The electronic replicates the real. Here are online books, magazines, historical and contemporary archives, reference works, creative tools, recordings, discussion forums and news round-ups. Many dedicate themselves entirely to poetry. Some of our national institutions, notably the BBC and the *Guardian*, have discovered that poetry makes for ideal Web content and allocated significant sections of their sites to verse. On the Internet, poetry is a consumer staple.

Journals

Online e-magazines range from those which mirror their print-based cousins (and in some cases are simply direct copies) to completely innovative, interactive compilations which mix sound and action with the text. The Net is no static place. Some magazines offer playable recordings in both sound and vision of their poets performing, others give space for readers to add criticism. More and more run forums where readers can exchange views. The difference between online and print-based magazines becomes more apparent when you discover that what you get when you call them up is not simply an enhanced version of the current issue but access to the entire back catalogue. All searchable, storable and, for most of the poetry world, entirely free.

Geography dissolves online. America is no further and no more costly to access than Britain. One of the great magazines, John Tranter's *Jacket,* is based in Australia. It's just as easy to read as George Simmers' UK *Snakeskin* or Rick

Lupert's Los Angeles *Poetry Super Highway*. In fact, half the time, the user has no idea precisely where the site being accessed is physically based. Place ceases to matter, language takes over. Online journals can range from the terrible to the terrific. For my money the aforementioned *Jacket, nth position,* Joan Houlihan's *Perihelion,* James Alsop's long-lived and hugely professional *Alsop Review*, and Rupert Loydell's *Stride Magazine* are some of the world's best. K.M. Dersley's *Ragged Edge*, a completely engaging assemblage of poems and comment shows that online the spirit of the little magazine is thoroughly alive. At Sarah Annetts and Peter Johnson's *Scriberazone* the whole world is waiting.

How do you contribute? Read first. Will you fit in? If you think so then send your poems by e-mail. More than likely you'll get an instant answer. No more waiting around for six weeks before your poems return, rejected and dog-eared. Online can be lightening fast.

Cyberspace is huge. Some of the sites which list online journals, such as Peter Howard's Poetry Contacts, or Patrick Martin's Poetry Resource seem to go on for days. On the Web it is easy to put up more, so in terms of quality of content that often means less. As in the real world not everything is even. Check the site's design. If thought has gone into it then it's likely that consideration has been given to the content as well.

Personal sites

If you tire of contributing to the websites of others or want to make an even bigger splash then why not start your own? Putting a whole collection of verse online will present relatively little difficulty. Most Internet Service Providers (ISPs) offer an amount of free Web space to users and building a site shouldn't be beyond anyone capable of writing poetry in the first place. If you'd like to see the kind of thing that's possible have a look at the site of poets Matthew Francis and Attila the Stockbroker, or for something more challenging, Tom Leonard's site which includes his amazing reading of 'The Six O'Clock News'. You might also care to look at my own, The Peter Finch Archive. If you are reticent, get a fan to set up a site devoted to your works. This has happened to David Gascoyne, to J.H. Prynne, Maya Angelou, Ivor Cutler, Benjamin Zephaniah and others. Most of us, however, seem to prefer the idea of self-build.

Hypertext

Naturally the Web has developed its own verse forms. Most of these straddle the boundaries between verse, sound and image much in the way that concrete poetry did fifty years ago. Many critics dismiss the new work as simply moving graphic art but protagonists see the world very differently. The subject is large and new. Check the Flash-driven examples on the BBC's poetry site as well as those created by poet and Web-watcher Peter Howard. Edward Picot's Hyperliterature Exchange, Rob Kendall's Word Circuits and the Electronic Literature Directory offer an ever increasing number of links to new developments.

Groups

To reduce the poet's traditional feeling of isolation the Net presents a number of opportunities. E-mail provides one vehicle. Here, bands of poets circulate their work, their criticisms and their views of world literature. Join a group and you'll find a daily delivery of e-mails in your in-box. Some groups are moderated which means that contributions are filtered by a controlling individual although most are free-for-alls. Discussion can range from the moronic to the stimulating. The British and Irish Poets group and Poetryetc are two worth trying.

A variant on e-mail discussion groups are Usenet Newsgroups. Newsgroups are open to contributions from anyone anywhere. Articles are delivered to your browser for consumption. If you want to contribute then type it up and it's done. The principle poetry newsgroups, rec.arts.poems and alt.arts.poetry.comments, offer pretty varied fare. By their world-wide nature they tend to be American dominated and standards of contribution are not always that high. There are also masterclasses out there with established poets offering online advice. The BBC and the Poetry Society are some the organisations which have offered virtual residencies with well-known bards.

Tools and resources

The Net offers a multitude of these. There are online spell-checkers (in many language), thesauri, an anagram creator, Shakespeare concordances, a rhyming dictionary. *TrAce* at Nottingham Trent offers new media writing, creative online courses, incisive articles, innovative Web design, and a broad range of resources, news, discussions and research. The archives of universities (particularly in America) offer the great poetry of the past in comprehensive quantity. Download facsimile editions of *The Germ* (the first ever poetry magazine from 1850) or hear Seamus Heaney recite. Read the complete works of Blake, find out what powered the Beat generation, discover how Hardy worked, check the roots of modern verse. See where it's all going at the *Electronic Poetry Center* at Buffalo or the *British Electronic Poetry Centre* at Southampton. Not only can you find the texts themselves but entire critical apparatuses, historical contexts, biographies, bibliographies, portraits, shoe sizes and names of lovers for most of the greats. You can access information on poetry readings locally and worldwide. Bill Griffith's *Lollipop* tells you all you need to know about the small presses. At the *Poetry Archive* you can hear what your favourites actually sound like. At *About Poetry* you can find a list of poets' blogs. Interested in a particular style? Haiku? Visual poetry? Traditional forms? They've all got their sites.

E-commerce

Shopping on the Net is now the preferred and often the only method for buying specialist material. The big Internet bookshop, Amazon, offers the hunter for that difficult-to-obtain poetry title searchable lists. Buying online is generally safe and swift although, as with all mail order, only as perfect as the van that brings the package to your door.

How to find it all

Use the search engines. The big ones – Google and Yahoo – can return enormous lists in response to keying in the word 'poetry'. I got 122,000,000 results out of Google, a tenfold increase on my results from a year ago, which does sound like verse is taking over the world. Much easier is to log on to a poetry resource site which runs clickable lists of relevant pages. The UK *Poetry Society*, the *Poetry Library* and Peter Howard's home page are worth consulting. Poetry Kit provides a large amount of poetry information, competition lists and resources.

Some Web addresses for poets

Academi	www.academi.org
Alsop Review (magazine)	www.alsopreview.com
Attila the Stockbroker	www.attilathestockbroker.com
BBC	www.bbc.co.uk/arts/books
British Electronic Poetry Centre	www.soton.ac.uk/~bepc
British Poets e-mail list	www.jiscmail.ac.uk/lists/ british-poets.html
Electronic Literature Directory	directory.eliterature.org
Electronic Poetry Center	wings.buffalo.edu/epc
Matthew Francis	www.7greenhill.freeserve.co.uk
The Hyperliterature Exchange	hyperex.co.uk
Jacket (magazine)	www.jacketmagazine.com
Tom Leonard	www.tomleonard.co.uk
Lollipop (List of Little Press Publications)	www.indigogroup.co.uk/llpp
Patrick Martin's Poetry Resource	www.pmpoetry.com
nth position (magazine)	www.nthposition.com
Peter Finch Archive	www.peterfinch.co.uk
Peter Howard's Poetry Page	www.hphoward.demon.co.uk/poetry
The Poetry Archive	www.poetryarchive.org
The Poetry Kit (magazine)	www.poetrykit.org
The Poetry Library	www.poetrylibrary.org.uk
The Poetry Society (UK)	www.poetrysociety.org.uk
Poetry Super Highway (magazine)	poetrysuperhighway.com/ PoetLinks.html
Poetryetc	www.jiscmail.ac.uk/lists/ poetryetc.html
Poetry Blogs	poetry.about.com/od/poetryblogs
ragged edge (magazine)	www.raggededge.btInternet.co.uk/ indexp.htm
The Scriberazone (magazine)	www.scriberazone.co.uk
Snakeskin (magazine)	homepages.nildram.co.uk/~simmers
Stride (magazine)	www.stridemagazine.co.uk
Trace	www.trace.ntu.ac.uk
Word Circuits	www.wordcircuits.com

Commercial publishers

The number of commercial publishers who deal in poetry is actually extremely small. Despite the apparent acceptability of verse, profit is easier turned elsewhere. Where once there were a multitude of mainstream poetry imprints there are now only three or four. Poetry is a commercial risk and the bookshops generally don't welcome it. If it appears on a publisher's list then it's there for decoration.

The obvious exception to this approach is long-term market leader and envy of the whole business **Faber & Faber**. Here editor Paul Keegan presides over a list which continues to be as important to the firm as when T.S. Eliot inaugurated it more than seventy years ago. This is the imprint most poets would like to join. The greats of the twentieth century are here – Pound, Eliot, Plath, Hughes, Larkin. Seamus Heaney sold half a million copies when he won the Nobel Prize. The imprint is built on distinctively designed class reflected even in their anthologies (e.g. *The Thunder Mutters – 101 Poems for the Planet*, ed. Alice Oswald). Their roster of contemporary poets include some of the best we have – Simon Armitage, Don Paterson, Andrew Motion, Christopher Logue, Alice Oswald, Hugo Williams, Paul Muldoon, Nick Laird, Douglas Dunn. The press publishes forty or so poetry titles each year although new editions to the list are rare. If you fancy your chances then send a brief covering letter and a sample of your writing (six to ten poems) not forgetting an s.a.e. if you think this is where you'll fit in. Visit www.faber.co.uk and sign up for their quarterly poetry e-newsletter.

At **Random House** a commercial editor with excellent taste is **Cape**'s Robin Robertson. Cape titles have won the Forward Prize for the best first collection two years in a row, been shortlisted for the T.S. Eliot Prize and won the Whitbread. Michael Symmons Roberts, Michael Longley, Sharon Olds, Matthew Sweeney and John Burnside are typical. Roberston produces four to six titles annually including some selecteds (Burnside, Olds, Crawford) and new first volumes (Leonita Flynn, Helen Farish, James Sheard) – all books, no anthologies. Worth trying? Yes, but potential contributors should never waste anyone's time by not looking at the list first. Poetry output at fellow Random House press, **Chatto & Windus**, is slightly lower than that at Cape and includes Gerard Woodward, Alan Jenkins, Ruth Padel and John Fuller. Anthologies are an increasing speciality. Their *Poems for the Day* sell in large quantities. Worth trying? No, unless supported by a strong recommendation from an established fellow practitioner Chatto does not want to see unsolicited manuscripts.

Also at Random House, **Harvill Secker** have an interest in European translation, Paul Durcan and Alan Ross. They will look at new manuscripts but chances are slim. New writers would be better off starting elsewhere. Random House's B-format paperbacker, **Vintage**, has published an anthology of refugee poetry and redone Ruth Padel's excellent primer *52 Ways of Looking at a Poem* but new poets should stay clear. **Hutchinson** mixes the old guard with the inspirational and has recently added Stephen Fry's *The Ode Less Travelled* but is not keen to see new work. **Everyman** produces generic anthologies on death and solitude. The Random House group is a rich mix.

   MQ Publications, who specialise in gift books, have launched their own series of generic anthologies using luminaries Marilyn Hacker, Mimi Khalvati, Michael Schmidt and others as compilers. *Poetry to Calm Your Soul* is typical. Scotland's **Canongate** publishes Alan Spence, Robbie Burns, Lemn Sissay and others and has a fine *Modern Scottish Women Poets* anthology. Among the other commercial houses activity appears to be limited to nominal titles, anthologies or back-list obligations. **HarperCollins** makes money from Daisy Goodwin's *Essential* anthologies and their own version of Purple Ronnie, Edward Monkton. **Virgin** does Charles Bukowski and Spike Milligan. **Duckworth** brings out Edith Sitwell and Horace's Odes. **Methuen** sells John Hegley and anthologies of cricket poetry and verse for everyday. **Allen Lane** does Patrick Kavanagh and anthologies from the First World War. **Bloomsbury** has Michael Ondaatje, Lewis Carroll and anthologies edited by Roger McGough. **Cassell** anthologises the poems from the London Underground. **Hamish Hamilton** does John Updike. **John Murray** recycles Betjeman and prints anthologies of old chestnuts although have recently had *The Night Before Christmas* recast by Carol Ann Duffy. **W.W. Norton** handles John Kinsella and a variety of Americans and now has the legendary **New Directions** as one of their imprints. **Virago** concentrates on women's verse – Maya Angelou, Margaret Atwood along with an expected range of generic anthologies. Do they take on new poets? Hardly ever. **Boxtree** keeps Purple Ronnie in the hands of those who don't like poetry. Some specialist interests are dealt with at **Lion Hudson** (Christian verse) but it isn't a lot.

   Authors of poetry aimed at children, a difficult but rewarding market, should look at the following imprints: A.&C. Black, Walker Books, Chrysalis, Macmillan, Young Picador, Red Fox, Puffin and Faber & Faber

The smaller operators

Not all commercial publishing is vast and conglomerate. A few independents still exist and on their lists poetry occasionally occurs. Northern Ireland general publisher, **Blackstaff Press**, brings out one or two poetry titles annually, including Michael Foley and Michael Longley's anthology of *Poems of Mayo*. Welsh family firm **Gwasg Gomer** produces neat editions of Menna Elfyn, Gillian Clarke, Nigel Jenkins and others although most of their verse publications are in Welsh. Check their site at www.gomer.co.uk **Polygon**, (which is an imprint of **Birlinn Ltd**) continues to mix Gaelic with English. The press has at least half a dozen poets on the list including Norman MacCaig, Roddy Gorman, Liz Lochhead and W.N. Herbert. Their own generic anthologies on birth and death have a Scottish flavour. At the **Onlywomen Press** editor Lilian Mohin publishes two or three poetry titles annually. Paula Jennings, Kate Foley and Suniti Namjoshi are typical. Check their anthology *Not for the Academy: Lesbian Poets*.

Universities

With **OUP**'s contemporary list gone to Carcanet, interest among the UK's university presses is sparse. Reprints and literary studies at **Cambridge**, the same at **Manchester**. At the **University of Wales Press**, who publish a splendid series of collected works from Welsh poets, you need to be dead. American university presses such as **Nebraska, Princeton, Louisiana, Wisconsin,** Calgary, **Chicago, Harvard, Michigan, North Carolina, Washington, Alabama** and **California** do an increasing amount of verse but exclusively by Americans. King's College, London has **MPT Books** which publishes modern poetry in translation. Wolfgang Görtschacher's **Poetry Salzburg** is an independent Anglophone operation run from the University of Salzburg in Austria. They publish six to eight titles annually concentrating on critical works, translations from European minorities and collections from neglected English-language poets including a number from the UK (Rose Flint, Glen Cavaliero). Their excellent and eclectic magazine is *Poetry Salzburg Review*. Their website is at www.poetrysalzburg.com

The mass-market paperback

The popular end is where many poets imagine the best starting place to be. Paperback houses were founded to publish inexpensive reprints of hard-covered originals and, despite years of innovation, to a large extent still fulfil this role. Being neither cheap nor (in sales terms) that popular, poetry does not really fit in. Among the carousels at airports you do not see it. Check the empires of **Arrow, Bantam, Corgi, Headline** and **Mills & Boon**. If you discount the inspirational, you won't find a book of verse between them. But there are exceptions. At **Penguin**, where things have always been different, poetry has a significant role. With its unfailing commercial ear the company continues to correctly assess the market for contemporary and traditional verse. Reprinting important volumes pioneered by less commercial poetry presses, originating historic and thematic anthologies, reviving classic authors and producing translations en route, Penguin provides an almost unrivalled introduction to the world of verse. But appearances aside, this is most certainly no place for the beginner. 'We publish almost no new or unknown poets. In fact we publish very little new poetry beyond a small circle of the established. We concentrate on selecteds and general anthologies,' publishing director Tony Lacey told me. The main thrust recently has been the re-packaging and expanding of their range of selecteds including Carol Ann Duffy, James Fenton, Derek Mahon, Roger McGough, Tony Harrison, Sophie Hannah, Linton Kwesi Johnson and Brian Patten. They also publish a good range of modern poets in translation along with larger collections from the likes of William Empson, Allen Ginsberg and Patrick Kavanagh. The company's poetry overview and thematic anthologies, notably their *Poems and Readings for Weddings* and *Poems and Readings for Funerals*, the Simon Armitage and Robert Crawford edited *British and Irish Poetry Since the War*, Peter Forbes' *Scanning the Century* and Paul Keegan's *New Penguin Book of English Poetry* are leaders. Despite these obvious winners Lacey sees the whole market for verse as small, despite the hype.

Penguin's nearest rival, **Picador**, the literary paperbacker from **Pan Macmillan**, has developed into one of the country's leading poetry publishers. Under the commanding eye of successful and non-metropolitan poet Don Paterson it has moved into high gear putting out a stream of successful collections from new poets such as Jacob Polley and Colette Bryce, along with established names such as Kathleen Jamie, Peter Porter, Carol Ann Duffy, Kate Clanchy, the late Michael Donaghy, American poet laureate Billy Collins and Sean O'Brien. With its reliable content Picador is a UK reference point. Paterson will bring out between four and six new titles annually. Worth trying here? The imprint reckons to receive about 700 book-length submissions annually and the rate of take-up from this slush pile is around zero.

The specialists

Despite a clear lack of success in the commercial marketplace poetry still gets published in quantity. But by whom? By the specialist independents. These are the many semi-commercial operations scattered across the country. They are run by poetry enthusiasts whose prime concern starts not with money but with the furtherance of their art. A number – but certainly not all – receive grant aid. They are models of what poetry publishing should be – active, involving, alert and exciting. They promote their lists through readings, tours, websites and broadcasts and they involve their authors in the production, promotion and sales of their books. Never before have new poets been faced with so many publishing opportunities. Just how does the reader see through the flood? By reputation. Two specialist publishers early on emerged well ahead of the pack – **Carcanet** and **Bloodaxe**. Along with **Faber**, **Cape** and **Picador** these two bring out and distribute more poetry books than any other British imprint. Distribution is a key here. The advent of print-on-demand technology has led to a considerable increase in the number of titles being published. But few of these reach the traditional market place – the shops.

Taking them alphabetically, Neil Astley's acclaimed **Bloodaxe Books** publishes at least thirty titles annually. Based in Northumberland and begun in Newcastle in the late '70s, the press is unhindered by a past catalogue of classical wonders or an overly regional concern. It relentlessly pursues the new. Astley presents the complete service from thematic anthologies, world greats and selecteds to slim volumes by total newcomers. The press has its own range of excellent handbooks to the scene including *Getting into Poetry* and *Writing Poems* along with an increasing range of critical volumes. Best poetry sellers are their anthologies: Neil Astley's own *Staying Alive* along with his *Being Alive* (both huge sellers), Edna Longley's *Bloodaxe Book of 20th Century Poetry* and their decade-framing anthology *The New Poetry*. Bloodaxe relishes the chance to publish work from outside the standard English mainstream – Ireland, Scotland and Wales are all well represented, as are our more traditional UK outsiders such as J.H. Prynne. Bestsellers include Jackie Kay, Simon Armitage, Benjamin Zephaniah, Tony Harrison and Brendan Kennelly. Bloodaxe with a combative, assured Astley at the helm will not go rusty with age. Check their site, one of the best poetry places on the Web, at www.bloodaxebooks.com

The second, **Carcanet Press**, has been the consistent recipient of critical accolades. Publishing four Nobel Prize-winning authors and six Pulitzers helps. It is once again almost exclusively a publisher of verse, though some volumes of literary criticism, fiction and related titles also emanate from the house. Carcanet currently has over 900 titles in print, reps in forty-two countries and pursues a programme that brings out thirty-five or so poetry titles annually. Managing director Michael Schmidt agrees with Auden's observation that most people who read verse read it for some reason other than the poetry. He fights the tide with his own mainstream journal *PN Review*, which celebrated its thirtieth year in 2006. Carcanet has a policy of serious quality. 'I am strongly aware of the anti-modernist slant in a lot of poetry publishing, and publish to balance this,' Schmidt comments. 'Most submissions we receive come from people ignorant of the list to which they are submitting. Nothing is more disheartening than to receive a telephone call asking whether Carcanet publishes poetry.' The press has a four-part editorial programme: to publish new writing, to dust down substantial but neglected figures of this and earlier centuries, to encourage the translation of poetry and to explore poets' prose and work relating to modern poetry. There is a bias against poetic nationalism and against Little Englandism. Typical of their list are John Ashbery, Sujata Bhatt, Eavan Boland, Alison Brackenbury, Gillian Clarke, Elaine Feinstein, Louise Gluck, Lorna Goodison, Jorie Graham, Sophie Hannah, Mimi Khalvati, Thomas Kinsella, Mervyn Morris, Togara Muzanenhamo. Christopher Middleton, Edwin Morgan, Sinead Morrissey, Les Murray, John Peck, Tom Raworth, Peter Scupham, Charles Tomlinson and others. Carcanet has an air of purpose about it. 'We avoid the technicolour and pyrotechnic media razzmatazz,' says Schmidt. Have a look at their website – www.carcanet.co.uk New poets are welcome to submit. Send six to ten pages of work and expect to wait six weeks for a reply. Carcanet's *New Poetries* and *Oxford Poets* series of anthologies give an idea where the taste of the press is going next.

There are other specialists with similar aims and style but perhaps with not quite the Carcanet/Bloodaxe reach.

Anvil Press Poetry, founded by Peter Jay in 1968, is England's longest-standing independent poetry publisher. It publishes the best of English language poets: Martina Evans, A.B. Jackson, Dennis O'Driscoll, Greta Stoddart, Dick Davis, James Harpur, Michael Hamburger and others. In addition, Anvil boasts a backlist containing four Nobel Prize Laureates and has a deserved reputation for the finest translations of the finest poets in the international canon (Apollinaire, Baudelaire, Bei Dao, Goethe, Hikmet, Lorca, Neruda, Seferis, Tagore, etc.). Anvil publishes about twelve new titles annually. For those who wish to familiarise themselves with the flavour of the list, Anvil's thirtieth anniversary anthology *The Spaces of Hope* gives a perfect starting point. Anvil's website is www.anvilpresspoetry.com

Enitharmon Press cares about presentation and publishes fine-quality literary editions with good bindings, quality paper and dust jackets. Enitharmon has little interest in fashion. The press is 'dedicated to a poetry of the human spirit in an age of rampant commercialism' (Anne Stevenson). Owner Stephen Stuart-Smith continues a policy of publishing new, established and unjustly neglected poets, with output now up to twenty volumes annually. Typical of the list are Alan Brownjohn, Jane Duran, Duncan Forbes, Seamus Heaney, Michael Longley, Paul Muldoon and Anthony Thwaite. The future looks bright and includes Kevin Crossley-Holland, Jeremy Hooker and Simon Rae. Visit www.enitharmon.co.uk for more information and samples of some of its poets reading.

Tony Ward's **Arc Publications**, based in Lancashire, brings out around twenty poetry titles annually. 'We publish work that we believe important, innovative, and of outstanding quality,' Ward told me. The imprint has Jean Boase-Beier, Jo Shapcott, Angela Jarman and John Kinsella on the board and maintains a backlist of in excess of 180 titles. Ivor Cutler, Julia Darling, Alison Croggan, Michael Haslam, Tony Curtis (Ireland), Inna Lisianskaya (Russia), Elizabeth Smither (New Zealand), Jackie Wills and the anthology *A Fine Line* are top sellers. Arc's policy is to publish the best in contemporary poetry and their list is particularly strong in translations in bilingual editions, authors from overseas whose first language/adopted tongue is English, and anthologies from Eastern and Central Europe. The Arc website is at www.arcpublications.co.uk Submissions from unpublished authors are not accepted. Poets should familiarise themselves with the list before sending anything and, unless accompanied by a publishing history and s.a.e. will not be considered. Electronic submissions are not accepted.

Ward has an excellent reputation as a printer to the poetry press community and over the years has done splendid job for David Tipton's **Redbeck Press**. Tipton, who came up the pamphlet route used by many a small press, drove Redbeck into the top echelon, publishing everything from Argentinean poets to Michael Tolkien, Alexis Lykiard and the British beats. His star title of recent times has been Debjani Chatterjee's 200-page *Redbeck Anthology of British South Asian Poetry*. At the end of 2006 Redbeck's grant was withdrawn and the future is now uncertain. A great loss.

Seren Books is a Welsh-based literary house publishing novels, art books, short fiction, biographies and critical texts. Although Welsh-interest comes first this is not Seren's exclusive focus. The imprint has a solid interest in verse and publishes six to ten new single-author volumes annually. Poetry editor Amy Wack reads *everything* submitted but admits she has only ever accepted one unsolicited manuscript in her entire tenure. Poets should read more, she says. Editions are quality productions. Typical recent poets include John Barnie, Tiffany Atkinson, Pascale Petit, Owen Sheers and Sheenagh Pugh. Their *Seren Selections* anthologies showcase groups of new voices. *Women's Work* (ed. Amy Wack) is an anthology of English poetry from the 1850s to the present day. Their website is www.seren-books.com

Rupert Loydell's **Stride** has gathered a good reputation for catholic taste and running risks. After thirty-three issues in hardcopy his eponymous magazine is now available on the Web at www.stridemagazine.co.uk This is an excellent sample of Stride's taste with an eclectic mix of verse, criticism and feature. Based in the south-west output is six to ten titles annually. The backlist now runs to more than 200 titles ranging from the totally unknown to the famous. Stride perfectly fills the gap between the avant-garde and the user-friendly. Recent successes include Tim Cumming, Peter Redgrove, Robert Lax, Rose Flint, Phil Bowen and Charles Wright. 'Poets expecting fame and fortune need not apply,' says Loydell. 'Those interested in promoting and publicising new, intriguing work should.' Visit their website at www.stridebooks.com for up-to-date information.

Peterloo Poets, based in Cornwall, represents poetry without frills, without fuss, and most definitely without the avant-garde. Run by Harry Chambers, the press aims to publish quality work by new and neglected poets, some of them late starters; to co-publish with other reputable presses; and to establish a Peterloo list of succeeding volumes by a core of poets of proven worth. Heaney described Chambers as one of the 'great hearers and hearteners of the work being done in British and Irish poetry'. Peterloo, which represents a stable centre for many people's idea of what poetry is, runs an active backlist of nearly 200 titles. Bestsellers include U.A. Fanthorpe, Dana Gioia, Elma Mitchell, and M.R. Peakcoke. Poets central to the list are Ann Drysdale, John Mole, William Scammell, David Sutton, and John Whitworth. Recent additions include R.V. Bailey, Brian Bartlett, Anne-Marie Fyfe, Kate Scott, Christine Webb and John Weston. Peterloo, now in its thirty-first year, runs its own poetry competition with prize money running to the thousands. Chambers insists that prospective contributors to the press have had at least six poems in reputable magazines. Send a full ms accompanied by an s.a.e. large enough to carry your ms back to you. Chambers currently takes a couple of months to reply, and is full to the year 2008. Peterloo are at www.peterloopoets.com

John Skelton has now joined the team at **Salt**, which comprises Linda Bennett, Chris Hamilton-Emery, Jen Hamilton-Emery and John Kinsella. This originally Australian business has successfully consolidated its operations in the UK. Salt has solid left-field leanings and an interest in contemporary poetics and culture. Sales from their booming list are doubling year on year. Stocks of their large, award-winning catalogue are held with major distributors in the UK, USA and Australia and sold in bookstores around the world. Salt has a diverse, pluralistic backlist which includes poets Charles Bernstein, Adam Czerniawski, Forrest Gander, Diane Glancy, Jill Jones, John Matthias, Peter Rose, Ron Silliman and John Wilkinson. Bestsellers include *Vanishing Points* – Rod Mengham and John Kinsella's modernist anthology, Eugenio Montejo, John James and John Tranter. Their excellent website, full of poetry news and reviews is at www.saltpublishing.com, a substantial online poetry shop is also available at the same location. Expect more titles, more collections and more criticism. An innovator to watch. There are other presses with less prodigious outputs but whose editions are still up there with the best of them. In Northumberland Margaret and Peter Lewis's **Flambard Press**, which also deals in northern fiction, publishes around four or five or so poetry titles annually in the Bloodaxe style. The press is interested in translations and in new and neglected poets especially from the North and the Borders. Paul Stubbs, Amanda White, Peter Bennet and William Radice are typical poets. Check www.flambardpress.co.uk

Tony Frazer's Exeter-based **Shearsman** grew out of his eclectic yet most regular little magazine of the same name. *Shearsman*, the magazine, was founded in 1981 expressing an interest in the left-field, the innovative and the new. Slightly bigger than when it started (108 pages as opposed to sixteen) it still does that work splendidly today. Shearsman Books have similar interests and a solid backlist of more than eighty titles. They bring out around twenty substantially-sized new books annually. Typical poets include Scott Thurston, Catherine Walsh, Frances Presley, Gael Turnbull, Maurice Scully, Peter Larkin, Ken Edwards, Roy Fisher, Lee Harwood, Andrew Duncan and Fred Beake. To leaven the bread they also publish anthologies of classic poets with a connection to the south-west of England. Range is strength and Frazer certainly exhibits that. Their site is at www.shearsman.com

Gladys Mary Coles has developed her **Headland Publications** into a regular Peterloo clone and is now producing upwards of nine fine books annually including an exciting range of anthologies. Her interest centres on north-west England and Wales, with the new **Headland: Wales** imprint. Typical poets include Herbert Williams, Cathy Grindrod (Derbyshire's first Poet Laureate), John Barnie, Richard Poole, David Woolley, P.C. Evans and Alison Chisholm. Headland publishes the *Dead Good Poets Society* anthology. Ken Edwards' **Reality Street Editions** specialises in contemporary, innovative writing in English and in translation from other languages. Publishing no more than three or four single-author volumes or anthologies each year, the press takes the new poetry seriously. Typical authors include Maggie O'Sullivan, Allen Fisher and Denise Riley. New authors are advised to check out the publication programme first – a number of subscription deals are on offer. No unsolicited submissions without prior e-mail enquiry, please. More information is at http://freespace.virgin.net/reality.street

Nicholas Johnson's **Etruscan Books** carries the flame for UK avant-garde poetry and performance with a series of readers, chapbooks and multi-contributor volumes along with a first-class anthology of contemporary material, *Foil*. If anyone is pushing the edge out then Johnson is, and he's doing it with style. His poets include Bob Cobbing, Gael Turnbull, Stuart Montgomery, Harriet Tarlo, John Daniel, Ed Dorn, Maurice Scully, Wendy Mulford, Sean Rafferty, Maggie O'Sullivan, Bill Griffiths and Tom Pickard. The press is on the Web at www.seaham.i12.com/etruscan

Paul Beasley's poetry agency (see *Organisations of Interest to Poets*) **57 Productions**, represents performance poetry heartland and, realising that most of his material works better on audio, has concentrated on editions on cassette and CD. Recent releases include John Hegley, *Poetry in Performance Volume 1* and *Volume 2* (the Jukebox Edition), Michael Rosen and Jean 'Binta' Breeze – with extant titles from R.S. Thomas, Christopher Logue and John Cooper Clarke. In Huddersfield Janet Fisher and Peter Sansom run **Smith/Doorstop** the poetry imprint of their enterprising **Poetry Business** (see *Organisations of Interest to Poets*). The press produces eight new titles annually. Pascale Petit, Patricia Debney and Catherine Smith are recent authors. Smith/Doorstop also runs an enterprising annual poetry-pamphlet competition as well as producing poetry on cassette. Their *Contemporary Poems* edited by Peter Sansom and Lesley Jeffries offers a good critical introduction to the scene. Their magazine is *The North*. On the Web they are at www.poetrybusiness.co.uk

With North American connections Jessie Lendennie runs **Salmon Publishing** from the Cliffs of Moher, Co. Clare, in Ireland. The press have been in the business for twenty-four years and publish some of the best designed titles in the West. An Irish connection is pretty useful when trying here although Salmon do look at material from further afield. Poets published include Adrienne Rich, Carol Ann Duffy, Ray Bradbury, Ben Howard, Catherine Byron, Rita Ann Higgins, Marvin Bell, Joan McBreen and Mary Dorcey. Recent books include poetry collections from Anne Le Marquand Hartigan, Maurice Harmon and Kevin Higgins, and a literary memoir by James Liddy. *Salmon: A Poetic Journey*, an anthology/memoir of Salmon's poets and history, will be published in 2006 to celebrate Salmon's twenty-fifth year. Salmon have an excellent website at www.salmonpoetry.com which includes discussion, advice, events listings, sound files and a complete bookshop.

Peepal Tree is the largest independent publisher of Caribbean and black British poetry. Founded in 1986 they now produce around twelve poetry titles annually. Typical poets include Dorothea Smartt, Raman Mundair, David Dabydeen and Anthony Kellman. Kwame Dawes has compiled *Red,* their anthology of new black British poetry. Press editor Jeremy Poynting reads over 1,000 submissions annually and is not known for speedy responses. You can view the Peepal Tree catalogue at www.peepaltreepress.com

John Lucas's Nottingham-based **Shoestring Press** brings out eighteen titles by established but unfashionable poets annually. Recent books include Nadine Brummer, Vernon Scannell, Alan Dent, Angela Leighton, Graham Holderness, J.C. Hall, Barbara Hardy, Arnold Rattenbury and Mandy Coe. Check Shoestring's website at www.shoestringpress.com Peter Fallon's **Gallery Press** in Co. Meath, after more than twenty-five years of publishing a veritable Irish institution, continues to produce substantial quality collections from the likes of Frank Orsmby, Paul Muldoon, Sean Dunne, Derek Mahon, Medbh McGuckian, Richard Murphy and everyone who is anyone on the Irish scene. They are proud to publish younger writers including Vona Groarke, John McAuliffe, Conor O'Callaghan, Justin Quinn and Peter Sirr and especially pleased to be bringing out Alan Gillis and David Wheatley, both poets younger than the press itself. Duncan Glen's amazingly long-lived and still exciting **Akros Publications** are at the forefront of Scotland's poetry pamphlet revolution with a range that includes Tessa Ransford, Ian Revie and Alexander Hutchison. Edinburgh's **Luath Press,** from the heart of Burns country, has spawned an increasing and impressive poetry roster. Under editor Gavin MacDougall the list includes Liz Niven, Alistair Findlay, Gerry Cambridge, Donald Smith, and Angus Calder, James Robertson's collection of poems and essays written as first resident poet at the Scottish Parliament, and Stuart McHardy's collection of *Scots Poems To Be Read Out Loud*. Their website it at www.luath.co.uk

In Wales **Parthian Books** under poetry editors Norman Schwenk and Jasmine Donahaye continues to publish around four collections annually. Typical poets include Jasmine Donahaye, Lynne Rees, Lloyd Robson, David Greenslade, Rhian Saadat and Ifor Thomas. A recent surprise best-seller is Schwenk's anthology *The Hare That Hides Within*. Parthian's *The Pterodactyl's Wing* collects the best of Welsh world poetry. Their website is well worth a visit at www.parthianbooks.co.uk

Now that technology, and in particular print on demand, has made life easier for publishers it's become harder and harder to draw the line between the poetry specialists and the classic small presses. The difference may simply be a matter of distribution although the new and much more stringent stocking policies adopted by chain booksellers may end up turning poetry into an entirely Amazon-sourced pursuit.

The regional anthologies

Running in parallel with the high-ground literary approach of much of the poetry world are empires largely unknown to the taste-makers and ignored by the critics. The biggest, Ian Walton's **Forward Press** in Peterborough, now turns over £2.2 million annually and has a back catalogue of 15,000 titles. Establishing itself in 1989 as the People's Publisher, and adopting a truly inclusive approach to poetry, the company's ethos has always been to act as a bridge to publication, rather than a barrier, and give anyone from any walk of life the opportunity to see their poems in print. Forward Press targets contributors who find much contemporary poetry 'over complex and difficult to understand'. All published poets are automatically entered for free into the company's annual Top 100 Poets of the Year Award which is currently in its ninth year. To date more than £80,000 has been awarded in prize money to competition entrants, with £10,000 awarded each year, £3,000 to the author of the best poem and ninety-nine other prizes.

The phenomenal success of Forward Press over the past seventeen years has meant it has moved from being a kitchen-table operation to a three-storey office block with more than seventy members of staff. Ian remains at the helm of the company, and, with son Chris, continues to champion original poetry and new avenues for aspiring poets to see their work in print.

Anthologies, the mainstay of Forward's operation, can include as many as 160 to 200 poems in each edition. No entry fee is asked, nor are there purchase requirements. Submissions under thirty lines are preferred. Costs are kept down by using in-house printing equipment coupled to serviceable bindings. But if you want to own a copy of your work in print, and for most contributors this is the whole raison d'être for writing, then you have to buy a copy. However, this is no traditional vanity operation. No one is actually being ripped off nor are the publishers raking in exorbitant profits. Page for page their titles are not much more expensive than those of Cape or Faber and are cheaper than the output of some little presses.

Critics claim that quality at Forward Press is being neglected in exchange for quantity. Dumb down your criteria for inclusion, cram the poems in, sell more copies. Undoubtedly the genuine literary achievement of appearing in one of Forward Press' books is questionable. In mitigation it must be said that for some writers this will be their much needed beginning (check Angela Macnab and Sally Spedding), but for others the only success they are ever going to get. In 2005 Forward launched a competition to find their one-millionth poem for publication.

Forward's range of imprints include **Young Writers** aimed at primary- and secondary-school-age children, **Writers' Bookshop** which publishes a most useful series of reference books including subject and genre guides, directories and handbooks, and **New Fiction** which publishes short stories. Forward's new website – www.forwardpress.co.uk – features useful information and an immensely popular message board with live-chat facilities The site attracted nearly 20,000 visitors in its first three weeks. Forward Press offer the complete poetry life. For more information telephone their approachable team on 01733 898105, e-mail info@forwardpress.co.uk or write to Forward Press, Remus House, Woodston, Peterborough, PE2 9JX.

Envious of Forward's success at catching the hearts and minds of most of the UK's poetry hobbyists a number of rival operators have risen in their wake. Regional poetry anthologies, Magic of the Muse, Best of Britain collections, compendiums of English, Scottish, Irish and Welsh verse abound. Contributions are sourced through notices on library walls, local free sheets, local radio and through direct mail. These operations vary from the glossy to the poorly pro-duced No actual rip-off occurs and contributors tend to get in whether they purchase or not. But if you want to see your work then you must buy and the books can cost a lot. Before agreeing to contribute, check the press's output. Do not submit blindly, research their backlist. It is what Faber would demand of you. The rule applies to the whole poetry scene.

The small press and the little magazine

Small publishing ventures have been with us since the dawn of print, and print is cheaper today than it ever was. Costs are down. Technology scores. For the past decade small-press and little-magazine publishing has seen a golden age. But there are signs of change. In the face of so-simple Internet could print-only little magazines be ending? Closures outnumber start-ups. Why bother with print? On the Web there are no distribution difficulties and size just doesn't matter. But the small magazine isn't dead, not yet.

Statistically, small presses and little magazines have been the largest UK pub-lishers of new poetry both in terms of range and circulation for decades, although this honour is now fast shifting to the Web. They operate in a bewildering blur of shapes and sizes everywhere from Brighton to Birmingham and from Aberystwyth to Aberdeen. For up to the moment data have a look at the address list maintained by the Poetry Library at www.poetrylibrary.org.uk/magazines

This country's best poetry magazines all began as classic titles. Between them *PN Review, Ambit, Orbis, Poetry Review,* Craig Raine's *Arete, The Rialto, Acumen, The North, Smiths Knoll, Magma* and *Envoi*, do not come up to even half the circulation of journals like *Shooting Times* and *All About Soap* – which says a lot about the way society values its poetry. Nonetheless, taken as a group, they will get to most everyone who matters. They represent poetry as a whole. Read these and you will get some idea of where the cutting edge is. In the second division in terms of kudos lie the regional or genre specialists such as *Raw Edge* (new writing from the West Midlands), *Poetry London, Banipal* (Arab literature), *The New Welsh Review, Poetry Wales, Poetry Ireland, Chapman* (Scotland's quality literary magazine), *Poetry Scotland, Haiku Scotland, Mslexia* (for women who write), *The Poetry Church* (Christian poetry), *Brando's Hat* (rare opportunities), *Akros* (an independent view of Scottish verse), Krax (served up on a plate), and *Haiku Quarterly (HQ Magazine)*. All these magazines are well produced, sometimes with the help of grants, and all represent a specific point of view. In Wales there is *Barddas* for poets using the strict meters and in Scotland *Lallans* for poets working in Lowland Scots. The vast majority of small magazines, however, owe no allegiance and range. From quality round-ups *The Reater, Smoke, Purple Patch, The Frogmore Papers,* former Rialto editor John Wakeman's splendid *SHOp*, Colin Shaddick's stapled *Saw* (poetry with an edge), *Zed20* (Duncan Glen's Scottish extravaganza), the Usk Valley's marvellously produced *Scintilla*, the enormously long-lived *Iota* (now managed by *Ragged Raven*), and Barry Tebb's notorious *Leeds Poetry Weekly*, to irregulars like *The Yellow Crane* (interesting new poems), *Sphinx* (a magazine with a mission), *Rubies in the Darkness* (high quality romantic), *Roundyhouse* (bards from both sides of the border), *Pulsar* (poems from the Ligden Poetry Society, *Linkway*, a publication for writers & friends), *Quattrocento* (an independent journal)*, Anon* (your work judged by what it says rather than your name), *Openwide* (high-octane writing) and *Skald* (the innovative and experimental). Some like *The Penniless Press* are for the poor of pocket and rich of mind, the long-established and excellent *Fire* goes for length and the otherwise unpublishable. If you can't find a magazine that suits you and your style then you can't be writing poetry. On the other hand, if you are really sure you are then start your own.

Among the small presses there is a similar range with increased production on all sides. Brian Wake and Tony Dash's enormously long-lived **Driftwood Publications** extends the Liverpool vision with David Bateman, Jim Mangnall and Henry Graham. Will Parfitt's **PS Avalon** publishes inspirational and contemplative poetry including Jay Ramsay, Owen Ahrmanian and Keith Hackwood. David Perman's excellent **Rockingham Press** is in the heart of it. Recent titles include Wendy French, Lotte Kramer and Judi Benson. They publish five books and a range of pamphlets annually. The press is at www.rockingham-press.co.uk **The Wrecking Ball Press** grew out of Shane Rhodes poetry cafe managing experiences to become a hot imprint – Geoff Hattersley, Brendan Cleary and

Eva Salzman are some of the quality writers attracted. Supplementing the magazine, **Rialto** brings out poetry-scene stalwarts Julia Casterton, Andrew Waterhouse and others. They have recently begun a series of booklets with the imprint **Bridge Pamphlets**. New start-up **Egg Box Publishing** majors on performances *Live from the Hellfire Club* along with a range of books by new poets. **Waywiser Press** under editorship of Peter Hoy is dedicated to modern poetry in English and has published fine editions by Al Alvarez, Anthony Hecht, Mark Strand, Richard Wilbur and others. A heavyweight future looks assured. **Iron Press** has been there since 1973 and still brings out five or so titles annually majoring in haiku. Alan Halsey's **West House Books** publishes the innovative Geraldine Monk, David Annwn, Kelvin Corcoran, Richard Caddel and others, and Keston Sutherland's **Barque Press** publishes an ambitious programme of often post-language poets including Chris Goode, John Tranter, Peter Manson, Andrew Duncan and Tom Jones. **Bluechrome**, a new gen start-up based in Portishead, produces excellent books and includes Roland John, Roger Harvey and Rupert M. Loydell among its roster. **The King's England Press** publishes poetry for children under their **The Potty Poets** imprint featuring Chris White, Gez Walsh, Andrew Collett and others. Janet Murch and Bob Mee's **Ragged Raven Press** steams on with Tony Petch, Bron Bateman, John Robinson, Chris Kinsey and others. Andy Croft's **Smokestack** magazine is no longer with us but the press of the same name has a list that includes Alison Fell, Sebastian Barker, John Goodby, Alan Dent, David Craig and Arnold Rattenbury. Their manifesto is delicious: Smokestack champions poets who are unconventional, unfashionable, radical or left-field and who are working a long way from the metropolitan centres of cultural authority. **Chapman New Writing** does the new gen from Scotland and includes Tom Bryan, Magi Gibson, Janet Paisley, Lydia Robb and Dilys Rose. For the new writer these kinds of presses are the obvious place to try first. Indeed it is where many have. Who put out T.S. Eliot's first? A small publisher. Dannie Abse, Peter Redgrove, James Fenton and Dylan Thomas, the same. R.S. Thomas, Ezra Pound and Edgar Allen Poe didn't even go that far – they published themselves.

Cash

Being a poet is not really much of an occupation. You get better wages delivering papers. There will be the odd £25 from the better-heeled magazine, perhaps even as much as £100 or so from those periodicals lucky enough to be in receipt of a grant, but generally it will be free copies of the issues concerned, thank you letters and little more. Those with collections published by a subsidised, specialist publisher can expect a couple of hundred as an advance on royalties. Those using the small presses can look forward to complimentary copies. On the Internet, published poets usually get nothing at all. The truth is that poetry itself is undervalued. You can earn money writing about it, reviewing it, lecturing on it, teaching it or, certainly, by giving public performances (£150 standard here, £1,000 plus if you are Roger McGough, much more if you are Seamus Heaney). But at bottom, most things in the poetry business will earn better money than the verse itself. This isn't capitalism, this is art.

Readings

Since the great 1964 Beat Generation readings at the Albert Hall, there has been an ever expanding phenomenon of poets on platforms, reading or reciting their stuff to an audience that can be anywhere between raptly attentive and fast asleep. Begin by attending and see how others manage. Watch out for local events advertised at your local library, ring your local arts council (in Wales look at www.academi.org). Poets with heavy reputations can often turn out to be lousy performers while many an amateur can really crack it out. Don't expect to catch every image as you listen. Readings are not places for total comprehension but rather for glancing blows. Treat it as fun and it will be. If you are trying things yourself for the first time, make sure you've brought along your books to sell, stand upright, drop the shoulders, gaze at a spot at the back of the hall and blow.

Competitions and awards

Poetry competitions have been the vogue for decades now with the most unlikely organisations sponsoring them. The notion here is that anonymity ensures fairness. Entries are made under pseudonyms so if your name does happen to be Andrew Motion, it won't help you much. Results seem to bear this out too. The big competitions run biennially by the **Arvon Foundation** with the help of commercial sponsors, the **Academi**'s Cardiff International and the **Poetry Society**'s National attract a large entry and usually throw up quite a number of complete unknowns among the winners. And why do people bother? Cash prizes can be large – thousands – but it costs at least a few pounds a poem to enter, and often much more than that. And there has been a trend for winners to come from places like Cape Girardeau, Missouri and Tibooburra, Australia. The odds are getting longer. Who won the last Arvon? I don't remember. But if you do fancy a try then it is a pretty innocent activity. You tie up a poem for a few months and you spend a little money. Winners' tips include reading the work of the judges to see how they do it, submitting non-controversial middle-of-the-road smiling things, and doing this just before the closing date so you won't have to wait too long. Try two or three of your best. Huge wodges are costly and will only convince the judges of your insecurity. Have a look at *The Ring of Words* (Sutton Publishing), an excellent historical anthology of Arvon contenders or the Arvon's own collections of their latest winners. For contests to enter watch the small magazines, write to your local arts council, consult Carole Baldock's regular *Competitions Bulletin* (17 Greenhow Avenue, West Kirby, Wirral CH48 5EL), check out *The New Writer*, *Poetry London* or *Writer's News*, look on the notice board at your local library, or check the regularly updated list at **The Poetry Library** in London (see *Organisations of Interest to Poets*). And be wary of those that are free to enter. Before trying be sure it's not a vanity-press scam

Poetry Awards are slightly different. These are usually made for published books and convention generally requires your publisher to make the nomination rather than yourself. These glittering prizes are increasing both in value and impact. Both the annual T.S. Eliot and Forward Prizes ('The Bardic Booker') are now worth £10,000 a time with the poetry section of the Whitbread Book Award offering £5,000. To win one of these your book needs to be pretty hot. In America The Emily Dickinson First Book Award is open only to poets over the age of fifty. The first winner was Landis Everson, who is seventy-nine. We could do with an award like this in the population-ageing UK.

Radio and TV

Poetry on television has never been much of a success. Verse is rarely visual. On TV, when it appears at all, it is usually Great Stuff read by actors whose over-trained voices relentlessly drive home the brightness, the melancholy or the laughter of their lines. Opportunities for the newcomer, even on Five or among the digital dross of Sky's outer reaches, are rare.

On radio, however, things can be different. In enlightened mode both Radio 3 and Radio 4 give over whole half hours to verse and use a fair smattering of contemporary voices. What is usually important here are the poets themselves. Listen out for *Poetry Please*, for *The Verb*, for the Radio Four dedicated poetry slot on Sunday afternoons, for programmes produced by Sue Roberts, Fiona Mclean, Julian May and others. The BBC's website (www.bbc.co.uk/arts/books) collects information on the Corporation's poetry interests.

Poetry on radio is a large but difficult market. The BBC are pretty definite about having no remit to use 'unpublished or amateur verse'. Programme ideas should always be directed to a programme-making department at the BBC rather than to Radio 4 or Radio 3 themselves. If you are determined to put your verse on air then local and regional radio offer better possibilities. Try sending in self-produced readings on CD (if you are any good at it) or topical poetry which regional magazine programmes could readily use. Don't expect to be paid much.

Starting up

Probably the best place will be locally. Find out through the library, your local arts council or check the Internet to find which writers groups gather in your area and attend. There you will meet others of a like mind, encounter whatever locally produced magazines there might be and get a little direct feedback on your work. 'How am I doing?' is a big question for the emerging poet and although criticism is not all that hard to come by, do not expect it from all sources. Magazine editors, for example, will rarely have the time to offer advice. It is also reasonable to be suspicious of that offered by friends and relations – they will no doubt only be trying to please. Writers groups present the best chance for poets to engage in honest mutual criticism. But if you'd prefer a more detached, written analysis of your efforts and are willing to pay a small sum, then you could apply to *Prescription,* the service operated nationally by the Poetry Society (22 Betterton Street, London WC2H 9BX), to the service run by Academi in Wales (see **Organisations of Interest to Poets**), The Literary Consultancy (Diorama Arts, 34 Osnaburgh Street, London NW1 3ND) or to those run on an area basis by your regional arts council. There are also a number of non-subsidised critical services which you will find advertised in writers' magazines.

Read: if it's all a mystery to you, try Tony Curtis' *How to Study Modern Poetry* (Macmillan); Matthew Sweeney and John Hartley Williams' *Teach Yourself Writing Poetry* (Teach Yourself), John Whitworth's *Writing Poetry* (A.&C. Black), John Redmond's *How To Write a Poem* (Blackwell), Stephen Fry's traditional approach with *The Ode Less Travelled* (Hutchinson) or my own *The Poetry Business* (Seren). How real poets actually work can be discovered by reading *Don't Ask Me What I Mean* (Picador), Don Paterson's collection of essays about modern British poets in their own words or *How Poets Work* (Seren). After all this, if you still think it's appropriate, try sending in.

How to do it

Increase your chances of acceptance by following simple, standard procedure:

- Type on a single side of the paper, A4 size, single-spacing with double between stanzas, exactly as you'd wish your poem to appear when published.
- Give the poem a title, clip multi-page works together, include your name and address at the foot of the final sheet. Avoid files, plastic covers, stiffeners and fancy clips of any sort.
- Keep a copy, make a record of what you send where and when, leave a space to note reaction.
- Send in small batches – six is a good number – with a brief covering letter saying who you are. Leave justification, apology and explanation for your writers group.
- Include a self-addressed, stamped envelope of sufficient size for reply and/or return of your work.
- Be prepared to wait some weeks for a response. Don't pester. Be patient. Most magazines will reply in the end.
- Never send the same poem to two places at the same time (and this includes

e-zine vs. hard copy). If you've entered the poem for a competition then make sure you *never* simultaneously send it elsewhere.

- If you are thinking of sending your submission electronically *check* first. Some journals and publishers in the *Writer's Handbook* survey don't accept materials sent this way.
- Send your best. Work which fails to fully satisfy even the author is unlikely to impress anyone else.

Where?

Try the list which follows. This is by no means the whole UK small-press scene but only some of those where potential contributors might stand a chance. Even here do not expect unrelenting positive responses: magazines get overstocked, editors change, addresses shift, policy alters, operators run out of steam. Be prepared to hunt around, and for a lot of your work to come back. You can help improve things by buying copies. Send in an s.a.e. asking how much. The total market is vast and if you want to go further then you could consult the handout produced by the *Poetry Library* (see **Organisations of Interest to Poets**) or *Light's List of Literary Magazines* which contains both UK and US addresses (John Light, Photon Press, The Lighthouse, 37 The Meadows, Berwick upon Tweed, Northumberland TD15 1NY).

The next step

Once you have placed a few poems you may like to consider publishing a booklet. There are as many small presses around as there are magazines. Start with the upmarket professionals by all means but be prepared for compromise. The specialists and the small presses are swifter and more open to new work.

If all else fails you could do it yourself. Blake did, so did Walt Whitman. Technology puts the process within the reach of us all and if you can put up a shelf, there is a fair chance you will be able to produce a book to go on it. Read my *How to Publish Yourself* (Allison & Busby). Remember that publishing the book may be as hard as writing it but marketing and selling it is quite something else. Check Alison Baverstock's *Marketing Your Book: An Author's Guide* (A.&C. Black) if you really want to get ahead.

The listings

The list of addresses which follows is not exhaustive. Publishers come and go with amazing frequency. For up to the minute information check with some of the **Organisations of Interest to Poets** (see page 160). Poetry has a huge market.

It pays to keep your ear to the ground. The magazines and presses listed here have all been active during the past eighteen months and most (although be warned, *not all*) have indicated a willingness to look at new work. But do check before sending. Ask to see a catalogue or a sample copy. Good luck.

Poetry Presses

Abraxas Press
13 Copthall Gardens, Mill House, London
NW7 2NG
✉ poetry@abraxas.fsnet.co.uk

Agenda Editions
The Wheelwrights, Fletching Street, Mayfield
TN20 6TL
✉ agendapoetry@lycos.co.uk

Contact *Patricia McCarthy*

See also **Agenda** magazine.

Akros Publications
33 Lady Nairn Avenue, Kirkcaldy KY1 2AW
☎01592 651522

Contact *Duncan Glen*

Publisher of Scottish poetry and literary criticism. See also *ZED2O* magazine and entry
under *UK Publishers*.

Allison Allison
Double Ddykes, Elm Road, Galashiels
TD1 3HT
☎01896 753728
✉ allisonallisondouble@yahoo.co.uk

Anvil Press Poetry Ltd
Neptune House, 70 Royal Hill, London
SE10 8RF
☎020 8469 3033 Fax 020 8469 3363
✉ anvil@anvilpresspoetry.com
www.anvilpresspoetry.com

Contact *Peter Jay*

Contemporary British poetry and poetry in
translation. See entry under *UK Publishers*.

Arc Publications
Nanholme Mill, Shaw Wood Road,
Todmorden OL14 6DA
☎01706 812338 Fax 01706 818948
✉ arc.publications@btconnect.com
www.arcpublications.co.uk

Contact *Tony Ward*

Contemporary poetry from new and established writers both in the UK and abroad. See
entry under *UK Publishers*.

Arrowhead Press
70 Clifton Road, Darlington DL1 5DX
✉ editor@arrowheadpress.co.uk
www.arrowheadpress.co.uk

Contact *Roger Collett*

Quality books and pamphlets of contemporary
poetry.

Atlantean Publishing
38 Pierrot Steps, 71 Kursal Way, Southend on
Sea SS1 2UY
✉ atlanteanpublishing@hotmail.com
www.geocities.com/dj_tyrer/atlantean-
pub.html

Contact *David John Tyrer*

Single author broadsheets and poetry/prose
booklets. See also **Awen, Monomyth, Bard,
Garbaj** and **The Supplement** magazines.

BB Books
Spring Bank, Longsight Road, Copster Green,
Blackburn BB1 9EU
☎01254 249128

Contact *Dave Cunliffe*

Post-Beat poetics and counterculture theoretic.
Iconoclastic rants and anarchic psycho–cultural
tracts. See also **Global Tapestry Journal**.

Beyond the Cloister Publications
74 Marina Street, St Leonards on Sea
TN38 0BJ
☎01424 444072

Contact *Hugh Hellicar*

Anthologies of poetry and slim volumes to
launch poets.

Big Little Poem Books
3 Park Avenue, Melton Mowbray LE13 0JB

Contact *Robert Richardson*

Effective contemporary approaches to the lyric
and epigram. See also **Door-To-Everywhere**
press.

Blinking Eye Publishing
PO Box 549, North Shields NE30 2WT
☎0191 257 3778
✉ jeanne@millview77.freeserve.co.uk

www.blinking-eye.co.uk
Contact *Jeanne Macdonald*
Launched to promote the work of poets over 50 – by annual competition.

Bloodaxe Books Ltd
Highgreen, Tarset NE48 1RP
☎01434 240500 Fax 01434 240505
✉ editor@bloodaxebooks.com
www.bloodaxebooks.com

Contact *Neil Astley*

Britain's leading publisher of new poetry. No submissions by e-mail attachments. See entry under **UK Publishers**.

Blue Butterfly Publishers
13 Irvine Way, Invermurie AB51 4ZR
☎01467 625986 Fax 01467 625986
✉ blue7butterfly@which.net
homepages.which.net/~david.madill

Contact *Betty Madill*

Christian poetry.

Bluechrome
PO Box 109, Portishead, Bristol BS20 7ZJ
www.bluechrome.co.uk

The Boho Press
Bluechrome, PO Box 109, Portishead, Bristol BS20 7ZJ
☎07092 273360 Fax 02092 273357
✉ info@bohopress.co.uk
www.bluechrome.co.uk

Contact *Anthony Delgrado*

Bradshaw Books
Tigh Fili, Thompson House, Maccurtain Street, Cork, Republic of Ireland
☎00 353 21 450 9274
Fax 00 353 21 455 1617
✉ admin@cwpc.ie
www.tighfili.com

Contact *M. Bradshaw*

Seen entry under **Irish Publishers**.

Bridge Pamphlets
PO Box 309, Aylsham, Norwich NR11 6LN
✉ mail@therialto.co.uk
www.therialto.co.uk

Contact *Michael Mackmin*

An imprint of **Rialto Publications**.

Paula Brown Publishing
26 Orkney Roadq, Corsham, Portsmouth PO6 3UE
☎01202 672173
✉ paulabrownpublishing@btinternet.com
www.thepeoplespoet.com

Contact *Paula Brown*

Online poetry and arts community which publishes anthologies and single author collections.

Bucephalus Press
67 Hady Crescent, Chesterfield S41 0EB
☎01246 276532

Contact *David Holliday*

Founded in 2004 to publish small collections of poetry.

Bullseye Publications
5 Camptoun, North Berwick EH39 5BA
☎01620 880311
✉ alancharlesgay@aol.com

Contact *Alan Gay*

Calder Wood Press
1 Beachmont Court, Dunbar EH42 1YF

Carcanet Press Ltd
4th Floor, Alliance House, 30 Cross Street, Manchester M2 7AQ
☎0161 834 8730 Fax 0161 832 0084
✉ info@carcanet.co.uk
www.carcanet.co.uk

Contact *Michael Schmidt*

Major poetry publisher. See entry under **UK Publishers**; also **PN Review** magazine.

Chapman Publishing
4 Broughton Place, Edinburgh EH1 3RX
☎0131 557 2207 Fax 0131 556 9565
✉ chapman-pub@blueyonder.co.uk
www.chapman-pub.co.uk

Contact *Joy Hendry*

Scottish writing, mainly from contributors to *Chapman* magazine. See entry under **UK Publishers**.

Cinnamon Press
Ty Meirion House, Glanyrafon, Tanygrisiau, Blaenau Festiniog LL4 3SU
☎01766 832112
✉ jan@coffeehousepoetry.co.uk
www.coffeehousepoetry.co.uk

Contact *Dr Jan Fortune-Wood*

Poetry, fiction, some non-fiction from Wales. See also **Coffee House Poetry** magazine.

Clutag Press
PO Box 154, Thame OX9 3RQ

The Collective Press
c/o Penlanlas Farm, Llantilio Pertholey, Y-fenni NP7 7HN
☎01873 856350 Fax 01873 859559
✉ jj@jojowales.co.uk
www.welshwriters.com

Contact *John Jones & Frank Olding*

Non-profit promoter and publishers of contemporary poetry.

Comma Poetry
3 Vale Bower, Mytholmroyd HX7 5EP
☎07792 564747
✉ commapress@yahoo.co.uk
www.commapress.co.uk/poetry

Contact *Ra Page*

Best in new British poetry.

Day Dream Press
39 Exmouth Street, Swindon SN1 3PU
☎01793 523927

Contact *Kevin Bailey*

Small poetry collections. See also *HQ, Haiku Quarterly*.

The Dedalus Press
13 Moyclare Road, Baldoyle, Dublin 13, Republic of Ireland
☎0870 127 2089
✉ office@dedaluspress.com
www.dedaluspress.com

Contact *Pat Boran*

Contemporary Irish poetry and poetry from around the world in English translation.

Diehard Publishers
91–93 Main Street, Callander FK17 8BQ
☎0131 229 7252

Contact *Ian W. King*

Poetry and drama, mainly Scottish. See also **Poetry Scotland** magazine.

Dionysia Press
127 Milton Road West, 7 Duddingston House Courtyard, Edinburgh EH7 1JG
☎0131 661 1156 Fax 0131 661 1156

Contact *Denise Smith*

Collections of poetry, short stories and translations. See also **Understanding** magazine.

DogHouse
PO Box 312, Tralee, Co. Kerry, Republic of Ireland
☎00 353 667 137547
✉ doghouse312@eircom.net
www.doghousebooks.ie

Contact *Noel King*

Poetry and short story collections by individuals (Irish born only).

Donut Press
PO Box 45093, London N4 1UZ
✉ donutchops@yahoo.co.uk
www.donutpress.co.uk

Contact *Andy Ching*

Door-To-Everywhere
3 Park Avenue, Melton Mowbray LE13 0JB

Contact *Robert Richardson*

Poem card series – imagination first! See also **Big Little Poem Books** press.

Dreadful Night Press
82 Kelvin Court, Glasgow G12 0AQ
☎0141 339 9150
✉ dreadfulnight1@aol.com

Dream Catcher
4 Church Street, Market Rasen LN8 3ET
☎01673 844325
✉ paulsuther@hotmail.com

Contact *Paul Sutherland*

Short fiction and poetry. See also *Dream Catcher* magazine.

Driftwood Publications
5 Timms Lane, Formby L37 7DW
☎01704 833911 Fax 0151 524 0216
✉ janet.speedy@tesco.net

Contact *Brian Wake*

New work by new and established poets more suited to the page than the stage.

Egg Box Publishing
25 Brian Avenue, Norwich NR1 2PH
☎01603 470191
✉ info@eggboxpublishing.com
www.eggboxpublishing.com

Contact *Gordon Smith*

New poetry, fiction and non-fiction. Submissions by post; translations considered.

Enitharmon Press
26B Caversham Road, London NW5 2DU
☎020 7482 5967 Fax 020 7284 1787
✉ books@enitharmon.co.uk
www.enitharmon.co.uk

Contact *Stephen Stuart-Smith*

Poetry and criticism. See entry under **UK Publishers**.

Erran Publishing
43 Willow Road, Carlton, Nottingham
NG4 3BH
✉ erranpublishing@hotmail.com
www.poetichours.homestead.com

Contact *Nick Clark*

Non-profit supporter of Third World charities.
See also **Poetic Hours** magazine.

Essence Press
8 Craiglea Drive, Edinburgh EH10 5PA
✉ jaj@essencepress.co.uk
www.essencepress.co.uk

Contact *Julie Johnstone*

Handbound editions of poetry, poetry post-cards. Interested in concrete poetry and nature.
See also **Island** magazine.

Etruscan Books
28 Fowler's Court, Fore Street, Buckfastleigh
TQ11 0AA
☎01364 643128 Fax 01364 643054
✉ etruscan@macunlimited.net
www.e-truscan.co.uk

Contact *Nicholas Johnson*

Modernist, sound, visual poetry, Gaelic, lyric poetry, US/UK poets.

Fal Publications
PO Box 74, Truro TR1 1XS
☎01208 851205
✉ info@falpublications.co.uk
www.falpublications.co.uk

Contact *Victoria Field*

Poetry and literature from Cornwall.

Feather Books
PO Box 438, Shrewsbury SY3 0WN
☎01743 872177 Fax 01743 872177
✉ john@waddysweb.freeuk.com
www.waddysweb.freeuk.com

Contact *Rev. J. Waddington-Feather*

Christian poetry, drama, hymns, novels. See entry under **Small Presses**; also **The Poetry Church** magazine.

Fire in the Head
PO Box 17, Yelverton PL20 6YF
☎01822 841081
✉ roselle.angwin@internet-today.co.uk
www.fire-in-the-head.co.uk

Contact *Roselle Angwin*

Five Leaves Publications
PO Box 8786, Nottingham NG5 4ER
☎0115 969 3597
✉ info@fiveleaves.co.uk
www.fiveleaves.co.uk

Contact *Ross Bradshaw*

Fiction, poetry, Jewish interest, social history.

Flambard
Stable Cottage, East Fourstones, Hexham
NE47 5DX
☎01434 674360 Fax 01434 674178
www.flambardpress.co.uk

Contact *Peter Elfed Lewis & Will Mackie*

Concentrates on poetry and literary fiction.

Flarestack Publishing
8 Abbot's Way, Pilton BA4 4BN
☎01749 890019
✉ cannula.dementia@virgin.net

Contact *Charles Johnson*

New poetry.

Forward Press
Remus House, Coltsfoot Drive, Woodston, Peterborough PE2 9JX
☎01733 898105 Fax 01733 313524
✉ info@forwardpress.co.uk
www.forwardpress.co.uk

Contact *Kerrie Pateman*

General poetry and short fiction anthologies.
See also **Triumph House** press.

Four Quarters Press
7 The Towers, Stevenage SG1 1HE
✉ octillion@ntlworld.com
www.fourquarterspress.co.uk

Contact *Eric Ratcliffe*

Commissioned work only for non-profit and charity purposes; mainly poetry.

Fras Publications
The Atholl Browse Bookshop, Blair Atholl
PH18 5SG

Contact *John Herdman & Walter Perrie*

The Frogmore Press
18 Neville Road, Lewes BN7 1PF
☎07751 251689
www.frogmorepress.co.uk

Contact *Jeremy Page*

A forum for contemporary poetry, prose and artwork. See also **The Frogmore Papers** magazine.

Galdragon Press
2b Church Road, Stromness, Orkney
KW16 3BT
✉ galdragon@ntlworld.com
homepage.ntlworld.com/galdragonpress
Contact *Anne Thomson*

The Gallery Press
Loughcrew, Oldcastle, Co. Meath, Republic of
Ireland
☎00 353 49 854 1779
Fax 00 353 49 854 1779
✉ gallery@indigo.ie
www.gallerypress.com
Contact *Peter Fallon*

Poems, plays and prose by contemporary Irish
writers.

The Goldsmith Press
Newbridge, Co. Kildare, Republic of Ireland
☎00 353 45 433613   Fax 00 353 45 434648
✉ viv1@aol.ie

Contact *Vivienne Abbott*

Gomer Press/Gwasg Gomer
Llandysul SA44 4JN
☎01559 363090   Fax 01559 363758
✉ ceri@gomer.co.uk
www.gomer.co.uk
Contact *Ceri Wyn Jones*

Welsh interest. See entry under **UK Publishers**.

Green Arrow Publishing
2 Chambers Cottages, Underlyn Lane,
Marden, Tonbridge TN12 9BD
☎01622 832485
✉ mail@johndench.demon.co.uk
Contact *John Dench*

Collaborative publishing scheme and other
services for writers. See also **Scriptor** magazine.

Gwasg Pantycelyn
Lôn Ddewi, Caernarfon LL55 1ER
☎01286 672018   Fax 01286 677823
✉ gwasgpantycelyn@ukonline.co.uk

Contact *R.M. Thomas*

Happenstance Press
21 Hatton Green, Glenrothes KY7 4SD
✉ nell@happenstancepress.com
www.happenstancepress.com

Contact *Helena Nelson*

Poetry chapbook collections; new and established poets. See also **Sphinx** magazine.

Harpercroft
24 Castle Street, Crail KY10 3SH
☎01333 451744
Contact *Gordon Jarvie*

Headland Publications
Ty Coch, Galltegfa, Ruthin LL15 2AR
☎0151 625 9128   Fax 0151 625 9128
Contact *Gladys Mary Coles*

Fine editions of poetry; anthologies.

Hearing Eye
Box 1, 99 Torriano Avenue, London
NW5 2RX
www.torriano.org/hearing_eye
Contact *John Rety*

Poetry/literature publishers based in Kentish
Town.

Heaventree Press
PO Box 3342, Coventry CV1 5YB
☎07833 150277
✉ info@heaventreepress.co.uk
www.heaventreepress.co.uk
Contact *Jon Morley*

'A new poetry press which already shows
immense promise.' See also **Avocado** magazine.

Hilltop Press
4 Nowell Place, Almondbury, Huddersfield
HD5 8PD
Contact *Steve Sneyd*

Specialist publisher of science fiction and dark
fantasy poetry, and background material.

Hippopotamus Press
22 Whitewell Road, Frome BA11 4EL
☎01373 466653   Fax 01373 466653
✉ rjhippopress@aol.com
Contact *Roland John*

First collections of verse from those with a
track record in the magazines. See also
Outposts magazine.

Honno Welsh Women's Press
Canolfan Merched Y Wawr, Vulcan Street,
Aberystwyth SY23 1JH
☎01970 623150   Fax 01970 623150
✉ post@honno.co.uk
www.honno.co.uk
Contact *Lindsay Ashford*

The Welsh women's press – novels, short stories,
poetry and autobiographical anthologies. Must

have a Welsh connection. See entry under **UK Publishers**.

I★D Books
Connah's Quay Library, Wepre Drive,
Connah's Quay, Deeside
☎0161 226 3419

Poetry, short fiction, local history – mainly self-publishing by associated writers' group.

Iron Press
5 Marden Terrace, Cullercoats, North Shields
NE30 4PD
☎0191 253 1901 Fax 0191 253 1901
✉ contact@ironpress.co.uk
www.ironpress.co.uk

Contact *Peter Mortimer*

Poetry and fiction.

Katabasis
10 St Martin's Close, London NW1 0HR
☎020 7485 3830
✉ katabasis@katabasis.co.uk
www.katabasis.co.uk

Contact *Dinah Livingstone*

Down-to-earth and Utopian poetry and prose from home an abroad – English and Latin American. No unsolicited mss.

Kates Hill Press
126 Watsons Green Road, Kates Hill, Dudley
DY2 7LG
www.kateshillpress.pwp.blueyonder.co.uk

Kettillonia
24 South Street, Newtyle PH12 8UQ
☎01828 650615
✉ james@kettillonia.co.uk
www.kettillonia.co.uk

Contact *James Robertson*

The King's England Press
Cambertown House, Commercial Road,
Goldthorpe, Rotherham S63 9BL
☎01226 270258 Fax 01484 663790
✉ steve@kingsengland.com
www.kingsengland.com
www.pottypoets.com

Contact *Steve Rudd*

History, folklore, children's poetry.

KT Publications
16 Fane Close, Stamford PE9 1HG
☎01780 754193

Contact *Kevin Troop*

Always looking for new material of the highest standard. See also **The Third Half** magazine.

Leaf Books
Gti Suite, Valleys Innovation, Navigation Park,
Abercynon CF45 4SN

Pocket-sized reads.

Leafe Press
4 Cohen Close, Chilwell, Nottingham
NG9 6RW
✉ leafepress@hotmail.com
www.leafepress.com

Contact *Alan Baker*

Pamphlets of contemporary poetry with occasional full-length collections.

Logan Press
Unit 11, 1a Bryson Street, Belfast BT5 4ES

Luath Press Ltd
543/2 Castlehill, The Royal Mile, Edinburgh
EH1 2ND
☎0131 225 4326 Fax 0131 225 4324
✉ gavin.macdougall@luath.co.uk
www.luath.co.uk

Contact *Gavin MacDougall*

Committed to publishing well-written books worth reading. Over 150 titles in print including poetry and fiction.

Ludovic Press
Heathfield, Horsewood Road, Bridge of Weir
PA11 3AU
☎01505 702906

Malfunction Press
Rose Cottage, 3 Tram Lane, Buckley CH7 3JB
✉ rosecot@presford.freeserve.co.uk

Contact *Peter E. Presford*

Mainly dedicated to science fiction, fantasy, light horror.

Mare's Nest
41 Addison Gardens, London W14 0DP
☎020 7603 3969
✉ maresnest@tesco.net
www.maresnest.co.uk

Contact *Pamela Cluines-Ross*

Icelandic.

Mariscat Press
10 Bell Place, Edinburgh EH3 5HT
☎0131 343 1070
✉ hamish.whyte@virgin.net

Contact *Hamish Whyte & Diana Hendry*
Currently publishing poetry pamphlets only.

Masque Publishing
PO Box 3257, Littlehampton BN16 9AF
✉ masque_pub@tiscali.co.uk
myweb.tiscali.co.uk/masquepublishing
Contact *Lisa Stewart*
For self-publishers. See also **Decanto** magazine.

Mews Press
English Department, Sheffield Hallam
University, Collegiate Crescent, Sheffield
S10 2BP
☎0114 225 2241
✉ s.l.earnshaw@shu.ac.uk
extra.shu.ac.uk/mews-press
Contact *Dr Steven Earnshaw*
Work by poets associated with Sheffield Hallam
University's MA in Writing.

Morning Star
(19) off Quay Building, Foundry Lane, Byker,
Newcastle upon Tyne NE6 1AF
☎0191 265 6699
✉ alexfinlay@yahoo.com
www.alecfinlay.com
Contact *Alec Finlay*
Pocketbooks, bookscapes and the small press
series.

The Moving Finger Press
PO Box 4867, Birmingham B3 3HD
Contact *Dave Reeves*
See also **Raw Edge** magazine.

Mudfog Press
Arts Development, The Stables, Stewart Park,
The Grove, Marton, Middlesborough
TS7 8AR
✉ mudfog@hodgeon.demon.co.uk
www.mudfog.co.uk
Community press publishing poetry and short
fiction only from writers in the Tees Valley.

New Fountainhead Press
10 Frenchlands Hatch, Ockham Road South,
East Horsley KT24 6SJ
☎01483 285396
✉ stanleyt5@aol.com
Stanley Trevor writ large.

New Hope International
20 Werneth Avenue, Gee Cross, Hyde
SK14 5NL

✉ england@spunge.org
www.geraldengland.org.uk
Contact *Gerald England*
Poetry booklet publisher. No longer considering unsolicited mss.

New Island
2 Brookside, Dundrum Road, Dublin 14,
Republic of Ireland
☎00 353 1 298 9937   Fax 00 353 1 298 2783
✉ edwin.higel@newisland.ie
www.newisland.ie
Contact *Edwin Higel*
See entry under **Irish Publishers**.

Northernsky Press
PO Box 21548, Stirling FK8 1YY
✉ northernsky@hush.com
www.northernskypress.com

nthposition
38 Allcroft Road, London NW5 4NE
☎020 7485 5002
✉ val@nthposition.com
www.nthposition.com
Eclectic mix of political opinion and arts, featuring contemporary Todd Swift (poetry).

Object Permanence
13 Buckingham Terrace, Glasgow G12 8EB
✉ petermanson@ntlworld.com
www.objectpermanence.co.uk
Contact *Robin Purves*

The Old Stile Press
Catchmays Court, Llandogo, Nr Monmouth
NP25 4TN
☎01291 689226
✉ oldstile@dircon.co.uk
www.oldstilepress.com
Contact *Frances & Nicolas McDowall*
Fine, hand-printed books with text and images.
No unsolicited mss.

The Once Orange Badge Poetry Press
PO Box 184, South Ockenden RM15 5WT
☎01708 852827
✉ orangebadge@poetry.fsworld.co.uk
Contact *D.M. Heath*
A4 and A5 pamphlets – ideal for first collections.
E-mail submissions preferred. See also **The
Once Orange Badge Poetry Supplement**
magazine.

The One Time Press
Model Farm, Linstead Magna, Halesworth
IP19 0DT
☎01986 785422
www.onetimepress.com

Contact *Peter Wells*

Poetry of the forties in limited editions.
Illustrated.

Original Plus
Flat 3, 18 Oxford Grove, Ilfracombe
EX34 9HQ
☎01271 862708
✉ smithsssj@aol.com
members.aol.com/smithsssj/index.html

Contact *Sam Smith*

Requires something extra – another language
or markedly original. See also **The Journal**
magazine.

Palores Publishing
1 Station Hill, Redruth TR15 2PP

Parthian
The Old Surgery, Napier Street, Cardigan
SA43 1ED
☎01239 612059 Fax 01239 612059
✉ parthianbooks@yahoo.co.uk
www.parthianbooks.co.uk

Contact *Richard Gwyn*

New Welsh writing. See entry under **UK
Publishers**.

Partners
289 Elmwood Avenue, Feltham TW13 7QB
✉ partners_writing_group@hotmail.com

Contact *Ian Deal*

Competitions and poetry pamphlets. See also **A
Bard Hair Day**, **Imagenation** and **Poet Tree**
magazines.

Peepal Tree Press Ltd
17 King's Avenue, Leeds LS6 1QS
☎0113 245 1703 Fax 0113 246 8368
✉ hannah@peepal.demon.co.uk
www.peepaltreepress.com

Contact *Jeremy Poynting*

Best in Caribbean, Black British and south
Asian writing from around the world.

Perjink Press
8a Leopold Place, Edinburgh EH7 5JW
✉ djlawrenson@hotmail.com

Contact *D.J. Lawrenson*

Peterloo Poets
The Old Chapel, Sand Lane, Calstock
PL18 9QX
☎01822 833473
✉ info@peterloopoets.com
www.peterloopoets.com

Contact *Harry Chambers*

Pigasus Press
13 Hazely Combe, Arreton, Isle of Wight
PO30 3AJ
✉ mail@pigasuspress.co.uk
www.pigasus.press.co.uk

Contact *Tony Lee*

Publisher of science fiction magazine and genre
poetry.

Pikestaff Press
Ellon House, Harpford, Sidmouth EX10 0NH
☎01395 568941

Contact *Robert Roberts*

Contemporary poetry belonging to the English
tradition, mainly 24-page pamphlets.

Pipers' Ash Ltd
Pipers Ash, Church Road, Christian Malford,
Chippenham SN15 4BW
☎01249 720563 Fax 0870 056 8916
✉ pipersash@supamasu.com
www.supamasu.com

Contact *Mr A. Tyson*

Collections of 60 poems arranged in their best
order, grouped on common themes, with an
appropriate title. See entry under **Small Presses**.

Poems in the Waiting Room
PO Box 488, Richmond TW9 4SW
✉ pitwr@blueyonder.co.uk

Contact *Michael Lee*

Pamphlets for medical waiting rooms.

Poetry Now
Remus House, Coltsfoot Drive, Woodston,
Peterborough PE2 8JX
☎01733 8998101 Fax 01733 313524
✉ poetrynow@forwardpress.co.uk
www.forwardpress.co.uk

Contact *Steve Twelvetree*

Lively, personal and contemporary; also deals
with womenswords. See also **Forward Press**.

Poetry Press Ltd
26 Park Grove, Edgware HA8 7SJ
☎020 8958 6499

poetrypress@yahoo.co.uk
www.poetrypress.co.uk

Contact *Judy Karbritz*

Anthologies – rhyming poetry welcome.

Poetry Salzburg
Dept. of English and American Studies,
University of Salzburg, Akademiestr. 24,
A–5020 Salzburg, Austria
✉ wolfgang.goertschacher@sbg.ac.at
www.poetrysalzburg.com

Contact *Wolfgang Görtschacher*

See also **Poetry Salzburg Review** magazine.

Poetry Wednesbury
25 Griffiths Road, West Bromwich B71 2EH
☎07950 591455
✉ ppatch66@hotmail.com
www.poetrywednesbury.co.uk

Contact *Geoff Stevens*

Occasional CDs, DVDs, leaflets and booklets.
See also **The Firing Squad** and **Purple
Patch** magazines.

Poets Anonymous
70 Aveling Close, Purley CR8 4DW
✉ poets@poetsanon.org.uk
www.poetsanon.org.uk

Contact *Peter L. Evans*

Anthologies and collections of predominantly
south London poets. See also **Poetic Licence**
magazine.

Poor Tom's Press
89a Winchester Avenue, Leicester LE3 1AY
☎0116 289 5400
✉ bfewster@gn.apc.org

Contact *Brian Fewster*

Precious Pearl Press
41 Grantham Road, Manor Park, London
E12 5LZ

Contact *Peter Geoffrey & Paul Thompson*

Romantic, lyrical, spiritual, inspirational and
mystical poetry; a traditionalist poetry press. See
also **Rubies in the Darkness** magazine.

Profitless Press
20 Princes Court, The Walk, Roath, Cardiff
CF24 3AU

Contact *J. Brookes*

PS Avalon
Box 1865, Glastonbury BA6 8YR
✉ info@psavalon
www.psavalon.com

Contact *Will Parfitt*

Quality books of contemplative, inspirational
and ecstatic poetry.

Puppet State Press
1 West Colinton House, 40 Woodhall Road,
Edinburgh EH13 0DU
☎0131 441 9693
✉ richard@puppetstate.com
www.puppetstate.com

QQ Press
York House, 15 Argyle Terrace, Rothesay, Isle
of Bute PA20 0BD

Contact *Alan Carter*

Collections of poetry plus poetry anthologies.
See also **Quantum Leap** magazine.

Rack Press
The Rack, Kinnerton, Presteigne LD8 2PF
☎01547 560411
✉ rackpress@britishlibrary.net
pages.britishlibrary.net/nicholas.murray/Rack
Press.htm

Contact *Nick Murray*

Welsh poetry pamphlet imprint with an international vision.

Ragged Raven Press
1 Lodge Farm, Snitterfield, Stratford upon
Avon CV37 0LR
☎01789 730358
✉ raggedravenpress@aol.com
www.raggedraven.co.uk

Contact *Bob Mee & Janet Murch*

Poetry. See also **Iota** magazine.

Raunchland Publications
26 Aldergrove, Dunfermline KY12 8RP
✉ raunchland@hotmail.com
www.raunchland.co.uk

Contact *John Mingay*

Limited edition poetry/graphics booklets and
online publications.

Reality Street Editions
63 All Saints Street, Hastings TN34 3BN
✉ reality.street@virgin.net
www.realitystreet.co.uk

Contact *Ken Edwards*

New poetry from Britain, Europe and America. No unsolicited mss.

Red Candle Press
50 Manbey Grove, London E15 1EX
✉ rcp@poetry7.fsnet.co.uk
www.members.tripod.com/redcandlepress
Contact *M.L. McCarthy*
Traditionalist poetry press. See also **Candelabrum Poetry Magazine**.

Rialto Publications
PO Box 309, Aylsham, Norwich NR11 6LN
✉ mail@therialto.co.uk
www.therialto.co.uk
Contact *Michael Mackmin*
'We want to publish first collections by poets of promise.' See also **The Rialto** magazine and **Bridge Pamphlets** press.

Rintoul Publishers
8 Rintoul Place, Edinburgh EH3 5JF

Rive Gauche Publishing
69 Lower Redland Road, Bristol BS6 6SP
☎0117 974 5106
✉ twinset1969@hotmail.com
Contact *PVT West*
Poetry by women writing and/or performing in Bristol.

Rogue Seeds
11 Gilbert Road, Hale, Altrincham WA15 9NR
☎01896 753728
✉ rogueseeds@lykos.co.uk
members.lycos.co.uk/rogueseeds

Route Publishing
PO Box 167, Pontefract WF8 4WW
☎01977 797695
✉ info@route-online.com
www.route-online.com
Contact *Ian Daley & Isabel Galan*
Contemporary fiction and performance poetry. Online magazine publishes downloadable books.

Salt Publishing
PO Box 937, Great Wilbraham, Cambridge CB1 5JX
☎01223 882220 Fax 01223 882260
✉ sales@saltpublishing.com
www.saltpublishing.com

Contact *Chris Hamilton-Emery*
International poetry and poetics.

Scriberazone
PO Box 3849, Sheffield S2 9AG
✉ peterjohnson@scriberazone.co.uk
www.scriberazone.co.uk
Contact *Peter Johnson & Sarah Annetts*
Poetry and other vibes.

Second Light Publications
9 Greendale Close, London SE22 8TG
☎020 8299 0088
✉ dilyswood@tiscali.co.uk
Contact *Dilys Wood*

The Seer Press
PO Box 29313, Glasgow G20 2AE
☎07743 307808
✉ admin@theseerpress.com
www.theseerpress.com

Seren
57 Nolton Street, Bridgend CF31 3AE
☎01656 663018 Fax 01656 649226
✉ seren@seren-books.com
www.seren-books.com
Contact *Mick Felton*
Poetry, fiction, lit crit, biography, essays. See entry under *UK Publishers*; also **Poetry Wales** magazine.

Shearsman Books
58 Velwell Road, Exeter EX4 4LD
☎01392 434511 Fax 01392 434511
✉ editor@shearsman.com
www.shearsman.com
Contact *Tony Frazer*
Publishes poetry almost exclusively. Contact editor before submitting. See also **Shearsman** magazine.

Sixties Press
89 Connaught Road, Sutton SM1 3PJ
☎020 8286 0419
Contact *Barry Tebb*
Small press concentrating on poetry and novellas. See also **Leeds Poetry Weekly** and **Literature and Psychoanalysis** magazines.

Smokestack Books
PO Box 408, Middlesbrough TS5 6WA
☎01642 813997
✉ info@smokestack-books.co.uk

Contact *Andy Croft*

Champions poets who are unconventional, unfashionable, radical or left-field.

Spectacular Diseases
83b London Road, Peterborough PE2 9BS

Contact *Paul Green*

Innovative poetry and some prose. Translations of both.

Stinging Fly Press
PO Box 6016, Dublin 8, Republic of Ireland
✉ stingingfly@gmail.com
www.stingingfly.org

New Irish and international writing. See also **The Stinging Fly** magazine.

Stride
4b Tremayne Close, Devoran, Truro TR3 6QE
✉ editor@stridebooks.co.uk
www.stridebooks.co.uk

Contact *Rupert Loydell*

Innovative poetry, criticism and music, essays and interviews. See entry under **Small Presses**.

Talking Pen
12 Derby Crescent, Moorside, Consett DH8 8DZ
☎01207 505724

Contact *Steve Urwin*

See also **Moodswing** magazine.

Tall Lighthouse Press
33 Longhurst Road, London SE13 5LR
www.tall-lighthouse.co.uk

Templar Poetry
PO Box 7082, Bakewell DE45 1FL
☎01629 810085
✉ info@templarpoetry.co.uk
www.templarpoetry.co.uk

Contact *Alexander McMillen*

New poets via national annual pamphlets collection competition. Committed to new emerging poets.

Terra Firma Press
11 Sinclair Drive, Glasgow G42 9PR

Contact *A. Murray*

Touch the Earth Publications
39 McKenzie Crescent, Lochgelly KY5 9LT
Contact *William Hershaw*

Triumph House
Remus House, Coltsfoot Drive, Woodston, Peterborough PE2 9JX
☎01733 898102   Fax 01733 313524
✉ triumphhouse@forwardpress.co.uk
www.forwardpress.co.uk

Contact *Steve Twelvetree*

A Christian poetry imprint publishing many anthologies annually. See also **Forward Press**.

Troubador Publishing Ltd
9 De Montfort Mews, Leicester LE1 7FW
☎0116 255 9311
www.troubador.co.uk

See entry under **UK Publishers**.

Tuba Press
Tunley Cottage, Tunley, Near Cirencester GL7 6LW
☎01285 760424

Contact *Charles Graham*

Vane Women Press
31 Garthorne Avenue, Darlington DL3 9XL
☎01325 468464
✉ marg.rule@ntl.com
www.vanewomen.co.uk

Contact *Margaret Rule*

Work by women of the North East.

Waterloo Press
126 Furze Croft, Hove BN3 1PF
☎01273 202876
www.waterloopresshove.com

Contact *Simon Jenner*

Poetry and periodical publisher; please phone for submissions. See also **Eratica** magazine.

Waywiser Press
9 Woodstock Road, London N4 3ET
☎020 8374 5526   Fax 020 8374 5736
✉ waywiserpress@aol.com
www.waywiser-press.com

Contact *Philip Hoy*

Specialises in modern poetry in English. See entry under **Small Presses**.

Wendy Webb Books
9 Walnut Close, Taverham, Norwich NR8 6YN
✉ tipsforwriters@yahoo.co.uk
www.webbw.freeserve.co.uk

Contact *Wendy Webb*

Poetry books with rules of new and traditional

forms; annual anthology. See also **Norfolk Poets and Writers – Tips Newsletter** magazine.

West House Books
40 Crescent Road, Nether Edge, Sheffield
S7 1HN
☎0114 258 6035
✉ alan@nethedge.demon.co.uk
www.westhousebooks.co.uk

Contact *Alan Halsey*

Contemporary poetry, poets' prose and related work.

Wild Women Press
Flat 10, The Common, Windermere
LA23 1JH

Woodburn Press
Kendalmere, Caledonian Road, Peebles
EH45 9DL

The Wordsworth Trust
Dove Cottage, Grasmere LA22 9SH

See entry under *Literary Societies*.

Worple Press
Achill Sound, 2b Dry Hill Road, Tonbridge
TN9 1LX
☎01732 368958
✉ theworpleco@aol.com
www.worplepress.co.uk

Contact *Amanda Knight & Peter Carpenter*

Contemporary UK and international poetry, pamphlets, literary essays, arts titles

Poetry Magazines

Acumen
6 The Mount, Higher Furzeham, Brixham TQ5 8QY
☎01803 851098   Fax 01803 851098
✉ patricia@acumen-poetry.co.uk
www.acumen-poetry.co.uk
Contact *Patricia Oxley*

Good poetry, intelligent articles and wide-ranging reviews.

Aesthetica
PO Box 371, York YO23 1WL
☎07756 170324
✉ info@aestheticamagazine.com
www.aestheticamagazine.com
Contact *Cherie Federico*

Contemporary glossy: poetry, fiction, scripts, artwork, reviews, interviews – ethos of arts for all.

Agenda
The Wheelwrights, Fletching Street, Mayfield TN20 6TL
✉ editor@agendapoetry.co.uk
Contact *Patricia McCarthy*

Poems, essays, reviews.

Aireings
Dean Head Farm, Scotland Lane, Horsforth, Leeds LS18 5HU
Contact *Lesley Quayle & Linda Marshall*

Biannual poetry mag: poetry, prose, reviews, b&w artwork.

The Amsterdam Review
Columbusplein 19-111, 1057 TT Amsterdam, The Netherlands
www.amsterdamreview.nl
Contact *Duncan Bush & P.C. Evans*

Magazine for European literature.

Anon
67 Learmouth Grove, Edinburgh EH4 1BL
✉ mike@volta1.fsworld.co.uk
www.blanko.org.uk/anon
Contact *Mike Stocks*

Poems selected anonymously; for submission guidelines see website or send s.a.e.

Aquarius
Flat 4, Room B, 116 Sutherland Avenue, London W9 2QP
☎020 7289 4338
www.geocities.com/eddielinden
Contact *Eddie S. Linden*

Literary magazine; prose and poetry.

Areopagus
48 Cornwood Road, Plympton, Plymouth PL7 1AL   Fax 0870 134 6384
✉ editor@areopagus.org.uk
www.areopagus.org.uk
Contact *Julian Barritt*

A Christian-based arena for creative writers.

Avocado
The Heaventree Press, PO Box 3342, Coventry CV1 5YB
✉ info@heaventreepress.co.uk
www.heaventreepress.co.uk
Contact *Jonathan Morley*

No first person whining, please. See also **Heaventree Press**.

Awen
38 Pierrot Steps, 71 Kursaal Way, Southend on Sea SS1 2UY
✉ atlanteanpublishing@hotmail.com
www.geocities.com/dj_tyrer/awen.html
Contact *David John Tyrer*

Poetry and vignette-length fiction of any style/ genre. See also **Bard**, **Monomyth**, **Garbaj** and **The Supplement** magazines and **Atlantean Publishing** press.

Banipal
PO Box 22300, London W13 8ZQ
☎020 8568 9747   Fax 020 8568 8509
✉ editor@banipal.co.uk
www.banipal.co.uk
Contact *Margaret Obank*

Contemporary Arab authors in English translation: poetry, fiction, interviews, reviews.

Bard
38 Pierrot Steps, 71 Kursal Way, Southend on Sea SS1 2UY

✉ atlanteanpublishing@hotmail.com
www.geocities.com/dj_tyrer/monomyth.html

Contact *David John Tyrer*

Short poetry. See also **Awen**, **Garbaj**, **Monomyth** and **The Supplement** magazines and **Atlantean Publishing** press.

A Bard Hair Day

289 Elmwood Avenue, Feltham TW13 7QB

Contact *Ian Deal*

Contemporary poetry magazine. See also **Partners** press, **Imagenation** and **Poet Tree** magazines.

Blithe Spirit

12 Eliot Vale, Blackheath, London SE3 0UW
☎020 8318 4677
www.britishhaikusociety.org

Contact *Graham High*

Journal of the British Haiku Society. Haiku and related forms.

Borderlines

Nant Y Brithyll, Llangynyw, Welshpool SY21 0JS
☎019388 810263

Contact *Angie Quinn & Kevin Bamford*

Open poetry mag with no axe to grind published by the Anglo-Welsh Poetry Society.

Brando's Hat

Flat 1a, 17 Mauldeth Road, Withington, Manchester M20 4NE
Contact *Steve Waling & Fran Pridham*

Braquemard

229 Hull Road, Hull HU6 8QZ
✉ braquemard@hotmail.com
www.braquemard.fsnet.co.uk

Contact *David Allenby*

A5, 52 pages, poetry and artwork. No doggerel.

Brittle Star

PO Box 56108, London E17 0AY
☎020 8802 1507
✉ magazine@brittlestar.org.uk
www.brittlestar.org.uk

Contact *Louise Hooper*

Poetry, short stories and articles on contemporary poetry.

Candelabrum Poetry Magazine

50 Manbey Grove, London E15 1EX
✉ rcp@poetry7.fsnet.co.uk

www.members.tripod.com/redcandlepress

Contact *M.L. McCarthy*

Formalist poetry magazine for people who like poetry rhythmic and shapely. See also **Red Candle Press**.

Cannon's Mouth

22 Margaret Grove, Harborne, Birmingham B17 9JH
☎0121 426 6413
✉ cannonmouth@yahoo.co.uk
www.cannonpoets.co.uk

Contact *Greg Cox*

New poetry, criticism, articles, information.

Carillon

19 Godric Drive, Bainsworth, Rotherham S60 5NA
✉ editor@carillonmag.org.uk
www.carillonmag.org.uk

Contact *Graham Rippon*

Eclectic poetry and prose.

Cauldron

10 Glyn Road, Wirral CH44 1AB
☎07775 645497   Fax 0151 200 9402
✉ terence.grogan50@ntlworld.com
www.thenewcauldron.co.uk

Contact *Terence Grogan*

Prose and poetry of all genres and styles, plus articles and regular features.

CFUK

105b Fidlas Road, Llanishen, Cardiff CF14 0LY
☎07786 988836
✉ cfuk@hotmail.co.uk
www.cfukmagazine.net

Contact *Dylan Moore*

Cardiff's brightest litzine: fiction, poetry, essays, interviews and reviews from Wales and the world.

Chanticleer Magazine

6/1 Jamaica Mews, Edinburgh EH3 6HN
✉ richard@livermore8304.freeserve.co.uk

Contact *Richad Livermore*

Poetry and ideas; not afraid to be different.

Chapman

4 Broughton Place, Edinburgh EH1 3RX
☎0131 557 2207
✉ chapman-pub@blueyonder.co.uk
www.chapman-pub.co.uk

Contact *Joy M. Hendry*

The best in Scottish and international writing, well-established writers and the up-and-coming. See entries under *UK Publishers* and *Magazines*.

Coffee House
Charnwood Arts, Loughborough Library, 31 Granby Street, Loughborough LE11 3DU
☎01509 822558   Fax 01509 822559
✉ charnwood-arts@ndirect.co.uk
www.charnwood-arts.org.uk

Contact *Deborah Tyler-Bennett*

A meeting place for the arts, poetry, prose and visual artwork.

Coffee House Poetry
Ty Meirion, Glanyrafon, Tanygrisiau, Blaenau Festiniog LL4 3SU
☎01766 832112
✉ jan@coffeehousepoetry.co.uk
www.coffeehousepoetry.co.uk

Contact *Dr Jan Fortune-Wood*

Contemporary poems of edge and depth from new voices and established writers. See also **Cinnamon Press**.

Connections
4 Shipwrights Lee, Island Wall, Whitstable CT5 1EW
☎01227 277773
✉ jane@hardy91.fsnet.co.uk

Contact *Jane Hardy*

Poetry and prose by new and established writers.

Cork Literary Review
Thompson's House, MacCurtain Street, Cork, Republic of Ireland
☎00 353 21 450 9274
Fax 00 353 21 455 1617
✉ fredjohnston_52@hotmail.com

Contact *Fred Johnston*

Current Accounts
16–18 Mill Lane, Horwich, Bolton BL6 6AT
✉ bswscribe@aol.com
hometown.ao.co.uk/bswscribe/myhome-page/writing.html

Contact *Rod Riesco*

Poetry, short fiction, articles. Magazine of the Bank Street Writers' Group.

Dandelion Arts Magazine
24 Frosty Hollow, East Hunsbury NN4 0SY
☎01604 701730   Fax 01604 701730

Contact *Jacqueline Gonzalez-Marina*

Literary magazine: poetry, articles, interviews, art, illustration. See also **The Student Magazine**.

The Dark Horse
3b Blantyre Mill Road, Bothwell G71 8DD
✉ gjctdh@freename.co.uk
www.star.ac.uk/darkhorse/abouthorse.html

Contact *Gerry Cambridge*

Poetry.

The David Jones Journal
The David Jones Society, 22 Gower Road, Sketty, Swansea SA2 9BY
☎01792 206144   Fax 01792 205305
✉ anne.price-owen@sihe.ac.uk
www.sihe.ac.uk/davidjones

Contact *Anne Price-Owen*

Articles, poetry, information, reviews and inspired works.

Decanto
PO Box 3257, Littlehampton BN16 9AF
✉ masque_pub@tiscali.co.uk
myweb.tiscali.co.uk/masquepublishing

Contact *Lisa Stewart*

Non-conformist poetry magazine; any style considered, not just contemporary. See also **Masque Publishing** press.

Dream Catcher
4 Church Street, Market Rasen LN8 3ET
☎01673 844325
✉ paulsuther@hotmail.com

Contact *Paul Sutherland*

Short fiction and poetry. See also **Dream Catcher** press.

Dreams That Money Can Buy
35 Michell Hey, College Bank, Rochdale OL12 6UL
☎01706 648040   Fax 01706 648040
✉ editorial@dreamsthatmoneycanbuy.co.uk
www.dreamsthatmoneycanbuy.co.uk

Contact *Benjamin Ware & Sarah Lomax*

Quaterly journal of avant-garde poetry, prose, satire and art.

Earthlove
PO Box 11219, Paisley PA1 2WH
homepage.ntlworld.com/earth.love/earthlove.htm

Contact *Tracy Patrick*

Poetry magazine for the environment; proceeds to conservation charities.

Eastern Rainbow

17 Farrow Road, Whaplode Drove, Spalding
PE12 0TS
✉ p_rance@yahoo.co.uk
uk.geocities.com/p_rance/pandf.htm

Contact *Paul Rance*

Focuses on 20th century culture via poetry,
prose and art. See also **Peace and Freedom**
magazine.

Echoes of Gilgamesh

18 Craighead Way, Barrhead, Glasgow
G78 2RS
✉ paul.mcdonagh@virgin.net
www.gilgamesh.fsworld.co.uk

Contact *Paul McDonagh*

Long poem magazine, short stories, community
groups, Barrhead and Neilston sports and arts
festival.

The Engine

3 Ardgreenan Drive, Belfast BT4 3FQ
☎028 9065 9866 Fax 028 9032 2767
✉ clitophon@yahoo.com
www.theengine.net

Contact *Paul Murphy*

Journal of art, poetry, reviews and short stories.

Envoi

44 Rudyard Road, Biddulph Moor, Stoke-on
Trent ST8 7JN
☎01782 517892

Contact *Roger Elkin*

Poetry, sequences, features, reviews, letters
pages, competitions.

Equinox

134b Joy Lane, Whitstable CT5 4ES
☎01227 282718
✉ dordi@baru.fsnet.co.uk
www.ctanaet.com/equinox

Contact *Barbara Dordi*

Contemporary poetry invited.

Eratica

126 Furze Croft, Hove BN3 1PF
☎01273 202876
✉ dr.jenner@virgin.net

Contact *Simon Jenner*

Biannual journal with colour plates – focus on
poetry, strong on music and art. See also
Waterloo Press.

Federation Magazine

Burslem School of Art, Queen Street, Stoke-
on-Trent ST6 3EJ
☎01792 822327
✉ fedmag@tiscali.co.uk
www.thefwwcp.org.uk

Articles, reviews, news for people working in
community publishing. 12-page broadsheet.

Fire

Field Cottage, Old Whitehill, Tackley,
Kidlington OX5 3AB
☎01869 331300
www.poetical.org

Contact *Jeremy Hilton*

Poetry: alternative, unfashionable, experimental,
spiritual, demotic; occasional experimental
prose.

Fire in the Head

PO Box 17, Yelverton PL20 6YF

Contact *Roselle Angwin*

The Firing Squad

36 Rooth Street, Wednesbury B71 2EH
☎077364 11089
www.purplepatchpoetry.co.uk

Contact *Alex Barzdo*

Protest poetry broadsheet. See also **Purple
Patch** magazine and **Poetry Wednesbury** press.

First Offense

Syringa, The Street, Stodmarsh, Canterbury
CT3 4BA
☎01227 721249
✉ tim@firstoffense.co.uk
www.firstoffense.co.uk

Contact *Tim Fletcher*

Magazine for contemporary poetry; not traditional but is received by most ground-breaking
poets.

Flaming Arrows

Sligo-Leitrim Arts, V E C, Riverside, Sligo,
Republic of Ireland
☎00 353 71 914 7304
Fax 00 353 71 914 3093
✉ leoregan@yahoo.ie

Contact *Leo Regan*

Poetry of the spirit: mystical, contemplative,
metaphysical, grounded in the senses.
Worldwide.

The Frogmore Papers
18 Nevill Road, Lewes BN7 1PF
www.frogmorepress.co.uk

Contact *Jeremy Page*

Founded 1983. Biannual. Poetry, prose and artwork. See also **The Frogmore Press**.

Gabriel
27 Headingley Court, North Grange Road, Leeds LS6 2QU

Contact *Thelma Laycock*

Annual Christian poetry magazine.

Garbaj
38 Pierrot Steps, 71 Kursaal Way, Southend on Sea SS1 2UY
atlanteanpublishing@hotmail.com
www.geocities.com/dj_tyrer/garbaj.html

Contact *D.J. Tyrer*

Humourous/non-pc poetry, vignette-length fiction, fake news, etc. See also **Awen**, **Bard**, **Monomyth** and **The Supplement** magazines and **Atlantean Publishing** press.

Global Tapestry Journal
Spring Bank, Longsight Road, Copster Green, Blackburn BB1 9EU
☎01254 249128

Contact *Dave Cunliffe*

Global Bohemia, post-Beat and counterculture orientation. See also **BB Books** press.

Green Queen
BM Box 5700, London WC1N 3XX
eandk@lineone.net

Contact *Elsa Wallace*

Occasional magazine, Green issues, lesbian & gay fiction, articles, poetry.

Haiku Scotland
2 Elizabeth Gardens, Stoneyburn EH47 8PB
haikuscotland@btinternet.com

Contact *Frazer Henderson*

Haiku, senryu, aphorism, epigram, reviews and articles.

Handshake
5 Cross Farm, Station Road North, Fearnhead, Warrington WA2 0QG

Contact *John Francis Haines*

Newsletter of **The Eight Hand Gang**, an association of UK sci-fi poets.

Harlequin
PO Box 23392, Edinburgh EH7 5GL
childoffolly@yahoo.co.uk
www.harlequinmagazine.com

Contact *Jim Sinclair*

High quality poetry and artwork of intense beauty, mysticism and wisdom.

HQ Poetry Magazine (Haiku Quarterly)
39 Exmouth Street, Swindon SN1 3PU
☎01793 523927

Contact *Kevin Bailey*

General poetry mag with slight bias towards imagistic/haikuesque work

Imagenation
289 Elmwood Avenue, Feltham TW13 7QB

Contact *Ian Deal*

Poetry and artwork magazine. See also **Partners** press, **A Bard Hair Day** and **Poet Tree** magazines.

Inclement
White Rose House, 8 Newmarket Road, Fordham, Ely CB7 5LL
inclement_poetry_magazine@hotmail.com

Contact *Michelle Foster*

All forms and styles of poetry. Responses within a month.

Interlude
Limehouse Town Hall, 646 Commercial Road, London E14 7HA
☎020 8673 2256
submissions@interludemagazine.co.uk
www.interludemagazine.co.uk

Contact *Francesca Ricci, Helen Nodding & Becky*

Poetry, writings and visual work; multidisciplinary projects and work in progress.

The Interpreter's House
19 The Paddox, Squitchey Lane, Oxford OX2 7PN

Contact *Merryn Williams*

Poems and stories up to 2500 words; new and established writers.

Iota
1 Lodge Farm, Snitterfield, Stratford upon Avon CV37 0LR
☎01789 730358
iotapoetry@aol.com

www.iotapoetry.co.uk
Contact *Bob Mee & Janet Murch*
Poetry, reviews; long and short poems welcome. No epics. See also **Ragged Raven Press**.

Irish Pages
The Linen Hall Library, 17 Donegall Square North, Belfast BT1 5GB
☎028 9064 1644
✉ irishpages@yahoo.co.uk
www.irishpages.org
Contact *Chris Agee*

Outstanding writing from Ireland and overseas: poetry, short fiction, essays, literary journalism, nature-writing, etc.

Island
8 Craiglea Drive, Edinburgh EH10 5PA
✉ jaj@essencepress.co.uk
www.essencepress.co.uk
Contact *Julie Johnstone*

A distinctive space for writing inspired by nature and exploring our place within the natural world. See also **Essence Press**.

The Journal
Flat 3, 18 Oxford Grove, Ilfracombe EX34 9HQ
☎01271 862708
✉ smithsssj@aol.com
Contact *Sam Smith*

Poems in translation alongside poetry written in English. See also **Original Plus** press.

Knight-Vision
103 Westminster Crescent, Lodge Moor, Sheffield S10 4EU
Contact *Richard Middlebrook*
Sheffield's poetry and art.

Krax
63 Dixon Lane, Wortley, Leeds LS12 4RR
Contact *Andy Robson*
Light-hearted, contemporary poetry, short fiction and graphics.

Leeds Poetry Weekly
89 Connaught Road, Sutton SM1 3PJ
☎020 8286 0419
Contact *Barry Tebb*

New poems, reviews, articles on literary and psychoanalytic matters. See also **Sixties Press** and **Literature and Psychoanalysis** magazine.

Linear B Publishing
PO Box 23614, 5/17 Saunders Street, Edinburgh EH3 6TT
☎0131 314 4527   Fax 0131 334 5353
✉ linearb26@hotmail.com
Contact *Jamie Kelly*
Poetry, literary fiction, short stories.

Linkway
The Shieling, The Links, Burry Port SA16 0HU
☎01554 834486   Fax 01554 834486
Contact *Fay C. Davies*

A publication for writers and friends; a general interest magazine for the whole family.

Literature and Psychoanalysis
89 Connaught Road, Sutton SM1 3PJ
☎020 8286 0419
Contact *Barry Tebb*

New poems, reviews, articles on literary and psychoanalytical matters. See also **Sixties Press** and **Leeds Poetry Weekly** magazine.

The London Magazine
32 Addison Grove, London W4 1ER
☎020 8400 5882   Fax 020 8994 1713
✉ admin@londonmagazine.net
www.londonmagazine.net
Contact *Sebastian Barker*

A review of literature and the arts. See entry under *Magazines*.

Magma
43 Keslake Road, London NW6 6DH
✉ magmapoetry@ntlworld.com
www.magmapoetry.com
Contact *David Boll*

New poetry plus poetry reviews and interviews.

Modern Poetry in Translation
Queen's College, Oxford OX1 4AW
☎01865 244701
✉ admin@mpt3.wanadoo.co.uk
www.mptmagazine.com
Contact *David & Helen Constantine*

Publishes and promotes poetry in English translation.

Monkey Kettle
PO Box 4616, Kiln Farm, Milton Keynes MK12 6XZ

✉ monkeykettle@hotmail.com
www.monkeykettle.co.uk

Contact *Matthew Taylor*

Quarterly poetry, prose, photos, articles in Milton Keynes and further afield.

Monomyth

38 Pierrot Steps, 71 Kursaal Way, Southend on Sea SS1 2UY
✉ atlanteanpublishing@hotmail.com
www.geocities.com/dj_tyrer/monomyth.html

Contact *David John Tyrer*

Poetry, prose and articles; all genres, styles and lengths considered. New writers welcome. See also **Awen, Bard, Garbaj** and **The Supplement** magazines and **Atlantean Publishing** press.

Moodswing

12 Derby Crescent, Moorside, Consett DH8 8DZ
☎01207 505724

Contact *Steve Urwin*

Short poems, short prose, light/dark psychologically charged. See also **Talking Pen** press.

Mslexia

PO Box 656, Newcastle upon Tyne NE99 1PZ
☎0191 261 6656   Fax 0191 261 6636
✉ postbag@mslexia.demon.co.uk
www.mslexia.co.uk

Contact *Debbie Taylor*

National quarterly magazine for women who write. Advice, inspiration, news, reviews, interviews, etc. See entry under *Magazines*.

Neon Highway

37 Grinshill Close, Liverpool L8 8LD
✉ poetshideout@yahoo.com
www.neonhighway.co.uk

Contact *Alice Lenkiewicz*

Innovative and experimental poetry/arts magazine.

Never Bury Poetry

Bracken Clock, Troutbeck Close, Hawkshaw, Bury BL8 4LJ
☎01204 884080
✉ n.b.poetry@zen.co.uk
www.nbpoetry.care4free.net

Contact *Jean Tarry*

Founded 1989. Quarterly. International reputation. Each issue has a different theme.

New Welsh Review

PO Box 170, Aberystwyth SY23 1WZ
☎01970 626230
✉ admin@newwelshreview.com
www.newwelshreview.com

Contact *Francesca Rhydderch*

Vibrant literary quarterly magazine which showcases the best new writing from Wales. Also includes features and reviews. See entry under *Magazines*.

Norfolk Poets and Writers – Tips Newsletter

9 Walnut Close, Taverham, Norwich NR8 6YN
✉ tipsforwriters@yahoo.co.uk
www.webbw.freeserve.co.uk

Contact *Wendy Webb*

Tips newsletter, quarterly mini comps, annual davidian – rules of poetry forms. See also **Wendy Webb Books** press.

The North

The Poetry Business, The Studio, Byram Arcade, Westgate, Huddersfield HD1 1ND
☎01484 434840   Fax 01484 426566
✉ edit@poetrybusiness.co.uk
www.poetrybusiness.co.uk

Contact *Peter Sansom & Janet Fisher*

Contemporary poetry and articles, extensive reviews.

The Once Orange Badge Poetry Supplement

PO Box 184, South Ockendon RM15 5WT
☎01708 852827
✉ onceorangebadge@poetry.fsworld.co.uk

Contact *D. Martyn Heath*

A4 poetry supplement for everyone whose life has been touched by disability in some way. See also **The Once Orange Badge Poetry Press**.

Open Wide

The Flat, Yew Tree Farm, Sealand Road, Chester CH1 6BS
☎07790 062317
✉ contact@openwidemagazine.co.uk
www.openwidemagazine.co.uk

Contact *James Quinton*

80 pages of punchy short fiction, poetry, reviews and interviews.

Other Poetry

29 Western Hill, Durham DH1 4RL

☎0191 386 4058
www.otherpoetry.com

Contact *Michael Standen & Others*

Thrice-yearly 60 – 70 poems per issue. Process of selection involves all four editors. Token payment.

Outposts
22 Whitewell Road, Frome BA11 4EL

☎01373 466653   Fax 01373 466653

✉ rjhippopress@aol.com

Contact *Roland John*

Longest-surviving independent poetry magazine in the UK. See also **Hippopotamus Press**.

Page 84's Pseudo-Chaotic Magazine
PEF Productions, 196 High Road, London N22 8HH

✉ page84direct@yahoo.co.uk
www.alienonthenet.freehosting.net

Contact *Mr Page 84*

Poetry, anti-poetry, aphorism, comment and artwork mag showing work of Page 84 and guest artists.

Parameter
48 New Street, Shrewsbury SY3 8JQ

✉ editor@parametermagazine.org
www.parametermagazine.org

Partners Annual Poetry Competition
289 Elmwood Avenue, Feltham TW13 7QB

✉ partners_writing_group@hotmail.com

Contact *Ian Deal*

Showcases poems entered into the Partners annual open poetry competitions.

Peace and Freedom
17 Farrow Road, Whaplode Drove, Spalding PE12 0TS

☎01406 330242

✉ p_rance@yahoo.co.uk
uk.geocities.com/p_rance/pandf.htm

Contact *Paul Rance*

Poetry, prose, art mag; humanitarian, environmental, animal welfare. See also **Eastern Rainbow** magazine.

Peer Poetry International
26 (wh) Arlington House, Bath Street BA1 1QN

☎01225 445298

✉ peerpoetry@msn.com
www.publish-your-poetry.com

Contact *Paul Amphlett*

Biannual; 60 poets per issue.

The Penniless Press
100 Waterloo Road, Ashton, Preston PR2 1EP

☎01772 736421

Contact *Alan Dent*

Quarterly for the poor pocket and the rich mind. Poetry, fiction, essays, reviews.

Pennine Ink Magazine
The Gallery, Mid-Pennine Arts, Yorke Street, Burnley BB11 1HD

☎01282 703657

✉ sheridansdandl@yahoo.co.uk

Contact *Laura Sheridan*

Quality poetry reflecting traditional and modern trends.

Pennine Platform
Frizingley Hall, Frizinghall Road, Bradford BD9 4LD

☎01274 541015

✉ nicholas.bielby@virgin.co.uk
www.pennineplatform.co.uk

Contact *Nicholas Bielby*

Biannual poetry magazine; eclectic and serious-minded.

Planet
PO Box 44, Aberystwyth SY23 3ZZ

☎01970 611255   Fax 01970 611197

✉ planet.enquiries@planetmagazine.org.uk
www.planetmagazine.org.uk

Contact *John Barnie*

The Welsh Internationalist: current affairs, arts, environment.

Poet Tree
289 Elmwood Avenue, Feltham TW13 7QB

Contact *Ian Deal*

Contemporary poetry magazine. See also **Partners** press, **A Bard Hair Day** and **Imagenation** magazines.

Poetic Hours
43 Willow Road, Carlton, Nottingham NG4 3BH

✉ erranpublishing@hotmail.com
www.poetichours.homestead.com

Contact *Nick Clark*

Non-profit supporter of Third World charities. See also **Erran Publishing**.

Poetic Licence
70 Aveling Close, Purley CR8 4DW
✉ poets@poetsanon.org.uk
www.poetsanon.org.uk

Contact *Peter L. Evans*

Original unpublished poems and drawings. See also **Poets Anonymous** press.

The Poetry Church
Feather Books, PO Box 438, Shrewsbury SY3 0WN
☎01743 872177   Fax 01743 872177
✉ john@waddysweb.freeuk.com
www.waddysweb.freeuk.com

Contact *Rev. J. Waddington-Feather*

Quarterly magazine of Christian poetry and prayers. See **Feather Books** under *Small Presses*.

Poetry Combination Module (PCM)
PEF Productions, 196 High Road, London N22 8HH
✉ page84direct@yahoo.co.uk
www.alienonthenet.freehosting.net

Contact *Mr Page 84*

Poetry Cornwall/ Bardhonyeth Kernow
11a Penryn Street, Redruth TR15 2SP
☎01209 218209
✉ poetrycornwall@yahoo.com
www.poetrycornwall.freeservers.com

Contact *Les Merton*

Poetry from around the world, including poems in Kernewek and dialect.

Poetry Express
Studio 11, Bickerton House, 25–27 Bickerton Road, London N19 5JT
☎020 7281 4654
✉ alan@survivorspoetry.org.uk
www.survivorspoetry.com

Contact *Alan Morrison & Others*

Quarterly newsletter from **Survivors' Poetry** (see entry under *Organisations of Interest to Poets*).

Poetry Ireland News
2 Proud's Lane, Dublin 2, Republic of Ireland
☎00 353 1 478 9974   Fax 00 353 1 478 0205

✉ publications@poetryireland.ie
www.poetryireland.ie

Contact *Paul Lenehan*

Bi-monthly newsletter. See also **Poetry Ireland Review** magazine.

Poetry Ireland Review/ Eigse Eireann
2 Proud's Lane, Dublin 2, Republic of Ireland
☎00 353 1 478 9974   Fax 00 353 1 478 0205
✉ poetry@iol.ie
www.poetryireland.ie

Contact *Peter Sirr*

Quarterly journal of poetry and reviews. See also **Poetry Ireland News** magazine.

Poetry London
1a Jewel Road, London E17 4QU
☎020 8521 0776   Fax 020 8521 0776
✉ editors@poetrylondon.co.uk
www.poetrylondon.co.uk

Contact *Maurice Riordan*

Poetry, listings, reviews, features and information.

Poetry Nottingham
11 Orkney Close, Stenson Fields, Derby DE24 3LW
✉ adrian.buckner@btopenworld.com

Contact *Adrian Buckner*

Poetry, articles, reviews, published quarterly.

Poetry Review
Poetry Society, 22 Betterton Street, London WC2H 9BU
☎020 7420 9883   Fax 020 7240 4818
✉ poetryreview@poetrysociety.org.uk
www.poetrysoc.org.uk

Contact *Fiona Sampson*

The senior review of contemporary poetry. Quarterly.

Poetry Salzburg Review
Dept of English and American Studies, University of Salzburg, Akademiestr. 24, A–5020 Salzburg, Austria
✉ wolfgang.goertschacher@sbg.ac.uk
www.poetrysalzburg.com

Contact *Wolfgang Görtschacher*

Poetry magazine, formerly *The Poet's Voice*. Published at the University of Salzburg.

Poetry Scotland
91–93 Main Street, Callander FK17 8BQ
www.poetryscotland.co.uk
Contact *Sally Evans*
All-poetry broadsheet with Scottish emphasis.
See also **Diehard Publishers** press.

Poetry Wales
57 Nolton Street, Bridgend CF31 3BN
☎01656 663018   Fax 01656 649226
✉ poetrywales@seren-books.com
www.poetrywales.co.uk
Contact *Robert Minhinnick*
An international magazine with a reputation
for fine writing and criticism. See also **Seren
Books** under *UK Publishers*.

Premonitions
13 Hazely Combe, Arreton, Isle of Wight
PO30 3AJ
☎01983 865668
✉ mail@pigasus.press.co.uk
www.pigasuspress.co.uk
Contact *Tony Lee*
Magazine of science fiction and horror stories,
with genre poetry and artwork. See also
Pigasus Press.

Presence
12 Grovehall Avenue, Leeds LS11 7EX
✉ martin.lucas2@btinternet.com
freespace.virgin.net/haiku.presence
Contact *Martin Lucas*
Haiku, senryu, tanka, renku and related poetry
in English.

Pulsar Poetry Magazine
34 Lineacre Close, Grange Park, Swindon
SN5 6DA
☎01793 875941
✉ pulsar.ed@btopenworld.com
www.pulsarpoetry.com
Contact *David Pike*
Hard hitting/inspirational poetry with a message and meaning. Biannual.

Purple Patch
25 Griffiths Road, West Bromwich B71 2EH
☎07950 591455
✉ ppatch66@hotmail.com
www.purplepatchpoetry.co.uk
Contact *Geoff Stevens*
Poetry mag founded 1976. Includes reviews and
gossip column. See also **The Firing Squad**
magazine and **Poetry Wednesbury** press.

Quantum Leap
York House, 15 Argyle Terrace, Rothesay, Isle
of Bute PA20 0BD
Contact *Alan Carter*
User-friendly magazine – encourages new
writers; all types of poetry – pays. See also **QQ
Press**.

Quattrocento
Bodnant, 11 Llwynon Gardens, Llandudno
LL30 2HP
☎07986 824336
✉ peter.barnes3@tesco.net
Contact *Malcolm Bradley*
An independent journal of the arts made in
Wales.

The Quiet Feather
St Mary's Cottage, Church Street, Dalton in
Furness LA15 8BA
☎01229 468967
✉ editors@thequietfeather.co.uk
www.thequietfeather.co.uk
Contact *Dominic Hall & Taissa Csaky*
Lively and eclectic quarterly: short stories,
poetry, travel, essays, cartoons, photographs, line
drawings; all welcome.

The Radiator
Flat 5, 48 Upper Parliament Street, Liverpool
L8 7LF
Contact *Scott Thurston*

Rainbow Poetry News
14 Lewes Crescent, Brighton BN2 1FH
☎01273 687053
Contact *Hugh C. Hellicar*
Quarterly with poems, articles and news of
poetry recitals in London and the South East.

Raw Edge
PO Box 4867, Birmingham B3 3HD
Contact *Dave Reeves*
New writing, free from outlets in ACE, West
Midlands area. Writers with a regional connec-
tion only. See also **The Moving Finger Press**.

Read the Music
20 Wharfedale Street, Wednesbury WS10 9AG
☎07970 441110
✉ mooncrow@tiscali.co.uk

www.poetrywednesbury.co.uk

Contact *Brendan Hawthorne*

Original poetry based on music and its influences.

The Reater
Wrecking Ball Press, 24 Cavendish Square, Hull HU3 1SS

☎01482 210226

✉ editor@wreckingballpress.com

www.wreckingballpress.com

Contact *Shane Rhodes*

No flowers, just blunt, chiselled poetry.

Red Poets – Y Beirdd Coch
26 Andrew's Close, Heolgerrig, Merthyr Tydfil CF48 1SS

☎01685 376726

✉ marc.jones@phonecoop.coop

Contact *Mike Jenkins & Marc Jones*

A magazine of left-wing poetry from Wales and beyond: socialist, republican and anarchist.

Reflections
PO Box 178, Sunderland SR1 1DU

✉ reflections1@fastmail.fm

Poetry by and for men and women of goodwill.

The Rialto
PO Box 309, Aylsham, Norwich NR11 6LN

✉ mail@therialto.co.uk

www.therialto.co.uk

Contact *Michael Mackmin*

Excellent poetry in a clear environment. Buy online at www.impressbooks.co.uk See also **Rialto Publications** press.

Roundyhouse
3 Crown Street, Port Talbot SA13 1BG

✉ srjones@alunbooks.co.uk

Contact *Sally R. Jones*

Poems and articles on poetry. Reviews. Eclectic approach.

Rubies In the Darkness
41 Grantham Road, Manor Park, London E12 5LZ

Contact *Peter Geoffrey & Paul Thompson*

Romantic, lyrical, spiritual, inspirational and mystical poetry. See also **Precious Pearl Press**.

Sable
PO Box 33504, London E9 7YE

✉ info@sablelitmag.org

Contact *Kadija Sesay*

Literary magazine for writers of African, Caribbean and Asian descent. Poetry, prose, memoirs, travel, etc.

Saw
4 Masefield Avenue, Pilton, Barnstaple EX31 1QJ

☎01271 342999

✉ sawpoems@btinternet.com

Contact *Colin Shaddick*

Poems that are radical, multicultural and international in outlook.

Scar Tissue
Pigasus Press, 13 Hazley Combe, Arreton, Isle of Wight PO30 3AJ

Contact *Tony Lee*

SF genre poetry, short fiction, cartoons and artwork.

Scribbler!
Remus House, Coltsfoot Drive, Woodston, Peterborough PE2 9JX

☎01733 890066 Fax 01733 313524

✉ youngwriters@forwardpress.co.uk

www.youngwriters.co.uk

Contact *Lynsey Hawkins*

Quarterly magazine by 7–11-year-olds: poetry, stories, guest authors, workshops, features.

Scriptor
2 Chambers Cottages, Underlyn Lane, Marden, Tonbridge TN12 9BD

☎01622 832485

✉ mail@johndench.demon.co.uk

Contact *John Dench*

Poetry, short stories, essays from the UK; publishes biennially. See also **Green Arrow Publishing** press.

Serenity
11 Stowe Croft, Lichfield WS13 6TW

Contact *Sharon Etton*

Christian poetry magazine. No free copies.

The Seventh Quarry
Dan-Y-Bryn, 74 Cwm Level Road, Brynhyfryd, Swansea SA5 9DY

Fax 01792 774070

Contact *Peter Thabit Jones*

Poetry from Swansea and beyond.

Shearsman
58 Velwell Road, Exeter EX4 4LD
☎01392 434511   Fax 01392 434511
✉ editor@shearsman.com
www.shearsman.com
Contact *Tony Frazer*

Mainly poetry, some prose, some reviews. Poetry in the modernist tradition. No fiction. See also **Shearsman Books** press.

The ShOp: A Magazine Of Poetry
Skeagh, Schull, Co. Cork, Republic of Ireland
✉ wakeman@iol.ie (not for submissions)
www.theshop-poetry-magazine.ie
Contact *John Wakeman*

International but with emphasis on Irish poetry.

Skald
6 Hill Street, Menai Bridge LL59 5AG
☎01248 712880
✉ editors@skald.co.uk
www.skald.co.uk
Contact *Zoe Skoulding*

Poetry, prose and artwork. Open to experimental/innovative writing.

Smiths Knoll
Goldings, Goldings Lane, Leiston IP16 4EB
Contact *Joanna Cutts & Michael Laskey*

Poems worth re-reading; two-week turnaround for submissions.

Smoke
The Windows Project, 96 Bold Street, Liverpool L1 4HY
☎0151 709 3688
✉ windows@windowsproject.demon.co.uk
www.windowsproject.demon.co.uk
Contact *Dave Ward*

Poetry, graphics, short prose. Biannual; 24pp.

South
PO Box 5369, Poole BH14 0XN
✉ south@martinblyth.co.uk
www.martinblyth.co.uk/south.htm
Contact *Martin Blyth*

Poetry magazine from the southern counties of England that welcomes poets from across the world.

Southword
84 Douglas Street, Cork, Republic of Ireland
www.munsterlit.ie
Contact *Frank O'Connor House*

Biannual, 120 pages of poetry, fiction, visual art and book reviews.

Sphinx
21 Hatton Green, Glenrothes KY7 4SD
✉ nell@happenstancepress.com
www.happenstancepress.com
Contact *Helena Nelson*

A magazine dedicated to the promotion, celebration and evaluation of chapbook poetry. See also **Happenstance Press**.

SPL Newsletter
Scottish Poetry Library, 5 Crichton's Close, Canongate, Edinburgh EH8 8DT
☎0131 557 2876   Fax 0131 557 8393
✉ inquiries@spl.org.uk
www.spl.org.uk
Contact *Duncan Glen*

Newsletter of the Scottish Poetry Library.

Springboard
Corrimbla, Ballina, Co. Mayo, Republic of Ireland
✉ bobgroom@eircom.net
Contact *Robert Groom*

Short fiction, poetry and articles.

Staple
74 Rangeley Road, Walkley, Sheffield S6 5DW
✉ e.barrett@shu.ac.uk
Contact *Elizabeth Barrett*

Poetry, short fiction, articles. Three issues a year.

The Stinging Fly
PO Box 6016, Dublin 8, Republic of Ireland
✉ stingingfly@gmail.com
www.stingingfly.org
Contact *Declan Meade*

New Irish and international writing. Poetry, short fiction, author interviews, essays and book reviews. See also **Stinging Fly Press**.

The Student Magazine
24 Frosty Hollow, East Hunsbury NN4 0SY
☎01604 701730   Fax 01604 701730
Contact *Jacqueline Gonzalez-Marina*

Poetry, articles, interviews, art and illustration. See also **Dandelion Arts Magazine**.

The Supplement
38 Pierrot Steps, 71 Kursaal Way, Southend on Sea SS1 2UY
✉ atlanteanpublishing@hotmail.com

www.geocities.com/dj_tyrer/DJ_TYRER.
html

Contact *D.J. Tyrer*

Non-fiction: articles, news, reviews, letters, etc.
See also **Awen**, **Bard**, **Garbaj** and **Monomyth**
magazines and **Atlantean Publishing** press.

Taliesin

Academi, 3rd Floor, Mount Stuart House,
Mount Stuart Square, Cardiff CV10 5FQ

☎029 2047 2266   Fax 029 2049 2930

✉ taliesin@academi.org
www.academi.org

Contact *Manon Rhys & Christine James*

Wales' leading Welsh language literary journal.

Tears in the Fence

38 Hod View, Stourpaine, Nr Blandford
Forum DT11 8TN

☎01258 456803   Fax 01258 454026

✉ david@davidcaddy.wanadoo.co.uk
www.thewordtravels.com

Contact *David Caddy*

A magazine looking for the unusual, perceptive,
risk-taking, lived and visionary literature.

10th Muse

33 Hartington Road, Southampton
SO14 0EW

✉ andyj@noplace.screaming.net

Contact *Andrew Jordan*

Poetry, prose and graphics. The main interest is
innovative poetry and the poetries influenced
by it.

The Third Half

16 Fane Close, Stamford PE9 1HG

☎01780 754193

Contact *Kevin Troop*

Searches for good poetry and fiction. See also
KT Publications press.

Time Haiku

105 King's Head Hill, London E4 7JG

☎020 8529 6478

✉ facey@aol.com

Contact *Doreen King*

Promotes haiku and haiku-related forms.

Tremenos Academy Review

PO Box 203, Ashford TN25 5ZT

✉ stephenovery@onetel.com

Understanding

127 Milton Road West, 7 Duddingston House
Courtyard, Edinburgh EH7 1JG

☎0131 661 1156   Fax 0131 661 1156

Contact *Denise Smith*

Original poetry, short stories, parts of plays,
reviews and articles. See also **Dionysia Press**.

The Unruly Sun

Rising Sun Arts Centre, 30 Silver Street,
Reading RG1 2ST

✉ submissions@hotmail.com
www.unrulysun.co.uk

Contact *Jennifer Hoskins & Others*

Contemporary poetry from the margins. 'If we
love it, we print it.'

Urthona

19 Mulberry Close, Cambridge CB4 2AS

☎01223 316019

✉ urthonamag@onetel.com
www.urthona.com

Contact *Ratnagarbha*

The only Buddhist arts magazine: artists, poetry,
essays, world culture from a Buddhist perspective.

Velvet Review Women Writing

154 Thornton Road, Manchester M14 7WS

✉ velvetreview@hotmail.co.uk

Contact *Becci Jackson*

Wasafiri

The Open University in London, 1–11
Hawley Crescent, Camden Town, London
NW1 8NP

☎020 7556 6110   Fax 020 7556 6187

✉ wasafiri@open.ac.uk
www.wasafiri.org

Literary journal of international and diasporic
writing with special focus on Asia, Africa and
the Caribbean.

Wordsmith

Remus House, Coltsfoot Drive, Woodston,
Peterborough PE2 9JX

☎01733 890066   Fax 01733 313524

✉ youngwriters@forwardpress.co.uk
www.youngwriters.co.uk

Contact *Allison Dowse*

Poetry, stories, guest authors, features in a quarterly magazine for 11–18-year-olds. See also
Scribbler! magazine.

The Yellow Crane
20 Princes Court, The Walk, Roath, Cardiff
CF24 3AU
Contact *J. Brookes*
Interesting new poems from S. Wales and beyond.

Zed 2 O
33 Lady Nairn Avenue, Kirkcaldy KY1 2AW
☎01592 651522
Contact *Duncan Glen*
See also **Akros Publications** press.

Organisations of Interest to Poets

A survey of some of the societies, groups and other bodies which may be of interest to practising poets. Organisations not listed should send details to the Editor for inclusion in future editions.

Academi – The Welsh National Literature Promotion Agency and Society for Writers

3rd Floor, Mount Stuart House, Mount Stuart Square, Cardiff Bay CF10 5FQ
☎029 2047 2266 Fax 029 2049 2930
✉ post@academi.org
www.academi.org

North Wales Office: Ty Newydd, Llanystumdwy, Cricieth, Gwynedd LL52 0LW

West Wales Office: Dylan Thomas Centre, Somerset Place, Swansea SA1 1RR

Glyn Jones Centre: Wales Millennium Centre, Cardiff

Chief Executive *Peter Finch*

The writers' organisation of Wales with special responsibility for literary activity, writers' residencies, writers on tour, festivals, writers' groups, readings, tours, exchanges and other development work. Academi awards financial bursaries annually, runs a criticism service and organises the **Welsh Book of the Year Awards**. Yr **Academi Gymreig/The Welsh Academy** operates the Arts Council of Wales franchise for Wales-wide literature development. It has offices in Cardiff and fieldworkers elsewhere in Wales. Publisher of the lottery-funded *Encyclopedia of Wales*, the Welsh-medium literary magazine *Taliesin*, the *Academi English-Welsh Dictionary*, co-publisher of *The New Welsh Review* along with a number of other projects. The Academi sponsors a range of annual contests including the John Tripp Award For Spoken Poetry and the prestigious **Cardiff International Poetry Competition**. Publishes *A470*, a bi-monthly literary information magazine.

Apples & Snakes

Battersea Arts Centre, Lavender Hill, London SW11 5TN
☎020 7924 3410 Fax 020 7924 3763
✉ info@applesandsnakes.org
www.applesandsnakes.org

Director *Geraldine Collinge*

Set up in 1982 as a platform for poetry which would be popular, relevant, cross-cultural and accessible to the widest possible range of people, A&S aims to stretch the boundaries of Poetry in Education and performance. Currently undergoing an extensive programme of expansion, bringing performance poetry to new places and new audiences across England.

The Arvon Foundation

See entry under *UK Writers' Courses*

The British Haiku Society

38 Wayside Avenue, Hornchurch RM12 4LL
☎01772 251827
www.britishhaikusociety.org

General Secretary *Doreen King*

Formed in 1990. Promotes the appreciation and writing within the British Isles of haiku, senyru, tanka, haibun and renku, and welcomes overseas members. It provides tutorials, workshops, readings, critical comment and information. The Society runs a haiku library and administers a haiku and haibun contest. The journal, *Blithe Spirit*, is produced quarterly. The Society has active local groups and issues a regular newsletter. Current membership details can be obtained from the website.

Contemporary Poetics Research Centre

School of English and Humanities, Birkbeck College, Malet Street, London WC1E 7HX
✉ w.rowe@bbk.ac.uk *or* c.watts@bbk.ac.uk
www.bbk.ac.uk/eh/research/contemppoeticscentre

Contact *Will Rowe*

Dedicated to fostering research and practice in all modes and formats of contemporary poetry. It runs a Creative Reading Workshop, holds readings, performances, talks and debates and organises conferences, the latest of which was E Poetry London 2005. It collaborates closely with Royal Holloway University of London and the Centre for Cultural Poetics at the University of

Southampton, e.g. on the British Electronic Poetry Centre at www.soton.ac.uk/~bepc Poets associated with the Centre include Ulli Freer, Caroline Bergvall and Bill Griffiths. The Centre publishes the web journal www.pores.bbk.ac.uk

The Eight Hand Gang
5 Cross Farm, Station Road North,
Fearnhead, Warrington WA2 0QG

Secretary *John F. Haines*

An association of SF poets. Publishes *Handshake*, a single-sheet newsletter of SF poetry and information available free in exchange for an s.a.e.

57 Productions
57 Effingham Road, Lee Green, London
SE12 8NT
☎020 8463 0866   Fax 020 8463 0866
✉ paul@57productions.com
www.57productions.com

Contact *Paul Beasley*

Specialises in the promotion of poetry and its production through an agency service, a programme of events and a series of audio publications. Services are available to event promoters, festivals, education institutions and the media. Poets represented include Jean 'Binta' Breeze, Adrian Mitchell, John Cooper Clarke and Liz Lochhead. 57 Productions' series of audio cassettes, CDs and Poetry in Performance compilations offer access to some of the most exciting poets working in Britain today – check their Poetry Jukebox on their excellent website.

The Football Poets
4 The Retreat, Butterow, Stroud GL5 2LS
☎01453 757376
✉ editors@footballpoets.org
www.footballpoets.org

Editor & Performance *Crispin Thomas*
Co-Editors *Stuart Butler, Simon Williams, Parry Maguire*

The Football Poets exist to promote and encourage the writing and performing of football poetry. Formed in 1995, they appear regularly at festivals and venues around the country. They also provide comprehensive and entertaining football poetry workshops in schools and communities. Their website is a fast, free and entertaining mix of literature and soccer poetry from around the world. Anyone may contribute.

The Poetry Archive
PO Box 286, Stroud GL6 1AL
☎01453 832090   Fax 01453 836450
✉ info@poetryarchive.org

Directors *Richard Carrington, Andrew Motion*

A permanent archive of audio recordings of work by poets who write in English. New 60-minute recordings are made for the Archive by a wide-ranging list of poets; extracts from those recordings are available on their website launched in 2005. The site also contains a wealth of educational and intepretative information and the full-length recordings are available on CD for purchase by mail order. A registered charity, the Archive intends to ensure that all significant poets are recorded for posterity and that their recordings are fully valued and enjoyed.

The Poetry Book Society
Fourth Floor, 2 Tavistock Place, London
WC1H 9RA
☎020 7833 9247   Fax 020 7833 5990
✉ info@poetrybooks.co.uk
www.poetrybooks.co.uk
www.poetrybookshoponline.com

Director *Chris Holifield*

For readers, writers, students and teachers of poetry. Founded in 1953 by T.S. Eliot and funded by the Arts Council, the PBS is a unique membership organisation and book club providing up-to-date and comprehensive information about poetry from publishers in the UK and Ireland. Members receive the quarterly *PBS Bulletin* packed with articles by poets, poems, news, listings and access to discounts of at least 25% off featured titles. These range from modern classics to contemporary works. Subscriptions start at £10. The relaunched PBS website has a recruitment area and a closed section for members. PBS also offers online a range of over 30,000 poetry titles. During 2005 the PBS relaunched the children's Poetry Bookshelf (www.childrenspoetrybookshelf.co.uk), a wider range of books and new membership schemes for parents, grandparents and libraries. Also runs the annual **T.S. Eliot Prize** for the best collection of new poetry. In 2004 it ran the Next Generation Poets promotion.

The Poetry Business
The Studio, Byram Arcade, Westgate,
Huddersfield HD1 1ND
☎01484 434840   Fax 01484 426566
✉ edit@poetrybusiness.co.uk
www.poetrybusiness.co.uk

Directors *Peter Sansom, Janet Fisher*

Founded in 1986, the Business publishes *The North* magazine and books, pamphlets and cassettes under the Smith/Doorstop imprint. It runs an annual competition and organises writing days and a Writing School. Send an s.a.e. for full details.

Poetry Can

Unit 11, 20–22 Hepburn Road, Bristol
BS2 8UD
0117 942 6976   Fax 0117 944 1478
✉ info@poetrycan.wanadoo.co.uk
www.poetrycan.co.uk

Founded in 1995, Poetry Can is a poetry development agency working predominantly across the Bristol, Bath & North East Somerset and South Gloucestershire areas. It organises events such as the annual **Bristol Poetry Festival**, lifelong learning projects and provides information and advice concerning all aspects of poetry to individuals, agencies and organisations. It also hosts the Literature South West website.

Poetry Ireland/Eigse Eireann

2 Proud's Lane, Dublin 2, Republic of Ireland
☎00 353 1 478 9974   Fax 00 353 1 478 0205
✉ poetry@iol.ie
www.poetryireland.ie

Education ☎00 353 671 4216 Writers in Schools scheme ☎00 353 1 475 8601

Director Joseph Woods

Poetry Ireland is the national organisation for poetry in Ireland, with its four core activities being readings, publications, education and an information and resource service. Organises readings by Irish and international poets countrywide. Through its website, telephone, post and public enquiries, Poetry Ireland operates as a clearing house for everything pertaining to poetry in Ireland. Operates the Writers in Schools scheme. Publishes *Poetry Ireland News*, a bi-monthly newsletter containing information on events, competitions and opportunities. *Poetry Ireland Review* appears quarterly and is the journal of record for poetry in Ireland; current editor: *Peter Sirr*.

The Poetry Library

Royal Festival Hall, Level 5, London SE1 8XX
☎020 7921 0943/0664   Fax 020 7921 0939
✉ info@poetrylibrary.org.uk
www.poetrylibrary.org.uk
www.poetrymagazines.org.uk

Librarian Simon Smith

Founded by the Arts Council in 1953. A collection of 60,000 titles of modern poetry since 1912, from Georgian to Rap, representing all English-speaking countries and including translations into English by contemporary poets. Two copies of each title are held, one for loan and one for reference. A wide range of poetry magazines and ephemera from all over the world are kept along with casettes, records and videos for consultation, with many available for loan. There is a children's poetry section with teacher's resource collection. An information service compiles lists of poetry magazines, competitions, publishers, groups and workshops which are available from the Library on receipt of a large s.a.e. or direct from the website. The main website also has a noticeboard for lost quotations through which it tries to identify lines or fragments of poetry which have been sent in by other readers. The Library is closed as part of the Royal Festival Hall refurbishment until June 2007 but the enquiry service still operates via e-mail, the phone and letter. The Library's website is one of the best poetry resources on the Net.

Poetry London

1a Jewel Road, London E17 4QU
✉ editors@poetrylondon.co.uk
www.poetrylondon.co.uk

Contacts *Kathryn Maris* (listings), *Maurice Riordan* (poetry editor), *Scott Verner* (reviews)

Published three times a year, *Poetry London* includes poetry by new and established writers, reviews of recent collections and anthologies, articles on issues relating to poetry, and an encyclopædic listings section of virtually everything to do with poetry in the capital and elsewhere in the UK.

The Poetry School

1a Jewel Road, London E17 4QU
☎020 8223 0401   Fax 020 8223 0401
✉ jacqueline@poetryschool.com
www.poetryschool.com

Administrator *Julia Bird*
Marketing Manager *Jacqueline Gabbitas*

Funded by Arts Council England, London, The Poetry School offers a wide range of courses and workshops on writing and reading poetry and is open to anyone regardless of experience or formal qualifications. Tutors include Graham Fawcett, Stephen Knight, Jane Draycott, Carole Satyamurti, Myra Schneider and Mimi Khalvati. The School provides a forum for practitioners to share experiences, develop skills and extend appreciation of the traditional and innovative aspects of their art. There are Special Events with visiting poets such as Marilyn Hacker, Jorie Graham, Molly Peacock, Galway

Kinnell, Paul Muldoon, Alfred Corn and August Kleinzahler. The Poetry School is a Registered Charity No. 1069314.

The Poetry Society

22 Betterton Street, London WC2H 9BX
☎020 7240 9881 Fax 020 7240 4818
✉ info@poetrysociety.org.uk
www.poetrysociety.org.uk
Director *Jules Mann*

Founded in 1909 which ought to make it venerable, the Society exists to help poets and poetry thrive in Britain. In the past decade it has undergone a renaissance, reaching out from its Covent Garden base to promote the national health of poetry in a range of imaginative ways. Membership costs £35 for individuals. *Poetry News* membership is £15. Current activities include:

- Quarterly magazine of new verse, views and criticism, *Poetry Review*.
- Quarterly newsletter, *Poetry News*, with lively relevant articles for members.
- Promotions, events and cooperation with Britain's many literature festivals, poetry venues and poetry publishers.
- **National Poetry Competition** with a £5000 first prize.
- A manuscript diagnosis service, *The Poetry Prescription*, which gives detailed reports on submissions. Reduced rates for members.
- Provides information and advice, publishes books, posters and resources for schools and libraries. Education membership costs £50 (secondary) or £30 (primary) which includes free poetry anthologies, lesson plans and a subscription to Poems on the Underground. Publications include *The Poetry Book For Primary Schools* and *Jumpstart Poetry for the Secondary School*, colourful poetry posters for Keystages 1, 2, 3 and 4. Many of Britain's most popular poets – including Michael Rosen, Roger McGough and Jackie Kay – contribute, offering advice and inspiration.
- The Society's online poetry classroom is at www.poetryclass.net
- The Poetry Café serving snacks and drinks to members, friends and guests, part of The Poetry Place, a venue for many poetry activities – readings, workshops and poetry launches. This space is available for bookings (☎020 7420 9887).
- *Poetry Landmarks of Britain*, a free resource on the Society's website, packed with regional poetry places, publishers, venues and regular events.

The Poetry Trust

The Cut, 9 New Cut, Halesworth IP9 8BY
☎01986 835950 Fax 01986 835949
✉ info@thepoetrytrust.org
www.thepoetrytrust.org
Director *Naomi Jaffa*

The flagship literature organisation for the East of England, funded by Arts Council England. The Trust promotes high quality contemporary poetry and works to increase people's enjoyment of reading, writing and teaching poetry. It organises the renowned international **Aldeburgh Poetry Festival**, held annually over the first weekend in November; the **Jerwood Aldeburgh First Collection Prize**; and a range of poetry events, workshops and residential writing courses. Its creative education programme, funded by the Paul Hamlyn Foundation, includes writing workshops for teachers and students and poetry tours to schools. The Poetry Trust, Registered Charity No. 1102893.

Point

Ithaca, Apdo. 125, E–03590 Altea, Spain
☎00 34 96 584 2350 Fax 00 34 96 688 2767
✉ elpoeta@point-editions.com
www.point-editions.com
Also at: Schapenstraat 157, B–1750 Lennik, Belgium
Director *Germain Droogenbroodt*

Founded as POetry INTernational in 1984, Point is based in Spain and Belgium. A multilingual publisher of contemporary verse from *established* poets, the organisation has brought out more than 80 titles in at least eight languages, including English. Point Editions runs the original work alongside a verse translation into Dutch made in cooperation with the poet. The organisation's website features the world's best known and unknown poets in English, Spanish and Dutch. Point also co-organises an annual international poetry festival.

Regional Arts Councils

See *Arts Councils and Regional Offices*, pages 540–1.

Scottish Pamphlet Poetry

No 4 Cottage, High Swinton, Masham HG4 4JH
✉ hazel@scottish-pamphlet-poetry.biz
www.scottish-pamphlet-poetry.com
Administrator *Hazel Cameron*

A publisher collective of more than 35 mainly

Scottish-based presses promoting poetry published as pamphlets. A pamphlet is defined as not less than six pages but no more than 30 and with a first edition of less than 300 copies. The organisation has an excellent website, publishes a video, runs book fairs and events, and administers the annual Callum Macdonald Memorial Award created to recognise publishing skill and effort in the pamphlet form.

Scottish Poetry Library

5 Crichton's Close, Canongate, Edinburgh
EH8 8DT
☎0131 557 2876
✉ inquiries@spl.org.uk
www.spl.org.uk
Director *Robyn Marsack*

A comprehensive reference and lending collection of work by Scottish poets in Gaelic, Scots and English, plus the work of British and international poets. Stock includes books, tapes, videos, news cuttings and magazines. Borrowing is free to all. Services include a postal lending scheme, for which there is a small fee; schools workshops throughout Scotland on application; exhibitions; bibliographies; publications; information and promotion in the field of poetry. Also available is an online catalogue and index to Scottish poetry periodicals. There is a Friends' scheme costing £20 annually. Friends receive a newsletter and other benefits and support the library.

Second Light

9 Greendale Close, London SE22 8TG
✉ dilyswood@tiscali.co.uk
Director *Dilys Wood*

A network of over 350 women poets, major names and less well-known. With its publishing arm, Second Light Publications, the network aims to develop and promote women's poetry. Issues a twice-yearly newsletter with poetry, articles and reviews; runs an annual poetry competition; holds residential workshops, readings; has published three anthologies of women's poetry.

Spiel Unlimited

20 Coxwell Street, Cirencester GL7 2BH
☎01285 640470/07814 830031
✉ spiel@arbury.freeserve.co.uk *or* info@spiel.wanadoo.co.uk
www.thepeoplespoet.com/spiel
Directors *Marcus Moore, Sara-Jane Arbury*

'Spoken word, written word, anywhere, everywhere' with two writers who put a positive charge in live literature by organising quirky and original events such as Slam!Fests, Spontaneity Days and Living Room Poetry performances, hosting UK poetry slams and running *word*shops for schools and adults. Also produce *SPIEL*, a monthly e-mail newsletter. Specialists in breathing new life into literature.

Survivors' Poetry

Studio 11, Bickerton House, 25–27 Bickerton Road, London N19 5JT
☎020 7281 4654 Fax 020 7272 9278
✉ info@survivorspoetry.org.uk
www.survivorspoetry.com
National Outreach
royb@survivorspoetry.org.uk
National Mentoring Scheme & *Poetry Express* alan@survivorspoetry.org.uk

A unique national literature organisation promoting poetry by survivors of mental distress through workshops, readings and performances to audiences all over the UK. It was founded in 1991 by four poets with first-hand experience of the mental health system. Survivors' community outreach work provides training and performance workshops and publishing projects. Survivors' Poetry National Mentoring Scheme continues to publish new survivor poets in solo pamphlets under the Survivors Press imprint until 2007. For the organisation's quarterly magazine, see *Poetry Express*. Survivors work with those who have survived mental distress and those who empathise with their experience.

Ty Newydd

Llanystumdwy, Criccieth LL52 0LW
☎01766 522811 Fax 01766 523095
✉ post@tynewydd.org
www.tynewydd.org
Executive Director *Sally Baker*

Run by the Taliesin Trust, an independent, Arvon-style residential writers centre established in the one-time home of Lloyd George in North Wales. The programme (in both Welsh and English) has a regular poetry content. (See also *UK Writers' Courses.*) Fees start at £200 for weekends and £400 for week-long courses. Among the many tutors to-date have been: Gillian Clarke, Owen Sheers, Robert Minhinnick, Liz Lochhead, Michael Longley, Ian Macmillan and Jo Shapcott. Send for the centre's descriptive leaflets and programme of courses.

The Virtual Writing School

Manchester Metropolitan University, Dept. of English, The Virtual Writing School, Geoffrey Manton Building, Rosamond Street West, off Oxford Road, Manchester M15 6LL
☎0161 247 1735
✉ h.beck@mmu.ac.uk
www.mmu.ac.uk/h–ss/eng

Contact *Heather Beck*

Manchester Metropolitan University's creative writing courses offer a virtual poetry strand with tutors Michael Symmons Roberts, Jeffrey Wainwright and others. The qualification is a MA/PgDip. Enquire early as places are strictly limited. The school also offers virtual novel writing. (See also *UK and Irish Writers' Courses*.)

Small Presses

Aard Press
c/o Aardverx, 31 Mountearl Gardens, London SW16 2NL
Managing Editors *Dawn Redwood, D. Jarvis*

Founded 1971. Publishes artists' bookworks, experimental/visual poetry and art theory, topographics, ephemera and international mail-art documentation. Very small editions. No unsolicited material or proposals.
ROYALTIES not paid. No sale-or-return deals.

Accent Press
PO Box 50, Pembroke Dock SA72 6WY
☎01646 681389 Fax 0870 130 6934
✉ info@accentpress.co.uk
www.accentpress.co.uk
Managing Editor *Hazel Cushion*

Founded 2002. Publishes fiction, health, humour and children's books. 11 titles in 2005. Visit the website for submission guidelines.
ROYALTIES twice-yearly.

Authors' Rating This regional publisher has been raising capital to take its first tentative steps into the mainstream. One to watch.

Allardyce, Barnett, Publishers
14 Mount Street, Lewes BN7 1HL
☎01273 479393
www.abar.net
Publisher *Fiona Allardyce*
Managing Editor *Anthony Barnett*

Founded 1981. Publishes art, literature and music. IMPRINT **Allardyce Book**. About 3 titles a year. Unsolicited mss and synopses cannot be considered.

Alphard Press
See **ignotus press**

Anglo-Saxon Books
25 Brocks Road, Swaffham PE37 7XG
☎0845 530 4200
✉ tony@asbooks.co.uk
www.asbooks.co.uk
Managing Editor *Tony Linsell*

Founded 1990 to promote a greater awareness of and interest in early English history, language and culture. Publishes Anglo-Saxon history, culture, language. Please phone before sending mss. About 5 titles a year.
ROYALTIES at standard rate.

Apex Publishing Ltd
PO Box 7086, Clacton on Sea CO15 5WN
☎001255 428500 Fax 0870 046 6536
✉ enquiry@apexpublishing.co.uk
www.apexpublishing.co.uk
Managing Editor *Susan Kidby*

Founded 2002. Subsidy publishing company for unknown and established authors. Publishes poetry, self-help, non-fiction, fiction, sci-fi, history, humour, sport, education and textbooks, economics, crime, children's books, biography, autobiography, academic, women's interests, medical, philosophy, law, pets, religion and travel. 42 titles in print. Welcomes unsolicited mss, synopses and ideas for books. Approach in writing to the address above.
ROYALTIES annually.

Ascendere Publishing
35 Anders Corner, Bracknell RG42 1PU
☎01344 307206
✉ books@ascendere.co.uk
www.ascendere.co.uk
Managing Editor *Carolyn Wilson*

Founded 2005. Publishes all categories apart from poetry. 12 titles in 2005 Unsolicited mss, synopses and ideas welcome. Approach in writing; send first three chapters, synopsis, author profile and return postage. General enquiries via e-mail/phone also welcome.

Authority Publishing
13 Coton Crescent, Shrewsbury SY1 2NY
☎01743 233563 Fax 08704 875827
✉ mail@authoritypublishing.co.uk
www.authoritypublishing.co.uk
Managing Editors *Kerri Miles, David Littlefield*

Founded 2004. Self-publishing service offered by a team of published authors, designers and production professionals. Publishes across a wide range of categories, working with individual authors and commercial organisations. 12

titles to date. Phone or e-mail for a brochure and submission form.

Authors retain all royalties.

M.&M. Baldwin
24 High Street, Cleobury Mortimer, Kidderminster DY14 8BY
☎01299 270110 Fax 01299 270110
✉ mb@mbaldwin.free-online.co.uk

Managing Editor *Dr Mark Baldwin*

Founded 1978. Publishes local interest/history, WW2 codebreaking and inland waterways books. Up to 5 titles a year. Unsolicited mss, synopses and ideas for books welcome (not general fiction).

ROYALTIES paid.

Barny Books
Hough on the Hill, near Grantham NG32 2BB
☎01400 250246/01522 790009
Fax 01400 251737

Managing Director/Editorial Head *Molly Burkett*
Business Manager *Jayne Thompson*

Founded with the aim of encouraging new writers and illustrators. Publishes mainly children's books but also adult fiction and non-fiction. Offers schools' projects where students help to produce books.

Too small a concern to have the staff/resources to deal with unsolicited mss. Writers with strong ideas should approach Molly Burkett by letter in the first instance. Also runs a readership and advisory service for new writers (£15 fee for short stories or illustrations; £40 for full-length stories).

Division of profits 50/50.

Authors' Rating Burkett is having problems with the duplication of the name of her company. Authors who want to contact Molly should make sure that they have the correct address for her Barny Books.

BB Books
See entry under *Poetry Presses*

The Better Book Company Ltd
Forum House, Chichester PO19 7DN
☎01243 530113 Fax 01243 531033
✉ betterbook@btconnect.com
www.better-book.co.uk

Managing Editor *Jill Field*
Business Manager *John Littlefield*

Founded 1996. Offers editorial, design and printing services together with a marketing advisory service to authors wishing to self-publish their work in all genre. Produces fiction, histories, memoirs, poetry, religious, scientific, company histories. A free booklet, *A Complete Guide to Self-Publishing*, is available on request. 45 titles in 2005.

Between the Lines
9 Woodstock Road, London N4 3ET
☎020 8374 5526 Fax 020 8374 5736
✉ btluk@aol.com
www.interviews-with-poets.com

Editorial Board *Peter Dale, Philip Hoy, J.D. McClatchy*
Editorial Assistant *Ryan Roberts*

Founded 1998. Publishes in book form extended interviews with leading contemporary poets. Thirteen volumes currently in print, featuring Peter Dale, John Ashbery, Charles Simic, Ian Hamilton, Donald Justice, Seamus Heaney, Richard Wilbur, Thom Gunn, Donald Hall, Anthony Hecht, Anthony Thwaite, Michael Hamburger and W.D. Snodgrass. Each volume includes a career sketch, a comprehensive bibliography and a representative selection of quotations from the poets' critics and reviewers. More recent volumes include photographs as well as previously uncollected poems. A second series, featuring slightly younger poets, is to be launched in 2006. The first of the volumes will feature Dick Davis, Rachel Hadas and Timothy Steele.

The Bewildered Publishing Company Ltd
Argoed Hall, Tregaron SY25 6JR
☎01974 298070
✉ john.wilson@virgin.net

Publisher *John Wilson*

Founded in 1999 'to provide a direct route to the book market for authors, with an unconventional approach to writing and publishing'. Publishes humorous paperbacks. No unsolicited material; initial inquiry by telephone, e-mail or letter.

ROYALTIES not paid.

Bitter Lemon Press
37 Arundel Gardens, London W11 2LW
☎020 7727 7927
✉ books@bitterlemonpress.com
www.bitterlemonpress.com

Managing Editor *Laurence Colchester*

Founded 2003. Publishes fiction only – mostly crime fiction. 6 titles in 2006. No unsolicited mss; welcomes synopses and ideas for books. Approach by e-mail in the first instance.

ROYALTIES annually.

Black Cat Books
See **Neil Miller Publications**

The Book Castle
12 Church Street, Dunstable LU5 4RU
☎01582 605670 Fax 01582 662431
✉ bc@book-castle.co.uk
www.book-castle.co.uk

Managing Editor *Paul Bowes*
Assistant Editor *Sally Siddons*

Founded 1986. Publishes non-fiction of local interest (Bedfordshire, Hertfordshire, Buckinghamshire, Oxfordshire, the Chilterns). Over 100 titles in print. 12 titles a year. Unsolicited mss, synopses and ideas for books welcome.

ROYALTIES paid.

Brilliant Publications
1 Church View, Sparrow Hall Farm,
Edlesborough, Dunstable LU6 2ES
☎01525 229720 Fax 01525 229725
✉ sales@brilliantpublications.co.uk
www.brilliantpublications.co.uk

Publisher *Priscilla Hannaford*

Founded 1993. Publishes practical resource books for teachers, parents and others working with 0–13-year-olds. About 10–15 titles a year. Submit synopsis and sample pages in the first instance. Most of the books have black and white insides and many have pupil sheets that may be photocopied. Potential authors are strongly advised to look at the format of existing books before submitting synopses. 'We do not publish children's picture books.'

ROYALTIES twice-yearly.

The Brodie Press
✉ thebrodiepress@hotmail.com
www.thebrodiepress.co.uk

Managing Editors *Hannah Sheppard,*
Tom Sperlinger

Founded 2002. Publishes poetry and anthologies. SERIES *The Brodie Poets*, launched in 2003, including Julie-ann Rowell, Poetry Book Society Pamphlet Choice, Winter 2003. Send synopses and proposals by e-mail in the first instance.

Charlewood Press
7 Weavers Place, Chandlers Ford SO53 1TU
☎023 8026 1192
✉ gponting@clara.net

www.home.clara.net/gponting/index-page11.html

Managing Editors *Gerald Ponting, Anthony Light*

Founded 1987. Publishes local history books and walks booklets on Hampshire and adjacent counties, especially around the Fordingbridge area. Mss in this field considered.

Chrysalis Press
7 Lower Ladyes Hills, Kenilworth CV8 2GN
☎01926 855223
✉ editor@margaretbuckley.com
www.margaretbuckley.com

Managing Editor *Brian Boyd*

Founded 1994. Publishes fiction, literary criticism and biography. No unsolicited mss.

ROYALTIES paid.

CNP Publications
See **Lyfrow Trelyspen**

Contact Publishing Ltd
Unit 346, 176 Finchley Road, London
NW3 6BT
☎020 7871 6990
✉ info@contact-publishing.co.uk
www.contact-publishing.co.uk

Managing Director *Anne Kontoyannis*

Founded 2003. Publishes general fiction, non-fiction, self help and New Age. No children's, political, sports or westerns. 3 titles in 2005. 'Interested in seeing mss by new authors with original angles and new ideas.' See website for author guidelines. Send synopsis, three sample chapters and outline in the first instance.

ROYALTIES twice-yearly.

The Cosmic Elk
68 Elsham Crescent, Lincoln LN6 3YS
☎01522 820922
✉ post@cosmicelk.co.uk
www.cosmicelk.co.uk

Contact *Heather Hobden*

Founded 1988. Publishes easily updated books on science, history and the history of science. Websites designed and maintained, with or without associated printed books. 'Authors and books always welcome.' Check the website first for information and contacts.

Crescent Moon Publishing and Joe's Press
PO Box 393, Maidstone ME14 5XU
☎01622 729593
✉ cresmopub@yahoo.co.uk

www.crescentmoon.org.uk

Managing Editor *Jeremy Robinson*

Founded 1988 to publish critical studies of figures such as D.H. Lawrence, Thomas Hardy, André Gide, Walt Disney, Rilke, Leonardo da Vinci, Mark Rothko, C.P. Cavafy and Hélène Cixous. Publishes literature, criticism, media, art, feminism, painting, poetry, travel, guidebooks, cinema and some fiction. Literary magazine, *Passion*, launched February 1994 (quarterly). *Pagan America*, twice-yearly anthology of American poetry. About 15–20 titles per year. Unsolicited synopses and ideas welcome but approach in writing first and send an s.a.e. Do not send whole mss.

ROYALTIES negotiable.

Crossbridge Books

345 Old Birmingham Road, Bromsgrove B60 1NX

☎0121 447 7897 Fax 0121 445 1063

✉ crossbridgebooks@btinternet.com

www.crossbridgebooks.com

Managing Director *Eileen Mohr*

Founded 1995. Publishes Christian books for adults and children. IMPRINT **Mohr Books**. 4–5 titles a year including Trevor Dearing's latest books. No New Age or books not biblically Christian.

ROYALTIES twice-yearly.

Culva House Publications

10 The Carrs, Sleights, Whitby YO21 1RR

☎01947 810819

✉ alan@culvahouse.co.uk

www.culvahouse.co.uk

Managing Editor *Alan Whitworth*

Founded in 1986 as a part-time self-publishing venture and grew into a full-time business in 2000. Publishes architecture and local history; biography. Unsolicited material welcome; approach by letter or e-mail.

ROYALTIES paid.

Day Books

Orchard Piece, Crawborough, Charlbury OX7 3TX

☎01608 811196 Fax 01608 811196

✉ diaries@day-books.com

www.day-books.com

Managing Editor *James Sanderson*

Founded in 1997 to publish a series of great diaries from around the world. Unsolicited mss, synopses and ideas welcome. Include postage if return of material is required.

Diggory Press

Three Rivers, Minions, Liskeard PL14 5LE

✉ publish@diggorypress.com

www.diggorypress.com

Managing Director *R. Franklin*

Founded 2005. Originally started as an imprint of **Meadow Books**, it has overtaken its parent company in terms of productivity and profit. Publishes mainly nursing, military and Christian titles and Cornish/Cornwall books. IMPRINT **Exposure Publishing** Christian-run self publishing service for all subjects (including other religious perspectives and alternative lifestyles): fiction, non-fiction, poetry, drama, biography, autobiography, children's picture books. 'Diggory Press will not publish anything that directly conflicts with traditional Christian beliefs and rarely publishes fiction.' Initial enquiries and submissions by e-mail only to Diggory Press; no telephone calls.

The Dragonby Press

4-A Enterprise Way, Roxby Road, Winterton DN15 9SU

☎01724 733011

✉ rich@rah2williams.freeserve.co.uk

freespace.virgin.net/rah.williams

Managing Editor *Richard Williams*

Founded 1987 to publish affordable bibliography for reader, collector and dealer. About 3 titles a year. Unsolicited mss, synopses and ideas welcome for bibliographical projects only.

ROYALTIES paid.

Dramatic Lines

PO Box 201, Twickenham TW2 5RQ

☎020 8296 9502 Fax 020 8296 9503

✉ mail@dramaticlinespublishers.co.uk

www.dramaticlines.co.uk

Managing Editor *John Nicholas*

Founded to promote drama for all. Publications with a wide variety of theatrical applications including classroom use and school assemblies, drama examinations, auditions, festivals, theatre group performance, musicals and handbooks. Unsolicited drama-related mss, proposals and synopses welcome; enclose s.a.e.

ROYALTIES paid.

DreamStar Books

Lasyard House, Underhill Street, Bridgnorth WV16 4BB

☎0870 777 3339 Fax 01746 765354

✉ enquiries@dreamstarbooks.com

www.dreamstarbooks.com

Owner *Dreamstar Books*
Managing Director *Mark Horton-Oliver*

Founded 2002. Assists new and unpublished authors gain recognition for their work by offering low cost self-publishing/printing. 'No royalty tie-ins; authors are free to pursue traditional publishing deal.' Mss, synopses and ideas welcome.

Edgewell Publishing

5A Front Street, Prudhoe NE42 5HJ
☎01661 835330 Fax 01661 835330
✉ keith@tynedale-languages.co.uk
www.tynedale-languages.co.uk

Editor *Keith Minton*

Quarterly short story and poetry magazine (*Lively Tales*) to encourage writing from new and established writers, also children. Writers from the North East especially welcome.

Educational Heretics Press

113 Arundel Drive, Bramcote Hills,
Nottingham NG9 3FQ
☎0115 925 7261 Fax 0115 925 7261
www.edheretics.gn.apc.org

Directors *Janet & Roland Meighan*

Non-profit venture which aims to question the dogmas of schooling in particular and education in general, and establish the logistics of the next personalised learning system. No unsolicited material. Enquiries only.

Royalties not paid but under review.

Eilish Press

4 Collegiate Crescent, Broomhall Park,
Sheffield S10 2BA
☎07973 353964
✉ eilishpress@hotmail.co.uk
eilishpress.tripod.com

Head of Marketing *Suzi Kapadia*

Specialises in academic work and popular non-fiction in the areas of women's studies, human rights and anti-racism. Also produces children's literature with humanitarian themes. No adult fiction. Unsolicited mss cannot be accepted at this time. However, ideas for children's books may be sent by e-mail.

Royalties annually.

Enable Enterprises

PO Box 1974, Coventry CV3 1YF
☎0800 358 8484 Fax 0800 358 8484
✉ writers@enableenterprises.com
www.enableenterprises.com

Chief Executive *Simon Stevens*

Enable Enterprises provides a wide range of accessibilty and disability services including publications on relevant issues. It welcomes unsolicited material related to accessibility and disability issues.

Exposure Publishing

See **Diggory Press**

Fand Music Press

Glenelg, 10 Avon Close, Petersfield
GU31 4LG
☎01730 267341 Fax 01730 267341
✉ Paul@fandmusic.com
www.fandmusic.com

Managing Editor *Peter Thompson*

Founded in 1989 as a sheet music publisher, Fand Music Press has expanded its range to include CD recordings and books on music. Also publishes poetry and short stories. 10 titles a year. No unsolicited mss. Write with ideas in the first instance.

Feather Books

PO Box 438, Shrewsbury SY3 0WN
☎01743 872177 Fax 01743 872177
✉ john@waddysweb.freeuk.com
www.waddysweb.freeuk.com

Managing Director *Rev. John Waddington-Feather*
Directors *David Grundy, Tony Reavill, Paul Evans*

Founded 1980 to publish writers' group work. All material has a strong Christian ethos. Publishes poetry (mainly, but not exclusively, religious); Christian mystery novels (the Revd. D.I. Blake Hartley series); Christian children's *Quill Hedgehog* novels; seasonal poetry collections and *The Poetry Church* quarterly magazine. Produces poetry, drama and hymn CD/cassettes; also the anthology 'Pilgrimages' ed. Professor Walter Nash ('a milestone in Christian poetry publishing'). About 20 titles a year. All correspondence to include s.a.e., please.

Fidra Books

60 Craigcrook Road, Edinburgh EH4 3PJ
☎0131 343 3118
✉ vanessa@fidrabooks.co.uk
www.fidrabooks.co.uk

Managing Editor *Vanessa Robertson*

Founded 2005. Publishes children's fiction, specialising in reprints of sought-after 20th century children's fiction. No unsolicited material; 'we would consider original work based on the characters or genres of our main list'. Approach by letter or e-mail.

ROYALTIES quarterly.

Five Leaves Publications

PO Box 8786, Nottingham NG1 9AW
☎0115 969 3597
✉ info@fiveleaves.co.uk
www.fiveleaves.co.uk

Contact *Ross Bradshaw*

Founded 1995 (taking over the publishing programme of Mushroom Bookshop). Publishes fiction, poetry, social history, politics and Jewish interest. Also publishes for the Anglo-Catalan Society. Titles normally commissioned. About 10 titles a year.

ROYALTIES paid.

Flambard

Stable Cottage, East Fourstones, Hexham NE47 5DX
☎01434 674360 Fax 01434 674178
✉ flambardpress@btinternet.com
www.flambardpress.co.uk

Also at: 43 Linskill Street, North Shields NE30 1DR

Managing Editors *Peter Lewis, Will Mackie*

Founded 1990. Publishes poetry and literary fiction. 8 titles in 2005. Welcomes unsolicited mss but essential to send preliminary letter (not fax or e-mail) with details of author and either a sample of 10 poems or a synopsis plus 2–3 chapters and s.a.e.

ROYALTIES paid.

Foxbury Press

15 St Michael's Road, Winchester SO23 9JE
☎01962 864037

Managing Editor *Robert Cross*

Founded 2000. 4 titles published.

Frontier Publishing

Windetts, Kirstead NR15 1EG
☎01508 558174
✉ frontier.pub@macunlimited.net
www.frontierpublishing.co.uk

Managing Editor *John Black*

Founded 1983. Publishes travel, photography, sculptural history and literature. 2–3 titles a year. No unsolicited mss; synopses and ideas.

ROYALTIES paid.

Galactic Central Publications

Imladris, 25A Copgrove Road, Leeds LS8 2SP
✉ gcp@philsp.com

www.philsp.com

Managing Editor *Phil Stephensen-Payne*

Founded 1982 in the US. Publishes science fiction bibliographies. All new publications originate in the UK. About 4 titles a year. Unsolicited mss, synopses and ideas (for bibliographies) welcome.

Galore Park Publishing Ltd

19/21 Sayer's Lane, Tenterden TN30 6BW
☎0870 234 2304 Fax 0870 234 2305
✉ info@galorepark.co.uk
www.galorepark.co.uk

Managing Director *Nicholas Oulton*

Founded 1999. Publishes school textbooks and children's books. 11 titles in 2005. No unsolicited mss. Synopses and ideas welcome; send by e-mail.

ROYALTIES twice-yearly.

GB Publishing Services

26 Percheron Drive, Spalding PE11 3GH
☎01775 768902
✉ garry.baker@btinternet.com
www.garrybaker.cjb.net

Managing Editor *Garry Baker*

Founded 2004. Publishes romance, fiction, non-fiction, history. Send first three chapters and synopsis (on A4 paper) with s.a.e.

ROYALTIES annually.

Glosa Education Organisation

PO Box 18, Richmond TW9 2GE
www.glosa.org

Managing Editor *Wendy Ashby*

Founded 1981. Publishes textbooks, dictionaries and translations for the teaching, speaking and promotion of Glosa (an international, auxiliary language); also a newsletter, *Plu Glosa Nota* and journal, *PGN*. Unsolicited mss and ideas for Glosa books welcome.

Godstow Press

60 Godstow Road, Wolvercote, Oxford OX2 8NY
☎01865 556215
✉ info@godstowpress.co.uk
www.godstowpress.co.uk

Managing Editors *Linda Smith, David Smith*

Founded in 2003 for the publication of creative work with a philosophical/spiritual content. 2–3 titles a year. Considers works self-published by the author for inclusion in the catalogue. The press works on a subscription scheme rather than through usual trade outlets. Synopses and ideas welcome but no unsolicited mss.

Graffeg
2 Radnor Court, 256 Cowbridge Road East, Cardiff CF5 1GZ
☎029 2037 7312   Fax 029 2039 8101
✉ info@graffeg.com
www.graffeg.com
Managing Editor *Peter Gill*

Founded 2002. Publishes travel, food and drink, Wales, landscapes, photography. 2 titles in 2005. Unsolicited material welcome by post.
    ROYALTIES annually.

Grant Books
The Coach House, New Road, Cutnall Green, Droitwich WR9 0PQ
☎01299 851588   Fax 01299 851446
✉ golf@grantbooks.co.uk
www.grantbooks.co.uk
Managing Editor *H.R.J. Grant*

Founded 1978. Publishes golf-related titles only: course architecture, history, biography, etc., but not instructional, humour or fiction material. New titles and old, plus limited editions. About 6 titles a year. Mss, synopses and ideas welcome.
    ROYALTIES paid.

Great Northern Publishing
PO Box 202, Scarborough YO11 3GE
☎01723 581329   Fax 01723 581329
✉ books@greatnorthernpublishing.co.uk
www.greatnorthernpublishing.co.uk
Production Manager *Mark Marsay*
Senior Editor *Diane Crowther*

Small, independent, award-winning, family-owned company founded in 1999. Publishers of books, magazines and journals. Also provides full book, magazine, print and Internet production services to individuals, businesses, charities, museums and other small publishers. Publishes non-fiction (mainly military), adult erotic material and, occasionally, fiction. No romance, religious, political, feminist, New Age, medical or children's books. Publishers of the bi-monthly magazines, *The Great War*, *The Second World War* and the monthly *Jade* (see entries under **Magazines**). Mail order and Internet-based bookshop stocking selected titles alongside its own. Website provides submission guidelines and current publishing requirements. No unsolicited mss; send letter or text-only e-mail in the first instance.
    ROYALTIES twice-yearly.

GSSE
11 Malford Grove, Gilwern, Abergavenny NP7 0RN
☎01873 830872
✉ GSSE@zoo.co.uk
www.gsse.org.uk
Owner/Manager *David P. Bosworth*

Publishes books and booklets describing classroom practice (at all levels of education and training). Ideas welcome – particularly from practising teachers, lecturers and trainers describing how they use technology in their teaching.
    ROYALTIES by arrangement.

Haunted Library
Flat 1, 36 Hamilton Street, Hoole, Chester CH2 3JQ
☎01244 313685
✉ pardos@globalnet.co.uk
www.users.globalnet.co.uk/~pardos/GS.html
Managing Editor *Rosemary Pardoe*

Founded 1979. Publishes the *Ghosts and Scholars M.R. James Newsletter* two or three times a year, featuring articles, news and reviews (no fiction).
    ROYALTIES not paid.

Headpress
Suite 306, The Colourworks, 2a Abbot Street, London E8 3DP
☎020 7249 1075   Fax 020 7249 6395
✉ info@headpress.com
www.headpress.com
Managing Editor *David Kerekes*

Founded 1991. Publishes *Headpress* journal and books devoted to film, music, popular culture, the strange and esoteric. No fiction or poetry. Unsolicited material welcome; send letter and outline in the first instance.
    ROYALTIES/flat fees vary.

Heart of Albion Press
2 Cross Hill Close, Wymeswold, Loughborough LE12 6UJ
☎01509 880725   Fax 01509 881715
✉ albion@indigogroup.co.uk
www.hoap.co.uk
Managing Editor *R.N. Trubshaw*

Founded 1990 to publish local history. Publishes folklore, local history and mythology. Synopses relating to these subjects welcome.
    ROYALTIES negotiable.

Hilmarton Manor Press
Calne SN11 8SB
☎01249 760208   Fax 01249 760379

✉ mailorder@hilmartonpress.co.uk
www.whoswhoinart.co.uk
Chairman/Managing Director *Charles Baile de Laperriere*
Publisher of fine art dictionaries and art reference only. Editor and publisher of *Who's Who In Art* (32nd edition).
ROYALTIES paid.

ignotus press
BCM-Writer, London WC1N 3XX
☎01530 831916   Fax 01530 831916
✉ ignotuspress@aol.com
www.ignotuspress.com
Publisher *Suzanne Ruthven*
Founded 1994. 'We are looking for positive, forward-looking material (fiction and non-fiction) on all aspects of British-based ritual magic, mysteries, spiritual development, traditional and hereditary witchcraft and other paths which demonstrate the writer's grasp of both traditional and contemporary esoteric practice. No New Age idealism, fantasy, pseudo-spirituality or neo-Hammer House of Horror fiction.' IMPRINTS **Moonraker Books** (fiction); **Alphard Press** (self-help and lifestyle). 'We are looking to extend these areas with the addition of compatible fiction and life-style titles).' About 20 titles a year. Send s.a.e. for authors' guidelines before submitting material for consideration.
ROYALTIES paid.

Immanion Press
8 Rowley Grove, Stafford ST17 9BJ
☎01785 613299
✉ editorial@immanionpress.wox.org
www.immanionpress.wox.org
Managing Editor *Storm Constantine*
Founded 2003. Publishes genre fiction (science fiction, fantasy, horror), slipstream fiction; esoteric non-fiction. Submissions by e-mail or post (enclose s.a.e.). Website gives full submission details.
ROYALTIES paid.

Infinity Junction
PO Box 64, Neston DO CH64 0WB
✉ infin-info@infinityjunction.com
www.infinityjunction.com
Managing Editor *Neil Gee*
Established originally as a self-publishing, self-help organisation in 1991, Infinity Junction became a publisher in 2001. Currently offers a variety of services to authors, including advice, free web display space and full commercial

publication. Authors are strongly advised to read the detailed information on the website before making contact. E-mail communication preferred. 'We cannot undertake to read unsolicited whole mss.'

Inner Sanctum Publications
75 Greenleaf Gardens, Polegate BN26 6PQ
☎01323 484058
✉ innersanctum@clara.co.uk
www.innersanctumpublications.com
Managing Editor *Mary Hession*
Founded in 1999 to publish spiritual books. Unsolicited mss, synopses and ideas welcome; initial approach via e-mail (address available on the website) or by post, including s.a.e.
ROYALTIES not paid.

Iolo
38 Chaucer Road, Bedford MK40 2AJ
☎01234 301718/07909 934866
Fax 01234 301718
✉ newplays@dedwyddjones.screaming.net
www.dedwyddjones.co.uk
Managing Director *Dedwydd Jones*
Publishes Welsh theatre-related material and campaigns for a Welsh National Theatre. Ideas on Welsh themes welcome; approach in writing.

Ivy Publications
72 Hyperion House, Somers Road, London SW2 1HZ
☎020 8671 6872
Proprietor *Ian Bruton-Simmonds*
Founded 1989. Publishes educational, science, fiction, philosophy, children's, travel, literary criticism, history, film scripts. No unsolicited mss; send two pages, one from the beginning and one from the body of the book, together with synopsis (one paragraph) and s.a.e. No cookery, gardening or science fiction.
ROYALTIES annually.

The Jupiter Press
The Coach House, Gatacre, Claverley, Nr Wolverhampton WV5 7AW
☎01746 710694   Fax 01746 710158
✉ gordonthomasdrury@btinternet.com
Managing Editor *Gordon Thomas Drury*
Founded 1995. Looking for niche market and information publications, also quiz and game subjects. Interested in holistic, clairvoyance and esoteric subjects. Synopses and ideas for books welcome. Send idea and sample chapter. Unsolicited mss welcome 'but may request a

reader's fee'. Currently seeking books for series entitled *How To Make Money At ....*
ROYALTIES paid.

Kinglake Publishing
61B Praed Street, London W2 1NS
✉ info@kinglakepublishing.co.uk
www.kinglakepublishing.co.uk
Managing Editor *James Farrell*

SERIES **Kinglake Short Classics** Shorter work of classic authors such as Joseph Conrad, Charles Dickens, R.L. Stevenson, Anthony Trollope; **Kinglake Academic Guides** Further and higher education: Shakespeare, English poets and novelists; politics and philosophy. 'Opportunities for living authors if they observe our strict guidelines. It is *essential* that initial contact be made by e-mail or through the website. No CD or floppy disk submissions initially. Definitely no hard copy. See website for genres considered.'

Kittiwake
3 Glantwymyn Village Workshops,
Glantwymyn, Nr Machynlleth SY20 8LY
☎01650 511314   Fax 01650 511314
✉ perrographics@btconnect.com
www.kittiwake-books.com
Managing Editor *David Perrott*

Founded 1986. Publishes guidebooks only, with an emphasis on careful design/production. Specialist research, writing, cartographic and electronic publishing services available. Unsolicited mss, synopses and ideas for guidebooks welcome.
ROYALTIES paid.

Legend Press Limited
13a Northwold Road, London N16 7HL
☎020 7249 6901
✉ info@legendpress.co.uk
www.legendpress.co.uk
Managing Editor *Tom Chalmers*

Founded 2005. Publishes original contemporary fiction, both novels and short story publications. Also runs year-round writing competitions for writers of all ages. 1 title in 2005. Send three chapters and synopsis with s.a.e. for return.
ROYALTIES twice-yearly.

The Lindsey Press
Unitarian Headquarters, 1–6 Essex Street,
Strand, London WC2R 3HY
☎020 7240 2384   Fax 020 7240 3089
✉ ga@unitarian.org.uk
Convenor *Kate Taylor*

Established at the end of the 18th century as a vehicle for disseminating liberal religion. Adopted the name of The Lindsey Press at the beginning of the 20th century (after Theophilus Lindsey, the great Unitarian Theologian). Publishes books reflecting liberal religious thought or Unitarian denominational history. Also worship material – hymn books, collections of prayers, etc. No unsolicited mss; synopses and ideas welcome.
ROYALTIES not paid.

Logaston Press
Logaston, Woonton, Almeley HR3 6QH
☎01544 327344
www.logastonpress.co.uk
Managing Editors *Andy Johnson, Ron Shoesmith*

Founded 1985. Publishes guides, archaeology, social history, rural issues and local history for Wales, the Welsh Border and West Midlands. 10–15 titles a year. Unsolicited mss, synopses and ideas welcome. Return postage appreciated.
ROYALTIES paid.

Luath Press Ltd
543/2 Castlehill, The Royal Mile, Edinburgh EH1 2ND
☎0131 225 4326   Fax 0131 225 4324
✉ gavin.macdougall@luath.co.uk
www.luath.co.uk
Managing Editor *G.H. MacDougall*

Founded 1981. Publishes mainly books with a Scottish connection. Current list includes fiction, poetry, guidebooks, walking and outdoor, history, folklore, politics and global issues, cartoons, biography, food and drink, environment, music and dance, sport and *On the Trail Of* and *The Quest For* SERIES. About 20–30 titles a year. Unsolicited mss, synopses and ideas welcome; 'committed to publishing well-written books worth reading'.
ROYALTIES paid.

Lyfrow Trelyspen
The Roseland Institute, Gorran, St Austell PL26 6NT
☎01726 843501   Fax 01726 843501
✉ trelispen@care4free.net
Managing Editor *Dr James Whetter*

Founded 1975. Publishes works on Cornish history, biography, essays, etc. Also **CNP Publications** which publishes the quarterly journal *The Cornish Banner/An Baner Kernewek*. 1–2 titles a year. Unsolicited mss, synopses and ideas welcome.
ROYALTIES not paid.

The Maia Press
82 Forest Road, London E8 3BH
☎020 7683 8141   Fax 020 7683 8141
✉ maggie@maiapress.com
www.maiapress.com

Contacts *Maggie Hamand, Jane Havell*

Founded 2002. Publishes fiction by known and new writers. 6 titles a year. No unsolicted mss, write with c.v. and synopsis only. S.a.e. essential.
ROYALTIES twice-yearly.

Maypole Editions
65 Mayfair Avenue, Ilford IG1 3DQ
☎020 8252 3937
www.maypoleeditions.co.uk

Contact *Barry Taylor*

Publisher of plays and poetry in the main. Catalogue available on the website. 2–3 titles a year. Unsolicited mss welcome provided return postage is included. Poetry always welcome for collected anthologies and should be approximately 30 lines of tight verse, broadly covering social concerns, ethnic minority issues, feminist incident, romance generally, travel and lyric rhyming verse. No politics except evenly comparative. The biannual collected anthology is designed as a small press platform for first-time poets who might not otherwise get into print, and a permanent showcase for those already published who want to break into the mainstream. Submissions must include A5 s.a.e. 'Please be patient when sending work because of the huge volume of submissions.' Exempt Charity Status.

Meadow Books
35 Stonefield Way, Burgess Hill RH15 8DW

Founded 1990. Publisher of nursing history books and nursing picture archive. IMPRINT **Diggory Press** (see entry). No longer taking on new titles; referring all contacts to Diggory Press instead.

Mercia Cinema Society
29 Blackbrook Court, Durham Road, Loughborough LE11 5UA
☎01509 218393
✉ Mervyn.Gould@virgin.net
www.merciacinema.org.uk

Managing Editor *Paul Smith*
Series Editor *Mervyn Gould*

Founded 1980 to foster research into the history of picture houses. Publishes books and booklets on the subject, including cinema circuits and chains. Books are often tied in with specific geographical areas. Quarterly journal: *Mercia Bioscope*, editor *Paul Smith*. 60 titles to date. Unsolicited mss (preferably on disk); synopses and ideas.
ROYALTIES not paid. Six free copies to the author.

Meridian Books
40 Hadzor Road, Oldbury B68 9LA
☎0121 429 4397
✉ meridian.books@btopenworld.com

Managing Editor *Peter Groves*

Founded 1985 as a small home-based enterprise following the acquisition of titles from Tetradon Publications Ltd. Publishes walking and regional guides. 4–5 titles a year. Unsolicited mss, synopses and ideas welcome if relevant. Send s.a.e. if mss to be returned.
ROYALTIES paid.

Neil Miller Publications
c/o Ormonde House, 49 Ormonde Road, Hythe CT21 6DW
www.webspawner.com/users/neilmillerpubs

Also at: 4 Rue D'Equiire Bergueneuse, Pas de Calais, France 62134
Managing Editor *Neil Miller*

Founded 1994. Publishes novels and collections of short stories on any subject: adventure mystery, horror, detective, romance, fantasy, comedy and tales with a twist. IMPRINT **Black Cat Books** Non-fiction: war memoirs, true tales, biographies, history and comedy. Interested in working with new and published writers. Evaluation and critique service available. 'Send £9.75 for latest book/authors pack giving details on being published by us plus large s.a.e. No unrequested tales, please.'

Millers Dale Publications
7 Weavers Place, Chandlers Ford, Eastleigh SO53 1TU
☎023 8026 1192
✉ gponting@clara.net
www.home.clara.net/gponting/index-
page10.html

Managing Editor *Gerald Ponting*

Founded 1990. Publishes books on local history related to central Hampshire. Also books related to slide presentations by Gerald Ponting. Ideas for local history books on Hampshire considered.

Mohr Books
See **Crossbridge Books**

Moonraker Books

See **ignotus press**

Natzler Enterprises (Entertainments)

1 Wakeford Cottages, Selden Lane, Worthing
BN11 2LQ
☎01903 211785 Fax 01903 211519
✉ info@natzler.com
www.natzler.com
www.paulgordon.net

Managing Editor *Paul Gordon*

Founded 1993. Publishes magic (entertainment) books only. No unsolicited mss; send synopses and ideas by post.

Need2Know

Remus House, Coltsfoot Drive, Woodston
PE2 9JX
☎01733 898105 Fax 01733 313524
✉ info@forwardpress.co.uk
www.n2kbooks.com

Founded 1995 'to fill a gap in the market for self-help books'. Need2Know is an imprint of **Forward Press** (see entry under *Poetry Presses*). Publishes contemporary health and lifestyle issues. No unsolicited mss. Call in the first instance.
ROYALTIES Advance plus 15% royalties.

Norvik Press Ltd

School of Language, Linguistic & Translation Studies, University of East Anglia, Norwich
NR4 7TJ
☎01603 593356 Fax 01603 250599
✉ norvik.press@uea.ac.uk
www.uea.ac.uk/llt/norvik_press

Managing Editors *Janet Garton, Michael Robinson, Neil Smith, C. Claire Thomson*

Small academic press. Publishes the journals *Scandinavica* and *Swedish Book Review* and both translations of and books related to Scandinavian literature. About 6 titles a year. Interested in synopses and ideas for books within its *Literary History and Criticism* SERIES. No unsolicited mss.
ROYALTIES paid.

The Nostalgia Collection

Silver Link Publishing Ltd, The Trundle, Ringstead Road, Great Addington, Kettering
NN14 4BW
☎01536 330588 Fax 01536 330588
✉ sales@nostalgiacollection.com
www.nostalgiacollection.com

Managing Editor *Will Adams*

Founded 1985. Small independent company specialising in nostalgia titles including illustrated books on towns and cities, villages and rural life, rivers and inland waterways, industrial heritage, railways, trams, ships and other transport subjects. Publishes post-war nostalgia on all aspects of social history under the **Past and Present Publishing** imprint.
FEES/ROYALTIES paid.

Nyala Publishing

4 Christian Fields, London SW16 3JZ
☎020 8764 6292/0115 981 9418
Fax 020 8764 6292/0115 981 9418
✉ nyala.publishing@geo-group.co.uk
www.geo-group.co.uk

Editorial Head *J.F.J. Douglas*

Founded 1996. Publishing arm of Geo Group. Publishes biography, travel and general non-fiction. Also offers a wide range of printing and publishing services. 'Quality low-cost printing a speciality.' No unsolicited mss; synopses and ideas considered.
ROYALTIES annually.

Orpheus Publishing House

4 Dunsborough Park, Ripley Green, Ripley, Guildford GU23 6AL
☎01483 225777 Fax 01483 225776
✉ orpheuspubl.ho@btinternet.com

Managing Editor *J.S. Gordon*

Founded 1996. Publishes 'well-researched and properly argued' books in the fields of occult science, esotericism and comparative philosophy/religion. 'Keen to encourage good (but sensible) new authors.' In the first instance, send maximum three-page synopsis with s.a.e.
ROYALTIES by agreement.

Packard Publishing Limited

Forum House, Stirling Road, Chichester
PO19 7DN
☎01243 537977 Fax 01243 537977
✉ info@packardpublishing.co.uk
www.packardpublishing.com

Chairman/Managing Director *Michael Packard*

Founded in 1977 to distribute overseas publishers' lists in biology, biochemistry and ecology. Publishes academic & professional: school/university interface, postgraduate – mainly in land management and applied ecology; agriculture, forestry, nature conservation, rural studies, landscape architecture and garden design; some languages (French, Arabic). SERIES Instructional books on garden and landscape design, and monographs or critical biographies in garden and landscape design and history. 30 titles to date. No unsolicited mss. Synopses and ideas in relevant areas welcome. Telephone first.

ROYALTIES twice-yearly in first year, then annually.

Palladour Books

23 Eldon Street, Southsea PO5 4BS
☎02392 826935 Fax 02392 826395
✉ jeremy.powell@ntlworld.com

Managing Editors *Jeremy Powell, Anne Powell*

Founded 1986. Started with a twice-yearly issue of catalogues on the literature and poetry of World War I. Occasional catalogues on World War II poetry have also been issued. No unsolicited mss.

ROYALTIES not paid.

Panacea Press Limited

86 North Gate, Prince Albert Road, London NW8 7EJ
☎020 7722 8464 Fax 020 7586 8187
✉ ebrecher@panaceapress.net
www.panaceapress.net

Managing Editor *Erwin Brecher, PhD*

Founded as a self-publisher but now open for non-fiction from other authors. Material of academic value considered provided it commands a wide general market. No unsolicited mss; synopses and ideas welcome. Approach by fax or letter. No telephone calls.

ROYALTIES annually.

Paperbooks Ltd

Neville House, Station Approach, Wendens Ambo CB11 4LB
☎01799 544657 Fax 01799 541747
✉ submissions@paperbooks.co.uk *or* info@paperbooks.co.uk
www.paperbooks.co.uk

Managing Editor *Keirsten Clark*

Founded 2004. Publishes literary and historical fiction, biography. 1 title in 2005. Unsolicited material welcome.

ROYALTIES twice-yearly.

Paradise Press

80 College Road, Isleworth TW7 5DS
☎020 8568 3777
✉ prdsprss@netscape.net

Founded 1995. Considers only high quality lesbian and gay fiction workshopped through **Gay Authors Workshop** (see entry under *Writers' Circles and Workshops*).

Parapress Ltd

The Basement, 9 Frant Road, Tunbridge Wells TN2 5SD
☎01892 512118 Fax 01892 512118
✉ office@parapress.eclipse.co.uk
www.parapress.co.uk

Managing Editor *Elizabeth Imlay*

Founded 1993. Publishes animals, autobiography, biography, history, literary criticism, military and naval, music, self-help. Some self-publishing. About 4 titles a year.

Past and Present Publishing

See **The Nostalgia Collection**

Paupers' Press

37 Quayside Close, Turney's Quay, Trent Bridge, Nottingham NG2 3BP
☎0115 986 3334 Fax 0115 986 3334
✉ books@pauperspress.com
www.pauperspress.com

Managing Editor *Colin Stanley*

Founded 1983. Publishes extended essays in booklet form (about 15,000 words) on literary criticism and philosophy. 'Sometimes we stray from these criteria and produce full-length books, but only to accommodate an exceptional ms.' Limited hardback editions of bestselling titles. About 6 titles a year. No unsolicited mss but synopses and ideas for books welcome.

ROYALTIES paid.

Peepal Tree Press Ltd

See entry under *Poetry Presses*

Pen Press Publishers Ltd

The Old School, 39 Chesham Road, Brighton BN2 1NB
☎0845 108 0530 Fax 01273 261434
✉ info@penpress.co.uk
www.penpress.co.uk

Managing Director *Lynn Ashman*

Founded 1996. Publishing across a wide range of categories, Pen Press helps new authors to self-publish. Distribution, promotion and marketing included in self-publishing deal. 300 titles to date. Write, phone or e-mail for submission form and full details. Return form with full ms (digital or hard copy).

ROYALTIES 45%, payable twice-yearly.

Perfect Publishers Ltd

23 Maitland Avenue, Cambridge CB4 1TA
☎01223 424422 Fax 01223 424414

✉ editor@perfectpublishers.co.uk
www.perfectpublishers.co.uk
Managing Editor *Dr Kal Karim*
Founded 2005. Publishes books of all genres. 6 titles in 2005. No unsolicited mss; send synopses and ideas for books by e-mail.
ROYALTIES: 'We pay 100% royalties twice-yearly.'

Pipers' Ash Ltd
'Pipers' Ash', Church Road, Christian Malford, Chippenham SN15 4BW
☎01249 720563   Fax 0870 0568916
✉ pipersash@supamasu.com
www.supamasu.com
Managing Editor *Mr A. Tyson*
Founded 1976. The company's publishing activities include individual collections of contemporary short stories, science fiction short stories, poetry, plays, short novels, local histories, children's fiction, philosophy, biographies, translations and general non-fiction. 12 titles a year. Synopses and ideas welcome; 'new authors with potential will be actively encouraged'. Offices in New Zealand and Australia.
ROYALTIES annually.

Planet
PO Box 44, Aberystwyth SY23 3ZZ
☎01970 611255   Fax 01970 611197
✉ planet.enquiries@planetmagazine.org.uk
www.planetmagazine.org.uk
Managing Editor *John Barnie*
Founded 1970 and relaunched in 1985 as publisher of the arts and current affairs magazine *Planet: The Welsh Internationalist* and branched out into book publishing in 1995. All books so far have been commissioned. Unsolicited synopses and ideas welcome.
ROYALTIES paid.

Playwrights Publishing Co.
70 Nottingham Road, Burton Joyce NG14 5AL
☎0115 931 3356
✉ playwrightspublishingco@yahoo.com
geocities.com/playwrightspublishingco
Managing Editors *Liz Breeze, Tony Breeze*
Founded 1990. Publishes one-act and full-length plays. Unsolicited scripts welcome. No synopses or ideas. Reading fees: £15 one act; £30 full length (waived if evidence of professional performance or if writer is unwaged).
ROYALTIES paid.

Pomegranate Press
Dolphin House, 51 St Nicholas Lane, Lewes BN7 2JZ
☎01273 470100   Fax 01273 470100
✉ pomegranatepress@aol.com
www.pomegranate-press.co.uk
Managing Editor *David Arscott*
Founded in 1992 by writer/broadcaster David Arscott, who also administers the **Sussex Book Club**. Specialises in books about Sussex. IMPRINT **Pomegranate Practicals** How-to books.
ROYALTIES twice-yearly.

Pond View
Remus House, Coltsfoot Drive, Woodston, Peterborough PE2 9JX
☎01733 898105   Fax 01733 313524
✉ info@forwardpress.co.uk

Pond View is an imprint of **Forward Press** (see entry under *Poetry Presses*). Publishes unrecorded biographies and novels, illustrated storybooks for children and educational titles.

David Porteous Editions
PO Box 5, Chudleigh, Newton Abbot TQ13 0YZ
☎01626 853310   Fax 01626 853663
✉ editorial@davidporteous.com
www.davidporteous.com
Publisher *David Porteous*
Founded 1992 to produce colour illustrated books on hobbies and leisure for the UK and international markets. Publishes crafts, hobbies, art techniques and needlecrafts. No poetry or fiction. 3–4 titles a year. Unsolicited mss, synopses and ideas welcome if return postage included.
ROYALTIES twice-yearly.

Praxis Books
Crossways Cottage, Walterstone HR2 0DX
☎01873 890695
✉ author@rebeccatope.fsnet.co.uk
www.rebeccatope.com
Proprietor *Rebecca Smith*
Founded 1992. Publishes reissues of the works of Sabine Baring-Gould, memoirs, diaries and local interest. 21 titles to date. Unsolicited mss accepted with s.a.e. No fiction. Editing and advisory service available. Funding negotiable. 'I am most likely to accept work with a clearly identifiable market.'

QueenSpark Books
49 Grand Parade, Brighton BN2 9QA
☎01273 571710   Fax 01273 571710

info@queensparkbooks.org.uk
www.queensparkbooks.org.uk

A community writing and publishing group. Since the early 1970s QueenSpark Books has published 80 titles, mainly featuring the lives of local people. Writing workshops and groups held on a regular basis. No unsolicited mss, please.

Radikal Phase Publishing House Ltd

Willow Court, Cordy Lane, Underwood NG16 5FD
☎01773 764288 Fax 01773 764282
sales@radikalbooks.com
www.radikalbooks.com

Joint Managing Directors *Philip Gardiner, Kevin Marks*

Founded 2001. Publishes radical revelation and technical electrical books. IMPRINTS **William Ernest** *Kevin Marks*; **Radikal Phase** *Philip Gardiner*. Welcomes unsolicited material; approach in writing in the first instance.
ROYALTIES twice-yearly.

Ravenhall Books

PO Box 357, Welwyn Garden City AL6 6WJ
Fax 01707 325230
info@ravenhallbooks.com
www.ravenhallbooks.com
Managing Editor *Eugenia North*

Founded 2004. Publishes history books. 5 titles in 2005. No unsolicited mss; send synopsis with sample chapter by post.
ROYALTIES twice-yearly.

Rickshaw Productions

See entry under *Audio Books*

Robinswood Press

30 South Avenue, Stourbridge DY8 3XY
☎01384 397475 Fax 01384 440443
info@robinswoodpress.com
www.robinswoodpress.com

Managing Editor *Christopher J. Marshall*

Founded 1985. Publishes children's, educational, teaching resources, SEN. Also collaborative publishing, e.g., with Camphill Foundation. About 12–15 titles a year. Unsolicited mss, synopses and ideas welcome. See website.
ROYALTIES paid.

St James Publishing

Suite 213 Parkway House, Sheen Lane, East Sheen, London SW14 8LS
☎0870 870 8797 Fax 0870 870 8798

www.stjamespublishing.co.uk
Managing Editors *Linda Smith, David Smith*

Founded 1995 to provide teaching materials with spiritual substance for St James Independent Schools: 'Good Books for Fine Minds'. Also many workbooks and textbooks for the study of English and mathematics. No unsolicited mss, synopses or ideas.

Serendipity

37/39 Victoria Road, Darlington DL1 5SF
☎0845 130 2434 Fax 0845 130 2434
info@serendipitypublishers.com
www.serendipitypublishers.com

Contact *Managing Director*

Founded 2001. Publishes fiction, academic, memoirs, poetry, children's and religion. About 40 titles a year. Unsolicited mss and synopses welcome.
ROYALTIES twice-yearly.

Serif

47 Strahan Road, London E3 5DA
☎020 8981 3990 Fax 020 8981 3990
stephen@serif.demon.co.uk
Managing Editor *Stephen Hayward*

Founded 1993. Publishes cookery, Irish and African studies, travel writing and modern history; no fiction. Ideas and synopses welcome; no unsolicited mss.
ROYALTIES paid.

Shield Publications

PO Box 5, Low Fell, Gateshead NE9 7YS
☎0191 4823222
Managing Director *Norman L. Middlemiss*

Founded 1977. Publishes nautical books only – the *Merchant Fleet* series (45 vols.). Unsolicited mss and fleet lists welcome.
ROYALTIES paid.

Spacelink Books

115 Hollybush Lane, Hampton TW12 2QY
☎020 8979 3148
www.spacelink.fsworld.co.uk
Managing Director *Lionel Beer*

Founded 1967. Named after a UFO magazine published in the 1960/70s. Publishes non-fiction titles connected with UFOs, Fortean phenomena and paranormal events. Publishers of *TEMS News* for the Travel and Earth Mysteries Society and *MWB Railway Society News Brief* newsletters. Distributors of a wide range of related titles and magazines. No unsolicited mss; send synopses and ideas.

ROYALTIES/FEES according to contract.

Stenlake Publishing Limited
54–58 Mill Square, Catrine KA5 6RD
☎01290 552233
✉ enquiries@stenlake.co.uk
www.stenlake.co.uk

Publishes illustrated local history, railways, shipping, aviation and industrial. 41 titles in 2005. Unsolicited mss, synopses and ideas welcome if accompanied by s.a.e. Freelance writers with experience in above fields also sought for specific commissions.

ROYALTIES or fixed fee paid.

Stone Flower Limited
PO Box 1513, Ilford IG1 3QU
✉ stoneflower10622@aol.com

Managing Editor *L. G. Norman*

Founded 1989. Publishes humour and general fiction. Will consider mss, synopses and ideas only if sent with s.a.e. or IRC ('this also means NO electronic submissions.') Approach in writing in the first instance. 'No anthropomorphism, illiteracy or anyone incapable of accepting any comment or criticism, please.'

Stride
4b Tremayne Close, Devoran, Truro TR3 3QE
✉ editor@stridebooks.co.uk
www.stridebooks.co.uk

Managing Editor *Rupert Loydell*

Founded in 1982 as a magazine and booklet series. Since the mid-1980s, the press has published paperback editions of imaginative new writing. Publishes poetry, prose-poems, criticism, reviews, interviews, arts (particularly experimental music and literary criticism). No unsolicited submissions required at this time.

ROYALTIES sometimes paid; free copies usually.

Superscript
404 Robin Square, Newtown SY16 1HP
☎01588 650452
✉ drjbford@yahoo.co.uk

Editor *Julie Ford*
Chair *Bernard Burgoyne*

Founded 2002. Publishes literary, philosophical and political fiction, humanities and social sciences. 10 titles in 2005. No unsolicited manuscripts. Initial enquiries by letter, telephone or e-mail to the editor.

ROYALTIES vary with each contract.

Tamarind Ltd
PO Box 52, Northwood HA6 1UN
☎020 8866 8808 Fax 020 8866 5627
✉ info@tamarindbooks.co.uk
www.tamarindbooks.co.uk

Managing Editor *Verna Wilkins*

Founded 1987 to publish picture books which give a high, positive profile to black children. They feature regularly on the SATs List for National Curriculum, on BBC Words and Pictures, CBBC and 'Balamory'. Regularly chosen among the Best Books of the Year. All titles sold into both trade and educational markets. Age range: 2–12.

Tarquin Publications
99 Hatfield Road, St Albans AL1 4JL
☎0870 143 2568 Fax 0845 456 6385
✉ sales@tarquinbooks.com
www.tarquinbooks.com

Managing Editor *Andrew Griffin*

Founded 1970 as a hobby which gradually grew and now publishes mathematical, cut-out models, teaching and pop-up books. Other topics covered if they involve some kind of paper cutting or pop-up scenes. About 5 titles a year. No unsolicited mss; letter with 1–2 page synopses welcome.

ROYALTIES paid.

Tartarus Press
Coverley House, Carlton-in-Coverdale, Leyburn DL8 4AY
☎01969 640399 Fax 01969 640399
✉ tartarus@pavilion.co.uk
www.tartaruspress.com

Proprietor *Raymond Russell*
Editor *Rosalie Parker*

Founded 1987. Publishes fiction, short stories, reprinted classic supernatural fiction and reference books. About 10 titles a year. 'Please do not send submissions. We cater to a small, collectable market and commission the fiction we publish.'

Tindal Street Press Ltd
217 The Custard Factory, Gibb Street, Birmingham B9 4AA
☎0121 773 8157 Fax 0121 693 5525
✉ emma@tindalstreet.co.uk
www.tindalstreet.co.uk

Managing Editor *Emma Hargrave*

Founded in 1998 to publish contemporary original fiction from the English regions. Publishes original fiction only – novels and

short story anthologies. No local history, memoirs or poetry. Published *Astonishing Splashes of Colour* by Clare Morrall, shortlisted for the 2003 **Man Booker Prize for Fiction**. 6 titles in 2005. Approach with a letter, synopsis and three chapters and include s.a.e. for return of ms.
ROYALTIES paid.

Wakefield Historical Publications
19 Pinder's Grove, Wakefield WF1 4AH
☎01924 372748
✉ kate@airtime.co.uk

Managing Editor *Kate Taylor*

Founded 1977 by the Wakefield Historical Society to publish well-researched, scholarly works of regional (namely West Riding) historical significance. 1–2 titles a year. Unsolicited mss, synopses and ideas for books welcome.
ROYALTIES not paid.

Watling Street Publishing Ltd
The Glen, Southrop, Nr Lechlade GL7 3NY
☎01367 850558
✉ chris.mclaren@saltwaypublishing.co.uk

Managing Director *Chris McLaren*
Editorial Head *Christine Kidney*

Founded 2001. Publishes non-fiction titles on London and its history; children's and adult. 14 titles in 2004. No unsolicited mss. Ideas and synopses welcome. Approach in writing or by e-mail with a one-page proposal. 'Not interested in anything not related to London.'

Waywiser Press
9 Woodstock Road, London N4 3ET
☎020 8374 5526 Fax 020 8374 5736
✉ waywiserpress@aol.com
www.waywiser-press.com

Managing Editor *Philip Hoy*
Editorial Advisers *Joseph Harrison, Clive Watkins, Greg Williamson*

Founded 2002. A literary press, publishing poetry and 'prose of distinction'. The list includes books by well-known figures such as Al Alvarez, Peter Dale, Mark Ford, Anthony Hecht, Mark Strand, Richard Wilbur and Richard Wollheim, as well as works by newcomers such as Neil Berry, Gregory Heath, Joseph Harrison, Eric McHenry, Dan Rifenburgh, Deborah Warren and Clive Watkins. 2005/6 saw the launch by Waywiser of a new literary award, the **Anthony Hecht Poetry Prize** (see entry under *Prizes*). Submissions, proposals and entries for the Prize are welcome; follow guidelines on website.
ROYALTIES paid.

Whitchurch Books Ltd
67 Merthyr Road, Whitchurch, Cardiff CF14 1DD
☎029 2052 1956 Fax 029 2062 3599
✉ whitchurchbooks@btconnect.com

Managing Director *Gale Canvin*

Founded 1994. Publishes local interest, particularly local history. Welcomes unsolicited mss, synopses and ideas on relevant subjects. Approach first by phone or in writing.
ROYALTIES twice-yearly.

White Ladder Press
Great Ambrook, Near Ipplepen TQ12 5UL
☎01803 813343 Fax 01803 813928
✉ enquiries@whiteladderpress.com
www.whiteladderpress.com

Publishers *Roni Jay, Richard Craze*

Founded 2002. Publishes non-fiction books which present a new angle on everyday living. Welcomes synopses and ideas by mail or e-mail. No fiction, poetry or children's titles.
ROYALTIES quarterly.

Whittles Publishing
Dunbeath Mains Cottages, Dunbeath KW6 6EY
☎01593 731333 Fax 01593 731400
✉ info@whittlespublishing.com
www.whittlespublishing.com

Publisher *Dr Keith Whittles*

Publisher in civil and structural engineering and geomatics disciplines plus maritime, military history, nature/outdoors writing and selected fiction. Unsolicited mss, synopses and ideas welcome on appropriate themes.
ROYALTIES annually.

William Ernest
See **Radikal Phase Publishing House Ltd**

Willow Bank Publishers Ltd
16A Bunters Road, Wickhambrook, Newmarket CB8 8XY
☎0800 7315258
✉ editorial@willowbankpublishers.co.uk
www.willowbankpublishers.co.uk

Managing Editor *Christopher Sims*

Founded 2005. Publishes all genres, fiction and non-fiction. Unsolicited mss, synopses and ideas for books welcome; send via post in the first instance.
ROYALTIES annually.

Witan Books

Cherry Tree House, 8 Nelson Crescent, Cotes
Heath, via Stafford ST21 6ST
☎01782 791673
✉ witan@mail.com

Managing Editor *Jeff Kent*

Founded in 1980 for self-publishing and commenced publishing other writers in 1991.
Publishes general books, including biography,
education, environment, geography, history,
politics, popular music and sport. 1 or 2 titles a
year. Unsolicited mss, synopses and ideas welcome (include s.a.e.)
    ROYALTIES paid.

Worple Press

PO Box 328, Tonbridge TN9 1WR
☎01732 368958
✉ theworpleco@aol.com

Managing Editors *Peter Carpenter, Amanda
    Knight*

Founded 1997. Independent publisher specialising in poetry, art and alternative titles. Write
or phone for catalogue and flyers. 4 titles a year.
    ROYALTIES paid.

Writers' Bookshop

Remus House, Coltsfoot Drive, Woodston,
Peterborough PE2 9JX
☎01733 898105   Fax 01733 313524
✉ info@forwardpress.co.uk
www.forwardpress.co.uk

Writers' Bookshop is an imprint of **Forward
Press** (see entry under *Poetry Presses*). Publishes writers' aids in the form of directories and
how-to guides.

Zymurgy Publishing

Hoults Estate, Walker Road, Newcastle upon
Tyne NE6 2HL
☎0191 276 2425   Fax 0191 276 2425
✉ martin.ellis@ablibris.com
zymurgypublishing.com

Chairman *Martin Ellis*

Founded 2000. Publishes adult non-fiction,
ranging from full colour illustrated hardbacks to
mass market paperbacks. Synopses and ideas for
books welcome but no unsolicited mss.
Contact by telephone or e-mail.
    ROYALTIES twice-yearly.

Electronic Publishing and Other Services

www.ABCtales.com

Unit 3N, Leroy House, 436 Essex Road, London N1 3QP
☎020 7682 1863 Fax 020 7682 1867
✉ markbrown@abctales.com
www.abctales.com

Owner *Burgeon Creative Ideas Ltd*
Editor *Mark Brown*

Founded by A. John Bird, MBE, co-founder of the *Big Issue* magazine, Tony Cook and Gordon Roddick. ABCtales is a free website dedicated to publishing and developing new writing. Content is predominantly short stories, autobiography and poetry. Anyone can upload creative writing to the website.

Arbour E-Books

2 Clonmel Road, Stirchley, Birmingham B30 2BU
☎0121 459 5659
✉ mike@arbour-ebooks.com
www.arbour-ebooks.com

Owner *Inspirational Web Help Ltd*
Sole Director/Editor *Mike Hill*

Electronic publisher. 'A small fee is charged for electronic submission checking by a specialist. If accepted, the e-book is produced, published and sold for a negotiated percentage of sales.' Short stories, serials or poems of social comedy/drama preferred. A negotiable fee is applicable to commercial artists and companies for catalogues and marketing e-books published. Some website work may be undertaken for all clients. Submissions must be Microsoft Word compatible, English and to a high standard of spelling and casual grammar. Paper submissions not accepted.

Authors OnLine

See entry under *UK Publishers*

BeWrite Books

32 Bryn Road South, Wigan WN4 8QR
☎00 334 9335 9531 (editorial base in France)
✉ info@bewrite.net
www.bewrite.net

Managing Director *Cait Myers*
Editorial Director *Neil Marr*

A multi-genre publishing house founded in 1999

and especially geared toward the encouragement and publication in electronic and print formats of first-time authors. About 20 titles a year. Unsolicited mss and synopses welcome (using the online form on the website). 'All offers promptly acknowledged ... draft manuscript-to-publication time shorter than most other publishing houses.'
ROYALTIES quarterly (no advance).

Books 4 Publishing

Grindle House, Grindle, Shifnal TF11 9JR
☎0870 777 3339 Fax 01952 750843
✉ editor@books4publishing.com
www.books4publishing.com

Owner *Dreamstar Books*
Managing Director *Mark Oliver*

Founded 2000. Specialises in helping new and unpublished authors gain recognition for their work by displaying synopses and up to 5000 words on the Books 4 Publishing website and promoting them to publishers and agents. Mss, synopses and ideas welcome; initial enquiries by e-mail or post.

Chameleon HH Publishing

The Quarry House, East End, Witney OX29 6QA
☎01993 880223 Fax 01993 880236
✉ marion@chameleonhh.co.uk *and* info@gc-database.co.uk (*One Step Further* series)
www.chameleonhh.co.uk
www.gc-database.co.uk

Directors *David Hall, Marion Hebblethwaite*

Founded 1997. CD-ROM publishers on behalf of commercial publishers, institutes, associations and government bodies. CD and DVD duplication, plus all artwork undertaken. SERIES *One Step Further – the George Cross*. Edits and arranges printing of self-distributed books.

Claritybooks.com

Colt Farm, Bromley Green Road, Ashford TN26 2EQ
✉ ed@claritybooks.com
www.claritybooks.com

Internet e-book publisher and distributor. Has proprietary e-book technology which simplifies the process of downloading and reading of purchased works for the reader while still providing authors with copyright protection/ encryption. Mss or synopses welcomed from new or published authors. No charges to authors. Will consider all works of a good standard. E-mail communication preferred. If paper submission, please include s.a.e.

50 Connect – www.50connect.co.uk
✉ admin@50connect.com
www.50connect.co.uk

Editor *Rachael Hannan*

Launched in 2000, www.50connect.co.uk is an over-45's web portal with a large community section. Daily updates. Check the website for topics covered. Approach with ideas by e-mail in the first instance.

Fledgling Press Limited
7 Lennox Street, Edinburgh EH4 1QB
☎0131 332 6867
✉ info@fledglingpress.co.uk
www.fledglingpress.co.uk

Director *Zander Wedderburn*

Founded 2000. Internet publisher, aiming to be 'a launching pad for new authors. Special interest in authentic writing about the human condition, including autobiography, diaries, poetry and fictionalised variations on these.' Monthly online competition (www.canyouwrite.com) with small prizes for short pieces. Also free books and reports in the areas of shiftwork and working time. Send mss and other details by e-mail from the website or by post. Links into short-run book production. 6 titles to date.

Justis Publishing Ltd
Grand Union House, 20 Kentish Town Road, London NW1 9NR
☎020 7267 8989   Fax 020 7267 1133
✉ enquiries@justis.com
www.justis.com

Founded 1986. Electronic publisher of UK and European legal and offical information on CD-ROM, online and the Internet.

Lulu
See entry under *UK Publishers*

The Male Alliance UK
Flat 440, 91 Western Road, Brighton BN1 2NW
✉ admin@themalealliance.info
www.themalealliance.info

Established in 2001. Non-profit Internet-based campaign devoted to serious gay male issues: politics, law, support, information, protest and male rights. Articles should promote positive images of gay men, challenge ignorance and stereotypical concepts of homosexual males. Unsolicited material from gay men will be considered for publication on the website as a free contribution.

New Authors Showcase
See **Barrie James Literary Agency** under *UK Literary Agents*

Online Originals
Priory Cottage, Wordsworth Place, London NW5 4HG
☎020 7267 4244
✉ editor@onlineoriginals.com
www.onlineoriginals.com

Managing Director *David Gettman*
Technical Director *Neill Sanders*

Publishes book-length works on the Internet and as print-on-demand. Acquires global electronic rights (including print-on-demand) in literary fiction, intellectual non-fiction, drama and youth fiction (ages 8–16). No poetry, fantasy, how-to, self-help, picture books, cookery, hobbies, crafts or local interest. TITLES *Being and Becoming* Christopher Macann (4 vols.); *Tamerlane's Grave* Patricia le Roy; *Quintet* Frederick Forsyth. 6 titles in 2005. Unsolicited mss, synopses and proposals for books welcome. *All* authors must have Internet access. Unique peer-review, automated submissions system, accessed via the website address above. No submissions on paper or disk.

ROYALTIES paid annually (50% royalties on e-book price of £6).

Research Bureau Digital Publishing
81 Hillhead Crescent, Belfast BT11 9FW
☎028 9087 4769/07849 020205
✉ info@researchbureau.co.uk
www.researchbureau.co.uk

Offers a range of book publishing services, including self-publishing, book promotion, print-on-demand from other publishers and e-book publishing. Primarily interested in non-fiction books, manuals and reports but also fiction considered. See website for further details. Text should be sent in electronic format (e-mail, pdf file) but will consider finished book or ms by post (include s.a.e).

WritersServices
See entry under *Useful Websites*

Useful Websites

Many of these and other useful websites for writers can be found in *The Internet for Writers* by Nick Daws (ISBN 1-84025-308-8), one of a series of books published by *Internet Handbooks*; *The Incredibly Indispensable Web Directory* by Clive and Bettina Zietman, published by Kogan Page (ISBN 0-7494-3617-4); *thegoodwebguide for writers* by Paul Chronnell, published by *The Good Web Guide Limited* (ISBN 1-903282-38-1).

A2A Access to Archives
www.a2a.org.uk
Database of UK archive catalogues dating from the 900s to the present day. Now contains '9.5 million records relating to 8.7 million items held in 396 record offices and other repositories'.

AbeBooks
www.abebooks.co.uk
Includes new and second-hand books search engine and 'The Rare Book Room' for antiquarian, rare and collectible titles online. 'Textbook Central' features a search engine specifically for textbooks and reference publications, both new and second-hand.

Academi (Welsh Academy/ Yr Academi Gymreig)
www.academi.org
News of events, publications and funding for Welsh-based literary events. (See entry under *Professional Associations and Societies*.)

Alibris
www.alibris.com
Over 40 million used, new and hard-to-find books online. Bargain books, text and reference listings and auction pages for rare books. ISBN search engine. Also movies and music.

Alliance of Literary Societies
www.sndc.demon.co.uk/als.htm
Details of societies and events. (See entry under *Professional Associations and Societies*.)

Amazon
www.amazon.co.uk
The online shop for books, music, videos and DVDs, electronics, software, photographic, toys and games, home and garden.

Ancestry
www.ancestry.com
Family history information – databases, articles and other sources of genealogical data.

Arts Council England
www.artscouncil.org.uk
Includes information on funding applications, publications and the National Lottery. (See entry under *Arts Councils and Regional Offices*.)

Arts Council of Northern Ireland
www.artscouncil-ni.org
Information on funding and awards, events and director of arts contacts. (See entry under *Arts Councils and Regional Offices*.)

Arts Council of Wales
www.acw-ccc.org.uk
Information on publications, council meetings, the arts in Wales. Links to other arts websites. (See entry under *Arts Councils and Regional Offices*.)

Arvon Foundation
www.arvonfoundation.org
(See entry under *UK Writers' Courses*.)

Association for Scottish Literary Studies
www.asls.org.uk
The educational charity promoting the languages and literature of Scotland. (See entry under *Professional Associations and Societies*.)

Association of Authors' Agents (AAA)

www.agentsassoc.co.uk

UK agents' organisation including list of current members. (See entry under *Professional Associations and Societies*.)

Association of Authors' Representatives (AAR)

www.aar-online.org

US agents' organisation including list of current members. (See entry under *Professional Associations and Societies*.)

Authorbank

www.authorbank.com

Registration for a fee enables authors to present book ideas to publishers online. Also offers assistance with publishers' contracts and a free advice service.

Author.co.uk

www.author.co.uk

Links to advice and information for writers.

Authors' Licensing and Collecting Society Limited (ALCS)

www.alcs.co.uk

Details of membership, news, publications, legal issues and rights. (See entry under *Professional Associations and Societies*.)

Author-Network

www.author-network.com

Writers' resource site run by Karen Scott and Diana Hayden.

Bartleby.com

www.bartleby.com

An ever-expanding list of books published online for reference, free of charge.

BBC

www.bbc.co.uk

Access to all BBC departments and services.

bibliofind

www.bibliofind.com

Over 20 million second-hand and rare books, periodicals and ephemera for sale online via Amazon.com.

Bibliomania

www.bibliomania.com

Over 2000 texts, study guides and reference resources available online for free. Also selected books for sale in the Bibliomania shop.

BOL

www.bol.com

Internet shopping; a database of over 1.5 million titles.

Book2Book

www.book2book.co.uk

Established by a group of publishers, booksellers, website developers and trade journalists to provide up-to-date news, features and useful information for the book trade.

Booktrust

www.booktrust.org.uk

Book information service, guide to prizes and awards, links to other book organisations, factsheets for writers. (See entry under *Professional Associations and Societies*.)

British Association of Picture Libraries and Agencies (BAPLA)

www.bapla.org.uk

Website includes the BAPLA Online Database with a search facility by category or name. (See under *Professional Associations and Societies*.)

British Centre for Literary Translation

www.literarytranslation.com

A joint website with the British Council containing workshops by leading translators, contacts and networks, and listings of translation conferences, seminars and events. (See entry under *Professional Associations and Societies*.)

The British Council

www.britishcouncil.org

Information on the Council's English Language services, education programmes, science and health links and information exchange. (See entry under *Professional Associations and Societies*.)

British Film Institute (bfi)

www.bfi.org.uk

Information on the services offered by the Institute. (See under *Professional Associations and Societies*.)

British Library

www.bl.uk

Reader service enquiries, access to main catalogues, information on collections, links to the various reading rooms and exhibitions. (See related entries under **Library Services**.)

Chapter One Promotions
www.chapteronepromotions.com

Provides services to writers at various stages of their writing career: workshops, annual competitions, plus story and poetry reading services. Register for free bi-monthly e-bulletin.

Children's Books UK Info
www.cbuk.info

Online information and resource website for children, parents, teachers, authors, illustrators and publishers. News on the current UK children's book market, links to websites of authors, book organisations, etc. Subscribers receive a monthly e-newsletter.

Children's Writing Resource Center
www.write4kids.com

US website for children's writers, whether published or beginners. Includes special reports, advice, chat links, news on the latest bestsellers and links to related sites.

CILIP
www.cilip.org.uk

The professional body for librarians and information professionals. (See entry under **Professional Associations and Societies**.)

Complete Works of William Shakespeare
www-tech.mit.edu/Shakespeare/works.html

Access to the text of the complete works with search facility, quotations and discussion pages.

Copyright Licensing Agency Ltd (CLA)
www.cla.co.uk

Copyright information, customer support and information on CLA services. (See entry under **Professional Associations and Societies**.)

Crime Writers' Association (CWA)
www.thecwa.co.uk

Website of the professional crime writers' association. (See entry under **Professional Associations and Societies**.)

Daily Mirror
www.mirror.co.uk

Daily Mirror online.

Dictionary of Slang
dictionaryofslang.co.uk

A guide to slang 'from a British perspective'. Research information and search facility.

The Eclectic Writer
www.eclectics.com/writing/writing.html

US website offering a selection of articles giving advice for writers and an online discussion board.

Electronic Telegraph
www.telegraph.co.uk

The Daily Telegraph online.

Encyclopædia Britannica
www.britannica.com

Subscription access to the entire *Encyclopædia Britannica*. EB online gives links to more than 130,000 sites, selected, rated and reviewed by Britannica editors.

The English Association
www.le.ac.uk/engassoc

News, publications, conference and membership information. (See entry under **Professional Associations and Societies**.)

Federation of Worker Writers and Community Publishers (FWWCP)
myweb.tiscali.co.uk/thefwwcp/Info.htm

Links to members of the FWWCP, the Federation magazine, information on membership. (See entry under **Professional Associations and Societies**.)

Film Angel
www.filmangel.co.uk

Established in conjunction with Hammerwood Films to create a shop window for writers and would-be film angels alike. Submitted synopses are displayed for a pre-determined period, for a fee, while would-be angels are invited to finance a production of their choice.

Filmmaker Store
www.filmmakerstore.com

US site giving scriptwriting resources, listings and advice.

Financial Times
www.ft.com

Financial Times online.

Frankfurt Book Fair
www.frankfurt-book-fair.com/en/portal.html

Provides latest news and market analysis of the book business plus information on the annual Book Fair.

The Froebel Archive for Childhood Studies

www.roehampton.ac.uk/froebel/archive/index.asp

Collection of children's literature. Supports courses at Roehampton University and is available to *bona fide* researchers. Catalogue available online.

The Good Web Guide Ltd

www.thegoodwebguide.co.uk

Guide to the best websites. Provides thousands of detailed and independent reviews of the best websites for travel, food and wine, interiors, antiques, genealogy, health, money and property, shopping, general reference, book lovers and writers.

The Guardian

www.guardian.co.uk

Website of *The Guardian* and the *Observer* newspapers online.

Guide to Grammar and Style

www.andromeda.rutgers.edu/~jlynch/Writing

A guide to grammar and style, organised alphabetically, plus articles and links to other grammatical reference sites.

Hansard

www.parliament.the-stationery-office.co.uk/pa/cm/cmhansrd.htm

The official record of debates and written answers in the House of Commons. The transcript of each day's business appears at noon on the following weekday.

House of Commons Research Library

www.parliament.uk/parliamentary_publications_and_archives/research_papers.cfm

Gives access to the text of research reports prepared for MPs on a wide range of current issues.

The HTML Writers Guild

www.hwg.org

US organisation offering resources, support, representation and education for Web authors. (See entry under *Professional Associations and Societies*.)

The Independent

www.independent.co.uk

The Independent newspaper online.

IngentaConnect

www.ingentaconnect.com

A comprehensive online UK academic research service. The site offers access to over 19 million articles, chapters and reports online.

Institute of Linguists

www.iol.org.uk

Discussion forum, news on regional societies, job opportunities, 'Find a Linguist' service and *The Linguist* magazine. (See entry under *Professional Associations and Societies*.)

Institute of Translation and Interpreting (ITI)

www.iti.org.uk

Website of the professional association of translators and interpreters, with the ITI Directory, publications, training and membership information. (See entry under *Professional Associations and Societies*.)

Internet Classics Archive

classics.mit.edu

Includes 441 works of classical literature by 59 different authors. Mostly Greek and Roman works with some Chinese and Persian. All are in English translation

Internet Movie Database (IMDb)

www.imdb.com

Essential resource for film buffs and researchers with search engine for cast lists, screenwriters, directors and producers; film and television news, awards, film preview information, video releases.

The Irish Arts Council/ An Chomhairle Ealaíon

www.artscouncil.ie

Monthly e-mail newsletter available giving latest information on grants and awards, news and events, etc. (See entry under *Arts Councils and Regional Offices*.)

Journalism UK

www.journalismuk.co.uk

A website for UK-based print journalists who write for text-based publications. Includes links to newspapers, magazines, e-zines, news sources plus information on jobs, training and organisations.

The Library Association see CILIP

Location Register of 20th-Century English Literary Manuscripts and Letters
www.library.rdg.ac.uk/colls/projects/
    locreg.html
Reference source for the study of English literature. Information about the manuscript holdings of repositories of all sizes, from the British Library to small-town museums, of literary authors – from major poets to minor science fiction writers.

Mr William Shakespeare and the Internet
shakespeare.palomar.edu
Guide to scholarly Shakespeare resources on the Internet.

National Union of Journalists (NUJ)
www.nuj.org.uk
Represents those journalists who work in all sectors of publishing, print and broadcasting. (See entry under *Professional Associations and Societies*.)

Newnovelist
www.newnovelist.com
Novel writing software. Embraces tuition used in university creative writing courses, helping experienced and novice writers alike. Aids research, characterisation, structure and plot, and breaks down the process of writing a novel into manageable chunks. Also 'Story Wizard', software to enable children to write creative stories (www.storywizard.co.uk).

News-Monkey.com
www.news-monkey.com
For newcomers to the journalism industry and to provide release for those already in the business. Advice, links, public forum and message boards.

New Writers Consultancy
www.new-writers-consultancy.com
Advice for writers and critiques, offered by Karen Scott and Diana Hayden.

New Writing North
www.newwritingnorth.com

Essentially for writers based in the north of England but also a useful source of advice and guidelines.

Novel Advice
www.noveladvice.com
A free US journal aimed at the fiction writer; full text of current and past issues online.

PEN
www.englishpen.org
Website of the English Centre of International PEN. News of events, information on prizes, membership details. (See under *Professional Associations and Societies*.)

PlaysOnTheNet
www.playsonthenet.com
Information and help for new playwrights. Launched in association with Oneword Radio in 2002, the site offers the chance to get involved, whether as a writer or someone who enjoys reading and listening to new plays. The site features new works that can be downloaded.

Poets and Writers, Inc
www.pw.org
A US site containing publishing advice, a directory of writers, online bookstore, literary links, newsletter, articles on aspects of writing, grants and awards.

Producers Alliance for Cinema and Television (PACT)
www.pact.co.uk
Publications, jobs in the industry, production companies, membership details. (See entry under *Professional Associations and Societies*.)

Publishers Association
www.publishers.org.uk
Information about the Association and careers in publishing; also 'Getting Published' pages. (See entry under *Professional Associations and Societies*.)

RefDesk.com
refdesk.com
Facts and statistics on every country in the world plus charts and maps, illustrations and related sources.

Royal Society of Literature
www.rslit.org
Information on lectures, discussions and read-

ings; membership details and prizes. (See entry under *Professional Associations and Societies*.)

Science Fiction Foundation Collection

www.liv.ac.uk/~asawyer/sffchome.html

The research library of the Science Fiction Foundation, based at the University of Liverpool. Includes links to the Foundation, the John Wyndham archive, the Foundation's journal and other SF collections and associations. (See entry under *Library Services*.)

Scottish Arts Council

www.sac.org.uk

Information on funding and events. (See entry under *Arts Councils and Regional Offices*.)

Scottish Book Trust

www.scottishbooktrust.com

Information on the Trust's activities and a link to their Book Information Service. (See entry under *Professional Associations and Societies*.)

Scottish Library Association (SLAINTE: Information & Libraries Scotland)

www.slainte.org.uk

Links to various services and major Scottish websites and information on people, organisations, libraries, events and resources of Scottish interest. (See entry under *Professional Associations and Societies*.)

Scottish Publishers Association

www.scottishbooks.org

Links to websites of members of the Association, information on activities and publications. (See entry under *Professional Associations and Societies*.)

Screenwriters Online

screenwriter.com/insider/news.html

Described as the 'only professional screenwriter's site run by major screenwriters who get their scripts and screenplays made into movies'. Contains screenplay analysis, expert articles and *The Insider Report*.

Shots Magazine

www.shotsmag.co.uk

Electronic magazine of crime and mystery fiction.

Society for Editors and Proofreaders (SfEP)

www.sfep.org.uk

Information about the Society including online directory of members. (See entry under *Professional Associations and Societies*.)

The Society of Authors

www.societyofauthors.org

Includes FAQs for new writers, diary of events, membership details, links to publishers' and other societies' websites. (See entry under *Professional Associations and Societies*.)

Society of Indexers

www.indexers.org.uk/

Indexing information for publishers and authors, `Indexers Available' pages. Membership information. (See entry under *Professional Associations and Societies*.)

South Bank Centre, London

www.sbc.org.uk

Links to the Royal Festival Hall, the Hayward Gallery and Poetry Library; news of literature events.

Story Wizard

See **Newnovelist**

The Sun

www.thesun.co.uk

Website of *The Sun* newspaper.

The Times

www.thetimes.co.uk

Website of *The Times* newspaper.

trAce Online Writing Centre

www.trace.ntu.ac.uk

Based at Nottingham Trent University, trAce is an online centre for writers and readers worldwide to share and critique their work, discuss favourite books and talk. Links to a wide range of sites for writers.

UK Children's Books Directory

www.ukchildrensbooks.co.uk

Website created by Steve and Diana Kimpton to 'increase the profile of UK children's books on the Internet'.

The UK Public Libraries Page

dspace.dial.pipex.com/town/square/ac940/
weblibs.html

Website links to public libraries throughout the UK, compiled by Sheila and Robert Harden.

Webster Dictionary/Thesaurus

www.m-w.com/home.htm

Merriam-Webster Online. Includes a search facility for words in the Webster Dictionary or Webster Thesaurus; word games and 'Word of the Day'.

Welsh Academy see Academi

Welsh Books Council (Cyngor Llyfrau Cymru)

www.cllc.org.uk

Information about books from Wales, editorial and design services, 'Wales Book Day'. (See entry under *Professional Associations and Societies*.)

The Word Pool

www.wordpool.co.uk

Children's book site with information on writing for children and a thriving discussion group for children's writers. Also Word Pool Design (www.wordpooldesign.co.uk): Web design for writers, illustrators and publishers.

WordCounter

www.wordcounter.com

Highlights the most frequently used words in a given text. Use as a guide to see what words are overused. Also Political Vocabulary Analysis: measures indications of political leanings in given text.

Writers' Guild of Great Britain

www.writersguild.org.uk

Information includes rates of pay, articles on topics such as copyright, news, writers' resources and industry regulations. (See entry under *Professional Associations and Societies*.)

Writers, Artists and their Copyright Holders (WATCH)

tyler.hrc.utexas.edu

Database of copyright holders in the UK and North America. (See entry under *Professional Associations and Societies*.)

Writers' Circles

www.writers-circles.com

Offers free pages to writers' circles. Listings and information.

Writernet

www.writernet.org.uk

Information, advice and guidance for writers on all aspects of live and recorded performance.

WritersNet

www.writers.net

A directory of writers, editors, publishers and literary agents.

Writers Nexus International

www.writersnexus.com

Enables writers to place their work online and for publishers, agents and readers to access the work quickly and effectively. Also contains a forum, listings page, link and resource directory, writers' Web directory.

WritersServices

www.WritersServices.com

Established in March 2000 by Chris Holifield, former deputy managing director and publisher at Cassell. Offers factsheets, book reviews, advice, links and other resources for writers including editorial services, contract vetting and self-publishing.

Writing-World.com

writing-world.com

'A world of writing tips ... for writers around the world.'

UK Packagers

Aladdin Books Ltd
2/3 Fitroy Mews, London W1T 6DF
☎020 7383 2084 Fax 020 7388 6391
Managing Director *Charles Nicholas*
Founded in 1979 as a packaging company but with joint publishing ventures in the UK and USA. Commissions children's fully illustrated, non-fiction reference books. IMPRINTS **Aladdin Books** *Bibby Whittaker* Children's reference; **Nicholas Enterprises** *Charles Nicholas* Adult non-fiction; **The Learning Factory** *Charles Nicholas* Early learning concepts 0–4 years. TITLES *World Issues*; *Science Readers*; *The Atlas of Animals*. About 40 titles a year. Will consider synopses and ideas for children's non-fiction with international sales potential only. No fiction.
FEES usually paid instead of royalties.

The Albion Press Ltd
Spring Hill, Idbury OX7 6RU
☎01993 831094 Fax 01993 831982
Chairman/Managing Director *Emma Bradford*
Founded 1984. Commissions illustrated trade titles, particularly children's. TITLES *The Great Circle: A History of the First Nations* Neil Philip; *Fairy Tales of Hans Christian Andersen* Isabelle Brent. About 2 titles a year. Unsolicited synopses and ideas for books not welcome.
ROYALTIES paid; fees paid for introductions and partial contributions.

Amber Books Ltd
Bradleys Close, 74–77 White Lion Street, London N1 9PF
☎020 7520 7600 Fax 020 7520 7606/7
✉ enquiries@amberbooks.co.uk
www.amberbooks.co.uk
Managing Director *Stasz Gnych*
Rights Director *Sara Ballard*
Publishing Manager *Charles Catton*
Founded 1989. Commissions history, encyclopedias, military, aviation, transport, sport, combat, survival and fitness, cookery, lifestyle, naval history, crime, childrens and general reference. No fiction, poetry or biography. 100 titles in 2005. No unsolicited material.
FEES paid.

Archival Facsimiles
See **Erskine Press**

BCS Publishing Ltd
2nd Floor, Temple Court, 109 Oxford Road, Cowley OX4 2ER
☎01865 770099 Fax 01865 770050
✉ bcs-publishing@dsl.pipex.com
Managing Director *Steve McCurdy*
Approx. Annual Turnover £150,000
Commissions general interest non-fiction for the international co-edition market.

Bender Richardson White
PO Box 266, Uxbridge UB9 5BD
☎01895 832444 Fax 01895 835213
✉ brw@brw.co.uk
Partners *Lionel Bender, Kim Richardson, Ben White*
Founded 1990 to produce illustrated non-fiction for children, adults and family reference for publishers in the UK and abroad. 80 titles in 2004. Unsolicited material not welcome.
FEES paid.

Book House
See **Salariya Book Company Ltd**

Book Packaging and Marketing
1 Church Street, Blakesley, Towcester NN12 8RA
☎01327 861300 Fax 01327 861300
✉ martin@marixevans.freeserve.co.uk
Contact *Martin F. Marix Evans*
Founded 1989. Essentially a project management service, handling books demanding close designer/editor teamwork or complicated multi-contributor administration, for publishers, business 'or anyone who needs one'. Illustrated adult non-fiction: mostly military history and other historical and reference books. No fiction or poetry. Proposals considered but rarely come to fruition; most books are bespoke by publishers. Additional writers are sometimes required for projects in development. TITLES *A Terrible Beauty: An Illustrated History of Irish Battlefields*; *The Fall of France*

1940; *Encyclopedia of the Boer War*; *The Military Heritage of Britain and Ireland*; *Guide to South Georgia*; *American Voices of World War I*; *Remarkable Maps*; *The World's Great Battlefields*. 2–4 titles a year.

Breslich & Foss Ltd
Unit 2A, Union Court, 20–22 Union Road, Clapham, London SW4 6JP
☎020 7819 3990   Fax 020 7819 3998
✉ sales@breslichfoss.com

Directors *Paula Breslich, K.B. Dunning*
Approx. Annual Turnover £650,000

Packagers of adult non-fiction titles, including interior design, crafts, gardening, health and children's non-fiction and picturebooks. Unsolicited mss welcome but synopses preferred. Include s.a.e. with all submissions.
ROYALTIES paid twice-yearly.

Brown Wells and Jacobs Ltd
Forresters Hall, 25–27 Westow Street, London SE19 3RY
☎020 8771 5115   Fax 020 8771 9994
✉ graham@bwj-ltd.com
www.bwj.org

Managing Director *Graham Brown*

Founded 1979. Commissions non-fiction, novelty, pre-school and first readers, natural history and science. About 40 titles a year. Unsolicited synopses and ideas for books welcome.
FEES paid.

Cameron & Hollis
PO Box 1, Moffat DG10 9SU
☎01683 220808   Fax 01683 220012
✉ info@cameronbooks.co.uk
www.cameronbooks.co.uk

Directors *Ian A. Cameron, Jill Hollis*
Approx. Annual Turnover £400,000

Commissions contemporary art, film (serious critical works only), design, collectors' reference, decorative arts, architecture and children's non-fiction About 6 titles a year.
PAYMENT varies with each contract.

Compendium Publishing Ltd
See entry under *UK Publishers*

Diagram Visual Information Ltd
195 Kentish Town Road, London NW5 2JU
☎020 7482 3633   Fax 020 7482 4932
✉ brucerobertson@diagramgroup.com

Managing Director *Bruce Robertson*

Founded 1967. Producer of library, school, academic and trade reference books. About 10 titles a year.
FEES paid; no payment for sample material/submissions for consideration.

Eddison Sadd Editions
St Chad's House, 148 King's Cross Road, London WC1X 9DH
☎020 7837 1968   Fax 020 7837 2025
✉ reception@eddisonsadd.co.uk
www.eddisonsadd.com

Managing Director *Nick Eddison*
Editorial Director *Ian Jackson*
Approx. Annual Turnover £2.5 million

Founded 1982. Produces a wide range of popular illustrated non-fiction – mind, body, spirit and complementary therapies are particular strengths – with books and interactive kits published in 30 countries. Many titles suit gift markets. Ideas and synopses, rather than mss, are welcome but titles must have international appeal.
ROYALTIES paid twice-yearly; fees paid when appropriate.

Erskine Press
The White House, Eccles, Quidenham, Norwich NR16 2PB
☎01953 887277   Fax 01953 888361
✉ erskpres@aol.com
www.erskine-press.com

Chief Executive *Crispin de Boos*

Specialist publisher of books on Antarctic exploration – facsimiles, diaries, previously unpublished works and first English translations of expeditions of the late 19th and early 20th centuries. Publisher of general interest biographies with special reference to Norfolk. Recent publications include a number of Second World War related subjects. Under the **Archival Facsimiles** imprint it produces scholarly reprints and limited edition publications for academic/business organisations ranging from period print reproductions to facsimiles of rare and important books no longer available. No unsolicited mss. Ideas welcome.
ROYALTIES paid twice-yearly.

Expert Publications Ltd
Sloe House, Halstead CO9 1PA
☎01787 474744   Fax 01787 474700
✉ expert@lineone.net

Chairman *Dr. D.G. Hessayon*

Founded 1993. Produces the *Expert* series of books by Dr. D.G. Hessayon. Currently 24 titles in the series, including *The Flower Expert*; *The*

Evergreen Expert; The Vegetable & Herb Expert; The Flowering Shrub Expert; The Container Expert. No unsolicited material.

Haldane Mason Ltd
PO Box 34196, London NW10 3YB
☎020 8459 2131 Fax 020 8728 1216
✉ info@haldanemason.com

Editorial Director *Samuel Francis*
Art Director *Ron Samuel*

Founded 1994. Commissions mainly children's illustrated non-fiction. Children's books are published under the **Red Kite Books** imprint. Adult list consists mainly of mind, body and spirit plus alternative health books under the Neal's Yard Remedies banner; children's age range 0–15. Unsolicited synopses and ideas welcome but approach by phone or e-mail first. No adult fiction.

FEES paid.

The Ilex Press Limited
The Old Candlemakers, West Street, Lewes BN7 2NX
☎01273 487440 Fax 01273 487441
✉ surname@ilex-press.com
www.ilex-press.com

Managing Director *Stephen Paul*

Founded 1999. Sister company of **The Ivy Press Limited**. Commissions titles on digital art, design and photography as well as on all aspects of website design and graphics software. No fiction. Unsolicited synopses and ideas welcome; send a *brief* idea outline (3 or 4 pages) and a letter.

FEES paid.

The Ivy Press Limited
The Old Candlemakers, West Street, Lewes BN7 2NZ
☎01273 487440 Fax 01273 487441
✉ surname@ivy-group.co.uk
www.ivy-press.com

Managing Director *Stephen Paul*

Founded 1996. Sister company of **The Ilex Press Limited**. Commissions illustrated non-fiction books covering subjects such as art, health, self-help, mind, body and spirit, and general reference. No fiction. Unsolicited synopses and ideas welcome; send a *brief* idea outline (3 or 4 pages) and a letter.

FEES paid.

The Learning Factory
See **Aladdin Books Ltd**

Lexus Ltd
60 Brook Street, Glasgow G40 2AB
☎0141 556 0440 Fax 0141 556 2202
✉ peterterrell@lexusforlanguages.co.uk
www.lexusforlanguages.co.uk

Managing/Editorial Director *P.M. Terrell*

Founded 1980. Compiles bilingual reference, language and phrase books. TITLES Rough Guide phrasebooks; Langenscheidt dictionaries; *HarperCollins English-Chinese*; *Oxford Italian Pocket Dictionary*. Own series of *Travelmates* published in 2004. About 5 titles a year. Unsolicited material considered although books are mostly commissioned. Freelance contributors employed for a wide range of languages.

PAYMENT Generally flat fee.

Lionheart Books
10 Chelmsford Square, London NW10 3AR
☎020 8459 0453 Fax 020 8451 3681
✉ Lionheart.Brw@btinternet.com

Senior Partner *Lionel Bender*
Partner *Madeleine Samuel*

A design/editorial packaging team. Titles are primarily commissioned from publishers. Highly illustrated non-fiction for children aged 8–14, mostly natural history, history and general science. See also **Bender Richardson White**. About 20 titles a year.

PAYMENT Generally flat fee.

M&M Publishing Services
33 Warner Road, Ware SG12 9JL
☎01920 466003
✉ MikeMoran@moran19.fsnet.co.uk
www.mikemoranphotography.co.uk

Proprietors *Mike Moran, Maggie Copeland*

Project managers, production and editorial, packagers and publishers. TITLES *MM Publisher Database; MM Printer Database* (available in UK, European and international editions).

Market House Books Ltd
2 Market House, Market Square, Aylesbury HP20 1TN
☎01296 484911 Fax 01296 437073
✉ books@mhbref.com
www.mhbref.com

Directors *Dr John Daintith, Peter Sapsed*

Founded 1970. Formerly Laurence Urdang Associates. Compiles dictionaries, encyclopedias and reference. TITLES *Collins English Dictionary*; Facts on File dictionaries; *Grolier Bibliographical Encyclopedia of Scientists* (10 vols);

Larousse Thematica (6 vols); *The Macmillan Encyclopedia*; Macmillan Dictionaries; Oxford Dictionaries of: *Business, Science, Medicine,* etc.; *Penguin Dictionary of Electronics; Penguin Rhyming Dictionary.* About 15 titles a year. Unsolicited material not welcome as most books are compiled in-house.

FEES paid.

Marshall Editions Ltd
See **Quarto Publishing**

Monkey Puzzle Media Ltd
Gissing's Farm, Fressingfield IP21 5SH
☎01379 588044   Fax 01379 588055
✉ info@monkeypuzzlemedia.com

Chairman/Managing Director *Roger Goddard-Coote*

Commissioning and List Development *Paul Mason*

Founded 1998. Packager of adult and children's non-fiction for trade, school, library and mass markets. No fiction or textbooks. About 80 titles a year. Synopses and ideas welcome. Include s.a.e. for return.

FEES paid; no royalties.

Nicholas Enterprises
See **Aladdin Books Ltd**

Orpheus Books Limited
6 Church Green, Witney OX28 4AW
☎01993 774949   Fax 01993 700330
✉ info@orpheusbooks.com
www.orpheusbooks.com

Chairman *Nicholas Harris*

Founded 1993. Commissions children's non-fiction. 20 titles in 2005. No unsolicited material.

FEES paid.

Playne Books Limited
Park Court Barn, Trefin, Haverfordwest SA62 5AU
☎01348 837073   Fax 01348 837063
✉ playne.books@virgin.net

Editorial Director *Gill Davies*
Design & Production *David Playne*

Founded 1987. Commissions early learning titles for young children – fun ideas with an educational slant and novelty books. Also highly illustrated and practical books on any subject. Synopses and ideas by prior arrangement only. Vanity publications considered.

ROYALTIES paid 'on payment from publishers'. Fees sometimes paid instead of royalties.

Mathew Price Ltd
The Old Glove Factory, Bristol Road, Sherborne DT9 4HP
☎01935 816010   Fax 01935 816310
✉ mathewp@mathewprice.com

Chairman/Managing Director *Mathew Price*
Approx. Annual Turnover £500,000

Commissions full-colour novelty and picture books and fiction for young children plus children's non-fiction for all ages. TITLES *Magnificent Mazes; Creepies; Tractor Factory; Join-In Stories for the Very Young; Treasure Hunt.* Mss should be double-spaced, typed on one side of paper. Enclose s.a.e. with submission and keep a copy of everything that is sent.

FEES sometimes paid instead of royalties.

Quarto Publishing plc
The Old Brewery, 6 Blundell Street, London N7 9BH
☎020 7700 6700   Fax 020 7700 4191
www.quarto.com

Chairman & CEO *Laurence Orbach*
Director of Co-edition Publishing *Piers Spence*

Founded 1976. Britain's largest book packager. Acquired Marshall Editions in 2002. Commissions illustrated non-fiction, including painting, graphic design, how-to, lifestyle, visual arts, history, cookery, gardening, crafts. Publishes under the Apple imprint. Unsolicited synopses/ideas for books welcome.

PAYMENT Flat fees paid.

Red Kite Books
See **Haldane Mason Ltd**

Regency House Publishing Limited
See entry under **UK Publishers**

Salariya Book Company Ltd
25 Marlborough Place, Brighton BN1 1UB
☎01273 603306   Fax 01273 693857
✉ salariya@salariya.com
www.salariya.com
www.book-house.co.uk

Managing Director *David Salariya*

Founded 1989. Children's information books – fiction, history, art, music, science, architecture, education and picture books. Publishes under its IMPRINT **Book House** Publisher *David*

Salariya Highly illustrated non-fiction in all subjects for children, from pre-school to teenage. No submissions.

PAYMENT by arrangement.

Savitri Books Ltd
25 Lisle Lane, Ely CB7 4AS
☎01353 654327 Fax 01353 654327
✉ munni@savitribooks.demon.co.uk

Managing Director *Mrinalini S. Srivastava*
Approx. Annual Turnover £200,000

Founded 1983 and since 1998, Savitri Books has also become a publisher in its own right (textile crafts). Keen to work 'very closely with authors/illustrators and try to establish long-term relationships with them, doing more books with the same team of people'. Commissions illustrated non-fiction: biography, history, travel. About 7 titles a year. Unsolicited synopses and ideas for books 'very welcome'.

Stonecastle Graphics Ltd
Highlands Lodge, Chartway Street, Sutton Valence ME17 3HZ
☎01622 844414 Fax 01622 844414
✉ paul@stonecastle-graphics.co.uk *or*
sue@stonecastle-graphics.co.uk
www.stonecastle-graphics.co.uk

Partner *Paul Turner*
Editorial Head *Sue Pressley*
Approx. Annual Turnover £300,000

Founded 1976. Formed additional design/packaging partnership, **Touchstone**, in 1983 (see entry). Commissions illustrated non-fiction general books – motoring, health, sport, leisure, lifestyle and children's non-fiction. TITLES *Birds of Prey*; *Spirit of the Wolf*; *Sharks*; *The Book of Crafts*; *Ultimate Sports-Utility Vehicle*; *Fun with Cartoons*. 20 titles in 2005. Unsolicited synopses and ideas for books welcome

FEES paid.

Templar Publishing
Pippbrook Mill, London Road, Dorking RH4 1JE
☎01306 876361 Fax 01306 889097
✉ editorial@templarco.co.uk
www.templarco.co.uk

Managing Director/Editorial Head *Amanda Wood*
Approx. Annual Turnover £14 million

Founded 1981. A division of The Templar Company plc. Commissions quality novelty and gift books, picture books and children's illustrated non-fiction. 100 titles a year. Synopses

and ideas for books welcome. 'We are particularly interested in picture book mss and ideas for new novelty concepts.'

ROYALTIES by arrangement.

Toucan Books Ltd
Third Floor, 89 Charterhouse Street, London EC1M 6HR
☎020 7250 3388 Fax 020 7250 3123

Managing Director *Ellen Dupont*

Founded 1985. Specialises in international co-editions and fee-based editorial, design and production services. Commissions illustrated non-fiction for children and adults. No fiction or non-illustrated titles.

About 5–10 titles a year.

ROYALTIES paid twice-yearly; fees paid in addition to or instead of royalties.

Touchstone Books Ltd
Highlands Lodge, Chartway Street, Sutton Valence ME17 3HZ
☎01622 844414 Fax 01622 844414
✉ paul@touchstone-books.com *or*
sue@touchstone-books.com
www.touchstone-books.com

Directors *Paul Turner, Sue Pressley, Nick Wigley, Trevor Legate*

Founded in 2006, Touchstone Books Ltd is an independent publisher of lavishly-illustrated books on motoring, art and general-interest subjects. TITLES *Cobra – The First 40 Years*; *100 Years of Grand Prix* and *The Very Best of Volkswagen*.

6 titles in 2006. Unsolicited synopses and ideas for books welcome.

FEES paid.

David West Children's Books
7 Princeton Court, 55 Felsham Road, London SW15 1AZ
☎020 8780 3836 Fax 020 8780 9313
✉ dww@btinternet.com
www.davidwestchildrensbooks.com

Founded 1992. Commissions children's illustrated reference books. No fiction or adult books. 70 titles in 2005. Unsolicited ideas and synopses welcome; approach in writing in the first instance

FEES/ROYALTIES paid annually.

Working Partners Ltd
1 Albion Place, London W6 0QT
☎020 8748 7477 Fax 020 8748 7450
✉ enquiries@workingpartnersltd.co.uk
www.workingpartnersltd.co.uk

Chairman *Ben Baglio*

Managing Director *Chris Snowdon*
Contact *James Noble*

Specialises in quality mass-market fiction for leading children's publishers including Bloomsbury, HarperCollins, Hodder, Macmillan, Orchard, OUP, Random House and Scholastic. First chapter books to young adult. No picture books. **Working Partners Two** handles adult fiction across all popular genres on a similar basis. Welcomes approaches from interested writers.

PAYMENT Both fees and royalties by arrangement.

Zoë Books

15 Worthy Lane, Winchester SO23 7AB
☎01962 851318
✉ enquiries@zoebooks.co.uk
www.zoebooks.co.uk

Managing Director *Imogen Dawson*

Founded 1990. Specialises in full-colour information and reference books for schools and libraries worldwide. Does *not* publish picture books or fiction. No freelance work available. Unsolicited material not considered.

FEES paid.

Book Clubs

David Arscott's Sussex Book Club
Dolphin House, 51 St Nicholas Lane, Lewes
BN7 2JZ
☎01273 470100 Fax 01273 470100
✉ sussexbooks@aol.com

Founded January 1998. Specialises in books about the county of Sussex. Represents all the major publishers of Sussex books and offers a wide range of titles. Free membership without obligation to buy.

Artists' Choice
PO Box 3, Huntingdon PE28 0QX
☎01832 710201 Fax 01832 710488
www.artists-choice.co.uk

Specialises in books for the amateur artist at all levels of ability.

Baker Books
Manfield Park, Cranleigh GU6 8NU
☎01483 267888 Fax 01483 267409
✉ bakerbooks@dial.pipex.com
www.bakerbooks.co.uk

Book clubs for schools: Funfare for ages 3—8 and Bookzone, ages 8–13. Four issues per year operated in the UK and overseas.

BCA (Book Club Associates)
Greater London House, Hampstead Road,
London NW1 7TZ
☎020 7760 6500 Fax 020 7760 6505

With two million members, BCA is Britain's largest book club organisation, consisting of over 20 book and software clubs as well as bol.com These include: Ancient & Medieval History Book Club, The Arts Guild, The Book Club of Ireland, Books For Children, Escape (female fiction), Fantasy Science Fiction, History Guild, Home Software World, Just Good Books, Mango, Military and Aviation Book Society, Mind, Body & Spirit, Mystery and Thriller Club, Quality Paperbacks Direct, Railway Book Club, Taste, TSP, World Books.

Bibliophile Books
5 Thomas Road, London E14 7BN
☎020 7515 9222 Fax 020 7538 4115
✉ orders@bibliophilebooks.com
www.bibliophilebooks.com

New books covering a wide range of subjects at discount prices. Write, phone or fax for free catalogue issued 10 times a year.

Cygnus Books
PO Box 15, Llandeilo SA19 6YX
☎01550 777701 Fax 01550 777569
✉ enquiries@cygnus-books.co.uk
www.cygnus-books.co.uk

'Bookseller offering books for your next step in spirituality and complementary health care. See website for over 1000 hand-picked titles.' Publishes *The Cygnus Review* magazine which features 30–40 reviews on new mind, body and spirit titles each month.

The Folio Society
44 Eagle Street, London WC1R 4FS
☎020 7400 4222 Fax 020 7400 4242
✉ enquiries@foliosoc.co.uk
www.foliosociety.com

Fine editions of classic fiction, history and memoirs; also some children's classics.

Letterbox Library
71–73 Allen Road, London N16 8RY
☎020 7503 4801 Fax 020 7503 4800
✉ info@letterboxlibrary.com
www.letterboxlibrary.com

Children's book cooperative. Hard and soft-cover specialist in inclusive books for children from one to teenage.

Poetry Book Society
See under *Organisations of Interest to Poets*

Readers' Union Ltd
Brunel House, Forde Close, Newton Abbot
TQ12 4PU
☎01626 323200 Fax 01626 323318

Book clubs with specific interests: Anglers' Book Club, The Craft Club, Craftsman's Book Club, Country Sports Book Club, Equestrian Society, The Gardeners Society, Needlecrafts with Cross Stitch, Painting for Pleasure, Photographers' Book Club, Puzzles Plus.

Scholastic Book Clubs
See **Scholastic Ltd** under *UK Publishers*

Six Scientists in
Search of an Author

Ann Lingard

Science is all around us: we live in a world increasingly dependent on science and technology. Yet readers and theatre audiences could be forgiven for failing to realise this, so rarely do modern plays and novels reflect the fact. Of course, it's easier for scientists to be literate and well read than for non-scientists to know about science.

If you are not a scientist, it is possible and probably forgivable that your knowledge of physics and chemistry is based on a hazy memory of Bunsen burners and test tubes in the early years of secondary school, and biology or bio-medicine is condensed into worrying headlines about GM, cloning and avian flu.

And as for scientists: the ubiquitous 'media tarts' (their words, not mine), the geeky microbiologist who extols the virtues of a yoghurt drink, the weirdly clad expert in consciousness or technology, the white-coated woman who is *always* pipetting something into vials . . . it is perhaps unsurprising that real scientists lie unrecognised in some corner of a foreign field.

But what a goldmine of topics, ideas and ethical dilemmas science can provide for a fiction writer. Scientists can provide characters for every fictional occasion. The problem for the writer is how to find out more – science can be daunting, and scientists are not always good at explaining what they do.

So here are four questions, four answers and four myths dispelled.

Who do you think scientists are?

Here is a thought experiment: read the following sentence and visualise the people and the situation in your mind. *Professor Smith rushed into the lab where Dr Jones was holding a rack of tubes.*

When I read this out to a large group of adults at a Café Scientifique meeting and asked what Jones and Smith looked like, a large majority admitted – with embarrassment – that the professor was a white male and at least middle aged; Dr Jones, also white and male, was holding test tubes. Yet there were female scientists in that audience, and not everyone was white and few people were old. And Dr Jones, possibly Japanese and married to an Englishman, could have been holding small plastic sterile tubes containing living cells.

Scientists have probably always thought the time they lived in was exciting, because science is always moving forwards and new insights are being gained. A good research scientist will have the questioning approach, always seeking the how and why and being aware that the answers may come from a totally different field;

scientists use metaphor, allusion and lateral thinking – and these days, boundaries between the disciplines have become blurred as information, techniques and communication have become rapid and global. So you might find an expert on fossil dinosaurs learning molecular genetic techniques, or a physical chemist collaborating with a zoologist on the adhesive properties of tree-frog feet, or an engineer working with a neurobiologist on persuading living nerve cells to grow along defined paths.

Physics has people working on 'big physics' with particle colliders and massive computing power as well as people working on solar plasmas or on interactions at a nano-scale. And nobody is a zoologist these days: there are ethologists, geneticists, parasitologists, marine ecologists, insect physiologists, comparative immunologists ... even evo-devo researchers who work on developmental biology from an evolutionary perspective.

Scientists work as full-time researchers in university departments; they may be lecturers who also manage research groups; they may be postgraduate students working all hours to get their PhD, or postdoctoral researchers on short-term funding. They may work in industry with its separate hierarchies and better pay. Or they may be science's foot-soldiers – the enormous numbers of people, the majority of them women with families, many of whom came to work in labs straight from school – who keep the labs running smoothly: checking equipment, making up solutions, carrying out basic tests and assays. There are also the technicians who breed and care for animals, look after the aquaria or insect-houses; and the people who run and use the big pieces of expensive and complicated equipment like electron-microscopes and robotic gene-sequencers.

And scientists talk! Science relies on communication and collaboration; scientists talk to each other, exchange ideas and learn from each other. They are also very competitive – they want the kudos of being the first, but also in order to get funding.

Where do you think scientists work?

In laboratories, standing in front of benches and shelves filled with bottles? In fact, the answer is simple: almost everywhere. Labs, museums, hospitals, offices with blackboards or boxes of rock samples, computer rooms, research vessels, the edges of volcanoes, ocean abysses, caves, islands, cliffs, observatories, in 'clean-rooms'. Few remain in one place. So, if you want to get rid of your fictional scientist for a month or a few days, send him or her off to an international conference, or out on field work (with all the opportunities that offers), or to carry out some collaborative research at another lab. She could even take a holiday! The possibilities are exciting and almost endless.

If your novel contains science, doesn't that make it science fiction?

No: science fiction and science fantasy belong to a completely different genre. If you wrote about mending a burst water pipe, your novel would not have to be about plumbing – or even about the plumber. Science and its practitioners do not have to be the main focus of the novel that contains science; indeed, unless you are entirely confident that you want the scientists to be central (as in William Boyd's *Brazzaville Beach* or Michael Frayn's *Copenhagen*) then you can have a lot more fun and flexibility by keeping the science peripheral and the scientist character as a person going about his or her normal business. 'Good day at the office, dear?' becomes 'Good day at the lab/animal house/estuary?' and 'Did you remember to pick up a pizza/packet of nappies/drain rods?' remains the same.

If you don't know much about science, will it be too daunting to try to find out more?

Scientists use jargon and acronyms; they assume everyone will understand the basics. 'They don't understand what it is like not to understand,' as one novelist said.

This, of course, is true: but there are also hundreds of scientists who love to explain what they do in simple terms. Most research councils these days run science communication courses for their grant-holders, and there is a plethora of awards and competitions to aid public understanding, aimed at reaching out to all ages from primary-school children to the University of the Third Age. But you may feel this is a little too impersonal and, to write convincingly about a character who is a scientist, you really need to watch and talk to a scientist at work and play.

SciTalk has been set up to help you do exactly that. It is a website (www.scitalk.org.uk) and database, set up by myself and my collaborator, physicist and information scientist Peter Normington, and funded during its start-up and development phase by NESTA (National Endowment for Science, Technology and the Arts). As a novelist and former scientist myself – and thus with an arm, a leg and half a brain in each of C.P. Snow's *Two Cultures* – I am not only excited by the possibilities which the sciences offer to the fiction writer, but also very aware of the difficulties that a non-scientist has in attempting to find out more. SciTalk is a free, easy-to-use resource, to help you – whether you are a novelist, playwright, poet or short-story writer – discover how the world around us works, and to write about it.

The SciTalk website has a database of scientists from all over the UK, self-selected enthusiasts and good communicators, who would love writers to contact them, question them, visit their labs and field-sites, talk to their research groups and experience the sights and sounds and the conversations that go on in their workplaces. There are scientists of all ages and stages in their careers (from PhD students to lecturers, to Fellows of the Royal Society and Emeritus Professors); there are academics and self-employed consultants, people working in industry or the NHS – and researching an extraordinary, exciting and inspiring range of topics.

The point of SciTalk lies in meeting and talking: writers find out about science and scientists, and scientists find out about writers. Both gain from the interaction, as the letters and comments received show very clearly.

So – browse the list of topics for inspiration, or search for something specific; read the relevant scientists' web pages and contact them by e-mail or phone to arrange a meeting.

Don't be daunted. Think pensions: none of us understand pensions, we would love someone to explain them simply, we don't mind asking simple-minded questions. Fortunately, for writers and for readers, science is much more thrilling.

And there is, of course, that all-important fifth question: who benefits?

Everyone benefits.

As a writer, you will explore new topics, be exposed to new ideas, new dramas and ethical dilemmas. You will discover the beauty of new images and the beauty of the simple, neat equation; you will find out about the busy sociability of research, the chatter in the tearoom and down at the pub; and you'll discover what drives people into science and to keep at it despite the drudgery and disappointments.

You'll find new ways of writing, and your work will stand out as different and relevant, so your agent and publisher will benefit.

Your readers or audience will benefit enormously too: we all like to be challenged, and to leave a book or play feeling we have gained new insights and been made to think. We talk about our experiences – and word of mouth is one of the best forms of publicity and helps increase sales.

If you can convey that sense of wonder that drives people into science, if you can write about science realistically, with inspiration, and sensitivity, then British science and scientists will benefit too.

Ann Lingard's fiction, science and enthusiasm for linking the so-called Two Cultures can be found by searching for scientist 'Lackie' on the SciTalk website, or visiting www.annlingard.com

UK Literary Agents

★ = Members of the **Association of Authors' Agents**

Sheila Ableman Literary Agency★

3rd Floor, Lymehouse Studios, 38 Georgiana Street, London NW1 0EB
☎020 7485 3409
✉ sheila@sheilaableman.co.uk

Contact *Sheila Ableman*

Founded 1999. Handles non-fiction including history, science, biography and autobiography. Specialises in TV tie-ins. No poetry, children's, gardening or sport. COMMISSION Home 15%; US & Translation 20%. Unsolicited mss welcome. Approach in writing with publishing history, c.v., synopsis, three chapters and s.a.e. for return. No reading fee.

The Agency (London) Ltd★

24 Pottery Lane, London W11 4LZ
☎020 7727 1346 Fax 020 7727 9037
✉ info@theagency.co.uk

Contacts *Stephen Durbridge, Leah Schmidt, Norman North, Julia Kreitman, Bethan Evans, Hilary Delamere, Katie Haines, Ligeia Marsh, Faye Webber, Nick Quinn*

Founded 1995. Handles writers and rights for TV, film, theatre, radio scripts and children's fiction. Only existing clients for adult fiction or non-fiction. COMMISSION Home 10%; US by arrangement. Send letter with s.a.e. No unsolicited mss. No reading fee.

Gillon Aitken Associates Ltd★

18–21 Cavaye Place, London SW10 9PT
☎020 7373 8672 Fax 020 7373 6002
✉ recep@gillonaitken.co.uk
www.gillonaitkenassociates.co.uk

Contacts *Gillon Aitken, Clare Alexander, Lesley Thorne* (also film/TV)
Associated Agents *Anthony Sheil, Mary Pachnos*

Founded 1977. Handles fiction and non-fiction. No plays, scripts or children's fiction unless by existing clients. CLIENTS include Caroline Alexander, Pat Barker, Nicholas Blincoe, Gordon Burn, Jung Chang, John Cornwell, Josephine Cox, Sarah Dunant, Susan Elderkin, Sebastian Faulks, Helen Fielding, Russell Grant, Jane Goldman, Germaine Greer, Mark Haddon, Susan Howatch, Liz Jensen, John Keegan, V.S. Naipaul, Jonathan Raban, Piers Paul Read, Michèle Roberts, Nicholas Shakespeare, Gillian Slovo, Matt Thorne, Colin Thubron, Sally Vickers, A.N. Wilson, Robert Wilson. COMMISSION Home 10%; US & Translation 20%; Film/TV 10%. Send preliminary letter, with half-page synopsis and first 30pp of sample material, and adequate return postage, in the first instance. No reading fee.

The Ampersand Agency

Ryman's Cottages, Little Tew OX7 4JJ
☎01608 683677 Fax 01608 683449
✉ peter@theampersandagency.co.uk
www.theampersandagency.co.uk

Contacts *Peter Buckman, Anne-Marie Doulton*

Founded 2003. Handles literary and commercial fiction and non-fiction; contemporary and historical novels, crime, thrillers, biography, women's fiction, history, cookery, memoirs. No scripts unless by existing clients. No poetry, science fiction or illustrated children's books. CLIENTS Georgette Heyer estate, Druin Burch, Will Davis, Cora Harrison, Michael Hutchinson, Beryl Kingston, Philip Purser, Vikas Swarup, Nick van Bloss, Michael Walters. COMMISSION Home 10–15%; US 15–20%; Translation 20%. Translation rights handled by The Buckman Agency. Unsolicited mss, synopses and ideas welcome, as are e-mail enquiries, but send sample chapters and synopsis by post (s.a.e. required if material is to be returned). No reading fee.

Darley Anderson Literary, TV & Film Agency★

Estelle House, 11 Eustace Road, London SW6 1JB
☎020 7385 6652 Fax 020 7386 5571
✉ enquiries@darleyanderson.com
www.darleyanderson.com

Contacts *Darley Anderson* (crime, mystery & thrillers), *Lucie Whitehouse* (women's fiction, non-fiction & foreign rights), *Julia Churchill* (children's fiction), *Emma White* (foreign rights, US, TV & film), *Elizabeth Wright* (agent), *Rosi Bridge* (finance), *Zoe King* (agency assistant)

Run by an ex-publisher with a knack for spotting talent and making great deals – many for six and seven figure advances. Handles commercial fiction and non-fiction, children's fiction; also selected scripts for film and TV. No academic books or poetry. Special fiction interests: all types of thrillers and crime (American/hard boiled/cosy/historical); women's fiction (sagas, chick-lit, contemporary, love stories, 'tear jerkers', women in jeopardy) and all types of American and Irish novels. Also comic fiction. Non-fiction interests: celebrity autobiographies, biographies, sports books, 'true life' women in jeopardy, revelatory history and science, popular psychology, self improvement, diet, beauty, health, finance, fashion, animals, humour/cartoon, gardening, cookery, inspirational and religious. CLIENTS Liz Allen, Anne Baker, Alex Barclay, Constance Briscoe, Paul Carson, Caroline Carver, Cathy Cassidy, Lee Child, Kira Cochrane, Martina Cole, John Connolly, Margaret Dickinson, Joan Jonker, Danny King, Freda Lightfoot, Rani Manicka, Carole Matthews, Lesley Pearse, Lynda Page, Adrian Plass, Sheila Quigley, Carmen Reid, Rebecca Shaw, Peter Sheridan, Kwong Kuen Shan, Elizabeth Waite, Patrick Woodrow. COMMISSION Home 15%; US & Translation 20%; Film/TV/Radio 20%. OVERSEAS ASSOCIATES APA Talent and Literary Agency (LA/Hollywood); Liza Dawson Literary Agency (New York); and leading foreign agents throughout the world. Send letter, synopsis and first three chapters; return postage/s.a.e. essential for reply. Disk and e-mailed submissions cannot be considered.

Anubis Literary Agency

7 Birdhaven Close, Lighthorne, Warwick CV35 0BE
☎01926 642588   Fax 01926 642588
Contact *Steve Calcutt*

Founded 1994. Handles genre fiction in the following categories: science fiction, fantasy and horror. No other material considered. COMMISSION Home 15%; US & Translation 20%. Works with the Marsh Agency on translation rights. In the first instance send 50 pages with a one-page synopsis (s.a.e. essential). No telephone calls. No reading fee.

Artellus Limited

30 Dorset House, Gloucester Place, London NW1 5AD
☎020 7935 6972   Fax 020 7487 5957
✉ artellus@artellusltd.co.uk
Chairman *Gabriele Pantucci*
Director *Leslie Gardner*
Associates *Darryl Samaraweera, Michael Kindellan*

Founded 1986. Full-length and short mss. Handles crime, science fiction, historical, contemporary and literary fiction; non-fiction: art history, current affairs, biography, general history, science. Charges reading fee 'selectively'. Works directly in the USA and with agencies internationally. COMMISSION Home 10%; Overseas 20%. Will suggest revision. Return postage essential.

Author Literary Agents

53 Talbot Road, London N6 4QX
☎020 8341 0442/07989 318245 (mobile)
Fax 020 8341 0442
✉ agile@authors.co.uk
Contact *John Havergal*

Founded 1997. 3-D, animation and graphics, plots, characters and games for digital media. COMMISSION (VAT extra) Book, Screen & Internet production rights – Home 15%; Overseas & Translation 25%. Send first chapter, scene or section plus half-page outline. S.a.e. essential for reply. No reading fee.

The Bell Lomax Agency

James House, 1 Babmaes Street, London SW1Y 6HF
☎020 7930 4447   Fax 020 7925 0118
✉ agency@bell-lomax.co.uk
Executives *Eddie Bell, Pat Lomax, Paul Moreton, June Bell*

Established 2002. Handles quality fiction and non-fiction, biography, children's, business and sport. No unsolicited mss without preliminary letter. No scripts. No reading fee.

Lorella Belli Literary Agency (LBLA)★

54 Hartford House, 35 Tavistock Crescent, Notting Hill, London W11 1AY
☎020 7727 8547   Fax 0870 787 4194
✉ info@lorellabelliagency.com
www.lorellabelliagency.com
Contact *Lorella Belli*

Founded 2002. Handles full-length fiction (from literary to genre) and general non-fiction. Particularly interested in first novelists, journalists, multi-cultural and international writing, books on or about Italy. No children's, fantasy, science fiction, poetry, plays, scripts or academic books. CLIENTS include Sean Bidder, Zöe Brân, Scott Capurro, Annalisa Coppolaro-Nowell, Sean Coughlan, Nino Filastò, Dario Fo, Jacopo Fo, Emily Giffin, Paul Martin, Nisha Minhas, Rick Mofina, Jennifer Ouellette,

Robet Ray, Grace Saunders, Dave Singleton, Rupert Steiner, Marcello Vannucci, Diana Winston. COMMISSION Home 15%; US, Translation & Dramatic Rights 20%. Works in conjunction with leading associate agencies in most countries and a film/TV agency in London. Also represents in the USA: The Imprint Agency, Sarah Lazin Books, Marmur Associates Ltd, Norris Literary Agency, LLC; Canada: The Harding Agency; Kathryn Mulders Literary Agency; Australia: Calidris Literary Agency; Italy: Boroli Editore Group; Nabu Literary Agency. Welcomes approaches from new authors. Send full proposal plus two chapters for non-fiction, and short synopsis plus first three chapters for fiction. S.a.e. essential. No reading fee. Revision suggested where appropriate.

Blake Friedmann
Literary Agency Ltd★
122 Arlington Road, London NW1 7HP
☎020 7284 0408 Fax 020 7284 0442
✉ firstname@blakefriedmann.co.uk
www.blakefriedmann.co.uk

Contacts *Carole Blake* (books), *Julian Friedmann* (film/TV), *Conrad Williams* (original scripts/radio), *Isobel Dixon* (books)

Founded 1977. Handles all kinds of fiction from genre to literary; a varied range of specialist and general non-fiction, plus scripts for TV, radio and film. No poetry, science fiction or short stories (unless from existing clients). Special interests: commercial women's fiction, intelligent thrillers, literary fiction, upmarket non-fiction. CLIENTS include Gilbert Adair, Jane Asher, Edward Carey, Elizabeth Chadwick, Anne de Courcy, Barbara Erskine, Ann Granger, Maeve Haran, Ken Hom, Billy Hopkins, Peter James, Glenn Meade, Deon Meyer, Lawrence Norfolk, Gregory Norminton, Joseph O'Connor, Sheila O'Flanagan, Siân Rees, Michael Ridpath, Craig Russell, Michael White. COMMISSION Books: Home 15%; US & Translation 20%. Radio/TV/Film: 15%. OVERSEAS ASSOCIATES 24 worldwide. Unsolicited mss welcome but initial letter with synopsis and first two chapters preferred. Letters should contain as much information as possible on previous writing experience, aims for the future, etc. No reading fee.

Luigi Bonomi Associates
Limited (LBA)★
91 Great Russell Street, London WC1B 3PS
☎020 7637 1234 Fax 020 7637 2111
✉ info@bonomiassociates.co.uk

Contacts *Luigi Bonomi, Amanda Preston*

Handles commercial and literary fiction, thrillers, crime and women's fiction; non-fiction: history, science, parenting, mind, body & spirit, lifestyle, diet, health; teen fiction. CLIENTS include James Barrington, Chris Beardshaw, John Humphrys, Gennaro Contaldo, Nick Foulkes, Vincent Gasnier, David Gibbins, Richard Hammond, Eamonn Holmes, John Humphrys, Graham Joyce, Simon Kernick, James May, Niki Monaghan, Dr Gillian McKeith, Richard Madeley & Judy Finnigan, Melanie Phillips, Jem Poster, Esther Rantzen, Prof. Bryan Sykes, Mitch Symons, Alan Titchmarsh, Kim Woodburn & Aggie MacKenzie, Sally Worboyes, Sir Terry Wogan. COMMISSION Home 15%; US & Translation 20%.

'We are very keen to find new authors and help them develop their careers.' No scripts, poetry, science fiction/fantasy, children's storybooks. Send preliminary letter, synopsis and first three chapters. Return postage/s.a.e. essential for reply. No reading fee.

BookBlast Ltd
PO Box 20184, London W10 5AU
☎020 8968 3089
www.bookblast.com

Contact *Address material to the Company*

Handles fiction and non-fiction. No scripts, horror, crime, children's, science fiction, fantasy, poetry, health, cookery, gardening, short stories, academic or articles. COMMISSION Home 12%; US & Translation 20%; TV & Radio 15%; Film 20%. No unsolicited approaches at present. No new authors taken on except by recommendation. Film, TV and radio rights mainly sold in works by existing clients. No reading fee.

Alan Brodie Representation Ltd
6th Floor, Fairgate House, 78 New Oxford Street, London WC1A 1HB
☎020 7079 7990 Fax 020 7079 7999
✉ info@alanbrodie.com
www.alanbrodie.com

Contacts *Alan Brodie, Sarah McNair, Lisa Foster*

Founded 1989. Handles theatre, film and TV scripts. No books. COMMISSION Home 10%; Overseas 15%. Preliminary letter plus professional recommendation and c.v. essential. No reading fee but s.a.e. required.

Jenny Brown Associates★
33 Argyle Place, Edinburgh EH9 1JT
☎0131 229 5334 Fax 0131 229 6695
✉ jenny-brown@blueyonder.co.uk

www.jennybrownassociates.com

Contacts *Jenny Brown, Mark Stanton*
Children's *Lucky Juckes*
Crime Noir *Allan Guthrie*

Founded 2002. Handles literary fiction, crime writing, writing for children; non-fiction: biography, history, sport, music, popular culture. No poetry, science fiction, fantasy or academic. CLIENTS include Lin Anderson, Jeff Connor, Mary Contini, Jennie Erdal, Alex Gray, Laura Hird, Laura Marney, Janet Morgan, Tom Pow, Suhayl Saadi, Paul Torday, Christopher Whyte. COMMISSION Home 12½%; US & Translation 20%. No unsolicited mss. Approach in writing with letter, synopsis and first two chapters. Include c.v. and s.a.e.

Felicity Bryan★

2A North Parade, Banbury Road, Oxford OX2 6LX
☎01865 513816   Fax 01865 310055

Agents *Felicity Bryan, Catherine Clarke*
Contact *Michele Topham*

Founded 1988. Handles fiction of various types and non-fiction with emphasis on history, biography, science and current affairs. No scripts for TV, radio or theatre. No crafts, how-to, science fiction or light romance. CLIENTS include Karen Armstrong, Simon Blackburn, Michael Buerk, Artemis Cooper, Isla Dewar, John Dickie, A.C. Grayling, Julie Hearn, Angela Huth, Colin Jones, Liz Kessler, Diarmaid MacCulloch, James Naughtie, John Julius Norwich, Gemma O'Connor, Iain Pears, Robin Pilcher, Rosamunde Pilcher, Matt Ridley, Meg Rosoff, Miriam Stoppard, Roy Strong, John Sulston, Eleanor Updale and the estates of Robertson Davies and Humphrey Carpenter. COMMISSION Home 15%; US & Translation 20%. OVERSEAS ASSOCIATES Andrew Nurnberg, Europe; several agencies in US. No unsolicited mss. Best approach by letter. No reading fee.

The Buckman Agency

Ryman's Cottages, Little Tew OX7 4JJ
☎01608 683677   Fax 01608 683449
✉ r.buckman@talk21.com *or*
j.buckman@talk21.com

Partners *Rosie Buckman, Jessica Buckman*

Founded in the early 1970s, the agency specialises in foreign rights and represents leading authors and agents from the UK and US. COMMISSON 20% (including sub-agent's commission). No unsolicited mss.

Brie Burkeman★

14 Neville Court, Abbey Road, London NW8 9DD
☎0870 199 5002   Fax 0870 199 1029
✉ brie.burkeman@mail.com

Contact *Brie Burkeman*

Founded 2000. Handles commercial and literary full-length fiction and non-fiction. Film and theatre scripts. No academic, text, poetry, short stories, musicals or short films. Also associated with Serafina Clarke Ltd and independent film/TV consultant to literary agents. CLIENTS include Richard Askwith, Alexandra Carew, Alastair Chisholm, Kitty Ferguson, Joanne Harris, Shaun Hutson, Robin Norwood, David Savage, Steven Sivell, Gerald Wilson. COMMISSION Home 15%; Overseas 20%. Unsolicited e-mail attachments will be deleted without opening. No reading fee but return postage essential.

Juliet Burton Literary Agency

2 Clifton Avenue, London W12 9DR
☎020 8762 0148   Fax 020 8743 8765
✉ juliet.burton@btinternet.com

Contact *Juliet Burton*

Founded 1999. Handles fiction and non-fiction. Special interests crime and women's fiction. No plays, film scripts, articles, poetry or academic material. COMMISSION Home 15%; US & Translation 20%. Approach in writing in the first instance; send synopsis and two sample chapters with s.a.e. No e-mail submissions. No unsolicited mss. No reading fee.

Campbell Thomson & McLaughlin Ltd★

11/12 Dover Street, London W1S 4LJ
☎020 7399 2808   Fax 020 7399 2801
✉ submissions@ctmcl.co.uk

Contact *Charlotte Bruton*

Founded 1931. Handles fiction and general non-fiction, excluding children's. No plays, film/TV scripts, articles, short stories or poetry. Translation rights handled by The Marsh Agency. No unsolicited mss or synopses. Preliminary enquiry essential, by letter or e-mail. No reading fee.

Capel & Land Ltd★

29 Wardour Street, London W1D 6PS
☎020 7734 2414   Fax 020 7734 8101
✉ robert@capelland.co.uk
www.capelland.com

Contact *Georgina Capel*

Handles fiction and non-fiction. Also film, TV, theatre and radio scripts. CLIENTS Kunal Basu, Julie Burchill, John Gimlette, Andrew Greig, Dr Tristram Hunt, Liz Jones, Andrew Roberts, Simon Sebag Montefiore, Stella Rimington, Diana Souhami, Louis Theroux, Fay Weldon. COMMISSION Home, US & Translation 15%. Send sample chapters and synopsis with covering letter and s.a.e. (if return required) in the first instance. No reading fee.

Casarotto Ramsay and Associates Ltd
National House, 60–66 Wardour Street, London W1V 4ND
☎020 7287 4450 Fax 020 7287 9128
✉ agents@casarotto.uk.com
www.casarotto.uk.com

Film/TV/Radio *Jenne Casarotto, Charlotte Kelly, Jodi Shields, Elinor Burns, Miriam James, Holly Nicholson*
Stage *Tom Erhardt, Mel Kenyon*

Handles scripts for TV, theatre, film and radio. CLIENTS include: **Theatre** Alan Ayckbourn, Caryl Churchill, Christopher Hampton, David Hare, Sarah Kane estate, Mark Ravenhill. **Film** Laura Jones, Neil Jordan, Nick Hornby, Shane Meadows, Purvis & Wade, Lynne Ramsay. **TV** Howard Brenton, Amy Jenkins, Susan Nickson, Jessica Stevenson. COMMISSION Home 10%. OVERSEAS ASSOCIATES worldwide. No unsolicited material without preliminary letter.

Celia Catchpole
56 Gilpin Avenue, London SW14 8QY
☎020 8255 4835
www.celiacatchpole.co.uk
Contact *Celia Catchpole*

Founded 1996. Handles children's books – artists and writers. No TV, film, radio or theatre scripts. No poetry. COMMISSION Home 10% (writers) 15% (artists); US & Translation 20%. Works with associate agents abroad. No unsolicited mss.

Chapman & Vincent★
The Mount, Sun Hill, Royston SG8 9AT
☎01763 245005 Fax 01763 243033
✉ info@chapmanvincent.co.uk
Contacts *Jennifer Chapman, Gilly Vincent*

A small agency whose clients come mainly from personal recommendation. The agency looks after only a limited number of predominantly non-fiction writers and is not actively seeking clients but happy to consider really original work. Does not handle thrillers, adventure or any othe kind of genre fiction, poetry, scripts or children's books. CLIENTS include George Carter, Leslie Geddes-Brown, Rowley Leigh and Eve Pollard. COMMISSION Home 15%; US & Europe 20%. Works with the Elaine Markson Agency. Please do not telephone or submit by fax or e-mail, or send disks. 'We regret we are also unable to respond by e-mail to submissions.' No reading fee. Write with two sample chapters and s.a.e.

Mic Cheetham Literary Agency
11–12 Dover Street, London W1S 4LJ
☎020 7495 2002 Fax 020 7399 2801
www.miccheetham.com
Contacts *Mic Cheetham, Simon Kavanagh*

Established 1994. Handles general and literary fiction, crime and science fiction, and some specific non-fiction. No film/TV scripts apart from existing clients. No children's, illustrated books or poetry. CLIENTS include Iain Banks, Carol Birch, Anita Burgh, Laurie Graham, M. John Harrison, Toby Litt, Ken MacLeod, China Miéville, Antony Sher, Janette Turner Hospital. COMMISSION Home 15%; US & Translation 20%. Works with The Marsh Agency for all translation rights. No unsolicited mss. Approach in writing with publishing history, first two chapters and return postage. No reading fee.

Judith Chilcote Agency★
8 Wentworth Mansions, Keats Grove, London NW3 2RL
☎020 7794 3717
✉ judybks@aol.com
Contact *Judith Chilcote*

Founded 1990. Handles commercial fiction, TV tie-ins, health and nutrition, popular psychology, biography and celebrity autobiography and current affairs. COMMISSION Home 15%; Overseas 20–25%. *No* academic, science fiction, children's, short stories, film scripts or poetry. *No approaches by e-mail.* Send letter with c.v., synopsis, three chapters and s.a.e. for return. No reading fee.

Teresa Chris Literary Agency Ltd★
43 Musard Road, London W6 8NR
☎020 7386 0633
Contacts *Teresa Chris, Charles Brudenell-Bruce*

Founded 1989. Handles crime, general, women's, commercial and literary fiction, and non-fiction: history, biography, health, cookery, lifestyle, sport and fitness, gardening, etc. Specialises in crime fiction and commercial women's fiction. No scripts. Film and TV rights handled by co-agent. No poetry, short stories, fantasy, science fiction or horror. CLIENTS include Stephen Booth, Martin Davies, Tamara McKinley, Marguerite Patten, Eileen Ramsay, Danuta Reah. COMMISSION Home 10%; US & Translation 20%. OVERSEAS ASSOCIATES Thompson & Chris Literary Agency, USA; representatives in all other countries. Unsolicited mss welcome. Send query letter with first two chapters plus two-page synopsis (s.a.e. *essential*) in first instance. No reading fee.

Mary Clemmey Literary Agency★
6 Dunollie Road, London NW5 2XP
☎020 7267 1290 Fax 020 7482 7360
Contact *Mary Clemmey*

Founded 1992. Handles fiction and non-fiction – high-quality work with an international market. No science fiction, fantasy or children's books. TV, film, radio and theatre scripts from existing clients only. US clients: Frederick Hill Bonnie Nadell Inc., Lynn C. Franklin Associates Ltd, The Miller Agency, Roslyn Targ, Weingel-Fidel Agency Inc, Betsy Amster Literary. COMMISSION Home 10%; US & Translation 20%. OVERSEAS ASSOCIATE Elaine Markson Literary Agency, New York. No unsolicited mss. Approach by letter only in the first instance giving a description of the work (include s.a.e.). No reading fee.

Jonathan Clowes Ltd★
10 Iron Bridge House, Bridge Approach, London NW1 8BD
☎020 7722 7674 Fax 020 7722 7677
Contacts *Ann Evans, Lisa Whadcock*

Founded 1960. Pronounced 'clewes'. Now one of the biggest fish in the pond, and not really for the untried unless they are true high-flyers. Fiction and non-fiction, plus scripts. No textbooks or children's. Special interests: situation comedy, film and television rights. CLIENTS include David Bellamy, Bill Dare, Len Deighton, Elizabeth Jane Howard, David Lawrence, Doris Lessing, David Nobbs, Gillian White and the estate of Kingsley Amis. COMMISSION Home & US 15%; Translation 19%. OVERSEAS ASSOCIATES Andrew Nurnberg Associates; Sane Töregard Agency. No unsolicited mss; authors come by recommendation or by successful follow-ups to preliminary letters.

Elspeth Cochrane Personal Management
16 Old Town, Clapham, London SW4 0JY
☎020 7819 6256 Fax 020 7819 4297
✉ info@elspethcochrane.co.uk
Contact *Elspeth Cochrane*

Founded 1960. Handles fiction, non-fiction, biographies, screenplays and plays. No children's fiction. CLIENTS include Alex Jones, Dominic Leyton, Royce Ryton, F.E. Smith, Robert Tanitch. COMMISSION 12½%. No unsolicited mss. Phone before submitting work.

Rosica Colin Ltd
1 Clareville Grove Mews, London SW7 5AH
☎020 7370 1080 Fax 020 7244 6441
Contact *Joanna Marston*

Founded 1949. Handles all full-length mss, plus theatre, film, television and sound broadcasting but few new writers being accepted. COMMISSION Home 10%; US & Translation 20%. Preliminary letter with return postage essential; writers should outline their writing credits and whether their mss have previously been submitted elsewhere. May take 3–4 months to consider full mss; synopsis preferred in first instance. No reading fee.

Conville & Walsh Limited★
2 Ganton Street, London W1F 7QL
☎020 7287 3030 Fax 020 7287 4545
✉ firstname@convilleandwalsh.com
Directors *Clare Conville, Patrick Walsh* (book rights), *Peter Tallack* (popular science)

Established in 2000 by Clare Conville (ex-A.P. Watt) and Patrick Walsh (ex-Christopher Little Literary Agency). Handles literary and commercial fiction plus serious and narrative non-fiction. Conville and Walsh also represents many successful children's authors. Particularly interested in first-time novelists, scientists, historians and journalists. No poetry, short stories or screenplays. CLIENTS John Burningham, Kate Cann, Helen Castor, Tom Conran, Michael Cordy, Mike Dash, Belle de Jour, Kevin Dutton, Professor John Emsley, Steve Erikson, Kitty Fitzgerald, Katy Gardner, Misha Glenny, Peadar O'Guilin, Sarah Hall, Christopher Hart, Dermot Healy, James Holland, Tom Holland, Sebastian Horsley, David Huggins, Dee Jarrett-Macauley, Richard T. Kelly, Guy Kennaway, Daren King, Manjit Kumar, P.J. Lynch, Hector Macdonald, Andrew Marshall, Hisham Matar, Harland Miller, Joshua Mowll, Jacqui Murhall, Ruth Padel, D.B.C. Pierre, Rebecca Ray, Patrick Redmond, Candace Robb,

Philip Robinson, Saira Shah, Tahir Shah, Nicky Singer, Simon Singh, Michael Smith, Steve Voake, Nick Wright, Dr Richard Wiseman, Adam Wishart, Isabel Wolff and the estate of Francis Bacon. COMMISSION Home 15%; US & Translation 20%. Send first three chapters, one-page synopsis, covering letter and s.a.e. No reading fee.

Jane Conway-Gordon Ltd★
1 Old Compton Street, London W1D 5JA
☎020 7494 0148 Fax 020 7287 9264
Contact *Jane Conway-Gordon*
Founded 1982. Works in association with Andrew Mann Ltd. Handles fiction and general non-fiction. No poetry, science fiction, children's or short stories. COMMISSION Home 15%; US & Translation 20%. OVERSEAS ASSOCIATES McIntosh & Otis, Inc., New York; plus agencies throughout Europe and Japan. Unsolicited mss welcome; preliminary letter and return postage essential. No reading fee.

Crawford & Pearlstine Associates Ltd★
31 Ashley Gardens, Ambrosden Avenue, London SW1P 1QE
☎0845 262 4212 Fax 0845 262 5546
www.pearlstine.co.uk
Contacts *Maggie Pearlstine, Jamie Crawford*
Founded 1989. Small, selective agency. Handles general non-fiction and fiction. Special interests: history, current affairs, biography, sport and health. No children's, poetry, horror, science fiction, short stories or scripts. Seldom takes on new authors. CLIENTS Matthew Baylis, Kate Bingham, Menzies Campbell, Frank Dobson, Kim Fletcher, Roy Hattersley, Charles Kennedy, Anders Larsen, Mark Leonard, Quentin Letts, Claire Macdonald, Prof. Raj Persaud, Prof. Lesley Regan, Winifred Robinson, Paul Rose, Henrietta Spencer-Churchill, Prof. Kathy Sykes, Gregor Townsend, Prof. Robert Winston. Translation rights handled by Gillon Aitken Associates Ltd. COMMISSION Home 12½% (fiction), 10% (non-fiction); US & Translation 20%; TV, Film & Journalism 20%. Prospective clients should write an explanatory letter and enclose s.a.e. and the first three chapters only. No submissions accepted by fax, e-mail or from abroad. No reading fee.

Rupert Crew Ltd★
1A King's Mews, London WC1N 2JA
☎020 7242 8586 Fax 020 7831 7914
✉ info@rupertcrew.co.uk (correspondence only)
www.rupertcrew.co.uk

Contacts *Doreen Montgomery, Caroline Montgomery*
Founded 1927. International representation, handling volume and subsidiary rights in fiction and non-fiction properties. No screenplays, plays or poetry, journalism or short stories, science fiction or fantasy. COMMISSION Home 15%; Elsewhere 20%. Preliminary letter and return postage essential. No reading fee.

Curtis Brown Group Ltd★
Haymarket House, 28/29 Haymarket, London SW1Y 4SP
☎020 7393 4400 Fax 020 7393 4401
✉ cb@curtisbrown.co.uk
www.curtisbrown.co.uk
CEO *Jonathan Lloyd*
Director of Operations *Ben Hall*
Directors *Jacquie Drewe, Jonny Geller, Nick Marston*
Books *Jonny Geller* (MD, Book Division), *Camilla Hornby, Jonathan Lloyd, Jonathan Pegg, Vivienne Schuster, Elizabeth Sheinkman, Janice Swanson, Gordon Wise*
Foreign Rights (books) *Kate Cooper, Carol Jackson, Diana Mackay, Betsy Robbins*
Film/TV/Theatre *Nick Marston* (MD, Media Division), *Tally Garner, Ben Hall, Joe Phillips, Sally Whitehill*
Actors *Grace Clissold, Maxine Hoffman, Sarah MacCormick, Sarah Spear, Kate Staddon, Claire Stannard, Frances Williams*
Presenters *Jacquie Drewe, Catherine Tapsell Jenkin*
Founded 1899. Agents for the negotiation in all markets of novels, general non-fiction, children's books and associated rights (including multimedia) as well as play, film, theatre, TV and radio scripts. OVERSEAS ASSOCIATES in Australia and the US. Send outline for non-fiction and short synopsis for fiction with two/three sample chapters and autobiographical note. No reading fee. Return postage essential. No submissions by e-mail. See further submission guidelines on website. Also represents playwrights, film and TV writers and directors, theatre directors and designers, TV and radio presenters and actors.

Judy Daish Associates Ltd
2 St Charles Place, London W10 6EG
☎020 8964 8811 Fax 020 8964 8966
Contacts *Judy Daish, Tracey Elliston, Howard Gooding*
Founded 1978. Theatrical literary agent. Handles scripts for film, TV, theatre and radio. No books. Preliminary letter essential. No unsolicited mss.

Caroline Davidson Literary Agency★

5 Queen Anne's Gardens, London W4 1TU
☎020 8995 5768 Fax 020 8994 2770
www.cdla.co.uk

Contact *Caroline Davidson*

Founded 1988. Handles fiction and non-fiction, including archaeology, architecture, art, astronomy, biography, design, gardening, health, history, medicine, natural history, reference, science. CLIENTS Peter Barham, Nigel Barlow, Andrew Beatty, Andrew Dalby, Emma Donoghue, Cindy Engel, Chris Greenhalgh, Tom Jaine, Paul Luff, Huon Mallalieu, Linda Sonntag, Simon Unwin, Caroline Williams. COMMISSION Home & Commonwealth, US, Translation 12½%; 20% if sub-agents are involved in foreign sales. Finished, polished first novels positively welcomed. No thrillers, crime, occult, short stories, children's, plays or poetry. Writers should send an initial letter giving details of their project and/or book proposal, including the first 50 pages of their novel if a fiction writer, together with c.v. and s.a.e. No response to submissions without return postage or to those sent by fax or e-mail.

Merric Davidson Literary Agency

See **MBA Literary Agents Ltd**

Felix de Wolfe

Kingsway House, 103 Kingsway, London WC2B 6QX
☎020 7242 5066 Fax 020 7242 8119
✉ info@felixdewolfe.com

Contact *Felix de Wolfe*

Founded 1938. Handles quality fiction only, and scripts. No non-fiction or children's. CLIENTS include Jan Butlin, Jeff Dowson, Brian Glover, Sheila Goff, Aileen Gonsalves, John Kershaw, Ray Kilby, Bill MacIlwraith, Angus Mackay, Gerard McLarnon, Julian Slade, Malcolm Taylor, David Thompson, Paul Todd, Dolores Walshe. COMMISSION Home 12½%; US 20%. No unsolicited mss. No reading fee.

The Dench Arnold Agency

10 Newburgh Street, London W1F 7RN
☎020 7437 4551 Fax 020 7439 1355
✉ contact@den07arnold.co.uk
www.dencharnold.co.uk

Contacts *Elizabeth Dench, Michelle Arnold*

Founded 1972. Handles scripts for TV and film. CLIENTS include Peter Chelsom. COMMISSION Home 10–15%. OVERSEAS ASSOCIATES include William Morris/Sanford Gross and C.A.A., Los Angeles. Unsolicited mss will be read, but a letter with sample of work and c.v. (plus s.a.e.) is required.

Dorian Literary Agency (DLA)★

Upper Thornehill, 27 Church Road, St Marychurch, Torquay TQ1 4QY
☎01803 312095 Fax 01803 312095

Contact *Dorothy Lumley*

Founded 1986. Handles popular genre fiction: romance, historicals, sagas; crime and thrillers; science fiction, fantasy, horror; some general fiction. No short stories, poetry, autobiography, film/TV scripts or plays. CLIENTS include Gillian Bradshaw, Gary Gibson, Kate Hardy, Stephen Jones, Brian Lumley, Amy Myers, Rosemary Rowe, Lyndon Stacey. COMMISSION Home 12½% for new clients; US 15%; Translation 20–25%. Works with agents in most countries for translation. Introductory letter with outline and 1–3 chapters (with return postage/s.a.e.) only, please. No enquiries or submissions by telephone, fax or e-mail. No reading fee.

Toby Eady Associates Ltd

9 Orme Court, London W2 4RL
☎020 7792 0092 Fax 020 7792 0879
✉ toby@tobyeady.demon.co.uk
www.tobyeadyassociates.co.uk

Contacts *Toby Eady*

Handles fiction, and non-fiction. Special interests: China, Middle East, Africa, India. CLIENTS include Nada Awar Jarrar, Mark Burnell, Chris Cleave, Bernard Cornwell, Yasmin Crowther, Rana Dasgupta, Fadia Faqir, Xiaolu Guo, Richard Lloyd Parry, Francesca Marciano, Rachel Seiffert, John Carey, Kuki Gallmann, Julia Lovell, Linda Polman, Fiammetta Rocco, Deborah Scroggins, Samia Serageldin, Xinran Xue. COMMISSION Home 15%; Elsewhere 20%. OVERSEAS ASSOCIATES France: La Nouvelle Agence; Holland: Jan Michael; Italy, Spain, Portugal and Scandinavia: The Buckman Agency; Eastern Europe/Russia: Prava I Prevodi; Czech Republic: Kristin Olson; Hungary: Katai & Bolza; Greece: JLM. Approach by personal recommendation. No film/TV scripts or poetry.

Eddison Pearson Ltd

West Hill House, 6 Swains Lane, London N6 6QS
☎020 7700 7763 Fax 020 7700 7866
✉ info@eddisonpearson.com

Contact *Clare Pearson*

Founded 1996. Small, personally run agency.

Handles children's books, literary fiction and non-fiction, poetry. CLIENTS include Sue Heap, Robert Muchamore, Valerie Bloom. COMMISSION Home 10%; US & Translation 15–20%. Please e-mail for up-to-date submission guidelines by return. Or post writing sample enclosing s.a.e. No reading fee.

Edwards Fuglewicz★

49 Great Ormond Street, London WC1N 3HZ
☎020 7405 6725 Fax 020 7405 6726

Contacts *Ros Edwards, Helenka Fuglewicz, Julia Forrest*

Founded 1996. Handles literary and commercial fiction (not children's, science fiction, horror or fantasy); non-fiction: biography, history, popular culture. COMMISSION Home 15%; US & Translation 20%. No unsolicited mss or e-mail submissions.

Faith Evans Associates★

27 Park Avenue North, London N8 7RU
☎020 8340 9920 Fax 020 8340 9410

Founded 1987. Small agency. CLIENTS include Melissa Benn, Shyam Bhatia, Cherie Booth, Eleanor Bron, Carolyn Cassady, Caroline Conran, Alicia Foster, Midge Gillies, Ed Glinert, Vesna Goldsworthy, Cate Haste, Jim Kelly, Helena Kennedy, Seumas Milne, Tom Paulin, Sheila Rowbotham, the estate of Lorna Sage, Rebecca Stott, Harriet Walter, Francesca Weisman, Elizabeth Wilson. COMMISSION Home 15%; US & Translation 20%. OVERSEAS ASSOCIATES worldwide. No unsolicited mss or phone calls, please.

Lisa Eveleigh Literary Agency★

c/o Pollinger Ltd, 9 Staple Inn, London WC1V 7QH
☎020 7404 0342 Fax 020 7242 5737
✉ lisaeveleigh@dial.pipex.com

Contact *Lisa Eveleigh*

Founded 1996. Handles literary and commercial fiction and non-fiction. No children's picture books, plays, scripts or poetry or horror. CLIENTS include Christina Balit, Robin Brooks, Samit Basu, Philip Casey, Jonathan Gornall, Jonathan Meres, Relate, Grace Wynne-Jones. COMMISSION Home 15%; US & Translation 20%. Send synopsis with covering letter and c.v. rather than full mss. No reading fee but return postage essential. Please restrict e-mail contact to preliminary letter only.

Laurence Fitch Ltd

Mezzanine, Quadrant House, 80–82 Regent Street, London W1B 5AU
☎020 7734 9911
✉ information@laurencefitch.com
www.laurencefitch.com

Contact *Brendan Davis*

Founded 1952, incorporating the London Play Company (1922) and in association with Film Rights Ltd (1932). Handles children's and horror books, scripts for theatre, film, TV and radio only. CLIENTS include Carlo Ardito, Hindi Brooks, John Chapman & Ray Cooney, Jeremy Lloyd, Dave Freeman, John Graham, Robin Hawdon, Glyn Robbins, Lawrence Roman, Gene Stone, the estate of Dodie Smith, Edward Taylor. COMMISSION UK 10%; Overseas 15%. OVERSEAS ASSOCIATES worldwide. No unsolicited mss. Send synopsis with sample scene(s)/first chapters in the first instance. No reading fee.

Jill Foster Ltd

9 Barb Mews, Brook Green, London W6 7PA
☎020 7602 1263 Fax 020 7602 9336
✉ agents@jflagency.com

Contacts *Jill Foster, Alison Finch, Simon Williamson, Dominic Lord, Gary Wild*

Founded 1976. Handles scripts for TV, drama and comedy. No fiction, short stories or poetry. CLIENTS include Ian Brown, Jan Etherington and Gavin Petrie, Phil Ford, Nev Fountain and Tom Jamieson, Rob Gittins, Jenny Lecoat, Jim Pullin and Fraser Steele, Pete Sinclair, Peter Tilbury, Susan Wilkins. COMMISSION Home 12½%; Books, US & Translation 15%. No unsolicited mss; approach by letter in the first instance. No approaches by e-mail. No reading fee.

Fox & Howard Literary Agency

4 Bramerton Street, London SW3 5JX
☎020 7352 8691 Fax 020 7352 8691

Contacts *Chelsey Fox, Charlotte Howard*

Founded 1992. A small agency, specialising in non-fiction, that prides itself on 'working closely with its authors'. Handles biography, history and popular culture, reference, business, mind, body and spirit, health and fitness. COMMISSION Home 15%; US & Translation 20%. No unsolicited mss; send letter and synopsis with s.a.e. for response. No reading fee.

FRA★

17 Deanhill Road, London SW14 7DQ
☎020 8255 7755 Fax 020 8286 4860
✉ guy@futermanrose.co.uk

www.futermanrose.co.uk
Biography/Non-Fiction/Screenplays *Guy Rose*
(guy@futermanrose.co.uk)
Adult Fiction *Betty Schwartz*
(betty@futermanrose.co.uk)
Teen Fiction *Alexandra Groom*
(alexandra@futermanrose.co.uk)
Founded 1984. Handles fiction; scripts for film and TV; biography; show business; current affairs and teenage fiction. No science fiction, fantasy or young children's. CLIENTS include Christian Piers Betley, Lesley Crewe, Joanne & Jerry Dryansky, Royston Ellis, Stephen Griffin, Brian Harvey, Paul Hendy, Keith R. Lindsay, Stephen Lowe, Eric MacInnes, Paul Marx, Francis Matthews, Max Morgan-Witts, Dr Ciarán O'Keeffe, Erin Pizzey, Paul Rattigan, Liz Rettig, Yvonne Ridley, Peter Sallis, Pat Silver-Lasky, Bill Tidy, Dr Mark White, Toyah Willcox, Simon Woodham, Allen Zeleski. COMMISSION 15–20%. No unsolicited mss. Send preliminary letter with brief resumé, detailed synopsis, first 20 pages (approx.) and s.a.e.

Fraser Ross Associates
6 Wellington Place, Edinburgh EH6 7EQ
☎0131 657 4412/0131 553 2759
✉ kjross@tiscali.co.uk *and*
   lindsey.fraser@tiscali.co.uk
Contact *Lindsey Fraser, Kathryn Ross*
Founded 2002. Handles children's books, adult literary and mainstream fiction. No poetry, short stories, adult fantasy and science fiction, academic, scripts. CLIENTS Thomas Bloor, Sally J Collins, Chris Fisher, Vivian French, Janey Louise Jones, Tanya Landman, Iain MacIntosh, Jack McLean, Michaela Morgan, Dugald Steer, Linda Strachan. COMMISSION Home 10%; USA & Translation 20%. Send preliminary letter, synopsis, first three chapters or equivalent, c.v. and s.a.e. No reading fee.

Futerman, Rose & Associates
See **FRA**

Jüri Gabriel
35 Camberwell Grove, London SE5 8JA
☎020 7703 6186   Fax 020 7703 6186
Contact *Jüri Gabriel*
Handles quality fiction and non-fiction and (almost exclusively for existing clients) film, TV and radio rights. Jüri Gabriel worked in television, wrote books for 20 years and is chairman of Dedalus publishers. No short stories, articles, verse or books for children. CLIENTS include

Maurice Caldera, Diana Constance, Miriam Dunne, Pat Gray, Mikka Haugaard, Robert Irwin, John Lucas, David Madsen, Richard Mankiewicz, Karina Mellinger, David Miller, Andy Oakes, John Outram, Philip Roberts, Dr Stefan Szymanski, Frances Treanor, Dr Terence White, Chris Wilkins, Dr Robert Youngson. COMMISSION Home 10%; US & Translation 20%. Unsolicited mss ('two-page synopsis and three sample chapters in first instance, please') welcome if accompanied by return postage and letter giving sufficient information about author's writing experience, aims, etc.

Eric Glass Ltd
25 Ladbroke Crescent, London W11 1PS
☎020 7229 9500   Fax 020 7229 6220
✉ eglassltd@aol.com
Contacts *Janet Glass, Sissi Lichtenstein*
Founded 1934. Handles fiction, non-fiction and scripts for publication or production in all media. No poetry, short stories or children's works. CLIENTS include Herbert Appleman, Pierre Chesnot, Charles Dyer, Henry Fleet, Tudor Gates, Philip Goulding and the estates of Rodney Ackland, Marc Camoletti, Jean Cocteau, Warwick Deeping, William Douglas Home, Philip King, Pauline Macaulay, Robin Maugham, Alan Melville, Brendan Murray, Beverley Nichols, Jack Popplewell, Jean-Paul Sartre. COMMISSION Home 15%; US & Translation 20%. OVERSEAS ASSOCIATES in the US, Australia, Czech Republic, France, Germany, Greece, Holland, Italy, Japan, Poland, Scandinavia, Slovakia, South Africa, Spain. No unsolicited mss. Return postage required. No reading fee.

David Godwin Associates
55 Monmouth Street, London WC2H 9DG
☎020 7240 9992   Fax 020 7395 6110
✉ assistant@davidgodwinassociates.co.uk
www.davidgodwinassociates.co.uk
Contact *David Godwin*
Founded 1996. Handles literary and general fiction, non-fiction, biography. No scripts, science fiction or children's. No reading fee. COMMISSION Home 10%; Overseas 20%. 'Please contact the office before making a submission.'

Annette Green Authors' Agency
1 East Cliff Road, Tunbridge Wells TN4 9AD
☎01892 514275   Fax 01892 518124
✉ annettekgreen@aol.com
www.annettegreenagency.co.uk
Contact *Address material to the Agency*

Founded 1998. Handles literary and general fiction and non-fiction, popular culture and current affairs, science, music, film, history, biography, children's and teenage fiction. No dramatic scripts or poetry. CLIENTS include Andrew Baker, Bill Broady, Meg Cabot, Simon Conway, Terry Darlington, Justin Hill, Anvar Khan, Maria McCann, Adam Macqueen, Ian Marchant, Professor Charles Pasternak, Kirsty Scott, Bernadette Strachan, Elizabeth Woodcraft. COMMISSION Home 15%; US & Translation 20%. Letter, synopsis, sample chapters and s.a.e. essential. No reading fee.

Christine Green Authors' Agent★
6 Whitehorse Mews, Westminster Bridge Road, London SE1 7QD
☎020 7401 8844   Fax 020 7401 8860
✉ info@christinegreen.co.uk
www.christinegreen.co.uk

Contact *Christine Green*

Founded 1984. Handles fiction (general and literary) and general non-fiction. No scripts, poetry or children's. COMMISSION Home 10%; US & Translation 20%. Initial letter, synopsis and first three chapters preferred. No reading fee but return postage essential.

Louise Greenberg Books Ltd★
The End House, Church Crescent, London N3 1BG
☎020 8349 1179   Fax 020 8343 4559
✉ louisegreenberg@msn.com

Contact *Louise Greenberg*

Founded 1997. Handles full-length literary fiction and serious non-fiction only. COMMISSION Home 15%; US & Translation 20%. DRAMATIC ASSOCIATE Micheline Steinberg Associates; CHILDREN'S ASSOCIATE Sarah Manson Literary Agent. *No telephone approaches.* No reading fee. S.a.e. essential.

Greene & Heaton Ltd★
37 Goldhawk Road, London W12 8QQ
☎020 8749 0315   Fax 020 8749 0318
www.greeneheaton.co.uk

Contacts *Carol Heaton, Judith Murray, Antony Topping, Linda Davis* (children's), *Will Francis*

A medium-sized agency with a broad range of clients. Handles all types of fiction and non-fiction. No original scripts for theatre, film or TV. CLIENTS include Mark Barrowcliffe, Bill Bryson, Jan Dalley, Marcus du Sautoy, Hugh Fearnley-Whittingstall, Michael Frayn, P.D. James, William Leith, Mary Morrissy, C.J.

Sansom, William Shawcross, Sarah Waters. COMMISSION Home 15%; US & Translation 20%. OVERSEAS ASSOCIATES worldwide. No reply to unsolicited submissions without s.a.e. and/or return postage.

Gregory & Company Authors' Agents★
(formerly **Gregory & Radice**)
3 Barb Mews, London W6 7PA
☎020 7610 4676   Fax 020 7610 4686
✉ info@gregoryandcompany.co.uk (general enquiries)
www.gregoryandcompany.co.uk

Contact *Jane Gregory*
Editorial Manager *Emma Dunford*
Rights Manager *Claire Morris*
Administration *Jemma McDonagh*

Founded 1987. Handles all kinds of fiction and general non-fiction. Special interest fiction – literary, commercial, women's fiction, crime, suspense and thrillers. 'We are particularly interested in books which will also sell to publishers abroad.' No original plays, film or TV scripts (only published books are sold to film and TV). No science fiction, fantasy, poetry, academic or children's books. No reading fee. Editorial advice given to own authors. COMMISSION Home 15%; US, Translation, Radio/TV/Film 20%. Is well represented throughout Europe, Asia and US. No unsolicited mss; send a preliminary letter with c.v., synopsis, first three chapters and future writing plans (plus return postage). Short submissions by fax or e-mail (maryjones@gregoryandcompany.co.uk) in the first instance; maximum five pages.

David Grossman Literary Agency Ltd
118b Holland Park Avenue, London W11 4UA
☎020 7221 2770   Fax 020 7221 1445

Contact *Submissions Dept.*

Founded 1976. Handles full-length fiction and general non-fiction – good writing of all kinds and anything healthily controversial. No verse or technical books for students. No original screenplays or teleplays (only works existing in volume form are sold for performance rights). Generally works with published writers of fiction only but 'truly original, well-written novels from beginners' will be considered. COMMISSION Rates vary for different markets. OVERSEAS ASSOCIATES throughout Europe, Asia, Brazil and the US. Best approach by preliminary letter giving full description of the work and, in the case of fiction, with the first 50 pages. 'Please ensure material is printed in at least 1½ spacing on one side of paper only; that all pages are numbered consecutively throughout and in minimum 11pt typeface.' All material must be accompanied by return postage. No approaches or submissions by fax or e-mail. No unsolicited mss. No reading fee.

Gunn Media Associates
8 Lower James Street, London W1F 9EL
✉ ali@gunnmedia.co.uk

Contacts *Ali Gunn, Alice Hart-Dyke*

Founded 2005. Handles commercial fiction and non-fiction. No scripts. CLIENTS include Jenny Colgan, Brian Freeman, Mil Millington, Gilda O'Neill. COMMISSION Home 15%; US & Translation 20%. ASSOCIATES Gelfman Schneider, LJK Literary, Fletcher Parry. Unsolicited mss, sample chapters and synopses welcome; approach in writing. No reading fee.

The Rod Hall Agency Limited
6th Floor, Fairgate House, 78 New Oxford Street, London W1A 1HB
☎ 020 7079 7987   Fax 020 7079 7988
✉ office@rodhallagency.com
www.rodhallagency.com

Contact *Charlotte Mann*

Founded 1997. Handles drama for film, TV and theatre and writers-directors. Does not represent writers of episodes for TV series where the format is provided but represents originators of series. CLIENTS include Simon Beaufoy (*The Full Monty*), Jeremy Brock (*Mrs Brown*), Liz Lochhead (*Perfect Days*), Martin McDonagh (*The Pillowman*), Simon Nye (*Men Behaving Badly*). COMMISSION Home 10%; US 15%; Translation 20%. No reading fee.

Margaret Hanbury Literary Agency★
27 Walcot Square, London SE11 4UB
☎ 020 7735 7680   Fax 020 7793 0316
✉ maggie@hanburyagency.demon.co.uk

Contact *Margaret Hanbury*

Personally run agency representing quality fiction and non-fiction. No plays, scripts, poetry, children's books, fantasy, horror. CLIENTS include George Alagiah, J.G. Ballard, Simon Callow, Jane Glover, Bernard Hare, Judith Lennox, Katie Price. COMMISSION Home 15%; Overseas 20%. No unsolicited approaches.

Roger Hancock Ltd
4 Water Lane, London NW1 8NZ
☎ 020 7267 4418   Fax 020 7267 0705
✉ info@rogerhancock.com

Contact *Material should be addressed to the Company*

Founded 1960. Special interests: comedy drama and light entertainment. Scripts only. No books. COMMISSION Home 10%; Overseas 15%. Unsolicited mss not welcome. Initial phone call required.

Antony Harwood Limited
103 Walton Street, Oxford OX2 6EB
☎ 01865 559615   Fax 01865 310660
✉ mail@antonyharwood.com
www.antonyharwood.com

Contacts *Antony Harwood, James Macdonald Lockhart*

Founded 2000. Handles fiction and non-fiction. CLIENTS Amanda Craig, Peter F. Hamilton, Alan Hollinghurst, A.L. Kennedy, Douglas Kennedy, Chris Manby, George Monbiot, Tim Parks. COMMISSION Home 15%; US & Translation 20%. Send letter and synopsis with return postage in the first instance. No reading fee.

A.M. Heath & Co. Ltd★
6 Warwick Court, London WC1R 5DJ
☎ 020 7242 2811   Fax 020 7242 2711
www.amheath.com

Contacts *Bill Hamilton, Sara Fisher, Sarah Molloy, Victoria Hobbs, Euan Thorneycroft*

Founded 1919. Handles fiction, general non-fiction and children's. No dramatic scripts, poetry or short stories. CLIENTS include Christopher Andrew, Bella Bathurst, Anita Brookner, Patricia Duncker, Geoff Dyer, Katie Fforde, Lesley Glaister, Graham Hancock, Conn Iggulden, Hilary Mantel, Hilary Norman, Susan Price, John Sutherland, Adam Thorpe, Barbara Trapido. COMMISSION Home 15%; US & Translation 20%; Film & TV 15%. OVERSEAS ASSOCIATES in the US, Europe, South America, Japan and the Far East. Preliminary letter and synopsis essential. No reading fee.

Rupert Heath Literary Agency
177a Old Winton Road, Andover SP10 2DR
☎ 020 7788 7807   Fax 020 7691 9331
✉ emailagency@rupertheath.com

Contact *Rupert Heath*

Founded 2000. Handles literary and general fiction and non-fiction, including history, biography and autobiography, current affairs, popular science, the arts and popular culture. No scripts or poetry. COMMISSION Home 15%; US & Translation 20%. OVERSEAS ASSOCIATES worldwide. Approach with e-mail or letter (sample chapter and s.a.e.). E-mail submission preferred. No reading fee.

Henser Literary Agency
174 Pennant Road, Llanelli SA14 8HN
☎01554 753520
✉ henserliteraryagency@btopenworld.com

Contact *Steve Henser*

Founded 2002. Handles mystery, mainstream, literary fiction, fantasy, science fiction. Also film, TV, radio and theatre scripts. No horror. Specialises in translations from Japanese into English – especially literary fiction. CLIENTS include John Campbell, Mary Matsumoto. COMMISSION Home 15%; Foreign & Translation 20%. No unsolicited mss, synopses or ideas as not looking for additional clients at this time.

hhb agency ltd
6 Warwick Court, London WC1R 5DJ
☎020 7405 5525
✉ heather@hhbagency.com
www.hhbagency.com

Contact *Heather Holden-Brown*

Founded in 2005 by Heather Holden-Brown, a publishing editor for 20 years with Waterstone's, Harrap, BBC Books and Headline. Handles non-fiction: history and politics, contemporary autobiography/biography, entertainment and TV, business, family memoir, food and cookery. No scripts. COMMISSION Home 15%. No unsolicited mss; please contact by e-mail or telephone before sending any material. No reading fee.

David Higham Associates Ltd★
5–8 Lower John Street, Golden Square, London W1F 9HA
☎020 7434 5900 Fax 020 7437 1072
✉ dha@davidhigham.co.uk
www.davidhigham.co.uk

Books *Anthony Goff, Bruce Hunter, Veronique Baxter, Lizzy Kremer, Caroline Walsh* (children's)
Scripts *Nicky Lund, Georgina Ruffhead, Gemma Hirst*

Founded 1935. Handles fiction, general non-fiction (biography, history, current affairs, etc.) and children's books. Also scripts. CLIENTS include John le Carré, J.M. Coetzee, Stephen Fry, Jane Green, James Herbert, Alexander McCall Smith, Lynne Truss, Jacqueline Wilson. COMMISSION Home 15%; US & Translation 20%; Scripts 10%. Preliminary letter with synopsis essential in first instance. No reading fee.

Vanessa Holt Ltd★
59 Crescent Road, Leigh-on-Sea SS9 2PF
☎01702 473787 Fax 01702 471890
✉ vanessa@holtlimited.freeserve.co.uk

Contact *Vanessa Holt*

Founded 1989. Handles general fiction, non-fiction and non-illustrated children's books. No scripts, poetry, academic or technical. Specialises in crime fiction, commercial and literary fiction, and particularly interested in books with potential for sales abroad and/or to TV. COMMISSION Home 15%; US & Translation 20%; Radio/TV/Film 15%. Represented in all foreign markets. No unsolicited mss. Representation by arrangement only.

Kate Hordern Literary Agency
18 Mortimer Road, Clifton, Bristol BS8 4EY
☎0117 923 9368 Fax 0117 973 1941
✉ katehordern@blueyonder.co.uk

Contact *Kate Hordern*

Founded 1999. Handles quality fiction and general non-fiction. CLIENTS Richard Bassett, Jeff Dawson, Leigh Eduardo, Kylie Fitzpatrick, Duncan Hewitt, J.T. Lees, Will Randall. COMMISSION Home 15%; US & Translation 20%. OVERSEAS ASSOCIATES VVV Agency, France; Carmen Balcells Agency, Spain; Synopsis Agency, Russia and various agencies in Asia. Approach in writing in the first instance with details of project. New clients taken on very selectively. Synopsis required for fiction; proposal/chapter breakdown for non-fiction. Sample chapters on request only. S.a.e. essential. No reading fee.

Valerie Hoskins Associates Limited
20 Charlotte Street, London W1T 2NA
☎020 7637 4490 Fax 020 7637 4493
✉ vha@vhassociates.co.uk

Contacts *Valerie Hoskins, Rebecca Watson*

Founded 1983. Handles scripts for film, TV and radio. Special interests feature films, animation and TV. COMMISSION Home 12½%; US 20% (maximum). No unsolicited scripts; preliminary letter of introduction essential. No reading fee.

ICM

Oxford House, 76 Oxford Street, London
W1D 1BS
☎020 7636 6565   Fax 020 7323 0101
www.icmlondon.co.uk

Contacts *Sue Rodgers, Jessica Sykes, Cathy King, Greg Hunt, Hugo Young, Michael McCoy, Duncan Heath, Paul Lyon-Maris*

Founded 1973. Specialises in scripts for film, theatre, TV and radio. No reading fee. OVERSEAS ASSOCIATES ICM, New York/Los Angeles.

ICM Books

International Creative Management Ltd, 4–6 Soho Square, London W1D 3PZ
☎020 7432 0800   Fax 020 7432 0808
www.icmtalent.com

Contacts *Kate Jones, Margaret Halton*

Handles fiction and non-fiction; no plays or scripts. OVERSEAS ASSOCIATE International Creative Management Inc., 40 West 57th Street, New York, NY 10019, USA. Submissions must include sample chapters and letter. No reading fee.

The Inspira Group

5 Bradley Road, Enfield EN3 6ES
☎020 8292 5163   Fax 0870 139 3057
✉ darin@theinspiragroup.com
www.theinspiragroup.com

Managing Director *Darin Jewell*

Founded 1996. Handles children's books, crime fiction, lifestyle/relationships, science fiction/fantasy. No scripts. CLIENTS Dominic Wyse, C.W. Reed, Mike Haskins, Steve Arnott, Stephanie Baudet. COMMISSION Home & US 15%. Unsolicited mss and synopses welcome; approach by e-mail or telephone. No reading fee but may ask authors to pay for editing, if required.

Intercontinental Literary Agency★

Centric House, 391 Strand, London
WC2R 0LT
☎020 7379 6611   Fax 020 7240 4724
✉ ila@ila-agency.co.uk

Contacts *Nicki Kennedy, Sam Edenborough*

Founded 1965. Handles translation rights only for, among others, the authors of PFD, London; PFD, New York; LAW Ltd, London; Harold Matson Co. Inc., New York.

International Scripts

1A Kidbrooke Park Road, London SE3 0LR
☎020 8319 8666   Fax 020 8319 0801
✉ internationalscripts@btinternet.com

Contacts *Bob Tanner, Pat Hornsey, Jill Lawson*

Founded 1979 by Bob Tanner. Handles most types of books (non-fiction and fiction) and scripts for most media. No poetry, articles or short stories. CLIENTS include Jane Adams, Zita Adamson, Ashleigh Bingham, Simon Clark, Ann Cliff, Dr James Fleming, June Gadsby, Julie Harris, Robert A. Heinlein, Anna Jacobs, Anne Jones, Richard Laymon, Trevor Lummis, Margaret Muir, Nick Oldham, Chris Pascoe, Christine Poulson, John and Anne Spencer, Janet Woods. COMMISSION Home 15%; US & Translation 20%. OVERSEAS ASSOCIATES include Ralph Vicinanza, USA; Thomas Schlück, Germany. Preliminary letter plus s.a.e. required. An editorial contribution plus return postage may be requested for reading mss.

Barrie James Literary Agency (including **New Authors Showcase**)

Rivendell, Kingsgate Close, Torquay
TQ2 8QA
☎01803 326617
✉ mail@newauthors.org.uk
www.newauthors.org.uk

Contact *Barrie James*

Founded 1997. No unsolicited mss. First approach should be made by sending s.a.e. or e-mail. No reading fee but small charge is made for display on the Internet.

Janklow & Nesbit (UK) Ltd

33 Drayson Mews, London W8 4LY
☎020 7376 2733   Fax 020 7376 2915
✉ queries@janklow.co.uk

Contacts *Tif Loehnis, Claire Paterson*

Founded 2000. Handles fiction and non-fiction; commercial and literary. (See also Janklow & Nesbit Associates, New York, under *US Literary Agents*.) No unsolicited mss. Send full outline (non-fiction), synopsis and three sample chapters (fiction) plus informative covering letter and return postage.

Johnson & Alcock★

Clerkenwell House, 45–47 Clerkenwell Green, London EC1R 0HT
☎020 7251 0125   Fax 020 7251 2172
✉ info@johnsonandalcock.co.uk

Contacts *Michael Alcock, Andrew Hewson, Anna Power, Merel Reinink*

Founded 1956. Handles literary and commercial fiction, children's fiction; general non-fiction including current affairs, biography and memoirs, history, lifestyle, health and personal development. No poetry, screenplays, science fiction, technical or academic material. COMMISSION Home 15%; US & Translation 20%. No unsolicited mss. For non-fiction only approach by letter in the first instance giving details of writing and other media experience, plus synopsis. S.a.e. essential for response. No reading fee.

Jane Judd Literary Agency★
18 Belitha Villas, London N1 1PD
☎020 7607 0273 Fax 020 7607 0623

Contact *Jane Judd*

Founded 1986. Handles general fiction and non-fiction: women's fiction, crime, thrillers, literary fiction, humour, biography, investigative journalism, health, women's interests and travel. 'Looking for good contemporary women's fiction but not Mills & Boon-type; also historical fiction and non-fiction.' No scripts, academic, gardening, short stories or DIY. CLIENTS include Andy Dougan, Cliff Goodwin, Jill Mansell, Jonathon Porritt, Rosie Rushton, Manda Scott, David Winner. COMMISSION Home 10%; US & Translation 20%. Approach with letter, including synopsis, first chapter and s.a.e. Initial telephone call helpful in the case of non-fiction.

Tamar Karet Literary Agency
56 Priory Road, London N8 7EX
☎020 8340 6460
✉ tamar.karet.agent@btinternet.com

Contact *Tamar Karet*

Specialises in fiction, literary travel, leisure, biography, history, social affairs and politics. No academic, children's, poetry, science fiction, horror, militaria or scripts. COMMISSION Home 15%; US & Translation 20%. No unsolicited mss; no submissions by e-mail. Send synopsis and brief sample in hard copy with e-mail address or s.a.e. if return requested

Michelle Kass Associates★
85 Charing Cross Road, London WC2H 0AA
☎020 7439 1624 Fax 020 7734 3394
✉ office@michellekass.co.uk

Contacts *Michelle Kass*

Founded 1991. Handles literary fiction, film and television primarily. COMMISSION Home 10%; US & Translation 15–20%. No mss accepted without preliminary phone call or e-mail. No reading fee.

Frances Kelly★
111 Clifton Road, Kingston upon Thames KT2 6PL
☎020 8549 7830 Fax 020 8547 0051

Contact *Frances Kelly*

Founded 1978. Handles non-fiction, including illustrated: biography, history, art, self-help, food & wine, complementary medicine and therapies, finance and business books; and academic non-fiction in all disciplines. No scripts except for existing clients. COMMISSION Home 10%; US & Translation 20%. No unsolicited mss. Approach by letter with brief description of work or synopsis, together with c.v. and return postage.

Knight Features
20 Crescent Grove, London SW4 7AH
☎020 7622 1467 Fax 020 7622 1522
✉ peter@knightfeatures.co.uk

Contacts *Peter Knight, Samantha Ferris, Gaby Martin, Andrew Knight*

Founded 1985. Handles motor sports, cartoon books, puzzles, business, history, factual and biographical material. No poetry, science fiction or cookery. CLIENTS include Frank Dickens, Gray Jolliffe, Angus McGill, Chris Maslanka, Barbara Minto. COMMISSION dependent upon authors and territories. OVERSEAS ASSOCIATES United Media, US; Auspac Media, Australia; Puzzle Co., New Zealand. No unsolicited mss and no e-mail submissions. Send letter accompanied by c.v. and s.a.e. with synopsis of proposed work.

LAW★
14 Vernon Street, London W14 0RJ
☎020 7471 7900 Fax 020 7471 7910

Contacts *Mark Lucas, Julian Alexander, Araminta Whitley, Alice Saunders, Lucinda Cook, Peta Nightingale, Lizzie Jones, Warsan Ali, Philippa Milnes-Smith* (children's), *Helen Norris* (children's)

Founded 1996. Handles full-length commercial and literary fiction, non-fiction and children's books. No fantasy (except children's), plays, poetry or textbooks. Film and TV scripts handled for established clients only. COMMISSION Home 15%; US & Translation 20%. OVERSEAS ASSOCIATES worldwide. Unsolicited mss considered; send brief covering letter, short synopsis and two sample chapters. S.a.e. essential. No e-mailed or disk submissions.

LBA
See **Luigi Bonomi Associates Limited**

Barbara Levy Literary Agency★
64 Greenhill, Hampstead High Street, London NW3 5TZ
☎020 7435 9046 Fax 020 7431 2063

Contacts *Barbara Levy, John Selby*

Founded 1986. Handles general fiction, non-fiction, and film and TV rights. COMMISSION Home 10%; US 20%; Translation by arrangement, in conjunction with The Buckman Agency. US ASSOCIATE Writers House, New York. No unsolicited mss. No reading fee.

Limelight Management★
33 Newman Street, London W1T 1PY
☎020 7637 2529 Fax 020 7637 2538
✉ limelight.management@virgin.net
www.limelightmanagement.com

Contacts *Fiona Lindsay, Linda Shanks*

Founded 1991. Handles general non-fiction: cookery, gardening, antiques, interior design, wine, art and crafts and health. No fiction, TV, film, radio or theatre. Specialises in illustrated books. COMMISSION Home 15%; US & Translation 20%. Unsolicited mss welcome; send preliminary letter (s.a.e. essential). No reading fee.

The Christopher Little Literary Agency★
10 Eel Brook Studios, 125 Moore Park Road, London SW6 4PS
☎020 7736 4455 Fax 020 7736 4490
✉ info@christopherlittle.net *or*
firstname@christopherlittle.net
www.christopherlittle.net

Contact *Christopher Little*

Founded 1979. Handles commercial and literary full-length fiction and non-fiction. No poetry, plays, science fiction, fantasy, textbooks, illustrated children's or short stories. Film scripts for established clients only. AUTHORS include Steve Barlow and Steve Skidmore, Paul Bajoria, Andrew Butcher, Will Daws, Janet Gleeson, Carol Hughes, Alastair MacNeill, Robert Mawson, Haydn Middleton, Andrew Quinnell, Christopher Matthew, Robert Radcliffe, J.K. Rowling, Darren Shan, Wladyslaw Szpilman, John Watson. COMMISSION Home 15%; US, Canada, Translation, Audio & Motion Picture 20%. Send detailed preliminary letter in the first instance with synopsis, first 2–3 chapters and s.a.e. No reading fee.

London Independent Books
26 Chalcot Crescent, London NW1 8YD
☎020 7706 0486 Fax 020 7724 3122

Proprietor *Carolyn Whitaker*

Founded 1971. A self-styled 'small and idiosyncratic' agency. Handles fiction and non-fiction reflecting the tastes of the proprietor. All subjects considered (except computer books and young children's), providing the treatment is strong and saleable. Scripts handled only if by existing clients. Special interests: boats, travelogues, commercial fiction, science fiction and fantasy, teenage fiction. COMMISSION Home 15%; US & Translation 20%. No unsolicited mss; letter, synopsis and first two chapters with return postage the best approach. No reading fee.

The Andrew Lownie Literary Agency★
17 Sutherland Street, London SW1V 4JU
☎020 7828 1274 Fax 020 7828 7608
✉ lownie@globalnet.co.uk
www.andrewlownie.co.uk

Contact *Andrew Lownie*

Founded 1988. Specialises in non-fiction, especially history, biography, current affairs, military history, UFOs, reference and packaging celebrities and journalists for the book market. No poetry, short stories or science fiction. Formerly a journalist, publisher and himself the author of 12 non-fiction books, Andrew Lownie's CLIENTS include Richard Aldrich, Juliet Barker, the Joyce Cary estate, Tom Divine, Jonathan Fryer, Laurence Gardner, Timothy Good, David Hasselhoff, Robert Holden, Lawrence James, Robert Jobson, Julian Maclaren-Ross estate, Patrick MacNee, Norma Major, Sir John Mills, Tom Pocock, Nick Pope, John Rae, Desmond Seward, David Stafford, Alan Whicker. COMMISSION Worldwide 15%. Preferred approach by e-mail in format suggested on website.

Lucas Alexander Whitley
See **LAW**

Lucy Luck Associates
20 Cowper Road, London W3 6PZ
☎020 8992 6142
✉ enquiries@lucyluck.com
www.lucyluck.com

Contact *Lucy Luck*

Founded 2006. Handles quality fiction and non-fiction. No TV, film, radio or theatre scripts; no illustrated or children's books. CLIENTS include Ewan Morrison, Jon Hotten, Doug Johnstone, Philip Ó Ceallaigh, Catherine O'Flynn, Lorelei Mathias. COMMISSION Home 10%; US & Translation 20% Send sample chapters by post. No reading fee.

Lutyens and Rubinstein★
231 Westbourne Park Road, London W11 1EB
☎020 7792 4855 Fax 020 7792 4833

Partners *Sarah Lutyens, Felicity Rubinstein*
Submissions *Susannah Godman*
Founded 1993. Handles adult fiction and non-fiction books. No TV, film, radio or theatre scripts. COMMISSION Home 15%; US & Translation 20%. Unsolicited mss accepted; send introductory letter, c.v., two chapters and return postage for all material submitted. No reading fee.

Duncan McAra
28 Beresford Gardens, Edinburgh EH5 3ES
☎0131 552 1558   Fax 0131 552 1558
✉ duncanmcara@hotmail.com
Contact *Duncan McAra*
Founded 1988. Handles fiction (literary fiction) and non-fiction, including art, architecture, archaeology, biography, military, travel and books of Scottish interest. COMMISSION Home 10%; Overseas 20%. Preliminary letter, synopsis and sample chapter (including return postage) essential. No reading fee.

McKernan Agency
6 Ann Street, Edinburgh EH4 1PJ
☎0131 332 6776
✉ maggie@mckernanagency.co.uk
Contact *Maggie McKernan*
Founded 2005. Works in conjunction with Capel & Land Ltd. Handles fiction, both literary and commercial; also TV, film, radio and theatre scripts. COMMISSION Home 15%; US & Translation 15%. Send s.a.e. for return of ms. No reading fee.

Bill McLean Personal Management Ltd
23B Deodar Road, London SW15 2NP
☎020 8789 8191
Contact *Bill McLean*
Founded 1972. Handles scripts for all media. No books. CLIENTS Dwynwen Berry, Graham Carlisle, Pat Cumper, Jane Galletly, Patrick Jones, Tony Jordan, Bill Lyons, John Maynard, Michael McStay, Les Miller, Ian Rowlands, Jeffrey Segal, Richard Shannon, Ronnie Smith, Barry Thomas, Garry Tyler, Frank Vickery, Laura Watson, Mark Wheatley. COMMISSION Home 10%. No unsolicited mss. Phone call or introductory letter essential. No reading fee.

Eunice McMullen Children's Literary Agent Ltd
Low Ibbotsholme Cottage, Off Bridge Lane, Troutbeck Bridge, Windermere LA23 1HU
☎01539 448551   Fax 01539 442289
✉ eunicemcmullen@totalise.co.uk
www.eunicemcmullen.co.uk
Contact *Eunice McMullen*
Founded 1992. Handles all types of children's fiction. Especially interested in 9plus and has 'an excellent' list of picture book authors and illustrators. CLIENTS include Wayne Anderson, Jon Berkeley, Sam Childs, Caroline Jayne Church, Jason Cockcroft, Ross Collins, Charles Fuge, Angela McAllister, David Melling, Angie Sage, Gillian Shields, Susan Winter, David Wood. COMMISSION Home 10%; US 15%; Translation 20%. *No unsolicited scripts*. Telephone enquiries only.

Andrew Mann Ltd★
1 Old Compton Street, London W1D 5JA
☎020 7734 4751   Fax 020 7287 9264
✉ manscript@onetel.com
Contacts *Anne Dewe, Tina Betts, Sacha Elliot*
Founded 1975. Handles fiction, general non-fiction, children's and film, TV, theatre, radio scripts. COMMISSION Home 15%; US & Translation 20%. OVERSEAS ASSOCIATES various. Unsolicited mss accepted only with preliminary letter, synopsis, first three chapters; s.a.e. essential. E-mail submissions for synopses only, but 'we do not open attachments'. No reading fee.

Sarah Manson Literary Agent
6 Totnes Walk, London N2 0AD
☎020 88442 0396
✉ info@sarahmanson.com
www.sarahmanson.com
Contact *Sarah Manson*
Founded 2002. Handles quality fiction for children and young adults. COMMISSION Home 10%; Overseas & Translation 20%. Please consult website for submission guidelines. No reading fee.

Marjacq Scripts Ltd
34 Devonshire Place, London W1G 6JW
☎020 7935 9499   Fax 020 7935 9115
✉ subs@marjacq.com
www.marjacq.com
Contact *Philip Patterson* (books), *Luke Speed* (film/TV)
Handles fiction and non-fiction, literary and commercial as well as film, TV, radio scripts. No poetry. COMMISSION Home 10%; Overseas 20%. New work welcome; send brief letter, synopsis and approx. first 50 pages plus s.a.e. No reading fee.

The Marsh Agency Ltd★
11/12 Dover Street, London W1S 4LJ
☎020 7399 2800 Fax 020 7399 2801
✉ submissions@marsh-agency.co.uk
www.marsh-agency.co.uk
Managing Director *Paul Marsh*
Contacts *Geraldine Cooke, Jessica Woollard, Leyla Moghadam, Caroline Hardman*
Foreign Rights *Camilla Ferrier*

Founded in 1994 as international rights specialist for British, American and Canadian agencies. Expanded to act as agents handling fiction and non-fiction. Specialises in authors with international potential. See website for further information on individual agents' areas of interest. COMMISSION Home 15%; Elsewhere 20%; Film & TV 15%. See also Paterson Marsh Ltd. No plays, scripts or poetry. Unsolicited mss considered. Brief e-mail enquiry preferred, with outline (non-fiction) synopsis and two chapters (fiction).

MBA Literary Agents Ltd★
62 Grafton Way, London W1T 5DW
☎020 7387 2076 Fax 020 7387 2042
✉ firstname@mbalit.co.uk
www.mbalit.co.uk
Contacts *Diana Tyler, John Richard Parker, Meg Davis, Laura Longrigg, David Riding, Sophie Gorell Barnes, Susan Smith, Jean Kitson*

Founded 1971. Handles fiction and non-fiction, TV, film, radio and theatre scripts. Works in conjunction with agents in most countries. Also UK representative for Donald Maass Agency, Frances Collin Literary Agency, Martha Millard Literary Agency and the JABberwocky Agency. In November 2006, the Merric Davidson Literary Agency became part of MBA. COMMISSION Home 15%; Overseas 20%; Theatre/TV/Radio 10%; Film 10–20%. See website for submission details.

Christy Moore Ltd
See **Sheil Land Associates Ltd**

William Morris Agency (UK) Ltd★
52/53 Poland Street, London W1F 7LX
☎020 7534 6800 Fax 020 7534 6900
www.wma.com
Managing Director *Caroline Michel*

London office founded in 1965. Worldwide theatrical and literary agency with offices in New York, Beverly Hills, Nashville, Miami and Shanghai. Handles fiction, general non-fiction, TV and film scripts. COMMISSION TV 10%; UK Books 15%; US Books & Translation 20%. Mss for books including covering letter to Book Department; single page synopsis, s.a.e. Limit submission to one title; sample to 50 pages or less. Telephone in the first instance for screenplay and TV submissions. No reading fee.

Michael Motley Ltd
The Old Vicarage, Tredington, Tewkesbury GL20 7BP
☎01684 276390 Fax 01684 297355
Contact *Michael Motley*

Founded 1973. Handles only full-length mss (adult: 60,000+; children's – all ages – and humour: length variable). No short stories or journalism. No science fiction, horror, poetry or original dramatic material. COMMISSION Home 10%; US 15%; Translation 20%. New clients by referral only: no unsolicited material considered. No reading fee.

Judith Murdoch Literary Agency★
19 Chalcot Square, London NW1 8YA
☎020 7722 4197
Contact *Judith Murdoch*

Founded 1993. Handles full-length fiction only, especially accessible literary and commercial women's fiction. No science fiction/fantasy, children's, poetry or short stories. CLIENTS include Anne Bennett, Alison Bond, Meg Hutchinson, Lisa Jewell, Pamela Jooste, Eve Makis. Translation rights handled by The Marsh Agency. COMMISSION Home 15%; US & Translation 20%. No unsolicited mss; approach in writing only enclosing first two chapters and brief synopsis. Submissions by e-mail cannot be considered. Return postage/s.a.e. essential. Editorial advice given. No reading fee.

The Narrow Road Company
182 Brighton Road, Coulsdon CR5 2NF
☎020 8763 9895 Fax 020 8763 2558
✉ richardireson@narrowroad.co.uk
Contact *Richard Ireson*

Founded 1986. Part of the Narrow Road Group. Theatrical literary agency. Handles scripts for TV, theatre, film and radio. No novels or poetry. CLIENTS include Ron Aldridge, Geoff Aymer, Steve Gooch, Joe Graham, David Halliwell, Ian Kershaw, Renny Krupinski, Simon McAllum, Tim Sanders. No unsolicited mss or e-mail attachments; approach by letter with c.v. only. Interested in writers with some experience in theatre, TV and radio

The Maggie Noach Literary Agency★

22 Dorville Crescent, London W6 0HJ
☎020 8748 2926 Fax 020 8748 8057
✉ m-noach@dircon.co.uk

Contact *Maggie Noach*

Founded 1982. Pronounced 'no-ack'. Recommended for promising young writers but very few new clients taken on as it is considered vital to give individual attention to each author's work. Will consider high quality full-length fiction; general non-fiction (especially travel and history); children's books (text only) for reading age eight and upwards. No short stories, poetry, plays, screenplays, cookery, gardening, mind, body & spirit, scientific/academic or specialist non-fiction. 'Absolutely *no* illustrated books.' COMMISSION Home 15%; US & Translation 20%. 'No submissions from authors resident outside the UK as we work very closely with our clients.' Initial approach should consist of a brief description of the book plus two/three sample chapters. Return postage essential. 'We do *not* open e-mail attachments or consider faxed submissions.' No reading fee.

Andrew Nurnberg Associates Ltd★

Clerkenwell House, 45–47 Clerkenwell Green, London EC1R 0QX
☎020 7417 8800 Fax 020 7417 8812
✉ all@nurnberg.co.uk

Directors *Andrew Nurnberg, Sarah Nundy, D. Roger Seaton, Vicky Mark*

Founded in the mid-1970s. Specialises in foreign rights, representing leading authors and agents. Branches in Moscow, Budapest, Prague, Sofia, Warsaw, Riga, Beijing and Taipei. COMMISSION Home 15%; US & Translation 20%.

Alexandra Nye

'Craigower', 6 Kinnoull Avenue, Dunblane FK15 9JG
☎01786 825114

Contact *Alexandra Nye*

Founded 1991. Handles fiction and topical non-fiction. Special interests: literary fiction and history. CLIENTS include Dr Tom Gallagher, Harry Mehta, Robin Jenkins. COMMISSION Home 10%; US 20%; Translation 15%. Unsolicited mss welcome (s.a.e. essential for return). No phone calls. Preliminary approach by letter, with synopsis, preferred. Reading fee for supply of detailed report.

David O'Leary Literary Agents

10 Lansdowne Court, Lansdowne Rise, London W11 2NR
☎020 7229 1623 Fax 020 7229 1623
✉ d.o'leary@virgin.net

Contact *David O'Leary*

Founded 1988. Handles fiction, both popular and literary, and non-fiction. Areas of interest include thrillers, history, popular science, Russia and Ireland (history and fiction). No poetry or science fiction. CLIENTS include David Crackanthorpe, James Kennedy, Nick Kochan, Jim Lusby, Derek Malcolm, Ken Russell. COMMISSION Home & US 10%. OVERSEAS ASSOCIATES Lennart Sane, Scandinavia/Spain/South America; Tuttle Mori, Japan. No unsolicited mss but happy to discuss a proposal. Ring or write in the first instance. No reading fee.

Deborah Owen Ltd★

78 Narrow Street, Limehouse, London E14 8BP
☎020 7987 5119/5441 Fax 020 7538 4004

Contact *Deborah Owen*

Founded 1971. Small agency specialising in only representing two authors direct around the world. *No new authors.* CLIENTS Amos Oz and Delia Smith. COMMISSION Home 10%; US & Translation 15%.

Paterson Marsh Ltd★

11/12 Dover Street, London W1S 4LJ
☎020 7399 2800 Fax 020 7399 2801
✉ submissions@patersonmarsh.co.uk
www.patersonmarsh.co.uk

Contact *Stephanie Ebdon*

Originally founded in 1961 as Mark Paterson & Associates. World rights representatives of authors and publishers with specialisation in psychoanalysis, psychotherapy and related fields. CLIENTS include the estates of Sigmund and Anna Freud, Donald Winnicott, Michael Balint and Wilfred Bion. Also interested in narrative non-fiction, health and neuroscience. Visit website for further information. COMMISSION 20% (including sub-agent's commission). See also The Marsh Agency Ltd. No fiction, scripts, poetry, children's, articles or short stories. Unsolicited mss considered. Brief enquiry preferred, with outline and synopsis.

John Pawsey

60 High Street, Tarring, Worthing BN14 7NR
☎01903 205167 Fax 01903 205167

Contact *John Pawsey*
Founded 1981. Experience in the publishing business has helped to attract some top names here, but the door remains open for bright, new ideas. Handles non-fiction: biography, politics, current affairs, popular culture, travel, sport, business; also fiction: crime, thrillers, suspense but not science fiction, fantasy or horror. Special interests: sport and biography. No children's, drama scripts, poetry, short stories, journalism or academic. CLIENTS include David Rayvern Allen, David Ashforth, Jennie Bond, Elwyn Hartley Edwards, William Fotheringham, Don Hale, Patricia Hall, Dr David Lewis, Anne Mustoe. COMMISSION Home 12½%; US & Translation 19–25%. OVERSEAS ASSOCIATES in the US, Japan, South America and throughout Europe. Preliminary letter with s.a.e. essential (no e-mail submissions). No reading fee.

Maggie Pearlstine Associates Ltd★
See **Crawford & Pearlstine Associates Ltd**

Peters Fraser & Dunlop Group Ltd
See **PFD**

PFD★
Drury House, 34–43 Russell Street, London WC2B 5HA
☎020 7344 1000
Fax 020 7836 9539/7836 9541
✉ postmaster@pfd.co.uk
www.pfd.co.uk
Joint Chairmen *St John Donald, Maureen Vincent*
Books *Caroline Dawnay, Michael Sissons, Pat Kavanagh, Charles Walker, Rosemary Canter, Robert Kirby, Simon Trewin, James Gill, Anna Webber*
Serial *Pat Kavanagh, Carol MacArthur*
Film/TV *Anthony Jones, Tim Corrie, Charles Walker, St. John Donald, Natasha Galloway, Jago Irwin, Louisa Thompson, Lynda Mamy, Andrew Naylor, Alice Dunne*
Actors *Maureen Vincent, Dallas Smith, Lindy King, Ruth Young, Lucy Brazier, Duncan Hayes, Hannah Begbie,*
Theatre *Kenneth Ewing, St John Donald, Nicki Stoddart, Rose Cobbe*
Children's *Rosemary Canter*
PFD represents authors of fiction and non-fiction, children's writers, screenwriters, playwrights, documentary makers, technicians, presenters and actors throughout the world. Consult the website for submission guidelines.

Pollinger Limited★
9 Staple Inn, London WC1V 7QH
☎020 7404 0342   Fax 020 7242 5737
✉ info@pollingerltd.com
www.pollingerltd.com
Managing Director *Lesley Pollinger*
Agents *Lesley Pollinger, Joanna Devereux, Tim Bates, Ruth Needham*
Permissions *electronic form available on website*
Rights Manager *rightsmanager@pollingerltd.com*
Consultants *Leigh Pollinger, Joan Deitch*

CLIENTS include Michael Coleman, Catherine Fisher, Philip Gross, Kelly McKain, Sue Mongredien, Gary Paulsen, Jeremy Poolman, Nicholas Rhea and Sue Welford. Also the estates of H.E. Bates, Louis Bromfield, Erskine Caldwell, Rachel Carson, D.H. Lawrence, John Masters, Carson McCullers, W. Heath Robinson, Eric Frank Russell, Clifford D. Simak and other notables. COMMISSION Home 15%; Translation 20%. Overseas, theatrical and media associates. No unsolicited material.

Shelley Power Literary Agency Ltd★
13 rue du Pré Saint Gervais, 75019 Paris, France
☎00 33 1 42 38 36 49
Fax 00 33 1 40 40 70 08
✉ shelley.power@wanadoo.fr
Contact *Shelley Power*
Founded 1976. Shelley Power works between London and Paris. This is an English agency with London-based administration/accounts office and the editorial office in Paris. Handles general commercial fiction, quality fiction, business books, self-help, true crime, investigative exposés, film and entertainment. No scripts, short stories, children's or poetry. COMMISSION Home 10%; US & Translation 19%. Preliminary letter with brief outline of project (plus return postage as from UK or France) essential. 'We do not consider submissions by e-mail.' No reading fee.

Puttick Agency★
46 Brookfield Mansions, Highgate Hill West, London N6 6AT
☎020 8340 6383   Fax 0870 751 8098
✉ enquiries@puttick.com
www.puttick.com
Contact *Liz Puttick*
Founded 1995. Handles general non-fiction (including illustrated books) with special interest in self-help, health and popular culture. Also

interested in current affairs, biography, history, philosophy, science. No fiction, poetry, scripts, drama or children's books. CLIENTS include William Bloom, Cornel Chin, Mike Fisher, Ann-Marie Gallagher, Nirmala Heriza, Diane Ladd, Martin Lewis, Steve Nobel, Emma Restall Orr, Lorraine Thomas. COMMISSION Home 15%; US & Translation 20%. Works with associates in the US for translation rights. Preliminary enquiries and c.v. by e-mail. No reading fee, but s.a.e. essential.

PVA Management Limited
Hallow Park, Worcester WR2 6PG
☎01905 640663 Fax 01905 641842
✉ pvamanltd@aol.com
Managing Director *Paul Vaughan*

Founded 1978. Handles non-fiction only. COMMISSION 15%. Send synopsis and sample chapters together with return postage.

Real Creatives Worldwide
14 Dean Street, London W1D 3RS
☎020 7437 4188
✉ malcolm.rasala@realcreatives.com
Contacts *Mark Maco, Malcolm Rasala*

Founded 1984. Specialises in drama, science, technology, factual and entertainment. Represents Hollywood TV/film writers and directors, as well as designers, editors, producers and composers. Has a production arm making motion pictures, television, etc. 'Send letter or e-mail requesting a writer's submission agreement covering libel, defamation, plagiarism, etc.' Reading fee: £125.

Redhammer
186 Bickenhall Mansions, Bickenhall Street, London W1U 6BX
☎020 7224 1748 Fax 020 7224 1802
✉ info@redhammer.biz
www.redhammer.biz
Vice President *Peter Cox*
Vice President *Barbara Gorna*

'Provides in-depth management for a small number of highly talented authors.' Willing to take on unpublished authors who are professional in their approach and who have major international potential, ideally for, book, film and/or tv. CLIENTS Martin Bell OBE, Mihir Bose, Brian Clegg, Caris Davis, Audrey Eyton, Senator Orrin Hatch, Gill Hudson, Amanda Lees, Josh McHugh, David McIntee, Michelle Paver, Fiona Ross, Carolyn Soutar, David Soul, Donald Trelford, Justin Wintle, David Yelland.

Submissions considered only if the guidelines given on the website have been followed. Do not send unsolicited mss by post. No radio or theatre scripts. No reading fee.

Rogers, Coleridge & White Ltd★
20 Powis Mews, London W11 1JN
☎020 7221 3717 Fax 020 7229 9084
Chairman *Deborah Rogers*
Managing Director *Peter Straus*
Directors *Gill Coleridge, Pat White, David Miller, Zoe Waldie, Laurence Laluyaux, Stephen Edwards*

Founded 1967. Handles full-length mss fiction, non-fiction and children's books. COMMISSION Home 10%; US & Translation 20%. No submissions by fax or e-mail.

Uli Rushby-Smith Literary Agency
72 Plimsoll Road, London N4 2EE
☎020 7354 2718 Fax 020 7354 2718
Contact *Uli Rushby-Smith*

Founded 1993. Handles fiction and non-fiction, commercial and literary, both adult and children's. Film and TV rights handled in conjunction with a sub-agent. No plays or poetry. COMMISSION Home 15%; US & Translation 20%. Represents UK rights for Curtis Brown, New York (children's), 2.13.61 USA and Columbia University Press. Approach with an outline, two or three sample chapters and explanatory letter in the first instance (s.a.e. essential). No disks. No reading fee.

Rosemary Sandberg Ltd
6 Bayley Street, London WC1B 3HB
☎020 7304 4110
✉ rosemary@sandberg.demon.co.uk
Contact *Rosemary Sandberg*

Founded 1991. In association with Ed Victor Ltd. Specialises in children's writers and illustrators. COMMISSION 10%. No unsolicited mss as client list is currently full.

The Sayle Literary Agency★
8b King's Parade, Cambridge CB2 1SJ
☎01223 303035 Fax 01223 301638
Contact *Rachel Calder*

Handles literary, crime and general fiction, current affairs, social issues, travel, biography, history, general non-fiction. No plays, poetry, children's, textbooks, technical, legal or medical books. COMMISSION Home 15%; US & Translation 20%. OVERSEAS ASSOCIATES Dunow & Carlson Literary Agency; Darhansoff, Verrill and Feldman; Anne Edelstein Literary Agency; New England Publishing Associates, USA; translation rights handled by The Marsh Agency; film rights by Sayle Screen Ltd. No unsolicited mss. Preliminary letter essential, including a brief biographical note and a synopsis plus two or three sample chapters. Return postage essential. No reading fee.

Sayle Screen Ltd
11 Jubilee Place, London SW3 3TD
☎020 7823 3883 Fax 020 7823 3363
✉ info@saylescreen.com
www.saylescreen.com
Agents *Jane Villiers, Matthew Bates, Toby Moorcroft*

Specialises in writers and directors for film and television. Also deals with theatre and radio. Works in association with The Sayle Literary Agency and Greene & Heaton Ltd representing film and TV rights in novels and non-fiction. CLIENTS include Shelagh Delaney, Marc Evans, Margaret Forster, John Forte, Rob Green, Mark Haddon, Christopher Monger, Paul Morrison, Gitta Sereny, Sue Townsend. No unsolicited material without preliminary letter. No e-mail submissions.

The Sharland Organisation Ltd
The Manor House, Manor Street, Raunds NN9 6JW
☎01933 626600 Fax 01933 624860
✉ tsoshar@aol.com
www.sharlandorganisation.co.uk
Contacts *Mike Sharland, Alice Sharland*

Founded 1988. Specialises in national and international film and TV negotiations. Also negotiates multimedia, interactive TV deals and computer game contracts. Handles scripts for film, TV, radio and theatre; also non-fiction. Markets books for film and handles stage, radio, film and TV rights for authors. No scientific, technical or poetry. COMMISSION Home 15%; US & Translation 20%. OVERSEAS ASSOCIATES various. No unsolicited mss. Preliminary enquiry by letter or phone essential.

Sheil Land Associates Ltd★
(incorporating **Richard Scott Simon Ltd 1971** and **Christy Moore Ltd 1912**)
52 Doughty Street, London WC1N 2LS
☎020 7405 9351 Fax 020 7831 2127
✉ info@sheilland.co.uk

Agents, UK & US *Sonia Land, Vivien Green, Ben Mason*
Film/Theatrical/TV *Emily Hayward, Sophie Janson*
Foreign *Gaia Banks, Sophie LeGrande*

Founded 1962. Handles full-length general, commercial and literary fiction and non-fiction, including: social politics, business, history, science, military history, gardening, thrillers, crime, romance, drama, biography, travel, cookery and humour, UK and foreign estates. Also theatre, film, radio and TV scripts. CLIENTS include Peter Ackroyd, Hugh Bicheno, Melvyn Bragg, David Cohen, Catherine Cookson estate, Anna del Conte, Seamus Deane, Greg Dyke, Bonnie Greer, Susan Hill, Richard Holmes, HRH The Prince of Wales, Mark Irving, Richard Mabey, Patrick O'Brian estate, Jean Rhys estate, Graham Rice, Martin Riley, Catherine Sampson, Diane Setterfield, Tom Sharpe, Martin Stephen, Brian Sykes, Jeffrey Tayler, Andrew Taylor, Rose Tremain, Barry Unsworth, John Wilsher, Toby Young. COMMISSION Home 15%; US & Translation 20%. OVERSEAS ASSOCIATES Georges Borchardt, Inc. (Richard Scott Simon). US film and TV representation: CAA, APA, and others. Welcomes approaches from new clients either to start or to develop their careers. Preliminary letter with s.a.e. essential. No reading fee.

Caroline Sheldon Literary Agency★
Thorley Manor Farm, Thorley, Yarmouth PO41 0SJ
☎01983 760205

Also at: 70–75 Cowcross Street, London EC1M 6EJ
Contacts *Caroline Sheldon, Penny Holroyde*

Founded 1985. Handles adult fiction, in particular women's (both commercial and literary) and human-interest non-fiction. Also full-length children's fiction, younger children's fiction, picture books and picture book artists. Actively handles TV and film rights on behalf of clients. COMMISSION Home 10–15%; US & Translation 20%. Submissions should be sent to the Thorley address and include a letter 'describing your ambitions', synopsis, the first three chapters of proposed book and an s.a.e. with sufficient postage for return. No e-mail submissions. No reading fee.

Dorie Simmonds Agency★
67 Upper Berkeley Street, London W1H 7QX
☎020 7569 8686 Fax 020 7569 8696
✉ dhsimmonds@aol.com

Contact *Dorie Simmonds*

Handles a wide range of subjects including commercial fiction and non-fiction, children's books and associated rights. Specialities include contemporary personalities and historical biographies, commercial women's fiction and children's books. COMMISSION Home & US 15%; Translation 20%. Outline required for non-fiction; a short synopsis for fiction with 2–3 sample chapters, and a c.v. with writing experience/publishing history. No reading fee. Return postage essential.

Jeffrey Simmons

15 Penn House, Mallory Street, London NW8 8SX
☎020 7224 8917
✉ jasimmons@btconnect.com

Contact *Jeffrey Simmons*

Founded 1978. Handles biography and autobiography, cinema and theatre, fiction (both quality and commercial), history, law and crime, politics and world affairs, parapsychology and sport (but not exclusively). No science fiction/fantasy, children's books, cookery, crafts, hobbies or gardening. Film scripts handled only if by book-writing clients. Special interest in personality books of all sorts and fiction from young writers (i.e. under 40) with a future. COMMISSION Home 10–15%; US & Foreign 15%. Writers become clients by personal introduction or by letter, enclosing a synopsis if possible, a brief biography, a note of any previously published books, plus a list of any publishers and agents who have already seen the mss.

Richard Scott Simon Ltd

See **Sheil Land Associates Ltd**

Sinclair-Stevenson

3 South Terrace, London SW7 2TB
☎020 7581 2550   Fax 020 7581 2550

Contact *Christopher Sinclair-Stevenson*

Founded 1995. Handles biography, current affairs, travel, history, fiction, the arts. No scripts, children's, academic, science fiction/fantasy. CLIENTS include Jennifer Johnston, J.D.F. Jones, Ross King, Christopher Lee, Andrew Sinclair and the estates of Alec Guinness, John Cowper Powys and John Galsworthy. COMMISSION Home 10%; US 15%; Translation 20%. OVERSEAS ASSOCIATE T.C. Wallace Ltd, New York. Translation rights handled by David Higham Associates. Send synopsis with s.a.e. in the first instance. No reading fee.

Robert Smith Literary Agency Ltd★

12 Bridge Wharf, 156 Caledonian Road, London N1 9UU
☎020 7278 2444   Fax 020 7833 5680
✉ robertsmith.literaryagency@virgin.net

Contact *Robert Smith*

Founded 1997. Handles non-fiction; biography, memoirs, current affairs, entertainment, true crime, cookery and lifestyle. No scripts, fiction, poetry, academic or children's books. CLIENTS Kate Adie (serialisations), Martin Allen, Amanda Barrie (serialisations), Kevin Booth, Stewart Evans, Neil and Christine Hamilton, James Haspiel, Judy Huxtable, Albert Jack, Muriel Jakubait, Lois Jenkins, Roberta Kray, Mike Reid, Professor Bill Rubinstein, Keith Skinner. COMMISSION Home 15%; US & Translation 20%. OVERSEAS ASSOCIATE Thomas Schlück Literary Agency (Germany). No unsolicited mss. Send a letter and synopsis in the first instance. No reading fee.

The Standen Literary Agency

41b Endymion Road, London N4 1EQ
☎020 8245 3053   Fax 020 8245 3053
✉ info@standenliteraryagency.com
www.standenliteraryagency.com

Contact *Mrs Yasmin Standen*

Founded 2004. Handles fiction, both adult and children's. 'We are interested in first time writers.' No TV/radio scripts. CLIENTS Jonathan Yeatman Biggs, Zara Kane, Zoe Marriott, Andrew Murray. COMMISSION Home 15%; Overseas 20%. Follow the submissions procedure on the website. 'With regard to non-fiction, please contact us in the first instance.' No reading fee.

Elaine Steel

110 Gloucester Avenue, London NW1 8HX
☎020 8348 0918   Fax 020 8341 9807
✉ ecmsteel@aol.com

Contact *Elaine Steel*

Founded 1986. Handles scripts, screenplays and books. No technical or academic. CLIENTS include Les Blair, Anna Campion, Michael Eaton, Pearse Elliott, Gwyneth Hughes, Brian Keenan, Troy Kennedy Martin, James Lovelock, Rob Ritchie, Albie Sachs, Ben Steiner. COMMISSION Home 10%; US & Translation 20%. Initial phone call preferred.

Abner Stein★

10 Roland Gardens, London SW7 3PH
☎020 7373 0456   Fax 020 7370 6316

Contact *Arabella Stein*

Founded 1971. Mainly represents US agents and authors but handles some full-length fiction and general non-fiction. No scientific, technical, etc. No scripts. COMMISSION Home 10%; US & Translation 20%.

Micheline Steinberg Associates

104 Great Portland Street, London W1W 6PE
☎020 7631 1310
✉ info@steinplays.com
www.steinplays.com

Contacts *Micheline Steinberg, Matt Connell, Helen MacAuley*

Founded 1988. Specialises in plays for stage, TV, film, animation and radio. Represents writers for film and TV rights in fiction and non-fiction on behalf of book agents. COMMISSION Home 10%; Overseas 15–20%. Works in association with agents in the USA and overseas. No reading fee. Return postage essential.

Shirley Stewart Literary Agency

3rd Floor, 21 Denmark Street, London WC2H 8NA
☎020 7836 4440 Fax 020 7836 3482

Director *Shirley Stewart*

Founded 1993. Handles fiction and non-fiction. No scripts, children's, science fiction, fantasy or poetry. COMMISSION Home 10–15%; US & Translation 20%. OVERSEAS ASSOCIATE Curtis Brown Ltd, New York; Carolyn Swayze Agency, Canada. Will consider unsolicited material; send letter with two or three sample chapters in the first instance. S.a.e. essential. Submissions by fax or on disk not accepted. No reading fee.

Sunflower Literary Agency

106 Mansfield Drive, Redhill RH1 3JN
✉ contact@sunflowerliteraryagency.com
www.sunflowerliteraryagency.com

Senior Editor *Philip Adams*
Correspondence Secretary *David Sherriff*

Founded 2003. Handles full-length fiction, especially thrillers (techno a plus); literary fiction, especially political and/or social satire (controversy a plus); erotica, in any of the above genres. No poetry, screenplays, non-fiction, short fiction, 'who–dunnits' or autobiography. COMMISSION Home 15% (first book), 10% (later books); USA & Translation: additional 5% to base rate. 'We *only* consider work from *unpublished* authors (or major changes of genre).' Electronic submissions preferred: contact via the website only. All requirements listed on the Web page must be fulfilled before e-mail contact is made. No fees charged.

The Susijn Agency Ltd

3rd Floor, 64 Great Titchfield Street, London W1W 7QH
☎020 7580 6341 Fax 020 7580 8626
✉ info@thesusijnagency.com
www.thesusijnagency.com

Contacts *Laura Susijn, Nicola Barr, Elaine Wishart*

Founded April 1998. Specialises in selling rights worldwide in literary fiction and non-fiction. Also represents non-English language authors and publishers for UK, US and translation rights worldwide. COMMISSION Home 15%; US & Translation 15–20%. Send preliminary letter, synopsis and first two chapters by post. No reading fee.

The Tennyson Agency

10 Cleveland Avenue, Wimbledon Chase, London SW20 9EW
☎020 8543 5939
✉ submissions@tenagy.co.uk
www.tenagy.co.uk

Contact *Christopher Oxford*

Founded 2001. Specialises in theatre, radio, television and film scripts. Related material considered on an ad hoc basis. No short stories, children's, poetry, travel, military/historical, academic, fantasy/science fiction or sport. CLIENTS Vivienne Allen, Tony Bagley, Alastair Cording, Caroline Coxon, Iain Grant, Jonathan Holloway, Julian Howell, Philip Hurd-Wood, Joanna Leigh, Antony Mann, John Ryan, Walter Saunders, Diane Speakman, Diana Ward. COMMISSION Home 12½–15%; Overseas 17½–20%. No unsolicited material; send introductory letter with résumé and proposal/outline of work. No reading fee.

Lavinia Trevor Literary Agency★

The Glasshouse, 49A Goldhawk Road, London W12 8QP
☎020 8749 8481 Fax 020 8749 7377

Contact *Lavinia Trevor*

Founded 1993. Handles general fiction (literary and commercial) and non-fiction, including popular science. No fantasy, science-fiction, poetry, academic, technical or children's books. No TV, film, radio, theatre scripts. COMMISSION rate by agreement with author. Approach with a preliminary letter, a brief autobiography and first 50–60 typewritten pages. 'For fiction, a short synopsis is helpful.' S.a.e. essential. No reading fee.

Jane Turnbull★

Mailing address: Barn Cottage, Veryan, Truro
TR2 5QA
☎01872 501317
✉ jane.turnbull@btinternet.com
London office: 58 Elgin Crescent, London
W11 2JJ
☎020 7727 9409
Contact *Jane Turnbull*
Founded 1986. Handles fiction and non-fiction
but specialises in biography, history, current
affairs, self-help and humour. Translation rights
handled by Gillon Aitken Associates Ltd.
COMMISSION Home 10%; US & Foreign 20%.
No unsolicited mss. Approach with letter in the
first instance. No reading fee.

Ed Victor Ltd★

6 Bayley Street, Bedford Square, London
WC1B 3HE
☎020 7304 4100 Fax 020 7304 4111
✉ mary@edvictor.com
Contacts *Ed Victor, Maggie Phillips, Sophie Hicks,
Grainne Fox, Charlie Campbell*
Founded 1976. Handles a broad range of material but leans towards the more commercial
ends of the fiction and non-fiction spectrums.
Excellent children's book list. No poetry, scripts
or academic. Takes on very few new writers and
does not accept unsolicited submissions. After
trying his hand at book publishing and literary
magazines, Ed Victor, an ebullient American,
found his true vocation. Strong opinions, very
pushy and works hard for those whose intelligence he respects. Loves nothing more than a
good title auction. CLIENTS include John
Banville, Herbie Brennan, Eoin Colfer,
Frederick Forsyth, A.A. Gill, Josephine Hart,
Jack Higgins, Nigella Lawson, Kathy Lette,
Allan Mallinson, Andrew Marr, Janet Street-
Porter and the estates of Douglas Adams,
Raymond Chandler, Dame Iris Murdoch, Sir
Stephen Spender and Irving Wallace.
COMMISSION Home & US 15%; Translation
20%. No unsolicited mss.

Wade & Doherty
Literary Agency Ltd

33 Cormorant Lodge, Thomas More Street,
London E1W 1AU
☎020 7488 4171 Fax 020 7488 4172
✉ rw@rwla.com *or* bd@rwla.com
www.rwla.com
Contacts *Robin Wade, Broo Doherty*
Founded 2001. Handles general fiction and non-

fiction including children's books. Specialises in
military history and crime books. No scripts,
poetry, plays or short stories. CLIENTS include
Louise Cooper, Adam Guillain, Georgina
Harding, Caroline Kington, Helen Oyeyemi,
Lance Price, Ewen Southby-Tailyour. COM-
MISSION Home 10%; Overseas & Translation
20%. 'Fees negotiable if a contract has already
been offered.' Send detailed synopsis and first
10,000 words by e-mail with a brief biography.
No reading fee.

Cecily Ware Literary Agents

19C John Spencer Square, London N1 2LZ
☎020 7359 3787 Fax 020 7226 9828
✉ info@cecilyware.com
Contacts *Cecily Ware, Gilly Schuster, Warren
Sherman*
Founded 1972. Primarily a film and TV script
agency representing work in all areas: drama,
children's, series/serials, adaptations, comedies,
etc. COMMISSION Home 10%; US 10–20% by
arrangement. No unsolicited mss or phone
calls. Approach in writing only. No reading fee.

Watson, Little Ltd★

Lymehouse Studios, 38 Georgiana Street,
London NW1 0EB
☎020 7485 5935 Fax 020 7485 6051
✉ office@watsonlittle.com
Contacts *Mandy Little, James Wills*
Handles fiction, commercial women's fiction,
crime and literary fiction. Non-fiction special
interests include history, science, popular psychology, self-help and general leisure books.
Also children's fiction and non-fiction. No
short stories, poetry, TV, play or film scripts. Not
interested in purely academic writers.
COMMISSION Home 15%; US & Translation
20%. OVERSEAS ASSOCIATES The Marsh Agency;
FILM & TV ASSOCIATES The Sharland
Organisation Ltd; MBA Literary Agents; USA
Howard Morhaim (adult); The Chudney
Agency (children). No e-mails or unsolicited
mss. Informative preliminary letter and synopsis
with return postage essential.

A.P. Watt Ltd★

20 John Street, London WC1N 2DR
☎020 7405 6774 Fax 020 7831 2154
✉ apw@apwatt.co.uk
www.apwatt.co.uk
Directors *Caradoc King, Linda Shaughnessy,
Derek Johns, Georgia Garrett, Natasha
Fairweather, Sheila Crowley*
Founded 1875. The oldest-established literary

agency in the world. Handles full-length type-scripts, including children's books, screenplays for film and TV. No poetry, academic or specialist works. CLIENTS include Trezza Azzopardi, David Baddiel, Sebastian Barry, Quentin Blake, Marika Cobbold, Helen Dunmore, Nicholas Evans, Giles Foden, Esther Freud, Janice Galloway, Martin Gilbert, Nadine Gordimer, Linda Grant, Reginald Hill, Michael Holroyd, Michael Ignatieff, Mick Jackson, Philip Kerr, Dick King-Smith, India Knight, John Lanchester, Alison Lurie, Jan Morris, Andrew O'Hagan, Susie Orbach, Tony Parsons, Caryl Phillips, Philip Pullman, Jancis Robinson, Jon Ronson, Elaine Showalter, Zadie Smith, Graham Swift, Fiona Walker and the estates of Graves and Maugham. COMMISSION Home 15%; US & Translation 20%. No unsolicited mss accepted.

Josef Weinberger Plays
12–14 Mortimer Street, London W1T 3JJ
☎020 7580 2827 Fax 020 7436 9616
✉ general.info@jwmail.co.uk
www.josef-weinberger.com
Contact *Michael Callahan*

Josef Weinberger is both agent and publisher of scripts for the theatre. CLIENTS include Ray Cooney, John Godber, Peter Gordon, Debbie Isitt, Arthur Miller, Sam Shepard, John Steinbeck. OVERSEAS REPRESENTATIVES in the USA, Canada, Australia, New Zealand, India, South Africa and Zimbabwe. No unsolicited mss; introductory letter essential. No reading fee.

John Welch, Literary Consultant & Agent
Mill Cottage, Calf Lane, Chipping Camden GL55 6JQ
☎01386 840237 Fax 01386 840568
✉ johnwelch@cyphus.co.uk
Contact *John Welch*

Founded 1992. Handles military aviation and naval history, and history in general. No fiction, poetry, children's books or scripts for radio, TV, film or theatre. Already has a full hand of authors so no new authors being considered. CLIENTS include Alexander Baron, Michael Calvert, Patrick Delaforce, Timothy Jenkins, Sybil Marshall, Ewart Oakeshott, Norman Scarfe, Anthony Trew, Peter Trew, David Wragg. COMMISSION Home 10%.

Eve White Literary Agent
Irish Hill House, Hamstead Marshall,
Newbury RG20 0JB
☎01488 657656

✉ evewhite@btinternet.com
www.evewhite.co.uk
Contact *Eve White*

Founded 2003. Handles full-length adult and children's fiction and non-fiction. No poetry, short stories or textbooks. CLIENTS Steve Emmerson, Shanta Everingtn, Marguerite Hann Syme, Peter J. Murray, Vijay Medtia, Gillian Rogerson, Carol Sinclair, Andy Stanton, Emma Tennant. COMMISSION Home 15%; US & Translation 20%. No unsolicited mss. Post introductory letter (enclose résumé, brief synopsis, e-mail address and phone number) and three chapters. No initial approach by e-mail or telephone. No reading fee.

Dinah Wiener Ltd★
12 Cornwall Grove, Chiswick, London W4 2LB
☎020 8994 6011 Fax 020 8994 6044
Contact *Dinah Wiener*

Founded 1985. Handles fiction and general non-fiction: auto/biography, popular science, cookery. No scripts, children's or poetry. CLIENTS include Valerie-Anne Baglietto, Malcolm Billings, Hugh Brune, Guy Burt, David Deutsch, Jenny Hobbs, Mark Jeffery, Michael Lockwood, Sarah Mason, Daniel Snowman, Mitchell Tonks, Rachel Trethewey, Marcia Willett. COMMISSION Home 15%; US & Translation 20%. Approach with preliminary letter in first instance, giving full but brief c.v. of past work and future plans. Mss submitted must include s.a.e. and be typed in double-spacing.

Rebecca Winfield Literary Agency
5B Walpole Court, Ealing Studios, London W5 5ED
☎020 8567 6738 Fax 020 8567 6738
✉ rebecca.winfield@btopenworld.com
Contact *Rebecca Winfield*

Founded 2003. Specialises in non-fiction; biography, popular culture, history and narrative non-fiction. No children's books, science fiction, fantasy, horror or poetry. COMMISSION Home 15%; US & Translation 20%. Send letter, synopsis and no more than three sample chapters in the first instance together with s.a.e. for return of material. Submissions on disk or by e-mail not accepted. No reading fee.

The Wylie Agency (UK) Ltd
17 Bedford Square, London WC1B 3JA
☎020 7908 5900 Fax 020 7908 5901
✉ mail@wylieagency.co.uk

Handles fiction and non-fiction. No scripts or children's books. COMMISSION Home 10%; US 15%; Translation 20%. The Wylie Agency does not accept unsolicited submissions. Enquire by letter or e-mail before submitting. Any submission must be accompanied by return postage/s.a.e.

AGENCY CONSULTANTS

Agent Research & Evaluation, Inc. (AR&E)
25 Barrow Street, New York, NY 10017 USA
☎001 212 924 9942   Fax 001 212 924 1864
✉ info@agentresearch.com
www.agentresearch.uk.net

Contact *Bill Martin*

US consultancy founded in 1996. Provides authors, editors and other professionals with data on clients and sales made by literary agents in the USA, UK and Canada, i.e. who sells what to whom for how much. Information is culled from the trade and general press, and collection has been continuous since 1980. Individual reports on specific agents and various forms of manuscript-agent match-up services are available. See website for pricing or send s.a.e. Publishes *Talking Agents*, the AR&E newsletter (10 p.a.). The website offers a free service of agent verification: information on whether or not the database reflects that a given agent has created a public record of sales.

UK Literary Scouts

Literary scouts gather information from UK agents, publishers and editors on behalf of foreign clients. They are not literary agents and work only with material that is already commissioned or being handled by an agent. They do **not** accept unsolicited material and do **not** deal directly with writers.

Louise Allen-Jones Literary Scouts
40 Lillieshall Road, Clapham Old Town, London SW4 0LP
☎020 7720 2453 Fax 020 7498 1818
Contacts *Louise Allen-Jones* (louise@louiseallenjones.com), *Mira Popken* (mira@louiseallenjones.com), *Lucy Abrahams* (lucy@louiseallenjones.com)
Scouts for Ullstein, Ullstein Taschenbuch, List, Claassen, Marion von Schröder, Econ, Propyläen, Germany; The English Agency, Japan; A.W. Bruna, Signature, VIP and J.M. Meulenhoff, De Boekerij, 'M', Forum, The Netherlands; Distribuidora Record, Brazil; Keter Books, Israel; Cairo Editore, Italy; BBC TV Drama, UK.

Badcock & Rozycki Literary Scouts
1 Old Compton Street, London W1D 5JA
☎020 7734 7997 Fax 020 7734 6886
Contacts *June Badcock* (june@badcock-rozycki.co.uk), *Barbara Rozycki* (barbara@badcock-rozycki.co.uk), *Claire Holt* (claire@badcock-rozycki.co.uk)
Scouts for Wilhelm Heyne Verlag and Diana Verlag, Germany; Unieboek BV, The Netherlands; RCS Libri Group, Italy; Editions Jean-Claude Lattès, France; Ediciones Salamandra, Spain; Ellinika Grammata, Greece; Werner Söderström Osakeyhtiö, Finland; Forum, Sweden; NW Damm & Son A/S, Norway; Aschehoug Dansk Forlag, Denmark; Edda Media, Iceland.

Natasha Farrant
77 Starfield Road, London W12 9SN
☎020 8746 1857
✉ natasha.farrant@btinternet.com
Contact *Natasha Farrant*
Scouts for children's fiction on behalf of Hachette Jeunesse, France; Edizione Piemme, Italy; Lerner Publishing Group, USA.

Anne Louise Fisher and Suzy Lucas
29 D'Arblay Street, London W1F 8EP
☎020 7494 4609 Fax 020 7494 4611
✉ annelouise@alfisher.co.uk
Contacts *Anne Louise Fisher, Catherine Eccles*
Scouts for Doubleday/Broadway Books/Nan Talese, US; Doubleday/Bond Street Books, Canada; Librarie Plon, Univers Poche//Pocket Jeunesse, France; Karl Blessing Verlag, C. Bertelsmann, Knaus, Siedler, Blanvalet, DVA, C. Bertelsmann Jugenbuch, Germany; Arnoldo Mondadori Editore and Mondadori Ragazzi, Italy; Albert Bonniers Forlag, Sweden; Otava, Finland; Gyldendal Norsk Forlag, Norway; Mouria, Holland; Random House Mondadori, Spain; Patakis Publications, Greece, Heyday Films, UK.

Koukla MacLehose
Arundel House, 3 Westbourne Road, London N7 8AR
☎020 7607 1336 Fax 020 7609 7775
✉ koukla@btopenworld.com
Contact *Koukla MacLehose*
Scouts for Tammi, Finland; Wåhlström & Widstrand, Sweden; Pax, Norway; Rosinante, Samlerens and Forum/Fremad, Denmark; De Bezige Bij, The Netherlands; Hanser, Zsolnay, Sans Souci and Nagel & Kimche, Germany; Gallimard and Denoël, France; Einaudi, Italy; Anagrama, Spain; Asa, Portugal; Psichogios, Greece.

Folly Marland, Literary Scout
6 Elmcroft Street, London E5 0SQ
☎020 8986 0111 Fax 020 8986 0111
✉ fmarland@pobox.com
Contact *Folly Marland*
Scouts for Scherz Verlag, Krüger Verlag, Germany; Sony Magazines, Japan; Livani, Greece.

Rosalind Ramsay Limited

First Floor, 2 Ingate Place, London SW8 3NS
☎020 7622 3336
✉ ros@rosalindramsay.com
www.rosalindramsay.com

Contact *Rosalind Ramsay*

Scouts for Ambo Anthos, The Netherlands; Kadokawa, Japan; Kiepenheuer and Witsch, Germany; Kinneret Zmora Bitan Dvir, Israel; Norstedts, Sweden; Sperling & Kupfer, Italy; Channel 4 and FilmFour, UK.

Heather Schiller

✉ heather.schiller@virgin.net

Contact *Heather Schiller*

Scouts for BZZTÔH, The Netherlands; Cappelen, Norway; Piper, Germany; Lindhardt & Ringhof, Denmark.

Petra Sluka

21 Denmark Street, London WC2H 8NA
☎020 7836 9028   Fax 020 7836 3982
✉ petrasluka@aol.com

Also at: 3 Dry Bank Road, Tonbridge TN10 3BS
☎01732 353694 Fax 01732 359225

Contact *Petra Sluka*

Scouts for Verlagsgruppe Lübbe, Gemany; De Fontein/De Kern, Holland; J'ailu, France; Bra Böcker, Sweden; Japan Uni Agency, Inc., Japan; Harlenic Hallas, Greece.

Jane Southern

11 Russell Avenue, Bedford MK40 3TE
☎01234 400147   Fax 01234 400146
✉ jane.southern@ntlworld.com

Contact *Jane Southern*

UK Scout for Hoffmann und Campe Verlag and Der Club, Germany; The House of Books, The Netherlands; Belfond, Presses de la Cité and France Loisirs, France; Newton & Compton, Italy.

Van Lear Limited

PO Box 21816, London SW6 5ZU
☎020 7385 1199   Fax 020 7385 6262
✉ evl@vanlear.co.uk

Contact *Liz Van Lear*

Scouts for Droemer Knaur, Germany; Planeta Group, Spain and Latin America; Damm, Sweden; Oceanida, Greece; Dom Quixote, Portugal; il Saggiatore, Italy; Veen Bosch & Keuning, The Netherlands.

Sylvie Zannier-Betts

114 Springfield Road, Brighton BN1 6DE
☎01273 557370   Fax 01273 557370
✉ szannier@lineone.net

Contact *Sylvie Zannier-Betts*

Scouts for Uitgeverij De Geus, The Netherlands; S. Fischer Verlag, Germany; Gummerus Publishers, Finland; Alfabeta Bokfoerlag, Sweden; Borgen Forlag, Denmark. Exclusive agent in the UK for S. Fischer Verlag, Germany.

National Newspapers

Departmental e-mail addresses are too numerous to include in this listing. They can be obtained from the newspaper's main switchboard or the department in question

The Business
292 Vauxhall Bridge Road, London
SW1V 1SS
☎020 7961 0000
Owner *Barclay Brothers*
Editor-in-Chief *Andrew Neil*
Circulation 148,774
Launched in 1998. Sunday national newspaper dedicated to business, finance and politics. No unsolicited material. All ideas must be discussed with the department's editor in advance.
Political Editor *Fraser Nelson*

Daily Express
The Northern & Shell Building, No. 10 Lower Thames Street, London EC3R 6EN
☎0871 434 1010
www.express.co.uk
Owner *Northern & Shell Media/Richard Desmond*
Editor *Peter Hill*
Circulation 832,462
Under owner Richard Desmond, publisher of *OK!* magazine, the paper features a large amount of celebrity coverage. The general rule of thumb is to approach in writing with an idea; all departments are prepared to look at an outline without commitment. Ideas welcome but already receives many which are 'too numerous to count'.
News Editor *Greg Swift*
Diary (Hickey Column) *Kathryn Spencer*
Features Editor *Heather Preen*
City Editor *Stephen Kahn*
Political Editor *Macer Hall*
Sports Editor *Bill Bradshaw*
Planning Editor (News Desk) should be circulated with copies of official reports, press releases, etc., to ensure news desk cover at all times.
Saturday magazine. Editor *Graham Bailey*
PAYMENT negotiable.

Daily Mail
Northcliffe House, 2 Derry Street, London
W8 5TT
☎020 7938 6000
Owner *Associated Newspapers/Lord Rothermere*

Editor *Paul Dacre*
Circulation 2.3 million
In-house feature writers and regular columnists provide much of the material. Photo-stories and crusading features often appear; it's essential to hit the right note to be a successful Mail writer. Close scrutiny of the paper is strongly advised. Not a good bet for the unseasoned. Accepts news on savings, building societies, insurance, unit trusts, legal rights and tax.
News Editor *Chris Evans*
City Editor *Alex Brummer*
'Money Mail' Editor *Tony Hazell*
Political Editor *David Hughes*
Education Correspondent *Sarah Harris*
Diary Editor *Richard Kay*
Features Editor *Leaf Kalfayan*
Literary Editor *Jane Mays*
Head of Sport *Tim Jotischky*
Femail *Lisa Collins*
Weekend Saturday supplement. Editor *Heather McGlone*

Daily Mirror
1 Canada Square, Canary Wharf, London
E14 5AP
☎020 7293 3000 Fax 020 7293 3409
www.mirror.co.uk
Owner *Trinity Mirror plc*
Editor *Richard Wallace*
Circulation 1.65 million
No freelance opportunities for the inexperienced, but strong writers who understand what the tabloid market demands are always needed.
Deputy Editor *Conor Hanna*
News Editor *Anthony Harwood*
Features Editor *Matt Kelly*
Political Editor *Kevin Maguire*
Business Editor *Clinton Manning*
Showbusiness Diary Editor *Eva Simpson*
Sports Editor *Dean Morse*

Daily Record
One Central Quay, Glasgow G3 8DA
☎0141 309 3000 Fax 0141 309 3340
www.record-mail.co.uk

Owner *Trinity Mirror plc*
Editor *Bruce Waddell*
Circulation 445,736

Mass-market Scottish tabloid. Freelance material is generally welcome.

News Editor *Tom Hamilton*
Features Editor *Melanie Harvey*
Business Editor *To be appointed*
Political Editor *Paul Sinclair*
Assistant Editor (Sport) *James Traynor*
Magazine Editor *Angela Dewar*

Scotland Means Business Quarterly business magazine, launched 2002. Editor *Magnus Gardham*

Daily Sport
19 Great Ancoats Street, Manchester
M60 4BT
☎0161 236 4466 Fax 0161 236 4535
www.dailysport.co.uk
Owner *Sport Newspapers Ltd*
Editor *David Beevers*
Circulation 200,000

Tabloid catering for young male readership. Unsolicited material welcome; send to News Editor, *Jane Field-Harris*

Sports Editor *Marc Fester*

Lads Mag Monthly glossy magazine. Editor *Mark Harris.*

Daily Star
The Northern & Shell Building, No. 10
Lower Thames Street, London EC3R 6EN
☎0871 434 1010
Owner *Northern & Shell Media/Richard Desmond*
Editor *Dawn Neesom*
Circulation 769,514

In competition with *The Sun* for off-the-wall news and features. Freelance opportunities available.

Deputy Editor *Jim Mansell*
Assistant Editor, Features *Ruth Hughes*
Sports Editor *Howard Wheatcroft*

Daily Star Sunday
The Northern & Shell Building, No. 10
Lower Thames Street, London EC3R 6EN
☎0871 434 1010 Fax 0871 434 2941
✉ michael.booker@dailystar.co.uk
www.dailystarsunday.co.uk
Owner *Northern & Shell Media/Richard Desmond*
Editor *Gareth Morgan*
Circulation 385,109

Launched in September 2002 in direct competition with *News of the World* and *The People*.

Supplement: *Take5* Lifestyle/showbiz magazine.

The Daily Telegraph
1 Canada Square, Canary Wharf, London
E14 5DT (relocating to: 111 Buckingham
Palace Road, London SW1W 0DT
☎020 7538 5000 Fax 020 7513 2506
www.telegraph.co.uk
Owner *Telegraph Media Group*
Editor-in-Chief *John Bryant*
Circulation 837,285

Unsolicited mss not generally welcome – 'all are carefully read and considered, but very few published'. Contenders should approach the paper in writing, making clear their authority for writing on that subject. No fiction.

Home News Editor *Richrd Preston* Tip-offs or news reports from *bona fide* journalists. Must phone the news desk in first instance. Maximum 200 words. Payment minimum £40 (tip).

Arts Editor *Sarah Crompton*
City Editor *Will Lewis*
Political Editor *George Jones*
Diary Editor *Celia Walden* Always interested in diary pieces.
Environment *Charles Clover*
Features Editor *Rachel Simhon* Most material supplied by commission from established contributors. New writers are tried out by arrangement with the features editor. Approach in writing. Maximum 1500 words.
Literary Editor *Sam Leith*
Sports Editor *Keith Perry* Occasional opportunities for specialised items.
Style Editor *Georgina Cover*
PAYMENT by arrangement.

Daily Telegraph Weekend Saturday supplement. Editor *Jon Stock*

Telegraph Magazine Editor *Michele Lavery*

Financial Times
1 Southwark Bridge, London SE1 9HL
☎020 7873 3000 Fax 020 7873 3076
✉ firstname.lastname@ft.com
www.ft.com
Owner *Pearson*
Editor *Lionel Barber*
Circulation 428,895

Founded 1888. UK and international coverage of business, finance, politics, technology, management, marketing and the arts. All feature ideas must be discussed with the department's editor in advance. Not snowed under with unsolicited contributions – they get less than any other national newspaper. Approach by e-mail with ideas in the first instance.

News Editor *Robert Shrimsley*
Features Editor *Brian Groom*

Arts Editor *Peter Aspden*
Financial Editor *Andrew Hill*
Literary Editor *Jan Dalley*
Education *Jon Boone*
Environment *Fiona Harvey*
Political Editor *James Blitz*
Sports Editor *David Owen*

Weekend FT Editor *Michael Skapinker*
How to Spend It Monthly magazine. Editor *Gillian de Bono*

The Guardian

119 Farringdon Road, London EC1R 3ER
☎020 7278 2332 Fax 020 7837 2114
✉ firstname.secondname@guardian.co.uk
www.guardian.co.uk
Owner *The Scott Trust*
Editor *Alan Rusbridger*
Circulation 359,303

Of all the nationals *The Guardian* probably offers the greatest opportunities for freelance writers, if only because it has the greatest number of specialised pages which use freelance work. Read specific sections before submitting mss.

Deputy Editor *Paul Johnson* No opportunities except in those regions where there is presently no local contact for news stories.

Literary Editor *Claire Armitstead*
City Editor *Julia Finch*
G2 Editor *Katharine Viner*
Technology Editor *Charles Arthur* Thursday supplement.
Diary Editor *Jon Henley*
Education Editor *Rebecca Smithers*
Environment *John Vidal*
Features Editor *Katherine Viner*
Guardian Society *Patrick Butler* Focuses on all public service activity.
Media Editor *Matt Wells*
Political Editor *Patrick Wintour*
Sports Editor *Ben Clissitt*
Women's Page *Clare Margetson* Runs three days a week.

The Guardian Weekend Glossy Saturday issue. Editor *Merope Mills*

The Guide Editor *Tim Lusher*

The Herald (Glasgow)

200 Renfield Street, Glasgow G2 3PR
☎0141 302 7000 Fax 0141 302 7007
www.theherald.co.uk
Owner *Gannett UK Ltd*
Editor *Charles McGhee*
Circulation 73,834

One of the oldest national newspapers in the

English-speaking world, *The Herald*, which dropped its 'Glasgow' prefix in February 1992, was bought by Scottish Television in 1996 and by Newsquest in 2003. Lively, quality, national Scottish daily broadsheet. Approach with ideas in writing or by phone in first instance.

News Editor *Magnus Llewellin*
Arts Editor *Keith Bruce*
Business Editor *Ian McConnell*
Diary *Ken Smith*
Education *Andrew Denholm*
Sports Editor *Donald Cowey*

Herald Magazine Editor *Kathleen Morgan*

The Independent

Independent House, 191 Marsh Wall, London E14 9RS
☎020 7005 2000 Fax 020 7005 2999
www.independent.co.uk
Owner *Independent Newspapers*
Editor *Simon Kelner*
Circulation 214,533

Founded 1986. Particularly strong on its arts/media coverage, with a high proportion of feature material. Theoretically, opportunities for freelancers are good. However, unsolicited mss are not welcome; most pieces originate in-house or from known and trusted outsiders. Ideas should be submitted in writing.

News Editor *John Mullin*
Features *Adam Leigh*
Arts Editor *Ian Irvine*
Business Editor *Jeremy Warner*
Education *Richard Garner*
Environment *Michael McCarthy*
The Independent Extra Editor *Ruth Metzstein*
Literary Editor *Boyd Tonkin*
Political Editor *Andrew Grice*
Sports Editor *Matt Tench*
Travel Editor *Simon Calder*

The Independent Magazine Saturday supplement. Editor *Laurence Earle*

The Independent Traveller 32-page Saturday magazine

The Information Editor *Jo Ellison*

Independent on Sunday

Independent House, 191 Marsh Wall, London E14 9RS
☎020 7005 2000 Fax 020 7005 2999
www.independent.co.uk
Owner *Independent Newspapers*
Editor *Tristan Davies*
Circulation 224,882

Founded 1986. Regular columnists contribute

most material but feature opportunites exist. Approach with ideas in first instance.

News Editor *Andy Malone*
Focus Editor *Cole Moreton*
Arts Editor *Ian Irvine*
Comment Editor *James Hanning*
Business Editor *Jason Nissé*
Literary Editor *Suzi Feay*
Environment *Geoffrey Lean*
Political Editor *Marie Woolf*
Sports Editor *Neil Morton*
Travel Editor *Kate Simon*

The Sunday Review supplement. Acting Editor *Bill Tuckey*

ABC Arts, books and culture supplement.

International Herald Tribune

6 bis, rue des Graviers, 92521 Neuilly, Paris
☎0033 1 4143 9322
Fax 0033 1 4143 9338 (editorial)
✉ iht@iht.com
www.iht.com

Executive Editor *Michael Oreskes*
Managing Editor *Alison Smale*
Features Editor *Katherine Knorr*
Circulation 245,223

Published in France, Monday to Saturday, and circulated in Europe, the Middle East, North Africa, the Far East and the USA. General news, business and financial, arts and leisure. Uses regular freelance contributors. Contributor policy can be found on the website at: www.iht.com/contributor.htm

The Mail on Sunday

Northcliffe House, 2 Derry Street, London W8 5TS
☎020 7938 6000 Fax 020 7937 3829

Owner *Associated Newspapers/Lord Rothermere*
Editor *Peter Wright*
Circulation 2.34 million

Sunday paper with a high proportion of newsy features and articles. Experience and judgement required to break into its band of regular feature writers.

News Editor *Sebastian Hamilton*
Financial Editor *Lisa Buckingham*
Diary Editor *Katie Nicholl*
Features Editor/Women's Page *Sian James*
Books *Marilyn Warnick*
Political Editor *Simon Walters*
Sports Editor *Malcolm Vallerius*
Live Night & Day Editor *Gerald Greaves*
Review Editor *Jim Gillespie*

You – The Mail on Sunday Magazine Colour sup-

plement. Many feature articles, supplied entirely by freelance writers. Editor *Sue Peart*. Features Editor *Rosalind Lowe*

Morning Star

William Rust House, 52 Beachy Road, London E3 2NS
☎020 8510 0815 Fax 020 8986 5694
✉ morsta@geo2.poptel.org.uk

Owner *Peoples Press Printing Society*
Editor *John Haylett*
Circulation 9000

Not to be confused with the *Daily Star*, the *Morning Star* is the farthest left national daily. Those with a penchant for a Marxist reading of events and ideas can try their luck, though feature space is as competitive here as in the other nationals.

News Editor *Dan Coysh*
Features & Arts Editor/Political Editor *Richard Bagley*
Foreign Editor *Dave Williams*
Sports Editor *Mark Barber*

News of the World

1 Virginia Street, London E98 1NW
☎020 7782 1000 Fax 020 7583 9504
www.newsoftheworld.co.uk

Owner *News International plc/Rupert Murdoch*
Editor *Andy Coulson*
Circulation 3.55 million

Highest circulation Sunday paper. Freelance contributions welcome. News and features editors welcome tips and ideas.

Deputy Editor *Neil Wallis*
Assistant Editor (News) *Ian Edmondson*
Features Editor *Douglas Wight*
Political Editor *Ian Kirby*
Sports Editor *Mike Dunn*

Sunday Magazine Colour supplement. Editor *Louise Oswald*. Showbiz interviews and strong human-interest features make up most of the content, but there are no strict rules about what is 'interesting'. Unsolicited mss and ideas welcome.

The Observer

3–7 Herbal Hill, London EC1R 5EJ
☎020 7278 2332 Fax 020 7837 7817
✉ editor@observer.co.uk
www.observer.co.uk

Owner *Guardian Newspapers Ltd*
Editor *Roger Alton*
Circulation 476,367

Founded 1791. Acquired by Guardian Newspapers from Lonrho in May 1993. Occupies the middle ground of Sunday newspaper politics.

Unsolicited material is not generally welcome, 'except from distinguished, established writers'. Receives far too many unsolicited offerings already. No news, fiction or special page opportunities. The newspaper runs annual competitions which change from year to year. Details are advertised in the newspaper.

Executive Editor, News *Kamal Ahmed*
Home News Editor *Lucy Rock*
Foreign News Editor *Tracy McVeigh*
Crime Correspondent *Mark Townsend*
Foreign Affairs Editor *Peter Beaumont*
Home Affairs Editor *Jamie Doward*
Investigations Editor *Antony Barnett*
Sports News and Social Affairs
    Correspondent *Denis Campbell*
Culture and Society Correspondent *Amelia Hill*
Political Editor *Gaby Hinsliff*
Chief Political Correspondent *Ned Temko*
Arts Editor *Sarah Donaldson*
Review Editor *Jane Ferguson*
Comment Editor *Barbara Gunnell*
Deputy Business Editor/City Editor *Richard Wachman*
Business Editor *To be appointed*
Personal Finance Editor *Jill Insley*
Science Editor *Robin McKie*
Education Correspondent *Anushka Asthana*
Environment and Transport Editor *Juliette Jowit*
Literary Editor *Robert McCrum*
Travel Editor *Joanne O'Connor*
Sports Editor *Brian Oliver*

The Observer Magazine Glossy arts and lifestyle supplement. Editor *Allan Jenkins*

The Observer Sport Monthly Magazine supplement launched in 2000. Editor *Jason Cowley*

The Observer Food Monthly Launched in 2001. Editor *Nicola Jeal*

The Observer Music Monthly Launched in 2003. Editor *Caspar Llewellyn Smith*

Observer Woman Launched in 2006. Editor *Nicola Jeal*

The People

1 Canada Square, Canary Wharf, London E14 5AP
☎020 7293 3437 Fax 020 7293 3517
www.people.co.uk

Owner *Trinity Mirror plc*
Editor *Mark Thomas*
Circulation 843,077

Slightly up-market version of *The News of the World*. Keen on exposés and big-name gossip. Interested in ideas for investigative articles. Phone in first instance.

News Editor *David Jeffs*
Features Editor *Chris Bucktin*
Political Editor *Nigel Nelson*
Sports Editor *Lee Horton*
Travel Associate Editor *Trisha Harbord*

Take It Easy Magazine supplement. Editor *Maria Coole* Approach by phone with ideas in first instance.

Scotland on Sunday

Barclay House, 108 Holyrood Road, Edinburgh EH8 8AS
☎0131 620 8620 Fax 0131 620 8491
www.scotlandonsunday.com

Owner *Scotsman Publications Ltd*
Editor *Iain Martin*
Circulation 75,240

Scotland's top-selling quality broadsheet. Welcomes ideas rather than finished articles.

News Editor *Peter Laing*
Arts Editor *Fiona Leith*

Spectrum Colour supplement. Features on personalities, etc. Editor *Clare Trodden*

The Scotsman

Barclay House, 108 Holyrood Road, Edinburgh EH8 8AS
☎0131 620 8620
Fax 0131 620 8616 (editorial)
www.scotsman.com

Owner *Johnston Press*
Editor *John McGurk*
Circulation 63,449

Scotland's national newspaper. Many unsolicited mss come in, and stand a good chance of being read, although a small army of regulars supply much of the feature material not written in-house. See website for contact details.

News Editor *James Hall*
Business Editor *Nick Bevens*
Education *Kevin Schofield*
Features Editor *Jackie Hunter*
Book Reviews *David Robinson*
Sports Editor *Donald Walker*

The Sun

1 Virginia Street, London E98 1SN
☎020 7782 4000 Fax 020 7782 4108
✉ firstname.lastname@the-sun.co.uk
www.the-sun.co.uk

Owner *News International Ltd/Rupert Murdoch*

Editor *Rebekah Wade*
Circulation 3.15 million

Highest circulation daily. Populist outlook; very keen on gossip, pop stars, TV soap, scandals and exposés of all kinds. No room for non-professional feature writers; 'investigative journalism' of a certain hue is always in demand, however.
Head of News *Chris Pharo*
Head of Features *Dominic Mohan*
Head of Sport *Steve Waring*
Woman's Editor *Sharon Hendry*
Health Editor *Jane Symons*
Fashion Editor *Erica Davies*

Sunday Express

The Northern & Shell Building, Number 10 Lower Thames Street, London EC3R 6EN
☎0871 434 1010 Fax 0871 434 7300

Owner *Northern & Shell Media/Richard Desmond*
Editor *Martin Townsend*
Circulation 789,363

The general rule of thumb is to approach in writing with an idea; all departments are prepared to look at an outline without commitment.
News Editor *James Murray*
Features Editor *Giulia Rhodes*
Business Editor *Lawrie Holmes*
Political Editor *Julia Hartley-Brewer*
Sports Editor *Scott Wilson*

S Fashion and lifestyle magazine for women. Editor *Louise Robinson* No unsolicited mss. All contributions are commissioned. Ideas in writing only.
PAYMENT negotiable.

Sunday Herald

200 Renfield Street, Glasgow G2 3QB
☎0141 302 7800 Fax 0141 302 7815
✉ editor@sundayherald.com
www.sundayherald.com
Owner *Newsquest*
Editor *Richard Walker*
Circulation 56,611

Also at: 9/10 St Andrew Square, Edinburgh EH2 2AF
☎0131 718 6040 Fax 0131 718 6105

Launched February 1999. Scottish seven-section compact.
Deputy Editor *David Milne*
News Editor *Charlene Sweeney*
Political Editor *Paul Hutcheon*
Sports Editor *Stephen Penman*
Entertainment Editor *Graeme Virtue*
Magazine Editor *Jane Wright*

Sunday Mail

One Central Quay, Glasgow G3 8DA
☎0141 309 3000 Fax 0141 309 3587
www.sundaymail.co.uk
Owner *Trinity Mirror plc*
Editor *Allan Rennie*
Circulation 527,221

Popular Scottish Sunday tabloid.
News Editor *Brendan McGinty*
Sports Editor *George Cheyne*

7Days Weekly supplement. Editor *Liz Cowan*

Sunday Mirror

1 Canada Square, Canary Wharf, London E14 5AP
☎020 7293 3000
Fax 020 7293 3939 (news desk)
www.sundaymirror.co.uk
Owner *Trinity Mirror*
Editor *Tina Weaver*
Circulation 1.46 million

In general terms contributions are welcome, though the paper patiently points out it has more time for those who have taken the - trouble to study the market. Initial contact in writing preferred, except for live news situations. No fiction.
News Editor *James Saville* The news desk is very much in the market for tip-offs and inside information. Contributors would be expected to work with staff writers on news stories. Approach by telephone or fax in the first instance.
Finance *Melanie Wright*
Features Editor *Nicky Dawson* 'Anyone who has obviously studied the market will be dealt with constructively and courteously.' Cherishes its record as a breeding ground for new talent.
Sports Editor *David Walker*

Celebs on Sunday Colour supplement. Editor *Mel Brodie*

Sunday Post

2 Albert Square, Dundee DD1 9QJ
☎01382 223131 Fax 01382 201064
✉ mail@sundaypost.com
www.sundaypost.com
Owner *D.C. Thomson & Co. Ltd*
Editor *David Pollington*
Circulation 468,414

Contributions should be addressed to the editor.

post plus Monthly colour supplement. Editor *Jan Gooderham*

Sunday Sport

19 Great Ancoats Street, Manchester
M60 4BT
☎0161 236 4466 Fax 0161 236 4535
www.sundaysport.com
Owner *David Sullivan*
Editor *Paul Carter*
Circulation 121,737

Founded 1986. Sunday tabloid catering for a particular sector of the male 15–35 readership. As concerned with 'glamour' (read: 'page 3') as with human interest, news, features and sport. Unsolicited mss are welcome; receives about 90 a week. Approach should be made by phone in the case of news and sports items, by letter for features. Address all material to the news editor.

News Editor *Nick Coal* Off-beat news, human interest, preferably with photographs.

Showbiz Editor *Tanya Jones* Regular items: showbiz, television, films, pop music and gossip.

Sports Editor *Marc Fester* Hard-hitting sports stories on major soccer clubs and their personalities, plus leading clubs/people in other sports. Strong quotations to back up the news angle essential.

PAYMENT negotiable and on publication.

The Sunday Telegraph

1 Canada Square, Canary Wharf, London
E14 5DT (relocating to 111 Buckingham
Palace Road, London SW1W 0DT)
☎020 7538 5000 Fax 020 7538 6065
www.telegraph.co.uk
Owner *Press Holdings Limited*
Editor *Patience Wheatcroft*
Circulation 646,141

Right-of-centre quality Sunday paper which, although traditionally formal, has pepped up its image to attract a younger readership. Unsolicited material from untried writers is rarely ever used. Contact with idea and details of track record.

News Editor *Tim Woodward*
Seven Editor *Susannah Herbert*
City Editor *Dan Roberts*
Political Editor *Patrick Hennessy*
Arts Editor *Lucy Tuck*
Environment Editor *David Harrison*
Literary Editor *Michael Prodger*
Diary Editor *Tim Walker*
Sports Editor *Jon Ryan*

Stella Magazine Colour supplement. Editor
Anna Murphy

The Sunday Times

1 Pennington Street, London E98 1ST
☎020 7782 5000 Fax 020 7782 5658

www.sunday-times.co.uk
Owner *News International plc/Rupert Murdoch*
Editor *John Witherow*
Circulation 1.32 million

Founded 1820. Tendency to be anti-establishment, with a strong crusading investigative tradition. Approach the relevant editor with an idea in writing. Close scrutiny of the style of each section of the paper is strongly advised before sending mss. No fiction. All fees by negotiation.

News Editor *Charles Hymas* Opportunities are very rare.

News Review Editor *Eleanor Mills* Submissions are always welcome, but the paper commissions its own, uses staff writers or works with literary agents, by and large. The features sections where most opportunities exist are *Style* and *The Culture*.

Culture Editor *Helen Hawkins*
Business Editor *John Waples*
City Editor *Richard Fletcher*
Education Correspondent *Geraldine Hackett*
Science and Environment Editor *Jonathan Leake*
Literary Editor *Caroline Gascoigne*
Sports Editor *Alex Butler*
Style Editor *Tiffanie Darke*

Sunday Times Magazine Colour supplement. Editor *Robin Morgan* No unsolicited material. Write with ideas in first instance.

The Times

1 Pennington Street, London E98 1TT
☎020 7782 5000 Fax 020 7488 3242
www.thetimes.co.uk
Owner *News International plc/Rupert Murdoch*
Editor *Robert Thomson*
Circulation 616,881

Generally right (though features can range in tone from diehard to libertarian). *The Times* receives a great many unsolicited offerings. Writers with feature ideas should approach by letter in the first instance. No fiction.

Deputy Editor *Ben Preston*
News Editor *John Wellman*
Features Editor *Michael Harvey*
City/Financial Editor *Patience Wheatcroft*
Diary Editor *Hugo Rifkind*
Arts Editor *Alex O'Connell*
Literary Editor *Erica Wagner*
Political Editor *Phil Webster*
Sports Editor *Tim Hallissey*

The Times Magazine Saturday supplement. Editor *Gill Morgan*

Times 2 Editor *Sandra Parsons*

Regional Newspapers

ENGLAND

Berkshire

Reading Evening Post
8 Tessa Road, Reading RG1 8NS
☎0118 918 3000 Fax 0118 959 9363
✉ editorial@reading-epost.co.uk
Owner *Guardian Media Group*
Editor *Andy Murrill*
Circulation 17,733

Unsolicited mss welcome; one or two received every day. Fiction rarely used. Interested in local news features, human interest, well-researched investigations. Special sections include holidays & travel (Mon); food page; children's page (Tues); style page (Wed); business (Wed & Fri); motoring and motorcycling; gardening; rock music (Thurs).

Cambridgeshire

Cambridge Evening News
Winship Road, Milton, Cambridge CB4 6PP
☎01223 434434 Fax 01223 434415
Owner *Cambridge Newspapers Ltd*
Editor *Murray Morse*
Circulation 30,224

    Deputy Editor *James Foster*
    News Editor *John Deex*
    Business Editor *Jenny Chapman*
    Sports Editor *Chris Gill*

Cheshire

Trinity Mirror Cheshire
Chronicle House, Commonhall Street, Chester CH1 2AA
☎01244 340151 Fax 01244 606498
✉ eric.langton@cheshirenews.co.uk
www.iccheshireonline.co.uk
Owner *Trinity Mirror Plc*
Editor-in-Chief *Eric Langton*

All unsolicited feature material will be considered.

Cleveland

Hartlepool Mail
New Clarence House, Wesley Square, Hartlepool TS24 8BX
☎01429 239333 Fax 01429 869024
✉ mail.news@northeast-press.co.uk
www.hartlepooltoday.co.uk
www.peterleetoday.co.uk
Owner *Johnston Press Plc*
Editor *To be appointed*
Circulation 20,199

    Deputy Editor *Brian Nuttney*
    News Editor *Pete McCusker*
    Sports Editor *Roy Kelly*

Cumbria

News & Star
Newspaper House, Dalston Road, Carlisle CA2 5UA
☎01228 612600 Fax 01228 612601
Owner *Cumbrian Newspaper Group Ltd*
Editor *Neil Hodgkinson*
Circulation 24,946

    Deputy Editor *Nick Turner*
    Sports Editor *Vic Gibson*
    Women's Page *Jane Loughran*

North West Evening Mail
Abbey Road, Barrow in Furness LA14 5QS
☎01229 821835 Fax 01229 840164
✉ news@nwemail.co.uk
www.nwemail.co.uk
Owner *Robin Burgess*
Editor *Stephen Brauner*
Circulation 19,314

All editorial material should be addressed to the editor.

    Sports Editor *Frank Cassidy*

Derbyshire

Derby Evening Telegraph
Northcliffe House, Meadow Road, Derby DE1 2DW
☎01332 291111

✉ newsdesk@derbytelegraph.co.ukA
Owner *Northcliffe Newspapers Group Ltd*
Editor *Steve Hall*
Circulation 47,809
> News Editor *Cheryl Hague*
> (newsdesk@derbytelegraph.co.uk)
> Sports Editor *Peter Green*
> (sports@derbytelegraph.co.uk)
> Motoring Editor *Bob Maddox*

Devon

Evening Herald
17 Brest Road, Derriford Business Park,
Derriford, Plymouth PL6 5AA
☎01752 765500 Fax 01752 765527
✉ news@eveningherald.co.uk
www.thisisplymouth.co.uk
Owner *Northcliffe Newspapers Group Ltd*
Editor *Bill Martin*
Circulation 40,736

All editorial material to be addressed to the editor or the News Editor *James Garnett*.

Express & Echo
Heron Road, Sowton, Exeter EX2 7NF
☎01392 442211
Fax 01392 442294 (editorial)
✉ echonews@expressandecho.co.uk
www.thisisexeter.co.uk
Owner *Westcountry Publications Limited*
Editor *Marc Astley*
Circulation 23,925

Weekly supplements: *Business Week*; *Property Echo*; *Wheels*; *Weekend Echo*.
> Head of Content *Sue Kemp*
> Features Editor *Lynne Turner*
> Sports Editor *Richard Davies* (Fax 01392 442416)

Herald Express
Harmsworth House, Barton Hill Road,
Torquay TQ2 8JN
☎01803 676000 Fax 01803 676228
(editorial)
✉ newsdesk@heraldexpress.co.uk
www.thisissouthdevon.co.uk
Owner *Northcliffe Newspapers Group Ltd*
Editor *B. Hanrahan*
Circulation 26,080

Drive scene, property guide, *On The Town* (leisure and entertainment guide), Monday sports, special pages, rail trail, Saturday surgery, nature and conservation column, dance scene,

shop scene, The Business. Supplements: *Gardening* (weekly); *Visitors Guide* and *Antiques & Collectables* (fortnightly). Unsolicited mss generally not welcome. All editorial material should be addressed to the editor in writing.

Western Morning News
17 Brest Road, Derriford Business Park,
Derriford, Plymouth PL6 5AA
☎01752 765500 Fax 01752 765535
✉ wmnnewsdesk@westernmorningnews.
co.uk
www.thisisplymouth.co.uk
Owner *Northcliffe Newspapers Group Ltd*
Editor *Alan Qualtrough*
Circulation 44,767

Unsolicited mss welcome, but must be of topical and local interest and addressed to the Deputy Editor *Philip Bowern*.
> Assistant Editor (News) *Mark Hughes*.
> Features Editor *Su Carroll*
> Sports Editor *Mark Stephens*

Dorset

Daily Echo
Richmond Hill, Bournemouth BH2 6HH
☎01202 554601 Fax 01202 299543
Owner *Newsquest Media Group Ltd (a Gannett company)*
Editor *Neal Butterworth*
Circulation 33,900

Founded 1900. Has a strong news and features content and invites specialist articles, particularly on unusual subjects, either contemporary or historical, but only with a local angle or flavour. Special review sections each day, including sport, property, entertainment and culture, heritage, motoring, gardening, the environment and the coastline. Also *Saturday Magazine* and monthly *Society* glossy magazine. All editorial material should be addressed to the Editor *Neal Butterworth*. Payment on publication.

Dorset Echo
Fleet House, Hampshire Road, Granby
Industrial Estate, Weymouth DT4 9XD
☎01305 830930 Fax 01305 830956
Owner *Newsquest Media Group Ltd (a Gannett company)*
Editor *David Murdock*
Circulation 19,444

By-gone days, films, arts, showbiz, brides, motoring, property, weekend leisure and entertainment including computers and gardening and weekend magazine.

News Editor *Paul Thomas*
Sports Editor *Paul Baker*

Durham

The Northern Echo
Priestgate, Darlington DL1 1NF
☎01325 381313 Fax 01325 380539
✉ echo@nne.co.uk
www.thisisthenortheast.co.uk
Owner *Newsquest (North East) Ltd (a Gannett company)*
Editor *Peter Barron*
Circulation 53,481

Founded 1870. Freelance pieces welcome but telephone first to discuss submission.
News Editor *Nigel Burton* Interested in reports involving the North East or North Yorkshire. Preferably phoned in.

Features Editor *Nick Morrison* Background pieces to topical news stories relevant to the area. Must be arranged with the features editor before submission of any material.
Business Editor *Julia Breen*
Sports Editor *Nick Loughlin*
PAYMENT and length by arrangement.

Essex

Echo Newspapers
Newspaper House, Chester Hall Lane, Basildon SS14 3BL
☎01268 522792 Fax 01268 469281
Owner *Newsquest Media Group (a Gannett company)*
Editor *Martin McNeill*
Circulation 38,081

Relies almost entirely on staff and regular outside contributors, but will very occasionally consider material sent on spec. Approach the editor in writing with ideas. Although the paper is Basildon-based, its largest circulation is in the Southend area.

Evening Gazette (Colchester)
Oriel House, 43–44 North Hill, Colchester CO1 1TZ
☎01206 506000 Fax 01206 508274
✉ gazette_newsdesk@nqe.com
www.thisisessex.co.uk
Owner *Newsquest (Essex) Ltd*
Editor *Irene Kettle*

Circulation 24,545

Monday to Friday daily newspaper servicing north and mid-Essex including Colchester, Harwich, Clacton, Braintree, Witham, Maldon and Chelmsford. Unsolicited mss not generally used. Relies heavily on regular contributors.
Features Editor *Iris Clapp*

Gloucestershire

The Citizen
St John's Lane, Gloucester GL1 2AY
☎01452 424442 Fax 01452 420664 (editorial)
Owner *Northcliffe Newspapers Group Ltd*
Editor *Ian Mean*
Circulation 27,828

News or features material should be addressed to News Editor, *Jenny Eastwood* or Features Editor, *Victoria Temple*.

Gloucestershire Echo
1 Clarence Parade, Cheltenham GL50 3NY
☎01242 271900 Fax 01242 271848
Owner *Northcliffe Newspapers Group Ltd*
Editor *Anita Syvret*
Circulation 22,496

All material, other than news, should be addressed to the editor.
News Editor *Sam Shepherd*

Hampshire

The News
The News Centre, Hilsea, Portsmouth PO2 9SX
☎023 9266 4488 Fax 023 9267 3363
✉ newsdesk@thenews.co.uk
www.portsmouth.co.uk
Owner *Portsmouth Printing & Publishing Ltd*
Editor *Mike Gilson*
Circulation 60,663

Unsolicited mss not generally accepted. Approach by letter.
Assistant Editor *Colin McNeill*
Features Editor *John Millard* General subjects of S.E. Hants interest. Maximum 600 words. No fiction.
Sports Editor *Colin Channon* Sports background features. Maximum 600 words.

The Southern Daily Echo
Newspaper House, Test Lane, Redbridge, Southampton SO16 9JX
☎023 8042 4777 Fax 023 8042 4545

www.thisishampshire.net
Owner *Newsquest Plc*
Editor *Ian Murray*
Circulation 41,469
Unsolicited mss 'tolerated'. Approach the editor in writing with strong ideas; staff supply almost all the material.

Kent

Kent Messenger
6 & 7 Middle Row, Maidstone ME14 1TG
☎01622 695666 Fax 01622 757227
✉ messengernews@thekmgroup.co.uk
www.kentonline.co.uk
Owner *Kent Messenger Group*
Editor *Bob Dimond*
Circulation 55,109
Very little freelance work is commissioned.

Medway Messenger
Medway House, Ginsbury Close, Sir Thomas Longley Road, Medway City Estate, Strood, Rochester ME2 4DU
☎01634 227800 Fax 01634 715256
✉ medwaymessenger@thekmgroup.co.uk
www.kentonline.co.uk
Owner *Kent Messenger Group*
Editor *Bob Dimond*
Circulation 12,914 (Mon)/20,000 (Fri)
Published Mondays and Fridays with the free *Medway Extra* on Wednesday.
  Business Editor *Trevor Sturgess*
  Community Editor *David Jones*
  Sports Editor *Mike Rees*

Lancashire

Bolton Evening News
Newspaper House, Churchgate, Bolton BL1 1DE
☎01204 522345 Fax 01204 365068
✉ bennewsdesk@boltoneveningnews.co.uk
www.thisisbolton.co.uk
Owner *Newsquest Media Group Ltd (a Gannett company)*
Editor *Steve Hughes*
Circulation 32,212
Business, children's page, travel, local services, motoring, fashion and cookery.
  News Editor *James Higgins*
  Features Editor/Women's Page *Andrew Mosley*

The Gazette (Blackpool)
PO Box 20, Avroe House, Avroe Crescent, Blackpool FY4 2DP
☎01253 400888 Fax 01253 361870
✉ editorial@blackpoolgazette.co.uk
www.blackpooltoday.co.uk
Owner *Johnston Press plc*
Managing Director *Philip Welsh*
Editor *David Helliwell*
Circulation 32,294
Unsolicited mss welcome in theory. Approach in writing with an idea. Supplements: *Eve* (women, Tues); *All Stars* (football, Wed); *Homes* (Thurs); *The Weekend* (entertainment, Fri); *Wheels* (motoring, Fri); *Life!* magazine (entertainment & leisure, Sat); *Jobs Plus* (jobs and careers, Sat).

Lancashire Evening Post
Olivers Place, Eastway, Fulwood, Preston PR2 9ZA
☎01772 254841 Fax 01772 880173
www.prestontoday.net
Owner *Johnston Press plc*
Editor *Simon Reynolds*
Circulation 34,877
Unsolicited mss are not generally welcome; many are received and not used. All ideas in writing to the editor.

Lancashire Evening Telegraph
Newspaper House, High Street, Blackburn BB1 1HT
☎01254 678678 Fax 01254 680429
✉ Let_editorial@lancashire.newsquest.co.uk
www.thisislancashire.co.uk
Owner *Newsquest Media Group Ltd (a Gannett company)*
Editor *Kevin Young*
Circulation 32,978
News stories and feature material with an East Lancashire flavour (a local angle, or written by local people) welcome. Approach in writing with an idea in the first instance. No fiction.
  News Editor *Andrew Turner*
  Features Editor *John Anson*
  Sports Editor *Paul Plunkett*
  Pictures Editor *Neil Johnson*

Oldham Evening Chronicle
PO Box 47, Union Street, Oldham OL1 1EQ
☎0161 633 2121 Fax 0161 652 2111
✉ editorial@oldham-chronicle.co.uk
Owner *Hirst Kidd & Rennie Ltd*
Editor *Jim Williams*
Circulation 24,644

Motoring, food and wine, lifestyle supplement, business page.

News Editor *Mike Attenborough*

Leicestershire

Leicester Mercury

St George Street, Leicester LE1 9FQ
☎0116 251 2512 Fax 0116 253 0645
www.thisisleicestershire.co.uk
Owner *Northcliffe Newspapers Group Ltd*
Editor *Nick Carter*
Circulation 78,075

News Editor *Mark Charlton*
Features Editor *Alex Dawson*

Lincolnshire

Grimsby Telegraph

80 Cleethorpe Road, Grimsby DN31 3EH
☎01472 360360 Fax 01472 372257
✉ newsdesk@grimsbytelegraph.co.uk
Owner *Northcliffe Newspapers Group Ltd*
Editor *Michelle Lalor*
Circulation 38,297

Sister paper of the *Scunthorpe Evening Telegraph*. Unsolicited mss generally welcome. Approach in writing. No fiction. Weekly supplements: *Business Telegraph*; *Property Telegraph*; *Motoring*; *Sports Telegraph* (Sat). All material to be addressed to the News Editor *Lucy Wood*. Particularly welcomes hard news stories; approach in haste by telephone.

Special Publications Editor *B. Farnsworth*

Lincolnshire Echo

Brayford Wharf East, Lincoln LN5 7AT
☎01522 820000 Fax 01522 804493
✉ news@lincolnshireecho.co.uk
Owner *Northcliffe Newspapers Group Ltd*
Editor *John Grubb*
Circulation 24,526

Best buys, holidays, motoring, dial-a-service, restaurants, sport, leisure, home improvement, record reviews, gardening corner, stars.

Scunthorpe Telegraph

4–5 Park Square, Scunthorpe DN15 6JH
☎01724 273273 Fax 01724 273101
Owner *Northcliffe Newspapers Group Ltd*
Editor *Jane Manning*
Circulation 20,699

All correspondence should go to the Deputy Editor *Dave Atkin*.

London

Evening Standard

Northcliffe House, 2 Derry Street, London W8 5EE
☎020 7938 6000 Fax 020 7937 2648
www.standard.co.uk/e-editions
Owner *Associated Newspapers/Lord Rothermere*
Editor *Veronica Wadley*
Circulation 334,144

Long-established evening paper, serving Londoners with both news and feature material. Genuine opportunities for London-based features. Produces a weekly colour supplement, *ES Magazine* (Fri) and *Homes & Property* (Wed).

Joint Deputy Editors *Andrew Bordiss, Ian MacGregor*
Executive Editor *Anne McElvoy*
Managing Editor *Doug Wills*
Assistant Editor (Features) *Guy Eaton*
News Editor *Ian Walker*
Assistant Editor (Arts) *Norman Lebrecht*
Assistant Editor (Sport) *Martin Chilton*
Editor, *ES Catherine Ostler*
Editor, *Homes & Property Janice Morley*

Manchester

Manchester Evening News

164 Deansgate, Manchester M60 2RD
☎0161 832 7200 Fax 0161 834 3814
www.manchesteronline.co.uk
Owner *Manchester Evening News Ltd*
Editor *Paul Horrocks*
Circulation 128,445

One of the country's major regional dailies. Initial approach in writing preferred. No fiction. *Personal Finance* (Mon); *Health*; *Holidays* (Tues); *Homes & Property* (Wed); *Small Business* (Thurs); *Lifestyle* (Fri/Sat).

News Editor *Ian Wood*
Features Editor *Deanna Delamotta* Regional news features, personality pieces and showbiz profiles considered. Maximum 1200 words.
Sports Editor *Peter Spencer*
Women's Page *Helen Tither*
PAYMENT based on house agreement rates.

Merseyside

Liverpool Daily Post

PO Box 48, Old Hall Street, Liverpool L69 3EB
☎0151 227 2000 Fax 0151 472 2506
www.icliverpool.co.uk
Owner *Trinity Mirror Plc*

Editor *Jane Wolstenholme*
Circulation 18,741

Unsolicited mss welcome. Receives about six a day. Approach in writing with an idea. No fiction. Local, national/international news, current affairs, profiles (with pictures). Maximum 800–1000 words.

Features Editor *Louise Douglas*
News Editor *Greg Fray*
Business Editor *Bill Gleeson*
Sports Editor *Richard Williamson*

Liverpool Echo

PO Box 48, Old Hall Street, Liverpool
L69 3EB
☎0151 227 2000   Fax 0151 236 4682
✉ letters@liverpoolecho.co.uk

Owner *Trinity Mirror Merseyside*
Editor *Alastair Machray*
Circulation 120,131

One of the country's major regional dailies. Unsolicited mss welcome; initial approach with ideas in writing preferred.

News Editor *Alison Gow*
Features Editor *Jane Haase*
Sports Editor *John Thompson*
Women's Editor *Susan Lee*

Norfolk

Eastern Daily Press

Prospect House, Rouen Road, Norwich
NR1 1RE
☎01603 628311   Fax 01603 623872
✉ EDP@archant.co.uk
www.EDP24.co.uk

Owner *Archant Regional*
Editor *Peter Franzen, OBE*
Circulation 69,355

Most pieces by commission only. Supplements: Centro (daily); rental, motoring, business, property pages, agriculture, employment (all weekly); *Event* full-colour magazine (Fri); *Saturday* full colour magazine; *Sunday* 24-page supplement.

Deputy Editor *James Ruddy*
Assistant Editor (News) *Paul Durrant*
Head of Feature Content *Sarah Hardy*
Sports Editor *David Thorpe*
Assistant Editor (*Saturday*) *Steve Snelling*

Evening News

Prospect House, Rouen Road, Norwich
NR1 1RE
☎01603 628311   Fax 01603 219060

✉ david.bourn@archant.co.uk
www.eveningnews24.co.uk

Owner *Archant Ltd*
Editor *David Bourn*
Circulation 26,014

Includes special pages on local property, motoring, pop, fashion, arts, entertainments and TV, gardening, local music scene, home and family.

Deputy Editor *Tim Williams*
(tim.williams@archant.co.uk)
Assistant Editor *Zoe Catchpole*
(zoe.catchpole@archant.co.uk)
Features Editor *Derek James*
(derek.james@archant.co.uk)

Northamptonshire

Chronicle and Echo

Upper Mounts, Northampton NN1 3HR
☎01604 467000   Fax 01604 467190

Owner *Northamptonshire Newspapers*
Editor *Mark Edwards*
Circulation 22,403

Unsolicited mss are 'not necessarily unwelcome but opportunities to use them are rare'. Approach in writing with an idea. No fiction. Supplements: *Sport on Monday*; *Business Week* (Tues); *Property Week* (Wed); *Job Search* (Thurs); *Weekend Motors* and *The Guide* (Friday); *TV Week* (Sat).

News Editor *Richard Edmondson*
Features Editor/Women's Page *Angela Pownall*
Sports Editor *Steve Pitts*

Evening Telegraph

Newspaper House, Ise Park, Rothwell Road, Kettering NN16 8GA
☎01536 506100   Fax 01536 506195
(editorial)
✉ et.newsdesk@northantsnews.co.uk
www.northantsnews.com

Owner *Johnston Press Plc*
Editor *Jeremy Clifford*
Circulation 24,995

Northamptonshire Business Guide (weekly); *Entertainment Guide* and *Jobs* supplements (Thurs); films and eating out (Fri); and *Home & Garden* – monthly lifestyle supplement including gardening, etc.

Assistant Editor *Nick Tite*
News Editor *Kristy Ward*
Sports Editor *Steve Pitts*

Nottinghamshire

Evening Post Nottingham

Castle Wharf House, Nottingham NG1 7EU
☎0115 948 2000 Fax 0115 964 4032
Owner *Northcliffe Newspapers Group Ltd*
Editor *Graham Glen*
Circulation 68,354

Unsolicited mss occasionally used. Good local interest only. Maximum 800 words. No fiction. Send ideas in writing.

News Editor *Steven Fletcher*
Deputy Editor *Martin Done*
Sports Editor *Dave Parkinson*

Oxfordshire

Oxford Mail

Osney Mead, Oxford OX2 0EJ
☎01865 425262 Fax 01865 425554
✉ nqonews@nqo.com
www.thisisoxfordshire.co.uk

Owner *Newsquest (Oxfordshire) Ltd*
Editor *Simon O'Neill*
Circulation 25,069

Unsolicited mss are considered but a great many unsuitable offerings are received. Approach in writing with an idea, rather than by phone. No fiction.

PAYMENT All fees negotiable.

Shropshire

Shropshire Star

Ketley, Telford TF1 5HU
☎01952 242424 Fax 01952 254605
Owner *Shropshire Newspapers Ltd*
Editor *Sarah-Jane Smith*
Circulation 77,457

No unsolicited mss; approach the editor with ideas in writing in the first instance. No news or fiction.

Head of Features *Carl Jones* Limited opportunities; uses mostly in-house or syndicated material. Maximum 1200 words.

Sports Editor *Dave Ballinger*

Somerset

The Bath Chronicle

Windsor House, Windsor Bridge Road, Bath
BA2 3AU
☎01225 322322 Fax 01225 322291
www.thisisbath.com

Owner *Northcliffe Newspapers Group Ltd*
Editor *Sam Holliday*
(s.holliday@bathchron.co.uk)
Circulation 13,017

Local news and features especially welcomed (news@bathchron.co.uk).

Deputy Editor *John McCready*
News Editor *Paul Wiltshire*
Features Editor *Georgette McCready*
Sports Editor *Julie Riegal*

Evening Post

Temple Way, Bristol BS99 7HD
☎0117 934 3000 Fax 0117 934 3575
✉ epnews@bepp.co.uk
www.thisisbristol.co.uk

Owner *Northcliffe Newspapers Group Ltd*
Editor *Mike Norton*
Circulation 56,250

News Editor *Robin Perkins*
Features Editor *David Webb*
Sports Editor *Chris Spittles*

Western Daily Press

Temple Way, Bristol BS99 7HD
☎0117 934 3000 Fax 0117 934 3574
✉WDEditor *or* WDNews *or*
WDFeats@bepp.co.uk
www.westpress.co.uk

Owner *Bristol Evening Post & Press Ltd*
Editor *Andy Wright*
Circulation 47,306

Sports Editor *Chris Spittles*
Women's Page *Susie Weldon* (Features Production)

Staffordshire

Burton Mail

65–68 High Street, Burton upon Trent
DE14 1LE
☎01283 512345 Fax 01283 515351
✉ editorial@burtonmail.co.uk

Owner *Staffordshire Newspapers Ltd*
Editor *Paul Hazeldine*
Circulation 15.454

Fashion, health, wildlife, environment, nostalgia, financial/money; consumer; women's world, rock; property; motoring, farming; what's on, leisure *Weekend Supplement* (Sat).

News *Steve Doohan*
Features *Louise Worrell*
Sports Editor *Rex Page*

The Sentinel/Sentinel Sunday

Sentinel House, Etruria, Stoke on Trent
ST1 5SS
☎01782 602525 Fax 01782 280781
(Sentinel)/201167 (Sentinel Sunday)
www.thisisthesentinel.co.uk

Owner *Staffordshire Sentinel Newspapers Ltd*
Editor-in-Chief *Mike Sassi*
Circulation 73,830 (Sentinel)/12,660 (Sentinel Sunday)

Weekly sports final supplement. All material should be sent to the Head of Content *Martin Tideswell*.

Suffolk

East Anglian Daily Times

Press House, 30 Lower Brook Street, Ipswich IP4 1AN
☎01473 230023 Fax 01473 324776
✉ eadt@eadt.co.uk
www.eadt.co.uk

Owner *Archant Ltd*
Editor *Terry Hunt*
Circulation 37,338

Founded 1874. Unsolicited mss generally not welcome; three or four received a week and almost none are used. Approach in writing in the first instance. No fiction. Supplements: sport (Mon); business (Tues); jobs (Wed); property (Thurs); motoring (Fri); magazine (Sat).

News Editor *Brad Jones* Hard news stories involving East Anglia (Suffolk, Essex particularly) or individuals resident in the area are always of interest.

Features *Julian Ford* Mostly in-house, but will occasionally buy in when the subject is of strong Suffolk/East Anglian interest. Photo features preferred (extra payment). Special advertisement features are regularly run. Some opportunities here. Maximum 1000 words.

Sports Editor *Nick Garnham*
Women's Page *Victoria Hawkins*

Evening Star

30 Lower Brook Street, Ipswich IP4 1AN
☎01473 230023 Fax 01473 324850

Owner *Archant Ltd*
Editor *Nigel Pickover*
Circulation 21,814

News Editor *Martin Davey*

Sussex

The Argus

Argus House, Crowhurst Road, Hollingbury, Brighton BN1 8AR
☎01273 544544 Fax 01273 505703
✉ editor@theargus.co.uk
www.theargus.co.uk

Owner *Newsquest (Sussex) Ltd*
Editor *Michael Beard*
Circulation 35,169

News Editor *Melanie Dowding*
Sports Editor *Chris Giles*

Teesside

Evening Gazette

Borough Road, Middlesbrough TS1 3AZ
☎01642 234242 Fax 01642 232014
www.gazettelive.co.uk

Owner *Trinity Mirror plc*
Editor *Darren Thwaites*
Circulation 55,545

Special pages: health, education, family, business, property, entertainment, leisure, motoring, recruitment.

News Editor *Jim Horsley*
Business Features/Commercial Features *Helen Logan*
Sports Editor *Phil Tallentire*
Councils *Sandy McKenzie*
Health *Audrey Forbes*
Crime *Mike Underwood*

Tyne & Wear

Evening Chronicle

Groat Market, Newcastle upon Tyne NE1 1ED
☎0191 232 7500 Fax 0191 232 2256
✉ ec.news@ncjmedia.co.uk
www.icnewcastle.co.uk

Owner *Trinity Mirror Plc*
Editor *Paul Robertson*
Circulation 83,425

Receives a lot of unsolicited material, much of which is not used. Family issues, gardening, pop, fashion, cooking, consumer, films and entertainment guide, home improvements, motoring, property, angling, sport and holidays. Approach in writing with ideas. Limited opportunities for features due to full-time feature staff.

News Editor *James Marley*
Sports Editor *Paul New*
Women's Interests *Jennifer Bradbury*

Gazette
Chapter Row, South Shields NE33 1BL
☎0191 427 4800 Fax 0191 456 8270
www.southtynesidetoday.co.uk
Owner *Northeast Press Ltd*
Editor *John Szymanski*
Circulation 20,335

News Editor *Gary Welford*
Sports Editor *Mick Worrall*
Feature's Editor *Janis Blower*

The Journal
Groat Market, Newcastle upon Tyne
NE1 1ED
☎0191 232 7500/201 6344 (Newsdesk)
Fax 0191 232 2256/201 6044
✉ jnl.newsdesk@ncjmedia.co.uk
www.icnewcastle.co.uk
Owner *Trinity Mirror Plc*
Editor *Brian Aitken*
Circulation 41,665

Daily platforms include farming and business.
Deputy Editor *Graham Pratt*
Sports Editor *Kevin Dinsdale*
Arts & Entertainment Editor *David Whetstone*
Environment Editor *Tony Henderson*
Business Editor *Iain Laing*

Sunday Sun
Newcastle Chronicle & Journal Ltd, Groat
Market, Newcastle upon Tyne NE1 1ED
☎0191 201 6158 Fax 0191 201 6180
✉ colin.patterson@ncjmedia.co.uk
Owner *Trinity Mirror Plc*
Editor *Colin Patterson*
Circulation 75,499

All material should be addressed to the appropriate editor (phone to check), or to the editor.
Sports Editor *Darren Kelso*

Sunderland Echo
Echo House, Pennywell, Sunderland SR4 9ER
☎0191 501 5800 Fax 0191 534 4861
✉ rob.lawson@northeast-press.co.uk
Owner *Johnston Press Plc*
Editor *Rob Lawson*
Circulation 45,783

All editorial material to be addressed to the
News Editor *Gavin Foster*(echo.news@northeast-press.co.uk).

Warwickshire
Coventry Evening Telegraph
Corporation Street, Coventry CV1 1FP
☎024 7663 3633 Fax 024 7655 0869
✉ news@coventry-telegraph.co.uk
www.IcCoventry.co.uk
Owner *Trinity Mirror Plc*
Editor *Alan Kirby*
Circulation 52,664

Unsolicited mss are read, but few are published.
Approach in writing with an idea. No fiction.
All unsolicited material should be addressed to
the editor. Maximum 600 words for features.
News Managers *Steve Chilton, Steve Williams*
Features Manager/Women's Page *Tara Cain*
Sports Editor *Rob Madill*
PAYMENT negotiable.

Leamington Spa Courier
32 Hamilton Terrace, Leamington Spa
CV32 4LY
☎01926 457755 Fax 01926 339960
✉ editorial@leamingtoncourier.co.uk
www.leamingtontoday.co.uk
Owner *Heart of England Newspapers (Johnston Press)*
Editor *Martin Lawson*
Circulation 15,337

One of the Leamington Spa Courier series
which also includes the Warwick Courier and
Kenilworth Weekly News. Unsolicited feature
articles considered, particularly matter with a
local angle. Telephone with idea first.
News Editor *Peter Ormerod*

West Midlands
Birmingham Evening Mail
PO Box 78, Weaman Street, Birmingham
B4 6AT
☎0121 234 5688
Fax 0121 234 5878 (editorial)
✉ Steve_dyson@mrn.co.uk
www.icbirmingham.co.uk
Owner *Trinity Mirror Plc*
Editor *Steve Dyson*
Circulation 94,339

Freelance contributions are welcome, particularly topics of interest to the West Midlands and
feature pieces offering original and lively comment on family issues, health or education. Also
news tips and community picture contributions.

Deputy Editor *Carole Cole*
Assistant Editor (Content) *Alf Bennett*
Features *Paul Fulford*
News *Andy Richards*
Sport *Ken Montgomery*
Pictures *Steve Murphy*
Business *Jon Griffin*

Birmingham Post
Weaman Street, Birmingham B4 6AT
☎0121 236 3366   Fax 0121 234 5667

Owner *Trinity Mirror Plc*
Editor *Marc Reeves*
Circulation 13,002

One of the country's leading regional newspapers. Freelance contributions are welcome. Topics of interest to the West Midlands and pieces offering lively, original comment are particularly welcome.

News Editor *Mo Ilyas*
Features Editor *Caroline Foulkes*

Express & Star
Queen Street, Wolverhampton WV1 1ES
☎01902 313131   Fax 01902 319721

Owner *Midlands News Association*
Editor *Adrian Faber*
Circulation 150,553

Deputy Editor *Keith Harrison*
Assistant Editor *Roy Williams*
Head of News *Mark Drew*
Features Editor *Emma Farmer*
Business Editor *Jim Walsh*
Sports Editor *Tim Walters*
Women's Editor *Eluned Bowen*

Sunday Mercury (Birmingham)
Weaman Street, Birmingham B4 6AY
☎0121 234 5567   Fax 0121 234 5877
✉ sundaymercury@mrn.co.uk
www.icbirmingham.co.uk

Owner *Trinity Mirror Plc*
Editor *David Brookes*
Circulation 66,007

Deputy Editor (Features) *Paul Cole*
Head of Content (News) *Tony Larner*
Assistant Editor (Sport) *Lee Gibson*
Lifestyle Editor *Zoe Chamberlain*

Wiltshire

Swindon Advertiser
100 Victoria Road, Swindon SN1 3BE
☎01793 528144   Fax 01793 501888
✉ editor@newswilts.co.uk

www.swindonadvertiser.co.uk

Owner *Newsquest (Wiltshire) Ltd*
Editor *Mark Waldron*
Circulation 22,116

Copy and ideas invited. 'All material must be strongly related or relevant to the town of Swindon or the county of Wiltshire.' Little scope for freelance work. Fees vary depending on material.

Deputy Editor *Pauline Leighton*
News Editor *Tom Morton*
Sports Editor *Steve Butt*

Worcestershire

Worcester News
Berrow's House, Hylton Road, Worcester WR2 5JX
☎01905 748200   Fax 01905 742277

Owner *Newsquest (Midlands South) Ltd*
Editor *Stewart Gilbert*
Circulation 18,851

Community (Tues); jobs (Wed); property (Thurs); entertainment and motoring (Fri).

News Editor *Stephanie Preece*
Features Editor *Stewart Gilbert*
Sports Editor *Paul Ricketts*

Yorkshire

The Doncaster Star
Sunny Bar, Doncaster DN1 1NB
☎01302 348500   Fax 01302 348528
✉ doncaster@sheffieldnewspapers.co.uk

Owner *Sheffield Newspapers Ltd*
Editor *David Kessen*
Circulation 5,099

All editorial material to be addressed to the editor.

Sports Writer *Steve Hossack*

Evening Press
PO Box 29, 76–86 Walmgate, York YO1 9YN
☎01904 653051   Fax 01904 612853
✉ newsdesk@ycp.co.uk
www.thisisyork.co.uk

Owner *Newsquest Media Group (a Gannett company)*
Editor *Kevin Booth*
Circulation 35,761

Unsolicited mss not generally welcome, unless submitted by journalists of proven ability. *Business Press Pages* (daily); *Property Press* (Thurs);

Twenty4Seven – entertainment (Sat).
Assistant Editor *Fran Clee*
News Editor *Scott Armstrong*
Picture Editor *Martin Oates*
Sports Editor *Martin Jarred*
PAYMENT negotiable.

Huddersfield Daily Examiner
Queen Street South, Huddersfield HD1 2TD
☎01484 430000 Fax 01484 437789
Owner *Trinity Mirror Plc*
Editor *Roy Wright*
Circulation 28,226
Home improvement, home heating, weddings, dining out, motoring, fashion, services to trade and industry.
Assistant Editor *Michael O'Connell*
Head of Content *Jenny Parkin*
News Editor *Neil Atkinson*
Features Editor *Andrew Flynn*
Sports Editor *Mel Booth*
Women's Page *Hilarie Stelfox*

Hull Daily Mail
Blundell's Corner, Beverley Road, Hull HU3 1XS
☎01482 327111 Fax 01482 315353
✉ news@hdmp.co.uk
www.thisishullandeastriding.co.uk
Owner *Northcliffe Newspapers Group Ltd*
Editor *John Meehan*
Circulation 62,960
News Editor *Jeremy Deacon*
Features Editor *Paul Johnson*

Scarborough Evening News
17–23 Aberdeen Walk, Scarborough YO11 1BB
☎01723 363636 Fax 01723 383825
✉ editorial@scarborougheveningnews.co.uk
www.scarboroughtoday.co.uk
Owner *Yorkshire Regional Newspapers Ltd*
Editor *Ed Asquith*
Circulation 14,690
Special pages include property (Mon); jobs (Thurs); motors (Fri).
Deputy Editor *Sue Wilkinson*
News Editor *Steven Hartley*
Sports Editor *Charles Place*
All other material should be addressed to the editor.

The Star
York Street, Sheffield S1 1PU
☎0114 276 7676 Fax 0114 272 5978

Owner *Sheffield Newspapers Ltd*
Editor *Alan Powell*
Circulation 59,733
Unsolicited mss not welcome, unless topical and local.
News Editor *Charles Smith* Contributions only accepted from freelance news reporters if they relate to the area.
Features Editor *John Highfield* Very rarely requires outside features, unless on specialised local subjects.
Sports Editor *Bob Westerdale*
Women's Page *Jo Davison*
PAYMENT negotiable.

Telegraph & Argus (Bradford)
Hall Ings, Bradford BD1 1JR
☎01274 729511 Fax 01274 723634
www.thisisbradford.co.uk
Owner *Newsquest Media Group Ltd (a Gannett company)*
Editor *Perry Austin-Clarke*
Circulation 42,044
No unsolicited mss – approach in writing with samples of work. No fiction.
Head of News *Martin Heminway*
Features Editor *David Barnett*
Local features and general interest. Showbiz pieces. 600–1000 words (maximum 1500).

Yorkshire Evening Post
Wellington Street, Leeds LS1 1RF
☎0113 243 2701 Fax 0113 238 8536
✉ eped@ypn.co.uk
Owner *Johnson Press*
Editor *Paul Napier*
Circulation 63,265
Evening sister of the Yorkshire Post.
News Editor *Gilian Haworth*
Features Editor *Anne Pickles*
Sports Editor *Phil Rostron*
Women's Page *Jayne Dawson*

Yorkshire Post
Wellington Street, Leeds LS1 1RF
☎0113 243 2701 Fax 0113 238 8537
✉ yp.editor@ypn.co.uk
Owner *Johnston Press*
Editor *Peter Charlton*
Circulation 54,730
A serious-minded, quality regional daily with a generally conservative outlook. Three or four unsolicited mss arrive each day; all will be considered but initial approach in writing preferred. All submissions should be addressed to the edi-

tor. No fiction, poetry or family histories.
Deputy Editor *Duncan Hamilton*
Acting Features Editor *Sarah Freeman* Open
to suggestions in all fields (though ordinarily
commissioned from specialist writers).
Sports Editor *Matt Reeder*

NORTHERN IRELAND

Belfast News Letter
46–56 Boucher Crescent, Belfast BT12 6QY
☎028 9068 0000 Fax 028 9066 9910
Owner *Johnson Press/Century Newspapers Ltd*
Editor *Austin Hunter*
Weekly supplements: *Farming Life*; *Business
News Letter*, *Female Times*; *Spectrum*; *Sports Ulster*.
News Editors *Ric Clark, Steven Moore, Karen
Quinn*
Features Editor *Geoff Hill*
Sports Editor *Brian Millar*
Business Editor *Adrienne McGill*
Agricultural Editor *David McCoy*
Political Editor *Stephen Dempster*

Belfast Telegraph
Royal Avenue, Belfast BT1 1EB
☎028 9026 4000 Fax 028 9055 4506/4540
✉ newseditor@belfasttelegraph.co.uk
www.belfasttelegraph.co.uk
Owner *Independent News & Media (UK)*
Editor *Martin Lindsay*
Circulation 93,786
Weekly business, property and recruitment
supplements.
News Editor *Paul Connolly*
Features Editor *Gail Walker*
Sports Editor *Steven Beacom*
Business Editor *Nigel Tilson*

The Irish News
113/117 Donegall Street, Belfast BT1 2GE
☎028 9032 2226 Fax 028 9033 7505
✉ newsdesk@irishnews.com
Owner *Irish News Ltd*
Editor *Noel Doran*
Circulation 48,323
All material to appropriate editor (phone to
check), or to the news desk.
Assistant Editor *Fiona McGarry*
Sports Editor *Thomas Hawkins*
Arts Editor/Women's Page *Joanna Braniff*

Sunday Life
124–144 Royal Avenue, Belfast BT1 1EB
☎028 9026 4300 Fax 028 9055 4739
✉ b.arnold@belfasttelegraph.co.uk
www.sundaylife.co.uk
Owner *Independent News & Media (UK)*
Editor *Jim Flanagan*
Circulation 77,688
Deputy Editor *Martin Hill*
Sports Editor *Jim Gracey*
Features Editor *Audrey Watson*

SCOTLAND

The Courier and Advertiser
80 Kingsway East, Dundee DD4 8SL
☎01382 223131 Fax 01382 454590
✉ courier@dcthomson.co.uk
www.thecourier.co.uk
Owner *D.C. Thomson & Co. Ltd*
Editor *Bill Hutcheon*
Circulation 78,010
Circulates in East Central Scotland. Features
occasionally accepted on a wide range of subjects, particularly local/Scottish interest, including finance, insurance, agriculture, motoring,
modern homes, lifestyle and fitness. Maximum
length, 500 words.
News Editor *Arliss Rhind*
Features Editor/Women's Page *Catriona
McInnes*
Sports Editor *Graeme Dey*

Daily Record (Glasgow)
See *National Newspapers*

Evening Express (Aberdeen)
PO Box 43, Lang Stracht, Mastrick, Aberdeen
AB15 6DF
☎01224 690222 Fax 01224 699575
✉ ee.news@ajl.co.uk
Owner *D.C. Thomson & Co. Ltd*
Editor *Damian Bates*
Circulation 56,868
Circulates in Aberdeen and the Grampian
region. Local, national and international news
and pictures, sport. Family platforms include
What's On, Counter (consumer news), *Eating
Out Guide, Family Days Out*. Unsolicited mss
welcome 'if on a controlled basis'.

Assistant Editor *Richard Prest* Freelance news contributors welcome. PAYMENT negotiable.

Evening News

Barclay House, 108 Holyrood Road, Edinburgh EH8 8AS
☎0131 620 8620 Fax 0131 620 8696
www.edinburghnews.com
Owner *Scotsman Publications Ltd*
Editor *John McLellan*
Circulation 56,646

Founded 1873. Circulates in Edinburgh, Fife, Central and Lothian. Coverage includes: entertainment, gardening, motoring, shopping, fashion, health and lifestyle, showbusiness. Occasional platform pieces, features of topical and/or local interest. Unsolicited feature material welcome. Approach the appropriate editor in writing.

News Editor *Euan McGrory*
Sports Editor *Graham Lindsay*
PAYMENT NUJ/house rates.

Evening Telegraph

80 Kingsway East, Dundee DD4 8SL
☎01382 223131 Fax 01382 454590
✉ general@eveningtelegraph.co.uk
www.eveningtelegraph.co.uk
Owner *D.C. Thomson & Co. Ltd*
Editor *Gordon Wishart*
Circulation 25,050

Circulates in Tayside, Dundee and Fife. All material should be addressed to the editor.

Evening Times

200 Renfield Street, Glasgow G2 3QB
☎0141 302 7000 Fax 0141 302 6677
✉ times@eveningtimes.co.uk
Owner *Newsquest*
Editor *Donald Martin*
Circulation 81,393

Circulates in Glasgow and the west of Scotland. Supplements: *Job Search*; *City Living*; *Drive times*; *Extra times*; *Times Out*; *et* magazine.

News Editor *Hugh Boag*
Features Editor *Garry Scott*
Sports Editor *David Stirling*

Greenock Telegraph

2 Crawfurd Street, Greenock PA15 1LH
☎01475 726511 Fax 01475 783734
Owner *Clyde & Forth Press Ltd*

Editor *Tom McConigley*
Circulation 18,156

Circulates in Greenock, Port Glasgow, Gourock, Kilmacolm, Langbank, Bridge of Weir, Inverkip, Wemyss Bay, Skelmorlie, Largs. Unsolicited mss considered 'if they relate to the newspaper's general interests'. No fiction. All material to be addressed to the editor.

The Herald/Sunday Herald (Glasgow)

See *National Newspapers*

Paisley Daily Express

14 New Street, Paisley PA1 1YA
☎0141 887 7911 Fax 0141 887 6254
✉ pde@s-un.co.uk
Owner *Scottish & Universal Newspapers Ltd*
Editor *Jonathan Russell*
Circulation 10,683

Circulates in Paisley, Linwood, Renfrew, Johnstone, Elderslie, Neilston and Barrhead. Unsolicited mss welcome only if of genuine local (Renfrewshire) interest. The paper does not commission work and will consider submitted material. Maximum 1000–1500 words. All submissions to the news editor.

News Editor *Anne Dalrymple*
Sports Reporter *Paul Behan*

The Press and Journal

PO Box 43, Lang Stracht, Mastrick, Aberdeen AB15 6DF
☎01224 690222 Fax 01224 663575
Owner *D.C. Thomson & Co. Ltd*
Editor *Derek Tucker*
Circulation 84,612

A well-established daily that circulates in Aberdeen, Grampians, Highlands, Tayside, Orkney, Shetland and the Western Isles. Most material is commissioned but will consider ideas.

News Editor *Andrew Hebden* Wide variety of hard or off-beat news and features relating especially, but not exclusively, to the north of Scotland.

Sports Editor *Alex Martin*
Women's Page *Victoria Banks*
Your Life *Sonja Cox* Saturday lifestyle tabloid pullout. Features food, fashion, travel, books, arts and lifestyle.
PAYMENT by arrangement.

Scotland on Sunday (Edinburgh)

See *National Newspapers*

The Scotsman (Edinburgh)
See *National Newspapers*

Sunday Mail (Glasgow)
See *National Newspapers*

Sunday Post (Dundee)
See *National Newspapers*

WALES

Daily Post

PO Box 202, Vale Road, Llandudno Junction,
Conwy LL31 9ZD
☎01492 574455 Fax 01492 574433
✉ welshnews@dailypost.co.uk
Owner *Trinity Mirror Plc*
Editor *Rob Irvine*
Circulation 39,595

Features Editor *Mark Brittain*
News Editor *Maria Breslyn*
Sports Editor *Steve Macmillan*

Evening Leader
Mold Business Park, Wrexham Road, Mold
CH7 1XY
☎01352 707707 Fax 01352 752180
✉ news@eveningleader.co.uk
Owner *North Wales Newspapers*
Editor-in-Chief *Barrie Jones*
Circulation 24,353

Circulates in Wrexham, Flintshire, Deeside and
Chester. Special pages/features: motoring,
travel, arts, women's, children's, local housing,
information and news for the disabled, music
and entertainment.
Deputy Editor *Martin Wright*
Assistant Editor *Jonathon Barnett*
Sports Editor *Nick Harrison*

South Wales Argus
Cardiff Road, Maesglas, Newport NP20 3QN
☎01633 810000 Fax 01633 777202
www.thisisgwent.co.uk
Owner *Newsquest*
Editor *Gerry Keighley*
Circulation 29,566

Circulates in Newport, Gwent and surrounding
areas.

News Editor *Maria Williams*
Sports Editor *Phil Webb*

South Wales Echo
Thomson House, Havelock Street, Cardiff
CF10 1XR
☎029 2058 3622 Fax 029 2058 3624
www.icwales.co.uk
Owner *Trinity Mirror Plc*
Editor *Richard Williams*
Circulation 54,635

Circulates in South and Mid Glamorgan and
Gwent.
Head of News *Cathy Owen*
Head of Features *Jonah Webb, Alison Stokes*
Head of Sport *Delme Parfitt*

South Wales Evening Post
Adelaide Street, Swansea SA1 1QT
☎01792 510000 Fax 01792 514697
✉ postbox@swwp.co.uk
www.thisissouthwales.co.uk
Owner *Northcliffe Newspapers Group Ltd*
Editor *Spencer Feeney*
Circulation 54,682

Circulates throughout south west Wales.
News Editor *Peter Slee*
Features Editor *Catherine Ings*
Sports Editor *David Evans*

Wales on Sunday
Thomson House, Havelock Street, Cardiff
CF10 1XR
☎029 2058 3733 Fax 029 2058 3725
Owner *Trinity Mirror plc*
Editor *Tim Gordon*
Circulation 47,724

Launched 1989. Tabloid with sports supple-
ment. Does not welcome unsolicited mss.
Head of Content *Laura Kemp*
Show Biz/Features Editor Rachel
Mainwaring
Sports Editor Nick Rippington

Western Mail
Thomson House, Havelock Street, Cardiff
CF10 1XR
☎029 2058 3583 Fax 029 2058 3652
www.icwales.co.uk
Owner *Trinity Mirror Plc*
Editor *Alan Edmunds*
Circulation 42,956

Circulates in Cardiff, Merthyr Tydfil, Newport,
Swansea and towns and villages throughout
Wales. Mss welcome if of a topical nature, of

Welsh interest. No short stories or travel. Approach in writing to the features editor. 'Usual subjects already well covered, e.g. motoring, travel, books, gardening. We look for the unusual.' Maximum 1000 words. Opportunities also on women's page. Supplements: *Saturday Magazine*; *Education*; *WM*; *Box Office*; *Welsh Homes*; *Business*; *Sport*; *Motoring*; *Country & Farming*.
Deputy Editor *Ceri Gould*
News Editor *Pal Carey*
Sports Editor *Philip Blanche*
Features Editor *Duncan Higgitt*

CHANNEL ISLANDS

Guernsey Press & Star
Braye Road, Vale, Guernsey GY1 3BW
☎01481 240240 Fax 01481 240235
✉ newsroom@guernsey-press.com
www.guernsey-press.com

Editor *Richard Digard*
Owner *Guiton Group*
Circulation 16,121
Special pages include children's and women's interest, gardening and fashion.
News Editor *James Falla*
Sports Editor *Rob Batiste*
Features Editor *Suzanne Heneghan*

Jersey Evening Post
PO Box 582, Jersey JE4 8XQ
☎01534 611611 Fax 01534 611622
✉ editorial@jerseyeveningpost.com
www.thisisjersey.com
Owner *Claverley Company*
Editor *Chris Bright*
Circulation 21,315
Special pages: gardening, motoring, property, boating, technology, young person's (16–25), women, food and drink, personal finance, rock reviews, health, business.
News Editor *Sue Le Ruez*
Features Editor *Elaine Hanning*
Sports Editor *Ron Felton*

Confessions of a Serial Buyer

Brian MacArthur reflects on two decades of selecting books for extracts in The Times

Over the past twenty years I have spent at least £10 million on books. Once I even offered £2 million for one book. But it wasn't my money: fortunately Rupert Murdoch was paying the bills. So I have been lucky in my career. One of my jobs at *The Times* and *Sunday Times* (and now the *Daily Telegraph*) since 1979 has been to buy books for use in the papers as serialisations or extracts. Any study of national newspapers will show that they rely heavily on books, not only for serials but also for interviews, features and news stories.

I was one of about ten serial buyers on national newspapers and my guess is that in total they spend between £5 and £10 million a year, paying from £500 to more than £150,000 for a celebrity author or a subject that will boost sales. The *Daily Mirror*, for instance, sold a million extra copies in the week it serialised Paul Burrell's account of his years as the Queen's footman and Princess Diana's butler. Insider gossip about the royals always sells newspapers. Ten years ago Sarah Bradford's book on the Queen sold an extra 100,000 copies of *The Times* on the first day of serialisation.

There is a symbiotic relationship between newspapers and publishers. On the one hand the money newspapers spend on serialisations helps publishers increase their bids to literary agents for books they are anxious to buy. Newspapers will also advertise a serial on radio or television and this helps boost sales. Meanwhile sampling the book through the serialisation will tempt readers to go out to buy it. Off-the-page sales from newspapers are also now significant. On the other hand, publishers help newspapers fill all the extra pages that have been created since Rupert Murdoch's Wapping revolution of 1986. Editors also benefit from the years of research that many authors have put into their books, time which most editors are no longer prepared to allow to their journalists. So this is a game in which all the players – editors, publishers, authors, agents and, of course, readers of newspapers and books – are winners.

It was not until a year-long study was done by Jeni Giffen two years ago that I realised how busy my job had become. In one year we received 810 books. More than half were obviously unsuitable for newspaper serialisation and were immediately rejected. But 365 were sent out to experienced readers, all former journalists, for reports on their suitability for newspaper publication. On the basis of those reports we bought 120. Yet that wasn't the end of *The Times'* association with books. Add interviews with authors, features based on books and reviews in the weekly literary pages to those 120 serials and *The Times* publicised about 1,200 books in a year. The story will be roughly the same at several other newspapers, including the *Daily Mail*, the *Daily Telegraph* and the *Guardian*. As Andrew Neil used to say when he was editing the

Sunday Times, publishers should be paying newspapers for all that free advertising.

The job has also changed significantly over the past three decades. When I first started in the late 1970s there were only two significant players – the *Sunday Times* and the *Observer* – and they concentrated heavily on political autobiographies and social history. Serials were the week's 'big read', usually lasting for two or three weeks – fourteen in the case of Field-Marshal Montgomery – and were an important part of Sunday papers that had only two or three sections. But it is the daily papers that are now the most prolific users of book serials, mainly because the serial is over within three to four days, instead of three to four Sundays. Newspapers with serialisations not only insist on exclusivity but also that rival newspapers do not receive the book until the serial is over. Some contracts even insist that books do not leave the warehouse until then. Serials in dailies therefore mean that publishers can get their books reviewed and on sale much more quickly.

The rivalry between British newspapers is probably the fiercest in the world with ten national dailies competing for readers in a declining market in an island not much bigger than California. So editors don't enjoy spending more than £100,000 on a serial only to be scooped by a rival newspaper's spoiler. When, several years ago, the *Daily Mail* had bought serialisation in a new book about the Duke of Windsor, the *Daily Express* simply walked into a bookshop, bought the book, used from it the number of words allowed by copyright law and had a front page splash – a brilliantly achieved spoiler – before the *Mail* even started its serialisation. If the *Daily Mirror* learns that the *Sun* is about to serialise David Beckham's latest book, it will create its own 'serial' from the cuttings library and splash it across the front page so that buyers cannot tell which paper has the genuine article.

It is such spoilers that have made lawyers essential parties in newspaper book deals. Publishers now insist that serial buyers sign confidentiality agreements in which they swear the contents of a book won't be used to spoil the deal agreed with the successful paper once the auction is over. Newspapers meanwhile insist on a quality control clause in any contract under which they get their money back if the author does not offer sufficient anecdotes, insights and insider gossip to make a worthwhile serial, preferably with a front-page story – the sort of anecdotes provided by Sir Christopher Meyer last year in his *DC Confidential* about George W. Bush and Tony Blair or the splash when *The Times* exposed the granny spy, Melita Norwood, as 'The Spy Who Walked in From the Co-op'.

The memoirs of Lord 'Willie' Whitelaw, the senior Tory who was Margaret Thatcher's deputy, were the worst disappointment of my career. Whitelaw was such a gentleman that he couldn't bring himself to spite his colleagues or, in particular, Lady Thatcher and there was no newsworthy material. The despairing solution was an interview in which the noble lord still failed to deliver. That was when Andrew Neil, editor of the *Sunday Times*, stipulated that contracts included a quality control clause.

But the serial that I shall never forget and in which all these factors came into play was Edwina Currie's *Diaries*. The first we knew of the diaries was when David Young, the chief executive of Time Warner Books, Ursula Mackenzie, the publisher, and Currie's agent and managing director of the literary agency Curtis Brown, Jonathan Lloyd, asked for a meeting with me and the editor Robert Thomson. The last time there had been such a request the meeting had been about Gita Sereny's highly controversial book on the child-killer Mary Bell. Both Thomson and I were required to sign confidentiality agreements. But our faces fell when we were told that the meeting was about Edwina Currie's diaries. Edwina Currie is a splendid woman, but so what? But our mood quickly changed when we were told they revealed that she and John Major, before he became prime minister, had enjoyed a four-year affair. Wow!

I read the diaries in an office at Time Warner next day, reported back to Thomson and we agreed a deal. Journalists love gossip: if you want to keep a secret the last place to do so is in a newsroom. This, moreover, was such a jaw-dropping story – as Andrew Marr, the BBC political editor was later to say on the *Today* programme – that it was vital our story did not leak. It had to remain a secret for thirty-eight days. Yet if the serial was to be edited and published the circle of those in the know had to be widened. The interviewer Ginny Dougary had to read the book and she was accompanied by a photographer when she met Currie, so the picture editor had to know. Barry Turner who edited the extracts obviously knew the import of the diaries as did Mary Fulton who was dealing with the press and broadcasters. On the day before publication our political writers and sub-editors were told about the story – but not the newsdesk.

There was also an element of nail-biting uncertainty about the story. What if Major denied the affair, threatened to sue, applied for an injunction or issued a statement to all newspapers thereby denying *The Times* its scoop? So it was a tense moment when Philip Webster, the political editor, tried to contact Major, only to discover that he was in America. It was another agonising two and a half hours before we heard back from him. Our luck held, however. Major issued a statement, only to *The Times*, saying that the affair was the incident of his life of which he was most ashamed. We had our scoop – but we used another newspaper trick to ensure that it remained a scoop: we did a front page without the story for the first edition which goes to other newspapers and is sold on the streets of London. After 18,000 of those had been printed, we switched to the Major-Currie story. Next day *The Times* was sold out in some areas by 9 a.m. We sold an extra 120,000 copies and could have doubled that if we had realised how much interest the story would generate. I was particularly pleased to find that our news editor was as surprised by the story as the rest of the world.

I have had the good fortune to be paid to read and buy books for a living and it has been an exciting life in which I have been part of teams bringing in sensational scoops – which is what newspapers are about. Those twenty years have also given me a huge admiration for the idealism, enthusiasm and professionalism of the British book trade.

Brian MacArthur was founder editor of The Times Higher Education Supplement *and* Eddie Shah's Today, *editor of the* Western Morning News *and held senior positions on* The Times *and* Sunday Times.

Magazines

Abraxas
57 Eastbourne Road, St Austell PL25 4SU
☎01726 64975 Fax 01726 64975
✉ lordcrashingbore@btinternet.com
www.stormloader.com/users/abrax7
Owner *Paul Newman*
Editors *Paul Newman, Pamela Smith-Rawnsley*
Founded 1991. Usually features a lead article by Colin Wilson combined with short stories, poems, translations and articles on philosophy, existentialism and ideas. Favours challenging essays on the new and radical slants on the old (e.g. Stefan Ball introducing Pablo Palacio). Contributors include Gary Lachman, D.M. Thomas, Ramond Tallis, Adam Daly and Colin Stanley. Abraxas is due to be published as a large-format POD paperback, obtainable both from the editor and Abraxas Storefront at Lulu Publishing (www.lulu.com/lord-crashingbore)
FICTION One story per issue; approx. 1000 words. 'Think of a writer like Wolfgang Borchert who wrote briefly, vividly and fiercely.'
POETRY Open to all styles, rhymed and irregular but prefers a creative, original use of language rather than prosy verse.
PAYMENT 'flattery'.

Acclaim
See **The New Writer**

Accountancy
145 London Road, Kingston Upon Thames KT2 6SR
☎020 8247 1389 Fax 020 8247 1424
www.accountancymagazine.com
Owner *Wolters Kluwer UK*
Editor *Chris Quick*
Circulation 51,579
Founded 1889. MONTHLY. Written ideas welcome.
FEATURES *Lesley Bolton* Accounting, tax, business-related articles of high technical content aimed at professional/managerial readers. Maximum 2000 words. PAYMENT by arrangement.

Accountancy Age
32–34 Broadwick Street, London W1A 2HG
☎020 7316 9190 Fax 020 7316 9250
✉ accountancy_age@vnu.co.uk
www.accountancyage.com
Owner *VNU Business Publications*
Editor-in-Chief *Damian Wild*
Editor *Gavin Hinks* (☎020 7316 9608)
Circulation 65,855
Founded 1969. WEEKLY. Unsolicited mss welcome. Ideas may be suggested in writing provided they are clearly thought out.
FEATURES *Rachel Fielding* Topics right across the accountancy, business and financial world. Max. 2000 words. PAYMENT negotiable.

ACE Tennis Magazine
IG House, Palliser Road, London W14 9EB
☎020 7381 7100 Fax 020 7610 2794
✉ Nigel.Billen@acemag.co.uk
Owner *Tennis GB*
Editor *Nigel Billen*
Circulation 47,020
Founded 1996. MONTHLY specialist tennis magazine. News (250 words max.) and features (2000 words max.). No unsolicited mss; send feature synopses by e-mail in the first instance. No tournament reports. PAYMENT £200 per 1000 words.

Acumen
See under *Poetry Magazines*

Aeroplane
IPC Media Ltd., King's Reach Tower, Stamford Street, London SE1 9LS
☎020 7261 5849 Fax 020 7261 5269
✉ aeroplane_monthly@ipcmedia.com
www.aeroplanemonthly.com
Owner *IPC Country & Leisure Media Ltd*
Editor *Michael Oakey*
Circulation 36,656
Founded 1973. MONTHLY. Historic aviation and aircraft preservation from its beginnings to the 1960s. No post-1960 aircraft types; no poetry. Will consider news items and features written with authoritative knowledge of the subject, illustrated with good quality photographs.
NEWS *Tony Harsmworth* Max. 500 words.
FEATURES *Michael Oakey* Max. 3000 words. Approach by letter or e-mail in the first instance.
PAYMENT £60 per 1000 words; £10–40 per picture used.

Air International

PO Box 100, Stamford PE9 1XQ
☎01780 755131 Fax 01780 757261
✉ malcolm.english@keypublishing.com
www.airinternational.com
Owner *Key Publishing Ltd*
Editor *Malcolm English*
Circulation 12,636

Founded 1971. MONTHLY. Civil and military aircraft magazine. Unsolicited mss welcome but initial approach by phone or in writing preferred.

AirForces Monthly

PO Box 100, Stamford PE9 1XQ
☎01780 755131 Fax 01780 757261
✉ edafm@keypublishing.com
Owner *Key Publishing Ltd*
Editor *Alan Warnes*
Circulation 19,582

Founded 1988. MONTHLY. Modern military aviation magazine. Unsolicited mss welcome but initial approach by phone or in writing preferred.

Amateur Gardening

Westover House, West Quay Road, Poole
BH15 1JG
☎01202 440840 Fax 01202 440860
Owner *IPC Media (A Time Warner Company)*
Editor *Tim Rumball*
Circulation 45,872

Founded 1884. WEEKLY. New contributions are welcome especially if they are topical and informative. All articles/news items should be supported by colour pictures (which may or may not be supplied by the author).

FEATURES Topical and practical gardening articles; will only consider those accompanied by photos. Max. 1000 words.

NEWS Compiled and edited in-house generally but all stories welcomed.

PAYMENT negotiable.

Amateur Photographer

IPC Media Ltd., King's Reach Tower,
Stamford Street, London SE1 9LS
☎020 7261 5100/0870 444 5000
(switchboard) Fax 020 7261 5404
✉ amateurphotographer@ipcmedia.com
Owner *IPC Media (A Time Warner Company)*
Editor *Garry Coward-Williams*
Circulation 26,869

Founded 1884. WEEKLY. For the competent amateur with a technical interest. Freelancers are used but writers should be aware that there is ordinarily no use for words without pictures.

Amateur Stage

Hampden House, 2 Weymouth Street, London
W1W 5BT
☎020 7636 4343 Fax 020 7636 2323
✉ cvtheatre@aol.com
Owner *Platform Publications Ltd*
Editor *Charles Vance*

Some opportunity here for outside contributions. Topics of interest include amateur premières, technical developments within the amateur forum and items relating to landmarks or anniversaries in the history of amateur societies. Approach in writing only (include s.a.e. for return of mss). No PAYMENT.

Ancestors

See **The National Archives** under
UK Publishers

Angler's Mail

IPC Media Ltd., King's Reach Tower,
Stamford Street, London SE1 9LS
☎020 7261 5778 Fax 020 7261 6016
✉ anglersmail@ipcmedia.com
www.anglersmail.com
Owner *IPC Media (A Time Warner Company)*
Editor *Tim Knight*
Circulation 45,237

Founded 1965. WEEKLY. Angling news and matches. Interested in pictures, stories, tip-offs and features. Approach the news desk by telephone.

PAYMENT £10–40 per 200 words; pictures, £20–40.

Angling Times Advanced

Emap Active, Bushfield House, Orton Centre,
Peterborough PE2 5UW
☎01733 465705 Fax 01733 465658
✉ lewis.murawski@emap.com
www.atadvanced.co.uk
Owner *Emap Active*
Editor *Lewis Murawski*
Circulation 15,665

Founded 1992. MONTHLY magazine aimed at match anglers and advanced pleasure anglers. Coarse fishing only.

FEATURES only. Please send relevant articles, with or without pictures, by e-mail to the editor. Max. 2500 words.

Animal Action

Wilberforce Way, Southwater, Horsham
RH13 9RS
☎0870 010 1181   Fax 0870 753 0048
✉ publications@rspca.org.uk
www.rspca.org.uk
Owner *RSPCA*
Editor *Sarah Evans*
Circulation 50,000

BI-MONTHLY RSPCA youth membership magazine. Articles (pet care, etc.) are written in-house. Good-quality animal photographs welcome.

Animals and You

D.C. Thomson & Co. Ltd, 2 Albert Square, Dundee DD1 9QJ
☎01382 223131   Fax 01382 322214
✉ animalsandyou@dcthomson.co.uk
Owner *D.C. Thomson & Co. Ltd*
Editor *Margaret Monaghan*
Circulation 65,000

Founded 1998. MONTHLY magazine aimed at girls, aged 7–11 years who love animals. Contains cute 'n' cuddly pin-ups, pet tips and advice, animal charity information, photo stories, puzzles, readers' pictures and drawings. Most work done in-house but will consider short features, photographic or with good illustrations. Approach by e-mail.

The Antique Dealer and Collectors' Guide

PO Box 805, Greenwich, London SE10 8TD
☎020 8691 4820   Fax 020 8691 2489
✉ antiquedealercollectorsguide@
   ukbusiness.com
www.antiquecollectorsguide.co.uk
Owner *Statuscourt Ltd*
Publisher *Philip Bartlam*
Circulation 12,500

Founded 1946. SIX ISSUES YEARLY. Covers all aspects of the antiques and fine art worlds. Unsolicited mss welcome.

FEATURES Practical but readable articles on the history, design, authenticity, restoration and market aspects of antiques and fine art. Max. 2000 words.

NEWS Items on events, sales, museums, exhibitions, antique fairs and markets. Max. 300 words.

PAYMENT rates for features by arrangement.

Antiquesnews incorporating

Antiques & Art Independent

1 Brambledean Road, Portslade, Brighton
BN41 1LP
✉ antiquesnews@hotmail.com
www.antiquesnews.co.uk
Owners *A.J. & M.K. Keniston*
Publisher/Editor *Tony Keniston*

Founded 1997. WEEKLY. Up-to-date information online for the British antiques and art trade. News, photographs, gossip and controversial views on all aspects of the fine art and antiques world welcome. Articles on antiques and fine arts themselves are not featured. Approach in writing with ideas.

Apex Advertiser

PO Box 7086, Clacton-on-Sea CO15 5WN
☎01255 428500   Fax 0870 046 6536
✉ apex@apexadvertiser.co.uk
www.apexadvertiser.co.uk
Owner *Apex Publishing Ltd*
Editor *Susan Kidby*
Circulation 12,000

Founded 2002. MONTHLY advertising magazine including guides and information, features, listings and reviews. Approach by post, only.

Apollo Magazine

20 Theobald's Road, London WC1X 8PF
☎020 7430 1900   Fax 020 7404 7386
✉ editorial@apollomag.com
www.apollo-magazine.com
Owner *The Spectator (1828) Ltd*
Publisher *Kimberly Quinn*
Editor *Michael Hall*

FOUNDED 1925. MONTHLY. Specialist articles on art and antiques, exhibition and book reviews, exhibition diary, information on dealers and auction houses. Unsolicited mss welcome. Interested in specialist, usually new research in fine arts, architecture and antiques.

The Architects' Journal

151 Rosebery Avenue, London EC1R 4GB
☎020 7505 6700   Fax 020 7505 6701
www.ajplus.co.uk
Owner *Emap Construct*
Editor *Isabel Allen*
Circulation 13,491

WEEKLY trade magazine dealing with all aspects of the industry. No unsolicited mss. Approach in writing with ideas.

Architectural Design

John Wiley & Sons, 3rd Floor, International House, Ealing Broadway Centre, London W5 5DB
☎020 8326 3800   Fax 020 8326 3801

Owner *John Wiley & Sons Ltd*
Editor *Helen Castle*
Development Editor *Mariangela Palazzi-Williams*
Circulation 5000

Founded 1930. BI-MONTHLY. Sold as a book and journal as well as online, *AD* charts theoretical and topical developments in architecture. Format consists of 128pp, the first part dedicated to a theme compiled by a specially commissioned guest-editor; the back section (AD+) carries series and more current one-off articles. Unsolicited mss not welcome generally, though journalistic contributions will be considered for the back section.

The Architectural Review

151 Rosebery Avenue, London EC1R 4GB
☎020 7505 6725 Fax 020 7505 6701
www.arplus.com

Owner *Emap Construct*
Editor *Paul Finch*
Circulation 21,583

MONTHLY international professional magazine dealing with architecture and all aspects of design. No unsolicited mss. Approach in writing with ideas.

Arena

Endeavour House, 189 Shaftesbury Avenue, London WC2H 8JG
☎020 7437 9011
✉ emma.kay@emap.com

Owner *Emap East*
Editor *William Drew*
Circulation 49,296

MONTHLY style and general interest magazine for men. Intelligent articles and profiles.

FEATURES Fashion, lifestyle, film, television, politics, business, music, media, design, art and architecture. Ideas for articles will be considered; send by e-mail.

Art Monthly

4th Floor, 28 Charing Cross Road, London WC2H 0DB
☎020 7240 0389 Fax 020 7497 0726
✉ info@artmonthly.co.uk
www.artmonthly.co.uk

Owner *Britannia Art Publications Ltd*
Editor *Patricia Bickers*
Circulation 6000

Founded 1976. TEN ISSUES YEARLY. News and features of relevance to those interested in modern and contemporary visual art. Unsolicited mss

welcome. Contributions should be addressed to the deputy editor, accompanied by s.a.e.

FEATURES Always commissioned. Interviews and articles of up to 2000 words on art theory, individual artists, contemporary art history and issues affecting the arts (e.g. funding and arts education). Exhibition and book reviews: 750–1000 words.

NEWS Brief reports (250–300 words) on art issues.

PAYMENT negotiable.

The Art Newspaper

70 South Lambeth Road, London SW8 1RL
☎020 7735 3331 Fax 020 7735 3332
✉ contact@theartnewspaper.com
www.theartnewspaper.com

Owner *Umberto Allemandi & Co. Publishing*
Editor *Cristina Ruiz*
Circulation 22,000

Founded 1990. MONTHLY. Tabloid format with hard news on the international art market, news, museums, exhibitions, archaeology, conservation, books and current debate topics. Length 250–2000 words. No unsolicited mss. Approach with ideas in writing. Commissions only.

Art Review

1 Sekforde Street, London EC1R 0BE
☎020 7107 2760 Fax 020 7107 2761
✉ info@art-review.co.uk
www.art-review.co.uk

Owner *Dennis Hotz*
Editor *Rebecca Wilson*
Deputy Editor *Matt Price*
Circulation 35,000

Founded 1949. MONTHLY magazine of international contemporary art. Features, profiles, previews and reviews of artists and exhibitions worldwide. 'We have a very international focus so it's important that the artist is exhibiting internationally and has good gallery representation.'

FEATURES *Rebecca Wilson, Charlotte Edwards* Max. 1500 words. E-mail pitch and c.v. to editor@art-review.co.uk at least three months in advance of related show/publication. PAYMENT £400–500.

NEWS All items written in-house.

The Artist

Caxton House, 63–65 High Street, Tenterden TN30 6BD
☎0158076 3673 Fax 0158076 5411
www.theartistmagazine.co.uk

Owner/Editor *Sally Bulgin*
Circulation 21,500
Founded 1931. MONTHLY. Art journalists, artists, art tutors and writers with a good knowledge of art materials are invited to write to the editor with ideas for practical and informative features about art, materials, techniques and artists.

Asian Times
Unit 2.01, 65 Whitechapel Road, London E1 1DU
☎020 7650 2000 Fax 020 7650 2001
✉ editor@asiantimesonline.co.uk
www.asiantimesonline.co.uk
Owner *Ethnic Media Group*
Editor *Burhan Ahmad*
Circulation 28,525
Founded 1981. WEEKLY community paper for the Asian community in Britain. Interested in relevant general, local and international issues. Approach in writing with ideas for submission.

Athletics Weekly
83 Park Road, Peterborough PE1 2TN
☎01733 898440 Fax 01733 898441
✉ results@athletics-weekly.co.uk
www.athleticsweekly.com
Owner *Descartes Publishing*
Editor *Jason Henderson*
Results Editor *Paul Halford*
Circulation 14,000
Founded 1945. WEEKLY. Covers track and field, road, fell, cross-country, race walking. Results, fixtures, interviews, technical coaching articles and news surrounding build up to 2012 Olympics.
NEWS *Jon Mulkeen* Max. 400 words.
FEATURES *Jason Henderson* Max. 2000 words.
Approach in writing.
PAYMENT negotiable.

Attitude
Northern & Shell Tower, City Harbour, 4 Selsdon Way, London E14 9GL
☎020 7308 5090 Fax 020 7308 5384
✉ attitude@attitudemag.co.uk
Owner *Remnant Media*
Editor *Adam Mattera*
Deputy Editor *Jamie Hakim*
Circulation 60,000
Founded 1994. MONTHLY. Style magazine aimed primarily, but not exclusively, at gay men. Celebrity, fashion and cultural coverage. Brief summaries of proposed features, together with details of previously published work, should be sent by post or e-mail only. 'It sounds obvious, but anyone wanting to contribute to the magazine should read it first.'

The Author
84 Drayton Gardens, London SW10 9SB
☎020 7373 6642
✉ theauthor@societyofauthors.org
Owner *The Society of Authors*
Editor *Andrew Taylor*
Manager *Kate Pool*
Circulation 8500
Founded 1890. QUARTERLY journal of the **Society of Authors**. Most articles are commissioned.

Auto Express
30 Cleveland Street, London W1T 4JD
☎020 7907 6200 Fax 020 7907 6234
✉ editorial@autoexpress.co.uk
www.autoexpress.co.uk
Owner *Dennis Publishing*
Editor *David Johns*
Associate Editor *Tom Johnston*
Circulation 101,013
Founded 1989. WEEKLY consumer motoring title with news, drives, tests, investigations, etc.
NEWS News stories and tip-offs welcome. Fillers 150 words max.; leads 300 words. Approach by e-mail.
Features Ideas welcome. No fully-written articles – features will be commissioned if appropriate. Max. 2000 words.
PAYMENT £350 per 1000 words.

Autocar
Haymarket Publishing, Teddington Studios, Broom Road, Teddington TW11 9BE
☎020 8267 5630 Fax 020 8267 5759
✉ autocar@haynet.com
www.autocar.co.uk
Owner *Haymarket Publishing Ltd*
Editor *Chas Hallett*
News Editor *Hilton Holloway*
Circulation 62,577
Founded 1895. WEEKLY. All news stories, features, interviews, scoops, ideas, tip-offs and photographs welcome. PAYMENT negotiable.

Aviation News
HPC, Drury Lane, St Leonards on Sea TN38 9BJ
☎01424 720477 Fax 01424 443693
✉ editor@aviation-news.co.uk

www.aviation-news.co.uk
Owner *Hastings Printing Company*
Editor *Barry C. Wheeler*
Circulation 21,000

Founded 1939. MONTHLY review of aviation for those interested in military, commercial and business aircraft and equipment – old and new. Will consider articles on military and civil aircraft, airports, air forces, current and historical subjects. No fiction.

FEATURES 'New writers always welcome and if the copy is not good enough it is returned with guidance attached.' Max. 5000 words.

NEWS Items are always considered from new sources. Max. 300 words.

PAYMENT negotiable.

Balance

Diabetes UK, 10 Parkway, London NW1 7AA
☎020 7424 1000　Fax 020 7424 1001
✉ balance@diabetes.org.uk

Owner *Diabetes UK*
Editor *Martin Cullen*
Circulation 250,000

Founded 1935. BI-MONTHLY. Unsolicited mss are not accepted. Writers may submit a brief proposal in writing. Only topics relevant to diabetes will be considered.

NEWS Short pieces about activities relating to diabetes and the lifestyle of people with diabetes. Max. 150 words.

FEATURES Medical, diet and lifestyle features written by people with diabetes or with an interest and expert knowledge in the field. General features are mostly based on experience or personal observation. Max. 1500 words.

PAYMENT NUJ rates.

The Banker

Tabernacle Court, 16–28 Tabernacle Street, London EC2A 4DD
☎020 7382 8507　Fax 020 7382 8586
✉ stephen.timewell@ft.com
www.thebanker.com

Owner *FT Business*
Editor-in-Chief *Stephen Timewell*
Circulation 26,089

Founded 1926. MONTHLY. News and features on banking, finance and capital markets worldwide and technology.

BBC Gardeners' World Magazine

Woodlands, 80 Wood Lane, London W12 0TT
☎020 8433 3959　Fax 020 8433 3986
✉ adam.pasco@bbc.co.uk
www.gardenersworld.com

Owner *BBC Worldwide Publishing Ltd*
Editor *Adam Pasco*
Deputy Editor *Lucy Hall*
Features Editor *Harriet Smith*
Commissioning Editor *Kevin Smith*
Circulation 235,792

Founded 1991. MONTHLY. Gardening advice, ideas and inspiration. No unsolicited mss. Approach by phone or in writing with ideas – interested in features about exceptional small gardens. Also interested in any exciting new gardens showing good design and planting ideas as well as new plants and the stories behind them. 'The magazine aims to be the first to bring news of new trends and developments, and always welcomes ideas from contributors.'

BBC Good Food

Woodlands, 80 Wood Lane, London W12 0TT
☎020 8433 2000　Fax 020 8433 3931
✉ goodfood.magazine@bbc.co.uk

Owner *BBC Worldwide Publishing Ltd*
Editor *Gillian Carter*
Circulation 344,434

Founded 1989. MONTHLY food and drink magazine with television and radio links. No unsolicited mss.

BBC History Magazine
(incorporating **Living History**)

14th Floor, Tower House, Fairfax Street, Bristol BS1 3BN
☎0117 927 9009

Owner *Bristol Magazines Ltd*
Editor *Dave Musgrove*
Circulation 54,067

Founded 2000. MONTHLY. General news and features on British and international history, with books and CD reviews, listings of history events, TV and radio history programmes and regular features for those interested in history and current affairs. Winner, British Society of Magazine Editors 'Editor of the Year Award', 2002, for general interest and current affairs titles. Will consider submissions from academic or otherwise expert historians/archaeologists as well as, occasionally, from historically literate journalists who include expert analysis and historiography with a well-told narrative. Ideas for regular features are welcome. Also publishes cartoons, quizzes and crosswords. 'We cannot guarantee to acknowledge all unsolicited mss immediately.'

FEATURES should be pegged to anniversaries or forthcoming books/TV programmes, current affairs topics, etc. 750–3000 words.

NEWS 400–500 words. Send short letter or

e-mail with synopsis, giving appropriate sources, pegs for publication dates, etc. PAYMENT negotiable.

BBC Homes & Antiques

14th Floor, Tower House, Fairfax Street, Bristol BS1 3BN
☎0117 927 9009
www.bbcworldwide.com/Antiques
Owner *BBC Worldwide Publishing Ltd*
Editor *Bernie Herlihy*
Circulation 120,141

Founded 1993. MONTHLY traditional home interest magazine with a strong bias towards antiques and collectibles. Opportunities for freelancers are limited; most features are commissioned from regular stable of contributors. No fiction, health and beauty, fashion or general showbusiness. Approach with ideas by phone or in writing.

FEATURES *Caroline Wheater* At-home features: inspirational houses – people-led items. Pieces commissioned on recce shots and cuttings. Guidelines available on request. Send cuttings of relevant work published. Max. 1500 words. PAYMENT negotiable.

BBC Music Magazine

14th Floor, Tower House, Fairfax Street, Bristol BS1 3BN
☎0117 927 9009
Owner *BBC Worldwide Publishing Ltd*
Editor *Oliver Condy*
Circulation 51,272

Founded 1992. MONTHLY. All areas of classical music. Not interested in unsolicited material. Approach with ideas by e-mail or fax.

BBC Top Gear Magazine

Room A1004, Woodlands, 80 Wood Lane, London W12 0TT
☎020 8433 3716 Fax 020 8433 3754
www.topgear.com
Owner *BBC Magazines*
Editor *Michael Harvey*
Circulation 175,218

Founded 1993. MONTHLY companion magazine to the popular TV series. No unsolicited material as most features are commissioned.

BBC Wildlife Magazine

14th Floor, Tower House, Fairfax Street, Bristol BS1 3BN
☎0117 927 9009 Fax 0117 927 9008
✉ wildlifemagazine@originpublishing.co.uk
Owner *Bristol Magazines Ltd*

Editor *Sophie Stafford*
Features Editor *Fergus Collins*
News & Travel Editor *James Fair*
Circulation 44,036

Founded 1963 (formerly *Wildlife*, née *Animals*). THIRTEEN ISSUES A YEAR. Welcomes idea pitches but not unsolicited mss. Read guidelines on website to improve chances of success.

FEATURES Most features commissioned from excellent writers with expert knowledge of wildlife or conservation subjects. Max. 2500 words.

NEWS Most news stories commissioned from known freelancers. Max. 400 words. PAYMENT features, £200–450; news, £80–120.

Bee World
See **Journal of Apicultural Research**

Bella

H. Bauer Publishing, Academic House, 24–28 Oval Road, London NW1 7DT
☎020 7241 8000 Fax 020 7241 8056
Owner *H. Bauer Publishing*
Editor-in-Chief *Jayne Marsden*
Circulation 380,973

Founded 1987. WEEKLY. Women's magazine specialising in real-life, human interest stories.

FEATURES *Clare Swatman* Contributions welcome for some sections of the magazine: readers' letters, 'Blush with Bella'.

FICTION *Linda O'Byrne* Max. 1000–1500 words. Send s.a.e. for guidelines.

Best

33 Broadwick Street, London W1F 0DQ
☎020 7339 4000 Fax 020 7339 4580
✉ best@acp-natmag.co.uk
Owner *National Magazine Company/ACP*
Editor *Michelle Hather*
Circulation 400,807

Founded 1987. WEEKLY women's magazine. Multiple features, news, short stories on all topics of interest to women. Important for would-be contributors to study the magazine's style which differs from many other women's weeklies. Approach in writing with s.a.e.

FEATURES *Helen Garston, Charlotte Seligman* Max. 1500 words. No unsolicited mss.

FICTION *Pat Richardson* Short story slot: 900–1200 words. Send s.a.e. for guidelines. PAYMENT negotiable.

Best of British

Church Lane Publishing Ltd, Bank Chambers, 27a Market Place, Market Deeping PE6 8EA

☎01778 342814
✉ mail@british.fsbusiness.co.uk
www.bestofbritishmag.co.uk

Owner *Church Lane Publishing Ltd*
Editor-in-Chief *Ian Beacham*
Assistant Editor *Linne Matthews*

Founded 1994. MONTHLY magazine celebrating all things British, both past and present. Emphasis on nostalgia – memories from the 1940s, 1950s and 1960s. Study of the magazine is advised in the first instance. All preliminary approaches should be made in writing.

The Big Issue

1–5 Wandsworth Road, London SW8 2LN
☎020 7526 3200   Fax 020 7526 3201
✉ editorialinfo@bigissue.com
www.bigissue.com

Editor-in-Chief *A. John Bird*
Acting Editor *Charles Howgego*
Circulation 154,932 (Group)

Founded 1991. WEEKLY. An award-winning campaigning and street-wise general interest magazine sold in London, the Midlands, the North East and South of England. Separate regional editions sold in Manchester, Scotland, Wales and the South West.

NEWS *Judy Kerr* Hard-hitting exclusive stories with emphasis on social injustice aimed at national leaders.

ARTS *Charles Howgego* Interested in interviews and analysis ideas. Reviews written in-house. Send synopses to arts editor.

FEATURES Interviews, campaigns, comment, opinion and social issues reflecting a varied and informed audience. Balance includes social issues but mixed with arts and cultural features. Freelance writers used each week – commissioned from a variety of contributors. Best approach is to e-mail or post synopses to acting editor *Charles Howgego* with examples of work in the first instance. Max. 1500 words. PAYMENT £165 for 1000 words.

The Big Issue Cymru

55 Charles Street, Cardiff CF10 2GD
☎029 2025 5670   Fax 029 2025 5672
✉ edit@bigissuecymru.fsnet.co.uk
www.bigissuecymru.co.uk

Editor *Cathryn Scott*
Circulation 8,408

Founded 1993. WEEKLY. Hard-hitting social and news features plus arts and entertainment.

FEATURES/NEWS *Cathryn Scott* Welcomes contributions but must be relevant to a Welsh readership. Approach by e-mail. Lead in of four to six weeks. Max. 1000 words (features); 550 (news). No poetry or fiction.

The Big Issue in Scotland

Mir Village, 71 Oxford Street, Glasgow
G5 9EP
☎0141 418 7000   Fax 0141 418 7061
✉ editorial@bigissuescotland.com
www.bigissuescotland.com

Editor *Clare Harris*
Circulation 32,008

WEEKLY. Coverage of social issues, arts and culture, sport, interviews; news and hard-hitting journalism.

The Big Issue in the North

135–141 Oldham Street, Manchester M4 1LN
☎0161 834 6300   Fax 0161 832 3237
✉ editorial@bigissueinthenorth.com
www.thebiglifecompany.com

Owner *The Big Life Company*
Editor *Matt Baker*
Circulation 32,000

Launched 1992. WEEKLY. Entertainment, celebrity interviews, environmental issues and issues from the social sector as well as homelessness. Welcomes news stories not covered by the national press; approach by e-mail.

The Big Issue South West

5 Brunswick Court, Brunswick Square, Bristol
BS2 8PT
☎0117 916 6593   Fax 0017 916 6599
✉ editorial@bigissuesouthwest.co.uk

Editor *Cathryn Scott*
Circulation 14,222

Founded 1994. WEEKLY. Hard-hitting, socially aware news and features, local arts and entertainment. Welcomes news features with a regional relevance. No poetry or fiction.

FEATURES/NEWS *Cathryn Scott* Items must be regionally specific, date pegged, new information and people-based. Approach by e-mail. Max. 1000 words (features); 550 (news).

Bike

Emap Automotive Ltd, Media House, Lynch Wood, Peterborough PE2 6EA
☎01733 468181   Fax 01733 468196
✉ bike@emap.com

Owner *Emap Plc*
Editor *Tim Thompson*
Circulation 89,325

Founded 1971. MONTHLY. Broad-based motorcycle magazine. Approach by e-mail.

Bird Life Magazine
The RSPB, UK Headquarters, The Lodge, Sandy SG19 2DL
☎01767 680551 Fax 01767 683262
✉ derek.niemann@rspb.org.uk
Owner *Royal Society for the Protection of Birds*
Editor *Derek Niemann*
Circulation 90,000
Founded 1965. BI-MONTHLY. Bird, wildlife and nature conservation for 8–12-year-olds (RSPB Wildlife Explorers members). No unsolicited mss. No 'captive/animal welfare' articles.
FEATURES Unsolicited material rarely used.
NEWS News releases welcome. Approach in writing in the first instance.

Bird Watching
Emap Active, Bretton Court, Peterborough PE3 8DZ
☎0870 062 0200 Fax 01733 465376
✉ kevin.wilmot@emap.com
www.birdwatching.co.uk
Owner *Emap Active*
Editor *Kevin Wilmot*
Circulation 20,266
Founded 1986. MONTHLY magazine for birdwatchers at all levels of experience. Offers practical advice of where and when to see birds, how to identify them, product reviews (particularly binoculars, telescopes and digiscoping equipment), extensive bird sightings, 'Go Birding' walks (10 each issue), news and general articles.
FEATURES Interested in authoratative articles on bird behaviour and bird watching/sites in the UK. Please send synopsis, not the whole piece. Max. 1000 words.
NEWS UK news pre-eminent, preferably with pictures. Max. 350 words.
FEES negotiable.

Birds
The RSPB, UK Headquarters, The Lodge, Sandy SG19 2DL
☎01767 680551 Fax 01767 683262
✉ rob.hume@rspb.org.uk
www.rspb.org.uk
Owner *Royal Society for the Protection of Birds*
Editor *R.A. Hume*
Circulation 620,780
QUARTERLY magazine which covers not only wild birds but also other wildlife and related conservation topics. No interest in features on pet birds or 'rescued' sick/injured/orphaned ones. Content refers mostly to RSPB work so opportunities for freelance work on other sub-

jects are limited but some freelance submissions are used in most issues. Phone or e-mail to discuss.

Birdwatch
B403A The Chocolate Factory, 5 Clarendon Road, London N22 6XJ
☎020 8881 0550 Fax 020 8881 0990
✉ editorial@birdwatch.co.uk
www.birdwatch.co.uk
Owner *Solo Publishing*
Editor *Dominic Mitchell*
Circulation 13,000
Founded 1992. MONTHLY magazine featuring illustrated articles on all aspects of birds and birdwatching, especially in Britain. No unsolicited mss. Approach in writing with synopsis of 100 words max. Annual **Birdwatch Bird Book of the Year** award (see entry under *Prizes*).
FEATURES *Dominic Mitchell* Unusual angles/personal accounts, if well-written. Articles of an educative or practical nature suited to the readership. Max. 2000 words.
FICTION *Dominic Mitchell* Very little opportunity although occasional short story published. Max. 1500 words.
NEWS *Simon Papps* Very rarely use external material.
PAYMENT £50 per 1000 words.

Bizarre
30 Cleveland Street, London W1T 4JD
☎020 7907 6000 Fax 020 7907 6516
✉ bizarre@dennis.co.uk
www.bizarremag.com
Owner *Dennis Publishing*
Editor *Alex Godfrey*
Circulation 90,750
Founded 1997. MONTHLY magazine featuring amazing stories and images from around the world. No fiction, poetry, illustrations, short snippets.
FEATURES *Kate Hodges* No unsolicited mss. Send synopsis by post or e-mail.
PAYMENT negotiable.

Black Beauty & Hair
2nd Floor, Culvert House, Culvert Road, Battersea, London SW11 5HD
☎020 7720 2108 Fax 020 7498 3023
✉ info@blackbeautyandhair.com
www.blackbeautyandhair.com
Owner *Hawker Consumer Publications Ltd*
Publisher *Pat Petker* (☎ext. 207)
Editor *Irene Shelley*
Circulation 19,697

BI-MONTHLY with one annual special: *The Hairstyle Book* in October; and a *Bridal Supplement* in the April/May issue. Black hair and beauty magazine with emphasis on authoritative articles relating to hair, beauty, fashion, health and lifestyle. Unsolicited contributions welcome.

FEATURES Beauty and fashion pieces welcome from writers with a sound knowledge of the Afro-Caribbean beauty scene plus bridal features. Minimum 1000 words.

PAYMENT £100 per 1000 words.

Black Static

5 Martins Lane, Witcham, Ely CB6 2LB
✉ andy@ttapress.demon.co.uk
www.ttapress.com

Owner *TTA Press*
Editor *Andy Cox*

Formerly *The Third Alternative*, founded 1993. BIMONTHLY colour horror magazine: short fiction, news and gossip, film and television, manga and anime books. Publishes talented newcomers alongside famous authors. Unsolicited mss welcome if accompanied by s.a.e. or e-mail address for overseas submissions (max. 8000 words). Fiction submissions as hard copy only; feature suggestions can be e-mailed. Potential contributors are advised to study the magazine. Contracts are exchanged upon acceptance; payment is upon acceptance. Winner of several British Fantasy Awards.

Bliss Magazine

Endeavour House, 189 Shaftesbury Avenue, London WC2H 8JG
☎ 020 7208 3478   Fax 020 7208 3591
✉ diana.best@emap.com

Owner *Emap élan*
Editor *Lisa Smosarski*
Deputy Editor *Chantelle Horton*
Circulation 277,165

Founded 1995. MONTHLY teenage lifestyle magazine for girls. No unsolicited mss; 'e-mail the Features Editor (*Emma Deeks*) with an idea and then follow up with a call.'

NEWS Worldwide teenage news. Max. 200 words.

FEATURES Real life teenage stories with subjects willing to be photographed. Reports on teenage issues. Max. 1500 words.

PAYMENT news, £50–100; feaures, up to £350.

Blueprint

6–14 Underwood Street, London N1 7JQ
☎ 020 7549 2548

✉ vrichardson@wilmington.co.uk
www.blueprintmagazine.co.uk

Owner *Wilmington Media*
Editor *Vicky Richardson*
Circulation 10,000

Founded 1983. MONTHLY. 'Crossing the boundaries of design and architecture (from graphics and product design to interiors and urban development), Blueprint examines their impact on society in general.' Features, news and reviews. Welcomes ideas and pitches for articles on topics relevant to the magazine; no completed features. Approach by e-mail.

The Book Collector

PO Box 12426, London W11 3GW
☎ 020 7792 3492   Fax 020 7792 3492
✉ editor@thebookcollector.co.uk (editorial)
www.thebookcollector.co.uk

Owner *The Collector Ltd*
Editor *Nicolas J. Barker*

Founded 1950. QUARTERLY magazine on bibliography and the history of books, book-collecting, libraries and the book trade.

Book World Magazine

2 Caversham Street, London SW3 4AH
☎ 020 7351 4995   Fax 020 7351 4995

Owner *Christchurch Publishers Ltd*
Editor *James Hughes*
Circulation 5500

Founded 1980. MONTHLY news and reviews for serious book collectors, librarians, antiquarian and other booksellers. No unsolicited mss. Interested in material relevant to literature, art and book collecting. Send letter in the first instance.

Bookdealer

11 Gainsborough Court, College Road, Dulwich, London SE21 7LT
☎ 020 8693 5685
✉ wernershawltd@btinternet.com

Editor *Barry Shaw*

WEEKLY trade paper which acts almost exclusively as a platform for people wishing to buy or sell rare/out-of-print books. Twelve-page editorial only; occasional articles and book reviews by regular freelance writers.

The Bookseller

Endeavour House, 5th Floor, 189 Shaftesbury Avenue, London WC2H 8TJ
☎ 020 7420 6006   Fax 020 7420 6103

www.thebookseller.com
Owner *VNU Entertainment Media*
Editor-in-Chief *Neill Denny*
Trade journal of the book trade, publishing, retail and libraries – the essential guide to the book business since 1858. Trade news and features, including special features, company news, publishing trends, bestseller data, etc. Unsolicited mss rarely used as most writing is either done in-house or commissioned from experts within the trade. Approach in writing first.

Boxing Monthly
40 Morpeth Road, London E9 7LD
☎020 8986 4141 Fax 020 8986 4145
✉ mail@boxing-monthly.demon.co.uk
www.boxing-monthly.co.uk
Owner *Topwave Ltd*
Editor *Glyn Leach*
Circulation 25,000
Founded 1989. MONTHLY. International coverage of professional boxing; previews, reports and interviews. Unsolicited material welcome. Interested in small hall shows and grass-roots knowledge. No big fight reports. Approach in writing in the first instance.

Boyz
18 Brewer Street, London W1F 0SH
☎020 7025 6120 Fax 020 7025 6109
✉ hudson@boyz.co.uk
Editor *David Hudson*
Circulation 55,000
Founded 1991. WEEKLY entertainment and features magazine aimed at a gay readership covering clubs, fashion, TV, films, music, theatre, celebrities and the UK gay scene in general. Unsolicited mss are looked at but not often used.

Brides
Vogue House, Hanover Square, London W1S 1JU
☎020 7499 9080 Fax 020 7152 3369
www.bridesuk.net
Owner *Condé Nast Publications Ltd*
Editor *Deborah Joseph*
Circulation 67,060
Founded 1955. BI-MONTHLY. Much of the magazine is produced in-house, but a good, relevant feature on cakes, jewellery, music, flowers, etc. is always welcome. Max. 1000 words. Prospective contributors should telephone with an idea in the first instance.

British Birds
The Banks, Mountfield, Robertsbridge TN32 5JY
☎01580 882039 Fax 01580 882038
✉ editor@britishbirds.co.uk
Editor *Dr R. Riddington*
Circulation 6,000
Founded 1907. MONTHLY ornithological journal. Features main papers on topics such as behaviour, distribution, ecology, identification and taxonomy; annual *Report on Rare Birds in Great Britain* and *Rare Breeding Birds in the UK*; sponsored competition for Bird Photograph of the Year. Unsolicited mss welcome from ornithologists.
FEATURES Well-researched, original material relating to Western Palearctic birds welcome.
NEWS *Adrian Pitches* (adrian.pitches@blueyonder.co.uk) Items ranging from conservation to humour. Max. 200 words.
PAYMENT for photographs, drawings, paintings and main papers.

British Chess Magazine
The Chess Shop, 44 Baker Street, London W1U 7RT
☎020 7486 8222 Fax 020 7486 3355
✉ bcmchess@compuserve.com
www.bcmchess.co.uk
Director/Editor *John Saunders*
Founded 1881. MONTHLY. Emphasis on tournaments, the history of chess and chess-related literature. Approach in writing with ideas. Unsolicited mss not welcome unless from qualified chess experts and players.

British Journalism Review
Sage Publications Ltd, 1 Oliver's Yard, 55 City Road, London EC1Y 1Sp
☎020 7324 8500 Fax 020 7324 8600
✉ bill.hagerty@btinternet.com
www.bjr.org.uk
Owner *BJR Ltd*
Editor *Bill Hagerty*
Founded 1988. QUARTERLY. Media magazine providing a forum for the news media. Freelance contributions welcome: non-academic articles on all aspects of the news media only. No academic papers. Approach by e-mail. Max. 2000 words.

British Medical Journal
BMA House, Tavistock Square, London WC1H 9JR
☎020 7387 4499 Fax 020 7383 6418
✉ editor@bmj.com

www.bmj.com
Owner *British Medical Association*
Editor *Dr Fiona Goodlee*
Circulation 122,982

One of the world's leading general medical journals.

British Philatelic Bulletin
Royal Mail, 148 Old Street, London
EC1V 9HQ
☎020 7250 2038 Fax 020 7250 2389

Owner *Royal Mail*
Editor *John Holman*
Circulation 22,000

Founded 1963. MONTHLY bulletin giving details of forthcoming British stamps, features on older stamps and postal history, and book reviews. Welcomes photographs of interesting, unusual or historic letter boxes.

FEATURES Articles on all aspects of British philately. Max. 1500 words.

NEWS Reports on exhibitions and philatelic events. Max. 500 words. Approach in writing in the first instance.

PAYMENT £65 per 1000 words.

British Railway Modelling
The Maltings, West Street, Bourne PE10 9PH
☎01778 391027 Fax 01778 425437
✉ johne@warnersgroup.co.uk
www.brmodelling.com

Owner *Warners Group Publications Plc*
Managing Editor *David Brown*
Editor *John Emerson*
Assistant Editor *Tony Wright*
Circulation 22,500

Founded 1993. MONTHLY. A general magazine for the practising modeller. No unsolicited mss but ideas are welcome. Interested in features on quality models, from individual items to complete layouts. Approach in writing.

FEATURES Articles on practical elements of the hobby, e.g. locomotive construction, kit conversions, etc. Layout features and articles on individual items which represent high standards of the railway modelling art. Max. length 6000 words (single feature).

NEWS News and reviews containing the model railway trade, new products, etc. Max. length 1000 words.

Broadcast
33-39 Bowling Green Lane, London
EC1R 0DA
☎020 7505 8045 Fax 020 7505 8050
Owner *Emap Communications*

Editor *Conor Dignam*
Circulation 11,468

Founded 1960. WEEKLY. Opportunities for freelance contributions. Write to the relevant editor in the first instance.

FEATURES *Lisa Campbell* Any broadcasting issue. Max. 1500 words.

NEWS *Colin Robertson* Broadcasting news. Max. 350 words.

PAYMENT £250 per 1000 words.

Build It
1 Canada Square, Canary Wharf, London
E14 5AP
☎020 7772 8440 Fax 020 7772 8584
✉ buildit@mrn.co.uk
www.buildit-online.co.uk

Owner *Inside Communications*
Editor *Catherine Monk*
Circulation 23,663

Founded 1990. MONTHLY magazine covering self-build, conversion and renovation. Unsolicited material welcome on self-build case studies as well as articles on technical construction, architecture and design and dealing with builders. Max. length 2500 words. Approach by phone, post or e-mail.

The Burlington Magazine
14–16 Duke's Road, London WC1H 9SZ
☎020 7388 1228 Fax 020 7388 1230
✉ editorial@burlington.org.uk
www.burlington.org.uk

Owner *The Burlington Magazine Publications Ltd*
Managing Director *Kate Trevelyan*
Editor *Richard Shone*
Deputy Editor *Bart Cornelis*
Associate Editors *Jane Martineau*

Founded 1903. MONTHLY. Unsolicited contributions welcome on the subject of art history provided they are previously unpublished. All preliminary approaches should be made in writing.

EXHIBITION REVIEWS Usually commissioned, but occasionally unsolicited reviews are published if appropriate. Max. 1000 words.

ARTICLES Max. 4500 words.

Shorter Notices Max. 2000 words.

PAYMENT articles, £140 (max.); shorter notices, £80 (max.).

Business Brief
PO Box 582, Five Oaks, St Saviour JE4 8XQ
☎01534 611600 Fax 01534 611610
✉ mspeditorial@msppublishing.com
Owner *MSP Publishing*

Editor *Peter Body*
Circulation 6500 (Jersey & Guernsey)
Founded 1989. MONTHLY magazine covering business developments in the Channel Islands and how they affect the local market. Styles itself as the magazine for business people rather than just a magazine about business. Interested in business-orientated articles only – 800 words max. Approach the editor by e-mail in the first instance with telephone follow-up.
PAYMENT negotiable.

Business Traveller
Perry Publications, 2nd Floor, 68–69 St Martin's Lane, London WC2N 4JS
☎020 7845 6533 Fax 020 7845 6512
✉ editorial@businesstraveller.com
www.businesstraveller.com
Owner *Panacea Publications*
Editorial Director *Tom Otley*
Circulation 500,000 (worldwide)
MONTHLY. Consumer publication. Opportunities exist for freelance writers but unsolicited contributions tend to be about leisure travel rather than business travel. Would-be contributors are strongly advised to study the magazine or the website first. Approach in writing with ideas.
PAYMENT varies.

Campaign
174 Hammersmith Road, London W6 7JP
☎020 8267 4683 Fax 020 8267 4914
✉ campaign@haynet.com
www.brandrepublic.com
Owner *Haymarket Publishing Ltd*
Editor *Claire Beale*
Circulation 11,062
Founded 1968. WEEKLY. Lively magazine serving the advertising and related industries. Freelance contributors are best advised to write in the first instance.
FEATURES Ideas welcome.
NEWS Relevant news stories of up to 320 words.
PAYMENT negotiable.

Camping and Caravanning
Greenfields House, Westwood Way, Coventry CV4 8JH
☎024 7647 5448 Fax 024 7647 5413
Owner *The Camping and Caravanning Club*
Editor *Nick Harding*
Circulation 197,802
Founded 1901. MONTHLY. Interested in jour-

nalists with camping and caravanning knowledge. Write with ideas for features in the first instance.
FEATURES Outdoor pieces in general, plus items on specific regions of Britain. Max. 1200 words. Illustrations to support text essential.

Canals and Rivers
PO Box 618, Norwich NR7 0QT
☎01603 708930
✉ chris@themag.fsnet.co.uk
www.canalsandrivers.com
Owner *A.E. Morgan Publications Ltd*
Editor *Chris Cattrall*
Circulation 14,000
Covers all aspects of waterways, narrow boats and cruisers. Contributions welcome. Make initial approach by post or e-mail.
FEATURES Waterways, narrow boats and motor cruisers, cruising reports, practical advice, etc. Unusual ideas and personal comments are particularly welcome. Max. 2000 words. Articles should be supplied in PC Windows format disk or e-mailed with JPEG images.
NEWS Items of up to 200 words welcome on the Inland Waterways System, plus photographs if possible.
PAYMENT features, around £60 per page; news, £20.

Candis
Newhall Lane, Hoylake CH47 4BQ
☎0151 632 7642 Fax 0870 745 3003
✉ editorial@candis.co.uk
Owner *Newhall Publications*
Editor *Jenny Campbell*
Circulation 312, 547
MONTHLY. General features on health and family life – no fashion or beauty items or first-person accounts of illness. No unsolicited contributions as most features are individually commissioned but fiction will be considered (max. 2000 words). Send by e-mail to Fiction Editor *John Jenkins*.

Car Mechanics
Kelsey Publishing Group, Cudham Tithe Barn, Berry's Hill, Cudham TN16 3AG
☎01959 541444/01733 771292 (editor)
Fax 01959 541400
✉ cm.mag@kelsey.co.uk
Owner *Kelsey Publishing Group*
Editor *Peter Simpson*
Circulation 35,000

MONTHLY. Practical guide to maintenance and repair of post-1978 cars for DIY and the motor trade. Unsolicited mss, with good-quality colour prints or transparencies, sent 'at sender's risk'. Initial approach by letter or phone strongly recommended, 'but please read a recent copy for style first'. No non-technical material, cartoons or fiction.

FEATURES Good, entertaining and well-researched technical material welcome, especially anything presenting complex matters clearly and simply. PAYMENT negotiable.

Caravan Magazine

IPC Media Ltd, Leon House, 233 High Street, Croydon CR9 1HZ
☎020 8726 8000 Fax 020 8726 8299
✉ caravan@ipcmedia.com
www.caravanmagazine.co.uk

Owner *IPC Media (A Time Warner Company)*
Editor *Steve Rowe*
Circulation 14,362

Founded 1933. MONTHLY. Unsolicited mss welcome. Approach in writing with ideas. All correspondence should go direct to the editor.

FEATURES Touring with strong caravan bias, technical/DIY features and how-to section. Max. 1500 words.

PAYMENT by arrangement.

Caribbean Times

Unit 2, 65 Whitechapel Road, London E1 1DU
☎020 7650 2000 Fax 020 7650 2001
✉ caribbeantimes@ethnicmedia.co.uk
www.ethnicmedia.co.uk

Owner *Ethnic Media Group*
Editor *Ron Shillingford*
Circulation 25,190

Founded 1981. WEEKLY community paper for the African and Caribbean communities in Britain. Interested in general, local and international issues relevant to these communities.

Cat World

Ancient Lights, 19 River Road, Arundel BN18 9EY
☎01903 884988 Fax 01903 885514
✉ editor@catworld.co.uk
www.catworld.co.uk

Owner *Ashdown Publishing Ltd*
Editor *Jess White*

Founded 1981. MONTHLY. Unsolicited mss welcome but initial approach in writing preferred. No poems or fiction.

FEATURES Lively, first-hand experience features

on every aspect of the cat. Breeding features and veterinary articles by acknowledged experts only. Preferred length 750 or 1700 words. Accompanying pictures should be good quality and sharp. Submissions by e-mail (MS Word attachment) if possible, or by disk with accompanying hard copy and s.a.e. for return.

The Catholic Herald

Lamb's Passage, Bunhill Row, London EC1Y 8TQ
☎020 7448 3603 Fax 020 7256 9728
✉ editorial@catholicherald.co.uk
www.catholicherald.co.uk

Editor *Luke Coppen*
Features Editor *Christina Farrell*
Literary Editor *Stav Sherez*
Circulation 22,000

WEEKLY. Interested mainly in straight Catholic issues but also in general humanitarian matters, social policies, the Third World, the arts and books. PAYMENT by arrangement.

Chapman

4 Broughton Place, Edinburgh EH1 3RX
☎0131 557 2207
✉ chapman-pub@blueyonder.co.uk
www.chapman-pub.co.uk

Owner/Editor *Joy Hendry*
Assistant Editor *Edmund O'Connor*
Circulation 2000

Founded 1970. Scotland's quality literary magazine. Features poetry, short works of fiction, criticism, reviews and articles on theatre, politics, language and the arts. Gives priority to Scottish writers but also has work from UK and international authors. Unsolicited material welcome if accompanied by s.a.e. Approach in writing unless discussion is needed. Priority is given to full-time writers.

FEATURES Topics of literary interest, especially Scottish literature, theatre, culture or politics. Max. 5000 words.

FICTION Short stories, occasionally novel extracts if self-contained. Max. 6000 words.

SPECIAL PAGES Poetry, both UK and non-UK in translation (mainly, but not necessarily, European).

PAYMENT by negotiation.

Chat

IPC Connect Ltd., King's Reach Tower, Stamford Street, London SE1 9LS
☎020 7261 6565 Fax 020 7261 6534
www.ipcmedia.com/pubs/chat.htm

Owner *IPC Media*

Editor *Gilly Sinclair*
Circulation 602,308

Founded 1985. WEEKLY general interest women's magazine. Unsolicited mss considered; approach in writing with ideas. Not interested in contributors 'who have never bothered to read *Chat* and therefore don't know what type of magazine it is. *Chat* does not publish fiction.'

FEATURES *Ingrid Millar* Human interest and humour. Max. 1000 words.

PAYMENT up to £1500 maximum.

Chemist & Druggist

Sovereign House, Sovereign Way, Tonbridge TN9 1RW
☎01732 377487 Fax 01732 367065
✉ chemdrug@cmpinformation.com
www.dotpharmacy.com

Owner *CMP Information*
Editor *Charles Gladwin*
Circulation 13,956

Founded 1859. WEEKLY news magazine for community pharmacy.

FEATURES practice, politics, professional matters, clinical articles and business advice. Contact by phone or e-mail to discuss features ideas.

NEWS Contact News Editor with news articles relating to local pharmacy matters, local pharmaceutical industry events and pharmacists in the news. Max. 200 words.

PAYMENT standard rates.

Child Education

Scholastic Ltd, Villiers House, Clarendon Avenue, Leamington Spa CV32 5PR
☎01926 887799 Fax 01926 883331
www.scholastic.co.uk

Owner *Scholastic Ltd*
Editor *Helen Freeman*
Circulation 21,121

Founded 1923. MONTHLY magazine aimed at teachers of children aged 4–7 years. Practical articles from teachers about education for this age group are welcome. Max. 900 words. Approach in writing with synopsis.

Choice

First Floor, 2 King Street, Peterborough PE1 1LT
☎01733 555123 Fax 01733 427500
✉ editorial@choicemag.co.uk

Owner *Choice Publishing Ltd*
Editor *Norman Wright*
Circulation 90,000

Monthly full-colour, lively and informative magazine for people aged 50 plus which helps them get the most out of their lives, time and money after full-time work.

FEATURES Real-life stories, hobbies, interesting (older) people, British heritage and countryside, involving activities for active bodies and minds, health, relationships, book/entertainment reviews. Unsolicited mss read (s.a.e. for return of material); write with ideas and copies of cuttings if new contributor. No phone calls, please.

RIGHTS/MONEY All items affecting the magazine's readership are written by experts. Areas of interest include pensions, state benefits, health, finance, property, legal. PAYMENT by arrangement.

Church Music Quarterly

Cleveland Lodge, Westhumble, Dorking RH5 6BW
☎01306 872800 Fax 01306 887260
✉ cmq@rscm.com
www.rscm.com

Owner *Royal School of Church Music*
Editor *Esther Jones*
Circulation 15,500

QUARTERLY. Contributions welcome. Phone in the first instance.

FEATURES Articles on church music or related subjects considered. Max. 2100 words.

PAYMENT £60 per page.

Church of England Newspaper

Central House, 142 Central Street, London EC1V 8AR
☎020 7417 5800 Fax 020 7216 6410
✉ cen@churchnewspaper.com
www.churchnewspaper.com

Owner *Religious Intelligence*
Editor *Colin Blakely*
Circulation 9,500

Founded 1828. WEEKLY. Almost all material is commissioned but unsolicited mss are considered.

FEATURES Preliminary enquiry essential. Max. 1200 words.

NEWS *Jonathan Wynne-Jones* Items must be sent promptly and should have a church/Christian relevance. Max. 200–400 words.

PAYMENT negotiable.

Church Times

33 Upper Street, London N1 0PN
☎020 7359 4570 Fax 020 7226 3073
✉ news@churchtimes.co.uk *or* features@churchtimes.co.uk

www.churchtimes.co.uk
Owner *Hymns Ancient & Modern*
Editor *Paul Handley*
Circulation 31,570
Founded 1863. WEEKLY. Unsolicited mss considered.
FEATURES *Christine Miles* Articles and pictures (any format) on religious topics. Max. 2000 words.
NEWS *Helen Saxbee* Occasional reports (commissions only) and up-to-date photographs.
PAYMENT features, £120 per 1000 words; news, by arrangement.

Classic & Sports Car
Teddington Studios, Broom Road, Teddington TW11 9BE
☎020 8267 5399   Fax 020 8267 5318
✉ letters.c&sc@haynet.com
www.classicandsportscar.com
Owner *Haymarket Publishing Ltd*
Editor *James Elliott*
Circulation 81,125
Founded 1982. MONTHLY. Best-selling classic car magazine covering all aspects of buying, selling, owning and maintaining historic vehicles. Will consider news stories and features involving classic cars but 'be patient because hundreds of unsolicited material received monthly'. Initial contact by e-mail (james.elliott@haynet.com).

Classic Bike
EMAP Automotive, Media House, Lynchwood, Peterborough Business Park, Peterborough PE2 6EA
☎01733 468465   Fax 01733 468466
✉ classic.bike@emap.com
Owner *Emap Automotive Ltd*
Editor *Hugo Wilson*
Circulation 40,241
Founded 1978. MONTHLY. Mainly pre-1980 classic motorcycles with a heavy bias to British marques. Freelancers must contact the editor before making submissions. Approach in writing.
NEWS Genuine news with good illustrations, if possible, suitable for a global audience. Max. 400 words.
FEATURES British motorcycle industry inside stories, technical features 'that can be understood by all', German, Spanish and French machine features, people. Max. 2000 words.
SPECIAL PAGES How-to features, oddball machines, stunning pictures, features with a fresh slant.

PAYMENT £100–125 per 1000 words, plus pictures.

Classic Boat
IPC Media Ltd, Leon House, 233 High Street, Croydon CR9 1HZ
☎020 8726 8000
✉ cb@ipcmedia.com
www.classicboat.co.uk
Owner *IPC Media (A Time Warner Company)*
Editor *Dan Houston*
Circulation 12,870
Founded 1987. MONTHLY. Traditional boats and classic yachts, old and new; maritime history. Unsolicited mss, particularly if supported by good photos, are welcome. Sail and power boat pieces considered. Approach in writing with ideas. Interested in well-researched stories on all nautical matters. News reports welcome. Contributor's notes available online.
FEATURES Boatbuilding, boat history and design, events, yachts and working boats. Material must be well-informed and supported where possible by good-quality or historic photos. Max. 3000 words. Classic is defined by excellence of design and construction – the boat need not be old and wooden!
NEWS New boats, restorations, events, boatbuilders, etc. Max. 500 words.
PAYMENT features, £75–100 per published page; news, according to merit.

Classic Cars
Media House, Peterborough Business Park, Lynchwood, Peterborough PE2 6EA
☎01733 468219   Fax 01733 468888
✉ classic.cars@emap.com
www.classiccarsmagazine.co.uk
Owner *Emap Automotive Ltd*
Editor *Phil Bell*
Circulation 43,833
Founded 1973. TWELVE ISSUES YEARLY. International classic car magazine containing entertaining and informative articles about classic cars, events and associated personalities. Contributions welcome. PAYMENT negotiable.

Classic Stitches
D.C. Thomson & Co. Ltd, 80 Kingsway East, Dundee DD4 8SL
☎01382 223131   Fax 01382 452491
✉ editorial@classicstitches.com
www.classicstitches.com
Owner *D.C. Thomson & Co. Ltd*
Editor *Mrs Bea Neilson*
Circulation 10,000

Founded 1994. BI-MONTHLY magazine with exclusive designs to stitch, textile-based features, designer profiles, book reviews and 'what's new shopping' information. Will consider features covering textiles – historical and modern, designer profiles and original designs in context with the style of the magazine (no items on knitting or crochet). Approach by e-mail or letter with short synopsis to avoid clashes. For designs, send sketches, swatches and brief description of the idea.

FEATURES *Bea Neilson* Three features per issue with accompanying photography. Max. 2000 words.

NEWS *Liz O'Rourke* Max. 300 words.

SPECIAL PAGES *Susan Kydd* Details only.

Classical Guitar

1 & 2 Vance Court, Trans Britannia Enterprise Park, Blaydon on Tyne NE21 5NH
☎0191 414 9000 Fax 0191 414 9001
✉ classicalguitar@ashleymark.co.uk
www.classicalguitarmagazine.com
Owner *Ashley Mark Publishing Co.*
Editor *Oliver McGhie*
Founded 1982. MONTHLY.

FEATURES *Oliver McGhie* Usually written by staff writers. Max. 1500 words.

NEWS *Thérèse Wassily Saba* Small paragraphs and festival concert reports welcome.

REVIEWS *Tim Panting* Concert reviews of up to 250 words are usually written by staff reviewers.

PAYMENT features, by arrangement; no payment for news.

Classical Music

241 Shaftesbury Avenue, London WC2H 8TF
☎020 7333 1742 Fax 020 7333 1769
✉ classical.music@rhinegold.co.uk
www.rhinegold.co.uk
Owner *Rhinegold Publishing Ltd*
Editor *Keith Clarke*
Founded 1976. FORTNIGHTLY. A specialist magazine using precisely targeted news and feature articles aimed at the music business. Most material is commissioned but professionally written unsolicited mss are occasionally published. Freelance contributors may approach in writing with an idea but should familiarise themselves beforehand with the style and market of the magazine. PAYMENT negotiable.

Climber

Warners Group Publications plc, West Street, Bourne PE10 9PH
☎01778 392425

✉ climber@bernardnewman.demon.co.uk
www.climber.co.uk
Owner *Warners Group Publications plc*
Editor *Bernard Newman*
Founded 1962. MONTHLY. Features articles and news on climbing and mountaineering in the UK and abroad. No unsolicited mss.

Closer

Endeavour House, 189 Shaftesbury Avenue, London WC2H 8JG
☎020 7437 9011 Fax 020 7859 8600
✉ closer@emap.com
Owner *Emap élan Ltd*
Editor *Jane Johnson*
Circulation 578,337
Launched 2002. WEEKLY celebrity magazine with a 'tongue-in-cheek' approach. No unsolicited material; approach by e-mail with idea in the first instance.

Club International

2 Archer Street, London W1D 7AW
☎020 7292 8000 Fax 020 7734 5030
✉ mattb@paulraymond.com
Owner *Paul Raymond*
Editor *Matt Berry*
Circulation 180,000
Founded 1972. MONTHLY. Features and short humorous items aimed at young male readership aged 18–30.

FEATURES Max. 1000 words.

SHORTS 200–750 words.

PAYMENT negotiable.

Coach and Bus Week

Rouncy Media, 3 The Office Village, Cygnet Park, Hampton, Peterborough PE7 8FD
☎01733 294240 Fax 0845 280 2927
✉ jacqui.grobler@rouncy.co.uk
www.cbwnet.co.uk
Owner *Rouncy Media*
Editor *Mark Williams*
Circulation 4575
WEEKLY magazine, aimed at coach and bus operators. Interested in coach and bus industry-related items only: business, financial and legal. Contact by letter, e-mail, telephone or via website.

Coin News

Token Publishing Ltd, Orchard House, Duchy Road, Heathpark, Honiton EX14 1YD
☎01404 46972 Fax 01404 44788
✉ info@tokenpublishing.com

www.tokenpublishing.com
Owners *J.W. Mussell, Carol Hartman*
Editor *J.W. Mussell*
Circulation 10,000
Founded 1964. MONTHLY. Contributions welcome. Approach by phone in the first instance.
FEATURES Opportunity exists for well-informed authors 'who know the subject and do their homework'. Max. 2000 words.
PAYMENT by arrangement.

Company

National Magazine House, 72 Broadwick Street, London W1F 9EP
☎020 7439 5000 Fax 020 7312 3797
✉ company.mail@natmags.co.uk
www.company.co.uk
Owner *National Magazine Co. Ltd*
Editor *Victoria White*
Circulation 283,429

MONTHLY. Glossy women's magazine appealing to the independent and intelligent young woman. A good market for freelancers: 'We look for great newsy features relevant to young British women'. Keen to encourage bright, new, young talent, but uncommissioned material is rarely accepted. Feature outlines are the only sensible approach in the first instance. Max. 1500–2000 words. Send to *Claire Askew*, Features Editor.
PAYMENT £250 per 1000 words.

Computer Arts

30 Monmouth Street, Bath BA1 2BW
☎01225 442244 Fax 01225 732295
✉ ca.mail@futurenet.co.uk
www.computerarts.co.uk
Owner *The Future Network*
Editor *Paul Newman*
Circulation 19,758

Founded 1995. MONTHLY. The world of computer arts – 3D, web design, photoshop, digital video. No unsolicited mss. Interested in tutorials, profiles, tips, software and hardware reviews. Approach by post or e-mail.

Computer Weekly

Quadrant House, The Quadrant, Sutton SM2 5AS
☎020 8652 3122 Fax 020 8652 8979
✉ computer.weekly@rbi.co.uk
www.computerweekly.com
Owner *Reed Business Information*
Editor *Hooman Bassirian*
Circulation 143,000

Founded 1966. Freelance contributions welcome.
FEATURES Always looking for good new writers with specialised industry knowledge. Max. 1800 words.
NEWS *Mike Simons* Some openings for regional or foreign news items. Max. 300 words.
PAYMENT negotiable.

Computeractive

VNU Business Publications, VNU House, 32–34 Broadwick Street, London W1A 2HG
☎020 7316 9000 Fax 020 7316 9520
✉ news@computeractive.co.uk
www.computeractive.co.uk
Owner *VNU Business Publications Ltd*
Editor *Dylan Armbrust*
Circulation 236,026

Launched 1998. FORTNIGHTLY. Consumer and computer technology magazine. No unsolicited material.

Computing, The IT Newspaper

VNU Business Publications, VNU House, 32–34 Broadwick Street, London W1A 2HG
☎020 7316 9000 Fax 020 7316 9160
✉ computing@vnu.co.uk
www.computing.co.uk
Owner *VNU Business Publications Ltd*
Editor-in-Chief *Toby Wolpe*
Managing Editor *Bryan Glick*
Circulation 115,000

Founded 1973. WEEKLY newspaper for IT professionals. Unsolicited articles welcome. Please enclose s.a.e. for return.
NEWS *Emma Nash*
PAYMENT up to £350 per 1000 words.

Condé Nast Traveller

Vogue House, Hanover Square, London W1S 1JU
☎020 7499 9080 Fax 020 7493 3758
✉ editorcntraveller@condenast.co.uk
www.cntraveller.co.uk
Owner *Condé Nast Publications*
Editor *Sarah Miller*
Circulation 84029

Founded 1997. MONTHLY travel magazine. Proposals rather than completed mss preferred. Approach in writing in the first instance. No unsolicited photographs. 'The magazine has a no freebie policy and no writing can be accepted on the basis of a press or paid-for trip.'

Construction News

Emap Construct, 151 Rosebery Avenue,
London EC1R 4GB
☎020 7505 6868 Fax 020 7505 6867
✉ cneditorial@emap.com
www.cnplus.co.uk
Editor *Aaron Morby*
Circulation 26,835

WEEKLY. Since 1871, *Construction News* has provided news to the industry. Readership ranges from construction site to the boardroom, from building and specialist construction through to civil engineering. Initial approach by e-mail.

FEATURES *Emma Crates*
NEWS *Grant Prior*

Contemporary Review

PO Box 1242, Oxford OX1 4FJ
✉ editorial@contemporaryreview.co.uk
www.contemporaryreview.co.uk
Owner *Contemporary Review Co. Ltd*
Editor *Dr Richard Mullen*

Founded 1866. MONTHLY. Covers international affairs and politics, literature and the arts, history and religion. No fiction. Max. 3000 words.

Literary Editor *Dr James Munson* Monthly book section with reviews which are always commissioned.

Coop Traveller

River Publishing, Victory House, 14 Leicester Place, London WC2H 7BZ
☎020 7413 9308 Fax 020 7306 0304
✉ cooptraveller@riverltd.co.uk
www.riverltd.co.uk
Owner *River Publishing*
Editor *Heather Farmborough*
Circulation 300,000

Founded 2001. BIANNUAL. Magazine for Co-op Travel customers. Travel articles and travel-related news for the independent traveller. No unsolicited material; approach by telephone, fax, letter or e-mail in the first instance.

FEATURES Ideas for exciting travel features, including destinations, accommodation, activities etc. Max. 1000 words.

NEWS Stories that reveal fascinating facts for holidaymakers, including interesting products, new destinations and developments in the travel market. Max. 300 words.

PAYMENT negotiable.

CosmoGIRL!

National Magazine House, 72 Broadwick Street, London W1F 9EP
☎020 7439 5000 Fax 020 7439 5400
✉ cosmogirl.mail@natmags.co.uk
www.cosmogirl.co.uk
Owner *National Magazine Co. Ltd*
Editor *Celia Duncan*
Circulation 173,135

Founded 2001. MONTHLY glossy magazine for teenagers aged 14–19-years-old. Fashion, beauty advice and boys.

FEATURES *Di Leeming* Interested in ideas – send synopsis by mail – no finished articles.

Cosmopolitan

National Magazine House, 72 Broadwick Street, London W1F 9EP
☎020 7439 5000 Fax 020 7439 5016
✉ cosmo.mail@natmags.co.uk
www.cosmopolitan.co.uk
Owner *National Magazine Co. Ltd*
Editor *Sam Baker*
Deputy Editor *Helen Daly*
Circulation 461,610

MONTHLY. Designed to appeal to the mid-twenties, modern-minded female. Popular mix of articles, with emphasis on relationships and careers, and hard news. No fiction. Will rarely use unsolicited mss but always on the look-out for 'new writers with original and relevant ideas and a strong voice'. All would-be writers should be familiar with the magazine. E-mail for submission guidelines.

Counselling at Work

Association for Counselling at Work, BACP, BACP House, 35–37 Albert Street, Rugby CV21 2SG
☎0870 443 5252 Fax 0870 443 5160
✉ acw@bacp.co.uk
www.counsellingatwork.org.uk
Owner *British Association for Counselling and Psychotherapy*
Editor *Rick Hughes*
Circulation 1600

Founded 1993. QUARTERLY official journal of the Association for Counselling at Work, a Division of BACP. Looking for well-researched articles (500–2400 words) about *any* aspect of workplace counselling. Mss from those employed as counsellors or in welfare posts are particularly welcome. Photographs accepted. No fiction or poetry. Send A4 s.a.e. for writer's guidelines and sample copy of the journal. No PAYMENT.

Country Homes and Interiors

IPC Media Ltd., King's Reach Tower, Stamford Street, London SE1 9LS

☎020 7261 6451 Fax 020 7261 6895
✉ countryhomes@ipcmedia.com
Owner *IPC Media*
Editor *Rhoda Parry*
Circulation 77,677

Founded 1986. MONTHLY. The best approach for prospective contributors is with an idea in writing as unsolicited mss are not welcome.

FEATURES *Jean Carr* Monthly personality interviews of interest to an intelligent, affluent readership (women and men), aged 25–44. Max. 1200 words.

HOUSES *Vivienne Ayers* Country-style homes with excellent design ideas. Length 1000 words.

PAYMENT negotiable.

Country Life

IPC Media Ltd., King's Reach Tower, Stamford Street, London SE1 9LS
☎020 7261 6400 Fax 020 7261 5139
www.countrylife.co.uk
Owner *IPC Media (A Time Warner Company)*
Editor-in-Chief *Mark Hedges*
Circulation 42,693

Established 1897. WEEKLY. *Country Life* features articles which relate to architecture, countryside, wildlife, rural events, sports, arts, exhibitions, current events, property and news articles of interest to town and country dwellers. Strong informed material rather than amateur enthusiasm. 'Uncommissioned material is rarely accepted. We regret we cannot be liable for the safe custody or return of any solicited or unsolicited materials.'

Country Living

National Magazine House, 72 Broadwick Street, London W1F 9EP
☎020 7439 5000 Fax 020 7439 5093
www.countryliving.co.uk
Owner *National Magazine Co. Ltd*
Editor *Susy Smith*
Circulation 191,225

Magazine aimed at both country dwellers and town dwellers who love the countryside. Covers people, conservation, wildlife, houses (gardens and interiors) and rural businesses. No unsolicited mss

Country Smallholding

Archant Publishing, Fair Oak Close, Exeter Airport Business Park, Clysts Honiton, Nr Exeter EX5 2UL
☎01392 888475 Fax 01392 888550
✉ editorial.csh@archant.co.uk
www.countrysmallholding.com

Owner *Archant Publishing*
Editor *Diane Cowgill*
Circulation 18,966

Founded 1975. MONTHLY magazine for small farmers, smallholders, practical landowners and for anyone interested in self sufficiency at all levels both in town and in the country. Articles welcome on organic growing, keeping poultry, livestock and other animals, crafts, cookery, herbs, building and energy. Articles should be detailed and practical, based on first-hand knowledge and experience. Approach in writing or by e-mail.

Country Walking

Bretton Court, Bretton, Peterborough PE3 8DZ
☎01733 282614 Fax 01733 282654
✉ country.walking@emap.com
Owner *Emap Plc*
Editor *Jonathan Manning*
Circulation 47,822

Founded 1987. MONTHLY magazine focused on walking in the finest landscapes of the UK and Europe. News, gear tests and profiles of celebrity walkers also feature. Special monthly pull-out section of 28 detailed walking routes. Original high quality photography and ideas for features considered, although very few unsolicited mss accepted. Approach by letter or e-mail.

FEATURES *Danny Hopkins*

SPECIAL PAGES 'Down your way' section of walk routes, including outline map and step-by-step directions. Accurately and recently researched walk and fact file including photographs and points of interest en route. Please contact *Jane Ward* for guidelines (unsolicited submissions generally not accepted for this section).

PAYMENT not negotiable.

The Countryman

PO Box 5956, Sherborne DT9 9AA
☎01935 812434
✉ editorial@thecountryman.co.uk
www.thecountryman.co.uk
Owner *Country Publications Ltd*
Editor *Bill Taylor*
Circulation 22,870

Founded 1927. MONTHLY. Feature ideas welcome by e-mail. Contributors are strongly advised to study the magazine's content in the first instance. Articles supplied with top quality illustrations (colour transparencies, archive b&w prints and line drawings) are far more likely to be used. Max. article length 1200 words.

The Countryman's Weekly (incorporating Gamekeeper and Sporting Dog)
Yelverton PL20 7PE
☎01822 855281 Fax 01822 855372
✉ editorial@countrymanswweekly.com
Owner *Diamond Publishing Ltd*
Editor *David Venner*
Founded 1895. WEEKLY. Unsolicited material welcome.
FEATURES on any country sports topic. Max. 1000 words.
PAYMENT rates available on request.

Countryside Alliance Campaign Update
The Old Town Hall 367 Kennington Road, London SE1 4PT
☎020 7840 9200 Fax 020 7793 8484
www.countryside-alliance.org
Owner *Countryside Alliance*
Editor *Georgina Kester*
Circulation 70,000
Founded 1996. QUARTERLY membership magazine on country sports and conservation issues. No unsolicited mss.

The Creative Writer
28 Howard Mews, Denmark Road, Norwich NR3 4JU
☎0870 240 9998
✉ WritersSociety@aol.com
www.societyofcreativewriters.org
Owner *The Society of Creative Writers*
Editor *Robin Barratt*
Circulation 3500
QUARTERLY journal of the Society of Creative Writers. Most items are commissioned from its members but articles on creative writing welcomed.

The Cricketer International
See **The Wisden Cricketer**

Crimewave
5 Martins Lane, Witcham, Ely CB6 2LB
✉ andy@ttapress.demon.co.uk
www.ttapress.com
Owner *TTA Press*
Editor *Andy Cox*
Founded 1998. QUARTERLY B5 colour magazine of crime fiction. 'The UK's only magazine specialising in crime short stories, publishing the very best from across the spectrum.' Every issue contains stories by authors who are household

names in the crime fiction world but room is found for lesser known and unknown writers. Submissions welcome (not via e-mail) with appropriate return postage. Potential contributors are advised to study the magazine. Contracts exchanged upon acceptance. PAYMENT on publication.

Crucible
See **Hymns Ancient & Modern Ltd** under *UK Publishers*

Cumbria
The Water Mill, Broughton Hall, Skipton BD23 3AG
☎01756 701381 Fax 01756 701326
✉ editorial@dalesman.co.uk
www.dalesman.co.uk
Owner *Country Publications Ltd*
Editor *Terry Fletcher*
Circulation 13,713
Founded 1951. MONTHLY. County magazine of strong regional and countryside interest, focusing on the Lake District. Unsolicited mss welcome. Max. 1500 words. Approach in writing, by phone or e-mail with feature ideas. PAYMENT negotiable.

Cycle Sport
IPC Media Ltd, Leon House, 233 High Street, Croydon CR9 1HZ
☎020 8726 8463 Fax 020 8726 8499
✉ cyclesport@ipcmedia.com *and* cycling@ipcmedia.com
www.cyclesport.co.uk
Owner *IPC Media (A Time Warner Company)*
Managing Editor *Robert Garbutt*
Deputy Editor *Nigel Wynn*
Circulation 21,198
Founded 1993. MONTHLY magazine dedicated to professional cycle racing. Unsolicited ideas for features welcome.

Cycling Weekly
IPC Media Ltd, Leon House, 233 High Street, Croydon CR9 1HZ
☎020 8726 8000
✉ cycling@ipcmedia.com
www.cyclingweekly.co.uk
Owner *IPC Media (A Time Warner Company)*
Publishing Director *Keith Foster*
Editor *Robert Garbutt*
Circulation 26,429
Founded 1891. WEEKLY. All aspects of cycle sport covered. Unsolicited mss and ideas for

features welcome. Approach in writing with ideas. Fiction rarely used.

FEATURES Cycle racing, coaching, technical material and related areas. Max. 2000 words. Most work commissioned but interested in seeing new work.

NEWS Short news pieces, local news, etc. Max. 300 words.

PAYMENT features, around £60–120 per 1000 words (quality permitting); news, £15 per story.

Dalesman
The Water Mill, Broughton Hall, Skipton BD23 3AG
☎01756 701381 Fax 01756 701326
✉ editorial@dalesman.co.uk
www.dalesman.co.uk
Owner *Country Publications Ltd*
Editor *Terry Fletcher*
Circulation 43,935

Founded 1939. Now the biggest-selling regional publication of its kind in the country. MONTHLY magazine with articles of specific Yorkshire interest. Unsolicited mss welcome; receives approximately ten per day. Initial approach in writing, by phone or e-mail. Max. 1500 words. PAYMENT negotiable.

Dance Theatre Journal
Laban, Creekside, London SE8 3DZ
☎020 8691 8600 Fax 020 8691 8400
✉ dtj@laban.org
www.laban.org
Owner *Laban*
Editor *Martin Hargreaves*
Circulation 2000

Founded 1982. QUARTERLY. Interested in features on every aspect of the contemporary dance scene, particularly issues such as the funding policy for dance, critical assessments of choreographers' work and the latest developments in the various schools of contemporary dance. Unsolicited mss welcome. Length 1000–3000 words

Dance Today
The Dancing Times Ltd, Clerkenwell House, 45–47 Clerkenwell Green, London EC1R 0EB
☎020 7250 3006 Fax 020 7253 6679
✉ dancetoday@dancing-times.co.uk
www.dancing-times.co.uk
Owner *The Dancing Times Ltd*
Editor *Katie Gregory*

Circulation 2500

Founded in 1956 as the *Ballroom Dancing Times* and relaunched as *Dance Today!* in 2001. MONTHLY magazine for anyone interested in ballroom, social and popular dance. Styles include ballroom and Latin American, salsa, tango, flamenco, tea dancing, sequence and urban dance (hip hop). Related topics covered include health and fitness and dance fashion. Contributions welcome; send c.v. with sample work by post or e-mail to the editor.

The Dancing Times
The Dancing Times Ltd, Clerkenwell House, 45–47 Clerkenwell Green, London EC1R 0EB
☎020 7250 3006 Fax 020 7253 6679
✉ editorial@dancing-times.co.uk
www.dancing-times.co.uk
Owner *The Dancing Times Ltd*
Editor *Mary Clarke*

Founded 1910. MONTHLY. Freelance suggestions welcome from specialist dance writers and photographers only. Approach in writing.

The Dandy
D.C. Thomson & Co. Ltd, Albert Square, Dundee DD1 8QJ
☎01382 223131 Fax 01382 322214
www.dandy.com
Owner *D.C. Thomson & Co. Ltd*
Editor *Morris Heggie*

Founded 1937. WEEKLY comic. Original, humorous comic strips for 7–12-year-olds, featuring established characters such as Desperate Dan as well as new ones like Jak. Generally, unsolicited contributions are welcome but 'please read the comic before sending any material. Try a one-off script for an established, current *Dandy* character. Send by e-mail or post but never send your only copy.' Include s.a.e. for reply. No non-script material such as puzzles, poetry, etc.

Darts World
81 Selwood Road, Croydon CR0 7JW
☎020 8650 6580 Fax 020 8654 4343
✉ dartsworld@blueyonder.co.uk
www.dartsworld.com
Owner *World Magazines Ltd*
Editor *A.J. Wood*
Circulation 12,263

FEATURES Single articles or series on technique and instruction. Max. 1200 words.

FICTION Short stories with darts theme. Max. 1000 words.

NEWS Tournament reports and general or personality news required. Max. 800 words. PAYMENT negotiable.

Day by Day

Woolacombe House, 141 Woolacombe Road, London SE3 8QP

☎020 8856 6249

Owner *Loverseed Press*

Editor *Patrick Richards*

Circulation 25,000

Founded 1963. MONTHLY. News commentary and digest of national and international affairs, with reviews of the arts (books, plays, art exhibitions, films, opera, musicals) and county cricket and Test reports among regular slots. Unsolicited mss welcome (s.a.e. essential). Approach in writing with ideas. Contributors are advised to study the magazine in the first instance. (Specimen copy £1.25) UK subscription £14.85; Europe £18.85; RoW £22.85.

NEWS *Ronald Mallone* Interested in themes connected with non-violence and social justice only. Max. 600 words.

FEATURES No scope for freelance contributions here.

POEMS *Michael Gibson* Short poems in line with editorial principles considered. Max. 20 lines.

PAYMENT negotiable.

Dazed & Confused

112 – 116 Old Street, London EC1V 1BG

☎020 7549 6816   Fax 020 7336 0966

✉ rod@confused.co.uk

www.confused.co.uk

Owner *Waddell Ltd*

Editor *Rod Stanley*

Circulation 80,000

Founded 1992. MONTHLY. Cutting edge fashion, music, film, art, interviews and features. No unsolicited material. Approach in writing with ideas in the first instance.

Decanter

First Floor, Broadway House, 2–6 Fulham Broadway, London SW6 1AA

☎020 7610 3929   Fax 020 7381 5282

✉ decanter_editorial@decanter.com

www.decanter.com

Editor *Amy Wislocki*

Circulation 35,000

FOUNDED 1975. Glossy wines magazine. Feature ideas welcome; send to editor by post or fax (not e-mail). No fiction.

NEWS/FEATURES All items and articles should concern wines, food and related subjects. PAYMENT £230 per 1000 words.

Delicious

Seven Publishing, 20 Upper Ground, London SE1 9PD

☎020 7775 7757   Fax 020 7775 7705

✉ info@deliciousmagazine.co.uk

www.deliciousmagazine.co.uk

Owner *Seven Publishing*

Editor *Mitzie Wilson*

Circulation 95,272

Launched 2003. MONTHLY publication for people who love food and cooking. Recipes – from the simple to the sophisticated – plus features on food and where it comes from. Welcomes freelance contributions; approach by e-mail.

Derbyshire Life and Countryside

61 Friar Gate, Derby DE1 1DJ

☎01332 227850   Fax 01332 227860

Owner *Archant Life*

Editor *Joy Hales*

Circulation 12,140

Founded 1931. MONTHLY county magazine for Derbyshire. Unsolicited mss and photographs of Derbyshire welcome, but written approach with ideas preferred.

Descent

Wild Places Publishing, PO Box 100, Abergavenny NP7 9WY

☎01873 737707   Fax 08717 505277

✉ descent@wildplaces.co.uk

www.caving.uk.com

Owner *Wild Places Publishing*

Editor *Chris Howes*

Assistant Editor *Judith Calford*

Founded 1969. BI-MONTHLY magazine for cavers and mine enthusiasts. Submissions welcome from freelance contributors who can write accurately and knowledgeably and in the style of existing content on any aspect of caves, mines or underground structures.

FEATURES General interest articles of under 1000 words welcome, as well as short foreign news reports, especially if supported by photographs/illustrations. Suitable topics include exploration (particularly British, both historical and modern), expeditions, equipment, techniques and regional British news. Max. 2000 words.

PAYMENT on publication according to page area filled.

Desire
9 Harmsworth Street, London SE17 3TJ
☎020 7820 8844 Fax 020 7820 9944
www.desire.co.uk
Owner *Moondance Media Ltd*
Editor *Ian Jackson*
Founded 1994. FIVE ISSUES YEARLY. Britain's only erotic magazine for both women and men, celebrating sex and sensuality with a mix of features, reviews, interviews, photography and erotic fantasy. For a sample copy of the magazine plus contributors' guidelines and rates, please enclose four first class stamps.

Destination France
151 Station Street, Burton on Trent
DE14 1BG
☎01283 742950 Fax 01283 742957
✉ alison.bell@wwonline.co.uk
Owner *Waterways World*
Editor *Alison Bell*
Circulation 10,000
Founded in 2005 as *Camping in France*. MONTHLY. Aimed at the Francophile – the British holidaymaker in France and for those who wish to move there. Features include sports, general tourism, property and regional information. Photographs to accompany articles. Approach in writing, preferably by e-mail, in the first instance.
PAYMENT negotiable.

Director
116 Pall Mall, London SW1Y 5ED
☎020 7766 8950 Fax 020 7766 8840
✉ director-ed@iod.com
Editor *Joanna Higgins*
Circulation 58,271
1991 Business Magazine of the Year. Published by Director Publications Ltd. for members of the Institute of Directors. Wide range of features from political and business profiles and management thinking to employment and financial issues. Also book reviews. Regular contributors used. Send letter with synopsis/published samples rather than unsolicited mss. PAYMENT negotiable.

Disability Now
6 Market Road, London N7 9PW
☎020 7619 7323 Fax 020 7619 7331
✉ editor@disabilitynow.org.uk
www.disabilitynow.org.uk
Owner *SCOPE*

Acting Editor *Sarah Hobson*
Circulation 19,022
Founded 1984. Leading MONTHLY newspaper with fortnightly supplement for disabled people in the UK – people with a wide range of physical disabilities, as well as their families, carers and relevant professionals. Freelance contributions welcome. No fiction. Approach in writing.
FEATURES Covering new initiatives and services, personal experiences and general issues of interest to a wide national readership. Max. 900 words. Disabled contributors welcome.
NEWS Max. 300 words.
SPECIAL PAGES Possible openings for cartoonists.
PAYMENT by arrangement.

Disabled Motorist
See **No Limit**

Diva, lesbian life and style
Spectrum House, 32–34 Gordon House Road, London NW5 1LP
☎020 7424 7400 Fax 020 7424 7401
✉ edit@divamag.co.uk
www.divamag.co.uk
Owner *Millivres-Prowler Ltd*
Editor *Jane Czyzselska*
Founded 1994. MONTHLY glossy magazine featuring lesbian news and culture including fashion, lifestyle and satire. Welcomes news, features and photographs. No poetry. Contact the news editor at the e-mail address above with news items and feature ideas and photo/fashion photographs.

Dog World
Somerfield House, Wotton Road, Ashford TN23 6LW
☎01233 621877 Fax 01233 645669
www.dogworld.co.uk
Owner *DW Media Holdings Ltd*
Editor *Stuart Baillie*
Circulation 19,826
Founded 1902. WEEKLY newspaper for people who are seriously interested in pedigree dogs. Unsolicited mss occasionally considered but initial approach in writing preferred.
FEATURES Well-researched historical items or items of unusual interest concerning dogs. Max. 1000 words. Photographs of unusual 'doggy' situations occasionally of interest.
NEWS Freelance reports welcome on court cases and local government issues involving dogs.
PAYMENT features, up to £50; photos, £15.

Dogs Monthly
Ascot House, High Street, Ascot SL5 7HG
☎0870 730 8433 Fax 0870 730 8431
✉ dm@rtc-mail.org.uk
www.dogsmonthly.co.uk
Owner *Mr D. Cavill*
Editor *Meriel France*
Circulation 11,000
Founded 1983. MONTHLY magazine suitable for serious dog owners whose dog is more than just a pet.
FEATURES Articles on breeds and topical news. Approach the editor first by e-mail. Max. length for features, news, fiction or other articles, 2000 words.
PAYMENT negotiable.

Eastern Eye
Unit 2, 65 Whitechapel Road, London E1 1DU
☎020 7650 2000 Fax 020 7650 2001
www.ethnicmedia.co.uk
Owner *Ethnic Media Group*
Editor *Hamant Verma*
Circulation 20,844
Founded 1989. WEEKLY community paper for the Asian community in Britain. Interested in relevant general, local and international issues. Approach in writing with ideas for submission.

Easy Gardening
BBC Worldwide, AG 192, 80 Wood Lane, London W12 0TT
☎020 8433 2000
✉ easygardening@bbc.co.uk
www.bbcworldwide.co.uk
Owner *BBC Worldwide Publishing Ltd*
Editor *Ceri Thomas*
Circulation 40,095
TEN ISSUES YEARLY. Down-to-earth and easy to follow gardening advice 'that gets results'. Will consider 'reader gardens' contributions; approach by e-mail. No transparencies; digital images only.

Easy Living
68 Old Bond Street, London W1S 4PH
☎020 7499 9080 Fax 020 7399 2625
✉ easylivingeditorial@condenast.co.uk
www.easylivingmagazine.com
Owner *Condé Nast*
Editor *Susie Forbes*
Circulation 182,146
Launched 2005. MONTHLY magazine aimed at women aged 30–50-plus. Focuses on aspects of home life, beauty and health, food, relationships; stylish and glossy with real-life, practical and useful items.

The Ecologist
Unit 18, Chelsea Wharf, 15 Lots Road, London SW10 0QJ
☎020 7351 3578 Fax 020 7351 3617
✉ editorial@theecologist.org
www.theecologist.org
Owner *Ecosystems Ltd*
Managing Editor *Harry Ram*
Editor *Zac Goldsmith*
Circulation 25,000
Founded 1970. MONTHLY. Unsolicited mss welcome but best approach is a brief proposal to the editor by e-mail (address above), outlining experience and background and summarising suggested article.
FEATURES Radical approach to political, economic, social and environmental issues, with an emphasis on rethinking the basic assumptions that underpin modern society. Articles of between 500 and 3000 words.
PAYMENT negotiable.

The Economist
25 St James's Street, London SW1A 1HG
☎020 7830 7000 Fax 020 7839 2968
www.economist.com
Owner *Pearson/individual shareholders*
Editor *John Micklethwait*
Circulation 158,142 (UK edition)
Founded 1843. WEEKLY. Worldwide circulation. Approaches should be made in writing to the editor. No unsolicited mss.

The Edge
65 Guinness Buildings, Hammersmith, London W6 8BD
☎0845 456 9337
✉ davec@theedge.abelgratis.co.uk
www.theedgeabelgratis.co.uk
Editor *Dave Clark*
QUARTERLY. Reviews and features: film (indie, arts), books, popular culture. Fiction: modern crime/horror/SF/erotica/slipstream. Sample issue £5 post-free (cheques payable to 'The Edge'). Writers' guidelines available on website, for s.a.e. or by e-mail.
PAYMENT up to £75 per 1000 words.

Electrical Times
Media House, Swanley BR8 8HU
☎01322 611276 Fax 01322 616376

✉ louise.frampton@nexusmedia.com
Owner *Nexus Media Communications*
Editor *Louise Frampton*
Circulation 10,613

Founded 1891. MONTHLY. Aimed at electrical contractors, designers and installers. Unsolicited mss welcome but initial approach preferred.

Elle
64 North Row, London W1K 7LL
☎020 7150 7000   Fax 020 7150 7670
Owner *Hachette Filipacchi*
Editor *Lorraine Candy*
Features Editor *Anna Pursglove*
Circulation 208,132

Founded 1985. MONTHLY fashion glossy. Prospective contributors should approach the relevant editor in writing in the first instance, including cuttings.
   FEATURES Max. 2000 words.
   HOT LIST Short articles on hot trends, events, fashion and beauty. Max. 500 words.
   PAYMENT negotiable.

Embroidery
PO Box 42B, East Molesley KT8 9BB
☎01260 295735
✉ jhall@embroiderersguild.com
www.embroiderersguild.com
Owner *Embroiderers' Guild*
Editor *Joanne Hall*
Circulation 12,000

Founded 1933. BI-MONTHLY. Features articles on historical and foreign embroidery, and contemporary artists' work with illustrations. Covers all forms of textile art, historical and contemporary. Also reviews. Unsolicited material welcome. Max. 1000 words.
   PAYMENT negotiable.

Empire
4th Floor, Mappin House, 4 Winsley Street, London W1W 8HF
☎020 7182 8781   Fax 020 7182 8703
✉ empire@emap.com
www.empireonline.co.uk
Owner *Emap East*
Editor-in-Chief *Colin Kennedy*
Circulation 190,224

Founded 1989. Launched at the Cannes Film Festival. MONTHLY guide to the movies which aims to cover the world of films in a 'comprehensive, adult, intelligent and witty package'. Although most of *Empire* is devoted to films and the people behind them, it also looks at the

developments and technology behind television and DVDs plus music, multimedia and books. Wide selection of in-depth features and stories on all the main releases of the month, and reviews of over 100 films and videos. Contributions welcome but approach in writing first.
   FEATURES Behind-the-scenes features on films, humorous and factual features.
   PAYMENT by agreement.

The Engineer
50 Poland Street, London W1F 7AX
☎020 7970 4000   Fax 020 7970 4123
✉ andrew.lee@centaur.co.uk
www.theengineer.co.uk
Owner *Centaur Communications*
Editor *Andrew Lee*
Circulation 31,224

FOUNDED 1856. FORTNIGHTLY news magazine for technology and innovation.
   FEATURES Most outside contributions are commissioned but good ideas are always welcome. Max. 2000 words.
   NEWS Scope for specialist regional freelancers, and for tip-offs. Max. 500 words.
   TECHNOLOGY Technology news from specialists, and tip-offs. Max. 500 words.
   PAYMENT by arrangement.

The English Garden
Archant Specialist, Jubilee House, 2 Jubilee Place, London SW3 3QT
☎020 7751 4800   Fax 020 7751 4848
✉ theenglishgarden@archant.co.uk
www.theenglishgarden.co.uk
Owner *Archant Specialist*
Editor *Janine Wookey*
Circulation 32,752

Founded 1996. MONTHLY. Features on beautiful gardens with practical ideas on design and planting. No unsolicited mss.
   FEATURES *Jackie Bennett* Max. 800 words. Approach in writing in the first instance; send synopsis of 150 words with strong design and planting ideas, feature proposals, or sets of photographs of interesting gardens.

English Nature Magazine
English Nature, Northminster House, Peterborough PE1 1UA
☎01733 455000   Fax 01733 455188
✉ amanda.giles@english-nature.org.uk
www.english-nature.org.uk
Owner *English Nature*

Editor *Amanda Giles*
Circulation 16,000

Founded 1992. BI-MONTHLY magazine which explains the work of English Nature, the government adviser on wildlife and conservation policies. No unsolicited material.

Erotic Review

500 Chiswick High Road, London W4 5RG
☎0870 383 1114
✉ info@erotic-review.co.uk
erotic-review.co.uk

Owner *Alton Russell International*
Circulation 20,000

Founded 1997 by The Erotic Print Society. Now produced independently as a QUARTERLY erotic literary magazine containing articles, humour, fiction, poetry and art work. Unsolicited material welcome, but please read magazine first. No clichéd pornography. Approach in writing in the first instance enclosing a brief sample of work and s.a.e.

FEATURES Esoteric, humorous or real-life experiences. Max. 2000 words.

FICTION Erotic short stories. Max. 2000 words.

PAYMENT features, £40–200; fiction, £50–200.

ES

See **Evening Standard** under *Regional Newspapers*

Esquire

National Magazine House, 72 Broadwick Street, London W1F 9EP
☎020 7439 5000 Fax 020 7439 5675

Owner *National Magazine Co. Ltd*
Editor *Simon Tiffin*
Circulation 54,548

Founded 1991. MONTHLY. Quality men's general interest magazine. No unsolicited mss or short stories.

Essentials

IPC Media Ltd., King's Reach Tower, Stamford Street, London SE1 9LS
☎020 7261 6970 Fax 020 7261 5262

Owner *IPC Media (A Time Warner Company)*
Editor *Julie Barton-Breck*
Circulation 118,853

Founded 1988. MONTHLY women's interest magazine. Unsolicited mss (not originals) welcome if accompanied by s.a.e. Initial approach in writing preferred. Prospective contributors

should study the magazine thoroughly before submitting anything. No fiction.

FEATURES Max. 2000 words (double-spaced on A4).

PAYMENT negotiable.

The Essex Magazine

See **The Journal Magazines**

Eve

Griffin House, 174 Hammersmith Road, London W6 7JP
☎020 8267 8223 Fax 020 8267 8222
✉ evemagazine@haynet.com
www.evemagazine.co.uk

Owner *Haymarket Publishing*
Editor *Sara Cremer*
Deputy Editor *Rachael Ashley*
Features Director *Sharon Bradley*
Circulation 163,671

Founded 2000. MONTHLY. Wide-ranging general interest – aimed at the intelligent 30+ woman. No unsolicited material. Send introductory letter, *recent* writings and outlines for ideas aimed at a specific section. It is essential that would-be contributors familiarise themselves with the magazine.

Eventing

See **Horse and Hound**

Evergreen

PO Box 52, Cheltenham GL50 1YQ
☎01242 537900 Fax 01242 537901

Editor *R. Faiers*
Circulation 75,000

Founded 1985. QUARTERLY magazine featuring articles and poems about Britain. Unsolicited contributions welcome.

FEATURES Britain's natural beauty, towns and villages, nostalgia, wildlife, traditions, odd customs, legends, folklore, crafts, etc. Length 250–2000 words.

PAYMENT £15 per 1000 words; poems £4.

Everything France

Westgate, 120–128 Station Road, Redhill RH1 1ET
☎01737 786800 Fax 01737 786801
✉ martin.hedges@brooklandsgroup.com
www.brooklandsgroup.com
www.everythingFrancemag.co.uk

Owner *Brooklands Group Limited*
Editor *Martin Hedges*

Founded 2001. MONTHLY. 'The premier maga-

zine for French property, travel, touring, food and drink.' Welcomes French-based features on property – buying, lifestyle and gardens; tourism, cities and regions, personalities and French culture. Words and picture packages welcome. Approach by e-mail. Max. 3000 words.
PAYMENT negotiable.

Executive Woman
2 Chantry Place, Harrow HA3 6NY
☎020 8420 1210　Fax 020 8420 1691
✉ info@execwoman.com
www.execwoman.com

Owner *Saleworld*
Managing Editor *Angela Giveon*
Circulation 85,000

Founded 1987. BI-MONTHLY magazine for female executives in the corporate field and female entrepreneurs.
FEATURES New and interesting business issues and 'Women to Watch'. Health and conferencing, profiles, technology, beauty, fashion, training and arts items. 700 words per page.
LEGAL/FINANCIAL Opportunities for lawyers/accountants to write on issues in their field. Max. 600 words.

Fairgame Magazine
The Baltic Business Centre, Gateshead NE8 3DA
☎0191 442 4001　Fax 0191 442 4002
www.fairgamemagazine.com

Editor *Jennifer O'Neill*
Circulation 15,000

Founded 2003. BI-MONTHLY magazine for women football players. Contributions welcome.
FEATURES *Jennifer O'Neill* International reports, player and team profiles, interviews, diet, health and fitness, tactics, training advice, play improvement, fund-raising. Max. 1500 words.
NEWS *Wilf Frith* Match reports, team news, transfers, injuries, results and fixtures. Max. 600 words.

Family Circle
IPC Media Ltd., King's Reach Tower, Stamford Street, London SE1 9LS
☎0870 444 5000　Fax 020 7261 5929

Owner *IPC Media (A Time Warner Company)*
Editor *Karen Livermore*
Circulation 112,597

Founded 1964. MONTHLY. Women's general interest. Little scope for freelancers as most material is produced in-house or by published journalists.

FEATURES *Emma Burstall*
HEALTH *Sarah Touquet*
FOOD & DRINK *Jennifer Mallinson*

Family Tree Magazine
61 Great Whyte, Ramsey, Huntingdon PE26 1HJ
☎01487 814050　Fax 01487 711361
✉ sue.f@family-tree.co.uk
www.family-tree.co.uk

Owner *ABM Publishing Ltd*
Editor *Peter Watson*
Circulation 50,000

Founded 1984. MONTHLY. News and features on matters of genealogy. Not interested in own family histories. Approach in writing with ideas. All material should be addressed to *Peter Watson*.
FEATURES Any genealogically related subject. Max. 2000 words. No puzzles or fictional articles.
PAYMENT news and features, negotiable.

Fancy Fowl
The Publishing House, Station Road, Framlingham IP13 9EE
☎01728 622030　Fax 01728 622031
✉ fancyfowl@todaymagazines.co.uk

Owner *TP Publications*
Editor *Liz Fairbrother*
Circulation 3000

Founded 1979. MONTHLY. Devoted entirely to poultry, waterfowl, turkeys, geese, pea fowl, etc. – management, breeding, rearing and exhibition. Outside contributions of knowledgeable, technical poultry-related articles and news welcome. Max. 1000 words. Approach by letter.
PAYMENT negotiable.

Farmers Weekly
Quadrant House, Sutton SM2 5AS
☎020 8652 4911　Fax 020 8652 4005
✉ farmers.weekly@rbi.co.uk
www.fwi.co.uk

Owner *Reed Business Information*
Editor *Jane King*
Circulation 73,890

WEEKLY. 1996 Business Magazine of the Year. For practising farmers and those in the ancillary industries. Unsolicited mss considered.
FEATURES A wide range of material relating to farmers' problems and interests: specific sections on arable and livestock farming, farm life, practical and general interest, machinery and business.
NEWS General farming news.
PAYMENT negotiable.

Fast Car

Future Publishing Ltd, 30 Monmouth Streeet, Bath BA1 2BW
www.fastcar.co.uk
Owner *Future Publishing Ltd*
Editor *Gez Jones*
Circulation 95,893

Founded 1987. THIRTEEN ISSUES YEARLY. Lad's magazine about performance tuning and modifying cars. Covers all aspects of this youth culture including the latest street styles and music. Features cars and their owners, product tests and in-car entertainment. Also includes a free reader ads section.

NEWS Any item in line with the above.

Features Innovative ideas in line with the above and in the *Fast Car* writing style. Generally four pages in length. No Kit-car features, race reports or road test reports of standard cars. Copy should be as concise as possible. PAYMENT negotiable.

FHM

Mappin House, 4 Winsley Street, London W1W 8HF
☎020 7182 8028   Fax 020 7182 8021
✉ general@fhm.com
www.fhm.com
Owner *Emap Plc*
Editor *Ross Brown*
Circulation 500,865

Founded in 1986 as a free fashion magazine, FHM evolved to become more male oriented but without much public acclaim until Emap bought the title in 1994. Since then it has become the best-selling men's magazine in the world covering all areas of men's lifestyle. Published MONTHLY with 18 international editions worldwide. No unsolicited mss. Synopses and ideas welcome by e-mail. PAYMENT negotiable.

The Field

IPC Media Ltd., King's Reach Tower, Stamford Street, London SE1 9LS
☎020 7261 5198   Fax 020 7261 5358
✉ beatrice_gray@ipcmedia.com
www.thefield.co.uk
Owner *IPC Media (A Time Warner Company)*
Editor-in-Chief *Jonathan Young*
Circulation 30,974

Founded 1853. MONTHLY magazine for those who are serious about the British countryside and its pleasures. Unsolicited mss (and transparencies) welcome but initial approach should be made in writing or by phone on 020 7261 6225.

FEATURES Exceptional work on any subject concerning the countryside. Most work tends to be commissioned. PAYMENT varies.

50 Connect – www.50connect.co.uk

See entry under *Electronic Publishing and Other Services*

Film Review

Visual Imagination Ltd, 9 Blades Court, Deodar Road, London SW15 2NU
☎020 8875 1520   Fax 020 8875 1588
✉ filmreview@visimag.com
www.visimag.com
Owner *Visual Imagination Ltd*
Editor *Nikki Baughan*
Circulation 50,000

FOUR-WEEKLY. Reviews, profiles, interviews and special reports on films. Unsolicited material considered. PAYMENT negotiable.

Fishing News

4th Floor, Albert House 1–4 Singer Street, London EC2A 4LQ
☎020 7017 4531   Fax 020 7017 4536
✉ tim.oliver@informa.com
www.fishingnews.co.uk
Owner *Informa Group Plc*
Editor *Tim Oliver*
Circulation 8739

Founded 1913. WEEKLY. All aspects of the commercial fishing industry in the UK and Ireland. No unsolicited mss; telephone inquiry in the first instance. Max. 600 words for news and 1500 words for features. PAYMENT £100 per 1000 words.

The Fix

5 Martins Lane, Witcham, Ely CB6 2LB
✉ andy@ttapress.demon.co.uk
www.ttapress.com
Owner *TTA Press*

Founded 1994. BI-MONTHLY. Features detailed contributors' guidelines and reviews of international short story publications, plus varied articles, news, views and interviews.

FEATURES Unsolicited articles welcome on any aspect of short story publishing: market information, writing, editing, illustrating, interviews and reviews. All genres. Submissions should include adequate return postage. 'Please study the magazine: this will greatly enhance your chances of acceptance.' No fiction or poetry.

Flight International

Quadrant House, The Quadrant, Sutton SM2 5AS
☎020 8652 3842   Fax 020 8652 3840
✉ flight.international@flightglobal.com
www.flightglobal.com
Owner *Reed Business Information*
Editor *Murdo Morrison*
Circulation 52,222

Founded 1909. WEEKLY. International trade magazine for the aerospace industry, including civil, military and space. Unsolicited mss considered. Commissions preferred – phone with ideas and follow up with letter. E-mail submissions encouraged.

FEATURES *Murdo Morrison* Technically informed articles and pieces on specific geographical areas with international appeal. Analytical, in-depth coverage required, preferably supported by interviews. Max. 1800 words.

NEWS *Andrew Doyle* Opportunities exist for news pieces from particular geographical areas on specific technical developments. Max. 350 words.

PAYMENT NUJ rates.

Flora International

The Fishing Lodge Studio, 77 Bulbridge Road, Wilton, Salisbury SP2 0LE
☎01722 743207   Fax 01722 743207
✉ floramag@aol.com
Publisher/Editor *Maureen Foster*
Circulation 16,000

Founded 1974. BI-MONTHLY magazine for flower arrangers and florists. Unsolicited mss welcome. Approach in writing with ideas. Not interested in general gardening articles.

FEATURES Fully illustrated: colour photographs, transparencies or CD. Flower arranging, flower arrangers' gardens and flower crafts. Floristry items written with practical knowledge and well illustrated are particularly welcome. Max. 1000 words.

PAYMENT £50 per 1000 words plus additional payment for suitable photographs.

FlyPast

PO Box 100, Stamford PE9 1XQ
☎01780 755131   Fax 01780 757261
✉ flypast@keypublishing.com
Owner *Key Publishing Ltd*
Editor *Ken Ellis*
Circulation 38,524

Founded 1981. MONTHLY. Historic aviation and aviation heritage, mainly military, Second World War period up to c.1970. Unsolicited mss welcome.

Focus

See **British Science Fiction Association** under *Professional Associations and Societies*

Focus

Origin Publishing, Tower House, Fairfax Street, Bristol BS1 3BN
☎0117 927 9009   Fax 0117 934 9008
✉ focus@originpublishing.co.uk
www.bbcfocusmagazine.co.uk
Owner *Origin Publishing*
Editor *Paul Parsons*
News & Features *Sally Palmer*
Reviews *Ian Taylor*
Circulation 57,306

Founded 1992. FOUR-WEEKLY. Popular science and discovery. Welcomes *relevant* summaries of original feature ideas by e-mail.

For Women

Fantasy Publications, PO Box 55723, The Northern and Shell Tower, London E14 1BE
☎020 7308 5363
Editor *Elizabeth Coldwell*
Circulation 60,000

Founded 1992. SIX-WEEKLY magazine of erotic and sex interest for women – health and sex, erotic fiction and erotic photography. No homes and gardens articles. Approach in writing in the first instance. Send s.a.e. for submission guidelines.

FICTION *Elizabeth Coldwell* Erotic short stories. Length: 2000 – 3000 words.

PAYMENT £150 total.

Fortean Times: The Journal of Strange Phenomena

PO Box 2409, London NW5 4NP
☎020 7907 6235   Fax 020 7907 6406
✉ david_sutton@dennis.co.uk
www.forteantimes.com
Editor *David Sutton*
Circulation 25,174

Founded 1973. THIRTEEN ISSUES YEARLY. Accounts of strange phenomena and experiences, curiosities, mysteries, prodigies and portents. Unsolicited mss welcome. Approach in writing with ideas. No fiction, poetry, rehashes or politics.

FEATURES Well-researched and referenced material on current or historical mysteries, or first-hand accounts of oddities. Max. 3000 words, preferably with good relevant photos/illustrations.

NEWS Concise copy with full source references essential.

PAYMENT negotiable.

FQ Magazine
Seymour House, South Street, Bromley
BR1 1RH
☎020 8460 6060 Fax 020 8460 6050
✉ matt@touchline.com
www.fqmagazine.co.uk

Owner *3D Media Ltd*
Editor *Matt Weiner*

Launched 2003. BI-MONTHLY. Lifestyle magazine for young fathers. Interviews, reviews, finance, kids' toys, child issues, parenting tips and general fatherhood advice. Ideas welcome; contact the editor by e-mail.

France Magazine
Archant House, Oriel Road, Cheltenham
GL50 1BB
☎01242 216050 Fax 01242 216074
✉ editorial@francemag.com
www.francemag.com

Owner *Archant (Life South) Ltd*
Editor *Nick Wall*
Circulation 38,641

FOUNDED 1989. MONTHLY magazine containing all things of interest to Francophiles – in English. Approach by e-mail in the first instance.

Freelance Market News
Sevendale House, 7 Dale Street, Manchester
M1 1JB
☎0161 228 2362, ext 210 Fax 0161 228 3533
✉ fmn@writersbureau.com
www.writersbureau.com/fmn

Editor *Angela Cox*

MONTHLY. News and information on the freelance writers' market, both inland and overseas. Includes market information, competitions, seminars, courses, overseas openings, etc. Short articles (700 words max.). Unsolicited contributions welcome.

PAYMENT by negotiation.

The Freelance
See **National Union of Journalists** under *Professional Associations and Societies*

Front Magazine
Jordan House, 47 Brunwick Place, London
N1 6EB
☎020 7608 6300 Fax 020 7608 6330
✉ front@hhc.co.uk

Owner *Higbury House*
Acting Editor *Johnny Sharp*
Circulation 85,000

Founded 1998. MONTHLY men's interest magazine. Includes features on sport (including extreme sport), crime, war, humour, sex, real life stories and irreverent celebrity interviews. Welcomes contributions but nothing on food, health and fitness, finance items or 'how to pull women' stories. Approach by e-mail.

FYi
Aspect Media, The Bake House, J108 TBBC, 100 Clements Road, London SE16 4DG
☎020 7064 8400 Fax 020 7231 1232
✉ FYi@aspectmediauk.com
www.aspectmediauk.com

Owner *Workplace Group Plc/Aspect Media*
Editor *Jackie Scully*
Circulation 5000

Founded 2003. QUARTERLY. Magazine for managing directors of small companies who lease property from Workspace Group. Business articles and London-focused material for the small business owner. No unsolicited material; approach by telephone, fax, letter or e-mail in the first instance.

FEATURES Ideas for business features directed at small to medium-sized enterprises, including issues such as HR, copyright, IT, pensions, etc. Max. 1000 words.

NEWS Stories to interest and inform business owners; latest technology, products, services and developments in the business sector. Max. 300 words.

PAYMENT negotiable.

Garden Answers
Bretton Court, Bretton, Peterborough
PE3 8DZ
☎01733 264666 Fax 01733 282695

Owner *Emap Active Publications Ltd*
Deputy Editor *Daniella Delaney*
Circulation 38,707

Founded 1982. MONTHLY. 'It is unlikely that unsolicited manuscripts will be used, as articles are usually commissioned and must be in the magazine style.' Prospective contributors should approach the editor in writing. Interested in hearing from gardening writers on any subject, whether flowers, fruit, vegetables, houseplants or greenhouse gardening.

Garden News
Bretton Court, Bretton, Peterborough
PE3 8DZ
☎01733 264666 Fax 01733 282695

Owner *Emap Active Publications Ltd*
Editor *Sarah Page*
Circulation 47,239

Founded 1958. Britain's biggest-selling, full-colour gardening WEEKLY. News and advice on growing flowers, fruit and vegetables, plus colourful features on all aspects of gardening especially for the committed gardener. News and features welcome, especially if accompanied by top-quality photos or illustrations. Contact the editor before submitting any material.

The Garden, Journal of the Royal Horticultural Society

RHS Publications, 4th Floor, Churchgate New Road, Peterborough PE1 1TT
☎01733 775775 Fax 01733 775819
✉ thegarden@rhs.org.uk
www.rhs.org.uk
Owner *The Royal Horticultural Society*
Editor *Ian Hodgson*
Circulation 352,735

Founded 1866. MONTHLY journal of the Royal Horticultural Society. Covers all aspects of the art, science and practice of horticulture and garden making. 'Articles must have depth and substance.' Approach by letter with a synopsis in the first instance. Max. 2500 words.

Gardens Illustrated

Origin Publishing, Tower House, Fairfax Street, Bristol BS1 3BN
☎0117 314 8774 Fax 0117 933 8032
www.gardensillustrated.com
Owner *BBC Worldwide Publishing Ltd*
Editor *Juliet Roberts*
Circulation 24,080

Founded 1993. MONTHLY. 'Britain's most distinguished garden magazine' with a worldwide readership. The focus is on garden design, with a strong international flavour. Unsolicited mss are rarely used and it is best that prospective contributors approach the editor with ideas in writing, supported by photographs.

Gardens Monthly

Berwick House, 8–10 Knoll Rise, Orpington BR6 0EL
☎01689 899297 Fax 01689 899266
✉ liz.dobbs@encanta.co.uk
www.gardening.co.uk
Owner *Encanta Media Ltd*
Editor *Liz Dobbs*
Circulation 32,978

Launched 2002. MONTHLY consumer magazine for amateur gardeners with some experience. Practical advice on plants, gardens, garden design and equipment. Welcomes big garden features with pictures; e-mail in the first instance.

Gay Times

Unit M, Spectrum House, 32–34 Gordon House Road, London NW5 1LP
☎020 7424 7400 Fax 020 7424 7401
✉ edit@gaytimes.co.uk
www.gaytimes.co.uk
Owner *Millivres-Prowler Group*
Editor *Vicky Powell*
Circulation 65,000

Covers all aspects of gay life, plus general interest likely to appeal to the gay community, art reviews and news. Regular freelance writers used. PAYMENT negotiable.

Gibbons Stamp Monthly

Stanley Gibbons, 7 Parkside, Christchurch Road, Ringwood BH24 3SH
☎01425 472363 Fax 01425 470247
✉ hjefferies@stanleygibbons.co.uk
www.gibbonsstampmonthly.com
Owner *Stanley Gibbons Ltd*
Editor *Hugh Jefferies*
Circulation 22,000

Founded 1890. MONTHLY. News and features. Unsolicited mss welcome. Make initial approach in writing by telephone or e-mail to avoid disappointment.

FEATURES *Hugh Jefferies* Unsolicited material of specialised nature and general stamp features welcome. Max. 3000 words but longer pieces can be serialised.

NEWS *John Moody* Any philatelic news item. Max. 500 words.

PAYMENT Features, £40–50 per 1000 words; news, no payment.

Glamour

6–8 Old Bond Street, London W1S 4PH
☎020 7499 9080 Fax 020 7491 2551
www.condenast.co.uk
Owner *Condé Nast*
Editor *Jo Elvin*
Circulation 585,984

Founded 2001. Handbag-size glossy women's magazine – fashion, beauty and celebrities. No unsolicited mss; send ideas for features in synopsis form to the Features Editor *Jade Beer*.

Golf Monthly

IPC Media Ltd., King's Reach Tower, Stamford Street, London SE1 9LS
☎020 7261 7237 Fax 020 7261 7240

✉ golfmonthly@ipcmedia.com
golf-monthly.co.uk
Owner *IPC Media (A Time Warner Company)*
Editor *Jane Carter*
Circulation 77,766
Founded 1911. MONTHLY. Player profiles, golf instruction, general golf features and columns. Not interested in instruction material from outside contributors. Unsolicited mss welcome. Approach in writing with ideas.
FEATURES Max. 1500–2000 words. PAYMENT by arrangement.

Golf World
Bushfield House, Orton Centre, Peterborough PE2 5UW
☎01733 237111 Fax 01733 288025
✉ paul.hamblin@emap.com
www.email.golfworldmagazine.co.uk
Owner *Emap Active Ltd*
Editor *Paul Hamblin*
Office Manager *Linda Manigan*
Circulation 42,696
Founded 1962. MONTHLY. No unsolicited mss. Approach in writing with ideas.

Good Holiday Magazine
27A High Street, Esher KT10 9RL
☎01372 468140 Fax 01372 470765
✉ info@goodholidayideas.com
Editor *John Hill*
Circulation 100,000
Founded 1985. QUARTERLY aimed at better-off holiday-makers rather than travellers. Worldwide destinations including Europe and domestic. No unsolicited material but approach in writing or by e-mail with ideas and/or synopsis. PAYMENT negotiable.

Good Homes Magazine
Woodlands, 80 Wood Lane, London W12 0TT
☎020 8433 2391 Fax 020 8433 2691
www.bbcgoodhomes.com
Owner *BBC Worldwide Publishing Ltd*
Editor *Lisa Allen*
Circulation 135,690
Founded 1998. MONTHLY. Decorating, interiors, readers' homes, shopping, makeovers, property and consumer information. No fiction.
FEATURES *Emily Peck*
PROPERTY & READERS' HOMES *Rachel Watson* Property features from specialists. Approach by letter with cuttings.

Good Housekeeping
National Magazine House, 72 Broadwick Street, London W1F 9EP
☎020 7439 5000 Fax 020 7439 5616
✉ firstname.lastname@natmags.co.uk
www.natmags.co.uk
Owner *National Magazine Co. Ltd*
Editor *Louise Chunn*
Circulation 468,579
Founded 1922. MONTHLY glossy. No unsolicited mss. Write with ideas in the first instance to the appropriate editor.
FEATURES *Lucy Moore* Most work is commissioned but original ideas are always welcome. No ideas are discussed on the telephone. Send short synopsis, plus relevant cuttings, showing previous examples of work published. No unsolicited mss.
HEALTH *Julie Powell.* Submission guidelines as for features; no unsolicited mss.

Good Motoring
Station Road, Forest Row RH18 5EN
☎01342 825676 Fax 01342 824847
✉ dh@motoringassist.com
www.roadsafety.org.uk
Owner *Gem Motoring Assist*
Editor *Derek Hainge*
Circulation 52,000
Founded 1932. QUARTERLY motoring, road safety, travel and general features magazine. 1500 words max. Prospective contributors should approach in writing only.

Good News
11 Pickford Road, Bournemouth BH9 2RR
☎01903 232208 Fax 01202 522177
✉ goodnews@pepr.co.uk
Owner *Good News Fellowship*
Editor *Paul Eddy*
Circulation 50,000
Founded 2001. MONTHLY evangelistic newspaper which welcomes contributions. No fiction. Send for sample copy of writers' guidelines in the first instance. No poetry or children's stories.
NEWS Items of up to 500 words (preferably with pictures) 'showing God at work, and human interest photo stories. "Churchy" items not wanted. Testimonies of how people have come to personal faith in Jesus Christ and the difference it has made are always welcome. They do not need to be dramatic!'
WOMEN'S PAGE Relevant items of interest welcome.
PAYMENT negotiable.

The Good Ski Guide
27A High Street, Esher KT10 9RL
☎01372 468140
✉ info@goodholidayideas.com
Owner *Good Holiday Group*
Editors *John Hill, Nick Dalton*
Circulation 250,000
Founded 1976. FOUR ISSUES YEARLY. Unsolicited mss welcome from writers with a knowledge of skiing and ski resorts. Prospective contributors are best advised to make initial contact in writing as ideas and work need to be seen before any discussion can take place. PAYMENT negotiable.

GQ
Vogue House, Hanover Square, London W1S 1JU
☎020 7499 9080 Fax 020 7495 1679
www.gq-magazine.co.uk
Owner *Condé Nast Publications Ltd*
Editor *Dylan Jones*
Circulation 126,275
Founded 1988. MONTHLY. Men's style magazine. No unsolicited material. Write or fax with an idea in the first instance.

Granta
2–3 Hanover Yard, Noel Road, London N1 8BE
☎020 7704 9776 Fax 020 7704 0474
✉ editorial@granta.com
www.granta.com
Editor *Ian Jack*
Deputy Editor *Matt Weiland*
QUARTERLY magazine of new writing, including fiction, memoirs, reportage and photography published in paperback book form. Highbrow, diverse and contemporary, with a thematic approach. Unsolicited mss (including fiction) considered. A lot of material is commissioned. Vital to read the magazine first to appreciate its very particular fusion of cultural and political interests. No reviews or news articles. No poetry. Access the website for submission guidelines.
PAYMENT negotiable.

Grazia
Emap Consumer Media, Endeavour House, 189 Shaftesbury Avenue, London WC2H 8JG
☎020 7437 9011
www.graziamagazine.co.uk
Owner *Emap Consumer Media*
Editor *Jane Bruton*

Circulation 170,783
Launched February 2005. Britain's first WEEKLY glossy aimed at women aged 25 to 45. Features articles on fashion, celebrity, news, beauty and lifestyle. Approach by e-mail.

The Great Outdoors
See **TGO**

The Great War
PO Box 202, Scarborough YO11 3GE
☎01723 581329 Fax 01723 581329
✉ books@greatnorthernpublising.co.uk
www.greatnorthernpublishing.co.uk
Owner *Great Northern Publishing*
Editor *Mark Marsay*
Founded 2001. BI-MONTHLY subscription only, non-academic magazine published in A5 format. 'The little magazine dedicated to the Great War (1914–19) and to those who perished and those who returned.' Articles, personal stories and accounts of those who served (men and women of all nationalities) and their families: diaries, anecdotes, letters, postcards, poetry, unit histories, events and memorials, etc. Absolutely no fiction or long academic works expounding historian's personal views. New material welcome but contact editor prior to sending. See website for submission guidelines and editorial content. 'Open door policy: all welcome regardless of ability to write to high standard as all work is carefully edited. No subject or topic excluded.' Sample copy £5.

Grow Your Own
25 Phoenix Court, Hawkins Road, Colchester CO2 8JY
☎01206 505979 Fax 01206 505945
✉ georgina.wroe@aceville.co.uk
www.growfruitandveg.co.uk
Owner *Helen Tudor*
Editor *Georgina Wroe*
Launched 2005. MONTHLY magazine aimed at aspiring self-sufficients giving information on the best ways to grow (and cook) seasonal produce. Contributions are welcome on anything relevant to fruit, vegetables and herbs. Approach by e-mail.
FEATURES *Georgina Wroe* (e-mail address above)
NEWS *Craig Drever* (craig.drever@aceville. co.uk)

Guardian Weekend
See **The Guardian** under *National Newspapers*

Guiding magazine
17–19 Buckingham Palace Road, London
SW1W 0PT
☎020 7834 6242 Fax 020 7828 5791
✉ guiding@girlguiding.org.uk
www.girlguiding.org.uk
Owner *The Guide Association*
Editor *Wendy Kewley*
Circulation 79,000

Founded 1914. MONTHLY. Unsolicited mss welcome provided topics relate to the Movement and/or women's role in society. Ideas in writing appreciated in first instance. No nostalgic, 'when I was a Guide', pieces, please.

ACTIVITY IDEAS Interesting, contemporary ideas and instructions for activities for girls aged 5 to 18+ to do during unit meetings – crafts, games (indoor/outdoor), etc.

FEATURES Topics relevant to today's girls and young women. 500 words.

NEWS Items likely to be of interest to members. Max. 100–150 words.

PAYMENT £70 per 1000 words.

H&E Naturist
Burlington Court, Carlisle Street, Goole
DN14 5EG
☎01405 760298/766769 Fax 01405 763815
✉ editor@henaturist.co.uk
www.healthandefficiency.co.uk
Owner *New Freedom Publications Ltd*
Editor *Sara Backhouse*
Circulation 20,000

Founded 1898. MONTHLY naturist magazine.

FEATURES Will consider short features on social nudism, longer features on nudist holidays and nudist philosophy. 90% of every issue is by freelance contributors. 800–1500 words.

NEWS 'We are always on the lookout for national and international nudist news stories.' 250–500 words. No soft porn, 'sexy' stories or sleazy photographs. Approach by post, e-mail or telephone.

Hair
IPC Media Ltd., King's Reach Tower,
Stamford Street, London SE1 9LS
☎020 7261 6975 Fax 020 7261 7382
Owner *IPC Media (A Time Warner Company)*
Editor *Zoe Richards*
Circulation 131,735

Founded 1977. TEN ISSUES YEARLY hair and beauty magazine. No unsolicited mss, but always interested in good photographs. Approach with ideas in writing.

FEATURES Fashion pieces on hair trends and styling advice.
PAYMENT negotiable.

Hairflair & Beauty
Hairflair Magazines Ltd, Freebournes House,
Freebournes Road, Witham CM8 3US
☎01376 534540 Fax 01376 534546
Owner *Hairflair Magazines Ltd*
Editor *Ruth Page*
Circulation 25,000

Founded 1982. BI-MONTHLY. Original and interesting hair and beauty-related features written in a young, lively style to appeal to a readership aged 16–35 years. Freelancers are not used.

Harper's Bazaar
National Magazine House, 72 Broadwick
Street, London W1F 9EP
☎020 7439 5000 Fax 020 7439 5506
harpersandqueen.co.uk
Owner *National Magazine Co. Ltd*
Editor *Lucy Yeomans*
Circulation 102,863

MONTHLY. Up-market glossy combining the stylish and the streetwise. Approach in writing (not phone) with ideas.

FEATURES *Harriet Green* Ideas only in the first instance.

NEWS Snippets welcome if very original.
PAYMENT negotiable.

Health & Fitness Magazine
2 Balcombe Street, London NW1 6NW
☎020 7042 4000
✉ mary.coomber@futurenet.co.uk
www.healthandfitnessonline.co.uk
Owner *Future Publishing Ltd*
Editor *Mary Comber*
Circulation 65,000

Founded 1983. MONTHLY. Target reader: active, health-conscious women aged 25–40.

FEATURES news and articles on nutrition, exercise, healthy eating, holistic health and well-being. Will consider ideas; approach in writing in the first instance.

Healthy
River Publishing, 14 Leicester Place, London
WC2H 7BZ
☎020 7413 9359 Fax 020 7306 0303
✉ hberesford@riverltd.co.uk
Owner *River Publishing*
Editor *Annabel Meggeson*
Circulation 266,538

NINE ISSUES YEARLY health magazine with authoritative and accessible information and advice. Will consider holistic health and lifestyle features; approach by e-mail.

Heat

Endeavour House, 189 Shaftesbury Avenue, London WC2H 8JG
☎020 7437 9011   Fax 020 7859 8670
✉ heat@emap.com
Owner *Emap Entertainment*
Editor *Mark Frith*
Circulation 575,267

Founded January 1999. WEEKLY entertainment magazine dealing with TV, film and radio information, fashion and features, with an emphasis on celebrity interviews and news. Targets 18 to 40-year-old readership, male and female. Articles written both in-house and by trusted freelancers. No unsolicited mss.

Hello!

Wellington House, 69–71 Upper Ground, London SE1 9PQ
☎020 7667 8700   Fax 020 7667 8716
www.hellomagazine.com
Owner *Hola! (Spain)*
Editor *Ronnie Whelan*
Commissioning Editor *Linda Newman*
Circulation 390,622

WEEKLY. Owned by a Madrid-based publishing family, *Hello!* has grown faster than any other British magazine since its launch here in 1988. The magazine has editorial offices both in Madrid and London. Major colour features plus regular news pages. Although much of the material is provided by regulars, good proposals do stand a chance. Approach the commissioning editor with ideas in the first instance. No unsolicited mss.

FEATURES Interested in celebrity-based features, with a newsy angle, and exclusive interviews from generally unapproachable personalities. PAYMENT by arrangement.

Hi-Fi News

IPC Media Ltd, Leon House, 233 High Street, Croydon CR9 1HZ
☎020 8726 8000   Fax 020 8726 8397
✉ hi-finews@ipcmedia.com
Owner *IPC Media (A Time Warner Company)*
Editor *Steve Fairclough*
Circulation 17,211

Founded 1956. MONTHLY. Write in the first instance with suggestions based on knowledge of the magazine's style and subject. All articles must be written from an informed technical or enthusiast viewpoint. PAYMENT negotiable, according to technical content.

High Life

37–43 Sackville Street, London W1S 3EH
☎020 7534 2400   Fax 020 7534 2555
✉ high.life@cedarcom.co.uk
www.cedarcom.co.uk
Owner *Cedar Communications*
Editor *Kerry Smith*
Circulation 216,946

Founded 1973. MONTHLY glossy. British Airways in-flight magazine. Almost all the content is commissioned. No unsolicited mss. Few opportunities for freelancers.

History Today

20 Old Compton Street, London W1D 4TW
☎020 7534 8000
✉ p.furtado@historytoday.com
www.historytoday.com
Owner *History Today Trust for the Advancement of Education*
Editor *Peter Furtado*
Circulation 27,070

Founded 1951. MONTHLY. General history and archaeology worldwide, history behind the headlines. Serious submissions only; no 'jokey' material. Approach by post only with s.a.e.

Home & Country

See **W.I. Life**

Home & Family

Mary Sumner House, 24 Tufton Street, London SW1P 3RB
☎020 7222 5533   Fax 020 7222 1591
Owner *MU Enterprises Ltd*
Editor *Jill Worth*
Circulation 54,450

Founded 1976. QUARTERLY. Unsolicited mss considered. No fiction or poetry. Features on family life, social problems, marriage, Christian faith, etc. Max. 1000 words. PAYMENT 'modest'.

Homes & Gardens

IPC Media Ltd., King's Reach Tower, Stamford Street, London SE1 9LS
☎020 7261 5000   Fax 020 7261 6247
www.homesand gardens.com
Owner *IPC Media (A Time Warner Company)*
Editor *Deborah Barker*
Circulation 136,088

Founded 1919. MONTHLY. Almost all published articles are specially commissioned. No fiction or poetry. Best to approach in writing with an idea, enclosing snapshots if appropriate.

Horse

Room 2914, IPC Country & Leisure Media Ltd, King's Reach Tower, Stamford Street, London SE1 9LS
☎020 7261 7969 Fax 020 7261 7979
✉ joanna_pyatt@ipcmedia.com
www.ipcmedia.com
Owner *IPC Media (A Time Warner Company)*
Editor *Jo Pyatt*
Circulation 24,302

Founded 1997. MONTHLY magazine aimed at dedicated leisure riders and keen competitors who are committed to improving their riding skills and horsecare knowledge. Also features veterinary developments and interviews with leading equestrian celebrities. Send feature ideas with a short synopsis to the editor.

Horse and Hound

IPC Media Ltd., King's Reach Tower, Stamford Street, London SE1 9LS
☎020 7261 6315 Fax 020 7261 5429
✉ jenny_sims@ipcmedia.com
www.horseandhound.co.uk
Owner *IPC Media (A Time Warner Company)*
Editor *Lucy Higginson*
Circulation 71,128

Founded 1884. WEEKLY. The oldest equestrian magazine on the market. Contains regular veterinary advice and instructional articles, as well as authoritative news and comment on fox hunting, international and national showjumping, horse trials, dressage, driving and endurance riding. Also weekly racing and point-to-points, breeding reports and articles. Regular books and art reviews, and humorous articles and cartoons are frequently published. Plenty of opportunities for freelancers. Unsolicited contributions welcome.

Also publishes a sister monthly publication, *Eventing*, which covers the sport of horse trials comprehensively; Editor *Julie Harding*.
PAYMENT NUJ rates.

Horse and Rider

Headley House, Headley Road, Grayshott GU26 6TU
☎01428 601020 Fax 01428 601030
✉ djm@djmurphy.co.uk
www.horseandridermagazine.co.uk
Owner *D.J. Murphy (Publishers) Ltd*

Editor *Alison Bridge*
Assistant Editor *Nicky Moffatt*
Circulation 46,000
Founded 1949. MONTHLY. Adult readership, largely horse-owning. News and instructional features, which make up the bulk of the magazine, are almost all written in-house or commissioned. New contributors and unsolicited articles are occasionally used. Approach the editor in writing with ideas.

Hotline

The River Group, Victory House, Leicester Square, London WC2H 7BZ
☎020 7306 0304
✉ arayner@riverltd.co.uk
Editor *Alex Rayner*
Circulation 179,669
Founded 1997. QUARTERLY on-board magazine for Virgin trains. UK celebrity and travel-based features. Ideas and outlines welcome by post or e-mail.

House & Garden

Vogue House, Hanover Square, London W1S 1JU
☎020 7499 9080 Fax 020 7629 2907
www.houseandgarden.co.uk
Owner *Condé Nast Publications Ltd*
Editor *Susan Crewe*
Circulation 140,361
Founded 1947. MONTHLY. Most feature material is produced in-house but occasional specialist features are commissioned from qualified freelancers, mainly for the interiors, wine and food sections and travel.

FEATURES *Liz Elliot* Suggestions for features, preferably in the form of brief outlines of proposed subjects, will be considered.

House Beautiful

National Magazine House, 72 Broadwick Street, London W1F 9EP
☎020 7439 5000 Fax 020 7439 5141
Owner *National Magazine Co. Ltd*
Editor *Julia Goodwin*
Circulation 198,112
Founded 1989 and relaunched in November 2003. MONTHLY. Lively magazine offering sound, practical information and plenty of inspiration for those who want to make the most of where they live. Over 100 pages of easy-reading editorial. Regular features about decoration, DIY, food, gardening and occasionally property, plus topical features with a newsy

slant to fit the 'Hot Topics' slot. Approach in writing with synopses in the first instance including a brief outline of areas of specialism and examples of previously published articles in a similar vein.

i-D Magazine
124 Tabernacle Street, London EC2A 4SA
☎020 7490 9710 Fax 020 7251 2225
✉ editor@i-dmagazine.co.uk
www.i-dmagazine.com

Owner *Levelprint*
Editor *Glenn Waldron*
Circulation 68,304

Founded 1980. MONTHLY lifestyle magazine for both sexes with a fashion bias. International. Very hip. Does not accept unsolicited contributions but welcomes new ideas from the fields of fashion, music, clubs, art, film, technology, books, sport, etc. No fiction or poetry. 'We are always looking for freelance non-fiction writers with new or unusual ideas.' A different theme each issue – past themes have included Green politics, taste, films, sex, love and loud dance music – means it is advisable to discuss feature ideas in the first instance.

Ideal Home
IPC Media Ltd., King's Reach Tower, Stamford Street, London SE1 9LS
☎020 7261 6474 Fax 020 7261 6697

Owner *IPC Media (A Time Warner Company)*
Editor *Susan Rose*
Circulation 245,729

Founded 1920. MONTHLY glossy. Unsolicited feature ideas are welcome only if appropriate to the magazine. Prospective contributors wishing to submit ideas should do so in writing to the editor. No fiction.

FEATURES Furnishing and decoration of houses, kitchens or bathrooms; interior design, soft furnishings, furniture and home improvements, lifestyle, consumer, gardening, property, food and readers' homes. Length to be discussed with editor.
PAYMENT negotiable.

Image Magazine
Upper Mounts, Northampton NN1 3HR
☎01604 467000 Fax 01604 467190
✉ image@northantsnews.co.uk
www.northantsnews.com

Owner *Northamptonshire Newspapers Ltd*
Editor *Ruth Supple*
Circulation 12,000

Founded 1905. MONTHLY general interest regional magazine. No unsolicited mss.

FEATURES Local issues, personalities, businesses, etc., of Northamptonshire, Bedfordshire, Buckinghamshire interest. Max. 500 words.
NEWS No hard news as such, just monthly diary column.
OTHER Regulars on motoring, fashion, beauty, lifestyle, travel and horoscopes. Max. 500 words.
PAYMENT for features negotiable.

In Britain
Jubilee House, 2 Jubilee Place, London SW3 3TQ
☎020 7751 4800 Fax 020 7751 4848
✉ inbritain@archant.co.uk

Editor *Andrea Spain*
Circulation 40,000

Founded in the 1930s. BI-MONTHLY. Travel magazine of 'VisitBritain'. Not much opportunity for unsolicited work – approach (by e-mail) with ideas and samples. Words and picture packages preferred (good quality transparencies only).

Independent Magazine
See **The Independent** under *National Newspapers*

Inspire
CPO, Garcia Estate, Canterbury Road, Worthing BN13 1BW
☎01903 821082 Fax 01903 821081
✉ russbravo@cpo.org.uk
www.inspiremagazine.org.uk

Owner *Christian Publishing & Outreach Ltd*
Editor *Russ Bravo*
Circulation 50,000

MONTHLY. Upbeat, good news Christian magazine featuring human interest stories, growing churches and community transformation. Limited freelance articles used. Contributor's guidelines available.

InStyle
IPC Media Ltd., 12th Floor, Kings Reach Tower, Stamford Street, London SE1 9LS
☎020 7261 5000 Fax 020 7261 6664
✉ firstname_lastname@instyleuk.com

Owner *IPC Media (A Time Warner Company)*
Senior Editor *Kate O'Donnell*
Editor *To be appointed*
Deputy Editor *Kate Bussmann*
Executive Fashion & Beauty Director *Sophie Hedley*
Fashion Director *Tamasin Doe*

Circulation 196,857

Launched March 2001. MONTHLY. UK edition of US fashion, beauty, celebrity and lifestyle magazine. Unsolicited material welcome; send by e-mail to individual editors.

Interlude

Limehouse Town Hall, 646 Commercial Road, London E14 7HA
☎020 8673 2256
✉ info@interludemagazine.co.uk
www.interludemagazine.co.uk

Editors *Helen Nodding, Becky Philip, Francesca Ricci*

Launched 2005. QUARTERLY magazine for writing and visual work with a focus on multi-disciplinary projects and 'work in progress'. Pages are formatted and illustrated by the author. Unsolicited contributions welcome by e-mail, particularly experimental writing (max. 2500 words); no extracts from published books. See website for submission guidelines.

Interzone: Science Fiction & Fantasy

TTA Press, 5 Martins Lane, Witcham, Ely CB6 2LB
✉ andy@ttapress.demon.co.uk
www.ttapress.com
Owner *TTA Press*
Editor *Andy Cox*
Circulation 10,000

Founded 1982. BI-MONTHLY magazine of science fiction and fantasy. Unsolicited mss are welcome 'from writers who have a knowledge of the magazine and its contents'. S.a.e. essential for return.

FICTION 2000–6000 words.

FEATURES Book/film reviews, interviews with writers and occasional short articles. Length by arrangement.

PAYMENT fiction, £30 per 1000 words; features, negotiable.

Investors Chronicle

Tabernacle Court, 16–28 Tabernacle Street, London EC2A 4DD
☎020 7382 8607 Fax 020 7382 8105
www.investorschronicle.co.uk
Owner *Pearson*
Editor *Matthew Vincent*
Deputy Editor *Rosie Carr*
Circulation 40,096

Founded 1860. WEEKLY. Opportunities for freelance contributors in the survey section

only. All approaches should be made in writing. Over forty surveys are published each year on a wide variety of subjects, generally with a financial, business or investment emphasis. Copies of survey list and synopses of individual surveys are obtainable from the surveys editor.

PAYMENT negotiable.

The Irish Book Review

Ashbrook House, 10 Main Street, Raheny, Dublin 5 Republic of Ireland
☎00 353 1 851 1459
✉ editor@irishbookreview.com
www.irishbookreview.com
Editor *Eugene O'Brien*
Publisher *David Givens*
Managing Editor *Brian Langan*

Founded 2005. QUARTERLY. Reviews books of Irish interest and/or by Irish authors. Also publishes features, extracts, articles relating to Irish books, publishing and the book trade. 'Would like to hear from potential reviewers/writers.'

Irish Pages

The Linen Hall Library, 17 Donegall Square North, Belfast BT1 5GB
✉ irishpages@yahoo.co.uk
www.irishpages.org
Editor *Chris Agee*
Circulation 1400

Founded 2002. BIANNUAL non-partisan, non-sectarian journal publishing writing from Ireland and abroad. 'The most important cultural journal in Ireland at the present moment' (Jonathan Allison, Director of the Yeats Summer School).

FEATURES Poetry, short fiction, essays, non-fiction, memoirs, nature-writing, translated work, literary journalism and other autobiographical, historical and scientific writing of literary distinction. Irish language and Ulster Scots writing are published in the original, with English translations. Equal editorial attention is given to established, emergent and new writers. Send submissions to the editor by post.

IRRV Valuer

IRRV, 41 Doughty Street, London WC1N 2LF
☎01992 505529 Fax 01992 505547
✉ katemiller@globalnet.co.uk
www.irrv.org.uk
Owner *Institute of Revenues, Rating and Valuation*
Managing Editor *Kate Miller*
Circulation 1322

Founded 2001. FOUR issues yearly for property valuation professionals. Well-qualified commentary, analysis and news covering issues affecting valuers, including reforms, legislation and technology. Small amount of appropriate lifestyle coverage. No unsolicited material; approach by telephone, fax, letter or e-mail in the first instance.
FEATURES Ideas for stories must be well sourced and informed. Max. 1000 words.
NEWS Stories relevant to property professionals. Max. 300 words.
PAYMENT negotiable.

It's Hot! Magazine
Rm A1136, BBC Worldwide, Woodlands, 80 Wood Lane, London W12 0TT
☎020 8433 3910 Fax 020 8433 2763
✉ itshotmail@bbc.co.uk
Owner *BBC Worldwide Publishing Ltd*
Editor *Rosalie Snaith*
Deputy Editor *Shelley Moulden*
Circulation 70,000

Founded 2002. MONTHLY magazine aimed at celebrity-mad 9–13 year old girls featuring music, film & TV gossip. Interested in exclusive celebrity interviews relevant to their market, and quizzes. Approach the deputy editor with ideas by e-mail (shelley.moulden@bbc.co.uk) but 'please read the magazine first for style'. PAYMENT negotiable.

Jade
PO Box 202, Scarborough YO11 3GE
☎01723 581329 Fax 01723 581329
✉ books@greatnorthernpublishing.co.uk
www.greatnorthernpublishing.co.uk
Owner *Great Northern Publishing*
Editor *Mark Marsay*

Founded 2002. BI-MONTHLY uncensored, adult subscription-only magazine in A5 format. Official magazine of the Guild of Erotic Artists. Features new and established international photographers, artists, sculptors and writers in all erotic genres from around the world. No editorial articles, features or advice columns. Contributors (photographers, artists, sculptors and writers) should consult the website for submission guidelines and current requirements; contact the editor prior to sending material. Sample copy £5 (contains strong adult content).

Jane's Defence Weekly
Sentinel House, 163 Brighton Road, Coulsdon CR5 2YH
☎020 8700 3700 Fax 020 8763 1007

✉ jdw@janes.com
www.janes.com
Owner *Jane's*
Editor *Peter Felstead*
Circulation 25,500

Founded 1984. WEEKLY. No unsolicited mss. Approach in writing with ideas in the first instance.
FEATURES Current defence topics of worldwide interest. No history pieces. Most features are commissioned. Max. 4000 words.

Jazz Journal International
3 & 3A Forest Road, Loughton IG10 1DR
☎020 8532 0456/0678 Fax 020 8532 0440
Owner *Jazz Journal Ltd*
Editor *Janet Cook*
Circulation 8000+

Founded 1948. MONTHLY. A specialised jazz magazine, for record collectors, principally using expert contributors whose work is known to the editor. Unsolicited mss not welcome, with the exception of news material (for which no payment is made). It is not a gig guide, nor a free reference source for students.

Jersey Now
PO Box 582, Five Oaks, St Saviour JE4 8XQ
☎01534 611743 Fax 01534 611610
✉ mspeditorial@msppublishing.com
Owner *MSP Publishing*
Managing Editor *Peter Body*
Circulation 24,000

Founded 1987. QUARTERLY lifestyle magazine for Jersey covering homes, gardens, the arts, Jersey heritage, motoring, boating, fashion, beauty, food and drink, health, travel and technology. Upmarket glossy aimed at an informed and discerning readership. Interested in Jersey-orientated articles only; 1200 words max. Approach the editor initially. PAYMENT negotiable.

Jewish Chronicle
25 Furnival Street, London EC4A 1JT
☎020 7415 1500 Fax 020 7405 9040
✉ editorial@thejc.com
www.thejc.com
Owner *Kessler Foundation*
Editor *David Rowan*
Circulation 35,427

WEEKLY. Unsolicited mss welcome if 'the specific interests of our readership are borne in mind by writers'. Approach in writing, except for urgent current news items. No fiction. Max. 1500 words for all material.

FEATURES *Gerald Jacobs*
LEISURE/LIFESTYLE *Alan Montague*
HOME NEWS *Barry Toberman*
FOREIGN NEWS *Joe Millis*
SUPPLEMENTS *Angela Kiverstein*
PAYMENT negotiable.

Jewish Quarterly

PO Box 37645, London NW7 1WB
☎020 8343 4675 Fax 020 8343 4675
✉ editor@jewquart.freeserve.co.uk
www.jewishquarterly.org

Publisher *Jewish Literary Trust Ltd*
Editor *Matthew Reisz*

Founded 1953. QUARTERLY illustrated magazine featuring Jewish literature and fiction, politics, art, music, film, poetry, history, dance, community, autobiography, Hebrew, Yiddish, Israel and the Middle East, Judaism, interviews, Zionism, philosophy and holocaust studies. Features a major books and arts section. Unsolicited mss welcome but letter or phone call preferred in first instance.

Jewish Telegraph Group of Newspapers

Telegraph House, 11 Park Hill, Bury Old Road, Prestwich, Manchester M25 0HH
☎0161 740 9321 Fax 0161 740 9325
✉ editor@jewishtelegraph.com
www.jewishtelegraph.com

Editor *Paul Harris* (☎0161 741 2633)
Circulation 16,000

Founded 1950. WEEKLY publication with local, national and international news and features. (Separate editions published for Manchester, Leeds, Liverpool and Glasgow.) Unsolicited features on Jewish humour and history welcome.

The Journal Magazines (Norfolk, Suffolk, Cambridgeshire)/The Essex Magazine

Cambridge Newspapers Ltd, Winship Road, Milton CB4 6PP
☎01223 434409 Fax 01223 434415

Owner *Cambridge Newspapers Ltd*
Editor *Debbie Tweedie*
Circulation 12,000 each

Founded 1990. MONTHLY magazines covering items of local interest – history, people, conservation, business, places, food and wine, fashion, homes and sport.

FEATURES 750–1500 words max., plus pictures. Approach the editor with ideas in the first instance.

Journal of Apicultural Research (including Bee World)

IBRA, 18 North Road, Cardiff CF10 3DT
☎029 2037 2409 Fax 029 2066 5522
✉ mail@ibra.org.uk
www.ibra.org.uk

Owner *International Bee Research Association*
Editor *Professor Keith Delaplane*
Circulation 1700

Bee World, founded 1919; Journal of Apicultural Research, 1962. QUARTERLY. High-quality factual journal, including peer-reviewed articles, with international readership. Features on apicultural science and technology. Unsolicited mss welcome but authors should write to the editor for guidelines before submitting material.

Kerrang!

Mappin House, 4 Winsley Street, London W1W 8HR
☎020 7182 8000 Fax 020 7182 8910
www.kerrang.com

Owner *Emap Performance*
Editor *Paul Brannigan*
Circulation 76,165

Founded 1980. WEEKLY rock, punk and metal magazine. 'Written by fans for fans.' Will consider ideas for features but not actively seeking new contributors unless expert in specialist fields such as black metal and hardcore, emo, etc.

The Lady

39–40 Bedford Street, London WC2E 9ER
☎020 7379 4717 Fax 020 7836 4620

Editor *Arline Usden*
Circulation 33,107

Founded 1885. WEEKLY. Unsolicited mss are accepted provided they are not on the subject of politics or religion, or on topics covered by staff writers or special correspondents, i.e. fashion and beauty, health, cookery, household, gardening, finance and shopping.

FEATURES Well-researched pieces on British and foreign travel, historical subjects or events; interviews and profiles and other general interest topics. Max. 1200 words for illustrated two-page articles; 900 words for one-page features; 430 words for first-person 'Viewpoint' pieces. All material should be addressed to the editor with s.a.e. enclosed. Photographs supporting features may be supplied as colour transparencies, b&w prints or on disk. Telephone enquiries about features are not encouraged.

Land Rover World

IPC Media Ltd, Leon House, 233 High Street, Croydon CR9 1HZ
☎020 8726 8371 Fax 020 8726 8398
✉ landroverworld@ipcmedia.co.uk
www.landroverworld.co.uk
Owner *IPC Media (A Time Warner Company)*
Editor *John Carroll*
Circulation 30,000

Founded 1994. MONTHLY. Incorporates *Practical Land Rover World* and *Classic Land Rover World*. Unsolicited material welcome, especially if supported by high-quality illustrations.
FEATURES All articles with a Land Rover theme of interest. Potential contributors are strongly advised to examine previous issues before starting work.
PAYMENT negotiable.

Let's Talk

Archant Norfolk, Prospect House, Rouen Road, Norwich NR1 1RE
☎01603 772455
✉ letstalk@archant.co.uk
Owner *Archant Regional*
Editor *Cathy Brown*
Circulation 30,000

Launched 2002. MONTHLY. Norfolk's biggest selling consumer magazine, aimed at the over-50s. Topical features, nostalgia, fiction and puzzles.
FEATURES 'Suggestions always welcome', particularly profiles of older people doing extraordinary things – adventurous hobbies, new businesses, community involvement, etc. No poetry or articles emphasising the problems of growing older. Max. 1500 words.
FICTION Short stories for the monthly magazine and seasonal fiction specials. All styles considered; regional themes preferred. Approach by letter or e-mail. Max. 1500 words.
PAYMENT From £50 upwards.

LG

Upper Mounts, Northampton NN1 3HR
☎01604 467043 Fax 01604 467190
Owner *Northamptonshire Newspapers Ltd*
Editor *Ruth Supple*
Circulation 10,000

Formerly *Looking Good*, founded 1984. Relaunched in 2002 as *LG*, a MONTHLY magazine aimed at women aged 18–30. Fashion and beauty, lifestyle, true life stories. Contributions

occasionally considered but majority of work is done in-house.

Lincolnshire Life

County Life Ltd, PO Box 81, Lincoln LN1 1HD
☎01522 527127 Fax 01522 560035
✉ editorial@lincolnshirelife.co.uk
www.lincolnshirelife.co.uk
Publisher *A.L. Robinson*
Executive Editor *Judy Theobald*
Circulation 10,000

Founded 1961. MONTHLY county magazine featuring geographically relevant articles on local culture, history, personalities, etc. Max. 1500 words. Contributions supported by three or four good-quality photographs welcome. Approach in writing. PAYMENT varies.

The Lincolnshire Poacher

County Life Ltd, PO Box 81, Lincoln LN1 1HD
☎01522 527127 Fax 01522 560035
✉ editorial@lincolnshirelife.co.uk
www.lincolnshirelife.co.uk
Publisher *C. Bingham*
Executive Editor *Judy Theobald*
Circulation 5000

QUARTERLY county magazine featuring geographically relevant but nostalgic articles on history, culture and personalities of Lincolnshire. Max. 2000 words. Contributions supported by three or four good-quality photographs/ illustrations appreciated. Approach in writing. PAYMENT varies.

The List

14 High Street, Edinburgh EH1 1TE
☎0131 558 1191 Fax 0131 550 3050
✉ editor@list.co.uk
www.list.co.uk
Owner *The List Ltd*
Publisher *Robin Hodge*
Editor *Nick Barley*
Circulation 17,500

Founded 1985. FORTNIGHTLY. Events guide covering Glasgow and Edinburgh. Interviews and profiles of people working in film, theatre, music and the arts. Max. 1200 words. No unsolicited mss. News material tends to be handled in-house.

Literary Review

44 Lexington Street, London W1F 0LW
☎020 7437 9392 Fax 020 7734 1844
✉ editorial@literaryreview.co.uk

www.literaryreview.co.uk
Editor *Nancy Sladek*
Circulation 15,000
Founded 1979. MONTHLY. Publishes book reviews (commissioned), features and articles on literary subjects. Prospective contributors are best advised to contact the editor in writing. Unsolicited mss not welcome. Runs a monthly competition for 'poems which rhyme, scan and make sense'.
PAYMENT 'minuscule'.

Living France Magazine
Archant House, Oriel Road, Cheltenham GL50 1BB
☎01242 216050 Fax 01242 216074
✉ editorial@livingfrance.com
www.livingfrance.com
Owner *Archant Life*
Editor *Lucy-Jane Cypher*
Founded 1989. MONTHLY. A magazine for people who are considering or actively purchasing a home in France. Editorial consists of practical, friendly information and advice on becoming an owner of French property. Will consider articles describing different regions of France, interviews with owners of property and aspects of living in France. Interested in hearing from professional writers who could do interviews. No unsolicited mss; approach in writing or by e-mail with an idea.

Living History
See **BBC History Magazine**

Loaded
IPC Media Ltd., King's Reach Tower, Stamford Street, London SE1 9LS
☎020 7261 5562 Fax 020 7261 5557
✉ andy_sherwood@ipcmedia.com
Owner *IPC Media (A Time Warner Company)*
Editor *Martin Daubney*
Features Editor *Andy Sherwood*
Circulation 232,001
Founded 1994. MONTHLY men's lifestyle magazine featuring music, sport, sex, humour, travel, fashion, hard news and popular culture. Will consider material which comes into these categories; approach the features editor in writing or by e-mail in the first instance. No fiction or poetry.

Logos
5 Beechwood Drive, Marlow SL7 2DH
☎01628 433871 Fax 01628 477577
✉ logos-marlow@dial.pipex.com

www.logos-journal.org
Owner *LOGOS International Educational Publishing Foundation*
Editor (New York) *Charles M. Levine* (Charlev@Nyc.rr.com)
Editor Emeritus *Gordon Graham* (Marlow address)
Business Manager *Betty Graham* (Marlow address)
Founded 1990. QUARTERLY. Aims to 'deal in depth with issues which unite, divide, excite and concern the world of books', with an international perspective. Each issue contains six to eight articles of between 3500 and 7000 words. 'Logos is a non-profit making professional forum, not a scholarly journal.' Suggestions and ideas for contributions are welcome, and should be addressed to the editor. 'Guidelines for Contributors' available. Contributors write from their experience as authors, publishers, booksellers, librarians, etc.
PAYMENT Contributors receive off-prints, a copy of the issue in which their article appears and a 50% concession on the subscription rate.

The London Magazine
Editorial office: 70 Wargrave Road, London N15 6UB
☎020 8400 5882 (Admin. office)
Fax 020 8994 1713
✉ admin@thelondonmagazine.net
www.londonmagazine.net
Publisher *Christopher Arkell*
Editor *Sebastian Barker*
Circulation 1200
Founded originally in 1732 and relaunched in 2002. BI-MONTHLY review of literature and the arts. Publishes poems, short stories, features, memoirs, and book and performance reviews. Not interested in overtly political material. Do *not* send anything by e-mail or fax. No phone-calls. All submissions should be made by post with an s.a.e. to the editorial office.
FEATURES Max. 6000 words.
FICTION Max. 6000 words.
POEMS 'Any length within reason.'
PAYMENT negotiable with the editor. Standard fees for most items.

London Review of Books
28 Little Russell Street, London WC1A 2HN
☎020 7209 1101 Fax 020 7209 1102
✉ edit@lrb.co.uk
www.lrb.co.uk
Owner *LRB Ltd*

Editor *Mary-Kay Wilmers*
Circulation 43,469
Founded 1979. FORTNIGHTLY. Reviews, essays and articles on political, literary, cultural and scientific subjects. Also poetry. Unsolicited contributions welcome (approximately 50 received each week). No pieces under 2000 words. Contact the editor in writing. Please include s.a.e.
PAYMENT £200 per 1000 words; poems, £125.

Looking Good
See **LG**

Lothian Life
Ballencrieff Cottage, Ballencrieff Toll, Bathgate EH48 4LD
☎01506 632728
✉ editor@lothianlife.co.uk
www.lothianlife.co.uk
Owner *Pages Editorial & Publishing Services*
Editor *Susan Coon*
QUARTERLY county magazine for people who live, work or have an interest in the Lothians. Twelve features on successful people, businesses or initiatives. A local walk takes up the centre spread. Regular articles by experts in the Lifestyle section including Homes & Gardens, Tastebuds, Out & About, The Arts and Health & Fitness. Freelance writers used only for main features. Phone first to discuss content and timing.
PAYMENT by arrangement.

Machine Knitting Monthly
PO Box 1479, Maidenhead SL6 8YX
☎01628 783080 Fax 01628 633250
✉ mail@machineknittingmonthly.net
www.machineknittingmonthly.net
Owner *RPA Publishing Ltd*
Editor *Anne Smith*
Founded 1986. MONTHLY. Unsolicited mss considered 'as long as they are applicable to this specialist publication. We have our own regular contributors each month but we're always willing to look at new ideas from other writers.' Approach in writing in the first instance.

MacUser
30 Cleveland Street, London W1T 4JD
☎020 7907 6000
✉ mailbox@macuser.co.uk
www.macuser.co.uk
Owner *Dennis Publishing*
Editor *Nik Rawlinson*

Circulation 18,906
Launched 1985. FORTNIGHTLY computer magazine.

Management Today
174 Hammersmith Road, London W6 7JP
☎020 8267 5000
✉ management.today@haynet.com
Owner *Haymarket Business Publications Ltd*
Managing Director *Nick Simpson*
Editor *Matthew Gwyther*
Circulation 99,198
General business topics and features. Ideas welcome. Send brief synopsis to the features editor.

marie claire
13th Floor, King's Reach Tower, Stamford Street, London SE1 9LS
☎020 7261 5240 Fax 020 7261 5277
✉ marieclaire@ipcmedia.com
www.ipcmedia.com
Owner *European Magazines Ltd*
Editor *Marie O'Riordan*
Circulation 371,444
Founded 1988. MONTHLY. An intelligent glossy magazine for women, with strong international features and fashion. No unsolicited mss. Approach with ideas in writing or by e-mail (marieclaireideas@ipcmedia.com). No fiction.
FEATURES *Charlotte Moore* Detailed proposals for feature ideas should be accompanied by samples of previous work.

Marketing Week
St Giles House, 50 Poland Street, London W1F 7AX
☎020 7970 4000 Fax 020 7970 6721
✉ mw.editorial@centaur.co.uk
www.mad.co.uk/publication/mw/
Owner *Centaur Communications*
Editor *Stuart Smith*
Circulation 38,171
WEEKLY trade magazine of the marketing industry. Features on all aspects of the business, written in a newsy and up-to-the-minute style. Approach with ideas in the first instance.
FEATURES *Daney Parker*
PAYMENT negotiable.

Match
Bushfield House, Orton Centre, Peterborough PE2 5UW
☎01733 237111 Fax 01733 288150
✉ match.magazine@emap.com
www.matchmag.co.uk

Owner *Emap Active Ltd*
Editor *Ian Foster*
Circulation 117,844

Founded 1979. WEEKLY. The UK's biggest-selling football magazine aimed at 10–15-year-olds. All material is generated in-house by a strong news and features team. Work experience placements often given to trainee journalists and students; the majority of staff are recruited through this route. Approach in writing or by phone.

Matrix

See **British Science Fiction Association** under *Professional Associations and Societies*

Maxim

30 Cleveland Street, London W1T 4JD
☎020 7907 6410 Fax 020 7907 6439
✉ editorial.maxim@dennis.co.uk
Owner *Dennis Publishing*
Editor *To be appointed*
Acting Editor *Eoin McSorley*
Circulation 190,438

Established 1995. MONTHLY glossy men's lifestyle magazine featuring sex, travel, health, motoring and fashion. No fiction or poetry. Approach in writing in the first instance, sending outlines of ideas only together with examples of published work.

Mayfair

2 Archer Street, Piccadilly Circus, London W1D 7AW
☎020 7292 8000 Fax 020 7734 5030
✉ mayfair@paulraymond.com
www.sexclub.co.uk
Owner *Paul Raymond Publications*
Editor *David Ryder*
Circulation 331,760

Founded 1966. THIRTEEN ISSUES YEARLY. Unsolicited material accepted if pertinent to the magazine and if accompanied by suitable illustrative material. 'We will *only* publish work if we can illustrate it.' Interested in features and humour aimed at men aged 18 to 80; 800–1000 words. Punchy, bite-sized humour, top ten features, etc. 'Must make the editor laugh.' Also considers erotica.

Mayfair Times

1 Blandel Bridge House, 56 Sloane Square, London SW1W 8AX
☎020 7259 1050 Fax 020 7901 9042
✉ erik.brown@pubbiz.com
www.pubbiz.com

Owner *Publishing Business Ltd*
Editor *Erik Brown*
Circulation 17,000

Founded 1985. MONTHLY. Features on Mayfair of interest to residents, local workers, visitors and shoppers.

Medal News

Orchard House, Duchy Road, Heathpark, Honiton EX14 1YD
☎01404 46972 Fax 01404 44788
✉ info@tokenpublishing.com
www.tokenpublishing.com
Owners *J.W. Mussell, Carol Hartman*
Editor *J.W. Mussell*
Circulation 5,500

Founded 1989. TEN ISSUES YEARLY. Unsolicited material welcome but initial approach by phone or in writing preferred.
FEATURES 'Opportunities exist for well-informed authors who know the subject and do their homework.' Max. 2500 words.
PAYMENT £30 per 1000 words.

Media Week

Griffin House, 161 Hammersmith Road, London W6 8BS
☎020 8267 5000 Fax 020 8267 8020
✉ firstname.surname@haynet.co.uk
www.mediaweek.co.uk
Owner *Haymarket Publishing Ltd*
Editor *Philip Smith*
Circulation 16,570

Founded 1986. WEEKLY trade magazine. UK and international coverage on all aspects of commercial media. Approach in writing with ideas. See website for e-mail addresses.

Melody Maker

See **New Musical Express**

Men's Health

National Magazine House, 72 Broadwick Street, London W1F 9EP
☎020 7339 4400 Fax 020 7339 4444
www.menshealth.co.uk
Owner *Natmag-Rodale Publishing*
Editor *Morgan Rees*
Circulation 233,445

Founded 1994. MONTHLY men's healthy lifestyle magazine covering health, fitness, nutrition, stress and sex issues. No unsolicited mss; will consider ideas and synopses tailored to men's health. No fiction or extreme sports. Approach in writing in the first instance.

MiniWorld Magazine

IPC Media Ltd, Leon House, 233 High Street, Croydon CR9 1HZ
☎020 8726 8000   Fax 020 8726 8399
✉ miniworld@ipcmedia.com
www.miniworld.co.uk
Owner *IPC Media (A Time Warner Company)*
Editor *Monty Watkins*
Circulation 37,000

Founded 1991. MONTHLY car magazine devoted to the Mini. Unsolicited material welcome but prospective contributors are advised to contact the editor.

FEATURES Maintenance, tuning, restoration, technical advice, classified, sport, readers' cars and social history of this cult car.
PAYMENT negotiable.

Mizz

Panini UK, Panini House, Coach & Horses Passage, Tunbridge Wells TN2 5UJ
☎01892 500100   Fax 01892 545666
✉ mizz@panini.co.uk
Owner *Panini UK Ltd*
Editor *Leslie Sinoway*
Circulation 60,425

Founded 1985. FORTNIGHTLY magazine for the 10–14-year-old girl.

FEATURES 'We have a full features team and thus do not accept freelance features.'

Model Collector

IPC Focus Network, Leon House, 233 High Street, Croydon CR9 1HZ
☎020 8726 8000   Fax 020 8726 8299
✉ modelcollector@ipcmedia.com
www.modelcollector.com
Owner *AOL Time Warner/IPC Media*
Editor *Lindsey Amrani*
Circulation 12,923

Founded 1987. THIRTEEN ISSUES YEARLY Britain's best selling die cast magazine. From the latest models to classic 1930's Dinkys. Interested in historical articles about particular models or ranges and reviews of the latest products. Photographs welcome. Not interested in radio controlled models or model railways.

FEATURES Freelancers should contact the editor. Unsolicited material may be considered.
NEWS Trade news welcome. Call *Lindsey Armrani* (☎020 8726 8238) to discuss details.

Mojo

Mappin House, 4 Winsley Street, London W1W 8HF
☎020 7182 8616   Fax 020 7182 8596
✉ mojo@emap.com
www.mojo4music.com
Owner *Emap Performance*
Editor-in-Chief *Phil Alexander*
Circulation 120,530

Founded 1993. MONTHLY magazine containing features, reviews and news stories about all types of music and its influences. Receives about five mss per day. No poetry, think-pieces on dead rock stars or similar fan worship.

FEATURES Amateur writers discouraged except as providers of source material, contacts, etc.
NEWS All verifiable, relevant stories considered.
REVIEWS Write to Reviews Editor *Jenny Bulley* with relevant specimen material.
PAYMENT negotiable.

Moneywise

1st Floor, Dashwood House, 69 Old Broad Street, London EC2M 1QS
☎020 7382 4300   Fax 020 7374 4520
www.moneywise.co.uk
Owner *Capital Accumulation Services Ltd*
Editor *Emma-Lou Montgomery*
Circulation 47,183

Founded 1990. MONTHLY. No unsolicited mss; ideas welcome. Make initial approach in writing to Editorial Department (c.v. preferred).

More!

Endeavour House, 189 Shaftesbury Avenue, London WC2H 8JG
☎020 7208 3165   Fax 020 7208 3595
✉ emma.patterson@emap.com
www.moremagazine.co.uk
Owner *Emap élan Publications*
Editor *Donna Armstrong*
Editorial Enquiries *Emma Patterson*
Circulation 277,862

Founded 1988. FORTNIGHTLY women's magazine aimed at the working woman aged 18–25. Features on sex and relationships plus celebrity news, style and fashion. Most items are commissioned; approach features director with idea. Prospective contributors are strongly advised to study the magazine's style before submitting anything.

Mother and Baby

Greater London House, Hampstead Road, London NW1 7EJ
☎020 7347 1869   Fax 020 7347 1888
✉ mother&baby@emap.com

Owner *Emap Esprit*
Editor *Elena Dalrymple*
Circulation 73,456
Founded 1956. MONTHLY. Welcomes suggestions for feature ideas about pregnancy, newborn basics, practical babycare, baby development and childcare subjects. Approaches may be made by telephone, e-mail or in writing to the Features Editor *Lucy Dimbylow*.

Motor Boat & Yachting
IPC Media Limited, King's Reach Tower, Stamford Street, London SE1 9LS
☎020 7261 5333 Fax 020 7261 5030
✉ mby@ipcmedia.com
www.mby.com
Owner *Time Warner*
Editor *Hugo Andreae*
Technical Editor *David Marsh*
Circulation 16,967
Founded 1904. MONTHLY for those interested in motor boats and motor cruising.

FEATURES *Hugo Andreae* Cruising features and practical features especially welcome. Illustrations/photographs (colour) are just as important as text. Max. 3000 words.

NEWS *Rob Peake* Factual pieces. Max. 200 words.

PAYMENT features: from £100 per 1000 words or by arrangement; news: up to £50 per item.

Motor Caravan Magazine
IPC Media Ltd, Leon House, 233 High Street, Croydon CR9 1HZ
☎020 8726 8000
✉ helen_avery@ipcmedia.com
www.motorcaravanmagazine.co.uk
Owner *IPC Media (A Time Warner Company)*
Editor *Simon Collis*
Circulation 12,000
Founded 1986. MONTHLY magazine with ideas about where to go in your caravan, expert advice to keep trips fun and practical advice on vans and kit. Interested in features on touring, unusual motorhomes, and activities people pursue while out and about in their van. E-mail the editor with ideas. PAYMENT £60 a page.

Motor Cycle News
Media House, Lynchwood, Peterborough Business Park, Peterborough PE2 6EA
☎01733 468000 Fax 01733 468028
✉ MCN@emap.com
www.motorcylenews.com
Owner *Emap plc*

Editor *Marc Potter*
Circulation 135,017
Founded 1955. WEEKLY. Interested in short news stories and features on motorcyles and motorcycle racing. No race reports. Contact relevant desks direct.

Motorcaravan Motorhome Monthly (MMM)
PO Box 88, Tiverton EX16 7ZN
✉ mmmeditor@warnersgroup.co.uk
www.mmmonline.co.uk
Owner *Warners Group Publications Plc*
Editor *Mike Jago*
Circulation 34,803
Founded 1966. MONTHLY. 'There's no money in motorcaravan journalism but for those wishing to cut their first teeth ...' Unsolicited mss welcome if relevant, but ideas in writing preferred in first instance.

FEATURES Caravan site reports. Max. 500 words.

TRAVEL Motorcaravanning trips (home and overseas). Max. 2000 words.

NEWS Short news items for miscellaneous pages. Max. 200 words.

FICTION Must be motorcaravan–related and include artwork/photos if possible. Max. 2000 words.

SPECIAL PAGES DIY – modifications to motorcaravans. Max. 1500 words.

OWNER REPORTS Contributions welcome from motorcaravan owners. Contact the editor for requirements. Max. 2000 words.

PAYMENT varies.

Mountain Magic
27A High Street, Esher KT10 9RL
☎01372 468140 Fax 01372 470765
✉ info@goodholidayideas.com
Editor *John Hill*
Circulation 250,000

New QUARTERLY magazine covering mountain travel worldwide. No unsolicited material but approach in writing or by e-mail with ideas and/or synopsis. PAYMENT negotiable.

Mslexia (For Women Who Write)
PO Box 656, Newcastle upon Tyne NE99 1PZ
☎0191 261 6656
✉ postbag@mslexia.demon.co.uk
www.mslexia.co.uk
Owner *Mslexia Publications Limited*
Editor *To be appointed*
Circulation 10,000

Founded 1997. QUARTERLY. Articles, advice, reviews, interviews, events for women writers plus new poetry and prose. Will consider fiction, poetry, features and letters but contributors *must* send for guidelines first.

Music Week

Ludgate House, 245 Blackfriars Road, London SE1 9UR
☎020 7921 5000 Fax 020 7921 8327
✉ mwletters@musicweek.com
www.musicweek.com

Owner *CMP Information*
Publisher *Ajax Scott*
Editor *Martin Talbot*
Group News Editor *Paul Williams*
Circulation 8,825

Britain's only WEEKLY music business magazine. Also produces a subscriber-only news and data website. Annual music industry contacts book – the *Music Week Directory*. Free Daily news e-mail. No unsolicited mss. Approach in writing with ideas.
FEATURES Analysis of specific music business events and trends.
NEWS Music industry news only.

Musical Opinion

2 Princes Road, St Leonards on Sea TN37 6EL
☎01424 715167 Fax 01424 712214
✉ musicalopinion2@aol.com
www.musicalopinion.com

Owner *Musical Opinion Ltd*
Editor *Denby Richards*
Circulation 8500

Founded 1877. Glossy, full-colour BI-MONTHLY magazine. Classical music content, with topical features on music, musicians, festivals, etc., and reviews (concerts, festivals, opera, ballet, jazz, CDs, DVDs, videos, books and printed music). International readership. No unsolicited mss; commissions only. Ideas always welcome though; approach by phone, fax or e-mail, giving telephone number. Visit the website for full information.
PAYMENT negotiable.

My Weekly

80 Kingsway East, Dundee DD4 8SL
☎01382 223131 Fax 01382 452491
✉ myweekly@dcthomson.co.uk
www.dcthomson.co.uk

Owner *D.C. Thomson & Co. Ltd*
Editor *Sally Hampton*

Deputy Editor *Fiona Brown*
(fbrown@dcthomson.co.uk)
Fiction Editor *Liz Smith*
(lsmith@dcthomson.co.uk)
Circulation 212,574

Weekly title aimed at women 55+. Mix of fiction, true-life stories, emotional features, fashion, food, craft, finance, gardening, travel. Ideas welcome. Approach in writing.
FEATURES Particularly interested in human interest pieces (1500 words approx.) which appeal to the 50-plus age-group.
FICTION Three stories a week, ranging in content from the emotional to the off-beat and unexpected. 1000–4000 words.
PAYMENT negotiable.

My Weekly Story Collection

D.C. Thomson & Co. Ltd, Albert Square, Dundee DD1 9QJ
☎020 7400 1030 Fax 020 7400 1089
✉ tsteele@dcthomson.co.uk

Owner *D.C. Thomson & Co. Ltd*
Editor *Tracey Steele*

MONTHLY. Publishes 25,000 – 30,000-word romantic stories aimed at the adult market. Send first three chapters and synopsis by mail.

The National Trust Magazine

Heelis, Kemble Drive, Swindon SN2 2NA
☎01793 817716 Fax 01793 817401
✉ magazine@nationaltrust.org.uk

Owner *The National Trust*
Editor *Sue Herdman*
Circulation 1.66 million

Founded 1968. THREE ISSUES YEARLY. Conservation of historic houses, coast and countryside in England, Northern Ireland and Wales. No unsolicited mss. Approach in writing with ideas.

The Naturalist

c/o University of Bradford, Bradford BD7 1DP
☎01274 234212 Fax 01274 234231
✉ m.r.d.seaward@bradford.ac.uk

Owner *Yorkshire Naturalists' Union*
Editor *Prof. M.R.D. Seaward*
Circulation 5000

Founded 1875. QUARTERLY. Natural history, biological and environmental sciences for a professional and amateur readership. Unsolicited mss and b&w illustrations welcome. Particularly interested in material – scientific papers – relating to the north of England. No PAYMENT.

Nature

The Macmillan Building, 4–6 Crinan Street,
London N1 9XW
☎020 7833 4000 Fax 020 7843 4596
✉ nature@nature.com
www.nature.com/nature
Owner *Nature Publishing Group*
Editor *Philip Campbell*
Circulation 65,000
Covers all fields of science, with articles and news on science and science policy only. Scope only for freelance writers with specialist knowledge in these areas.

NB

105 Judd Street, London WC1H 9NE
☎020 7388 1266
www.rnib.org.uk/nbmagazine
Owner *Royal National Institute of the Blind*
Editor *Ann Lee*
Circulation 5000
Founded 1917. MONTHLY (except August). Published in print, braille and on audio, disk and e-mail. Unsolicited mss accepted. Authoritative items by professionals or volunteers working in the field of sight loss welcome. Max. 1500 words.
PAYMENT negotiable.

New Beacon

See **NB**

New Humanist

1 Gower Street, London WC1E 6HD
☎020 7436 1151
✉ editor@newhumanist.org.uk
Owner *Rationalist Association*
Editor *Caspar Melville*
Circulation 5000
Founded 1885. BI-MONTHLY. Unsolicited mss welcome. No fiction.
FEATURES Articles with a humanist perspective welcome in the following fields: religion (critical), humanism, human rights, philosophy, current events, literature, history and science. 2000 words.
BOOK REVIEWS 750–1000 words, by arrangement with the editor.
PAYMENT for features is nominal, but negotiable.

New Internationalist

55 Rectory Road, Oxford OX4 1BW
☎01865 811400 Fax 01865 793152
✉ ni@newint.org

www.newint.org/
Owner *New Internationalist Trust*
Co-Editors *Vanessa Baird, David Ransom, Katharine Ainger, Adam Ma'anit*
Circulation 80,000
Radical and broadly leftist in approach, but unaligned. Concerned with world poverty and global issues of peace and politics, feminism and environmentalism, with emphasis on the Third World. Difficult to use unsolicited material as they work to a theme each month and features are commissioned by the editor on that basis. The way in is to send examples of published or unpublished work; writers of interest are taken up.

New Musical Express

IPC Media Ltd., King's Reach Tower,
Stamford Street, London SE1 9LS
☎020 7261 6472 Fax 020 7261 6022
www.nme.com
Owner *IPC Media (A Time Warner Company)*
Editor *Conor McNicholas*
Circulation 76,792
Britain's best-selling musical WEEKLY. Now incorporates *Melody Maker*. Freelancers used, but always for reviews in the first instance. Specialisation in areas of music (or film, which is also covered) is a help.
REVIEWS: LPs *Anthony Thornton*; LIVE *Pat Long*. Send in examples of work, either published or specially written samples.

New Nation

Unit 2, 65 Whitechapel Road, London
E1 1DU
☎020 7650 2000 Fax 020 7650 2004
www.newnation.co.uk
Owner *Ethnic Media Group*
Editor *Michael Eboda*
Circulation 21,630
Founded 1996. WEEKLY community paper for the black community in Britain. Interested in relevant general, local and international issues. Approach in writing with ideas for submission.

New Scientist

8th Floor, Lacon House, 84 Theobalds Road,
London WC1X 8NS
☎020 8652 3500 Fax 020 7611 1200 (News)
www.newscientist.com
Owner *Reed Business Information Ltd*
Editor *Jeremy Webb*
Circulation 163,724 (worldwide)

Founded 1956. WEEKLY. No unsolicited mss. Approach with ideas – one A4-page synopsis – by fax or e-mail.
FEATURES Commissions only, but good ideas welcome. Max. 3500 words.
NEWS *Matt Walker* Mostly commissions, but ideas for specialist news welcome. Max. 1000 words.
REVIEWS *Michael Bond* Reviews are commissioned.
OPINION *Michael Bond* Unsolicited material welcome if of general/humorous interest and related to science. Max. 1000 words.
PAYMENT negotiable.

The New Shetlander

Market House, 14 Market Street, Lerwick ZE1 0JP
☎01595 743902 Fax 01595 696787
✉ scss@shetland.org
www.shetlandcss.co.uk
Owner *Shetland Council of Social Service*
Editors *Brian Smith, Laureen Johnson*
Circulation 1400

Founded 1947. QUARTERLY literary magazine containing short stories, essays, poetry, historical articles, literary criticism, political comment, arts and books. The magazine has two editors and an editorial committee who all look at submitted material. Interested in considering short stories, poetry, historical articles with a northern Scottish or Scandinavian flavour, literary pieces and articles on Shetland. As a rough guide, items should be between 1000 and 2000 words although longer mss are considered. Initial approach in writing, please.
PAYMENT Complimentary copy.

New Statesman

3rd Floor, 52 Grosvenor Gardens, London SW1W 0AU
☎020 7730 3444 Fax 020 7259 0181
✉ info@newstatesman.co.uk
www.newstatesman.com
Publisher *Spencer Neal*
Editor *John Kampfner*
Deputy Editor *Sue Matthias*
Circulation 24,740

WEEKLY magazine, the result of a merger (1988) of *New Statesman* and *New Society*. Coverage of news, book reviews, arts, current affairs, politics and social reportage. Unsolicited contributions with s.a.e. will be considered. No short stories.
Arts Editor *Alice O'Keefe*
Books Editor *William Skidelsky*

New Theatre Quarterly

Oldstairs, Kingsdown, Deal CT14 8ES
☎01304 373448
✉ simontrussler@btinternet.com
www.uk.cambridge.org
Publisher *Cambridge University Press*
Editors *Simon Trussler, Maria Shevtsova*

Founded 1985 (originally launched in 1971 as *Theatre Quarterly*). Articles, interviews, documentation and reference material covering all aspects of live theatre. Recommend preliminary e-mail enquiry before sending contributions. No theatre reviews or anecdotal material.

New Welsh Review

PO Box 170, Aberystwyth SY23 1WZ
☎01970 628410 Fax 01970 626230
✉ editor@newwelshreview.co.uk
www.newwelshreview.co.uk
Owner *New Welsh Review Ltd*
Editor *Francesca Rhydderch*
Circulation 900

Founded 1988. QUARTERLY Welsh literary magazine in the English language. Welcomes material of literary and cultural relevance to Welsh readers and those with an interest in Wales. Approach in writing in the first instance.
FEATURES Max. 3000 words.
FICTION Max. 5000 words.
REVIEWS Max. 800 words.
PAYMENT average of £150 (features); £75 (fiction); £40 (reviews); £25 per poem.

New Woman

Endeavour House, 189 Shaftesbury Avenue, London WC2H 8JG
☎020 7437 9011 Fax 020 7208 3585
✉ sarah.williams@emap.com
www.newwoman.co.uk
Owner *Emap élan Ltd*
Editor *Helen Johnston*
Circulation 231,066

MONTHLY women's interest magazine. 'The only magazine to combine gorgeous fashion and beauty pages, glamorous celebrity features and real life experiences with a sense of humour. All our core subjects – fashion, beauty, relationships, money, work – are covered in a witty tone and style.'

The New Writer

PO Box 60, Cranbrook TN17 2ZR
☎01580 212626 Fax 01580 212041
✉ editor@thenewwriter.com
www.thenewwriter.com

Publisher *Merric Davidson*
Editor *Suzanne Ruthven*

Founded 1996. Published BI-MONTHLY following the merger between *Acclaim* and *Quartos* magazines. Available by subscription only, TNW continues to offer practical 'nuts and bolts' advice on creative writing but with the emphasis on *forward-looking* articles and features on all aspects of the written word that demonstrate the writer's grasp of contemporary writing and current editorial/publishing policies. Plenty of news, views, competitions, reviews; writers' guidelines available with s.a.e. Monthly e-mail News bulletin is included free of charge in the subscription package.

FEATURES Unsolicited mss welcome. Interested in lively, original articles on writing in its broadest sense. Approach with ideas in writing in the first instance. No material is returned unless accompanied by s.a.e.

FICTION Publishes short-listed entries from competitions and subscriber-only submissions.

POETRY Unsolicited poetry welcome. Both short and long unpublished poems, providing they are original and interesting.

PAYMENT features, £20 per 1000 words; fiction, £10 per story; poetry, £3 per poem.

Full guidelines and details of annual Prose & Poetry Prizes at the website.

New Writing Scotland

Association for Scottish Literary Studies, c/o Department of Scottish History, 9 University Gardens, University of Glasgow G12 8QH
☎0141 330 5309 Fax 0141 330 5309
✉ nws@asls.org.uk
www.asls.org.uk

Contact *Duncan Jones*

ANNUAL anthology of contemporary poetry and prose in English, Gaelic and Scots, produced by the **Association for Scottish Literary Studies** (see entry under *Professional Associations and Societies*). Will consider poetry, drama, short fiction or other creative prose but not full-length plays or novels, though self-contained extracts are acceptable. Contributors should be Scottish by birth or upbringing, or resident in Scotland. Max. length of 3500 words is suggested. Send no more than two short stories and six poems. Submissions should be accompanied by two s.a.e.s (one for receipt, the other for return of mss). Mss, which must be sent by 30 September, should be typed, double-spaced, on one side of the paper only with the sheets secured at top left-hand corner. Provide covering letter with full contact details but do not put name or address on individual work(s). Prose pieces should carry an approximate word count.

newbooks

4 Froxfield Close, Winchester SO22 6JW
✉ guy@newbooksmag.com
www.newbooksmag.com
Owner/Editor *Guy Pringle*
Circulation 80,000

Founded 2000. BI-MONTHLY magazine for readers and reading groups with extracts from the best new fiction and free copies to be claimed. No unsolicited contributions. Also publishes *myBOOKSmag* for 5–7-year-olds and *tBkmag* for 8–12-year-olds.

No Limit

Mobilise Organisation, Cottingham Way, Thrapston NN14 4PL
☎01832 734724 Fax 01832 733816
✉ info@ddmc.org.uk
www.ddmc.org.uk
Owner *Mobilise Organisation*
Editor *Alex Mead*
Circulation 30,000

MONTHLY publication of the Mobilise Organisation, which aims to promote and protect the interests and welfare of disabled people and help and encourage them in gaining increased mobility. Various discounts available for members; membership costs £14 p.a. (single), £18 (joint). The magazine includes information for members plus members' letters. Approach in writing with ideas. Unsolicited mss welcome.

The North

See under *Poetry Magazines*

Now

IPC Media Ltd., King's Reach Tower, Stamford Street, London SE1 9LS
☎020 7261 6274
Owner *IPC Media (A Time Warner Company)*
Editor *Jane Ennis*
Circulation 577,818

Founded 1996. WEEKLY magazine of celebrity gossip, news and topical features aimed at the working woman. Unlikely to use freelance contributions due to specialist content – e.g. exclusive showbiz interviews – but ideas will be considered. Approach in writing; no faxes.

Nursery Education

Scholastic Ltd, Villiers House, Clarendon Avenue, Leamington Spa CV32 5PR
☎01926 887799 Fax 01926 883331

✉ earlyyears@scholastic.co.uk
www.scholastic.co.uk
Owner *Scholastic Ltd*
Managing Editor *Helen Freeman*
Circulation 20,000

Founded 1997. MONTHLY magazine for early years professionals. Welcomes contributions from freelance journalists specialising in education.
FEATURES Early years issues explored. Max. 1500 words.
NEWS Relevant and timely news for the early years sector. Max. 400 words.
PRACTICAL IDEAS Themed activities that support the Foundation Stage curriculum and Birth-to-Three activites. Max. 800 words. Approach by letter or e-mail.

Nursing Times

Greater London House, Hampstead Road, London NW1 7EJ
☎020 7874 0500 Fax 020 7874 0505
www.nursingtimes.net
Owner *Emap Healthcare*
Editor *Rachel Downey*
Circulation 72,166

Some of *Nursing Times'* feature content is from unsolicited contributions sent on spec. Articles on all aspects of nursing and health care, including clinical information, written in a contemporary style, are welcome.

Nuts

IPC Media Ltd., King's Reach Tower, Stamford Street, London SE1 9LS
☎020 7261 5660 Fax 020 7261 5480
✉ nutsmagazine@ipcmedia.com
www.nuts.co.uk
Owner *IPC Media (A Time Warner Company)*
Editor *Phil Hilton*
Circulation 306,802

Launched 2004. WEEKLY magazine for men aged 16–45 'who like chat, women, gossip, cars and football'. Welcomes true life stories and items on gadgets. Approach by e-mail in the first instance.

OK! Magazine

The Northern & Shell Building, 10 Lower Thames Street, London EC3R 6EN
☎0871 434 1010 Fax 0871 434 7305
✉ firstname.lastname@express.co.uk
Owner *Northern & Shell Media/Richard Desmond*
Editor *Lisa Palta*
Circulation 649,777

Founded 1996. WEEKLY celebrity-based magazine. Welcomes interviews and pictures on well known personalities, and ideas for general features. Approach the editor by phone or fax in the first instance.

Old Glory

Mortons Heritage Media, Mortons Way, Horncastle LN9 6JR
☎01507 529300 Fax 01507 529495
✉ editor@oldglory.co.uk
www.oldglory.co.uk
Owner *Mortons Media Ltd*
Editor *Colin Tyson*

Founded 1988. MONTHLY magazine covering all aspects of transport and industrial heritage both in the UK and overseas. Specialises in vintage vehicles and steam preservation. Unsolicited articles are welcome. Approach by letter addressed to the editor.
FEATURES Restoration projects from steam rollers to windmills. Max. 1000 words.
NEWS Steam and transport rally reports. News concerning industrial and heritage sites and buildings.

The Oldie

65 Newman Street, London W1T 3EG
☎020 7436 8801 Fax 020 7436 8804
✉ theoldie@theoldie.co.uk
www.theoldie.co.uk
Owner *Oldie Publications Ltd*
Editor *Richard Ingrams*
Circulation 25,785

Founded 1992. MONTHLY general interest magazine with a strong humorous slant for the older person. Submissions welcome; enclose s.a.e. No poetry.

Olive

BBC Worldwide, 80 Wood Lane, London W12 0TT
☎020 8433 1389
✉ firstname.surname@bbc.co.uk
www.olivemagazine.co.uk
Owner *BBC Worldwide Publishing Ltd*
Editorial Coordinator *Paula Stain*
Deputy Editor/Food Editor *Lulu Grimes*
Circulation 60,680

Launched 2003. MONTHLY food magazine. Recipes, restaurants and food lovers' travel. Unsolicited contributions not welcome; 'generally only commission features from regular freelancers. It's impossible to respond to all the pitches we receive.'

Opera
36 Black Lion Lane, London W6 9BE
☎020 8563 8893 Fax 020 8563 8635
✉ editor@opera.co.uk
www.opera.co.uk
Owner *Opera Magazine Ltd*
Editor *John Allison*
Circulation 11,500
Founded 1950. MONTHLY review of the current opera scene. Almost all articles are commissioned and unsolicited mss are not welcome. All approaches should be made in writing.

Opera Now
241 Shaftesbury Avenue, London WC2H 8TF
☎020 7333 1740 Fax 020 7333 1769
✉ opera.now@rhinegold.co.uk
www.rhinegold.co.uk
Publisher *Rhinegold Publishing Ltd*
Editor-in-Chief *Ashutosh Khandekar*
Deputy Editor *Antonia Couling*
Founded 1989. BI-MONTHLY. News, features and reviews aimed at those involved as well as those interested in opera. No unsolicited mss. All work is commissioned. Approach with ideas in writing.

Organic Gardening
Sandvoe, North Roe, Shetland ZE2 9RY
☎01806 533319 Fax 01806 533319
✉ organic.gardening@virgin.net
Editor *Gaby Bartai Bevan*
Circulation 12,000
Founded 1988. MONTHLY. Articles and features on all aspects of gardening based on organic methods. Unsolicited material welcome; 800–2000 words for features and 100–300 for news items. Poetry not published. Prefers 'hands-on' accounts of projects, problems, challenges and how they are dealt with. Approach in writing.
PAYMENT by arrangement.

OS (Office Secretary) Magazine
15 Grangers Place, Witney OX28 4BS
☎01993 775545 Fax 01993 778884
Owner *Peebles Media Group Ltd*
Editor *Cath Janes*
Sponsorship & Promotions Manager *Paul Ormond*
Circulation 27,681
Founded 1986. BI-MONTHLY. Features articles of interest to secretaries and personal assistants aged 25–60. No unsolicited mss.
FEATURES Informative pieces on technology

and practices, office and employment-related topics. Length 1000 words. Approach with ideas by telephone or in writing.
PAYMENT by negotiation.

Palmtop User Magazine
Palmtop Publications, PO Box 188, Bicester OX26 6GP Fax 01869 246043
✉ editor@palmtop.co.uk
www.palmtop.co.uk
Owners *Mr S. Clack, Miss R.A. Rolfe*
Editor *Mr S. Clack*
Circulation 8,000
Founded 1994. Users' magazine for hand-held computers. No unsolicited mss; approach by e-mail in the first instance.

Park Home & Holiday Caravan
IPC Media Ltd, Leon House, 233 High Street, Croydon CR9 1HZ
☎020 8774 0600
✉ em_bartlett@ipcmedia.com
www.phhc.co.uk
Owner *IPC Country & Leisure Media*
Editor *Emma Bartlett*
Circulation 15,000
Founded 1960. THIRTEEN ISSUES YEARLY. News of parks, models, legislation, accessories, lifestyle for those living in residential park homes or owning holiday caravans. Welcomes material specifically related to park home and holiday caravan sites; no general touring features. Approach by letter or telephone.

PC Format
Future Publishing, 30 Monmouth Street, Bath BA1 2BW
☎01225 442244 Fax 01225 732295
✉ pcfmail@futurenet.co.uk
www.futurenet.co.uk
Owner *Future Publishing*
Publisher *James Binns*
Editor *Adam Oxford*
Circulation 36,320
Founded 1991. FOUR-WEEKLY magazine covering everything for the consumer PC – games, software and hardware. Welcomes feature and interview ideas in the first instance; approach by telephone or e-mail.

Pensions World
2 Addiscombe Road, Croydon CR9 5AF
☎020 8212 1946 Fax 020 8212 1970
Owner *Reed Elsevier*
Editor *Stephanie Hawthorne*

Circulation 6817

Launched 1972. MONTHLY magazine for pensions professionals. Pensions, law, investment and retirement issues. Specialist contributors only. No consumer pension stories. Approach by e-mail.
FEATURES Max. 1500 words.
NEWS Max. 400 words.
PAYMENT negotiable.

People Management
Personnel Publications Limited, 1 Benjamin Street, London EC1M 5EA
☎020 7880 6200   Fax 020 7296 4215
✉ editorial@peoplemanagement.co.uk
www.peoplemanagement.co.uk
Editor *Steve Crabb*
Deputy Editor *Rima Manocha*
Circulation 120,110

FORTNIGHTLY magazine on human resources, industrial relations, employment issues, etc. Welcomes submissions but apply for 'Guidelines for Contributors' in the first instance.
FEATURES *Jane Pickard/Claire Warren*
NEWS *Anna Scott*
LAW AT WORK *Jill Evans*

The People's Friend
80 Kingsway East, Dundee DD4 8SL
☎01382 223131   Fax 01382 452491
✉ peoplesfriend@dcthomson.co.uk
Owner *D.C. Thomson & Co. Ltd*
Editor *Margaret McCoy*
Circulation 359,104

The *Friend* is a fiction magazine, with two serials and several short stories each week. Founded in 1869, it has always prided itself on providing 'a good read for all the family'. Stories should be about ordinary, identifiable characters with the kind of problems the average reader can understand and sympathise with. 'We look for the romantic and emotional developments of characters, rather than an over-complicated or contrived plot. We regularly use period serials and, occasionally, mystery/adventure.' Guidelines on request with s.a.e.
SHORT STORIES Can vary in length from 1000 words or less to 4000.
SERIALS Serials of 8–12 instalments.
ARTICLES Short fillers welcome.
PAYMENT on acceptance.

Period Living
St Giles House, 50 Poland Street, London W1F 7AX
☎020 7970 4433   Fax 020 7970 4438
✉ period.living@centaur.co.uk

Owner *Centaur*
Editor-in-Chief *Michael Holmes*
Circulation 48,792
Founded 1992. Formed from the merger of *Period Living* and *Traditional Homes*. Covers interior decoration in a period style, period house profiles, traditional crafts, renovation of period properties.
PAYMENT varies according to length/type of article.

The Philosopher
6 Craighall Dane Avenue, Newcastle upon Tyne NE3 1OR
✉ thephilosophicalsociety@yahoo.co.uk
www.the-philosopher.co.uk
Owner *The Philosophical Society*
Editor *Martin Cohen*

Founded 1913. BIANNUAL journal of the Philosophical Society of Great Britain with an international readership made up of members, libraries and specialist booksellers. Wide range of philosophical interests, but leaning towards articles that present philosophical investigation which is relevant to the individual and to society in our modern era. Accessible to the non-specialist. Will consider articles and book reviews. Notes for Contributors available; see website. As well as short philosophical papers, will accept:
NEWS about lectures, conventions, philosophy groups. Ethical issues in the news. Max. 1000 words.
REVIEWS of philosophy books (max. 600 words); discussion articles of individual philosophers and their published works (max. 2000 words).
MISCELLANEOUS items, including graphics, of philosophical interest and/or merit.
PAYMENT Free copies.

Piano
241 Shaftesbury Avenue, London WC2H 8TF
☎020 7333 1724   Fax 020 7333 1769
✉ piano@rhinegold.co.uk
www.rhinegold.co.uk
Owner *Rhinegold Publishing*
Editor *Jeremy Siepmann*
Deputy Editor *Sarah Smith*
Circulation 11,000

Founded 1993. BI-MONTHLY magazine containing features, profiles, technical information, news, reviews of interest to those with a serious amateur or professional concern with pianos or their playing. No unsolicited material. Approach with ideas in writing only.

Picture Postcard Monthly

15 Debdale Lane, Keyworth, Nottingham
NG12 5HT
☎0115 937 4079 Fax 0115 937 6197
✉ reflections@postcardcollecting.co.uk
www.postcardcollecting.co.uk
Owners *Brian & Mary Lund*
Editor *Brian Lund*
Circulation 4000

Founded 1978. MONTHLY. News, views, clubs, diary of fairs, sales, auctions, and well-researched postcard-related articles. Might be interested in general articles supported by postcards. Unsolicited mss welcome. Approach by phone, e-mail or in writing with ideas.

Pilot

Archant Specialist, The Mill, Bearwalden
Business Park, Wendens Ambo, Saffron Walden
CB11 4GB
☎01799 544200 Fax 01799 544201
✉ nick.bloom@pilotweb.aero
www.pilotweb.co.uk
Publisher *Archant Specialist*
Editor *Nick Bloom*
Circulation 19,811

Founded 1966. MONTHLY magazine for private plane pilots. Much of the magazine is written by outside contributors – mostly regulars. Unsolicited mss welcome but ideas in writing preferred. Perusal of any issue of the magazine will reveal the type of material bought. 700 words of 'Advice to would-be contributors' sent on receipt of s.a.e. (mark envelope 'Advice'), or see the website for details.

NEWS Contributions, preferably with photographs, need to be as short as possible. See *Pilot Notes* and *Old-Timers* in the magazine.

FEATURES Many articles are unsolicited personal experiences/travel accounts from pilots of private planes; good photo coverage is very important. Max. 5000 words.

Pink Paper

Unit M, Spectrum House, 32–34 Gordon
House Road, London NW5 1LP
☎020 7424 7400 Fax 020 7424 7401
✉ editorial@pinkpaper.com
Owner *Millivres Prowler Group*
Editor *Tris Reid-Smith*
Circulation 39,758

Founded 1987. FORTNIGHTLY. Only national newspaper for lesbians and gay men covering politics, social issues, health, the arts, celebrity interviews and all areas of concern to lesbian/gay

people. Unsolicited mss welcome. Initial approach by post with an idea preferred. Interested in profiles, reviews, in-depth features and short news pieces.
PAYMENT by arrangement.

Poetry Ireland Review

See under *Poetry Magazines*

Poetry Review

See under *Poetry Magazines*

Poetry Scotland

See under *Poetry Magazines*

Poetry Wales

See under *Poetry Magazines*

Pony

D.J. Murphy (Publishers) Ltd, Headley House,
Headley Road, Grayshott GU26 6TU
☎01428 601020 Fax 01428 601030
✉ djm@djmurphy.co.uk (text only)
www.ponymag.com
Owner *D.J. Murphy (Publishers) Ltd*
Editor *Janet Rising*
Assistant Editor *Zoe Cannon*
Circulation 35,857

Founded 1948. Lively MONTHLY aimed at 10–16-year-olds. News, instruction on riding, stable management, veterinary care, interviews. Approach in writing with an idea.

FEATURES welcome. Max. 900 words.

NEWS Written in-house. Photographs and illustrations (serious/cartoon) welcome.
PAYMENT £65 per 1000 words.

post plus

See **Sunday Post** under *National Newspapers*

PR Week

174 Hammersmith Road, London W6 7JP
☎020 8267 4429 Fax 020 8267 4509
✉ prweek@haynet.com
www.prweek.com
Owner *Haymarket Business Publications Ltd*
Editor *Daniel Rodgers*
Circulation 16,326

Founded 1984. WEEKLY. Contributions accepted from experienced journalists. Approach in writing with an idea.
PAYMENT negotiable.

Practical Boat Owner

IPC Media Ltd, Westover House, West Quay
Road, Poole BH15 1JG

☎01202 440820
✉ sarah_norbury@ipcmedia.com
www.pbo.co.uk

Owner *IPC Media (A Time Warner Company)*
Editor *Sarah Norbury*
Circulation 50,013

Britain's biggest selling boating magazine. MONTHLY magazine of practical information for cruising boat owners. Receives about 1500 mss per year.

FEATURES Technical articles about maintenance, restoration, modifications to cruising boats, power and sail up to 45ft. European and British regional pilotage articles and cruising guides. Approach in writing with synopsis in the first instance.

PAYMENT negotiable.

Practical Caravan

Teddington Studios, Teddington Lock, Broom Road, Teddington TW11 9BE
☎020 8267 5629   Fax 020 8267 5725
✉ practical.caravan@haynet.com
www.practicalcaravan.com

Owner *Haymarket Magazines Ltd*
Editor *Alex Newby*
Circulation 44,062

Founded 1967. MONTHLY. Contains caravan reviews, travel features, investigations, products, park reviews. Unsolicited mss welcome on travel relevant only to caravanning/touring vans. No motorcaravan or static van stories. Approach with ideas by phone, letter or e-mail.

FEATURES Must refer to caravanning. Written in friendly, chatty manner. Pictures essential. Max. length 2000 words.

PAYMENT negotiable.

Practical Fishkeeping

Bretton Court, Bretton, Peterborough PE3 8DZ
☎01733 264666   Fax 01733 465246
✉ karen.youngs@emap.com
www.practicalfishkeeping.co.uk

Owner *Emap Active Publications Ltd*
Editor *Karen Youngs*
Circulation 15,103

THIRTEEN ISSUES YEARLY. Practical articles on all aspects of fishkeeping. Unsolicited mss welcome; approach in writing with ideas. Quality photographs of fish always welcome. No fiction or verse.

Practical Parenting

IPC Media Ltd., King's Reach Tower, Stamford Street, London SE1 9LS
☎020 7261 5058   Fax 020 7261 6542

Owner *IPC Media (A Time Warner Company)*
Editor *Mara Lee*
Circulation 50,456

Founded 1987. MONTHLY. Practical advice on pregnancy, birth, babycare and childcare, 0–4 years. Submit ideas in writing with synopsis or send mss on spec. Interested in feature articles of up to 3000 words in length, and in readers' experiences/personal viewpoint pieces of between 750–1000 words. All material must be written for the magazine's specifically targeted audience and in-house style. Submissions to: *Amy Benson* (amy_benson@ipcmedia.com).

PAYMENT negotiable.

Practical Photography

Bretton Court, Bretton, Peterborough PE3 8DZ
☎01733 264666   Fax 01733 465246
✉ practical.photography@emap.com
www.practicalphotography.co.uk

Owner *Emap Active Publications Ltd*
Editor *Andrew James*
Circulation 57,359

MONTHLY All types of photography, particularly technique-orientated pictures. No unsolicited mss. Preliminary approach may be made by e-mail. Always interested in new, especially unusual, ideas.

FEATURES Anything relevant to the world of photography, but not 'the sort of feature produced by staff writers. Features on technology, digital imaging techniques and humour are three areas worth exploring. Bear in mind that there is a three-month lead-in time.' Max. 2000 words.

PAYMENT varies.

Practical Wireless

Arrowsmith Court, Station Approach, Broadstone BH18 8PW
☎0870 224 7810   Fax 0870 224 7850
✉ rob@pwpublishing.ltd.uk
www.pwpublishing.ltd.uk

Owner *PW Publishing Ltd*
Editor *Rob Mannion (G3XFD)*
Circulation 20,000

Founded 1932. MONTHLY. News and features relating to amateur radio, radio construction and radio communications. Unsolicited mss welcome. Author's guidelines available and are essential reading (send s.a.e.). Approach by phone or e-mail with ideas in the first instance. Only interested in hearing from people with a thorough knowledge of amateur radio. Copy (typed only) should be supported where possi-

ble by artwork, either illustrations, diagrams or photographs.
PAYMENT £54–70 per page.

Practical Woodworking

Encanta Media Ltd, Berwick House,
8–10 Knoll Rise, Orpington BR6 0EL
☎01442 831128 Fax 01442 831128
✉ practicalwoodworking@encanta.co.uk
www.getwoodworking.com
Owner *Encanta Media Ltd*
Editor *Mark Chisholm*
Circulation 9,500

Founded 1965. THIRTEEN ISSUES YEARLY. Contains articles relating to woodworking: projects, techniques, new products, tips, letters, etc. Unsolicited mss welcome. No fiction. Approach with ideas in writing, by phone or e-mail.

FEATURES Projects, techniques, etc.
PAYMENT by arrangement.

The Practitioner

245 Blackfriars Road, London SE1 9UY
☎020 7921 8113
✉ gmatkin@cmpinformation.com
www.practitioner-i.co.uk
Owner *CMPi*
Editor *Gavin Atkin*
Circulation 43,000

Founded 1868. MONTHLY publication that keeps General Practitioners up to date on clinical issues. Freelance material from specialist doctors only. Send synopsis by e-mail.

Prediction

IPC Media Ltd, Leon House, 233 High Street, Croydon CR9 1HZ
☎020 8726 8000
✉ prediction@ipcmedia.com
www.predictionmagazine.co.uk
Owner *IPC Media (A Time Warner Company)*
Editor *Tania Ahsan*
Circulation 14,326

Founded 1936. MONTHLY. Covering astrology and mind, body, spirit topics. Unsolicited material in these areas welcome (about 200–300 mss received every year). Writers' guidelines available on request.

ASTROLOGY Pieces should be practical and of general interest.

FEATURES Articles on divination, shamanism, alternative healing, psychics and other supernatural phenonema considered. Please read a recent copy of the magazine before sending unsolicited material.

Pregnancy & Birth

Greater London House, Hampstead Road, London NW1 7EJ
☎020 7347 1885 Fax 020 7347 1888
Owner *Emap Esprit*
Editor *Sarah Hart*
Features Editor *Tatty Good*
Circulation 50,307

MONTHLY magazine covering all aspects of pregnancy from health to fashion. Regularly commissions features from health journalists. Freelancers should approach by post in the first instance.

PAYMENT varies.

Pregnancy, Baby & You

2 Balcombe Street, London NW1 6NW
☎020 7042 4000
✉ claire.roberts@futurenet.co.uk
Owner *Future Publishing Ltd*
Editor *Claire Roberts*
Deputy Editor *Emma Hartfield*

MONTHLY publication that focuses on issues affecting the family as a whole. No unsolicited mss; e-mail the editor with ideas only.

Press Gazette

10 Old Bailey, London EC4M 7NG
☎020 7038 1055 Fax 020 7039 1155
✉ pged@pressgazette.co.uk
www.pressgazette.co.uk
Owner *Press Gazette Limited*
Editor *Ian Reeves*
Deputy Editor *Jon Slattery*
Circulation 5609

WEEKLY magazine for all journalists – in regional and national newspapers, magazines, broadcasting and online – containing news, features and analysis of all areas of journalism, print and broadcasting. Unsolicited mss welcome; interested in profiles of magazines, broadcasting companies and news agencies, personality profiles, technical and current affairs relating to the world of journalism. Approach with ideas by phone, e-mail, fax or post.

Pride

Pride House, 55 Battersea Bridge Road, London SW11 3AX
☎020 7228 3110 Fax 020 7228 3121
✉ info@pridemagazine.com
Owner *Carl Cushnie Junior*
Editor *Sherry Dixon*
Circulation 40,000

Founded 1991. MONTHLY lifestyle magazine

for Black women with features, beauty, arts and fashion. Approach in writing or by e-mail with ideas.

FEATURES Issues pertaining to the Black community. 'Ideas and solicited mss are welcomed from new freelancers.' Max. 2000 words.
FICTION Publishes the occasional short story. Max. 3000 words.
HEALTH, BEAUTY, LIFESTYLE *Sherry Dixon* Freelancers used for short features. Max. 1000 words.

Prima

National Magazine House, 72 Broadwick Street, London W1F 9EP
☎020 7439 5000
✉ prima@natmags.co.uk
www.natmags.co.uk

Owner *National Magazine Company*
Editor *Maire Fahey*
Circulation 331,715

Founded 1986. MONTHLY women's magazine.
HEALTH & FEATURES Coordinator *Ruth Tierney* Mostly practical and written by specialists, or commissioned from known freelancers. Unsolicited mss not welcome.

Private Eye

6 Carlisle Street, London W1D 3BN
☎020 7437 4017 Fax 020 7437 0705
✉ strobes@private-eye.co.uk
www.private-eye.co.uk
Owner *Pressdram*
Editor *Ian Hislop*
Circulation 204,847

Founded 1961. FORTNIGHTLY satirical and investigative magazine. Prospective contributors are best advised to approach the editor in writing. News stories and feature ideas are always welcome, as are cartoons. All jokes written in-house.
PAYMENT in all cases is 'not great', and length of piece varies as appropriate.

Prospect

2 Bloomsbury Place, London WC1A 2QA
☎020 7255 1935 (editorial)/1281 (publishing)
Fax 020 7255 1279
✉ editorial@prospect-magazine.co.uk *or* publishing@prospect-magazine.co.uk
www.prospect-magazine.co.uk
Owner *Prospect Publishing Limited*
Editor *David Goodhart*
Circulation 26,553

Founded 1995. MONTHLY. Essays, reviews, short fiction and research on current/international

affairs and cultural issues. No news features. Unsolicited contributions welcome, although more useful to approach in writing with ideas in the first instance.

Psychic News

The Coach House, Stansted Hall, Stansted CM24 8UD
☎01279 817050 Fax 01279 817051
✉ pnadv@snu.org.uk
www.psychicnewsbookshop.co.uk
Owner *Psychic Press 1995 Ltd*
Editor *Tony Ortzen*
Circulation 40,000

Founded 1932. *Psychic News* is the world's only WEEKLY spiritualist newspaper. It covers subjects such as psychic research, hauntings, ghosts, poltergeists, spiritual healing, survival after death and paranormal gifts. Unsolicited material considered.

Publishing News

7 John Street, London WC1N 2ES
☎0870 870 2345 Fax 0870 870 0385
✉ mailbox@publishingnews.co.uk
www.publishingnews.co.uk
Editor *Liz Thomson*

WEEKLY newspaper of the book trade. Hardback and paperback reviews and extensive listings of new paperbacks and hardbacks. Interviews with leading personalities in the trade, authors, agents, and features on specialist book areas. 'Almost no submissions accepted.'

Q

Mappin House, 4 Winsley Street, London W1W 8HF
☎020 7436 1515 Fax 020 7182 8547
✉ firstname.surname@emap.com
www.q4music.com
Owner *Emap Consumer Media*
Editor *Paul Rees*
Circulation 168,547

Founded 1986. MONTHLY. Glossy aimed at educated popular music enthusiasts of all ages. Few opportunities for freelance writers. Unsolicited mss are strongly discouraged. Prospective contributors should approach in writing only.

Q-News, The Muslim Magazine

PO Box 4295, London W1A 7YH
☎07985 143263
✉ info@q-news.com
www.q-news.com
Owner *Fuad Nahdi*

Editor *Fareena Alam*
Circulation 40,000

Founded 1992. MONTHLY British Muslim community magazine concerned with shaping the debate about Muslims in Britain. Covers recruitment, news, opinion and reviews.

FEATURES *Abdul-Rehman Malik* 'Writers wishing to focus on areas of interest to our readership will gain access and credibility among the relevant people.' Max. 3000 words.

OTHER *Fareena Alam* Analysis on news and current affairs – alternative rather than mainstream viewpoint preferred. Max. 2000 words.

PAYMENT None.

Quartos Magazine
See **The New Writer**

QWF Magazine
PO Box 1768, Rugby CV21 4ZA
☎01788 334302
✉ jo@qwfmagazine.co.uk
www.qwfmagazine.co.uk

Editor *Jo Good*

QUARTERLY small press magazine. Founded in 1994, as a showcase for the best in women's short story writing – original and thought-provoking. Only considers stories that are previously unpublished and of less than 4000 words; articles must be less than 1000 words and of interest to the writer. Include covering letter, s.a.e. and brief biography with mss. Before submission of material send s.a.e. (50p stamp) with request for free back copy. Also runs script appraisal service and regular short story competitions. For further information and detailed guidelines for contributors please access the website or contact the editor at the address above. Submissions should be sent to Assistant Editor, *Sally Zigmond* (18 Warwick Crescent, Harrogate HG2 8JA) with s.a.e.

RA Magazine (Royal Academy of Arts Magazine)
Royal Academy of Arts, Burlington House, Piccadilly, London W1J 0BD
☎020 7300 5820 Fax 020 7300 5032
✉ ramagazine@royalacademy.org.uk
www.ramagazine.org.uk

Owner *Royal Academy of Arts*
Editor *Sarah Greenberg*
Circulation 100,000

Founded 1983. QUARTERLY visual arts, architecture and culture magazine distributed to Friends of the RA, promoting exhibitions and publishing articles on art shows, books and news worldwide. 'There are opportunities for freelancers who can write about art in an accessible way. Most articles need to be tied in to forthcoming exhibitions, books and projects.' No unsolicited contributions. Approach by telephone or e-mail.

Racecar Engineering
IPC Media Ltd, Leon House, 233 High Street, Croydon CR9 1HZ
☎020 8726 8000 Fax 0208 726 8399
✉ racecar@ipcmedia.com
www.racecar-engineering.co.uk

Owner *IPC Media (A Time Warner Company)*
Editor *Charles Armstrong-Wilson*
Circulation 15,000

Founded 1990. MONTHLY. In-depth features on motorsport technology plus news and products. Interested in receiving news and features from freelancers.

FEATURES Informed insight into current motorsport technology. 3000 words max.

NEWS New cars, products or business news relevant to motorsport. No items on road cars or racing drivers. 500 words max. Call or e-mail to discuss proposal.

Racing Post
1 Canada Square, Canary Wharf, London E14 5AP
☎020 7293 3000 Fax 020 7293 3758
✉ editor@racingpost.co.uk
www.racingpost.co.uk

Owner *Trinity Mirror Plc*
Editor *Chris Smith*
Circulation 69,114

Founded 1986. DAILY horse racing paper with some general sport. In 1998, following an agreement between the owners of *The Sporting Life* and the *Racing Post*, the two papers merged.

Radio Times
80 Wood Lane, London W12 0TT
☎020 8433 3400 Fax 020 8433 3160
✉ radio.times@bbc.co.uk
www.radiotimes.com

Owner *BBC Worldwide Limited*
Editor *Gill Hudson*
Circulation 1.09 million

WEEKLY. UK's leading broadcast listings magazine. The majority of material is provided by freelance and retained writers, but the topicality of the pieces means close consultation with editors is essential. Very unlikely to use unsolicited material. Detailed BBC, ITV, Channel 4, Channel 5 and satellite television and radio listings are accompanied by feature material relevant to the week's output.

PAYMENT by arrangement.

Radio User

Arrowsmith Court, Station Approach,
Broadstone BH18 8PW
☎0870 224 7810 Fax 0870 224 7850
✉ elaine@pwpublishing.ltd.uk
www.pwpublishing.ltd.uk
Owner *PW Publishing Ltd*
Editor *Elaine Richards*
Circulation 19,000

Founded 1937. In 2006, *Shortwave Magazine* merged with *Radio Active* magazine to become *Radio User*. MONTHLY. Specialist electronics and radio enthusiasts' magazine covering all aspects of listening to radio signals. Features, news, regular columns and projects. Will consider contributions but recommends that contact be made prior to submission to check publishing plans.

Rail

Bretton Court, Bretton, Peterborough
PE3 8DZ
☎01733 264666 Fax 01733 282720
✉ rail@emap.com
www.rail-magazine.co.uk
Owner *Emap Active Publications Ltd*
Managing Editor *Nigel Harris*
Circulation 27,087

Founded 1981. FORTNIGHTLY magazine dedicated to modern railway. News and features, and topical newsworthy events. Unsolicited mss welcome. Approach by phone with ideas. Not interested in personal journey reminiscences. No fiction.

FEATURES By arrangement with the editor. All modern railway British subjects considered. Max. 2000 words.

NEWS Any news item welcome. Max. 500 words.

PAYMENT features, varies/negotiable; news, up to £100 per 1000 words.

Railway Gazette International

Quadrant House, Sutton SM2 5AS
☎020 8652 8608 Fax 020 8652 3738
✉ railway.gazette@rbi.co.uk
www.railwaygazette.com
Owner *Reed Business Information*
Editor *Murray Hughes*
Deputy Editor *Chris Jackson*
Industry Editor *Andrew Gratham*
Circulation 9752

Founded 1835. MONTHLY magazine for senior railway, metro and tramway managers, engineers and suppliers worldwide. 'No material for railway enthusiast publications.' Telephone to discuss ideas in the first instance.

The Railway Magazine

IPC Media Ltd., King's Reach Tower,
Stamford Street, London SE1 9LS
☎020 7261 5533/5821 Fax 020 7261 5269
✉ railway@ipcmedia.com
www.ipcmedia.com
Owner *IPC Media (A Time Warner Company)*
Editor *Nick Pigott*
Circulation 30,783

Founded 1897. MONTHLY. Articles, photos and short news stories of a topical nature, covering modern railways, steam preservation and railway history, welcome. Max. 2000 words, with sketch maps of routes, etc., where appropriate. Unsolicited mss welcome. No poetry.

PAYMENT negotiable.

Reader's Digest

11 Westferry Circus, Canary Wharf, London
E14 4HE
☎020 7715 8000 Fax 020 7715 8716
www.readersdigest.co.uk
Owner *Reader's Digest Association Ltd*
Editor-in-Chief *Katherine Walker*
Circulation 735,138

Although in theory, a good market for general interest features of around 2500 words very few are ever accepted. However, 'a tiny proportion' comes from freelance writers, all of which are specially commissioned. Opportunities exist for short humorous contributions to regular features – 'Life's Like That', 'Laughter, the Best Medicine', 'All in a Day's Work'. Issues a helpful booklet called 'Writing for Reader's Digest', available by post at £4.50.

PAYMENT up to £100.

The Reader

Reader Office, 19 Abercromby Square,
Liverpool L69 7ZG
☎0151 794 2830
✉ readers@liv.co.uk
www.thereader.co.uk
Editor *Jane Davis*
Circulation 1200

Founded 1997. QUARTERLY. Poetry, short fiction, literary articles and essays, thought, reviews, recommendations. Contributions from internationally lauded and new voices. Welcomes articles/essays about reading, max.

2000 words. Recommendations for good reading, max. 1000 words. Short stories, max. 2500 words. No theoretical style literary discourses. Approach in writing. PAYMENT negotiable.

Readers' Review Magazine

9 De Montfort Mews, Leicester LE1 7FW
☎0116 255 9311 Fax 0116 255 9323
✉ readersreview@troubador.co.uk
www.troubador.co.uk/readersreview
Owner *Troubador Publishing Ltd*
Editor *Jane Rowland*
Circulation 2000

Launched 2005. THRICE-YEARLY. Revews of author-financed books; articles on self publishing. Articles welcome on aspects of authors publishing their own books (design, production, editing, print, marketing). Approach by e-mail. Max. 2000 words.
BOOK REVIEWS Self-published books only. Max. 300 words.

Real

Essential Publishing, Phoenix Square, Colchester CO4 9HU
☎01206 851117
www.essentialpublishing.co.uk
Owner *Essential Publishing Ltd*
Editor *Sally Narraway*
Circulation 183,042

FORTNIGHTLY women's magazine. Real life stories

Record Collector

Unit 101, 140 Wales Farm Road, Acton, London W3 6UG
☎0870 732 8080 Fax 0870 732 6060
✉ alan.lewis@metropolis.co.uk
www.recordcollectormag.com
Owner *Metropolis*
Editor *Alan Lewis*

Founded 1979. MONTHLY. Detailed, well-researched articles welcome on any aspect of record collecting or any collectable artist in the field of popular music (1950s to present day), with complete discographies where appropriate. Unsolicited mss welcome. Approach with ideas by phone or e-mail.
PAYMENT negotiable.

Red

64 North Row, London W1K 7LL
☎020 7150 7000 Fax 020 7150 7684
✉ harriet.cooper@hf-uk.com

www.redmagazine.co.uk
Owner *Hachette Filipacchi UK Ltd*
Editor *Trish Halpin*
Circulation 219,689

Founded 1998. MONTHLY magazine aimed at the 30-something woman. Will consider ideas sent in 'on spec' but tends to rely on regular contributors.

Report

ATL, 7 Northumberland Street, London WC2N 5RD
☎020 7930 6441 Fax 020 7782 1618
www.atl.org.uk
Owner *Association of Teachers and Lecturers*
Joint Editors *Guy Goodwin, Victoria Poskitt*
Circulation 160,000

Founded 1978. TEN ISSUES YEARLY during academic terms. Contributions welcome. All submissions should go directly to the editor. Articles should be no more than 800 words and must be of practical interest to the classroom teacher and F.E. lecturers.

Reveal

National Magazine Co., National Magazine House, 33 Broadwick Street, London W1F 0DQ
☎020 7339 4500 Fax 020 7339 4529
✉ michael@acp-natmag.co.uk
www.natmags.co.uk
Owner *ACP – Natmag*
Editor *Michael Butcher*
Circulation 345,502

Launched 2004. WEEKLY glossy lifestyle magazine with celebrities, real-life stories, cookery, beauty and seven-day TV guide. No unsolicited contributions.

Right Now!

Box 361, 78 Marylebone High Street, London W1U 5AP
☎0845 601 3243 Fax 0845 601 3243
✉ editor@right-now.org
www.right-now.org
Owner *Right Now! Press Ltd*
Editor *Derek Turner*
Circulation 3000

Founded 1993. BI-MONTHLY right-wing conservative commentary. Welcomes well-documented disputations, news stories and features about British heritage ('the more politically incorrect, the better!'). No fiction or poems. Initial approach in writing.
No PAYMENT.

Rugby World

IPC Media Ltd., 23rd Floor, King's Reach Tower, Stamford Street, London SE1 9LS
☎020 7261 6830   Fax 020 7261 5419
www.rugbyworld.com
Owner *IPC Media (A Time Warner Company)*
Editor *Paul Morgan*
Circulation 45,244

Founded 1960. MONTHLY. Features of special rugby interest only. Unsolicited contributions welcome but s.a.e. essential for return of material. Prior approach by phone or in writing preferred.

Runner's World

33 Broadwick Street, London W1F 0AD
☎020 7339 4400   Fax 020 7339 4220
✉ rwedit@natmag-rodale.co.uk
www.runnersworld.co.uk
Owner *Natmag – Rodale Press*
Editor *Steven Seaton*
Circulation 83,527

Founded 1979. MONTHLY magazine giving practical advice on all areas of distance running including products and training, travel features, news and cross-training advice. Personal running-related articles, famous people who run or off-beat travel articles are welcome. No elite athlete or training articles. Approach with ideas in writing in the first instance.

Running Fitness

1st Floor, South Wing, Broadway Court, Broadway, Peterborough PE1 1RP
☎01733 347559   Fax 01733 891342
✉ rf.ed@kelsey.pb.co.uk
www.runningfitnessmag.com
Owner *Kelsey Publishing*
Editor *Paul Larkins*
Circulation 26,000

Founded 1985. MONTHLY. Instructional articles on running, fitness, and lifestyle, plus running-related activities and health.

FEATURES Specialist knowledge an advantage. Opportunities are wide, but approach with ideas in first instance.

NEWS Opportunities for people stories, especially if backed up by photographs.

Saga Magazine

Saga Publishing Ltd, Middelburg Square, Folkestone CT21 1AZ
☎01303 771523   Fax 01303 776699
✉ editor@saga.co.uk
www.saga.co.uk
Owner *Saga Publishing Ltd*

Editor *Emma Soames*
Circulation 1.23 million

Founded 1984. MONTHLY magazine that sets out to celebrate the role of older people in society, reflecting their achievements, promoting their skills, protecting their interests, and campaigning on their behalf. A warm personal approach, addressing the readership in an up-beat and positive manner. It has a hard core of celebrated commentators/writers (e.g. Keith Waterhouse, Alexander Chancellor, Sally Brampton) as regular contributors. Articles mostly commissioned or written in-house but exclusive celebrity interviews welcome if appropriate/relevant. Length 1000–1200 words (max. 1600). No short stories or poems, please.

Sailing Today

Swanwick Marina, Lower Swanwick, Southampton SO31 1ZL
☎01489 585225   Fax 01489 565054
✉ john.goode@sailingtoday.co.uk
www.sailingtoday.co.uk
Owner *Edisey Ltd*
Editor *John Goode*

Founded 1997. MONTHLY practical magazine for cruising sailors. *Sailing Today* covers owning and buying a boat, equipment and products for sailing and is about improving readers' skills, boat maintenance and product tests. Most articles are commissioned but will consider practical features and cruising stories with photos. Approach by telephone or in writing in the first instance.

Sainsbury's Magazine

20 Upper Ground, London SE1 9PD
☎020 7633 0266   Fax 020 7401 9423
✉ edit@newcrane.co.uk
Owner *New Crane Ltd*
Editor *Sue Robinson*
Consultant Director *Delia Smith*
Circulation 414,337

Founded 1993. MONTHLY featuring a main core of food and cookery with features, health, beauty, home and gardening. No unsolicited mss. Approach in writing with ideas only in the first instance.

The Salisbury Review

33 Canonbury Park South, London N1 2JW
☎020 7226 7791   Fax 020 7354 0383
✉ salisburyreview@tiscali.co.uk
www.salisburyreview.co.uk
Editor *Dennis O'Keefe*
Managing Editor *Merrie Cave*

Consulting Editors *Roger Scruton, Sir Richard Body, Myles Harris*
Circulation 1700

Founded 1982. QUARTERLY magazine of conservative thought. Editorials and features from a right-wing viewpoint. Unsolicited material welcome. No fiction or poetry.
FEATURES Max. 2000 words.
REVIEWS Max. 1000 words.
Small PAYMENT.

Scotland in Trust
91 East London Street, Edinburgh EH7 4BQ
☎0131 556 2220 Fax 0131 556 3300
✉ trust@cmyk-design.co.uk
www.scotlandintrust.co.uk
Owner *National Trust for Scotland*
Editor *Iain Gale*
Contact *Neil Braidwood*
Circulation 158,378

Founded 1983. THREE ISSUES YEARLY. Magazine containing heritage/conservation features. No unsolicited mss.

Scotland on Sunday Magazine
See **Scotland on Sunday** under *National Newspapers*

The Scots Magazine
D.C. Thomson & Co., 2 Albert Square, Dundee DD1 9QJ
☎01382 223131 Fax 01382 322214
✉ mail@scotsmagazine.com
www.scotsmagazine.com
Owner *D.C. Thomson & Co. Ltd*
Editor *John Methven*
Circulation 41,698

Founded 1739. MONTHLY. Covers a wide field of Scottish interests ranging from personalities to wildlife, climbing, reminiscence, history and folklore. Outside contributions welcome; 'staff delighted to discuss in advance by letter or e-mail'.
EVENTS LISTING *Christina Dolan*
PHOTOGRAPHY/MUSIC *Ian Neilson*
Books *Alison Cook*

The Scottish Farmer
Newsquest Magazines, 200 Renfield Street, Glasgow G2 3PR
☎0141 302 7727 Fax 0141 302 7799
✉ ken.fletcher@thescottishfarmer.co.uk
Owner *Newsquest Magazines*
Editor *Alasdair Fletcher*
Circulation 21,220

Founded 1893. WEEKLY. Farmer's magazine

covering most aspects of Scottish agriculture. Unsolicited mss welcome. Approach with ideas in writing, by fax or e-mail.
FEATURES *Ken Fletcher* Technical articles on agriculture or farming units. 1000–2000 words.
NEWS *Ken Fletcher* Factual news about farming developments, political, personal and technological. Max. 800 words.
WEEKEND FAMILY PAGES Rural and craft topics.

Scottish Field
Special Publications, Craigcrook Castle, Craigcrook Road, Edinburgh EH4 3PE
☎0131 312 4550 Fax 0131 312 4551
✉ editor@scottishfield.co.uk
www.scottishfield.co.uk
Owner *Oban Times*
Editor *Claire Grant*
Circulation 14,091

Founded 1903. MONTHLY. Scotland's quality lifestyle magazine. Unsolicited mss welcome but writers should study the magazine first.
FEATURES Articles of general interest on Scotland and Scots abroad with good photographs or, preferably, e-mailed images at 300 dpi. Approx. 1000 words.
PAYMENT negotiable.

Scottish Home & Country
42 Heriot Row, Edinburgh EH3 6ES
☎0131 225 1724 Fax 0131 225 8129
✉ magazine@swri.demon.co.uk
Owner *Scottish Women's Rural Institutes*
Editor *Liz Ferguson*
Circulation 11,000

Founded 1924. MONTHLY. Scottish or rural-related issues, health, travel, women's issues and general interest. Unsolicited mss welcome. Commissions are rare and tend to go to established contributors only.

Scouting Magazine
Gilwell House, Gilwell Park, Chingford E4 7QW
☎020 8433 7100 Fax 020 8433 7103
✉ scouting.magazine@scout.org.uk
www.scouts.org.uk
Owner *The Scout Association*
Editors *Chris James, Hilary Galloway, Matthew Oakes*
Circulation 72,000+

BI-MONTHLY magazine for adults connected to or interested in the Scout Movement. Interested in Scouting-related submissions only.
PAYMENT by negotiation.

Screen

Gilmorehill Centre for Theatre, Film and
Television, University of Glasgow, Glasgow
G12 8QQ
☎0141 330 5035 Fax 0141 330 3515
✉ screen@arts.gla.ac.uk
www.screen.arts.gla.ac.uk

Publisher *Oxford University Press*
Editors *Annette Kuhn, John Caughie, Simon
Frith, Karen Lury, Jackie Stacey, Sarah Street*
Editorial Assistant *Caroline Beven*
Circulation 1200

QUARTERLY, refereed academic journal of film
and television studies for a readership ranging
from undergraduates to screen studies academics and media professionals. There are no specific qualifications for acceptance of articles.
Straightforward film reviews are not normally
published. Check the magazine's style and market in the first instance.

Screen International

33–39 Bowling Green Lane, London
EC1R 0DA
☎020 7505 8000
✉ michael.gubbins@emap.com
www.screendaily.com

Owner *Emap Communications*
Editor *Michael Gubbins*
Circulation 7107

The voice of the international film industry.
Expert freelance writers used in all areas. No
unsolicited mss. Approach by e-mail.
FEATURES *Louise Tutt*
INTERNATIONAL *Finn Halligan*
PAYMENT negotiable on NUJ basis.

Screentrade Magazine

Screentrade Media Ltd, PO Box 144,
Orpington BR6 6LZ
☎01689 833117 Fax 01689 833117
✉ philip@screentrademagazine.co.uk
www.screentrademagazine.co.uk

Owner *Screentrade Media Ltd*
Editor *Philip Turner*
Circulation 3000+

Founded 2002. QUARTERLY journal for British,
European and American exhibitors and film
distributors.
FEATURES Items on cinema management,
technical, cinema building history, nostalgia,
showmanship, book reviews, concession supply,
ticketing issues, trade articles including seating,
screening, projection/career tips and other managerial matters. Also film and producer/director

opinions. Some film reviews but no 'film star'
interviews. Most contributions are from within
the industry. Items on the state of cinema exhibition, film distribution, cinema architecture, interviews with key industry personnel frequently
undertaken. 1500–3000 words.
NEWS Topical items (if substantiated) welcome. Events coverage (e.g. festivals, premières)
from an exhibitor's viewpoint preferred.

ScriptWriter Magazine

2 Elliott Square, London NW3 3SU
☎020 7586 4853 Fax 020 7586 4853
✉ info@scriptwritermagazine.com
www.scriptwritermagazine.com

Owner *Scriptease Ltd*
Editor *Julian Friedmann*
Circulation 1500

Launched November 2001. SIX ISSUES PER
YEAR. Magazine for professional scriptwriters
covering all aspects of the business and craft of
writing for the small and large screen.
Interested in serious, in-depth analysis; max.
1500–3500 words. E-mail with synopsis sample
material and c.v.

Sea Breezes

Mannin Media Group Ltd, Media House,
Cronkbourne IM4 4SB
☎01624 696566 Fax 01624 661655
✉ seabreezes@manninmedia.co.im
www.seabreezes.co.im

Owner *Print Centres*
Editor *Captain A.C. Douglas*
Circulation 17,000

Founded 1919. MONTHLY. Covers virtually
everything relating to ships and seamen.
Unsolicited mss welcome; they should be thoroughly researched and accompanied by relevant
photographs. No fiction, poetry, or anything
which 'smacks of the romance of the sea'.
FEATURES Factual tales of ships, seamen and
the sea, Royal or Merchant Navy, sail or power,
nautical history, shipping company histories, epic
voyages, etc. Length 1000–4000 words. 'The most
readily acceptable work will be that which shows
it is clearly the result of first-hand experience or
the product of extensive and accurate research.'
PAYMENT £14 per page (about 800 words).

The Second World War
– WWII (1939–1945)

PO Box 202, Scarborough YO11 3GE
☎01723 581329 Fax 01723 581329
✉ books@greatnorthernpublishing.co.uk
www.greatnorthernpublishing.co.uk

Owner *Great Northern Publishing*
Editor *Mark Marsay*
Launched October 2005. BI-MONTHLY subscription only, non-academic magazine published in A5 format (sister magazine to *The Great War*). 'The magazine dedicated to the struggle for freedom – the voice and record of those who served between 1939 and 1945.' Articles, personal stories and accounts of those who served (men and women of all nationalities) on the war and home fronts and their families; diaries, anecdotes, letters postcards, poetry, unit histories, events and memorials, etc. Absolutely no fiction or academic works expounding historian's personal views. New material welcome; contact the editor prior to sending. Submission guidelines and editorial content on the website. 'Open door policy: all welcome regardless of ability to write to a high standard as all work is carefully edited. No subject or topic excluded.' Sample copy £5.

She Magazine
National Magazine House, 72 Broadwick Street, London W1F 9EP
☎020 7439 5000 Fax 020 7312 3940
www.shemagazine.co.uk
Owner *National Magazine Company Ltd*
Editor *To be appointed*
Circulation 156,674

Glossy MONTHLY for the 35-plus woman, addressing her needs as a modern individual, a parent and a homemaker. Talks to its readers in an intelligent, humorous and informative way.

Approach with feature ideas in writing or e-mail to Features Director *Bernice Davison* (bernice.davison@natmags.co.uk). No unsolicited material. PAYMENT negotiable.

Ships Monthly
IPC Country & Leisure Media Ltd, 222 Branston Road, Burton-upon-Trent DE14 3BT
☎01283 542721 Fax 01283 546436
✉ shipsmonthly@ipcmedia.com
www.shipsmonthly.com
Owner *IPC Country & Leisure Media Ltd*
Editor *Iain Wakefield*
Deputy Editor *Nicholas Leach*
Circulation 22,000

Founded 1966. MONTHLY A4 format magazine for ship enthusiasts and maritime professionals. News, photographs and illustrated articles on all kinds of ships – mercantile and naval, past and present. No yachting. Most articles are commissioned; prospective contributors should telephone or e-mail in the first instance.

Shoot Monthly Magazine
IPC Media Ltd., King's Reach Tower, Stamford Street, London SE1 9LS
☎020 7261 6287 Fax 020 7261 6019
✉ shoot@ipcmedia.com
www.shoot.co.uk
Owner *IPC Media (A Time Warner Company)*
Editor *Colin Mitchell*
Circulation 30,316

Founded 1969. MONTHLY football magazine. No unsolicited mss. Present ideas for news, features or colour photo-features to the editor by letter or e-mail.

FEATURES Hard-hitting, topical and off-beat. Very limited opportunities for freelance work. PAYMENT negotiable.

Shooting and Conservation
BASC, Marford Mill, Rossett, Wrexham LL12 0HL
☎01244 573000 Fax 01244 573001
✉ jeffrey.olstead@basc.org.uk
Owner *The British Association for Shooting and Conservation (BASC)*
Editor *Jeffrey Olstead*
Circulation 120,000

SIX ISSUES PER YEAR. Good articles and stories on shooting, conservation and related areas may be considered although most material is produced in-house. Max. 1500 words. PAYMENT negotiable.

The Shooting Gazette
PO Box 225, Stamford PE9 2HS
Fax 01780 485390
✉ will_hetherington@ipcmedia.com
Owner *IPC Media (A Time Warner Company)*
Editor *Will Hetherington*
Circulation 20,000

Launched 1989. MONTHLY aimed at those who enjoy driven game shooting in the UK and around the world.

FEATURES *Will Hetherington* Welcomes articles directly related to interesting or unusual game shooting stories; max. 2000 words. Approach by e-mail.

NEWS *Darren Crush* Max. 2000 words.

Shooting Times & Country Magazine
IPC Media Ltd., King's Reach Tower, Stamford Street, London SE1 9LS
☎020 7261 6180 Fax 020 7261 7179
✉ steditorial@ipcmedia.com
www.shootingtimes.co.uk

Owner *IPC Media (A Time Warner Company)*
Editor *Camilla Clark*
Circulation 28,178

Founded 1882. WEEKLY. Covers shooting, fishing and related countryside topics. Unsolicited contributions considered.
PAYMENT negotiable.

Shout Magazine

D.C. Thomson & Co., Albert Square, Dundee DD1 9QJ
☎01382 223131 Fax 01382 200880
✉ shout@dcthomson.co.uk

Owner *D.C. Thomson Publishers*
Editor *Maria T. Welch*
Circulation 74,409

Founded 1993. FORTNIGHTLY. Pop music, quizzes, emotional, beauty, fashion, soap features.
FICTION *Maria Welch* Supernatural/spooky stories welcome. Approach by telephone in the first instance. Max. 1500 words. PAYMENT £100.

Shout!

PO Box YR46, Leeds LS9 6XG
☎0113 248 5700 Fax 0113 295 6097
✉ shout.magazine@ntlworld.com
www.shoutweb.co.uk

Owner/Editor *Mark Michalowski*
Circulation 7000

Founded 1995. MONTHLY lesbian/gay and bisexual news, views, arts and scene for Yorkshire; lgb health and politics. Interested in reviews of Yorkshire lgb events, happenings, news, analysis – 300 to 1000 words max. No fiction, fashion or items with no reasonable relevance to Yorkshire and the north.
PAYMENT £40 per 1000 words.

Showing World

The Publishing House, Station Road, Framlingham IP13 9EE
☎01728 622030 Fax 01728 622031
✉ todaymagazine@btopeworld.com

Owner *T.P. Publications*
Editor *Charlotte Knight*
Circulation 3000

Founded 1991. Features every aspect of showing horses and ponies plus natives, miniatures and donkeys. Knowledgeable and how-to-do-it articles welcome. Photos essential.
PAYMENT negotiable.

Shropshire Magazine

Waterloo Road, Telford TS1 5HU
☎01952 288822 Fax 01952 288820

Owner *Shropshire Newspapers Ltd*
Editor *Henry Carpenter*

Founded 1950. MONTHLY. Unsolicited mss welcome but ideas in writing preferred.
FEATURES Personalities, topical items, historical (e.g. family) of Shropshire; also general interest: homes, weddings, antiques, etc. Max. 1000 words.
PAYMENT negotiable 'but modest'.

Sight & Sound

British Film Institute, 21 Stephen Street, London W1T 1LN
☎020 7255 1444 Fax 020 7436 2327
www.bfi.org.uk/sightandsound

Owner *British Film Institute*
Editor *Nick James*

Founded 1932. MONTHLY. Topical and critical articles on international cinema, with regular columns from the USA and Europe. Length 1000–5000 words. Relevant photographs appreciated. Also book, film, DVD and video release reviews. Approach in writing with ideas.
PAYMENT by arrangement.

Ski and Board

The White House, 57–63 Church Road, Wimbledon, London SW19 5SB
☎020 8410 2000 Fax 020 8410 2001
✉ info@skiandboard.co.uk
www.skiclub.co.uk

Owner *Ski Club of Great Britain*
Editor *Arnie Wilson*

Founded 1903. FOUR ISSUES YEARLY. Features from established ski/snowboard writers only.

The Skier and Snowboarder Magazine

Mountain Marketing Ltd., PO Box 386, Sevenoaks TN13 1AQ
☎0845 310 8303
✉ skierandsnowboarder@hotmail.com

Publisher *Mountain Marketing Ltd*
Editor *Frank Baldwin*
Circulation 30,000

SEASONAL (from July to May). FIVE ISSUES YEARLY. Outside contributions welcome.
FEATURES Various topics covered, including race reports, resort reports, fashion, equipment update, dry slope, club news, new products, health and safety. Crisp, tight, informative copy of 800 words or less preferred.
NEWS All aspects of skiing news covered.
PAYMENT negotiable.

Slightly Foxed:
The Real Reader's Quarterly

67 Dickinson Court, 15 Brewhouse Yard,
London EC1V 4JX
☎020 7549 2121/2111 Fax 0870 199 1245
✉ all@foxedquarterly.com
www.foxedquarterly.com

Owner *Slightly Foxed Ltd*
Editors *Gail Pirkis, Hazel Wood*
Circulation 4000

Founded 2004. 'Reviews of books (fiction and non-fiction) that have stood the test of time or books that have been published recently and are of real quality but which have been overlooked by reviewers and bookshops.' Unsolicited contributions of 'lively, personal, idiosyncratic writing of real quality' are welcome but it is recommended that would-be contributors read the magazine first to gauge its approach. Send e-mail with sample work in the first instance. Not interested in anything that is not actually a review of a book or author.

Smallholder

Hook House, Wimblington March PE15 0QL
☎01354 741538 Fax 01354 741182
✉ liz.wright1@btconnect.com
www.smallholder.co.uk

Owner *Newsquest Plc*
Editor *Liz Wright*
Circulation 20,000

Founded 1982. MONTHLY. Outside contributions welcome. Send for sample magazine and editorial schedule before submitting anything. Follow up with samples of work to the editor so that style can be assessed for suitability. No poetry or humorous, unfocused personal tales; no puzzles.

FEATURES New writers always welcome, but must have high level of technical expertise – 'not textbook stuff'. 'How to do it' articles with photos welcome. Illustrations and photos paid for. Length 750–1500 words.

NEWS All agricultural and rural news welcome. Length 200–500 words.

PAYMENT negotiable.

SmartLife International

21–23 Phoenix Court, Hawkins Road,
Colchester CO2 8JY
☎01206 505924 Fax 01206 505929
✉ stuart@smartlifeint.com
www.smartlifeint.com

Owner *Aceville Publications Ltd*
Editor *Stuart Pritchard*

Circulation 18,789

Launched 2000. TEN ISSUES YEARLY. High-end lifestyle magazine: consumer technology, interior design, luxury cars, travel, fashion and grooming. Welcomes proposals by e-mail.

FEATURES *Hamish McNair-Wilson* 'No good feature ideas that fit the remit are ruled out.' Max. 2000 words.

NEWS *Jake Stow* Generally compiled in-house.

Sneak Magazine

Mappin House, 4 Winsley Street, London
W1W 8HF
☎020 7182 8000 Fax 020 7182 8529
✉ michelle.garnett@emap.com
www.sneakmagazine.com

Owner *EMAP*
Editor *Michelle Garnett*
Editorial Director *Jennifer Cawthron*
Circulation 74,299

Founded 2002. WEEKLY magazine for teenagers providing gossip and entertainment. Unsolicited material welcome.

FEATURES *Laura Atkinson*
NEWS *Rowan Erlam*

Snooker Scene

Hayley Green Court, 130 Hagley Road,
Halesowen, Birmingham B63 1DY
☎0121 585 9188 Fax 0121 585 7117
✉ clive.everton@talk21.com
www.snookersceneonline.com

Owner *Everton's News Agency*
Editor *Clive Everton*
Circulation 10,000

Founded 1971. MONTHLY. No unsolicited mss. Approach in writing with an idea.

The Spectator

56 Doughty Street, London WC1N 2LL
☎020 7405 1706 Fax 020 7242 0603
✉ editor@spectator.co.uk
www.spectator.co.uk

Owner *The Spectator (1828) Ltd*
Editor *Matthew d'Ancona*
Deputy Editor *Stuart Reid*
Books *Mark Amory*
Circulation 68,415

Founded 1828. WEEKLY political and literary magazine. Prospective contributors should write in the first instance to the relevant editor. Unsolicited mss welcome, but no 'follow up' phone calls, please. (Relocation due 2007. Check website for new address.) PAYMENT nominal.

The Sportsman

1 Riverside, Manbre Road, London W6 9WA
☎020 8846 3000   Fax 020 8846 9660
✉ info@thesportsman.co.uk
www.thesportsman.co.uk
Owner *Sports Betting Media Ltd*
Editor *Charlie Methven*

Sports betting and racing DAILY newspaper, launched in March 2006. 'In-depth reports, results and inside information from those closest to the sport.' Contributions by e-mail are welcome.

Staffordshire Life

The Publishing Centre, Derby Street, Stafford ST16 2DT
☎01785 257700   Fax 01785 253287
✉ editor@staffordshirelife.co.uk
www.staffordshirelife.co.uk
Owner *Staffordshire Newspapers Ltd*
Editor *Philip Thurlow-Craig*
Circulation 17,000

Founded 1982. ELEVEN ISSUES YEARLY. Full-colour county magazine devoted to Staffordshire, its surroundings and people. Contributions welcome. Approach in writing with ideas.
FEATURES Max. 1200 words.
PAYMENT NUJ rates.

The Stage

Stage House, 47 Bermondsey Street, London SE1 3XT
☎020 7403 1818   Fax 020 7357 9287
✉ editor@thestage.co.uk
www.thestage.co.uk
Owner *The Stage Newspaper Ltd*
Editor *Brian Attwood*
Circulation 27,247

Founded 1880. WEEKLY. No unsolicited mss. Prospective contributors should write with ideas in the first instance.
FEATURES Preference for middle-market, tabloid-style articles. 'Puff pieces', PR plugs and extended production notes will not be considered. Max. 800 words. Profiles: 1200 words.
NEWS News stories from outside London are always welcome. Max. 300 words.
PAYMENT £100 per 1000 words.

Stamp Lover

National Philatelic Society, 107 Charterhouse Street, London EC1M 6PT
☎020 7490 9610
✉ nps@ukphilately.org.uk

www.ukphilately.org.uk/nps
Owner *National Philatelic Society*
Editor *David Alford*
Circulation 1000

Founded 1908. SIX ISSUES YEARLY. Magazine of the National Philatelic Society. Welcomes articles about the hobby; stamps, old and new. Approach by e-mail or letter.
NEWS Information about worldwide philately. Max. 1000 words.

Stamp Magazine

IPC Media Ltd, Leon House, 233 High Street, Croydon CR9 1HZ
☎020 8726 8000
✉ guy_thomas@ipcmedia.com
Owner *IPC Media (A Time Warner Company)*
Editor *Guy Thomas*
Circulation 12,000

Founded 1934. MONTHLY news and features on the world of stamp collecting from the past to the present day. Interested in articles by experts on particular countries or themes such as subject matter illustrated on stamps – dogs, politics, etc. Approach in writing.
NEWS *Julia Lee* News of latest stamp issues or industry news. Max. 500 words.
FEATURES *Guy Thomas* Any features welcome on famous stamps, rarities, postmarks, postal history, exhibitions, postcards, personal collections, auctions. Must be illustrated with colour images ('we can arrange for photography of original stamps'). Max. 2500 words, or 5000 for 2-part expert piece.
PAYMENT negotiable.

Staple

See under *Poetry Magazines*

Steam Railway Magazine

Bretton Court, Bretton, Peterborough PE3 8DZ
☎01733 264666   Fax 01733 282720
✉ steam.railway@emap.com
Owner *Emap Active Limited*
Editor *Tony Streeter*
Circulation 32,831

Founded 1979. FOUR-WEEKLY magazine targeted at all steam enthusiasts interested in the modern preservation movement. Unsolicited material welcome. News reports, photographs, steam-age reminiscences. Approach in writing or by e-mail.

The Strad

Orpheus Publications, Newsquest Specialist Media Ltd, 2nd Floor, 30 Cannon Street, London EC4M 6YJ
☎020 7618 3095 Fax 020 7618 3483
✉ thestrad@orpheuspublications.com
www.thestrad.com
Owner *Newsquest Specialist Media Group*
Editor *Naomi Sadler*
Circulation 17,500
Founded 1890. MONTHLY for classical string musicians, makers and enthusiasts. Unsolicited mss accepted occasionally 'though acknowledgement/return not guaranteed'.
FEATURES Profiles of string players, teachers, luthiers and musical instruments, also relevant research. Max. 2000 words.
REVIEWS *Ariane Todes, Catherine Nelson*
PAYMENT £150 per 1000 words.

Stuff

Teddington Studios, Broom Road, Teddington TW11 9NT
☎020 8267 5036
✉ stuff@haynet.com
www.stuffmag.co.uk
Owner *Haymarket Publishing Ltd*
Editor *Michael Brook*
Circulation 90,750
Launched 1998. MONTHLY guide to new technology with information on all the latest gadgets and gear. Includes a 'Buyers' Guide' with information about the top tried and tested items. No unsolicited contributions.

Suffolk and Norfolk Life

The Publishing House, Framlingham IP13 9EE
☎01728 622030 Fax 01728 622031
Owner *Today Magazines Ltd*
Editor *Kevin Davis*
Circulation 17,000
Founded 1989. MONTHLY. General interest, local stories, historical, personalities, wine, travel, food. Unsolicited mss welcome. Approach by phone or in writing with ideas. Not interested in anything which does not relate specifically to East Anglia.
FEATURES *Kevin Davis* Max. 1500 words, with photos.
NEWS *Kevin Davis* Max. 1000 words, with photos.
SPECIAL PAGES *William Locks* Study the magazine for guidelines. Max. 1500 words.
PAYMENT £40–60.

Sugar Magazine

64 North Row, London W1K 7LL
☎020 7150 7050 Fax 020 7150 7678
www.sugarmagazine.co.uk
Owner *Hachette Filipacchi (UK)*
Editor *Annabel Brog*
Editorial Director *Lysanne Currie*
Circulation 250,099
Founded 1994. MONTHLY. Everything that might interest the teenage girl. No unsolicited mss. Will consider ideas or contacts for real-life features. No fiction. Approach in writing in the first instance.

Sunday Times Magazine

See **The Sunday Times** under *National Newspapers*

SuperBike Magazine

IPC Media Ltd, Leon House, 233 High Street, Croydon CR9 1HZ
☎020 8726 8419
www.superbikes.com
Owner *IPC Media (A Time Warner Company)*
Publishing Director *Keith Foster*
Editor *Kenny Pryde*
Circulation 54,642
Founded 1977. MONTHLY. Dedicated to all that is best and most exciting in the world of high-performance motorcycling. Unsolicited mss, synopses and ideas welcome.

Sussex Life

Baskerville Place, 28 Teville Road, Worthing BN11 1UG
☎01903 218719 Fax 01903 820193
✉ jonathan.keeble@sussexlife.co.uk
www.sussexlife.com
Owner *Archant Life*
Editor *Jonathan Keeble*
Circulation 42,000
Founded 1965. MONTHLY. Sussex and general interest magazine. Regular supplements on education, fashion, homes and gardens. Interested in investigative, journalistic pieces relevant to the area and celebrity profiles. Unsolicited mss, synopses and ideas welcome but approach by telephone in the first instance.

Swimming Magazine

41 Granby Street, Loughborough LE11 3DU
☎01509 632230 Fax 01509 632233
Owner *Amateur Swimming Association*
Editor *P. Hassall*
Circulation 20,000

Founded 1923. MONTHLY about competitive swimming and associated subjects. Unsolicited mss welcome.
FEATURES Technical articles on swimming, water polo, diving or synchronised swimming. Length and payment negotiable.

The Tablet
1 King Street Cloisters, Clifton Walk, London W6 0QZ
☎020 8748 8484 Fax 020 8748 1550
✉ thetablet@tablet.co.uk
www.thetablet.co.uk
Owner *The Tablet Publishing Co Ltd*
Editor *Catherine Pepinster*
Circulation 23,071
Founded 1840. WEEKLY. Quality international Roman Catholic periodical featuring articles (political, social, cultural, theological or spiritual) of interest to concerned Christian laity and clergy. 'We welcome ideas for articles; please send a brief outline in advance, setting out what you propose to write about and explaining your credentials.' Unsolicited material is not accepted.
PAYMENT negotiable.

Take a Break
Academic House, 24–28 Oval Road, London NW1 7DT
☎020 7241 8000
✉ tab.features@bauer.co.uk
Owner *H. Bauer Publishing Ltd*
Editor *John Dale*
Circulation 1.16 million
Founded 1990. WEEKLY. True-life feature magazine. Approach with ideas in writing.
NEWS/FEATURES Always on the look-out for good, true-life stories. Max. 1200 words.
FICTION Sharp, succinct stories which are well told and often with a twist at the end. All categories, provided it is relevant to the magazine's style and market. Max. 1000 words.
PAYMENT negotiable.

Tate Etc
Millbank, London SW1P 4RG
☎020 7887 8030 Fax 020 7887 8729
✉ tateetc@tate.org.uk
www.tate.org.uk
Owner *Tate*
Editorial Director *Bice Curiger*
Editor *Simon Grant*
Circulation 90,000
Relaunched May 2004. THREE ISSUES YEARLY.

Visual arts magazine aimed at a broad readership with articles blending the historic and the contemporary. Please send material by post.

Tatler
Vogue House, Hanover Square, London W1S 1JU
☎020 7499 9080 Fax 020 7493 1641
www.tatler.co.uk
Owner *Condé Nast Publications Ltd*
Editor *Geordie Greig*
Features Director *Vassi Chamberlain*
Circulation 88,189
Up-market glossy from the Condé Nast stable. New writers should send in copies of either published work or unpublished material; writers of promise will be taken up. The magazine works largely on a commission basis: they are unlikely to publish unsolicited features, but will ask writers to work to specific projects.

The Teacher
Hamilton House, Mabledon Place, London WC1H 9BD
☎020 7380 4708 Fax 020 7383 7230
✉ teacher@nut.org.uk
www.teachers.org.uk
Owner *National Union of Teachers*
Editor *Mitch Howard*
Circulation 300,000
Journal of the National Union of Teachers, published EIGHT TIMES YEARLY. News, advice, information and special features on educational matters relating to classroom teaching. Will consider 'anything on spec'. Approach by letter or e-mail.

Textualities
Main Point Books, 8 Lauriston Street, Edinburgh EH3 9DJ
☎0131 228 4837
✉ the.editor@textualities.net
www.textualities.net
Editor *Jennie Renton*
Circulation 1000
Fomerly *Scottish Book Collector*, launched in 1986. ANNUAL. Literature and book collecting, with a Scottish slant. No unsolicited contributions. Telephone or check the website in the first instance.

TGO (The Great Outdoors)
Newsquest Magazines, 200 Renfield Street, Glasgow G2 3QB
☎0141 302 7700 Fax 0141 302 7799

✉ cameron.mcneish@tgomagazine.co.uk

Owner *Newsquest*
Editor *Cameron McNeish*
Circulation 11,569

Founded 1978. MONTHLY. Deals with walking, backpacking and wild country topics. Unsolicited mss are welcome.

FEATURES Well-written and illustrated items on relevant topics. Max. 2500 words. Quality high resolution digital colour images only, please.

NEWS Short topical items (or photographs). Max. 300 words.

PAYMENT negotiable.

That's Life!

3rd Floor, Academic House, 24–28 Oval Road, London NW1 7DT
☎020 7241 8000 Fax 020 7241 8008
✉ firstname.lastname@bauer.co.uk

Owner *H. Bauer Publishing Ltd*
Editor *Jo Checkley*
Circulation 550,036

Founded 1995. WEEKLY. True-life stories, puzzles, health, homes, parenting, cookery and fun.

FEATURES *Karen Bryans* Max. 1600 words.
FICTION *Emma Fabian* 1200 words.
PAYMENT features, varies; fiction, £300.

Therapy Weekly

Emap Healthcare, Greater London House, Hampstead Road, London NW1 7EJ
☎020 7874 0367 Fax 020 7874 0368
www.therapyweekly.co.uk

Owner *Emap Healthcare*
Editor *Richard Evans*
Circulation 15,000

Founded 1974. WEEKLY professional magazine for physiotherapists, occupational therapists and speech and language therapists. Will consider topical articles of professional interest to the reader. No fiction. Approach by telephone.

The Third Alternative

See **Black Static**

This England

PO Box 52, Cheltenham GL50 1YQ
☎01242 537900 Fax 01242 537901

Owner *This England Ltd*
Editor *Roy Faiers*
Circulation 200,000

Founded 1968. QUARTERLY, with a strong overseas readership. Celebration of England and all things English: famous people, natural beauty,

towns and villages, history, traditions, customs and legends, crafts, etc. Generally a rural basis, with the 'Forgetmenots' section publishing readers' recollections and nostalgia. Up to a hundred unsolicited pieces received each week. Unsolicited mss/ideas welcome. Length 250–2000 words. PAYMENT £25 per 1000 words.

Time

Brettenham House, Lancaster Place, London WC2E 7TL
☎020 7499 4080
✉ edit_office@timemagazine.com
www.timeeurope.com

Owner *Time Warner*
International Editor *Michael Elliott*
Circulation 142,464 (UK)

Founded 1923. WEEKLY current affairs and news magazine. There are few opportunities for freelancers on *Time* as almost all the magazine's content is written by staff members from various bureaux around the world. No unsolicited mss.

Time Out

Universal House, 251 Tottenham Court Road, London W1T 7AB
☎020 7813 3000 Fax 020 7813 6001
www.timeout.com

Publisher *Lesley Gill*
Editor *Gordon Thomson*
Circulation 89,503

Founded 1968. WEEKLY magazine of news, arts, entertainment and lifestyle in London plus listings.

FEATURES *Alan Rutter* 'Usually written by staff writers or commissioned, but it's always worth submitting an idea by post if particularly apt to the magazine.' Word length varies; up to 2000 max.

CONSUMER SECTION Food and drink, shopping, travel, design, property.

PAYMENT negotiable.

The Times Educational Supplement

Admiral House, 66–68 East Smithfield, London E1W 1BX
☎020 7782 3000 Fax 020 7782 3200
✉ newsdesk@tes.co.uk *or* editor@tes.co.uk
www.tes.co.uk

Owner *Exponent*
Editor *Judith Judd*
Circulation 69,448

Founded 1910. WEEKLY. New contributors are

welcome and should fax or e-mail ideas on one sheet of A4 for news, features or reviews, or e-mail the editor or newsdesk.The main newspaper accepts contributions in the following sections:

OPINION 'Platform': a weekly slot for a well-informed and cogently argued viewpoint. Max. 1200 words. 'Another Voice': a shorter comment on an issue of the day by non-education professionals. Max. 700 words.

LEADERSHIP Weekly pages on practical issues for school governors and managers. Max. 800 words.

FE FOCUS Weekly pull-out section covering post-16 education and training in colleges, work and the wider community. Aimed at everyone from teachers/lecturers to leaders and opinion formers in lifelong learning. News, features, comment and opinion on all aspects of college life welcome. Length from 350 words (news) to 1000 max. (features). Contact ian.nash@tes.co.uk

Friday A weekly magazine with *The TES* which focuses on whole school issues, good practice, teaching as a career and the work/life balance (friday@tes.co.uk):

FEATURES Unsolicited features are rarely accepted but ideas are welcome accompanied by cuttings and/or c.v. Length from 1000–2000 words. Strong storylines are expected.

TALKBACK Short, first person pieces, max. 650 words, are welcome for consideration. Humour from teachers is encouraged, especially for the 'Thank God it's Friday' column.

TES Teacher Weekly magazine for classroom teachers focusing on what individual teachers do in the classroom to teach pupils and subjects. Specific subject section each week. Max. 800 words. (teacher@tes.co.uk)

Online (Computers in Education) A magazine devoted to information and communications technology appearing with *The TES* six times a year. (merlin.john@tes.co.uk)

SPECIAL ISSUES Occasional pull-out magazines on topics including newly qualified teachers (fiona.flynn@tes.co.uk); business links (ian.nash@tes.co.uk); *Go Global* (brendan.o'malley@tes.co.uk); school visits – *Going Places* (thomas.watson@tes.co.uk).

The Times Educational Supplement Scotland

Scott House, 10 South St Andrew Street, Edinburgh EH2 2AZ
☎0131 557 1133 Fax 0131 558 1155
✉ scoted@tes.co.uk
www.tes.co.uk/scotland
Owner *TSL Education Ltd*

Editor *Neil Munro*
Circulation 6,076
Founded 1965. WEEKLY. Unsolicited mss welcome.

FEATURES Articles on education in Scotland. Max. 1000 words.

NEWS Items on education in Scotland. Max. 600 words.

The Times Higher Education Supplement

Admiral House, 66–68 East Smithfield, London E1W 1BX
☎020 7782 3000 Fax 020 7782 3300
✉ editor@thes.co.uk
www.thes.co.uk
Owner *News International*
Editor *John O'Leary*
Circulation 23,902

Founded 1971. WEEKLY. Unsolicited items are welcome but most articles and almost all book reviews are commissioned. 'In most cases it is better to write or e-mail, but in the case of news stories it is all right to phone.'

FEATURES *Mandy Garner* Most articles are commissioned from academics in higher education.

News *Lee Eliot-Major* Freelance opportunities very occasionally.

BOOKS *Andrew Robinson*
SCIENCE *Steve Farrar*
SCIENCE BOOKS *Andrew Robinson*
FOREIGN *David Jobbins*
PAYMENT by negotiation.

The Times Literary Supplement

Times House, 1 Pennington Street, London E98 1BS
☎020 7782 5000 Fax 020 7782 4966
www.the-tls.co.uk
Owner *The Times Literary Supplement Ltd*
Editor *Peter Stothard*
Circulation 33,323

Founded 1902. WEEKLY review of literature, history, philosophy, science and the arts. Contributors should approach in writing and be familiar with the general level of writing in the *TLS*.

LITERARY DISCOVERIES *Alan Jenkins*
POEMS *Mick Imlah*

News Reviews and general articles concerned with literature, publishing and new intellectual developments anywhere in the world. Length by arrangement.

PAYMENT by arrangement.

Titbits

2 Caversham Street, London SW3 4AH
☎020 7351 4995 Fax 020 7351 4995
Owner *Sport Newspapers Ltd*
Editor *James Hughes*
Circulation 150,000

Founded 1895. MONTHLY. Consumer magazine for men covering show business and general interests. Ideas in writing welcome. Max. 3000 words. News, features, particularly photofeatures (colour) and fiction. Always send letter or telephone first.
PAYMENT negotiable.

Today's Golfer

Bushfield House, Orton Centre, Peterborough PE2 5UW
☎01733 237111 Fax 01733 288014
Owner *Emap Active Ltd*
Editor *Andy Calton*
Deputy Editor *Chris Jones*
Circulation 104,000

Founded 1988. MONTHLY. Golf instruction, features, player profiles and news. Most features written in-house but unsolicited mss will be considered. Approach in writing with ideas. Not interested in instruction material from outside contributors.
FEATURES/NEWS *Kevin Brown* Opinion, player profiles and general golf-related features.

Top of the Pops Magazine

Room A1136, Woodlands, 80 Wood Lane, London W12 0TT
☎020 8433 3910 Fax 020 8433 2694
Owner *BBC Worldwide Publishing Ltd*
Editor *Peter Hart*
Circulation 96,576

Founded 1995. MONTHLY teenage pop music magazine with a lighthearted and humorous approach. No unsolicited material apart from pop star interviews.

Total Film

1 Balcombe Street, London NW1 6LY
☎020 7042 4830 Fax 020 7042 4839
✉ totalfilm@futurenet.co.uk
Owner *Future Publishing*
Editor *Mark Dinning*
Circulation 90,642

Founded 1997. MONTHLY reviews-based movie magazine. Interested in ideas for features, not necessarily tied in to specific releases, and humour items. No reviews or interviews with celebrities/directors. Approach by post or e-mail.

Total TV Guide

H. Bauer Publishing, Academic House, 24–28 Oval Road, London NW1 8DT
☎020 7241 8000 Fax 020 7241 8042
✉ barbara.miller@bauer.co.uk
www.bauer.co.uk
Owner *H. Bauer Publishing*
Editor *Jon Peake*
Circulation 92,004

Founded 2003. WEEKLY TV listings for those with access to multichannel television, covering everything from movies to sport, drama to children's programmes.

FEATURES *Ben Lawrence* Commissions features relating to current TV programmes; chiefly celebrity interviews and set visits. No unsolicited contributions.

Total Vauxhall

Future Publishing, 30 Monmouth Street, Bath BA1 2BW
☎01225 442244 Fax 01225 446019
✉ info@totalvauxhall.co.uk
www.totalvauxhall.co.uk
Owner *Future Publishing*
Editor *Barton Brisland*
Circulation 20,000

Founded 2001. MONTHLY independent newsstand magazine aimed at the Vauxhall enthusiast. Covers new, modified, historical/classic, race and rally Vauxhalls of all kinds. Substantial amount of technical content. Also covers the more interesting parts of the GM family, particularly Opel and Holden. Uses a lot of freelance contributors; 'those who hit deadlines and fulfill the brief get regular work and lots of it.' Feature ideas, news items, historical pieces and potential feature cars welcome but must have a Vauxhall/GM tilt. Call the editor directly for an informal discussion on style, approach and angle.
PAYMENT 'surprisingly generous'.

Traditional Woodworking

151 Station Street, Burton on Trent DE14 1BG
☎01283 742950 Fax 01283 742957
✉ enquiries@twonline.co.uk
Owner *Waterways World*
Editor *Alison Bell*
Circulation 8,034

Founded 1988. MONTHLY. Features workshop projects, techniques, reviews of the latest woodworking tools and equipment, general articles on woodworking and furniture making. Supplement: *Power Tool Guide*.

FEATURES Technical features and furniture projects welcome.The latter must include drawings and cutting lists.A photograph of the piece is required before commissioning. Approach in writing in the first instance.

PAYMENT negotiable.

Trail
Bretton Court, Bretton, Peterborough PE3 8DZ
☎01733 264666 Fax 01733 282653
✉ trail@emap.com
www.trailroutes.com
Owner *Emap Active Publishing Ltd*
Editor *Guy Procter*
Circulation 41,245

Founded 1990. MONTHLY. Gear reports, where to walk and practical advice for the hillwalker and long distance walker. Inspirational reads on people and outdoor/walking issues. Health, fitness and injury prevention for high level walkers and outdoor lovers. Approach by phone or in writing in the first instance.

FEATURES *Simon Ingram* Very limited requirement for overseas articles, 'written to our style'. Ask for guidelines. Max. 2000 words. Limited requirement for guided walks articles. Specialist writers only. Ask for guidelines. 750–2000 words (depending on subject).

PAYMENT £100 per 1000 words.

Traveller
45–49 Brompton Road, London SW3 1DE
☎020 7589 0500 Fax 020 7581 1357
www.traveller.org.uk
Owner *Wexas International Ltd*
Editor *Amy Sohanpaul*
Circulation 28,831

Founded 1970. QUARTERLY travel magazine.

FEATURES High quality, personal narratives of remarkable journeys. Articles should be off-beat, adventurous, authentic. For guidelines, see website. Articles may be accompanied by professional quality, original slides. Freelance articles considered. Max. 1000 words. Initial contact by e-mail.

PAYMENT £200 per 1000 words.

Tribune
9 Arkwright Road, London NW3 6An
☎020 7433 6410 Fax 020 7433 6410
✉ tribuneweb@btconnect.com
Owner *Tribune Publications*
Editor *Chris McLaughlin*

Founded 1937. WEEKLY. Independent Labour publication covering parliament, politics, trade unions, public policy and social issues, international affairs and the arts. Welcomes freelance contributions; approach by telephone or e-mail.

FEATURES *George Osgerby* Anything in line with the topics above. Max. 1000 words.

NEWS *Barckley Sumner* Breaking or forthcoming news events/stories. Max. 480 words.

OTHER Interviews, reviews, cartoons.

Trout Fisherman
EMAP Active Ltd, Bushfield House, Orton Centre, Peterborough PE2 5UW
☎01733 237111 Fax 01733 465820
✉ russell.hill@emap.com
www.troutfisherman.co.uk
Owner *Emap Active Ltd*
Editor *Russell Hill*
Circulation 27,734

Founded 1977. MONTHLY instructive magazine on trout fishing. Most of the articles are commissioned, but unsolicited mss and quality colour transparencies welcome.

FEATURES Max. 2500 words.

PAYMENT varies.

TVTimes
IPC Media Ltd., King's Reach Tower, Stamford Street, London SE1 9LS
☎020 7261 7000 Fax 020 7261 7888
Owner *IPC Media (A Time Warner Company)*
Editor *Ian Abbott*
Circulation 407,878

Founded 1955. WEEKLY magazine of listings and features serving the viewers of independent television, BBC, satellite and radio. Freelance contributions by commission only. No unsolicited contributions.

Ulster Business
5b Edgewater Business Park, Belfast Harbour Estate, Belfast BT3 9JQ
☎028 9078 3200 Fax 028 9078 3210
✉ russellcampbell@greerpublications.com
www.ulsterbusiness.com
Owner *James Greer*
Editor *Russell Campbell*
Circulation 8,274

Founded 1987. MONTHLY. General business content with coverage of all sectors: ICT, retail, agriculture, commercial property, etc. 'Opportunities exist for well-written local orientated features, particularly those dealing with local firms or the issues they face; local business personality interviews also useful.' Contact the editor by e-mail. Max. 1000 words.

Ulster Tatler
39 Boucher Road, Belfast BT12 6UT
☎028 9066 3311 Fax 028 9038 1915
✉ edit@ulstertatler.com
www.ulstertatler.com
Owner/Editor *Richard Sherry*
Circulation 11,995
Founded 1965. MONTHLY. Articles of local interest and social functions appealing to Northern Ireland's ABC1 population. Welcomes unsolicited material; approach by phone or in writing in the first instance.
FEATURES *Noreen Dorman* Max. 1500 words.
FICTION *Richard Sherry* Max. 3000 words

Ultimate Advertiser
PO Box 7086, Clacton on Sea CO15 5WN
☎01255 428500 Fax 0870 046 6536
✉ sales@ultimateadvertiser.co.uk
www.ultimateadvertiser.co.uk
Owner *Apex Publishing Ltd*
Editor *Susan Kidby*
Circulation 5000
Founded 2005. MONTHLY advertising magazine including guides and information, features, listings and reviews. Approach by post, only.

Uncut
25th Floor, King's Reach Tower, Stamford Street, London SE1 9LS
☎020 7261 6992 Fax 020 7261 5573
✉ farah_ishaq@ipcmedia.com
www.uncut.co.uk
Owner *IPC Media (A Time Warner Company)*
Editor *Allan Jones*
Deputy Editor *Paul Lester*
Associate Editor (Film) *Michael Bonner*
Music Editor *John Mulvey*
First Cuts Editor *Simon Goddard*
Online Editor *Ben Perreau*
Circulation 110,052
Launched 1997. MONTHLY music and film magazine with free CD each issue. Welcomes music and film reviews; approach by e-mail.

The Universe
St James's Buildings, Oxford Street, Manchester M1 6FP
☎0161 237 4350 Fax 0161 237 4381
✉ joseph.kelly@totalcatholic.com
www.totalcatholic.com
Owner *Gabriel Communications Ltd*
Editor *Joseph Kelly*
Circulation 60,000
Occasional use of new writers, but a substantial network of regular contributors already exists. Interested in a very wide range of material: all subjects which might bear on Christian life. Fiction not normally accepted. PAYMENT negotiable.

Vector
See **British Science Fiction Association** under *Professional Associations and Societies*

The Vegan
Donald Watson House, 7 Battle Road, St Leonards on Sea TN37 7AA
☎01424 427393 Fax 01424 717064
✉ editor@vegansociety.com
www.vegansociety.com
Owner *Vegan Society*
Editor *Catriona Toms*
Circulation 7000
Founded 1944. QUARTERLY. Deals with the ecological, ethical and health aspects of veganism. Unsolicited mss welcome. Max. 2000 words. PAYMENT negotiable.

Verbatim The Language Quarterly
PO Box 156, Chearsley, Aylesbury HP18 0DQ
☎01844 208474
✉ verbatim.uk@tesco.net
www.verbatimmag.com
Owner *Word, Inc.*
Editor *Erin McKean*
Founded in 1974 by Laurence Urdang. QUARTERLY journal devoted to what is amusing, interesting and engaging about the English language and languages in general. Will consider unsolicited material but send for writer's guidelines in the first instance. For a sample copy of the magazine, send 50p (stamp or IRC).
PAYMENT ranges from £20–300, 'depending on length, wit and other merit'.

Vogue
Vogue House, Hanover Square, London W1S 1JU
☎020 7499 9080 Fax 020 7408 0559
www.vogue.co.uk
Owner *Condé Nast Publications Ltd*
Editor *Alexandra Shulman*
Circulation 214,348
Launched 1916. Condé Nast Magazines tend to use known writers and commission what's needed, rather than using unsolicited mss. Contacts are useful.
FEATURES *Harriet Quick* Upmarket general interest rather than 'women's'. Good proportion of highbrow art and literary articles, as well as travel, gardens, food, home interest and reviews.

The Voice Newspaper
Blue Star House, 234–244 Stockwell Road, London SW9 9UG
☎020 7737 7377 Fax 020 7274 8994
✉ newsdesk@gvmedia.co.uk
www.voice-online.co.uk
Managing Director *Kingsley Thomas*
Chief Editor *Deidre Forbes*
Circulation 40,000
Founded 1982. Leading WEEKLY newspaper for black Britons and other minority communities. Includes news, features, arts, sport and a comprehensive jobs section. Also includes a weekly glossy entertainment section. Illustrations: colour and b&w photos. Open to ideas for news and features on sport, business, community events and the arts.

VW Golf+
IPC Media Ltd, Leon House, 233 High Street, Croydon CR9 1HZ
☎020 8726 8000
✉ thegolfmag@ipcmedia.com
www.thegolf.co.uk
Owner *IPC Media (A Time Warner Company)*
Editor *Fabian Cotter*
Circulation 25,000
Founded 1995. MONTHLY. Features Volkswagen Golfs and other VAG cars. Articles on tuning, styling, performance, technical and potential feature cars. 'Not interested in anything to do with the game of golf.' Submissions should be made directly to the editor. Articles must show excellent specialist knowledge of the subject matter. PAYMENT by negotiation.

W.I. Life
104 New Kings Road, London SW6 4LY
☎020 7731 5777 Fax 020 7736 4061
Owner *National Federation of Women's Institutes*
Editor *Joanna Grey*
Circulation 200,000
Founded 1919. EIGHT ISSUES YEARLY. Official full-colour journal of the Federation of Women's Institutes, containing articles on a wide range of subjects of interest to women. Strong environmental country slant with crafts and cookery plus gardening. Unsolicited mss, photos and illustrations welcome. PAYMENT by arrangement.

walk
2nd Floor, Camelford House, 87–90 Albert Embankment, London SE1 7TW
☎020 7339 8500 Fax 020 7339 8501
✉ ramblers@london.ramblers.org.uk
Owner *Ramblers' Association*
Editor *Christopher Sparrow*
Circulation 106,068
QUARTERLY. Official magazine of the Ramblers' Association, available to members only. Unsolicited mss welcome. S.a.e. required for return.
FEATURES Freelance features are invited on any aspect of walking in Britain. Length up to 1,000 words, preferably with good photographs. No general travel articles.

The War Cry
101 Newington Causeway, London SE1 6BN
☎020 7367 4900 Fax 020 7367 4710
✉ warcry@salvationarmy.org.uk
www.salvationarmy.org.uk/warcry
Owner *The Salvation Army*
Editor *Major Nigel Bovey*
Circulation 58,000
Founded 1879. WEEKLY full-colour magazine containing Christian comment on current issues. Unsolicited mss welcome if appropriate to contents. No fiction or poetry. Approach by phone with ideas.
NEWS relating to Christian Church or social issues. Max. length 500 words.
FEATURES Human interest articles aimed at the 'person-in-the-street'. Max. 500 words.
PAYMENT negotiable.

Waterways World
151 Station Street, Burton on Trent DE14 1BG
☎01283 742950 Fax 01283 742957
✉ admin@wwonline.co.uk
Owner *Waterways World Ltd*
Editor *Richard Fairhurst*
Circulation 16,782
Founded 1972. MONTHLY magazine for inland waterway enthusiasts. Unsolicited mss welcome, provided the writer has a good knowledge of the subject. No fiction.
FEATURES *Richard Fairhurst* Articles (preferably illustrated) are published on all aspects of inland waterways in Britain and abroad, including recreational and commercial boating on rivers and canals.
NEWS *Chris Daniels* Max. 500 words.
PAYMENT £42 per 1000 words.

Web User
IPC Media, Room 0305, King's Reach Tower, Stamford Street, London SE1 9LS
☎020 7261 7294 Fax 020 7261 7878
✉ letters@web-user.co.uk

www.web-user.co.uk
Owner *IPC Media (A Time Warner Company)*
Editor *Andrew Craig*
Circulation 31,886
Founded 2001. FORTNIGHTLY bestseller Internet magazine for all users of the Internet. No unsolicited material; send e-mail or letter of enquiry in the first instance.

Wedding
IPC Media Ltd., King's Reach Tower, Stamford Street, London SE1 9LS
☎020 7261 7471 Fax 020 7261 7459
✉ wedding@ipcmedia.com
Owner *IPC Media (A Time Warner Company)*
Editor *To be appointed*
Circulation 50,000
Founded 1985. BI-MONTHLY offering ideas and inspiration for women planning their wedding. Most features are written in-house or commissioned from known freelancers. Unsolicited mss are not welcome, but approaches may be made in writing.

Weekly News
D.C. Thomson & Co. Ltd., Albert Square, Dundee DD1 9QJ
☎01382 223131 Fax 01382 201390
✉ dburness@dcthomson.co.uk
Owner *D.C. Thomson & Co. Ltd*
Editor *David Burness*
Circulation 89,106
Founded 1855. WEEKLY. Newsy, family-orientated magazine designed to appeal to the busy housewife. Regulars include true-life stories told in the first person, showbiz, royals and television. One or two general interest fiction stories each week. Usually commissions, but writers of promise will be taken up. PAYMENT negotiable.

Welsh Country Magazine
Aberbanc, Llandysul SA44 5NP
☎01559 372010 Fax 01559 371995
✉ editor@welshcountry.co.uk
www.welshcountry.co.uk
Owner *Equine Marketing Limited*
Editor *Kath Rhodes*
Circulation 19,195
Founded 2004. BI-MONTHLY. Outside contributions welcome. Contact the editor with samples of work before submitting full article. The magazine contains a couple of pages in Welsh but is predominantly written in English.
FEATURES Pesonal experiences or view-

points, historical or modern, but there needs to be a strong Welsh connection in some form.
NEWS All Welsh news welcome; anything at all commercial is not paid for.
PAYMENT negotiable.

What Car?
Teddington Studios, Teddington Lock, Broom Road, Teddington TW11 9BE
☎020 8267 5688
✉ editorial@whatcar.com
www.whatcar.com
Owner *Haymarket Motoring Publications Ltd*
Editor *David Motton*
Circulation 122,532
MONTHLY. The car buyer's bible, *What Car?* concentrates on road test comparisons of new cars, news and buying advice on used cars, as well as a strong consumer section. Some scope for freelancers. No unsolicited mss.
PAYMENT negotiable.

What Hi-Fi? Sound & Vision
Teddington Studios, Teddington Lock, Broom Road, Teddington TW11 9BE
☎020 8943 5000 Fax 020 8267 5019
www.whathifi.com
Owner *Haymarket Magazines Ltd*
Managing Director *Kevin Costello*
Editor *Clare Newsome*
Circulation 67,531
Founded 1976. THIRTEEN ISSUES YEARLY. Features on hi-fi and home cinema. No unsolicited contributions. Prior consultation with the editor essential.
FEATURES General or more specific items on hi-fi and home cinema pertinent to the consumer electronics market.
REVIEWS Specific product reviews. All material is now generated by in-house staff. Freelance writing no longer accepted.

What Investment
4th Floor, Arnold House, 36–41 Holywell Lane, London EC2A 3SF
☎020 7827 5454 Fax 020 7827 0567
Owner *Charterhouse Communications*
Editor-in-Chief *Keiron Root*
Editor *Martin Fagan*
Circulation 25,000
Founded 1982. MONTHLY. Features articles on a variety of savings and investment matters. E-mail any ideas to: mfagan@ccplcemail.co.uk
FEATURES Max. 2500 words.
PAYMENT £200 per 1000 words.

What Mortgage

Arnold House, 36–41 Holywell Lane, London EC2A 3SF
☎020 7827 5454   Fax 020 7827 0567
✉ vhartley@charterhouse-communications.co.uk
www.whatmortgage.co.uk
Owner *Charterhouse Communications*
Editor *Victoria Hartley*

Founded 1982. MONTHLY magazine on property purchase and finance. No unsolicited material; prospective contributors may make initial contact with ideas either by telephone or in writing.

FEATURES Particularly welcomes new angles, ideas or specialities relevant to mortgages.
PAYMENT varies.

What Satellite and Digital TV

2 Balcombe Street, London NW1 6NW
☎020 7042 4000
✉ wotsat@futurenet.co.uk
www.wotsat.com
Owner *Future Publishing Ltd*
Editor *Alex Lane*
Circulation 40,000

Founded 1986. MONTHLY including news, technical information, equipment tests, programme background, listings. Contributions welcome – phone first.

FEATURES Unusual installations and users. In-depth guides to popular/cult shows. Technical tutorials.
NEWS Industry and programming. Max. 250 words.

What's New in Building

Ludgate House, 245 Blackfriars Road, London SE1 9UY
☎020 7921 8228   Fax 020 7921 8247
✉ mpennington@cmpinformation.com
Owner *CMP Information*
Editor *Mark Pennington*
Circulation 29,000

MONTHLY. Specialist magazine covering new products for building. Unsolicited mss not generally welcome. The only freelance work available is rewriting press release material. This is offered on a monthly basis of 25–50 items of about 150 words each. PAYMENT £5.25 per item.

What's On in London

Unit 9 & 10, Brooks Court, Cringle Street, London SW8 5BX
☎0845 225 9720   Fax 0845 225 9739

www.whatsoninlondon.co.uk
Owner *Remnant Media Ltd*
Managing Editor *To be appointed*
Circulation 40,000

WEEKLY entertainment-based guide and information magazine. Features, celebrity interviews, listings and reviews. Always interested in well-thought-out and well-presented mss. Articles should have London/Home Counties connection, except during the summer when they can be of much wider tourist/historic interest, relating to unusual traditions and events. Approach the managing editor by telephone in the first instance.

FEATURES *Graham Hassell*
CINEMA *Jim Healy*
POP MUSIC *John Coleman*
CLASSICAL MUSIC *Michael Darvell*
THEATRE *Contact the Theatre Desk*
EVENTS *Adam Lay*
EATING OUT *Michael Darvell*
PAYMENT by arrangement.

Which Caravan

Warners Group Publications plc, The Maltings, West Street, Bourne PH10 9PH
☎01778 391165   Fax 01778 425437
✉ marks@warnersgroup.co.uk
Editor *Mark Sutcliffe*

Founded 1987. Magazine for experienced caravanners and enthusiasts providing practical and useful information and product evaluation. Opportunities for caravanning, relevant touring and travel material, also monthly reviews of the best tow cars, all with good-quality colour photographs.

Wild Times

The RSPB, UK Headquarters, The Lodge, Sandy SG19 2DL
☎01767 680551   Fax 01767 683262
✉ derek.niemann@rspb.org.uk
Owner *Royal Society for the Protection of Birds*
Editor *Derek Niemann*

Founded 1965. BI-MONTHLY. Bird, wildlife and nature conservation for under 8-year-olds (RSPB Wildlife Explorers members). No unsolicited mss. No 'captive/animal welfare' articles.

FEATURES Unsolicited material rarely used.
NEWS News releases welcome. Approach in writing in the first instance.

Wine & Spirit

William Reed Publishing, Broadfield Park, Crawley RH11 9RT
☎01293 613400

✉ wine@wineint.com
www.wineint.com
Owner *William Reed Publishing Ltd*
Editor *Graham Holter*
Circulation 35,000
MONTHLY. New owner, William Reed, has merged *Wine Magazine* with its sister title *Wine & Spirit International* to create *Wine & Spirit*. Still a consumer/specialist magazine, covering wine, spirit and beer, plus food and food/wine-related travel. No unsolicited mss. Prospective contributors should approach in writing or by e-mail.

Wingbeat
The RSPB, UK Headquarters, The Lodge, Sandy SG19 2DL
☎01767 680551 Fax 01767 683262
✉ derek.niemann@rspb.org.uk
Owner *Royal Society for the Protection of Birds*
Editor *Derek Niemann*
Founded 1965. BI-MONTHLY. Bird, wildlife and nature conservation for 14–18-year-olds (RSPB Wildlife Explorers members). No unsolicited mss. No 'captive/animal welfare' articles.
FEATURES Unsolicited material rarely used.
NEWS News releases welcome. Approach in writing in the first instance.

The Wisden Cricketer
1.4 Shepherds Building, Charecroft Way, London W14 0EE
☎020 7471 6900 Fax 020 7471 6901
✉ twc@wisdengroup.com
Owner *Wisden Cricketer Publishing Ltd*
Editor *John Stern*
Circulation 35,000
Founded 2003. MONTHLY. Result of a merger between *The Cricketer International* (1921) and *Wisden Cricket Monthly* (1979). Very few uncommissioned articles are used, but would-be contributors are not discouraged. Approach in writing. PAYMENT varies.

Woman
IPC Media Ltd, King's Reach Tower, Stamford Street, London SE1 9LS
☎020 7261 7023 Fax 020 7261 5997
Owner *IPC Media (A Time Warner Company)*
Editor *Jackie Hatton*
Deputy Editor *Abigail Blackburn*
Circulation 456,524
Founded 1937. WEEKLY. Long-running, popular women's magazine which boasts a readership of over 2.5 million. No unsolicited mss.

Most work commissioned. Approach with ideas in writing.
FEATURES *Judy Yorke* Max. 1250 words.
BOOKS *Lori Miles*

Woman and Home
IPC Media Ltd., King's Reach Tower, Stamford Street, London SE1 9LS
☎020 7261 5176 Fax 020 7261 7346
Owner *IPC Media (A Time Warner Company)*
Editor *Sue James*
Circulation 335,922
Founded 1926. MONTHLY. No unsolicited mss. Prospective contributors are advised to write with ideas, including photocopies of other published work or details of magazines to which they have contributed. S.a.e. essential for return of material. All freelance work is specially commissioned.

Woman's Own
IPC Media Ltd., King's Reach Tower, Stamford Street, London SE1 9LS
☎020 7261 5500 Fax 020 7261 5346
Owner *IPC Media (A Time Warner Company)*
Editor *Elsa McAlonan*
Features Editor *Michelle Maynard*
Circulation 409,616
Founded 1932. WEEKLY. Prospective contributors should contact the features editor *in writing* in the first instance before making a submission. No unsolicited fiction.

Woman's Weekly
IPC Media Ltd., King's Reach Tower, Stamford Street, London SE1 9LS
☎0870 444 5000 Fax 020 7261 6322
✉ womansweeklypostbag@ipcmedia.com
Owner *IPC Media (A Time Warner Company)*
Editor *Sheena Harvey*
Deputy Editor *Geoffrey Palmer*
Features Editor *Sue Pilkington*
Fiction Editor *Gaynor Davies*
Circulation 414,778
Founded 1911. Mass-market WEEKLY for the mature woman.
FEATURES General features covering anything and everything of interest to women of forty-plus. Can be newsy and\or emotional but should be informative. Could be campaigning, or nostalgic, first or third person. Words: ranging from 800 to 2000. Only experienced journalists. Synopses and ideas should be submitted by e-mail to susan_archer@ipcmedia.com
FICTION Short stories, 1000–2500 words;

serials, 12,000–30,000 words. Guidelines for serials: 'a strong emotional theme with a conflict not resolved until the end'; short stories should have warmth and originality. Short stories up to 5000 words considered for *Woman's Weekly Fiction Specials* (see entry). E-mails to maureen_street@ipcmedia.com

Woman's Weekly Fiction Special

IPC Media Ltd., King's Reach Tower, Stamford Street, London SE1 9LS
☎020 7261 6701

Owner *IPC Media (A Time Warner Company)*
Editor *Olwen Rice*
Fiction Editor *Gaynor Davies*

Launched 1998. BI-MONTHLY. Welcomes short stories of between 1000 and 5000 words. Guidelines are available from the Fiction Department. See also *Woman's Weekly*.

Women & Golf

24th Floor, IPC Media Ltd., King's Reach Tower, Stamford Street, London SE1 9LS
☎020 7261 7237 Fax 020 7261 7240
✉ women&golf@ipcmedia.com

Owner *IPC Media (A Time Warner Company)*
Editor *Jane Carter*
Circulation 24,000

Founded 1991. NINE ISSUES YEARLY. Consumer magazine aimed at amateur lady golfers of all ability levels. Features and photography and news welcome; approach by e-mail or post.

The Woodworker

Encanta Media Ltd, Berwick House, 8–10 Knoll Rise, Orpington BR6 0EL
☎01689 899256
www.getwoodworking.com

Owner *Encanta Media Ltd*
Editor *Mark Ramuz*
Circulation 45,000

Founded 1901. MONTHLY. Contributions welcome; approach with ideas in writing.
FEATURES Articles on woodworking with good photo support appreciated. Max. 2000 words.
PAYMENT £150+ per 1000 words.

World Fishing

Media House, Azalea Drive, Swanley BR8 8HU
☎01322 660070 Fax 01322 616376

Owner *Nexus Media Communications Ltd*
Editor *Pilar Santamaria*

Circulation 3384

Founded 1952. MONTHLY. Unsolicited mss welcome; approach by phone or in writing with an idea.
NEWS/FEATURES of a technical or commercial nature relating to the commercial fishing and fish processing industries worldwide (the magazine is read in over 100 different countries). Max. 1500 words.
PAYMENT by arrangement.

The World of Interiors

Vogue House, Hanover Square, London W1S 1JU
☎020 7499 9080 Fax 020 7493 4013
✉ interiors@condenast.co.uk
www.worldofinteriors.co.uk

Owner *Condé Nast Publications Ltd*
Editor *Rupert Thomas*
Circulation 64,656

Founded 1981. MONTHLY. Best approach by fax or letter with an idea, preferably with reference snaps or guidebooks.
FEATURES *Rupert Thomas* Most feature material is commissioned. 'Subjects tend to be found by us, but we are delighted to receive suggestions of interiors, archives, little-known museums, collections, etc. unpublished elsewhere, and are keen to find new writers.'

World Ski and Wintersports Guide

27a High Street, Esher KT10 9RL
☎01372 468140 Fax 01372 470765
✉ info@goodholidayideas.com

Editor *John Hill*
Circulation 65,000

Founded 2002. BIANNUAL destination guide for skiers and winter sports enthusiasts covering the top 100 ski and winter sports resorts. No unsolicited mss. Approach with ideas and/or synopsis in writing or by e-mail.
PAYMENT negotiable.

World Soccer

IPC Media Ltd., King's Reach Tower, Stamford Street, London SE1 9LS
☎020 7261 5737 Fax 020 7261 7474
✉ world_soccer@ipcmedia.com
www.worldsoccer.com

Owner *IPC Media (A Time Warner Company)*
Editor *Gavin Hamilton*
Circulation 45,497

Founded 1960. MONTHLY. Unsolicited material welcome but initial approach by e-mail or in writing. News and features on world soccer.

Writers' Forum incorporating World Wide Writers

PO Box 3229, Bournemouth BH1 1ZS
☎01202 589828 Fax 01202 587757
✉ editorial@writers-forum-com
www.worldwidewriters.com
Owner *Writers International Ltd*
Editor *John Jenkins*
Deputy Editor *Mary Hogarth*

Founded 1993. MONTHLY. Magazine covers all aspects of the craft of writing. Well written articles welcome.Write to the editor in the first instance.

Writers Forum Short Story Competition Prizes: £300 (1st), £150 (2nd), £100 (3rd) with an annual trophy and a cheque for £1000 for the best story of the year. Entrance fee: non-subscribers: £10; subscribers: £7. Winners published in every issue.

Writers' Forum Poetry Competition First prize £100; runners up receive a dictionary. Entrance fee: £5 for one poem or £7 for two. Winners published in every issue. Annual subscription: £33 UK; £44 Worldwide. Send s.a.e. with 66p in stamps for free back issue.

Writers' News/Writing Magazine

First Floor,Victoria House, 143–144 The Headrow, Leeds LS1 5RL
☎0113 200 2929 Fax 0113 200 2928
www.writersnews.co.uk
Owner *Warners Group Publications plc*
Publishing Editor *Derek Hudson*

Founded 1989. MONTHLY magazines containing news and advice for writers. *Writers' News* is exclusive to mail-order members who also receive *Writing Magazine*, a full-colour glossy publication, which is available on newsstands. No poetry or general items on 'how to become a writer'. Receive 1000 mss each year. Approach in writing or by e-mail.

NEWS Exclusive news stories of interest to writers. Max. 350 words.

FEATURES How-to articles of interest to professional writers. Max. 1000 words.

Yachting Monthly

IPC Media Ltd., King's Reach Tower, Stamford Street, London SE1 9LS
☎020 7261 6040 Fax 020 7261 7555
✉ paul_gelder@ipcmedia.com
www.yachtingmonthly.com
Owner *IPC Media (A Time Warner Company)*
Editor *Paul Gelder*
Circulation 35,740

Founded 1906. MONTHLY magazine for yachting and cruising enthusiasts – not racing. Unsolicited mss welcome, but many are received and not used. Prospective contributors should make initial contact in writing.

FEATURES A wide range of features concerned with maritime subjects and cruising under sail; well-researched and innovative material always welcome, especially if accompanied by high resolution digital images. Max. 1800 words.

PAYMENT £80–110 per 1000 words.

Yachting World

IPC Media Ltd., King's Reach Tower, Stamford Street, London SE1 9LS
☎020 7261 6800 Fax 020 7261 6818
✉ yachting_world@ipcmedia.com
www.yachtingworld.com
Owner *IPC Media (A Time Warner Company)*
Editor *Andrew Bray*
Circulation 29,152

Founded 1894. MONTHLY with international coverage of yacht racing, cruising and yachting events. Will consider well researched and written sailing stories. Preliminary approaches should be by phone for news stories and in writing for features.

PAYMENT by arrangement.

Yorkshire Women's Life Magazine

PO Box 113, Leeds LS8 2WX
✉ ywlmagenquiries@btinternet.com
www.yorkshirewomenslife.co.uk
Editor/Owner *Dawn Maria France*
Fashion *Sky Taylor*
Magazine PA *Anna Jenkins*
Diary *Giles Smith*
Circulation 15,000

Founded 2001. THREE ISSUES YEARLY. Features of interest to women along with regional, national, international news and lifestyle articles. Past issues have covered anorexia nervosa, mental health, stress management, children in US chain gangs, women living in pain, Windrush awards. 'It is important to study the style of the magazine before submitting material. Send A4 s.a.e. with 46p stamp for copy of submission guidelines. Unsolicited mss and new writers actively encouraged; approach in writing in the first instance with s.a.e.' Magazine available on subscription.

You & Your Wedding

National Magazine Company, 72 Broadwick Street, London W1F 9EP
☎020 7439 5000 (editorial)

Fax 020 7439 2985
www.youandyourwedding.co.uk
Owner *The National Magazine Company Ltd*
Editor *To be appointed*
Circulation 59,583

Founded 1985. BI-MONTHLY. Anything relating to weddings, setting up home, and honeymoons. No unsolicited mss. Submit ideas by e-mail only, especially travel features. No phone calls.

You - The Mail on Sunday Magazine

See **The Mail on Sunday** under *National Newspapers*

Young Voices

GV Media Ltd, Blue Star House, 234–244 Stockwell Road, London SW9 9UG
☎020 7737 7377   Fax 020 7274 8894
www.young-voices.co.uk
Editor-in-Chief *Deidre Forbes*
Editor *Emelia Kenlock*

Founded 2003. MONTHLY glossy magazine aimed at 11–19-year-olds. 'Provides a new outlet for today's youth.' Latest news features, showbiz insight and reviews. Also covers current affairs topics that affect readers' lives.

Young WriterS

Glebe House, Weobley, Hereford HR4 8SD
☎01544 318901   Fax 01544 318901
✉ editor@youngwriter.org
www.youngwriter.org
Editor *Kate Jones*

Describing itself as 'The Magazine for Children with Something to Say', *Young Writer* is issued three times a year, at the back-to-school times of September, January and April. A forum for young people's writing – fiction and non-fiction, prose and poetry – the magazine is an introduction to independent writing for young writers aged five to 18. PAYMENT from £20 to £100 for freelance commissioned articles (these can be from adult writers).

Your Cat Magazine

Roebuck House, 33 Broad Street, Stamford PE9 1RB
☎01780 766199   Fax 01780 766416
✉ yourcat@bournepublishinggroup.co.uk
www.yourcat.co.uk
Owner *BPG (Stamford) Ltd*
Editor *Sue Parslow*

Founded 1994. MONTHLY magazine giving practical information on the care of cats and

kittens, pedigree and non-pedigree, plus a wide range of general interest items on cats. Will consider 'true life' cat stories (max. 900 words) and quality fiction. Send synopsis in the first instance. 'No articles written as though by a cat and no poetry.'

Your Dog Magazine

Roebuck House, 33 Broad Street, Stamford PE9 1RB
☎01780 766199   Fax 01780 766416
✉ s.wright@bournepublishinggroup.co.uk
www.yourdog.co.uk
Owner *BPG (Stamford) Ltd*
Editor *Sarah Wright*
Editorial Secretary *Lisa Leftley*
Circulation 28,044

Founded 1995. MONTHLY. Practical advice for pet dog owners. Will consider practical features and some personal experiences (no highly emotive pieces or fiction). Telephone in the first instance.

NEWS Max. 300–400 words.

FEATURES Max. 2500 words; limited opportunities.

PAYMENT negotiable.

Your Horse

Bretton Court, Bretton, Peterborough PE3 8DZ
☎01733 264666   Fax 01733 465200
www.yourhorse.co.uk
Owner *Emap Active Ltd*
Editor *Nicola Dela-Croix*
Circulation 50,785

'The magazine that aims to make owning and riding horses more rewarding.' Most writing produced in-house but well-targeted articles will always be considered.

Yours Magazine

Emap Esprit, Bretton Court, Bretton, Peterborough PE3 8DZ
☎01733 264666   Fax 01733 465266
Owner *Emap Esprit*
Editor *Valery McConnell*
Circulation 421,438

Founded 1973. MONTHLY plus various special issues. Aimed at a readership aged 50 and over. Submission guidelines on request.

FEATURES Unsolicited mss welcome but must enclose s.a.e. Max. 1400 words.

FICTION One or two short stories used in each issue. Max. 1500 words.

PAYMENT negotiable.

Zembla Magazine

2nd Floor, 31 Maddox Street, London
W1S 2PB
✉ info@zemblamagazine.com
www.zemblamagazine.com
Owners *Simon Finch, Dan Crowe*
Editor *Dan Crowe*
Circulation 30,000

Founded 2003. BI-MONTHLY literary magazine featuring fiction, non-fiction, reviews, interviews and 'all sorts of fun with words'. Welcomes fiction and non-fiction ideas and review material. Approach by e-mail in the first instance.

Zest

National Magazine House, 72 Broadwick Street, London W1F 9EP
☎020 7439 5000 Fax 020 7312 3750
✉ zest.mail@natmags.co.uk
www.zest.co.uk

Owner *National Magazine Company*
Editor *Alison Pylkkanen*
Deputy Editors *Rebecca Frank, Charlotte Bradshaw*
Circulation 97,428

Founded 1994. MONTHLY. Health, beauty, fitness, nutrition and general well-being. No unsolicited mss. Prefers ideas in synopsis form; approach in writing.

Zoo

Emap Consumer Media, Endeavour House, 189 Shaftesbury Avenue, London WC2H 8JG
☎020 7437 9011 Fax 0207 208 3586
www.zooweekly.co.uk

Owner *Emap Consumer Media*
Editor *Anthony Noguera*
Circulation 260,470

Launched 2004. WEEKLY men's lifestyle magazine featuring showbiz, sport, humour, sex, fashion and news. Will consider ideas; see 'Work for Us' page on the website for freelance guidelines.

News Agencies

Associated Press Limited
12 Norwich Street, London EC4A 1BP
☎020 7353 1515
Fax 020 7353 8118 (Newsdesk)
Material is either generated in-house or by regulars. Hires the occasional stringer. No unsolicited mss.

Dow Jones Newswires
10 Fleet Place, London EC4M 7QN
☎020 7842 9900   Fax 020 7842 9361
A real-time financial and business newswire operated by Dow Jones & Co., publishers of *The Wall Street Journal*. No unsolicited material.

National News Press and Photo Agency
4–5 Academy Buildings, Fanshaw Street, London N1 6LQ
☎020 7684 3000
Fax 020 7684 3030
✉ news@nationalnews.co.uk
All press releases are welcome. Most work is ordered or commissioned. Coverage includes courts, tribunals, conferences, general news, etc. – words and pictures – as well as PR.

The Press Association Ltd
292 Vauxhall Bridge Road, London SW1V 1AE
☎020 7963 7000
Fax 020 7963 7090
✉ copy@pa.press.net
www.pressassociation.co.uk
No unsolicited material. Most items are produced in-house though occasional outsiders may be used. A phone call to discuss specific material may lead somewhere 'but this is rare'.

Reuters
30 South Colonnade, Canary Wharf, London E14 5EU
☎020 7250 1122
No unsolicited material.

Solo Syndication Ltd
17–18 Hayward's Place, London EC1R 0EQ
☎020 7566 0360   Fax 020 7566 0388
✉ tyork@solosyndication.com
www.solosyndication.com
Founded 1978. Specialises in worldwide newspaper syndication of photos, features and cartoons. Professional contributors only.

South Yorkshire Sport
6 Sharman Walk, Apperknowle, Sheffield S18 4BJ
☎01246 414767/07970 284848 (mobile)
Fax 01246 414767
✉ Nicksport1@aol.com
Contact *Nick Johnson*
Provides written/broadcast coverage of sport in the South Yorkshire area.

Space Press News and Pictures
Bridge House, Blackden Lane, Goostrey CW4 8PZ
☎01477 533403   Fax 01477 535756
✉ Scoop2001@aol.com
Editor *John Williams*
Pictures *Emma Williams*
Founded 1972. Press and picture agency covering Cheshire and the North West, North Midlands, including Knutsford, Macclesfield, Congleton, Crewe and Nantwich, Wilmslow, Alderley Edge, serving national, regional and local press, TV, radio, and digital picture transmission. Copy and pictures produced for in-house publications and PR. Property, countryside and travel writing. A member of the National Association of Press Agencies (NAPA).

Television and Radio

For the latest information on broadcast rates for freelancers access the following websites: the National Union of Journalists' 'The Rate for the Job' database link (www.gn.apc.org/media); the Producers Alliance for Cinema and Television (www.pact.co.uk); the Society of Authors (www.societyofauthors.org); and the Writers' Guild (www.writersguild.org.uk).

BBC TV and Radio

www.bbc.co.uk

Director-General *Mark Thompson*
Deputy Director-General *Mark Byford*
The BBC structure consists of the following: Television Division - responsible for the network television channels and for commissioning in most genres; Drama, Entertainment and Children's; Factual and Learning; Radio and Music; News; Sport; Nations and Regions; and the New Media division which develops the BBC's interactive television and online activities.

TV & Radio Commissioning: www.bbc.co.uk/commissioning

TELEVISION
BBC Television Centre, Wood Lane, London W12 7RJ
☎020 8743 8000
Director, Television *Jana Bennett*
Controller, BBC ONE *Peter Fincham*
Controller, BBC TWO *Roly Keating*
Controller, Daytime *Jay Hunt*
DIGITAL TELEVISION
Controller, BBC THREE *Julian Bellamy*
Controller, BBC FOUR *Janice Hadlow*
Launched in 2003, BBC THREE broadcasts a wide range of entertainment aimed at a 25–34-year-old audience. BBC FOUR, launched in 2002, is devoted solely to the arts. Programmes include *Readers and Writers*, a weekly book programme.

RADIO
Broadcasting House, Portland Place, London W1A 1AA
☎020 7580 4468
Director of Radio & Music *Jenny Abramsky*
Controller, Radio 1 *Andy Parfitt*
Radio 1 documentary submission enquiries:
   Sam Steele, Executive Producer, Speech & Campaigns (sam.steele@bbc.co.uk)

Controller, Radio 2 & 6 Music *Lesley Douglas*
   Radio 2 commissioning enquiries: *Robert Gallacher*, Editor, Planning & Station Sound (robert.gallacher@bbc.co.uk)
Controller, Radio 3 *Roger Wright*
   Radio 3 commissioning enquiries: *David Ireland*, Commissions & Schedules Manager (david.ireland@bbc.co.uk)
Controller, Radio 4 & BBC 7 *Mark Damazer*
   Radio 4 proposals must be submitted through an in-house department or a registered independent production company (lists of departments and companies are available at www.bbc.co.uk/commissioningradio/network/radio4. shtml).
Controller, Radio 5 Live *Bob Shennan*
   Radio 5 Live commissioning enquiries: *Moz Dee*, Commissioning Editor (moz.dee@bbc. co.uk)

DIGITAL RADIO
BBC 1Xtra
BBC Five Live Sports Extra
BBC 6 Music
BBC 7 (comedy, drama and books)
BBC Asian Network

Drama, Entertainment and Children's Division

Creative Director *Alan Yentob*

BBC *writersroom* champions new writers across all BBC platforms for Drama, Comedy and CBBC, running targeted schemes and workshops linked directly to production. It accepts and assesses unsolicited scripts for film, TV drama, narrative comedy and radio drama. The *writersroom* website (www.bbc.co.uk/writersroom) offers a diary of events, opportunities, competitions, interviews with established writers, submission guidelines and free formatting software. BBC *writersroom* also runs *northern exposure* which focuses on new writing in the north of England. Writers should address hard copies of original, completed scripts to: Development Manager, BBC *writersroom*, 1 Mortimer Street, London W1T 3JA. Before sending in scripts, please log on to the website, or send a large s.a.e. to *writersroom* at the Mortimer Street address above for the latest guidelines on submitting unsolicited work. See also www. bbc.co.uk/commissioning/structure/public .shtml

DRAMA
Controller, Drama Commissioning *Jane Tranter*
Controller, Continuing Drama Series/Head of Independent Drama *John Yorke*
Head of Development, Continuing Drama Series *Belinda Campbell*
Head of Drama Series and Serials *Laura Mackie*
Acting Head of Development, Drama Series and Serials *Lisa Osborne*
Head of Films and Single Drama *David Thompson*
Creative Director, New Writing *Kate Rowland*
Head of Radio Drama *Alison Hindell*
Executive Producer (Birmingham) & Editor, The Archers *Vanessa Whitburn*
Executive Producer (World Service Drama) *Marion Nancarrow*
Executive Producer (Manchester) *Sue Roberts*

ENTERTAINMENT
Controller, Entertainment Commissioning *Jon Beazley*
Head of Comedy Commissioning *Lucy Lumsden*
Commissioning Executive, London *Simon Wilson*
Commissioning Executive, Nations & Regions *Cheryl Taylor*
Head of Comedy *Jon Plowman*
Head of Radio Entertainment *Paul Schlesinger*

CBBC (CHILDREN'S)
Controller, CBBC *Richard Deverell*
Executive Editor, Independents & Events *Anne Gilchrist*
Head of CBBC Drama *John East*
Head of Acquisitions and Animation *Michael Carrington*
Head of Entertainment *Joe Godwin*
Head of CBBC Pre-school *Clare Elstow*
Head of CBBC Education *Sue Nott*
Channel Executive *Amanda Gabbitas*

Factual and Learning Division
Director, Factual TV & Learning *John Willis*
Controller, Learning & Interactive *Liz Cleaver*
Controller, Documentaries and Contemporary Factual *Anne Morrison*
Controller, Specialist Factual *Keith Scholey*

News Division
www.bbc.co.uk/news
news.bbc.co.uk
BBC News is the world's largest news-gathering organisation with over 2500 journalists, 45 bureaux worldwide and 15 networks and services across TV, radio and new media.

Director, News *Helen Boaden*
Controller of Production/Deputy Director, News *Adrian Van Klaveren*
Head of Current Affairs *George Entwistle*
Head of Newsgathering *Fran Unsworth*
Head of News Interactive *Peter Clifton*
Head of Political Programmes, Analysis and Research *Sue Inglish*
Head of Radio News *Stephen Mitchell*
Head of Television News *Peter Horrocks*
Deputy Head of Television News *Rachel Attwell*
Controller, BBC News 24 *Kevin Bakhurst*

TELEVISION
Editor, Daytime *Amanda Farnsworth*
Editor, 10 o'clock News *Craig Oliver*
Editor, Newsnight *Peter Barron*
Editor, Breakfast *David Kermode*
Editor, This World *Karen O'Connor*

RADIO
Editor, Today *Ceri Thomas*
Editor, The World at One/World This Weekend *Colin Hancock*
Editor, PM/Broadcasting House *Peter Rippon*
Head of News, Five Live *Matt Morris*
Editor, The World Tonight *Alistair Burnett*
Editor, World Service News Programmes & Current Affairs *Mary Hockaday*

CEEFAX
Room 7540, BBC Television Centre, Wood Lane, London W12 7RJ
☎020 8576 1801
Editor, Ceefax *Paul Brannan*

SUBTITLING
Now supplied by Red Bee Media (formerly BBC Broadcast Ltd), Broadcast Centre, 201 Wood Lane, London W12 7TP www. redbeemedia.com
A rapidly expanding service available via Ceefax page 888.

Sport Division
Director, Sport *Roger Mosey*
Sports news and commentaries across television and Radios 1, 4 and 5 Live, with the majority of output on Radio 5 Live.

BBC Religion
New Broadcasting House, Oxford Road,
Manchester M60 1SJ
☎0161 200 2020   Fax 0161 244 3183
Head of Religion and Ethics *Alan Bookbinder*

Regular programmes for television include *Heaven & Earth; Songs of Praise.* Radio output includes *Good Morning Sunday; Sunday Half Hour; Thought for the Day; The Daily Service.*

BBC New Talent
www.bbc.co.uk/newtalent

The BBC's search for new talent covers a constantly changing range of outlets that has included radio producers, presenters, young storytellers, filmmakers and comedy writers. Access the website for latest information.

BBC World Service
PO Box 76, Bush House, Strand, London
WC2B 4PH
☎020 7240 3456   Fax 020 7557 1900
www.bbc.co.uk/worldservice

Director, World Service *Nigel Chapman*
Director, English Networks & News, BBCWS *Phil Harding*

The World Service broadcasts in English and 32 other languages. The English service is round-the-clock, with news and current affairs as the main component. With over 140 million listeners, excluding countries where research is not possible, it reaches a bigger audience than its five closest competitors combined. The World Service is increasingly available throughout the world on local FM stations, via satellite and online as well as through short-wave frequencies. Coverage includes world business, politics, people/events/opinions, development issues, the international scene, developments in science and technology, sport, religion, music, the arts. BBC World Service broadcasting is financed by a grant-in-aid voted by Parliament amounting to £239 million for 2005/2006.

BBC writersroom
See **Drama, Entertainment and Children's Division**

BBC Nations

BBC Northern Ireland
Broadcasting House, Ormeau Avenue, Belfast
BT2 8HQ
☎028 9033 8000

www.bbc.co.uk/northernireland

Controller *Anna Carragher*
Head of Broadcasting *Peter Johnston*
Head of Production Planning & Development *Stephen Beckett*
Head of News & Current Affairs *Andrew Colman*
Head of Interactive and Learning *Kieran Hegarty*
Head of Drama *Patrick Spence*
Head of Entertainment, Events & Sport *Mike Edgar*
Head of Radio *Susan Lovell*
Head of Factual TV *Paul McGuigan*
Commissioning Editor Broadcasting *Fergus Keeling*
Editor Learning *Jane Cassidy*
Editor New Media *David Sims*
Senior Producer Irish Language *Antaine O'Donnaile*
Editor, TV News *Angelina Fusco*
Editor, Radio News *Kathleen Carragher*
Editor, News Gathering *Michael Cairns*
Editor TV Current Affairs *Jeremy Adams*
Editor News Online *Eddie Fleming*
Editor - Foyle *Paul McCauley*

Regular television programmes include *BBC Newsline 6.30* and a wide range of documentary, popular factual and entertainment programmes. Radio stations: BBC Radio Foyle and BBC Radio Ulster (see entries). For further details on television and film scripts contact: *Susan Carson,* Development Co-ordinator Television, BBC Northern Ireland Drama, Room 3.07, Blackstaff House, Great Victoria Street, Belfast, BT2 7BB. (☎028 9033 8498 ✉ tvdrama.ni@bbc.co.uk) Radio scripts contact: *Anne Simpson,* Manager, Radio Drama at the same address.

BBC Scotland
Broadcasting House, Queen Margaret Drive,
Glasgow G12 8DG
☎0141 338 2000
www.bbc.co.uk/scotland

Controller *Ken MacQuarrie*
Head of Programme and Services *Donalda MacKinnon and Maggie Cunningham*
Head of Drama, Television *Anne Mensah*
Head of Drama, Radio *Patrick Rayner*
Head of Factual Programmes *Andrea Miller*
Head of Gaelic *Margaret Mary Murray*
Head of Radio *Jeff Zycinski*
Head of News and Current Affairs *Blair Jenkins*
Commissioning Editor, Television *Ewan Angus*
Headquarters of BBC Scotland with centres in Aberdeen, Dundee, Edinburgh, Dumfries,

Inverness, Orkney, Shetland and Stornaway. Regular and recent programmes include *Reporting Scotland*, *Sportscene* and *River City* on television and *Good Morning Scotland* and *Macaulay and Co.* on radio.

Aberdeen
Broadcasting House, Beechgrove Terrace, Aberdeen AB9 2ZT
☎01224 625233

Dundee
Nethergate Centre, 66 Nethergate, Dundee DD1 4ER
☎01382 202481

Edinburgh
The Tun, Holyrood Road, Edinburgh EH8 8JF
☎0131 557 5677

Dumfries
Elmbank, Lover's Walk, Dumfries DG1 1NZ

Inverness
7 Culduthel Road, Inverness IV2 4ADT
☎01463 720720
Editor *Ishbel MacLennan*

Orkney
Castle Street, Kirkwall, Orkney KW15 1DF

Shetland
Pitt Lane, Lerwick, Shetland ZE1 0DW

Stornaway
Rosebank, Church Street, Stornoway, Isle of Lewis PA87 2LS
☎01851 705000

Radio Nan Gaidheal
Rosebank, Church Street, Stornoway, Isle of Lewis PA87 2LS
☎01851 705000

BBC Wales
Broadcasting House, Llandaff CF5 2YQ
☎029 2032 2000 Fax 029 2055 2973
www.bbc.co.uk/wales
Controller *Menna Richards*
Head of Programmes (Welsh Language) *Keith Jones*
Head of Programmes (English Language) *Clare Hudson*
Head of News & Current Affairs *Mark O'Callaghan*
Head of Drama *Julie Gardner*
Commissioning Editor, Independents and BBC2W *Martyn Ingram*

Producer, Pobol y Cwm *Bethan Jones*
Editor, New Media *Iain Tweedale*
Headquarters of BBC Wales, with regional centres in Bangor, Aberystwyth, Carmarthen, Wrexham and Swansea. BBC Wales television produces up to 12 hours of English language programmes a week, 12 hours in Welsh for transmission on **S4C** and an increasing number of hours on network services. BBC2W, the digital channel, was launched in 2001. Regular programmes include *Wales Today*; *Newyddion* (Welsh-language daily news); *Week In Week Out*, *X-Ray* and *Pobol y Cwm* (Welsh-language soap) on television and *Good Morning Wales*; *Good Evening Wales*; *Post Cyntaf* and *Post Prynhawn* on Radio Wales and Radio Cymru. Ideas for programmes should be submitted either by post to *Martyn Ingram*, Commissioning Editor, Room 3021 at the address above or by e-mail to commissioning @bbc.co.uk

Bangor
Broadcasting House, Meirion Road, Bangor LL57 2BY
☎01248 370880 Fax 01248 351443
Head of Centre *Marian Wyn Jones*

BBC Regions

BBC Asian Network
The Mailbox, Birmingham B1 1RF
☎0121 567 6767
✉ asian.network@bbc.co.uk
www.bbc.co.uk/asiannetwork
Managing Editor *Vijay Sharma*
Commenced broadcasting in November 1996. Broadcasts nationwide. Programmes in English, Bengali, Gujerati, Hindi, Punjabi and Urdu.

BBC Birmingham
The Mailbox, Birmingham B1 1RF
☎0121 567 6767 Fax 0121 567 6875
✉ birmingham@bbc.co.uk
www.bbc.co.uk/birmingham
Head of Regional and Local Programmes *David Holdsworth*
Output Editor *Dave Hart*
BBC Birmingham's Documentaries & Contemporary Factual Department produces a broad range of programming for BBC ONE, BBC TWO and BBC THREE, including *Gardener's World*; *Coast*; *Pay off your mortgage in two years*; *Bunking Off*, *Conflicts*; *Pakistani Actually*; *Mind Your Own Business*; *Desi DNA*; and *To Buy or Not to*

Buy. Network radio includes: Radio 2: Janice Long, Paul Jones, Alex Lester, Mo Dutta. Radio 4: *The Archers*; *Farming Today*; *Ramblings*; *On the Ropes*. Radio 5 Live: *The Stephen Nolan Show*. The Asian Network: Adil Ray. Regional & Local Programmes: TV: *Midlands Today*; *Inside Out*; *The Politics Show*; Radio: BBC WM (see entry).

BBC Birmingham is the headquarters for BBC English Regions. There is a television Drama Village at the University of Birmingham.

BBC Birmingham Drama
Archibald House, 1059 Bristol Road, Selly Oak, Birmingham B29 6LT
☎0121 567 7350
Programmes produced include *Dalziel and Pascoe*; *Doctors*; *The Afternoon Play* and *Brief Encounters* (which champions new writers).

BBC East Midlands (Nottingham)
East Midlands Broadcasting Centre, London Road, Nottingham NG2 4UU
☎0115 955 0500 Fax 0115 902 1983
www.bbc.co.uk/nottingham
Head of Regional Programming *Mike Bettison*
Output Editor *Sally Bowman*

BBC East (Norwich)
The Forum, Millennium Plain, Norwich NR2 1AW
☎01603 284700 Fax 01603 284399
www.bbc.co.uk/norfolk
Head of Regional Programming *Tim Bishop*
Output Editor *Dave Betts*

BBC Bristol
Broadcasting House, Whiteladies Road, Bristol BS8 2LR
☎0117 973 2211
bbc.co.uk/bristol
Managing Editor *Jenny Lacey*
Head of Programmes Leisure and Factual Entertainment *Tom Archer*
Head of Natural History Unit *Neil Nightingale*
BBC Bristol is the home of the BBC's Natural History Unit, producing programmes such as *Blue Planet*; *Life of Mammals*; *British Isles, A Natural History*; *Abyss* and *The Really Wild Show* for BBC ONE and BBC TWO. It also produces natural history programmes for Radio 4 and Radio 5 Live. The Factual department produces a wide range of television programmes, including *DIY SOS*; *Antiques Roadshow*; *Soul Deep* and *Ray Mears* in addition to radio programmes specialising in history, travel, literature and human interest features for Radio 4.

BBC London
35 Marylebone High Street, London W1U 4QA
☎020 7224 2424
www.bbc.co.uk/london
Executive Editor *Mike MacFarlane*
(Responsible for BBC tri-media: BBC London News, BBC London 94.9FM and the BBC London website)
Planning Editor *Duncan Williamson*

BBC South East (Tunbridge Wells)
The Great Hall, Mount Pleasant Road, Tunbridge Wells TN1 1QQ
☎01892 670000
Head of Regional and Local Programmes *Mike Hapgood* (Responsible for BBC South East [TV], BBC Radio Kent and BBC Southern Counties Radio)
Editor, South East Today *Quentin Smith*
Managing Editor, Southern Counties Radio *Nicci Holiday*
Managing Editor, Radio Kent *Paul Leaper*
Editor, Newsgathering *Mark Hayman*
Producer, Inside Out *Linda Bell*

BBC West/BBC South/ BBC South West
The three regional television stations, BBC West, BBC South and BBC South West produce the lunchtime and nightly news magazine programmes, as well as regular 30-minute local current affairs programmes and parliamentary programmes. Each of the regions operates a comprehensive local radio service as well as a range of correspondents specialising in subjects such as health, education, business, home affairs and the environment.

BBC West (Bristol)
Broadcasting House, Whiteladies Road, Bristol BS8 2LR
☎0117 973 2211
Head of Regional and Local Programmes Andrew Wilson (Responsible for the BBC West region. TV: BBC Points West (regional news programme), Inside Out West (regional current affairs series) and The Politics Show West. Local Radio: BBC Radio Bristol, BBC Somerset Sound, BBC Radio Gloucestershire, BBC Radio Wiltshire, BBC Radio Swindon and the regional BBC Where I Live websites)
Daily TV Output Editors *Jane Kinghorn, Stephanie Marshall*

TV Features Editor *Roger Farrant*
Political Editor *Dave Harvey*

BBC South (Southampton)
Broadcasting House, Havelock Road,
Southampton SO14 7PU
☎023 8022 6201

Head of BBC South Eve Turner (Responsible
for BBC South TV, BBC Radio Berkshire,
BBC Radio Oxford, BBC Radio Solent
and online content for the region)
Output Editor, BBC South Today *Lee Desty*
Newsgathering Editor *Cathy Burnett*
Series Producer, Inside Out *Andrew Head*

BBC South West (Plymouth)
Broadcasting House, Seymour Road,
Mannamead, Plymouth PL3 5BD
☎01752 229201

Head of BBC South West John Lilley
(Responsible for the BBC South West
region. TV: BBC Spotlight (regional news
programme), Spotlight Channel Islands
(regional news programme), Inside Out
(regional current affairs series) and The
Politics Show South West. Local Radio: BBC
Radio Devon, BBC Radio Cornwall, BBC
Radio Guernsey, BBC Radio Jersey and the
regional BBC Where I Live websites)
Output Editor *Simon Read*
Series Producer *Simon Willis*
Political Editor *Chris Rogers*

BBC Yorkshire/BBC North West/ BBC North East & Cumbria

The regional centres at Leeds, Manchester and
Newcastle make their own programmes on a
bi-media approach, each centre having its own
head of regional and local programmes.

BBC Yorkshire
Broadcasting Centre, 2 St Peter's Square, Leeds
LS9 8AH
☎0113 244 1188

Head of Regional and Local Programmes
Tamsin O'Brien
Editor, Newsgathering *Kate Watkins*
Output Editor, Look North Yorkshire *Jake Fowler*
Output Editor, Look North East Yorkshire and
Lincolnshire *Steve Punter*
Assistant News Editors, Look North *Denise Wallace*/ Acting Editor *Graham Moorby*
Political Editor, North of Westminster *Len Tingle*
Senior Broadcast Journalist, North of
Westminster *Rod Jones*

Weeklies Editor, Close Up North *Ian Cundall*
Producers, Close Up North *Richard Taylor, Paul Greenan*

BBC North West (Manchester)
New Broadcasting House, Oxford Road,
Manchester M60 1SJ
☎0161 200 2020

Head of Regional and Local Programmes *Leo Devine*
Editor, Newsgathering *Michelle Mayman*
Output Editor *Cerys Griffiths*
Producer, Northwest Tonight *Jim Clarke*
Producer, Inside Out *Deborah van Bishop*
Producer, The Politics Show *Liam Fogarty*

BBC North East & Cumbria (Newcastle upon Tyne)
Broadcasting Centre, Barrack Road, Newcastle
Upon Tyne NE99 2NE
☎0191 232 1313

Head of Regional and Local Programmes
Wendy Pilmer
Editor, Newsgathering *Andy Cooper*
Output Editor, Look North *Jeff Milburn*

BBC Local Radio

bbc.co.uk/england

There are 40 local BBC radio stations across
England transmitting on FM and medium wave.
These present local news, information and entertainment to local audiences and reflect the life of
the communities they serve. Each has its own
newsroom which supplies local bulletins and
national news service. Many have specialist producers. A comprehensive list of programmes for
each is unavailable and would soon be out of
date. For general information on programming
visit the website or contact the relevant station
direct.

BBC Radio Berkshire
PO Box 104.4, Reading RG4 8FH
☎0118 9464200 Fax 0118 9464555
www.bbc.co.uk/berkshire
Editor *Marianne Bell*

BBC Radio Bristol
PO Box 194, Bristol BS99 7QT
☎0117 974 1111 Fax 0117 923 8323
✉ radio.bristol@bbc.co.uk
www.bbc.co.uk/england/radiobristol
Managing Editor *Jenny Lacey*
Wide range of feature material used.

BBC Radio Cambridgeshire
104 Hills Road, Cambridge CB2 1LD
☎01223 259696 Fax 01223 460832
✉ cambs@bbc.co.uk
www.bbc.co.uk/radiocambridgeshire
Editor *Jason Horton*
Commenced broadcasting in May 1982.

BBC Radio Cleveland
PO Box 95FM, Broadcasting House, Newport
Road, Middlesbrough TS1 5DG
☎01642 225211 Fax 01642 211356
✉ cleveland.studios@bbc.co.uk (programmes)
and cleveland.news@bbc.co.uk (news)
www.bbc.co.uk/england/radiocleveland
Managing Editor *Peter Cook*
Assistant Editor *Ken Snowdon*
Material used is local to Teesside, Co. Durham
and North Yorkshire. News, current affairs and
features about life in the north east.

BBC Radio Cornwall
Phoenix Wharf, Truro TR1 1UA
☎01872 275421 Fax 01872 240679
✉ radio.cornwall@bbc.co.uk
www.bbc.co.uk/radiocornwall
Editor *Pauline Causey*
On air from 1983 serving Cornwall and the
Isles of Scilly. Broadcasts 117 hours of local programmes weekly including news, phone-ins
and specialist music.

BBC Coventry and Warwickshire
Priory Place, Coventry CV1 5SQ
☎024 7655 1000
✉ coventry@bbc.co.uk *and*
warwickshire@bbc.co.uk
www.bbc.co.uk/coventrywarwickshire
Editor *David Clargo*
Commenced broadcasting in January 1990 as
CWR. News, current affairs, public service
information and community involvement, relevant to its broadcast area.

BBC Radio Cumbria
Annetwell Street, Carlisle CA3 8BB
☎01228 592444 Fax 01228 511195
✉ radio.cumbria@bbc.co.uk
bbc.co.uk/cumbria
Editor *Nigel Dyson*
Occasional opportunities for plays and short
stories are advertised on-air.

BBC Radio Cymru
Broadcasting House, Llandaff, Cardiff
CF5 2YQ
☎029 20 322018 Fax 029 20 322473
✉ radio.cymru@bbc.co.uk
www.bbc.co.uk/radiocymru
Editor *Aled Glynne Davies*
Welsh language station serving Welsh speaking
communities. Rich mix of news, music, sport,
features, current affairs, drama, comedy, religion
and education. Writing opportunities: DRAMA
Daily 10 minute soap *Rhydeglwys* and over nine
further hours of new radio drama each year.
COMEDY Occasional series during the year (for
details of independent commissions see www.
bbc.co.uk/wales/commissioning/).

BBC Radio Derby
PO Box 104.5, Derby DE1 3HL
☎01332 361111 Fax 01332 290794
✉ radio.derby@bbc.co.uk
www.bbc.co.uk/derby
Editor *Simon Cornes*
News, sport, information and entertainment.

BBC Radio Devon
PO Box 1034, Plymouth
☎01752 260323 Fax 01752 234599
✉ radio.devon@bbc.co.uk
www.bbc.co.uk/devon
Also at: Walnut Gardens, St David's Hill, Exeter
EX4 4DB
☎01392 215651 Fax 01392 425570
Managing Editor *Robert Wallace*
Head of Programmes *Ian Timms*
Head of News *Sarah Solftley*
On air since 1983.

BBC Essex
PO Box 765, Chelmsford CM2 9XB
☎01245 616000 Fax 01245 492983
✉ essex@bbc.co.uk
www.bbc.co.uk/essex
Managing Editor *Margaret Hyde*
Programmes are a mix of news, interviews, expert contributors, phone-ins, sport and special
interest such as gardening.

BBC Radio Foyle
8 Northland Road, Londonderry BT48 7GD
☎028 7137 8600 Fax 028 7137 8666
www.bbc.co.uk/northernireland
Managing Editor *Paul McCauley*
News Producer *Paul McFadden*

Features *Michael Bradley*

Radio Foyle broadcasts about seven hours of original material a day, seven days a week to the north west of Northern Ireland. Other programmes are transmitted simultaneously with Radio Ulster. The output ranges from news, sport, and current affairs to live music recordings and arts reviews.

BBC Radio Gloucestershire

London Road, Gloucester GL1 1SW
☎01452 308585   Fax 01452 309491
✉ radio.gloucestershire@bbc.co.uk
www.bbc.co.uk/radiogloucestershire
Managing Editor *Mark Hurrell*
Assistant Editor *Mark Jones*

News and information covering the large variety of interests and concerns in Gloucestershire. Leisure, sport and music, plus African Caribbean and Asian interests. Regular book reviews and interviews with local authors in the *Trish Campbell Show*.

BBC GLR

See **BBC London**

BBC GMR

See **BBC Radio Manchester**

BBC Guernsey

Broadcasting House, Bulwer Avenue, St Sampson's, Guernsey GY2 4LA
☎01481 200600   Fax 01481 200361
✉ radio.guernsey@bbc.co.uk
www.bbc.co.uk/guernsey
Managing Editor *David Martin*

Opened with its sister station, BBC Radio Jersey, in March 1982. Broadcasts 80 hours of local programming a week.

BBC Hereford & Worcester

Hylton Road, Worcester WR2 5WW
☎01905 748485   Fax 01905 748006
✉ bbchw@bbc.co.uk
www.bbc.co.uk/herefordworcester

Also at: 43 Broad Street, Hereford HR4 9HH
☎01432 355252 Fax 01432 356446
Managing Editor *James Coghill*

Has an interest in writers/writing with local connections

BBC Radio Humberside

Queen's Court, Queen's Gardens, Hull HU1 3RH
☎01482 323232   Fax 01482 621403

✉ radio.humberside@bbc.co.uk
www.bbc.co.uk/radiohumberside
Managing Editor *Simon Pattern*

On air since 1971. BBC Radio Humberside has broadcast short pieces by local writers. Interested in ideas for longer form comedy from local writing talent. A short series has been commissioned for transmission later in 2006.

BBC Radio Jersey

18 & 21 Parade Road, St Helier, Jersey JE2 3PL
☎01534 870000   Fax 01534 732569
✉ radiojersey@bbc.co.uk
www.bbc.co.uk/jersey
Managing Editor *Denzil Dudley*
Assistant Editor *Matthew Price*

Local news, current affairs and community items.

BBC Radio Kent

The Great Hall, Mount Pleasant Road, Tunbridge Wells TN1 1QQ
☎01892 670000   Fax 01892 549118
✉ radio.kent@bbc.co.uk
www.bbc.co.uk/radiokent
Managing Editor *Paul Leaper*

Occasional commissions are made for local interest documentaries and other one-off programmes.

BBC Radio Lancashire

20–26 Darwen Street, Blackburn BB2 2EA
☎01254 262411
✉ lancashire@bbc.co.uk
www.bbc.co.uk/radiolancashire
Editor *John Clayton*

Journalism-based radio station, interested in interviews with local writers. Contact *Alison Brown*, Daily Programmes Producer, Monday to Friday (alison.brown.01@bbc.co.uk).

BBC Radio Leeds

2 St Peters Square, Leeds LS9 8AH
☎0113 244 2131   Fax 0113 224 7316
✉ radio.leeds@bbc.co.uk
www.bbc.co.uk/radioleeds
Managing Editor *Phil Roberts*

BBC Radio Leeds is the station for West Yorkshire, serving 1.3 million potential listeners since 1968. Broadcasts a mix of news, sport, talk, music and entertainment, 24 hours a day.

BBC Radio Leicester
9 St Nicholas Place, Leicester LE1 5LB
☎0116 251 6688 Fax 0116 251 1463
✉ radioleicester@bbc.co.uk
www.bbc.co.uk/radioleicester
Managing Editor *Kate Squire*

The first local station in Britain. Occasional interviews with local authors.

BBC Radio Lincolnshire
PO Box 219, Newport, Lincoln LN1 3XY
☎01522 511411 Fax 01522 511058
✉ radio.lincolnshire@bbc.co.uk
www.bbc.co.uk/radiolincolnshire
Managing Editor *Charlie Partridge*

Unsolicited material considered only if locally relevant. Maximum 1000 words: straight narrative preferred, ideally with a topical content.

BBC London
PO Box 94.9, Marylebone High Street,
London W1A 6FL
☎020 7224 2424 Fax 020 7208 9661 (news)
✉ yourlondon@bbc.co.uk
www.bbc.co.uk/london
Managing Editor *David Robey*

Formerly Greater London Radio (GLR), launched in 1988, BBC London 94.9 broadcasts news, information, travel bulletins, sport and music to Greater London and the Home Counties.

BBC Radio Manchester
PO Box 951, Oxford Road, Manchester
M60 1SD
☎0161 200 2000 Fax 0161 228 6110
✉ radio.manchester@bbc.co.uk
www.bbc.co.uk/radiomanchester
Managing Editor *John Ryan*
News Editor *Mark Elliot*

One of the largest of the BBC local radio stations, broadcasting news, current affairs, phone-ins, help, advice and sport.

BBC Radio Merseyside
55 Paradise Street, Liverpool L1 3BP
☎0151 708 5500 Fax 0151 794 0988
✉ radio.merseyside@bbc.co.uk
www.bbc.co.uk/radiomerseyside
www.bbc.co.uk/liverpool
Acting Editor *Mick Ord*

First Friday – a monthly poetry slot between 1.30 pm and 2.00 pm on the first Friday of every month in the Roger Phillips lunchtime programme. Merseyside writers can offer poetry by e-mailing roger.phillips@bbc.co.uk or send copies with name/address attached, to 'First Friday Poetry', c/o BBC Radio Merseyside at the address above. Only the poets used will be acknowledged and contacted.

BBC Radio Newcastle
Broadcasting Centre, Barrack Road, Newcastle upon Tyne NE99 1RN
☎0191 232 4141
✉ radionewcastle.news@bbc.co.uk
www.bbc.co.uk/tyne
www.bbc.co.uk/wear
Editor *Graham Moss*
Senior Producer (Programmes) *Sarah Miller*

Commenced broadcasting in January 1971. One of the BBC's big city radio stations in England, Radio Newcastle reaches an audience of 233,000.

BBC Radio Norfolk
The Forum, Millennium Plain, Norwich
NR2 1BH
☎01603 617411 Fax 01603 633692
✉ radionorfolk@bbc.co.uk
www.bbc.co.uk/radionorfolk
Editor *David Clayton*

Good local ideas and material welcome for features and documentaries *if* directly related to Norfolk.

BBC Radio Northampton
Broadcasting House, Abington Street,
Northampton NN1 2BH
☎01604 239100 Fax 01604 230709
✉ northampton@bbc.co.uk
www.bbc.co.uk/northamptonshire
Managing Editor *Laura Moss*

Books of local interest are regularly featured. Authors and poets are interviewed on merit. Poems and short stories are reviewed occasionally, but not broadcast. Runs occasional competitions for local writers.

BBC Radio Nottingham
London Road, Nottingham NG2 4UU
☎0115 955 0500 Fax 0115 902 1983
✉ radio.nottingham@bbc.co.uk
www.bbc.co.uk/radionottingham
Editor *Sophie Stewart*

Rarely broadcasts scripted pieces of any kind but interviews with authors form a regular part of the station's output.

BBC Radio Orkney

Castle Street, Kirkwall KW15 1DF
☎01856 873939 Fax 01856 872908
✉ radio.orkney@bbc.co.uk

Senior Producer *John Fergusson*

Regular programmes include *Around Orkney* (news magazine programme), *Bruck* (swapshop and general features) and *Orky-Ology* (archaeology magazine). As a BBC Community station, all Radio Orkney's programme material is generated from within the Orkney Islands.

BBC Radio Oxford

269 Banbury Road, Oxford OX2 7DW
☎08459 311444 Fax 08459 311555
✉ oxford@bbc.co.uk
www.bbc.co.uk/oxford/local_radio

Executive Editor *Steve Taschini*

Restored to its original name in 2000 having been merged with BBC Radio Berkshire in 1995 to create BBC Thames Valley. The station frequently carries interviews with local authors and offers books as prizes.

BBC Radio Scotland (Dumfries)

Elmbank, Lover's Walk, Dumfries DG1 1NZ
☎01387 268008 Fax 01387 252568
✉ dumfries@bbc.co.uk

Senior Producer *Willie Johnston*

Previously Radio Solway. The station mainly outputs news bulletins (four daily) although it has become more of a production centre with programmes being made for Radio Scotland as well as BBC Radio 2 and 5 Live. Freelancers of a high standard, familiar with Radio Scotland, should contact the producer.

BBC Radio Scotland (Selkirk)

Unit 1, Ettrick Riverside, Dunsdale Road, Selkirk TD7 5EB
☎01750 724 567 Fax 01750 724555

Senior Broadcaster *Cameron Buttle*

Formerly BBC Radio Tweed. Local news bulletins only.

BBC Radio Sheffield

54 Shoreham Street, Sheffield S1 4RS
☎0114 273 1177 Fax 0114 267 5454
✉ radio.sheffield@bbc.co.uk
www.bbc.co.uk/radiosheffield

Managing Editor *Gary Keown*
Programmes Editor *Angus Morat*
News Editor *Michael Woodcock*

Writer interviews, writing-related topics and readings on the Rony Robinson Show at 11.00 am.

BBC Radio Shetland

Pitt Lane, Lerwick ZE1 0DW
☎01595 694747 Fax 01595 694307
✉ radio.shetland@bbc.co.uk

Senior Producer *Caroline Moyes*

Regular programmes include *Good Evening Shetland*. An occasional books programme highlights the activities of local writers and writers' groups.

BBC Radio Shropshire

2–4 Boscobel Drive, Shrewsbury SY1 3TT
☎01743 248484 Fax 01743 237018
✉ radio.shropshire@bbc.co.uk
bbc.co.uk/shropshire

Managing Editor *Tim Beech*

On air since 1985. Unsolicited literary material rarely used, and then only if locally relevant.

BBC Radio Solent

Broadcasting House, Havelock Road, Southampton SO14 7PW
☎023 8063 2811 Fax 023 8033 9648 (news)
✉ radio.solent@bbc.co.uk
www.bbc.co.uk/radiosolent

Managing Editor *Mia Costello*

Broadcasting since 1970.

BBC Somerset Sound

Broadcasting House, Park Street, Taunton TA1 4DA
☎01823 348920 Fax 01823 332539
✉ somerset.sound@bbc.co.uk
www.bbc.co.uk/somerset

Managing Editor *Jenny Lacey*
Assistant Editor *Simon Clifford*

Informal, speech-based programming with strong news and current affairs output and regular local interest features, including local writing. Poetry and short stories on the *Adam Thomas Programme*.

BBC Southern Counties Radio

Broadcasting House, 40–42 Queens Road, Brighton BN1 3XB
☎01483 306306
✉ southern.counties.radio@bbc.co.uk
www.bbc.co.uk/southerncounties

Also at: Broadcasting Centre, Guildford GU2 7AP

Managing Editor *Nicci Holliday*

Regular programmes include three individual breakfast shows: *Breakfast Live in Surrey with Fred Maden/in Sussex with Neil Pringle*.

BBC Radio Stoke

Cheapside, Hanley, Stoke on Trent ST1 1JJ
☎01782 208080 Fax 01782 289115
✉ radio.stoke@bbc.co.uk
www.bbc.co.uk/radiostoke

Editor *Sue Owen*

On air since 1968, one of the first eight 'experimental' BBC stations. Emphasis on news, current affairs and local topics. Music represents one fifth of total output. Unsolicited material of local interest is welcome – send to *Tim Wedgwood*.

BBC Radio Suffolk

Broadcasting House, St Matthew's Street, Ipswich IP1 3EP
☎01473 250000 Fax 01473 210887
✉ radiosuffolk@bbc.co.uk
www.bbc.co.uk/suffolk

Managing Editor *Gerald Main*

Strongly locally speech-based, dealing with news, current affairs, community issues, the arts, agriculture, commerce, travel, sport and leisure. Programmes sometimes carry interviews with writers.

BBC Radio Swindon

BBC Broadcasting House, Prospect Place, Swindon SN1 3RW
☎01793 513626 Fax 01793 513650
✉ radio.swindon@bbc.co.uk
www.bbc.co.uk/england/radiowiltshire

Managing Editor *Tony Worgan*

Local news and current affairs. Local authors are interviewed on Mark Seaman's *Afternoon Show*.

BBC Three Counties Radio

1 Hastings Street, Luton LU1 5XL
☎01582 637400 Fax 01582 401467
✉ threecounties@bbc.co.uk
www.bbc.co.uk/threecounties

Managing Editor *Mark Norman*

Encourages freelance contributions from the community across a wide range of radio output, including interview and feature material. Interested in local history topics (five minutes maximum).

BBC Radio Ulster

Broadcasting House, Ormeau Avenue, Belfast BT2 8HQ

☎028 9033 8000

Managing Editor *Susan Lovell*

Programmes broadcast from 6.30 am to midnight weekdays and from 6.55 am to midnight at weekends. Programmes include: *Good Morning Ulster*; *Gerry Anderson*; *Talk Back*; *Just Jones*; *Evening Extra*; *On Your Behalf*; *Your Place and Mine* and *Saturday Magazine*.

BBC Radio Wales

Broadcasting House, Llandaff, Cardiff CF5 2YQ
☎029 2032 2000 Fax 029 2032 2674
✉ radio.wales@bbc.co.uk
www.bbc.co.uk/radiowales

Editor *Julie Barton*

Editor, Radio Wales News *Geoff Williams*

Broadcasts news on the hour and half hour throughout weekday daytime programmes; hourly bulletins in the evenings and at weekends. Programmes include *Good Morning Wales*; *Roy Noble & Nicola Heywood-Thomas*. Access line number: 08700 100110.

BBC Radio Wiltshire

BBC Broadcasting House, Prospect Place, Swindon SN1 3RW
☎01793 513626 Fax 01793 513650
✉ radio.wiltshire@bbc.co.uk
www.bbc.co.uk/england/radiowiltshire

Editor *Tony Worgon*

Sister company of BBC Radio Swindon. Regular programmes include Mark Seaman's *Afternoon Show* (reviews and author interviews).

BBC WM

The Mailbox, Birmingham B1 1RF
☎08453 009956 Fax 0121 567 6025
✉ bbcwm@bbc.co.uk
www.bbc.co.uk/radiowm

Managing Editor *Keith Beech*

Commenced broadcasting in November 1970 as BBC Birmingham and has won four gold Sony awards in recent years. Speech-based station broadcasting to the West Midlands, South Staffordshire and North Worcestershire.

BBC Radio York

20 Bootham Row, York YO30 7BR
☎01904 641351 Fax 01904 610937
✉ radio.york@bbc.co.uk
www.bbc.co.uk/northyorkshire

Editor *Matt Youdale*

Books of local interest are sometimes previewed.

Independent Television

Carlton
See **ITV London**

Channel 4
124 Horseferry Road, London SW1P 2TX
☎020 7396 4444 Fax 020 7306 8356
www.channel4.com

Chief Executive *Andy Duncan*
Director of Television *Kevin Lygo*
Head of E4 and Factual Entertainment *Danny Cohen*
Head of Features *Sue Murphy*
Head of History, Science, Religion and Arts *Hamish Mykura*
Head of News, Current Affairs *Dorothy Byrne*
Head of Commissioning Management (Managing Editor, Commissioning) *Janey Walker*
Director of Acquisitions *Jeff Ford*
Head of Education *Heather Rabbatts*
Head of More4 and Documentary Events *Peter Dale*

COMMISSIONING EDITORS
Head of Drama and Film Four *Tessa Ross*
Head of Comedy and Films *Caroline Leddy*
Head of Entertainment *Andrew Newman*
Head of Sport *Andrew Thompson*
Controller of Broadcasting *Rosemary Newell*
Head of Schedules, Music, Youth and T4 *Julie Oldroyd*
Commissioning Editor, Daytime *Adam McDonald*
Head of Documentaries *Angus Macqueen*

Channel 4 started broadcasting as a national channel in November 1982. It enjoys unique status as the world's only major public service broadcaster funded entirely by its own commercial activities. All programmes are commissioned from independent production companies and are broadcast across the whole of the UK except those parts of Wales covered by S4C. Its FilmFour channel, launched in 1998, is a premium pay-TV channel featuring modern independent cinema. A second digital entertainment channel, E4, was launched in January 2001, focusing on young audiences, and More4 launched in October 2005, featuring news, current affairs, documentaries and drama targeted at older audiences.

Channel Television
Television Centre, La Pouquelaye, St Helier, Jersey JE1 3ZD
☎01534 816816 Fax 01534 816817

www.channelonline.tv
Also at: Television House, Bulwer Avenue, St Sampsons, Guernsey GY2 4LA
☎01481 241888 Fax 01481 241878

Managing Director *Michael Lucas*
Director of Programmes *Karen Rankine*
Director of Sales *Don Miller*
Director of Resources & Transmission *Kevin Banner*

Channel Television is the independent television broadcaster to the Channel Islands, serving 150,000 residents, most of whom live on the main islands, Jersey, Guernsey, Alderney and Sark. The station has a weekly reach of more than 83% with local programmes (in the region of five and a half hours each week) at the heart of the ITV service to the islands.

Five
22 Long Acre, London WC2E 9LY
☎020 7550 5555
www.five.tv

CEO *Jane Lighting*
Director of Programmes *Dan Chambers*
Controller of Children's Programmes *Nick Wilson*
Senior Programme Controller (News & Current Affairs) *Chris Shaw*
Drama Editor *Abigail Webber*

Channel 5 Broadcasting Ltd won the franchise for Britain's third commercial terrestrial television station in 1995 and came on air at the end of March 1997. Regular programmes include *The Wright Stuff* (weekday morning chat show), *The Trisha Goddard Show* (talk show), *CSI: NY* (drama) and *House* (drama).

GMTV
The London Television Centre, Upper Ground, London SE1 9TT
☎020 7827 7000 Fax 020 7827 7249
✉ talk2us@gm.tv
www.gmtv.co.uk

Managing Director *Paul Corley*
Director of Programmes *Peter McHugh*
Managing Editor *John Scammell*
Editor *Martin Frizell*

Winner of the national breakfast television franchise. Jointly owned by ITV plc and Disney. GMTV took over from TV-am on 1 January 1993, with live programming from 6.00 am to 9.25 am. Regular news bulletins, current affairs, topical features, showbiz and lifestyle. Plus competitions, travel and weather reports. Launched its digital service, GMTV2, in January 1999, with daily broadcasts from 6.00 am to 9.25 am. News reports, travel, health and lifestyle features, some simulcast with GMTV1. Children's programming on Saturdays. The week's news and political issues reviewed on Sundays, followed by children's programming.

Grampian TV

Television Centre, Craigshaw Business Park, West Tullos, Aberdeen AB12 3QH
☎01224 848848
www.stv.tv.co.uk
In 2006 Grampian TV and Scottish TV were merged to form **stv** (see entry). Extensive regional news and reports including farming, fishing and sports, interviews and leisure features, various light entertainment, Gaelic and religious programmes, and live coverage of the Scottish political, economic and industrial scene. Serves the area stretching from Fife to Shetland. Regular programmes include *North Tonight* and other varied genre shows strongly reflecting the regionality of the north of Scotland.

HTV

See **ITV West**

ITN (Independent Television News Ltd)

200 Gray's Inn Road, London WC1X 8XZ
☎020 7833 3000 Fax 020 7430 4868
✉ contact@itn.co.uk
www.itn.co.uk
Chief Executive *Mark Wood*
Editor-in-Chief, ITV News *David Mannion*
Editor, Channel 4 News *Jim Gray*
Provider of the main national and international news for ITV and Channel 4 and radio news for IRN. Programmes on ITV: *Lunchtime News*; *London Today*; *Evening News*; *London Tonight*; *News at 10.30*, plus regular news summaries and three programmes a day at weekends. Programmes on Channel 4 include the in-depth news analysis programmes *Channel 4 News at Noon* and *Channel 4 News*.

ITV plc

The London Television Centre, Upper Ground, London SE1 9LT
☎020 7620 1620
www.itvplc.com
Chief Executive *Charles Allen*

ITV Broadcasting

200 Gray's Inn Road, London WC1X 8HF
☎020 7843 8000
www.itv.com
Chief Executive *Mick Desmond*
See listings below for ITV Anglia, ITV Border, ITV Central, ITV Granada, ITV London, ITV Meridian, ITV Tyne Tees, ITV Wales, ITV West, ITV Westcountry and ITV Yorkshire.

ITV Network

ITV1 comprises 15 regional channel with ITV plc holding the English and Welsh regional ITV licences (Anglia, Border, Central, Granada, London, Meridian, Tyne Tees, Wales, West, Westcountry and Yorkshire) as well as the digital channels, ITV2, ITV3 and ITV4. The remaining ITV licences belong to: SMG plc (Grampian and Scottish), Ulster Television plc (UTV) and Channel Television. Granada is the production arm of ITV plc.

ITV Anglia Television

Anglia House, Norwich NR1 3JG
☎01603 615151
www.angliatv.com
Managing Director *Neil Thompson*
Broadcasting to the east of England, Anglia Television is a major producer of programmes for the ITV network. Its network factual department currently boasts the largest portfolio of North American documentary commissions for a UK-based production company.

ITV Border Television

Television Centre, Durranhill, Carlisle CA1 3NT
☎01228 525101 Fax 01228 541384
www.border-tv.com
Managing Director *Douglas Merrall*
Border's region covers three different cultures – English, Scottish and Manx. Programming concentrates on documentaries rather than drama. Most scripts are supplied in-house but occasionally there are commissions. Apart from notes, writers should not submit written work until their ideas have been fully discussed.

ITV Central

Gas Street, Birmingham B1 2JT
☎0121 643 9898/0808 100 7888 (newsdesk)
Managing Director *Ian Squires*
Formed in 2004 by the merger of Carlton and Granada, ITV Central is the largest of the UK

commercial television networks outside of London.

ITV Granada

Quay Street, Manchester M60 9EA
☎0161 832 7211 Fax 0161 827 2180
www.granadatv.com

Director of Production *Claire Poyser*
Controller of Regional Programmes *Kieron Collins*
Controller of Drama *Carolyn Reynolds*
Controller of Current Affairs and Features *Jeff Anderson*
Controller of Documentaries, History and Science *Bill Jones*

The longest continuous ITC licence holder, broadcasting for over 40 years. Programmes include *Coronation Street* and *Disappearing World*. See also **ITV Productions** under **Film, TV and Radio Producers**.

ITV London

London Television Centre, Upper Ground, London SE1 9LT
☎020 7261 8163
✉ newsdesk@itvlondon.com

Managing Director *Christy Swords*

ITV London, formed in February 2004 by the merger of Carlton and LWT, broadcasts to the Greater London region, extending into the counties on its border.

ITV Meridian

Solent Business Park, Whiteley PO15 7PA
☎01489 442000
www.meridiantv.com

Managing Director *Lindsay Charlton*
Controller of Regional Programmes *Mark Southgate*

Serves five and a half million listeners spread across the South Coast, Thames Valley, Sussex and Kent. Long-running programmes include *Country Ways* and *Monkey Business*.

ITV Tyne Tees

Television House, The Watermark, Gateshead NE11 9SZ
☎0191 404 8700 Fax 0191 404 8710
www.tynetees.tv

Managing Director/Controller of Programmes *Graeme Thompson*
Head of Features *Jane Bolesworth*
Head of News & Sport *Graham Marples*
Executive Producer & Head of Development, Yorkshire Tyne Tees Features *Mark Robinson*

Head of Regional Affairs *Norma Hope*
Programming covers religion, politics, news and current affairs, regional documentaries, business, entertainment, sport and arts. Regular programmes include *North East Tonight with Mike Neville* and *Around the House* (politics).

ITV Wales

The Television Centre, Culverhouse Cross, Cardiff CF5 6XJ
☎029 2059 0590 Fax 029 2059 7183
✉ info@itvwales.com

Managing Director *Roger Lewis*

Formerly HTV Wales. Programmes include the consumer affairs magazine, *The Ferret* and current affairs series, *Wales this Week*. The company also makes Welsh language programming for S4C, including the series voted the most popular with viewers on the Welsh channel – *Cefn Gwlad* and the current affairs series, *Y Byd ar Bedwar*.

ITV West

Television Centre, Bath Road, Bristol BS4 3HG
☎0117 972 2722 Fax 0117 971 7685
✉ itvwestnews@itv.com (newsdesk)

Managing Director *Mark Haskell*
Director of Programmes *Jane McCloskey*

Formerly HTV. Broadcasts to over two million listeners in the West of England.

ITV West Country

Langage Science Park, Western Wood Way, Plymouth PL7 5BQ
☎01752 333333 Fax 01752 333444

Managing Director *Mark Haskell*
Director of Programmes *Jane McCloskey*

Broadcasts to Cornwall, Devon, Somerset and west Dorset. Produces regional news, current affairs and features programmes.

ITV Yorkshire

The Television Centre, Leeds LS3 1JS
☎0113 243 8283 Fax 0113 244 5107
www.itv.com

Managing Director *David Croft*
Controller of Drama, Leeds *Keith Richardson*
Controller of Comedy Drama and Drama Features *David Reynolds*

Drama series, comedy drama, single drama, adaptations and long-running series like *Emmerdale* and *Heartbeat*. Always looking for strong writing in these areas, but prefers to find it through an agent. Documentary/current affairs material tends to be supplied by producers; opportunities in these areas are rare but adaptations of published work as a documentary subject are considered. In theory, opportunity exists within series, episode material but the best approach is through a good agent.

LWT
See **ITV London**

S4C
Parc Ty Glas, Llanishen CF14 5DU
☎029 2074 7444 Fax 029 2075 4444
✉ s4c@s4c.co.uk
www.s4c.co.uk
Chief Executive *Iona Jones*
Director of Programmes *Rhian Gibson*
The Welsh 4th Channel, established by the Broadcasting Act 1980, is responsible for a schedule of Welsh and English programmes on the Fourth Channel in Wales. Known as S4C, the analogue service is made up of about 34 hours per week of Welsh language programmes and more than 85 hours of English language output from Channel 4. S4C digidol broadcasts in Welsh exclusively for 80 hours per week. Ten hours a week of the Welsh programmes are provided by the BBC; the remainder are purchased from ITV1 Wales and independent producers. Drama, comedy and documentary are all part of S4C's programming. Commissioning guidelines can be viewed on the website given above.

stv
Pacific Quay, Glasgow G51 1PQ
☎0141 300 3000 Fax 0141 300 3030
www.stv.tv
Also at: Television Centre, Craigshaw Business Park, West Tullos, Aberdeen AB12 3QH
☎01224 848848 Fax 01224 848800
Managing Director, Broadcasting, SMG Television Bobby Hain
Deputy Managing Director, Broadcasting, SMG Television *Derrick Thomson*
Head of News & Current Affairs (Glasgow) *Gordon Macmillan*
Head of News & Current Affairs (Aberdeen) *Craig Wilson*
Head of Sport *Henry Eagles*
stv is the ITV (Channel 3) licence holder for the north and central regions of Scotland. The company produces a range of television programmes, covering current affairs, sport, entertainment, documentary and drama, as well as flagship news programmes *Scotland Today* and *North Tonight*.

Teletext Ltd
Building 10, Chiswick Park, 566 Chiswick High Road, London W4 5TS
☎0870 731 3000 Fax 0870 731 3001
www.teletext.co.uk
Managing Director *Mike Stewart*
Editor-in-Chief *John Sage*
Broadcasts TV text services on analogue TV on ITV, Channel 4 and Five. Also broadcasts digital text services on Freeview and satellite on Channel 4 and, since 2005, on ITV. In addition, Teletext runs a holidays website and mobile services.

UTV (Ulster Television)
Havelock House, Ormeau Road, Belfast BT7 1EB
☎028 9032 8122 Fax 028 9024 6695
✉ info@u.tv
www.u.tv
Head of Television *Michael Wilson*
Head of News, Current Affairs and Sport *Rob Morrison*
Regular programmes on news and current affairs, sport and entertainment.

Cable and Satellite Television

British Sky Broadcasting Ltd (BSkyB)
6 Centaurs Business Park, Grant Way, Isleworth TW7 5QD
☎020 7705 3000 Fax 020 7705 3030
www.sky.com
Chief Executive *James Murdoch*
Managing Director, Sky Networks *Dawn Airey*
Chief Operating Officer *Richard Freudenstein*
Head of Sky News *Nick Pollard*
Managing Director, Sky Sports *Vic Wakeling*
Launched in 1989, British Sky Broadcasting gives over 21 million viewers (in more than eight million households) access to movies, news, entertainment and sports channels, and interactive services on Sky digital. Launched in October 1998, Sky digital has more than 400 channels and offers a range of innovative interactive services. 2006 saw the introduction of high definition television (HDTV).

WHOLLY-OWNED SKY CHANNELS
Sky Movies 1–9/Sky Cinema 1&2
Largest TV movie service outside the US. Sky Movies 1–9 show over 90% of the top 100 grossing box-office films of the previous year.

Sky Cinema 1&2 show classic films, from Westerns to Film Noir, Chaplin to Chevy Chase, as well as a World Cinema strand that includes UK premières of new and old movies.

Sky News

Award winning 24-hours news service with hourly bulletins and expert comment.

Sky One/Sky Two/Sky Three

One of the most frequently watched non-terrestrial channel with the accent on entertainment for 16–34-year-olds.

Sky Sports 1/Sky Sports 2/Sky Sports 3/ Sky Sports News/Sky Sports Extra

Around 40,000 hours of sport are broadcast every year across the five Sky Sports channels. Sky Sports 1, 2 and 3 are devoted to live events, support programmes and in-depth sports coverage seven days a week. Sky Sports News provides sports news and the latest results and information 24 hours a day. Sky Sports Extra carries additional sports programming including the award-winning live interactive coverage.

Sky Travel/Sky Travel Extra

Magazine shows, documentaries and teleshopping.

Artsworld

Wholly-owned Sky channel showcasing the best of the world's arts programmes, 18 hours a day, seven days a week.

JOINT VENTURES

National Geographic; Nickelodeon; Nick Jr; The History Channel; Paramount Comedy Channel; MUTV; Adventure One; The Biography Channel; Attheraces; Chelsea Digital Media.

CNBC Europe

10 Fleet Place, London EC4M 7QS
☎020 7653 9300 Fax 020 7653 5956
www.cnbceurope.com

Managing Director *Mick Buckley*

A service of NBC and Dow Jones. 24-hour business and financial news service. Programmes include *Today's Business*; *Morning Exchange*; *Capital Ideas*; *Europe Squawk Box*.

CNN International

Turner House, 16 Great Marlborough Street, London W1P 1DF
☎020 7693 1000 Fax 020 7693 1552
edition.cnn.com

Managing Editor, CNN International Europe, Middle East & Africa *Nick Wrenn*

CNN, the leading global 24-hour news network, is available to one billion people worldwide via the 26 CNN branded TV, Internet, radio and mobile services produced by CNN News Group, a Time Warner company. CNN has major production centres in Atlanta, New York, Los Angeles, London, Hong Kong and Mexico City. The London bureau, the largest outside the USA, is CNN's European headquarters and produces over 50 hours of programming per week. Live business and news programmes, including *Business International*; *World News* and *World Business Today*.

MTV Networks Europe

180 Oxford Street, London W1D 1DS
☎020 7284 7777 Fax 020 7284 7788
www.mtv.co.uk

President & Chief Executive *Brent Hansen*

Established 1987. Europe's 24-hour music and youth entertainment channel, available on cable, via satellite and digitally. Transmitted from London in English across Europe.

Travel Channel

66 Newman Street, London W1T 3EQ
☎020 7636 5401 Fax 020 7636 6424
www.travelchannel.co.uk

Launched in February 1994. Broadcasts programmes and information on the world of travel. Destinations reports, lifestyle programmes plus food and drink, sport and leisure pursuits.

National Commercial Radio

Classic FM

30 Leicester Square, London WC2H 7LA
☎020 7343 9000 Fax 020 7766 6100
www.classicfm.com

Station Manager *Darren Henley*

Classic FM, Britain's largest national commercial radio station, started broadcasting in September 1992. Plays accessible classical music 24 hours a day and broadcasts news, weather, travel, business information, political/ celebrity/ general interest talks, features and interviews. Winner of the 'Station of the Year' Sony Award in 2000.

Digital One

7 Swallow Place, London W1B 2AG
☎020 7288 4600 Fax 020 7288 4601
✉ info@digitalone.co.uk
www.ukdigitalradio.com

The UK's only national commercial digital radio multiplex operator. Backed by GCap Media and Arqiva, Digital One began broadcasting on 15 November 1999. Stations include **Classic FM, Virgin Radio, talkSPORT**and digital-only stations, **Oneword**, Planet Rock, Core, PrimeTime Radio and Life.

Oneword Radio

50 Lisson Street, London NW1 5DF
☎020 7976 3030   Fax 020 7930 9460
✉ info@oneword.co.uk
www.oneword.co.uk

Station Manager *Simon Blackmore*
Head of Programmes *Paul Kent*

The first commercial radio station dedicated solely to the transmission of plays, books, comedy and reviews. Broadcasts on Sky Digital (channel 877), Freeview (channel 717), ntl (channel 893) in Europe, DAB Digital Radio (Digital One – 18 hours a day) in the UK and worldwide on the Internet. Programmes include *Between the Lines*, a twice-daily conversation by Paul Blezard with different authors; *Cinemascope*, a weekly film review, *The Children's Good Book Guide* and *The Gallery*, a weekly guide to the UK arts scene. Winner of the 'Station of the Year' Sony Radio Awards in 2001 and 2002, the NTL Commercial Radio Award in 2003 and the Clarion Broadcast Radio Award in 2005.

talkSPORT

PO Box 1089, London SE1 8WQ
☎020 7959 7800
✉ pressreleases@talksport.co.uk
www.talksport.net

Programme Director *Bill Ridley*

Commenced broadcasting in February 1995 as Talk Radio UK. Re-launched January 2000 as TalkSport, the UK's first sports radio station. Acquired by Ulster Television in 2005. Broadcasts 24 hours a day. News items can be e-mailed via the website.

Virgin Radio

1 Golden Square, London W1F 9DJ
☎020 7434 1215   Fax 020 7434 1197
www.virginradio.co.uk

Programme Director *Paul Jackson*

Music-based station launched in 1973, bought by Chris Evans' Ginger Media Group in December 1997 and acquired by the Scottish Media Group in March 2000.

Independent Local Radio

Capital Radio London

30 Leicester Square, London WC2H 7LA
☎020 7766 6000   Fax 020 7766 6012
www.capitalradio.com

Programme Director *Scott Muller*

Commenced broadcasting in October 1973 as the country's second commercial radio station (the first being LBC, launched a week earlier). Europe's largest commercial radio station.

Central FM Ltd

201–203 High Street, Falkirk FK1 1DU
☎01324 611164   Fax 01324 611168
✉ email@centralfm.co.uk
www.centralfm.co.uk

Programme Controller *Tom Bell*

Broadcasts music, sport and local news to central Scotland, 24 hours a day.

Clyde 1/Clyde 2

Clydebank Business Park, Clydebank G81 2RX
☎0141 565 2200   Fax 0141 565 2265
www.clyde1.com
www.clyde2.com

Owner *Radio Clyde*
Managing Director *Paul Cooney*

Programmes usually originate in-house or by commission. All documentary material is made in-house. Good local news items always considered. There are three book programmes presented by Alex Dickson each week on Clyde 2 at 10.00 pm – 10.30 pm: *Authors* (Monday) features author interviews while *Hardback Bookcase* (Tuesday) and *Paperback Bookcase* (Wednesday) review latest titles.

Cool FM

See **Downtown Radio**

Downtown Radio/Cool FM

Newtownards, Co. Down BT23 4ES
☎028 9181 5555   Fax 028 9181 5252
✉ programmes@downtown.co.uk
www.downtown.co.uk

Managing Director *David Sloan*

Downtown Radio first ran a highly successful short story competition in 1988, attracting over 400 stories. The competition is now an annual event and writers living within the station's transmission area are asked to submit material during the winter and early spring. The competition is promoted in association with Eason

Shops. For further information, write to *Anita Downey* at the station.

Forth One/Forth 2

Forth House, Forth Street, Edinburgh
EH1 3LF
☎0131 556 9255 Fax 0131 475 1221
✉ scott@forth2.com
www.forthonline.co.uk

Controller, Forth One & Forth 2 *Luke McCullough*
Programme Producer, Forth 2 *Moira Millar*
News Editor *Paul Robertson*
Book Reviewer *Lesley Fraser-Taylor*

News stories welcome from freelancers. Music-based programming.

Isle of Wight Radio

Dodnor Park, Newport PO30 5XE
☎01983 822557 Fax 01983 821690
www.iwradio.co.uk

Station Manager *Andy Shier*
Programme Controller *Tom Stroud*

Part of The Local Radio Company, Isle of Wight Radio is the island's only radio station broadcasting local news, music and general entertainment including phone-ins and interview based shows. Music, television, film, popular culture are the main areas of interest.

KMfm

Head Office: Express House, 34–36 North Street, Ashford TN24 8JR
☎01233 895825
www.kmfm.co.uk

Group Programme Controller *Steve Fountain*

A wide range of music programming plus news, views and local interest. Part of the Kent Messenger Group.

LBC Radio Ltd

The Chrysalis Building, Bramley Road, London W10 6SP
☎020 7314 7300
www.lbc.co.uk

Programme Director *Scott Solder*
Editorial Director *Jonathan Richards*

LBC 97.3 FM is a talk-based station broadcasting 24 hours a day, providing entertainment, interviews, celebrity guests, music, chat shows, local interest, news and sport. LBC News 1152 AM, the sister station of LBC 97.3 FM, provides 24-hour rolling news.

NorthSound Radio

Abbotswell Road, Aberdeen AB12 3AJ
☎01224 337000
www.northsound1.com
andwww.northsound2.com

Managing Director *Ken Massie*
Programme Controller *Chris Thomson*

Features and music programmes 24 hours a day including, mid-morning (9.00 am – midday), *Northsound 2* feature programme.

Premier Radio

22 Chapter Street, London SW1P 4NP
☎020 7316 1300 Fax 020 7233 6706
✉ premier@premier.org.uk
www.premier.org.uk

Managing Director *Peter Kerridge*

Broadcasts programmes that reflect the beliefs and values of the Christian faith, 24 hours a day on 1305, 1413, 1332 MW, Sky digital 0123, ntl 886, Freeview channel 725 and on the Web.

Radio XL 1296 AM

KMS House, Bradford Street, Birmingham B12 0JD
☎0121 753 5353 Fax 0121 753 3111

Managing Director *Arun Bajaj*

Asian broadcasting for the West Midlands, 24 hours a day. Broadcasts *Love Express* featuring love stories and poems. Writers should send material for the attention of *Sukhjinder Ghataore*.

Sabras Radio

Radio House, 63 Melton Road, Leicester LE4 6PN
☎0116 261 0666 Fax 0116 266 7776
www.sabrasradio.com

Programme Controller *Don Kotak*

Programmes for the Asian community, broadcasting 24 hours a day.

Spectrum Radio

4 Ingate Place, London SW8 3NS
☎020 7627 4433 Fax 020 7627 3409
✉ enquiries@spectrumradio.net
www.spectrumradio.net

Managing Director *Toby Aldrych*

Programmes for a broad spectrum of ethnic groups in London.

Spire FM

City Hall Studios, Malthouse Lane, Salisbury SP2 7QQ
☎01722 416644 Fax 01722 416688

www.spirefm.co.uk
Station Director *Ceri Herford-Jones*
Music, news current affairs, quizzes and sport. Broadcasts to south Wiltshire and west Hampshire.

Sunrise Radio (Yorkshire)

Sunrise House, 30 Chapel Street, Bradford BD1 5DN
☎01274 735043 Fax 01274 728534
www.sunriseradio.fm
Programme Controller, Chief Executive & Chairman *Usha Parmar*
Programmes for the Asian community in West Yorkshire.

Swansea Sound 1170 MW/ 96.4 FM The Wave

Radio House, Victoria Road, Gowerton, Swansea SA4 3AB
☎01792 511170 (MW)/ 511964 (FM)
Fax 01792 511171 (MW)/511965 (FM)
www.swanseasound.co.uk
Station Director *Carrie Mosley*

Programme Controller *Steve Barnes*
News Editor *Emma Thomas*
Music-based programming on FM while Swansea Sound is interested in a wide variety of material, though news items must be of local relevance. An explanatory letter, in the first instance, is advisable.

Talk 107

9 South Gyle Crescent, Edinburgh Park, Edinburgh EH12 9EB
☎0131 316 3107
✉ studio@talk107.co.uk
www.talk107.co.uk
Station Director *Peter Gillespie*
News Editor *Gwen Lawrie*
Talk 107 is the first commercial speech radio station to be launched in the UK outside London. Commenced broadcasting in February 2006. Serves Edinburgh, Fife and the Lothians in Scotland. News, sport and debate.

96.4 FM The Wave

See **Swansea Sound 1170 MW**

Film, TV and Radio Producers

Aardman
Gas Ferry Road, Bristol BS1 6UN
☎0117 984 8485 Fax 0117 984 8486
www.aardman.com
Development Executive (Features) *Cath Hall*
Script Editor (Television) *Dick Hansom*
Founded 1972. Award-winning animation studio producing films, television series, videos, commercials and new media properties. OUTPUT includes: *Rex the Runt; Morph Files; Creature Comforts; Wallace and Gromit; Angry Kid; Chicken Run; The Presenters.* No unsolicited submissions.

Above The Title
Level 2, 10/11 St Georges Mews, London
NW1 8XE
☎020 7916 1984 Fax 020 7722 5706
✉ mail@abovethetitle.com
www.abovethetitle.com
Contacts *Bruce Hyman, Helen Chattwell*
Producer of radio drama, comedy and factual programmes. OUTPUT includes *Clive Anderson's Chat Room* and *Till the End of the Day – The Kinks Story* (Radio 2); *Unreliable Evidence; The Glittering Prizes* and *The Hitchhiker's Guide to the Galaxy* (Radio 4); *The Joy of Sax* and *Features Like Mine* (Radio 3). Unsolicited mss and ideas welcome. See website for details of how to approach in the first instance by e-mail. 'We encourage and support new writing in every way we can.'

Abstract Images
117 Willoughby House, Barbican, London
EC2Y 8BL
☎020 7638 5123
✉ productions@abstract-images.co.uk
Contact *Howard Ross*
Television documentary and drama programming. Also theatre productions. OUTPUT includes *Balm in Gilead* (drama); *Road* (drama); *Bent* (drama); *God: For & Against* (documentary); *This Is a Man* (drama/doc). New writers should send synopsis in the first instance.

Acacia Productions Ltd
80 Weston Park, London N8 9TB
☎020 8341 9392 Fax 020 8341 4879
✉ acacia@dial.pipex.com
www.acaciaproductions.co.uk
Contact *J. Edward Milner*
Producer of award-winning television and video documentaries; also news reports, corporates and programmes for educational charities. Undertakes basic video training and has a video manual in preparation. OUTPUT includes documentary series entitled *Last Plant Standing; A Farm in Uganda; Montserrat: Under the Volcano; Spirit of Trees* (8 progs.); *Vietnam: After the Fire; Macroeconomics – the Decision-makers; Greening of Thailand; A Future for Forests.* No unsolicited mss.

Actaeon Films Ltd
49 Blenheim Gardens, London NW2 4NR
☎020 8830 7990 Fax 0870 134 7980
✉ info@actaeonfilms.com
www.actaeonfilms.com
Producer *Daniel Cormack*
Head of Development *Becky Connell*
Founded 2004. Specialises in short and feature length theatrical motion pictures and micro-short films for distribution via new media (3G mobile phones, Internet). OUTPUT includes *Amelia and Michael* (short drama starring Anthony Head). In development: *Golden Apples* (feature-length drama), *The Dead Letters* (feature-length psychological thriller), *My Brother's Keeper* (feature-length psychological thriller). Actaeon Films is a member of the **New Producers Alliance, The Script Factory** and the London Filming Partnership. 'We actively encourage new writers and new writing. However, we can only give feedback on scripts with strong potential for developments (all mss are read by a professional reader within four weeks of submission). Scripts returned only if accompanied by s.a.e.'

All Out Productions
50 Copperas Street, Manchester M4 1HS
☎0161 834 9955 Fax 0161 834 6978
✉ mail@allout.co.uk
www.allout.co.uk
Contact *David Cook*
Producer of documentaries, features and current affairs programmes for radio. OUTPUT includes

Five Live Report (BBC Five Live – weekly news documentary); *Lamacq Live* (BBC Radio One – music and social affairs). Ideas welcome but not mss. Approach by e-mail.

Anglo/Fortunato Films Ltd
170 Popes Lane, London W5 4NJ
☎020 8932 7676   Fax 020 8932 7491

Contact *Luciano Celentino*

Film, television and video producer/director of action comedy and psych-thriller drama. No unsolicited mss.

Arlington Productions Limited
Cippenham Court, Cippenham Lane,
Cippenham, Nr Slough SL1 5AU
☎01753 516767   Fax 01753 691785

Television producer. Specialises in popular international drama, with *occasional* forays into other areas. 'We have an enviable reputation for encouraging new writers but only accept unsolicited submissions via agents.'

Art & Training Films Ltd
PO Box 3459, Stratford upon Avon CV37 6ZJ
☎056 0043 3970
✉ andrew.haynes@atf.org.uk
www.atf.org.uk

Contacts *Andrew Haynes, Gary Vernon*

Producer of documentaries, drama and corporate films and video. Submissions via agents considered.

The Ashford Entertainment Corporation Ltd
20 The Chase, Coulsdon CR5 2EG
☎020 8660 9609   Fax 087 0116 4142
✉ info@ashford-entertainment.co.uk
www.ashford-entertainment.co.uk

Managing Director *Frazer Ashford*

Founded in 1996 by award-winning film and TV producer Frazer Ashford whose credits include *Great Little Trains* (Mainline Television for Westcountry/Ch4, starring the late Willie Rushton); *Street Life* and *Make Yourself at Home* (both for WTV). Produces theatrical films and television – drama, lifestyle and documentaries. Happy to receive ideas for documentaries but submit a one-page synopsis only in the first instance, enclosing s.a.e. 'Be patient, allow up to four weeks for a reply. Be precise with the idea; specific details rather than vague thoughts. Attach a back-up sheet with credentials and supporting evidence, i.e., can you ensure that your idea is feasible?'

Beckmann International
Milntown Lodge, Lezayre Road, Ramsey
IM8 2TG
☎01624 816585   Fax 01624 816589
✉ sales@beckmanngroup.co.uk
www.beckmanngroup.co.uk

Contacts *Jo White, Stuart Semark*

Isle of Man-based company. Video and television documentary distributor. OUTPUT *Practical Guide to Europe* (travel series); *Maestro* (12-part series on classical composers); *Above and Beyond – The Story of British Aviation* (a celebration of aviation technology).

Big Heart Media
✉ info@bigheartmedia.com
www.bigheartmedia.com

Contacts *Colin Izod, Beth Newell*

Producer of drama and documentaries for television, radio and video. Ideas/outlines welcome by e-mail, but not unsolicited mss. 'We will respond as soon as we can. We're very keen to enourage new writing – particularly for radio drama.'

Blackwatch Productions Limited
2/1, 104 Marlboro Avenue, Glasgow G11 7LE
☎0141 339 9996
✉ info@blackwatchtv.com
www.blackwatchtv.com

Company Director *Nicola Black*
Production Manager *Anke Hilt*

Film, television, video producer of drama and documentary programmes. OUTPUT includes *The Paranormal Peter Sellers*; *Snorting Coke with the BBC*; *When Freddie Mercury Met Kenny Everett*; *Designer Vaginas*; *Bonebreakers*; *Luv Bytes*; and *Can We Carry On, Girls?* for Ch4. Also coordinates *Mesh*, animation scheme. Does not welcome unsolicited mss.

Bona Broadcasting Ltd
3rd Floor, 21 Albert Square, Dundee DD1 1DJ
☎01382 225403   Fax 01382 225408
✉ ideas@bonabroadcasting.com
www.bonabroadcasting.com

Contact *Turan Ali*

Producer of award winning-drama and documentary programmes for BBC Radio, TV and film projects. No unsolicted mss but send a one-paragraph summary by e-mail in the first instance. 'Writers new to BBC radio should expect to write a whole script on spec to win a commission.' Runs radio and TV drama training courses in the UK and internationally.

Buccaneer Films
5 Rainbow Court, Oxhey WD19 4RP
☎01923 254000
✉ michael@gosling.com
Contact *Michael Gosling*

Corporate video production and still photography specialists in education and sport. No unsolicited mss.

Calon Limited
3 Mount Stuart Square, Butetown, Cardiff
CF10 5EE
☎029 2048 8400   Fax 029 2048 5962
✉ enquiries@calon.tv
Contact *Andrew Offiler*

Animated series, mainly for children. OUTPUT includes *Meeow; Hilltop Hospital; The Hurricanes; Tales of the Toothfairies; Billy the Cat; The Blobs*, as well as the feature films, *Under Milk Wood* and *The Princess and the Goblin*. Write with ideas and sample script in the first instance.

Carnival (Films & Theatre) Ltd
12 Raddington Road, Ladbroke Grove,
London W10 5TG
☎020 8968 0968   Fax 020 8968 0155
✉ info@carnival-films.co.uk
www.carnival-films.co.uk
Contacts *Brian Eastman, Gareth Neame*

Film, TV and theatre producer. OUTPUT FILM: *The Mill on the Floss* (BBC); *Firelight* (Hollywood Pictures/Wind Dancer Productions); *Up on the Roof* (Rank/Granada); *Shadowlands* (Savoy/Spelling); *The Infiltrator* (Home Box Office); *Under Suspicion* (Columbia/Rank/LWT). TELEVISION: *Hotel Babylon* (BBC); *Rosemary & Thyme* (ITV/Granada); *The Grid* (BBC/TNT); *As If* (Ch4/Columbia); *Lucy Sullivan is Getting Married* (ITV); *The Tenth Kingdom* (Sky/NBC); *Agatha Christie's Poirot* (ITV/LWT/A&E); *Every Woman Knows a Secret* and *Oktober* (both for ITV Network Centre); *The Fragile Heart* (Ch4); *Crime Traveller* and *Bugs 1–4* (BBC); *Anna Lee* and *All Or Nothing At All* (LWT); *Head Over Heels* (Carlton); *Jeeves & Wooster I–IV* (Granada); *Traffik* and *Porterhouse Blue* (Ch4); *Blott on the Landscape* (BBC). THEATRE: *What a Performance; Juno & the Paycock; Murder is Easy; Misery; Ghost Train; Map of the Heart; Shadowlands; Up on the Roof.*

Cartwn Cymru
32 Wordsworth Avenue, Roath, Cardiff
CF24 3FR
☎029 2046 3556/07771 640400
✉ production@cartwn-cymru.com

Contact *Naomi Jones*

Animation production company. OUTPUT *Toucan 'Tecs* (YTV/S4C); *Funnybones* and *Turandot: Operavox* (both for S4C/BBC); *Testament: The Bible in Animation* (BBC2/S4C); *The Miracle Maker* (S4C/BBC/British Screen/Icon Entertainment International); *Faeries* (HIT Entertainment plc for CITV); *Otherworld* (animated feature film for S4C Films, British Screen, Arts Council of Wales).

Celador Films
39 Long Acre, London WC2E 9LG
☎020 7845 6988   Fax 020 7845 6979
✉ sbaker@celador.co.uk
www.celador.co.uk
Story Editor *Sarah Baker*

Producer of feature films. OUTPUT includes *Dirty Pretty Things*, Julian Fellowes-helmed romantic drama, *Separate Lives* and Neil Marshall's second feature, *The Descent*. No unsolicited mss.

Celador Productions
39 Long Acre, London WC2E 9LG
☎020 7240 8101   Fax 020 7845 6979
✉ tvhits@celador.co.uk
www.celador.co.uk
Head of Entertainment *Colman Hutchinson*
Development Executive, Comedy *Humphrey Barclay*
Head of Comedy Development *Vanessa Haynes*
Head of Radio *Liz Anstee*

Producer of TV and radio comedy and light entertainment. OUTPUT *You Are What You Eat; Who Wants to be a Millionaire; Winning Lines; Commercial Breakdown; Britain's Brainiest ...; All About Me; It's Been a Bad Week.* 'We are interested in original comedy and radio scripts but do not accept unsolicited entertainment formats. As a relatively small company our script-reading capacity is limited.'

Celtic Films Entertainment Ltd
31 Sackville Street, London W1S 3DZ
☎020 7734 4434   Fax 020 7734 4744
✉ info@celticfilms.co.uk
www.celticfilms.co.uk
Contact *Stuart Sutherland*

Film and television drama producer. OUTPUT includes 14 feature-length *Sharpe* TV films for Carlton and *A Life for a Life – The True Story of Stefan Kiszko* TV film for ITV. Devised *Hornblower* series for ITV. Supports new writing and welcomes unsolicited material: features and TV pilots/features.

Chameleon Television Ltd

Great Minster House, Lister Hill, Horsforth, Leeds LS18 5DL
☎0113 205 0040   Fax 0113 281 9454
✉ allen@chameleontv.com
Contacts *Allen Jewhurst, Qyuen Muu, Julia Kirby-Smith*

Film and television drama and documentary producer. OUTPUT includes *Edge of the City*; 'Dispatches' – *Killing for Honour; College Girls; Ken Dodd in the Dock* (all for Ch4); *Divorces From Hell; Shipman; Love to Shop; The Marchioness* (all for ITV); *Ted & Sylvia – Love, Loss; Hamas Bombers* (BBC); *Liverpool Poets* (Ch5). Scripts not welcome unless via agents but new writing is encouraged.

The Children's Film & Television Foundation Ltd

✉ annahome@cftf.org
Chief Executive *Anna Home*

Involved in the development and co-production of films for children and the family, both for the theatric market and for TV.

Cinécosse

North Meadows, Oldmeldrum AB51 OGQ
☎01651 873311   Fax 01651 873300
✉ admin@cinecosse.co.uk
www.cinecosse.co.uk
Contact *Graeme Mowat*

Television and video documentary and corporate productions. OUTPUT includes *Scotland's Larder* and *Rising to the Challenge* (Scottish and Grampian TV); safety and training videos for industry; tourism promotional and sales information, interactive multimedia and DVD authoring. All scripts are commissioned; no unsolicited material.

Cinema Verity Productions Ltd

11 Addison Avenue, London W11 4QS
☎020 7460 2777   Fax 020 7371 3329
Contact *Verity Lambert*

Leading television drama producer whose credits include *She's Out* by Lynda la Plante; *Class Act* by Michael Aitkens; *May to December* (BBC series); *Running Late* by Simon Gray (Screen 1); *The Cazalets* adapt. of *The Cazalet Chronicle* by Elizabeth Jane Howard (BBC).

Cleveland Productions

5 Rainbow Court, Oxhey, Near Watford WD19 4RP
☎01923 254000

✉ michael@gosling.com
Contact *Michael Gosling*

Communications in sound and vision A/V production and still photography specialists in education and sport. No unsolicited mss.

COI

Hercules Road, London SE1 7DU
☎020 7928 2345

Government advertising and marketing communications, and public information films.

Collingwood O'Hare Entertainment Ltd & Convergence Productions Ltd

10–14 Crown Street, London W3 8SB
☎020 8993 3666   Fax 020 8993 9595
✉ info@crownstreet.co.uk
Producer (Collingwood O'Hare Entertainment) *Christopher O'Hare*
Producer (Convergence Productions) *Terence Clegg*
Head of Development *Helen Stroud*

Film and TV. Convergence Productions produces live action, drama documentaries; Collingwood O'Hare Entertainment specialises in children's animation. OUTPUT **Convergence**: *Theo* (film drama series); *Plastic Fantastic* (UK cosmetic surgery techniques, Ch5); *David Starkey's Henry VIII* (Ch4 historical documentary) and *On the Road Again* (BBC2 documentary travel series). **Collingwood**: *RARG* (award-winning animated film); *Yoko! Jakamoko! Toto!* (CITV); *Daisy-Head Mayzie* (Dr Seuss animated series for Turner Network and Hanna-Barbera); *Gordon the Garden Gnome* (CBBC); *Eddy and the Bear* (CITV) and *The King's Beard* (CITV). Unsolicited mss not welcome 'as a general rule as we do not have the capacity to process the sheer weight of submissions this creates. We therefore tend to review material from individuals recommended to us through personal contact with agents or other industry professionals. We like to encourage new writing and have worked with new writers but our ability to do so is limited by our capacity for development. We can usually only consider taking on one project each year, as development/finance takes several years to put in place.'

The Comedy Unit

Glasgow TV & Film Studios, Glasgow Media Park, Craigmont Street, Glasgow G20 9BT
☎0141 305 6666   Fax 0141 305 6600
✉ comedyunit@comedyunit.co.uk

www.comedyunit.co.uk

Managing Directors *April Chamberlain, Colin Gilbert*

Producers of comedy entertainment for children's TV, radio, video and film. OUTPUT *Still Game*; *Karen Dunbar Show*; *Offside*; *Chewin' the Fat*; *Only An Excuse*; *Yo! Diary* and *Watson's Wind Up*. Unsolicited mss welcome by post or e-mail.

Convergence Productions Ltd
See **Collingwood O'Hare Entertainment Ltd & Convergence Productions Ltd**

Cosgrove Hall Films
8 Albany Road, Chorlton–cum–Hardy M21 0AW
☎0161 882 2500 Fax 0161 882 2555
✉ animation@cosgrovehall.com

Contact *Lee Marriott*

Children's animation producer; film video and television. OUTPUT includes *Noddy* and *Rotten Ralph* (both for BBC); *Lavender Castle* by Gerry Anderson; *The Fox Busters*; *Animal Shelf*; *Rocky & the Dodos*; Alison Uttley's *Little Grey Rabbit* (all for children's ITV); Terry Pratchett's *Discworld* (Ch4). 'We try to select writers on a project-by-project basis.'

Creative Channel Ltd
Channel TV, Television Centre, St Helier, Jersey JE1 3ZD
☎01534 816873 Fax 01534 816889
✉ david@channeltv.co.uk
www.creativechannel.co.uk

Senior Producer *David Evans*

Producer of TV commercials and corporate material: information, promotional, sales, training and events coverage. CD and DVD production; promotional videos for all types of businesses throughout Europe. No unsolicited mss; new writing/scripts commissioned as required. Interested in hearing from local writers resident in the Channel Islands.

The Creative Partnership
13 Bateman Street, London W1D 3AF
☎020 7439 7762
✉ sallyc@thecreativepartnership.co.uk
www.thecreativepartnership.co.uk

Contacts *Christopher Fowler, Sally Chapman*

'Europe's largest "one-stop shop" for advertising and marketing campaigns for the film and television industries.' Clients include most major and independent film companies. No

scripts. 'We train new writers in-house, and find them from submitted c.v.s. All applicants must have previous commercial writing experience.'

Cricket Ltd
Medius House, 63–69 New Oxford Street, London WC1A 1EA
☎020 7845 0300 Fax 020 7845 0303
✉ team@cricket-ltd.com
www.cricket-ltd.com

Head of Production (Film & Video) *Jonathan Freer*

Film and video, live events and conferences, print and design. 'Communications solutions for business clients wishing to influence targeted external and internal audiences.'

CSA Word
6A Archway Mews, 241A Putney Bridge Road, London SW15 2PE
☎020 8871 0220 Fax 020 8877 0712
✉ victoria@csaword.co.uk
www.csaword.co.uk

Contacts *Victoria Williams, Clive Stanhope*

Producer of drama, documentaries and readings for radio. OUTPUT *Alfie Elkins & His Little Life* (drama for BBC World Service); *The Hungry Years* (reading for BBC R4); *A Stable Relationship* (feature for BBC R4); *Bob Dylan's Chronicles 1* (reading for BBC R2); *It's a Girl*; *Chat Snaps*; *Videotape – Two* (documentaries for BBC World Service Learning); *The Glenn Miller Story* (documentary for BBC Radio 2). Unsolicited drama ideas welcome by post or e-mail. 'We encourage new drama, and documentary/feature ideas.'

Cutting Edge Productions Ltd
27 Erpingham Road, London SW15 1BE
☎020 8780 1476 Fax 020 8780 0102
✉ juliannorridge@btconnect.com

Contact *Julian Norridge*

Corporate and documentary video and television. OUTPUT includes US series on evangelicalism, 'Dispatches' on US tobacco and government videos. No unsolicited mss; 'we commission all our writing to order, but are open to ideas.'

Dakota Films Ltd
4a Junction Mews, London W2 1PN
☎020 7402 1300 Fax 020 7402 6111
✉ info@o-spi.com

Managing Director *Jonathan Olsberg*

Film and television drama. Feature films

include: *Head in the Clouds; Me Without You; Janice Beard 45wpm; Let Him Have It; Othello.* Currently developing a slate of films including John Sayles' *Fade to Black* and a number of projects by new writers. Interested in working with new talent but does not consider unsolicited material.

Diverse Production Limited

6 Gorleston Street, London W14 8XS
☎020 7603 4567 Fax 020 7603 2148
www.diverse.tv

Independent production company specialising in popular prime-time formats, strong documentaries, specialist factual, historical, cultural, religious, arts, music and factual entertainment. Recent OUTPUT includes *Musicality; Operatunity; Who Wrote the Bible; Who You Callin' Nigger?; In Search of Tony Blair; Britain AD; Shock Treatment; Beyond Boundaries; Escape to the Legion.*

DMS Films Ltd

89 Sevington Road, London NW4 3RU
☎020 8203 5540 Fax 0870 762 5871
✉ danny@dmsfilms.co.uk

Producer *Daniel San*

Film producer. OUTPUT includes *Understanding Jane; Hard Edge; Popcorn.* Unsolicited screenplays not welcome: phone, fax or e-mail synopsis or outline in first instance.

Double Exposure

See **Flashback Television Limited**

DoubleBand Films

3 Crescent Gardens, Belfast BT7 1NS
☎028 9024 3331 Fax 028 9023 6980
✉ info@doublebandfilms.com
www.doublebandfilms.com

Contacts *Michael Hewitt, Dermot Lavery*

Specialises in documentaries and drama. Recent productions include *Seven Days that Shook the World* and *War in Mind* (both for Ch4); *Christine's Children* (BBC Northern Ireland; nominated for both the RTS and Celtic Film Festival); *D-Day: Triumph and Tragedy* (BBC NI).

Drake A-V Video Ltd

89 St Fagans Road, Fairwater, Cardiff CF5 3AE
☎029 2056 0333 Fax 029 2055 4909
www.drakeav.com

Contact *Ian Lewis*

Corporate A-V film and video, mostly promotional, training or educational. Scripts in these fields welcome. Design and installation of AV systems.

Charles Dunstan Communications Ltd

42 Wolseley Gardens, London W4 3LS
☎020 8994 2328 Fax 020 8994 2328

Contact *Charles Dunstan*

Producer of film, video and TV for documentary and corporate material. OUTPUT *Renewable Energy* for broadcast worldwide in 'Inside Britain' series; *The Far Reaches* travel series; *The Electric Environment.* No unsolicited scripts.

Electric Airwaves Ltd (Ladbroke Radio)

Essel House, 29 Foley Street, London W1W 7JW
☎020 7323 2770 Fax 020 7079 2080
✉ neil@electricairwaves.com
www.electricairwaves.com

Contacts *Neil Gardner, Richard Bannerman*

Producer of radio drama, documentary, corporate, music, music documentaries and readings. OUTPUT includes *The Woman in White; The Darling Buds of May; The True History of British Pop; The World on a String; The Colour of Music* (all for BBC Radio 2); *Don Carlos; In the Company of Men* (BBC Radio 3 drama); *Sitting in Limbo* (BBC World Service drama); *Your Vote Counts* (Electoral Commision audio CDs). Unsolicited mss and ideas welcome; send letter in the first instance. 'We are willing to help develop for possible submission to the BBC.'

Fairline Productions Ltd

15 Royal Terrace, Glasgow G3 7NY
☎0141 331 0077 Fax 0141 331 0066
✉ fairprods@aol.com
www.fairlineproductions.com

Contact *Mr R. Walker*

Television and video producer of documentary and corporate programmes and commercials. OUTPUT includes *Hooked*, a 15-part angling series (Discovery Channel) plus training and instructional videos for Forbo-Nairn Ltd, Royal Bank of Scotland, and Health & Safety Executive. No unsolicited scripts.

Farnham Film Company Ltd

34 Burnt Hill Road, Lower Bourne, Farnham GU10 3LZ
☎01252 710313 Fax 01252 725855
www.farnfilm.com

Contact *Ian Lewis*

Television and film: children's drama and documentaries. Unsolicited mss usually welcome but prefers a letter to be sent in the first instance. Check website for current requirements.

Fast Films
Christmas House, 213 Chester Road, Castle Bromwich, Solihull B36 0ET
☎0121 749 7147/4144
✉ gavinprime@mac.com
Contact *Gavin Prime*

Film and television: comedy, entertainment and animation. No unsolicited mss.

Festival Film and Television Ltd
Festival House, Tranquil Passage, Blackheath, London SE3 0BJ
☎020 8297 9999   Fax 020 8297 1155
✉ info@festivalfilm.com
www.festivalfilm.com
Managing Director *Ray Marshall*
Producer *Matt Marshall*
Development *Johanna Devereaux*

Television drama and feature films. Best known for its Catherine Cookson Dramas, which became one of ITV's long-running brands. Now developing both TV drama and features. Generally accept material submitted through an agent. However, will consider unsolicited material but prefers a treatment or synopsis in the first instance.

Fiction Factory
14 Greenwich Church Street, London SE10 9BJ
☎020 8853 5100   Fax 020 8293 3001
✉ radio@fictionfactory.co.uk
www.fictionfactory.co.uk
Creative Director *John Taylor*

Producer of drama and documentaries for radio. OUTPUT includes Proust's *A La Recherche du Temps Perdu*; H.G. Wells' *Kipps* (BBC R4 Classic Serial); *Abrogate* by Larry Gebart (BBC R4 Friday Play); *The Fringe of Fame* (BBC R4 feature). Ideas considered if sent by e-mail. Mss only from agents or writers with a professional track record in the broadcast media.

Film and General Productions Ltd
4 Bradbrook House, Studio Place, London SW1X 8EL
☎020 7235 4495   Fax 020 7245 9853
✉ cparsons@filmgen.co.uk
Contacts *Clive Parsons, Davina Belling*

Film and television drama. Feature films include

True Blue, Tea with Mussolini and *I Am David*. Also *Seesaw* (ITV drama), *The Greatest Store in the World* (family drama, BBC) and *The Queen's Nose* (children's series, BBC). Interested in considering new writing but subject to prior telephone conversation.

Firehouse Productions
42 Glasshouse Street, London W1B 5DW
☎020 7439 2220   Fax 020 7439 2210
✉ postie@firehouse.biz
www.firehouse.biz
Contacts *Julie-Anne Edwards, Gavin Knight*

Corporate films and websites, commercials and DRTV. OUTPUT includes work for De Beers; Prudential; government and various agencies.

The First Film Company Ltd
3 Bourlet Close, London W1W 7BQ
☎020 7436 9490   Fax 020 7637 1290
✉ info@firstfilmcompany.com
Producers *Roger Randall-Cutler, Robert Cheek*

Founded 1984. Cinema screenplays. All submissions should be made through an agent.

First Writes Theatre Company
Lime Kiln Cottage, High Starlings, Banham, Norwich NR16 2BS
☎01953 888525   Fax 01953 888974
✉ ellen@firstwrites.fsnet.co.uk
www.first-writes.co.uk
Contact *Ellen Dryden*

Producer of numerous afternoon, Friday and Saturday plays, classic serials and comedy narrative series for BBC Radio 3, 4 and World Service. Welcomes unsolicited mss or ideas by post. 'As an independent company it is difficult to obtain commissions for new writers and inhouse should be your first port of call. However, we are committed to producing new work by established writers.'

Flannel
21 Berwick Street, London W1F 0PZ
☎020 7287 9277   Fax 020 7287 7785
✉ mail@flannel.net
Contact *Kate Haldane*

Producer of drama, documentaries and comedy for television and radio. OUTPUT includes *Women's Hour* (BBC R4); *The Hendersons' Christmas Party* (five-part Christmas drama, BBC R4). No unsolicited mss. 'Keen to encourage new writing, but must come via an agent. Particularly interested in 45–50 minute dramas for radio. Not in a position to produce plays for stage, but very happy to consider adaptations. Welcomes comedy with some track record.'

Flashback Television Limited
11 Bowling Green Lane, London EC1R 0BG
☎020 7490 8996 Fax 020 7490 5610
✉ mailbox@flashbacktv.co.uk
www.flashbacktelevision.com

Contact *Tim Ball*

Producer of documentaries and factual entertainment since 1982. Based in London and Bristol. Acquired education producer Double Exposure in 2004. Recent credits include *Married to the Prime Minister* and *The Hiroshima Pictures* (both for Ch4); *Discovery Superhomes* and *Top Tens* (both for Discovery).

Focus Films Ltd
The Rotunda Studios, Rear of 116–118 Finchley Road, London NW3 5HT
☎020 7435 9004 Fax 020 7431 3562
✉ focus@focusfilms.co.uk
www.focusfilms.co.uk

Contacts *David Pupkewitz, Malcolm Kohll* (Head of Development)

Film producer. OUTPUT *The Book of Eve* (Canadian drama); *The Bone Snatcher* (Horror, UK/Can/SA); *Julia's Ghost* (German co-production); *The 51st State* (feature film); *Secret Society* (comedy drama feature film); *Crimetime* (feature thriller); *Diary of a Sane Man; Othello.* Projects in development include *Heaven and Earth; Tainted Desert; The Complete History of the Breast; Triomf.* No unsolicited scripts.

Mark Forstater Productions Ltd
27 Lonsdale Road, London NW6 6RA
☎020 7624 1123 Fax 020 7624 1124

Contact *Mark Forstater*

Active in the selection, development and production of material for film and TV. OUTPUT *Monty Python and the Holy Grail; The Odd Job; The Grass is Singing; Xtro; Forbidden; Separation; The Fantasist; Shalom Joan Collins; The Silent Touch; Grushko; The Wolves of Willoughby Chase; Between the Devil and the Deep Blue Sea; Doing Rude Things.* No unsolicited scripts.

FremantleMedia Ltd
1 Stephen Street, London W1T 1AL
☎020 7691 6000 Fax 020 7691 6100
www.fremantlemedia.com

CEO *Tony Cohen*
CEO, talkbackTHAMES *Lorraine Heggessey*

FremantleMedia, formerly known as Pearson Television, is the production arm of the RTL Group, Europe's largest TV and radio company. Acquired Thames Television in 1993 (producer of *The Bill*) and Grundy Worldwide (*Neighbours*) in 1995. Further acquisitions were Witzend Productions (*Lovejoy*) and Alomo Productions in 1996 and TalkBack Productions in 2000. FremantleMedia produces more than 260 programmes in over 40 countries and territories a year.

Gaia Communications
Sanctuary House, 35 Harding Avenue, Eastbourne BN22 8PL
☎01323 734809/727183 Fax 01323 734809
✉ production@gaiacommunications.co.uk
www.gaiacommunications.co.uk

Producer *Robert Armstrong*
Script Editor *Loni Webb*

Established 1987. Video and TV corporate and documentary. OUTPUT *Discovering* (south east regional tourist and local knowledge series); *Holistic* (therapies and general information); local interest audiobooks.

Noel Gay Television
Shepperton Studios, Studios Road, Shepperton TW17 0QD
☎01932 592569 Fax 01932 592172
✉ charles.armitage@virgin.net

CEO *Charles Armitage*

OUTPUT *The Fear* (BBC Choice); *Second Chance* (Ch4); *Hububb* Series 1–5 (BBC); *I-Camcorder* (Ch4); *Frank Stubbs Promotes* and *10%ers* Series 2 (both for Carlton/ITV); *Call Up the Stars* (BBC1); *Smeg Outs* (BBC video); *Red Dwarf; Dave Allen* (ITV); *Windrush* (BBC2). Joint ventures and companies include a partnership with Odyssey, a leading Indian commercials, film and TV producer, and the Noel Gay Motion Picture Company, whose credits include *Virtual Sexuality; Trainspotting* (with Ch4 and Figment Films); *Killer Tongue; Dog Soldiers; Fast Sofa* and *Pasty Faces.* Associate NGTV companies are Grant Naylor Productions and Pepper Productions. NGTV is willing to accept unsolicited material from writers but 1–2-page treatments only. No scripts, please.

Ginger Television
See **SMG & Ginger TV Productions Ltd**

Goldcrest Films International Ltd
65–66 Dean Street, London W1D 4PL
☎020 7437 8696 Fax 020 7437 4448
✉ mailbox@goldcrestfilms.com

www.goldcrestfilms.com

Chairman *John Quested*

Contact *Wayne Godfrey*

Since it was established in 1977, Goldcrest Films has become a leading independent film production company winning many prizes at international festivals including 19 Academy Awards. Finances, produces and distributes films and television programmes. OUTPUT includes *Chariots of Fire*; *Gandhi*; *The Killing Fields*; *A Room With a View*; *Local Hero*; *The Mission*; *To End All Wars*. 'We are currently seeking film projects to invest equity in through our Finishing Fund in return for International Sales Rights.' Scripts via agents only.

The Good Film Company Ltd

The Studio, 5–6 Eton Garages, Lambolle Place, London NW3 4PE

☎020 7794 6222 Fax 020 7794 4651

✉ yanina@goodfilms.co.uk

www.goodfilms.co.uk

Contact *Yanina Barry*

Commercials and pop videos. Clients include Suzuki, Burberry, Totally London, Hugo Boss, Cadbury's. *No* unsolicited mss.

Granite Film & Television Productions Ltd

Vigilant House, 120 Wilton Road, London SW1V 1JZ

☎020 7808 7230 Fax 020 7808 7231

Contact *Simon Welfare*

Producer of television documentary programmes such as *Nicholas & Alexandra*; *Victoria & Albert* and *Arthur C. Clarke's Mysterious Universe*.

Green Umbrella Ltd

59 Cotham Hill, Stoke Bishop, Bristol BS6 6JR

☎0117 906 4336 Fax 0117 923 7003

✉ postmaster@umbrella.co.uk

www.umbrella.co.uk

Film producers specialising in science and natural history documentaries. OUTPUT includes episodes for *The Natural World*, *Wildlife on One* and original series such as *Living Europe* and *Triumph of Life*. Unsolicited treatments relating to natural history and science subjects are welcome.

Greenwich Village Productions

14 Greenwich Church Street, London SE10 9BJ

☎020 8853 5100 Fax 020 8293 3001

✉ tv@fictionfactory.co.uk

www.fictionfactory.co.uk

Contact *John Taylor*

Producer of drama documentaries, arts features and educational programmes. OUTPUT *An Arundel Tomb* (video treatment of Philip Larkin's poem); *Adlestrop* (video treatment of Edward Thomas' poem); and *The Secret Places of the Four Quartets*. Welcomes ideas by e-mail. Mss only from agents or writers with a professional track record in the chosen medium.

H2 Business Communications

Shepperton Studios, Shepperton TW17 0QD

☎01932 593717 Fax 01932 593718

✉ mail@h2bc.co.uk

www.h2bc.co.uk

Contact *Julie Knight*

Conferences, videos, awards presentations and speaker training.

Hammerwood Film Productions

110 Trafalgar Road, Portslade BN41 1GS

☎01273 277333 Fax 01273 705451

✉ filmangels@freenetname.co.uk

www.filmangel.co.uk

Contacts *Ralph de Straet von Kollman, Petra Ginman*

Film, video and TV drama. OUTPUT *Iceni* (film; co-production with Pan-European Film Productions and Boudicca Film Productions Ltd); *Boudicca – A Celtic Tragedy* (TV series). In pre-production: *The Black Egg* (witchcraft in 17th century England); *The Ghosthunter, Iceni* (documentary of the rebellion of AD61); *No Case to Answer* (legal series). 'Authors are recommended to access www.filmangel.co.uk' (see *Useful Websites*).

Hartswood Films Ltd

Twickenham Studios, The Barons, St Margarets TW1 2AW

☎020 8607 8736 Fax 020 8607 8744

✉ films.tv@hartswoodfilms.co.uk

Contact *Elaine Cameron*

Film and TV production for drama, comedy and documentary. OUTPUT *Men Behaving Badly*; *Border Cafe*; *Coupling*; *Carrie & Barry* (all for BBC); *After Thomas* (ITV drama).

Hat Trick Productions Ltd

10 Livonia Street, London W1F 8AF

☎020 7434 2451 Fax 020 7287 9791

www.hattrick.com

Managing Director *Jimmy Mulville* Television programmes.

Healthcare Productions Limited

The Great Barn, Godmersham, Canterbury CT4 7DT
☎01227 738279 Fax 01227 732145
✉ penny@healthcareproductions.co.uk
www.healthcareproductions.co.uk
Contact *Penny Webb*

Television and video: documentary and drama. Produces training and educational material, in text, video, CD-ROM and DVD, mostly health-related, social care issues, law and marriage.

Heritage Theatre Ltd

Unit 1, 8 Clanricarde Gardens, London W2 4NA
☎020 7243 2750 Fax 020 7792 8584
✉ rm@heritagetheatre.com
www.heritagetheatre.com
Contact *Robert Marshall*

Video recordings of successful stage plays for distribution on DVD and broadcast.

David Hill

107 Wellington Road North, Stockport SK4 2LP
☎0161 477 9090 Fax 0161 477 9191
✉ david.hill@acrobat-tv.co.uk
Contacts *David Hill*

All script genres for broadcast and coporate television, including training and promotional scripts, comedy and drama-based material. OUTPUT includes *Make a Stand* (Jack Dee, Gina Bellman and John Thompson for Video Arts); *The Customer View* (Roy Barraclough for Air Products); *Serious About Waves* series (Peter Hart for the Royal Yachting Association). No unsolicited mss.

Holmes Associates

The Studio, 37 Redington Road, London NW3 7QY
☎020 7813 4333
✉ holmesassociates@blueyonder.co.uk
Contact *Andrew Holmes*

Prolific originator, producer and packager of documentary, drama and music television and films. See also **Open Road Films**. OUTPUT has included *Ashes and Sand* (Film 4); *Chunky Monkey* (J&V Films); *Prometheus* (Ch4 'Film 4'); *The Shadow of Hiroshima* (Ch4 'Witness'); *The House of Bernarda Alba* (Ch4/WNET/Amaya);

Piece of Cake (LWT); *The Cormorant* (BBC/Screen 2); *John Gielgud Looks Back*; *Rock Steady*; *Well Being*; *Signals*; *Ideal Home?* (all Ch4); *Timeline* (with MPT, TVE Spain & TRT Turkey); *Seven Canticles of St Francis* (BBC2). Unsolicited drama project outlines accepted, but not scripts.

Hourglass Productions

27 Prince's Road, London SW19 8RA
☎020 8540 8786
✉ productions@hourglass.co.uk
www.hourglass.co.uk
Directors *Martin Chilcott, Jacqueline Chilcott*

Film and video; documentary and drama. OUTPUT BAFTA nominated scientific television documentaries and educational programming. Also current affairs, health and social issues.

Icon Films

10 Redland Terrace, Bristol BS6 6TD
☎0117 924 8535 Fax 0117 974 4971
✉ info@iconfilms.co.uk
www.iconfilms.co.uk
Contact *Harry Marshall*

Film and TV documentaries. OUTPUT *Holy Cow!* (WNET); *The King Cobra & I* (BBC 'Natural World'); *The Riddle of Einstein's Brain* (Ch4/National Geographic Channels International). Specialises in factual documentaries. Open-minded to new documentary proposals.

Imari Entertainment Ltd

PO Box 158, Beaconsfield HP9 1AY
☎01494 677147 Fax 01494 677147
✉ info@imarientertainment.com
Contact *Jonathan Fowke*

TV and video producer, covering all areas of drama, documentary and corporate productions.

Isis Productions

106 Hammersmith Grove, London W6 7HB
☎020 8748 3042 Fax 020 8748 3046
✉ isis@isis-productions.com
www.isisproductions.co.uk
Directors *Nick de Grunwald, Jamie Rugge-Price*
Production Coordinator *Catriona Lawless*

Formed in 1991, Isis Productions focuses on the production of music and documentary programmes. OUTPUT *Ray Davies – The World from My Window*; *James Brown – Soul Survivor* (Ch4); *Bernie Taupin* (ITV 'South Bank Show'); *Iron Maiden, Judas Priest* (Five 'Rock Classics'); Films on *Deep Purple, Metallica, Def Leppard, Lou Reed, Elton John, Elvis Presley, Sex Pistols* (ITV 'Classic Albums 3'); *Simply Red, Nirvana, Cream, Pink Floyd, Motorhead* ('Classic Albums 4'); *England's Other Elizabeth – Elizabeth Taylor* (BBC 'Omnibus').

Isolde Films
28 Twyford Avenue, London W3 9QB
☎020 8896 2860
✉ isolde@btinternet.com
www.tonypalmer.org
Contact *Michela Antonello*

Film and TV documentaries. OUTPUT *Wagner; Margot; Menuhin; Maria Callas; Testimony; In From the Cold; Pushkin; England, My England* (by John Osborne). Unsolicited material is read, but please send a written outline first.

ITV Productions
The London Television Centre, Upper Ground, South Bank, London SE1 9LT
☎020 7620 1620   Fax 020 7261 3041
www.granadamedia.com/sf/gm/
Controller of ITV Productions (Drama), London *Michele Buck*
Director *John Whiston*

ITV Productions is the largest commercial TV production company in the UK. Produces original programmes, co-productions and TV movies for ITV channels and other broadcasters, both in the UK and abroad. OUTPUT includes *Hornblower; Poirot; Miss Marple; Touching Evil; Where the Heart Is; The Last Detective; Jericho.*

JAM Pictures and Jane Walmsley Productions
8 Hanover Street, London W1S 1YE
☎020 7290 2676   Fax 020 7256 6818
✉ producers@jampix.com
Contacts *Jane Walmsley, Michael Braham*

JAM Pictures was founded in 1996 to produce drama for film, TV and stage. Projects include: *Hillary's Choice* (TV film, A&E Network); *Son of Pocahontas* (TV film, ABC); *Rudy: the Rudy Giuliani Story* (TV film, USA Network); *One More Kiss* (feature, directed by Vadim Jean); *Bad Blood* (UK theatre tour). Jane Walmsley Productions, formed in 1985 by TV producer, writer and broadcaster, Jane Walmsley, has completed award-winning documentaries and features such as *Hot House People* (Ch4). No unsolicited mss. 'Letters can be sent to us, asking if we wish to see mss; we are very interested

in quality material, from published or produced writers only, please'

Justice Entertainment Ltd
PO Box 4377, London W1A 7SX
☎020 7467 5450   Fax 020 7467 5451
✉ info@timwestwood.com
www.timwestwood.com

Producer of shows for Radio 1. No unsolicited material.

Keo Films.com Ltd
101 St John Street, London EC1M 4AS
☎020 7490 3580   Fax 020 7490 8419
✉ keo@keofilms.com
www.keofilms.com
Contact *Katherine Perry*

Television documentaries and factual entertainment. OUTPUT includes *Atlantic Britain* and *Surviving Extremes* (both for Ch4/NatGeo Europe); *Beyond River Cottage; Where's Your F★★★ing Manners?; Road Trip; Tales From River Cottage; How To Be a Man; Running for God; Heavy; My Body My Business; A Dangerous Obsession; Sperm Bandits* (all for Ch4); *10 Years Younger* (Discovery Health). No unsolicited mss.

Kingfisher Television Productions Ltd
Martindale House, The Green, Ruddington, Nottingham NG11 6HH
☎0115 945 6581   Fax 0115 921 7750
Contact *Tony Francis*
Broadcast television production.

Kudos Film and Televison Ltd
12–14 Amwell Street, London EC1R 1UQ
☎020 7812 3270   Fax 020 7812 3271
✉ info@kudosfilmandtv.com
www.kudosfilmandtv.com
Joint Managing Directors *Jane Featherstone, Stephen Garrett*
General Manager *Daniel Isaacs*

Television dramas include *Life on Mars; Spooks; Hustle* and *The Magician's House* (BBC1 series); *Psychos* (Ch4 series); *Comfortably Numb* and *Pleasureland* (Ch4); *Child of Mine* (ITV). Feature films such as *Among Giants* and *Pure*. No unsolicited mss.

Lagan Pictures Ltd
21 Tullaghbrow, Tullaghgarley, Ballymena BT42 2LY
☎028 2563 9479/077 9852 8797
Fax 028 2563 9479

✉ laganpictures@tullaghbrow.freeserve.co.uk
Producer/Director *Stephen Butcher*
Film, video and TV: drama, documentary and corporate. OUTPUT *A Force Under Fire* (Ulster TV). In development: *Into the Bright Light of Day* (drama-doc); *The £10 Float* (feature film); *The Centre* (drama series). 'We are always interested in hearing from writers originating from or based in Northern Ireland or anyone with, preferably unstereotypical, projects relevant to Northern Ireland. We do not have the resources to deal with unsolicited mss, so please write with a brief treatment/synopsis in the first instance.'

Landseer Productions Ltd
140 Royal College Street, London NW1 0TA
☎020 7485 7333
✉ mail@landseerfilms.com
www.landseerfilms.com
Directors *Derek Bailey, Ken Howard*

Film and video production: documentary, drama, music and arts. OUTPUT *Swinger* (BBC2/Arts Council); *Auld Lang Syne* and *Retying the Knot – The Incredible String Band* (both for BBC Scotland); *Benjamin Zander* ('The Works', BBC2); *Zeffirelli, Johnnie Ray, Petula Clark, Bing Crosby, Maxim Vengerov* (all for 'South Bank Show', LWT); *Death of a Legend – Frank Sinatra* ('South Bank Show' special); *Routes of Rock* (Carlton); *See You in Court* (BBC); *Nureyev Unzipped, Gounod's Faust, The Judas Tree, Ballet Boyz, 4Dance* and *Bourne to Dance* (all for Ch4), *Proms in the Park* (Belfast).

Lilyville Screen Entertainment Ltd
7 Lilyville Road, London SW6 5DP
☎020 7471 8989
✉ tony.cash@btclick.com
Contact *Tony Cash*

Drama and documentaries for TV. OUTPUT *Poetry in Motion* (series for Ch4); 'South Bank Show': *Ben Elton* and *Vanessa Redgrave; Musique Enquête* (drama-based French language series, Ch4); *Sex and Religion* (ITV); *Landscape and Memory* (arts documentary series for the BBC); Jonathan Miller's production of the *St Matthew Passion* for the BBC; major documentary on the BeeGees for the 'South Bank Show'. Scripts with an obvious application to TV may be considered. Interested in new writing for documentary programmes.

Loftus Productions Ltd
2A Aldine Street, London W12 8AN
☎020 8740 4666

✉ ask@loftusproductions.co.uk
www.loftusproductions.co.uk
Contact *Nigel Acheson*

Producer of radio documentaries, readings (mostly non-fiction) and drama, as well as audio guides for museums and galleries. OUTPUT includes *Swimming with My Father* and *Tales from the Country Matchmaker* for Radio 4's 'Book of the Week'. 'We are interested in new, commissioned non-fiction titles suitable for abridgement for R4's Book of the Week.' Send e-mail with brief synopsis for radio feature or documentary ideas; also advance information on commissioned non-fiction titles.

London Scientific Films Ltd
Dassels House, Dassels, Braughing, Ware SG11 2RW
☎01763 289905
✉ lsf@londonscientificfilms.co.uk
Contact *Mike Cockburn*

Film and video documentary and corporate programming. No unsolicited mss.

Lucida Productions
5 Alleyn Crescent, London SE21 8BN
☎020 8761 4344
✉ paul.lucida@ntlworld.com
Contact *Paul Joyce*

Television and cinema: arts, adventure, current affairs, documentary, drama and music. OUTPUT has included *Motion and Emotion: The Films of Wim Wenders; Dirk Bogarde – By Myself; Sam Peckinpah – Man of Iron; Kris Kristofferson – Pilgrim; Wild One: Marlon Brando; Stanley Kubrick: 'The Invisible Man'; 2001: the Making of a Myth* (Ch4); *Mantrap – Straw Dogs, the final cut* (with Dustin Hoffman). Restoration of the Director's Cut of *The Devils* plus the documentary *Hell on Earth* with Ken Russell and Vanessa Redgrave. Currently in development for documentary and drama projects.

Malone Gill Productions Ltd
27 Campden Hill Road, London W8 7DX
☎020 7937 0557 Fax 020 7376 1727
✉ malonegill@aol.com
Contact *Georgina Denison*

Mainly documentary but also some drama. OUTPUT includes *The Face of Russia* (PBS); *Vermeer* ('South Bank Show'); *Highlanders* (ITV); *Storm Chasers; Nature Perfected* and *The Feast of Christmas* (all for Ch4); *The Buried Mirror: Reflections on Spain and the New World* by Carlos Fuentes (BBC2/Discovery Channel).

Approach by letter with proposal in the first instance.

Marchmont Films
24 Three Cups Yard, Sandland Street, London WC1R 4PZ
✉ office@marchmontfilms.com
www.marchmonfilms.com

Development Executives *Beverley Hills, Daniel Hayes, Andrew Cussens*

Producer of short films and feature projects. OUTPUT includes *Out In the Cold*; *Platinum*; *Murdering Howard*. Welcomes new writers. See website for current submission criteria.

Jane Marshall Productions
The Coach-House, Westhill Road, Blackdown, Leamington Spa CV32 6RA
☎01926 831680
✉ jane@jmproductions.freeserve.co.uk

Contact *Jane Marshall*

Producer of readings of published work both fiction and non-fiction for BBC Radio. Published work only.

Maverick Television
Progress Works, Heath Mill Lane, Birmingham B9 4AL
☎0121 771 1812 Fax 0121 771 1550
✉ mail@mavericktv.co.uk
www.mavericktv.co.uk

Contact *Clare Welch*

Established in 1994, Maverick has a strong reputation for popular factual programming as well as drama. It is now one of network television's most prolific independent suppliers. OUTPUT includes *10 Years Younger*; *Who'll Age Worst?*; *Bollywood Star*; *Fat Chance*; *Born Too Soon*; *VeeTV*; *Trade Secrets*; *Embarrassing Illnesses*; *10 Things You Didn't Know About …*; *How To Live Longer*; *The Property Chain*; *Male, 33, Seeks Puberty*; *Extreme Engineering*; *Picture This*: *Accidental Hero*; *Up Your Street*; *The Property Chain*; *Motherless Daughters*; *Highland Bollywood*: *Black Bag*; *Health Alert: My Teenage Menopause*; *Long Haul*; *Learning to Love the Grey*.

Maya Vision International Ltd
6 Kinghorn Street, London EC1A 7HW
☎020 7796 4842 Fax 020 7796 4580
www.mayavisionint.com

Contact *John Cranmer*

Film and TV: drama and documentary. OUTPUT *Saddam's Killing Fields* (for 'Viewpoint', Central TV); *3 Steps to Heaven* and *A Bit of Scarlet* (feature films for BFI/Ch4); *A Place in the Sun* and *North*

of Vortex (dramas for Ch4/Arts Council); *The Real History Show* (Ch4); *In Search of Myths and Heroes*; *In Search of Shakespeare*; *In the Footsteps of Alexander the Great*; *Conquistadors* (BBC documentaries); *Hitler's Search for the Holy Grail* (Ch4 documentary). Absolutely no unsolicited material; commissions only.

MBP TV
Saucelands Barn, Coolham, Horsham RH13 8QG
☎01403 741620 Fax 01403 741647
✉ info@mbptv.com
www.mbptv.com

Contact *Phil Jennings*

Maker of film and video specialising in programmes covering equestrianism and the countryside. No unsolicited scripts, but always looking for new writers who are fully acquainted with the subject.

Melendez Films
Julia House, 44 Newman Street, London W1T 1QD
☎020 7323 5273 Fax 020 7323 5373

Contact *Steven Melendez*

Independent production company specialising in 2D animation. Also involved in production and film design for clients in England, Spain, Sweden, India and the US, plus website design and 3D animation on the Web. Clients include book publishers, TV companies and advertisers. Winner of international awards for films, particularly of classic books, stories and comic characters. 'We will look at unsolicited projects in outline or synopsis form only. Enclose s.a.e.'

Mendoza Film Productions
3–5 Barrett Street, London W1U 1AY
☎020 7935 4674 Fax 020 7935 4417
✉ office@mendozafilms.com
www.mendozafilms.com

Contacts *Wynn Wheldon, Debby Mendoza*

Commercials, title sequences (e.g. Alan Bleasdale's *G.B.H.*); party political broadcasts. Currently in pre-production on a feature-length comedy film. Involved with the **Screenwriters' Workshop**. Unsolicited mss welcome but 'comedies only, please'. Material will not be returned without s.a.e.

Merseyfilm
Tirley Garth, Utkinton, Near Tarporley CW6 0LZ
☎01829 732301 Fax 01829 732265
www.merseytv.com

Chairman *Prof. Phil Redmond*
The best known of the independents in the north of England. Creators of television dramas *Brookside, Hollyoaks, The Courtroom* (Ch4) and *Grange Hill* (BBC).

Moonstone Films Ltd
5 Linkenholt Mansions, Stamford Brook Avenue, London W6 0YA
☎020 8846 8511 Fax 0870 005 6839
✉ info@moonstonefilms.co.uk
www.moonstonefilms.co.uk
Contact *Tony Stark*

Television: current affairs, science and history documentaries. OUTPUT *Arafat's Authority* and *Arafat Investigated*, both for BBC 'Correspondent'. Plus various Ch4 News commissions. Unsolicited mss welcome.

Neon
Studio Two, 19 Marine Crescent, Glasgow G51 1HD
☎0141 429 6366 Fax 0141 429 6377
✉ stephy@go2neon.com
www.go2neon.com
Contact *Stephanie Pordage*

Television and radio: drama and documentary producers. OUTPUT includes *Brand New Country; Asian Overground; Peeking Past the Gates of Skibo*. Supports and encourages new writing 'at every opportunity'. Welcomes unsolicited material but telephone in the first instance.

Number 9 Films
Linton House, 24 Wells Street, London W1T 3PH
☎020 7323 4060 Fax 020 7323 0456
✉ info@number9films.co.uk
Contacts *Stephen Woolley, Elizabeth Karlsen*

Leading feature film producer. OUTPUT includes *Breakfast on Pluto; Stoned; Mrs Harris*. Forthcoming productions: *How to Lose Friends and Alienate People; Edith and the Lonely Doll; Ford Dagenham Strike Project*. No unsolicited material.

Odyssey Productions Ltd
72 Tay Street, Newport-on-Tay DD6 8AP
☎01382 542070 Fax 01382 542070
✉ billykay@sol.co.uk
www.sol.co.uk/b/billy
Contact *Billy Kay*

Producer of radio documentaries. OUTPUT includes *Scotland's Black History; Gentle Shepherds* (oral history); *Street Kids* (Scottish missionaries working with street kids in Brazil).

Ideas for radio documentaries welcome; send letter with one page outlining the idea and programme content.

Omnivision
Pinewood Studios, Iver Heath SL0 0NH
☎01753 656329 Fax 01753 631146
✉ info@omnivision.co.uk
www.omnivision.co.uk
Contacts *Christopher Morris, Nick Long*

TV and video producers of documentary, corporate, news and sport programming. Also equipment and facilities hire. Interested in ideas; approach by letter or e-mail.

Open Road Films
The Studio, 37 Redington Road, London NW3 7QY
☎020 7813 4333
✉ openroadfilms@blueyonder.co.uk
Development Executive *Elizabeth King*
Producer *Andrew Holmes*

Company, formed by **Holmes Associates**, to produce low to medium budget British feature films. OUTPUT *Chunky Monkey; Ashes & Sand*. Four projects in development. Unsolicited treatments/synopses by e-mail will be considered but may take some time for response. No unsolicited scripts will be accepted.

Orlando TV Productions
Up-the-Steps, Little Tew, Chipping Norton OX7 4JB
☎01608 683218 Fax 01608 683364
✉ info@orlandomedia.co.uk
www.orlandomedia.co.uk
Contact *Mike Tomlinson*

Producer of TV documentaries and digital multimedia content, with science, health and information technology subjects as a specialisation. Approaches by established writers/journalists to discuss proposals for collaboration are welcome.

Orpheus Productions
6 Amyand Park Gardens, Twickenham TW1 3HS
☎020 8892 3172 Fax 020 8892 4821
✉ richard-taylor@blueyonder.co.uk
Contact *Richard Taylor*

Television documentaries and corporate work. OUTPUT has included programmes for the BBC, ITV and Ch4 as well as documentaries for the United Nations, the Shell Film Unit and Video Arts. Unsolicited scripts are welcomed with caution. 'Our preference is for the more classically structured documentary that, while being hard-hitting, explores the subtleties and the paradox of an issue – and is not presented by unqualified celebrities.'

Outcast Production
92 Buckhold Road, London SW18 4AP
✉ andythewise@aol.com

Contact *Andreas Wisniewski*

Low-budget feature films. No unsolicited mss; send synopsis or treatment only.'We are actively searching for and encouraging new writing.'

Ovation
Upstairs at the Gatehouse, Highgate, London N6 4BD
☎020 8340 4256   Fax 020 8340 3466

Contact *John Plews*

Corporate video and conference scripts. Unsolicited mss not welcome. 'We talk to new writers from time to time.' Ovation also runs the fringe theatre, 'Upstairs at the Gatehouse'.

Paper Moon Productions
Wychwood House, Burchetts Green Lane, Littlewick Green, Nr. Maidenhead SL6 3QW
☎01628 829819   Fax 01628 825949
✉ david@paper-moon.co.uk

Contact *David Haggas*

Broadcast documentaries and corporate communications. Recent OUTPUT includes *Bilbo & Beyond*, an affectionate glimpse into the life and work of the dedicated philologist and fantasy writer J.R.R. Tolkien.

Parallax Independent Ltd
St Runwald Street, Colchester CO1 1HF
☎01206 574909   Fax 01206 575311
www.parallaxindependent.co.uk

Contact *Sally Hibbin*

Feature films/television drama. OUTPUT *A Very British Coup*; *Riff-Raff*; *Bad Behaviour*; *Raining Stones*; *Ladybird, Ladybird*; *i.d.*; *Land and Freedom*; *The Englishman Who Went up a Hill But Came Down a Mountain*; *Bliss*; *Jump the Gun*; *Carla's Song*; *The Governess*; *My Name Is Joe*; *Stand and Deliver*; *Dockers*; *Hold Back the Night*; *Bread and Roses*; *Princesa*; *The Navigators*; *Sweet Sixteen*; *Innocence*; *The Intended*; *Blind Flight*; *Yasmin*; *Almost Adult*.

Passion Pictures
3rd Floor, 33–34 Rathbone Place, London W1T 1JN
☎020 7323 9933   Fax 020 7323 9030

✉ info@passion-pictures.com

Managing Director *Andrew Ruhemann*

Documentary and drama includes: *One Day in September* (Academy Award-winner for Best Feature Documentary, 2000); also commercials and music videos: Carphone Warehouse, Mini, Aero, Gorillaz, Coldplay and Robbie Williams. Unsolicited mss welcome.

Pathé Pictures
14–17 Kenthouse, Market Place, London W1W 8AR
☎020 7323 5151   Fax 020 7631 3568

Head of Creative Affairs *Celine Haddad*
Creative Development Executive *Erol Arguden*

Produces 4–6 theatrical feature films each year. 'We are pleased to consider all material that has representation from an agent or production company.'

Pearson Television
See **FremantleMedia Ltd**

Pelicula Films
59 Holland Street, Glasgow G2 4NJ
☎0141 287 9522

Contact *Mike Alexander*

Television producer. Maker of drama documentaries and music programmes for the BBC and Ch4. OUTPUT *As an Eilean (From the Island)*; *The Trans-Atlantic Sessions 1 & 2*; *Nanci Griffith, Other Voices 2*; *Follow the Moonstone*.

Pennine Productions LLP
Kilmagadwood Cottage, Scotlandwell, Kinross KY13 9HY
☎05600 472247
✉ mike@pennine.biz
www.pennine.biz

Contact *Mike Hally*

Producer of radio documentaries, features and short story readings. OUTPUT includes *Red Games*; *Still Angry After All These Years*; *After the Silver* (all for Radio 4). No unsolicited material.

Photoplay Productions Ltd
21 Princess Road, London NW1 8JR
☎020 7722 2500   Fax 020 7722 6662
✉ photoplay@compuserve.com

Contact *Patrick Stanbury*

Documentaries for film, television and video plus restoration of silent films and their theatrical presentation. OUTPUT includes *The Cat and the Canary*; *Orphans of the Storm*; *Cecil B.*

DeMille: American Epic and the 'Channel 4 Silents' series of silent film restoration, including *The Wedding March* and *The Iron Mask*. Recently completed *Garbo* and *I'm King Kong!* No unsolicited mss; 'we tend to create and write all our own programmes.'

Picardy Media & Communication
1 Park Circus, Glasgow G3 6AX
☎0141 333 5554   Fax 0141 332 6002
✉ jr@picardy.co.uk
www.picardy.co.uk
Head of Production *John Rocchiccioli*

Produces screen-based content for education, training, sales and marketing, HR and induction. Operates in a variety of areas including health, education, social policy, etc. 'Aims to inform through entertainment.' Unsolicited mss welcome; 'keen to encourage new writing.'

Picture Palace Films Ltd
13 Egbert Street, London NW1 8LJ
☎020 7586 8763   Fax 020 7586 9048
✉ info@picturepalace.com
www.picturepalace.com
Contacts *Malcolm Craddock, Katherine Hedderly*

Leading independent producer of film and TV drama. OUTPUT *Rebel Heart* (BBC1); *Sharpe's Challenge*; *Extremely Dangerous*; *A Life for A Life* and *Frances Tuesday* (all for ITV); *Sharpe's Rifles* (14 films for Carlton TV); *Little Napoleons* (comedy drama, Ch4); *The Orchid House* (drama serial, Ch4); *Tandoori Nights*; *4 Minutes*; *When Love Dies* (all for Ch4); *Ping Pong* (feature film); *Acid House* (Picture Palace North). Material will only be considered if submitted through an agent.

Plantagenet Films Limited
Ard-Daraich Studio B, Ardgour, Nr Fort William PH33 7AB
☎01855 841384   Fax 01855 841384
✉ plantagenetfilms@aol.com
Contact *Norrie Maclaren*

Film and television: documentary and drama programming such as *Dig* (gardening series for Ch4); various 'Dispatches' for Ch4 and 'Omnibus' for BBC. Keen to encourage and promote new writing; unsolicited mss welcome.

Portobello Pictures
Eardley House, 4 Uxbridge Street, London W8 7SY
Contact *Eric Abraham*

Film, TV and theatre production. Past credits include Jan Sverak's *Dark Blue World* and *Kolya*; Jez Butterworth's *Birthday Girl* and *Mojo*; Tim Roth's *The War Zone*, Roald Dahl's *Danny the Champion of the World*; BBC1's *Dalziel & Pascoe* (series 1–3). First theatre production, *Embers* by Christopher Hampton from the novel by Sandor Marai, opened in London's West End in March 2006.

Pozzitive Television
Paramount House, 162–170 Wardour Street, London W1F 8AB
☎020 7734 3258   Fax 020 7437 3130
✉ david@pozzitive.co.uk
Contact *David Tyler*

Producer of comedy and entertainment for television and radio. OUTPUT *Dinner Ladies*; *Coogan's Run*; *The 99p Challenge*; *The Comic Side of 7 Days*; Armando Iannucci's *Charm Offensive*. Unsolicited mss of TV and radio comedy welcome. 'No screenplays or stage plays or novels, please. Send hard copy of full sample script. We read everything submitted this way. Sorry, we don't return scripts unless you send an s.a.e.'

Promenade Enterprises Limited
6 Russell Grove, London SW9 6HS
☎020 7582 9354   Fax 020 7587 1564
✉ info@promenadeproductions.com
www.promenade productions.com
Contact *Nicholas Newton*

Producer of drama for radio and theatre predominantly. Supports new writing but only accepts unsolicited mss via agents or producers.

Redweather
Easton Business Centre, Felix Road, Easton BS5 0HE
☎0117 941 5854   Fax 0117 941 5851
✉ production@redweather.co.uk
www.redweather.co.uk

Broadcast documentaries on arts and disability, corporate video and CD-ROM, Water Aid, British Oxygen, etc.

Renaissance Vision
256 Fakenham Road, Taverham, Norwich NR8 6QW
☎01603 260280   Fax 01603 864853
✉ bfg@renvision.co.uk
Contact *B. Gardner*

Video: full range of corporate work (training, sales, promotional, etc.). Producers of educational and special-interest video publications. Willing to consider good ideas and proposals.

Richmond Films & Television Ltd
PO Box 33154, London NW3 4AZ
☎020 7722 6464 Fax 020 7722 6232
✉ mail@richmondfilms.com
Contact *Development Executive*

Film and TV: drama and comedy. OUTPUT *Press Gang*; *The Lodge*; *The Office*; *Wavelength*; *Privates*; *in2minds*. No unsolicited scripts.

RS Productions
191 Trewhitt Road, Newcastle upon Tyne NE6 5DY
☎0191 224 4301/00 49 89 5111 5895/07710 064632 (Mobile) Fax 0191 224 4301
✉ enquiries@rsproductions.co.uk
www.rsproductions.co.uk
Contact *Mark Lavender*

Feature films and television: drama series/serials and singles. TV documentaries and series. Working with established and new talent.

Sands Films
119 Rotherhithe Street, London SE16 4NF
☎020 7231 2209 Fax 020 7231 2119
✉ sands@sandsfilms.co.uk
www.sandsfilms.co.uk
Contacts *Christine Edzard, Olivier Stockman*

Film and TV drama. OUTPUT *Little Dorrit*; *The Fool*; *As You Like It*; *A Dangerous Man*; *The Long Day Closes*; *A Passage to India*; *Topsy Turvy*; *Nicholas Nickleby*; *The Gangs of New York*; *The Children's Midsummer Night's Dream*. No unsolicited scripts.

Scala Productions Ltd
4th Floor, Portland House, 4 Great Portland Street, London W1W 8QJ
☎020 7612 0060 Fax 020 7612 0031
✉ scalaprods@aol.com
Contacts *Ian Prior*

Production company set up by ex-Palace Productions Nik Powell and Stephen Woolley, who have an impressive list of credits including *Company of Wolves*; *Absolute Beginners*; *Mona Lisa*; *Scandal*; *The Crying Game*; *Backbeat*; *Neon Bible*; *24:7*; *Little Voice*; *Divorcing Jack*; *The Last September*; *Wild About Harry*; *Last Orders*; *A Christmas Carol – The Movie*; *Black and White*; *Leo*; *One Love*; *The Night We Called It A Day*; *Ladies in Lavender*; *Stoned*. In development: *The Queen & I*; *Meek*; *The Coat*; *Train to Glory*; *Du Cane's Boys*; *Shang-a-*

Lang; *Johnny Bollywood*; *English Passengers*; *He Kills Coppers*; *Eden's Team*.

Scope Productions Ltd
123 Blythswood Street, Glasgow G2 4EN
☎0141 332 7720 Fax 0141 332 1049
✉ laurakingwell@scopeproductions.co.uk
www.scopeproductions.co.uk
Corporate *Laura Kingwell*

Corporate film and video; broadcast documentaries and sport; TV commercials.

Screen First Ltd
The Studios, Funnells Farm, Down Street, Nutley TN22 3LG
☎01825 712034 Fax 01825 713511
✉ paul.madden@virgin.net
Contacts *M. Thomas, P. Madden*

Television dramas, documentaries, arts and animation programmes. Developing major drama series, feature films, animated specials and series. No unsolicited scripts.

Screen Ventures Ltd
49 Goodge Street, London W1T 1TE
☎020 7580 7448
✉ info@screenventures.com
Contacts *Christopher Mould, Michael Evans*

Film and TV sales and production: documentary, music videos and drama. OUTPUT *Life and Limb* (documentary, Discovery Health Channel); *Pavement Aristocrats* (SABC); *Woodstock Diary*; *Vanessa Redgrave* and *Genet* (both for LWT 'South Bank Show'); *Mojo Working*; *Burma: Dying for Democracy* (Ch4); *Dani Dares* (Ch4 series on strong women); *Pagad* (Ch4 news report).

Screenhouse Productions Ltd
Chapel Allerton House, 114 Harrogate Road, Leeds LS7 4NY
☎0113 266 8881 Fax 0113 266 8882
✉ paul.bader@screenhouse.co.uk
www.screenhouse.co.uk
Contacts *Paul Bader, Barbara Govan*

Specialises in science TV, documentary, stunts and events, including outside broadcasts. Science prop. and demo workshop supplying working models to, e.g., BBC History *What the Past Did For Us*; ITV, Discovery and museums. Output includes *Stardate* (BBC2 astronomy series); *Zapped* (Discovery/US/Canada); *The Man Who Invented the Aeroplane* (UKTV/BBC North); *Science Shack*, *Local Heroes*, BBC2, presented by Adam Hart-Davis. 'More likely to consider written up proposals.'

Screenprojex.com – a division of Screen Production Associates Ltd

☎020 7287 1170
✉ info@screenprojex.com
screenprojex.com

Contacts *Doug Abbott, John Jaquiss*

Feature films: *The Fourth Man*; *The Case*; *Black Badge*; *The Truth Game*; *Club Le Monde*; *Midnight Warriors*; *Strong Language*; *Holding On*; *Chunky Monkey*; *Sixty-three Closure*. No unsolicited mss. Send preliminary letter outlining project and c.v.

September Films Ltd

Glen House, 22 Glenthorne Road, London W6 0NG
☎020 8563 9393 Fax 020 8741 7214
✉ september@septemberfilms.com
www.septemberfilms.com

Director of Production *Elaine Day*

Factual entertainment and documentary specialists. Feature film OUTPUT includes *Breathtaking*; *House of America*; *Solomon & Gaenor*.

Serendipity Picture Company

Media Centre, Emma-Chris Way, Abbeywood Park, Bristol BS34 7JU
☎0117 906 6541
✉ tony@serendipitypictures.com

Contacts *Tony Yeadon, Nick Dance*

Television and video; corporate and documentary programming. Encourages new writing; will consider proposals for documentaries only.

Shell Like

81 Whitfield Street, London W1T 4HG
☎020 7255 5204 Fax 020 7255 5255
✉ enquiries@shellike.com
www.shelllike.com

Contact *Nicola Warman-Johnston*

Produces radio commercials. Unsolicited mss and ideas welcome; send by e-mail.

Sianco Cyf

36 Y Maes, Caernarfon LL55 2NN
☎01286 676100/07831 726111 (mobile)
Fax 01286 677616
✉ post@sianco.tv

Contact *Siân Teifi*

Children's, youth and education programmes, children's drama, people-based documentaries for adults. '*Please note that we do not accept any unsolicited scripts.*'

Silent Sound Films Ltd

Cambridge Court, Cambridge Road, Frinton on Sea CO13 9HN
☎01255 676381 Fax 01255 676381
✉ thj@silentsoundfilms.co.uk
www.silentsoundfilms.co.uk
www.londonfoodfilmfiesta.co.uk

Contact *Timothy Foster*

Active in European film co-production with mainstream connections in the USA. Special interest in developing stage and film musicals, art house and documentaries on the arts. Synopses considered via e-mail or post.

Skyline Productions

10 Scotland Street, Edinburgh EH3 6PS
☎0131 557 4580 Fax 0131 556 4377
✉ leslie@skyline.uk.com
www.skyline.uk.com

Producer/Writer *Leslie Hills*

Produces film and television drama and documentary.

SMG & Ginger TV Productions Ltd

SMG: 200 Renfield Street, Glasgow G2 3PR
☎0141 300 3000
www.smgproductions.tv

Also: Ginger TV Productions, 3 Waterhouse Square, 138–142 Holborn London EC1N 2NY
☎020 7882 1020 www.ginger.tv

Managing Director (SMG TV Productions & Ginger TV Productions) *Elizabeth Partyka*
Head of Drama *Eric Coulter*
Head of Business Development *Helen Alexander*

SMG TV Productions, which incorporates Ginger Television, makes programmes for the national television networks, including ITV, Ch4 and Sky. Specialises in drama, factual entertainment and children's programming. OUTPUT includes *Taggart*; *Rebus*; *Our Daughter Holly*; *Club Reps*.

Somethin Else

Units 1–4, 1A Old Nichol Street, London E2 7HR
☎020 7613 3211 Fax 020 7739 9799
✉ info@somethin-else.com
www.somethin-else.com

Contact *Jez Nelson*

Producer of television, video and radio documentaries, DVD and interactive content. Ideas for TV shows welcome; send letter in the first instance.

Soundplay
17 Gleneagles Drive, Henbury, Bristol
BS10 7PS
☎07818 271659
✉ enquiries@soundplay.co.uk
www.soundplay.co.uk
Contact *Tom Bennett*

Producer of radio drama and documentaries. OUTPUT includes *In Search of the Picturesque* (dramatised radio feature by Tom Bennett); *The Hearts and Lives of Men* (radio drama by Fay Weldon); *Remember the Day* (radio thriller by Tom Bennett).

Specific Films
25 Rathbone Street, London W1T 1NQ
☎020 7580 7476   Fax 020 7494 2676
✉ info@specificfilms.com
Contact *Michael Hamlyn*

Founded 1991. OUTPUT includes *Mr Reliable* (feature film co-produced by PolyGram and the AFFC); *The Adventures of Priscilla, Queen of the Desert*, co-produced with Latent Image (Australia) and financed by PolyGram and AFFC; *U2 Rattle and Hum*, full-length feature – part concert film/part cinema verité documentary; *Paws* (executive producer); *The Last Seduction 2* (Polygram); and numerous pop promos for major international artists.

Spellbound Productions Ltd
90 Cowdenbeath Path, Islington, London
N1 0LG
☎020 7713 8066   Fax 020 7713 8066
✉ phspellbound@hotmail.com
Contact *Paul Harris*

Specialises in feature films for cinema and drama for television. Keen to support and encourage new writing. Material will only be considered if in correct screenplay format and accompanied by s.a.e.

Spice Factory (UK) Ltd
14 Regent Hill, Brighton BN1 3ED
☎01273 739182   Fax 01273 749122
✉ shirine@spicefactory.co.uk
www.spicefactory.co.uk
Contacts *Lucy Shuttleworth, Shirine Best*

Founded 1995. Film producers. OUTPUT *Plots With a View* (Christopher Walken, Brenda Blethyn, Alfred Molina, Lee Evans); *Bollywood Queen* (Preeya Kallidas, James McAvoy, Ian McShane); *The Bridge of San Luis Rey* (Robert De Niro, Kathy Bates, Harvey Keitel); *A Different Loyalty* (Sharon Stone, Rupert Everett); *Head in the Clouds* (Charlize Theron, Penelope Cruz);

The Merchant of Venice (Al Pacino, Jeremy Irons, Joseph Fiennes, Lynn Collins). No unsolicited material accepted.

'Spoken' Image Ltd
8 Hewitt Street M15 4GB
☎0161 236 7522   Fax 0161 236 0020
✉ info@spoken-image.com
www.spoken-image.com
Contacts *Geoff Allman, Steve Foster*

Film, video and TV production for documentary and corporate material. Specialises in high-quality brochures and reports, CD-ROMs, exhibitions, conferences, film and video production for broadcast, industry and commerce.

Starz! – Film and Theatre Performing Arts
See entry under **UK Writers' Courses**

Tony Staveacre Productions
Channel View, Blagdon BS40 7TP
☎01761 462161   Fax 01761 462161
✉ newstaving@btinternet.com
Contact *Tony Staveacre*

Producer of dramas and documentaries as well as music, arts and comedy progammes. OUTPUT *The Wodehouse Notebooks*; *The Liberation of Daphne*, *Speaking from the Belly* (Radio 4); *The Very Thought of You* (theatre); *Tango Maestro* (BBC4). No unsolicited mss.

Stirling Film & TV Productions Limited
137 University Street, Belfast BT7 1HP
☎028 9033 3848   Fax 028 9043 8644
✉ anne@stirlingtelevision.co.uk
Contact *Anne Stirling*

Producer of broadcast and corporate programming – documentary, sport, entertainment and lifestyle programmes.

Straight Forward Film & Television Productions Ltd
Building 2, Lesley Office Park, 393
Hollywood Road, Belfast BT4 2LS
☎028 9065 1010   Fax 028 9065 1012
✉ enquiries@straightforwardltd.co.uk
Contacts *John Nicholson, Ian Kennedy*

Northern Ireland-based production company specialising in documentary, feature and lifestyle series for both regional and network transmission. OUTPUT includes *We Shall Overcome* (winner of Best Documentary at 1999 Celtic Television Festival for BBC); *Conquering the*

Normans (Ch4 Learning – history of Normans in Ireland); *Gift of the Gab* (Ch4 Learning – contemporary Irish writing); *Fire School* (BBC NI – training of a team of fire-fighters); *On Eagle's Wing* (full stage musical/TV material; story of the Scots/Irish in America); *Just Jones* (BBC Radio Ulster daily show); *Sportsweek* (BBC Radio Ulster); *School Challenge* (3rd series, BBC NI); *World Indoor Bowls* (BBC NI); *Awash With Colour* (series, BBC Daytime).

Strawberry Productions Ltd
36 Priory Avenue, London W4 1TY
☎020 8994 4494   Fax 020 8742 7675
Contact *John Black*

Film, video and TV: drama and documentary; corporate and video publishing.

Sunset + Vine Productions Ltd
30 Sackville Street, London W1S 3DY
☎020 7478 7300   Fax 020 7478 7403
www.sunsetvine.co.uk

Sports, children's and music programmes for television. No unsolicited mss. 'We hire freelancers only upon receipt of a commission.'

Table Top Productions
1 The Orchard, Chiswick, London W4 1JZ
☎020 8742 0507   Fax 020 8742 0507
✉ alvin@tabletopproductions.com
Contact *Alvin Rakoff*

TV and film. OUTPUT *Paradise Postponed; The Adventures of Don Quixote; A Voyage Round My Father; The First Olympics 1896; Dirty Tricks; A Dance to the Music of Time; Too Marvellous for Words*. Also Dancetime Ltd. No unsolicited mss.

talkbackTHAMES
20–21 Newman Street, London W1T 1PG
☎020 7861 8000   Fax 020 7861 8001
✉ reception@talkbackthames.tv
www.talkbackthames.tv

Chief Executive Officer *Lorraine Heggessey*
Chief Operating Officer *Alex Mahon*

talkackTHAMES Productions is a **Fremantle-Media** company. OUTPUT includes: comedy, comedy drama , drama, entertainment, documentary and lifestyle programmes. OUTPUT *Green Wing; The Bill; The X Factor; They Think It's All Over; Never Mind the Buzzcocks; Grand Designs; Look Around You; The Lost Prince; Unteachables; Property Ladder*.

Talkingheads Production Ltd
2–4 Noel Street, London W1F 8GB
☎020 7292 7575   Fax 020 7292 7576

✉ johnsachs@talkingheadsproductions.com
www.talkingheadsproductions.com
Contact *John Sachs*

Feature films. OUTPUT includes *The Merchant of Venice* starring Al Pacino. Will consider scripts; contact by e-mail. 'Somewhere out there is the new Tom Stoppard.'

Tandem TV & Film Ltd
Suite 206, Charleston House, Hemel Hempstead HP1 3AA
☎01442 261576   Fax 01442 219250
✉ info@tandemtv.com
www.tandemtv.com
Contact *Barbara Page*

Internal and external communications, documentaries, drama-documentaries, public relations, sales, marketing and training programmes for, amongst others, the construction, civil engineering, transport, local government and charitable sectors. Welcomes unsolicited mss.

Taylor Made Broadcasts Ltd
3B Cromwell Park, Chipping Norton OX7 5SR
☎01608 677777
✉ post@tmtv.co.uk
Contact *Trevor Taylor*

Producer of corporate videos and documentaries for television and radio. OUTPUT includes *Gardeners' Question Time* (BBC Radio 4). No unsolicited mss.

Telemagination Ltd
Royalty House, 72–74 Dean Street, London W1D 3SG
☎020 7434 1551   Fax 020 7434 3344
✉ mail@tmation.co.uk
www.telemagination.co.uk
Contact *Beth Parker*

Animation production company. CREDITS include *The Animals of Farthing Wood; Noah's Island; The Last Polar Bears; Little Ghosts; Ponguiffy; Heidi, The Cramp Twins ll; Pettson and Findus*. In production: *Rudi and Trudi*.

Tern Television Productions Ltd
73 Crown Street, Aberdeen AB11 6EX
☎01224 211123   Fax 01224 211199
✉ aberdeen@terntv.com
www.terntv.com

Also at: 4th Floor, 114 Union Street, Glasgow G1 3QQ
☎0141 204 1717   Email glasgow@terntv.com

Contacts *David Strachan, Gwyneth Hardy*
(Aberdeen), *Harry Bell* (Glasgow)

Broadcast, television and corporate video productions. Specialises in factual entertainment.
Currently developing drama.

Testimony Films

12 Great George Street, Bristol BS1 5RS
☎0117 925 8589 Fax 0117 925 7608
✉ steve.humphries@testimonyfilms.com

Contact *Steve Humphries*

TV documentary producer. Specialises in social
history exploring Britain's past using living
memory. OUTPUT includes *Hooked: History of
Addictions*; *Married Love* (both Ch4 series); *A
Secret World of Sex* (BBC series); *The 50s & 60s
in Living Colour*; *Some Liked It Hot* (both ITV
series). Welcomes ideas from those working on
life stories and oral history.

Theatre of Comedy Company

See *Theatre Producers*

Tiger Aspect Productions

7 Soho Street, London W1D 3DQ
☎020 7434 6700 Fax 020 7434 1798
✉ general@tigeraspect.co.uk
www.tigeraspect.co.uk

Contact *Charles Brand*

Part of IMG Media. Television producer for
comedy, drama, documentary and entertainment. OUTPUT *Births, Marriages & Deaths*; *Kid in
the Corner*; *Country House*; *Gimme Gimme
Gimme*; *Harry Enfield & Chums*; *Howard Goodalls'
Big Bangs*; *Playing the Field I, II & III*; *Streetmate I
& II*; *Let Them Eat Cake*; *The Vicar of Dibley*. Only
considers material submitted via an agent or
from writers with a known track record.

Touch Productions Ltd

18 Queen Square, Bath BA1 2HN
☎01225 484666 Fax 01225 483620
✉ erica@touchproductions.co.uk

Contacts *Erica Wolfe-Murray, Malcolm
Brinkworth*

Over the past 18 years has produced 'investigative documentary films, history-based films
with a strong contemporary relevance, powerful
observational series and innovative films that
stretch the form.' Television documentaries
such as *Separating Twins*; *Paris in the Sun*; *Brit
School*; *Thanks for the Memories*; *Angela's Story*;
Afghan Warrior, the Life and Death of Abdul Haq.
Also has a drama section based on real-life stories and unsolicited mss are welcome.

Transatlantic Films Production and Distribution Company

Studio One, 3 Brackenbury Road, London
W6 0BE
☎020 8735 0505 Fax 020 8735 0605
✉ mail@transatlanticfilms.com
www.transatlanticfilms.com

Executive Producer *Revel Guest*

Producer of TV documentaries. OUTPUT
Belzoni (Ch4 Schools); *Science of Sleep and
Dreams*; *Science of Love* and *Extreme Body Parts*
(all for Discovery Health); *Legends of the Living
Dead* (Discovery Travel/S4C International);
2025 (Discovery Digital); *How Animals Tell the
Time* (Discovery); *Trailblazers* (Travel Channel).
No unsolicited scripts. Interested in new writ-
ers to write 'the book of the series', e.g. for
Greek Fire and *The Horse in Sport*, but not usu-
ally drama script writers.

TV Choice Ltd

PO Box 597, Bromley BR2 OYB
☎020 8464 7402 Fax 020 8464 7845
✉ tvchoiceuk@aol.com
www.tvchoice.uk.com

Contact *Norman Thomas*

Produces a range of educational videos for
schools and colleges on subjects such as history,
geography, business studies and economics. No
unsolicited mss; send proposals only.

Twentieth Century Fox Film Co

Twentieth Century House, 31–32 Soho
Square, London W1D 3AP
☎020 7437 7766 Fax 020 7734 3187
www.fox.co.uk

London office of the American giant.

Twofour Group Limited

Twofoour Studios, Estover, Plymouth
PL6 7RG
☎01752 727400 Fax 01752 727450
✉ enq@twofour.co.uk
www.twofour.co.uk

Managing Director *Charles Wace*
Director of Broadcast *Melanie Leach*

One of the largest broadcast television and corporate communications producers in the UK,
comprising Twofour Broadcasting, Twofour
Communications and Twofour Digital. The
Group produces over 200 hours of factual
entertainment broadcast programming and 100
hours of corporate communications each year.
Content is distributed over a range of multimedia platforms including websites, intranets,

CD-ROM, DVD, mobile devices and Internet video streaming.

Tyburn Film Productions Limited

Cippenham Court, Cippenham Lane, Cippenham, Nr Slough SL1 5AU
☎01753 516767 Fax 01753 691785

Feature films. Subsidiary of **Arlington Productions Limited**. No unsolicited submissions.

UBA Ltd

c/o 21 Alderville Road, London SW6 2EE
☎01984 623619 Fax 01984 623733
✉ peterjshaw@btinternet.com

Contacts *Peter Shaw, Joanna Shaw*

Feature films and TV for an international market. OUTPUT includes *Windprints; The Lonely Passion of Judith Hearne* (co-production with HandMade Films Ltd); *Taffin; Castaway; Turtle Diary; Sweeney Todd; Keep the Aspidistra Flying*. In development: *Kinder Garden; Rebel Magic; No Man's Land*. Prepared to commission new writing whether adapted from another medium or based on a short outline/treatment. Concerned with the quality of the script (*Turtle Diary* was written by Harold Pinter) and breadth of appeal. 'Exploitation material' not welcome.

UK Film and TV Production Company Plc

3 Colville Place, London W1T 2BH
☎020 7255 1650

Contact *Henrietta Fudakowski*

Film producers. Currently looking for feature films, with a preference for stories with humour. No TV, please. Return postage and list of credits essential. Please phone before submitting material.

Vera Productions

66–68 Margaret Street, London W1W 8SR
☎020 7436 6116 Fax 020 7436 6117

Contact *Cree Jones*

Produces television comedy such as *Bremner, Bird and Fortune*.

Video Enterprises

12 Barbers Wood Road, High Wycombe HP12 4EP
☎01494 534144/07831 875216 (mobile)
Fax 01494 534145
✉ videoenterprises@ntlworld.com
www.videoenterprises-uk.co.uk

Contact *Maurice R. Fleisher*

Video and TV, mainly corporate: business and industrial training, promotional material and conferences. No unsolicited material 'but always ready to try out good new writers'.

VIP Broadcasting

8 Bunbury Way, Epsom KT17 4JP
☎01372 721196 Fax 01372 726697
✉ mail@vipbroadcasting.co.uk

Contact *Chris Vezey*

Produces a wide range of radio programmes, particularly interviews, documentaries, music programmes and live concerts. Won award for 'Best Sound' at New York Festival 2000. Approach with idea by e-mail in the first instance; no unsolicited mss.

Wall to Wall

8–9 Spring Place, London NW5 3ER
☎020 7485 7424 Fax 020 7267 5292
www.walltowall.co.uk

Chief Executive *Alex Graham*

Factual and drama programming. OUTPUT includes *Who Do You Think You Are?; New Tricks; A Rather English Marriage; Glasgow Kiss; Sex, Chips & Rock 'n' Roll; The 1940s House; Body Story; Neanderthal; The Mafia; Not Forgotten; H. G. Wells*.

Jane Walmsley Productions

See **JAM Pictures**

Walsh Bros. Limited

4 The Heights, London SE7 8JH
☎020 8858 6870
✉ john@walshbros.co.uk
www.walshbros.co.uk

Producer/Director *John Walsh*
Producer/Head of Finance *David Walsh, ACA*
Producer/Head of Development *Maura Walsh*

Producer of television, film drama and documentaries. OUTPUT *Monarch* (feature film); *Don't Make Me Angry* (Ch 4); *Headhunting the Homeless* (BBC programme on the perception of homeless people in the work place); *Trex* (factual series on teenagers at work in China, Mexico, Vancouver and Alaska); *Trex2* (follow-up series covering Romania, India, Iceland and Louisiana); *Boyz & Girlz*, (Derbyshire dairy farm documentary series); *Cowboyz & Cowgirlz* (US sequel to hit series of Brit teens working on a ranch in Montana). Also arts documentaries: *The Comedy Store* and *Ray Harryhausen* (the work of Hollywood special effects legend). Drama: *The Sleeper; The Sceptic and the Psychic; A State of Mind*.

Paul Weiland Film Company

14 Newburgh Street, London W1F 7RT
☎020 7287 6900   Fax 020 7434 0146
✉ action@paulweiland.com
www.paulweiland.com

Television commercials and pop promos.

Whistledown Productions Ltd

66 Southwark Bridge Road, London SE1 0AS
☎020 7922 1120   Fax 020 7261 0939
✉ david.prest@whistledown.net
www.whistledown.net

Contact *David Prest*

Producer of Sony Award Winning Landmark Series for BBC Radio 4: *Evacuation, The Child Migrants.* Features and documentaries on a wide range of social and historical subjects, contemporary issues and popular culture. OUTPUT includes *Questions Questions* and *The Reunion* (Radio 4); music-based documentaries for Radio 2. 'We welcome contributions and ideas, but phone or e-mail first.'

Wise Buddah Creative Ltd

74 Great Titchfield Street, London W1W 7QP
☎020 7307 1600   Fax 020 7307 1602
✉ info@wisebuddah.com
www.wisebuddah.com

Contacts *Chris North, Paul Plant*

Radio production company: documentaries and commercials. Also studio facilities, sound-to-picture/sound design, talent management. No unsolicited material.

Working Title Films Ltd

Oxford House, 76 Oxford Street, London W1D 1BS
☎020 7307 3000   Fax 020 7307 3001/2/3
Co-Chairmen (Films) *Tim Bevan, Eric Fellner*
Head of Development (Films) *Natascha Wharton*
Executive Producer (Films) *Debra Hayward*
Development Executives (Films) Amelia Granger, Rachael Prior, Dan MacRae
Development Coordinator (Films) Hannah Farrell
Television *Simon Wright*

Feature films OUTPUT *Nanny McPhee; Pride & Prejudice; The Interpreter; Wimbledon; Bridget Jones 2; Edge of Reason; Shaun of the Dead; Love Actually; Thunderbirds; Ned Kelly; Johnny English; Bridget Jones's Diary; Captain Corelli's Mandolin; Ali G Indahouse; Billy Elliot; Notting Hill;* *Elizabeth; Fargo; Dead Man Walking; French Kiss; Four Weddings and a Funeral; The Hudsucker Proxy; The Tall Guy; Wish You Were Here; My Beautiful Laundrette.* Television (drama, family/children's entertainment, comedy) OUTPUT *More Tales of the City; The Borrowers I & II; Armisted Maupin's Tales of the City; News Hounds; Randall & Hopkirk.* No unsolicited mss at present.

Wortman Productions UK

48 Chiswick Staithe, London W4 3TP
☎020 8994 8886/07976 805976 (mobile)
✉ nevillewortman@beeb.net

Producer *Neville Wortman*

Co-producers with Polestar Pictures Ltd. Feature film and TV production for drama, documentary, entertainment and corporate. OUTPUT 'Lost Ships' series: *White Gold of the Dragon Sea* (Discovery Channel, US); *Neffertiti; Resurrected; Who Killed Julius Caesar* (Discovery Channel, US/Ch 5, UK); 'Days That Shook the World' series: *Conspiracy to Kill; Hitler Bomb Plot; Assassinate De Gaulle* (BBC); 'Surviving Disaster' series: *Munich Air Crash; Eruption at Mount St Helen.* Open to new writing, preferably through agents; single page outline, some pages of dialogue; s.a.e. for reply.

WT2

Oxford House, 76 Oxford Street, London W1D 1BS
☎020 7307 3000   Fax 020 7307 3004

Head of WT2 *Natascha Wharton*
Head of Development *Rachael Prior*
Development Coordinator *Hannah Farrell*

Lower budget film division of **Working Title Films**. Feature films only. OUTPUT includes *Billy Elliot; Long Time Dead; Ali G Indahouse; My Little Eye; Shaun of the Dead; Inside I'm Dancing.* No unsolicited screenplays at present.

Zenith Entertainment Ltd

43–45 Dorset Street, London W1U 7NA
☎020 7224 2440   Fax 020 7224 3194
✉ general@zenith-entertainment.co.uk

Head of Drama *Adrian Bate*

Feature films and TV drama. OUTPUT: FILMS Todd Haynes' *Velvet Goldmine; Wisdom of Crocodiles;* Nicole Holofcener's *Walking and Talking.* TELEVISION *Hamish Macbeth; Rhodes; Bodyguards; Bomber; Two Thousand Acres of Sky; Hear the Silence; Roman Road; 55 Degrees North; Class of '76.* No unsolicited scripts.

Theatre Producers

For latest minimum rates for writers of plays for subsidised repertory theatres (not Scotland) access the following websites: Theatrical Management Association at www.tmauk.org; and the Writers' Guild at www.writersguild.org.uk

Almeida Theatre Company

The Almeida Theatre, Almeida Street, London N1 1TA
☎020 7288 4900   Fax 020 7288 4901
www.almeida.co.uk

Artistic Director *Michael Attenborough*

Founded 1980. Now in its fifteenth year as a full-time producing theatre, presenting a year-round theatre and music programme in which international writers, composers, performers, directors and designers are invited to work with British artists on challenging new and classical works. Previous productions: *Ivanov; Naked; The Iceman Cometh; The Jew of Malta; Celebration; Richard II; Coriolanus; The Shape of Things; King Lear, The Lady from the Sea; The Goat, or Who is Sylvia?; The Mercy Seat; Festen*. No unsolicited mss: 'our producing programme is very limited and linked to individual directors and actors'.

Alternative Theatre Company Ltd

Bush Theatre, Shepherds Bush Green, London W12 8QD
☎020 7602 3703   Fax 020 7602 7614
✉ info@bushtheatre.co.uk
www.bushtheatre.co.uk

Literary Manager *Abigail Gonda*

Founded 1972. Trading as The Bush Theatre. Produces nine new plays a year (principally British) including up to three visiting companies also producing new work: 'we are a writer's theatre'. Previous productions include: *Kiss of the Spiderwoman* Manuel Puig; *Raping the Gold* Lucy Gannon; *The Wexford Trilogy* Billy Roche; *Love and Understanding* Joe Penhall; *This Limetree Bower* Conor McPherson; *Discopigs* Enda Walsh; *The Pitchfork Disney* Philip Ridley; *Caravan* Helen Blakeman; *Beautiful Thing* Jonathan Harvey; *Killer Joe* Tracy Letts; *Shang-a-Lang* Catherine Johnson; *Howie the Rookie* Mark O'Rowe; *The Glee Club* Richard Cameron; *Adrenalin ... Heart* Georgia Fitch. Scripts are read by a team of associates, then discussed with the management, a process which takes about four months. The theatre offers a small number of commissions, recommissions to ensure further drafts on promising plays, and a guarantee against royalties so writers are not financially penalised even though the plays are produced in a small house. Writers should send scripts (full-length plays only) with small s.a.e. for acknowledgement and large s.a.e. for return of script.

ATC (Actors Touring Company)

15–16 Nassau Street, London W1W 7AB
☎020 7580 7723   Fax 020 7580 7724
✉ info@atc-online.com
www.atc-online.com

Artistic Director *Gordon Anderson*

Collaborates with writers on adaptation and/or translation work and unsolicited mss will be considered in this category as well as new writing. 'We endeavour to read mss but do not have the resources to do so quickly.' As a small-scale company, all plays must have a cast of six or less.

Birmingham Repertory Theatre

Centenary Square, Broad Street, Birmingham B1 2EP
☎0121 245 2000   Fax 0121 245 2100
www.birmingham-rep.co.uk

Literary Assistant *Ben Musgrave*

The Birmingham Repertory Theatre aims to provide a platform for the best work from new writers from both within and beyond the West Midlands region. The Rep is committed to the production of new work which reflects both the diversity of contemporary experience and of approaches to writing for the stage. The commissioning of new plays takes place across the full range of the theatre's activities: in the Main House, The Door (which is a dedicated new writing space) and on tour to community venues in the region. The theatre runs a programme of writers' attachments every year in addition to its commissioning policy and maintains close links with *Script* (the regional writers' training agency) and the MPhil in Playwriting Studies at the University of

Birmingham. For more information contact the Literary Assistant.

Black Theatre Co-op
See **NITRO**

Bootleg Theatre Company
23 Burgess Green, Bishopdown, Salisbury
SP1 3El
☎01722 421476
✉ colin281@btinternet.com
Contact *Colin Burden*

Founded 1984. Tries to encompass as wide an audience as possible and has a tendency towards plays with socially relevant themes. A good bet for new writing since unsolicited mss are very welcome. 'Our policy is to produce new and/or rarely seen plays and anything received is given the most serious consideration.' Actively seeks to obtain grants to commission new writers for the company. Productions include: *Clubland* by Giles, Harris, Suthers and Mordell; *Hanging Hanratty* Michael Burnham; *The Truth About Blokes* Trevor Suthers; *Cool Blokes: Decent Suits* Russell Mardell; *Rainy Night in Soho* Stephen Giles.

Borderline Theatre
Darlington New Church, North Harbour Street, Ayr KA8 8AA
☎01292 281010   Fax 01292 263825
✉ enquiries@borderlinetheatre.co.uk
www.borderlinetheatre.co.uk
Producer *Eddie Jackson*

Founded 1974. Borderline is one of Scotland's leading touring companies. Tours to main-house theatres and small venues throughout Scotland. Productions include the world pre-mières of *The Angels' Share* by Chris Dolan; *The Prince and the Pilot* Anita Sullivan. Previous writers have included Dario Fo, Liz Lochhead and John Byrne. Borderline is also committed to commissioning and touring new plays for young people. Please contact the company before submitting synopsis or script.

Bristol Old Vic Theatre Company (Old Vic, Studio & Basement)
King Street, Bristol BS1 4ED
☎0117 949 3993   Fax 0117 949 3996
✉ admin@bristol-old-vic.co.uk
www.bristol-old-vic.co.uk

Bristol Old Vic actively seeks new writers for development and commission. 'We do not offer a formal reading service but are keen to build relationships with local writers in particular.'

Bush Theatre
See **Alternative Theatre Company Ltd**

Carnival (Films & Theatre) Ltd
See entry under *Film, TV and Radio Producers*

Guy Chapman Associates Ltd
33 Southampton Street, London WC2E 7HE
☎020 7379 7474   Fax 020 7379 8484
✉ admin@g-c-a.co.uk
Contact *Guy Chapman*

Performs to young audiences with innovative, experimental theatre. Productions include: *Shopping and Fucking*; *Love Upon the Throne*; *Crave*; *Disco Pigs*; *Resident Alien*; *Corpus Christi*; *New Boy*.

Citizens Theatre
Gorbals, Glasgow G5 9DS
☎0141 429 5561   Fax 0141 429 7374
✉ info@citz.co.uk
www.citz.co.uk
Artistic Director *Jeremy Raison*
General Manager *Anna Stapleton*

No formal new play policy. The theatre has a play reader but opportunities to do new work are limited.

Clwyd Theatr Cymru
Mold, Flintshire CH7 1YA
☎01352 756331   Fax 01352 701558
✉ drama@celtic.co.uk
www.clwyd-theatr-cymru.co.uk
Literary Manager *William James*
   (william.james@clwyd-theatr-cymru.co.uk)

Clwyd Theatr Cymru produces plays per-formed by a core ensemble in Mold and tours them throughout Wales (in English and Welsh). Productions are a mix of classics, revivals and contemporary drama. Recent new writing includes: *Stone City Blue* Ed Thomas; *The Rabbit* Meredydd Barker; *The Journey of Mary Kelly* Siân Evans; *And Now What?* Tim Baker and Sarah Argent; *The Way It Was, Flights of Fancy*; *Pocketful of Memories*; *The Ballad of Megan Morgan*; *Flora's War/Rhyfel Flora*; *Word for Word/Gair am Air* and *The Secret/Y Gyfrinach*: all Tim Baker. Plays by Welsh writers or on Welsh themes will be considered.

Michael Codron Plays Ltd
Aldwych Theatre Offices, Aldwych, London WC2B 4DF
☎020 7240 8291   Fax 020 7240 8467

Michael Codron Plays Ltd manages the Aldwych Theatre in London's West End. The plays it produces don't necessarily go into the Aldwych but always tend to be big-time West End fare. Previous productions: *Bedroom Farce*; *Blue Orange*; *Copenhagen*; *The Invention of Love*; *Hapgood*; *Uncle Vanya*; *Rise and Fall of Little Voice*; *Arcadia*; *Dead Funny*; *My Brilliant Divorce*; *Dinner*. No particular rule of thumb on subject matter or treatment. The acid test is whether 'something appeals to Michael'. Straight plays rather than musicals.

Colchester Mercury Theatre Limited
Balkerne Gate, Colchester CO1 1PT
☎01206 577006 Fax 01206 769607
✉ info@mercurytheatre.co.uk
www.mercurytheatre.co.uk
Chief Executive *Dee Evans*
Associate Director *Adrian Stokes*

Producing theatre with a wide-ranging audience. New writing encouraged. The theatre has a free playwright's group for adults with a serious commitment to writing plays.

The Coliseum, Oldham
Fairbottom Street, Oldham OL1 3SW
☎0161 624 1731 Fax 0161 624 5318
Chief Executive/Artistic Director *Kevin Shaw*

The artistic policy of the theatre is to present a high quality and diverse theatre programme with the ambition to commission a new play each year. Unsolicited scripts will be read; please enclose s.a.e.

Concordance
Finborough Theatre, 118 Finborough Road, London SW10 9ED
☎020 7244 7439 Fax 020 7835 1853
✉ admin@concordance.org.uk
www.concordance.org.uk
Artistic Director *Neil McPherson*

Founded in 1981, Concordance is the resident company based at the **Finborough Theatre** (see entry). Presents world premières of new writing and revivals of neglected work with a special commitment to music theatre as well as integrating music into its work and productions featuring the writing of non-theatrical artists – poets, artists, novelists, etc. – presenting their work in a theatrical setting. Unsolicited scripts not welcome, 'although we offer dramaturgical services through our website'.

Contact Theatre Company
Oxford Road, Manchester M15 6JA
☎0161 274 3434 Fax 0161 274 0640
✉ info@contact-theatre.org.uk
www.contact-theatre.org
Artistic Director *John E. McGrath*

The RAW Theatre Department at Contact looks at new writing and new work. The title RAW: Rhythm and Words in Theatre emphasises the fact that the new writing department will concentrate on all forms of writing for theatre – including lyrical writing, and experiments with other artists as well as plays. Works primarily with the 13–30 age group and is particularly interested in materials that relate to the lives and culture of young people. 'We guarantee to read the first ten pages of whatever you send at Pitch Party, which comprises a group of people from Contact and the BBC. From there your writing could be entered into Flip the Script (our monthly no-holds-barred playwriting "slam" night where professional actors and directors put 5–7 minutes of your script on stage), BBC Writers Room, or you can access our RAW writing workshop programme.'

Crucible Theatre
55 Norfolk Street, Sheffield S1 1DA
☎0114 249 5999 Fax 0114 249 6003
Artistic Director *Sam West*
Literary Associate *Matthew Byam Shaw*

Although we are interested in all new writing, most of the new work we present will be the result of commissions or prolonged script development with writers in whom we have expressed an interest.'

CV Productions
Hampden House, 2 Weymouth Street, London W1W 5BT
☎020 7636 4343 Fax 020 7636 2323
✉ cvtheatre@aol.com
Contact *Charles Vance*

In the market for medium-scale touring productions and summer-season plays. Hardly any new work and no commissions but writing of promise stands a good chance of being passed on to someone who might be interested in it. Occasional try-outs for new work in the Sidmouth repertory theatre. Send s.a.e. for return of mss.

Derby Playhouse
Eagle Centre, Derby DE1 2NF
☎01332 363271 Fax 01332 547200
www.derbyplayhouse.co.uk

Chief Executive *Karen Hebden*
Creative Producer *Stephen Edwards*

Derby Playhouse is interested in new work and has produced several world premières over the last year. 'We have a discrete commissioning budget but already have several projects under way. Due to the amount of scripts we receive, we now ask writers to send a letter accompanied by a synopsis of the play, a résumé of writing experience and any ten pages of the script they wish to submit. We will then determine whether we think it is suitable for the Playhouse, in which case we will ask for a full script.' Writers are welcome to send details of rehearsed readings and productions as an alternative means of introducing the theatre to their work.

Druid Theatre Company

Flood Street, Galway, Republic of Ireland
☎00 353 91 568660   Fax 00 353 91 563109
✉ info@druidtheatre.com
www.druidtheatre.com

New Writing Manager *Thomas Conway*

Founded 1975. Based in Galway and playing nationally and internationally, the company operates a major programme for the development of new writing. While focusing on Irish work, the company also accepts unsolicited material from outside Ireland.

The Dukes

Moor Lane, Lancaster LA1 1QE
☎01524 598505   Fax 01524 598519
✉ info@dukes-lancaster.org
www.dukes-lancaster.org

Chief Executive *Amanda Belcham*
Artistic Director *Ian Hastings*

Founded 1971. The only producing house in Lancashire. Wide target market for cinema and theatre. Plays in a 313-seater end-on auditorium and in a 198-seater in-the-round studio. Host for **Litfest** – Lancaster's annual festival of literature. In the summer months open-air promenade performances are held in Williamson Park. Also, community based Youth Arts Centre.

Dundee Repertory Theatre

Tay Square, Dundee DD1 1PB
☎01382 227684   Fax 01382 228609
✉ hwatson@dundeereptheatre.co.uk
www.dundeereptheatre.co.uk

Artistic Directors *Dominic Hill, James Brining*

Founded 1939. Plays to a varied audience. Translations and adaptations of classics, and new local plays. Most new work is commissioned.

Interested in contemporary plays in translation and in new Scottish writing. No scripts except by prior arrangement.

Eastern Angles Theatre Company

Sir John Mills Theatre, Gatacre Road, Ipswich IP1 2LQ
☎01473 218202   Fax 01473 384999
✉ admin@easternangles.co.uk
www.easternangles.co.uk

Artistic Director *Ivan Cutting*
General Manager *Jill Streatfeild*

Founded 1982. Plays to a rural audience for the most part. New work only: some commissioned, some devised by the company, some researched documentaries. Unsolicited mss welcome but scripts or writers need to have some connection with East Anglia. 'We are always keen to develop and produce new writing, especially that which is germane to a rural area.'

Edinburgh Royal Lyceum Theatre

See **Royal Lyceum Theatre Company**

English Touring Theatre

25 Short Street, London SE1 8LJ
☎020 7450 1990   Fax 020 7450 1991
✉ admin@ett.org.uk
www.ett.org.uk

Artistic Director *Stephen Unwin*

Founded 1993. National touring company visiting middle-scale receiving houses and arts centres throughout the UK. Mostly mainstream. Largely classical programme, but with increasing interest to tour one modern English play per year. Strong commitment to education work. No unsolicited mss.

Finborough Theatre

118 Finborough Road, London SW10 9ED
☎020 7244 7439   Fax 020 7835 1853
✉ admin@finboroughtheatre.co.uk
www.finboroughtheatre.co.uk

Artistic Director *Neil McPherson*

Founded 1980. 'One of London's leading new writing venues' (*Time Out*). Presents revivals of neglected work from 1850 onwards, music theatre and UK premières of foreign work, particularly from Ireland, the United States and Canada. The theatre is available for hire and the fee is sometimes negotiable to encourage interesting work, though unsolicted mss are no longer accepted. Premièred work by Chris Lee, Anthony Neilson, Naomi Wallace, Tony Marchant, Diane Samuels and Mark Ravenhill.

Gate Theatre Company Ltd

11 Pembridge Road, London W11 3HQ
☎020 7229 5387 Fax 020 7221 6055
✉ gate@gatetheatre.co.uk
www.gatetheatre.co.uk

Artistic Director *Thea Sharrock*

Founded 1979. Plays to a mixed, London-wide audience, depending on production. Aims to produce British premières of plays which originate from abroad and translations of neglected classics. Most work is with translators. Runs a biennial Translation Award. Recent productions: *Tshepang* by Lara Foot Newton; *Woyzeck* by George Büchner, adapted by Daniel Kramer; *Tejas Verdes* by Fermín Cabal, transl. by Robert Shaw. Positively encourages writers from abroad to send in scripts or translations. Most unsolicited scripts are read but it is extremely unlikely that new British plays will have any future at the theatre due to emphasis on plays translated from foreign languages. Please address submissions to the Literary Associate. Always enclose s.a.e. if play needs returning.

Graeae Theatre Company

LVS Resource Centre, 356 Holloway Road, London N7 6PA
☎020 7700 2455 Fax 020 7609 7324
✉ info@graeae.org
www.graeae.org
Minicom 020 7700 8184

CEO/Artistic Director *Jenny Sealey*

Europe's premier theatre company of disabled people, the company tours nationally and internationally with innovative theatre productions highlighting both historical and contemporary disabled experience. Graeae also runs educational programmes available to schools, youth clubs, students and disabled adults nationally and provides vocational training in theatre arts (including playwriting). Unsolicited scripts, from disabled writers, welcome. New work is commissioned.

Hampstead Theatre

Eton Avenue, Swiss Cottage, London NW3 3EU
☎020 7449 4200 Fax 020 7449 4201
✉ literary@hampsteadtheatre.com
www.hampsteadtheatre.com

Contact *Holly Hughes*

A brand new Hampstead Theatre opened in 2003. The building is an intimate space with a flexible stage and an auditorium capable of expanding to seat 325. The artistic policy continues to be the production of British and international new plays and the development of important young writers. 'We are looking for writers who recognise the power of theatre and who have a story to tell. All plays are read and discussed. We give feedback to all writers with potential.' Writers produced at Hampstead include Michael Frayn, Roy Williams, Shelagh Stephenson, Simon Block, Philip Ridley, Frank McGuinness, Rona Munro, Brad Fraser, Tim Firth and Abi Morgan.

Harrogate Theatre

Oxford Street, Harrogate HG1 1QF
☎01423 502710 Fax 01423 563205
✉ firstname.surname@harrogatetheatre.co.uk

Artistic Director *To be appointed*

Produces four to five productions a year on the main stage, one of which may be a new play but is most likely to be commissioned. Annual mainstage Youth Theatre production may also be commissioned. (Policy on new writing unknown at the time of going to press as a new artistic director had not been appointed.)

Heritage Theatre Ltd

See entry under *Film, TV and Radio Producers*

The Hiss & Boo Company Ltd

1 Nyes Hill, Wineham Lane, Bolney RH17 5SD
Fax 01444 882057
✉ hissboo@msn.com
www.hissboo.co.uk

Contact *Ian Liston*

Particularly interested in new thrillers, comedy thrillers, comedy and melodrama – must be commercial full-length plays. Also interested in plays/plays with music for children. No one-acts. Previous productions: *The Shakespeare Revue*; *Come Rain Come Shine*; *Sleighrider*; *Beauty and the Beast*; *An Ideal Husband*; *Mr Men's Magical Island*; *Mr Men and the Space Pirates*; *Nunsense*; *Corpse!*; *Groucho: A Life in Revue*; *See How They Run*; *Christmas Cat and the Pudding Pirates*; *Pinocchio* and traditional pantos written by Roy Hudd for the company. 'We are keen on revue-type shows and compilation shows but *not* tribute-type performances.' No unsolicited scripts; no telephone calls. Send synopsis and introductory letter in the first instance.

Hull Truck Theatre Company

Spring Street, Hull HU2 8RW
☎01482 224800 Fax 01482 581182
✉ admin@hulltruck.co.uk

www.hulltruck.co.uk
Executive Director *Joanne Gower*
General Manager *Nigel Penn*
Artistic Director *John Godber*
Associate Artistic Director *Gareth Tudor-Price*

John Godber, of *Teechers, Bouncers* and *Up 'n' Under* fame (the artistic director of this high-profile Northern company since 1984), has very much dominated the scene in the past with his own successful plays. The emphasis is still on new writing but Godber's works continue to be toured extensively. Recent premieres include *Going Dutch, Reunion, Men of the World* and *Black Tie and Tales*. Most new plays are commissioned. Recent Commissions: *Confessions of a City Supporter* Alan Plater; *A Kick in the Baubles* and *Kissing Married Women* Gordon Steel; *Ladies Day* Amanda Whittington; *Up on Roof* Richard Bean; *1984* adapted by Nick Lane and *I Want That Hair* Jane Thornton, plus various family shows by Nick Lane. The company receives a large number of unsolicited scripts but cannot guarantee a quick response. Bear in mind the artistic policy of Hull Truck, which is 'accessibility and popularity'. In general they are not interested in musicals, or in plays with casts of more than seven.

Stephen Joseph Theatre
Westborough, Scarborough YO11 1JW
☎01723 370540   Fax 01723 360506
www.sjt.uk.com
Artistic Director *Alan Ayckbourn*
Literary Manager *Laura Harvey*

A two-auditoria complex housing a 165-seat end stage theatre/cinema (the McCarthy) and a 400-seat theatre-in-the-round (the Round). Positive policy on new work. For obvious reasons, Alan Ayckbourn's work features quite strongly but a new writing programme ensures plays from other sources are actively encouraged. Also runs a lunchtime season of one-act plays each summer. Writers are advised however that the SJT is very unlikely to produce an unsolicited script – synopses are preferred. Recent commissions and past productions include: *Soap* Sarah Woods; *Fields of Gold* Alex Jones; *For Starters* Nick Warburton; *Bedtime Stories* Lesley Bruce; *Making Waves* Stephen Clark; *Larkin with Women* Ben Brown; *Amaretti Angels* Sarah Phelps; *Something Blue* Gill Adams; *Clockwatching* and *A Listening Heaven* Torben Betts; *The Star Throwers* Paul Lucas; *Safari Party* Tim Firth; *Drowning on Dry Land*; *Private Fears in Public Places* and *My Sister Sadie* Alan Ayckbourn. 'Writers are welcome to send details of rehearsed readings and productions as

an alternative means of introducing the theatre to their work.' Submit to *Laura Harvey* enclosing an s.a.e. for return of mss.

Bill Kenwright Ltd
BKL House, 106 Harrow Road, London W2 1RR
☎020 7446 6200   Fax 020 7446 6222
Contact *Bill Kenwright*

Presents both revivals and new shows for West End and touring theatres. Although new work tends to be by established playwrights, this does not preclude or prejudice new plays from new writers. Scripts should be addressed to Bill Kenwright with a covering letter and s.a.e. 'We have enormous amounts of scripts sent to us although we very rarely produce unsolicited work. Scripts are read systematically. Please do not phone; the return of your script or contact with you will take place in time.'

Komedia
Gardner Street, North Lane, Brighton BN1 1UN
☎01273 647101   Fax 01273 647102
✉ info@komedia.co.uk
www.komedia.co.uk
Contact *David Lavender*

Founded in 1994, Komedia promotes, produces and presents new work. Mss of new plays welcome.

Leicester Haymarket Theatre
Belgrave Gate, Leicester LE1 3YQ
☎0116 253 0021   Fax 0116 251 3310
✉ enquiries@lhtheatre.co.uk
www.lhtheatre.co.uk
Artistic Directors *Kully Thiarai, Paul Kerryson*

Leicester Haymarket Theatre aims for a balanced programme of original and established works. It is a multi-cultural integrated company with educational projects that support all productions and areas of work. The company will move to new theatre spaces in a newly designed, state-of-the-art performance building in 2007. Current programme includes work by Brecht and Stephen Sondheim. There is a thriving young peoples theatre company, *Young Blood*, plus a New Writing Theatre initiative.

Library Theatre Company
St Peter's Square, Manchester M2 5PD
☎0161 234 1920   Fax 0161 228 6481
✉ ltc@m.barnett.manchester.gov.uk
www.librarytheatre.com

Artistic Director *Chris Honer*

Produces new and contemporary work, as well as the classics. No unsolicited mss. Send outline of the nature of the script first. Encourages new writing through the commissioning of new plays and through a programme of rehearsed readings to help writers' development.

Live Theatre Company

7/8 Trinity Chare, Newcastle upon Tyne NE1 3DF
☎0191 261 2694 Fax 0191 232 2224
✉ info@live.org.uk
www.live.org.uk

Artistic Director *Max Roberts*
Executive Director *Jim Beirne*

Founded 1973. Produces shows at its refurbished 200-seat venue, and also tours regionally and nationally. Company policy is to produce work that is rooted in the culture of the region, particularly for those who do not normally get involved in the arts. The company is particularly interested in promoting new writing. As well as full-scale productions the company organises workshops, rehearsed readings and other new writing activities. The company also enjoys a close relationship with **New Writing North** and is funded to support new writing through the BBC's *Northern Exposure* project. Productions include *Falling Together* Tom Hadaway; *Cooking With Elvis* Lee Hall; *Bones* Peter Straughan; *ne1* and *Tales From the Backyard* Alan Plater; *Double Lives* Julia Darling and Sean O'Brien; *Smack Family Robinson* Richard Bean; *Keepers of the Flame* and *Laughter When We're Dead* Sean O'Brien.

London Bubble Theatre Company

5 Elephant Lane, London SE16 4JD
☎020 7237 4434 Fax 020 7231 2366
✉ admin@londonbubble.org.uk
www.londonbubble.org.uk

Artistic Director *Jonathan Petherbridge*

Produces workshops, plays and events for a mixed audience of theatregoers and non-theatregoers, wide-ranging in terms of age, culture and class. Previous productions: *Punchkin, Enchanter, You Can't Say You Can't Play*. Unsolicited mss are received but 'our reading service is extremely limited and there can be a considerable wait before we can give a response'. Commissions approximately one new project a year, often inspired by a promenade site, specific community of interest or workshop group.

Lyric Hammersmith

Lyric Square, King Street, London W6 0QL
☎08700 500 5111 Fax 020 8741 5965
✉ enquiries@lyric.co.uk
www.lyric.co.uk

Artistic Director *David Farr*
Executive Director *Jessica Hepburn*

The main theatre stages an eclectic programme of new and revived classics. Interested in developing projects with writers, translators and adaptors. The Lyric does not accept unsolicited scripts. Its 110-seat studio focuses on work for children, young people and families.

mac

Cannon Hill Park, Birmingham B12 9QH
☎0121 440 3838 Fax 0121 446 4372
✉ info@mac-birmingham.org.uk
www.macarts.co.uk
Minicom: 0121 440 4923

Director *Dorothy Wilson*

Innovative creative arts activities, including theatre, music, comedy, plays for children, literature and poetry events, courses and workshops, family show at Christmas, films and free exhibitions.

Manchester Library Theatre

See **Library Theatre Company**

New Vic Theatre

Etruria Road, Newcastle under Lyme ST5 0JG
☎01782 717954 Fax 01782 712885
✉ admin@newvictheatre.org.uk
www.newvictheatre.org.uk

Artistic Director *Gwenda Hughes* (to Dec. 2006)

The New Vic is a purpose-built theatre-in-the-round. Produces ten in-house plays each year and is active within the education sector and community. New plays produced are the result of specific commissions. Send synopses *not* unsolicited scripts. 'We cannot guarantee that unsolicited scripts will be read; they will be returned on receipt of an s.a.e.'

Newpalm Productions

26 Cavendish Avenue, London N3 3QN
☎020 8349 0802 Fax 020 8346 8257

Contact *Lionel Chilcott*

Very rarely produces new plays (*As Is* by William M. Hoffman, which came from Broadway to the Half Moon Theatre, was an exception to this). National tours and West End productions such as *Peter Pan (The Musical)*; *Noises Off; Seven Brides for Seven Brothers* and *Rebecca*, at regional repertory theatres, are more typical examples of Newpalm's work. Both plays and musicals are, however, welcome; synopses are preferable to scripts.

Nimax Theatres

1 Lumley Court, off 402 Strand, London
WC2R 0NB
☎0845 434 9290
CEO *Nica Burns*

West End theatre managers of the Apollo, Duchess, Garrick, Lyric and Vaudeville theatres. Unsolicited scripts are not considered.

NITRO

6 Brewery Road, London N7 9NH
☎020 7609 1331   Fax 020 7609 1221
✉ info@nitro.co.uk
www.nitro.co.uk
Artistic Director *Felix Cross*

Founded 1978. Formerly Black Theatre Co-op. Plays to a mixed audience, approximately 65% female. Usually tours nationally twice a year. 'A music theatre company, we are committed in the first instance to new writing by Black British writers and work which relates to the Black culture and experience throughout the Diaspora.' Unsolicited mss welcome.

Northcott Theatre

Stocker Road, Exeter EX4 4QB
☎01392 223999   Fax 01392 223996
www.northcott-theatre.co.uk
Artistic Director *Ben Crocker*

Founded 1967. The Northcott is the Southwest's principal subsidised producing theatre, situated on the University of Exeter campus. Describes its audience as 'geographically diverse, with a core audience of AB1s (40–60 age range)'. Continually looking to broaden the base of its audience profile, targeting younger and/or non-mainstream theatregoers. Aims to develop, promote and produce quality new writing which reflects the life of the region and addresses the audience it serves. Generally works on a commission basis but occasionally options existing new work. Unsolicited mss welcome – current turnaround on script-reading service is approximately three months and no mss can be returned unless a correct value s.a.e. is included with the original submission.

Norwich Puppet Theatre

St James, Whitefriars, Norwich NR3 1TN
☎01603 615564   Fax 01603 617578
✉ info@puppettheatre.co.uk
www.puppettheatre.co.uk
Artistic Director *Luis Boy*
General Manager *Ian Woods*

Plays to a young audience (aged 3–12) but developing shows for adult audiences interested in puppetry. All year round programme plus tours to schools and arts venues. Most productions are based on traditional stories but unsolicited mss welcome if relevant.

Nottingham Playhouse

Nottingham Playhouse Trust, Wellington Circus, Nottingham NG1 5AF
☎0115 947 4361   Fax 0115 947 5759
www.nottinghamplayhouse.co.uk
Artistic Director *Giles Croft*

Aims to make innovation popular, and present the best of world theatre, working closely with the communities of Nottingham and Nottinghamshire. Unsolicited mss will be read. It normally takes about six months, however, and 'we have never yet produced an unsolicited script. All our plays have to achieve a minimum of 60 per cent audiences in a 732-seat theatre. We have no studio.'

Nottingham Playhouse Roundabout Theatre in Education

Wellington Circus, Nottingham NG1 5AF
☎0115 947 4361
✉ andrewb@nottinghamplayhouse.co.uk
www.nottinghamplayhouse.co.uk
Contact *Andrew Breakwell*

Founded 1973. Theatre-in-Education company of the **Nottingham Playhouse**. Plays to a young audience aged 5–18 years of age. 'We are committed to the encouragement of new writing and commission at least two new plays for young people each year. With other major producers in the East Midlands we share the resources of the *Theatre Writing Partnership* which is based at the Playhouse. See website for philosophy and play details. Please make contact before submitting scripts.'

N.T.C. Touring Theatre Company

The Playhouse, Bondgate Without, Alnwick NE66 1PQ
☎01665 602586   Fax 01665 605837
✉ admin@ntc-touringtheatre.co.uk
www.ntc-touringtheatre.co.uk

Contact *Gillian Hambleton*
General Manager *Anna Flood*

Founded 1978. Formerly Northumberland Theatre Company. An Arts Council England revenue funded organisation. Predominantly rural, small-scale touring company, playing to village halls and community centres throughout the Northern region, the Scottish Borders and countrywide. Productions range from established classics to new work and popular comedies, but must be appropriate to their audience. Unsolicited scripts welcome but are unlikely to be produced. All scripts are read and returned with constructive criticism within six months. Writers whose style is of interest may then be commissioned. The company encourages new writing and commissions when possible. Financial constraints restrict casting to a *maximum* of six.

Nuffield Theatre
University Road, Southampton SO17 1TR
☎023 8031 5500 Fax 023 8031 5511
✉ alison.thurley@nuffieldtheatre.co.uk
www.nuffieldtheatre.co.uk
Artistic Director *Patrick Sandford*
Script Executive *John Burgess*

Well known as a good bet for new playwrights, the Nuffield gets an awful lot of scripts. Produces two new main stage plays every season. Previous productions: *Exchange* by Yuri Trifonov (transl. Michael Frayn) which transferred to the Vaudeville Theatre; *The Floating Light Bulb* Woody Allen (British première); *Nelson*, a new play by Pam Gems; *Dogspot* and *The Dramatic Attitudes of Miss Fanny Kemble* Claire Luckham; and *The Winter Wife* by Claire Tomalin. Open-minded about subject and style, producing musicals as well as straight plays. Also opportunities for some small-scale fringe work. Scripts preferred to synopses in the case of writers new to theatre. All will, eventually, be read 'but please be patient. We do not have a large team of paid readers. We read everything ourselves.'

Octagon Theatre Trust Ltd
Howell Croft South, Bolton BL1 1SB
☎01204 529407 Fax 01204 556502
✉ info@octagonbolton.co.uk
www.octagonbolton.co.uk
Executive Director *John Blackmore*

Founded in 1967, the award-winning Octagon Theatre stages at least eight main auditorium home-produced shows a year, and hosts UK touring companies such as the National

Theatre, John Godber's Hull Truck Theatre Company, Peshkar Productions and Alan Ayckbourn's Stephen Joseph Theatre. Also hosts the work of partner companies as part of its commitment to creative partnerships. The theatre boasts a thriving and constantly developing participatory department, activ8, which operates a highly successful Youth Theatre as well as initiating and facilitating exciting education and outreach programmes. The theatre is keen to encourage new writing but, due to the lack of a dedicated literary department, is unable to accept and process new and unsolicited scripts; the theatre uses **North West Playwrights** as a reading service instead.

Orange Tree Theatre
1 Clarence Street, Richmond TW9 2SA
☎020 8940 0141 Fax 020 8332 0369
✉ admin@orange-tree.demon.co.uk
www.orangetreetheatre.co.uk
Artistic Director *Sam Walters*

The Orange Tree, a theatre-in-the-round venue, presents a broad cross section of work. Past productions have included plays by Rodney Ackland, John Galsworthy and a new translation of Lorca as well as new plays by Oliver Ford Davies, David Lewis, Ben Brown and Kenneth Jupp. The theatre no longer considers unsolicited mss; writers who may wish to approach the theatre are asked to write first. The Theatre currently has a young 'trainee' writer in residence.

Out of Joint
7 Thane Works, Thane Villas, London
N7 7NU
☎020 7609 0207 Fax 020 7609 0203
✉ ojo@outofjoint.co.uk
www.outofjoint.co.uk
Director *Max Stafford-Clark*
Producer *Graham Cowley*
Literary Associate *Alex Roberts*

Founded 1993. Award-winning theatre company with new writing central to its policy. Produces new plays which reflect society and its concerns, placing an emphasis on education activity to attract young audiences. Welcomes unsolicited mss. Productions include: *Blue Heart* Caryl Churchill; *Our Lady of Sligo*, *The Steward of Christendom* and *Hinterland* Sebastian Barry; *Shopping and Fucking* and *Some Explicit Polaroids* Mark Ravenhill; *Rita, Sue and Bob Too* Andrea Dunbar; *A State Affair* and *Talking to Terrorists* Robin Soans; *Sliding with Suzanne* Judy Upton; *The Positive Hour* and *A Laughing Matter* April de Angelis; *Duck* and *Oh go my Man* Stella Feehily; *The Permanent Way* David Hare.

Oxford Stage Company

Chertsey Chambers, 12 Mercer Street, London WC2H 9QD
☎020 7438 9940 Fax 020 7438 9941
www.oxfordstage.co.uk
Artistic Director *Rupert Goold*

A middle-scale touring company producing established and new plays. On average, one new play or new adaptation a year. Due to forthcoming projects the company is not considering unsolicited scripts at present.

Paines Plough

4th Floor, 43 Aldwych, London WC2B 4DN
☎020 7240 4533 Fax 020 7240 4534
✉ office@painesplough.com
www.painesplough.com
Artistic Director *Roxana Silbert*
Literary Manager *Pippa Ellis*

Tours new plays nationally and internationally. Works with writers to develop their skills and voices through workshops, rehearsed readings and playwriting projects. Provides a supportive environment for commissioned writers to push themselves and challenge their craft. Will consider unsolicited material from UK writers (please send s.a.e. for return of script).

Perth Repertory Theatre Ltd

185 High Street, Perth PH1 5UW
☎01738 472700 Fax 01738 624576
✉ info@horsecross.co.uk
www.horsecross.co.uk
Creative Directors *Ian Grieve, Graham McLaren*
General Manager *Paul Hackett*

Founded 1935. Combination of one to four-weekly repertoire of plays and musicals, incoming tours and studio productions. Unsolicited mss are read when time permits, but the timetable for return of scripts is lengthy. New plays staged by the company are usually commissioned under the SAC scheme.

Plymouth Theatre Royal

See **Theatre Royal**

Polka Theatre for Children

240 The Broadway, Wimbledon SW19 1SB
☎020 8545 8320 Fax 020 8545 8365
✉ info@polkatheatre.com
www.polkatheatre.com
Artistic Director *Annie Wood*

Executive Director *Stephen Midlane*
Associate Director, New Writing *Richard Shannon*

Founded in 1967 and moved into its Wimbledon base in 1979. Leading children's theatre committed to commissioning and producing new plays. Programmes are planned two years ahead and at least three new plays are commissioned each year. 'Many of our scripts are commissioned from established writers. We are, however, keen to develop work from writers new to children's and young people's theatre. We run a new writing programme which includes master classes and workshops. Potential new writers' work is read and discussed on a regular basis; thus we constantly add to our pool of interesting and interested writers. This department is headed by *Richard Shannon*, Associate Director for New Writing.'

Queen's Theatre, Hornchurch

Billet Lane, Hornchurch RM11 1QT
☎01708 462362 Fax 01708 462363
✉ info@queens-theatre.co.uk
www.queens-theatre.co.uk
Artistic Director *Bob Carlton*

The Queen's Theatre is a 503-seat theatre producing up to nine in-house productions per year, including pantomime. Aims for distinctive and accessible performances in an identifiable house style focused upon actor/musician shows but, in addition, embraces straight plays, classics and comedies. 'New play/musical submissions are welcome but should be submitted in treatment and not script form.' Also runs a writers' group which meets on the first Thursday of each month, and playwright Paul Miller runs the 'Beginning Writers' Group' for adults (contact the Education Manager for information). These groups have close links with the Queen's community company which workshops and showcases the groups' work. Summer 2006 saw the staging of a large-scale community play by a local writer.

The Really Useful Group Ltd

22 Tower Street, London WC2H 9TW
☎020 7240 0880 Fax 020 7240 1204
www.reallyuseful.com

Commercial/West End, national and international theatre producer/co-producer/licensor whose output has included *Joseph and the Amazing Technicolor Dreamcoat*; *Jesus Christ Superstar*; *Cats*; *Evita*; *Song & Dance*; *Daisy Pulls It Off*; *Lend Me a Tenor*; *Starlight Express*; *The Phantom of the Opera*; *Aspects of Love*; *Sunset*

Boulevard; *By Jeeves*; *Whistle Down the Wind*; *The Beautiful Game*; *Tell Me On a Sunday*; *Bombay Dreams*; *The Woman in White*.

Red Ladder Theatre Company

3 St Peter's Buildings, York Street, Leeds
LS9 8AJ
☎0113 245 5311 Fax 0113 245 5351
✉ rod@redladder.co.uk
www.redladder.co.uk

Artistic Director/Literary Manager *Rod Dixon*
Administrator *Layla Asadi*

Founded 1968. Commissioning company touring 2–3 shows a year with a strong commitment to new work and new writers. Aimed at an audience of young people aged between 13–25 years who have little or no access to theatre. Performances held in youth clubs and theatre venues. Recent productions: *Kaahini* Maya Chowdhry; *Worlds Apart* Mick Martin; *Free Falling* Madani Younis; *Silent Cry* Madani Younis. The company is particularly keen to enter into a dialogue with writers with regard to creating new work for young people. E-mail the artistic director for more information at the address above.

Red Shift Theatre Company

TRG2 Trowbray House, 108 Weston Street, London SE1 3QB
☎020 7378 9787 Fax 020 7378 9789
✉ mail@redshifttheatreco.co.uk
www.redshifttheatreco.co.uk

Contact *Jonathan Holloway* (Artistic Director)
General Manager *Emma Rees*

Founded 1982. Small-scale touring company which plays to a theatre-literate audience. Welcomes contact with writers – 'we try to see their work' – and receipt of c.v.s and treatments. Occasionally runs workshops bringing new scripts, writers and actors together. These can develop links with a reservoir of writers who may feed the company. Interested in new plays with subject matter which is accessible to a broad audience and concerns issues of importance; also new translations and adaptations. Recent productions: *The Third Man*; *Get Carter* and *Vertigo*.

Ridiculusmus

BAC, Lavender Hill, London SW11 5TN
✉ enquiries@ridiculusmus.com
www.ridiculusmus.com

Artistic Directors *Jon Haynes, David Woods*

Founded 1992. Touring company which plays to a wide range of audiences. Productions have included adaptations of *The Importance of Being Earnest*; *Three Men In a Boat*; *The Third Policeman*; *At Swim Two Birds* and original work: *The Exhibitionists*; *Yes, Yes, Yes*; *Say Nothing* and *Ideas Men*. Unsolicited scripts not welcome.

Royal Court Theatre

Sloane Square, London SW1W 8AS
☎020 7565 5050 Fax 020 7565 5002
(Literary office)
www.royalcourttheatre.com

Literary Manager *Graham Whybrow*

The Royal Court is a leading international theatre producing up to 17 new plays each year in its 400-seat proscenium theatre and 80-seat studio. In 1956 its first director George Devine set out to find 'hard-hitting, uncompromising writers whose plays are stimulating, provocative and exciting'. This artistic policy helped transform post-war British theatre, with new plays by writers such as John Osborne, Arnold Wesker, John Arden, Samuel Beckett, Edward Bond and David Storey, through to Caryl Churchill, Jim Cartwright, Kevin Elyot and Timberlake Wertenbaker. Since 1994 it has produced a new generation of playwrights such as Joe Penhall, Rebecca Prichard, Sarah Kane, Jez Butterworth, Martin McDonagh, Mark Ravenhill, Ayub Khan-Din, Conor McPherson, Roy Williams and many other first-time writers. The Royal Court has programmes for young writers and international writers, and it is always searching for new plays and new playwrights.

Royal Exchange Theatre Company

St Ann's Square, Manchester M2 7DH
☎0161 615 6709 Fax 0161 832 0881
✉ jo.combes@royalexchange.co.uk
www.royalexchange.co.uk

Associate Artistic Director *Sarah Frankcom*
Associate Director (Literary) *Jo Combes*

Founded 1976. The Royal Exchange has developed a new writing policy which it finds is attracting a younger audience to the theatre. The company has recently produced new plays by Nick Leather, Chloe Moss, Simon Stephens, Shelagh Stephenson, Brad Fraser, Jim Cartwright and Owen McCafferty. Currently has Gurpreet Bhatti, Linda Marshall Griffiths, Owen McCafferty, Abi Morgan, Sharif Samad, Simon Stephens and Roy Williams on commission. 'Not currently accepting unsolicited work as we are running a National Playwriting Competition [The Bruntwood Playwriting

Competition for the Royal Exchange], details of which are available on our website.'

Royal Lyceum Theatre Company

Grindlay Street, Edinburgh EH3 9AX
☎0131 248 4800 Fax 0131 228 3955
www.lyceum.org.uk

Artistic Director *Mark Thomson*
Administration Manager *Ruth Butterworth*

Founded 1965. Repertory theatre which plays to a mixed urban Scottish audience. Produces classic, contemporary and new plays. Would like to stage more new plays, especially Scottish. No full-time literary staff to provide reports on submitted scripts.

Royal National Theatre

South Bank, London SE1 9PX
☎020 7452 3333 Fax 020 7452 3344
www.nationaltheatre.org.uk

Literary Manager *Jack Bradley*

The majority of the National's new plays come about as a result of direct commission or from existing contacts with playwrights. There is no quota for new work, though many of the plays presented have been the work of living playwrights especially in the Cottesloe Theatre which is dedicated to new plays. Writers new to the theatre would need to be of exceptional talent to be successful with a script here, however the Royal National Theatre Studio helps a limited number of playwrights, through readings, workshops and discussions. Scripts considered but not by e-mail (send s.a.e).

Royal Shakespeare Company

1 Earlham Street, London WC2H 9LL
☎020 7845 0515
✉ Daniel.Usztan@rsc.org.uk
www.rsc.org.uk

Literary Manager *Jeanie O'Hare*

The RSC is a classical theatre company based in Stratford upon Avon. As well as Shakespeare, the RSC produces English classics, foreign classics in translation and new plays. The literary department is proactive rather than reactive and seeks out the plays and playwrights it wishes to commission. 'We can only read contemporary works where the writer is known. Sadly we are unable to read unsolicited work from less established writers but we do monitor the work of emerging playwrights in production nationally and internationally.' From April 2006 to April 2007 the Company is presenting the Complete Works of Shakespeare Festival.

7:84 Theatre Company Scotland

333 Woodlands Road, Glasgow G3 6NG
☎0141 334 6686 Fax 0141 334 3369
✉ admin@784theatre.com
www.784theatre.com

Artistic Director *Lorenzo Mele*

Founded 1973. One of Scotland's foremost touring theatre companies committed to producing work that addresses current social, cultural and political issues. Recent productions include commissions by Scottish playwrights such as Stephen Greenhorn, Rona Munro and Martin McArdie (*Reasons to be Cheerful*); Christopher Dean (*Boiling a Frog*); Peter Arnott (*A Little Rain*); Stephen Greenhorn (*Dissent*); David Greig (*Caledonia Dreaming*) and the Scottish premières of Tony Kushner's *Angels in America* and Athol Fugard's *Valley Song*. 'The company is committed to a new writing policy that encourages and develops writers at every level of experience, to get new voices and strong messages on to the stage.' New writing development has always been central to 7:84's core activity and has included Summer Schools and rehearsed readings. The company continues to be committed to this work and its development.

Shared Experience

The Soho Laundry, 9 Dufour's Place, London W1F 7SJ
☎020 7434 9248 Fax 020 7287 8763
✉ admin@sharedexperience.org.uk
www.sharedexperience.org.uk

Joint Artistic Directors *Nancy Meckler, Polly Teale*

Founded 1975. Varied audience depending on venue, since this is a touring company. Recent productions have included: *Anna Karenina, Mill on the Floss*, and *War and Peace* (all adapt. by Helen Edmundson); *Jane Eyre* (adapt. Polly Teale); *The House of Bernarda Alba* (transl. Rona Munro); *Mother Courage* (transl. Lee Hall); *A Doll's House* (transl. Michael Meyer); *The Magic Toyshop* (adapt. Bryony Lavery); *The Clearing* and *Gone to Earth* Helen Edmundson; *A Passage to India* (adapt. Martin Sherman); *After Mrs Rochester* and *Brontë* Polly Teale. No unsolicited mss. Primarily not a new writing company. New plays always commissioned.

Sherman Theatre Company

Senghennydd Road, Cardiff CF24 4YE
☎029 2064 6901 Fax 029 2064 6902
www.shermantheatre.co.uk

Artistic Director *Phil Clark*

Founded 1973. Theatre for Young People, with main house and studio. Encourages new writing; has produced 86 new plays in the last ten years. Previous productions include a David Wood adaptation of Roald Dahl's *Danny the Champion of the World*, plays by Frank Vickery (*Pullin the Wool*); Helen Griffin (*Flesh and Blood*); Patrick Jones (*Everything Must Go*); Terry Deary (*Horrible Histories Crackers Christmas*); Mike Kenny (*Puff the Magic Dragon*); Brendan Murray (*Something Beginning With ...*); Roald Dahl (*The Enormous Crocodile*); Roger Williams (*Pop*); Arnold Wesker (*Break, My Heart*). Runs a new scheme called WriteHere for which scripts can be submitted. Interesting ideas go through to ScriptSlam during which an audience votes for their favourite excerpt to be developed further.

Show of Strength

74 Chessel Street, Bedminster, Bristol
BS3 3DN
☎0117 902 0235 Fax 0117 902 0196
✉ info@showofstrength.org.uk
www.showofstrength.org.uk

Creative Producer *Sheila Hannon*

Founded 1986. Plays to an informal, younger than average audience. Aims to stage at least one new play each season with a preference for work from Bristol and the South West. Will read unsolicited scripts but a lack of funding means they are unable to provide written reports. Output: *The Wills Girls* Amanda Whittington; *Lags* Ron Hutchinson; *So Long Life* and *Nicholodeon* Peter Nichols. Also, rehearsed readings of new work.

Soho Theatre Company

21 Dean Street, London W1D 3NE
☎020 7287 5060 Fax 020 7287 5061
✉ writers@sohotheatre.com
www.sohotheatre.com

Artistic Director *To be appointed*

Dedicated to new writing, the company has an extensive research and development programme consisting of a free script-reading service, workshops and readings. Also runs many courses for new writers. Soho Young Writers hold free 'Taster Workshops' and longer courses for promising playwrights aged 15–25. The company produces around four plays a year. Recent productions include: *Other Hands* and *Colder than Here* Laura Wade (recipient of the Critics' Circle Most Promising New Playwright and Olivier Award nominated for Outstanding Achievement); *On Ego* by Mick Gordon with Paul Broks; *Shoreditch Madonna* Rebecca Lenkiewicz.

Runs the **Verity Bargate Award**, a biennial competition (see entry under *Prizes*).

Sphinx Theatre Company

25 Short Street, London SE1 8LJ
☎020 7401 9993 Fax 020 7401 9995
✉ info@sphinxtheatre.co.uk
www.sphinxtheatre.co.uk

Artistic Director *Sue Parrish*
General Manager *Susannah Kraft Levene*
Administrator *Bonnie Mitchell*

'Sphinx is a feminist theatre company that places women at the centre of its artistic endeavour.' Since 1973 the company has toured ground-breaking productions to small and mid-scale venues. Synopses and ideas are welcome by e-mail or post with s.a.e.

Talawa Theatre Company Ltd

3rd Floor, 23–25 Great Sutton Street, London
EC1V 0DN
☎020 7251 6644 Fax 020 7251 5969
✉ hq@talawa.com
www.talawa.com

Founded 1985. 'Aims to provide high quality productions that reflect the significant creative role that Black theatre plays within the national and international arena and also to enlarge theatre audiences from the Black community.' Previous productions include all-Black performances of *The Importance of Being Earnest* and *Antony and Cleopatra*; plus Jamaican pantomime *Arawak Gold*; *The Gods Are Not to Blame*; *The Road* Wole Soyinka; *Beef, No Chicken* Derek Walcott; *Flying West* Pearl Cleage; *Othello* William Shakespeare. Seeks to provide a platform for new work from up and coming Black British writers. Send synopsis in the first instance. Runs a black script development project. Talawa is funded by the Arts Council England, London.

Theatre Absolute

57–61 Corporation Street, Coventry
CV1 1GQ
☎024 7625 7380 Fax 024 7655 0680
✉ julia@theatreabsolute.co.uk
www.theatreabsolute.co.uk

Artistic Director/Writer *Chris O'Connell*
Producer *Julia Negus*

Founded 1992. An independent theatre company which commissions, produces and tours new plays based on a strong narrative text and aimed at audiences aged 15 and upwards. Productions include: *Car*, winner of an

Edinburgh Fringe First Award 1999 and a *Time Out* Live Award – Best New Play on the London Fringe 1999; and most recently, *Kid*, Edinburgh Fringe 2003. In 2005, produced *Street Trilogy*, bringing all three plays together for the first time. The company also runs The Writing House, a script development scheme.

Theatre of Comedy Company

210 Shaftesbury Avenue, London WC2H 8DP
☎020 7379 3345 Fax 020 7836 8181
Executive Producer *James Williams*

Produces new work and revivals for the commercial stage, with a focus on comedy in the widest sense. Scripts welcome, as are treatments for television comedy series and entertainment.

Theatre Royal Plymouth & Drum Theatre Plymouth

Royal Parade, Plymouth PL1 2TR
☎01752 230347 Fax 01752 230499
✉ d.prescott@theatreroyal.com
www.theatreroyal.com
Artistic Director *Simon Stokes*
Artistic Associate *David Prescott*

Stages small, middle and large-scale drama and music theatre. Commissions and produces new plays. The theatre no longer accepts unsolicited playscripts but will consider plays through known channels, i.e. theatre practitioners, regional and national scriptwriters' groups and agents.

Theatre Royal Stratford East

Gerry Raffles Square, London E15 1BN
☎020 8279 1104 Fax 020 8534 8381
✉ asohoye@stratfordeast.com *and* sramamurphy@stratfordeast.com
www.stratfordeast.com
New Writing Associates *Ashmeed Sohoye, Sita Ramamurphy*

In the heart of the East End, catering for a very mixed audience, in terms of both culture and age range. Produces plays and musicals, youth theatre and local community plays/events, all of which is new work. Special interest in plays and musicals reflecting the culturally diverse communities of London and the UK. New initiatives in developing contemporary British musicals. No longer accepts unsolicited scripts but instead asks for a) synopsis of script, b) sample ten pages of writing, c) brief writer's biography. 'From this information we will decide whether or not to ask for full-length script.'

Theatre Royal Windsor

Windsor SL4 1PS
☎01753 863444 Fax 01753 831673
✉ info@theatreroyalwindsor.co.uk
www.theatreroyalwindsor.co.uk
Executive Producer *Bill Kenwright*
Executive Director *Mark Piper*

Plays to a middle-class, West End-type audience. Produces thirteen plays a year and 'would be disappointed to do fewer than two new plays in a year; always hope to do half a dozen'. Modern classics, thrillers, comedy and farce. Only interested in scripts along these lines.

Theatre Workshop Edinburgh

34 Hamilton Place, Edinburgh EH3 5AX
☎0131 225 7942 Fax 0131 220 0112
www.theatre-workshop.com
Artistic Director *Robert Rae*

First ever professional producing theatre to fully include disabled actors in all its productions. Plays to a young, broad-based audience with many pieces targeted towards particular groups or communities. Output has included *D.A.R.E.*; *Threepenny Opera*; *Black Sun Over Genoa*. Particularly interested in issues-based work for young people and minority groups. Frequently engages writers for collaborative work and devised projects. Commissions a significant amount of new writing for a wide range of contexts, from large-scale community plays to small-scale professional productions. Favours writers based in Scotland, producing material relevant to a contemporary Scottish audience.

The Torch Theatre

St Peter's Road, Milford Haven SA73 2BU
☎01646 694192 Fax 01646 698919
✉ info@torchtheatre.co.uk
www.torchtheatre.co.uk
Artistic Director *Peter Doran*

Founded 1977. Stages a mixed programme of in-house and middle-scale touring work. Unsolicited scripts will be read and guidance offered but production unlikely due to restricted funding. Please include s.a.e. for return of script and notes; mark clearly, 'FAO Peter Doran'. Torch Theatre Company productions include: *Dancing at Lughnasa*; *Neville's Island*; *The Woman in Black*; *Abigail's Party*; *Taking Steps*; *Blue Remembered Hills*; *A Prayer for Wings*; *Little Shop of Horrors*; *The Caretaker*; *One Flew Over the Cuckoo's Nest*; *One for the Road* plus annual Christmas musicals.

Traverse Theatre

Cambridge Street, Edinburgh EH1 2ED
☎0131 228 3223 Fax 0131 229 8443
✉ dave@traverse.co.uk
www.traverse.co.uk

Artistic Director *Philip Howard*
Literary Manager *Katherine Mendelsohn*
Literary Assistant *Dave Overend*

The Traverse is Scotland's only new writing theatre, with a particular commitment to producing new Scottish plays. However, it also has a strong international programme of work in translation and visiting companies. Previous productions include *The People Next Door* Henry Adam; *Dark Earth* David Harrower; *15 Seconds* François Archambarlt, version by Isabel Wright; *Iron* Rona Munro; *Outlying Islands* David Greig; *Gagarin Way* Gregory Burke; *Perfect Days* Liz Lochhead. Please address unsolicited scripts to *Dave Overend*, Literary Assistant.

Trestle Theatre Company

Trestle Arts Base, Russet Drive, St Albans
AL4 0JQ
☎01727 850950 Fax 01727 855558
✉ admin@trestle.org.uk
www.trestle.org.uk

Artistic Director *Emily Gray*

Founded 1981. Some devised work, but increasing collaboration with writers to create new writing for touring visual/physical performance work and also local community projects. No unsolicited scripts.

Tricycle Theatre

269 Kilburn High Road, London NW6 7JR
☎020 7372 6611 Fax 020 7328 0795
www.tricycle.co.uk

Artistic Director *Nicolas Kent*

Founded 1980. Plays to a very mixed audience, in terms of both culture and class. Previous productions: *Stones in his Pockets* Marie Jones; *The Stephen Lawrence Enquiry – The Colour of Justice* adapt. from the enquiry transcripts by Richard Norton-Taylor; *Nuremberg* adapt. from transcripts of the trials by Richard Norton-Taylor; *Joe Turner's Come and Gone*, *The Piano Lesson* and *Two Trains Runnin'* all by August Wilson; *Kat and the Kings* David Kramer. New writing welcome from women and ethnic minorities (particularly Black, Asian and Irish). Looks for a strong narrative drive with popular appeal, not 'studio' plays. Fee: £12 per script. Supplies written reader's report. Can only return scripts if postage coupons or s.a.e. are enclosed with original submission.

Tron Theatre Company

63 Trongate, Glasgow G1 5HB
☎0141 552 3748 Fax 0141 552 6657
✉ ali.curran@tron.co.uk
www.tron.co.uk

Director *Ali Curran*

Founded 1981. Plays to a broad cross-section of Glasgow and beyond, including international tours. Recent productions: *Pyrenees* David Greig (co-production with Paines Plough); *Half Life* John Mighton (co-production with Necessary Angel Theatre Company, Canada and Perth Rep); *Ubu the King* adapted by David Greig (co-production with Dundee Rep, BITE05, Barbican and the Young Vic as part of 'Young Genius'). Interested in ambitious plays by UK and international writers. No unsolicited scripts.

Unicorn Theatre for Children

147 Tooley Street, More London, London SE1 2HZ
☎020 7645 0500 Fax 020 7645 0550
✉ stagedoor@unicorntheatre.com
www.unicorntheatre.com

Artistic Director *Tony Graham*
Literary Manager *Carl Miller*

Founded 1947, resident at the Arts Theatre from 1967 to 1999 and now based at the new Unicorn Children's Centre with two theatres. Produces full-length professionally performed plays for children, aged 4–12, their teachers and families. Recent work includes *Old King Cole* by Ken Campbell; *Rama and Sita: Path of Flames* and *Clockwork* by Philip Pullman, adapt. David Wood and Stephen McNeff. Does not produce unsolicited scripts but works with commissioned writers. Writers interested in working with the company should e-mail artistic@unicorntheatre.com, requesting further information.

Upstairs at the Gatehouse

See **Ovation Productions** under *Film, TV and Radio Producers*

Charles Vance Productions

See **CV Productions**

Warehouse Theatre

Dingwall Road (adjacent to East Croydon Station), Croydon CR0 2NF
☎020 8681 1257
✉ info@warehousetheatre.co.uk
www.warehousetheatre.co.uk

Artistic Director *Ted Craig*

South London's new writing theatre seats 90–100 and produces up to six new plays a year. Also co-produces with, and hosts, selected touring companies who share the theatre's commitment to new work. The theatre continues to build upon a tradition of discovering and nurturing new writers through the **International Playwriting Festival** (see entry under *Festivals*). Also runs a vigorous writers' workshop at the end of each month and hosts youth theatre workshops and Saturday morning children's theatre. Scripts will get a faster response if submitted through the International Playwriting Festival.

Watford Palace Theatre
Clarendon Road, Watford WD17 1JZ
☎01923 235455 Fax 01923 819664
✉ enquiries@watfordtheatre.co.uk
www.watfordtheatre.co.uk

Artistic Director *Lawrence Till*
Literary Director *Joyce Branagh*

Reopened in Autumn 2004, following an £8.7 million refurbishment. An important part of artistic and cultural policy is the commissioning of new plays and to discover major new playwrights and new plays of enduring stature to be produced in the region. Recent new plays: *One Last Card Trick* Stewart Permutt; *Queen's English* Vanessa Brooks; *Flying Under Bridges* Sarah Daniels; *Get Ken Barlow* Ian Kershaw; *Elton John's Glasses* David Farr (1997 Writers' Guild Best Regional Play award); *The Talented Mr Ripley* Phyllis Nagy; *The Dark* Jonathan Holloway; *The Late Middle Classes* Simon Gray (1999 Barclays/TMA Best New Play Award); *Big Night Out at the Little Palace Theatre* Sandi Toksvig and Dillie Keane.

West Yorkshire Playhouse
Playhouse Square, Leeds LS2 7UP
☎0113 213 7800 Fax 0113 213 7250
✉ alex.chisholm@wyp.org.uk
www.wyp.org.uk
Literary Manager *Alex Chisholm*

Committed to working with new writing originating from or set in the Yorkshire and Humberside region. New writing from outside the region is programmed usually where writer or company is already known to the theatre. The Playhouse runs workshops, courses and writers' events including Thursday Night Live, an open platform held at the theatre for local writers and performers. For more information contact the Literary Manager, ☎0113 213 7286 or e-mail to address above. Scripts should be submitted with s.a.e. for return. 'Not all submitted scripts will be read. You are strongly advised

to check guidelines on the website *before* submitting.'

Whirligig Theatre
14 Belvedere Drive, Wimbledon, London SW19 7BY
☎020 8947 1732 Fax 020 8879 7648
✉ whirligig-theatre@virgin.net
Contact *David Wood*

Occasional productions and tours to major theatre venues, usually a musical for primary school audiences and weekend family groups. Interested in scripts which exploit the theatrical nature of children's tastes. Previous productions: *The See-Saw Tree*; *The Selfish Shellfish*; *The Gingerbread Man*; *The Old Man of Lochnagar*; *The Ideal Gnome Expedition*; *Save the Human*; *Dreams of Anne Frank*; *Babe, the Sheep-Pig*.

White Bear Theatre Club
138 Kennington Park Road, London SE11 4DJ
Administration: 3 Dante Road, Kennington, London SE11 4RB
☎020 7793 9193 Fax 020 7793 9193
Contact *Michael Kingsbury*
Administrator *Julia Parr*

Founded 1988. Output primarily new work for an audience aged 20–35. Unsolicited scripts welcome, particularly new work with a keen eye on contemporary issues, though not agitprop. *Absolution* by Robert Sherwood was nominated by the Writers' Guild for 'Best Fringe Play' and *Spin* by the same author was the *Time Out* Critics' Choice in 2000. The theatre received the *Time Out* award for Best Fringe Venue in 2001 and a Peter Brook award for best up-and-coming venue. In 2004 *Round the Horne ... Revisited* transferred to The Venue, Leicester Square.

Windsor Theatre Royal
See **Theatre Royal Windsor**

The Young Vic
66 The Cut, London SE1 8LZ
☎020 7820 3350 Fax 020 7820 3355
✉ info@youngvic.org
www.youngvic.org
Artistic Director *David Lan*
Executive Director *Kevin Fitzmaurice*

Founded 1970. The Young Vic is a theatre for everyone but, above all, for younger artists and audiences. Produces revivals of classics – old and new – as well as new plays and annual events that embrace both young people and adults.

Festivals

Aberdeen Arts Carnival
Aberdeen Arts Centre, 33 King Street,
Aberdeen AB24 5AA
☎01224 635208
www.aberdeenartscentre.org.uk
Venue Manager *Arthur Deans*

Performances – mainly by local amateurs and arts workshops in drama, music, art, dance and creative writing – take place each summer during the school holidays.

University of Aberdeen Writers Festival
See **Word**

The Aldeburgh Literary Festival
44 High Street, Aldebugh IP15 5AB
☎01728 452389 Fax 01728 452389
✉ johnandmary@aldeburghbookshop.co.uk
www.aldeburghbookshop.co.uk
Festival Organisers *John and Mary James*

Founded 2002. Held on the first weekend in March. The programme includes literary workshops, a literary dinner, and talks. Previous speakers have included Beryl Bainbridge, Alan Bennett, Craig Brown, Richard Dawkins, Lady Antonia Fraser, Michael Frayn, Anthony Horowitz, P.D. James, Doris Lessing, David Lodge, Ian McEwan, Harold Pinter, Matt Ridley, Alexander McCall Smith, Claire Tomalin, Salley Vickers, A.N. Wilson.

Aldeburgh Poetry Festival
The Poetry Trust, The Cut, 9 New Cut,
Halesworth IP19 8BY
☎01986 835950 Fax 01986 835949
✉ info@thepoetrytrust.org
www.thepoetrytrust.org
Director *Naomi Jaffa*

Founded 1989. An annual celebration of international contemporary poetry, held annually on the first weekend in November. Features poetry readings, performances, talks, public masterclass, workshops, discussions, Writer-in-Residence and a children's event. Also includes a reading by the winner of the annual **Jerwood Aldeburgh First Collection Prize** (see entry under **Prizes**).

Aspects Literature Festival
North Down Borough Council, Town Hall,
The Castle, Bangor BT20 4BT
☎028 9127 8032 Fax 028 9127 1370
✉ gail.prentice@northdown.gov.uk
Festival Coordinator/Arts Officer *Gail Prentice*

Founded 1992. 'Ireland's Premier Literary Festival' is held at the end of September and celebrates the richness and diversity of living Irish writers with occasional special features on past generations. It draws upon all disciplines – fiction (of all types), poetry, theatre, non-fiction, cinema, song-writing, etc. It also includes a day of writing for young readers and sends writers to visit local schools during the festival. Highlights of recent festivals include appearances by Bernard MacLaverty, Marion Keyes, Alice Taylor, Frank Delaney, Seamus Heaney, Brian Keenan and Fergal Keane.

Bath Literature Festival
Administration Office: Bath Festivals Trust, 5 Broad Street, Bath BA1 5LJ
☎01225 462231 Fax 01225 445551
✉ info@bathfestivals.org.uk
www.bathlitfest.org.uk

Box Office: Bath Festivals Box Office, 2 Church Street, Abbey Green, Bath BA1 1NL
☎01225 463362
✉ boxoffice@bathfestivals.org.uk
Artistic Director *Sarah LeFanu*

Founded 1995. This annual festival (held in March) programmes over 100 different literary events from debates and lectures to readers' groups and workshops in venues throughout the city. In addition there are a number of events for children and young people. Previous featured writers Tony Benn, Kazuo Ishiguro, Andrea Levy, Peter Porter, Oliver Sacks, Sue Townsend.

Bay Lit
Academi, Mount Stuart House, Mount Stuart Square, Cardiff CF10 5FQ
☎029 2047 2266 Fax 029 2049 2930
✉ post@academi.org
www.academi.org
Chief Executive *Peter Finch*

Annual literature festival held in Cardiff Bay, featuring writers from Wales and beyond. Lectures, readings, performances, workshops and book launches in English and Welsh. Dates and further details available on the Academi website. Writers who appeared in recent festivals include: Ian McMillan, Fay Weldon, Simon Singh, Helen Oyeyemi and Will Self.

Belfast Festival at Queen's
8 Fitzwilliam Street, Belfast BT9 6AW
☎028 9097 1034 Fax 028 9097 1336
✉ g.farrow@qub.ac.uk
www.belfastfestival.com

Director *Graeme Farrow*

Founded 1964. Annual three-week festival held in October/November. Organised by Queen's University, the festival covers a wide variety of events, including literature. Programme available in September.

Beverley Literature Festival
Wordquake, Libraries and Information, Council Offices, Skirlaugh HU11 5HN
☎01482 392745 Fax 01482 392710
✉ john@bevlit.org
www.beverley-literature-festival.org

Festival Director *John Clarke*

Founded 2002. Annual October festival which has acquired 'a national reputation for commissioning and hosting quality poetry events'. Also covers all other literary genres and mixes readings and performanes with author-led readers' groups and creative writing workshops. Held in intimate and historic venues across Beverley.

Birmingham Book Festival
See **Orange Birmingham Book Festival**

Book Now!
The Arts Team, Orleans House Gallery, Riverside, Twickenham TW1 3DJ
✉ artsinfo@richmond.gov.uk
www.richmond.gov.uk/arts

Founded 1992. Annual three-week festival held in November, administered by the Arts Section of Richmond Council. Previous guests include U.A. Fanthorpe, Andrew Lambert, Sally Gardner, Kate Adie, Michelle Paver, David Attenborough, David McDowall, John Harding, Carl Honoré, Anna Swan, Clive Aslet, Anthony Majanlahti.

Bradford Book Festival
Central Library, Princes Way, Bradford BD1 1NN
☎01274 433915
✉ paula.truman@bradford.gov.uk

Contact *Paula Truman*

Founded in 1999, the festival is organised by Bradford Libraries and held during first two weeks in June.

Brighton Festival
Festival Office, 12a Pavilion Buildings, Castle Square, Brighton BN1 1EE
☎01273 700747 Fax 01273 707505
✉ info@brightonfestival.org
www.brightonfestival.org

Contact *General Manager*

Founded 1966. For 24 days every May, Brighton hosts England's largest mixed arts festival. Music, dance, theatre, film, opera, literature, comedy and exhibitions. Literary enquiries will be passed to the literature officer. Deadline October for following May.

Bristol Poetry Festival
The Poetry Can, Unit 11, 20–23 Hepburn Road, Bristol BS2 8UD
☎0117 942 6976 Fax 0117 944 1478
✉ info@poetrycan.co.uk
www.poetrycan.co.uk

Festival Director *Colin Brown*

Founded 1995. Annual festival taking place across the city every September (7–17th in 2006). A celebration of the best in local, national and international contemporary poetry, from readings and performances to cabaret and slam and open mic. 'Where words mean more than a spin in the dark.'

Broadstairs Dickens Festival
10 Lanthorne Road, Broadstairs CT10 3NH
☎01843 861827 Fax 01843 861827
www.broadstairs.gov.uk/DickensFestival.html

Organiser *Sylvia Hawkes*

Founded 1937 to commemorate the 100th anniversary of Charles Dickens' first visit to Broadstairs in 1837, which he continued to visit until 1859. The Festival lasts for nine days in June and events include an opening gala concert, a parade, a performance of a Dickens play (*Hard Times* in 2006), duels, melodramas, Dickens readings, a Victorian cricket match, Victorian bathing parties, talks, music hall, three-day Victorian country fair. Costumed Dickensian ladies in crinolines with top-hatted escorts promenade during the week.

Cambridge History Festival
Indicombe, West Buckland, Barnstaple EX32 0SE
☎01598 760367

✉ wh@histfest.com
www.histfest.com
Contacts *Derek Wilson, Ruth Wilson*
Annual three-day festival held in August in the heart of the university. The major networking event for all popular history enthusiasts – academics, historical novelists, popular historians, TV producers and presenters, museum and gallery staff. Varied programme includes talks, presentations, displays, discussions, concerts of period music, publishers' receptions, etc. Programmes available from April. Among the speakers who have appeared are David Starkey, Beryl Bainbridge, Louis de Bernières, Timothy West, Tracy Chevalier, Diarmaid MacCulloch, John Guy, Richard Holmes, Felipe Fernández-Armesto, Conn Iggulden, Lisa Jardine, Prunella Scales and Terry Jones.

Cambridge Wordfest

☎01223 264404
✉ cam.wordfest@btinternet.com
www.cambridgewordfest.co.uk
Festival Director *Cathy Moore*

An annual spring festival for writers as well as readers which takes place at various venues across Cambridge and the surrounding area. A weekend event packed with the best of contemporary writing, poetry, political debate, events for children and writing workshops.

Camelford Poetry Festival Workshops

The Indian King, Garmoe Cottage, 2 Trefrew Road, Camelford PL32 9TP
☎01840 212161
✉ indianking@btconnect.com
www.indianking.org.uk
Director *Helen Wood*
Founded 1997 as the Jon Silkin Memorial Poetry Festival. Jon Silkin taught annual poetry workshops and readings to raise funds for the Centre, and the festival was held to honour his life and work. Held annually close to Easter in Camelford, the central town in North Cornwall, the festival consists of workshops, readings and performances, and a dinner in memory of Jon Silkin. Previous guests have included Fred d'Aguilar, Sara Jane Arbury, John Branfield, Ann Gray, John Greening, Philip Gross, Derrek Hines, Christopher Logue, William Oxley, Ian Parks, Fiona Sampson, Myra Schneider and Dilys Wood. Book for individual events or buy a ticket for the whole festival.

Canterbury Festival

Christ Church Gate, The Precincts,
Canterbury CT1 2EE
☎01227 452853 Fax 01227 781830
✉ info@canterburyfestival.co.uk
Festival Director *Rosie Turner*

Canterbury provides a unique location for the largest festival of arts and culture in the region, showcasing local, national and international talent in classical and contemporary music, world theatre, opera, comedy, dance, talks, walks and community events.

Centre for Creative & Performing Arts Spring Literary Festival at UEA

University of East Anglia, School of Literature and Creative Writing, Norwich NR4 7TJ
☎01603 592810
✉ v.striker@uea.ac.uk
www.uea.ac.uk/eas/events/intro.shtml
Contact *Val Striker*

Founded 1993. Annual event held in the spring and autumn.

Charleston Festival

The Charleston Trust, Charleston, Nr Firle,
Nr Lewes BN8 6LL
☎01323 811626
✉ info@charleston.org.uk
www.charleston.org.uk
Festival Programmer *Diana Reich*

Annual literary festival held in May over nine days. Novelists, biographers, travel writers, broadcasters, poets, food writers, actors and artists gather at Charleston, the country home of the Bloomsbury Group. Past speakers include Margaret Atwood, Alan Bennett, Jeanette Winterson, Louis de Bernières, Patti Smith, Paula Rego, Clive James, Ali Smith, Roger McGough, Germaine Greer and Harold Pinter.

The Cheltenham Festival of Literature

Town Hall, Imperial Square, Cheltenham
GL50 1QA
☎01242 263494 Fax 01242 256457
✉ clair.greenaway@cheltenham.gov.uk
www.cheltenhamfestivals.co.uk
Festival Manager *Clair Greenaway*

Founded 1949. Annual festival held in October. The first purely literary festival of its kind, this festival has over the past decade developed from an essentially local event into the largest and most popular in Europe. A wide range of events including talks and lectures, poetry readings, novelists in conversation, exhibitions, discussions and a large bookshop.

Chester Literature Festival

Viscount House, River Lane, Saltney, Chester CH4 8RH
☎01244 674020 Fax 01244 680037
✉ info@chesterlitfest.org.uk
www.chester-literary-festival.org.uk
Chairman *Bill Hughes*

Founded 1989. Annual festival (30th September–27th October in 2006). Events include international and nationally known writers, as well as events by local literary groups. There is a Literary Lunch and a Festival Dinner, events for children, workshops and competitions. Free mailing list.

Children's Books Ireland – Annual Festival

See **Children's Books Ireland** under *Professional Associations and Societies*

Dartington Literary Festival

See **Ways With Words**

Derby's Festival of Words

Derby City Council, Roman House, Friar Gate, Derby DE1 1XB
☎01332 715434
✉ alex.davis@derby.gov.uk
Literature Development Officer *Alex Davis*

A biannual celebration of words in all their forms. Derby's Festival of Words takes in poetry, novels, storytelling, graphic novels, children's writing, reading and games. Runs for ten days in mid-October.

Derbyshire Literature Festival

c/o Arts Office, Derbyshire County Council, Cultural & Community Services Department, Alfreton Library, Severn Square, Alfreton DE55 7BQ
☎01773 832497 Fax 01773 831359
✉ ann.wright@derbyshire.gov.uk
www.derbyshire.gov.uk
Festival Organiser *Ann Wright*

Founded 2000. The festival takes place in June every two years and covers the whole county. The festival programming includes all types of live literature events; performance poetry, theatre, talks, readers' groups, workshops, dramatised readings, signings, storytelling and literary trails,

as well as a number of cross-art form events. The festival takes place in libraries and many other community venues including heritage centres, industrial buildings, stately homes, parks and moors, churches and schools and is specifically designed to reach as many different communities and geographical areas in the county as possible.

Dorchester Festival

Dorchester Arts Centre, School Lane, The Grove, Dorchester DT1 1XR
☎01305 266926 Fax 01305 266143
✉ enquiries@dorchesterarts.org.uk
www.dorchesterarts.org.uk
Artistic Director *Sharon Hayden*

Founded 1996. A biennial five-day international festival held over early May Bank Holiday (next takes place in 2007) which includes performance, live music and visual arts with associated educational and community projects. Also three days of free events various venues around the town, including literature and poetry.

The Daphne du Maurier Festival of Arts & Literature

Restormel Borough Council, Penwinnick Road, St Austell PL25 5DR
☎01726 223535
www.dumaurierfestival.co.uk

Founded 1997. Annual festival, held in Fowey over ten days in May (10–19th in 2007). Guests at the 2006 Festival included Jonathan Miller, Kate Adie, Germaine Greer, Cathy Lette, Miles Kington, Sir David Frost, Carol Drinkwater and Tony Hawks.

Dumfries and Galloway Arts Festival

Gracefield Arts Centre, 28 Edinburgh Road, Dumfries DG1 1JQ
☎01387 260447 Fax 01387 260447
✉ info@dgartsfestival.org.uk
www.dgartsfestival.org.uk
Festival Organiser *Mrs Barbara Kelly*

Founded 1980. Annual week-long festival held at the end of May with a variety of events including classical and folk music, theatre, dance, literary events, exhibitions and children's events.

Durham Literature Festival

Durham City Arts, 2 The Cottages, Fowlers Yard, Back Silver Street, Durham DH1 3RA
☎0191 301 8245 Fax 0191 301 8821
✉ info@durhamcityarts.demon.co.uk
Festival Coordinator *Alison Lister*

Founded 1989. Annual 2–3-week festival now held in September/October at various locations in the city. Performances and readings plus workshops, cabaret, exhibitions and other events.

Edinburgh International Book Festival

5a Charlotte Square, Edinburgh EH2 4DR
☎0131 718 5666 Fax 0131 226 5335
✉ admin@edbookfest.co.uk
www.edbookfest.co.uk

Director *Catherine Lockerbie*

Founded 1983. 'The world's largest and most dynamic annual book event.' Takes place over 17 days in Edinburgh each August. An extensive programme showcases the work of the world's top authors and thinkers to an audience of over 200,000 adults and children. Featuring workshops, readings, lectures and a high profile debate and discussion series.

Falmouth Festival of Literature & Arts

56 Killigrew Street, Falmouth TR11 3PP
☎01326 211522
✉ admin@falmouthfestival.co.uk
www.falmouthfestival.co.uk

Festival Director *Kirsten Whiting*

Founded 2003. Held annually in October, the Festival brings together international and local authors for adults and children alike at various venues in the seaside town of Falmouth. Talks, readings, workshops, music, discussion, art and performance make up three full days and nights of literary and artistic celebration.

Fife Festival of Authors

Fife Council Libraries – Central Area,
Libraries HQ, East Fergus Place, Kirkcaldy KY1 1XT
☎01592 412938
✉ fife.libraries@fife.gov.uk

Contact *June Souter*

Founded 1996. Annual festival running in March/April for adults and children (not held in 2005). Aims to bring the best of modern writing to the public as well as stimulate and foster creative writing within the local communities. Author readings, poetry events, writing workshops, literary competitions and dramatic presentations feature in the programme.

Folkestone Literary Festival

The Metropole Arts Centre, The Leas,
Folkestone CT20 2LS

☎01303 244706
✉ info@folkestonelitfest.com
www.folkestonelitfest.com

Festival Director *Nick Ewbank*

Annual festival. Tours, discussions, talks and readings. 2006 festival: 10–18th November.

Frome Festival

25 Market Place, Frome BA11 1AH
☎01373 453889
✉ office@fromefestival.co.uk
www.fromefestival.co.uk

Festival Director *Martin Bax*

An annual festival held from the first Friday in July for ten days celebrating all aspects of visual and performing arts and entertainment and with a strong literary element. Features music, film, dance, drama and visual arts plus readings, talks and workshops. Previous literary guests have included nationally renowned writers as well as local authors.

Graham Greene Festival

See **Graham Greene Birthplace Trust** under *Literary Societies*

The Guardian Hay Festival

25 Lion Street, Hay-on-Wye HR3 5AD
☎0870 787 2848 Fax 01497 821066
www.hayfestival.com

Festival Director *Peter Florence*

Founded 1988. Annual May festival sponsored by *The Guardian*. Also has a children's programme which began in 2003. The event coincides with half term and caters for young children through to teenage. Guests have included Paul McCartney, Bill Clinton, Salman Rushdie, Toni Morrison, Stephen Fry, Joseph Heller, Carlos Fuentes, Maya Angelou, Amos Oz, Arthur Miller.

Guildford Book Festival

c/o Tourist Information Centre, 15 Tunsgate,
Guildford GU1 3QT
☎01483 444334
✉ deputy@guildfordbookfestival.co.uk
www.guildfordbookfestival.co.uk

Book Festival Director *Glenis Pycraft*

Founded 1990. Patrons: Elizabeth Buchan, Michael Buerk, Sandi Toksvig, Fay Weldon, Timothy West and Jacqueline Wilson. Held annually, during October in venues throughout the ancient town of Guildford. The festival includes events with established and new writers, workshops, poetry performances, children's events, adult short story competition and the **Goss First**

Novel Award (see entry under *Prizes*). This diverse festival aims to involve, instruct and entertain all who care about literature. Guest authors in 2005 included Nicholas Evans, Simon Hoggart, Penny Vincenzi, Richard Holmes, Tom Holland, Ian McMillan, Joanne Harris, Ned Sherrin, Ian Rankin, Michael Connelly, Mark Billingham, Bettany Hughes.

Haringey Literature

Collage Arts, The Chocolate Factory, Clarendon Road, London N22 6XJ
☎020 8829 1317 Fax 020 8365 8686/020 8829 8962 (ticket office)
✉ dana@collage-arts.org
www.collage-arts.org

Programme Organiser *Dana Captainino*

Founded 1995. An annual literature programme which is a mixture of poetry and literature in the form of readings, discussions, workshops and residencies. A regular feature is *Poetry and Poppadums* featuring top and up-and-coming poets in the setting of the Karamel Club next to La Kera, Indian restaurant in Chocolate Factory 2. Writers who have appeared in the past include Lemn Sissay, Zena Edwards, Tim Turnbull, Kat Francois, Matthew Sweeney, Fay Weldon.

Harrogate Crime Writing Festival

See **Theakston's Old Peculier Harrogate Crime Writing Festival**

Harrogate International Festival

1 Victoria Avenue, Harrogate HG1 1EQ
☎01423 562303 Fax 01423 521264
✉ info@harrogate-festival.org.uk
www.harrogate-festival.org.uk

Festival Director *William Culver-Dodds*
Festival Manager *Sharon Canavar*

Founded 1966. Annual two-week festival at the end of July and beginning of August. Events include international symphony orchestras, chamber concerts, ballet, celebrity recitals, contemporary dance, opera, drama, jazz and comedy.

Harwich Festival of the Arts

2A Kings Head Street, Harwich CO12 3EG
☎01255 503571
✉ anna@rendell-knights.freeserve.co.uk
Contact *Anna Rendell-Knights*

Founded 1980. Annual ten-day summer festival held in June/July. Events include concerts, drama, film, dance, art, exhibitions, historic town walks. The 2006 Festival commemorated

Christopher Newport and the founding of James Town, Virginia.

The Hay Festival

See **The Guardian Hay Festival**

Hebden Bridge Arts Festival

New Oxford House, Albert Street, Hebden Bridge HX7 4AH
☎01422 842684
✉ hbartsfestival@hotmail.com *or* enid.stephenson@3-c.coop
www.hebdenbridge.co.uk/festival

Contact *Enid Stephenson*

Founded 1994. Annual arts festival with increasingly strong adult and children's literature events. Previous guest writers include Roger McGough, Benjamin Zephaniah, Anne Fine, Juliet Barker, Jacqueline Wilson, Pete McCarthy, Ian McMillan, Adele Geras.

Humber Mouth –
Hull Literature Festival

City Arts Unit, Central Library, Albion Street, Kingston upon Hull HU1 3TF
☎01482 616961 Fax 01482 616827
✉ humbermouth@gmail.com
www.humbermouth.org.uk

Contact *Maggie Hannan*, City Arts Unit

Founded 1992. Hull's largest festival, held in the summer, and one of the region's liveliest events. Features readings, talks, performances and workshops by writers and artists from around the world and from the city.

Ilkley Literature Festival

The Manor House, 2 Castle Hill, Ilkley LS29 9DT
☎01943 601210 Fax 01943 817079
✉ admin@ilkleyliteraturefestival.org.uk
www.ilkleyliteraturefestival.org.uk

Director *Rachel Feldberg*

Founded 1973. Major literature festival in the north held over 17 days every October. Includes children's literature weekend and Festival fringe. Recent guests include Maya Angelou, Alan Bennett, Benjamin Zephaniah, P.D. James, Donna Tartt, Kate Adie, Liz Lochhead, Ian Rankin. Telephone or e-mail to join free mailing list.

Imagine: Writers and Writing for Children

See **Royal Festival Hall Literature & Talks**

The International Festival of Mountaineering Literature

15 Ednaston Court, Ednaston, Ashbourne DE6 3BA
☎01335 360581 Fax 01333 439148
✉ terrygifford@gonuts4free.com
www.festivalofmountaineeringliterature.co.uk
Director *Terry Gifford*
Founded 1987. Annual one-day festival held at the University of Leeds, Bretton Hall Campus in Wakefield. Taking place in March, the Festival celebrates recent books, commissions new writing, gives overviews of national literatures, holds debates of issues, book signings and discussion with the Chair of Judges of the adjudication of the annual **Boardman Tasker Award** for the best mountaineering book of the year. Announces the winner of the festival writing competition run in conjunction with *Climb* magazine. Write to join free mailing list.

International Playwriting Festival

Warehouse Theatre, Dingwall Road, Croydon CR0 2NF
☎020 8681 1257 Fax 020 8688 6699
✉ info@warehousetheatre.co.uk
www.warehousetheatre.co.uk
Festival Administrator *Rose Marie Vernon*
Founded 1985. Annual competition for full-length unperformed plays, judged by a panel of theatre professionals. Finalists given rehearsed readings during the festival week in November. Entries welcome from all parts of the world. Scripts plus two s.a.e.s (one script-sized) should reach the theatre by the end of June, accompanied by an entry form (available online or from the theatre). Previous winners produced at the theatre include: Kevin Hood *Beached*; Ellen Fox *Conversations with George Sandburgh After a Solo Flight Across the Atlantic*; Guy Jenkin *Fighting for the Dunghill*; James Martin Charlton *Fat Souls*; Peter Moffat *Iona Rain*; Dino Mahoney *YoYo*; Simon Smith *Fat Janet is Dead*; Dominic McHale *The Resurrectionists*; Philip Edwards *51 Peg*; Roumen Shomov *The Dove*; Maggie Nevill *The Shagaround*; Andrew Shakeshaft *Just Sitting*. Shares plays with its partner festival in Italy, the Premio Candoni Arta Terme.

Isle of Man Literature Festival

Isle of Man Arts Council, 10 Villa Marina Arcade, Douglas IM1 2HN
☎01624 611316 Fax 01624 615423
✉ dawn.maddrell@iomartscouncil.dtl.gov.im

Contact *Arts Development Manager*
Founded 1997. Regular programme of literature events throughout the year.

King's Lynn, The Fiction Festival

19 Tuesday Market Place, King's Lynn PE30 1JW
☎01553 691661 (office hours) or 761919
Fax 01553 691779
Contact *Anthony Ellis*
Founded 1989. Annual weekend festival held in March. Over the weekend there are readings and discussions, attended by guest writers of which there are usually eight. Previous guests have included Beryl Bainbridge, Louis de Bernière, John Buchan, Jane Gardam, Maggie Gee, Adele Geras, Julian Rathbone, William Riviere, Toby Litt and David Mitchell.

King's Lynn, The Poetry Festival

19 Tuesday Market Place, King's Lynn PE30 1JW
☎01553 691661 (office hours) or 761919
Fax 01553 691779
Contact *Anthony Ellis*
Founded 1985. Annual weekend festival held at the end of September, with guest poets (usually eight). Previous guests have included Alan Brownjohn, Clive James, Les Murray, Peter Porter, D.M. Thomas and Kit Wright.

Knutsford Literature Festival

☎01565 722738/07050 183417
✉ knutsfordlitfest@yahoo.co.uk
www.knutsfordlitfest.blogspot.com
Contact *Charlotte Peters Rock*
An annual two-week festival, held at the beginning of October to celebrate writing and performance by distinguished national, international and local authors. Events include readings and discussions, a literary lunch and theatrical performances.

Lancaster LitFest

PO Box 751, Lancaster LA1 9AS
☎01524 62166
✉ andy.darby@litfest.org
www.litfest.org

Founded 1978. Regional Literature Development Agency, organising workshops, readings, residencies, publications. Year-round programme of literature-based events and annual festival in November featuring a wide range of writers from the UK and overseas.

Ledbury Poetry Festival

Church Lane, Ledbury HR8 1DH
☎0845 458 1743
✉ info@poetry-festival.com
www.poetry-festival.com
Contact *Dr Charles Bennett*

Founded 1997. Annual ten-day festival held in July. Includes readings, discussions, workshops, exhibitions, music and walks. There is also an extensive year-round community programme and a national poetry competition. Past guests have included Andrew Motion, Benjamin Zephaniah, Simon Armitage, Roger McGough, John Hegley and Germaine Greer. Full programme available in May.

Lewes Live Literature Festival

PO Box 2766, Lewes BN7 2WF
☎01273 401100   Fax 01273 401100
✉ info@leweslivelit.co.uk
www.leweslivelit.co.uk
Artistic Director *Mark Hewitt*

Founded 1995. Lewes Live Literature Festival is a three-day intensive event, held in late October/early November. Areas of programming include poetry, fiction, non-fiction, art, art history, music, theatre, film, TV. Events include readings, performances, lectures, workshops, screenings of film and video, exhibitions. LLL also runs year-round creative writing workshops and courses led by established professionals.

Lichfield Festival

7 The Close, Lichfield WS13 7LD
☎01543 306270   Fax 01543 306274
✉ lichfield.fest@lichfield-arts.org.uk
www.lichfieldfestival.org
Festival Director *Richard Hawley*

Founded 1982. Annual July festival with events taking place in the 13th century Cathedral, the new Lichfield Garrick Theatre, and various country churches and outdoor venues. Mainly music but a growing programme of literary events such as poetry, plays and talks.

City of London Festival

12–14 Mason's Avenue, London EC2V 5BB
☎020 7796 4949
✉ admin@colf.org
www.colf.org
Director *Ian Ritchie*

Founded 1962. Annual three-week festival held in June and July. Features over fifty classical and popular music events alongside poetry and prose readings, street theatre and open-air

extravaganzas, in some of the most outstanding performance spaces in the world.

Lowdham Book Festival

The Bookcase, 50 Main Street, Lowdham NG14 7BE
☎0115 966 4143
✉ janestreeter@thebookcase.co.uk
www.lowdhambookfestival.co.uk
Contact *Jane Streeter*

Founded 1999. Annual nine-day festival combining a village fête atmosphere with that of a major literature festival. Guests have included Carol Ann Duffy, Polly Toynbee, Ian McMillan, Alan Sillitoe, Jackie Kay, Gary Younge and Carole Blake. Talks on everything from St Kilda to the Jewish roots of rock 'n' roll.

Ludlow Festival

Castle Square, Ludlow SY8 1AY
☎01584 875070 (Admin)/872150 (Box Office)   Fax 01584 877673
✉ admin@ludlowfestival.co.uk
www.ludlowfestival.co.uk
Contact *Festival Manager*

Now in its 47th year, the 2006 Festival ran for two weeks with an open-air Shakespeare production held at Ludlow Castle, street events and a varied programme including recitals, opera, dance, popular and classical concerts, literary and historical lectures.

Manchester Literature Festival

3rd Floor, 24 Lever Street, Manchester M1 1DZ
☎0161 236 5725
✉ admin@mlfestival.co.uk
www.mlfestival.co.uk
Contact *Festival Manager*

Held in October, Manchester Literature Festival offers 'unique and imaginative literature experiences to its audiences' with a programme that features readings by some of the world's finest authors, freshly commissioned work, and a series of cutting-edge events exploring the crossover between new technology and literature.

Mere Literary Festival

Lawrence's, Old Hollow, Mere BA12 6EG
☎01747 860475/861211 (Tourist Information)
www.merewilts.org.uk
Contact *Adrienne Howell*

Founded 1997. Annual festival held in the second week of October in aid of registered charity, The Mere & District Linkscheme. Events include readings, quiz, workshop, writer's lunch and talks. Finale is adjudication of the festival's writing competition (see entry under *Prizes*) and presentation of awards.

Arthur Miller Centre Literary Festival at UEA

University of East Anglia, School of American Studies, Norwich NR4 8TJ
☎01603 592810
✉ v.striker@uea.ac.uk
www.uea.ac.uk/eas/events/intro.shtml
Contact *Val Striker*
Founded 1991. Annual autumn festival.

National Association of Writers' Groups (NAWG) Open Festival of Writing

The Arts Centre, Washington NE38 2AB
☎01262 609228
✉ nawg@tesco.net
www.nawg.co.uk
Festival Administrator *Mike Wilson*
Founded 1995. Annual Festival held at St Aidan's College, University of Durham, 1st–3rd September 2006. Three days of creative writing tuition covering poetry, short and long fiction, playwriting, journalism, TV sitcom and many other subjects all led by professional writer-tutors. Workshops, one-to-one tutorials and fringe events. Saturday gala dinner and awards ceremony. Full or part-residential weekend, or single workshops only. Open to all, no qualifications or NAWG membership required.

National Eisteddfod of Wales

40 Parc Ty Glas, Llanishen, Cardiff CF14 5WU
☎029 2076 3777 Fax 029 2076 3737
www.eisteddfod.org.uk

The National Eisteddfod, held in August, is the largest arts festival in Wales, attracting over 170,000 visitors during the week-long celebration of more than 800 years of tradition. Competitions, bardic ceremonies and concerts.

National Student Drama Festival

See **University of Hull** under *UK Writers' Courses*

New Hall School Festival of Literature

New Hall School, Chelmsford CM3 3HS
✉ library@newhallschool.co.uk
www.newhallschool.co.uk
Contact *Jenny Bignold*
Founded 1992, the festival is open to parents, staff and friends. The aim is to widen students' horizons and students from other schools in the town are invited to join in an array of events.

Northern Children's Book Festival

Schools Library Service, Sandhill Centre, Grindon Lane, Sunderland SR3 4EN
☎0191553 8866/7/8 Fax 0191 553 8869
✉ schools.library@sunderland.gov.uk
www.ncbf.org.uk
Secretary *Eleanor Dowley*
Founded 1984. Annual two-week festival during November. Events in schools and libraries for children in the North East region. One Saturday during the festival sees the staging of a large book event hosted by one of the local authorities involved.

Off the Page Literature Festival

County Library Support Services, Glaisdale Parkway, Nottingham NG8 4GP
☎0115 928 6029 Fax 0115 928 6400
✉ alison.hirst@nottscc.gov.uk
Contact *Alison Hirst*
Author visits aimed at making authors accessible to readers. Programme is available from late summer/early autumn.

Off the Shelf Literature Festival

Central Library, Surrey Street, Sheffield S1 1XZ
☎0114 273 4716/4400 Fax 0114 273 5009
✉ offtheshelf@sheffield.gov.uk
www.offtheshelf.org.uk
Festival Organisers *Maria de Souza, Susan Walker, Lesley Webster*
Founded 1992. Annual two-week festival held during the last fortnight in October. Lively and diverse mix of readings, workshops, children's events, storytelling and competitions. Previous guests have included Nick Hornby, Doris Lessing, Benjamin Zephaniah, Terry Pratchett, Michael Palin, Carol Ann Duffy and Louis de Bernières.

Orange Birmingham Book Festival

c/o Book Communications, Unit 116, The Custard Factory, Gibb Street, Birmingham B9 4AA
☎0121 246 2770 Fax 0121 246 2771
✉ jonathan@bookcommunications.co.uk

www.orangebirminghambookfestival.org
Contact *Jonathan Davidson*
Founded 1999. Annual nine-day festival held during October at venues around Birmingham. Also promotes events throughout the year. Includes performances, lectures, discussion events and workshops.

Oundle Festival of Literature

Amherst, 2 Herne Road, Oundle PE8 4BS
☎01832 274960
✉ enquiries@oundlelitfest.org.uk
www.oundlelitfest.org.uk
Festival Deputy Chair *Liz Dillarstone*
Founded 2002. Annual festival running in the first two weeks of March for adults and children. Features talks by high profile authors and poets, writing workshops, poetry and prose showcases for local writers, children's writing competitions, school events, drama productions and community readings for young and old.

Oxford Literary Festival

See **The** *Sunday Times* **Oxford Literary Festival**

Poetry Otherwise

Emerson College, Forest Row RH18 5JX
☎01342 822238   Fax 01342 826055
✉ mail@emerson.org.uk
www.emerson.org.uk
www.poetryotherwise.org
Director *Paul Matthews*

Held in August. A summer gathering of poets, writers and all lovers of language. Workshops, readings, talks, conversation, practice in the art of speaking poetry. Contributors have included Andrea Hollander Budy, John Freeman, Ashley Ramsden, Andie Lewenstein, Paul Matthews, Peter Abbs, Katherine Pierpoint, Fiona Owen, Lee Harwood, Jay Ramsay, Mimi Khalvati and Roselle Angwin. 'Wholesome food, wonderful Sussex countryside.'

ProudWords Writing Festival

PO Box 181, Newcastle upon Tyne NE6 5XG
☎07973 8949 12
✉ pwcwf@hotmail.com
www.proudwords.org.uk
Contact *Mary Lowe*
Founded 1998. The only writing festival in the UK to celebrate the diversity of literary talent that exists within the gay community. Held annually, the festival includes workshops, bus trips, walking tours, readings, discussions and

performances of both writing and music. ProudWords encourages participation, lively debate, an interest in literature-related activity and offers opportunities for gay people to express themselves in writing in a supportive, friendly atmosphere. Writers at past festivals include Jackie Kay, Julia Darling, Sarah Waters, Jake Arnott, P-P Hartness, Emma Donaghue, Paul Magrs, Stella Duffy, Julia Bell, Val McDermid, Chrissie Glazebrook and Cathal O Searcaigh. 'Lesbians, gay men and bisexuals are invited to Newcastle to discover for themselves the thriving writing culture that exists here.' Other events and courses held throughout the year; contact for further details.

Purple Patch Poetry Convention

25 Griffiths Road, West Bromwich B71 2EH
✉ ppatch66@hotmail.com
www.purplepatchpoetry.co.uk
Contact *Geoff Stevens*
Held at the Barlow Theatre near Birmingham this event celebrates the strength of small press poets. The next Purple Patch Poetry Convention, due to take place in 2007, is a three-day event of poetry readings, talks, workshops and discussions. Admission charges are kept very low, payments to participants being low to non-existent. The Convention's aims are quality and an opportunity to participate. Poets at past festivals have included Ray Avery, R.G. Bishop, Tilla Brading, Gerald England, J.F. Haines, Brendan Hawthorne, Martin Holroyd, Mike Hoy, Eamer O'Keeffe, Carolyn King, Paul McDonald, Bob Mee, Les Merton, Michael Newman, Simon Pitt, Andy Robson, Sam Smith and Steve Sneyd. Monthly poetry readings are held at the Barlow Theatre with open mic, guest poet, music and residents Unleaded Petrels.

Redbridge Book and Media Festival

Arts Team, Culture, Sport and Community Learning, 8th Floor, Lynton House, 255–259 High Road, Ilford IG1 1NY
☎020 8708 3532   Fax 020 8708 3178
www.redbridge.gov.uk
Contact *Arts Development Officer*
Founded in 2003, the festival celebrates literature in all its forms, and takes place annually over two weeks in April/May. Features a programme of author readings, book signings, creative writing classes, school-based workshops, community events, performance poetry evenings, competitions, exhibitions and panel debates.

Royal Court Young Writers Programme

The Site, Royal Court Theatre, Sloane Square, London SW1W 8AS
☎020 7565 5050 Fax 020 7565 5001
✉ ywp@royalcourttheatre.com
www.royalcourttheatre.com

Associate Director *Ola Animashawun*

Open to young people up to the age of 25. The YWP focuses on the process of playwriting by running a series of writers' groups throughout the year at its base in Sloane Square. Additionally the YWP welcomes unsolicited scripts from all young writers from across the country. 'We are always looking for scripts for development and possible production (not film scripts).'

Royal Festival Hall Literature & Talks

Performing Arts Department, Royal Festival Hall, London SE1 8XX
☎020 7921 0906 Fax 020 7921 0700
✉ awhitehead@rfh.org.uk
www.rfh.org.uk

Head of Literature & Talks *Ruth Borthwick*

The Royal Festival Hall presents a year-round literature programme covering all aspects of writing. Regular series range from A Life Indeed! to Fiction International and there are two biennial festivals: Poetry International and Imagine: Writers and Writing for Children. Literature events are now programmed in the Purcell Room and Queen Elizabeth Hall. To join the free mailing list, call 020 7921 0971 or e-mail: Literature&Talks@rfh.org.uk

Rye Festival

PO Box 33, Rye TN31 7YB
☎01797 224442
✉ info@ryefestival.co.uk
www.ryefestival.co.uk

Director *Tony Clamp*

Founded 1972. Annual two-week September arts event, plus short winter series. Covers music, visual arts, theatre and literature. Write or phone for more information.

The Scottish Book Town Festival

Wigtown Book Town Company, County Buildings, Wigtown DG8 9JH
☎01988 402036 Fax 01988 402506
✉ info@wigtown-booktown.co.uk
www.wigtown-booktown.co.uk

Contact *Jennifer Bradley*

Founded 1999. A rural literary festival which takes place annually at the end of September in Wigtown town centre, many of the town's bookshops and the nearby Bladnoch Distillery. Authors' readings, including children's authors, debates, poetry, music and film.

Southwold Festival

See **Ways with Words**

StAnza: Scotland's Poetry Festival

Registered Office: 57 Lade Braes, St Andrews KY16 9DA
☎01333 360491
✉ info@stanzapoetry.org
www.stanzapoetry.org

Festival Director *Brian Johnstone*
(admin@stanzapoetry.org)
Artistic Director *Eleanor Livingstone*
(arts@stanzapoetry.org)
Children's Programme Manager Jane Petegree
(kids@stanzapoetry.org)

The only regular festival dedicated to poetry in Scotland, StAnza is international in outlook. Held annually in the ancient university town of St Andrews, the festival is an opportunity to hear world class poets reading in exciting and atmospheric venues. The 2006 festival themes were 'Poetry & the Land' and 'Celtic Voices'. The festival, held in March, featured, readings, discussions, conversations, performance poetry, poetry in exhibition, workshops and children's poetry. It also had a strong showing of Irish and Welsh poets and leading Scottish poets as well as the festival's signature foreign language readings. Tickets can be purchased from the Byre Theatre box office on 01334 475000 early in 2007. Free programmes can be ordered from Fife Council Arts on 01592 414714 or by e-mail to arts.development@fife.gov.uk

Stratford-upon-Avon Poetry Festival

The Shakespeare Centre, Henley Street, Stratford-upon-Avon CV37 6QW
☎01789 204016/292176 (box office)
Fax 01789 296083
✉ director@shakespeare.org.uk

Festival Director *Roger Pringle*

Sponsored by the Shakespeare Birthplace Trust, this Festival, now in its 53rd year, features well known actors presenting poetry of past periods, leading contemporary poets reading their own work, a Local Poets evening and a Poetry Mass. The 2006 Festival, held in the summer, included poems by Shakespeare and poetry of later times inspired by his works; a celebration of two major Poet Laureates, Alfred Tennyson and John Betjeman; and verse written by local children for National Poetry Day. Most of the readings take place on Sunday evenings, in Stratford venues.

Strokestown International Poetry Festival
See **Strokestown International Poetry Prize** under *Prizes*

The Sunday Times Oxford Literary Festival
301 Woodstock Road, Oxford OX2 7NY
☎01865 514149 Fax 01865 514804
✉ angela@sundaytimes-oxfordliteraryfestival.co.uk
www.sundaytimes-oxfordliteraryfestival.co.uk
Directors *Sally Dunsmore, Angela Prysor-Jones*
Founded 1997. Annual week-long festival held two weekends prior to Easter. Authors speaking about their books, covering a wide variety of writing: fiction, poetry, biography, travel, food, gardening, children's art. Previous guests have included William Boyd, Andrew Motion, Beryl Bainbridge, Sophie Grigson, Philip Pullman, Doris Lessing, Seamus Heaney, Richard Dawkins, Zandra Rhodes, Kazuro Ishiguro.

Swansea Festivals
Dylan Thomas Centre, Somerset Place, Swansea SA1 1RR
☎01792 463980 Fax 01792 463993
✉ dylanthomas.lit@swansea.gov.uk
www.dylanthomas.com
Contacts *David Woolley, Jo Furber*
Wordplay (held in October): numerous events held throughout the year to celebrate literature and arts for young people. The Dylan Thomas Celebration (October–November) is two weeks of performances, talks, lectures, films, music, poetry, exhibitions and celebrity guests. The Dylan Thomas Centre also runs a year-round programme of literary events; please e-mail for details.

Swindon Festival of Literature
Lower Shaw Farm, Shaw, Swindon SN5 5PJ
☎01793 771080 Fax 01793 771080
✉ swindonlitfest@lowershawfarm.co.uk
www.swindonfestivaloliterature.co.uk
Festival Director *Matt Holland*
Founded 1994. Annual festival held in May, starting with 'Dawn Chorus' at sunrise on May Day. Includes a wide range of authors, speakers,

discussions, performances and workshops, plus the Clive Brain Memorial Lecture and the Swindon Performance Poetry Slam competition. Guests at th 2006 Festival included Kate Adie, Matthew Parris, Anne Widdecombe, Satish Kumar, Bettany Hughes, Melvin Burgess, Marina Lewyzka, Christian Wolmar and John Carey.

Tears in the Fence Festival
38 Hod View, Stourpaine, Blandford Forum DT11 8TN
☎01258 456803
www.thewordtravels.com
Festival Director *David Caddy*
Festival Manager *Jonathan Ward*
Founded 1995. Annual international poetry festival based in London with readings, talks, discussions and workshops continuing the work begun by the Wessex Poetry Festivals, 1995–2001. Previous guests have included Lee Harwood, Elizabeth Cook, Jeremy Reed, Alice Notley, Fred Voss, Joan Jobe Smith, Irina Ratushinskaya, Michele Roberts, Edwin Morgan and Kim Taplin.

Theakston's Old Peculier Harrogate Crime Writing Festival
1 Victoria Avenue, Harrogate HG1 1EQ
☎01423 562303 Fax 01423 521264
✉ crime@harrogate-festival.org.uk
www.harrogate-festival.org.uk
Festival Director *William Culver Dodds*
Festival Manager *Sharon Canavar*
Launched 2003. Weekend of events at the end of July each year featuring the best of British and American crime writers. The inaugural winner of the **Theakston's Old Peculier Prize for the Crime Novel of the Year** was announced at the 2005 Festival (see entry under *Prizes*). Events also include industry 'How to ...' sessions, social events and late night shows. Part of the **Harrogate International Festival**.

The Dylan Thomas Celebration
See **Swansea Festivals**

Ty Newydd Festival
Ty Newydd, Llanystumdwy, Cricieth LL52 0LW
☎01766 522811 Fax 01766 523095
✉ post@tynewydd.org
www.tynewydd.org
Director *Sally Baker*
Biennial, bilingual literature festival held on

alternate years with the Academi's **Bay Lit Festival**. Held in April and run by the National Writers' Centre for Wales, it is located at Ty Newydd Writers' Centre and other venues near Cricieth. Features writers and poets from Wales (working in both English and Welsh) and worldwide. Ty Newydd also holds an annual weekend festival in November devoted solely to Cynghanedd – Welsh strict meter poetry.

Warwick Words
The Court House, Jury Street, Warwick
CV34 4EW
☎01926 427056
✉ info@warwickwords.co.uk
www.warwickwords.co.uk

Founded 2002. Annual venture featuring both living writers and those who have had connections with Warwick – Tolkien, Larkin and Landor in particular. Also workshops and an education programme. A weekend festival of literature and spoken word for all the family. Events at the Bridge House Theatre, St Mary's Church, the Lord Leycester Hospital and other historic buildings around Warwick over the first weekend in October. 2006 Festival: 5–8th October.

Ways with Words
Droridge Farm, Dartington, Totnes TQ9 6JG
☎01803 867373 Fax 01803 863688
✉ admin@wayswithwords.co.uk
www.wayswithwords.co.uk
Festival Director Kay Dunbar

Ways With Words runs three major annual literature festivals. Dartington Hall in south Devon for ten days in July, features over 200 writers giving lectures, readings, interviews, discussions, performances, masterclasses and workshops. Words by the Water is a ten-day festival held in Keswick in March. Southwold, Suffolk, a five-day festival (9–13th Nov. 2006). Also organises writing, reading and painting courses in Italy.

Wellington Literary Festival
Civic Offices, Larkin Way, Tan Bank,
Wellington, Telford TF1 1LX
☎01952 222935 Fax 01952 222936
✉ welltowncl@aol.com
www.wellington-shropshire.gov.uk
Contact Derrick Drew

Founded 1997. Annual festival held throughout October. Events include storytelling, writers' forum, 'Pints and Poetry', children's poetry competition, story competition, theatre review and guest speakers.

Wells Festival of Literature
25 Chamberlain Street, Wells BA5 2PQ
☎01749 670929
www.somersite.co.uk/wellsfest.htm

Founded 1992. Annual weekend-plus festival held at the end of October. Main venue is the historic, moated Bishop's Palace. A wide range of speakers caters for different tastes in reading. Recent guests include: Sir Roy Strong, Kate Adie, Libby Purves, Melvyn Bragg, Margaret Drabble, William Dalrymple, Timothy West. Short story and poetry competitions and writing workshops are run in conjunction with the Festival.

Wessex Poetry Festival
See **Tears in the Fence Festival**

Westwords
Arts Team, Room M25, Civic Centre, Station Road, Harrow HA1 2UW
☎020 8424 1803

Currently under development; telephone for further information.

Winchester Writers' Conference, Bookfair & Workshops
See entry under *UK Writers' Courses*

Wonderful Words Book Festival
c/o Penzance Library, Morrab Road, Penzance TR18 4EY
☎01736 363954
✉ agunderson@cornwall.gov.uk
www.cornwall.gov.uk/library
Festival Organiser Rebecca Rowland

Founded 1994. Biennial literature festival hosted throughout Cornwall. The next and seventh Festival will be in September 2006. Organised by the Cornwal Library Service, the Festival has grown into a prestigious event for children and adults, offering author talks, writers' workshops, poetry performances, theatre and storytelling. Guest authors have included Doris Lessing, Ruth Rendell, Margaret Drabble and Dick King-Smith.

Word – University of Aberdeen Writers Festival
Office of External Affairs, University of Aberdeen, King's College, Aberdeen BA24 3FX
☎01224 284444
www.abdn.ac.uk/word
Artistic Director Alan Spence

Festival Producer *Elly Rothnie*

Held annually in May, the Festival takes place over four days at the historic King's College Campus and at venues throughout the city. Attracts over 50 authors and over 6000 visitors to a weekend of readings, lectures, debates, music, art exhibitions and film screenings. Also includes an extended schools' and children's programme and a Festival of Gaelic.

Word Market Festival

PO Box 150, Barrow-in-Furness LA14 3WF
☎07834 150523
✉ admin@word-market.co.uk
www.word-market.co.uk
Contact *Linda Graham*

A new writing project designed to support and develop writers, readers and audiences in south Cumbria and beyond. As well as the annual February Festival and a year-round programme of training and events, also manages projects such as Pub Scripts, South Cumbria Poet Laureate and Song Furnace. Also organises tailor-made activities with community groups. Readings, workshops, competitions and performances.

Wordplay

See **Swansea Festivals**

Words by the Water

See **Ways with Words**

WordStar

Leicester City Council, Libraries, A12 New Walk Centre, Leicester LE1 6ZG
☎0116 252 7347
✉ damien.walter@leicester.gov.uk

Literature Development Officer *Damien Walter*

Year-round programme of live literature including author events, poetry, storytelling, graphic novels and new media.

Wordsworth Trust

The Wordsworth Trust, Dove Cottage, Grasmere LA22 9SH
☎015394 35544 Fax 015394 35748
✉ enquiries@wordsworth.org.uk
www.wordsworth.org.uk
Contact *Arts Officer*

Ongoing contemporary poetry programme held over 30 weeks. Readers include Seamus Heaney, Paul Muldoon, Philip Pullman, Simon Armitage and Don Paterson. The Trust also operates an artists-in-residence programme throughout the year, giving time and space for important new artists to develop their work. Past poets in residence include Henry Shukman, Owen Sheers, Paul Farley, Helen Farish, Rebecca O'Connor, Jacob Polley and Jack Mapanje

Writing on the Wall

60 Duke Street, Liverpool L1 5AA
☎0151 707 4313
✉ info@writingonthewall.org.uk
Festival Coordinator *Madeline Heneghan*

Annual festival held in Liverpool that works alongside schools, young people, local communities and broader audiences to celebrate writing, diversity, tolerance, story-telling and humour through controversy, inquiry and debate. Performances, readings, workshops, screenings, high profile debates and discussions. Guest speakers have included Noam Chomsky, Irvine Welsh, Howard Marks, Roddy Doyle.

European Publishers

Austria

Springer-Verlag GmbH
Postfach 89, A–1201 Vienna
☎00 43 1 3302415 Fax 00 43 1 3302426
✉ springer@springer.at
www.springer.at
Founded 1924. Austria's largest scientific publisher. Publishes academic and textbooks, journals and translations: architecture, art, chemistry, computer science, economics, engineering, geosciences, law, life sciences, mathematics, medicine, philosophy, psychotherapy.

Verlag Carl Ueberreuter GmbH
Alser Strasse 24, A–1090 Vienna
☎00 43 1 404440 Fax 00 43 1 404445
www.ueberreuter.de
Founded 1548. Publishes fiction and general non-fiction; art, astrology, biography, children's, government, history, economics, political science, general science, health and nutrition, science fiction, fantasy, music and dance.

Paul Zsolnay Verlag GmbH
Prinz Eugen Strasse 30, A–1040 Vienna
☎00 43 1 50576610 Fax 00 43 1 505766110
✉ info@zsolnay.at
www.zsolnay.at
Founded 1923. Publishes biography, fiction, general non-fiction, history, poetry.

Belgium

Brepols Publishers NV
Begijnhof 67, B–2300 Turnhout
☎00 32 14 448020 Fax 00 32 14 428919
✉ info@brepols.net
www.brepols.net
Founded 1796. Publishes academic – architecture, archaeology, art, interior design, Asian studies, history, language arts, linguistics, literature, literary criticism, essays, philosophy, religion and biblical studies.

Facet NV
Willem Linnigstr 13, B–2060 Antwerp
☎00 32 3 2274028 Fax 00 32 3 2273792
Founded 1986. Publishes children's books.

Uitgeverij Lannoo NV
Kasteelstr 97, B–8700 Tielt
☎00 32 51 424211 Fax 00 32 51 401152
✉ lannoo@lannoo.be
www.lannoo.be
Founded 1909. Publishes general non-fiction, art, architecture and interior design, cookery, biography, economics, gardening, health and nutrition, history, management, photography, self-help, poetry, government, political science, religion, travel.

Standaard Uitgeverij
Mechelsesteenweg 203, B–2018 Antwerp
☎00 32 3 2857200 Fax 00 32 3 2857299
✉ info@standaarduitgeverij.be
www.standaarduitgeverij.be
Founded 1919. Publishes education, fiction, poetry, humour, children's and young adult.

Denmark

Forlaget Apostrof ApS
Postboks 2580, DK–2100 Copenhagen OE
☎00 45 39 208420 Fax 00 45 39 208453
✉ apostrof@apostrof.dk
www.apostrof.dk
Founded 1980. Publishes psychology and psychiatry.

Aschehoug Dansk Forlag A/S
Vognmagergade 11, DK–1048 Copenhagen K
☎00 45 36 156600
✉ info@aschehoug.dk
www.aschehoug.dk
Founded 1977. Merged with Egmont Lademann A/S in 2003. Publishes reference, directories, dictionaries, encyclopedias, young adult, textbooks, fiction, biography, cookery, children's, how-to, health and nutrition, maritime.

Blackwell Munksgaard
1 Rosenørns Alle, DK–1970 Frederiksberg C
☎00 45 77 333333 Fax 00 45 77 333377
✉ info@msk.blackwellpublishing.com
www.blackwellmunksgaard.com
Founded 1917. Part of **Blackwell Publishing**.

Publishes academic books and journals for higher education, research and professional markets.

Borgens Forlag A/S
Valbygardsvej 33, DK–2500 Valby
☎00 45 36 153615   Fax 00 45 36 153616
✉ post@borgen.dk
www.borgen.dk
Founded 1948. Publishes fiction and general non-fiction: bibliography, children's and young adult, illustrated, journals, textbooks, literature, literary criticism, essays.

Forlaget Forum
PO Box 2252, DK–1019 Copenhagen K
☎00 45 33 411800   Fax 00 45 33 411801
✉ kontakt@forlagetforum.dk
www.forlagetforum.dk
Founded 1940. Part of **Gyldendalske Boghandel-Nordisk Forlag A/S**. Publishes fiction, bibliography, history, humour, mysteries, children's and young adults.

Gyldendal
Klareboderne 3, DK–1001 Copenhagen K
☎00 45 33 755555   Fax 00 45 33 755556
✉ gyldendal@gyldendal.dk
www.gyldendal.dk
Founded 1770. Publishes fiction, children's and young adult, directories, art, biography, dance, dentistry, education, history, how-to, medicine, music, poetry, nursing, philosophy, psychology, psychiatry, reference, general and social sciences, sociology, textbooks.

Høst & Søn Publishers Ltd
Købmagergade 62, DK–1150 Copenhagen K
☎00 45 33 411800   Fax 00 45 33 411801
✉ gb@gb-forlagene.dk
Founded 1836. Imprint of **Gyldendal**. Publishes fiction, children's, crafts, environmental studies, games, hobbies, history.

Lindhardt og Ringhof
Pilestræde 52, DK–1112 Copenhagen K
☎00 45 33 695000   Fax 00 45 33 695001
www.lrforlag.dk
Founded 1971. Publishes fiction and general non-fiction.

Nyt Nordisk Forlag Arnold Busck A/S
Landemærket 11, DK–1119 Copenhagen K
☎00 45 33 733575   Fax 00 45 33 733576
www.nytnordiskforlag.dk
Founded 1896. Publishes fiction, architecture,

art, biography, dance, dentistry, directories, history, how-to, music, philosophy, reference, religion, medicine, nursing, psychology, psychiatry, general and social sciences, sociology, textbooks.

Samlerens Forlag A/S
Postboks 2252, DK–1019 Copenhagen K
☎00 45 33 411800   Fax 00 45 33 411801
✉ gb@gb-samleren.dk
www.samleren.dk
Founded 1943. Imprint of **Gyldendal**. Publishes essays, translations, fiction, government, history, literature, literary criticism, political science.

Det Schønbergske Forlag
Landemærket 11, DK–1119 Copenhagen K
☎00 45 33 733585   Fax 00 45 33 733586
www.nytnordiskforlag.dk
Founded 1857. Part of **Nyt Nordisk Forlag Arnold Busck A/S**. Publishes art, biography, careers, directories, fiction, history, humour, philosophy, poetry, psychology, psychiatry, reference, textbooks, travel

Spektrum Forlagsaktieselskab
PO Box 2252, DK–1019 Copenhagen K
☎00 45 33 147714   Fax 00 45 33 147791
Founded 1990. Publishes general non-fiction.

Tiderne Skifter Forlag A/S
Laederstraede 5, 1, DK–1201 Copenhagen K
☎00 45 33 186390   Fax 00 45 33 186391
✉ tiderneskifter@tiderneskifter.dk
www.tiderneskifter.dk
Founded 1973. Publishes fiction, literature and literary criticism, essays, poetry, drama, translations, politics, psychoanalysis, sexual politics, ethnicity, photography.

Finland

Gummerus Publishers
PO Box 749, SF–00101 Helsinki
☎00 358 9 584301   Fax 00 358 9 58430200
www.gummerus.fi
Founded 1872. Publishes fiction and general non-fiction.

Karisto Oy
PO Box 102, SF–13101 Hämeenlinna
☎00 358 3 63151   Fax 00 358 3 6161565
✉ kustannusliike@karisto.fi
www.karisto.fi

Founded 1900. Publishes fiction (including crime, thrillers and fantasy), general non-fiction (including health, history, family and childcare, pets, fishing), juvenile and young adult.

Kirjayhtymä Oy
Urho Kekkosen Katu 4–6E,
SF–00100 Helsinki
☎00 358 9 6937641   Fax 00 358 9 69376366
Founded 1958. Publishes fiction and general non-fiction, textbooks.

Kustannusosakeyhtiö Tammi
PL 410, SF–00101 Helsinki
☎00 358 9 6937621   Fax 00 358 9 69376266
www.tammi.net
Founded 1943. Publishes fiction, general non-fiction, children's and young adult, illustrated. Part of the Bonnier Group.

Otava Publishing Co. Ltd
Uudenmaankatu 8–12, SF–00120 Helsinki
☎00 358 9 19961
✉ otava@otava.fi
www.otava.fi
Founded 1890. Publishes fiction, translations, general non-fiction, children's and young adult, education, textbooks, art, architecture and interior design, history, natural history, food, how-to.

Werner Söderström Osakeyhtiö (WSOY)
PO Box 222, SF–00121 Helsinki
☎00 358 9 61681   Fax 00 358 9 61683560
www.wsoy.fi
Founded 1878. Publishes fiction, translation, general non-fiction, education, dictionaries, encyclopedias, textbooks, children's and young adult.

France

Éditions Arthaud
Flammarion Groupe, 87 quai Panhard-et-Levassor, F–75647 Paris Cedex 13
☎00 33 1 4051 3100
✉ contact@arthaud.fr
www.arthaud.fr
Founded 1890. Imprint of **Flammarion SA**.

Éditions Belfond
12 avenue d'Italie, F–75627 Paris Cedex 13
☎00 33 1 4416 0500
www.belfond.fr
Founded 1963. Publishes fiction and general non-fiction.

Éditions Bordas
89 blvd Auguste-Blanqui, F–75013 Paris
☎00 33 1 4439 5445   Fax 00 33 1 4439 4350
www.editions-bordas.com
Founded 1945. Publishes education and general non-fiction: dictionaries, directories, encyclopedias, reference.

Éditions Calmann-Lévy
31 rue de Fleurus, F–75006 Paris
☎00 33 1 4954 3600   Fax 00 33 1 4544 8632
www.editions-calmann-levy.com
Founded 1836. Publishes fiction, science fiction, fantasy, biography, history, humour, economics, philosophy, psychology, psychiatry, social sciences, sociology, sport.

Éditions Denoël
9 rue du Cherche-Midi,
F–75278 Paris Cedex 06
☎00 33 1 4439 7373   Fax 00 33 1 4439 7390
www.denoel.fr
Founded 1932. Part of **Editions Gallimard**. Publishes fiction, science fiction, fantasy, art, directories, economics, government, history, illustrated, philosophy, political science, psychology, psychiatry, reference.

Librairie Arthème Fayard
75 rue des Saints-Pères,
F-75279 Paris Cedex 6
☎00 33 1 4549 8200   Fax 00 33 1 4222 4017
www.editions-fayard.fr
Founded 1854. Publishes fiction, biography, directories, maps, atlases, history, dance, music, philosophy, religion, reference, social sciences, sociology, general science, technology.

Flammarion SA
87 quai Panhard-et-Levassor, F–75647 Paris Cedex 13
☎00 33 1 4051 3100
www.flammarion.com
Founded 1875. Publishes general fiction and non-fiction, art, architecture, children's, gardening, plants, CD-ROMs, bilingual, literature, literary criticism, essays, medicine, nursing, dentistry, wine and spirits.

Éditions Gallimard
5 rue Sébastien-Bottin,
F–75328 Paris Cedex 07
☎00 33 1 4954 4200   Fax 00 33 1 4544 9403
www.gallimard.fr
Founded 1911. Publishes fiction, poetry, art,

biography, dance, history, music, philosophy, young adult.

Éditions Grasset et Fasquelle
61 rue des Saints-Pères, F–75006 Paris
☎00 33 1 4439 2200 Fax 00 33 1 4222 6418
www.edition-grasset.fr
Founded 1907. Publishes fiction and general non-fiction, essays, literature, literary criticism, philosophy.

Hachette-Livre
43 quai de Grenelle, F–75905 Paris Cedex 15
☎00 33 1 4392 3000 Fax 00 33 1 4392 3030
www.hatchette.com
Founded 1826. With the acquisition of Time Warner Book Group, Hachette, already the owner of Hodder Headline and Orion, is now the biggest publisher in the British market and the third largest publisher in the world behind Pearson and Bertelsmann. Publishes fiction and general non-fiction, bibliographies, bilingual, directories, education, general engineering, government, language and linguistics, reference, general science, textbooks.

Éditions Robert Laffont
24 ave Marceau, F–75381 Paris Cedex 08
☎00 33 1 5367 1400 Fax 00 33 1 5367 1414
www.laffont.fr
Founded 1987. Publishes fiction.

Éditions Larousse
21 rue de Montparnasse,
F–75283 Paris Cedex 06
☎00 33 1 4439 4400
www.larousse.fr
Founded 1852. Publishes animals, bilingual, children's and young adult, childcare, cookery, dictionaries, directories, encyclopedias, gardening, history, medicine, nursing, dentistry, music, dance, self-help, psychology, psychiatry, reference, general science, social sciences, sociology, language arts, linguistics, sport, technology, textbooks.

Éditions Jean-Claude Lattès
17 rue Jacob, F–75006 Paris
☎00 33 1 4441 7400 Fax 00 33 1 4325 3047
www.editions-jclattes.fr
Founded 1968. Part of **Hachette-Livre**. Publishes fiction and general non-fiction.

Magnard SA
20 rue Berbier-du-Mets,
F–75647 Paris Cedex 13
☎00 33 1 4408 8585 Fax 00 33 1 4408 4979
www.magnard.fr
Founded 1933. Publishes education, foreign language and bilingual books, juvenile and young adults, textbooks.

Michelin Éditions des Voyages
46 ave de Breteuil, F–75007 Paris
☎00 33 1 4566 1170
Founded 1900. Publishes travel: maps and atlases.

Les Éditions de Minuit SA
7 rue Bernard-Palissy, F–75006 Paris
☎00 33 1 4439 3920 Fax 00 33 1 4544 8236
✉ contact@leseditionsdeminuit.fr
www.leseditionsdeminuit.fr
Founded 1942. Publishes fiction, essays, literature, literary criticism, philosophy, social sciences, sociology.

Éditions Fernand Nathan
9 rue Méchain, F–75686 Paris
☎00 33 1 4587 5000 Fax 00 33 1 4587 5757
www.nathan.fr
Founded 1881. Publishes dictionaries, directories, education, encyclopedias, history, philosophy, psychology, psychiatry, reference, general and social sciences, sociology, textbooks.

Presses de la Cité
12 ave d'Italie, F–75627 Paris Cedex 13
☎00 33 1 4416 0500 Fax 00 33 1 4416 0505
www.pressesdelacite.com
Founded 1947. Imprint of **Editions Belfond**. Publishes fiction and general non-fiction, science fiction, fantasy, history, mysteries, romance, biography.

Presses Universitaires de France (PUF)
6 ave Reille, F–75685 Paris Cedex 14
☎00 33 1 5810 3100 Fax 00 33 1 5810 3182
www.puf.com
Founded 1921. Publishes art, biography, dance, dentistry, dictionaries, directories, encyclopedias, government, general engineering, geography, geology, history, journals, law, medicine, music, nursing, philosophy, psychology, psychiatry, religion, political science, reference, social science, sociology, textbooks.

Éditions du Seuil
27 rue Jacob, F–75006 Paris
☎00 33 1 4046 5050 Fax 00 33 1 4046 4300
✉ contact@seuil.com

www.seuil.com
Founded 1935. Publishes fiction, literature, literary criticism, essays, poetry, art, biography, dance, government, illustrated, political science, history, how-to, music, photography, philosophy, psychology, psychiatry, religion, general and social sciences, sociology, textbooks.

Les Editions de la Table Ronde
14 rue Séguier, F–75006 Paris
☎00 33 1 4046 7070
Founded 1944. Publishes fiction and general non-fiction, biography, history, psychology, psychiatry, religion.

Librairie Vuibert
20 rue Berbier-du-Mets,
F–75647 Paris Cedex 13
☎00 33 1 4408 4900   Fax 00 33 1 4408 4969
www.vuibert.com
Founded 1877. Publishes biological and earth sciences, chemistry, chemical engineering, children's, economics, law, mathematics, physics, textbooks.

Germany

Verlag C.H. Beck (OHG)
Postfach 40 03 40, 80703 Munich
☎00 49 89 381890   Fax 00 49 89 38189398
www.beck.de
Founded 1763. Publishes general non-fiction, anthropology, archaeology, art, CD-ROMs, dance, dictionaries, directories, economics, essays, encyclopedias, history, illustrated, journals, language arts, law, linguistics, literature, literary criticism, music, philosophy, professional, reference, social sciences, sociology, textbooks, theology.

Bertelsmann
Verlagsgruppe Random House, Neumarkter Strasse 28, 81673 Munich
☎00 49 89 41360
www.randomhouse.de
Founded 1835. Part of the **Random House Group**. Publishes fiction and general non-fiction, art, biography, government and political science.

Carlsen Verlag GmbH
Postfach 50 03 80, 22703 Hamburg
☎00 49 40 398040   Fax 00 49 40 39804390
✉ info@carlsen.de
www.carlsen.de

Founded 1953. Publishes children's and comic books.

Deutscher Taschenbuch Verlag GmbH & Co. KG (dtv)
Friedrichstrasse 1a, 80704 Munich
☎00 49 89 38167-0   Fax 00 49 89 346428
www.dtv.de
Founded 1961. Publishes fiction and general non-fiction; biography, child care and development, children's, dictionaries, directories, education, encyclopedias, government, health and nutrition, history, poetry, psychiatry, psychology, philosophy, political science, reference, religion, literature, literary criticism, essays, translations, travel, young adult.

Econ-Verlag GmbH
Friedrichstrasse 126, 10117 Berlin
☎00 49 30 23456-300
Fax 00 49 30 23456-303
✉ info@econ-verlag.de
www.econ-verlag.de
Founded 1950. Publishes general non-fiction and fiction, CD-ROMs, directories, economics, professional, reference and general science.

S Fischer Verlag GmbH
Hedderichstrasse 114, 60596 Frankfurt am Main
☎00 49 69 6062-0   Fax 00 49 69 6062-214
www.fischerverlage.de
Founded 1886. Part of the **Holtzbrinck Group**. Publishes fiction, general non-fiction, directories, essays, literature, literary criticism, reference.

Carl Hanser Verlag GmbH & Co. KG
Postfach 86 04 20, 81631 Munich
☎00 49 89 998300   Fax 00 49 89 984809
✉ info@hanser.de
www.hanser.de/verlag
Founded in 1928. Publishes international and German contemporary literature; children's and juveniles; specialist books on engineering, natural science, plastics, computers and computer science, economics and management, dentistry; CD-ROMs, journals, academic, textbooks, translations.

Heyne Verlag
Bayerstrasse 71–73, 80335 Munich
☎00 49 89 4136-0
www.heyne.de

Founded 1934. Part of **Random House Group**. Publishes fiction, mystery, romance, humour, science fiction, fantasy, astrology, biography, cookery, film, history, how-to, occult, psychology, psychiatry, video, illustrated.

Hoffmann und Campe Verlag GmbH

Harvestehuder Weg 42, 20149 Hamburg
☎00 49 40 441880 Fax 00 49 40 44188-202
✉ email@hoca.de
www.hoca.de
Founded 1781. Publishes fiction and general non-fiction; art, biography, dance, history, illustrated, music, poetry, philosophy, psychology, psychiatry, general science, social sciences, sociology.

Verlagsgruppe Georg von Holtzbrinck GmbH

Gänsheidestrasse 26, 70184 Stuttgart
☎00 49 711 2150-0
Fax 00 49 711 2150-269
✉ info@holtzbrinck.com
www.holtzbrinck.com
Founded 1948. One of the world's largest publishing groups with 12 book publishing houses and 40 imprints. Also publishes the newspapers, *Handelsblatt* and *Die Zeit*.

Hüthig GmbH & Co. KG

Postfach 10 28 69, 69018 Heidelberg
☎00 49 6221 489-0
Fax 00 49 6221 489-279
✉ info@huethig.de
www.huethig.de
Founded 1925. Germany's fourth largest professional publisher: CD-ROMs, journals, academic, textbooks, translations.

Ernst Klett Verlag GmbH

Rotebühlstrasse 77, 70178 Stuttgart
☎00 49 711 6672 1333
Fax 00 49 711 6672 2080
www.klett.de
Founded 1897. Publishes dictionaries, encyclopedias, maps and atlases, education, geography, geology; textbooks.

Verlagsgruppe Lübbe GmbH & Co. KG

Scheidtbachstrasse 23–31, 51469 Bergisch Gladbach
☎00 49 2202 121-069

Fax 00 49 2202 121928
www.lubbe.de
Founded 1963. Publishes fiction and general non-fiction, audio, archaeology, biography, history, how-to.

Rowohlt Verlag GmbH

Hamburgerstr 17, 21465 Reinbeck
☎00 49 40 72720 Fax 00 49 40 7272-319
✉ info@rowohlt.de
www.rowohlt.de
Founded 1908. Publishes general non-fiction.

Springer GmbH

Tiergartenstrasse 17, 69121 Heidelberg
☎00 49 6221 4870
Fax 00 49 6221 487-8366
www.springer.de

Also at: Heidelberger Platz 3, 14197 Berlin
☎00 49 30 827870 Fax 00 49 30 8214091
Founded 1842. Part of Springer Science+ Business Media. Leading scientific publisher. Subjects range from natural sciences, mathematics, engineering and computer science, medicine, psychology, economics, law, arts and social sciences – with eighty per cent of publications in English.

Suhrkamp Verlag

Postfach 101945, 60019 Frankfurt am Main
☎00 49 69 75601-0
Fax 00 49 69 75601-314
www.suhrkamp.de
Founded 1950. Publishes fiction, poetry, biography, cinema, film, theatre, philosophy, psychology, psychiatry, general science.

Taschen GmbH

Hohenzollernring 53, 50672 Cologne
☎00 49 221 201800 Fax 00 49 221 254919
✉ contact@taschen.com
www.taschen.com
Founded 1980. Publishes photography, art, erotica, architecture and interior design.

WEKA Firmengruppe GmbH & Co KG

Postfach 13 31, 86438 Kissing
☎00 49 8233 23-0 Fax 00 49 8233 23-195
✉ info@weka-holding.de
www.weka-holding.de
Founded 1973. Germany's largest professional publisher.

Italy

Adelphi Edizioni SpA
Via S. Giovanni sul Muro 14, 20121 Milan
☎00 39 2 725731 Fax 00 39 2 89010337
✉ info@adelphi.it
www.adelphi.it
Founded 1962. Publishes literature, literary criticism, anthropology, autobiography, archaeology, architecture, biography, biology, economics, history, mathematics, medicine, music, philosophy, photography, physics, politics, psychology, religion, general science, translation.

Bompiani
Via Mecenate 91, 20138 Milan
☎00 39 2 50951 Fax 00 39 2 5065361
www.rcslibri.it
Founded 1929. Part of RCS Libri publishing group. Publishes fiction and general nonfiction, dictionaries, encyclopedias, juvenile and young adult.

Bulzoni Editore SRL (Le Edizioni Universitarie d'Italia)
Via Dei Liburni 14, 00185 Rome
☎00 39 6 4455207 Fax 00 39 6 4450355
✉ bulzoni@bulzoni.it
www.bulzoni.it
Founded 1969. Publishes fiction, literature, literary criticism, essays, art, drama, general engineering, film, law, language, linguistics, philosophy, general science, social sciences, sociology, textbooks, theatre, video.

Cappelli Editore
Via Farini 14, 40124 Bologna
☎00 39 51 239060 Fax 00 39 51 239286
✉ info@cappellieditore.com
www.cappellieditore.com
Founded 1851. Publishes fiction, art, biography, drama, film, government, history, music, dance, directories, poetry, medicine, nursing, dentistry, juvenile and young adult, philosophy, political science, psychology, psychiatry, reference, religion, general science, social sciences, sociology, textbooks, theatre, video.

Garzanti Libri SpA
Via Gasparotto 1, 20124 Milan
☎00 39 2 674171 Fax 00 39 2 67417323
www.garzantilibri.it
Founded 1861. Publishes fiction, literature, literary criticism, essays, art, biography, dictionaries, directories, encyclopedias, history, poetry,

government, political science, reference, textbooks.

Giunti Gruppo Editoriale
Via Bolognese 165, 50139 Florence
☎00 39 55 5062376 Fax 00 39 55 5062397
www.giunti.it
Founded 1840. Publishes fiction, literature, literary criticism, essays, art, chemistry, chemical engineering, dictionaries, directories, education, encyclopedias, history, how-to, language arts, linguistics, mathematics, psychology, psychiatry, reference, general science. Italian publishers of National Geographical Society books.

Gremese Editore
Via Virginia Agnelli 88, 00151 Rome
☎00 39 6 657 40507 Fax 00 39 6 657 40509
✉ gremese@gremese.com
www.gremese.com
Founded 1954. Publishes fiction, art, erotica, astrology, cookery, crafts, dance, drama, film, video, fashion, games, hobbies, illustrated, essays, literature, literary criticism, bilingual, dictionaries, directories, encyclopedias, health and nutrition, house and home, how-to, music, occult, reference, sport, travel, theatre, television, radio, wine and spirits.

Casa Editrice Longanesi SpA
Via Gherardini 10, 20145 Milan
☎00 39 2 34597620 Fax 00 39 2 34597212
✉ info@longanesi.it
www.longanesi.it
Founded 1946. Mass market paperback publisher of fiction, art, biography, dance, history, how-to, medicine, nursing, dentistry, music, philosophy, psychology, psychiatry, religion, general and social sciences, sociology.

Arnoldo Mondadori Editore SpA
Via Mondadori 1, 20090 Segrate (Milan)
☎00 39 2 75421 Fax 00 39 2 75422302
www.mondadori.it
Founded 1907. Italy's largest publisher. Publishes fiction, mystery, romance, art, biography, children's, dance, directories, history, how-to, medicine, music, poetry, philosophy, psychology, psychiatry, reference, religion, general science, education, textbooks.

Società Editrice Il Mulino
Strada Maggiore 37, 40125 Bologna
☎00 39 51 256011 Fax 00 39 51 256034
✉ info@mulino.it
www.mulino.it

Founded 1954. Publishes economics, government, history, law, language arts, linguistics, philosophy, political science, psychology, psychiatry, social sciences, sociology, textbooks, journals.

Gruppo Ugo Mursia Editore SpA
Via Melchiorre Gioia 45, 20124 Milan
☎00 39 2 6737 8500 Fax 00 39 2 6737 8605
✉ info@mursia.com
www.mursia.com
Founded 1922. Publishes fiction, poetry, art, biography, directories, education, history, maritime, philosophy, reference, religion, sport, general science, social sciences, sociology, textbooks, juvenile and young adult.

Rizzoli Editore
Via Mecenate 91, 20138 Milan
☎00 39 2 50951 Fax 00 39 2 5065361
www.rcslibri.it
Founded 1945. Part of RCS Libri publishing group. Publishes art, crafts, dance, business, dictionaries, directories, encyclopedias, games, hobbies, history, music, medicine, nursing, dentistry, general science, textbooks, juvenile and young adult.

Società Editrice Internazionale – SEI
Corso Regina Margherita 176, 10152 Turin
☎00 39 11 52271 Fax 00 39 11 5211320
www.seieditrice.com
Founded 1908. Publishes literature, literary criticism, essays, children's, dictionaries, encyclopedias, education, geography, geology, history, mathematics, philosophy, physics, religion, psychology, psychiatry, textbooks.

Sonzogno
Via Mecenate 91, 20138 Milan
☎00 39 2 50951 Fax 00 39 2 5065361
www.rcslibri.it
Founded 1818. Part of RCS Libri publishing group. Publishes fiction, mysteries, and general non-fiction.

Sperling e Kupfer Editori SpA
Via Durazzo 4, 20134 Milan
☎00 39 2 217211 Fax 00 39 2 21721277
www.sperling.it
Founded 1899. Publishes fiction and general non-fiction.

Sugarco Edizioni SRL
Via don Gnocchi 4, 21048 Milan
☎00 39 2 407 8370 Fax 00 39 2 407 8493

✉ info@sugarcoedizioni.it
www.sugarcoedizioni.it
Founded 1956. Publishes fiction, biography, history, how-to, philosophy.

Todariana Editrice
Via Gardone 29, 20139 Milan
☎00 39 2 56812953 Fax 00 39 2 55213405
www.todariana-eurapress.it
Founded 1967. Publishes fiction, poetry, science fiction, fantasy, literature, literary criticism, essays, language arts, linguistics, psychology, psychiatry, social sciences, sociology, travel.

The Netherlands

A.W. Bruna Uitgevers BV
Postbus 40203, 3504 AA Utrecht
☎00 31 30 247 0411 Fax 00 31 30 241 0018
✉ info@awwbruna.nl
www.awbruna.nl
Founded 1868. Publishes fiction and general non-fiction; mysteries, thrillers, computer science, CD-ROMs, history, philosophy, psychology, psychiatry, general science, social sciences, sociology.

BZZTÔH Publishers
Laan van Meerdervoort 10, 2517 AJ The Hague
☎00 31 70 363 2934 Fax 00 31 70 363 1932
✉ info@bzztoh.nl
www.bzztoh.nl
Founded 1970. Publishes fiction, mysteries, romance, literature, literary criticism, essays, foreign language, bilingual, general non-fiction, animals, astrology, biography, cookery, dance, humour, journals, music, philosophy, self-help, health and nutrition, occult, pets, religion (Buddhist, Hindhu, Jewish), sport, thrillers, translations, travel, women's studies.

Elsevier Science BV
Postbus 152, 1055 AD Amsterdam
☎00 31 20 515 9944 Fax 00 31 20 515 9900
www.elsevier.nl
Founded 1946. Parent company Reed Elsevier. Publishes sciences (all fields), medicine, nursing, dentistry, economics, engineering (chemical and general), mathematics, physics, technology.

Uitgeversmaatschappij J. H. Kok BV
PO Box 5019, 8260 GA Kampen
☎00 31 38 339 2555

www.kok.nl
Founded 1894. Publishes fiction, poetry, history, religion, directories, reference, general science, social sciences, sociology, textbooks, journals, juvenile and young adult.

J.M. Meulenhoff BV

Postbus 100, 1000 AC Amsterdam
☎00 31 20 553 3500 Fax 00 31 20 625 1135
✉ info@meulenhoff.nl
www.meulenhoff.nl

Founded 1895. Publishes international co-productions, fiction and general non-fiction. Specialises in Dutch and translated literature.

Pearson Education Benelux

Postbus 75598, 1070 AN Amsterdam
☎00 31 20 575 5800 Fax 00 31 20 664 5334
www.pearsoneducation.nl

Founded 1942. Publishes education, business, computer science, directories, economics, management, reference, textbooks, technology.

Uitgeverij Het Spectrum BV

Postbus 2073, 3500 GB Utrecht
☎00 31 30 265 0650 Fax 00 31 30 262 0850
www.spectrum.nl

Founded 1935. Publishes science fiction, fantasy, literature, literary criticism, essays, mysteries, criminology, general non-fiction, computer science, dictionaries, encyclopedias, history, illustrated, astrology, occult, management, environmental studies, travel.

Springer Science+Business Media BV

Van Godewijckstraat 30, 3311 GX Dordrecht
☎00 31 78 657 6000 Fax 00 31 78 657 6555
www.springer.com

Publishes ebooks, CD-ROMs, databases and journals; computer science, economics, engineering, humanities, medicine, social sciences, mathematics, physics.

Uitgeverij Unieboek BV

Postbus 97, 3990 DB Houten
☎00 31 30 799 8300 Fax 00 31 30 799 8398
✉ info@unieboek.nl
www.unieboek.nl

Founded 1891. Publishes fiction: mysteries, romance, thrillers; general non-fiction, reference and children's books.

Uniepers BV

Postbus 69, 1390 AB Abcoude
☎00 31 29 428 5111 Fax 00 31 29 428 3013

✉ info@uniepers.nl
www.uniepers.nl
Founded 1961. Publishes (mostly in co-editions) antiques, anthropology, archaeology, architecture and interior design, art, dance, history, music, natural history, photography.

Norway

H. Aschehoug & Co (W. Nygaard)

Postboks 363 Sentrum, N–0102 Oslo
☎00 47 22 400400
✉ epost@aschehoug.no
www.aschehoug.no

Founded 1872. Publishes fiction and general non-fiction, children's, reference, popular science, hobbies, education and textbooks.

J.W. Cappelens Forlag AS

Postboks 350 Sentrum, N–0101 Oslo
☎00 47 22 365000 Fax 00 47 22 365040
www.cappelen.no

Founded 1829. Publishes fiction, general non-fiction, maps and atlases, juvenile and young adult, dictionaries, directories, encyclopedias, reference, religion, textbooks.

N.W. Damm & Søn AS

Fridtjof Nansens vei 14, N–0055 Oslo
☎00 47 24 051000 Fax 00 47 24 051290
www.damm.no

Founded 1845. Owned by the Egmont Group. Publishes fiction, children's and young adult, general non-fiction, reference and translated fiction.

Gyldendal Norsk Forlag

Postboks 6860, St Olavs Plass, N–0130 Oslo
☎00 47 22 034100 Fax 00 47 22 034105
✉ gnf@gyldendal.no
www.gyldendal.no

Founded 1925. Publishes fiction, science fiction, fantasy, art, dance, biography, children's, dictionaries, directories, encyclopedias, government, journals, political science, history, how-to, music, social sciences, sociology, poetry, philosophy, psychology, psychiatry, reference, religion, textbooks.

Tiden Norsk Forlag

Postboks 6704, St Olavs Plass, N–0130 Oslo
☎00 47 22 2332 7660
Fax 00 46 22 2332 7697
✉ tiden@tiden.no
www.tiden.no

Founded 1933. Part of **Gyldendal Norsk**

Forlag group. Publishes Norwegian and translated fiction and general non-fiction.

Portugal

Bertrand Editora Lda
Rua Anchieta 29–1, 1200 Lisbon
☎00 351 21 320084
Founded 1727. Publishes art, essays, literature, literary criticism, bilingual, dictionaries, encyclopedias, juvenile and young adult, social sciences, sociology.

Editorial Caminho SARL
Al Santo Antonio dos Capuchos 6B, 1100 Lisbon
☎00 351 1 3152683   Fax 00 351 1 534346
Founded 1977. Publishes fiction, government, political science, juvenile and young adult.

Livraria Civilização (Américo Fraga Lamares & Ca Lda)
Rua Dr Alberto Aires de Gouveia 27, 4050–023 Porto
☎00 351 22 6062286
Founded 1921. Publishes fiction, art, economics, history, political science, government, sociology, social sciences, juvenile and young adult.

Publicações Europa-América Lda
Estrada Nacional No. 249 (Lisboa–Sintra), ao Km 14, Apartardo 8, 2725 Mem Martins
☎00 351 21 926 7700
Fax 00 351 21 926 7771
Founded 1945. Publishes fiction, poetry, art, anthropology, architecture, biography, children's, cookery, ecology, education, history, humour, literature, medicine, parenting, philosophy, politics, psychology, psychiatry, reference, social sciences, sociology, textbooks, theatre, thrillers.

Gradiva–Publicações Lda
Rua Almeida e Sousa 21 R/C Esq, 1399–041 Lisbon
☎00 351 21 3974067
Fax 00 351 21 3953470
www.gravida.pt
Founded 1981. Publishes fiction, literature, literary criticism, essays, science fiction, fantasy, romance, anthropology, Asian studies, astronomy, behavioural sciences, biological science, children's, communications, computer science, crafts, directories, earth sciences, education, games, hobbies, economics, general engineering, geography, geology, government, political

studies, journalism, natural history, history, humour, environmental studies, human relations, illustrated, management, mathematics, philosophy, general science, physics, psychology, psychiatry, reference, self-help, social sciences, sociology, translations.

Livros Horizonte Lda
Rua Chagas 17–1 Dto, 1200–106 Lisbon
☎00 351 1 3466917
Founded 1953. Publishes art, children's, education, history, psychology, psychiatry, social sciences, sociology, textbooks.

Editorial Verbo SA
Av António Augusto de Aguiar 148, 1069–019 Lisbon
☎00 351 21 380 1100   Fax 00 351 21 386 5397
www.editorialverbo.pt
Founded 1959. Publishes dictionaries, education, encyclopedias, history, general science, juvenile and young adult.

Spain

Alianza Editorial SA
Juan Ignacio Luca de Tena 15, 28027 Madrid
☎00 34 91 393 8890   Fax 00 34 91 320 4408
www.alianzaeditorial.es
Founded 1966. Publishes fiction, poetry, art, history, mathematics, dance, music, philosophy, government, political science, social sciences, sociology, general science.

Ediciones Anaya SA
Juan Ignacio Luca de Tena 15, 28027 Madrid
☎00 349 1 393 8600   Fax 00 349 1 742 6631
www.anaya.es
Founded 1959. Educational publisher.

EDHASA (Editora y Distribuidora Hispano – Americana SA)
Av Diagonal 519–521, 2 piso, 08029 Barcelona
☎00 349 3 494 9720   Fax 00 349 3 419 4584
✉ info@edhasa.es
www.edhasa.es
Founded 1946. Publishes fiction, literature, literary criticism, essays, history.

Editorial Espasa-Calpe SA
Apdo de correos 547, Carreterade Irún Km 12, 200, 28049 Madrid
☎00 349 1 358 9689

www.espasa.com
Founded 1925. Publishes fiction, children's, biography, essays, education, literature, CD-ROMs, dictionaries, encyclopedias, reference, maps and atlases.

Grijalbo Mondadori SA
Arago 385, 08013 Barcelona
☎00 349 3 476 7110
www.grijalbo.com
Founded 1962. Publishes fiction, general non-fiction, children's, dictionaries, directories, encyclopedias, humour, illustrated, literature, literary criticism, essays, politics, reference, self-help, spirituality.

Ediciónes Hiperión SL
Calle de Salustiano Olózaga 14, 28001 Madrid
☎00 349 1 557 6015   Fax 00 349 1 435 8690
✉ info@hiperion.com
www.hiperion.com
Founded 1976. Publishes literature, literary criticism, essays, poetry, bilingual, language arts and linguistics, children's, religion (Islamic and Jewish), translations.

Editorial Luis Vives (Edelvives)
Xaudaró 25, 28034 Madrid
☎00 349 1 334 4883
www.edelvives.es
Founded 1890. Educational publisher.

Editorial Molino
Calabria 166, 08015 Barcelona
☎00 349 3 226 0625   Fax 00 349 3 226 6998
www.editorialmolino.com
Founded 1933. Publishes children's, education, mysteries, sport, fiction.

Pearson Educacion SA
Nunez de Balboa 120, 28006 Madrid
☎00 349 1 590 3432   Fax 00 349 1 590 3448
Founded 1942. Educational publishers.

Editorial Planeta
Edifici Planeta Diagonal 662–664, 08034 Barcelona
☎00 349 3 228 5800
www.planeta.es
Founded 1952. Part of Groupo Planeta SA. Publishes fiction and general non-fiction.

Editorial Seix Barral SA
Avda Diagonal 662–664, 7a, 08034 Barcelona
☎00 349 3 496 7003   Fax 00 349 3 496 7004

✉ editorial@seix-barral.es
www.seix-barral.es
Founded 1911. Part of Grupo Planeta. Foreign language publisher of literature.

Tusquets Editores
Cesare Cantù 8, 08017 Barcelona
☎00 349 3 253 0400   Fax 00 349 3 417 6703
www.tusquets-editores.com
Founded 1969. Publishes fiction, biography, history, essays, literature, literary criticism, general science.

Sweden

Albert Bonniers Förlag
PO Box 3159, SE-103 63 Stockholm
☎00 46 8 696 8620   Fax 00 46 8 696 8369
✉ info@abforlag.bonnier.se
www.albertbonniersforlag.com
Founded 1837. Publishes fiction and general non-fiction.

Bokförlaget Bra Böcker AB
PO Box 892, SE-20180 Malmö
☎00 46 40 665 4600   Fax 00 46 40 665 4622
www.bbb.se
Founded 1965. Publishes fiction, dictionaries, encyclopedias, geography, geology, history, illustrated.

Brombergs Bokförlag AB
PO Box 12 886, SE-112 98 Stockholm
☎00 46 8 5626 2080   Fax 00 46 8 5626 2085
✉ info@brombergs.se
www.brombergs.se
Founded 1973. Publishes fiction and general non-fiction.

Bokförlaget Forum AB
PO Box 70321, SE-107 23 Stockholm
☎00 46 8 696 8440   Fax 00 46 8 696 8367
Founded 1944. Publishes fiction and general non-fiction.

Bokförlaget Natur och Kultur
PO Box 27 323, SE-102 54 Stockholm
☎00 46 8 453 8600   Fax 00 46 8 453 8790
✉ info@nok.se
www.nok.se
Founded 1922. Publishes fiction and general non-fiction; education and textbooks.

Norstedts Förlag

Box 2052, SE-103 12 Stockholm
☎00 46 8 769 8850 Fax 00 46 8 769 8864
✉ info@norstedts.se
www.norstedts.se
Founded 1823. Publishes fiction and general non-fiction.

Rabén och Sjögren Bokförlag

PO Box 2052, SE-103 12 Stockholm
☎00 46 8 769 8800 Fax 00 46 8 769 8813
www.raben.se
Founded 1942. Part of Norstedts Förlagsgrupp. Publishes children's and young adult books.

Richters Förlag AB

Sallerupsvaegen 9, SE-205 75 Malmö
☎00 46 40 380600 Fax 00 46 40 930820
www.egmont.com
Founded 1942. Part of Egmont International Holding A/S. Publishes fiction and non-fiction; children's, dictionaries, directories, reference.

B. Wählströms Bokförlag AB

PO Box 30022, SE-104 25 Stockholm
☎00 46 8 6198600 Fax 00 46 8 6189761
✉ info@wahlstroms.se
www.wahlstroms.se
Founded 1911. Publishes fiction and general non-fiction, juvenile and young adult.

Switzerland

Arche Verlag AG

Niederdorfstr 90, CH-8001 Zurich
☎00 41 1 2522410 Fax 00 41 1 2611115
✉ info@arche-verlag.com
www.arche-verlag.com
Founded 1944. Publishes literature and literary criticism, essays, biography, fiction, poetry, music, dance, travel.

Diogenes Verlag AG

Sprecherstr 8, CH-8032 Zurich
☎00 41 1 2548511 Fax 00 41 1 2528407
✉ info@diogenes.ch
www.diogenes.ch
Founded 1952. Publishes fiction, essays, literature, literary criticism, illustrated, mysteries, art, children's, drama, theatre, philosophy.

Larousse (Suisse) SA

c/o Acces-Direct, 3 Route du Grand-Mont,
CH-1052 Le Mont-sur-Lausanne
☎00 41 21 335336
Publishes dictionaries, directories, encyclopedias, reference and textbooks. Part of **Librairie Larousse**, France.

Neptun-Verlag

Erlenstrasse 2, CH-8280 Kreuzlingen
☎00 41 71 6779655 Fax 00 41 72 6779650
✉ neptun@bluewin.ch
www.neptunart.ch
Founded 1946. Publishes non-fiction and children's books.

Orell Füssli Verlag

Dietzingerstr 3, CH-8036 Zurich
☎00 41 1 466 7711 Fax 00 41 1 466 7412
✉ info@ofv.ch
www.ofv.ch
Founded 1519. Publishes accountancy, architecture, art, art history, business, leisure, photography, politics, psychology.

Editions Payot Lausanne

CP 529, CH-1001 Lausanne
☎00 41 21 329 0264 Fax 00 41 21 329 0266
Founded 1875. Publishes general non-fiction, academic, anthropology, archaeology, architecture and interior design, dance, history, law, medicine, music, philosophy, literature, literary criticism, essays, general science, social sciences and sociology, textbooks.

Sauerländer Verlage AG

Ausserfeldstr. 9, CH-5036 Oberentfelden
☎00 41 64 2836 8686 Fax 00 41 64 2836 8620
✉ verlag@sauerlaender.ch
www.sauerlaender.ch
Founded 1807. Publishes education and general non-fiction.

Scherz Verlag AG

Postfach 850, CH-3000 Berne 7
☎00 41 31 3277117 Fax 00 41 31 3277171
✉ scherz@scherzverlag.ch
Founded 1938. Publishes biography, fiction, history, psychology, psychiatry, philosophy, parapsychology.

European Television Companies

Austria

ORF (Österreichisher Rundfunk)
Würzburggasse 30, A–1136 Vienna
☎00 43 1 87 878-0
www.orf.at

Belgium

Radio-Télévision Belge de la Communauté Française (RTBF)
Boulevard Auguste Reyers 52, B–1044 Brussels
☎00 32 2 737 2111
www.rtbf.be

Vlaamse Radio en Televisieomroep (VRT)
Auguste Reyerslaan 52, B–1043 Brussels
☎00 32 2 741 3111
www.vrt.be

Vlaamse Televisie Maatschappij (VTM) (cable)
Medialaan 1, B–1800 Vilvoorde
☎00 32 2 255 3211
✉ info@vtm.be
www.vtm.be

Denmark

Danmarks Radio–TV
TV-Byen, DK–2860 Søborg
☎00 45 35 20 3040
✉ dr@dr.dk
www.dr.dk

TV Danmark
Mileparken 20A, DK–2740 Skovlunde
☎00 45 70 10 1010
✉ info@tvdanmark.dk
www.tvdanmark.dk

TV–2 Danmark
Rugaardsvej 25, DK–5100 Odense C
☎00 45 65 91 9191
✉ tv2@tv2.dk
www.tv2.dk

Finland

MTV3 Finland
Ilmalantori 2, FIN–00033 Helsinki
☎00 358 10 300300
www.mtv3.fi

Yleisradio Oy (YLE)
PO Box 90, FIN–00024 Yleisradio
☎00 358 9 14801
www.yle.fi

France

Arte France (cable & satellite)
8 rue Marceau, 92785 Issy les Moulineaux Cedex 9
☎00 33 1 55 00 77 77
www.artefrance.fr

Canal + (pay TV)
85–89 quai André Citroën, 75711 Paris Cedex 15
☎00 33 1 44 25 10 00
www.cplus.fr

France 5
10–12 rue Horace-Vernet, 92785 Issy-les-Moulineaux Cedex 9
☎00 33 1 56 22 91 91
www.france5.fr

France Télévision (France 2/ France 3)
7 Esplanade Henri de France, 75907 Paris Cedex 15
☎00 33 1 56 22 42 42(France 2)/ 30 30 (France 3)
www.france2.fr
www.france3.fr

M6 (Métropole Télévision)
89 ave Charles de Gaulle, 92575 Neuilly-sur-Seine Cedex
☎00 33 1 41 92 66 66
www.m6.fr

RFO (Radio Télévision Française d'Outre-mer)
35 rue Danton, 92240 Malakoff

☎00 33 1 55 22 71 00
www.rfo.fr

TF1 (Télévision Française 1)
1 quai du Pont du Jour, 92656 Boulogne
☎00 33 1 41 41 12 34
www.tf1.fr

Germany

ARD – Das Erste
Arnulfstrasse 42, 80335 Munich
☎00 49 89 5900 3344
✉ info@daserste.de
www.daserste.de

Arte Germany (cable & satellite)
Postfach 10 02 13, 76483 Baden-Baden
☎00 49 7221 93690
www.arte.de

ZDF (Zweites Deutsches Fernsehen)
Postfach 40 40, 55100 Mainz
☎00 49 61 31/701
✉ info@zdf.de
www.zdf.de

Republic of Ireland

Radio Telefís Éireann (RTÉ One – RTÉ Two)
Donnybrook, Dublin 4
☎00 353 1 208 3111
✉ info@rte.ie
www.rte.ie

TG4 (Teilefís na Gaelige) (Irish language TV)
Baile na hAbhann, Co. na Gaillimhe
☎00 353 91 505050
www.tg4.ie

Italy

RAI (RadioTelevisione Italiana)
Viale Mazzini 14, 00195 Rome
☎00 39 06 3878-1
www.rai.it

The Netherlands

AVRO (Algemene Omroep Vereniging)
Postbus 2, 1200 JA Hilversum
☎00 31 35 671 79 11
✉ info@avro.nl
www.central.avro.nl/index.asp

IKON
Postbus 10009, 1201 DA Hilversum
☎00 31 35 672 72 72
✉ ikon@ikon.nl
www.omroep.nl/ikon

NCRV (Nederlandse Christelijke Radio Vereniging)
Postbus 25000, 1202 HB Hilversum
☎00 31 35 671 99 11
info.omroep.nl/ncrv

NOS (Nederlandse Omroep Stichting)
Sumatralaan 45, 1217 GP Hilversum
☎00 31 35 677 92 22
www.nos.nl

NPS (Nederlandse Programma Stichting)
Postbus 29000, 1202 MA Hilversum
☎00 31 35 677 9333
✉ publiek@nps.nl
www.omroep.nl/nps

VARA
Postbus 175, 1200 AD Hilversum
☎00 31 35 671 19 11
www.omroep.nl

VPRO
Postbus 11, 1200 JC Hilversum
☎00 31 35 671 29 11
✉ info@vpro.nl
www.vpro.nl

Norway

NRK (Norsk Rikskringkasting), N–0340 Oslo
☎00 47 23 04 7000
✉ info@nrk.no
www.nrk.no

TvNorge
Postboks 11, Sentrum, N–0101 Oslo
☎00 47 21 02 2000
✉ tvnorge@tvnorge.no
www.tvnorge.no

TV2
Postboks 7222, N–5020 Bergen
☎00 47 55 90 8070
✉ info@tv2.no
www.tv2.no

Portugal

Radiotelevisão Portuguesa (RTP)
Avenida Marechal, Gomes da Costa 37,
1849–030 Lisbon
☎00 351 21 794 7000
www.rtp.pt

TVI (Televisão Independente)
Rua Mário Castelhano 40, Queluz de Baixo,
2734–502 Barcarena
☎00 351 21 434 7500
www.tvi.pt

Spain

RTVE (RadioTelevision Española)
Edificio Prado del Rey, E–28223 Madrid
☎00 349 1 581 7000
www.rtve.es

Sweden

Sveriges Television AB–SVT
Oxenstierngatan 26–34, S–105 10 Stockholm
☎00 46 8 784 0000
www.svt.se

TV4
Tegeluddsvägen 3, S–115 79 Stockholm
☎00 46 8 459 4000
www.tv4.se

Switzerland

RTR (Radio e Televisiun Rumantscha)
(Romansch language TV)
Via dal Teater 1, CH–7000 Cuira
☎00 41 81 255 7575
✉ contact@rtr.ch
www.rtr.ch

RTSI (Radiotelevisione svizzera di lingua Italiana) (Italian language TV)
Casella postale, CH–6903 Lugano
☎00 41 91 803 51 11
✉ info@rtsi.ch
www.rtsi.ch

Schweizer Fernsehen (SF) (German language TV)
Postfach, CH–8052 Zurich
☎00 41 1 305 66 11
✉ sf@sf.tv
www.sf.tv

SRG SSR idée suisse (Swiss Broadcasting Corp.)
Postfach 26, CH-3000 Berne15
☎00 41 31 350 91 11
✉ info@srgssrideesuisse.ch
www.srg-ssr.ch

TSR (Télévision Suisse Romande)
Quai Ernest Ansermet 20,
CH–1211 Geneva 8
☎00 41 22 708 20 20
www.tsr.ch

US Publishers

Anyone corresponding with the big American publishers should know that following the terrorist attacks of 2001 they are wary of any package or letter that looks in any way suspicious. This, of course, begs the question what is or what is not suspicious which is as difficult to answer as what makes or does not make a good novel. The best policy is to make an initial enquiry by e-mail.

International Reply Coupons (IRCs)

For return postage, send IRCs, available from post offices. Letters, 60 pence; mss according to weight. For current postal rates to the UK, go to the United States Postal Service website at www.usps.com and click on 'Calculate Postage'.

ABC–CLIO

PO Box 1911, Santa Barbara CA 93116–1911
☎001 805 968 1911 Fax 001 805 685 9685
www.abc-clio.com
CEO *Ronald J. Boehm*

Founded 1953. Publishes academic and reference, focusing on history and social studies; books and multimedia. UK SUBSIDIARY **ABC-Clio Ltd**, Oxford. No unsolicited mss; synopses and ideas welcome.
ROYALTIES annually.

Abingdon Press

PO Box 801, Nashville TN 37202–0801
☎001 615 749 6290 Fax 001 615 749 6056
www.abingdonpress.com
Snr. VP/Editorial Director *Harriett Jane Olson*

Founded 1789. Publishes non-fiction: religious (Protestant), reference, professional and academic texts. Over 100 titles a year.

Harry N. Abrams, Inc.

100 Fifth Avenue, New York NY 10011
☎001 212 206 7715 Fax 001 212 645 8437
www.abramsbooks.com
VP/Editor-in-Chief *Eric Himmel*

Founded 1950. Publishes illustrated books: art, natural history, photography. No fiction. About 200 titles a year.

Academy Chicago Publishers

363 W. Erie Street, Chicago IL 60610
☎001 312 751 7300 Fax 001 312 751 7306
www.academychicago.com
President & Senior Editor *Anita Miller*

Founded 1975. Publishes mainstream fiction; non-fiction: art, history, mysteries. No romance, children's, young adult, religious, sexist or avant-garde.
ROYALTIES twice-yearly.

Ace Books

See **Penguin Group (USA) Inc.**

Addison Wesley

75 Arlington Street, Suite 300, Boston MA 02116
☎001 617 848 7500 Fax 001 617 848 6016
✉ firstname.lastname@pearsoned.com
www.aw-bc.com

A division of Pearson Education. Publishes academic textbooks, multimedia and learning programs in computer science, economics, finance, mathematics and statistics. See the website for submission guidelines.

University of Alabama Press

Box 870380, Tuscaloosa AL 35487–0380
☎001 205 348 5180 Fax 001 205 348 9201
www.uapress.ua.edu
Director *Daniel J.J. Ross*

Founded 1945. Publishes American history, Latin American history, American religious history; African-American and Native American studies, Judaic studies, archaeology, anthropology, ethnohistory and American letters. About 60 titles a year. Submissions are not invited in poetry, fiction or drama.

Aladdin Books

See **Simon & Schuster Children's Publishing**

University of Alaska Press

PO Box 756240, University of Alaska,
Fairbanks AK 99775–6240
☎001 907 474 5831 Fax 001 907 474 5502
✉ fypress@uaf.edu
www.uaf.edu/uapress
Editorial *Erica Hill*

Publishes scholarly works about Alaska and the North Pacific rim, with a special emphasis on circumpolar regions, history, anthropology, natural history. No fiction or poetry.

DIVISIONS **Rasmuson Library Historical Translation Series**; **Oral Biography Series**; **Classic Reprint Series** Informal non-fiction covering Northern interest. 10 titles a year. Queries and proposals welcome (see website for proposal guidelines).

Alpha – See **Penguin Group (USA) Inc.**

AMACOM Books

1601 Broadway, New York NY 10019–7406
☎001 212 586 8100 Fax 001 212 903 8168
www.amacombooks.org
President & Publisher *Harold V. Kennedy*

Founded 1972. Owned by American Management Association. Publishes business books only, including general management, business communications, sales and marketing, finance, computers and information systems, human resource management and training, career/personal growth skills. About 80 titles a year.

Amistad

See **HarperCollins Publishers, Inc.**

Anchor Books

See **Doubleday Broadway Publishing Group**

Julie Andrews Collection

See **HarperCollins Publishers, Inc.**

Anvil

See **Krieger Publishing Co.**

Shaye Areheart Books

See **Crown Publishing Group**

University of Arizona Press

355 S. Euclid Avenue, Suite. 103, Tucson
AZ 85719–6654
☎001 520 621 1441 Fax 001 520 621 8899
✉ uapress@uapress.arizona.edu
www.uapress.arizona.edu
Director *Christine Szuter*

Founded 1959. Publishes academic non-fiction, particularly with a regional/cultural link, plus Native-American and Hispanic literature. About 50 titles a year.

University of Arkansas Press

McIlroy House, 201 Ozark Avenue,
Fayetteville AR 72701
☎001 479 575 3246 Fax 001 479 575 6044
www.uapress.com
Director *Lawrence J. Malley*

Founded 1980. Publishes scholarly monographs, poetry and general trade books. Particularly interested in scholarly works in history, politics and literary criticism.

ROYALTIES annually.

ASM Press

1752 N. Street NW, Washington
DC 20036–2904
☎001 202 737 3600 Fax 001 202 942 9342
www.asmpress.org
Director *Jeffrey Holtmeier*

Founded 1899. The book publishing division of the American Society for Microbiology. Publishes monographs, texts, reference books and manuals in microbiological sciences.

Atheneum Books for Young Readers

See **Simon & Schuster Children's Publishing**

Atlantic Monthly Press

See **Grove/Atlantic Inc.**

Atria Books

See **Simon & Schuster Adult Publishing Group**

Avalon Publishing Group

1400 65th Street, Suite 250, Emeryville
CA 94608
www.avalonpub.com
Also at: 245 West 17th Street, 11th floor, New York, NY 10011–5300
Chairman *Charlie Winton*

Founded 1994. Leading independent publisher of fiction and non-fiction; current affairs, history, politics, psychology, self-help, health, science, women's studies, gay and lesbian, travel, music, mystery and popular culture.

DIVISIONS **Avalon Publishing Group California** IMPRINTS **Avalon Travel Publishing** (guide books); **Seal Press** (books by and about women); **Shoemaker & Hoard Publishers** (literature, fiction, history, biography); **Avalon Publishing Group New York** IMPRINTS **Carroll & Graf Publishers** (history, current affairs, literature, fiction, mystery); **Thunder's Mouth Press** (current affairs, popular culture, film, music, fiction, science); **Nation Books** (current world affairs, politics, cultural studies); **Marlowe & Company** (psychology, self-help, health). 581 titles in 2005. No unsolicited material.

Avery
375 Hudson Street, New York NY 10014
☎001 212 366 2000 Fax 001 212 366 2643
www.penguinputnam.com
Publisher *Megan Newman*
Founded 1976. Imprint of **Penguin Group (USA) Inc.** Publishes alternative and complementary health care, nutrition, disease prevention, diet, supplements, functional foods, mind/body therapies, holistic healing. About 30 titles a year. No unsolicited mss; synopses and ideas welcome if accompanied by s.a.e./IRCs.
ROYALTIES twice-yearly.

Avon
See **HarperCollins Publishers, Inc.**

Ballantine Books
See **Random House Publishing Group**

Bantam Dell Publishing Group
1745 Broadway, New York NY 10019
☎001 212 782 9000 Fax 001 212 302 7985
www.randomhouse.com/bantamdell
President & Publisher *Irwyn Applebaum*
Founded 1945. The largest mass market paperback publisher in the USA. A division of the **Random House Publishing Group.** Publishes general commercial fiction and non-fiction, young readers and children's: mysteries, science fiction and fantasy, romance, health and nutrition, self-help. DIVISIONS/IMPRINTS **Bantam Classics; Delacorte Press; Dell; Delta Books; Dial Press.**

Barron's Educational Series, Inc.
250 Wireless Boulevard, Hauppauge
NY 11788–3917
☎001 631 434 3311 Fax 001 631 434 3723
www.barronseduc.com
Chairman/CEO *Manuel H. Barron*
President *Ellen Sibley*
Acquisitions Editor *Wayne Barr*
Founded 1942. *Publishes* adult non-fiction, children's fiction and non-fiction, test preparation materials and language materials, cookbooks, pets, hobbies, sport, photography, health, business, law, computers, travel, business, art and painting. No adult fiction. 400 titles a year. Unsolicited mss, synopses and ideas for books welcome.
ROYALTIES twice-yearly.

Basic Books
See **Perseus Books Group**

Beacon Press
25 Beacon Street, Boston MA 02108
☎001 617 742 2110 Fax 001 617 723 3097
www.beacon.org
Director *Helene Atwan*
Founded 1854. Publishes general non-fiction. About 60 titles a year. Does not accept unsolicited mss. For further information, refer to the website.

Belknap Press
See **Harvard University Press**

Berkley
See **Penguin Group (USA) Inc.**

Bison Books
See **University of Nebraska Press**

Blackbirch Press
See **Thomson Gale**

Blackwell Publishing
2121 State Avenue, Ames IA 50014
☎001 515 292 0140 Fax 001 515 292 3348
✉ acquisitions@blackwellprofessional.com
www.blackwellprofessional.com
www.blackwellpublishing.com
Vice President, Professional Publishing *Antonia Seymour*
Formerly Iowa State Press. Founded 1934 as an offshoot of the Iowa State University's journalism department. Publishes reference books and textbooks on plant science, applied chemistry, food science, human dentistry, aquaculture, agriculture, animal science and veterinary medicine. No fiction, trade books or poetry. 60 titles a year. If within subject areas listed above, submit to acquisitions@blackwellprofessional.com
ROYALTIES annually

Boyds Mills Press
815 Church Street, Honesdale PA 18431
☎001 570 253 1164 Fax 001 570 253 0179

www.boydsmillspress.com

Publisher *Kent Brown*

A subsidiary of Highlights for Children, Inc. Founded 1990 as a publisher of children's trade books. Publishes children's and young adult's fiction, non-fiction and poetry. About 60 titles a year.

Brassey's, Inc.
See **Potomac Books, Inc.**

Caedmon
See **HarperCollins Publishers, Inc.**

University of California Press
2120 Berkeley Way, Berkeley CA 94704
☎001 510 642 4247   Fax 001 510 643 7127
✉ askucp@ucpress.edu
www.ucpress.edu

Director *Lynne Withey*

Founded 1893. Publishes scholarly and scientific non-fiction; some fiction in translation. Preliminary letter with outline preferred.

Canongate US
See **Grove/Atlantic Inc.**

Carolrhoda Books, Inc.
241 First Avenue N, Minneapolis MN 55401
☎001 612 332 3344   Fax 001 612 332 7615
www.lernerbooks.com

VP & Editor-in-Chief *Mary M. Rodgers*

Founded 1969. A division of the **Lerner Publishing Group**. Publishes: animals, biography, earth sciences, ethnology, history, geography, geology, general science, historical fiction and picture books. Please send s.a.e. for author guidelines, making sure guideline requests are clearly marked on the envelope or they will be returned. 'We are *only* accepting submissions once a year – November 1st–30th only. Submissions postmarked with other dates will be returned unopened. Also, only submissions with s.a.e./IRCs will receive a response.'

Carroll & Graf Publishers
See **Avalon Publishing Group**

Chamberlain Bros.
See **Penguin Group (USA) Inc.**

Charlesbridge Publishing
85 Main Street, Watertown MA 02472
☎001 617 926 0329   Fax 001 617 926 5720
✉ books@charlesbridge.com

www.charlesbridge.com

President/Publisher *Brent Farmer*
Vice President, School Division *Elena Dworkin Wright*

Founded 1980 as an educational publisher focused on a strategic approach to reading, writing, maths and science. Publishes children's educational programmes, non-fiction picture books and fiction for 3 to 12-year-olds. School division publishes mathematical fiction, *Maths Adventures*, in picture-book format and astronomy-related picture books.

University of Chicago Press
1427 East 60th Street, Chicago IL 60637
☎001 773 702 7700   Fax 001 773 702 9756
www.press.uchicago.edu

Founded 1891. Publishes academic non-fiction only.

Children's Press
See **Scholastic Library Publishing**

Chronicle Books LLC
85 Second Street, Sixth Floor, San Francisco CA 94105
☎001 415 537 4200   Fax 001 415 437 4460
www.chroniclebooks.com

President/Publisher *Jack Jensen*

Founded 1966. Publishes illustrated and non-illustrated adult trade and children's books as well as stationery and gift items. About 200 titles a year. Query or submit outline/synopsis and sample chapters and artwork. Guidelines for ms submissions on the website.
   ROYALTIES twice-yearly.

Clarkson Potter
See **Crown Publishing Group**

Columbia University Press
61 West 62nd Street, New York NY 10023
☎001 212 459 0600   Fax 001 212 459 3678
www.columbia.edu/cu/cup

Managing Director *James D. Jordan*
Editorial Director *Jennifer Crewe*

Founded 1893. Publishes scholarly and general interest non-fiction, reference, translations of Asian literature. No fiction or poetry. Welcomes unsolicited material if the subject fits their programme (see website). Approach by regular mail only.

Joanna Cotler Books
See **HarperCollins Publishers, Inc.**

Counterpoint Press
See **Perseus Books Group**

Crocodile Books, USA
See **Interlink Publishing Group, Inc.**

Crown Publishing Group
1745 Broadway, New York NY 10019
☎001 212 782 9000   Fax 001 212 940 7408
www.randomhouse.com/crown

Founded 1933. Division of the **Random House Publishing Group**. Publishes popular trade fiction and non-fiction.

IMPRINTS **Clarkson Potter** *Lauren Shakely* Illustrated books: cookery, gardening, style, decorating and design; **Crown Business** *Steve Ross* Business books; **Crown** *Steve Ross* General fiction and non-fiction; **Harmony Books** *Shaye Areheart* New Age, spirituality, religion, some fiction; **Shaye Areheart Books** *Shaye Areheart* Fiction; **Three Rivers Press** *Steve Ross* Non-fiction paperbacks.

Currency
See **Doubleday Broadway Publishing Group**

Da Capo Press
See **Perseus Books Group**

DAW Books, Inc.
375 Hudson Street, 3rd Floor, New York NY 10014–3658
☎001 212 366 2096   Fax 001 212 366 2090
✉ daw@penguingroup.com
www.dawbooks.com
Publishers *Elizabeth R. Wollheim, Sheila E. Gilbert*
Associate Editor *Peter Stampfel*

Founded 1971 by Donald and Elsie Wollheim as the first mass-market publisher devoted to science fiction and fantasy. An imprint of **Penguin Group (USA) Inc.** Publishes science fiction/fantasy, and some horror. No short stories, anthology ideas or non-fiction. Unsolicited mss, synopses and ideas for books welcome. About 36 titles a year.
ROYALTIES twice-yearly.

DD Equestrian Library
See **Doubleday Broadway Publishing Group**

Dearborn Trade Publishing
30 S. Wacker Drive, Chicago IL 60606–1719
☎001 312 836 4400   Fax 001 312 836 1021
www.dearborn.com
President *Roy Lipner*

Founded 1967. Publishes professional, textbooks, finance, law, business, marketing and investment reference for the consumer (personal finance, real estate) and small business owner. About 200 titles a year.

Del Rey
See **Random House Publishing Group**

Delacorte Press
See **Bantam Dell Publishing Group**

Dell
See **Bantam Dell Publishing Group**

Delta Books
See **Bantam Dell Publishing Group**

Dial Books for Young Readers
345 Hudson Street, New York NY 10014–3657
☎001 212 366 2800
Queries *Submissions Coordinator*

Founded 1961. A division of Penguin Books for Young Readers. Publishes children's books, including picture books, beginning readers, fiction and non-fiction for middle grade and young adults.

IMPRINTS Hardcover only: **Dial Books for Young Readers**; **Dial Easy-to-Read**. 50 titles a year. Accepts unsolicited picture book mss and up to ten pages for longer works with query letter. 'Do not send self-addressed envelope with submissions. Dial will respond within four months if interested in a manuscript.'
ROYALTIES twice-yearly.

Dial Press
See **Bantam Dell Publishing Group**

Doubleday Broadway Publishing Group
1745 Broadway, New York NY 10019
☎001 212 782 9000   Fax 001 212 302 7985
www.randomhouse.com
President & Publisher *Stephen Rubin*

The Doubleday Broadway Publishing Group, a division of the **Random House Publishing Group**, was formed by a merger of Doubleday and Broadway Books in 1999. Publishes fiction and non-fiction. DIVISION/IMPRINTS **The**

Anchor Bible; Anchor Books; Currency; DD Equestrian Library; Galilee Books; Image Books; Made Simple Books; Main Street/Back List; New Jerusalem Bible; Nan A. Talese Books; Outdoor Bible Series. No unsolicited material.

Downtown Press
See **Simon & Schuster Adult Publishing Group**

Lisa Drew Books
See **Simon & Schuster Adult Publishing Group**

Thomas Dunne Books
See **St Martin's Press LLC**

Dutton/Dutton's Children's Books
See **Penguin Group (USA) Inc.**

East Gate Books
See **M.E. Sharpe, Inc.**

Ecco
See **HarperCollins Publishers, Inc.**

William B. Eerdmans Publishing Co.
255 Jefferson Avenue SE, Grand Rapids MI 49503
☎001 616 459 4591 Fax 001 616 459 6540
www.eerdmans.com
President *William B. Eerdmans Jr*
Vice President/Editor-in-Chief *Jon Pott*
Founded 1911 as a theological and reference publisher. Gradually began publishing in other genres with authors like C.S. Lewis, Dorothy Sayers and Malcolm Muggeridge on its lists. Publishes religious: theology, biblical studies, ethical and social concern, social criticism and children's, religious history, religion and literature. DIVISIONS **Children's** *Judy Zylstra* Picture books, novels and biographies for the general trade market; **Other** *Jon Pott.* About 120 titles a year. Unsolicited mss, synopses and ideas welcome.
ROYALTIES twice-yearly.

Eos
See **HarperCollins Publishers, Inc.**

M. Evans & Co., Inc.
216 East 49th Street, New York NY 10017
☎001 212 688 2810 Fax 001 212 486 4544
✉ editorial@mevans.com
www.mevans.com
Associate Publisher *Harry McCullough*
Founded 1954 as a packager. Began publishing in 1962. Best known for its popular psychology and health books, with titles like *Dr Atkins' New Diet Revolution, This is How Love Works* and *Robert Crayhon's Nutrition Made Simple.* Publishes general non-fiction and fiction. About 30 titles a year. No unsolicited mss; query first. See website for ms submission guidelines.

Faber & Faber, Inc.
19 Union Square West, New York NY 10003
☎001 212 741 6900 Fax 001 212 633 9385
www.fsgbooks.com/faberandfaber.htm
Senior Editor *Denise Oswald*
Founded 1976. An affiliate of **Farrar, Straus & Giroux, Inc.** Publishes primarily non-fiction books for adults with a focus on film, theatre, music, popular culture and literary and cultural criticism. Unsolicited mss accepted; please query first and include IRCs with letter.

Farrar, Straus & Giroux, Inc.
19 Union Square West, New York NY 10003
☎001 212 741 6900 Fax 001 212 741 6973
www.fsgbooks.com
Founded 1946. Publishes general fiction, non-fiction, poetry, juveniles. No unsolicited material.

Fireside
See **Simon & Schuster Adult Publishing Group**

First Avenue Editions
See **Lerner Publishing Group**

Five Star
See **Thomson Gale**

Free Press
See **Simon & Schuster Adult Publishing Group**

Samuel French, Inc.
45 West 25th Street, New York NY 10010–2751
☎001 212 206 8990 Fax 001 212 206 1429
✉ info@samuelfrench.com
www.samuelfrench.com
Editor *Roxanne Heinz-Bradshaw*
Founded 1830. Publishes plays in paperback: London, Broadway and off-Broadway hits, light comedies, mysteries, one-act plays and plays for

young audiences. Unsolicited mss welcome. No synopses. OVERSEAS ASSOCIATES in London, Toronto, Sydney and Johannesburg.

ROYALTIES annually (books); twice-yearly (amateur productions); monthly (professional productions).

Gale
See **Thomson Gale**

Galilee Books
See **Doubleday Broadway Publishing Group**

Laura Geringer Books
See **HarperCollins Publishers, Inc.**

The Globe Pequot Press
PO Box 480, Guilford CT 06437–0480
☎001 203 458 4500 Fax 001 203 458 4601
✉ info@gobepequot.com
www.globepequot.com

Founded 1947. Publishes regional and international travel, how-to, regional and outdoor recreation. Also publishes the *Insiders'* guides. About 500 titles a year. Unsolicited mss, synopses and ideas welcome, particularly for travel and outdoor recreation books.

Gotham
See **Penguin Group (USA) Inc.**

Graham & Whiteside
See **Thomson Gale**

Great Source Education Group
See **Houghton Mifflin Co.**

Greenhaven Press
See **Thomson Gale**

Greenlight Readers
See **Harcourt Trade Publishers**

Greenwillow
See **HarperCollins Publishers, Inc.**

Griffin
See **St Martin's Press LLC**

Grolier Educational
See **Scholastic Library Publishing**

Grosset & Dunlap
See **Penguin Group (USA) Inc.**

Grove/Atlantic Inc.
841 Broadway, 4th Floor, New York
NY 10003–4793
☎001 212 614 7850 Fax 001 212 614 7886
www.groveatlantic.com
President/Publisher *Morgan Entrekin*
Managing Editor *Michael Hornburg*
Founded 1952. Publishes general fiction and non-fiction. IMPRINTS **Atlantic Monthly Press; Canongate US; Grove Press**.

Hachette Book Group USA
1271 Avenue of the Americas, New York
NY 10020
☎001 212 522 7200 Fax 001 212 522 7991
www.twbookmark.com
Chairman/CEO *David Young*
Formerly Time Warner Book Group. Acquired by Hachette Livre in 2006. Publishes fiction, non-fiction and children's. No unsolicited mss.

G.K. Hall
See **Thomson Gale**

Harcourt School Publishers
6277 Sea Harbor Drive, Orlando FL 32887
☎001 407 345 2000 Fax 001 407 345 3016
www.harcourtschool.com
President/CEO *Jan Spalding*
A division of Harcourt Inc., founded 1919. Publishes education materials – books, CD-ROMs, Internet and audio.

Harcourt Trade Publishers
525 'B' Street, Suite 1900, San Diego
CA 92101
☎001 619 231 6616
www.harcourtbooks.com
Also at: 15 East 26th Street, 15th Floor, New York, NY 10010 Tel 001 212 592 1000
President/CEO *Dan Farley*
A division of Harcourt Inc. Publishes fiction, poetry and non-fiction covering a wide range of subjects: biography, history, humour, music, dance, philosophy, psychology, religion, science, social sciences and sociology, sport, wine and spirits, women's studies.
    IMPRINTS **Greenlight Readers; Harvest Books; Libros Viajeros; Magic Carpet Books; Odyssey Classics; Red Wagon Books; Voyager Books**. About 300 titles a year. No unsolicited mss.

Harmony Books
See **Crown Publishing Group**

HarperCollins Publishers, Inc.
10 East 53rd Street, New York NY 10022
☎001 212 207 7000 Fax 001 212 207 7145
www.harpercollins.com
President/Chief Executive Officer *Jane Friedman*
Founded 1817. Subsidiary of News Corporation. Publishes general and literary fiction, general non-fiction, business, children's, reference and religious books.
GENERAL BOOKS GROUP IMPRINTS
Amistad; Avon; Caedmon; Collins; Collins Design; Ecco; Eos; Harper; Harper Paperbacks; Harper Perennial; Harper Perennial Modern Classics; HarperAudio; HarperEntertainment; HarperLargePrint; HarperSanFrancisco; PerfectBound; Rayo; ReganBooks; Smithsonian Books; William Morrow; William Morrow Cookbooks.
CHILDREN'S IMPRINTS
Amistad; Collins; Eos; Greenwillow; HarperChildren's Audio; HarperCollins Children's Books; HarperFestival; Harper-KidsEntertainment; HarperTempest; HarperTrophy; Joanna Cotler Books; Julie Andrews Collection; Katherine Tegen Books; Laura Geringer Books; Rayo. About 1700 titles a year. No unsolicited material.

Harvard University Press
79 Garden Street, Cambridge
MA 02138–1499
☎001 617 495 2600 Fax 001 617 495 5898
www.hup.harvard.edu
Director *William P. Sisler*
Founded 1913. Publishes scholarly non-fiction only; humanities, social sciences, sciences.
IMPRINT **Belknap Press**.

Harvest Books
See **Harcourt Trade Publishers**

University of Hawai'i Press
2840 Kolowalu Street, Honolulu HI 96822
☎001 808 956 8255 Fax 001 808 988 6052
✉ uhpbooks@hawaii.edu
www.uhpress.hawaii.edu
Director *William Hamilton*
Executive Editor *Patricia Crosby*
Founded 1947. Publishes scholarly books pertaining to East Asia, Southeast Asia, Hawaii and the Pacific. IMPRINT **Latitude 20**. Unsolicited

synopses and ideas welcome; approach by mail. No poetry, children's books or any topics other than Asia and the Pacific.
ROYALTIES twice-yearly.

HiddenSpring
See **Paulist Press**

Hill Street Press LLC
191 E. Broad Street, Suite 209, Athens
GA 30601–2848
☎001 706 613 7200 Fax 001 706 613 7204
www.hillstreetpress.com
Senior Editor *Patrick Allen*
Founded 1998. Publishes books on the American South – fiction and non-fiction. No poetry, erotica, romance, children's or young adults. Unsolicited material welcome; approach in writing in the first instance.

Hippocrene Books, Inc.
171 Madison Avenue, New York NY 10016
☎001 212 685 4371 Fax 001 212 779 9338
✉ hippocrene.books@verizon.net
www.hippocrenebooks.com
President/Editorial Director *George Blagowidow*
Founded 1971. Publishes general non-fiction and reference books. Particularly strong on foreign language dictionaries, language studies and international cookbooks. No fiction. Send brief summary, table of contents and one chapter for appraisal. S.a.e. essential for response. For manuscript return include sufficient postage cover (IRCs).

Holiday House, Inc.
425 Madison Avenue, New York NY 10017
☎001 212 688 0085 Fax 001 212 421 6134
www.holidayhouse.com
Vice President/Editor-in-Chief *Regina Griffin*
Publishes children's general fiction and non-fiction (pre-school to secondary). About 50 titles a year. Send query letters only. IRCs for reply must be included.

Henry Holt & Company, Inc.
175 Fifth Avenue, New York NY 10010
☎001 646 307 5095 Fax 001 212 633 0748
www.henryholt.com
President/Publisher *John Sterling*
Editor-in-Chief *Jennifer Barth*
Founded in 1866, Henry Holt is one of the oldest publishers in the United States. Part of Holtzbrinck Publishing Holdings. Publishes fiction, by both American and international

authors, biographies, children's and books on history and politics, ecology and psychology. DIVISIONS/IMPRINTS **Adult Trade; Books for Young Readers; Metropolitan Books; Owl Books; Times Books.** About 250 titles a year.

Houghton Mifflin Co.
222 Berkeley Street, Boston MA 02116–3764
☎001 617 351 5000   Fax 001 617 351 1125
www.hmco.com
Contact *Submissions Editor*

Founded 1832. Acquired by Vivendi in June 2001. Publishes literary fiction and general non-fiction, including autobiography, biography and history. Also school and college textbooks; children's fiction and non-fiction.

DIVISIONS/SUBSIDIARY COMPANIES
Houghton Mifflin College Division; Houghton Mifflin School Division; Houghton Mifflin Trade & Reference Division; Great Source Education Group; McDougal Littell Inc.; The Riverside Publishing Co.; Promissor Inc. About 100 titles a year. Unsolicited adult mss no longer accepted. Send synopses, outline and sample chapters for children's non-fiction; complete mss for children's fiction. Do not include s.a.e. 'You will not hear from us regarding the status of your submission unless we are interested, in which case you can expect to hear back from us within 12 weeks. We regret that we cannot respond personally to each submission, but we do consider each and every submission we receive.'

HPBooks
See **Penguin Group (USA) Inc.**

Hudson Street Press
See **Penguin Group (USA) Inc.**

Humanity Books
See **Prometheus Books**

Hydra
See **Northwestern University Press**

University of Illinois Press
1325 South Oak Street, Champaign IL 61820–6903
☎001 217 333 0950   Fax 001 217 244 8082
✉ uipress@uillinois.edu
www.press.uillinois.edu
Director *Willis Regier*

Publishes non-fiction, scholarly and general, with special interest in Americana, women's

studies, African–American studies, film, religion, American music and regional books. About 140–150 titles a year.

Image Books
See **Doubleday Broadway Publishing Group**

Indiana University Press
601 North Morton Street, Bloomington IN 47404–3797
☎001 812 855 8817   Fax 001 812 855 8507
✉ iupress@indiana.edu
www.indiana.edu/~iupress
Director *Janet Rabinowitch*

Publishes scholarly non-fiction in the following subject areas: African studies, anthropology, Asian studies, African-American studies, bioethics, environment and ecology, film, folklore, history, Jewish studies, Middle East studies, military history, music, paleontology, philanthropy, philosophy, politics, religion, Russian and East European studies, women's studies. Query in writing in first instance.

Interlink Publishing Group, Inc.
46 Crosby Street, Northampton MA 01060
☎001 413 582 7054   Fax 001 413 582 7057
✉ info@interlinkbooks.com
www.interlinkbooks.com
Publisher *Michel Moushabeck*
Editor *Pam Thompson*

Founded 1987. Publishes international fiction, travel, politics, cookbooks. Specialises in Middle East titles and ethnicity. IMPRINTS **Crocodile Books, USA** Editorial Head *Ruth Lane Moushabeck* Children's books; **Olive Branch Press** Editorial Head *Phyllis Bennis* Political books. About 50-60 titles a year. See submission guidelines on the website before making an approach.
ROYALTIES annually.

University of Iowa Press
100 Kuhl House, 119 West Park Road, Iowa City IA 52242–1000
☎001 319 335 2000   Fax 001 319 335 2055
✉ uipress@uiowa.edu
www.uiowapress.org
Director *Holly Carver*

Founded 1969 as a small scholarly press publishing about five books a year. Now publishing about 35 annually in a variety of scholarly fields, plus local interest, short stories, creative non-fiction and poetry anthologies. No unso-

licited mss; query first. Unsolicited ideas and synopses welcome.
ROYALTIES annually.

Jove
See **Penguin Group (USA) Inc.**

University Press of Kansas
2502 Westbrooke Circle, Lawrence KS 66045-4444
☎001 785 864 4154 Fax 001 785 864 4586
✉ upress@ku.edu
www.kansaspress.ku.edu
Director *Fred M. Woodward*
Founded 1946. Became the publishing arm for all six state universities in Kansas in 1976. Publishes scholarly books in American history, legal studies, presidential studies, American studies, political philosophy, political science, military history and environmental history. About 55 titles a year. Proposals welcome.
ROYALTIES annually.

Kar-Ben Publishing
See **Lerner Publishing Group**

Kent State University Press
307 Lowry Hall, Terrace Drive, Kent OH 44242
☎001 330 672 7913 Fax 001 330 672 3104
www.kentstateuniversitypress.com
Director *Will Underwood*
Editor-in-Chief *Joanna Hildebrand Craig*
Founded 1965. Publishes scholarly works in history, literary studies and general non-fiction with an emphasis on American history and literature. 30–40 titles a year. Queries welcome; no mss.
ROYALTIES annually.

The University Press of Kentucky
663 South Limestone Street, Lexington Kentucky 40508
☎001 859 257 8434 Fax 001 859 323 1873
✉ joyce.harrison@uky.edu
www.kentuckypress.com
Director *Stephen M. Wrinn*
Editor-in-Chief *Joyce Harrison*
Approx. Annual Turnover $2 million
Founded 1943. Publishes scholarly and general interest books in thehumanities and social sciences. 50 titles in 2005. No unsolicited mss; send synopses and ideas for books by post or e-mail. No fiction, drama, poetry, translations, memoirs or children's books.
ROYALTIES annually.

KidHaven Press
See **Thomson Gale**

Krieger Publishing Co.
PO Box 9542, Melbourne FL 32902–9542
☎001 321 724 9542 Fax 001 321 951 3671
✉ info@krieger-publishing.com
www.krieger-publishing.com
VEO *Robert E. Krieger*
President *Donald E. Krieger*
Vice-President *Maxine D. Krieger*
Founded 1970. Publishes science, education, ecology, humanities, history, mathematics, chemistry, space science, technology and engineering.
IMPRINTS/SERIES **Anvil; Exploring Community History; Orbit; Professional Practices; Public History.** Unsolicited mss welcome. Not interested in synopses/ideas or trade type titles.
ROYALTIES annually.

Large Print Press
See **Thomson Gale**

Latino Voices
See **Northwestern University Press**

Latitude 20
See **University of Hawai'i Press**

Lerner Publishing Group
241 First Avenue N., Minneapolis MN 55401
☎001 612 332 3344 Fax 001 612 332 7615
✉ info@lernerbooks.com
www.lernerbooks.com
Chairman *Harry J. Lerner*
President & Publisher *Adam M. Lerner*
Founded 1959. Publishes children's non-fiction, fiction and curriculum material for all grade levels.
DIVISIONS/IMPRINTS **Lerner Publications; Carolrhoda Books** (see entry); **Lerner-Classroom; First Avenue Editions; Millbrook Press; Twenty-First Century Books; Kar-Ben Publishing.** No puzzle, song or alphabet books, text books, workbooks, religious subject matter or plays. Submissions accepted only during the month of November; all others returned unopened. S.a.e./IRCs required for return of authorised submission material. Allow eight months for a response. No phone calls.
ROYALTIES annually.

Libros Viajeros
See **Harcourt Trade Publishers**

Little Simon
See **Simon & Schuster Children's Publishing**

Llewellyn Publications
PO Box 64383, St Paul MN 55164–0383
☎001 651 291 1970 Fax 001 612 291 1908
✉ lwlpc@llewellyn.com
www.llewellyn.com
President *Carl L. Weschcke*

Division of Llewellyn Worldwide Ltd. Founded 1901. Publishes self-help and how-to: astrology, alternative health, tantra, Fortean studies, tarot, yoga, Santeria, dream studies, metaphysics, magic, witchcraft, herbalism, shamanism, organic gardening, women's spirituality, graphology, palmistry, parapsychology. Also fiction with an authentic magical or metaphysical theme. About 100 titles a year. Unsolicited mss welcome; proposals preferred. IRCs essential in all cases.

Louisiana State University Press
PO Box 25053, Baton Rouge
LA 70894–5053
☎001 225 578 6295 Fax 001 225 578 6461
✉ lsupress@lsu.edu
www.lsu.edu/lsupress
Director *MaryKatherine Callaway*

Publishes non-fiction: Southern history, American history, Southern literary criticism, American literary criticism, biography, Atlantic World studies, environmental studies, political science and music (jazz). About 80 titles a year. See website for mss guidelines.

Lucent Books
See **Thomson Gale**

The Lyons Press Inc.
246 Goose Lane, Guilford CT 06347
☎001 203 458 4500
www.lyonspress.com
Associate Publisher *Gene Brissie*
Managing Editor *Alicia Solis*
Editor-in-Chief *Maureen Graney*
Executive Editor *Tom McCarthy*

Founded 1978. Imprint of The Globe Pequot Press. Publishes non-fiction; outdoor skills, hunting, fishing, sports, animals/pets, equestrian, history/current affairs, military history, nature, games, reference, health and fitness and

self-reliant living. About 200 titles a year. Unsolicited mss, synopses and book proposals welcome.
ROYALTIES twice-yearly.

McDougal Littell Inc.
See **Houghton Mifflin Co.**

Margaret K. McElderry Books
See **Simon & Schuster Children's Publishing**

McFarland & Company, Inc., Publishers
PO Box 611, Jefferson NC 28640
☎001 336 246 4460 Fax 001 336 246 5018
✉ info@mcfarlandpub.com
www.mcfarlandpub.com
President *Robert Franklin*
Executive Vice President *Rhonda Herman*
Executive Editor *Steve Wilson*
Editorial Development Chief *Virginia Tobiassen*

Founded 1979. A library reference and upper-end speciality market press publishing scholarly books in many fields: international studies, performing arts, popular culture, sports, automotive history, women's studies, music and fine arts, chess, history and librarianship. Specialises in general reference. Especially strong in cinema studies. No fiction, poetry, children's, New Age or inspirational/devotional works. About 275 titles a year. No unsolicited mss; send query letter first. Synopses and ideas welcome; submissions by mail preferred.
ROYALTIES annually.

The McGraw-Hill Companies, Inc.
1221 Avenue of the Americas, 50th Floor,
New York NY 10020
☎001 212 512 2000
www.mcgraw-hill.com
Chairman/President/CEO *Harold W. McGraw*

Founded 1888. Parent of **McGraw-Hill Education** which has offices in the UK (see entry under **UK Publishers**). Publishes a wide range of educational, professional, business, science, engineering and computing books.

Macmillan Reference USA
See **Thomson Gale**

Made Simple Books
See **Doubleday Broadway Publishing Group**

Magic Carpet Books
See **Harcourt Trade Publishers**

Main Street
See **Doubleday Broadway Publishing Group**

Marlowe & Company
See **Avalon Publishing Group**

University of Massachusetts Press
PO Box 429, Amherst MA 01004–0429
☎001 413 545 2217 Fax 001 413 545 1226
✉ info@umpress.umass.edu
www.umass.edu/umpress
Director *Bruce Wilcox*
Senior Editor *Clark Dougan*
Founded 1964. Publishes scholarly, general interest, African-American, ethnic, women's and gender studies, cultural criticism, economics, fiction, literary criticism, poetry, philosophy, biography, history. About 40 titles a year. Unsolicited mss considered but query letter preferred in the first instance. Synopses and ideas welcome.

Metropolitan Books
See **Henry Holt & Company, Inc.**

The University of Michigan Press
839 Greene Street, Ann Arbor
MI 48104–3209
☎001 734 764 4388 Fax 001 734 615 1540
✉ um.press@umich.edu
www.press.umich.edu
Founded 1930. Publishes scholarly non-fiction, fiction, textbooks, translation, literary criticism, theatre, music, current affairs, economics, political science, history, classics, anthropology, law studies, gender studies, English as a second language.

Milet Publishing LLC
333 North Michigan Avenue, Suite 530,
Chicago IL 60601
✉ info@milet.com
www.milet.com
Managing Directors *Sedat Turhan, Patricia Billings*
Founded 1995. Publishes children's picture books in English and dual language, and language learning books. Welcomes synopses and ideas for books. Queries may be made by e-mail but all submissions – proposal, outline or synopsis with sample text and/or artwork – by post only. 'Please review submission guidelines and existing titles on our website before submitting. We like bold, original stories and artwork, universal and/or multicultural.'

Millbrook Press
See **Lerner Publishing Group**

University of Minnesota Press
111 Third Avenue South, Suite 290,
Minneapolis MN 55401–2520
☎001 612 627 1970
www.upress.umn.edu
Director *Douglas Armato*
Founded 1927. Publishes academic books for scholars and selected general interest titles: American studies, anthropology, art and aesthetics, cultural theory, film and media studies, gay and lesbian studies, geography, literary theory, political and social theory, race and ethnic studies, sociology and urban studies. No original fiction or poetry. About 110 titles a year. No unsolicited mss. Welcomes synopses and proposals sent by mail (*no e-mails*). See website for submission details.

Minotaur
See **St Martin's Press LLC**

University Press of Mississippi
3825 Ridgewood Road, Jackson
MS 39211–6492
☎001 601 432 6205 Fax 001 601 432 6217
✉ press@ihl.state.ms.us
www.upress.state.ms.us
Director *Seetha Srinivasan*
Assistant Director/Editor-in-Chief *Craig Gill*
Founded 1970. Non-profit book publisher partially supported by the eight state universities. Publishes scholarly and trade titles in literature, history, American culture, Southern culture, African-American studies, women's studies, popular culture, folklife, ethnic, performance, art, architecture, photography and other liberal arts. REPRESENTED worldwide. UK representative: **Roundhouse Publishing Group**. About 60 titles a year. Send letter of enquiry, prospectus, table of contents and sample chapter prior to submission of full mss. ROYALTIES annually.

University of Missouri Press
2910 LeMone Boulevard, Columbia
MO 65201
☎001 573 882 7641 Fax 001 573 884 4498
www.system.missouri.edu/upress
Director *Beverly Jarrett*

Founded 1958. Publishes academic: history, intellectual history, journalism, literary criticism and related humanities disciplines, and occasional volumes of short stories. About 70 titles a year. Best approach is by letter. Send synopses for academic work together with author c.v.

Modern Library
See **Random House Publishing Group**

William Morrow
See **HarperCollins Publishers, Inc.**

NAL
See **Penguin Group (USA) Inc.**

Nation Books
See **Avalon Publishing Group**

University of Nebraska Press
233 North 8th Street, Lincoln
NE 68588–0255
☎001 402 472 3581 Fax 001 402 472 0308
www.nebraskapress.unl.edu
Director *Paul Royster*
Founded 1941. Publishes scholarly, Native American studies, history of the American West, literary and cultural studies, music, Jewish studies, military history, sports history, environmental history. IMPRINT **Bison Books**. No unsolicited mss; welcomes synopses and ideas for books. Send enquiry letter in the first instance with description of project and sample material. No original fiction, children's books or poetry.
ROYALTIES annually.

University of Nevada Press
MS 166, Reno NV 89557–0076
☎001 775 784 6573 Fax 001 775 784 6200
www.nvbooks.nevada.edu
Director & Editor-in-Chief *Joanne O'Hare*
Founded 1961. Publishes scholarly and popular books; serious fiction, Native American studies, natural history, Western Americana, Basque studies and regional studies. Unsolicited material welcome if it fits in with areas published, or offers a 'new and exciting' direction.

University Press of New England
One Court Street, Suite 250, Lebanon
NH 03766
☎001 603 448 1533 Fax 001 603 448 7006
www.upne.com
Director *Richard Abel*
Editor-in-Chief *Phyllis Deutsch*

Founded 1970. A scholarly books publisher sponsored by six institutions of higher education in the region: Brandeis, Dartmouth, University of Vermont, Tufts, the University of New Hampshire and Northchestern. Publishes general and scholarly non-fiction and Hardscrabble Books fiction of New England. OVERSEAS ASSOCIATES Canada: University of British Columbia; UK, Europe, Middle East: Eurospan University Press Group; Australia, New Zealand, Asia & the Pacific: East-West Export Books. About 80 titles a year. Unsolicited material welcome.
ROYALTIES annually.

University of New Mexico Press
1601 Randolph Road SE, Albuquerque
NM 87106
☎001 505 277 2346 Fax 001 505 277 9270
www.unmpress.com
Director *Luther Wilson*
Senior Acquisition Editor *William 'Clark' Whitehorn*
Founded 1929. Publishes scholarly, regional books and fiction. No how-to, humour, self-help or technical.

North Castle Books
See **M.E. Sharpe, Inc.**

University of North Texas Press
PO Box 311336, Denton TX 76203–1336
☎001 940 565 2142 Fax 001 940 565 4590
✉ rchrisman@unt.edu
www.unt.edu/untpress
Director *Ronald Chrisman*
Managing Editor *Karen DeVinney*
Founded 1987. Publishes folklore, regional interest, contemporary, social issues, Texas history, military history, women's issues, multcultural. Publishes annually the winners of the Vassar Miller Poetry Prize and the Katherine Anne Porter Prize in Short Fiction. About 15 titles a year. No unsolicited mss; synopses and ideas welcome.
ROYALTIES annually.

Northwestern University Press
629 Noyes Street, Evanston IL 60208
☎001 847 491 2046 Fax 001 847 491 8150
✉ nupress@northwestern.edu
www.nupress.northwestern.edu
Chairman *Peter Hayes*
Managing Director *Donna Shear*
Publishes general and academic books: philosophy, theatre and performance studies, Slavic

studies, Latino fiction and biography, contemporary fiction, poetry. No children's, art books. IMPRINTS **Hydra**; **Latino Voices** Editorial Head *Susan Betz*. 60 titles in 2005. Unsolicited mss, synopses and ideas welcome; approach by mail.
ROYALTIES annually.

W.W. Norton & Company, Inc.
500 Fifth Avenue, New York NY 10110–0017
☎001 212 354 5500 Fax 001 212 869 0856
www.wwnorton.com
Vice-President/Managing Editor *Nancy K. Palmquist*
Founded 1923. Publishes fiction and non-fiction, college textbooks and professional books. About 400 titles a year.

Odyssey Classics
See **Harcourt Trade Division**

Ohio University Press
19 Circle Drive, The Ridges, Athens OH 45701
☎001 740 593 1155 Fax 001 740 593 4536
www.ohiou.edu/oupress
Director *David Sanders*
Founded 1964. Publishes academic, regional and general trade books. IMPRINT **Swallow Press**. 50 titles in 2005. Synopses and ideas for books welcome. Send detailed synopsis, sample chapters and c.v. with covering letter. See website for author guidelines. No children's, how-to or genre fiction.
ROYALTIES twice-yearly.

University of Oklahoma Press
2800 Venture Drive, Norman OK 73069–8216
☎001 405 325 2000 Fax 001 405 325 4000
www.oupress.com
Director *John N. Drayton*
Founded 1928. Publishes general scholarly non-fiction only: American Indian studies, American West, classical studies, anthropology, natural history and political science. About 100 titles a year.

Olive Branch Press
See **Interlink Publishing Group, Inc.**

One World
See **Random House Publishing Group**

Orbit
See **Krieger Publishing Co.**

Outdoor Bible Series
See **Doubleday Broadway Publishing Group**

Owl Books
See **Henry Holt & Company, Inc.**

Palgrave
See **St Martin's Press LLC**

Paragon House
1925 Oakcrest Avenue, Suite 7, St Paul MN 55113–2619
☎001 651 644 3087 Fax 001 651 644 0997
✉ paragon@paragonhouse.com
www.paragonhouse.com
VP/Executive Director *Dr Gordon L. Anderson*
Founded 1982. Publishes non-fiction: reference and academic. Subjects include history, religion, philosophy, spirituality, Jewish interest, political science, international relations, psychology.
ROYALTIES twice-yearly.

Paulist Press
997 Macarthur Boulevard, Mahwah NJ 07430
☎001 201 825 7300 Fax 001 201 825 8345
✉ sales@paulistpress.com
www.paulistpress.com
Owner *Missionary Society of St Paul the Apostle, New York*
Publisher *Fr. Lawrence Boadt, C.S.P.*
Managing Editor *Paul McMahon*
Founded in 1866 by the Paulist Fathers as the Catholic Publication Society, it is now one of the largest Catholic publishing houses in the world. Publishes religious, spiritual, theology and children's religious books. IMPRINTS **Paulist Press** *Paul McMahon* Spirituality, ministry resources, ethics and social issues, ecumenical and inter-religious; *Nancy de Flon* Theology and philosophy; *Susan O'Keefe* Children's religious. **HiddenSpring** *Paul McMahon* General religious trade books. 90 titles a year. Unsolicited mss, synopses and ideas welcome; approach through direct mail with IRCs for return postage of material and/or letter. Mainstream Christian religious material; no New Age, Evangelical Christian books.

Pearson Scott Foresman
1900 E Lake Avenue, Glenview IL 60025
☎001 847 729 3000
✉ firstname.lastname@scottforesman.com
www.scottforesman.com
President *Paul McFall*

Founded 1896. Part of Pearson Education. Publishes elementary education materials. No unsolicited material.

Pelican Publishing Company

1000 Burmaster Street, Gretna LA 70053
☎001 504 368 1175
www.pelicanpub.com
Editor-in-Chief *Nina Kooij*

Publishes general non-fiction: popular history, cookbooks, travel, art, business, biography, children's, editorial cartoon, architecture, Scottish interest, collectibles guides and motivational. About 75 titles a year. Initial enquiries required for all submissions.

Penguin Group (USA) Inc.

375 Hudson Street, New York NY 10014
☎001 212 366 2000   Fax 001 212 366 2666
www.penguingroup.com
CEO *David Shanks*
President *Susan Petersen Kennedy*

The second-largest trade book publisher in the world. Publishes fiction and non-fiction in hardback and paperback; adult and children's.

ADULT DIVISION IMPRINTS Hardcover: **Avery** (see entry); **Chamberlain Bros.**; **Dutton**; **G.P. Putnam's Sons**; **Gotham**; **Hudson Street Press**; **Jeremy P. Tarcher/Putnam**; **The Penguin Press**; **Portfolio**; **Riverhead Books**; **Sentinel**; **Viking**; Trade Paperback: **Ace Books**; **Alpha Books**; **Berkley**; **HPBooks**; **NAL**; **Perigee**; **Penguin Books**; **Plume**; **Riverhead**; **Roc**. Mass Market Paperback: **Ace**; **Berkley**; **DAW Books** (see entry); **Jove**.

YOUNG READERS DIVISION Hardcover: **Dial Books for Young Readers** (see entry); **Dutton Children's Books**; **Frederick Warne**; **G.P. Putnam's Sons** (see entry); **Philomel Books**; **Viking Children's Books**. Paperback: **Firebird**; **Puffin Books**; **Razorbill**; **Speak**. Mass Merchandise: **Grosset & Dunlap**; **Price Stern Sloan**.

No unsolicited mss.
ROYALTIES twice-yearly.

University of Pennsylvania Press

3905 Spruce Street, Philadelphia
PA 19104–4112
☎001 215 898 6261   Fax 001 215 898 0404
✉ custserv@pobox.upenn.edu
www.upenn.edu/pennpress
Director *Eric Halpern*
Founded 1890. Publishes serious non-fiction:

scholarly, reference, professional, textbooks and semi-popular trade. No original fiction or poetry. About 100 titles a year. No unsolicited mss but synopses and ideas for books welcome.
ROYALTIES vary according to sales prospects and other relevant factors.

Perennial

See **HarperCollins Publisers, Inc.**

PerfectBound

See **HarperCollins Publishers, Inc.**

Perigee

See **Penguin Group (USA) Inc.**

Perseus Books Group

387 Park Avenue S, 12th Floor, New York
NY 10016
☎001 212 340 8100   Fax 001 212 340 8115
www.perseusbooksgroup.com
President/CEO *David Steinberger*

Founded 1997. Publishes general, academic and professional. IMPRINTS **Basic Books**; **Counterpoint Press**; **Da Capo Press**; **PublicAffairs**; **Westview Press**. No unsolicited mss.

Phantom-Players Press

See **Players Press**

Philomel Books

See **Penguin Group (USA) Inc.**

Picador USA

See **St Martin's Press LLC**

Players Press

PO Box 1132, Studio City CA 91614–0132
☎001 818 789 4980
CEO *William-Alan Landes*

Founded 1965 as a publisher of plays; now publishes across the entire range of performing arts: plays, musicals, theatre, film, cinema, television, costume, puppetry, plus technical theatre and cinema material. IMPRINT **Phantom-Players Press** Music: choral, percussions, musicals. OVERSEAS SUBSIDIARIES in Canada, Australia, Germany and the UK. No unsolicited mss; synopses/ideas welcome. Send query letter s.a.e. for response.
ROYALTIES twice-yearly.

Plume

See **Penguin Group (USA) Inc.**

Pocket Books
See **Simon & Schuster Adult Publishing Group**

Portfolio
See **Penguin Group (USA) Inc.**

Potomac Books, Inc.
22841 Quicksilver Drive, Dulles VA 20166
☎001 703 661 1548 Fax 001 703 661 1547
www.potomacbooksinc.com
Publisher *Don McKeon*
Marketing & Subsidiary Rights *Sam Dorrance*
Formerly Brassey's, Inc., founded 1984 (acquired in 1999 by Books International of Dulles, Virginia). Publishes non-fiction titles on topics of history (especially military and diplomatic history), world and US affairs, US foreign policy, defence, intelligence, biography and sports. About 80 titles a year. No unsolicited mss; synopses and ideas welcome.
ROYALTIES annually.

Presidio Press
See **Random House Publishing Group**

Price Stern Sloan
See **Penguin Group (USA) Inc.**

Primary Source Microfilm
See **Thomson Gale**

Princeton University Press
41 William Street, Princeton NJ 08540
☎001 609 258 4900
www.pup.princeton.edu
Editor-in-Chief *Sam Elworthy*
Founded 1905. Publishes academic and trade books. About 200 titles a year. No unsolicited mss. Synopses and ideas considered. Send letter to editor-in-chief in the first instance. No fiction. OVERSEAS ASSOCIATE Princeton University Press, 3 Market Place, Woodstock OX20 1SY, UK.
ROYALTIES annually.

Professional Practices
See **Krieger Publishing Co.**

Prometheus Books
59 John Glenn Drive, Amherst NY 14228–2197
☎001 800 421 0351 Fax 001 716 691 0137
✉ marketing@prometheusbooks.com
www.prometheusbooks.com
www.pyrsf.com
Chairman *Paul Kurtz*
Editor-in-Chief *Steven L. Mitchell*
Founded 1969. Publishes books and journals: educational, scientific professional, library, popular science, science fiction and fantasy, philosophy and young readers. IMPRINTS **Humanity Books**; **Pyr™**. About 100 titles a year. Unsolicited mss, synopses and ideas for books welcome.
ROYALTIES twice-yearly.

Promissor Inc
See **Houghton Mifflin Co.**

Public History
See **Krieger Publishing Co.**

PublicAffairs
See **Perseus Books Group**

Puffin Books
See **Penguin Group (USA) Inc.**

G.P. Putnam's Sons (Children's)
345 Hudson Street, New York NY 10014
☎001 212 366 2000
www.penguingroup.com
President/Publisher *Nancy Paulsen*
Executive Editor *Kathryn Dawson*
A children's book imprint of Penguin Young Readers Group, a member of **Penguin Group (USA) Inc.** Publishes picture books, middle-grade fiction and young adult fiction.

Pyr™
See **Prometheus Books**

Rand McNally
PO Box 7600, Chicago IL 60680
☎001 847 329 8100 Fax 001 847 673 0539
www.randmcnally.com
President/CEO *Rob Apatoff*
Founded 1856. Publishes world atlases and maps, road atlases of North America and Europe, city and state maps of the United States and Canada, educational wall maps, atlases and globes, plus children's products. Includes electronic multimedia products. IMPRINT **Rand McNally for Kids**.

Random House Publishing Group
1745 Broadway, New York NY 10019
☎001 212 782 9000
www.randomhouse.com
President/Publisher *Gina Centrello*

Publishes fiction, non-fiction, science fiction in hardcover, trade paperback and mass market.

IMPRINTS **Ballantine Books; Del Rey; Modern Library; One World; Presidio Press; Random House; Random House Trade Paperbacks; Villard.** 720 titles in 2005. No unsolicited mss.

Rayo
See **HarperCollins Publishers, Inc.**

Razorbill
See **Penguin Group (USA) Inc.**

Reader's Digest Association Inc
Reader's Digest Road, Pleasantville NY 10570–7000
☎001 914 238 1000 Fax 001 914 238 4559
www.rd.com
Chairman/CEO *Thomas Ryder*

Publishes home maintenance reference, cookery, DIY, health, gardening, children's books; videos and magazines.

Red Wagon Books
See **Harcourt Trade Division**

ReganBooks
See **HarperCollins Publishers, Inc.**

Riverhead Books
See **Penguin Group (USA) Inc.**

The Riverside Publishing Co.
See **Houghton Mifflin Co.**

The Rosen Publishing Group, Inc.
29 East 21st Street, New York NY 10010
☎001 212 777 3017 Fax 001 212 777 0277
www.rosenpublishing.com
President *Roger Rosen*
Vice-President *Gina Strazzabosco-Hayn*

Founded 1950. Publishes non-fiction books (supplementary to the curriculum, reference and self-help) for a young adult audience. Reading levels are years 7–12, 4–6 (books for teens with literacy problems), and 5–9. Subjects include conflict resolution, character building, health, safety, drug abuse prevention, self-help and multicultural titles. For all imprints, write with outline and sample chapters.

Rutgers University Press
100 Joyce Kilmer Avenue, Piscataway NJ 08854–8099
☎001 732 445 7762 Fax 001 732 445 7039
rutgerspress.rutgers.edu
Director *Marlie Wasserman*
Associate Director/Editor-in-Chief *Leslie Mitchner*

Founded 1936. Publishes scholarly books, regional, social sciences and humanities. About 80 titles a year. Unsolicited mss, synopses and ideas for books welcome. No original fiction or poetry.

St James Press
See **Thomson Gale**

St Martin's Press LLC
175 Fifth Avenue, New York NY 10010
☎001 212 674 5151 Fax 001 212 420 9314
✉ inquiries@stmartins.com
www.stmartins.com
CEO (Holtzbrinck) *John Sargent*
President/Publisher (Trade Division) *Sally Richardson*

Founded 1952. A subsidiary of **Macmillan Publishers** (UK), St Martin's Press made its name and fortune by importing raw talent from the UK to the States and has continued to buy heavily in the UK. Publishes general fiction, especially mysteries and crime; and adult non-fiction: history, self-help, political science, travel, biography, scholarly, popular reference, college textbooks.

IMPRINTS **Picador USA; Griffin** (trade paperbacks); **St Martin's Paperbacks** (mass market); **Thomas Dunne Books; Minotaur; Palgrave; Truman Talley Books.** All submissions via legitimate literary agents only.

K.G. Saur
See **Thomson Gale**

Scarecrow Press Inc.
4501 Forbes Boulevard, Suite 200, Lanham MD 20706
☎001 301 459 3366 Fax 001 301 429 5747
www.scarecrowpress.com
President *Jed Lyons*
Vice President/Publisher *Edward Kurdyla*

Founded 1950 as a short-run publisher of library reference books. Acquired by **University Press of America, Inc.** in 1995 which is now part of Rowman and Littlefield Publishing Group. Publishes reference, scholarly and monographs (all levels) for libraries. Reference books in all areas except sciences, specialising in the performing arts, music, cinema and library science. About 160 titles a year. Unsolicited mss welcome but material will not be returned unless requested and accompanied by return postage. Unsolicited synopses and ideas for books welcome.

Schirmer Reference
See **Thomson Gale**

Scholarly Resources, Inc.
See **Thomson Gale**

Scholastic Library Publishing
90 Old Sherman Turnpike, Danbury CT 06816
☎001 203 797 3500 Fax 001 203 797 3657
www.scholasticlibrary.com
President *Greg Worrell*

Publishes juvenile non-fiction, encyclopedias, speciality reference sets and picture books.
DIVISIONS/IMPRINTS **Children's Press**; **Grolier Educational**; **Franklin Watts**. About 500 titles a year.

Scribner
See **Simon & Schuster Adult Publishing Group**

Charles Scribner's Sons
See **Thomson Gale**

Seal Press
See **Avalon Publishing Group**

Sentinel
See **Penguin Group (USA) Inc.**

Seven Stories Press
140 Watts Street, New York NY 10013
☎001 212 226 8760 Fax 001 212 226 1411
www.sevenstories.com
Publisher *Daniel Simon*
Subsidiary Rights *Anna Lui*

Founded 1995. Named by *Publishers Weekly* in 1999 as the fastest growing independent publisher in America. Publishes, literature, politics, media studies, popular culture, health. About 50 titles a year. No unsolicited mss; synopses and ideas from agents welcome or send query letter. No e-mail submissions. No children's or business books. OVERSEAS SUBSIDIARIES Turnaround Publishing Services, UK and EU; Palgrave Macmillan, Australia; Macmillian Publishers NZ Ltd., New Zealand; Liberty Books (Pte.) Ltd., Pakistan; Pen International Pte. Ltd., Singapore; Stephan Phillips (Pty.) Ltd., Southern Africa; Publishers Group Canada, Canada.

M.E. Sharpe, Inc.
80 Business Park Drive, Suite 202, Armonk NY 10504
☎001 914 273 1800 Fax 001 914 273 2106
✉ info@mesharpe.com
www.mesharpe.com
Chairman *M.E. Sharpe*
Managing Director *Vincent Fuentes*

Founded 1958. Publishes books and journals in the social sciences and humanities, both original works and translations in Asian and East European studies. IMPRINTS **East Gate Books**; **North Castle Books**; **Sharpe Reference** *Patricia Kolb*. 80 titles in 2005. No unsolicited material.
ROYALTIES annually.

Shoemaker & Hoard Publishers
See **Avalon Publishing Group**

Simon & Schuster Adult Publishing Group (Division of Simon & Schuster, Inc)
1230 Avenue of the Americas, New York NY 10020
☎001 212 698 7000 Fax 001 212 698 7007
www.simonsays.com
President *Carolyn K. Reidy*

Publishes fiction and non-fiction.
DIVISIONS
Atria Books VP & Executive Editorial Director *Emily Bestler*, **Free Press** VP & Editorial Director *Dominick Anfuso*; **Fireside/ Touchstone** VP & Editor-in-Chief Trish Todd; **Pocket Books** VP & Editorial Director *Maggie Crawford*; **Scribner** VP & Editor-in-Chief *Nan Graham*; **Simon and Schuster** VP & Editorial Director *Alice Mayhew*.
IMPRINTS
Atria Books; Downtown Press; Lisa Drew Books; Fireside; Free Press; Pocket Books; Scribner; Scribner Classics; S&S Libros eñ Espanol; Simon & Schuster; Strebor Books; Threshold Editions; Touchstone; Washington Square Press. No unsolicited mss.
ROYALTIES twice-yearly.

Simon & Schuster Children's Publishing
1230 Avenue of the Americas, New York NY 10020
☎001 212 698 7200
www.simonsayskids.com
President/Publisher *Rick Richter*

A division of the Simon & Schuster Consumer Group. Publishes pre-school to young adult, picture books, hardcover and paperback fiction, non-fiction, trade, library and mass-market titles.
IMPRINTS
Aladdin Books Picture books, paperback fiction and non-fiction reprints and originals, and limited series for ages pre-school to young adult; **Atheneum Books for Young Readers** Picture books, hardcover fiction and non-fiction books across all genres for ages three to young adult; **Little Simon** Mass-market novelty books (pop-ups, board books, colouring & activity) and merchandise (book and audio cassette) for ages birth through eight; **Margaret K. McElderry Books** Picture books, hardcover fiction and non-fiction trade books for children ages three to young adult; **Simon & Schuster Books for Young Readers** Picture books, hardcover fiction and non-fiction for children ages three to young adult. **Simon Spotlight** Devoted exclusively to children's media tie-ins and licensed properties. About 480 titles a year. No unsolicited material.

Simon Spotlight
See **Simon & Schuster Children's Publishing**

Sleeping Bear Press
See **Thomson Gale**

Smithsonian Books
See **HarperCollins Publishers, Inc.**

Southern Illinois University Press
PO Box 3697, Carbondale IL 62902–3697
☎001 618 453 2281 Fax 001 618 453 1221
www.siu.edu/~siupress
Director *Lain Adkins*
Founded 1956. Publishes scholarly and general interest non-fiction books and educational materials. 50 titles a year.

Stackpole Books
5067 Ritter Road, Mechanicsburg PA 17055
☎001 717 796 0411 Fax 001 717 796 0412
www.stackpolebooks.com
President *David Ritter*
Vice President/Editorial Director *Judith Schnell*
Founded 1933. Publishes outdoor sports, fishing, hunting, nature, crafts, Pennsylvania and regional, military reference, history. About 100 titles a year.
ROYALTIES twice-yearly.

Stanford University Press
1450 Page Mill Road, Palo Alto
CA 94304–1124
☎001 650 723 9434 Fax 001 650 725 3457
✉ info@www.sup.org
www.sup.org
Managing Director *Geoffrey R.H. Burn*
Founded 1925. Publishes non-fiction: scholarly works in all areas of the humanities, social sciences, history and literature, also professional lists in business, economics and law. About 150 titles a year. No unsolicited mss; query in writing first.

State University of New York Press
194 Washington Avenue, Suite 305, Albany
NY 12210–2384
☎001 518 472 5000 Fax 001 518 472 5038
✉ info@sunypress.edu
www.sunypress.edu
Director *James Peltz*
Editor-in-Chief *Jane Bunker*
Founded 1966. Part of the Research Foundation of SUNY. Publishes scholarly and trade books in the humanities and social sciences. 175 titles in 2005. Send submissions to the Editor-in-Chief.
ROYALTIES annually.

Sterling Publishing Co. Inc.
387 Park Avenue South, 5th Floor, New York
NY 10016–8810
☎001 212 532 7160 Fax 001 212 213 2495
www.sterlingpub.com
VP/Publisher *Andrew Martin*
President/CEO *Charles Nurnberg*
VP, Editorial *Steve Magnuson*
Executive VP/COO *Macus Leaver*
Founded 1949. Publishes illustrated non-fiction: reference and information books, science, business, nature, arts and crafts, home improvement, history, photography, children's humour, complementary health, wine and food, sports, music, psychology, Mind, Body & Spirit, woodworking, pets, hobbies, gardening, games and puzzles, general non-fiction. Submission guidelines available.

Strebor Books
See **Simon & Schuster Adult Publishing Group**

Swallow Press
See **Ohio University Press**

Syracuse University Press

621 Skytop Road, Suite 110, Syracuse
NY 13244–5290
☎001 315 443 5534 Fax 001 315 443 5545
www.SyracuseUniversityPress.syr.edu

Director *Peter B. Webber*

Founded 1943. Publishes scholarly books in the following areas: Middle East studies, Middle East literature in translation,Irish studies, Jewish studies, sports, gender and globalisation, Iroquois studies, women and religion, medieval studies, religion and politics, television, geography and regional books. Distributes for the Moshe Dayan Center, Jusoor. About 50 titles a year. No unsolicited mss. Send query letter with IRCs.
ROYALTIES annually.

The TAFT Group

See **Thomson Gale**

Nan A. Talese

See **Doubleday Broadway Publishing Group**

Jeremy P. Tarcher

See **Penguin Group (USA) Inc.**

Katherine Tegan Books

See **HarperCollins Publishers, Inc.**

Temple University Press

1601 N. Broad Street, 083–42, Philadelphia
PA 19122–6099
☎001 215 204 8787 Fax 001 215 204 4719
www.temple.edu/tempress

Editor-in-Chief *Janet M. Francendese*

Founded 1969. Publishes scholarly books. Authors generally academics. Letter of inquiry with brief outline. Include fax/e-mail address. About 60 titles a year.

University of Tennessee Press

110 Conference Center Bldg., Knoxville
TN 37996–4108
☎001 865 974 3321 Fax 001 865 974 3724
www.utpress.org

Managing Editor *Stan Ivester*
Acquisitions Editor *Scott Danforth*

Founded 1940. Publishes scholarly and regional non-fiction. Submission guidelines are posted on the website.

University of Texas Press

PO Box 7819, Austin TX 78722
☎001 512 471 7233/471 4278 (editorial)
Fax 001 512 232 7178
✉ utpress@uts.cc.utexas.edu
www.utexas.edu/utpress/
www.utexaspress.com

Director *Joanna Hitchcock*
Assistant Director/Editor-in-Chief *Theresa J. May*

Publishes scholarly and regional non-fiction: anthropology, architecture, classics, environmental studies, humanities, social sciences, geography, language studies, literary modernism; Latin American/Latino/Mexican American/Middle Eastern/Native American studies, natural history and ornithology, regional books (Texas and the southwest). Unsolicited material welcome in above subject areas only. Author guidelines available on the website. About 90 titles a year and 11 journals.
ROYALTIES annually.

Thomson Gale

27500 Drake Road, Farmington Hills
MI 48331–3535
☎001 248 699 4253 Fax 001 248 699 8070
www.gale.com

President *Gordon Macomber*

Part of The Thomson Corporation, Thomson Gale is a world leader in information and educational publishing. Addresses all types of information needs, from homework help to health questions and business profiles, in a variety of formats: books, Web-based material and microfilm.

BRANDS/IMPRINTS **Blackbirch Press**; **Five Star**; **Graham & Whiteside**; **Greenhaven Press**; **G.K. Hall**; **KidHaven Press**; **Large Print Press**; **Lucent Books**; **Macmillan Reference USA**; **Primary Source Microfilm**; **K.G. Saur**; **Schirmer Reference**; **Scholarly Resources, Inc.**; **Charles Scribner's Sons**; **Sleeping Bear Press**; **St James Press**; **The TAFT Group**; **Thorndike Press**; **Twayne Publishers**; **UXL**; **Walker Large Print**; **Wheeler Publishing**.

Thorndike Press

See **Thomson Gale**

Three Rivers Press

See **Crown Publishing Group**

Threshold Editions

See **Simon & Schuster Adult Publishing Group**

Thunder's Mouth Press

See **Avalon Publishing Group**

Times Books
See **Henry Holt & Company, Inc.**

Touchstone
See **Simon & Schuster Adult Publishing Group**

Transaction Publishers Ltd
c/o Rutgers – The State University of New Jersey, 35 Berrue Circle, Piscataway NJ 08854–8042
☎001 732 445 2280   Fax 001 732 445 3138
✉ ihorowitz@transactionpub.com
www.transactionpub.com

Chairman *I.L. Horowitz*
President *Mary E. Curtis*
Vice President *Scott B. Bramson*

Founded 1962. Independent publisher of academic social scientific books, periodicals and serials. Publisher of record in international social research. 170 titles in 2005. All unsolicited material should be submitted in hard copy and full draft. E-mail submissions are not accepted. 'Decision-making is rapid.'

Truman Talley Books
See **St Martin's Press LLC**

Twayne Publishers
See **Thomson Gale**

Twenty-First Century Books
See **Lerner Publishing Group**

Tyndale House Publishers, Inc.
PO Box 80, Wheaton IL 60189–0080
☎001 630 668 8303
www.tyndale.com
President *Mark D. Taylor*

Founded 1962. Books cover a wide range of categories from non-fiction to gift books, theology, doctrine, Bibles, fiction, children's and youth. Also produces video material, calendars and audio books for the same market. No poetry. Non-denominational religious publisher of around 300 titles a year for the evangelical Christian market. No unsolicited mss. Synopses and ideas considered. Writer's guidelines available on the website.

University Press of America, Inc.
4501 Forbes Boulevard, Suite 200, Lanham MD 20706
☎001 301 459 3366   Fax 001 301 429 5748
www.univpress.com

President/Publisher *James E. Lyons*
VP/Editorial Director *Judith L. Rothman*
Founded 1974. Publishes scholarly monographs, college and graduate level textbooks. No children's, elementary or high school. About 300 titles a year. Submit outline or request proposal questionnaire.

UXL
See **Thomson Gale**

Viking/Viking Children's Books
See **Penguin Group (USA) Inc.**

Villard
See **Random House Publishing Group**

University of Virginia Press
PO Box 400318, Charlottesville VA 22904–4318
☎001 434 924 3468   Fax 001 434 982 2655
✉ vapress@virginia.edu
www.upress.virginia.edu

Director *Penelope J. Kaiserlian*

Founded 1963. Publishes academic books in humanities and social science with concentrations in American history, African-American studies, architecture, Victorian literature, Caribbean literature and ecocriticism. No unsolicited mss; will consider synopses and ideas for books if in their specific areas of concentration. Approach by mail for full proposal; e-mail for short inquiry. No fiction, children's, poetry or academic books outside interests specified above.
ROYALTIES annually.

Voyager Books
See **Harcourt Trade Division**

J. Weston Walch, Publisher
PO Box 658, Portland ME 04104
☎001 207 772 2846   Fax 001 207 772 3105
www.walch.com

President *John Thoreson*
Editor-in-Chief *Susan Blair*

Founded 1927. Publishes supplementary educational materials for middle and secondary schools across a wide range of subjects, including English/language arts, literacy, special needs, mathematics, social studies, science and school-to-career. Always interested in ideas from secondary school teachers who develop materials in the classroom. Proposal letters, synopses and ideas welcome.

Walker & Co.

104 Fifth Avenue, 7th Floor, New York NY 10011
☎001 212 727 8300 Fax 001 212 727 0984
✉ firstinitiallastname@walkerbooks.com
www.walkerbooks.com (trade non-fiction)
www.walkeryoungreaders.com (BFYR)
Contact *Submissions Editor*

Founded 1959. A division of **Bloomsbury Publishing**. Publishes children's fiction and non-fiction and adult non-fiction. Please contact the following editors in advance before sending any material to be sure of their interest, then follow up as instructed: **Trade Non-fiction** *George Gibson* Permission and documentation must be available with mss. Submit prospectus first, with sample chapters and marketing analysis. **Books for Young Readers** *Emily Easton* Fiction and non-fiction for all ages. Query before sending non-fiction proposals. Especially interested in picture books – fiction and non-fiction, historical and contemporary fiction for middle grades and young adults. BFYR will consider unsolicited submissions.

Walker Large Print
See **Thomson Gale**

Frederick Warne
See **Penguin Group (USA) Inc.**

Washington Square Press
See **Simon & Schuster Adult Publishing Group**

Washington State University Press
PO Box 645910, Pullman WA 99164–5910
☎001 509 335 3518 Fax 001 509 335 8568
✉ wsupress@wsu.edu
wsupress.wsu.edu
Editor-in-Chief *Glen Lindeman*

Founded 1928. Publishes hardcover originals, trade paperbacks and reprints. Publishes mainly on the history, prehistory, culture, politics and natural history of the Northwest United States (Washington, Idaho, Oregon, Montana, Alaska) and British Columbia, but works that focus on national topics or other regions may also be considered if they have a Northwest connection. Subjects include history, biography, cooking/food history, nature/environment, politics. 8–10 titles a year. Queries welcome.

Franklin Watts
See **Scholastic Library Publishing**

Westview Press
See **Perseus Books Group**

Wheeler Publishing
See **Thomson Gale**

John Wiley & Sons, Inc.

111 River Street, Hoboken NJ 07030–5774
☎001 201 748 6000 Fax 001 201 748 6088
✉ info@wiley.com
www.wiley.com
President/CEO *William J. Pesce*

Founded 1807. Wiley's core publishing programme includes scientific, technical and medical journals, encyclopedias, books and online products and services; professional and consumer books and subscription services; and educational materials for undergraduate, graduate students and life-long learners. About 1700 titles a year. Submission guidelines available on the website under 'Resources for Authors'.

The University of Wisconsin Press

1930 Monroe Street, 3rd Floor, Madison WI 53711
☎001 608 263 1110 Fax 001 608 263 1120
✉ uwiscpress@uwpress.wisc.edu
www.wisc.edu/wisconsinpress

Founded 1936. Publishes scholarly, general interest non-fiction and regional books about Wisconsin and the mid-west. About 50 titles a year. No unsolicited mss. Detailed author guidelines available on the website.

Zondervan

5300 Patterson Avenue SE, Grand Rapids MI 49530
☎001 616 698 6900 Fax 001 616 698 3439
www.zondervan.com
President/Chief Executive *Doug Lockhart*

Founded 1931. Subsidiary of **HarperCollins Publishers, Inc.** Publishes Protestant religion, Bibles, books, audio & video, computer software, calendars and speciality items.

US Literary Agents

★ = Members of the **Association of Authors' Representatives, Inc.**

Dominick Abel
Literary Agency, Inc★
146 West 82nd Street, Suite 1B, New York
NY 10024
☎001 212 877 0710   Fax 001 212 595 3133
Contact *Dominick Abel*

Established 1975. No scripts, children's books
or poetry. COMMISSION Home 15%; Translation
20%. No unsolicited material. Send query letter
with s.a.e. in the first instance. No reading fee.

Miriam Altshuler
Literary Agency★
53 Old Post Road North, Red Hook
NY 12571
☎001 845 758 9408

Founded 1994. Handles literary and commercial fiction; general non-fiction, narrative non-
fiction, memoirs, psychology, biography. No
romance, science fiction, mysteries, poetry,
westerns, fantasy, how-to, techno thrillers or
self-help. COMMISSION Home 15%; Foreign/
Translation 20%. Send query letter and synopsis in the first instance with return postage or
s.a.e. (no e-mail or fax queries). No reading fee.

Bart Andrews & Associates Inc
7510 Sunset Boulevard, Suite 100, Los Angeles
CA 90046–3418
☎001 310 271 9916
Contact *Bart Andrews*

Founded 1982. General non-fiction: show business, biography and autobiography, film books,
trivia, TV and nostalgia. No scripts. No fiction,
poetry, children's or science. No books of less
than major commercial potential. Specialises in
working with celebrities on autobiographies.
COMMISSION Home & Translation 15%.
OVERSEAS ASSOCIATE **Abner Stein**, UK. No
unsolicited mss. 'Send a brilliant letter (with
IRCs for response) extolling your manuscript's
virtues. Sell me!' No reading fee.

Malaga Baldi Literary Agency
233 West 99th Street, Suite 19C, New York
NY 10025
☎001 212 222 3213

Contact *Malaga Baldi*

Founded 1986. Handles quality fiction and non-
fiction. No scripts. No westerns, men's adventure,
science fiction/fantasy, romance, how-to, young
adult or children's. COMMISSION 15%. OVERSEAS
ASSOCIATES **Abner Stein**, UK; Owl Agency;
Eliane Benisti, France; **Marsh Agency**. Writers
of fiction should send query letter describing the
novel plus IRCs. For non-fiction, approach in
writing with a proposal, table of contents and two
sample chapters. No reading fee.

The Balkin Agency, Inc.★
PO Box 222, Amherst MA 01004
☎001 413 548 9835   Fax 001 413 548 9836
✉ rick62838@crocker.com
Contact *Richard Balkin*

Founded 1973. Handles adult non-fiction only.
COMMISSION Home 15%; Foreign 20%. No
reading fee for outlines and synopses.

Loretta Barrett Books, Inc.★
101 Fifth Avenue, New York NY 10003
☎001 212 242 3420   Fax 001 212 807 9579
Contacts *Loretta Barrett, Nick Mullendore*

Founded 1990. Handles all non-fiction and fiction genres except children's, poetry, science
fiction/fantasy. Specialises in women's fiction,
history, spirituality. No scripts. COMMISSION
Home 15%; Foreign 20%. No e-mail submissions. Send query letter with biography and
return postage only in the first instance.

Meredith Bernstein
Literary Agency, Inc.★
2095 Broadway, Suite 505, New York
NY 10023
☎001 212 799 1007   Fax 001 212 799 1145
Contacts *Meredith Bernstein*

Founded 1981. Handles commercial and literary fiction, mysteries and non-fiction (women's
issues, business, memoirs, health, current affairs,
crafts). COMMISSION Home & Dramatic 15%;
Translation 20%. OVERSEAS ASSOCIATES **Abner
Stein**, UK; Lennart Sane, Holland, Scandinavia
and Spanish language; Thomas Schluck,
Germany; Bardon Chinese Media Agency;

William Miller, Japan; Frederique Porretta, France; Agenzia Letteraria, Italy.

Bleecker Street Associates, Inc.★

532 LaGuardia Place, #617, New York NY 10012
☎001 212 677 4492 Fax 001 212 388 0001

Founded 1984. Handles fiction: women's, mystery, suspense, literary; non-fiction: history, women's interests, parenting, health, relationships, psychology, sports, sociology, current events, biography, spirituality, New Age, business. No poetry, children's, westerns, science fiction, professional, academic. COMMISSION Home 15%; Foreign 25%. Send query letter in the first instance. Will only respond if envelope and return postage enclosed. No phone calls, faxes or e-mails. No reading fee.

The Blumer Literary Agency★

350 Seventh Avenue, Suite 2003, New York NY 10001
☎001 212 947 3040 Fax 001 212 947 0460
Contact *Olivia Blumer*

Founded 2002. Handles a broad range of commercial and literary fiction and non-fiction. Strong background in memoir, inspiration, commercial, literary fiction, illustrated and non-fiction. Specialist subject: cookery. No TV, film, radio or theatre scripts. No children's, science fiction and fantasy or romances. COMMISSION Home 15%; Foreign & Translation 20%. Send initial introductory letter. No reading fee.

Georges Borchardt, Inc.★

136 East 57th Street, New York NY 10022
☎001 212 753 5785 Fax 001 212 838 6518

Founded 1967. Works mostly with established/published authors. Specialises in fiction, biography, and general non-fiction of unusual interest. COMMISSION Home, UK & Dramatic 15%; Translation 20%. UK ASSOCIATE **Sheil Land Associates Ltd** (Richard Scott Simon), London. Unsolicited mss not read.

Brandt & Hochman Literary Agents, Inc.★

1501 Broadway, Suite 2310, New York NY 10036
☎001 212 840 5760
Contacts *Carl D. Brandt, Gail Hochman, Marianne Merola, Charles Schlessiger*

Founded 1914. Handles non-fiction and fiction. No poetry. COMMISSION Home & Dramatic 15%; Foreign 20%. UK ASSOCIATE

A.M. Heath & Co. Ltd. No unsolicited mss. Approach by letter describing background and ambitions; include return postage. No reading fee.

Barbara Braun Associates, Inc★

104 Fifth Avenue, 7th Floor, New York NY 10011
☎001 212 604 9023 Fax 001 212 604 9041
✉ bba.230@earthlink.net
www/barbarabraunagency.com
Contacts *Barbara Braun, John Baker*

Founded 1995. Handles literary and mainstream, women's and historical fiction, also serious non-fiction, including psychology and biography. Also young adult and mystery books. Specialises in art history, archaeology, architecture and cultural history. No scripts, self-help, science fiction. COMMISSION Home 15%; Foreign 20%. OVERSEAS ASSOCIATE Chandler Crawford Literary Agency. No unsolicited mss; send query letter in the first instance. No reading fee.

Browne & Miller Literary Associates★

410 S. Michigan Avenue, Suite 460, Chicago IL 60605
☎001 312 922 3063 Fax 001 312 922 1905
✉ mail@browneandmiller.com
www.browneandmiller.com
President *Danielle Egan-Miller*

Founded 1971. Formerly known as Multimedia Product Development. Handles commercial and literary fiction, and practical non-fiction with wide appeal. No scripts, juvenile, science fiction or poetry. COMMISSION Home 15%; Foreign & Translation 20%. OVERSEAS ASSOCIATES in Europe, Latin America, Japan and Asia. In the first instance, send query letter with return postage. No unsolicited material. No reading fee.

Pema Browne Ltd, Illustration and Literary Agents

11 Tena Place, Valley Cottage NY 10989
✉ ppbltd@optonline.net
www.pemabrowneltd.com
Contacts *Pema Browne, Perry Browne*

Founded 1966. ('Pema rhymes with Emma.') Handles mass-market mainstream and hardcover fiction: romance, business, children's picture books and young adult; non-fiction: how-to and reference. COMMISSION Home 15%; Translation 20%; Overseas authors 20%. No unsolicited mss; send query letter with

IRCs. No fax or e-mail queries. Also handles illustrators' work. No longer accepting screenplays. 'We are accepting very few new clients at this time.'

Sheree Bykofsky Associates, Inc.★
16 West 36th Street, 13th Floor, New York NY 10018
☎001 212 244 4144
✉ shereebee@aol.com
Contact *Sheree Bykofsky*
Founded 1991. Handles adult fiction and non-fiction. No scripts. No children's, young adult, horror, science fiction, romance, westerns, occult or supernatural. COMMISSION Home 15%; UK (including sub-agent's fee) 20%. No unsolicited mss. Send query letter first with brief synopsis or outline and writing sample (1–3 pp) for fiction. IRCs essential for reply or return of material. 'Please do not send material via methods that require signature, such as FedEx, etc.' No phone calls. No reading fee.

Maria Carvainis Agency, Inc.★
1350 Avenue of the Americas, Suite 2905, New York NY 10019
☎001 212 245 6365   Fax 001 212 245 7196
✉ mca@mariacarvainisagency.com
President *Maria Carvainis*
Founded 1977. Handles fiction: literary and mainstream, contemporary women's, mystery, suspense, historical, young adult novels; non-fiction: business, finance, women's issues, politics, film, memoirs, reportage, biography, medicine, psychology and popular science. No film scripts unless from writers with established credits. No science fiction. COMMISSION Domestic & Dramatic 15%; Translation 20%. No faxed or e-mailed queries. No unsolicited mss; they will be returned unread. Queries only, with IRCs for response. No reading fee.

Castiglia Literary Agency★
1155 Camino del mar, Suite 510, Del Mar CA 92014
☎001 858 755 8761   Fax 001 858 755 7063
✉ jaclagency@aol.com
Contacts *Julie Castiglia, Winifred Golden*
Founded 1993. Handles fiction: literary, mainstream, ethnic; non-fiction: narrative, biography, science, health, parenting, memoirs, psychology, women's and contemporary issues. Specialises in science, biography and literary fiction. No scripts, horror or true crime. COMMISSION Home 15%; Foreign & Translation 25%. No

unsolicited material; send query letter only in the first instance. No reading fee.

The Catalog Literary Agency
PO Box 2964, Vancouver WA 98668
☎001 360 694 8531
Contact *Douglas Storey*
Founded 1986. Handles popular, professional and textbook material in all subjects, especially business, health, money, science, technology, computers, electronics and women's interests; also how-to, self-help. No fiction. No scripts, articles, screenplays, plays, poetry or short stories. COMMISSION 15%. No unsolicited mss. Query with an outline and sample chapters, and include IRCs. No reading fee.

Jane Chelius Literary Agency, Inc.★
548 Second Street, Brooklyn, New York NY 11215
☎001 718 499 0236   Fax 001 718 832 7335
✉ queries@janechelius.com
www.janechelius.com
Contacts *Jane Chelius, Mark Chelius*
Founded 1995. No children's, young adult, screenplays, scripts and poetry. COMMISSION Home 15% Foreign 20%. Submission guidelines available on the website.

Linda Chester & Associates★
Rockefeller Center, 630 Fifth Avenue, New York NY 10111
☎001 212 218 3350   Fax 001 212 218 3343
✉ lcassoc@mindspring.com
www.lindachester.com
Contact *Linda Chester*
Founded 1978. Handles literary and commercial fiction and non-fiction in all subjects. No scripts, children's or textbooks. COMMISSION Home & Dramatic 15%; Translation 25%. No unsolicited mss or queries. No reading fee for solicited material.

William Clark Associates★
154 Christopher Street, Suite 3C, New York NY 10014
☎001 212 675 2784   Fax 001 646 349 1658
✉ query@wmclark.com
www.wmclark.com
Contact *William Clark*
Founded 1997. Handles non-fiction, mainstream literary fiction and some young adult books. No scripts, horror, science fiction, fantasy, diet or mystery. COMMISSION Home 15%; Foreign & Translation 20%. OVERSEAS ASSOCI-

ATES **Ed Victor Ltd; Andrew Nurnberg Associates Ltd** (translation rights). Synopses should be part of query letter; sample chapters, complete mss on request only. Contact via e-mail only with concise description of work, synopsis/outline, biographical information and publishing history, if any. No reading fee.

Frances Collin Literary Agent★
PO Box 33, Wayne PA 19087–0033
☎001 610 254 0555 Fax 001 610 254 5029
Contact *Frances Collin*

Founded 1948. Successor to Marie Rodell. Handles general fiction and non-fiction. No scripts. OVERSEAS ASSOCIATES worldwide. No unsolicited mss. Send query letter only, with IRCs for reply, for the attention of *Sarah Yake*. No fax or telephone queries, please. No reading fee. Rarely accepts non-professional writers or writers not represented in the UK.

Don Congdon Associates, Inc.★
156 Fifth Avenue, Suite 625, New York NY 10010–7002
☎001 212 645 1229 Fax 001 212 727 2688
Contacts *Don Congdon, Michael Congdon, Susan Ramer, Cristina Concepcion*

Founded 1983. Handles fiction and non-fiction. No academic, technical, romantic fiction or scripts. COMMISSION Home 15%; UK & Translation 19%. OVERSEAS ASSOCIATES worldwide. No unsolicited mss. Query letter with return postage in the first instance. No reading fee.

Curtis Brown Ltd★
10 Astor Place, New York NY 10003
☎001 212 473 5400
Book Rights *Laura Blake Peterson, Peter L. Ginsberg, Emilie Jacobson, Ginger Knowlton, Maureen Walters, Mitchell Waters, Elizabeth Harding, Ginger Clark, Michele Beno, Nathan Bransford*
Film & TV Rights *Timothy Knowlton, Edwin Wintle, Holly Frederick*
Translation *Dave Barbor*

Founded 1914. Handles general fiction and non-fiction. Also some scripts for film, TV and theatre. OVERSEAS ASSOCIATES Representatives in all major foreign countries. No unsolicited mss; queries only, with IRCs for reply. No reading fee.

Sandra Dijkstra Literary Agency★
PMB 515, 1155 Camino Del Mar, Del Mar CA 92014
☎001 858 755 3115 Fax 001 858 794 2822

Contact *Taryn Fagerness*

Founded 1981. Handles quality and commercial non-fiction and fiction, including some genre fiction. No scripts. No westerns, contemporary romance or poetry. Willing to look at children's projects. Specialises in quality fiction, mystery/thrillers, narrative non-fiction, psychology, self-help, science, health, business, memoirs, biography, current affairs. 'Dedicated to promoting new and original voices and ideas.' COMMISSION Home 15%; Translation 20%. OVERSEAS ASSOCIATES **Abner Stein**, UK; Ursula Bender, Agence Hoffman, Germany; Licht & Burr, Scandinavia; Luigi Bernabo, Italy; Sandra Bruna, Spain; Caroline Van Gelderen, Netherlands; M. Kling (La Nouvelle Agence), France; The English Agency, Japan; Bardon-Chinese Media Agency, China/Taiwan; Prava I Prevodi, Eastern Europe. For fiction send brief synopsis (one page) and first 50 pages; for non-fiction send proposal with overview, chapter outline, author biog, two sample chapters and profile of competition. All submissions should be accompanied by IRCs. No reading fee.

Dunham Literary Inc★
156 Fifth Avenue, Suite 625, New York NY 10010
☎001 212 929 0994 Fax 001 212 929 0904
www.dunhamlit.com
Contacts *Jennie Dunham, Ashley Johnston*

Founded 2000. Handles literary fiction and non-fiction, New Age spirituality and children's (from picture books through young adult). No scripts, romance, westerns, horror, science-fiction/fantasy or poetry. COMMISSION Home 15%; Foreign & Translation 20%. OVERSEAS ASSOCIATE UK & Europe: **A.M. Heath & Co. Ltd.** The Rhoda Weyr Agency is now a division of Dunham Literary Inc. No unsolicited material. Send query letter (with return postage) giving information on the author and ms. No e-mail or faxed queries; see the website for further contact information. No reading fee.

Dystel & Goderich Literary Management★
One Union Square West, Suite 904, New York NY 10003
☎001 212 627 9100 Fax 001 212 627 9313
www.dystel.com
Contacts *Jane Dystel, Miriam Goderich, Stacey Glick, Michael Bourret, Jim McCarthy, Kate McKean, Lauren Abramo*

Founded 1991. Handles non-fiction and fiction. Specialises in politics, history, biography, cookbooks, current affairs, celebrities, commercial and literary fiction. No reading fee.

Anne Edelstein
Literary Agency LLC★
20 West 22nd Street, Suite 1603, New York NY 10010
☎001 212 414 4923 Fax 001 212 414 2930
✉ info@aeliterary.com
www.aeliterary.com

Contact *Emilie Stewart*

Founded 1990. No film, TV, theatre or radio scripts. COMMISSION Home 15%; Translation 20%. OVERSEAS ASSOCIATES Ulf Toregard; Eliane Benisti; Caroline van Gelderen; Luigi Bernabo; Rachel Calder, **The Sayle Literary Agency**; Mercedes Casanovas; Petra Eggers; Lucia Riff, BMSR. Unsolicited material welcome; send query letter in the first instance.

Educational Design Services, Inc.
7238 Treviso Lane, Boynton Beach FL 33437
☎001 561 739 9402

President *Bertram Linder*

Founded 1979. Specialises in educational material and textbooks for sale to school markets. COMMISSION Home 15%; Foreign 25%. IRCs must accompany submissions.

Ethan Ellenberg Literary Agency★
548 Broadway, Suite 5E, New York NY 10012
☎001 212 431 4554 Fax 001 212 941 4652
✉ agent@ethanellenberg.com
www.ethanellenberg.com

Contact *Ethan Ellenberg*

Founded 1984. Handles fiction: commercial, genre, literary and children's; non-fiction: history, biography, business, science, health, cooking, current affairs. Specialises in commercial fiction, thrillers, suspense and romance. No scripts, poetry or short stories. COMMISSION Home 15%; Translation 20%. Prefers submissions by mail with return postage. For fiction send synopsis and three chapters; for non-fiction send proposal and sample chapters, if available. No reading fee. For e-mail submissions send query letter only; no attachments.

Ann Elmo Agency, Inc.★
60 East 42nd Street, New York NY 10165
☎001 212 661 2880/1
Fax 001 212 661 2883

Contacts *Lettie Lee, Mari Cronin, Andree Abecassis*

Founded in the 1940s. Handles literary and romantic fiction, mysteries and mainstream; also non-fiction in all subjects, including biography and self-help. Some children's (8–12-year-olds). COMMISSION Home 15–20%. Query letter with outline of project in the first instance. No reading fee.

The Fogelman Literary Agency★
5420 LBJ Freeway, Suite 1900, Dallas TX 75240
☎001 972 661 5114 Fax 001 972 661 5691
✉ info@fogelman.com
www.fogelman.com

Also at: 445 Park Avenue, 9th Floor, New York, NY 10022

Contacts Evan Fogelman, Linda Kruger

Founded 1989. Handles non-fiction and fiction: romance (including historical and contemporary) and some mystery/suspense. No scripts, poetry, westerns, science fiction/fantasy or children's books. COMMISSION Home 15%; Foreign & Translation 10%. OVERSEAS ASSOCIATES Thomas Schluck Agency; Shin Won Literary Agency; Bastei Lubbe Taschenbucher; Big Apple Tuttle-Mori Agency. No unsolicited material. Published authors are welcome to call but unpublished authors should send query by e-mail or letter with return postage. No reading fee.

Jeanne Fredericks
Literary Agency, Inc.★
221 Benedict Hill Road, New Canaan CT 06840
☎001 203 972 3011 Fax 001 203 972 3011

Contact *Jeanne Fredericks*

Founded 1997. Handles quality adult non-fiction, usually of a practical and popular nature by authorities in their fields. Specialises in health, gardening, business, self-help, reference. No fiction, juvenile, poetry, essays, politics, academic or textbooks. COMMISSION Home 15%; Foreign 25% (with co-agent) or 20% (direct). No unsolicited material; send query by e-mail (no attachments) or letter with return postage in the first instance. No reading fee.

Robert A. Freedman
Dramatic Agency, Inc.★
Suite 2310, 1501 Broadway, New York NY 10036
☎001 212 840 5760

President *Robert A. Freedman*
Senior Vice-President *Selma Luttinger*

Vice-President *Robin Kaver*
Associate *Marta Praeger*
Founded 1928 as Brandt & Brandt Dramatic Department, Inc. Took its present name in 1984. Works mostly with established authors. Send letter of enquiry first with s.a.e. Specialises in plays, film and TV scripts. COMMISSION Dramatic 10%. Unsolicited mss not read.

Gelfman Schneider Literary Agents, Inc.★
250 West 57th Street, Suite 2515, New York NY 10107
☎001 212 245 1993 Fax 001 212 245 8678
Contacts *Deborah Schneider, Jane Gelfman*
Founded 1919 (London), 1980 (New York). Formerly John Farquharson Ltd. Works mostly with established/published authors. Specialises in general trade fiction and non-fiction. No poetry, short stories or screenplays. COMMISSION Home 15%; Dramatic 15%; Foreign 20%. OVERSEAS ASSOCIATE **Curtis Brown Group Ltd**, UK. No reading fee for outlines. Submissions must be accompanied by IRCs. No e-mail queries please.

Sanford J. Greenburger Associates, Inc.★
55 Fifth Avenue, 15th Floor, New York NY 10003
☎001 212 206 5600 Fax 001 212 463 8718
www.greenburger.com
Contacts *Heide Lange, Faith Hamlin, Daniel Mandel, Matt Bialer, Peter McGuigan, Jeremy Katz*
Handles fiction and non-fiction. No unsolicited mss. First approach with query letter, sample chapter and synopsis. No reading fee.

Joy Harris Literary Agency, Inc.★
156 Fifth Avenue, Suite 617, New York NY 10010
☎001 212 924 6269 Fax 001 212 924 6609
Contacts *Joy Harris, Leslie Daniels*
Handles adult non-fiction and fiction. COMMISSION Home 15%; Foreign 20%. No unsolicited mss. Query letter in the first instance. No reading fee.

John Hawkins & Associates, Inc.★
71 West 23rd Street, Suite 1600, New York NY 10010
☎001 212 807 7040 Fax 001 212 807 9555
Contacts *John Hawkins, William Reiss*

Founded 1893. Handles film and TV rights. COMMISSION Apply for rates. No unsolicited mss; send queries with 1–3-page outline and one-page c.v. IRCs necessary for response. No reading fee.

The Jeff Herman Agency, LLC
PO Box 1522, Stockbridge MA 01262
☎001 413 298 0077 Fax 001 413 298 8188
✉ jeff@jeffherman.com
www.jeffherman.com
Contact *Jeffrey H. Herman*
Handles all areas of non-fiction, textbooks and reference, business, spiritual and psychology. No scripts. COMMISSION Home 15%; Translation 10%. No unsolicited mss. Query letter with IRCs in the first instance. No reading fee. Jeff Herman publishes a useful reference guide to the book trade called *Herman's Guide to Book Editors, Publishers & Literary Agents* (Kalmbach).

Frederick Hill Bonnie Nadell Inc.
1842 Union Street, San Francisco CA 94123
☎001 415 921 2910 Fax 001 415 921 2802
Contacts *Fred Hill, Bonnie Nadell, Elise Proulx*
Founded 1979. General fiction and non-fiction. No scripts. COMMISSION Home & Dramatic 15%; Foreign 20%. OVERSEAS ASSOCIATE **Mary Clemmey Literary Agency**, UK.

Janklow & Nesbit Associates
445 Park Avenue, New York NY 10022
☎001 212 421 1700 Fax 001 212 980 3671
Partners *Morton L. Janklow, Lynn Nesbit*
Senior Vice-President *Anne Sibbald*
Agents *Tina Bennett, Luke Janklow, Richard Morris, Eric Simonoff*
Founded 1989. Handles fiction and non-fiction; commercial and literary. See also **Janklow & Nesbit (UK) Ltd** under *UK Literary Agents*. No unsolicited mss.

JCA Literary Agency, Inc★
174 Sullivan Street, New York NY 10012
☎001 212 807 0888
Contacts *Tom Cushman, Melanie Meyers-Cushman*
Founded 1978. Handles general fiction and non-fiction. No scripts, poetry, science fiction /fantasy or children's books. COMMISSION Home 15%; Foreign 20%. OVERSEAS ASSOCIATE **Vanessa Holt Ltd**, UK. No unsolicited mss; send query letter with return postage. No reading fee.

The Karpfinger Agency
357 West 20th Street, New York NY 10011
☎001 212 691 2690 Fax 001 212 691 7129
Agent *Barney M. Karpfinger*

Founded 1985. Handles quality fiction and non-fiction. No scripts, poetry, romance, horror, science fiction/fantasy, children's picture books. COMMISSION Home 15%; Foreign & Translation 20%. No unsolicited mss. Send query letter with synopsis and writing samples (not exceeding 30 pages). No reading fee.

Kirchoff/Wohlberg, Inc.★
866 United Nations Plaza, Suite 525, New York NY 10017
☎001 212 644 2020 Fax 001 212 223 4387
www.kirchoffwohlberg.com
Authors' Representative *Liza Pulitzer-Voges*

Founded 1930. Handles books for children and young adults, specialising in children's picture books. No adult material. No scripts for TV, radio, film or theatre. Send letter of enquiry with synopsis or outline and writing sample plus IRCs for reply or return. No reading fee.

Harvey Klinger, Inc.★
301 West 53rd Street, New York NY 10019
☎001 212 581 7068 Fax 001 212 315 3823
✉ queries@harveyklinger.com
www.harveyklinger.com
Contact *Harvey Klinger*

Founded 1977. Handles mainstream fiction and non-fiction. Specialises in commercial and literary fiction, psychology, health and science. No scripts, poetry, computer or children's books. COMMISSION Home 15%; Foreign 25%. OVERSEAS ASSOCIATES in all principal countries. Welcomes unsolicited material; send by e-mail or post (no faxes). No reading fee.

Linda Konner Literary Agency★
10 West 15 Street, Suite 1918, New York NY 10011
☎001 212 691 3419
Contact *Linda Konner*

Founded 1996. Handles non-fiction only, specialising in health, self-help, diet/fitness, pop psychology, relationships, parenting, personal finance. Also some pop culture/celebrities. COMMISSION Home 15%; Foreign 25%. Books must be written by or with established experts in their field. No scripts, fiction, poetry or children's books. No unsolicited material; send one-page query with return postage. No reading fee.

Peter Lampack Agency, Inc.
551 Fifth Avenue, Suite 1613, New York NY 10176
☎001 212 687 9106
Contact *Andrew Lampack*

Founded in 1977. Handles commercial fiction: male action and adventure, contemporary relationships, historical, mysteries and suspense, literary fiction; also non-fiction from recognised experts in a given field, plus biographies, autobiographies. Handles theatrical, motion picture, and TV rights from book properties. No original scripts or screenplays, series or episodic material. COMMISSION Home & Dramatic 15%; Translation & UK 20%. Best approach by letter in first instance. No reply without s.a.e. 'We will respond within three weeks and invite the submission of manuscripts which we would like to examine.' No reading fee. No unsolicited mss.

Michael Larsen/Elizabeth Pomada Literary Agency★
1029 Jones Street, San Francisco CA 94109
☎001 415 673 0939
www.larsenpomada.com
Contact (non-fiction) *Michael Larsen*
Contact (fiction) *Elizabeth Pomada*

Founded 1972. Handles adult fiction and non-fiction – literary and commercial. No scripts, poetry, children's, science fiction. COMMISSION Home 15%; Foreign 20–30%. OVERSEAS ASSOCIATES **David Grossman Literary Agency Ltd**, British rights; Chandler Crawford (foreign rights). Fiction: send first ten pages with 2-page synopsis and s.a.e.; non-fiction: e-mail title and promotion plan. Consult website for guidelines.

Sarah Lazin Books★
126 Fifth Avenue, Suite 300, New York NY 10011
☎001 212 989 5757 Fax 001 212 989 1393
Contact *Sarah Lazin*

Handles adult narrative non-fiction in pop culture, biography, social issues, music reference, photography, fiction. Specialises in music and biography. COMMISSION Home 15%; Foreign 10%. Send query letter with references and writing sample.

The Ned Leavitt Agency★
70 Wooster Street, Suite 4F, New York NY 10012
www.nedleavittagency.com
President *Ned Leavitt*
Agent *Britta Steiner Alexander*

Ned Leavitt specialises in creativity, spirituality, health and literary fiction; Britta Alexander specialises in smart non-fiction for 20 and 30-somethings (dating, relationships, business) and commercial ficton. No screenplays or genre fiction. COMMISSION Home 15%. Send 2–3 sample chapters with synopsis, by post, with s.a.e. See submission guidelines on the website. No reading fee.

Lescher & Lescher Ltd★
47 East 19th Street, New York NY 10003
☎001 212 529 1790 Fax 001 212 529 2716
Contact *Robert Lescher*
Founded 1964. Handles a broad range of serious non-fiction including current affairs, history, biography, memoir, politics, law, contemporary issues, popular culture, food and wine, literary and commercial fiction including mysteries and thrillers; some children's books. Specialises in wine books and cookbooks. No poetry, science fiction, New Age, spiritual, romance. COMMISSION Home 15%; Foreign 20%. No unsolicited manuscripts – please query first. No reading fee.

Sterling Lord Literistic, Inc.
65 Bleecker Street, New York NY 10012
☎001 212 780 6050 Fax 001 212 780 6095
www.sll.com
Contacts *Philippa Brophy, Chris Calhoun*
Founded 1979. Handles all genres, fiction and non-fiction, plus scripts for TV and film. COMMISSION Home 15%; UK & Translation 20%. No unsolicited mss. Prefers letter outlining all non-fiction. No reading fee.

Lowenstein–Yost Associates Inc★
121 West 27th Street, Suite 601, New York NY 10001
☎001 212 206 1630 Fax 001 212 727 0280
www.lowensteinyost.com
Agents *Barbara Lowenstein, Nancy Yost, Julie Culver, Rachel Vater*
Founded 1976. Handles fiction: upmarket, commercial and multicultural, thrillers, mysteries, women's fiction of all kinds including historicals, paranormals and romantic suspense, fantasy and young adult. Non-fiction: narrative, business, health, spirituality, psychology, relationships, politics, history, memoirs, natural science, women's issues, social issues, pop culture, parenting, personal finance. COMMISSION Home 15%; Foreign & Translation 20%. OVERSEAS ASSOCIATES in all major countries.

Fiction: send query letter with short synopsis, first chapter and s.a.e. Include any prior literary credits (previously published titles and reviews, writing courses, awards/grants); non-fiction: send query letter, project overview, list of credentials, media appearances, previous titles, reviews and s.a.e. No reading fee.

The Margret McBride Literary Agency★
7744 Fay Avenue, Suite 201, La Jolla CA 92037
☎001 858 454 1550 Fax 001 858 454 2156
✉ staff@mcbridelit.com
www.mcbrideliterary.com
Submissions Manager *Michael Daly*
Assistant to Margret McBride *Faye Atchison*
Vice President/Agent *Donna DeGutis*
Founded 1981. Handles non-fiction mostly, plus business and some fiction. No scripts, science fiction, fantasy. romance or children's books. Specialises in business and management. COMMISSION Home 15%; Overseas 15–25%; Translation 25%. No unsolicited mss. Send query letter with synopsis and s.a.e. only. Check the submission guidelines on the website before making contact.

Carol Mann Agency★
55 Fifth Avenue, New York NY 10003
☎001 212 206 5635 Fax 001 212 675 4809
✉ carol.mann@carolmannagency.com *or*
  kristy@carolmannagency.com *or*
  emily@carolmannagency.com
Contacts *Carol Mann, Emily Nurkin, Kristy Mayer*
Founded 1977. Handles literary fiction and narrative non-fiction, including psychology, biography, memoirs, history, pop culture, spirituality. No scripts or genre fiction. COMMISSION Home 15%; Foreign 20%. No unsolicited material; send query letter with return postage. No reading fee.

Manus & Associates Literary Agency, Inc.★
425 Sherman Avenue, Suite 200, Palo Alto CA 94306
✉ ManusLit@ManusLit.com
www.ManusLit.com
Also at: 445 Park Avenue, New York, NY 10022
Contacts (California) *Jillian Manus, Jandy Nelson, Stephanie Lee*
Contact (New York) *Janet Manus*

Handles commercial and literary fiction; non-fiction, including true crime, self-help, memoirs, history, pop culture and popular science. No scripts, science fiction/fantasy, westerns, romance, horror, poetry or children's books. COMMISSION Home 15%; Foreign 25%. No unsolicited mss. Fiction: send query letter and first 30 pages; non-fiction: query letter and proposal. Include return postage. All submissions must be made to the California office. No reading fee.

The Evan Marshall Agency*

Six Tristam Place, Pine Brook NJ 07058–9445
☎001 973 882 1122 Fax 001 973 882 3099
www.publishersmarketplace.com/members/
evanmarshall

Contact *Evan Marshall*

Founded 1987. Handles general adult fiction. COMMISSION Home 15%; UK & Translation 20%. No unsolicited mss; send query letter first. No reading fee.

Mews Books Ltd

c/o Sidney B. Kramer, 20 Bluewater Hill,
Westport CT 06880
☎001 203 227 1836 Fax 001 203 227 1144
✉ mewsbooks@aol.com (initial contact only;
submission by regular mail)

Contacts *Sidney B. Kramer, Fran Pollak*

Founded 1970. Handles adult fiction and non-fiction, children's, pre-school and young adult. No scripts, short stories or novellas (unless by established authors). Specialises in cookery, medical, health and nutrition, scientific non-fiction, children's and young adult. COMMISSION Home 15%; Film & Translation 20%. Unsolicited material welcome. Presentation must be professional and should include summary of plot/characters, one or two sample chapters, personal credentials and brief on target market, all suitable for forwarding to a publisher. No reading fee. Charges for photocopying, postage expenses, telephone calls and other direct costs. Principal agent is an attorney and former publisher (a founder of Bantam Books, Corgi Books). Offers consultation service through which writers can get advice on a contract or on publishing problems.

Doris S. Michaels
Literary Agency Inc.*

1841 Broadway, Suite 903, New York
NY 10023
☎001 212 265 9474 Fax 001 212 265 9480
www.dsmagency.com

Contact *Doris Michaels*

Handles literary fiction that has a commercial appeal and strong screen potential and women's fiction; non-fiction: current affairs, biography and memoirs, self-help, business, history, health, classical music, sports, women's issues, computers and pop culture. No action/adventure, suspense, science fiction, romance, New Age, religion/spirituality, gift books, art books, fantasy, thrillers, mysteries, westerns, occult and supernatural, horror, historical fiction, poetry, children's literature, humour or travel books. COMMISSION Home 15% Send query letter via e-mail with a one-page synopsis and include a short paragraph detailing credentials. No reading fee. .

Howard Morhaim
Literary Agency*

11 John Street, Suite 407, New York
NY 10038
☎001 212 529 4433 Fax 001 212 995 1112

Contact *Howard Morhaim*

Founded 1979. Handles general adult fiction and non-fiction. No scripts. No children's or young adult material, poetry or religious. COMMISSION Home 15%; UK & Translation 20%. OVERSEAS ASSOCIATES worldwide. No unsolicited mss. Send query letter with synopsis and sample chapters for fiction; query letter with outline or proposal for non-fiction. Include return postage. No reading fee.

Henry Morrison, Inc.

PO Box 235, Bedford Hills NY 10507–0235
☎001 914 666 3500 Fax 001 914 241 7846

Contact *Henry Morrison*

Founded 1965. Handles general fiction, crime and science fiction, and non-fiction. No scripts unless by established writers. COMMISSION Home 15%; UK & Translation 25%. Unsolicited material welcome but send query letter with outline (1–5 pp) in the first instance. No reading fee.

The Jean V. Naggar
Literary Agency*

216 East 75th Street, Suite 1-E, New York
City NY 10021

Contacts *Jean Naggar, Alice Tasman, Mollie Glick,
Jennifer Weltz*

Founded 1978. Handles strong mainstream fiction, literary fiction, memoir, biography, sophisticated self-help, popular science and psychology. No scripts. COMMISSION Home

15%; Foreign 20%. No unsolicited material; send query letter *only* with return postage initially. No reading fee.

B.K. Nelson Literary Agency
84 Woodland Road, Pleasantville NY 10570
☎001 914 741 1322 Fax 001 914 741 1324
✉ bknelson4@cs.com
www.bknelson.com

Also at: 1565 Paseo Vida, Palm Springs, CA 92264
☎001 760 880 8800 Fax 001 914 741 1324
President *Bonita K. Nelson*
Vice President *Leonard 'Chip' Ashbach*
Editorial Director *John W. Benson*

Founded 1979. Specialises in novels, business, self-help, how-to, political, autobiography, celebrity biography. Major motion picture and TV documentary success. COMMISSION 20%. Lecture Bureau for Authors founded 1994; Foreign Rights Catalogue established 1995; BK Nelson Infomercial Marketing Co. 1996, primarily for authors and endorsements, and BKNelson, Inc. for motion picture production in 1998. Signatory to Writers Guild of America, West (WGAW). No unsolicited mss. Letter of inquiry. Reading fee charged.

New England Publishing Associates, Inc.★
Box 5, Chester CT 06412
☎001 860 345 7323 Fax 001 860 345 3660
✉ nepa@nepa.com
www.nepa.com

Contacts *Elizabeth Frost-Knappman, Edward W. Knappman, Kris Schiavi, Ron Formica, Victoria S. Harlow* (photo/research editor)

Founded 1983. Handles non-fiction. Specialises in current affairs, business, history, science, women's studies, reference, psychology, politics, biography, true crime and literature. No textbooks or anthologies. No scripts, poetry or fiction. COMMISSION Home 15%. OVERSEAS ASSOCIATES throughout Europe and Japan; Rachel Calder, UK. Dramatic rights: Joel Gotler, Intellectual Property Group, Los Angeles. Unsolicited mss considered but query letter or phone call preferred first. No reading fee.

Richard Parks Agency★
PO Box 693, Salem NY 12865
☎001 518 854 9466 Fax 001 518 854 9466
✉ rp@richardparksagency.com
Contact *Richard Parks*
Founded 1989. Handles general trade fiction

and non-fiction: literary novels, mysteries and thrillers, commercial fiction, science fiction, biography, pop culture, psychology, self-help, parenting, medical, cooking, gardening, history, etc. No scripts. No technical or academic. COMMISSION Home 15%; UK & Translation 20%. OVERSEAS ASSOCIATES **The Marsh Agency; Barbara Levy Literary Agency**. No unsolicited mss. Fiction read by referral only. Non-fiction query with s.a.e. Faxed or e-mail queries will *not* be considered. No reading fee.

Alison J. Picard Literary Agent
PO Box 2000, Cotuit MA 02635
☎001 508 477 7192
Fax 001 508 477 7192 (notify before faxing)
✉ ajpicard@aol.com
Contact *Alison Picard*

Founded 1985. Handles mainstream and literary fiction, contemporary and historical romance, children's and young adult, mysteries and thrillers; plus non-fiction. No short stories or poetry. Rarely any science fiction and fantasy. Particularly interested in expanding non-fiction titles. COMMISSION 15%. OVERSEAS ASSOCIATE **John Pawsey**, UK. Approach with written query. No reading fee.

Pinder Lane & Garon-Brooke Associates Ltd★
159 West 53rd Street, Suite 14–E, New York NY 10019
☎001 212 489 0880 Fax 001 212 489 7104
Owner Agents *Dick Duane, Robert Thixton*

Founded 1951. Fiction and non-fiction. No category romance, westerns or mysteries. COMMISSION Home 15%; Dramatic 10–15%; Foreign 30%. OVERSEAS ASSOCIATES **Abner Stein**, UK; Translation: Rights Unlimited. No unsolicited mss. First approach by query letter. No reading fee.

PMA Literary & Film Management, Inc.
PO Box 1817, Old Chelsea Station, New York NY 10013
☎001 212 929 1222 Fax 001 212 206 0238
✉ queries@pmalitfilm.com
www.pmalitfilm.com
President *Peter Miller*
Associate *Scott Hoffman*

Founded 1976. Commercial fiction and non-fiction. Specialises in books with motion picture and television potential, and in true crime. No poetry, pornography, non-commercial or academic. COMMISSION Home 15%; Dramatic 10–15%; Foreign 20–25%. No unsolicited mss. Approach by letter with one-page synopsis.

The Aaron M. Priest Literary Agency★
708 Third Avenue, 23rd Floor, New York NY 10017
☎001 212 818 0344   Fax 001 212 373 9417

Founded 1974. Handles literary and commercial fiction. No scripts, children's fantasy or sci-fi. Submissions by mail only. No reading fee.

Susan Ann Protter Literary Agent★
110 West 40th Street, Suite 1408, New York NY 10018
☎001 212 840 0480

Contact *Susan Ann Protter*

Founded 1971. Handles general fiction, mysteries, thrillers, science fiction and fantasy; non-fiction: history, general reference, biography, science, health and parenting. No romance, poetry, westerns, religious, children's or sport manuals. No scripts. COMMISSION Home & Dramatic 15%. OVERSEAS ASSOCIATES **Abner Stein**, UK; agents in all major markets. First approach with letter, including IRCs. No reading fee.

Quicksilver Books, Literary Agents
508 Central Park Avenue, Suite 5101, Scarsdale NY 10583
☎001 914 722 4664   Fax 001 914 722 4664

President *Bob Silverstein*

Founded 1973. Handles literary fiction and mainstream commercial fiction: blockbuster, suspense, thriller, contemporary, mystery and historical; and general non-fiction, including self-help, psychology, holistic healing, ecology, environmental, biography, fact crime, New Age, health, nutrition, cookery, enlightened wisdom and spirituality. No scripts, science fiction and fantasy, pornography, children's or romance. COMMISSION Home & Dramatic 15%; Translation 20%. UK material being submitted must have universal appeal for the US market. Unsolicited material welcome but must be accompanied by IRCs for response, together with biographical details, covering letter, etc. No reading fee.

Raines & Raines★
103 Kenyon Road, Medusa NY 12120
☎001 518 239 8311   Fax 001 518 239 6029

Contacts *Theron Raines, Joan Raines, Keith Korman*

Founded 1961. Handles general non-fiction. No scripts. COMMISSION Home 15%; Foreign & Translation 20%. No unsolicited material; send one-page letter in the first instance. No reading fee.

Reece Halsey North★
98 Main Street, #704, Tiburon CA 94920
☎001 415 789 9191   Fax 001 415 789 9177
✉ info@reecehalseynorth.com
www.kimberleycameron.com

Also: Reece Halsey Agency, 8733 Sunset Blvd. #101, Los Angeles, CA 90069
☎001 310 652 2409 Fax 001 310 652 7595
Contact (Tiburon) *Kimberley Cameron, Adam Marsh, Elizabeth Evans*
Contact (Los Angeles) *Dorris Halsey*

Founded 1957. Represents literary and mainstream fiction, non-fiction. No scripts, poetry or children's books. COMMISSION Home 15%; Foreign 20%. Send query letter with first ten pages together with return postage. No e-mail submissions. No reading fee.

Helen Rees Literary Agency★
376 North Street, Boston MA 02113–2103
☎001 617 227 9014   Fax 001 617 227 8762
✉ agent10702@aol.com

Contact *Helen Rees*

Associates *Ann Collette, Lorin Rees*

Founded 1982. Specialises in books on health and business; also handles biography, autobiography and history; quality fiction. No scholarly or technical books. No scripts, science fiction, children's, poetry, photography, short stories, cookery. COMMISSION Home 15%; Foreign 20%. No unsolicited mss; no e-mail queries or attachments. Send query letter with IRCs. No reading fee.

Rights Unlimited, Inc.★
6 West 37th Street, 4th Floor, New York NY 10018
☎001 212 246 0900   Fax 001 212 246 2114
✉ submissions@rightsunlimited.com

Contact *Albert T. Longden*

Founded 1985. Handles adult fiction, non-fiction. No scripts, poetry, short stories, educational or literary works. COMMISSION Home & Translation 20%. Query letter with synopsis preferred in the first instance. No reading fee.

The Angela Rinaldi Literary Agency★
PO Box 7877, Beverly Hills CA 90212–7877
☎001 310 842 7665   Fax 001 310 837 8143

✉ amr@rinaldiliterary.com

Contact *Angela Rinaldi*

Founded 1995. Handles commercial and literary fiction; narrative non-fiction, practical and pro-active self-help. No scripts, cookery, science fiction, westerns, romance, poetry, children's/young adult. COMMISSION Home 15%; Foreign 20%. Send brief e-mail or query letter with return postage in the first instance. No reading fee.

Ann Rittenberg Literary Agency, Inc.★

30 Bond Street, New York NY 10012

☎001 212 684 6936 Fax 001 212 684 6929

www.rittlit.com

Contacts *Ann Rittenberg, Penn Whaling*

Founded 1991. Handles literary fiction, serious narrative non-fiction, biography/memoir, cultural history, upmarket women's fiction and thrillers. No scripts, romance, science fiction, self-help, inspirational and nothing at genre level. COMMISSION Home 15%; Foreign 20%. Send query letter, sample chapters and synopses by post; no e-mails. Enclose s.a.e. No reading fee.

B.J. Robbins Literary Agency★

5130 Bellaire Avenue, North Hollywood CA 91607

☎001 818 760 6602 Fax 001 818 760 6616

Contact *B.J. Robbins*

Founded 1992. Handles literary fiction, narrative and general non-fiction. No scripts, genre fiction, romance, horror, science fiction or children's books. COMMISSION Home 15%; Foreign & Translation 20%. OVERSEAS ASSOCIATES **Abner Stein** and **The Marsh Agency**, UK. Send covering letter with first three chapters or e-mail query in the first instance. No reading fee.

Linda Roghaar Literary Agency, Inc.★

133 High Point Drive, Amherst MA 01002

☎001 413 256 1921 Fax 001 413 256 2636

✉ contact@LindaRoghaar.com

www.lindaroghaar.com

Contact *Linda L. Roghaar*

Founded 1997. Handles fiction and non-fiction, specialising in religious titles. No science fiction or horror. COMMISSION Home 15%; Foreign & Translation rate varies. Send query by e-mail or letter with return postage (for fic-

tion, include the first five pages). No reading fee.

The Rosenberg Group★

23 Lincoln Avenue, Marblehead MA 01945

www.rosenberggroup.com

Contact *Barbara Collins Rosenberg*

Founded 1998. Handles non-fiction (please see website for areas of interest), fiction, specialising in romance (single title and category) and women's; non-fiction, specialising in college textbooks. No scripts, science fiction, true crime, inspirational fiction, children's and young adult. COMMISSION Home 15%; Foreign 25%. No unsolicited material; send query letter by post only. No reading fee.

Rosenstone/Wender★

38 East 29th Street, 10th Floor, New York NY 10016

☎001 212 725 9445 Fax 001 212 725 9447

Contacts *Phyllis Wender, Susan Perlman Cohen, Sonia E. Pabley*

Founded 1981. Handles fiction, non-fiction, children's, and scripts for film, TV and theatre. No material for radio. COMMISSION Home 15%; Dramatic 10%; Foreign 20%. OVERSEAS ASSOCIATES La Nouvelle Agence, France; Andrew Nurnberg, Netherlands; The English Agency, Japan; Mohrbooks, Germany; Ole Licht, Scandinavia. No unsolicited mss. Send letter outlining the project, credits, etc. No reading fee.

The Sagalyn Literary Agency★

7201 Wisconsin Avenue, Suite 675, Bethesda MD 20814

☎001 301 718 6440 Fax 001 301 718 6444

✉ info@sagalyn.com

www.sagalyn.com

Founded 1980. Handles mostly upmarket non-fiction with some fiction. No screenplays, romance, science fiction/fantasy, children's literature. No unsolicited material. See website for submissions procedure. No reading fee.

Victoria Sanders & Associates LLC★

241 Avenue of the Americas, Suite 11H, New York NY 10014

☎001 212 633 8811 Fax 001 212 633 0525

✉ queriesvsa@hotmail.com

www.victoriasanders.com

Contacts *Victoria Sanders, Diane Dickensheid*

Founded 1993. Handles general trade fiction and non-fiction, plus ancillary film and television rights. COMMISSION Home & Dramatic 15%; Translation 20%. Please send all queries via e-mail.

Jack Scagnetti Talent & Literary Agency
5118 Vineland Avenue, Suite 102, North Hollywood CA 91601
☎001 818 762 3871
www.jackscagnetti.com

Contact *Jack Scagnetti*

Founded 1974. Works mostly with established/published authors. Handles non-fiction, fiction, film and TV scripts. No reading fee. COMMISSION Home & Dramatic 10% (scripts), 15% (books); Foreign 15%.

Schiavone Literary Agency, Inc.
236 Trails End, West Palm Beach FL 33413–2135
☎001 561 966 9294   Fax 001 561 966 9294
✉ profschia@aol.com
www.publishersmarketplace.com/members/profschia

Branch office (June/July/Aug. only): 3671 Hudson Manor Terrace, Suite 11H, Bronx, NY 10463
☎/Fax 001 718 548 5332

President *James Schiavone*
Vice-President *Jennifer Duvall*

Founded 1996. Handles fiction and non-fiction (all genres). Specialises in biography, autobiography, celebrity memoirs. No poetry. COMMISSION Home 15%; Foreign & Translation 20%. OVERSEAS ASSOCIATES in Europe and Asia. No unsolicited mss; send query letter only with s.a.e. and IRCs. No response without s.a.e. For fastest response, e-mail queries of one page (no attachments) are acceptable and encouraged. No reading fee.

Susan Schulman, A Literary Agency★
454 West 44th Street, New York NY 10036
☎001 212 713 1633   Fax 001 212 581 8830

Submissions Editor (books) *Emily Uhry*
Submissions Editor (plays) *Linda Migalti*

Founded 1979. Specialises in non-fiction of all types but particularly in health and psychology-based self-help for men, women and families. Other interests include business, memoirs, the social sciences, biography, language and international law. Fiction interests include contemporary fiction, including women's, mysteries, historical and thrillers 'with a cutting edge'. Always looking for 'something original and fresh'. Represents

properties for film and theatre, and works with agents in appropriate territories for translation rights. COMMISSION Home & Dramatic 15%; Translation 20%. OVERSEAS ASSOCIATES Plays: **Rosica Colin Ltd** and **The Agency Ltd**, UK; Commercial fiction: Laura Morris, UK. No unsolicited mss. Query first, including outline and three sample chapters with IRCs. No reading fee.

Scovil Chichak Galen Literary Agency, Inc.★
381 Park Avenue South, Suite 1020, New York NY 10016
☎001 212 679 8686   Fax 001 212 679 6710
✉ info@scglit.com
www.scglit.com

Contacts *Russell Galen, Anna M. Ghosh, Jack Scovil*

Founded 1993. Handles all categories of books. No scripts. COMMISSION Home 15%; Foreign 20%. No unsolicited material; send query by e-mail or letter. No reading fee.

Scribblers House LLC Literary Agency
PO Box 1007 Cooper Station, New York NY 10276–1007
✉ query@scribblershouse.net
www.scribblershouse.net

Agents *Stedman Mays, Garrett Gambino*

Founded 2003 by Stedman Mays, founding member of Clausen, Mays & Tahan Literary Agency. Handles health, medical, diet, nutrition, the brain, psychology, self-help, how-to, business, personal finance, memoirs, biography, history, politics, writing books, language, relationships, sex, pop culture, spirituality, gender issues, parenting. No fiction, young adult or screenplays. COMMISSION 15%. Send e-mail query letter with brief description of the book, what's fresh and new about it, and a brief author biog including credentials for writing it. Consult the website for more submission information.

Rosalie Siegel, International Literary Agency, Inc.★
1 Abey Drive, Pennington NJ 08534
☎001 609 737 1007   Fax 001 609 737 3708

Contact *Rosalie Siegel*

Founded 1978. A one-woman, highly selective agency that takes on only a limited number of new projects. Handles fiction and non-fiction (especially narrative). Specialises in French history and literature; Europe in general; American history, social history. No science fiction, photography, illustrated art books or children's. COMMISSION Home 15%; Foreign 20%. OVERSEAS ASSOCIATE **Louise Greenberg**, UK; plus associates worldwide. No unsolicited material; send query letter citing background, previously published books and brief description of current book. Include return postage. No reading fee.

Michael Snell Literary Agency
PO Box 1206, Truro MA 02666–1206
☎001 508 349 3718

President *Michael Snell*
Vice President *Patricia Smith*

Founded 1980. Adult non-fiction, especially psychology, health, parenting, science, business and women's issues. Specialises in business and pet and animal books (professional and reference to popular trade how-to); general how-to and self-help on all topics, from diet and exercise to parenting, relationships, health, sex, psychology, personal finance, and dogs, cats and horses, plus literary and suspense fiction. COMMISSION Home 15%. No unsolicited mss. Send outline and sample chapter with return postage for reply. No reading fee for outlines. Brochure available on how to write a book proposal. Model proposal also for sale directly to prospective clients. Author of *From Book Idea to Bestseller*, published by Prima. Rewriting, developmental editing, collaborating and ghostwriting services available on a fee basis. Send IRCs.

Spectrum Literary Agency★
320 Central Park West, Suite 1-D, New York NY 10025
☎001 212 362 4323
www.spectrumliteraryagency.com

President and Agent *Eleanor Wood*
Agent *Lucienne Diver*

Founded 1976. Handles science fiction, fantasy, mystery, suspense and romance. No scripts. Not interested in self-help, New Age, religious fiction/non-fiction, children's books, poetry, short stories, gift books or memoirs. COMMISSION Home 15%; Translation 20%. Send query letter in first instance with s.a.e. Faxed or electronic submissions are not accepted. No reading fees.

The Spieler Agency
154 West 57th Street, Room 135, New York NY 10019
☎001 212 757 4439

The Spieler Agency/West, 4096 Piedmont Avenue, Oakland, CA 94611

☎001 510 985 1422 Fax 001 510 985 1323

Contacts *Joseph Spieler, John Thornton, Lisa M. Ross, Dierdre Mullane* (NY); *Victoria Shoemaker* (Oakland)

Founded 1980. Handles literary fiction and non-fiction. No how-to, genre romance, humour or science fiction. Specialises in history, science, ecology, social and political issues and business. No scripts. COMMISSION Home 15%; Translation 20%. OVERSEAS ASSOCIATES **Abner Stein**; **The Marsh Agency**, UK. Approach in writing with IRCs. No reading fee.

Philip G. Spitzer Literary Agency, Inc.★
50 Talmage Farm Lane, East Hampton NY 11937
☎001 631 329 3650 Fax 001 631 329 3651

Contact *Philip Spitzer*

Founded 1969. Works mostly with established/published authors. Specialises in general non-fiction and fiction – thrillers. COMMISSION Home & Dramatic 15%; Foreign 20%. No reading fee for outlines.

Gloria Stern Agency
12535 Chandler Boulevard, Suite 3, North Hollywood CA 91607
☎001 818 508 6296 Fax 001 818 508 6296

Contact *Gloria Stern*

Founded 1984. Handles film scripts, genre (romance, detective, thriller and sci-fi) and mainstream fiction; electronic media. Accepts interactive material, games and electronic data. COMMISSION Home 15%; Offshore 20%. Currently not accepting unsolicited material. Fee required for critique.

Stimola Literary Studio★
308 Chase Court, Edgewater NJ 07020
☎001 201 945 9353 Fax 001 201 945 9353
✉ LtryStudio@aol.com

Contact *Rosemary B. Stimola*

Founded 1997. Handles children's books – preschool through young adult – fiction and non fiction. Specialises in picture books, middle/young adult novels. No adult fiction. COMMISSION Home 15%; Foreign 20%. No unsolicited material; send query e-mail. No reading fee.

Barbara W. Stuhlmann Author's Representative
PO Box 276, Becket MA 01223–0276
☎001 413 623 5170

Contact *Barbara Ward Stuhlmann*

Founded 1954. COMMISSION Home 10%; Foreign 15%; Translation 20%. Query first with IRCs, including sample chapters and synopsis of project. No reading fee.

Mary M. Tahan Literary Agency LLC★

PO Box 1060 Gracie Station, New York NY 10028–1060
☎001 646 375 2483
Contact *Mary M. Tahan*

Founded 2004 by Mary M. Tahan who is also co-owner of Clausen, Mays & Tahan Literary Agency since 1997. Specialises in mainstream commercial fiction: thrillers, suspense, romance, mysteries, science fiction; narrative non-fiction: history, biography, autobiography, heroic true stories, entrepreneurial business books, health and nutrition (prospective authors must have expertise in their field). No scripts, children's, fundamental religious, humour. COMMISSION Home 15%; Foreign 25%. For non-fiction submissions send proposal and sample chapters; for fiction, synopsis and first three chapters. Include s.a.e for return of material. Initial approach should be by e-mail or post; no phone calls.

Roslyn Targ★

105 West 13th Street, Suite 15-E, New York NY 10011
☎001 212 206 9390   Fax 001 212 989 6233
Contact *Roslyn Targ*

Founded 1970. Handles non-fiction, particularly biography, self-help, and literary fiction. No screenplays or cookbooks. COMMISSION Home 15%; Foreign 20%. No unsolicited material; send query e-mail or letter describing the work. No reading fee.

Patricia Teal Literary Agency★

2036 Vista del Rosa, Fullerton CA 92831
☎001 714 738 8333   Fax 001 714 738 8333
Contact *Patricial Teal*

Founded 1978. Handles women's fiction: series and single-title works; commercial and popular non-fiction. Specialises in romantic fiction. No scripts, science fiction, fantasy, horror, academic texts. COMMISSION Home 15%; Foreign 20%. No unsolicited material. Send query letter in the first instance. No reading fee.

S©ott Treimel NY★

434 Lafayette Street, New York NY 10003
☎001 212 505 8353   Fax 001 212 505 0664

Founded 1995. Handles children's books only,

from concept/board books to teen fiction. No filmscripts. COMMISSION Home 15%; Foreign 20%. No unsolicited material. 'Not accepting anyone unless recommended by professional authors or editors.' No reading fee.

2M Communications Ltd★

121 West 27th Street, Suite 601, New York NY 10001
☎001 212 741 1509   Fax 001 212 691 4460
✉ morel@bookhaven.com
www.2mcommunications.com
Contact *Madeleine Morel*

Founded 1982. Handles non-fiction only: specialises in representing ghostwriters. No scripts. No fiction, children's, computers or science. COMMISSION Home & Dramatic 15%; Translation 20%. OVERSEAS ASSOCIATES Thomas Schluck Agency, Germany; Asano Agency, Japan; EAIS, France; Living Literary Agency, Italy; Nueva Agencia Literaria Internacional, Spain. No unsolicited mss; send letter with sample pages and IRCs. No reading fee.

Wales Literary Agency, Inc.★

PO Box 9428, Seattle WA 98109–0428
☎001 206 284 7114
✉ waleslit@waleslit.com
www.waleslit.com
Contacts *Elizabeth Wales, Josie Di Bernardo*

Founded 1988. Handles quality fiction and non-fiction. No genre fiction, westerns, romance, science fiction or horror. Special interest in 'Pacific Rim', West Coast and Pacific Northwest stories. COMMISSION Home 15%; Dramatic & Translation 20%. No unsolicited mss; send query letter with publication list and writing sample. No e-mail queries longer than one page and no attachments. No reading fee.

John A. Ware Literary Agency

392 Central Park West, New York NY 10025
☎001 212 866 4733   Fax 001 212 866 4734
Contact *John Ware*

Founded 1978. Specialises in non-fiction: biography, history, current affairs, investigative journalism, science, nature, inside looks at phenomena, medicine and psychology (academic credentials required). No personal memoirs. Also handles literary fiction, mysteries/thrillers, sport, oral history, Americana and folklore. COMMISSION Home & Dramatic 15%; Foreign 20%. Unsolicited mss not read. Send query letter first with IRCs to cover return postage. No reading fee.

Cherry Weiner Literary Agency
28 Kipling Way, Manalapan NJ 07726
☎001 732 446 2096 Fax 001 732 792 0506
Contact *Cherry Weiner*
Founded 1977. Handles all types of fiction: science fiction and fantasy, mainstream, romance, mystery, westerns. COMMISSION 15%. No submissions except through referral. No reading fee.

Wieser & Elwell, Inc.★
80 Fifth Avenue, Suite 1101, New York NY 10011
☎001 212 260 0860
President *Jake Elwell*
Founded 1976. Works mostly with established/published authors. Specialises in literary and mainstream fiction, serious and popular historical fiction, and general non-fiction: business, finance, aviation, sports, travel and popular medicine. No poetry, children's, science fiction or religious. COMMISSION Home & Dramatic 15%; Foreign 20%. No unsolicited mss. First approach by letter with IRCs. No reading fee for outlines.

Ann Wright Representatives
165 West 46th Street, Suite 1105, New York NY 10036–2501
☎001 212 764 6770 Fax 001 212 764 5125
Contact *Dan Wright*
Founded 1961. Specialises in material with strong film potential. Handles screenplays and novels, drama and fiction. No academic, scientific or scholarly. COMMISSION Literary 10–20%; Screenplays 10% of gross. Approach by letter; no reply without IRCs. Include outline and credits only. 'Has reputation for encouraging new writers.' No reading fee. Signatory to the Writers Guild of America Agreement.

Writers House, LLC.★
21 West 26th Street, New York NY 10010
☎001 212 685 2400 Fax 001 212 685 1781
www.writershouse.com
Contacts *Albert Zuckerman, Amy Berkower, Merrilee Heifetz, Susan Cohen, Susan Ginsburg, Robin Rue, Simon Lipskar, Steven Malk, Jodi Reamer*
Founded 1974. Handles all types of fiction, including children's and young adult, plus narrative non-fiction: history, biography, popular science, pop and rock culture as well as how-to, business and finance, and New Age. Specialises in popular and literary fiction, women's novels, thrillers and children's. No scripts. No professional or scholarly. COMMISSION Home & Dramatic 15%; Foreign 20%. Albert Zuckerman is author of *Writing the Blockbuster Novel*, published by Little, Brown & Co. and Warner Paperbacks. For consideration of unsolicited mss, send one-page letter of enquiry, 'explaining why your book is wonderful, briefly what it's about and outlining your writing background'. No reading fee.

Susan Zeckendorf Associates, Inc★
171 West 57th Street, Suite 11B, New York NY 10019
☎001 212 245 2928
Contact *Susan Zeckendorf*
Founded 1979. Handles non-fiction of all kinds: self help, social history, biography; fiction. No scripts, romance, science fiction or children's books. COMMISSION Home 15%; Foreign & Translation 20%. ASSOCIATES Rosemarie Buckman (translation); **Abner Stein**, UK. No unsolicited material; send query letter with s.a.e. in the first instance. No reading fee.

AGENCY CONSULTANTS

Agent Research & Evaluation, Inc. (AR&E)
See entry under *Agency Consultants*, page 229

US Media Contacts in the UK

ABC News Intercontinental Inc.
3 Queen Caroline Street, London W6 9PE
☎020 8222 5000 Fax 020 8222 5020
Director of News Coverage, Europe, Middle
East & Africa *Marcus Wilford*

The Associated Press
12 Norwich Street, London EC4A 1BP
☎020 7353 1515 Fax 020 7353 8118 (news)
Vice President – Global Business for Europe,
Africa & Middle East *Barry Renfrew*

The Baltimore Sun
11 Kensington Court Place, London W8 5BJ
☎020 7460 2200
Bureau Chief *Todd Richissin*

Bloomberg Business News
City Gate House, 39–45 Finsbury Square,
London EC2A 1PQ
☎020 7330 7500 Fax 020 7330 7797
Print – London Bureau Chief *Chris Collins*

Boston Globe
6 Holly Mount, London NW3 6SG
☎020 7431 5797 Fax 020 7431 5807
✉ sennott@globe.com
Bureau Chief *Charles Sennott*

Business Week
20 Canada Square, Canary Wharf, London
E14 5LH
☎020 7176 6060 Fax 020 7176 6070
Bureau Chief *Stanley Reed*

CBC Television and Radio
43/51 Great Titchfield Street, London
W1P 8DD
☎020 7412 9200 Fax 020 7412 9226
London Bureau Manager *Ann Macmillan*

CBS News
68 Knightsbridge, London SW1X 7LL
☎020 7581 4801 Fax 020 7581 4431
Deputy Bureau Chief *Laura Dubowski*

Chicago Tribune Press Service
116 Brompton Road, London SW3 1JJ

☎020 7225 0345 Fax 020 7225 0345
Chief European Correspondent *Tom Hundley*

CNBC
10 Fleet Place, Limeburner Lane, London
EC4M 7QS
☎020 7653 9451 Fax 020 7653 9393
Assignments Editor *Jennifer Callegher*

CNN International
See entry under *Television and Radio*

Dallas Morning News
5 Rylett Crescent, London W12 9RP
☎020 8248 4924
European Bureau Chief *Tod Robberson*

Dow Jones Newswires
10 Fleet Place, Limeburner Lane, London
EC4M 7QN
☎020 7842 9300
Editor (Europe, Middle East, Africa) *Jan Boucek*

Fairchild Publications of New York
20 Shorts Gardens, London WC2H 9AU
☎020 7240 0420
Bureau Chief *Samantha Conti*

Forbes Magazine
Malta House, 36/38 Picadilly, London
W1J 0DP
☎020 7534 3900
Managing Director & Publisher (Europe,
Middle East & Africa) *Bob Crozier*

Fortune
Brettenham House, Lancaster Place, London
WC2E 7TL
☎020 7322 1000
Europe Editor *Nelson Schwartz*

Fox News Channel
6 Centaurs Business Park, Grant Way,
Isleworth TW7 5QD
☎020 7805 7143 Fax 020 7805 1111
Bureau Chief *Scott Norvell*

International Herald Tribune
40 Marsh Wall, London E14 9TP
☎020 7510 5718 Fax 020 7987 3470
London Correspondent *Eric Pfanner*
See entry under **National Newspapers**

Los Angeles Times
Moreau House, 116–118 Brompton Road,
London SW3 1JJ
☎020 7823 7315 Fax 020 7823 7308
Bureau Chief *John Daniszewski*

Market News International
Ocean House, 10–12 Little Trinity Lane,
London EC4A 2AR
☎020 7634 1655 Fax 020 7236 7122
✉ ukeditorial@marketnews.com
Senior UK Political Correspondent *David
Robinson*

National Public Radio
Room G-10 East Wing, Bush House, Strand,
London WC2B 4PH
☎020 7557 1087 Fax 020 7379 6486
Bureau Chief *Robert Gifford*

NBC News
4th Floor, 3 Shortlands, Hammersmith,
London W6 8HX
☎020 8600 6600 Fax 020 8600 6601
Deputy Bureau Chief *Suzette Knittl*

The New York Times
66 Buckingham Gate, London SW1E 6AU
☎020 7799 5050 Fax 020 7799 2962
Acting Bureau Chief *Alan Cowell*

Newsweek
Academy House, 36 Poland Street, London
W1F 7LU
☎020 7851 9750 Fax 020 7851 9762
Bureau Chief *Stryker McGuire*

People Magazine
Brettenham House, Lancaster Place, London
WC2E 7TL
☎020 7499 4080
Bureau Chief *Bryan Alexander*

Reader's Digest Association Ltd
11 Westferry Circus, Canary Wharf, London
E14 4HE
See entries under **UK Publishers** and
Magazines

Time Magazine
Brettenham House, Lancaster Place, London
WC2E 7TL
☎020 7322 1000 Fax 020 7322 1261
Bureau Chief *Jef McAllister*
See entry under **Magazines**

Voice of America
London News Centre, 167 Fleet Street,
London EC4A 2EA
☎020 7410 0960
Bureau Chief *Michael Drudge*

Wall Street Journal
10 Fleet Place, Limeburner Lane, London
EC4M 7QN
☎020 7842 9200
London Bureau Chief *Paul Beckett*

Washington Post
17 Dartmouth Street, London SW1H 9BL
☎020 7222 8512 Fax 020 7233 4597
Bureau Chiefs *Mary Jordan/Kevin Sullivan*

US Writers' Courses

In general, courses are open to students from overseas though the financial aid situation varies for international students.

Arizona

University of Arizona
MFA Program in Creative Writing, Department of English, Modern Languages 445, PO Box 210067, Tucson AZ 95721–0067
☎001 520 621 3880
✉ creativewriting@english.arizona.edu
www.arizona.edu/~cwp

Established in 1974, the MFA in *Creative Writing* is a two-year programme with concentrations in Poetry, Fiction and Creative Non-Fiction. 'It boasts a faculty of 14 distinguished writers who share an uncommon commitment to teaching and supporting their students in the completion of publishable manuscripts.'

Arkansas

University of Arkansas
Programs in Creative Writing & Translation, Department of English, 333 Kimpel Hall, Fayetteville AR 72701
✉ mfa@uark.edu
www.uark.edu/depts/english/PCWT.html
Contact *Course Director*

MFA in *Creative Writing*, offering small, intensive workshops and innovative classes in fiction and poetry.

California

American Film Institute
2021 N. Western Avenue, Los Angeles CA 90027
☎001 323 856 7628   Fax 001 323 856 7720
✉ jjackman@afi.com
www.afi.com
Admissions Manager *J.J. Jackman*

Screenwriting at AFI focuses on narrative storytelling in an environment designed to stimulate the world of the professional screenwriter. Screenwriting Fellows in the First Year are immersed in the production process in order to learn how screenplays are visualised.

Initially writing short screenplays – one of which will be the basis for a first year production – writers collaborate with Producing and Directing Fellows to see their work move from page to screen. The remainder of the first year is devoted to the completion of a feature-length screenplay. Second Year Fellows may write a second feature-length screenplay, or develop materials for television, including biopics, television movies and spec scripts for sitcoms and one-hour dramas. They also have the opportunity to work closely with other disciplines by writing a Second Year thesis script.

California Institute for the Arts
MFA Writing Program, School of Critical Studies, 24700 McBean Parkway, Valencia CA 91355–2397
☎001 661 253 7701
✉ writing@calarts.edu
www.calarts.edu/schools/critical_studies/index.html
Contact *Program Coordinator*

The two-year MFA *Writing Programme* is rooted in principles of critical thought, experimentation and innovation. It is intended as an alternative to traditional programmes, with a founding premise that distinctions between creative and critical writing should be suspended. Students are encouraged to work across genres and often work in various multi-media forms in addition to their literary production.

Chapman University
Master of Fine Arts Degree, Dept. of English and Comparative Literature, Office of Admissions, One University Drive, Orange CA 92866
☎001 714 997 6750
www.chapman.edu
Contact *Admissions*

Three-year Master of Fine Arts (MFA) degree in *Creative Writing* is intended for graduate students who wish to pursue writing as a career and is aimed toward publishing as well as development of writing techniques.

Saint Mary's College of California

MFA Program in Creative Writing, PO Box 4686, Moraga CA 94575–4686
☎001 925 631 4762
✉ writers@stmarys-ca.edu
www.stmarys-ca.edu

Programme Coordinator *Thomas Cooney*

Two-year MFA course in *Fiction, Non-Fiction* or *Poetry*. The core of the programme is the Writing Workshop which provides the opportunity for students to work with established writers.

San Francisco State University

Creative Writing Department, College of Humanities, 1600 Holloway Avenue, San Francisco CA 94132
☎001 415 338 1891
✉ cwriting@sfsu.edu
www.sfsu.edu/~cwriting

Offers BA and MA in *English:* with a concentration on *Creative Writing*; and MFA in *Creative Writing*. Undergraduate classes include feature writing, short story writing, the craft of poetry and the craft of playwriting while graduate classes include advanced story writing, advanced poetry writing, advanced playwriting, experimental fiction, playwright's theatre workshop and workshops in fiction, poetry and playwriting.

University of Southern California (USC)

School of Cinema-Television, University Park, LUC 301, Los Angeles CA 90089–2211
☎001 213 740 3303 Fax 001 213 740 8035
✉ writing@cinema.usc.edu
www-cntv.usc.edu

Offers a Bachelor of Fine Arts or Master of Fine Arts degree in *Writing for Screen and Television*. Each spring, the most advanced graduating students have the opportunity to pitch their best scripts to industry professionals at a special Writing Division event called 'First Pitch'. The Division has a strong international presence, having accepted students from over 44 countries.

Colorado

Colorado State University

Creative Writing Program, 1773 Campus Delivery, 359 Eddy Hall, Fort Collins CO 80523–1773
☎001 970 491 2403
✉ english@lamar.colostate.edu

www.colostate.edu/Depts/English/programs/mfa.htm

Contact *Assistant to the Director of Creative Writing or Director of Creative Writing*

Three-year Master of Fine Arts (MFA) programme in creative writing with concentrations in fiction or poetry. The programme offers a balance of intimate and intensive writing and translation. Course work culminates in a thesis – a collection of poetry or short stories or a novel. Students have the opportunity to teach introductory creative-writing courses, intern with literary journals including the *Colorado Review* and be a part of a thriving community.

District of Columbia

American University

Department of Literature, 4400 Massachusetts Avenue, N.W., Washington DC 20016
☎001 202 885 2973
www.american.edu/cas/lit/mfa-lit.cfm

Contact *Kristin Toburen* (Graduate Programs Assistant)

The MFA in *Creative Writing* is a 48-credit hour programme allowing students to concentrate in Poetry, Fiction or Creative Non-Fiction. Cross-genre experimentation is encouraged. All students complete a book-length thesis before graduating in two to three years. The programme is literature intensive and also exposes students to Literary Journalism and the Art of Translation. Students can elect to follow the Internship Track or the Teaching Track. The Visiting Writers Series brings writers of international renown to the campus, often to lead a workshop.

Florida

University of West Florida

Department of English and Foreign Languages, 11000 University Parkway, Building 50, Room 211, Pensacola FL 32514
☎001 850 474 2923 Fax 001 850 474 2935
uwf.edu/english

BA in *English (Writing Specialization)*: students who choose to develop their creative writing skills or editing can take courses in poetry, fiction, creative non-fiction, magazine writing and editing, and feature writing. *MA in English (Creative Writing Specialization)*: workshop courses in the specialisation include fiction, creative non-fiction, poetry, editing, teaching creative writing and special topics in creative writing. Students also have the opportunity to work on the literary magazine *Bayou*.

Illinois

Chicago State University
MFA Program in Creative Writing, Department of English, 9501 South King Drive, SCI 320, Chicago IL 60628
☎001 773 995 2189
www.csu.edu/GraduateSchool
Program Coordinator *Dr Kelly Norman Ellis*

Offers a two-year MFA with courses in Creative Writing; writing workshops in fiction, poetry, creative non-fiction, playwriting and scriptwriting. Students undertake coursework in African American Literature and non-African American Literature. Students will show competency in the genre of their choice, choosing from fiction, creative non-fiction and poetry.

Southern Illinois University at Carbondale
Department of English, Carbondale
IL 62901–4503
☎001 618 453 6849
✉ aljoseph@siu.edu
Contact *Professor Allison Joseph*

Three-year MFA in *Creative Writing*. The programme accepts a maximum of eight students each year, so workshops are small and faculty members work closely with students.

Indiana

University of Notre Dame
Creative Writing Program, Department of English, Notre Dame IN 46556
☎001 574 631 7526
✉ creativewriting@nd.edu
www.nd.edu/~alcwp

The MFA in *Creative Writing* is a two-year degree programme centred around workshops in poetry and fiction, offering literature courses, translation, a literary publishing course and twelve credits of thesis preparation with an individual faculty adviser.

Purdue University
MFA Program in Creative Writing, Department of English, West Lafayette
IN 47907
☎001 765 494 3740
www.cla.purdue.edu/mfacw

Program Director *Porter Shreve*

MFA in *Creative Writing* offering 'full funding, generous stipends and editorial experience with the award-winning literary journal *Sycamore Review*'. The three-year programme in either fiction or poetry is small and intensive and includes workshops, literature and craft courses, and thesis tutorials toward a book-length manuscript.

Taylor University
Department of English, 1025 West Rudisill Blvd, Fort Wayne IN 46807–2170
☎001 260 744 8647
✉ DNHensley@TaylorU.edu
Contact *Dr Dennis E. Hensley*

Summer Honours Programme one-week seminars in *Professional Writing*; evening courses in *Freelance Writing* and *Fiction Writing*; one year college certificate in *Professional Writing*. Dr Hensley is a professor of English and director of the professional writing major.

Louisiana

Louisiana State University
English Department, 260 Allen Hall, Baton Rouge LA 70803
www.english.lsu.edu
Director of Creative Writing *James Wilcox*

Master of *Fine Arts* (MFA) course with a focus in Poetry, Fiction, Playwriting, Screenwriting or Creative Non-Fiction. Includes opportunity to edit literary journals.

Maryland

Goucher College
Welch Center for Graduate Studies, 1021 Dulaney Valley Road, Baltimore
MD 21204–2794
☎001 800 697 4646 Fax 001 410 337 6085
✉ center@goucher.edu
Programme Director *Patsy Sims* (☎001 800 697 4646)

The two-year MFA Program in *Creative Nonfiction* is a limited-residency programme that allows students to complete most of the requirements off campus while developing their skill as non-fiction writers under the close supervision of a faculty mentor. Provides instruction in the following areas: the personal essay, memoir, literary journalism, travel/nature/science writing, biography/profiles and narrative non-fiction.

Massachusetts

Boston University

Creative Writing Program, 236 Bay State
Road, Boston MA 02215
☎001 617 353 2510 Fax 001 617 353 3653
✉ crwr@bu.edu
www.bu.edu/writing

Director *Leslie Epstein*

Contact *Matthew Yost*

One-year Master of Arts in *Creative Writing*:
Fiction, Poetry or Drama. The Boston
University Creative Writing Program is one of
the oldest in the country. Students participate in
workshops or seminars concentrating on their
chosen specialisation and are expected to balance that work with an equal number of graduate literature courses. Internships at the
literary journal *AGNI*, assistantships at the
Boston Arts Academy, as well as teaching fellowships are available on a limited basis.

Emerson College

120 Boylston Street, Boston MA 01226–4624
☎001 617 824 8610
✉ gradapp@emerson.edu
www.emerson.edu/graduate_admission

Graduate Program Director *Douglas Whynott*

Offers MFA in *Creative Writing* with a focus on
writing fiction, non-fiction and poetry. Includes
writing workshops, internship opportunities, a
student reading series and student teaching
opportunities. Publishes literary magazines,
Ploughshares and *Redivider*. Contact the Graduate
Admission Office for more information.

Michigan

Western Michigan University

Department of English, 1903 W. Michigan
Avenue, Kalamazoo MI 49008-5331
☎001 269 387 2584
✉ larson@wmich.edu
www.wmich.edu/english

Director of Graduate Studies *Jill Larson*

BA English Major/Minor with *Creative Writing
Emphasis* (poetry, fiction, playwriting). The
English Major aims at giving students intensive
practice in writing and criticism in various
genres in a workshop format; for general writing careers or for prospective candidates for the
MFA in Creative Writing.

MFA in *Creative Writing* (poetry, fiction, playwriting, non-fiction) For students who wish to
become professional writers of poetry, fiction,
drama or non-fiction. Qualifies them to teach
the craft at college or university level.

Minnesota

Minnesota State University Moorhead

Graduate Studies Office, MSUM, 1104 7th
Avenue South, Moorhead MN 56563
☎001 218 477 2344
✉ early@mnstate.edu
www.mnstate.edu/finearts

Program Coordinator *John Early*

MFA in *Creative Writing* (Fiction, Non-fiction,
Playwriting, Poetry, Screenwriting). The programme offers the opportunity to take workshops, seminars and tutorials in chosen areas
and to work with New Rivers Press (www.
newriverspress.com) or with *Red Weather*, the
campus literary magazine.

Minnesota State University, Mankato

Department of English, 230 Armstrong Hall,
Mankato MN 56001
☎001 507 389 2117
✉ richard.robbins@mnsu.edu
www.english.mnsu.edu/web/gradCreativeWri
ting.htm

Programme Director *Richard Robbins*

The MFA programme in *Creative Writing* meets
the needs of students who want to strike a balance between the development of individual
creative talent and the close study of literature
and language. The programme gives appropriate
training for careers in freelancing, college-level
teaching, editing and publishing and arts
administration.

Missouri

University of Missouri-Columbia

Creative Writing Program, Department of
English, 107 Tate Hall, Columbia
MO 65211–1500
☎011 573 884 7773
✉ creativewriting@missouri.edu
www.missouri.edu/~cwp

Contact *Sharon Fisher*

Creative Writing MA and PhD in English programmes in fiction, poetry and non-fiction.
Access the website for further information.

New York

Brooklyn College of the City University of New York

MFA Program in Creative Writing, Department of English, Brooklyn NY 11210
☎001 718 951 5914
academic.brooklyn.cuny.edu/english/
index.html

Deputy Chair for English Graduate Programs
Mark Patkowski

The MFA in *Creative Writing* is a small, highly personal two-year programme which confers degrees in fiction, poetry and playwriting. Admission is highly competitive. Students must complete 12 courses (four workshops, four tutorials and four literature courses), submit a book-length work in their chosen genre near the end of the second year and pass a comprehensive examination that tests their knowledge and expertise in literature. The workshops, seminars and one-on-one tutorials with established writers particularly emphasise relationships between instructors and students. 'We think of ourselves as helping the next generation of writers find the voices and visions that are uniquely their own.

New York University

19 University Place, Room 219, New York NY 10003
✉ creative.writing@nyu.edu
www.nyu.edu/gsas/program/cwp

Contact *Russell Carmony*

Director *Melissa Hammerle*

Offers MFA in *Creative Writing* and MA in *English* with focus in *Creative Writing* in poetry and fiction. Includes writing workshops and craft courses, literary outreach programmes, a public reading series, student readings, special literary seminars and student teaching opportunities. Publishes a literary journal, *Washington Square*. Contact the department via e-mail.

North Carolina

University of North Carolina at Greensboro

MFA Writing Program, English Department, 134 McIver Building, UNCG, PO Box 26170, Greensboro NC 27402-6170
☎001 336 334 5459
www.uncg.edu/eng/mfa

Contact *Jim Clark, Director*

MFA in Creative Writing (Poetry, Fiction) One of the oldest of its kind in the country, the MFA

Writing Program at Greensboro is a two-year residency with an emphasis on providing students with studio time in which to study the writing of poetry or fiction. Gives a flexibility that permits students to develop their particular talents through small classes in writing, literature and the arts.

University of North Carolina at Wilmington

Department of Creative Writing, 601 S. College Road, Wilmington NC 28403
☎001 910 962 7711
✉ mfa@uncw.edu
www.uncw.edu/mfa

Contact *MFA Coordinator*

An intensive studio-academic programme in the writing of fiction, poetry and creative non-fiction leading to either the Master of Fine Arts or Bachelor of Fine Arts degree in *Creative Writing*. Courses include workshops in the three genres, special topics and forms courses as well as a range of courses in literature. Course work in publishing and editing is also offered in the Publishing Laboratory, a university press imprint which supports local, regional and national publishing projects.

Ohio

Bowling Green State University

Creative Writing Program, English Department, Bowling Green OH 43403
☎001 419 372 8370 Fax 001 419 372 6805
www.bgsu.edu/departments/creative-writing/

Undergraduate BFA programme: a four-year programme which offers comprehensive and rigorous training in the art of writing and develops students' skills in preparation for numerous post-graduate careers.

Graduate MFA programme: a two-year studio/academic composite, mostly work in writing itself in either poetry or fiction. Also offers ten new teaching assistantships each autumn. See the website for details on both programmes.

Philadelphia

Seton Hill University

1 Seton Hill Drive, Greensburg PA 15601
☎001 724 838 4221
✉ gadmit@setonhill.edu
www.setonhill.edu

Contact *Dane Zimmer*

The MA in *Writing Popular Fiction* programme

at Seton Hill University allows students to earn a graduate degree by writing fiction that people *actually* read. Students attend week-long residencies in January and June and complete writing projects off-campus, working with a faculty mentor who is a published author in the chosen genre. Students can choose to specialise in science fiction, fantasy, horror, children's literature, romance or mystery. Programmes can be completed in 24 months.

Rhode Island

Brown University
Literary Arts, Box 1923, Providence RI 02912
☎001 401 863 3260
✉ Writing@brown.edu
www.brown.edu/cw
Contact *Director of Literary Arts*

Two-year MFA in *Fiction, Poetry, Playwriting and Electronic Writing*. Students take three workshops, four electives and one independent study (through which they complete a thesis project). Application deadline: 15 December.

Virginia

George Mason University
English Department, MSN 3E4, 4400 University Drive, Fairfax VA 22030
☎001 703 993 1180
✉ writing@gmu.edu
creativewriting.gmu.edu
Contact *Graduate Coordinator*

The MFA in *Creative Writing* is a 48-credit hour programme with flexibility for students to tailor their studies to their interests and craft development. At least 12 hours are in writing seminars in the major genre (fiction, non-fiction or poetry), including a course in the historic forms of that genre. At least 12 hours are in literature and at least three hours are in a genre other than the concentration. Six hours are in thesis. The distribution of the remaining hours is generally up to the students with consultation from the faculty. 'Students study on a campus that is a major part of the Washington DC literary community and work with prominent writers.'

Virginia Commonwealth University
Department of English, PO Box 842005, Richmond VA 23284–2005
☎001 804 828 1329
✉ jalodge@vcu.edu
www.has.vcu.edu/eng

Graduate Programs Coordinator *Jeff Lodge*

Three-year MFA in *Creative Writing* with tracks in fiction and poetry and workshops in short fiction, the novel, poetry, drama, screenwriting and creative non-fiction. Opportunities to work with *Blackbird*: an online journal of literature and the arts (www.blackbird.vcu.edu), *Stand Magazine*, the Levis Reading Prize and the First Novelist Award.

Washington

Eastern Washington University
Inland Northwest Center for Writers, Creative Writing, 705 W. 1st Avenue, Spokane WA 99201
☎001 509 623 4221
✉ writing@mail.ewu.edu
www.creativewriting.ewu.edu
Director *Jonathan Johnson*

The MFA Program is an intensive two-year, pre-professional course of study with an emphasis on the practice of literature as a fine art. Includes course work in the study of literature from the vantage point of its composition and history, but the student's principal work is done in advanced workshops and in the writing of a book-length thesis of publishable quality in fiction, literary non-fiction or poetry. Students have the opportunity to work as interns on several projects: the literary magazine, *Willow Springs*; the community outreach programme, Writers in the Community; and Eastern Washington University Press. The MFA is a terminal degree programme.

Wyoming

University of Wyoming
MFA in Creative Writing, Department of English – 3353, 1000 E. University Avenue, Laramie WY 82071–2000
☎001 307 766 2867
✉ cw@uwyo.edu
www.uwyo.edu/creativewriting
Contact *Kris DeForest* (Program Assistant)

The two-year Master of Fine Arts in *Creative Writing* is an intensive 40-hour studio degree in Poetry, Fiction or Creative Non-Fiction. Special features include opportunities for interdisciplinary study, supported by a wide range of university departments, and a required professional internship on campus, in the community or further afield, ensuring the acquisition or polishing of 'real-life' writing skills.

Commonwealth Publishers

Australia

ACER Press
Private Bag 55, Camberwell Victoria 3124
☎00 61 3 9277 5555 Fax 00 61 3 9277 5500
www.acer.edu.au
Founded 1930. Publishes education, human resources, psychology, parent education, occupational therapy.

Allen & Unwin Pty Ltd
PO Box 8500, St Leonards, Sydney
NSW 1590
☎00 61 2 8425 0100 Fax 00 61 2 9906 2218
www.allenandunwin.com
Founded 1976. Publishes fiction, crime, literature; general non-fiction, academic, biography, business, children's, cookery, environment, health and nutrition, history, how-to, military history, humanities, humour, popular science, social science, women's and men's studies, professional, reference, textbooks.

Edward Arnold (Australia) Pty Ltd
PO Box 885, Kew Victoria 3101
☎00 61 3 985 9011 Fax 00 61 3 985 9141
Founded 1966. Part of Hodder & Stoughton (Australia) Pty Ltd. Publishes general non-fiction: accountancy, Asian studies, behavioural sciences, career development, computer science, cookery, geography, geology, government, political science, health and nutrition, law, mathematics, psychology and psychiatry, technology, textbooks.

Blackwell Publishing Asia
550 Swanston Street, Carlton South
Victoria 3053
☎00 61 3 8359 1011 Fax 00 61 3 8359 1120
✉ info@blackwellpublishingasia.com
Founded 1971. Part of Blackwell Science Ltd, UK. Publishes academic books, journals and CD-ROMs; business, economics, finance, general science, humanities, law, medicine, mathematics, professional, reference, textbooks.

Currency Press Pty Ltd
PO Box 2287, Strawberry Hills NSW 2012
☎00 61 2 9319 5877 Fax 00 61 2 9319 3649
✉ enquiries@currency.com.au
www.currency.com.au
Founded 1971. Performing arts publisher – directories and reference – drama, theatre, music, dance, film and video.

Dangaroo Press
GPO Box 1209, New Lambton NSW 2001
☎00 61 2 4565 6011 Fax 00 61 2 4951 7430
Founded 1978. Publishes general non-fiction, art, literature, literary criticism, essays, poetry, social sciences, sociology, women's studies.

Hachette Livre Australia
Level 17, 207 Kent Street, Sydney NSW 2000
☎00 61 2 8248 0800 Fax 00 61 2 8248 0810
www.hha.com.au
Founded 1958. Part of the **Hachette Livre Publishing Group**. Publishes popular fiction, literature, general non-fiction, autobiography, biography, current affairs, health, history, humour, self-help, sport, travel.

HarperCollins Publishers (Australia) Pty Ltd
PO Box 321, Pymble NSW 2073
☎00 61 2 9952 5000 Fax 00 61 2 9952 5555
www.harpercollins.com.au
Founded 1872. Part of the HarperCollins Publishers Group. Publishes fiction and non-fiction, children's and illustrated books.

Thomas C. Lothian Pty Ltd
Level 5, 132–136 Albert Road, South
Melbourne Victoria 3205
☎00 61 3 9694 4900 Fax 00 61 3 9645 0705
✉ books@lothian.com.au
www.lothian.com.au
Founded 1888. Publishes general non-fiction: biography, self-help, sport and children's and young adult fiction.

Macmillan Education Australia Pty Ltd
627 Chapel Street, South Yarra Victoria 3141
☎00 61 3 9825 1025 Fax 00 61 3 9825 1010
www.macmillan.com.au
Founded 1896. Part of **Macmillan Publishers**,

UK. Educational publisher for primary and secondary schools.

Mcgraw-Hill Australia Pty Ltd
Locked Bag 2233, Business Centre, North Ryde NSW 1670
☎00 61 2 9900 1800 Fax 00 61 2 9878 8280
www.mcgraw-hill.com.au
Founded 1964. Owned by **McGraw-Hill Inc.**, USA. Publishes accountancy, education, health and nutrition, advertising, aeronautics, aviation, anthropology, architecture and interior design, art, behavioural sciences, chemistry, chemical engineering, child care and development, computer science, criminology, disability, earth sciences, economics, electronics, electrical engineering, general engineering, English as a second language, environmental studies, film and video, geography, geology, journalism, industrial relations, labour, language arts, linguistics, management, marketing, maritime, mathematics, mechanical engineering, medicine, nursing, dentistry, philosophy, photography, physics, professional, psychology, psychiatry, sport, social sciences and sociology, textbooks.

Melbourne University Publishing Ltd
187 Grattan Street, Carlton South Victoria 3053
☎00 61 3 9342 0300 Fax 00 61 3 9342 0399
✉ mup-info@unimelb.edu.au
www.mup.unimelb.edu.au
Founded 1922. Academic publishers; general non-fiction, biography, essays, history, literature, literary criticism, natural history, psychology, psychiatry, travel.

Oxford University Press (Australia, New Zealand, Singapore & the Pacific)
GPO Box 2784Y, Melbourne Victoria 3001
☎00 61 3 9934 9123 Fax 00 61 3 9934 9100
www.oup.com.au
Founded 1908. Owned by **Oxford University Press**, UK. Publishes for the college, school and trade markets.

Pan Macmillan Australia Pty Ltd
Level 25, 1 Market Street, Sydney NSW 2000
☎00 61 2 9285 9100 Fax 00 61 2 9285 9190
www.panmacmillan.com.au
Founded 1983. Part of **Macmillan Publishers**, UK. Publishes fiction, essays, literature, literary criticism; general non-fiction,

biography, children's, health and nutrition, humour, self-help, travel.

Pearson Education Australia Pty Ltd
Locked Bag 507, Frenchs Forest NSW 1640
☎00 61 3 9454 2200 Fax 00 61 3 9453 0089
www.pearson.com.au
Australia's largest educational publisher, formed in 1998 from a merger of Addison Wesley Longman Australia and Prentice Hall Australia.

Penguin Group (Australia)
PO Box 701, Hawthorn Victoria 3122
☎00 61 3 9811 2400 Fax 00 61 3 9870 6086
www.penguin.com.au
Founded 1946. Publishes general non-fiction and fiction; biography, children's, cookery, humour, literature, literary criticism, essays, science fiction, fantasy, self-help, travel.

University of Queensland Press
PO Box 6042, St Lucia Queensland 4067
☎00 61 7 3365 2127
✉ uqp@uqp.uq.edu.au
www.uqp.uq.edu.au
Founded 1948. Publishes academic, textbooks, children's, general non-fiction and fiction, literature, literary criticism, essays, poetry, biography, history, sport, travel.

Random House Australia
20 Alfred Street, Milsons Point NSW 2061
☎00 61 2 9954 9966 Fax 00 61 2 9954 4562
✉ random@randomhouse.com.au
www.randomhouse.com.au
Subsidiary of **Bertelsmann AG**. Publishes fiction and non-fiction.

Scholastic Australia Pty Limited
PO Box 579, Gosford NSW 2250
☎00 61 2 4328 3555
www.scholastic.com.au
Founded 1968. Educational publisher.

Science Press
Unit 16, 102 Edinburgh Road, Marrickville NSW 2204
☎00 61 2 9516 1122 Fax 00 61 2 9550 1915
Founded 1945. Educational publisher.

Simon & Schuster Australia Pty Ltd
PO Box 33, Pymble NSW 2073
☎00 61 2 9983 6600 Fax 00 61 2 9988 4293

Founded 1987. Part of **Simon & Schuster Inc.**, USA. Publishes general non-fiction; animals and pets, anthropology, childcare, children's, cookery, crafts, games and hobbies, health and nutrition, history, how-to, management, natural history, self-help.

UWA Press
University of Western Australia, 35 Stirling Highway, Crawley WA 6009
☎00 61 8 9380 3670 Fax 00 61 8 9380 1027
✉ admin@uwapress.uwa.edu.au
www.uwapress.uwa.edu.au
Founded 1954. Publishes general non-fiction, essays, literature, literary criticism, science fiction, fantasy, history, social sciences, sociology, natural history, children's, directories, biography, reference, textbooks, women's studies.

John Wiley & Sons Australia Ltd
PO Box 1226, Milton Queensland 4064
☎00 61 7 3859 9755 Fax 00 61 7 3859 9715
✉ brisbane@johnwiley.com.au
www.johnwiley.com.au
Founded 1954. Owned by **John Wiley & Sons Inc.**, USA. Publishes general non-fiction and education books, dictionaries, encyclopedias, maps and atlases, textbooks.

Canada

Canadian Scholars' Press, Inc
180 Bloor Street W, Suite 801, Toronto
Ontario M5S 2V6
☎001 416 929 2774 Fax 001 416 929 1926
✉ info@cspi.org
www.cspi.org
Founded 1987. Publishes academic books in English and French.

Fenn Publishing
34 Nixon Road, Bolton Ontario L7E 1W2
☎001 905 951 6600 Fax 001 905 951 6601
www.hbfenn.com
Founded 1977. Publishes fiction and non-fiction, children's.

Firefly Books Ltd
66 Leek Crescent, Richmond Hill
Ontario L4B 1H1
☎001 416 499 8412 Fax 001 416 499 8313
www.fireflybooks.com
Founded 1976. Publishes children's and young

adult, encyclopedias, general non-fiction, astronomy, cookery, crafts, gardening, health, how-to, natural history, reference, science, sport, transport, travel.

Fitzhenry and Whiteside Limited
195 Allstate Parkway, Markham
Ontario L3R 4T8
☎001 905 477 9700
✉ godwit@fitzhenry.ca
www.fitzhenry.ca
Founded 1966. Publishes reference, biography, history, poetry, photography, sport, children's and young adult books.

Harlequin Enterprises Ltd
225 Duncan Mill Road, Don Mills
Ontario M3B 3K9
☎001 416 445 5860 Fax 001 416 445 8655
www.eharlequin.com
Founded 1949. Canada's second largest publishing house. Publishes romantic and women's fiction.

HarperCollins Publishers Limited
2 Bloor Street E, 20th Floor, Toronto
Ontario M4W 1A8
☎001 416 975 9334 Fax 001 416 975 9884
www.harpercanada.com
Founded 1989. Publishes commerical and literary fiction, non-fiction, children's, reference and religious books.

LexisNexis Canada Ltd
123 Commerce Valley Drive E, Suite 700,
Markham Ontario L3T 7W8
☎001 905 479 2665 Fax 001 905 479 2826
www.lexisnexis.ca
Founded 1912. Publishes law books, CD-ROMs, journals, newsletters, law reports.

McClelland & Stewart Ltd
75 Sherbourne Street, Fifth Floor, Toronto
Ontario M5A 2P9
☎001 416 598 1114 Fax 001 416 598 7764
✉ mail@mcclelland.com
www.mcclelland.com
Founded 1906. Publishes fiction and general non-fiction, poetry.

McGraw-Hill Ryerson Ltd
300 Water Street, Whitby Ontario L1N 9B6
☎001 905 430 5000
www.mcgrawhill.ca
Founded 1944. Subsidiary of **McGraw-Hill**

Education. Publishes education, professional and medical.

New Star Books Ltd
107–3477 Commercial Street, Vancouver
BC V5N 4E8
☎001 604 738 9429 Fax 001 604 738 9332
✉ info@newstarbooks.com
www.newstarbooks.com
Founded 1974. Publishes fiction, literature, poetry, government and political science, history, sociology, social sciences.

Oxford University Press, Canada
70 Wynford Drive, Don Mills
Onatario M3C 1J9
☎001 416 441 2941 Fax 001 416 444 0427
www.oup.com/ca
Founded 1904. Owned by **Oxford University Press**, UK. Publishes for college, school and trade markets.

Pearson Canada
26 Prince Andrew Place, Don Mills
Ontario M3C 2T8
☎001 416 447 5101 Fax 001 416 443 0948
www.pearsoned.com
Founded 1966. A division of Pearson Plc and Canada's largest publisher. Publishes fiction, non-fiction and educational material in English and French.

Penguin Group Canada
90 Eglinton Avenue East, Suite 700, Toronto
Ontario M4P 2Y3
☎001 416 925 2249 Fax 001 416 925 0068
✉ info@penguin.ca
www.penguin.ca
Founded 1974. Publishes fiction and non-fiction books and audio cassettes.

Random House of Canada Ltd
One Toronto Street, Unit 300, Toronto
Ontario M5C 2V6
☎001 416 364 4449 Fax 001 416 364 6863
www.randomhouse.ca
Founded 1944. Publishes fiction and non-fiction and children's.

Scholastic Canada Ltd
175 Hillmount Road, Markham
Ontario L6C 1Z7
☎001 905 887 7323 Fax 001 905 887 1131
www.scholastic.ca
Founded 1957. Publishes (in English and French) children's books and educational material.

Thomson Nelson
1120 Birchmount Road, Scarborough
Ontario M1K 5G4
☎001 416 752 9448 Fax 001 416 752 8101
✉ inquire@nelson.com
www.nelson.com
Part of the Thomson Corporation. Publishes directories, education, professional, reference, textbooks.

University of Toronto Press
10 St Mary Street, Suite 700, Toronto
Ontario M4Y 2W8
☎001 416 978 2239 Fax 001 416 978 4738
✉ info@utpress.utoronto.ca
www.utpress.utoronto.ca
Founded 1901. Publishes scholarly books and journals.

Tundra Books
75 Sherbourne Street, Suite 700, Toronto
Ontario M5A 2P9
☎001 416 598 4786
✉ tundra@mcclelland.com
www.tundrabooks.com
Founded 1967. Division of **McClelland & Stewart Ltd**. Publishes (in English and French) children's and young adult books.

John Wiley & Sons Canada Ltd
6045 Fremont Blvd, Mississauga
Ontario L5R 4J3
☎001 416 236 4433
✉ canada@wiley.com
www.wiley.ca
Founded 1968. Subsidiary of **John Wiley & Sons Inc.**, USA. Publishes professional, reference and textbooks.

India

Affiliated East West Press Pvt Ltd
105 Nirmal Tower, 26 Barakhamba Road, New Delhi 110 001
☎00 91 11 2331 5398
Founded 1962. Publishes textbooks, CD-ROMs, electronic books.

Arnold Heinemann Publishers (India) Pvt Ltd
AB-9, 1st Floor, Safdaoung Enclave, New Delhi 110 029
☎00 91 11 2638 3422
Fax 00 91 11 2687 7571

Founded 1969. Associate company of Edward Arnold (Publishers) Ltd, UK. Publishes fiction, directories, reference and textbooks.

S. Chand & Co Ltd
7361 Ram Nagar, Qutub Road, Tourist Hotel Complex, New Delhi 110 055
☎00 91 11 2367 2080
Fax 00 91 11 2367 7446
✉ info@schandgroup.com
www.schandgroup.com
Founded 1917. Publishes computer science, dictionaries, encyclopedias, engineering, reference, textbooks.

Hind Pocket Books Pvt. Ltd
18–19 Dilshad Garden, G.T. Road, Shahadara, Delhi 110 032   Fax 00 91 11 2228 2332
Founded 1957. Publishes fiction and general non-fiction; literature, health and self-help.

Jaico Publishing House
127 M.G. Road, Mumbai 400 023
☎00 91 22 267 6702   Fax 00 91 22 265 6412
✉ jaicobom@bom5.vsnl.net.in
www.jaicobooks.com/home.asp
Founded 1946. Publishes computer science, engineering, finance, health and nutrition, information technology, law, reference, literature, self-help, philosophy, religion, history, government, political science, sociology.

LexisNexis India
14th Floor, Vijaya Building, 17 Barakhamba Road, New Delhi 110 001
☎00 91 11 2373 9614
Fax 00 91 11 2332 6456
✉ info@lexisnexis.co.in
www.lexisnexis.co.in
Publishes law, taxation and business books in print form, online and CD-ROM.

Macmillan India Ltd
315/316 Raheja Chambers, 12 Museum Road, Bangalore 560 011
☎00 91 80 558 7878   Fax 00 91 80 558 8713
www.macmillanindia.com
Founded 1893. Part of **Macmillan Publishers**, UK. Publishes education, non-fiction, reference, dictionaries, encyclopedias.

Munshiram Manoharlal Publishers Pvt Ltd
PO Box 5715, 54 Rani Jhansi Road, New Delhi 110 055

☎00 91 11 2367 1668
Fax 00 91 11 2361 2745
✉ mrml@mrmlbooks.com
www.mrmlbooks.com
Founded 1952. Publishes academic, dictionaries, art and art history, architecture and interior design, anthropology, archaeology, occult, religion, philosophy, geography, history, humanities, language arts and linguistics, law, literature, medicine, numismatics, music, dance, drama, theatre, Asian studies, sociology, social sciences, travel.

National Publishing House
23 Daryaganj, New Delhi 110 002
☎00 91 11 2327 4161
✉ info@nationalpublishinghouse.com
www.nationalpublishinghouse.com
Founded 1950. Publishes non-fiction, social sciences, sociology.

Orient Paperbacks
5 A/8 Ansari Road, First Floor, Darya Ganj, Delhi 110 002
☎00 91 11 2327 8877
Fax 00 91 11 2327 8879
✉ mail@orientpaperbacks.com
www.orientpaperbacks.com
Founded 1977. Publishes fiction and general non-fiction; autobiography, biography, business, career development, current affairs, education, games, hobbies, humour, health and nutrition, literature, New Age, politics, puzzles, reference, religion, self-help.

Oxford University Press India
YMCA Library Building, 1st Floor, 1 Jai Singh Road, New Delhi 110 001
☎00 91 11 2374 7124
Fax 00 91 11 2374 2312
Founded 1912. Owned by **Oxford University Press**, UK. Academic publishers.

Rajpal & Sons
1590 Madarasa Road, Kashmere Gate, Delhi 110 006
☎00 91 11 296 3904   Fax 00 91 11 296 7791
Founded 1947. Publishes fiction, general science, children's, dictionaries, encyclopedias, textbooks.

Tata McGraw-Hill India
7 West Patel Nagar, New Delhi 110 008
☎00 91 11 2588 2743
Fax 00 91 11 2588 5154

www.tatamcgrawhill.com
Founded 1970. Educational publisher.

Vidyarthi Mithram Press
Bakar Road, Kottayarn 686 001
☎00 91 481 563281
Founded 1928. Publishes children's and young adult, CD-ROMs, dictionaries, directories, encyclopedias, computer science, reference.

A.H. Wheeler & Co Ltd
23 Lal Bahadur Shasti Marg,
Allahabad 211 001
☎00 91 11 331 2629
Founded 1879. Publishes CD-ROMs, professional, textbooks; computer science, communications.

New Zealand

Auckland University Press
University of Auckland, Private Bag 92019, Auckland
☎00 64 9 373 7528 Fax 00 64 9 373 7465
✉ aup@auckland.ac.nz
www.auckland.ac.nz/aup
Founded 1966. Publishes academic, biography, government, political science, history, social sciences, sociology, poetry, literature, literary criticism, Maori studies.

Canterbury University Press
University of Canterbury, Private Bag 4800, Christchurch
☎00 64 3 364 2914 Fax 00 64 3 364 2044
✉ mail@cup.canterbury.ac.nz
www.cup.canterbury.ac.nz
Founded 1964. Academic publishers; general non-fiction; history, marine biology, natural history.

The Caxton Press
113 Victoria Street, Christchurch
☎00 64 3 353 0734 Fax 00 64 3 365 7840
www.caxton.co.nz
Founded 1935. Publishes general non-fiction.

Hachette Livre New Zealand Ltd
4 Whetu Place, Mairangi Bay, Auckland 1330
☎00 64 9 478 1000 Fax 00 64 9 478 1010
✉ admin@hachette.co.nz
Founded 1971. Part of the **Hachette Livre Publishing Group**. Publishes fiction and general non-fiction; biography, business, cookery, humour, sport.

HarperCollins Publishers (New Zealand) Ltd
31 View Road, Glenfield, Auckland
☎00 64 9 443 9400 Fax 00 64 9 443 9403
✉ editors@harpercollins.co.nz
www.harpercollins.co.nz
Founded 1888. Publishes fiction, literature, children's, business, cookery, gardening, reference, religion.

Huia Publishers
PO Box 17-335, Wellington, Aotearoa
☎00 64 4 473 9262 Fax 00 64 4 473 9265
✉ books@huia.co.nz
www.huia.co.nz
Founded 1991. Publishes Maori cultural history and language, children's books in Maori and English, fiction.

LexisNexis New Zealand
PO Box 472, Wellington 1
☎00 64 4 385 1479 Fax 00 64 4 385 1598
www.lexisnexis.co.nz
Founded 1914. Publishes law, professional and textbooks in book and electronic formats.

Macmillan Publishers New Zealand Ltd
6 Ride Way, Albany, Auckland
☎00 64 9 414 0350 Fax 00 64 9 414 0351
www.macmillan.co.nz
Education publishers – general, school and academic books; fiction and non-fiction for all ages.

Pearson Education New Zealand Ltd
Private Bag 102908, North Shore Mail Centre, Auckland 1310
☎00 64 9 414 9980 Fax 00 64 9 414 9981
www.pearson.co.nz
Founded 1968. Educational publishers.

Penguin Books (NZ) Ltd
Private Bag 102–902, North Shore Mail Centre, Auckland
☎00 64 9 415 4700 Fax 00 64 9 415 4701
www.penguin.co.nz
Founded 1976. Owned by **Penguin UK**. Adult and children's fiction and non-fiction.

Random House New Zealand
Private Bag 102950, North Shore Mail Centre, Auckland

☎00 64 9 444 7197 Fax 00 64 9 444 7524
www.randomhouse.co.nz
Publishes fiction and non-fiction (cooking, gardening, art, natural history) and children's.

Reed Publishing (NZ) Ltd
Private Bag 34901, Birkenhead, Auckland
☎00 64 9 441 2960 Fax 00 64 9 480 4999
✉ info@reed.co.nz
www.reed.co.nz
Founded 1988. Publishes fiction and general non-fiction, biography, children's, cookery, directories, history, natural history, regional interests, reference, textbooks, travel.

Tandem Press
PO Box 34–272, Birkenhead, Auckland
☎00 64 9 480 1452
www.tandempress.co.nz
Founded 1990. Publishes fiction and general non-fiction.

Victoria University Press
PO Box 600, Wellington
☎00 64 4 463 6580 Fax 00 64 4 463 6581
✉ victoria-press@vuw.ac.nz
www.vuw.ac.nz/vup
Founded 1979. Publishes new fiction and, poetry, literature, essays, New Zealand history, Maori topics.

Viking Sevenseas NZ Ltd
PO Box 152, Paraparaumu, Wellington
☎00 64 4 902 8240
Founded 1957. Publishes natural history and ethnicity.

Bridget Williams Books Ltd
PO Box 5482, Wellington
☎00 64 4 494 6054 Fax 00 64 4 499 8942
✉ info@bwb.co.nz
www.bwb.co.nz
Founded 1990. Independent publisher of New Zealand history, Maori experience, contemporary issues and women's studies.

South Africa

Heinemann International Southern Africa
PO Box 781940, Sandton 2146
☎00 27 11 322 8600 Fax 00 27 11 322 8716
www.heinemann.co.za
Founded 1986. Educational publisher.

University of Kwa-Zulu–Natal Press
Private Bag X01, Scottsville 3209
☎00 27 33 260 5226 Fax 00 27 33 260 5801
✉ books@ukzn.ac.za
www.ukznpress.co.za
Founded 1947. Publishes academic and general books; children's, government, political science, African literature, poetry, economics, military history, natural sciences, social sciences.

LexisNexis Butterworths South Africa
PO Box 792, Durban 4000
☎00 27 31 268 3111
www.lexisnexis.co.za
Publishes professional, accountancy, finance, business, law, taxation, economics books in print form, online and CD-ROM.

Macmillan South Africa
PO Box 32484, Braamfontein 2017
☎00 27 11 731 3300 Fax 00 27 11 731 3500
✉ info@macmillan.co.za
www.macmillan.co.za/southafrica.html
Founded 1972. Part of **Macmillan Publishers Ltd**, UK. Educational publisher.

Maskew Miller Longman
PO Box 396, Cape Town 8000
☎00 27 21 532 6000 Fax 00 27 21 531 8103
www.mml.co.za
Founded 1893. Publishes education and teacher support books.

Oxford University Press Southern Africa (Pty) Ltd
PO Box 12119, N1 City, Cape Town 7463
☎00 27 21 596 2300 Fax 00 27 21 596 1234
✉ oxford.za@oup.com
www.oup.com/za
Founded 1915. Parent company: **Oxford University Press**, UK. Publishes academic, educational and general books.

Shuter & Shooter (Pty) Ltd
PO Box 13016, Cascades,
Pietermaritzburg 3202
☎00 27 33 347 6100 Fax 00 27 33 346 6120
www.shuter.co.za
Founded 1925. Publishes educational material.

Struik Publishers (Pty) Ltd

PO Box 1144, Cape Town 8000
☎00 27 21 462 4360 Fax 00 27 21 462 4379
✉ admin@struik.co.za
www.struik.co.za

Founded 1962. Publishes general non-fiction, illustrated, art and culture, lifestyle, natural history, travel.

Wits University Press

PO Wits, Johannesburg 2050
☎00 27 11 717 1000 Fax 00 27 11 717 1065
witspress.wits.ac.za

Founded 1922. Publishes academic, art, biography and memoirs, economics, theatre studies, history, business, anthropology, archaeology, politics, law, popular science, medicine, women's writing.

Professional Associations and Societies

ABSW

Wellcome Wolfson Building, 165 Queen's Gate, London SW7 5HE
☎0870 770 3361
✉ absw@absw.org.uk
www.absw.org.uk
Chairman *Ted Nield*
Administrator & EUSJA Board Member *Barbara Drillsma*
MEMBERSHIP £40 (full) p.a.; £36 (associate); £5 (student)

ABSW has played a central role in improving the standards of science journalism in the UK over the last 40 years. The Association seeks to improve standards by means of networking, lectures and organised visits to institutional laboratories and industrial research centres. Puts members in touch with major projects in the field and with experts worldwide. A member of the European Union of Science Journalists' Associations, ABSW is able to offer heavily subsidised places on visits to research centres in most other European countries, and hosts reciprocal visits to Britain by European journalists. Membership open to those who are considered to be *bona fide* science writers/editors, or their film/TV/radio equivalents, who earn a substantial part of their income by promoting public interest in and understanding of science. Runs the administration and judging of the **Glaxo Science Writers' Awards**, for outstanding science journalism in newspapers, journals and broadcasting and, with The Wellcome Trust, awards bursaries for science undergraduates taking a science communication course.

Academi (Yr Academi Gymreig)

3rd Floor, Mount Stuart House, Mount Stuart Square, Cardiff CF10 5FQ
☎029 2047 2266 Fax 029 2049 2930
✉ post@academi.org
www.academi.org

Glyn Jones Centre, Wales Millenium Centre, Cardiff Bay, Cardiff

North West Wales office: Ty Newydd, Llanystumdwy, Criccieth, Gwynedd LL52 0LW
☎01766 522817 Fax 01766 523095
✉ olwen@academi.org

West Wales office: Dylan Thomas Centre, Somerset Place, Swansea SA1 1RR
☎01792 463980 Fax 01792 463993
✉ academi.dylan.thomas@business.ntl.com
☎Chief Executive *Peter Finch*

Academi is the trading name of Yr Academi Gymreig, the Welsh National Literature Promotion Agency and Society for Writers. Yr Academi Gymreig was founded in 1959 as an association of Welsh language writers. An English language section was established in 1968. Membership, for those who have made a significant contribution to the literature of Wales, is by invitation. Membership currently stands at 500. The Academi runs courses, competitions (including the **Cardiff International Poetry Competition**), conferences, tours by authors, festivals, and represents the interests of Welsh writers and Welsh writing both inside Wales and beyond. Its publications include *Taliesin*, a quarterly literary journal in the Welsh language, *The Oxford Companion to the Literature of Wales*, *The Welsh Academy English-Welsh Dictionary* and a variety of translated works.

The Academi won the franchise from the Arts Council of Wales to run the Welsh National Literature Promotion Agency. The new, much enlarged organisation now administers a variety of schemes including bursaries, the annual **Book of the Year Award**, critical services, writers' mentoring, Writers on Tour, Writers Residencies and a number of literature development projects. It promotes an annual literary festival alternating between North and South Wales, runs its own programme of literary activity and publishes *A470*, a bi-monthly literature information magazine. The Academi is also in receipt of a lottery grant to publish the first Welsh National Encyclopedia. This is expected to be ready in 2006.

Those with an interest in literature in Wales can become an associate of the Academi (which carries a range of benefits). Rates are £15 p.a. (waged); £7.50 (unwaged).

ALCS

See **Authors' Licensing & Collecting Society Limited**

Alliance of Literary Societies

22 Belmont Grove, Bedhampton, Havant
PO9 3PU
☎023 9247 5855
✉ rosemary@sndc.demon.co.uk
www.allianceofliterarysocieties.org

Honorary Secretary *Rosemary Culley*

Founded 1974. Aims to help and support its 100+ member societies and, when necessary, to act as a pressure group. Produces a handbook which holds useful information that is deemed important for the successful running of a literary society. It also contains details of the member societies to publicise them to the ALS members and the wider public. In addition, the Alliance produces two newsletters and *The Open Book*, an annual publication.

Arts & Business (A&B)

Nutmeg House, 60 Gainsford Street, Butlers Wharf, London SE1 2NY
☎020 7378 8143 Fax 020 7407 7527
✉ head.office@AandB.org.uk
www.AandB.org.uk

Acting Director of Communications *Jonathan Tuchner*
Media Manager *Rachel Balfour*

A&B enables business and its people to be more successful by engaging with the arts and to increase resources for the arts from business and its people. It provides a wide range of services to over 400 business members and 1100 arts organisations through the Development Forum. Programmes include professional development for arts and business people through the skills bank, board bank and mentoring schemes, and the New Partners programme which invests funds to foster innovative long term partnerships. With the support of its President, HRH The Prince of Wales, it explores and develops new ways for business, the arts and society to interact. Arts & Business has 17 regional offices offering a range of services throughout the UK.

Arvon Foundation

See entry under *UK Writers' Courses*

ASLS

See **Association for Scottish Literary Studies**

Association for Scottish Literary Studies

c/o Department of Scottish History, 9 University Gardens, University of Glasgow, Glasgow G12 8QH

☎0141 330 5309 Fax 0141 330 5309
✉ office@asls.org.uk
www.asls.org.uk

Contact *Duncan Jones*
SUBSCRIPTION £38 (individual); £67 (institutional)

Founded 1970. ASLS is an educational charity promoting the languages and literature of Scotland. Publishes works of Scottish literature; essays, monographs and journals; and *Scotnotes*, a series of comprehensive study guides to major Scottish writers. Also produces *New Writing Scotland*, an annual anthology of contemporary poetry and prose in English, Gaelic and Scots (see entry under *Magazines*).

Association of American Correspondents in London

c/o People Magazine, Brettenham House, Lancaster Place, London WC2E 7TL
☎020 7322 1155 Fax 020 7322 1125
www.theaacl.co.uk

Secretary/Treasurer *Monique Jessen*
SUBSCRIPTION £100 (organisations)

Founded 1919 to serve the professional interests of its member organisations, promote social cooperation among them, and maintain the ethical standards of the profession. (An extra £40 is charged for each department of an organisation which requires separate listing in the Association's handbook and a charge of £10 for each full-time editorial staff listed, up to a maximum of £120 regardless of the number listed.)

Association of American Publishers, Inc

71 Fifth Avenue, 2nd Floor, New York, NY 10003–3004, USA
☎001 212 255 0200 Fax 001 212 255 7007
www.publishers.org

Also at: 50 F Street, NW, Suite 400, Washington, DC 20001
☎001 202 347 3375 Fax 001 202 347 3690

Founded 1970. For information, visit the Association's website.

Association of Authors' Agents (AAA)

Gillon Aitken Associates Ltd, 18–21 Cavaye Place, London SW10 9PT
☎020 7373 8672
✉ aaa@gillonaitken.co.uk
www.agentsassoc.co.uk

President *Clare Alexander*

MEMBERSHIP £50 p.a.

Founded 1974. Membership voluntary. The AAA maintains a code of practice, provides a forum for discussion and represents its members in issues affecting the profession. For a full list of members and a list of frequently asked questions visit the AAA website. The AAA is a voluntary body and unable to operate as an information service to the public.

Association of Authors' Representatives (AAR)
✉ info@aar-online.org
www.aar-online.org
Administrative Secretary *Leslie Carroll*

Founded in 1991 through the merger of the Society of Authors' Representatives and the Independent Literary Agents Association. Membership of this US organisation is restricted to agents of at least two years' operation. Provides information, education and support for its members and works to protect their best interests.

Association of British Editors
See **Society of Editors**

Association of British Science Writers
See **ABSW**

Association of Canadian Publishers
161 Eglinton Avenue East, Suite 702, Toronto, Ontario M4P 1J5, Canada
☎001 416 487 6116   Fax 001 416 487 8815
✉ admin@canbook.org
www.publishers.ca
Executive Director *Margaret Eaton*

Founded 1971. ACP represents over 140 Canadian-owned book publishers countrywide from the literary, general trade, scholarly and education sectors. Aims to encourage the writing, publishing, distribution and promotion of Canadian books and to support the development of a 'strong, independent and vibrant Canadian-owned publishing industry'. The organisation's website has information on getting published and links to many of their member publishers' websites.

Association of Christian Writers
All Saints Vicarage, 43 All Saints Close,
London N9 9AT
☎020 8884 4348   Fax 020 8884 4348
✉ admin@christianwriters.org.uk

www.christianwriters.org.uk
Administrator *Mrs Jenny Kyriacou*
SUBSCRIPTION single: £20 (£17 Direct Debit); joint husband/wife: £23 (£20 DD); overseas: £27 (£24 DD on UK a/c)

Founded in 1971 'to inspire and equip men and women to use their talents and skills with integrity to devise, write and market excellent material which comes from a Christian worldview. In this way we seek to be an influence for good and for God in this generation.' Publishes a quarterly magazine. Runs three training events each year, biennial conference, competitions, postal workshops, area groups, prayer support and manuscript criticism. Charity No. 1069839.

Association of Freelance Editors, Proofreaders & Indexers (Ireland)
3 The Lawn, Oldtown Mill, Celbridge, Co. Kildare, Republic of Ireland
☎00 353 1 601 2846/1 295 2194
www.afepi.ie
Contacts *Priscilla O'Connor, Brenda O'Hanlon*
SUBSCRIPTION €40 p.a. (full); €20 (associate)

The organisation was established in Ireland to protect the interests of its members and to provide information to publishers on freelancers working in the relevant fields. Full membership is restricted to freelancers with experience and/or references (but the association does not test or evaluate the skills of members). A new category of membership, Associate Member, is available for trainees in proofreading/editing who are taking the Publishing Training Centre correspondence courses in Proofreading and Copy-editing.

Association of Freelance Writers
Sevendale House, 7 Dale Street, Manchester M1 1JB
☎0161 228 2362, ext 210
Fax 0161 228 3533
✉ fmn@writersbureau.com
www.writersbureau.com/fmn
Contact *Angela Cox*
SUBSCRIPTION £29 p.a.

Founded in 1995 to help and advise new and established freelance writers. Members receive a copy of *Freelance Market News* each month which gives news, views and the latest advice and guidelines about publications at home and abroad. Other benefits include one free appraisal of prose or poetry each year, reduced entry to **The Writers Bureau** writing competition, reduced fees for writing seminars and discounts on books for writers.

Association of Golf Writers
1 Pilgrims Bungalow, Mulberry Hill, Chilham CT4 8AH
☎01227 732496 Fax 01227 732496
✉ andyfarrell@compuserve.com
Honorary Secretary *Andy Farrell*
Founded 1938. Aims to cooperate with golfing bodies to ensure best possible working conditions.

Association of Illustrators
2nd Floor, Back Building, 150 Curtain Road, London EC2A 3AT
☎020 7613 4328 Fax 020 7613 4417
✉ info@theaoi.com
www.theaoi.com
Contact *Membership Coordinator*
Founded 1973 to promote illustration, protect illustrators' rights, and encourage professional standards. The AOI is a non-profit-making trade association dedicated to its members, to protecting their interests and promoting their work. Talks, seminars, tri-monthly journal, legal and portfolio advice as well as a number of related publications such as *Rights, The Illustrator's Guide to Professional Practice*; *Contact Directories*; *Survive, The Illustrator's Guide to a Professional Career* and *Images*, the only jury-selected annual of British contemporary illustration.

Association of Independent Libraries
Leeds Library, 18 Commercial Street, Leeds LS1 6AL
☎0113 245 3071
www.independentlibraries.co.uk
Chairman *Geoffrey Forster*
Secretary *Krystyna Smithers*
Established to 'further the advancement, conservation and restoration of a little-known but important living portion of our cultural heritage'. Members include the **London Library, Devon & Exeter Institution, Linen Hall Library** and **Plymouth Proprietary Library**.

Association of Learned and Professional Society Publishers
South House, The Street, Clapham, Worthing BN13 3UU
☎01903 871686 Fax 01903 871457
✉ sally.morris@alpsp.org
www.alpsp.org

Chief Executive *Ian Russell* (from Oct. 2006)
Member Services Manager *Nick Evans*
Editor, Learned Publishing *Robert Welham*
(editor@alpsp.org)
The Association of Learned and Professional Society Publishers (ALPSP) is the international trade association for not-for-profit publishers and those who work with them. It currently has over 300 members in more than 30 countries. ALPSP provides representation of its sector, cooperative services such as the award-winning ALPSP Learned Journals Collection, professional development activities and a wealth of information and advice.

Association of Scottish Motoring Writers
c/o Scottish and Universal Newspapers, 5/15 Bank Street, Airdrie ML6 6AF
☎01236 748048 Fax 01236 748098
✉ jmurdoch@s-un.co.uk
Secretary *John Murdoch*
SUBSCRIPTION £45 (full); £25 (associate)
Founded 1961. Aims to co-ordinate the activities of, and provide shared facilities for, motoring writers resident in Scotland. Membership is by invitation only.

Audiobook Publishing Association
c/o 18 Green Lanes, Hatfield AL10 9JT
☎07971 280788
✉ charlotte.mccandlish@ntlworld.com
www.theapa.net
Chair *Jo Forshaw*
Administrator *Charlotte McCandlish* (at address above)
Founded 1994. The Audiobook Publishing Association (formerly the Spoken Word Publishing Association) is the UK trade association for the audiobook industry with membership open to all those involved in the publishing of spoken word audio. Publishes *APA Resources Directory*, available from the address above.

Australian Copyright Council
PO Box 1986, Strawberry Hills, NSW 2016, Australia
☎00 612 9318 1788 Fax 00 612 9698 3536
✉ info@copyright.org.au
www.copyright.org.au
Contact *Customer Service* (☎00 612 9699 3247)
Founded 1968. The Council's activities and services include a range of publications, organising and speaking about copyright at seminars,

research, consultancies and free legal advice. Aims include assistance for copyright owners to exercise their rights effectively, raising awareness about the importance of copyright and seeking changes to the law of copyright.

Australian Publishers Association

60/89 Jones Street, Ultimo, NSW 2007, Australia
☎00 612 9281 9788   Fax 00 612 9281 1073
✉ apa@publishers.asn.au
www.publishers.asn.au

Chief Executive *Susan Bridge*
SUBSCRIPTION Annual membership subscription open to Australian publishers

Founded 1948. The APA initiates programmes that contribute to the development of publishing in Australia, virgorously protects and furthers the interests of copyright owners, agents and licensees and actively represents members' interests to government and other organisations as appropriate. The Association encourages excellence in writing, editing, design, production, marketing and distribution of published works in Australia, protects freedom of expression and manages members' funds to further the interests of the industry.

Australian Society of Authors

PO Box 1566, Strawberry Hills, NSW 2012, Australia
☎00 612 9318 0877   Fax 00 612 9318 0530
✉ asa@asauthors.org
www.asauthors.org

Executive Director *Dr Jeremy Fisher*

Founded 1963. The ASA aims to promote and protect the professional interests of Australian authors. Provides contract advice and assists authors on industry standards and practices. Publishes *Australian Author* magazine.

Authors' Club

40 Dover Street, London W1S 4NP
☎020 7499 8581   Fax 020 7409 0913
✉ stella@theauthorsclub.co.uk
www.authorsclub.co.uk

Secretary *Stella Kane*

Founded in 1891 by Sir Walter Besant, the Authors' Club welcomes as members writers, agents, publishers, critics, journalists, academics and anyone involved with literature and the written word. Administers the **Authors' Club Best First Novel Award**, the **Dolman Best First Travel Book Award** and **Sir Banister Fletcher Award**, and organises regular talks

and dinners with well-known guest speakers. Membership fee: apply to secretary.

Authors' Licensing & Collecting Society Limited (ALCS)

Marlborough Court, 14–18 Holborn, London EC1N 2LE
☎020 7395 0600   Fax 020 7395 0660
✉ alcs@alcs.co.uk
www.alcs.co.uk

Chief Executive *Owen Atkinson*
SUBSCRIPTION £10.00 incl. VAT (UK; free to members of Society of Authors, Writers' Guild, NUJ, BAJ and CIOJ)

Founded 1977. The UK collective rights management society for writers and their successors, ALCS is a non-profit organisation whose principal purpose is to ensure that hard-to-collect revenues due to writers are efficiently collected and speedily distributed. Established to give assistance to writers through the protection and exploitation of collective rights, ALCS has distributed over £105 million in secondary royalties to writers since its creation.

ALCS represents all types of writer, fiction and non-fiction, including educational, research and academic authors, scriptwriters, playwrights, poets, editors and freelance journalists across the print and broadcast media. On joining, members give ALCS a mandate to administer on their behalf those rights which the law determines must be received or which are best handled collectively. Chief among these are: photocopying, cable retransmission (including the fees for BBC Prime and BBC World Service programming), rental and lending rights (but not British Public Lending Right), off-air recording, electronic rights, the performing right and public reception of broadcasts. The society is a prime resource and a leading authority on copyright matters and writers' collective interests. It maintains a watching brief on all matters affecting copyright both in Britain and abroad, making representations to UK government authorities and the EU. Visit the ALCS website or contact the office for registration forms and further information.

BAPLA (British Association of Picture Libraries and Agencies)

18 Vine Hill, London EC1R 5DZ
☎020 7713 1780   Fax 020 7713 1211
✉ enquiries@bapla.org.uk
www.bapla.org

Everything you need to know about finding, buying and selling pictures. Represents over 450 members.

The Bibliographical Society

c/o Institute of English Studies, University of London, Senate House, Malet Street, London WC1E 7HU
☎020 7862 8679 Fax 020 7862 8720
✉ secretary@bibsoc.org.uk
www.bibsoc.org.uk
President *J.L. Flood*
Honorary Secretary *M.L. Ford*
SUBSCRIPTION £33 p.a.

Aims to promote and encourage the study and research of historical, analytical, descriptive and textual bibliography, and the history of printing, publishing, bookselling, bookbinding and collecting; to hold meetings at which papers are read and discussed; to print and publish works concerned with bibliography; to form a bibliographical library. Awards grants and bursaries for bibliographical research. Publishes a quarterly magazine called *The Library*.

Booksellers Association of the UK & Ireland Ltd

Minster House, 272 Vauxhall Bridge Road, London SW1V 1BA
☎020 7802 0802 Fax 020 7802 0803
✉ mail@booksellers.org.uk
www.booksellers.org.uk
Chief Executive *Tim Godfray*

Founded 1895. The BA helps 3200 independent, chain and multiple members to sell more books, reduce costs and improve efficiency. It represents members' interests to the UK Government, European Commission, publishers, authors and others in the trade as well as offering marketing assistance, conferences, seminars and exhibitions. Together with **The Publishers Association**, coordinates World Book Day. Publishes directories, catalogues, surveys and various other publications connected with the book trade and administers the **Whitbread Book Awards**.

Booktrust

Book House, 45 East Hill, London SW18 2QZ
☎020 8516 2977 Fax 020 8516 2978
✉ query@booktrust.org.uk
www.booktrust.org.uk
www.booktrusted.com
Director *Chris Meade*
Head of Promotions *Helen Hayes*

Founded 1925. Booktrust is an independent national charity that encourages readers of all ages and cultures to discover and enjoy reading.

The reader is at the heart of everything they do. Their children's books website, booktrusted. com, also includes information about National Children's Book Week and the **Children's Laureate**, both of which Booktrust administers. Booktrust also administers literary prizes, including the **Orange Prize for Fiction** and the **Booktrust Teenage Prize** (see entries under *Prizes*), and promotes reading through campaigns such as Get London Reading (www. getlondonreading.com). Booktrust runs Bookstart (www. bookstart.org.uk), the acclaimed national scheme that works through locally based organisations to give a free pack of books to babies and guidance materials for parents and carers.

British Academy of Composers and Songwriters

2nd Floor, British Music House, 25–27 Berners Street, London W1T 3LR
☎020 7636 2929 Fax 020 7636 2212
✉ info@britishacademy.com
www.britishacademy.com
Head of Membership *Fran Matthews*

The Academy represents the interests of music writers of all genres, providing advice on professional and artistic matters. Publishes bi-monthly magazines and administers the annual Ivor Novello Awards and British Composer Awards.

British Association of Communicators in Business (CiB)

Suite GA2, Oak House, Woodlands Business Park, Linford Wood, Milton Keynes MK14 6EY
☎01908 313755 Fax 01908 313661
✉ enquiries@cib.uk.com
www.cib.uk
Secretary General *Kathie Jones*

The professional body for in-house, freelance and agency staff involved in internal and corporate communications. Services to members include a business support helpline, an online forum, a monthly e-zine, the CiB Freelance Directory, an annual conference and gala dinner, automatic eligibility to FEIEA, a European network of 5000 communicators.

British Association of Journalists

89 Fleet Street, London EC4Y 1DH
☎020 7353 3003 Fax 020 7353 2310
✉ office@bajunion.org.uk
www.bajunion.org.uk
General Secretary *Steve Turner*
SUBSCRIPTION National newspaper staff,

national broadcasting staff, national news agency staff: £17.50 per month. Other seniors, including magazine journalists, PRs and freelances who earn the majority of their income from journalism: £10 p.m. Journalists under 24: £7.50 p.m.

Founded 1992. Aims to protect and promote the industrial and professional interests of journalists.

British Association of Picture Libraries and Agencies
See **BAPLA**

British Centre for Literary Translation
University of East Anglia, Norwich NR4 7TJ
☎01603 592785   Fax 01603 592737
✉ bclt@uea.ac.uk
www.literarytranslation.com
www.uea.ac.uk

Contact *Catherine Fuller*

Founded 1989, BCLT is funded jointly by Arts Council England and the University of East Anglia. It aims to raise the profile of literary translation in the UK through events, publications, activities and research aimed at professional translators, students and the general reader. Member of the international RECIT literary translation network. Activities include the annual Sebald Lecture, Summer School, translator in residence scheme and a joint website with the British Council. BCLT has a PhD programme in literary translation as well as an MA in Literary Translation and other units at undergraduate and postgraduate level. Joint sponsor with BCLA of the **John Dryden Translation Prize**. Publishes a journal *In Other Words* and *New Books in German*. Free mailing list.

British Copyright Council
Copyright House, 29–33 Berners Street, London W1T 3AB
☎01986 788122   Fax 01986 788847
✉ secretary@britishcopyright.org
www.britishcopyright.org

Contact *Janet Ibbotson*

Works for the national and international acceptance of copyright and acts as a lobby/watchdog organisation on behalf of creators, publishers and performers on copyright and associated matters. Publications include *Guide to the Law of Copyright and Rights in Performances*.

The British Council
10 Spring Gardens, London SW1A 2BN
☎020 7389 3166 (Literature Dept)
Fax 020 7839 6347
www.britishcouncil.org

The British Council promotes Britain abroad. It provides access to British ideas, expertise and experience in education, the English language, literature and the arts, science and technology and governance. Works in 110 countries running a mix of offices, libraries, resource centres and English teaching operations.

British Equestrian Writers' Association
Priory House, Station Road, Swavesey, Cambridge CB4 5QJ
☎01954 232084   Fax 01954 231362
✉ gnewsumn@aol.com

Contact *Gillian Newsum*
SUBSCRIPTION £15

Founded 1973. Aims to further the interests of equestrian sport and improve, wherever possible, the working conditions of the equestrian press. Membership is by invitation of the committee. Candidates for membership must be nominated and seconded by full members and receive a majority vote of the committee.

British Film Institute
21 Stephen Street, London W1T 1LN
☎020 7255 1444   Fax 020 7436 0439
www.bfi.org.uk

Chair *Anthony Minghella CBE*
Director *Amanda Nevill*

Established in 1933 to champion moving image culture in all its richness and diversity across the UK, for the benefit of as wide an audience as possible and to create and encourage debate. Visit the website for more information on *bfi* services or ring the enquiry line on the main switchboard between 10.00 am and 6.00 pm.

British Guild of Beer Writers
Lee Farm, Winsford TA24 7HX
✉ tierneyjones@btinternet.com
www.beerwriters.co.uk
Secretary *Adrian Tierney-Jones*
SUBSCRIPTION £40 p.a.

Founded 1988. Aims to improve standards in beer writing and at the same time extend public knowledge of beers and brewing. Publishes a directory of members with details of their publications and their particular areas of expertise; this is then circulated to newspapers, magazines, trade press and broadcasting organisations. Also publishes a monthly newsletter, the *BGBW Newsletter*. As part of the plan to improve writing standards and to achieve a higher profile for beer, the Guild offers annual awards, The Gold and Silver Tankard Awards, to writers and broadcasters judged to have made the most valuable contribution towards this end in their work. Meetings are held regularly.

British Guild of Travel Writers

51b Askew Crescent, London W12 9DN
☎020 8749 1128   Fax 020 8181 6663
✉ charlotte.c@virtualnecessities.com
www.bgtw.org
Chairman *Mary Anne Evans*
Secretariat *Charlotte Copeman*

The professional association of travel writers, broadcasters, photographers and editors which aims to serve its members' professional interests by acting as a forum for debate, discussion and 'networking'. The Guild publishes an annual Year Book and has a website giving full details of all its members and useful trade contacts, holds monthly meetings and has a monthly newsletter. Members are required to spend a significant proportion of their working time on travel.

British Science Fiction Association

39 Glyn Avenue, New Barnet EN4 9PJ
☎07876 682310
✉ bsfachair@gmail.com
www.bsfa.co.uk
Chair *Pat McMurray and Julie Rigby*
SUBSCRIPTION £26 p.a. (reduction for unwaged)

Founded originally in 1958 by a group of authors, readers, publishers and booksellers interested in science fiction. With a worldwide membership, the Association aims to promote the reading, writing and publishing of science fiction and to encourage SF fans to maintain contact with each other. Publishes *Matrix* bi-monthly newsletter with comment and opinions, news of conventions, etc. Contributions from members welcomed; *Vector* bi-monthly critical journal – reviews of books and magazines; *Focus* biannual magazine with articles, original fiction and letters column. Also offers postal and online writer's workshop. For further information, contact the Membership Secretary *Peter Wilkinson* at the postal address above or via e-mail.

British Society of Comedy Writers

61 Parry Road, Ashmore Park,
Wolverhampton WV11 2PS
☎01902 722729   Fax 01902 722729
✉ comedy@bscw.co.uk
www.bscw.co.uk
Contact *Ken Rock*

Founded 1999. The Society aims to develop good practice and professionalism among comedy writers while bringing together the best creative professionals, and working to standards of excellence agreed with the light entertainment industry. Offers a network of industry contacts and a range of products, services and training initiatives including specialised workshops, an annual international conference, script assessment service and opportunities to visit international festivals.

British Society of Magazine Editors (BSME)

137 Hale Lane, Edgware HA8 9QP
☎020 8906 4664   Fax 020 8959 2137
✉ admin@bsme.com
www.bsme.com
Contact *Gill Branston*

Holds regular industry forums and events as well as an annual awards dinner.

British Universities Film & Video Council

See **Learning on Screen**

Broadcasting Press Guild

Tiverton, The Ridge, Woking GU22 7EQ
☎01483 764895   Fax 01483 765882
✉ torin.douglas@bbc.co.uk
www.broadcastingpressguild.org
Membership Secretary *Richard Last*
Lunch Secretary *Torin Douglas*
SUBSCRIPTION £15 p.a.

Founded 1974 to promote the professional interests of journalists specialising in writing or broadcasting about the media. Organises monthly lunches addressed by leading industry figures, and annual TV and radio awards. Membership by invitation.

BSME

See **British Society of Magazine Editors**

Bureau of Freelance Photographers

Focus House, 497 Green Lanes, London
N13 4BP

☎020 8882 3315   Fax 020 8886 5174
✉ info@thebfp.com
Membership Secretary *Angela Kidd*
SUBSCRIPTION £49 p.a. (UK); £65 p.a.
(overseas)

Founded 1965. Assists members in selling their pictures through monthly *Market Newsletter*, and offers advisory, legal assistance and other services.

Campaign for Press and Broadcasting Freedom

Second Floor, 23 Orford Road, London
E17 9NL
☎020 8521 5932
✉ freepress@cpbf.org.uk
www.cpbf.org.uk
SUBSCRIPTION £15 p.a. (concessions available);
£25 p.a. (institutions/organisations)

Broadly based pressure group working for more accountable and accessible media in Britain. Advises on right of reply and takes up the issue of the portrayal of minorities. Members receive *Free Press* (bi-monthly), discounts on publications and news of campaign progress.

Canadian Authors Association

National Office: Box 419, 320 South Shores Road, Campbellford, Ontario K0L 1L0, Canada
☎001 705 653 0323   Fax 001 705 653 0593
✉ admin@canauthors.org
www.canauthors.org
Contact *The Administrator*

Founded 1921. The CAA was founded to promote recognition of Canadian writers and their works, and to foster and develop a climate favourable to the creative arts. It is Canada's national association for writers of every kind; for those actively seeking to become writers and for those who want to support writers. The Association has branches across the country providing support to local members in the form of advice, local contests, publications and writers' circles. Publishes *National Newsline* (quarterly) and *The Canadian Writer's Guide*.

Canadian Federation of Poets

78 Wheeler Avenue, Toronto, Ontario M4L 3V2, Canada
☎001 416 694 6347
✉ info@federationofpoets.com
www.federationofpoets.com
Contact *Tracy Repchuk*
SUBSCRIPTION $35 (Canada); $45 (USA); $60 (International)

Founded 2003. Federations and members from around the world can post messages, 'meet' via forums and live chats and learn about themselves and their international colleagues with regard to poetry. Membership includes poetry workshops, anthologies, publishing opportunities, online forums, free book promotion, calendar of events and free subscription to *Poetry Canada* magazine (www.poetrycanada.com). Also offers an online 52-week poetry certification programme to help educate on the various types of poetry and promote the diversity of poetry.

Canadian Publishers' Council

250 Merton Street, Suite 203, Toronto, Ontario M4S 1B1, Canada
☎001 416 322 7011   Fax 001 416 322 6999
✉ pubadmin@pubcouncil.ca
www.pubcouncil.ca
Executive Director, External Relations *Jacqueline Hushion*

Founded 1910. Trade association of English-language publishers which represents the domestic and international interests of member companies.

Careers Writers' Association

www.careerswriters.co.uk

Founded 1979. 'An association of professional careers writers whose work in careers writing reaches high standards of accuracy and impartiality. Membership is open only to writers with an established reputation for providing objective and up-to-date careers information.' See website for details.

Chartered Institute of Journalists

2 Dock Offices, Surrey Quays Road, London SE16 2XU
☎020 7252 1187   Fax 020 7232 2302
✉ memberservices@cioj.co.uk
www.cioj.co.uk
General Secretary *Dominic Cooper*
SUBSCRIPTION £195 p.a.; £16 (monthly)

Founded 1884. The Institute is concerned with professional journalistic standards and with safeguarding the freedom of the media. It is open to writers, broadcasters and journalists (including self-employed) in all media. Affiliate membership (£133) is available to part-time or occasional practitioners and to overseas journalists who can join the Institute's International Division. Non employing members also belong to the IOJ (TU), an independent trade union which protects, advises and represents them in their employment or freelance work; negotiates on their behalf and provides legal assistance and support. The IOJ (TU) is a certificated independent trade union which represents members' interests in the workplace, and the CIOJ is also a constituent member of the Media Society, the **British Copyright Council** and the Journalists Copyright Fund. Editor of the Institute's quarterly magazine is *Andrew Smith*.

Chartered Institute of Linguists (IoL)

Saxon House, 48 Southwark Street, London SE1 1UN
☎020 7940 3100 Fax 020 7940 3101
✉ info@iol.org.uk
www.iol.org.uk

Acting Chief Executive Officer & Legal Counsel *John Hammond*
Membership Services Manager *Stephen Eden*
SUBSCRIPTION Rates on application

Founded 1910. Professional association for translators, interpreters and trainers; examining body for languages at degree level and above for vocational purposes; the National Register of Public Service Interpreters is managed by NRPSI Limited, an IoL subsidiary. The Institute's limited company, Language Services Ltd, provides customised assessments of language-oriented requirements, skills, etc.

Children's Book Circle

✉ childrensbookcircle@hotmail.co.uk
www.childrensbookcircle.org.uk

Membership Secretary *Katie Jennings*

The Children's Book Circle provides a discussion forum for anybody involved with children's books. Regular meetings are addressed by a panel of invited speakers and topics focus on current and controversial issues. Administers the **Eleanor Farjeon Award** and the Patrick Hardy lecture.

Children's Books Ireland

17 North Great George's Street, Dublin 1, Republic of Ireland
☎00 353 1 872 7475 Fax 00 353 1 872 7476
✉ info@childrensbooksireland.com
www.childrensbooksireland.com

Contact *Mags Walsh*
SUBSCRIPTION €30 p.a. (individual); €50 (institution); €20 (student); €45/US$40 (overseas)

Aims to promote quality children's books and reading. Holds annual summer school as well as

other occasional seminars and events. Quarterly magazine, *Inis* and bi-monthly newsletter, *Children's Book News*. Annual children's book festival in October; **CBI Bisto Book of the Year Award** (see entry under *Prizes*). Partners other organisations to promote and develop ways of bringing young people and books together.

CiB

See **British Association of Communicators in Business**

CILIP in Scotland

1st Floor, Building C, Brandon Gate, Leechlee Road, Hamilton ML3 6AU
☎01698 458888 Fax 01698 283170
✉ cilips@slainte.org.uk
www.slainte.org.uk

Director *Elaine Fulton*

CILIP in Scotland (Chartered Institute of Library and Information Professionals in Scotland) – formerly the Scottish Library Association – aims to bring together everyone engaged in or interested in library work in Scotland. The Association has over 2300 members, covering all aspects of library and information work. Its main aims are the promotion of library services and the qualifications and status of librarians.

CILIP: The Chartered Institute of Library and Information Professionals

7 Ridgmount Street, London WC1E 7AE
☎020 7255 0500 Fax 020 7255 0501
✉ info@cilip.org.uk
www.cilip.org.uk

Chief Executive *Bob McKee*

The leading membership body for library and information professionals, formed in 2002 following the unification of The Library Association and the Institute of Information Scientists. **Facet Publishing** (successor to LA Publishing) produces 25–30 new titles each year and has over 150 titles in print from the LA's back catalogue. Further information from Marketing & External Relations, CILIP.

Circle of Wine Writers

6 Albion Road, Chalfont St Giles HP8 4EW
☎01494 589201 Fax 01494 589201
✉ administrator@winewriters.org
www.winewriters.org

Administrator *Andrea Warren*
MEMBERSHIP £35 p.a.

Founded 1960. Membership is open to all those

professionally engaged in communicating about wines and spirits, with the exception of people primarily doing so for promotional purposes. Aims to improve the standard of writing, broadcasting and lecturing about wines, spirits and beers; to contribute to the growing knowledge and interest in wine; to promote wines and spirits of quality and to comment adversely on faulty products or dubious practices; to establish and maintain good relations with the news media and the wine trade; to provide members with a strong voice with which to promote their views; to provide a programme of workshops, meetings, talks and tastings.

CLÉ – Irish Book Publishers' Association

25 Denzille Lane, Dublin 2, Republic of Ireland
☎00 353 1 639 4868
✉ info@publishingireland.com
www.publishingireland.com

President *Tony Farmar*
Administrator *Jolly Ronan*

Founded 1970 to promote Irish publishing, protect members' interests and train the industry.

Comhairle nan Leabhraichean/ The Gaelic Books Council

22 Mansfield Street, Glasgow G11 5QP
☎0141 337 6211 Fax 0141 341 0515
✉ brath@gaelicbooks.net
www.gaelicbooks.net

Chairman *Professor Roibeard ÓMalalaigh*
Director *Ian MacDonald*

Founded 1968 and now a charitable company with its own bookshop. Encourages and promotes Gaelic publishing by giving grants to publishers and writers; providing editorial and word-processing services; retailing Gaelic books; producing a catalogue of all Gaelic books in print and answering enquiries about them; mounting occasional literary evenings and training courses.

Commercial Radio Companies Association

See **RadioCentre**

The Copyright Licensing Agency Ltd

Saffron House, 6–10 Kirby Street, London EC1N 8TS
☎020 7400 3100/0800 085 6644 (new licences) Fax 020 7400 3101
✉ cla@cla.co.uk
www.cla.co.uk

Chief Executive *Peter Shepherd*

CLA is the UK's reproduction rights organisation which looks after the interests of authors, publishers and artists in the photocopying and scanning of extracts from books, journals and periodicals. Founded in 1982 by the **Authors' Licensing and Collecting Society Limited (ALCS)** and the **Publishers Licensing Society Ltd (PLS)** to promote and enforce intellectual property rights of UK rightsholders both at home and abroad. CLA works closely with Reproductive Rights Organizations (RROs) from other countries and has an agency agreement with the Design and Artists Copyright Society (DACS) which represents artists and illustrators. A not-for-profit organisation, CLA licenses the use of copyright text by business, education and government and distributes fees collected via authors', publishers' and artists' collective societies. CLA has also developed licences which enable digitisation of existing print material. The licence enables users to scan and electronically send extracts from copyright works. Scanning and e-mail distribution is only available for UK works at present. Since its inception in 1982, CLA has distributed over £100 million.

Council for British Archaeology

St Mary's House, 66 Bootham, York YO30 7BZ
☎01904 671417 Fax 01904 671384
✉ info@britarch.ac.uk
www.britarch.ac.uk

Information Officer *Jonathan Bateman*
Publications Officer *Jane Thorniley-Walker*

Founded 1944 to represent and promote archaeology at all levels. Its aims are to improve the public's awareness in and understanding of Britain's past; to carry out research; to survey, guide and promote the teaching of archaeology at all levels of education; to publish a wide range of academic, educational, general and bibliographical works (see **CBA Publishing** under *UK Publishers*).

Crime Writers' Association (CWA)

PO Box 273, Boreham Wood WD6 2XA
✉ secretary@thecwa.co.uk
www.thecwa.co.uk

Hon. Secretary *Liz Evans*
Membership Secretary *Rebecca Tope* (Crossways Cottage, Walterstone HR2 0DX)
MEMBERSHIP £45, £60 (associate)

Full membership is limited to professional

crime writers, but publishers, literary agents, booksellers, etc. who specialise in crime, are eligible for Associate membership. The Association has regional chapters throughout the country, including Scotland. Meetings are held regularly with informative talks frequently given by police, scenes of crime officers, lawyers, etc., and a weekend conference is held annually in different parts of the country. Produces a monthly newsletter for members called *Red Herrings* and presents various annual awards (see entries under *Prizes*).

The Critics' Circle

c/o Catherine Cooper, 69 Marylebone Lane, London W1U 2PH
☎020 7224 1410
www.criticscircle.org.uk

President *Mike Dixon*
Honorary General Secretary *Charles Hedges*
SUBSCRIPTION £25 p.a.

Membership by invitation only. Aims to uphold and promote the art of criticism (and the commercial rates of pay thereof) and preserve the interests of its members: professionals involved in criticism of film, drama, music, dance and art.

Cyngor Llyfrau Cymru

See **Welsh Books Council**

Data Publishers Association

Queen's House, 28 Kingsway, London WC2B 6JR
☎020 7405 0836
✉ christine.scott@dpassoc.org
www.directory-publisher.co.uk

Contact *Christine Scott*
SUBSCRIPTION £395 to £2100 p.a.

Since 1970, the DPA has existed to serve, promote and protect the interests of all companies operating in the directory, data and search publishing sector. Today, the industry contributes well over £1 billion to the UK economy. The DPA membership not only includes mainstream data providers but also a whole host of organisations providing services and products to the data provision and publishing sector, such as printers, software solution providers and contract directory publishers. The DPA's members are predominantly UK companies but it also offers membership to overseas companies with UK interests. It provides its members with opportunities to develop their businesses by providing a complete and diverse range of services, including communications, networking, training and seminars, statistics, representation

to government, publicity and promotion, legal support and recognition.

Department for Culture, Media and Sport

2–4 Cockspur Street, London SW1Y 5DH
☎020 7211 6000 Fax 020 7211 6270
✉ lauren.mcgovern@culture.gsi.gov.uk
Head of News & Communications *Linda Martin*

The Department for Culture, Media and Sport has responsibilities for Government policies relating to the arts, museums and galleries, public libraries, sport, gambling, broadcasting, Press standards, the built heritage, the film and music industries, tourism and the National Lottery. It funds the **Arts Council**, national museums and galleries, the **British Library**, the **Public Lending Right** and the Royal Commission on Historical Manuscripts. It is responsible within Government for the public library service in England, and for library and information matters generally, where they are not the responsibility of other departments.

DOI Registration Agency

3rd Floor, Midas House, 62 Goldsworth Road, Woking GU21 6LQ
☎0870 777 8712 Fax 0870 777 8714
✉ doi@nielsenbookdata.co.uk
www.doi.nielsenbookdata.co.uk

DOIs (Digital Object Identifiers) are used to identify ebooks and other digital publications on the Internet. They are used instead of a URL to enable links to be made to a publication that will still work even if the publication is moved to a different Internet address or the file is renamed. The DOI Registration Agency operates a complete service enabling publishers to allocate and maintain DOIs for their publications and enabling Internet users to access publications via these DOIs.

Drama Association of Wales

The Old Library Building, Singleton Road, Splott, Cardiff CF24 2ET
☎029 2045 2200 Fax 029 2045 2277
✉ aled.daw@virgin.net
www.amdram.co.uk/daw

Contact *Teresa Hennessy*

Runs a large playscript lending library; holds an annual playwriting competition (see entry under *Prizes*); offers a script-reading service (£15 per script) which usually takes three months from receipt of play to issue of reports. From plays submitted to the reading service, selected scripts are considered for publication of a short run (70–200 copies). Writers receive a percentage of the cover price on sales and a percentage of the performance fee.

Edinburgh Bibliographical Society

National Library of Scotland, George IV Bridge, Edinburgh EH1 1EW
✉ warrenmcdougall@aol.com
www.edbibsoc.lib.ed.ac.uk
Honorary Secretary *Warren McDougall*
SUBSCRIPTION £10; £15 (institution); £7 (student)

Founded 1890. Organises lectures on bibliographical topics and visits to libraries. Publishes an occasional journal, which is free to members, and other occasional publications.

Educational Publishers Council

See **The Publishers Association**

Electronic Publishers' Forum

See **The Publishers Association**

The English Association

University of Leicester, University Road, Leicester LE1 7RH
☎0116 252 3982 Fax 0116 252 2301
✉ engassoc@le.ac.uk
www.le.ac.uk/engassoc

Chief Executive *Helen Lucas*
Contact *Julia Hughes*

Founded 1906 to promote understanding and appreciation of the English language and its literatures. Activities include sponsoring a number of publications and organising lectures and conferences for teachers, plus annual sixth-form conferences. Publications include *The Year's Work in Critical and Cultural Theory*; *English, The Use of English*; *English 4–11*; *Essays and Studies* and *The Year's Work in English Studies*.

English PEN

6–8 Amwell Street, London EC1R 1UQ
☎020 7713 0023 Fax 020 7837 7838
✉ enquiries@englishpen.org
www.englishpen.org

Director *Jonathan Heawood*
MEMBERSHIP Cheque/standing order: £45/£40 (London/overseas); £40/£35 (country); £15 (students)

English PEN is part of International PEN, a worldwide association of writers and other literary professionals which promotes literature, fights for freedom of expression and speaks out for writers who are imprisoned or harassed for having criticised their governments, or for publishing other unpopular views.

Founded in London in 1921, International PEN now consists of over 130 centres in almost 100 countries. PEN originally stood for poets, essayists and novelists, but membership is now open to all literary professionals. It is also possible to become a 'Friend of English PEN'. A programme of talks and discussions, and other activities such as social gatherings, is supplemented by mailings, website and annual congress at one of the centre countries.

Federation of Entertainment Unions

1 Highfield, Twyford, Nr Winchester SO21 1QR
☎01962 713134 Fax 01962 713134
✉ harris.s@btconnect.com

Secretary *Steve Harris*

Plenary meetings six times annually. Additionally, there are Training & European Committees. Represents the following unions: British Actors' Equity Association; Broadcasting Entertainment Cinematograph and Theatre Union; Musicians' Union; AMICUS; Professional Footballers' Association; **National Union of Journalists**; **The Writers' Guild of Great Britain**.

The Federation of Worker Writers and Community Publishers (FWWCP)

Burslem School of Art, Queen Street, Stoke on Trent ST6 3EJ
☎01782 822327
✉ thefwwcp@tiscali.co.uk
www.thefwwcp.org.uk

Administrator/Coordinator *Tim Diggles*

The FWWCP is a federation of writing groups committed to writing and publishing based on working-class experience and creativity. The FWWCP is the membership's collective national voice and has for some time been given funding by the Arts Council. Founded in 1976, it comprises around 80 member groups, each one with its own identity, reflecting its community and membership. These groups represent over 5000 people who regularly (often weekly) meet to offer constructive criticism, produce books and tapes, perform and share skills, offering creative and critical support. There are writers' workshops of long standing; adult literacy organisations; groups working mainly in oral and local history; groups and local networks of writers who come together to publish, train or perform; groups with a specific remit to further the aims of a section of the community such as the homeless or disabled.

Although diverse in nature, member organisations share the aim of making writing and publishing accessible to people and encourage them to take an active, cooperative and democratic role in writing, performing and publishing. The main activities include training days and weekends to learn and share skills, a quarterly magazine, a quarterly broadsheet of members' writing, a major annual festival of writing and networking between member organisations.

The FWWCP has published a number of anthologies and is willing to work with other organisations on publishing projects. Membership is open only to groups but individuals will be put in touch with groups which can help them, and become friends of the Federation. Contact the address above for an information leaflet.

Fellowship of Authors and Artists

PO Box 158, Hertford SG13 8FA
☎0870 747 2514 Fax 0870 116 3398
✉ fellowship@compassion-in-business.co.uk
www.author-fellowship.co.uk

Contact *Graham Irwin*

Founded in 2000 to promote and encourage the use of writing and all art forms as a means of therapy and self healing; to provide a valuable resource and meeting point for all interested parties including, but not limited to, writers, artists, counsellors and healers; to publish as Web pages or e-books any suitable works that may help to support or promote the aims of the fellowship.

Foreign Press Association in London

11 Carlton House Terrace, London SW1Y 5AJ
☎020 7930 0445 Fax 020 7925 0469
✉ programmemanager@foreign-press.org.uk
www.foreign-press.org.uk

Director *Gerry McCrudden*
ANNUAL SUBSCRIPTION Details available on the website

Founded 1888. Non-profit-making service association for foreign correspondents based in London, providing a variety of press-related services.

The Gaelic Books Council

See **Comhairle nan Leabhraichean**

The Garden Writers' Guild

c/o Institute of Horticulture, 14/15 Belgrave Square SW1X 8PS
☎020 7245 6943
✉ gwg@horticulture.org.uk
www.gardenwriters.co.uk

Contact *Angela Clarke*
SUBSCRIPTION £50; (£45 to Institute of Horticulture members); £60 (associate members)

Founded 1990. Aims to raise the quality of gardening communication, to help members operate efficiently and profitably, to improve liaison between garden communicators and the horticultural industry. Administers an annual awards scheme. Operates a mailing service and organises press briefing days.

Guild of Agricultural Journalists

Isfield Cottage, Church Road, Crowborough TN6 1BN
☎01892 611618 Fax 01892 613394
✉ don.gomery@farmingline.com
www.gaj.org.uk

Honorary General Secretary *Don Gomery*
SUBSCRIPTION £40 p.a.

Founded 1944 to promote a high professional standard among journalists who specialise in agriculture, horticulture and allied subjects. Represents members' interests with representative bodies in the industry; provides a forum through meetings and social activities for members to meet eminent people in the industry; maintains contact with associations of agricultural journalists overseas; promotes schemes for the education of members and for the provision of suitable entrants into agricultural journalism.

Guild of Editors

See **Society of Editors**

The Guild of Food Writers

9 Colman House, High Street, London SE20 7EX
☎020 8659 0422
✉ gfw@gfw.co.uk
www.gfw.co.uk

Administrator *Jonathan Woods*
SUBSCRIPTION £70

Founded 1985. The objects of the Guild are to bring together professional food writers including journalists, broadcasters and authors, to extend the range of members' knowledge and experience by arranging discussions, tastings and visits, and to encourage new writers through competitions and awards. The Guild aims to contribute to the growth of public interest in, and knowledge of, the subject of food and to campaign for improvements in the quality of food.

Guild of Motoring Writers

39 Beswick Avenue, Ensbury Park, Bournemouth BH10 4EY
☎01202 518808 Fax 01202 518808
✉ gensec@gomw.co.uk
www.guildofmotoringwriters.co.uk

General Secretary *Patricia Lodge*

Founded 1944. Represents members' interests and provides a forum for members to exchange information.

Horror Writers Association

UK Contact: 24 Pearl Road, London E17 4QZ
✉ hwa@horror.org
www.horror.org

US Contact: HWA Membership, 244 Fifth Avenue, Suite 2767, New York, NY 10001

Contact (UK) Jo Fletcher

Founded 1987. Worldwide organisation of writers and publishers dedicated to promoting the interests of writers of horror and dark fantasy. Publishes a monthly newsletter, issues e-mail bulletins, gives access to lists of horror agents, reviewers and bookstores; and keys to the 'Members Only' area of the HWA website. Presents the annual **Bram Stoker Awards** (see entry under *Prizes*).

HWA

See **Horror Writers Association**

Independent Publishers Guild

PO Box 93, Royston SG8 5GH
☎01763 247014 Fax 01763 246293
✉ info@ipg.uk.com
www.ipg.uk.com

Executive Director *Bridget Shine*

Founded 1962. Membership open to independent publishers, packagers and suppliers, i.e. professionals in allied fields. Regular meetings, annual conference, seminars, mailings and e-mail bulletin.

Independent Theatre Council

12 The Leathermarket, Weston Street, London SE1 3ER
☎020 7403 1727 Fax 020 7403 1745
✉ admin@itc-arts.org

www.itc-arts.org

Chief Executive *Charlotte Jones*

The Independent Theatre Council (ITC) is the UK management association for the performing arts. Since 1974 it has empowered and supported its diverse membership by providing management, legal and financial advice; developing tailored arts management training; creating networking opportunities and representing the sector. Publications available from ITC include *The ITC Practical Guide for Writers and Companies*. ITC negotiates contracts and has established standard agreements for theatre professionals with Equity. The rights and fee structure agreement, reached with **The Writers' Guild** in 1991, was updated in December 2002 and rates of pay are reviewed annually. Contact The Writers' Guild or visit ITC's website for further details.

Institute of Copywriting

Overbrook Business Centre, Poolbridge Road, Blackford, Wedmore BS28 4PA
☎0800 781 1715 Fax 0800 781 1715
✉ copy@inst.org
www.inst.org/copy

Secretary *Lynn Hall*

Founded 1991 to promote copywriters and copywriting (writing publicity material). Maintains a code of practice. Membership is open to students as well as experienced practitioners. Runs training courses (see entry under *UK Writers' Courses*). Has a list of approved copywriters. Answers queries relating to copywriting. Contact the Institute for a free booklet.

Institute of Translation and Interpreting (ITI)

Fortuna House, South Fifth Street, Milton Keynes MK9 2EU
☎01908 325250 Fax 01908 325259
✉ info@iti.org.uk
www.iti.org.uk

Founded 1986. The ITI is an association of translators and interpreters to promote the highest standards in their field. It has strong corporate membership and runs professional development courses and conferences. Membership is open to those with a genuine and proven involvement in translation and interpreting (including students). ITI's bimonthly *Bulletin* and other publications are available from the Secretariat, which also offers a free referral service for those in need of a professional translator/interpreter. ITI's *Directory of Members* is available online. ITI is a full and active member of FIT (International Federation of Translators).

IoL
See **Chartered Institute of Linguists**

Irish Book Publishers' Association
See **CLÉ**

Irish Copyright Licensing Agency Ltd
25 Denzille Lane, Dublin 2, Republic of Ireland
☎00 353 1 662 4211 Fax 00 353 1 662 4213
✉ info@icla.ie
www.icla.ie
Executive Director *Samantha Holman*

Founded 1992 by writers and publishers in Ireland to provide a scheme through which rights holders can give permission, and users of copyright material can obtain permission, to copy.

Irish Playwrights and Screenwriters Guild
Irish Writers' Centre, 19 Parnell Square, Dublin 1, Republic of Ireland
☎00 353 1 492 3808
✉ david.cavanagh@script.ie
www.script.ie
Contact *David Cavanagh*
SUBSCRIPTION details available on request
Founded in 1969 to safeguard the rights of scriptwriters for radio, stage and screen.

Irish Translators' & Interpreters' Association (ITIA)
Irish Writers' Centre, 19 Parnell Square, Dublin 1, Republic of Ireland
☎00 353 1 872 1302 Fax 00 353 1 872 6282
✉ itiasecretary@eircom.net
www.translatorsassociation.ie
Chairperson *Annette Schiller*
Honorary Secretary *Mary Phelan*
Treasurer *Mirian Watchorn*
Annual Membership €120 (corporate); €75 (professional); €40 (ordinary); €20 (student)
Founded 1986. The Association is open to all translators: technical, commercial, literary and cultural, and to all classes of interpreters. It is also for those with an interest in translation such as teachers and third-level students. Information on the profession of interpreting and translation and a Register of members are available on the website. Publishes a newsletter,

Translation Ireland and an eZine, the *ITIA Bulletin*.

Irish Writers' Union
Irish Writers' Centre, 19 Parnell Square, Dublin 1, Republic of Ireland
☎00 353 1 872 1302
✉ iwu@ireland-writers.com
www.ireland-writers.com
Chairman *Conor Costick*
SUBSCRIPTION €50 p.a.; €30 (associate)
Founded 1986 to promote the interests and protect the rights of writers in Ireland.

ISBN Agency
3rd Floor, Midas House, 62 Goldsworth Road, Woking GU21 6LQ
☎0870 777 8712 Fax 0870 777 8714
✉ isbn@nielsenbookdata.co.uk
www.isbn.nielsenbookdata.co.uk
ISBNs are product numbers used by all sections of the book trade for ordering and listing purposes. The ISBN Agency is responsible for issuing ISBNs to publishers based in the UK and Republic of Ireland and can provide help and advice on changing from 10 to 13-digits.

Isle of Man Authors
11 Christian Close, Ballastowell Gardens, Ramsey IM8 2AU
☎01624 815634
Secretary *Mrs Beryl Sandwell*
SUBSCRIPTION £5 p.a.
An association of writers living on the Isle of Man, which has links with the **Society of Authors**.

ITC
See **Independent Theatre Council**

ITI
See **Institute of Translation and Interpreting**

IVCA (International Visual Communication Association)
19 Pepper Street, Glengall Bridge, London E14 9RP
☎020 7512 0571 Fax 020 7512 0591
✉ info@ivca.org
www.ivca.org
Chief Executive *Wayne Drew*
Publications and Information Officer *Philip Fey*
The IVCA is a professional association repre-

senting the interests of the users and suppliers of visual communications. In particular it pursues the interests of producers, commissioners and manufacturers involved in the non-broadcast and independent facilities industries and also business event companies. It represents all sizes of company and freelance individuals, offering information and advice services, publications, a professional network, special interest groups, a magazine and a variety of events including the UK's Film and Video Communications Festival.

Learning on Screen (British Universities Film & Video Council)

77 Wells Street, London W1T 3QJ
☎020 7393 1512   Fax 020 7393 1555
www.bufvc.ac.uk/learningonscreen.ac.uk

Learning on Screen is the title which was used by the Society for Screen-Based Learning (SSBL) for its courses and conferences. In January 2004 the SSBL merged with the British Universities Film & Video Council (BUFVC). The title Learning on Screen, now adopted by the BUFVC, will continue for a range of practical, 'hands-on' one-day courses and events around the country as well as the annual Learning on Screen conference and Awards. The BUFCV promotes the production, study and use of moving images and related media for learning, teaching and research. It offers a specialist information service, publications, online services and the unique Off-Air Recording Back-Up Service, recording 44,000 hours per year of UK television.

Lewes Live Literature

See **Lewes Live Literature Festival** under *Festivals*

The Library Association

See **CILIP: The Chartered Institute of Library and Information Professionals**

literaturetraining

PO Box 23595, Leith, Edinburgh EH6 7YX
☎0131 476 4039
✉ info@literaturetraining.com
www.literaturetraining.com

Director *Philippa Johnston*

A group of eight literature organisations working in partnership to provide information, advice and guidance on professional development for writers and others involved with new writing and literature. Their easy to use, fully searchable website provides a central source of information on literature training and professional development opportunities in the UK and is supported by a range of advisory services. The literaturetraining partners are **The National Association of Writers in Education**, **The National Association for Literature Development**, **Writernet**, **The Federation of Worker Writers and Community Publishers**, Lapidus, **Survivors' Poetry**, **Apples & Snakes** and **Scottish Book Trust**. literaturetraining is a partner in the CreativePeople Network.

Medical Journalists' Association

Fairfield, Cross in Hand, Heathfield
TN21 0SH
☎01435 868786   Fax 01435 865714
✉ pigache@tiscali.co.uk
www.mja-uk.org

Chairman *Oliver Gillie*
Honorary Secretary *Philippa Pigache*
SUBSCRIPTION £40 p.a. (full); £30 (associate); £10 (junior)

Founded 1967. Aims to improve the quality and practice of medical and health journalism and to improve relationships and understanding between medical and health journalists and the health and medical professions. Regular meetings with senior figures in medicine and medico politics; educational workshops on important subject areas or issues of the day; debates; awards for medical journalists from commercial sponsors, plus the MJA's own annual awards for journalism and books. Publishes a newsletter five times a year.

Medical Writers' Group

The Society of Authors, 84 Drayton Gardens, London SW10 9SB
☎020 7373 6642   Fax 020 7373 5768
✉ info@societyofauthors.org
www.societyofauthors.org/medical

Contact *Dorothy Sym*

Founded 1980. A specialist group within the **Society of Authors** offering advice and help to authors of medical books.

Mystery Writers of America, Inc.

17 East 47th Street, 6th Floor, New York, NY 10017, USA
☎001 212 888 8171   Fax 001 212 888 8107
✉ mwa@mysterywriters.org
www.mysterywriters.org

Office Manager *Margery Flax*
SUBSCRIPTION $95 (US)

Founded 1945. Aims to promote and protect

the interests of writers of the mystery genre in all media; to educate and inform its membership on matters relating to their profession; to uphold a standard of excellence and raise the profile of this literary form to the world at large. Holds an annual banquet at which the 'Edgars' are awarded (named after Edgar Allan Poe).

National Association for Literature Development
☎01524 62166
www.nald.org
Contact *Andy Darby*

NALD is the largest membership organisation for literary professionals. The only national body for all those involved in developing writers, readers and literary audiences. Offers individual, organisational or corporate membership.

National Association of Writers Groups
The Arts Centre, Biddick Lane, Washington NE38 2AB
☎01262 609228
✉ nawg@tesco.net
www.nawg.co.uk
Secretary *Diane Wilson*
SUBSCRIPTION £25 p.a. + £5 registration (group); £12 p.a. (individual)

Founded 1995 with the object of furthering the interests of writers' groups throughout the UK. A registered charity, No. 1059047, NAWG is strictly non-sectarian and non-political. Publishes a bi-monthly newsletter, distributed to member groups; gives free entry to competitions for group anthologies, poetry, short stories, articles, novels and sketches; holds an annual open festival of writing with 36 workshops, seminars, individual surgeries led by professional, high-profile writers. Membership is open to all writers' groups and individual writers – there are no restrictions or qualifications required for joining; 160 groups are affiliated to-date.

National Association of Writers in Education
PO Box 1, Sheriff Hutton, York YO60 7YU
☎01653 618429
✉ info@nawe.co.uk
www.nawe.co.uk
Contact *Paul Munden*

SUBSCRIPTION £20 p.a. (individual); £10 (student); £60 (institution); £30 (overseas)

Founded 1991. Aims to promote the contribution of living writers to education and to encourage both the practice and the critical appreciation of creative writing. Has over 800 members. Organises national conferences and training courses. A directory of writers who work in schools, colleges and the community is available online. Publishes a magazine, *Writing in Education*, issued free to members three times per year.

National Campaign for the Arts
1 Kingly Street, London W1B 5PA
☎020 7287 3777 Fax 020 7287 4777
✉ nca@artscampaign.org.uk
www.artscampaign.org.uk
Director *Victoria Todd*

The UK's only independent lobbying organisation representing the arts. Founded in 1984 it seeks to safeguard, promote and develop the arts and win public and political recognition for the importance of the arts as a key element in the national culture. As a membership organisation it relies on subscription to sustain its work, receiving no public subsidy. Members have access to the NCA's information, advice, networks, seminars, conferences and publications. Membership is open to organisations and individuals working in or with an interest in the arts. Literature subscriptions available.

National Centre for Research in Children's Literature (NCRCL)
Roehampton University, Froebel College, London SW15 5PJ
☎020 8392 3008 Fax 020 8392 3819
✉ ncrcl@roehampton.ac.uk
www.ncrcl.ac.uk

The National Centre for Research in Children's Literature facilitates and supports research exchange in the field of children's literature. Runs an internationally acclaimed distance learning MA Programme, an annual conference in association with the International Board on Books for Young People (IBBY) and the biennial Children's Literature International Summer School.

National Literacy Trust
Swire House, 59 Buckingham Gate, London SW1E 6AJ
☎020 7828 2435 Fax 020 7931 9986
✉ contact@literacytrust.org.uk

www.literacytrust.org.uk
www.rif.org.uk
www.readon.org.uk
Director *Neil McClelland*
Founded 1993. Independent registered charity (No. 1015539) 'dedicated to building a literate nation in which everyone enjoys the skills, confidence and pleasures that literacy can bring.' The only organisation concerned with raising literacy standards for all age groups throughout the UK. Maintains an extensive website with literacy news, summaries of key issues, research and examples of practice nationwide; organises conferences, courses and training events and runs a range of initiatives to turn promising ideas into effective action. These include the National Reading Campaign, funded by the government; Reading Is Fundamental, UK, which provides free books to children; Reading The Game, involving the professional football community and the Talk To Your Baby campaign.

National Union of Journalists
Headland House, 308 Gray's Inn Road, London WC1X 8DP
☎020 7278 7916 Fax 020 7837 8143
✉ acorn.house@nuj.org.uk
www.nuj.org.uk
General Secretary *Jeremy Dear*
SUBSCRIPTION £182 p.a. (freelance) or 1% of annual income if lower; or 0.5% if income less than £13,600 p.a.
Represents journalists in all sectors of publishing, print, broadcast and online media. Responsible for wages and conditions agreements which apply across the industry. Provides advice and representation for its members, as well as administering unemployment and other benefits. Publishes various guides and magazines: *On-Line Freelance Directory; Fees Guide; The Journalist* and *The Freelance*.

NCRCL
See **National Centre for Research in Children's Literature**

New Playwrights Trust
See **Writernet**

New Producers Alliance (NPA)
1.07 The Tea Building, 56 Shoreditch High Street, London E1 6JJ
☎020 7613 0440 Fax 020 7729 1852
✉ queries@npa.org.uk
www.npa.org.uk

Founded 1993. National membership and training organisation for independent new filmmakers, the NPA provides a forum and focus for over 800 members, ranging from students and first timers to highly experienced feature filmmakers and industry affiliates. Services include: producer training from 'entrance' to 'advanced' levels; seminars, masterclasses, business breakfasts, themed networking evenings and preview screenings; in addition the NPA supports its members at film festivals including Cannes and Edinburgh with events and industry receptions. Provides free advice services including Legal and Tax & Accounting; the NPA also publishes a monthly newsletter and online members directory included in the website.

The New SF Alliance (NSFA)
c/o BBR, PO Box 625, Sheffield S1 3GY
www.bbr-online.com/catalogue
Contact *Chris Reed*
Founded 1989. Committed to supporting the work of new writers and artists by promoting independent and small press publications worldwide. 'Helps with finding the right market for your material by providing a mail-order service which allows you to sample magazines, quickly and conveniently from a single address, to help you to find the ones best suited to your needs.' Provides ueful information about many more outlets in the review pages of these magazines, while *Light's List* supplies contact addresses for a host of small press publications.

New Writing North
2 School Lane, Whickham, Newcastle upon Tyne NE16 4SL
☎0191 488 8580 Fax 0191 488 8576
✉ mail@newwritingnorth.com
www.newwritingnorth.com
Director *Claire Malcolm*
Administrator *Catherine Lancaster*
New Writing North is the literature development agency for the Arts Council England, North East region and offers many useful services to writers, organising events, readings and workshops. NWN has a website and mailing list by which members of the public can receive news of literary events, courses and work opportunities. Administers the **Northern Rock Foundation Writer's Award** (see entry under *Bursaries, Fellowships and Grants*) and the Northern Writers' Awards, which include tailored development packages (mentoring and financial help) for local writers at different stages of their careers. NWN works to develop theatre writing and cre-

ative radio writing projects within the region, as well as a strong education and community-based programme, working with schools, LEAS and both public and private sector organisations..

The Newspaper Society

Bloomsbury House, 74–77 Great Russell Street, London WC1B 3DA
☎020 7636 7014 Fax 020 7631 5119
✉ ns@newspapersoc.org.uk
www.newspapersoc.org.uk

Director *David Newell*

The Newspaper Society is the voice of Britain's regional press – a £3 billion advertising medium read by over 40 million adults a week, It promotes the interests of the regional and local press, provides legal advice and lobbying services, holds a series of conferences and seminars, and runs the annual Local Newspaper Week.

NPA

See **New Producers Alliance**

NSFA

See **The New SF Alliance**

Outdoor Writers' Guild

PO Box 118, Twickenham TW1 2XB
☎020 8538 9468 Fax 020 8538 9468
✉ sec@owg.org.uk
www.owg.org.uk

Secretary *Hazelle Jackson*
SUBSCRIPTION £66 p.a.

Founded 1980 to promote, encourage and assist the development and maintenance of professional standards among those involved in all aspects of outdoor journalism. Members include writers, photographers, broadcasters, filmmakers, editors, publishers and illustrators. Publishes a quarterly journal, *Bootprint*, and an annual *Directory* (£30; free to members). Presents five Awards for Excellence plus other awards in recognition of achievement. Maintains a website of members' details; informal members' e-mail 'chatline' to exchange news and information; sends out regular media press releases; organises press trips.

PACT (Producers Alliance for Cinema and Television)

Procter House, 2nd Floor, 1 Procter Street, London WC1V 6DW
☎020 7067 4367 Fax 020 7067 4377
✉ enquiries@pact.co.uk
www.pact.co.uk

Chief Executive *John McVay*
Information Manager *David Alan Mills*

Founded 1991. PACT is the trade association of the UK independent feature film, television, animation and interactive media production sector and is a key contact point for foreign producers seeking British co-production, co-finance partners and distributors. Works for producers in the industry at every level and operates a members' regional network throughout the UK with a divisional office in Scotland. Membership services include: a dedicated industrial relations unit; discounted legal advice; a varied calendar of events; business advice; representation at international film and television markets; a comprehensive research programme; various publications: a monthly magazine, an annual members' directory; affiliation with European and international producers' organisations; extensive information and production advice. Lobbies actively with broadcasters, financiers and governments to ensure that the producer's voice is heard and understood in Britain and Europe on all matters affecting the feature film, television, animation and interactive production industry.

PEN

See **English PEN**

Performing Right Society

29–33 Berners Street, London W1T 3AB
☎020 7580 5544 Fax 020 7306 4455
✉ info@prs.co.uk
www.prs.co.uk

PRS collects licence fees for the public performance and broadcast of musical works and distributes this money to its members –writers and publishers of music.

Periodical Publishers Association (PPA)

Queens House, 28 Kingsway, London WC2B 6JR
☎020 7404 4166 Fax 020 7404 4167
✉ info1@ppa.co.uk
www.ppa.co.uk

Founded 1913 to promote and protect the interests of its members in particular and the magazine industry as a whole.

The Personal Managers' Association Ltd

1 Summer Road, East Molesey KT8 9LX
☎020 8398 9796 Fax 020 8398 9796
✉ info@thepma.com

Co-chairs *Michelle Kass, Alan Brodie, Nicholas Young*

Secretary *Angela Adler*
SUBSCRIPTION £275 p.a.

An association of artists' and dramatists' agents (membership not open to individuals). Monthly meetings for exchange of information and discussion. Maintains a code of conduct and acts as a lobby when necessary. Applicants screened. A high proportion of play agents are members of the PMA.

The Picture Research Association
c/o 1 Willow Court, off Willow Street, London EC2A 4QB
☎020 7739 8544 Fax 020 7782 0011
✉ chair@picture-research.org.uk
www.picture-research.org.uk

Chair *Veneta Bullen*
Membership Secretary *Wendy Wilders*
SUBSCRIPTION Members: £45 (introductory); £55 (full); £50 (associate). Magazine only: £16 (inland); £20 (overseas)

Founded 1977 as the Society of Picture Researchers & Editors. The Picture Research Association is a professional body for picture researchers, managers, picture editors and all those involved in the research, management and supply of visual material to all forms of the media. The Association's main aims are to promote the interests and specific skills of its members internationally; to promote and maintain professional standards; to bring together those involved in the research and publication of visual material; to provide a forum for the exchange of information and to provide guidance to its members. Free advisory service for members, regular meetings, quarterly magazine, monthly newsletter and Freelance Register.

Player–Playwrights
9 Hillfield Park, London N10 3QT
☎020 8883 0371
✉ P-P@dial.pipex.com
www.playerplaywrights.co.uk

Presidents *Laurence Marks, Maurice Gran*
Contact *Peter Thompson* (at the address above)
SUBSCRIPTION Members: £10 (joining fee); £6 p.a. thereafter, plus £2 per attendance

Founded 1948. A society giving opportunity for writers new to stage, radio, television and film, as well as others finding difficulty in achieving results, to work with writers established in those media. At weekly meetings (7.30 pm–10.00 pm, Mondays, upstairs at the Horse and Groom, 128 Great Portland Street, London W1), members' scripts are read or performed by actor members and afterwards assessed and dis-

sected in general discussion. New writers and new acting members are always welcome.

PLR
See **Public Lending Right**

PLS
See **Publishers Licensing Society Ltd**

PMA
See **The Personal Managers' Association Ltd**

Poetry Book Society
See under *Organisations of Interest to Poets*

Poetry Ireland
See under *Organisations of Interest to Poets*

The Poetry Society
See under *Organisations of Interest to Poets*

Press Complaints Commission
Halton House, 20/23 Holborn, London EC1N 2JD
☎020 7831 0022 Fax 020 7831 0025
✉ pcc@pcc.org.uk
www.pcc.org.uk

Director *Tim Toulmin*
Information Officer *Tonia Milton*

Founded in 1991 to deal with complaints from members of the public about the editorial content of newspapers and magazines. Administers the editors' Code of Practice covering such areas as accuracy, privacy, harrassment and intrusion into grief. Publications available: *Code of Practice, How to Complain* and *Annual Review*.

Producers Alliance for Cinema and Television
See **PACT**

Public Lending Right
Richard House, Sorbonne Close, Stockton-on-Tees TS17 6DA
☎01642 604699 Fax 01642 615641
✉ authorservices@plr.uk.com
www.plr.uk.com

Registrar *Jim Parker*

Founded 1979. Public Lending Right is funded by the Department for Culture, Media and Sport to recompense authors for books borrowed from public libraries. Authors and books can be registered for PLR only when application is made during the author's lifetime. To qualify, an author must be resident in a

European Union member state, or in Iceland, Liechtenstein or Norway, and the book must be printed, bound and put on sale with an ISBN. In 2006, £6.59 million was distributed to over 18,500 authors (£6.54 million in the previous year) with 281 authors reaching the maximum payment threshold of £6000. The Rate Per Loan was raised in 2006 to 5.57 pence, its highest level to date. Consult the website for further information.

The Publishers Association

29B Montague Street, London WC1B 5BW
☎020 7691 9191   Fax 020 7691 9199
✉ mail@publishers.org.uk
www.publishers.org.uk

Chief Executive *Ronnie Williams, OBE*

The national UK trade association for books, learned journals, and electronic publications, with around 200 member companies in the industry. Very much a trade body representing the industry to Government and the European Commission, and providing services to publishers. Publishes the *Directory of Publishing* in association with **Continuum**. Also home of the Educational Publishers Council (school books), PA's International Division (BDCI), the Academic and Professional Division, the Trade Publishers Council and the Electronic Publishers' Forum.

Publishers' Association of South Africa

PO Box 15277, Vlaberg 8018, Cape Town, South Africa
☎00 27 21 426 1726   Fax 00 27 21 426 1733
✉ pasa@publishsa.co.za
www.publishsa.co.za

Founded in 1992 to represent publishing in South Africa, a key industry sector. With a membership of 162 companies, the Association includes commercial organisations, university presses, one-person privately-owned publishers as well as importers and distributors.

Publishers Licensing Society Ltd

37–41 Gower Street, London WC1E 6HH
☎020 7299 7730   Fax 020 7299 7780
✉ pls@pls.org.uk
www.pls.org.uk

Chief Executive *Alicia Wise*
Operations Manager *Caroline Elmslie*

Founded in 1981, the PLS obtains mandates from publishers which grant PLS the authority to license photocopying of pages from published

works. Some licences for digitisation of printed works are available. PLS aims to maximise revenue from licences for mandating publishers and to expand the range and repertoire of mandated publishers available to licence holders. It supports the **Copyright Licensing Agency Ltd (CLA)** in its efforts to increase the number of legitimate users through the issuing of licences and vigorously pursues any infringements of copyright works belonging to rights' holders.

Publishers Publicity Circle

65 Airedale Avenue, London W4 2NN
☎020 8994 1881
✉ ppc-@lineone.net
www.publisherspublicitycircle.co.uk

Contact *Heather White*

Enables book publicists from both publishing houses and freelance PR agencies to meet and share information regularly. Meetings, held monthly in central London, provide a forum for press journalists, television and radio researchers and producers to meet publicists collectively. A directory of the PPC membership is published each year and distributed to over 2500 media contacts.

The Radio Academy

5 Market Place, London W1W 8AE
☎020 7255 2010   Fax 020 7255 2029
✉ info@radioacademy.org
www.radioacademy.org

Director *John Bradford*
SUBSCRIPTIONS £18 p.a., payable by direct debit at £1.50 per month, or a one-off payment of £55 by cheque or credit card

Founded 1983. The professional body for people working in the radio industry, the Academy is dedicated to the encouragement, recognition and promotion of excellence throughout the UK radio industry. Membership ranges from students to Governors of the BBC. Hosts the annual Radio Festival which features speakers from all aspects of the industry; holds events in London and the regions; runs masterclasses for those who aspire to enter the radio industry, and seminars for the further development of professionals within the industry at various levels. Services include a directory covering all aspects of the industry, a quarterly newsletter and the Academy website.

RadioCentre

77 Shaftesbury Avenue, London WC2D 5DU
☎020 7306 2603   Fax 020 7470 0062

Chairman *Paul Brown, CBE*

Research and Communications Manager *Alison Winter*
External Affairs Manager *Lisa Kerr*
The CRCA, to be known from summer 2006 as RadioCentre, is the trade body for UK commercial radio companies. It represents members' interests to government, Ofcom, the European Commission, the European Parliament, copyright organisations and other bodies concerned with radio and broadcasting.

Romance Writers of America

16000 Stuebner Airline Road, Suite 140, Spring, TX 77379, USA
☎001 832 717 5200   Fax 001 832 717 5201
✉ info@rwanational.org
www.rwanational.org
PR Coordinator *Nicole Kennedy*
MEMBERSHIP $75 p.a. plus $25 joining fee

Founded 1980. RWA, a non-profit association with more than 9000 members worldwide, provides a service to authors at all stages of their careers as well as to the romance publishing industry and its readers. Anyone pursuing a career in romantic fiction may join RWA. Holds an annual conference, and provides contests for both published and unpublished writers through the RITA Awards and Golden Hearts Awards.

The Romantic Novelists' Association

3 Bywater Street, London SW3 4XD
✉ jennyhaddon@dial.pipex.com
www.rna–uk.org
Contact *Jenny Haddon* (Chairman)
SUBSCRIPTION £40 p.a. (full members); £45 (full, non-EU); £50 (associate); full and associate members who pay by standing order receive a £3 discount

Membership is open to published writers of romantic fiction (modern or historical), or those who have had one or more full-length serials published. Associate membership is open to publishers, editors, literary agents, booksellers, librarians and others having a close connection with novel writing and publishing. Membership in the New Writers' Scheme is available to a limited number of writers who have not yet had a full-length novel published. New Writers must submit a manuscript each year. The mss receive a report from experienced published members and the reading fee is paid with the annual subscription of £90 (£95 for non-EU members). Meetings are held in London and the regions with guest speakers.

The *RNA News* is published quarterly and issued free to members. The Association makes three annual awards: **The Romantic Novel of the Year**; Joan Hessayon New Writers Award for the best published novel by a new writer who has gone through the New Writers' Scheme, and the Romance Prize for category romances.

Royal Festival Hall Literature & Talks

See entry under *Festivals*

Royal Society of Literature

Somerset House, Strand, London WC2R 1LA
☎020 7845 4676   Fax 020 7845 4679
✉ info@rslit.org
www.rslit.org
Chairman *Maggie Gee, FRSL*
SUBSCRIPTION £40 p.a.

Founded 1820. Membership by application to the Secretary. Fellowships are conferred by the Society on the proposal of two Fellows. Membership benefits include lectures, discussion meetings and poetry readings. Lecturers have included Julian Barnes, Michael Holroyd, Don Paterson, Zadie Smith and Tom Stoppard. Presents the **Royal Society of Literature Ondaatje Prize**, the **Royal Society of Literature/Jerwood Awards** and the **V.S. Pritchett Memorial Prize**.

Royal Television Society

Kildare House, 3 Dorset Rise, London EC4Y 8EN
☎020 7822 2810   Fax 020 7822 2811
✉ info@rts.org.uk
www.rts.org.uk
Membership Manager *Deborah Halls* (membership@rts.org.uk)
MEMBERSHIP from £65 p.a.

Founded 1927. Covers all disciplines involved in the television industry. Provides a forum for debate and conferences on technical, social and cultural aspects of the medium. Presents various awards including journalism, programmes, technology and design. Publishes *Television Magazine* nine times a year for members and subscribers.

SAN Agency

3rd Floor, Midas House, 62 Goldsworth Road, Woking GU21 6LQ
☎0870 777 8712   Fax 0870 777 8714
✉ san@nielsenbookdata.co.uk
www.san.nielsenbookdata.co.uk

The SAN Agency issues Standard Address Numbers and Global Location Numbers (GLNs) to organisations such as booksellers, libraries or publishers, enabling commercial transactions to be made more efficient and accurate. The numbers identify specific geographic locations and are recognised throughout the bookselling and publishing industries.

Science Fiction Foundation

37 Coventry Road, Ilford IG1 4QR
✉ sff.chair@gmail.com
www.sf-foundation.org

Founded 1970. The SFF is an international academic body for the furtherance of science fiction studies. Publishes a thrice-yearly magazine, *Foundation* (see entry under *Magazines*), which features academic articles and reviews of new fiction. Publishes a series of books on critical studies of science fiction, and arranges conferences, lectures and seminars on related topics. It also has a reference library (see entry under *Library Services*), housed at Liverpool University.

Scottish Book Trust

Sandeman House, Trunk's Close, 55 High Street, Edinburgh EH1 1SR
☎0131 524 0160 Fax 0131 524 0161
✉ info@scottishbooktrust.com
www.scottishbooktrust.com

Contact *Marc Lambert*

Founded 1956. Scottish Book Trust exists to serve readers and writers in Scotland. Works to ensure that everyone has access to good books and to related resources and opportunities. Operates 'Live Literature Scotland' which funds over 1400 visits a year by Scottish writers to a variety of institutions and groups; supports Scottish writing through a programme of professional training opportunities for writers; publishes a wide variety of resources and leaflets to support readership; promotes initiatives such as World Book Day and other readership development opportunities. Their Book Information Service provides free advice and support to readers and writers and the general public.

Scottish Daily Newspaper Society

48 Palmerston Place, Edinburgh EH12 5DE
☎0131 220 4353 Fax 0131 220 4344
✉ info@sdns.org.uk

Director *Mr J.B. Raeburn*

Founded 1915. Trade association representing publishers of Scottish daily and Sunday newspapers including the major Scottish editions of UK national newspapers.

Scottish Library Association

See **CILIP in Scotland**

Scottish Newspaper Publishers Association

48 Palmerston Place, Edinburgh EH12 5DE
☎0131 220 4353 Fax 0131 220 4344
✉ info@snpa.org.uk
www.snpa.org.uk

Director *Mr J.B. Raeburn*

The representative body for the publishers of paid-for weekly and associated free newspapers in Scotland. Represents the interests of the industry to government, public and other bodies and provides a range of services including marketing of *The Scottish Weekly Press*, industrial relations, and education and training. It is an active supporter of the Press Complaints Commission.

Scottish Print Employers Federation

48 Palmerston Place, Edinburgh EH12 5DE
☎0131 220 4353 Fax 0131 220 4344
✉ info@spef.org.uk
www.spef.org.uk

Director *Mr J.B. Raeburn*

Founded 1910. Employers' organisation and trade association for the Scottish printing industry. Represents the interests of the industry to government, public and other bodies and provides a range of services including industrial relations, education, training and commercial activities. Negotiates a national wages and conditions agreement with Amicus GPM Sector. The Federation is a member of Intergraf, the international confederation for employers' associations in the printing industry, which represents its interests at European level.

Scottish Publishers Association

Scottish Book Centre, 137 Dundee Street, Edinburgh EH11 1BG
☎0131 228 6866 Fax 0131 228 3220
✉ carol.lothian@scottishbooks.org
www.scottishbooks.org

Director *Lorraine Fannin*
Member Services Manager *Liz Small*
Financial and Office Administrator *Carol Lothian*
Information and Professional Development Administrator *Katherine A. Naish*

The Association represents over 70 Scottish publishers, from multinationals to small presses, in a number of capacities, but primarily in the cooperative promotion and marketing of their books. The SPA also acts as an information and advice centre for both the trade and general public. Publishes membership lists and the annual *Directory of Publishing in Scotland*. Represents members at international book fairs; runs an extensive training programme in publishing skills; carries out market research; and encourages export initiatives.

Scottish Screen

2nd Floor, 249 West George Street, Glasgow G2 4QE
☎0141 302 1700 Fax 0141 302 1711
✉ info@scottishscreen.com
www.scottishscreen.com

Contact *Francis Lopez*

Founded 1997. Scottish Screen develops, encourages and promotes every aspect of film, television and new media in Scotland through script development, short film production, distribution of national lottery film production finance, training, education, exhibition funding, film commission locations support and the Scottish Screen Archive.

Society for Editors and Proofreaders (SfEP)

Riverbank House, 1 Putney Bridge Approach, London SW6 3JD
☎020 7736 3278/7736 0901 (training dept.)
Fax 020 7736 3318
✉ administration@sfep.org.uk
www.sfep.org.uk

Chair *Penny Williams*
Vice-Chair *Shena Deuchars*

Company Secretary *Val Rice*
SUBSCRIPTION £75 p.a. (individuals) plus £25 joining fee; corporate membership available.

Founded 1988 in response to the growing number of freelance editors and their increasing importance to the publishing industry. Aims to promote high editorial standards by disseminating information through advice and training, and to achieve recognition of the professional status of its members. The Society also supports moves towards recognised standards of training and accreditation for editors and proofreaders. It launched its own Accreditation in Proofreading test in 2002.

Society for Technical Communications (STC)

901 N. Stuart Street, Suite 904, Arlington, Virginia 22203, USA
☎001 703 522 4114 Fax 001 703 522 2075
www.stc.org
www.stcuk.org

UK Chapter Contact *David S. Farbey*(dfarbey@yahoo.co.uk)

Dedicated to advancing the arts and sciences of technical communication, the STC has 18,000 members worldwide, including technical writers, editors, graphic designers, videographers, multimedia artists, Web and intranet page information designers, translators and others whose work involves making technical information available to those who need it. Publishes a quarterly scholarly journal, *Technical Communications* and the magazine, *Intercom*, ten times a year (both available to members only). The UK Chapter, which has about 140 members, hosts meetings and seminars, runs an annual technical publications competition, and publishes its own newsletter six times a year.

The Society of Authors

84 Drayton Gardens, London SW10 9SB
☎020 7373 6642 Fax 020 7373 5768
✉ info@societyofauthors.org
www.societyofauthors.org

General Secretary *Mark Le Fanu*
Deputy General Secretary *Kate Pool*
SUBSCRIPTION £85/80 p.a.

The Society of Authors is an independent trade union, chaired by Helen Dunmore in 2006, with some 7900 members. As well as campaigning for the profession, it advises members on negotiations with publishers, agents, broadcasting organisations, theatre managers and film companies and on queries or concerns members may have about the business aspects of their writing. The Society assists with complaints and takes action for breach of contract, copyright infringement, etc. Among the Society's publications are *The Author* (quarterly) and the *Quick Guides* series to various aspects of writing (all free of charge to members). Other services include vetting of contracts, emergency funds for writers, and various special discounts. There are groups within the Society for broadcasters, children's writers and illustrators, educational writers, academic writers, medical writers and translators, as well as some regional groups. Authors under 35 or over 65, not earning a significant income from their writing, may apply for lower subscription rates (after their first year, in the case of over-65s). Contact the Society for a free booklet and a copy of *The Author* or visit the website.

The Society of Authors in Scotland

8 Briar Road, Kirkintilloch, Glasgow G66 3SA
☎0141 776 4280 Fax 0141 776 4280

✉ brian@bdosborne.fsnet.co.uk
www.writersorg.co.uk
Secretary *Brian D. Osborne*
The Scottish branch of the **Society of Authors**, which organises business meetings, social and bookshop events throughout Scotland.

Society of Children's Book Writers & Illustrators

36 Mackenzie Road, Beckenham BR3 4RU
✉ ra@britishscbwi.org
www.britishscbwi.org
British Isles Regional Adviser *Natascha Biebow*
Founded in 1968 by a group of Los Angeles-based writers, the SCBWI is the only international professional organisation for the exchange of information between writers, illustrators, editors, publishers, agents and others involved with literature for young people. With a membership of 18,000 worldwide, it holds three annual international conferences plus a number of regional events, publishes a bi-monthly journal and awards grants for works in progress. The British Isles region sponsors workshops and speaker events to help authors and illustrators develop their craft and market their work. Events include the bi-monthly Professional Series in London, the Agents' Party and two conferences – an Illustrator's Day in the spring and a Writer's Day in the autumn. It also facilitates local critique groups and publishes a quarterly regional newsletter. For membership enquiries, visit the website or contact membership@british scbwi.org

Society of Civil and Public Service Writers

17 The Green, Corby Glen, Grantham NG33 4NP
✉ joan@lewis5634.fsnet.co.uk
www.scpsw.co.uk
Membership Secretary *Mrs Joan Lewis*
SUBSCRIPTION £15 p.a.

Founded 1935. Welcomes serving and retired members of the Civil Service, armed forces, Post Office, BT, nursing profession and other public servants who are aspiring or published writers. Offers competitions for short story, article and poetry; postal folios for short story and article; AGM, occasional meetings and luncheon held in London; quarterly magazine, *Civil Service Author*, to which members may submit material; Poetry Workshop (extra £3) offers annual weekend outside London, anthology, newsletter, postal folio, competitions. S.a.e. to Secretary for details.

The Society of Creative Writers

28 Howard Mews, Denmark Road, Norwich NR3 4JU
☎0870 240 9998
✉ WritersSociety@aol.com
www.societyofcreativewriters.org
Secretary *Inna Zabrodskaya*
SUBSCRIPTION £45 (full); £39 (concessions)
'The Society of Creative Writers does not represent the writing profession but has been formed exclusively to promote creativity, originality and literary exploration and to help introduce and market individual writers and their work to a global audience.' Publishes a quarterly journal, *The Creative Writer* (see entry under **Magazines**). Membership is open to novelists, journalists, editors, ghost-writers, broadcasters, academics, illustrators and translators, regardless of whether or not published.

Society of Editors

University Centre, Granta Place, Mill Lane, Cambridge CB2 1RU
☎01223 304080 Fax 01223 304090
✉ info@societyofeditors.org
www.societyofeditors.org
Executive Director *Bob Satchwell*
Contact *Lyn Disley*
Formed by a merger of the Association of British Editors and the Guild of Editors, the Society of Editors has nearly 500 members in national, regional and local newspapers, magazines, broadcasting, new media, journalism education and media law. Campaigns for media freedom and self-regulation. For further information call *Bob Satchwell* (☎07860 562815).

Society of Indexers

Woodbourn Business Centre, 10 Jessell Street, Sheffield S9 3HY
☎0114 244 9561 Fax 0114 244 9563
✉ admin@indexers.org.uk
www.indexers.org.uk
Secretary *Ann Kingdom*
Administrator *Wendy Burrow*
SUBSCRIPTION £84 p.a.; Institutions: from £168
Founded 1957. Publishes *The Indexer* (biannual, April and October), a quarterly newsletter, an online directory and *Indexers Available (IA)*, which lists members and their subject expertise. In addition, the Society runs an open-learning course entitled *Training in Indexing* and recommends rates of pay (currently £17.50–30 per hour or £2–£5 per page). Awards annually **The Wheatley Medal** and **The Bernard Levin Award** (see entries under **Prizes**).

Society of Picture Researchers & Editors

See **The Picture Research Association**

Society of Women Writers & Journalists

Flat D, 49 Christchurch Street,, London
SW3 4AS
☎020 7351 6377
✉ birl33@onetel.com
www.swwj.co.uk

Acting Secretary *Pamela Birley*
SUBSCRIPTION £35 (town); £30 (country);
£25 (overseas). £15 joining fee

Founded 1894. The first of its kind to be run as
an association of women engaged in journalism. Aims to encourage literary achievement,
uphold professional standards, and establish
social contacts with other writers. Offers advice
to members and has regular seminars, etc.
Publishes a society journal, *The Woman Writer*.

Society of Young Publishers

c/o The Bookseller, Endeavour House, 189
Shaftesbury Avenue, London WC2H 8TJ
www.thesyp.org.uk

Contact *Membership Secretary*
SUBSCRIPTION £30 p.a.; £20
(student/unwaged)

Provides facilities whereby members can
increase their knowledge and widen their experience of all aspects of publishing, and holds
regular social events. Run entirely by volunteers,
it is open to those in related occupations, students, and associate membership is available for
over-35s. Publishes a monthly newsletter called
InPrint and holds meetings on the last Wednesday
of each month featuring trade professionals. For
other events see the website. Please enclose an
s.a.e. when writing to the Society.

Spoken Word Publishing Association

See **Audiobook Publishing Association**

Sports Journalists' Association of Great Britain

c/o Sport England Events, 3rd Floor, Victoria
House, Bloomsbury Square, London
WC1B 4SE
☎020 7273 1789   Fax 020 7383 0273
✉ stevenwdownes@btinternet.com
www.sportsjournalists.co.uk

Secretary *Steven Downes* (80 Southbridge
   Road, Croydon CR0 1AE ☎020 8604

1166 (home)/020 7782 7612 (work)/07710
428562
SUBSCRIPTION £23.50 p.a. incl. VAT
(London); £11.75 (regional)

Founded in 1948 as the Sports Writers'
Association of Great Britain to promote and
maintain a high professional standard among
journalists who specialise in sport in all its
branches and to serve members' interests. Publishes a biannual bulletin, a quarterly *Newsletter*
and a Yearbook for members, and promotes
jointly with Sport England the annual British
Sports Personalities of the Year Awards, the British
Sports Journalism Awards and the Sports
Photographer of the Year award.

Tees Valley Arts

Third Floor, Melrose House, Melrose Street,
Middlesbrough TS1 2HZ
☎01642 264651   Fax 01642 264955
✉ info@teesvalleyarts.org.uk
www.teesvalleyarts.org.uk

Contact *Director*

Tees Valley Arts is a cultural education agency
working throughout the Tees Valley. The company works in partnership with local authorities, public agencies, the business sector, schools,
colleges, individuals and organisations to coor-
dinate, promote and develop the arts – crafts,
film, video, photography, music, drama, dance,
literature, public arts, disability, diverse arts,
community arts.

Theatre Writers' Union

See **The Writers' Guild of Great Britain**

Trade Publishers Council

See **The Publishers Association**

The Translators Association

84 Drayton Gardens, London SW10 9SB
☎020 7373 6642   Fax 020 7373 5768
✉ info@societyofauthors.org
www.societyofauthors.org/translators

Secretary *Dorothy Sym*

Founded 1958 as a subsidiary group within the
Society of Authors to deal exclusively with
the special problems of literary translators into
the English language. Benefits to members
include free legal and general advice and assistance on all business matters relating to translators' work, including the vetting of contracts
and advice on rates of remuneration. Membership is normally confined to translators who
have had their work published in volume or
serial form or produced in this country for

stage, television or radio. The Association administers several prizes for translators of published work (see **Prizes**) and maintains an on-line database of members' details for the use of publishers who are seeking a translator for a particular work.

UK Film Council
10 Little Portland Street, London W1W 7JG
☎020 7861 7861   Fax 020 7861 7862
✉ info@ukfilmcouncil.org.uk
www.ukfilmcouncil.org.uk

The UK's leading film body. Uses lottery money and Government Grant-in-Aid to encourage the development of new talent, skills and creative and technological innovation in UK film; help new and established filmmakers make distinctive British films; support the creation and growth of stable businesses in the film sector; provide access to finance and help the UK film industry to compete in the global marketplace. Also promotes enjoyment and understanding of the cinema and ensures that film's economic and creative and cultural interests are properly represented in public policy making.

Voice of the Listener & Viewer Ltd (VLV)
101 Kings Drive, Gravesend DA12 5BQ
☎01474 352835   Fax 01474 351112
✉ info@vlv.org.uk
www.vlv.org.uk
Chairman *Jocelyn Hay*
Administrative Secretary *Sue Washbrook*

VLV represents the citizen and consumer interests in broadcasting. It is an independent, non-profit-making society working to ensure independence, quality and diversity in broadcasting. VLV is the only consumer body speaking for listeners and viewers on the full range of broadcasting issues. It is funded by its members and is free from sectarian, commercial and political affiliations. Holds public lectures, seminars and conferences throughout the UK, and has frequent contact with MPs, civil servants, the BBC and independent broadcasters, regulators, academics and other consumer groups. Provides an independent forum where all with an interest in broadcasting can speak on equal terms. Produces a quarterly news bulletin and regular briefings on broadcasting issues. Holds its own archive and those of the former Broadcasting Research Unit (1980–90) and BACTV (British Action for Children's Television). Maintains a panel of speakers, the VLV Forum for Children's Broadcasting, the VLV Forum for Educational Broadcasting, and acts as secretariat for the European Alliance of Listeners' and Viewers' Associations (EURALVA). VLV has responded to all major public enquiries on broadcasting since 1984. The VLV does not handle complaints.

W.A.T.C.H.
See **Writers, Artists and their Copyright Holders**

Welsh Academy
See **Academi**

Welsh Books Council (Cyngor Llyfrau Cymru)
Castell Brychan, Aberystwyth SY23 2JB
☎01970 624151   Fax 01970 625385
✉ castellbrychan@cllc.org.uk
www.cllc.org.uk
www.gwales.com
Director *Gwerfyl Pierce Jones*

Founded 1961 to stimulate interest in books from Wales and to support publishing in Wales. The Council distributes publishing grants and promotes and fosters all aspects of book production in Wales in both Welsh and English. Its Editorial, Design, Marketing and Children's Books departments and wholesale distribution centre offer central services to publishers in Wales. Writers in Welsh and English are welcome to approach the Editorial Department for advice on how to get their manuscripts published.

Welsh National Literature Promotion Agency
See **Academi**

West Country Writers' Association
6 The Beals, Greenway, Woodbury, Exmouth EX5 1LU
☎01392 233753
www.westcountrywriters.co.uk
Honorary Secretary *Sarah Hughes*

Founded 1951 in the interest of published authors with an interest in the West Country. Meets to discuss news and views and to listen to talks. Conference and newsletters.

Women in Publishing
Membership Secretary: Basement Flat, 17 Leigh Street, London WC1H 9EW
☎020 7388 2672/07985 105169
✉ janey_burton@dsl.pipex.com
www.wipub.org.uk

Membership Secretary *Janey Burton*

Aims to promote the status of women working in publishing and related trades by helping them to develop their careers. Through WiP there are opportunities for members to learn more about their area of work, share information and expertise, give and receive support and partake in a practical forum for the exchange of information about different industry sectors. Monthly meetings provide a forum for discussion on various topics of interest within the industry. Meetings are held on the second Wednesday of each month. See website for further information. Publishes monthly newsletter, *WiPlash* and *Women in Publishing Directory*.

Women Writers Network (WWN)

23 Prospect Road, London NW2 2JU
☎020 7794 5861
www.womenwriters.org.uk
Membership Secretary *Cathy Smith*
SUBSCRIPTION £45 p.a. (incl. meeting admissions & 6 newsletters p.a., WWN website and online directory access); £35 p.a. (overseas); £30 p.a. ('newsletter only' UK membership')

Founded 1985. Provides a forum for the exchange of information, support, career and networking opportunities for working women writers. Meetings, seminars, excursions, newsletter and directory. Full membership includes free admission to monthly meetings and a monthly newsletter. Details from the Membership Secretary at the address above.

Writernet (formerly New Playwrights Trust)

Cabin V, Clarendon Buildings, 25 Horsell Road, London N5 1XL
☎020 7609 7474 Fax 020 7609 7557
✉ info@writernet.org.uk
www.writernet.org.uk
Director *Jonathan Meth*
Chair *Bonnie Greer*
Administrator *Anne-Marie Draycott*
SUBSCRIPTION Information on rates available by post or on website

Provides writers for all forms of live and recorded performance (at any stage in their career) with a range of services that enable them to pursue their careers more effectively. These include: a network connecting dramatic writers to the industry and to each other; online resources to support dramatic writers and those who work with them; a script-read-

ing service, publications and guides. Aims to help writers from all parts of the country and a wide diversity of backgrounds to fulfil their potential both inside and outside the new-writing mainstream.

The Writers' Guild of Great Britain

15 Britannia Street, London WC1X 9JN
☎020 7833 0777 Fax 020 7833 4777
✉ admin@writersguild.org.uk
www.writersguild.org.uk
President *David Nobbs*
Chair *Katharine Way*
General Secretary *Bernie Corbett*
Assistant General Secretaries *Anne Hogben, Christine Paris*
SUBSCRIPTION Full member: 1% of earnings from professional writing (min. £150, max. £1500); Candidate member: £90; Student member: £20; Affiliate member (agent or writers' group): £275; Life member: voluntary contribution

Founded in 1959 as the Screenwriters' Guild, the Writers' Guild is a trade union, affiliated to the TUC, representing professional writers in television, radio, theatre, film, books and new media. It negotiates Minimum Terms Agreements governing writers' contracts and covering minimum fees; advances; repeat fees; royalties and residuals; rights; credits; number of drafts; script alterations and the resolution of disputes. The most important MTAs cover BBC TV Drama; BBC Radio Drama; ITV Companies; **PACT** (independent TV and film producers); TAC (Welsh language independent TV producers); Theatrical Management Association; **Independent Theatre Council**; and an agreement covering the **Royal National Theatre**, **Royal Shakespeare Company**, and **Royal Court Theatre**. These agreements are regularly renegotiated and in most cases the minimum fees are reviewed annually.

The Guild advises members on all aspects of their working lives, including contract vetting, legal advice, help with copyright problems and representation in disputes with producers, publishers or other writers.

Events organised by the Guild include a seminar on writing sitcoms, a networking evening for TV soap writers, a panel discussion on marketing theatre plays and lectures on forensic science aimed at TV series writers. *UK Writer*, the Guild's quarterly magazine, is free to members and contains features about professional writing, Guild news and details of work opportunities, training courses, literary competitions, etc. A detailed e-mail of news, opportunities and other information is sent to members every Friday.

Full Membership is open to anyone who has received payment for a piece of written work under a contract with terms not less than those negotiated by the Guild. Writers who do not qualify can join as Candidate Members and those on accredited writing courses or theatre attachments can become Student Members. Aged writers and those with long service in the Guild are entitled to free Life Membership.

Writers, Artists and their Copyright Holders (W.A.T.C.H.)

The Library, The University of Reading, PO Box 223, Whiteknights, Reading RG6 6AE
☎0118 378 8783   Fax 0118 378 6636
www.watch-file.com

Contact *Dr David Sutton*

Founded 1994. Provides an online database of information about the copyright holders of literary authors and artists. The database is available free of charge on the Internet and the Web. W.A.T.C.H. is the successor project to the Location Register of English Literary Manuscripts and Letters, and continues to deal with location register enquiries.

Yachting Journalists' Association

22 St Johns Road, Woking GU21 7SA
☎01483 751506   Fax 01243 751021
✉ tom@yja.co.uk
www.yja.co.uk
Membership Secretary *Tom Willis*
SUBSCRIPTION £40 p.a.

To further the interest of yachting, sail and power, and to provide support and assistance to journalists in the field; current membership is just over 260 with 31 from overseas. A handbook, listing details of members and subscribing PR organisations, press facility recommendations, forthcoming events and other useful information, is published annually at a cost to non-members and non-advertisers of £10. Information for inclusion should be submitted by the end of August. The YJA organises the Yachtsman of the Year and Young Sailor of the Year Awards, presented annually at the beginning of January.

Yr Academi Gymreig

See **Academi**

The Words Complained Of . . .

*David Hooper gives advice on how to avoid
an expensive court appearance*

The main area of risk in libel is in non-fiction. The best working test is whether the tendency of the words used is to diminish the reputation of the claimant. If you were in the claimant's position, could you validly object to what was written about you? It is sensible to ask yourself who might complain about what you have written and how you would respond to that complaint bearing in mind that the burden of proving the facts by legally admissible evidence will be upon you. There is unfortunately no substitute for careful research and checking. Some errors pass into mythology. A British police officer called Morton collected damages on no less than three occasions from W.H. Allen, Secker & Warburg and Weidenfeld & Nicolson for the repetition of the canard that he was responsible for the shooting in cold blood of Abram Stern head of the Stern gang in Palestine. The Court of Appeal has rejected attempts to use the freedom of expression principles under the European Convention of Human Rights Article 10, to reduce the strict application of the repetition rule in libel. If you repeat someone else's libel you are liable to have to prove that it is true even if you believed your source of information was reliable. If you repeat what someone told you or what they suspected, you are likely to have to prove the underlying truth of what was said or the facts which give rise to justifiable suspicion.

The issue is what readers would reasonably conclude that the words meant. The fact that the author did not intend to libel the claimant is not a defence. The reader is in any event unlikely to know what the author's intention was and would form his own view on the interpretation of the words on the page. The fact that a libel was the result of an honest mistake rather than deliberate would be relevant to the amount of damages awarded. Unhappily, experience shows that libel is, particularly in the area of publishing, the product of mistake rather than the result of a failed exposé. Publishers are in any event increasingly reluctant to run the risk of publishing investigative books. Cases involving the exposure of the wrongdoing of footballers, policemen or doctors normally involve newspapers or television companies. Writers need therefore to check the accuracy of what they write. They would do well, for example, not to emulate the mistake of confusing the Chancellor of Glasgow University, Sir Alec Cairncross, with his brother a suspected member of the Cambridge spy ring. Nor is it wise to suggest that a Nigerian-born singer had said that 'it was time to support apartheid' when in reality she had said nothing more sinister than 'it was time to support a party'.

The writer should focus on all people who might bring a claim. Often controversial books successfully avoid an action from the principal target only to invite a claim from some minor character over a relatively trivial indiscretion. Claims can come from unlikely sources. The *Sunday Telegraph* can scarcely have expected to be sued by the son of Gaddafi, but when he turned up at court he obtained an apology although no damages. A Russian businessman Grigori Loutchansky successfully sued *The Times* over a report linking him with money laundering even though the paper may have felt such a claim was unlikely as he was banned from this country because his presence was deemed undesirable by the Home Secretary and he had served a lengthy prison sentence for dishonesty in the USSR. The Loutchansky case was a salutary reminder of the severity of English libel law. Although it is the case that the limitation period for bringing libel actions is one year, the courts upheld – which is bad news for writers of books – what is known as the single publication rule – a rule dating back to a case involving a nineteenth century duke who sent his butler out to buy a book published many years previously in order to be able to establish an act of publication within the limitation period – namely that each book sale or downloading from the Internet is a fresh act of publication with its own one-year limitation period. Journalists whose material might be published electronically in an archive or otherwise accessible on a website should take care to ensure that if there is a valid libel complaint steps are taken to stop any further publication of the material electronically, otherwise they may face another claim. Unfortunately, the libel laws in this country have attracted a number of libel tourists wishing to impress on the world their spotless reputation. Writers should bear in mind that the libel laws in the United States are unfavourable to plaintiffs with the result that people like Dr Armand Hammer sued the English edition of a hostile biography in this country whereas he had decided not to bring a claim in the USA. The fact that a book has been cleared for libel in America does not remove the risk of a claim in this country. US law requires proof of fault to establish a claim for libel – knowledge of falsity in the case of a public figure or fault amounting to negligence in the case of a private figure. One notable setback in 2005 was to a Sudanese diplomat who was ordered to lodge £375,000 in court if he wished to contravene his libel action against Time Warner Books.

If a claim for libel is notified, advice should be sought from a specialist lawyer, preferably one recommended by the publisher. An outraged response can raise the level of damages. If a claim is made immediate consideration must be given as to whether any amendment or footnote is required in respect of any electronic version of the article which can be accessed by third parties. Section 2 of the Defamation Act 1996 has significantly amended the defence of offer of amends which enables a swift and less expensive resolution of a claim where a mistake has been made. It involves an admission of liability and, if the parties cannot agree, an assessment of damages by the judge, but it can stop the greed of the claimant in its tracks. Recent cases have established that the court will give a 35 to 45 per cent discount on the level of damages if this procedure is promptly used. Writers need to discover whether they are covered by the publisher's insurance and, if so, what excess attaches to any claim. If the writer believes that the claim may be covered by insurance, he or she must ensure that the insurers are promptly notified and that any letter of complaint is forwarded to them and that no admission of liability is made without the authority of the insurers. Increasingly libel insurance only cuts in after the claim has cost five figures – scant consolation for the author who is likely to have warranted in the publishing contract that the book is free from libel.Very often publishers will not enforce that indemnity in the absence of serious blameworthy conduct on the part of the writer but again that is little consolation as publishers will not commit themselves in advance to their probable reaction to a libel claim. It is important therefore to consider whether the book should be read for libel and, if so, whether it is necessary to have it all or simply part of it read.

Many publishing contracts are silent on the question of who pays for the libel reading. Writers who try to modify the standard form indemnity given to publishers normally face a thankless task, but it is worth considering whether there is scope for agreeing that the writer's liability should be modified in respect of potential defamations of which the publisher is aware where the writer has complied with all the requirements of the lawyer reading the book for libel. Practical steps which can be taken include considering whether a particular passage should be sent to the person written about. If it can be shown that the person consented to what was written that is a defence to a claim for libel. The problem, however, is that normally such persons will not give consent.

Libel actions cannot be brought on behalf of those who are dead. The death of a plaintiff in the course of a libel action, as happened with Robert Maxwell's claim against Faber, brings the claim to an immediate halt, but each side is left bearing their own legal costs. Writers are sometimes well advised to consult a helpful volume called Who Was Who.

Another defence is justification, which involves the author proving that what was written was true. If it was fair comment on a matter of public interest based on facts which were substantially true, the writer will have a defence. The 2005 case of Lowe v. Associated Newspapers has shown a greater willingness of the court to enable this defence to be successfully put forward. By virtue of the Human Rights Act 1998 the English courts will increasingly take note of the decisions made under Article 10 of the European Convention of Human Rights which upholds the freedom of speech and which has a greater tendency to rule that criticisms made of a claimant were matters of comment rather than allegations of fact which have to be justified. If a court is told that the disputed passage in a libel claim will be defended, the court will not grant an interim injunction pending trial. The downside is that if the defence fails the damages are likely to be that much greater. Consideration often has to be given as to whether it would be appropriate and less expensive to deal with the claim at an early stage possibly by altering the disputed passage, if that can still be done, or revising it in a later edition.

One of the most promising developments has been the expansion of the defence of qualified privilege in the libel action brought by the former Irish Prime Minister Albert Reynolds against the *Sunday Times*. If the writer can prove that on a matter of public interest there was a duty to inform the public who had a corresponding interest in receiving that information, there will be a defence which does not require proving that the particular allegation was true. The Court will, however, look very carefully at the research carried out, the language used and the attempt to put both sides of the matter.

Qualified privilege was the issue in the Loutchansky case where the newspaper argued that it required the protection of qualified privilege to write about the alleged activities of Loutchansky which were by their nature very difficult to prove. The judge concluded, however, that the paper had made insufficient attempts to contact Loutchansky and should not have published until it had done so.

The most helpful development for writers is the recognition by the courts of the importance of freedom of speech. The press has to discharge vital functions as a bloodhound as well as a watchdog and any lingering doubts should be resolved in favour of publication. The courts have recognised that freedom of speech is essential to informed political debate and that restrictions imposed upon that freedom must be proportionate and no more than is necessary to promote the legitimate object of the restriction. The courts also recognise that news is a perishable commodity and that the decision to publish must be assessed in the light of the facts then known. To date, however, despite all the ringing endorsements of the freedom of the press, the courts have often been unwilling to uphold defences of qualified privilege. Too often they have found that there was some step which ought to have been taken before going into print. Journalists with publication deadlines are likely to have a better prospect of establishing qualified privilege than authors who may be expected to undertake more research to get to the truth of the matter. The existence of the defence and the unpredictability of the view which the judge may take of the research carried out is likely to deter many claimants particularly those in public life. The Court of Appeal has held that a balanced account of the allegations, which it termed neutral reportage, made by a Saudi dissident was protected by qualified privilege. The Reynolds qualified privilege has been instrumental in the decrease in the number of libel actions brought. However, in practice it seldom succeeds and often it spawns satellite litigation where the responsibility or otherwise of the journalism is pored over in minute but expensive detail. If the coverage is considered by the court to be partisan the defence will fail as in the case George Galloway brought against the *Telegraph*. The House of Lords will consider the ambit of this defence in 2006 in a libel claim brought by a Saudi against the American *Wall Street Journal* – another striking example of how attractive our libel laws are to foreigners seeking to sue foreign publications in this country.

Writers of fiction face fewer libel problems. However, their use of autobiographical material can lead to some of their characters being identifiable. The inadvertent use of the name of a real peer with fictitious sexual predilections has led to a novel being pulped. Directories should, where possible, be consulted to ensure there are no similarly named people in a comparable occupation. Care should be taken to see on whom characters are based and whether any of the surrounding events actually happened. Often there is much to be said for a carefully worded disclaimer of reference to living individuals. Compton Mackenzie used to pick names from old telephone directories. Unfortunately, even when this expedient was used by the novelist Paul Watkins, who wrote a fictionalised account of his experiences at Eton in the early 1980s in his book *Stand Before Your God*, a randomly chosen name of a villainous character was by ill-fortune the name of one of his contemporaries at the College. Damages had to be paid as checks in the school directories could have avoided this error. Choosing the names of friends or acquaintances and involving them in defamatory escapades may be very difficult to defend and could result in the payment of damages and costs. A novelist who recently used the name and some identifying features of a film producer believing his friend would not object found himself paying libel damages and even being threatened with a baseball bat – the latter a novel risk for novelists.

The growth of faction and the introduction of living people into works of fiction do increase the risk of libel claims by blurring the distinction between fact and imagination. A roman-à-clef can present significant libel problems and it was perhaps not surprising that recently a publisher could not be found for a novel featuring unattractive characteristics of a person described as the wife of a Labour Prime Minister who as 'a young chap with a phoney smile' was felt not to be sufficiently unrecognisable.

Changes introduced by the Defamation Act 1996 and procedural changes regarding the conduct of libel actions to make them less tortuous and expensive and to require each side to disclose the strengths and weaknesses of their cases at an earlier stage certainly are an improvement. Libel nevertheless remains a very costly pitfall even if the damages awarded are much less. Damages are now capped but are slowly moving upwards for the most serious libels. Two nursery workers accused of child abuse were awarded £200,000 each and a company that was falsely linked to Al Quaeda was reputed to have recovered £500,000 from the BBC although part of those damages may have related to loss of business contracts. On top of that there are the legal costs. £200,000 is the cap on general damages for libel and is reserved for the worst cases. In the last year the Chairman of Southampton Football Club was awarded £250,000 damages by a jury but this was reduced by agreement to £75,000 to settle the appeal. Damages can be higher if there is a financial loss directly attributable to the libel. This enabled the stockbrokers Collins Stewart to recover £300,000 damages against the *Financial Times*. Most cases settle for a fraction of that. There are fast-track procedures where libel damages will be capped at £10,000. This is little consolation to writers as these changes together with the willingness of lawyers to bring libel claims on a conditional fee basis – that is to say the lawyer does not get paid unless he wins the case, but can recover from the defendant a success fee on top of his not inconsiderable normal legal fees – serve only to encourage the bringing of smaller, but nevertheless expensive, claims. This has resulted in some lawyers seeking to charge £800 or more per hour and senior judges have referred to the blackmailing effect of such fees in the sense that claims have to be settled in the face of potentially astronomic fees set against the impossibility of recovering costs from an impecunious defendant. In Naomi Campbell's privacy case she recovered £3,500 damages, but her lawyers sought £1 million in legal costs. One saving in costs has been an increasing tendency of the courts to favour trial by judge alone rather than by jury. When Orion Books were sued by a police officer accused in a book of corruption, the judge considered the action involving a detailed reading of the book by a jury was best heard by a judge alone. If this gloomy assessment of the reading skills of jurors is followed, trial by jury in libel cases concerning books may become a thing of the past. Things are improving, but at present the only certainty about libel is its expense.

Article 8 of the European Convention of Human Rights protects the right to respect for private and family life. Initially, claims related either to intrusive tabloid exposés or to celebrities exploiting publicity rights, such as Michael Douglas in his spat with *Hello!* magazine which published unauthorised paparazzi photographs. That case was really about the right to control publicity. The court felt that there was no public interest in such intrusive behaviour on the part of *Hello!* and the Douglas's were entitled to £7,250 damage each for distress. Damages for privacy tend to be low, but legal costs can be enormous particularly if there is a conditional fee involved. Initially privacy involved intrusive behaviour by tabloid newspapers. A recent case brought by the Canadian folksinger Loreena McKennitt against the publication of an unauthorised biography by a former friend secured her an award of £5,000 damages but more importantly an injunction against the intrusive parts of the book which included details of her home, business contacts, her personal relationships and her health and diet. It is a developing area of law and the McKennitt case shows how it can impact on writers. The test is whether the information is private information and whether the complainant has a reasonable expectation of privacy. If so, a balancing exercise has to be carried out to weigh up the right to privacy against freedom of speech. Factors favouring publication would include whether the information is in the public domain (particularly if put there by the claimant), the triviality of the information or of any possible infringement or some genuine public interest in the sense of raising a matter of legitimate public interest. The mere fact that the public would be interested in such material is not sufficient. Naomi Campbell recovered £3,500 in respect of photographs of her leaving a drugs rehabilitation clinic and Amanda Holden and her husband received £40,000 from the *Daily Star* which had published intrusive pictures of them on holiday.

The English courts are beginning to enforce the rights of privacy recognised elsewhere in Europe most notably in Germany where the award of damages to Princess Caroline of Monaco for breach of her privacy was upheld by the European Court of Human Rights. The next year is likely to see an increasing number of privacy claims.

David Hooper is media partner of Reynolds Porter Chamberlain and author of Reputations under Fire, *published by Little Brown (2001).*

Literary Societies

Margery Allingham Society

2B Higham Green, Winchelsea TN36 4HB
☎01797 222363 Fax 01797 222363
www.margeryallingham.org.uk
Contact *Mrs Pamela Bruxner*
SUBSCRIPTION £14 p.a.

Founded 1988 to promote interest in and study of the works of Margery Allingham. The Society publishes two issues of the journal, *The Bottle Street Gazette*, per year. Contributions welcome. Two social events a year. Open membership.

Jane Austen Society

9 Nicola Close, South Croydon CR2 6NA
www.janeaustensociety.org.uk
Membership Secretary *Mrs Rosemary Culley*
SUBSCRIPTION UK: £7.50 (student); £15 (annual); £20 (joint); £45 (corporate); £250 (life); Overseas: £18 (annual by credit card or UK banker's order only); £50 (corporate); overseas membership £50/€75 (for 3 years); £300/€450 (life)

Founded 1940 to promote interest in and enjoyment of Jane Austen's novels and letters. The society has branches in Bath and Bristol, the Midlands, London, Oxford, Norfolk, Kent, Hampshire, Isle of Wight and northern Scotland. There are independent Societies in North America and Australia.

The Baskerville Hounds (The Dartmoor Sherlock Holmes Study Group)

6 Bramham Moor, Hill Head, Fareham PO14 3RU
☎01329 667325
✉ baskervillehounds@acd-221b.info
www.acd-221b.info
Chairman *Philip Weller*
SUBSCRIPTION Nil for members receiving newsletters and study material by e-mail

Founded 1989. An international Sherlock Holmes society specialising solely in studies of *The Hound of the Baskervilles* and its Dartmoor associations. Organises many study functions, mostly on Dartmoor. Currently involved in several large-scale research projects. Member- ship is open only to those who are willing to be actively involved, by correspondence and/or attendance at functions, in the group's study activities.

The BB Society

Secretary: 8 Park Road, Solihull B91 3SU
☎0121 704 1002
✉ enquiries@rosenworldproductions.com
Chairman *Brian Mutlow*
Secretary *Bryan Holden*
SUBSCRIPTION £10 (individual); £17.50 (family); £50 (corporate); £5 (student); £17.50 (overseas)

Founded in 2000 to bring together devotees of the writer/illustrator BB (Denys Watkins-Pitchford). BB's oeuvre included books on wildfowling, angling, children's fantasy and the countryside. The Society holds two meetings a year and publishes newsletters and an annual journal, *Sky Gypsy*.

The Beckford Society

The Timber Cottage, Crockerton, Warminster BA12 8AX
☎01985 213195
✉ Sidney.Blackmore@btinternet.com
Secretary *Sidney Blackmore*
SUBSCRIPTION £10 (minimum) p.a.

Founded 1995 to promote an interest in the life and works of William Beckford (1760–1844) and his circle. Encourages Beckford studies and scholarship through exhibitions, lectures and publications, including an annual journal, *The Beckford Journal* and occasional newsletters.

Thomas Lovell Beddoes Society

9 Amber Court, Belper DE56 1HG
☎01773 828066 Fax 01773 828066
✉ john@beddoes.demon.co.uk
www.beddoes.org
Chairman *John Lovell Beddoes*
Secretary *Christine Hunkinson*

Formed to research the life, times and work of poet Thomas Lovell Beddoes (1803–1849), encourage relevant publications, further the reading and appreciation of his works by a wider public and liaise with other groups and organisations. Publishes an annual journal.

The Adrian Bell Society

3 The Maltings, Church Close, Coltishall
NR12 7DZ
☎01603 737168
Secretary *Moya Leighton*
SUBSCRIPTION £5 p.a.

Founded 1995, the Society aims to promote the study and enjoyment of the writing of Adrian Bell (1901–80); to publish journals twice a year and hold meetings to help members obtain copies of out of print titles; to assemble a collection of photocopies of his 1500 *Countryman's Notebooks* that appeared in the *Eastern Daily Press* and to index them; to commemorate his career as *The Times* first crossword compiler; to share knowledge of the places and factual background mentioned in his books. The society has 250 members worldwide who keep in touch through the journal *A Centenary Countryman's Notebook*, published 2001 (£7 + p&p).

Hilaire Belloc Society

1 Hillview, Elsted, Midhurst GU29 0JX
☎01730 825575
✉ HilaireBelloc1@aol.com
Contact *Dr Grahame Clough*

Founded in 1996 to promote the life and work of Hilaire Belloc through the publication of newsletters containing rare and previously unpublished material. Organises walks, social events, a Belloc weekend and a three-day conference. Currently 70 members, of which 30% are from overseas.

Arnold Bennett Society

4 Field End Close, Trentham, Stoke on Trent
ST4 8DA
✉ arnoldbennettsociety@btinternet.com
www.arnoldbennettsociety.org.uk
Secretary *Mrs Carol Gorton*
SUBSCRIPTION £12 p.a. (single); £14 (family) plus £2 for membership outside the UK

Aims to promote interest in the life and works of 'Five Towns' author Arnold Bennett and other North Staffordshire writers. Annual dinner. Regular functions and talks in and around Burslem, plus annual seminar at Wedgwood College, Barlaston and annual conference at Staffordshire University.

E.F. Benson Society

The Old Coach House, High Street, Rye
TN31 7JF
☎01797 223114
www.efbensonsociety.org
Secretary *Allan Downend*
SUBSCRIPTION £7.50 (UK/Europe); £12.50 (overseas)

Founded 1985 to promote the life and work of E.F. Benson and the Benson family. Organises social and literary events, exhibitions, talks and Benson interest walks in Rye. Publishes a quarterly newsletter and annual journal, *The Dodo*, postcards and reprints of E.F. Benson articles and short stories in a series called 'Bensoniana' plus other books of Benson interest. Holds an archive which includes the Seckersen Collection (transcriptions of the Benson collection at the Bodleian Library in Oxford).

The Betjeman Society

6 St Annes Road, Shrewsbury SY3 6AU
☎01743 350372
✉ colin@colin-wright.freeserve.co.uk
www.johnbetjeman.com
Honorary Secretary *Colin Wright*
Chairman *John Heald*
SUBSCRIPTION £10 (individual); £12 (family); £3 (student); £3 additional for overseas members

Aims to promote the study and appreciation of the work and life of Sir John Betjeman. Annual programme includes poetry readings, lectures, discussions, visits to places associated with Betjeman, and various social events. Meetings are held in London and other centres. Regular newsletter and annual journal, *The Betjemanian*.

The Bewick Society

c/o The Hancock Museum, Newcastle upon Tyne NE2 4PT
☎01207 562196
✉ juneholmes@lineone.net
www.bewicksociety.org
Membership Secretary *June Holmes*
SUBSCRIPTION £7 p.a. (individual); £10 (family)

Founded 1988 to promote an interest in the life and work of Thomas Bewick, wood-engraver and naturalist (1753–1828). Organises related events and meetings, and is associated with the Bewick birthplace museum at Cherryburn, Northumberland.

Birmingham Central Literary Association

23 Arden Grove, Ladywood, Birmingham
B16 8HG
☎0121 454 9352
✉ bruce@bakerbrum.co.uk.

Contact *The Secretary*

Holds fortnightly meetings in central Birmingham to discuss the lives and work of authors and poets. Holds an annual dinner to celebrate Shakespeare's birthday.

The George Borrow Society

60 Upper Marsh Road, Warminster BA12 9PN
www.clough5.fsnet.co.uk/gb.html
Chairman/Bulletin Editor *Dr Ann M. Ridler*
Membership Secretary *Michael Skillman*
Honorary Treasurer *David Pattinson*
Bulletin Editor: St Mary's Cottage, 61 Thame Road, Warborough, Wallingford, Oxford OX10 7EA ☎01865 858379 Fax 01865 858575
SUBSCRIPTION £15 p.a.

Founded 1991 to promote knowledge of the life and works of George Borrow (1803–81), traveller, linguist and writer. The Society holds biennial conferences (with published proceedings) and informal intermediate gatherings, all at places associated with Borrow. Publishes the *George Borrow Bulletin* twice yearly, containing scholarly articles, reviews of publications relating to Borrow, reports of past events and news of forthcoming events. Member of the **Alliance of Literary Societies** and corporate associate member of the Centre of East Anglian Studies (CEAS) at the University of East Anglia, Norwich (Borrow's home city for many years).

Elinor Brent-Dyer

See **Friends of the Chalet School** and **The New Chalet Club**

British Fantasy Society

201 Reddish Road, South Reddish, Stockport SK5 7HR
☎0161 476 5368 (after 6pm)
✉ faliol@yahoo.com
www.britishfantasysociety.org.uk
President *Ramsey Campbell*
Chairman *Marie O'Regan*
Secretary *Robert Parkinson*
SUBSCRIPTION from £25 p.a.

Founded 1971 for devotees of fantasy, horror and related fields in literature, art and the cinema. Publishes a regular newsletter with information and reviews of new books and films, plus related fiction and non-fiction magazines. Annual conference at which the **British Fantasy Awards** are presented. These awards are voted on by the membership and are not an open competition.

The Brontë Society

Brontë Parsonage Museum, Haworth, Keighley BD22 8DR
☎01535 640195   Fax 01535 647131
✉ bronte@bronte.org.uk
www.bronte.info
Contact *Membership Officer*
SUBSCRIPTION Contact Membership Officer for details

Founded 1893. Aims and activities include the preservation of manuscripts and other objects related to or connected with the Brontë family, and the maintenance and development of the museum and library at Haworth. The Society holds regular meetings, lectures and exhibitions; publishes information relating to the family and a triannual *Gazette*. Freelance contributions for either publication should be sent to the Publications Secretary at the address above. Members can receive the journal, *Brontë Studies*, at a reduced subscription of £15.60 p.a.

The Rupert Brooke Society

The Orchard, 45/47 Mill Way, Grantchester CB3 9ND
☎01223 551118   Fax 01223 551119
✉ rbs@callan.co.uk
www.rupertbrooke.com
Contacts *Claire Pidoux, Karen Smith*
SUBSCRIPTION £7.50 (UK); £10.50 (overseas)

Founded in 1999 to foster an interest in the work of Rupert Brooke, help preserve places associated with him and to increase the knowledge and appreciation of the village of Grantchester. Members receive a newsletter with information about events, new books and activities.

The Browning Society

9 Duncan Terrace, London N1 8BZ
☎020 7833 4228   Fax 020 7833 5834
✉ anneke.berrill@btconnect.com
Honorary Secretary *Anneke Berrill*
SUBSCRIPTION £15 p.a.

Founded 1969 to promote an interest in the lives and poetry of Robert and Elizabeth Barrett Browning. Meetings are arranged in the London area, one of which occurs in December at Westminster Abbey to commemorate Robert Browning's death.

The John Buchan Society

Greenmantle, Main Street, Kings Newton, Melbourne DE73 8BX
☎01332 865315
✉ kenhbsoc@moonfleet69.freeserve.co.uk

Secretary *Kenneth Hillier*
SUBSCRIPTION £12 (full/overseas); £5 (associate); £6 (junior); £20 (corporate); £100 (10 years)

To perpetuate the memory of John Buchan and to promote a wider understanding of his life and works. Holds regular meetings and social gatherings, publishes a journal, and liaises with the John Buchan Centre at Broughton in the Scottish borders.

The Robert Burns World Federation Ltd

Dean Castle Country Park Dower House, Kilmarnock KA3 1XB
☎01563 572469 Fax 01563 572469
✉ member@kilmarnock26.freeserve.co.uk
www.worldburnsclub.com
Chief Executive *Shirley Bell*
Office Administrator *Margaret Craig*
SUBSCRIPTION £23 p.a.(individual); £25 (family); £46 (club subscription)

Founded 1885 to encourage interest in the life and work of Robert Burns and keep alive the old Scottish Tongue. The Society's interests go beyond Burns himself in its commitment to the development of Scottish literature, music and arts in general. Publishes the triannual *Burns Chronicle*.

Randolph Caldecott Society

Clatterwick House, Little Leigh, Northwich CW8 4RJ
☎01606 891303 (day)/781731 (evening)
Honorary Secretary *Kenneth N. Oultram*
SUBSCRIPTION £10–15 p.a.

Founded 1983 to promote the life and work of artist/book illustrator Randolph Caldecott. Meetings held in the spring and autumn in Caldecott's birthplace, Chester. Guest speakers, outings, newsletter, exchanges with the Society's American counterpart. (Caldecott died and was buried in St Augustine, Florida.) A medal in his memory is awarded annually in the US for children's book illustration.

Lewis Carroll Society

69 Cromwell Road, Hertford SG13 7DP
☎01992 584530
✉ alanwhite@tesco.net
www.lewiscarrollsociety.org.uk
Secretary *Alan White*
SUBSCRIPTION Refer to website for details

Founded 1969 to bring together people with an interest in Charles Dodgson and promote

research into his life and works. Publishes bi-annual journal *The Carrollian*, featuring scholarly articles and reviews; a newsletter (*Bandersnatch*) which reports on Carrollian events and the Society's activities; and *The Lewis Carroll Review*, a book-reviewing journal. Regular meetings held in London with lectures, talks, outings, etc.

Lewis Carroll Society (Daresbury)

Clatterwick House, Little Leigh, Northwich CW8 4RJ
☎01606 891303 (day)/781731 (evening)
Honorary Secretary *Kenneth N. Oultram*
SUBSCRIPTION £5 p.a.

Founded 1970. To promote the life and work of Charles Dodgson, author of the world-famous *Alice's Adventures*. Holds meetings in the spring and autumn in Carroll's birthplace, Daresbury, Cheshire. Guest speakers and theatre visits.

The New Chalet Club

18 Nuns Moor Crescent, Newcastle upon Tyne NE4 9BE
www.newchaletclub.co.uk
Membership Secretary *Mrs Rona S.S. Falconer*
SUBSCRIPTION £6 p.a. (UK under 18); £10 (UK adult & Europe); £12 (RoW)

Founded 1995 for all those with an interest in the books of Elinor Brent-Dyer. Publishes a quarterly journal and occasional supplements, including *Children's Series Fiction*, and regularly holds local and national meetings.

Friends of the Chalet School

4 Rock Terrace, Coleford, Bath BA3 5NF
☎01373 812705
✉ focs@rockterrace.demon.co.uk
www.rockterrace.demon.co.uk/FOCS
Contacts *Ann Mackie-Hunter, Clarissa Cridland*
SUBSCRIPTION Details on website or on application

Founded 1989 to promote the works of Elinor Brent-Dyer. The society has members world-wide; publishes four magazines a year and runs a lending library.

The Chesterton Society UK

11 Lawrence Leys, Bloxham, Near Banbury OX15 4NU
☎01295 720869/07766 711984 (mobile) Fax 01295 720869
Honorary Secretary *Rev. Deacon Robert Hughes, KCHS*
SUBSCRIPTION £12.50 p.a.

Founded 1964 to promote the ideas and writings of G.K. Chesterton.

The Children's Books History Society

26 St Bernards Close, Buckfast, Buckfastleigh TQ11 0EP
☎01364 643568
✉ cbhs@abcgarrett.demon.co.uk
Chair/Membership Secretary *Mrs Pat Garrett*
SUBSCRIPTION £10 p.a. (UK/Europe); write for overseas subscription details

Established 1969. Aims to promote an appreciation of children's books and to study their history, bibliography and literary content. The Society holds approximately five meetings per year in London and a summer meeting to a collection, or to a location with a children's book connection. Three substantial newsletters issued annually, sometimes with an occasional paper. Review copies should be sent to Newsletter co-editor *Mrs Pat Garrett* (address above). The Society constitutes the British branch of the Friends of the Osborne and Lillian H. Smith Collections in Toronto, Canada, and also liaises with **CILIP** (formerly The Library Association). In 1990, the Society established its biennial Harvey Darton Award for a book, published in English, which extends our knowledge of some aspect of British children's literature of the past. 2006 winner: Lawrence Darton for *The Dartons. An Annotated Check-List of Children's Books Issued by Two Publishing Houses 1787–1876.*

The John Clare Society

9 The Chase, Ely CB6 3DR
☎01353 668438
www.johnclare.org.uk
human.ntu.ac.uk/clare/clare.html
Honorary Secretary *Miss Sue Holgate*
SUBSCRIPTION £10 (individual); £13 (joint); £8 (fully retired); £10 (joint retired); £13 (group); £15 (library); £5 (student, full-time); £15 sterling draft/$30/€25 (eurocheque) (overseas)

Founded 1981 to promote a wider appreciation of the life and works of the poet John Clare (1793–1864). Organises an annual festival in Helpston in July; arranges exhibitions, poetry readings and conferences; and publishes an annual society journal and quarterly newsletter.

William Cobbett Society

10 Grenehurst Way, Petersfield GU31 4AZ
☎01730 262060
✉ williamcobbett@fsmail.net

Chairman *Molly Townsend*
Also: Boynell House, Outlands Lane, Curdridge, Southampton SO30 2HR
☎01489 782453
Contact *David Chun*
SUBSCRIPTION £8 p.a.

Founded in 1976 to bring together those with an interest in the life and works of William Cobbett (1763–1835) and to extend the interest to a wider public. Society activities include an annual Memorial Lecture; publication of an annual journal (*Cobbett's New Register*) containing articles on various aspects of his life and times; an annual expedition retracing routes taken by Cobbett on his Rural Rides in the 1820s; visits to his birthplace and his tomb in Farnham, Surrey. In association with the Society, the Museum of Farnham holds bound volumes of *Cobbett's Political Register*, a large collection of Cobbett's works, books about Cobbett, and has various Cobbett artefacts on display.

The Friends of Coleridge

87 Richmond Road, Montpelier, Bristol BS6 5EP
☎0117 942 6366
✉ gcdd@blueyonder.co.uk
www.friendsofcoleridge.com
Membership Secretary *Paul Cheshire* (74 Wells Road, Bath BA2 3AR email paul.cheshire@btclick.com)
Editor (*Coleridge Bulletin*) *Graham Davidson*
SUBSCRIPTION Refer to website for details

Founded in 1987 to advance knowledge about the life, work and times of Samuel Taylor Coleridge and his circle, and to support his Nether Stowey Cottage, with the National Trust, as a centre of Coleridge interest. Holds literary evenings, study weekends and a biennial international academic conference. Publishes *The Coleridge Bulletin* biannually. Short articles on Coleridge-related topics may be sent to the editor at the (Bristol) address above.

Wilkie Collins Society

4 Ernest Gardens, London W4 3QU
☎020 8747 0115
✉ paul@wilkiecollins.org
www.wilkiecollins.org
Chairman *Andrew Gasson*
Membership Secretary *Paul Lewis* (at address above)
SUBSCRIPTION £10 (UK/Europe); £18 (RoW; remittance must be made in UK sterling or by PayPal to paul@paullewis.co.uk)

Founded 1980 to provide information on and promote interest in the life and works of Wilkie Collins, one of the first English novelists to deal with the detection of crime. *The Woman in White* appeared in 1860 and *The Moonstone* in 1868. Publishes newsletters, reprints of Collins' work and an annual academic journal.

The Arthur Conan Doyle Society

PO Box 1360, Ashcroft, British Columbia, Canada V0K 1A0
☎001 250 453 2045   Fax 001 250 453 2075
✉ ashtree@ash-tree.bc.ca
www.ash-tree.bc.ca/acdsocy.html
Joint Organisers *Christopher Roden, Barbara Roden*

Founded 1989 to promote the study and discussion of the life and works of Sir Arthur Conan Doyle. Occasional meetings, functions and visits. Publishes an occasional journal together with reprints of Conan Doyle's writings.

Joseph Conrad Society (UK)

c/o The Polish Social and Cultural Association (POSK), 238–246 King Street, London W6 0RF
✉ theconradian@aol.com
www.josephconradsociety.org
Honorary Secretary *Hugh Epstein*
Treasurer/Editor (*The Conradian*) *Allan Simmons*
SUBSCRIPTION £20 p.a. (individual)

Founded in 1973 to promote the study of the works and life of Joseph Conrad (1857–1924). A scholarly society, supported by the Polish Library at the Polish Cultural Association where a substantial library of Conrad texts and criticism is held in the Study Centre. Publishes a journal of Conrad studies (*The Conradian*) biannually and holds an annual International Conference in the first week of July. Awards an essay prize and travel and study grants to scholars on application.

The Rhys Davies Trust

10 Heol Don, Whitchurch, Cardiff CF14 2AU
☎029 2062 3359
Contact *Professor Meic Stephens*

Founded 1990 to perpetuate the literary reputation of the Welsh prose writer, Rhys Davies (1901–78), and to foster Welsh writing in English. Organises competitions in association with other bodies such as the **Welsh Academy**, puts up plaques on buildings associated with Welsh writers, offers grant-aid for book production, etc.

The Walter de la Mare Society

Flat 15, Trinity Court, Vicarage Road, Twickenham TW2 5TY
www.bluetree.co.uk/wdlmsociety
Honorary President *Professor John Bayley, CBE*
Honorary Secretary & Treasurer *Julie de la Mare*
SUBSCRIPTION £15 p.a.

Founded in 1997 to honour the memory of Walter de la Mare; to promote the study and deepen the appreciation of his works; to widen the readership of his works; to facilitate research by making available the widest range of contacts and information about de la Mare; and to encourage and facilitate new Walter de la Mare publications. Produces a regular newsletter and organises events. Membership information from the address above.

Warwick Deeping Appreciation Society

23 Merton Road, Enfield EN2 0LS
☎020 8367 0263
✉ geoffrey@gillam.fsworld.co.uk
Secretary *Geoffrey Gillam*
SUBSCRIPTION £3.50 p.a.

Open to all with an interest in the life and work of Warwick Deeping who produced 70 novels and many short stories. A quarterly newsletter includes reviews of his books and results of research into his life.

The Dickens Fellowship

48 Doughty Street, London WC1N 2LX
☎020 7405 2127
✉ dickens.fellowship@btinternet.com
www.dickens.fellowship.btinternet.co.uk
Joint Honorary General Secretaries *Mrs Thelma Grove, Dr Tony Williams*
SUBSCRIPTION £6 (first year); £12 (renewal)

Founded 1902. The Society's particular aims and objectives are: to bring together lovers of Charles Dickens; to spread the message of Dickens, his love of humanity ('the keynote of all his work'); to remedy social injustice for the poor and oppressed; to assist in the preservation of material and buildings associated with Dickens. Annual conference. Publishes journal called *The Dickensian* (founded 1905 and available at special rate to members) and organises a full programme of lectures, discussions, visits and conducted walks throughout the year. Branches worldwide.

Dymock Poets

See **The Friends of the Dymock Poets**

Early English Text Society

Lady Margaret Hall, Oxford OX2 6QA Fax
01865 286581
www.eets.org.uk
Executive Secretary *Professor Vincent Gillespie*
(at address above)
Editorial Secretary *Dr H.L. Spencer* (at Exeter
College, Oxford OX1 3DP)
Membership Secretary *Mrs J.M. Watkinson* (at
12 North End, Durham DH1 4NJ)
SUBSCRIPTION £20 p.a. (UK); $30 (US);
$35 (Canada)

Founded 1864. Concerned with the publication of early English texts. Members receive
annual publications (one or two a year) or may
select titles from the backlist in lieu.

The George Eliot Fellowship

71 Stepping Stones Road, Coventry CV5 8JT
☎024 7659 2231
www.george-eliot-fellowship.com
Contact *Mrs Kathleen Adams*
SUBSCRIPTION £10 p.a.; £100 (life);
concession for pensioners

Founded 1930. Exists to honour George Eliot
and promote interest in her life and works.
Readings, memorial lecture, birthday luncheon
and functions. Issues a quarterly newsletter and
an annual journal. Awards an annual prize for a
George Eliot essay.

Rev. G. Bramwell Evens

See **The Romany Society**

The John Meade Falkner Society

Greenmantle, Main Street, Kings Newton,
Melbourne DE73 8BX
☎01332 865315
✉ kenjmfsoc@moonfleet69.freeserve.co.uk
Secretary *Kenneth Hillier*
SUBSCRIPTION £5 (UK); $10 (overseas)

Founded in 1999 to promote the appreciation
and study of John Meade Falkner's life, times
and works. Produces three newsletters a year
and an annual journal.

Folly (Fans of Light Literature for the Young)

21 Warwick Road, Pokesdown, Bournemouth
BH7 6JW
☎01202 432562
✉ folly@sims.abel.co.uk
Contact *Mrs Sue Sims*
SUBSCRIPTION £9 p.a. (UK); £11 (Europe);
£14 (worldwide)

Founded 1990 to promote interest in a wide
variety of children's authors – with a bias towards
writers of girls' books and school stories.
Publishes three magazines a year.

The Ford Madox Ford Society

c/o Dr Sara Haslam, Dept of Literature, The
Open University, Milton Keynes MK7 6AA
☎01908 653453 Fax 01908 653750
✉ s.j.haslam@open.ac.uk
www.rialto.com/fordmadoxford_society
Chairman *Professor Max Saunders*
Treasurer *Dr Sara Haslam*
SUBSCRIPTION £12 or £6 concession

Founded 1996 to promote the works of Ford
Madox Ford and to increase knowledge of his
writing and impact on writing in the 20th century. Meets for academic conferences and more
popular events annually. Distributes *International
Ford Madox Ford Studies* free to members.
Welcomes all with an interest in Ford and his
works. Has members in the UK, USA, Italy,
France and Germany and holds events in as
many different places as possible.

C.S. Forester Society

Flats 1 & 2, Moore Place, 103 Banbury Road,
Oxford OX2 6JX
☎01865 512111 Fax 01865 515292
✉ csforester@hotmail.com
www.csforester.com
Contact *Colin Blogg*
SUBSCRIPTION £15 p.a.

Founded in 1999 to provide an informal forum
to promote knowledge and enjoyment of the
works and life of C.S. Forester; to write a definitive bibliography and, ultimately, a biography.
Publishes a newsletter three or four times a year
containing contributions from members, and
holds meetings for film shows, readings and
lectures and a literary supplement, *Reflections*
(Editor: *David Stead* ☎0114 233 1255).

The Franco–Midland Hardware Company

6 Bramham Moor, Hill Head, Fareham
PO14 3RU
☎01329 667325
✉ fmhc@acd-221b.info
www.acd-221b.info
Chairman *Philip Weller*
SUBSCRIPTION £5 p.a. (UK); £10 (Europe);
£15 (RoW)

Founded 1989. A federation of societies in four
continents.   Two   core   groups,   '221B'

(Holmesian/Sherlockian) and 'The Arthur Conan Doyle Study Group' (Doylean), form the UK base. Membership is open only to those interested in being actively involved in the programme of correspondence studies and/or functions. Arranges certificated self-study projects and assists group and individual research programmes, plus scholarly gatherings.

The Friars' Club

33 Grenville Court, Chorleywood WD3 5PZ
☎01923 283795
✉ henry.quelch@westlodge.ed-i.net
Secretary *Frances-Mary Blake*
SUBSCRIPTION £10 (first year); £8.50 (renewals)

Founded in 1982 to promote the writings of Frank Richards (Charles Hamilton), author of of the Greyfriars School stories in *The Magnet* and creator of Billy Bunter. The club prtoduces a quarterly magazine for members; articles ans comments are welcomed.

The Friends of Shandy Hall (The Laurence Sterne Trust)

Shandy Hall, Coxwold, York YO61 4AD
☎01347 868465 Fax 01347 868465
www.asterisk.org.uk
Curator *Patrick Wildgust*
SUBSCRIPTION £7 (annual); £70 (life)

Promotes interest in the works of Laurence Sterne and aims to preserve the house in which they were created (open to the public). Publishes annual journal, *The Shandean*. An Annual Memorial Lecture is delivered each summer.

The Friends of the Dymock Poets

Burgage House, 19 The Southend, Ledbury HR8 2EY
☎01531 634796
✉ cateluck2003@yahoo.com
www.dymockpoets.co.uk
Chairman *Roy Palmer*
Hon. Secretary *Catharine Luck*
Membership Secretary *Jeff Cooper*
SUBSCRIPTION £7 (individual); £12 (couple); £3 (student); £12 (society/family)

Founded 1993. Established to foster an interest in the work of the Dymock Poets – Edward Thomas, Robert Frost, Wilfrid Gibson, Rupert Brooke, John Drinkwater, Lascelles Abercrombie; help preserve places and things associated with them; keep members informed of literary and other matters relating to the poets; increase

knowledge and appreciation of the landscape between May Hill (Gloucestershire) and the Malvern Hills. Members are offered lectures, poetry readings, social meetings, newsletters and annual journal, guided walks in the countryside around Dymock; links with other literary societies; and annual event to commemorate the first meeting between Edward Thomas and Robert Frost on 6 October 1913.

The Gaskell Society

Far Yew Tree House, Chester Road, Tabley, Knutsford WA16 0HN
☎01565 634668
✉ joanleach@aol.com
gaskellsociety.users.btopenworld.com
lang.nagoya-u.ac.jp/~matsuoka/EG-Society.html
Honorary Secretary *Joan Leach*
SUBSCRIPTION £15 p.a.; £20 (corporate & overseas)

Founded 1985 to promote and encourage the study and appreciation of the life and works of Elizabeth Cleghorn Gaskell. Meetings held in Knutsford, Manchester, Bath and London; annual journal and biannual newsletter. On alternate years holds either a residential weekend conference or overseas visit.

The Ghost Story Society

PO Box 1360, Ashcroft, British Columbia, Canada V0K 1A0
☎001 250 453 2045 Fax 001 250 453 2075
✉ nebuly@telus.net
www.ash-tree.bc.ca/GSS.html
Joint Organisers *Barbara Roden, Christopher Roden*
SUBSCRIPTION UK: £25 (airmail); $40 (US$); $45 (Canadian$)

Founded 1988. Devoted mainly to supernatural fiction in the literary tradition of M.R. James, Walter de la Mare, Algernon Blackwood, E.F. Benson, A.N.L. Munby, R.H. Malden, etc. Publishes a thrice-yearly journal, *All Hallows*, which includes new fiction in the genre and non-fiction of relevance to the genre.

Graham Greene Birthplace Trust

Rhenigidale, Ivy House Lane, Berkhamsted HP4 2PP
☎01442 865158
✉ secretary@grahamgreenebt.org
www.grahamgreenebt.org
Secretary *Ken Sherwood*
SUBSCRIPTION £8 (UK, £20 for 3 years); £11 (Europe, £27); £15 (RoW, £40)

Founded on 2 October 1997, the 93rd anniversary of Graham Greene's birth, to promote the appreciation and study of his works. Publishes a quarterly newsletter, occasional papers, videos and compact discs. Organises the annual four-day Graham Greene Festival during the weekend nearest to the writer's birthday (2nd October) and administrates the Graham Greene Memorial Awards.

The Ivor Gurney Society
2 Turrall Street, Barbourne, Worcester
WR3 8AJ
☎01497 831038
✉ jp-hay@beeb.net
www.ivor.gurney.net
SUBSCRIPTION £12.50 (individual);
£5 (student); £12.50 (group/library); rates for joint & retired memberships set out on membership leaflet

To promote interest in Ivor Gurney and his context and to make his music and poetry available to a wider audience by way of performances, readings, conferences, recordings and publications. To enhance and promote informed scholarship on all aspects of his life and work through the publication of a regular newsletter and an annual journal, available to society members. To maintain and expand the Gurney archive at Gloucester Record Office.

Rider Haggard Society
27 Denehalm, Whitley Bay NE25 9AU
☎0191 252 4516 Fax 0191 252 4516
✉ RB27Allen@aol.com
www.riderhaggardsociety.org.uk
Contact *Roger Allen*
SUBSCRIPTION £9 p.a. (UK); £12 (overseas)

Founded 1985 to promote appreciation of the life and works of Sir Henry Rider Haggard, English novelist, 1856–1925. News/books exchange and meetings every 18 months.

James Hanley Network
Old School House, George Green Road,
George Green, Wexham SL3 6BJ
☎01753 578632
✉ gostick@london.com
www.jameshanley.mcmail.com/index.htm
Network Coordinator *Chris Gostick*

An informal international association founded in 1997 for all those interested in exploring and publicising the works and contribution to literature of the novelist and dramatist James Hanley (1901–1985). Publishes an annual newsletter.

Occasional conferences are planned for the future. All enquiries welcome.

The Thomas Hardy Society
PO Box 1438, Dorchester DT1 1YH
☎01305 251501 Fax 01305 251501
✉ info@hardysociety.org
www.hardysociety.org
Honorary Secretary *Mike Nixon*
SUBSCRIPTION £18 (individual); £25 (corporate); £22.50 (individual, overseas); £30 (corporate, overseas)

Founded 1967 to promote the reading and study of the works and life of Thomas Hardy. Thrice-yearly journal, events and a biennial conference. An international organisation.

The Henty Society
Hayfield, Bourne Fields, Twyford, Winchester
SO21 1NY
☎01962 713164
Honorary Secretary *Bruce Lees*
SUBSCRIPTION £13 p.a. (UK); £16 (overseas)

Founded 1977 to study the life and work of George Alfred Henty, and to publish research, bibliographical data and lesser-known works, namely short stories. Organises conferences and social gatherings in the UK and North America, and publishes bulletins to members. Published in 1996: *G.A. Henty (1832–1902) a Bibliographical Study* by Peter Newbolt (2nd edition with addenda and corrigenda 2005).

James Hilton Society
49 Beckingthorpe Drive, Bottesford,
Nottingham NG13 0DN
www.jameshiltonsociety.co.uk
Honorary Secretary *J.R. Hammond*
SUBSCRIPTION £10 (UK/EU); £7 concession

Founded 2000 to promote interest in the life and work of novelist and scriptwriter James Hilton (1900–1954). Publishes *The Hiltonian* (annually) and *The James Hilton Newsletter* (quarterly) and organises meetings and conferences.

The Dartmoor Sherlock Holmes Study Group
See **The Baskerville Hounds**

Sherlock Holmes Society (The Musgraves)
Hallas Lodge, Greenside Lane, Cullingworth,
Bradford BD13 5AP
☎01535 273468
✉ hallaslodge@btinternet.com

Contacts *John Hall, Anne Jordan*
SUBSCRIPTION £10 p.a.; £12 (joint)
Founded 1987 to promote enjoyment and study of Sir Arthur Conan Doyle's Sherlock Holmes through publications and meetings. One of the largest Sherlock Holmes societies in Great Britain. Honorary members include Bert Coules, Edward Hardwicke, Clive Merrison and Douglas Wilmer. Past honorary members: Dame Jean Conan Doyle, Peter Cushing, Jeremy Brett, Michael Williams and Richard Lancelyn Green. Open membership. Lectures, presentations and consultation on matters relating to Holmes and Conan Doyle available.

Sherlock Holmes
See **The Baskerville Hounds** and **The Franco-Midland Hardware Company**

Hopkins Society
41 North Drive, Rhyl LL18 4SW
☎01745 354151
✉ bill&meljones@aol.com
www.hopkinsoc.freeserve.co.uk
Contact *Imelda Jones*
SUBSCRIPTION £7 p.a. (UK); £10 (overseas)
Founded 1990 to celebrate the life and work of Gerard Manley Hopkins; to inform members of any publications, courses or events about the poet. Holds an annual lecture on Hopkins in the spring; produces two newsletters a year; sponsors and organises educational projects based on Hopkins' life and works.

Housman Society
80 New Road, Bromsgrove B60 2LA
☎01527 874136
✉ info@housman-society.co.uk
www.housman-society.co.uk
Contact *Jim Page*
SUBSCRIPTION £10 (UK); £12.50 (overseas)
Founded 1973 to promote knowledge and appreciation of the lives and work of A.E. Housman and other members of his family, and to promote the cause of literature and poetry. Sponsors a lecture at the **Hay Festival** each year under the title of 'The Name and Nature of Poetry'. Publishes an annual journal and biannual newsletter.

W.W. Jacobs Appreciation Society
3 Roman Road, Southwick BN42 4TP
☎01273 596217
Contact *A.R. James*
Founded 1988 to encourage and promote the enjoyment of the works of W.W. Jacobs, and stimulate research into his life and works. No subscription charge. Material available for purchase includes *W.W. Jacobs*, a biography published in 1999, price £12, post paid, and *WWJ Book Hunter's Field Guide*, a narrative bibliography published in 2001, price £6, post paid.

Richard Jefferies Society
Pear Tree Cottage, Longcot SN7 7SS
☎01793 783040
✉ R.Jefferies_Society@tiscali.co.uk
www.bath.ac.uk/~lissmc/rjeffs.htm
Honorary Secretary *Jean Saunders*
Membership Secretary *Mrs Margaret Evans*
SUBSCRIPTION £7 p.a. (individual); £8 (joint); life membership for those over 50
Founded 1950 to promote understanding of the work of Richard Jefferies, nature/country writer, novelist and mystic (1848–87). Produces newsletters, reports and an annual journal; organises talks, discussions and readings. Library and archives. Assists in maintaining the museum in Jefferies' birthplace at Coate near Swindon. Membership applications should be sent to *Margaret Evans*, 23 Hardwell Close, Grove, Nr Wantage OX12 0BN.

Jerome K. Jerome Society
c/o Fraser Wood, Mayo and Pinson, 15/16 Lichfield Street, Walsall WS1 1TS
☎01922 629000 Fax 01922 721065
✉ tonygray@jkj.demon.co.uk
www.jeromekjerome.com
Honorary Secretary *Tony Gray*
SUBSCRIPTION £7.50 p.a. (ordinary); £25 (corporate); £3.75 (under 21/over 65)
Founded 1984 to stimulate interest in Jerome K. Jerome's life and works (1859–1927). One of the Society's principal activities is the support of a small museum in the author's birthplace, Walsall. Meetings, lectures, events and a newsletter, *Idle Thoughts*. Annual dinner in Walsall near Jerome's birth date (2nd May).

The Captain W.E. Johns Appreciation Society
221 Church Road, Northolt UB5 5BE
✉ brian@zhong-ding.com
Contact (Notts. meeting) *Brian Woodruff* (at address above Tel 07843 680048)
Contact (Twyford) *Joy Tilley* (☎01785 240299)
Society for the appreciation of W.E. Johns, creator of Biggles. Meets twice a year in Nottingham and Twyford, near Reading (see

above for contacts). Biannual magazine, *Biggles Flies Again* (Editor, *Jennifer Schofield* ☎/fax 01243 671209).

Johnson Society

Johnson Birthplace Museum, Breadmarket Street, Lichfield WS13 6LG
☎01543 264972
✉ sjmuseum@lichfield.gov.uk
www.lichfieldrambler.co.uk
Chairman *Mary Baker*
SUBSCRIPTION £10 p.a.; £15 (joint); £100/£150 (life: individual/joint)
Founded 1910 to encourage the study of the life, works and times of Samuel Johnson (1709–1784) and his contemporaries. The Society is committed to the preservation of the Johnson Birthplace Museum and Johnson memorials.

Johnson Society of London

255 Baring Road, Grove Park, London SE12 0BQ
☎020 8851 0173
✉ JSL@nbbl.demon.co.uk
www.nbbl.demon.co.uk/index.html
President *Lord Harmsworth*
Honorary Secretary *Mrs Z.E. O'Donnell*
SUBSCRIPTION £15 p.a.; £18 (joint)
Founded 1928 to promote the knowledge and appreciation of Dr Samuel Johnson and his works. Publishes an annual journal, *New Rambler* and occasional newsletter. Regular meetings from October to April in the meeting room of Wesley's Chapel, City Road, London EC1 on the second Saturday of each month, and a commemoration ceremony around the anniversary of Johnson's death (December) held in Westminster Abbey.

The David Jones Society

22 Gower Road, Sketty, Swansea SA2 9BY
☎01792 206144 Fax 01792 475037
✉ anne.price-owen@sihe.ac.uk
www.sihe/ac/uk/davidjones
Contact *Anne Price-Owen*
SUBSCRIPTION £18 (individual); £30 (corporate)
Founded 1996, the Society aims to promote and encourage knowledge of the painter-poet David Jones. The Society hosts annual scholarly meetings. The annual subscription includes a copy of the *David Jones Journal*. Unsolicited material relating to David Jones, art, literature or any of his philosophies may be sent for consideration for publication in the journal.

The Just William Society

Easter Badbea, Dundonnell IV23 2QX
✉ philandpaula@easter-badbea.co.uk
Secretary/Treasurer *Paula Cross*
SUBSCRIPTION £7 p.a. (UK); £10 (overseas); £5 (juvenile/student); £15 (family)
Founded 1994 to further knowledge of Richmal Crompton's *William* and *Jimmy* books. The *Just William Society Magazines* are published throughout the year and an annual 'William' meeting is held in April.

The Keats–Shelley Memorial Association (Inc)

Registered office: 1 Satchwell Walk, Royal Priors, Leamington Spa CV32 4QE
☎01926 427400 Fax 01926 335133
Contact *Honorary Secretary*
SUBSCRIPTION £10 p.a.
Founded 1903 to promote appreciation of the works of Keats and Shelley, and their circle. One of the Society's main tasks is the preservation of 26 Piazza di Spagna in Rome as a memorial to the British Romantic poets in Italy, particularly Keats and Shelley. Publishes an annual review of Romantic Studies called the *Keats-Shelley Review*, arranges events and lectures for Friends and promotes bursaries and competitive writing on Romantic Studies (see **Keats–Shelley Prize** under *Prizes*). The *Review* is edited by *Angus Graham-Campbell*, c/o Wordsworth Trust, Dove Cottage, Grasmere LA22 9SH

The Kenny/Naughton Society

Aghamore, Ballyhaunis, Co. Mayo, Republic of Ireland
✉ paulwdr@gofree.indigo.ie
www.aghamoreireland.com/kennynaughton/society.htm
Chairman *Paul W.D. Rogers*
Patron *Mrs Erna Naughton*
Founded in 1993 to commemorate two writers who had links with Aghamore: P.D. Kenny (1862–1944), who wrote under the pseudonym 'Pat' and Bill Naughton (1910–1992), best known as the author of *Alfie*. Holds an annual school over the October bank holiday weekend which includes lectures, drama, debate and competition (**Bill Naughton Short Story Competition** – see entry under *Prizes*).

Kent & Sussex Poetry Society

39 Rockington Way, Crowborough TN6 2NJ
☎01892 662781
✉ john@kentandsussexpoetrysociety.org

www.kentandsussexpoetrysociety.org

Publicity Secretary *John Arnold*

SUBSCRIPTION £10 p.a. (full); £6 (concessionary; country members living farther afield, senior citizen, under-16, unemployed)

Founded 1946 to promote the enjoyment of poetry. Monthly meetings are held in Tunbridge Wells, including readings by major poets, a monthly workshop and an annual writing retreat week. Publishes an annual folio of members' work based on Members' Competition, adjudicated and commented upon by a major poet. Runs an annual **Open Poetry Competition** (see entry under **Prizes** and details on website) and Saturday workshops twice a year with leading poets.

The Kilvert Society

Sandalwood, North End Road, Steeple Claydon, Buckingham MK18 2PG

☎01296 730498

Secretary *Mr D. Elvins*

SUBSCRIPTION £12 p.a.; £15 (two persons at same address)

Founded 1948 to foster an interest in the Diary, the diarist and the countryside he loved. Publishes three journals each year; during the summer holds three weekends of walks, commemoration services and talks.

The Kipling Society

6 Clifton Road, London W9 1SS

☎020 7286 0194 Fax 020 7286 0194

✉ jane@keskar.fsworld.co.uk

www.kipling.org.uk

Honorary Secretary *Jane Keskar*

SUBSCRIPTION £22 p.a. (£20 p.a. by standing order)

Founded 1927. The Society's main activities are: maintaining a specialised library in London; answering enquiries from the public (schools, publishers, writers and the media); arranging a regular programme of lectures, especially in London and in Sussex, and an annual luncheon with guest speaker; maintaining a small museum and reference at The Grange, in Rottingdean near Brighton; issuing a quarterly journal. (For the Kipling mailbox discussion list, e-mail to Rudyard-Kipling@jiscmail.ac.uk) This is a literary society for all who enjoy the prose and verse of Rudyard Kipling (1865–1936) and are interested in his life and times. Please contact the Secretary by letter, telephone, fax or e-mail for further information.

The Kitley Trust

Woodstock, Litton Dale, Litton SK17 8QL

☎01298 871564

✉ stottie2@waitrose.com

Contact *Rosie Ford*

Founded 1990 by a teacher in Sheffield to promote the art of creative writing, in memory of her mother, Jessie Kitley. Activities include: biannual poetry competitions; a 'Get Poetry' day (distribution of children's poems in shopping malls); annual sponsorship of a writer for a school; campaigns; organising conferences for writers and teachers of writing. Funds are provided by donations and profits (if any) from competitions.

The Charles Lamb Society

BM EC1A, London WC1N 3XX

Chairman *Nicholas Powell*

SUBSCRIPTION UK: £12 (single); £18 (double); £18 (corporate)

Founded 1935. Publishes studies of the life, works and times of Charles Lamb and his circle. Holds meetings in London five times a year. *The Charles Lamb Bulletin* is published four times a year (Editor: *Professor Richard S Tomlinson* email romanticism@insightbb.com).

Lancashire Authors' Association

Heatherslade, 5 Quakerfields, Westhoughton, Bolton BL5 2BJ

☎01942 791390

✉ eholt@cwctv.net

General Secretary *Eric Holt*

SUBSCRIPTION £10 p.a.; £13 (joint); £1 (junior)

Founded 1909 for writers and lovers of Lancashire literature and history. Aims to foster and stimulate interest in Lancashire history and literature as well as in the preservation of the Lancashire dialect. Meets three times a year on Saturday at various locations. Publishes a quarterly journal called *The Record*, which is issued free to members, and holds eight annual competitions (open to members only) for both verse and prose. Comprehensive library with access for research to members.

The Landor Society of Warwick

11 Watersfield Gardens, Sydenham, Leamington Spa CV31 1NT

☎01926 337874

Honorary Secretary *Mrs Jean Field*

SUBSCRIPTION £7 p.a. (UK/EU); £10 (joint); £12 (overseas)

Founded 2000 to promote interest in the life and works of the Warwick-born writer Walter Savage Landor (1775–1864). Holds a Landor Birthday Lunch each year, and reading and discussion meetings most months. Publishes newsletter twice a year.

The Philip Larkin Society
16 Mere View Avenue, Hornsea HU18 1RR
☎01964 533324
✉ andreweastwood@talktalk.net
www.philiplarkin.com
General Secretary *Andrew Eastwood*
SUBSCRIPTION £18 (full rate); £12 (unwaged/senior citizen); £4 (student)

Founded in 1995 to promote awareness of the life and work of Philip Larkin (1922–1985) and his literary contemporaries; to bring together all those who admire Larkin's work as a poet, writer and librarian; to bring about publications on all things Larkinesque. Organises a programme of events ranging from lectures to rambles exploring the countryside of Larkin's schooldays and publishes a biannual journal, *About Larkin*.

The D.H. Lawrence Society
24 Briarwood Avenue, Nottingham NG3 6JQ
☎0115 950 3008
Secretary *Ron Faulks*
SUBSCRIPTION £14; £12 (concession); £16 (European); £19 (RoW)

Founded 1974 to increase knowledge and the appreciation of the life and works of D.H. Lawrence. Monthly meetings, addressed by guest speakers, are held in the library at Eastwood (birthplace of DHL). Organises visits to places of interest in the surrounding countryside, supports the activities of the D.H. Lawrence Centre at Nottingham University, and has close links with DHL Societies worldwide. Publishes two newsletters and one journal each year, free to members.

The T.E. Lawrence Society
PO Box 728, Oxford OX2 9ZJ
✉ info@telsociety.org
www.telsociety.org
www.telawrence.net
Chairman *Jeremy Wilson*
Honorary Secretary *Ian Heritage*
SUBSCRIPTION £13/18 (UK); £18/23 (overseas) Higher price includes newsletter.

Founded 1985, an educational charity, formed to advance awareness of the life and work of Thomas Edward Lawrence and to promote research into his life and work. Publishes two journals and issues four internal newsletters a year. There is a biennial symposium, usually in Oxford. The Society also hosts the telawrence.net project, an online archive of works and letters by Lawrence now out of copyright. Regional groups include three in England (Northwest, London, Dorset), one in Europe (Netherlands), two in the USA (Eastern and Western States) and one in Japan.

The Leamington Literary Society
52 Newbold Terrace East, Leamington Spa CV32 4EZ
☎01926 425733
Honorary Secretary *Mrs Margaret Watkins*
SUBSCRIPTION £10 p.a.

Founded 1912 to promote the study and appreciation of literature and the arts. Holds regular meetings every second Tuesday of the month (from September to June) at the Royal Pump Rooms, Leamington Spa. Also smaller groups which meet regularly to study poetry and the modern novel. The Society has published various books of local interest.

Lewes Monday Literary Club
c/o 1c Prince Edward's Road, Lewes BN7 1BJ
☎01273 478512
✉ chris.lutrario@btinternet.com
Contact *Christopher Lutrario*
SUBSCRIPTION £20 p.a.; £5 (guest, per meeting)

Founded in 1948 for the promotion and enjoyment of literature. Seven meetings are held during the winter generally on the last Monday of each month (from October to April) at the Pelham House Hotel in Lewes. The Club attracts speakers of the highest quality and a balance between all forms of literature is aimed for. Guests are welcome to attend meetings.

The George MacDonald Society
4 Hereford Drive, Handforth, Wilmslow SK9 3BB
☎ 01625 527327
✉ partridge@dsl.pipex.com
www.macdonaldsociety.org *linked with*
www.george-macdonald.com
Contact *Mike Partridge*
SUBSCRIPTION £10 p.a. (individual); £13 (joint); £7 (unwaged); £11 (overseas)

Founded 1981 to increase awareness of 'the uniqueness and importance of MacDonald's writings'. Notable among Victorian writers for his radical mixture of genres: MacDonald's fantasy works influenced H.G. Wells, C.S. Lewis and J.R.R. Tolkien, among many others, and his 'realistic' novels offered a fascinating glimpse into Victorian Scottish life. The Society organises conferences and workshops in Britain and abroad, often in association with other societies with related interests. Publishes an annual journal, *North Wind*, with contributions from most of the leading MacDonald scholars worldwide and a newsletter, *Orts*.

The Friends of Arthur Machen

Apt 5, 26 Hervey Road, Blackheath, London SE3 8BS
www.machensoc.demon.co.uk
Contact *Jeremy Cantwell*
SUBSCRIPTION £17 p.a. (UK); £20 (Europe/RoW); $36 (US)

Brings together those who appreciate Machen's writings and generally promotes discussion and research. Publishes two journals and two newsletters annually, plus occasional publications for the membership only.

The Marlowe Society

9 Middlefield Gardens, Hurst Green Road, Halesowen B62 9QH
☎0121 421 1482 Fax 0121 421 1482
✉ marsocpt@aol.com
www.marlowe-society.org
Membership Secretary *Frieda Barker*
Treasurer *Bruce Young*
SUBSCRIPTION £12 p.a. (individual); £7 p.a. (pensioner/student/unwaged); £15 p.a. (overseas); £200 (group); £100 (individual life membership)

Founded 1955. Holds meetings, lectures and discussions, stimulates research into Marlowe's life and works, encourages production of his plays and publishes a biannual newsletter. At a ceremony on 11th July 2002 the Society celebrated their success in establishing a memorial to the playwright and poet in Poets' Corner in Westminster Abbey.

The John Masefield Society

The Frith, Ledbury HR8 1LW
☎01531 631647 Fax 01531 631647
✉ pcarter2@wanadoo.fr
www2.sas.ac.uk/ies/cmps/Projects/Masefield/Society/jms1.htm
Chairman *Peter Carter*
SUBSCRIPTION £5 p.a. (individual); £8 (family, institution, library); £10 (overseas); £2.50 (junior, student)

Founded in 1992 to stimulate the appreciation of and interest in the life and works of John Masefield (Poet Laureate 1930–1967). The Society is based in Ledbury, the Herefordshire market town of his birth and holds various public events in addition to publishing a journal and occasional papers.

William Morris Society

Kelmscott House, 26 Upper Mall, Hammersmith, London W6 9TA
☎020 8741 3735 Fax 020 8748 5207
✉ william.morris@care4free.net
www.morrissociety.org
Contact *Helen Elletson*
SUBSCRIPTION £18 p.a.

Founded 1955 to promote interest in the life, work and ideas of William Morris (1834–1896), English poet and craftsman.

The Neil Munro Society

8 Briar Road, Kirkintilloch, Glasgow G66 3SA
☎0141 776 4280
✉ brian@bdosborne.fsnet.co.uk
www.neilmunro.co.uk
Secretary *Brian D. Osborne*
SUBSCRIPTION £12 (annual); £7 (unwaged); £15 (institutional)

Founded in 1996 to encourage interest in the works of Neil Munro (1863–1930), the Scottish novelist, short story writer, poet and journalist. An annual programme of meetings is held in Glasgow and Munro's home-town of Inveraray. Publishes *ParaGraphs*, a twice-yearly magazine, sponsors reprints of Munro's work and is developing a Munro archive.

Bill Naughton

See **The Kenny/Naughton Society**

Violet Needham Society

c/o 19 Ashburnham Place, London SE10 8TZ
☎020 8692 4562
✉ richardcheffins@aol.com
Honorary Secretary *R.H.A. Cheffins*
SUBSCRIPTION £7.50 p.a. (UK & Europe); £11 (RoW)

Founded 1985 to celebrate the work of children's author Violet Needham and stimulate critical awareness of her work. Publishes thrice-yearly *Souvenir*, the Society journal with an accompanying newsletter; organises meetings and excursions to places associated with the author and her books. The journal includes articles about other children's writers of the 1940s and 1950s and on ruritanian fiction. Contributions welcome.

The Edith Nesbit Society
21 Churchfields, West Malling ME19 6RJ
www.the-railway-children.co.uk
Chairman *Margaret McCarthy*
SUBSCRIPTION £7 p.a.; £9 (joint); £80 (life)

Founded in 1996 to celebrate the life and work of Edith Nesbit (1858–1924), best known as the author of *The Railway Children*. The Society's activities include a regular newsletter, booklets, talks and visits to relevant places.

The Wilfred Owen Association
c/o 17 Belmont, Shrewsbury SY1 1TE
☎01743 460089
www.1914-19.co.uk/owen
Chairman *Michael Grayer*
SUBSCRIPTION Adults £6 (£10 overseas); £4 (senior citizen/student/unemployed); £15 (UK group/institution); £25 (overseas group/institution)

Founded 1989 to commemorate the life and works of Wilfred Owen by promoting readings, visits, talks and performances relating to Owen and his work. The Association offers practical support for students of literature and future poets through links with education, support for literary foundations and information on historical and literary background material. Membership is international with 700 members. Publishes a regular newsletter and annual journal. Speakers are available.

The Elsie Jeanette Oxenham Appreciation Society
32 Tadfield Road, Romsey SO51 5AJ
☎01794 517149
✉ abbey@bufobooks.demon.co.uk
www.bufobooks.demon.co.uk/abbeylnk.htm
Membership Secretary/Treasurer *Ms Ruth Allen*
Editor (*The Abbey Chronicle*) *Fiona Dyer* (fionadyer@btopenworld.com)
SUBSCRIPTION £7.50 p.a.; enquire for overseas rates

Founded 1989 to promote the works of Elsie J. Oxenham. Publishes a newsletter for members, *The Abbey Chronicle*, three times a year. 500+ members.

Thomas Paine Society
43 Eugene Gardens, Nottingham NG2 3LF
☎0115 986 0010
President *The Rt. Hon. Michael Foot*

Honorary Secretary *R. W. Morrell, MBE* (at address above)
Treasurer *Stuart Wright*
SUBSCRIPTION (minimum) £15 p.a. (UK); $35 (overseas); £5 (unwaged/pensioner/student)

Founded 1963 to promote the life and work of Thomas Paine, and continues to expound his ideals. Meetings, newsletters, lectures and research assistance. The Society has members worldwide and keeps in touch with American and French Thomas Paine associations. Publishes magazine, *The Journal of Radical History*, twice yearly (Editor, *R. W. Morrell*) and a newsletter. Holds occasional exhibitions and lectures, including the biannual Thomas Paine Memorial Lecture and the annual Eric Paine Memorial Lecture.

The Beatrix Potter Society
The Lodge, Salisbury Avenue, Harpenden AL5 2PS
☎01582 769755
✉ beatrixpottersociety@tiscali.co.uk
www.beatrixpottersociety.org.uk
Membership Secretary *Jenny Akester*
SUBSCRIPTION UK: £20 p.a. (individual); £25 (institution); Overseas: £25 (individual); £30 (institution)

Founded 1980 to promote the study and appreciation of the life and works of Beatrix Potter (1866–1943). Potter was not only the author of *The Tale of Peter Rabbit* and other classics of children's literature; she was also a landscape and natural history artist, diarist, farmer and conservationist, and was responsible for the preservation of large areas of the Lake District through her gifts to the National Trust. The Society upholds and protects the integrity of the unique work of Potter, her aims and bequests; holds regular talks and meetings in London and elsewhere with visits to places connected with Beatrix Potter. International Study Conferences are held in the UK and the USA. The Society has an active publishing programme. (UK Registered Charity No. 281198.)

Anthony Powell Society
76 Ennismore Avenue, Greenford UB6 0JW
☎020 8864 4095 Fax 020 8864 6109
✉ secretary@anthonypowell.org
www.anthonypowell.org
Patron *John M. A. Powell*
Honorary Secretary *Dr Keith C. Marshall*
SUBSCRIPTION £20 p.a. (individual); £30 (joint/gold); £12 (student); £100 (organisation)

Founded in June 2000 to advance education and interest in the life and works of the English author Anthony Powell (1905–2000). The Society's major activity is a biennial Powell conference, the first three of which were at Eton College (2001), Balliol College, Oxford (2003) and the Powell Centenary conference at The Wallace Collection, London (2005). The Society organises events for members, ranging from 'pub meets' to talks and visits to places of Powell interest as well as publishing a quarterly *Newsletter*. Member of the **Alliance of Literary Societies**.

The Powys Society

25 Mansfield Road, Taunton TA1 3NJ
☎01823 278177
✉ peter_lazare@hotmail.com
www.powys-society.org
Honorary Secretary *Peter Lazare*
SUBSCRIPTION £18.50 (UK); £22 (overseas); £10 (student)

The Society (with a membership of 300) aims to promote public education and recognition of the writings, thought and contribution to the arts of the Powys family; particularly of John Cowper, Theodore and Llewelyn, but also of the other members of the family and their close associates. The Society holds two major collections of Powys published works, letters, manuscripts and memorabilia. Publishes the *Powys Society Newsletter* in April, June and November and *The Powys Journal* in August. Organises an annual conference as well as lectures and meetings in Powys places.

The J.B. Priestley Society

Eldwick Crag Farm, Otley Road, Bingley BD16 3BB
☎01274 563078
✉ reavill@globalnet.co.uk
www.jbpriestley-society.com
President *Tom Priestley*
Chairman *Dr Ken Smith*
Honorary Secretary *R.E.Y. Slater*
Membership Secretary *Tony Reavill*
SUBSCRIPTION £12 (individual); £7 (concession); £18 (group/family)

Founded 1997 to widen the knowledge and understanding of Priestley's works; promote the study of his life and his social, cultural and political influences; provide members of the Society with lectures, seminars, films, journals and stimulate education projects; promote public performances of his works and the distribution of material associated with him. For further information, contact the Membership Secretary at the address above.

The Barbara Pym Society

St Hilda's College, Oxford OX4 1DU
☎01865 276867 Fax 01865 276820
✉ eileen.roberts@st-hildas.oxford.ac.uk
www.pym.org
Chairman *Deirdre Bryan-Brown*
SUBSCRIPTION £15 p.a. (individual); £22 p.a. (household); £8 p.a. (concession)

Aims to promote interest in and scholarly research into the works of Barbara Pym; to bring together like-minded people to enjoy the exploration of all aspects of her novels and to continue to encourage publishers to keep her novels in print. Annual weekend conference at St. Hilda's College in September, focusing on a theme or a particular novel. Annual North American Conference at Harvard Law School. Annual one-day spring meeting in London, with speaker. Publishes a newsletter, *Green Leaves*, biannually. In addition to reports on conferences and society activities, the newsletter includes scholarly papers and various unpublished items from the Pym archives at the Bodleian Library (i.e. short stories).

The Queen's English Society

Honorary Secretary: The Clergy House, Hide Place, London SW1P 4NJ
☎020 7630 1819
✉ enquiries@queens-english-society.com
www.queens-english-society.com
Honorary Secretary *Mr G.J. Hardwick*
SUBSCRIPTION £12 p.a. (ordinary); £15 (family/corporate)

Founded in 1972 to promote and uphold the use of good English and to encourage the enjoyment of the language. Holds regular meetings and conferences to which speakers are invited, an annual luncheon and publishes a quarterly journal, *Quest*, for which original articles are welcome.

Rainbow Poetry Recitals

14 Lewes Crescent, Brighton BN2 1FH
☎01424 444072
Administrator *Hugh Hellicar*
SUBSCRIPTION £6.50/€10 (individual); £10/€15 (joint/family); £12 (school)

Founded 1994. Regular recitals of poetry and other literature are held in Sussex, Kent and London. Seminars in some branches. Research library in Sussex. Quarterly magazine with overseas distribution.

The Arthur Ransome Society Ltd

Abbot Hall Art Gallery & Museum, Kendal
LA9 5AL
☎01539 722464
✉ tarsinfo@arthur-ransome.org
www.arthur-ransome.org/ar
Trustee Chairman *Geraint Lewis*
Company Secretary *Mike Glover*
SUBSCRIPTION UK: £5 (junior); £10
(student); £15 (adult); £20 (family);
£40 (corporate); Overseas: £5 (junior);
£10 (student); £20 (adult); £25 (family)
Payable in local currency in US, Canada,
Australia, Japan and New Zealand

Founded in 1990 to celebrate the life and to promote the works and ideas of Arthur Ransome, author of *Swallows and Amazons* titles for children, biographer of Oscar Wilde, works on the Russian Revolution and extensive articles on fishing. TARS seeks to encourage children and adults to engage in adventurous pursuits, to educate the public about Ransome and his works, and to sponsor research into his literary works and life.

The Romany Society

10 Haslam Street, Bury BL9 6EQ
☎0161 764 7078
✉ phil_shelley@btopenworld.com
www.romanysociety.org.uk
Honorary Secretary *John Thorpe* (at address above)
Publications Officer *Phil Shelley*
SUBSCRIPTION £5 (individual); £9 (family);
£10 (institution); £3.50 (student/unwaged)

Promotes the life, work and conservation message of the Rev. G. Bramwell Evens – 'Romany' – the first broadcasting naturalist who influenced generations of listeners with his *Out With Romany* radio programmes on the BBC during the 1930s and 1940s and with his series of natural history books. The Romany Society was established originally following Evens' death at the age of 59 in 1943 and ran until 1965. Revived in 1996, the Society holds an annual members' weekend in areas of significance in the Romany story, erects memorial plaques where appropriate, encourages media coverage of Romany and supports young naturalists with the Romany Memorial Grant.

The Followers of Rupert

31 Whiteley, Windsor SL4 5PJ
☎01753 865562

✉ followersofrupert@hotmail.com
www.rupertthebear.org.uk
Membership Secretary *Mrs Shirley Reeves*
SUBSCRIPTION UK: £18; £20 (joint); Europe,
airmail: £21 (individual); £23 (joint); RoW,
airmail: £23 (individual); £25 (joint)

Founded in 1983. The Society caters for the growing interest in the Rupert Bear stories, past, present and future. Publishes the *Nutwood Newsletter* quarterly which gives up-to-date news of Rupert and information on Society activities. A national get-together of members – the Followers Annual – is held during the autumn.

The Ruskin Society of London

20 Parmoor Court, Summerfield, Oxford
OX2 7XB
☎01865 310987   Fax 01865 240448
Honorary Secretary *Miss O.E. Forbes-Madden*
SUBSCRIPTION £15 p.a.

Founded 1986 to promote interest in John Ruskin (1819–1900) and his contemporaries. All aspects of Ruskinia are introduced. Functions are held in London. Publishes the annual *Ruskin Gazette*, a journal concerned with Ruskin's influence. Affiliated to other literary societies.

The Ruskin Society

49 Hallam Street, London W1W 6JP
☎020 7580 1894
✉ cgamble@britishlibrary.net
www.lancs.ac.uk/depts/ruskin/links.htm
Chairman *Professor Michael Wheeler*
Honorary Secretary *Dr Cynthia. J. Gamble*
SUBSCRIPTION £10 p.a. (payable on 1st Jan.)

Founded in 1997 to encourage a wider understanding of John Ruskin and his contemporaries. Organises lectures and events which seek not only to explain to the public at large the nature of Ruskin's theories but also to place these in a modern context.

The Malcolm Saville Society

78a Windmill Road, Mortimer RG7 3RL
✉ mystery@witchend.com
www.witchend.com
Chairman *Richard Griffiths*
SUBSCRIPTION £7.50 p.a. (UK/EU);
£12 (overseas)

Founded in 1994 to remember and promote interest in the work of the popular children's author. Regular social activities, booksearch, library, contact directory and four magazines per year.

The Dorothy L. Sayers Society

Rose Cottage, Malthouse Lane, Hurstpierpoint BN6 9JY
☎01273 833444 Fax 01273 835988
www.sayers.org.uk
Contact *Christopher Dean*
SUBSCRIPTION £14 p.a. (UK); £16.50 (Europe); $34 (US)

Founded 1976 to promote the study of the life, works and thoughts of Dorothy Sayers; to encourage the performance of her plays and publication of her books and books about her; to preserve original material and provide assistance to researchers. Acts as a forum and information centre, providing material for study purposes which would otherwise be unavailable. Annual conventions, usually in August and other meetings. Co-founder of the Dorothy L. Sayers Centre in Witham. Publishes bi-monthly bulletin, annual proceedings and other papers.

The Shaw Society

Flat F, 10 Compton Road, London N1 2PA
☎020 7226 4266
✉ shawsociety@blueyonder.so.uk
Honorary Secretary *Alan Knight*
SUBSCRIPTION £15 p.a. (individual); £22 (joint)

Founded 1941 to promote interest in the life and works of G. Bernard Shaw. Meetings are held on the last Friday of every month (except July, August and December) at Conway Hall, Red Lion Square, London WC1 (6.30 pm for 7.00 pm) at which speakers are invited to talk on some aspect of Shaw's life or works. Monthly playreadings are held on the first Friday of each month (except August). Over 40 years ago the Society began the annual open-air performance held at Shaw's Corner, Ayot St Lawrence in Hertfordshire, on the weekend nearest to Shaw's birthday (26th July). Publishes a quarterly newsletter and a biannual magazine, *The Shavian.* (No payment for contributors.)

The Robert Southey Society

1 Lewis Terrace, Abergarwed, Neath SA11 4DL
☎01639 711480
Contact *Robert King*
SUBSCRIPTION £10 p.a.

Founded 1990 to promote the work of Robert Southey. Publishes an annual newsletter and arranges talks on his life and work. Open membership.

The Laurence Sterne Trust

See **The Friends of Shandy Hall**

Robert Louis Stevenson Club

12 Dean Park, Longniddry EH32 0QR
☎01875 852976 Fax 01875 853328
✉ alan@amarchbank.freeserve.co.uk
www.rlsclub.org.uk
Secretary *Alan Marchbank*
SUBSCRIPTION £20 p.a. (individual); £26 p.a. (overseas); £150 (10-year)

Founded in 1920 to foster interest in Robert Louis Stevenson's life and works. The Club organises an annual lunch and other events. Publishes *RLS Club News* twice a year.

The R.S. Surtees Society

Manor Farm House, Nunney, Near Frome BA11 4NJ
☎01373 836937 Fax 01373 836574
✉ rssurtees@fsmail.net
www.r.s.surteessociety.org
Contact *Orders and Membership Secretary* (☎01373 302155)

Founded 1979 to republish the works of R.S. Surtees and others.

The Tennyson Society

Central Library, Free School Lane, Lincoln LN2 1EZ
☎01522 552862 Fax 01522 552858
✉ kathleenjefferson@lincolnshire.gov.uk
www.tennysonsociety.org.uk
Honorary Secretary *Miss K. Jefferson*
SUBSCRIPTION £10 p.a. (individual); £12 (family); £15 (corporate); £160 (life)

Founded 1960. An international society with membership worldwide. Exists to promote the study and understanding of the life and work of Alfred, Lord Tennyson. The Society is concerned with the work of the Tennyson Research Centre, 'probably the most significant collection of mss, family papers and books in the world'. Publishes annually the *Tennyson Research Bulletin*, which contains articles and critical reviews; and organises lectures, visits and seminars. Annual memorial service at Somersby in Lincolnshire.

The Angela Thirkell Society

54 Belmont Park, London SE13 5BN
☎020 8244 9339
✉ penny.aldred@ntlworld.com
www.angelathirkellsociety.com
www.angelathirkell.org (N. American branch)

Honorary Secretary *Mrs. P. Aldred*
SUBSCRIPTION £10 p.a.

Founded in 1980 to honour the memory of Angela Thirkell as a writer and to make her works available to new generations. Publishes an annual journal, holds an AGM in the autumn and a spring meeting which usually takes the form of a visit to a location associated with Thirkell. Has a flourishing North American branch which has frequent contact with the UK parent society.

The Dylan Thomas Society of Great Britain
Fern Hill, 24 Chapel Street, Mumbles, Swansea SA3 4NH
☎01792 363875

Contact *Mrs Cecily Hughes*
SUBSCRIPTION £5 (individual); £8 (two adults from same household)

Founded 1977 to foster an understanding of the work of Dylan Thomas and to extend members' awareness of other 20th century writers, especially Welsh writers in English. Meetings take place monthly, mainly in Swansea.

The Edward Thomas Fellowship
1 Carfax, Undercliff Drive, St Lawrence, Isle of Wight PO38 1XG
☎01983 853366
✉ colingthornton@btopenworld.com
www.edward-thomas-fellowship.org.uk

Hon. Secretary *Colin G. Thornton*
SUBSCRIPTION £7 p.a. (single); £10 p.a. (joint)

Founded 1980 to perpetuate and promote the memory of Edward Thomas and to encourage an appreciation of his life and work. The Fellowship holds a commemorative birthday walk on the Sunday nearest the poet's birthday (3rd March); issues newsletters and holds various events.

The Tolkien Society
65 Wentworth Crescent, Ash Vale GU12 5LF
Fax 0870 0525569
✉ membership@tolkiensociety.org
www.tolkiensociety.org
Membership Secretary *Trevor Reynolds*
SUBSCRIPTION £20 p.a. (UK); £22 (overseas)

An international organisation which aims to encourage and further interest in the life and works of the late Professor J.R.R. Tolkien, CBE, author of *The Hobbit* and *Lord of the Rings*. Current membership stands at 1200. Publishes *Mallorn* annually and *Amon Hen* bi-monthly.

The Trollope Society
Maritime House, Old Town, Clapham, London SW4 0JW
☎020 7720 6789 Fax 020 7627 2965
✉ info@trollopesociety.org
www.trollopesociety.org

Contacts *John Letts, Phyllis Eden*

Founded 1987 to study and promote Anthony Trollope's works. Publishes the complete works of Trollope's novels and travel books.

Wainwright Society
Kendal Museum, Station Road, Kendal LA9 6BT
☎01539 721374 Fax 01539 737976
✉ membership@wainwright.org.uk
www.wainwright.org.uk

Membership Secretary *Morag Clement*
SUBSCRIPTION £10 p.a. (per household, from 1st Jan.)

Founded in 2002 'to keep alive the things that Alfred Wainwright (1907–1991) promoted through his guidebooks (*Pictorial Guides to the Lakeland Fells*), started 50 years ago, and the many other publications which were the "labour of love" of a large portion of his life'. Produces a newsletter three times per year, organises walks, events, annual dinner and lecture.

The Walmsley Society
April Cottage, No 1 Brand Road, Hampden Park, Eastbourne BN22 9PX
☎01323 506447
✉ walmsley@haughshw.demon.co.uk

Honorary Secretary *Fred Lane*
SUBSCRIPTION £12 p.a.; £14 (family); £11 (student/senior citizen); £17 (overseas, £27 for 2 years)

Founded 1985 to promote interest in the writings of Leo Walmsley and to foster an appreciation of the work of his father, the artist Ulric Walmsley. Two annual meetings – one held in Robin Hood's Bay on the East Yorkshire coast, spiritual home of the author Leo Walmsley. Publishes a journal twice-yearly and newsletters, and is involved in other publications which benefit the aims of the Society. A biography of Leo Walmsley is now available.

Sylvia Townsend Warner Society
2 Vicarage Lane, Fordington, Dorchester DT1 1LH
☎01305 266028
✉ judith@bond.vispa.com
www.townsendwarner.com

Contact *Eileen Johnson*
SUBSCRIPTION £10 p.a.; $20 (overseas)
Founded in 2000 to promote a wider readership and better understanding of the writings of Sylvia Townsend Warner.

Mary Webb Society
8 The Knowe, Willaston, Neston CH64 1TA
☎0151 327 5843
✉ suehigginbotham@yahoo.co.uk
www.marywebb.VZE.com
Secretary *Sue Higginbotham*
SUBSCRIPTION UK: £10 p.a. (individual);
£13 p.a. (joint); Overseas: £13 p.a.
(individual); £15 p.a. (joint)
Founded 1972. Attracts members from the UK and overseas who are devotees of the literature of Mary Webb and of the beautiful Shropshire countryside of her novels. Publishes biannual journal, organises summer schools in various locations related to the authoress's life and works. Archives; lectures; tours arranged for individuals and groups.

H.G. Wells Society
51 Riseholme Road, Gainsborough
DN21 1YT
hgwellsusa.50megs.com
Honorary Secretary *Dr S. McLean*
SUBSCRIPTION £16 (UK/EU); £19 (overseas);
£20 (corporate); £10 (concessions)
Founded 1960 to promote an interest in and appreciation of the life, work and thought of Herbert George Wells. Publishes *The Wellsian* (annual) and *The H.G. Wells Newsletter* (three issues yearly). Organises meetings and conferences.

The Oscar Wilde Society
100 Peacock Street, Gravesend DA12 1EQ
✉ vanessasalome68@aol.com
Honorary Secretary *Vanessa Harris*
Founded 1990 to promote knowledge, appreciation and study of the life, personality and works of the writer and wit Oscar Wilde. Activities include meetings, lectures, readings and exhibitions, and visits to locations associated with Wilde. Members receive a journal, *The Wildean*, twice-yearly and a newsletter, *Intentions* (six per year).

The Charles Williams Society
35 Broomfield, Stacey Bushes, Milton Keynes
MK12 6HA
✉ charles_wms_soc@yahoo.co.uk

www.geocities.com/charles_wms_soc
Contact *Honorary Secretary*
Founded 1975 to promote interest in, and provide a means for the exchange of views and information on the life and work of Charles Walter Stansby Williams (1886–1945).

The Henry Williamson Society
7 Monmouth Road, Dorchester DT1 2DE
☎01305 264092
✉ zseagull@aol.com
www.henrywilliamson.org
General Secretary *Mrs Sue Cumming*
Membership Secretary *Mrs Margaret Murphy*
(16 Doran Drive, Redhill RH1 6AX
☎01737 763228;
mm@misterman.freeserve.co.uk)
SUBSCRIPTION £12 p.a.; £15 (family);
£5 (student)
Founded 1980 to encourage, by all appropriate means, a wider readership and deeper understanding of the literary heritage left by the 20th-century English writer Henry Williamson (1895–1977). Publishes annual journal.

The P.G. Wodehouse Society (UK)
26 Radcliffe Road, Croydon CR0 5QE
✉ christinehewitt@waitrose.com
www.pgwodehousesociety.org.uk
www.eclipse.co.uk/wodehouse
Membership Secretary *Christine Hewitt*
SUBSCRIPTION £15 p.a. (£20 Dec. to March, for membership extended to May the following year)
Formed in 1997 to promote enjoyment of the works of P.G. Wodehouse, author, lyricist, playwright and journalist, creator of Lord Emsworth, Jeeves & Wooster and many more. Membership of 1000+. Publications include the quarterly journal, *Wooster Sauce* and regular *By The Way* papers. Meetings and events are held in London and around the country. The Society is allied to Wodehouse societies around the world.

The Parson Woodforde Society
22 Gaynor Close, Wymondham NR18 0EA
☎01953 604124
✉ mabrayne@supanet.com
www.parsonwoodforde.org.uk
Membership Secretary *Mrs Ann Elliott*
SUBSCRIPTION £12.50 (UK); £25 (overseas)
Founded 1968. Aims to extend and develop knowledge of James Woodforde's life and the society in which he lived and to provide the

opportunity for fellow enthusiasts to meet together in places associated with the diarist. Publishes a quarterly journal and newsletter. The Society is producing a complete edition of the diary of James Woodforde. To date, fifteen volumes of diary material have been published covering the period 1759–1797.

The Virginia Woolf Society of Great Britain

Fairhaven, Charnleys Lane, Banks, Southport PR9 8HJ
✉ stuart.n.clarke@btinternet.com
www.virginiawoolfsociety.co.uk
Contact *Stuart N. Clarke*
SUBSCRIPTION £15 p.a.; £20 (overseas)

Founded 1998 to promote interest in the life and work of Virginia Woolf, author, essayist and diarist. The Society's activities include trips away, walks, reading groups and talks. Publishes a literary journal, *Virginia Woolf Bulletin*, three times a year.

The Wordsworth Trust

Dove Cottage, Grasmere LA22 9SH
☎015394 35544 Fax 015394 35748
✉ enquiries@wordsworth.org.uk
www.wordsworth.org.uk
Contacts *Allan King, Ann Pease*

Founded in 1890, the Trust is a living memorial to the life and poetry of William Wordsworth and his contemporaries. As Centre for British Romanticism, the Wordsworth Trust, with its wealth of manuscripts, books, drawings and pictures, provides 'the full context for understanding and celebrating a major cultural moment in history in which Britain played a profound role'. (Registered Charity No. 1066184.)

WW2 HMSO PPBKS Society

3 Roman Road, Southwick BN42 4TP
☎01273 596217
Contact *A.R. James*

Founded 1994 to encourage collectors and to promote research into HMSO's World War II series of paperbacks. Most of them were written by well-known authors, though in many cases anonymously. No subscription charge. Available for purchase: Collectors' Guide (£5); Handbook, *Informing the People* (£10).

The Yeats Society Sligo

Yeats Memorial Building, Hyde Bridge, Sligo, Republic of Ireland
☎00 353 71 914 2693
Fax 00 353 71 914 2780
✉ info@yeats-sligo.com
www.yeats-sligo.com
President *Aleck Crichton*
SUBSCRIPTION €25 (single); €40 (couple)

Founded in 1958 to promote the heritage of W.B. Yeats and the Yeats family. Attractions include continuous updated Yeats exhibitions for public viewing, annual Yeats International Summer School in July/August and Yeats Winter School in January. The Yeats Summer Festival is held each August and lectures are held in the winter and spring, sponsored by the Institute of Technology, Sligo. Poetry readings and workshops aimed at local writers are held on a regular basis in conjunction with Arts Officer, Sligo Co. Council.

The Charlotte M. Yonge Fellowship

8 Anchorage Terrace, Durham DH1 3DL
☎0191 384 7857
www.cmyf.org.uk
Contact *Dr C.E. Schultze*
SUBSCRIPTION £9 p.a.

Founded 1996 to provide the opportunity for all those who enjoy and admire the work of Charlotte M. Yonge (1823–1901), author of *The Heir of Radclyffe*, to learn more about her life and writings. Holds two meetings annually, one in November in London and the other, the spring AGM, at venues associated with Yonge's life, works or interests, or where buildings or gallery and museum collections relate to to Victorian history, art and society. Publishes a review twice-yearly and an occasional journal. A loan collection of Yonge's worrks enables members to borrow publications that are hard to obtain. The Fellowship's archive is held at St Hugh's College, Oxford and material is available to members and bona fide researchers.

Yorkshire Dialect Society

51 Stepney Avenue, Scarborough YO12 5BW
Secretary *Michael Park*
SUBSCRIPTION £10 p.a.

Founded 1897 to promote interest in and preserve a record of the Yorkshire dialect. Publishes dialect verse and prose writing. Two journals to members annually. Details of publications are available from YDS at address above.

Francis Brett Young Society

92 Gower Road, Halesowen B62 9BT
☎0121 422 8969
www.fbysociety.co.uk

Honorary Secretary *Mrs Jean Hadley*
SUBSCRIPTION £7 p.a. (individual);
£10 (couple sharing a journal);
£5 (student); £7 (organisation/overseas);
£70 (life); £100 (joint, life)

Founded 1979. Aims to provide a forum for those interested in the life and works of English novelist Francis Brett Young and to collate research on him. Promotes lectures, exhibitions and readings; publishes a regular newsletter.

Arts Councils and Regional Offices

Arts Council England
14 Great Peter Street, London SW1P 3NQ
☎0845 300 6200 Textphone 020 7973 6564
✉ enquiries@artscouncil.org.uk
www.artscouncil.org.uk
Chairman *Professor Sir Christopher Frayling*
Chief Executive *Peter Hewitt*
Director of Literature *Gary McKeone*

Founded 1946. Arts Council England is the national development agency for the arts in England, distributing public money from government and the National Lottery to artists and arts organisations. ACE works independently and at arm's length from government. Information about Arts Council England funding is available on the website, by e-mail or by contacting the enquiry line on 0845 300 6200.

Arts Council England has 9 regional offices:

Arts Council England, East
Eden House, 48–49 Bateman Street, Cambridge CB2 1LR
☎0845 300 6200 Fax 0870 242 1271
Textphone 01223 306893

Arts Council England, East Midlands
St Nicholas Court, 25–27 Castle Gate, Nottingham NG1 7AR
☎0845 300 6200 Fax 0115 950 2467

Arts Council England, London
2 Pear Tree Court, London EC1R 0DS
☎0845 300 6200 Fax 020 7608 4100
Textphone 020 7973 6564

Arts Council England, North East
Central Square, Forth Street, Newcastle upon Tyne NE1 3PJ
☎0845 300 6200 Fax 0191 230 1020
Textphone 0191 255 8585

Arts Council England, North West
Manchester House, 22 Bridge Street, Manchester M3 3AB
☎0845 300 6200 Fax 0161 834 6969
Textphone 0161 834 9131

Arts Council England, South East
Sovereign House, Church Street, Brighton BN1 1RA
☎0845 300 6200 Fax 0870 242 1257
Textphone 01273 710659

Arts Council England, South West
Senate Court, Southernhay Gardens, Exeter EX1 1UG
☎0845 300 6200 Fax 01392 229229
Textphone 01392 433503

Arts Council England, West Midlands
82 Granville Street, Birmingham B1 2LH
☎0845 300 6200 Fax 0121 643 7239
Textphone 0121 643 2815

Arts Council England, Yorkshire
21 Bond Street, Dewsbury WF13 1AX
☎0845 300 6200 Fax 01924 466522
Textphone 01924 438585

The Arts Council/
An Chomhairle Ealaíon
70 Merrion Square, Dublin 2
Republic of Ireland
☎00 353 1 618 0200   Fax 00 353 1 676 1302
✉ artistsservices@artscouncil.ie
www.artscouncil.ie
Director *Mary Cloake*
Literature Specialist (English language)
Bronwen Williams
Literature Specialist (Irish language) *Róisin Ní Mhianáin*
Artists' Services Manager *Paul Johnson*

The Arts Council is the Irish government agency for developing the arts. It provides financial assistance to artists, arts organisations, local authorities and others for artistic purposes. It offers advice and information on the arts to Government and to a wide range of individuals and organisations. As an advocate for the arts and artists, the Arts Council undertakes projects and research, often in new and emerging areas of arts practice, and increasingly in cooperation with partner organisations. Its funding from government for 2006 was €72.3 million.

Of particular interest to individual writers is the Council's free booklet, *Support for Artists 2006*, which describes bursaries, awards and schemes on offer and how to apply for them.

Applicants to these awards must have been born in, or be resident in, the Republic of Ireland.

The Arts Council of Northern Ireland

MacNeice House, 77 Malone Road, Belfast BT9 6AQ
☎028 9038 5200 Fax 028 9066 1715
✉ dsmyth@artscouncil-ni.org
www.artscouncil-ni.org
Literature and Language Arts Officer *Damian Smyth*

Funds book production by established publishers, programmes of readings, literary festivals, writers-in-residence schemes and literary magazines and periodicals. Occasional schools programmes and anthologies of children's writing are produced. Annual awards and bursaries for writers are available. Holds information also on various groups associated with local arts, workshops and courses.

Scottish Arts Council

12 Manor Place, Edinburgh EH3 7DD
☎0131 226 6051 Fax 0131 225 9833
✉ help.desk@scottisharts.org.uk
www.scottisharts.org.uk
Chief Executive *Graham Berry*
Head of Literature *Gavin Wallace*
Literature Officers *Jenny Attala, Aly Barr, Emma Turnbull*
Literature Administrator *Catherine Allan*

Principal channel for government funding of the arts in Scotland. The Scottish Arts Council is funded by the Scottish Executive and National Lottery. It aims to develop and improve the knowledge, understanding and practise of the arts, and to increase their accessibility throughout Scotland. It offers grants to artists and arts organisations concerned with the visual arts, crafts, dance and mime, drama, literature, music, festivals and traditional, ethnic and community arts. Scottish Arts Council's support for Scottish-based writers with a track record of publication includes bursaries, writing fellowships and book awards (see entries under **Bursaries, Fellowships and Grants** and **Prizes**). Information offered includes lists of literature awards, literary magazines, agents and publishers.

The Arts Council of Wales/ Cyngor Celfyddydau Cymru

9 Museum Place, Cardiff CF10 3NX
☎029 2037 6500 Fax 029 2022 1447
www.artswales.org.uk
www.celfcymru.org.uk

The Arts Council of Wales (ACW) is the development body for the arts in Wales. ACW's Creative Wales Awards offer substantial grants for established writers and playwrights. Funds the **Welsh Academy** and **Ty Newydd Writers' Centre** to provide services to individual writers, including bursaries, mentoring, the critical writers services and writers in residence/on tour. Responsibility for promoting the publishing and sales of books from Wales and funding literary magazines rests with the **Welsh Books Council**.

UK and Irish Writers' Courses

ENGLAND

Berkshire

University of Reading
The School of Continuing Education, London Road, Reading RG1 5AQ
☎0118 378 8347
✉ Cont-Ed@reading.ac.uk
www.reading.ac.uk/ContEd

An expanding programme of creative writing courses, including *Life into Fiction*; *Poetry Workshop*; *Getting Started*; *Writing Fiction*; *Publishing Poetry*; *Scriptwriting*; *Playwriting*, *Travel Writing*; *Comedy Writing* and *Writing for Radio*. There is also a public lecture by a writer and a reading by students of their work, and various Saturday workshops. Tutors include novelist Leslie Wilson and poets Jane Draycott, Susan Utting, David Grubb and Paul Bavister. Fees vary depending on the length of course. Concessions available.

The Write Coach
2 Rowan Close, Wokingham RG41 4BH
☎0118 978 4904
✉ enquiries@thewritecoach.co.uk
www.thewritecoach.co.uk

Contact *Bekki Hill*

Workshops and one-to-one coaching (both in person and by telephone) 'to assist both professional and aspiring writers to become more successful, break through their blocks, build confidence, increase motivation and expand creativity, define direction and find time and space to write'. Free e-zine and free initial consultation available. See website for details.

Buckinghamshire

Missenden Abbey
Evreham Adult Learning Centre, Swallow Street, Iver SL0 0HS
☎0845 045 4040
✉ dcevreham@buckscc.gov.uk
www.arca.uk.net/missendenabbey

Residential and non-residential weekend workshops, Easter and summer school.

Programmes have included *Writing Stories for Children*; *Short Story Writing*; *Poetry Workshop*; *Writing Comedy for Television*; *Life Writing*; *Travel Tales*.

National Film & Television School
Beaconsfield Studios, Station Road, Beaconsfield HP9 1LG
☎01494 731425 Fax 01494 674042
✉ info@nftsfilm-tv.ac.uk
www.nftsfilm-tv.ac.uk

Two-year programme covering all aspects of screenwriting from the development of ideas through to final production. Studying alongside other filmmaking students allows writers to have their work tested in workshops and productions. Unlike a Screenwriting MA set in an academic institution, this course is set in a working studio and emphasises practical filmmaking and contact with industry personnel through seminars and pitching sessions. The course requires and encourages a high level of dedication and a prolific output. Year One deals with the basic principles of storytelling, the craft of screenwriting for film and television and the collaborative nature of production, and includes several short writing assignments. Year Two focuses on longer writing assignments, with students writing a feature script and TV project as well as their MA dissertation. Opportunities may be available to write short fiction or animation scripts for production. A five-week *Feature Development* course is also offered at intervals during the year – details available from the website. In partnership with **The Script Factory**, The NFTS also offers an 18-month, part-time Diploma in *Script Development*.

Cambridgeshire

National Extension College
Michael Young Centre, Purbeck Road, Cambridge CB2 2HN
☎0800 389 2839 Fax 01223 400325
✉ info@nec.ac.uk
www.nec.ac.uk/courses

Contact *Customer Relationship Adviser*

Runs a number of home-study courses on

writing which include: *Essential Editing; Creative Writing* (which leads to an OCN Level 2 Cert.); *Writing for Money*. Contact the NEC for a free copy of the *Guide to Courses* which includes details of fees and course enrolment. 'You can enrol at any time, study at home, work at your own pace and fit learning into your lives.' The NEC is accredited by the Open Distance Learning Quality Council.

University of Cambridge Institute of Continuing Education

Madingley Hall, Madingley, Cambridge CB3 8AQ
☎01954 280399 Fax 01954 280200
www.cont-ed.cam.ac.uk

A wide range of weekend, five-day and week-long creative writing courses for adults is offered by the University at the Institute of Continuing Education's residential headquarters at Madingley Hall. Evening courses are also available in Cambridgeshire and surrounding areas. Details of all courses can be found on the website or phone for a brochure.

Cheshire

Burton Manor

The Village, Burton, Neston CH64 5SJ
☎0151 336 5172 Fax 0151 336 6586
✉ enquiry@burtonmanor.com
www.burtonmanor.com

Wide variety of short courses, residential and non-residential, on writing and literature, including *Creative Writing Workshop; Writing for Pleasure* and *Features Journalism*. Full details in brochure.

Cornwall

University College Falmouth

Woodlane, Falmouth TR11 4RH
☎01326 211077
www.falmouth.ac.uk
www.bloc-online.com (magazine)

Contact *Admissions*

PgDip/MA professional writing programme. An intensive vocational writing programme developing skills in fiction, magazine journalism/features, screenwriting. Students work on an extended writing project and form links with other PgDips such as television production and broadcast journalism.

Cumbria

Higham Hall College

Bassenthwaite Lake, Cockermouth CA13 9SH
☎01768 776276 Fax 01768 776013
✉ admin@highamhall.com
www.highamhall.com

Winter and summer residential courses. Programme includes *Creative Writing; Writing for Radio and TV*. Brochure available.

Derbyshire

Real Writers

PO Box 170, Chesterfield S40 1FE
☎01246 520834 Fax 01246 520834
✉ info@real-writers.com
www.real-writers.com

Correspondence service with personal tuition from working writers. Send s.a.e. for details.

Swanwick – The Writers' Summer School

The Hayes Conference Centre, Nr Alfreton
✉ jean.sutton@lineone.net
www.wss.org.uk

Secretary *Jean Sutton*

Offers six-days of informal talks, discussion groups, interactive workshops and quizzes. Competitions and 'a lot of fun'. All levels welcome. Held mid-August from Saturday to Friday morning. Cost (2006) £295–420 per person, all inclusive. S.a.e. to the Secretary at 10 Stag Road, Lake, Sandown, Isle of Wight PO36 8PE (Tel 01983 406759/e-mail as above).

University of Derby

Admissions Office, Kedleston Road, Derby DE22 1GB
☎01332 622236 Fax 01332 622754
✉ J.Bains@derby.ac.uk
www.derby.ac.uk

Contact *Carl Tighe*

With upwards of 300 students, this is one of the oldest *Creative Writing* operations at degree level in the UK. The subject offers a BA Hons *Creative Writing* with particular strengths in Short Stories, Writing and New Technologies and Storytelling. All teaching is done through practical workshops led by established and experienced writers. In the final year students produce an independent research project on a subject of their choice. The subject also contributes to the BA Hons Combined Studies.

Devon

Arvon Foundation (Devon)
See entry under **Greater London**

Dartington College of Arts
Totnes TQ9 6EJ
☎01803 862224   Fax 01803 861666
✉ registry@dartington.ac.uk
www.dartington.ac.uk

BA (Hons) *Writing* or *Writing (Contemporary Practices)* or *Writing (Scripted Media)*: exploratory approaches to writing as it relates to performance, visual arts, sound arts and contemporary culture. Encourages the interdisciplinary, with minor awards and electives in arts and cultural management, choreography, music, theatre, visual performance. Contact Director of Writing: see www.dartington.ac.uk/pw/

Exeter Phoenix
Bradninch Place, Gandy Street, Exeter
EX4 3LS
☎01392 667080   Fax 01392 667599
www.exeterphoenix.org.uk

Regular literature events, focusing on performances by living poets and writers, often linked to wider programmes including the annual tExt festival in May. Tutors in a wide range of writing skills run classes and workshops. 'Uncut Poets' group holds monthly meetings.

Fire in the Head
Creative Writing Programme
PO Box 17, Yelverton PL20 6YF
☎01822 841081
✉ roselle.angwin@internet-today.co.uk
www.fire-in-the-head.co.uk

Contact *Roselle Angwin*

Imaginative and comprehensive year-round writing programme in poetry, fiction (short and novel-writing), reflective writing and creative development. Roselle Angwin, director and tutor, is a poet and author whose courses have been featured in *The Guardian* and *The Sunday Times*. Also available are online and snailmail correspondence courses.

University of Exeter
Room 206, School of English, Queen's Building, Queen's Drive, Exeter EX4 4QH
☎01392 264352   Fax 01392 264594
✉ soe.pgoffice@ex.ac.uk
www.ex.ac.uk/english

Offers BA (Hons) in *English* with 2nd and 3rd-

year options in creative writing, poetry, short fiction, screenwriting and creative non-fiction. MA *English*; MA *Creative Writing*: poetry, novella, screenwriting, life writing and novel. PhD *Creative Writing*.

Dorset

Bournemouth University
Bournemouth Media School, Weymouth House, Talbot Campus, Fern Barrow, Poole BH12 5BB
☎01202 595553   Fax 01202 595530
Programme Administrator *Katrina King*

Three-year, full-time BA(Hons) course in *Scriptwriting for Film and Television*.

Essex

National Council for the Training of Journalists
The New Granary, Station Road, Newport, Saffron Walden CB11 3PL
☎01799 544014   Fax 01799 544015
✉ info@nctj.com
www.nctj.com

For details of journalism courses, both full-time and via distance learning, please write to the NCTJ enclosing a large s.a.e. or visit the website.

Writing Life
PO Box 4065, Braintree CM7 9RJ
☎01376 343759
✉ info@creativewritinglife.co.uk
www.creativewritinglife.co.uk

Contact *Mrs Bernie Ross*

Home study course. Postal tuition in *Creative Writing*, from anywhere in the world. Fiction speciality: one-off critiques and on-going mentoring. Economy e-mail-only version also available.

Gloucestershire

Chrysalis – The Poet In You with Jay Ramsay, BA Hons (Oxon), PGDip, UKCP member
5 Oxford Terrace, Uplands, Stroud GL5 1TW
☎01453 759436/020 7794 8880
✉ jay@ramsay3892.fsnet.co.uk
www.lotusfoundation.org.uk

Offers postal courses, day and weekend workshops (including 'The Sacred Space of the

Word'), an on-going poetry group based in London and Gloucestershire and individual therapy related to the participant's creative process. The Chrysalis course itself consists of Part 1, 'for those who feel drawn to reading more poetry as well as wanting to start to write their own', and Part 2, 'a more in-depth course designed for those who are already writing and who want to go more deeply into its process and technique, its background and cultural history'. Both courses combine course notes with in-depth individual correspondence and feedback. Editing and information about publication also provided. Brochure and workshop dates available from the address above.

Wye Valley Arts Centre

The Coach House, Mork, St Briavel's, Lydney GL15 6QH
☎01594 530214/01291 689463
Fax 01594 530321
✉ wyeart@cwcom.net
www.wyeart.cwc.net

Residential courses (Monday to Friday and weekends), held at The Coach House, 'a country house near Tintern Abbey and at our house in Cornwall', include *Creative Writing* and *Fiction Workshop*. All styles and abilities. Companions and other guests not taking the courses are welcome to stay.

Hampshire

Highbury College, Portsmouth

Dovercourt Road, Cosham, Portsmouth PO6 2SA
☎023 9238 3131 Fax 023 9237 8382
✉ media.journalism@highbury.ack.uk
www.highbury.ac.uk

Course Administratory *Joy Young* (☎0023 9231 3287)

The 20-week fast-track Postgraduate courses include: *Pre-entry Magazine Journalism*; *Pre-entry Newspaper Journalism*; and Diploma in *Broadcasting Journalism*, run under the auspices of the Periodicals Training Council, the National Council for Training of Journalists and the Broadcast Journalism Training Council respectively.

Southampton Solent University

East Park Terrace, Southampton SO14 0YN
☎023 8031 9000
✉ Richard.Hudson@Solent.ac.uk
www.solent.ac.uk

Contact *Rick Hudson* (☎023 8031 9097)

Courses offered: BA(Hons) *Media Writing*; BA(Hons) *Writing Fashion & Culture*; BA(Hons) *Journalism*. Writing may be taken as a specialism in MA *Media* or BA *Popular Fiction* and BA *Screenwriting*; BA *Magazine Journalism and Feature Writing*.

University of Portsmouth

School of Creative Arts, Film and Media, Portsmouth PO1 2DZ
☎023 9284 6132 Fax 023 9284 3082
✉ creative@port.ac.uk
www.port.ac.uk/departments/academic/scafm

Contact *School of Creative Arts, Film and Media*

Offers creative writing and combined creative writing degrees across a wide range of undergraduate programmes, and in all genre. BA, MA and PhD study is available. The School is a key partner in a national AHRC Research training project in Creative Writing. Staff include a number of national and/or international award-winning writers, short story writers/novelists, playwrights, screenwriters, new-media writers and poets. The School runs an annual international creative writing conference and regular national and international creative writing events.

University of Winchester, Winchester SO22 4NR

☎01962 841515 Fax 01962 842280
www.winchester.ac.uk

Contact *Enquiries* (☎01962 827252)

Offers a range of courses for budding writers both at undergraduate and postgraduate level. The three-year degree course in *Creative Writing* is available as a Single, Combined or Joint Honours programme. It covers a range of genres including writing for films, TV, short stories, fiction and poetry. Other three-year courses of possible interest include *English*; *English and English Literature*; *Journalism*; *Drama, Community Theatre and Media*.

MA courses in *Writing for Children* and *Creative and Critical Writing* are available on a one or two-year basis.

Winchester Writers' Conference, Bookfair & Workshops

Faculty of Arts, University of Winchester, Winchester SO22 4NR
☎01962 827238
✉ barbara.large@winchester.ac.uk
www.writersconference.co.uk

Conference Director *Barbara Large, MBE, FRSA, FUW*
Administrator *Christian Francis* (☎01962 827107)
Honorary Patron *Dame Beryl Bainbridge*
29th June to 1st July 2007. This Festival of Writing, now in its 27th year, attracts international authors, playwrights, poets, agents and editors who give workshops, mini courses, editor appointments, lectures and seminars to help writers harness their creativity and develop their writing, editing and marketing skills. Fifteen writing competitions are attached to the conference. All first-place winners are published in *The Best of* series annually. The Bookfair offers delegates a wide choice of exhibits including Internet author services, publishers, booksellers, printers and trade associations. See also **Pitstop Refuelling Writers' Weekend Workshops** under *Writers' Circles and Workshops*.

Hertfordshire

Liberato Breakaway Writing Courses
9 Bishop's Avenue, Bishop's Stortford CM23 3EJ
☎01279 833690
✉ liberato@tesco.net
www.liberato.co.uk
Contact *Maureen Blundell*

Specialises in beginner fiction writers with weekend and week-long courses. Emphasis on individual writing with written ms critiques and one-to-one sessions. Weekends held at Polstead in Suffolk throughout the year. Greek weeks in June on the Saronic island of Agistri, near Aegina – a relaxing, informal holiday with five-session fiction course and B&B accommodation included. Also offers postal and e-mail ms critiques on all fiction/autobiography.

✳ Isle of Wight

Annual Writers' Writing Courses & Workshops
F ✱ F Productions, 39 Ranelagh Road, Sandown PO36 8NT
☎01983 407772 Fax 01983 407772
✉ felicity@writeplot.co.uk
www.writeplot.co.uk
Contact *Felicity Fair Thompson*

Regular residential weeks and weekends on

Creative Writing for beginners and experienced writers – individual advice and workshops. Also offers postal ms critiques and one-to-one advice on fiction and film scripts

Kent

North West Kent College
Oakfield Lane, Dartford DA1 2JT
☎01322 629436/0800 074 1447 (Freephone helpline) Fax 01322 629468
www.nwkcollege.ac.uk
Contact *Neil Nixon*, Head of School, Media & Communications

Two-year, full-time course that explores writing from a number of angles, teaching essential skills, market and academic aspects of the subject. Successful students progress to work or the University of Greenwich, the latter option allowing them to gain a BA(Hons) in Humanities from a further year of study. Staff include scriptwriters, novelists and a book publisher. Students compile a portfolio in the final year.

University of Kent
Information, Advice & Guidance Unit, APS, The Registry, Canterbury CT2 7NZ
☎01227 827272
✉ information@kent.ac.uk
www.kent.ac.uk

Undergraduate certificate courses in *Practical Writing* and *Imaginative Writing*. Also combined studies – *English and Creative Writing*.

Lancashire

Alston Hall College
Alston Lane, Longridge, Preston PR3 3BP
☎01772 784661 Fax 01772 785835
✉ alston.hall@ed.lancscc.gov.uk
www.alstonhall.com

Holds regular day and residential *Creative Writing* workshops. Full colour brochure available.

Edge Hill College of Higher Education
St Helen's Road, Ormskirk L39 4QP
☎01695 575171
✉ sheppard@edgehill.ac.uk
Contact *Dr R. Sheppard*

Offers a two-year, part-time MA in *Writing Studies*. Combines advanced-level writers' workshops with closely related courses in the poetics of writing and contemporary writing in English. There is also provision for MPhil and PhD-level research in writing and poetics. A full range of creative writing courses is available at undergraduate level, in poetry and fiction writing which may be taken as part of a modular BA.

Lancaster University

English & Creative Writing, Bowland College, Bailrigg, Lancaster LA1 4YN
☎01524 594169 Fax 01524 594247
✉ l.kellett@lancaster.ac.uk
Contact *Lyn Kellett*

Offers practical graduate and undergraduate courses in writing fiction, poetry and scripts. All based on group workshops – students' work-in-progress is circulated and discussed. Distance learning MA now available. Graduates include Andrew Miller, Justin Hill, Monique Roffey, Alison MacLeod, Jacob Polley.

Leicestershire

Leicester Adult Education College, Writing School

2 Wellington Street, Leicester LE1 6HL
☎0116 233 4343 Fax 0116 233 4344
✉ vm1@laec.ac.uk
www.laec.ac.uk
Contact *Valerie Moore*

Offers a wide range of part time creative writing and journalism courses throughout the year. The programme offers a mix of critical workshops, one-day and term-length courses, and short craft modules. Supports writers through to publication and has strong links with local media.

London

Arvon Foundation

National Administration: 2nd Floor, 42A Buckingham Palace Road, London SW1W 0RE
☎020 7931 7611 Fax 020 7963 0961
www.arvonfoundation.org

Devon: Totleigh Barton, Sheepwash, Beaworthy EX21 5NS
☎01409 231338 Fax 01409 231144
✉ t-barton@arvonfoundation.org

Yorkshire: Lumb Bank, Heptonstall, Hebden Bridge HX7 6DF

☎01422 843714 Fax 01422 843714
✉ l-bank@arvonfoundation.org

Inverness-shire: Moniack Mhor, Teavarran, Kiltarlity, Beauly IV4 7HT
☎01463 741675
✉ m-mhor@arvonfoundation.org

Shropshire: The Hurst, Clunton, Craven Arms SY7 0JA
☎01588 640658 Fax 01588 640509
✉ hurst@arvonfoundation.org
Joint Presidents *Terry Hands, Sir Robin Chichester-Clark*
Chairman *Nigel Partling*
National Director *Stephanie Anderson*

Founded 1968. Offers people of any age (over 16) and any background the opportunity to live and work with professional writers. Four-and-a-half-day residential courses are held throughout the year at Arvon's four centres, covering poetry, fiction, drama, writing for children, songwriting and the performing arts. Bursaries towards the cost of course fees are available for those on low incomes, the unemployed, students and pensioners. Runs a biennial poetry competition (see entry under *Prizes*).

Birkbeck College, University of London

School of English and Humanities, Malet Street, London WC1E 7HX
☎020 77079 0689
✉ A.Whiting@bbk.ac.uk
www.bbk.ac.uk/eh/eng
Contact *Anne Marie Whiting*

Taught by published writers, Birkbeck offers an MA course in *Fiction Writing*. The course will extend and cultivate existing writing skills, help develop writing to a professional level and is supported by masterclasses and readings from visiting professionals. All classes are held in the evening. Study part-time over two years or full-time over one year. Applications must be supported by a portfolio of creative writing. Download an application form from the website.

The Central School of Speech and Drama

Embassy Theatre, Eton Avenue, London NW3 3HY
☎020 7722 8183 Fax 020 7722 4132
✉ n.wood@cssd.ac.uk
Contact *Nick Wood*, Course Leader

MA in *Advanced Theatre Practice*. One-year, full-time course aimed at providing a grounding in principal areas of professional theatre practice – *Writing for Performance, Dramaturgy, Directing, Performance, Puppetry* and *Design*, with an emphasis on collaboration between the various strands. *Writing for Performance* students have the opportunity of working with companies to create new and innovative work for the theatre. Prospectus available. Nick Wood is also editor of the Dramaturgy Forum website (www.dramforum.com). Also MA in *Writing for Stage & Broadcast* Course Leader: *Dymphna Callery* (✉ d.callery@cssd.ac.uk).

City Lit
Keeley Street, Covent Garden, London WC2B 4BA
☎020 7492 2652   Fax 020 7492 8256
✉ humanities@citylit.ac.uk

The Writing School offers a wide range of courses: *Ways Into Creative Writing; Writing for Children; Playwriting; Writing Short Stories; Screenwriting; Comedy Writing* and *Poetry*. Various lengths of course available. The Department offers information and advice during term time.

City University
Education and Lifelong Learning, Northampton Square, London EC1V 0HB
☎020 7040 8268   Fax 020 7040 8256
✉ conted@city.ac.uk
www.city.ac.uk/ell/cfa/write

The Courses for Adults evening programme includes: *Certificate in Novel Writing* (three-term course); *Novel Writing and Longer Works; Towards Publication; Writing Crime Fiction; Writing Television Drama; Writing Situation Comedy; Food Writing; Feature Writing*.

The Complete Creative Writing Course at the Groucho Club
☎020 7249 3711   Fax 020 7683 8141
✉ creative-writing@blueyonder.co.uk
www.writingcourses.org.uk
Contact *Maggie Hamand*

Courses of ten two-hour sessions held at the Groucho Club in London's Soho, starting in January, April and September, Monday or Saturday afternoons, 2.30 pm – 4.30 pm. Beginners and advanced courses offered. Courses include stimulating exercises, discussion and weekly homework. Fee: £195 for whole course.

The Drill Hall
16 Chenies Street, London WC1E 7EX
☎020 7307 5061   Fax 020 7307 5062
✉ admin@drillhall.co.uk
www.drillhall.co.uk

Holds a number of writing classes and workshops. Regular tutors include Carol Burns.

The Intensive Course
5 Queen Elizabeth Close, London N16 0HL
☎020 8809 4725
✉ henrietta@writtenwords.net
www.writtenwords.net
Contact *Henrietta Soames*

One-year course for writers working on a novel or collection of short stories. Eight classes from 10.00 am to 4.00 pm spread throughout the year. Also private one-to-one fiction tutorials for students who require concentrated attention and feedback on their work. These can be held monthly or as required.

London College of Communication
Elephant & Castle, London SE1 6SB
☎020 7514 6500
✉ info@lcc.arts.ac.uk
www.lcctraining.co.uk
www.lcc.arts.ac.uk

Intensive courses in journalism. Short courses, run by ARTSCOM at the Elephant & Castle address above, include: *News Writing; Feature Writing; Sub-editing; Adapting Fiction for Film or TV*. Also offers five-day specialist journalism courses in newswriting, subediting, print journalism, radio journalism and online journalism plus a three-week course in broadcast TV journalism. In addition, *Effective Copywriting, Effective Writing Techniques for Public Relations*. For individuals and companies 'tailor-made training' services can be provided. Prospectus and information leaflets available; telephone 020 7514 8193 or access the website.

London School of Journalism
126 Shirland Road, London W9 2BT
☎020 7289 7777   Fax 020 7432 8141
✉ info@lsjournalism.com
www.home-study.com
www.lsj.org
Contact *Student Administration Office*

Distance learning courses with an individual and personal approach. Students remain with the same tutor throughout the course. Options include: *Novel Writing; Short Story Writing;*

Writing for Children; *Poetry*; *Freelance Journalism*; *Media Law*; *Improve Your English*; *Cartooning*; *Thriller Writing*. Fees vary but range from £295 for *Enjoying English Literature* to £395 for *Journalism and Newswriting*. NUJ-recognised Postgraduate Diploma Courses taught in London (three month full-time, six month part-time, nine month evening classes). Online postgraduate diploma course also available.

Middlesex University

Trent Park, Bramley Road, London N14 4YZ
☎020 8411 5000 Fax 020 8411 6652
✉ tpadmissions@mdx.ac.uk
www.mdx.ac.uk

The UK's longest established writing degree offers a Single or Joint Honours programme in *Creative and Media Writing* (full or part-time). This modular programme gives an opportunity to explore journalism, poetry, prose fiction and dramatic writing for a wide range of genres and audiences. Option for work experience in the media and publishing industries. Contact Admissions or *David Rain*, Programme Leader (d.rain@mdx.ac.uk)

MA in *Writing* (full-time, part-time; day and evening classes) includes writing workshops; critical seminars; lectures and workshops from established writers; introduction to agents and publishers. Options available: Fiction, Poetry or Scriptwriting. Contact *Sue Gee* ☎020 8411 5941 (s.gee@mdx.ac.uk)

Also offer research degrees M.Phil/PhD in *Creative Writing*. The University has a thriving Writing Centre running an annual literary festival, weekly talks, community projects and writers in residence. 'All of our writing courses take place in the setting of a beautiful country park, within easy reach of central London.'

PMA Training

The PMA Centre for Media Excellence, 10 Cynthia Street, London N1 9JF
☎020 7278 0606 Fax 01480 496022
✉ training@pma-group.com
www.pma-group.com
www.becomeajournalist.co.uk

Contacts *Vicky Chandler, Melanie Gilbert*

Fast-track nine-week Postgraduate Diploma and more than 150 one and two-day editorial, PR, design and publishing courses held in central London. Intensive workshops run by top journalists, print and online, designers and PR professionals. All short courses are designed to lead to the PMA Gold Standard qualification.

Special discount for freelances. See website for dates and fees.

Roehampton University

Roehampton Lane, London SW15 5PUH
☎020 8392 3000
www.roehampton.ac.uk

Three-year BA(Hons) programmes in *Drama, Theatre and Performance Studies*; *Television Studies*; *Film Studies and Screen Practice* include courses on writing for stage and screen, creative writing, cultural and news studies and journalism. Also offers an MA, Postgraduate Certificate, Postgraduate Diploma in *Children's Literature*; MA in *Creative and Professional Writing*; MPhil, PhD in *English, (Literature and Language)*.

The Script Factory

66–67 Wells Street, London W1T 3PY
☎020 7323 1414
✉ general@scriptfactory.co.uk
www.scriptfactory.co.uk

Established in 1996, The Script Factory is a screenwriter and script developer organisation set up to bridge the gap between writers and the industry, and to promote excellence in screenwriting. Specialising in training, screenings, masterclasses and various services from its base in central London, The Script Factory operates throughout the UK and internationally. For the best source of information on upcoming activities, courses and latest news, and to join the free mailing list, check out the website

Soho Theatre Company

See entry under *Theatre Producers*

Travellers' Tales

92 Hillfield Road, London NW6 1QA
✉ info@travellers-tales.org
www.travellers-tales.org

Travellers' Tales is Britain's foremost provider of travel writing and travel photography training for non-professionals. Offers practical courses with top professionals. Tutors include award-winning authors William Dalrymple and Colin Thubron, foreign correspondent Fergal Keane, travel editors Simon Calder (*The Independent*), Lyn Hughes (*Wanderlust*) and Jonathan Lorie (*Traveller*). Courses include beginners' weekends, longer masterclasses and creative retreats.

University of Westminster

School of Media, Arts and Design, Harrow Campus, Watford Road, Harrow HA1 3TP

☎020 7911 5903 Fax 020 7911 5955
✉ harrow-admissions@wmin.ac.uk
www.wmin.ac.uk

Courses include part-time MAs available in *Journalism Studies*; *Film and Television Studies*; *Screenwriting and Producing*; *Public Communication and Public Relations*; *Communication and Communication Policy*.

Greater Manchester

Manchester Metropolitan University – The Writing School

Department of English, Geoffrey Manton Building, Rosamond Street West, off Oxford Road, Manchester M15 6LL
☎0161 247 1732/1 Fax 0161 247 6345
✉ a.biswell@mmu.ac.uk

Course Convenors *Andrew Biswell* (campus address), *Heather Beck* (online)

Closely associated with **Carcanet Press Ltd** and *PN Review*, The Writing School offers two 'routes' for students to follow: *Poetry* and *The Novel*. A key feature of the programme is regular readings, lectures, workshops and masterclasses by writers, publishers, producers, booksellers, librarians and agents. Tutors include Simon Armitage, Carol Ann Duffy, Jeffrey Wainwright, Heather Beck, Paul Magrs, Michael Symmons Roberts and Tiffany Murray. The course is available online as well as through the campus (contact *Heather Beck*, Online Convenor: h.beck@mmu.ac.uk).

University of Manchester

English & American Studies, School of Arts, Histories and Cultures, Humanities Lime Grove, Oxford Road, Manchester M13 9PL
☎0161 306 1259 Fax 0161 275 5987
✉ englishpg@manchester.ac.uk
www.manchester.ac.uk/english

Course Director *John McAuliffe*

Offers a one-year MA in *Creative Writing*.

University of Salford

Postgraduate Admissions, School of Media, Music & Performance, Adelphi Building, Peru Street, Salford M3 6EQ
☎0161 295 6027 Fax 0161 295 6023
✉ r.humphrey@salford.ac.uk
www.smmp.salford.ac.uk

MA in *Television and Radio Scriptwriting*. Two-year, part-time course taught by professional writers and producers. Also offers masterclasses

with leading figures in the radio and television industry.

The Writers Bureau

Sevendale House, 7 Dale Street, Manchester M1 1JB
☎0161 228 2362 Fax 0161 236 9440
✉ studentservices@writersbureau.com
www.writersbureau.com

Comprehensive home-study writing course with personal tuition service from professional writers. Fiction, non-fiction, articles, short stories, novels, TV, radio and drama all covered in detail. Trial period, guarantee and no time limits. Writing for children, using the Internet to sell your writing and biographies, memoirs and family history courses also available. ODLQC accredited. Quote Ref. EH07. Free enquiry line: 0800 856 2008.

The Writers Bureau College of Journalism

Address etc. as The Writers Bureau above

Home-study course covering all aspects of journalism. Real-life assignments assessed by qualified tutors with the emphasis on getting into print. Comprises 28 modules and three handbooks. Ref: EHJ07. Free enquiry line: 0800 298 7008.

The Writers College

Address etc. as The Writers Bureau above

The Art of Writing Poetry Course from The Writers Bureau sister college. A home-study course with a more 'recreational' emphasis. The 60,000-word course has 17 modules and lets you complete six written assignments for tutorial evaluation. Quote Ref. EHP07. Free enquiry line: 0800 856 2008.

Merseyside

University of Liverpool

Continuing Education, 126 Mount Pleasant, Liverpool L69 3GR
☎0151 794 6900/6952 (24 hours) Fax 0151 794 2544
✉ conted@liverpool.ac.uk
www.liv.ac.uk/conted

Course Organiser *Dr John Redmond*

Courses include: *Introduction to Creative Writing*; *Scriptwriting*; *Journalism*; *Writing for Children*; *Writing Your Life Story* and a series of Saturday courses on aspects of writing. Most courses take place on one evening or daytime meeting weekly, with some Saturdays and linked days. Courses may be taken to pursue a personal interest or to gain university credit towards an award. CE offers a Certificate in Higher Education (*Creative Writing*) – 120 credits. For most courses no previous knowledge is required. There are fee concessions for those who are receiving certain benefits or are retired. Free prospectus on request or see the website.

Norfolk

University of East Anglia
School of Literature and Creative Writing, Norwich NR4 7TJ
☎01603 592154 Fax 01603 250599
✉ pgt.hum@uea.ac.uk
www.uea.ac.uk/eas

Contact *Jack Camplin*, Postgraduate Admissions
UEA has a history of concern with contemporary literary culture. Among its programmes is the MA in *Creative Writing* (founded by Angus Wilson and Malcolm Bradbury in 1970/71). The course has three parallel entry points: Prose fiction, poetry and scriptwriting. A series of weekly workshops provide intensive examination of students' own work, and also draw on aspects of teaching in nineteenth and twentieth century literature, literary theory and film and cultural studies.

Northamptonshire

Knuston Hall Residential College for Adult Education
Irchester, Wellingborough NN29 7EU
☎01933 312104 Fax 01933 357596
✉ enquiries@knustonhall.org.uk
www.knustonhall.org.uk

Writing courses being held in 2006 included: *Writing and Illustration for Children*; *Writer's Workshops* and *Creative Writing*.

Northumberland

Community Creative Writing
'Sea Winds', 2 St Helens Terrace, Berwick-upon-Tweed TD15 1RJ
☎01289 305213
✉ mavismaureen@aol.com

Contact/Tutor *Maureen Raper, MBE*

The courses, which are held at the Community Centre College, Berwick-upon-Tweed as well as by distance learning for those unable to travel

into class, include: *Creative Writing for Beginners*; *Writing for Children*; *Writing Comedy*; *Writing for Radio and Television*; *Writing Crime and Mystery*. All courses are verified by North East Open College Networks.

Nottinghamshire

The Nottingham Trent University
School of Arts, Communication and Culture, Clifton Campus, Nottingham NG11 8NS
☎0115 848 3111
✉ acc.postgrad@ntu.ac.uk
www.human.ntu.ac.uk/writing

MA in *Creative Writing*. Hands-on and workshop-based, the course concentrates primarily on the practice and production of writing. A choice of options from *Fiction*, *Poetry*, *Creative Non-Fiction*, *New Media Writing*, *Children's Writing* and *Scriptwriting*. Assignments and a dissertation, but no formal exams. There is a full programme of visiting speakers. Study either full-time or part-time – all classes held in the evenings.

Oxfordshire

University of Oxford Department for Continuing Education
Rewley House, 1 Wellington Square, Oxford OX1 2JA
☎01865 280356 Fax 01865 270309
✉ pp@conted.ox.ac.uk
www.conted.ox.ac.uk

Creative writing classes held during the autumn and spring terms. There are also one-week summer school courses, a two-year part-time Diploma and a two-year part-time MSt in *Creative Writing*. Early booking is advised.

Shropshire

Arvon Foundation (Shropshire)
See entry under **Greater London**

Somerset

Ammerdown Conference and Retreat Centre
Ammerdown Park, Radstock, Bath BA3 5SW
☎01761 433709 Fax 01761 433094
✉ centre@ammerdown.org
www.ammerdown.org

Courses include a five-day creative writing course. En suite residential facilities. Brochure available or full details on the website.

Bath Spa University

Newton Park, Bath BA2 9BN
☎01225 875875   Fax 01225 875444
✉ enquiries@bathspa.ac.uk
www.bathspa.ac.uk

Contact *Admissions Officer* (☎01225 875821)

MA in *Creative Writing*. A course for creative writers wanting to develop their work. Teaching is by published writers in the novel, poetry, short stories and scriptwriting. In recent years, several students from this course have received contracts from publishers for novels, awards for poetry and short stories and have had work produced on BBC Radio. MA in *Writing for Young People*. A course for writers for children of all ages, from the picture-book age through to adolescent and 'crossover' writing, which aims at markets among adults as well as young people. An experienced teaching team helps and encourages students to create a significant body of writing, with practical plans for its place in the real world of publishing.

Dillington House

Ilminster TA19 9DT
☎01460 52427/Minicom: 01460 258640
Fax 01460 52433
✉ dillington@somerset.gov.uk
www.dillington.co.uk

Dillington House is one of the finest historic houses in Somerset. Provides short residential courses across a wide range of subjects, including writing and literary appreciation. Full details of the programme are available in the free brochure and on the website.

Institute of Copywriting

Overbrook House, Poolbridge Road,
Blackford, Wedmore BS28 4PA
☎0800 781 1715   Fax 0800 781 1715
✉ copy@inst.org
www.institute.org/copy

Comprehensive copywriting home-study course, including advice on becoming a self-employed copywriter. Each student has a personal tutor who is an experienced copywriter and who provides detailed feedback on the student's assignments. Other courses include: Diploma in *Creative Writing* and Diploma in *Screenwriting*.

University of Bristol

Department of English, 3/5 Woodland Road,
Bristol BS8 1TB
☎0117 954 6969

www.bris.ac.uk/english

Contact *Lifelong Learning Organiser*

A variety of short courses and day schools designed for both experienced writers and for absolute beginners, including courses exploring writing for therapeutic purposes. Also offers *Diploma in Creative Writing*. Detailed brochure available.

Staffordshire

Keele University

The Centre for Continuing and Professional Education, Keele University, (Freepost ST1666), Newcastle under Lyme ST5 5BR
☎01782 583436

Evening and weekend courses on literature and creative writing. The 2005/6 programme included courses on novel writing, writers workshops and sessions on poetry writing.

Surrey

The Guildford Institute of the University of Surrey

Guildford Institute of the University of Surrey,
Ward Street, Guildford GU1 4LH
☎01483 562142   Fax 01483 451034
✉ guildford-institute@surrey.ac.uk
www.guildford-institute.org.uk

The Guildford Institute is the venue for various creative writing courses. It also hosts Guildford Writers, a writers' circle meeting on alternate Tuesday evenings from 7.30 pm to 9.30 pm. Members of the group are writing short stories, poetry or novels, and bring their work to read aloud to the group for other members' advice, constructive criticism and general comments. New members are always welcome.

Royal Holloway University of London

Department of Drama and Theatre, Egham
Hill, Egham TW20 0EX
☎01784 443922   Fax 01784 431018
✉ drama@rhul.ac.uk
www.rhul.ac.uk/Drama
www.rhul.ac.uk/english

Contacts *Dan Rebellato, David Wiles*

Three-year BA courses in *Drama and Creative Writing* or *English and Creative Writing*, during which students progressively specialise in playwriting, poetry or fiction. Playwriting can be studied as part of the BA *Drama and Creative*

Writing degree and poetic practice is an option in the *English* programme. Playwriting can be studied at postgraduate level in the MA in *Theatre* and there is an MA in *Poetic Practice*.

University of Surrey
Department of Culture, Media and Communication, University of Surrey, Guildford GU2 7XH
☎01483 686237 Fax 01483 562142
✉ cmc@surrey.ac.uk
www.surrey.ac.uk

The certificate programme includes several *Creative Writing* courses. For autumn 2006 these will be held at the **Guildford Institute**. The courses carry credits and can build to a university award. For details, contact *Anita Valente*, Course Secretary on the number above.

Sussex
The Earnley Concourse
Earnley, Chichester PO20 7JL
☎01243 670392 Fax 01243 670832
✉ info@earnley.co.uk
www.earnley.co.uk

Offers a range of residential and non-residential courses throughout the year. Previous programme has included *Creative Writing: Getting Started*; *Secrets of a Professional Novelist*. Brochure available.

Lewes Live Literature
See entry under *Festivals*

The University of Chichester
Bishop Otter Campus, College Lane, Chichester PO19 6PE
☎01243 816000 Fax 01243 816080
✉ S.Norgate@chi.ac.uk
www.chi.ac.uk

MA Programme Coordinator (Creative Writing) *Stephanie Norgate* (01243 816296)

Postgraduate Certificate/Diploma/MA in *Creative Writing*, both full and part-time.

University of Sussex
Centre for Continuing Education, The Sussex Institute, Essex House, Brighton BN1 9QQ
☎01273 877888/877001
✉ cce@sussex.ac.uk
www.sussex.ac.uk/cce

Contact *Richard Crane*

MA in *Dramatic Writing*: the student is treated as a commissioned writer working in theatre, TV,

radio or film with professional directors and actors. Includes workshops, masterclasses, a residential weekend and a showcase of new work. Two years, part-time. Convenor: *Richard Crane*. Certificate in *Creative Writing*: short fiction, novel and poetry for imaginative writers. Two-year, part-time. Convenors: *Richard Crane, Mark Slater*.

Tyne & Wear
University of Sunderland
Centre for Lifelong Learning, Joseph Cowen House, Newcastle upon Tyne NE1 7RU
☎0191 515 2800 Fax 0191 515 2890
www.sunderland.ac.uk/cll

Courses, held in Newcastle, Durham and Blyth, include: *Creative Writing: Feature Writing, Screenwriting, Writing for Children* and *Writing From the Inside Out*, a workshop for women. Contact the Secretary, Adult Education Programme.

West Midlands
National Academy of Writing
(based at the **University of Central England**)
University of Central England, School of English, Perry Barr Campus, Birmingham B42 2SU
☎0121 331 5540 Fax 0121 331 6692
✉ nicola.monaghan@uce.ac.uk
www.thenationalacademyofwriting.org.uk
Diploma in *Writing*. First intake will be January 2007. The course will have a strong professional focus and aims to produce working writers. Modules will be available in a number of disciplines, including fiction and screenwriting. Teaching will include regular modules and supervision by UCE staff, all of whom are established writers. There will also be masterclasses taught by Academy patrons. Applications are welcome from all, regardless of previous academic experience. Admission will be based on talent and commitment to a career in writing. (See also **University of Central England**).

Starz! – Film and Theatre Performing Arts
Christmas House, Chester Road, Castle Bromwich, Solihull B36 0ET
☎0121 749 7147
www.gavinprime.mac.com

Creative Director *Gavin Prime*

Teaching disabled, disadvantaged and mainstream children. The only totally free theatre and film school of this type in England. Students range in age from eight to 23 and work in all ways connected to performing arts. This includes writing and showing them the structure of the business and how to try and get work accepted.

University of Birmingham

Department of Drama and Theatre Arts, Edgbaston, Birmingham B15 2TT
☎0121 414 3344 Fax 0121 414 3971
✉ e.m.braekkanpayne@bham.ac.uk

The MPhil in *Playwriting Studies*, established by playwright David Edgar in 1970, was the UK's first postgraduate course in playwriting. An intensive course which encourages students to think critically about dramatic writing, assisting them to put these insights into practice in their own plays.

University of Central England

School of English, Perry Barr Campus, Birmingham B42 2SU
☎0121 331 5540 Fax 0121 331 6692
✉ ruth.page@uce.ac.uk
www.lhds.uce.ac.uk/english/
   index.php?page=ma_creative_writing

The *Creative Writing* MA is staffed entirely by established writers and can be studied full or part time. The course has core modules of *Prose Fiction* and *Scriptwriting*, but there is also the opportunity to study within the wider context of reading and literature. With opportunities to get feedback in small groups and from staff, participants receive invaluable editorial advice. (See also **National Academy of Writing**).

University of Warwick

Open Studies, Centre for Lifelong Learning, Coventry CV4 7AL
☎024 7657 3739
✉ k.rainsley@warwick.ac.uk *or*
l.downs@warwick.ac.uk
www.warwick.ac.uk.cll/OpenStudies

Creative writing courses held at the university or in regional centres. Subjects include: *Creative Writing*; *Publishing and Editing*; *Creative Writing for All* and *Writing for Pleasure*. One-year certificates in *Creative Writing* and *Journalism* are available; individual modules can be taken.

Wiltshire

Marlborough College Summer School

Marlborough SN8 1PA
☎01672 892388 Fax 01672 892476
✉ admin@mcsummerschool.org.uk
www.mcsummerschool.org.uk

Summer School with literature and creative writing included in its programme. Caters for residential and day students. Brochure available giving full details and prices.

Urchfont Manor College

Urchfont, Devizes SN10 4RG
☎01380 840495 Fax 01380 840005
✉ urchfontmanor@wiltshire.gov.uk

Short courses – days, residential weeks and weekends – offered in a varied programme which includes literature and creative writing. 'Beautiful location; historic environment; delicious home cooking.' Send for a brochure.

Yorkshire

Arvon Foundation (Yorkshire)

See entry under **Greater London**

Leeds Metropolitan University

H505, City Site, Calverley Street, Leeds LS1 3HE
☎0113 283 2600 ext 3860
✉ c.j.pugh@leedsmet.ac.uk
www.leedsmet.ac.uk

Administrator *Chris Pugh*

Offers a Postgraduate Certificate/Diploma/MA in *Screenwriting (Fiction)*.

Open College of the Arts

Unit 1B, Redbrook Business Park, Wilthorpe Road, Barnsley S75 1JN
☎01226 730495 Fax 01226 730838
✉ open.arts@ukonline.co.uk
www.oca-uk.com

The OCA correspondence course, *Starting to Write*, offers help and stimulus from experienced writers/tutors. Emphasis is on personal development rather than commercial genre. Subsequent levels available include specialist poetry, fiction and autobiographical writing courses. OCA writing courses are accredited by the University of Glamorgan. Prospectus and Guide to Courses available on request.

Sheffield Hallam University

Faculty of Development & Society, Sheffield Hallam University, Collegiate Crescent, Sheffield S10 2BP
☎0114 225 2543 Fax 0114 225 2430
✉ fdsenquiries@shu.ac.uk
www.shu.ac.uk

Offers MA in *Creative Writing* (one-year, full-time; also part-time).

University of Hull

Scarborough Campus, Filey Road, Scarborough YO11 3AZ
☎01723 362392 Fax 01723 370815
✉ s.andrews@hull.ac.uk
www.hull.ac.uk

Director of Studies *Dr Stuart Andrews*

BA Single Honours in *Theatre and Performance Studies* incorporates opportunities in writing and other media across each level of the programme. Works closely with the Stephen Joseph Theatre and its artistic director Alan Ayckbourn. The theatre sustains a policy for staging new writers (see entry under *Theatre Producers*). The campus hosts the annual National Student Drama Festival which includes the International Student Playscript Competition (details from The National Information Centre for Student Drama; nsdf@hull.ac.uk).

University of Leeds

Lifelong Learning Centre, Leeds LS2 9JT
☎0113 343 3212
✉ part-time@leeds.ac.uk
www.leeds.ac.uk/lifelonglearningcentre

Contacts *Rebecca O'Rourke, Pat Owens*

The Lifelong Learning Centre provides accredited part-time courses in creative writing on the Leeds campus during the day and evening. Introductory workshop courses are offered each year with follow-on and advanced courses providing the opportunity to focus on particular aspects of creative writing. These more specialised courses change from year to year and can include poetry, fiction, script and lifewriting or themed work. These courses form part of the Lifelong Learning Centre's Open Studies programme, which is designed to provide adults with opportunities for continuing education and to create routes into higher education. The Centre also offers a dedicated Part-time Degree in Combined Arts, which currently includes a creative writing strand. Tutors include: Rosanna Blagg, Ian Parks, Rebecca O'Rourke and Rommi Smith.

University of Leeds, Bretton Hall Campus

School of Performance and Cultural Industries, Bretton Hall Campus, West Bretton, Wakefield WF4 4LG
☎0113 343 9022/9241
✉ g.f.lyons@leeds.ac.uk

Contact *Garry Lyons* or *Linda Smith*, Secretary (pculs@leeds.ac.uk)

MA in *Writing for Performance and Publication* due to start, subject to validation, in September, 2006. The course is particularly relevant to aspiring writers and students with professional ambitions, particularly in the areas of theatre, film and television and radio, as well as the published novel and other culturally significant genres. Studies are offered over one-year full-time and two-year part-time, and the tutors are established authors in their chosen fields. The MA is one of a new portfolio of post-graduate degrees to be offered by Leeds University's School of Performance and Cultural Industries, which is due to relocate to the main Leeds campus in the autumn of 2007.

University of Sheffield

Institute for Lifelong Learning, 196–198 West Street, Sheffield S1 4ET
☎0114 222 7000 Fax 0114 222 7001
www.shef.ac.uk/till

Certificate in *Creative Writing* (Degree Level 1) and a wide range of courses, from foundation level to specialist writing areas, open to all. Courses in poetry, journalism, scriptwriting, comedy, short story writing, travel writing. Brochures and information available from the address above.

Yorkshire Art Circus

School Lane, Glasshoughton, Castleford WF10 4QH
☎01977 550401
✉ admin@artcircus.org.uk
www.artcircus.org.uk

Administrator *Angela Sibbit*

Yorkshire Art Circus is a community arts organisation and a registered charity. Runs courses, forums and masterclasses that aim to meet the needs of writers and artists who are looking to learn more about creative writing, ICT and publishing. All tutors are professional writers and artists who make a living working in the field of arts that they teach. Also runs outreach projects and sessions for groups on request. An annual training brochure is available.

IRELAND

Dingle Writing Courses Ltd
Ballintlea, Ventry Co. Kerry
☎00 353 66 915 9815
Fax 00 353 66 915 9815
✉ info@dinglewritingcourses.ie
www.dinglewritingcourses.ie
Directors *Abigail Joffe, Nicholas McLachlan*

An autumn programme of weekend residential courses for beginners and experienced writers alike. Tutored by professional writers the courses include poetry, fiction, starting to write and writing for theatre as well as special themed courses. Past tutors have included Michael Donaghy, Paul Durcan, Anne Enright, Nuala Ni Dhomhnaill, Carlo Gébler, Jennifer Johnston, Paula Meeham. Also organises tailor-made courses for schools, writers' groups or students on a *Creative Writing* programme.

Queen's University of Belfast
Institute of Lifelong Learning, Belfast BT7 1NN
☎028 9097 3323   Fax 028 9097 1084
✉ ill@qub.ac.uk
www.qub.ac.uk/ill

Courses have included *Creative Writing; Writing for Profit and Pleasure* and *Scriptwriting.*

University of Dublin (Trinity College)
Graduate Studies Office, Arts Building, Trinity College, Dublin 2
☎00 353 1 608 1166   Fax 00 353 1 671 2821
✉ gradinfo@tcd.ie
www.tcd.ie/owc

Contact *Admissions*

Offers an MPhil *Creative Writing* course. A one-year, full-time course intended for students who are seriously committed to writing or prospective authors.

The Writer's Academy
Carrig-on-Bannow, Co. Wexford
☎00 353 51 561789
✉ thewritersacademy@eircom.net
www.thewritersacademy.net

Distance learning freelance article writing and short story writing courses, critique service and marketing advice. Personal tuition plus expert information and support for writers of all abilities.

SCOTLAND

Arvon Foundation (Inverness-shire)
See entry under **Greater London**

Edinburgh University
Office of Lifelong Learning, 11 Buccleuch Place, Edinburgh EH8 9LW
☎0131 650 4400   Fax 0131 667 6097
✉ oll@ed.ac.uk
www.lifelong.ed.ac.uk

Several writing-orientated courses and summer schools. Full course information available on the website.

Learning Curve Home Study Limited
Leader Cottage, Nether Blainslie, Galashiels TD1 2PR
☎01896 860661   Fax 01896 860367
✉ edesk@learningcurve.uk.com
www.learningcurve-uk.com

Contact *Enquiry Desk*

Offers a selection of flexible distance learning courses, each of which includes adaptable assignments enabling students either to follow the set exercises or work on their own writing project with the help of a tutor. Thirteen courses are available, including: *Writing for Children; Short Story Writing; Novel Writing; Freelance Journalism; Writing for Radio and Television; Autobiography.* Prices range from £195.

7:84 Summer School
See **7:84 Theatre Company Scotland** under *Theatre Producers*

University of Dundee
Continuing Education, Nethergate, Dundee DD1 4HN
☎01382 344809   Fax 01382 386713
www.dundee.ac.uk/learning/conted

Various creative writing courses held at the University and elsewhere in Tayside. Detailed course brochure available from end of June.

University of Glasgow
Department of Adult and Continuing Education, 11 Eldon Street, Glasgow G3 6NH
☎0141 330 1835   Fax 0141 330 1821
✉ enquiry@ace.gla.ac.uk
www.gla.ac.uk/adulteducation

Runs writers' workshops and courses at all levels; all friendly and informal. Daytime and evening meetings. Tutors are all experienced published writers. Call 0141 330 1829 for course brochure.

University of St Andrews

School of English, The University, St Andrews KY16 9AL
☎01334 462666 Fax 01334 462655
✉ english@st-andrews.ac.uk
www.st-andrews.ac.uk

Offers postgraduate study in *Creative Writing*. Modules in Writing Fiction and Writing Poetry. Students submit a dissertation of original writing – prose fiction of 15,000 words or a collection of around 30 short poems. Taught by Professor Douglas Dunn, John Burnside, Kathleen Jamie, A.L. Kennedy, Meaghan Delahunt and Don Paterson. Also offers PhD in *Creative Writing*.

WALES

Ty Newydd Writers' Centre

Llanystumdwy, Cricieth LL52 0LW
☎01766 522811 Fax 01766 523095
✉ post@tynewydd.org
www.tynewydd.org

Residential writers' centre set up by the Taliesin Trust with the support of the **Arts Council of Wales** to encourage and promote writing in both English and Welsh. Most courses run from Monday evening to Saturday morning. Each course has two tutors and a maximum of 16 participants. A wide range of courses for all levels of experience. Early booking essential. Fees from £400 inclusive. People on low incomes may be eligible for a grant or bursary. Course leaflet available. (See also *Organisations of Interest to Poets*.)

University of Glamorgan

Treforest, Pontypridd CF37 1DL
☎01443 483598
www.glam.ac.uk

Director, The National Centre for Writing
Professor Tony Curtis, FRSL

MPhil in *Writing*: a two-year part-time Masters degree for writers of fiction and poets. Established 1993. Contact *Professor Tony Curtis* at the School of Humanities, Law and Social Sciences.

MA in *Scriptwriting (Theatre, TV or Radio)*: a two-year part-time Masters degree for scriptwriters. Contact *Dr Lewis*.

BA in *Creative and Professional Writing*: a three-year course for undergraduates. Contact *Sheenagh Pugh*.

University of Wales, Aberystwyth

Department of English, Hugh Owen Building, Aberystwyth SY23 3DY
☎01970 622534 Fax 01970 622530
www.aber.ac.uk/english

BA in *English and Creative Writing*, a three-year course taught in part by practising writers: Director of Creative Writing, novelist and poet, Jem Poster and poets Tiffany Atkinson, Matthew Francis and Kelly Grovier. Also offers PhD and taught MA in *Writing* with modules in narratology and poetry, writing and publication.

University of Wales, Bangor

Department of English, College Road, Bangor LL57 2DG
☎01248 382102
✉ els029@bangor.ac.uk *or* postgrad-english@bangor.ac.uk
www.bangor.ac.uk

The Department of English offers: MPhil/PhD *Creative and Critical Writing*; Diploma/MA *Creative Studies (Creative Writing)*; BA (Hons) *English with Creative Writing*; BA (Hons) *English with Journalism*. The Centre for Creative and Performing Arts offers *Creative Writing* courses from undergraduate level to MA and PhD.

John Wilson's Writing Courses

Argoed Hall, Tregaron SY25 6JR
☎01974 298070
✉ john.wilson@virgin.net

Residential writing intensives ranging from basic skills to workshops in creative and business writing and journalism. For advanced writers an opportunity to understand and develop the creative process is provided. The courses normally run from Thursday evening to Sunday afternoon, with B&B accommodation and lunch at Argoed Hall, with evening meals (or full board) at nearby hotels. Phone or e-mail for details.

Writers' Holiday at Caerleon

School Bungalow, Church Road, Pontnewydd, Cwmbran NP44 1AT
☎01633 489438
✉ writersholiday@lineone.net
www.writersholiday.net
Contact *Anne Hobbs*

Annual six-day comprehensive conference

including 12 courses for writers of all standards held in the summer at the University of Wales' Caerleon Campus. Courses, lectures, concert and excursion all included in the fee. Private, single and en-suite, full board accommodation. Courses have included *Writing for Publication*; *Writing Poetry*; *Writing Romantic Fiction* and *Writing for the Radio.*

Writers' Circles and Workshops

Directory of Writers' Circles, Courses and Workshops

39 Lincoln Way, Harlington LU5 6NG
☎01525 873197
✉ diana@writers-circles.com
www.writers-circles.com

Directory of UK writers' circles, courses and workshops, edited by Diana Hayden. Contains contact details and information about meetings in the UK and Republic of Ireland. Updated twice annually.

Battersea Writers' Group at Battersea Arts Centre

Lavender Hill, London SW11 5TN
☎07970 715080
✉ info@batterseawriters.co.uk
www.writers-circles.com/battersea.html
Contacts *Jason Young, Rupert Davies-Cooke*

Formerly the Tooting and Balham Writers' Circle, which was founded in 2003, the Battersea Writers' Group is a group of writers who meet on the first Wednesday of each month at 7.30 pm in the Family Room at Battersea Arts Centre. E-mail for membership details.

Carmarthen Writers' Circle

Lower Carfan, Tavernspite, Whitland SA34 0NP
☎01994 240441
Contact *Jenny White*

Founded 1989. The Circle meets monthly on the second Monday of the month at the Indoor Bowls Centre, Carmarthen. All levels and genres welcome.

Caron Writers

Argoed Hall, Tregaron SY25 6JR
☎01974 298070
✉ john.wilson@virgin.net
Contact *John Wilson*

Founded in 2002, the group meets from 2.00 pm to 4.00 pm on the second Sunday of most months (not July or August). Each session comprises announcements and a writing/reading workshop. Emphasis is on fun, discussion and achievement. 'Outstanding results have been achieved and members are gaining considerable success in creative writing competitions and independent publishing.' All genres welcome. Fee: £15 p.a. and £3.50 per session (includes light refreshments). Phone or e-mail for details.

Chiltern Writers' Group

151 Chartridge Lane, Chesham HP5 2SE
☎01494 772308
chilternwriters.netfirms.com
SUBSCRIPTION £15 p.a.; £10 (concessions); £3 (non-members meetings)

Guest speakers, workshops, manuscript critiques and monthly meetings, held at Wendover Library every second Thursday of the month. Regular newsletter and competitions.

The Cotswold Writers' Circle

Bliss's Cottage, Lower Chedworth, Cheltenham GL54 4AN
☎01285 720668
✉ elaine@pandelunt.co.uk
Patron *Elizabeth Webster*
Membership Secretary *Elaine Lunt*
Competition Secretary *Mrs Anne Brookes*

The Circle meets every Tuesday morning (except second Tuesday of the month) in Cirencester. Activities include workshops with well-known authors and an International Open Writing Competition; closing date 31 January annually (send s.a.e. for details). Winners published in the Circle's anthology, *Pen Ultimate*.

Cumbrian Literary Group

'Calgarth', The Brow, Flimby, Maryport CA15 8TD
☎01900 813444
✉ elaine@pandelunt.co.uk
President *Glyn Matthews*
Secretary *Joyce E. Fisher*

Founded 1946 to provide a meeting place for readers and writers in Cumbria. The Group meets once a month (April to November) in Keswick. Invites speakers to meetings and holds annual competitions for poetry band prose. Publishes *Bookshelf* magazine. Further details from the Secretary at the address above.

'Sean Dorman' Manuscript Society

3 High Road, Britford, Salisbury SP5 4DS
Director *Jan Smith*

Founded 1957. Provides mutual help among writers and aspiring writers in England, Wales and Scotland. By means of circulating manuscript parcels, members receive constructive comment on their own work and read and comment on the work of others. Full details and application forms available on receipt of s.a.e.

East Anglian Writers

77 Marlborough Road, Norwich NR3 4PL
✉ chair@eastanglianwriters.org.uk
www.eastanglianwriters.org.uk
Chairman *Benjamin Scott*

A group for professional writers living in Norfolk, Suffolk, Essex, Cambridgeshire and Bedfordshire. Affiliated to the **Society of Authors**. Aims to help writers socialise and promote their work. Informal social events, speakers' evenings and contact point for professional writers in the area.

Eastbourne's Anderida Writers

20 Vian Avenue, Eastbourne BN23 6EY
☎01323 737677
Secretary *Stella Freshney*

Creative workshops for Sussex authors. Talks and competitions.

eQuinoxe – Screenwriters' Workshops

c/o Costes K, 81 Avenue Kleber, 75116 Paris, France
☎00 33 1 44 05 74 12
Fax 00 33 1 44 05 85 57
✉ equinoxetbc@equinoxetbc.fr
www.equinoxetbc.fr
Contacts *Yoann de Birague d'Apremont, Marianne Lére*

Week-long intensive screenwriting workshops, held twice a year in English and French, open to experienced European screenwriters. Participants are selected by an international jury: candidates must have written a script for a feature film, which is sufficiently developed and ready to go into production.

Euroscript

☎0780 336 9414
✉ scriptcounsel121@blueyonder.co.uk
www.euroscript.co.uk

Script development organisation offering cre-ative and editorial input to professional writers and producers. Develops screenplays through an intensive consultancy programme, including residential script workshops; also provides script reports. Open to writers of any nationality. E-mail, telephone, or access the website for further information.

Foyle Street Writers Group

See **See Sunderland City Library and Arts Centre** under *Library Services*

Gay Authors Workshop

BM Box 5700, London WC1N 3XX
Contact *Kathryn Byrd*

Established 1978 to encourage and support lesbian/gay writers. Regular meetings and a newsletter. GAW gave rise to **Paradise Press** (see entry under *Small Presses*).

Guildford Writers

See **The Guildford Institute of the University of Surrey** under *UK and Irish Writers' Courses*

Historical Novel Folio

17 Purbeck Heights, Mount Road, Parkstone, Poole BH14 0QP
☎01202 741897
Contact *Doris Myall-Harris*

An independent postal workshop – single folio dealing with any period before World War II. Send s.a.e. for details.

'How to Self-Publish Your Book' Workshops

Faculty of Arts, University of Winchester, Winchester SO22 4NR
☎01962 827238
✉ barbara.large@winchester.ac.uk
www.writersconference.co.uk
Contact *Barbara Large, MBE, FRSA, FUW*

One-day workshops to inform writers who wish to self-publish their books about the digital and lithographic processes. Participants will learn the skills of researching, writing and revising their mss; the use of photographs, maps, diagrams, illustrations, design and formatting; types of paper, fonts, sizes, ISBN numbers and costs, and marketing their books. 2007 workshops: Friday, 11th May and Friday, 21st September.

Janus Writers

See **See Sunderland City Library and Arts Centre** under *Library Services*

Kops and Ryan Advanced Playwriting Workshops

41B Canfield Gardens, London NW6 3JL
☎020 7624 2940/7263 8740

Tutors *Bernard Kops, Tom Ryan*

Three ten-week terms per year from September. Small group writing and improvisation workshops. Instruction in film technique and private tutorials. Call for details.

Lewes Live Literature

See entry under *Festivals*

London Writers' Circle

54 Rokeby Gardens, Woodford Green
IG8 9HR
☎020 8504 2506
✉ colleenmcmath@amserve.com

Membership Secretary *Colleen McMath*
SUBSCRIPTION £20 (London); £10 (country);
£6 (overseas)

Founded 1924. Encourages writers of all grades in poetry, short story and feature writing. Monthly meetings, social events and quarterly magazine.

New Writing South

9 Jew Street, Brighton BN1 1UT
☎01273 735353
✉ admin@pierplaywrights.co.uk
www.newwritingsouth.com

Contact *Chris Taylor*
SUBSCRIPTION £25 (individual);
£15 (unwaged); £50 (company)

Formerly Pier Playwrights. Run by playwrights for playwrights throughout the South East region. Workshops by visiting professionals, script reading, courses, residencies, etc. and a monthly newsletter.

North West Playwrights (NWP)

18 Express Networks, 1 George Leigh Street, Manchester M4 5DL
☎0161 237 1978
✉ newplaysnw@hotmail.com
www.newplaysnw.com

Founded 1982. Operates a script-reading service, classes and script development scheme and *The Lowdown* newsletter. Services available to writers in the region only.

Pier Playwrights

See **New Writing South**

Pitstop Refuelling Writers' Weekend Workshops

Faculty of Arts, University of Winchester, Winchester SO22 4NR
☎01962 827238
✉ barbara.large@winchester.ac.uk
www.writersconference.co.uk

Director *Barbara Large, MBE, FRSA, FUW*

Following on from the **Annual Writers' Conference** in Winchester, these are small-group writing workshops under the guidance of professional writers. 2006 workshop: 27–29th October; 2007: 16–18th March and 26–28th October.

Player–Playwrights

See under *Professional Associations and Societies*

Scribo

1/31 Hamilton Road, Bournemouth
BH1 4EQ
☎01202 302533

Contacts *K. & P. Sylvester*

Scribo (established over 20 years ago) is a postal workshop for novelists dealing with both manuscript folios (e.g. fantasy/sci-fi, mainstream, women's fiction, crime, literary) and forum folios (discussion, information exchange). No annual subscription. Send s.a.e. for further details.

Script Yorkshire

Membership: 9 Barker's Road, Sheffield S7 1SD
✉ members@scriptyorkshire.co.uk
www.scriptyorkshire.co.uk
Membership *Caroline Small*

Formerly known as Yorkshire Playwrights. Relaunched in 2005 as Script Yorkshire. A support and advocacy organisation for scriptwriters across performance and broadcast media which aims to empower Yorkshire's scriptwriters by giving them the skills and insights they need to develop their own careers. Open to professional or aspiring scriptwriters (theatre, radio, TV and film) who live or work in Yorkshire. Company membership also available. Visit the website for further information or write to the address above.

Short Story Writers' Folio/ Children's Novel Writers' Folio

5 Park Road, Brading, Sandown, Isle of Wight
PO36 0HU
☎01983 407697
✉ nott.wortley-dawn@tiscali.co.uk

Contact *Mrs Dawn Wortley-Nott*

Postal workshops; members receive constructive criticism of their work and read and offer advice on fellow members' contributions. Send an s.a.e. for further details.

Society of Sussex Authors

3 Dolphin House, 51 St Nicholas Lane, Lewes BN7 2JZ

☎01273 470100 Fax 01273 470100

✉ sussexbooks@aol.com

Contact *Michael Legat*

Founded 1968. Six meetings per year, held in Lewes, plus social events. Membership restricted to Sussex-based writers only.

Southwest Scriptwriters

☎0117 909 5522

✉ info@southwest-scriptwriters.co.uk

www.southwest-scriptwriters.co.uk

Secretary *John Colborn*

Founded 1994 to offer support to regional writers for all media. The group meets at the Bristol Old Vic.

Speakeasy – Milton Keynes Writers' Group

46 Wealdstone Place, Springfield, Milton Keynes MK6 3JG

☎01908 663860

✉ speakeasy@writerbrock.co.uk

www.mkweb.co.uk/speakeasy

Contact *Martin Brocklebank*

Monthly meetings on the first Friday of each month at 8.00 pm. Full and varied programme includes Local Writer Nights where work can be read and peformed and Guest Nights where writers, poets and journalists are invited to speak. Mini-workshops and information nights are also in the programme. Invites entries to Open Creative Writing Competitions. Phone, e-mail or send s.a.e. for details to address above.

Spread the Word

77 Lambeth Walk, London SE11 6DX

☎020 7735 3111 Fax 020 7735 2666

✉ info@spreadtheword.org.uk

www.spreadtheword.org.uk

General Manager *Nick Murza*

Develops new writing and writers in London throughout their careers through creative writing workshops, talks, reading groups, cross arts projects, advice sessions and one-to-one surgeries.

Sussex Playwrights' Club

2 Brunswick Mews, Hove BN3 1HD

☎01273 730106

www.newventure.org.uk

Secretary *Dennis Evans*

Founded 1935. Monthly readings of members' work by experienced actors. Membership open to all. Meetings held at New Venture Theatre, Bedford Place, Brighton.

Tooting and Balham Writers' Circle

See **Battersea Writers' Group at Battersea Arts Centre**

Ver Poets

15 Brampton Road, St Albans AL1 4PP

☎01727 864898

✉ daphne.schiller@virgin.net

Secretary *Daphne Schiller*

Founded 1966. Postal and local members. Meets in St Albans, runs evening meetings and daytime workshops and organises competitions.

Walton Wordsmiths

27 Braycourt Avenue, Walton on Thames KT12 2AZ

☎01932 702874

✉ words@stickler.org.uk

www.cajunmoon.co.uk

Contact *Wendy Hughes*

Founded in 1999 by Wendy Hughes. Supports writers of all grades and capabilities by offering constructive criticism and advice.

Workers' Educational Association

National Office: Quick House, 65 Clifton Street, London EC2A 4JE

☎020 7426 3450

✉ national@wea.org.uk

www.wea.org.uk

Founded in 1903, the WEA is a charitable provider of adult education with students drawn from all walks of life. It runs writing courses and workshops in many parts of the country which are open to everyone. Contact your local WEA office for details of courses in your region.

Eastern Botolph House, 17 Botolph Lane, Cambridge CB2 3RE

☎01223 350978 ✉ eastern@wea.org.uk

East Midlands 39 Mapperley Road, Mapperley Park, Nottingham NG3 5AQ

☎0115 962 8400
✉eastmidlands@wea.org.uk

London 4 Luke Street, London EC2A 4XW
☎020 7613 7550 ✉ london@wea.org.uk

North East 1st Floor, Unit 6, Metro
Riverside Park, Delta Bank Road, Gateshead
NE11 9DJ
☎0191 461 8100
✉northeast@wea.org.uk

North West Suite 405–409, The Cotton
Exchange, Old Hall Street, Liverpool L3 9JR
☎0151 243 5340
✉northwest@wea.org.uk

Southern Unit 57 Riverside 2, Sir Thomas
Longley Road, Rochester ME2 4DP
☎01634 730101 ✉ southern@wea.org.uk

South West Bradninch Court, Castle Street,
Exeter EX4 3PL
☎01392 490970 ✉ southwest@wea.org.uk

West Midlands 78/80 Sherlock Street,
Birmingham B5 6LT
☎0121 666 6101
✉westmidlands@wea.org.uk

Yorkshire and Humber 6 Woodhouse
Square, Leeds LS3 1AD
☎0113 245 3304
✉yorkshumber@wea.org.uk

Scottish Association Riddle's Court,
322 Lawnmarket, Edinburgh EH1 2PG
☎0131 226 3456
✉ hq@weascotland.org.uk

Northern Ireland 1 Fitzwilliam Street,
Belfast BT9 6AW
☎028 9032 9718 ✉ info@wea-ni.com

South Wales 11 Station Terrace, Cowbridge
Road West, Ely, Cardiff CF5 4AA
☎029 2055 2277 www.swales.wea.org.uk

North Wales Coleg Harlech WEA, Harlech
LL46 2PU
☎01766 781900 ✉ info@fc.harlech.ac.uk

Writers in Oxford
www.writersinoxford.org
Membership Secretary *Donna Dickenson*
Chair *Julie Summers*
SUBSCRIPTION £20 p.a.
Founded 1992. Open to published authors,
playwrights, poets and journalists. Literary sem-
inars and social functions. Publishes *The Oxford
Writer* newsletter.

Yorkshire Playwrights
See **Script Yorkshire**

Miscellany

Apple Coaching (inc. CoachingWriters.co.uk)
8 Feering Road, Billericay CM11 2DR
☎01277 632085
✉ eve@coachingwriters.co.uk
www.CoachingWriters.co.uk
Contact *Eve Menezes Cunningham*

Life coaching, business coaching and NLP (Neuro Linguistic Programming) for aspiring and professional writers (fiction and non-fiction). For help setting writing goals, building self-esteem and confidence, improving communication, getting organised and 'much more'. Editorial services also available. Rates negotiable.

Arjay Research
20 Rookery View, Little Thurrock, Grays RM17 6AS
☎01375 372199 Fax 01375 372199
✉ RogWJ@aol.com
www.copy-editing.net
Contact *Roger W. Jordan*

All aspects of international merchant shipping and naval research undertaken by former shipping archivist and editor. Extensive maritime library and comprehensive databases on *inter alia* ships wrecked/lost and passenger and cruise ships. Terms by arrangement.

Combrógos
10 Heol Don, Whitchurch, Cardiff CF14 2AU
☎029 2062 3359
Contact *Professor Meic Stephens*

Founded 1990. Arts and media research, editorial services, specialising in books about Wales or by Welsh authors. 'Encyclopaedic knowledge of Welsh history, language, literature and culture.'

Jacqueline Edwards
104 Earlsdon Avenue South, Coventry CV5 6DQ
✉ twigsbranches@yahoo.co.uk
Contact *Jacqueline Edwards, MA, LLB(Hons)*

Historical research: family, local and 19th and 20th century legal history. Covers Warwickshire, Gloucestershire, Wiltshire, Worcestershire, Cambridgeshire and the National Archive, Kew, London.

Firefly Media, Publishing Consultancy & Coaching
PO Box 3703, Trowbridge
☎01380 871331 Fax 01380 871331
✉ info@ffmedia.co.uk
www.ffmedia.co.uk
Contact *Julia McCutchen*

Following 20 years of working in-house as a director and publisher of non-fiction, Firefly Media was founded in 2001 by publishing consultant and creativity coach Julia McCutchen, author of *The Writer's Journey: From Inspiration to Publication*. A one-to-one coaching service provides writers with individual advice, feedback and guidance on any aspect of writing and the publishing process. 'Primary areas of expertise include how to write a first-class book proposal and approach the right people in the right way for the best possible chance of success.' A range of talks and in-depth workshops covering the key stages to publication as well as self-publishing options are also available throughout the year. See website for details.

Impressions of Monmouth
Unit 3, The New Building, Ellwood Road, Milkwall, Coleford GL16 7LE
☎01594 839407 Fax 01594 839287
✉ dave@impresscoleford.demon.co.uk
www.impressionsofmonmouth.com
www.wedderburnart.co.uk
Contacts *David Walker, Peter T. Wilson*

Self-publishing and school year books advice and technical assistance for those wishing to self-publish with full design, printing and binding services. Yearbooks, commemorative books, personal, family, local histories, etc. Print runs as low as 25 copies. Fixed prices.

The Indepublishing Agency
✉ enquiries@indepublishing.com
www.indepublishing.com
Contact *Jo Anthony*

Acts as an agent for authors, specialising in finding the best independent or self-published authors in the market today and selling rights under a contracted agreement. Fiction (women's, crime, romance, fantasy, children's) and non-fiction, especially self-help, biography, travelogue and business guides.

International Booksearch Service
☎020 7639 8900
✉ sarah.fordham@btinternet.com
www.scfordham.com
Contact *S.C. Fordham*

Founded 1992. International book search service for out-of-print books. A free service with no obligation to buy the book when found. Experienced in finding books for authors, researchers, TV and film companies, newspapers, magazines, etc.

Caroline Landeau
6 Querrin Street, London SW6 2SJ
☎07050 600420
✉ winmacweb@hotmail.com
Contact *Caroline Landeau*

Experienced research and production – films, multimedia, books, magazines, exhibitions, animation, general interest, art, music, crime, travel, food, film, theatre.

M-Y Books Ltd
1187 Ware Road, Hertford SG13 7EQ
☎01992 586279
✉ jonathan@m-ybooks.co.uk
www.m-ybooks.co.uk
Contact *Jonathan Miller*

Offers promotional and marketing services for authors or small publishers; also distribtution services within the UK and English-speaking Europe.

Murder Files
Dommett Hill Farm, Hare Lane, Buckland St. Mary, Chard TA20 3JS
☎01460 234065
✉ enquiry@murderfiles.com
www.murderfiles.com
Contact *Paul Williams*

Founded 1994. Crime writer and researcher specialising in British murders. Holds information on thousands of well-known and less well-known murders dating from 1400 to the present day. Copies of press cuttings available from 1920 onwards. Details of executions, particularly at the Tyburn and Newgate. Information on British hangmen. Specialist in British police murders since 1700. CD-ROM *The Ultimate Price – The Unlawful Killing of British Police Officers*, Part 1 (1700–1899) &

Part 2 (1900–2000) available. Service available to general enquirers, writers, researchers, TV, radio, video, etc.

Nielsen BookNet (BookData's transactional services)
3rd Floor, Midas House, 62 Goldsworth Road, Woking GU21 6LQ
☎0870 777 8710   Fax 0870 777 8711
✉ sales@nielsenbookdata.co.uk
www.nielsenbooknet.co.uk

BookNet provides a range of e-commerce services that allows electronic trading between booksellers, publishers/distributors, libraries and other suppliers. Services include BookNet Web for booksellers and publishers/distributors, TeleOrdering and EDI messaging.

Nielsen BookScan
3rd Floor, Midas House, 62 Goldsworth Road, Woking GU21 6LQ
☎01483 712222   Fax 01483 712220
✉ info@nielsenbookscan.co.uk
www.nielsenbookscan.co.uk
UK Business Director *Ann Betts*
Publisher Account Manager *Reeta Windsor*

Nielsen BookScan collects transactional data at the point of sale from tills and despatch systems of all the major book retailers in the UK, Ireland, USA and South Africa. Each week data is coded and analysed, producing complete market information for retailers, publishers, libraries, agents and the media within 72 hours of the week ending Saturday.

Ormrod Research Services
Weeping Birch, Burwash TN19 7HG
☎01435 882541
✉ richardormrod@aol.com
www.writeonservices.co.uk
Contact *Richard Ormrod*

Established 1982. Comprehensive research service: literary, historical, academic, biographical, commercial. Verbal quotations available. Also editing, indexing, ghost-writing and critical reading.

Patent Research
Dachsteinstr. 12a, D–81825 Munich, Germany
☎00 49 89 430 7833
Contact *Gerhard Evenwyn*

All world, historical patents for researchers, authors, archives, museums and publishers. Rates on application.

The United Kingdom Copyright Bureau

110 Trafalgar Road, Portslade BN41 1GS
☎01273 277333 Fax 01273 705451
✉ info@copyrightbureau.co.uk
www.copyrightbureau.co.uk

Contacts *Ralph de Straet von Kollman, Petra Ginman*

The UKCB provides a secure copyright service at reasonable cost, enabling multiple copyrights to be registered nominally when required. Prices are advertised on the website including the UKCB's solicitors, etc. Copyrights preferred on floppy disk or CD-ROM; mss are not accepted due to storage space.

Melanie Wilson

72 High Street, Syston LE7 1GQ
☎0116 260 4442 Fax 0116 260 1396
✉ MelanieWilson@dragonflight.co.uk

Contact *Melanie Wilson*

Comprehensive research service for books, magazines, newspapers, documentaries, films, radio, education, TV drama. Includes free worldwide booksearch service and groundwork for all media presentations, particularly in historical research, costume and textiles, crafts, food and cooking, weapons and uniforms, traditional storytelling, past technology, living history displays and exhibitions.

Press Cuttings Agencies

Durrants

Discovery House, 28–42 Banner Street,
London EC1Y 8QE
☎020 7674 0200   Fax 020 7674 0222
✉ contact@durrants.co.uk
www.durrants.co.uk

Wide coverage of all print media sectors including foreign press plus Internet, newswire and broadcast monitoring. High speed, early morning press cuttings from the national press by Web or e-mail. Overnight delivery via courier to most areas or first-class mail. Well presented, laser printed, A4 cuttings. Rates on application.

International Press-Cutting Bureau

224–236 Walworth Road, London SE17 1JE
☎020 7708 2113   Fax 020 7701 4489
✉ info@ipcb.co.uk
www.ipcb.co.uk

Contact *Robert Podro*

Covers national, provincial, trade, technical and magazine press. Cuttings are normally sent twice weekly by first-class post. Basic charges are £70 per month + £1 per cutting.

Romeike Ltd

Romeike House, 16–22 Baltic Street, London EC1Y 0UL
☎0870 726 0010   Fax 020 7490 5640
✉ info@romeike.com
www.romeike.com

Monitors national and international dailies and Sundays, provincial papers, consumer magazines, trade and technical journals, teletext services as well as national radio and TV networks. Back research, advertising checking and Internet monitoring, plus analysis and editorial summary service available.

We Find It (Press Clippings)

40 Galwally Avenue, Belfast BT8 7AJ
☎028 9064 6008   Fax 028 9064 6008

Contact *Avril Forsythe*

Specialises in Northern Ireland press and magazines, both national and provincial. Rates on application.

Bursaries, Fellowships and Grants

The Authors' Contingency Fund

The Society of Authors, 84 Drayton Gardens, London SW10 9SB
☎020 7373 6642 Fax 020 7373 5768
✉ info@societyofauthors.org
www.societyofauthors.org

This fund makes modest grants to published authors who find themselves in sudden financial difficulties. Contact the **Society of Authors** for an information sheet and application form.

The Authors' Foundation

The Society of Authors, 84 Drayton Gardens, London SW10 9SB
☎020 7373 6642 Fax 020 7373 5768
✉ info@societyofauthors.org
www.societyofauthors.org

Grants to writers whose publisher's advance is insufficient to cover the costs of research involved. Application by letter to The Authors' Foundation giving details, in confidence, of the advance and royalties, together with the reasons for needing additional funding. Grants are sometimes given even if there is no commitment by a publisher, so long as the applicant has had a book published and the new work will almost certainly be published. About £80,000 is distributed each year. Contact the **Society of Authors** for full entry details. Final entry dates: 30 April and 30 September.

The K. Blundell Trust

The Society of Authors, 84 Drayton Gardens, London SW10 9SB
☎020 7373 6642 Fax 020 7373 5768
✉ info@societyofauthors.org
www.societyofauthors.org

Grants to writers whose publisher's advance is insufficient to cover the costs of research. Author must be under 40, has to submit a copy of his/her previous book and the work must 'contribute to the greater understanding of existing social and economic organisation'. Application by letter. Contact the **Society of Authors** for full entry details. Final entry dates: 30 April and 30 September.

Alfred Bradley Bursary Award

c/o BBC Radio Drama, Room 2130, New Broadcasting House, Oxford Road, Manchester M60 1SJ
☎0161 244 4253 Fax 0161 244 4248
Contact *Coordinator*

Established 1992. Biennial award in commemoration of the life and work of the distinguished radio producer Alfred Bradley. Aims to encourage and develop new radio writing talent in the BBC North region. There is a change of focus for each award, e.g. previous years have targeted comedy drama, verse drama, etc. Entrants must live in the north of England. The award is given to help writers to pursue a career in writing for radio. Further information can be found on bbc.co.uk/writersroom Previous winners: Anthony Cropper, Julia Copus, Michael Stewart, Ben Tagoe, Katie Douglas.
AWARD Up to £6000 over two years and a BBC Radio Drama commission, the opportunity to develop further ideas with Radio Drama.

British Academy Small Research Grants

10 Carlton House Terrace, London SW1Y 5AH
☎020 7969 5217 Fax 020 7969 5414
✉ grants@britac.ac.uk
www.britac.ac.uk

Contact *Assistant Secretary, Research Grants*

Award to further original academic research at postdoctoral level in the humanities and social sciences. Entrants must be resident in the UK. See website for final entry dates. Three competitions a year.
AWARD £7500 (maximum).

Cholmondeley Awards

The Society of Authors, 84 Drayton Gardens, London SW10 9SB
☎020 7373 6642 Fax 020 7373 5768
✉ info@societyofauthors.org
www.societyofauthors.org

Founded 1965 by the late Dowager Marchioness of Cholmondeley. Annual honorary awards to recognise the achievement and

distinction of individual poets. 2005 winners: Jane Duran, Christopher Logue, M.R. Peacocke, Neil Rollinson.
AWARD £8000 (total).

Olive Cook Prize
See **Tom–Gallon Trust Award**

The Economist/Richard Casement Internship
The Economist, 25 St James's Street, London SW1A 1HG
☎020 7830 7000
✉ casement@economist.com
www.economist.com

Contact *Geoffrey Carr* Science Editor (re. Casement Internship)

For an aspiring journalist under 25 to spend three months in the summer writing for *The Economist* about science and technology. Applicants should write a letter of introduction along with an article of approximately 600 words suitable for inclusion in the Science and Technology Section. 'Our aim is more to discover writing talent in a young science student than scientific aptitude in a budding journalist.' Competition details normally announced in the magazine late January or early February and 4–5 weeks allowed for application.

European Jewish Publication Society
PO Box 19948, London N3 3ZJ
Fax 020 8346 1776
✉ cs@ejps.org.uk
www.ejps.org.uk
Contact *Dr Colin Shindler*

Established in 1995 to help fund the publication of books of European Jewish interest which would otherwise remain unpublished. Helps with the marketing, distribution and promotion of such books. Publishers who may be interested in publishing works of Jewish interest should approach the Society with a proposal and manuscript in the first instance. Books which have been supported recently include: *The History of Zionism* Walter Laqueur; *Photographing the Holocaust* Janina Struk; *Isaac Rosenberg: Selected Poems and Letters* ed. Jean Liddiard; *Migrations* Gloria Gervitz; *The Arab-Israeli Cookbook* Robin Soans. Also supports the publication of poetry, and translations from and into other European languages.
GRANT £3000 (maximum).

Fulbright Awards
The Fulbright Commission, Fulbright House, 62 Doughty Street, London WC1N 2JZ
☎020 7404 6880 Fax 020 7404 6834
✉ programmes@fulbright.co.uk
www.fulbright.co.uk

Contact *British Programme Manager*

The Fulbright Commission offers a number of scholarships given at postgraduate level and above, open to any field (science and the arts) of study/research to be undertaken in the USA. Length of award is typically an academic year. Application deadline for postgraduate awards is usually late October/early November of preceding year of study; and mid-March/early April for postdoctoral awards. Further details and application forms are available on the Commission's website. Alternatively, send A4 envelope with sufficient postage for 100g with a covering letter explaining which level of award is of interest.

Tony Godwin Memorial Trust
c/o 38 Lyttelton Court, Lyttelton Road, London N2 0EB
☎020 8209 1613
✉ info@tgmt.org.uk
www.tgmt.org.uk
Chairman *Iain Brown*

Biennial award established to commemorate the life of Tony Godwin, a prominent publisher in the 1960s/70s. Open to all young people (under 35 years old) who are UK nationals and working, or intending to work, in publishing. The award provides the recipient with the means to spend at least one month as the guest of an American publishing house in order to learn about international publishing. The recipient is expected to submit a report upon return to the UK. Next award: 2007; final entry date: 31 December 2006. Previous winners: George Lucas (Hodder), Clive Priddle (Fourth Estate), Richard Scrivener (Penguin), Lisa Shakespeare (Weidenfeld & Nicolson), Fiona Stewart (HarperCollins).
AWARD Bursary of approx. US$5000.

Eric Gregory Trust Fund
The Society of Authors, 84 Drayton Gardens, London SW10 9SB
☎020 7373 6642 Fax 020 7373 5768
✉ info@societyofauthors.org
www.societyofauthors.org

Annual awards of varying amounts are made for the encouragement of poets under the age of

30 on the basis of a submitted collection. Open only to British-born subjects resident in the UK. Final entry date: 31 October. Contact the **Society of Authors** for full entry details. 2005 winners: Melanie Challenger, Carolyn Jess, Luke Kennard, Jaim Smith.
AWARD £20,000 (total).

The Guardian Research Fellowship
Nuffield College, Oxford OX1 1NF
☎01865 278542 Fax 01865 278666
Contact *The Administrative Officer*

One-year fellowship endowed by the Scott Trust, owner of *The Guardian*, to give someone working in the media the chance to put their experience into a new perspective, publish the outcome and give a *Guardian* lecture. Applications welcomed from journalists and management members, in newspapers, periodicals or broadcasting. Research or study proposals should be directly related to experience of working in the media. Accommodation and meals in college will be provided and a stipend. Advertised biennially in November.

Hawthornden Literary Institute
Hawthornden International Retreat for Writers, Lasswade EH18 1EG
☎0131 440 2180 Fax 0131 440 1989
Contact *The Administrator*

Established 1982 to provide a peaceful setting where published writers can work in silence. The Castle houses up to six writers at a time, who are known as Hawthornden Fellows. Writers from any part of the world may apply for the fellowships. No monetary assistance is given, nor any contribution to travelling expenses, but once arrived at Hawthornden, the writer is the guest of the Retreat. Applications on forms provided must be made by the end of November for the following calendar year. Previous winners include: Les Murray, Alasdair Gray, Helen Vendler, David Profumo, Hilary Spurling.

Francis Head Bequest
The Society of Authors, 84 Drayton Gardens, London SW10 9SB
☎020 7373 6642 Fax 020 7373 5768
✉ info@societyofauthors.org
www.societyofauthors.org

Provides grants to published British authors over the age of 35 who need financial help during a period of illness, disablement or temporary financial crisis. Contact the **Society of**

Authors for an information sheet and application form.

Jerwood Awards
See **The Royal Society of Literature/ Jerwood Awards**

Journalists' Charity
Dickens House, 35 Wathen Road, Dorking RH4 1JY
☎01306 887511 Fax 01306 888212
✉ enquiries@journalistscharity.org.uk
www.journalistscharity.org.uk
Director/Secretary *David Ilott*

Aims to relieve distress among journalists and their dependants. Continuous and/or occasional financial grants; also retirement homes for eligible beneficiaries. Further information and subscription details available from the Director.

Ralph Lewis Award
University of Sussex Library, Brighton BN1 9QL
☎01273 678158 Fax 01273 678441
✉ a.timoney@sussex.ac.uk

Established 1985. Occasional award set up by Ralph Lewis, a Brighton author and art collector who left money to fund awards for promising manuscripts which would not otherwise be published. The award would be given in the form of a grant to a UK-based publisher in respect of a publication of literary works by new authors. No direct applications from writers. Previous winners: **Peterloo Poets**; **Serpent's Tail**; **Stride Publications**.

The Elizabeth Longford Grants
The Society of Authors, 84 Drayton Gardens, London SW10 9SB
☎020 7373 6642 Fax 020 7373 5768
✉ info@societyofauthors.org
www.societyofauthors.org

Biannual grant, sponsored by Flora Fraser and Peter Soros, to a historical biographer whose publisher's advance is insufficient to cover the costs of research involved. Contact the **Society of Authors** for full details. Final entry dates: 30 April and 30 September.
GRANT £2500.

The John Masefield Memorial Trust
The Society of Authors, 84 Drayton Gardens, London SW10 9SB
☎020 7373 6642 Fax 020 7373 5768

✉ info@societyofauthors.org
www.societyofauthors.org

This trust makes occasional grants to professional poets (or their immediate dependants) who are faced with sudden financial problems. Contact the **Society of Authors** for an information sheet and application form.

Somerset Maugham Trust Fund

The Society of Authors, 84 Drayton Gardens, London SW10 9SB
☎020 7373 6642 Fax 020 7373 5768
✉ info@societyofauthors.org
www.societyofauthors.org

Annual awards designed to encourage writers under the age of 35 to travel. Given on the basis of a published work of fiction, non-fiction or poetry. Open only to British-born subjects resident in the UK. Final entry date: 20 December. 2005 winners: Justin Hill *Passing Under Heaven*; Maggie O'Farrell *The Distance Between Us*.

AWARDS £10,000 (total).

The Airey Neave Trust

PO Box 36800, 40 Bernard Street, London WC1N 1WJ
☎020 7833 4440
✉ hanthoc@aol.com
www.aireyneavetrust.org.uk
Contact *Hannah Scott*

Initiated 1989. Annual research fellowships for up to three years – towards a book or paper – for serious research connected with national and international law, and human freedom. Preferably attached to a particular university in Britain.

North East Literary Fellowship

Arts Council England, North East, Central Square, Forth Street, Newcastle upon Tyne NE1 3PJ
☎0191 255 8542 Fax 0191 230 1020
www.artscouncil.org.uk
Contact *Literature Officer*

A competitive fellowship in association with the Universities of Durham and Newcastle upon Tyne. Contact **Arts Council England, North East**, for details.

Northern Rock Foundation Writer's Award

New Writing North, 2 School Lane, Whickham, Newcastle upon Tyne NE16 4SL
☎0191 488 8580 Fax 0191 488 8576
✉ mail@newwritingnorth.com

www.nr-foundationwriters.com
Contact *Catherine Lancaster*

Annual award established in 2002 with the aim of liberating established writers who live in the region from work other than writing. Applicants must have at least two books published by a recognised publisher and *must* live and work in Northumberland, Tyne and Wear, County Durham, Cumbria or Teesside. 2006 winner: Andrew Crumey.

AWARD £60,000 (£20,000 a year for three years).

Northern Writers' Awards

See **New Writing North** under *Professional Associations and Societies*

PAWS (Public Awareness of Science) Drama Fund

The PAWS Office, OMNI Communications, First Floor, 155 Regents Park Road, London NW1 8BB
✉ pawsomni@btconnect.com
www.pawsdrama.com
Contacts *Andrew Millington, Andree Molyneux*

Established 1994. PAWS encourages and supports television drama drawing on science, engineering and technology. It offers a range of activities to bring science and technology to TV drama writers and producers in an easily accessible way.

Events: covering the latest science and technology topics and enabling writers to meet scientists and engineers; Contacts & Information Service: aims to put writers and producers in 'one-to-one' contact with specialists who can help them develop their TV drama ideas; New Funding Scheme: rolling funding support primarily intended to help writers and producers who have a recent track record of successful TV drama experience to bring their ideas closer to production. People with lesser experience may also apply. Contact the PAWS Office or check out the website for further information.

Pearson Playwrights' Scheme

c/o Pearson Plc, 80 Strand, London WC2R 0RL
✉ playwrightscheme@tiscali.co.uk
www.pearson.com
Administrator *Jack Andrews, MBE*

Awards five bursaries to playwrights annually, each worth £6500. Applicants must be sponsored by a theatre which then submits the play for consideration by a panel. Each award allows the playwright a 12-month attachment. Applications invited via theatres in October each year. E-mail for up-to-date information.

Charles Pick Fellowship

School of Literature and Creative Writing, University of East Anglia, University Plain, Norwich NR4 7TJ
☎01603 592286 Fax 01603 507728
✉ Charlespickfellowship@uea.ac.uk
www.uea.ac.uk/eas/fellowships/pick.shtml

Contact *Shawn Alexander*

An annual award, founded in 2001 by the Charles Pick Consultancy in memory of the publisher and literary agent who died in 2000, to support a new unpublished writer of fictional or non-fictional prose. Award of the Fellowship, which is residential from August to January, is judged on the quality of writing and reference from a literary agent, editor or accredited creative writing teacher. Previous winner: Sam Fletcher. Deadline for applications: 31 January each year.

AWARD £10,000 plus free campus accommodation.

Peggy Ramsay Foundation

Hanover House, 14 Hanover Square, London W1S 1HP
☎020 7667 5000 Fax 020 7667 5100
✉ laurence.harbottle@harbottle.com
www.peggyramsayfoundation.org

Contact *G. Laurence Harbottle*

Founded 1992 in accordance with the will of the late Peggy Ramsay, the well-known agent. Grants are made to writers for the stage who have some experience and who need time and resources to make writing possible. Grants are also made for writing projects by organisations connected with the theatre. The Foundation does not support production costs or any project that does not have a direct benefit to playwriting. Writers must have some record of successful writing for the stage.

GRANTS total £150,000 to £200,000 per year.

The Royal Literary Fund

3 Johnson's Court, off Fleet Street, London EC4A 3EA
☎020 7353 7150 Fax 020 7353 1350
✉ egunnrlf@globalnet.co.uk
www.rlf.org.uk

Secretary *Eileen Gunn*

Grants and pensions are awarded to published authors of several works in financial need, or to their dependants. Examples of author's works are needed for assessment by Committee. Contact the Secretary for further details and application form.

The Royal Society of Literature/Jerwood Awards

The Royal Society of Literature, Somerset House, Strand, London WC2R 1LA
☎020 7845 4676 Fax 020 7845 4679
✉ paulaj@rslit.org
www.rslit.org

Submissions *Paula Johnson*

The awards offer financial assistance to authors engaged in writing their first major commissioned works of non-fiction. Three awards: one of £10,000 and two of £5000 will be offered annually to writers working on substantial non-fiction projects. Open to UK and Irish writers and writers who have been resident in the UK for at least three years. Applications for the awards should be submitted by end August. Further details available on the website.

Scottish Arts Council Creative Scotland Awards

Scottish Arts Council, 12 Manor Place, Edinburgh EH3 7DD
☎0131 226 6051/ Help Desk: 0845 603 6000
Fax 0131 225 9833
✉ help.desk@scottisharts.org.uk
www.scottisharts.org.uk

The scheme offers awards of £30,000. Available to established artists based in Scotland working in any medium, including writing.

Scottish Arts Council New Writers' Bursaries

Scottish Arts Council, 12 Manor Place, Edinburgh EH3 7DD
☎0131 226 6051 Fax 0131 225 9833
✉ gavin.wallace@scottisharts.org.uk
www.scottisharts.org.uk

Contact *Gavin Wallace*, Head of Literature

Ten bursaries of £2000 awarded annually to enable previously unpublished writers of literary work more time to devote to their writing. Applicants should be based in Scotland.

Scottish Arts Council Writers' and Playwrights' Bursaries

Scottish Arts Council, 12 Manor Place, Edinburgh EH3 7DD
☎0131 226 6051 Fax 0131 225 9833
✉ gavin.wallace@scottisharts.org.uk

www.scottisharts.org.uk

Contact *Gavin Wallace*, Head of Literature

Bursaries to enable published writers of literary work and recognised playwrights to devote more time to their writing. Around 20 bursaries of up to £15,000 awarded annually; deadline for applications in July and January. Application open to writers based in Scotland.

Laurence Stern Fellowship

Department of Journalism, City University, Northampton Square, London EC1V 0HB
☎020 7040 4036 Fax 020 7040 8594
✉ a.r.mckane@city.ac.uk
www.city.ac.uk/journalism

Contact *Anna McKane*

Founded 1980. Awarded each year to a young journalist experienced enough to work on national stories. It gives a chance to work on the national desk of the *Washington Post*. A senior executive from the newspaper selects from a shortlist drawn up in February/March. 2005 winner: Sam Coates of *The Times*. Full details about how to apply available on the City University website in January.

Tom-Gallon Trust Award and the Olive Cook Prize

The Society of Authors, 84 Drayton Gardens, London SW10 9SB
☎020 7373 6642 Fax 020 7373 5768
✉ info@societyofauthors.org
www.societyofauthors.org

An award of £1000 is made on the basis of a submitted story to fiction writers of limited means who have had at least one short story accepted for publication. Both awards are biennial and are awarded in alternate years. Contact the **Society of Authors** for an entry form. Final entry date 31 October.

The Betty Trask Awards

The Society of Authors, 84 Drayton Gardens, London SW10 9SB

☎020 7373 6642 Fax 020 7373 5768
✉ info@societyofauthors.org
www.societyofauthors.org

These annual awards are for authors who are under 35 and Commonwealth citizens, awarded on the strength of a first novel (published or unpublished) of a traditional or romantic nature. The awards must be used for a period or periods of foreign travel. Final entry date: 31 January. Contact the **Society of Authors** for an entry form. 2005 winners: Susan Fletcher *Eve Green*; Diana Evans *26a*; Helen Walsh *Brass*.
AWARD £20,000 (total).

The Travelling Scholarships

The Society of Authors, 84 Drayton Gardens, London SW10 9SB
☎020 7373 6642 Fax 020 7373 5768
✉ info@societyofauthors.org
www.societyofauthors.org

Annual honorary grants to established British writers. No submissions. 2005 winners: Anna Crowe, Lavinia Greenlaw.
AWARD £5000 (total).

David T.K. Wong Fellowship

School of Literature and Creative Writing, University of East Anglia, University Plain, Norwich NR4 7TJ
☎01603 592286 Fax 01603 507728
✉ davidtkwongfellowship@uea.ac.uk
www.uea.ac.uk/eas/fellowships/wong/wong.shtml

Contact *Shawn Alexander*

Founded 1998. An annual endowment to enable a writer of promise to spend a year at the University writing a work of fiction on some aspect of life in the Far East. Judged on the basis of submitted written work, the award is open to all nationalities. Final entry date: 31 January. 2005/6 winner: Linh Dinh.
AWARD £25,000.

Prizes

Academi Book of the Year Awards

Academi, 3rd Floor, Mount Stuart House, Mount Stuart Square, Cardiff CF10 5FQ
☎029 2047 2266 Fax 029 2047 0691
✉ post@academi.org
www.academi.org

Contacts *Peter Finch* (Chief Executive), *Lleucu Siencyn* (Deputy)

Annual non-competitive prizes awarded for works of exceptional literary merit written by Welsh authors (by birth or residence), published in Welsh or English during the previous calendar year. There is one major prize in English, the Book of the Year Award, and one major prize in Welsh, Gwobr Llyfr y Flwyddyn.
PRIZES £10,000 to each winner.

J.R. Ackerley Prize

English PEN, 6–8 Amwell Street, London EC1R 1UQ
☎020 7713 0023 Fax 020 7837 7838
✉ enquiries@englishpen.org
www.englishpen.org

Commemorating the novelist/autobiographer J.R. Ackerley, this prize is awarded for a literary autobiography, written in English and published in the year preceding the award. Entry restricted to nominations from the Ackerley Trustees only ('please do not submit books'). 2005 winner: Jonathan Gathorne-Hardy *Half An Arch*.
PRIZE £1000, plus silver pen.

Aldeburgh Poetry Festival Prize

See **Jerwood Aldeburgh First Collection Prize**

Alexander Prize

Royal Historical Society, University College London, Gower Street, London WC1E 6BT
☎020 7387 7532 Fax 020 7387 7532
✉ rhs.info@sas.ac.uk
www.rhs.ac.uk/prizes

Contact *Executive Secretary*

Established 1897. Awarded for a published journal article or essay based upon original research. The article/essay must have been published during the period 1 January 2006–31 December 2006. Competitors may choose their own subject for the essay. Closing date: 31 December.
PRIZE £250.

ALPSP Awards *and* ALPSP/Charlesworth Awards

ALPSP, 47 Vicarage Road, Old Moulsham, Chelmsford CM2 9BS
☎01245 260571 Fax 01245 260935
✉ events@alpsp.org
www.alpsp.org

Contact *Lesley Ogg*

Presented in recognition of significant achievement and innovation in the field of learned and professional publishing by the **Association of Learned and Professional Society Publishers** and the Charlesworth Group. The awards are international and open to publishers, organisations and individuals. Closing date: 31 May. Details available on the Association's website.

Hans Christian Andersen Awards

IBBY, Nonnenweg 12, Postfach, CH-4003 Basel, Switzerland
☎00 41 61 272 2917 Fax 00 41 61 272 2757
✉ ibby@ibby.org
www.ibby.org

Administrative Director *Liz Page*

The highest international prizes for children's literature: The Hans Christian Andersen Award for Writing, established 1956; The Hans Christian Andersen Award for Illustration, established 1966. Candidates are nominated by National Sections of IBBY (The International Board on Books for Young People). Biennial prizes are awarded, in even-numbered years, to an author and an illustrator whose body of work has made a lasting contribution to children's literature. 2006 winners: Award for Writing: Margaret Mahy (New Zealand); Award for Illustration: Wolf Erlbruch (Gemany).
AWARD Gold medals.

Angus Book Award

Angus Council Cultural Services, County Buildings, Forfar DD8 3WF
☎01307 461460 Fax 01307 462590
✉ cultural.services@angus.gov.uk

www.angus.gov.uk/bookaward
Contact *Moyra Hood*, Educational Resources Librarian

Established 1995. Designed to try to help teenagers develop an interest in and enthusiasm for reading. Eligible books are read and voted on by third-year schoolchildren in all eight Angus secondary schools. 2005 winner: Terence Blacker *Boy2Girl*.

PRIZE £500 cheque, plus trophy in the form of a replica Pictish stone.

Annual Theatre Book Prize
See **The Society for Theatre Research Annual Theatre Book Prize**

Arts Council Children's Award
Arts Council England, 14 Great Peter Street, London SW1P 3NQ
☎020 7973 6480
✉ charles.hart@artscouncil.org.uk
www.artscouncil.org.uk
Contact *Theatre Writing Section*

Founded 2000. An annual award for playwrights who write for children up to the age of 12. The plays, which must have been produced professionally, should be suitable for children up to the age of 12 and be at least 45 minutes long. The playwright must be resident in the UK. Contact the Theatre Writing Section for full details and application form. 2006 winner: Neil Duffield *The Lost Warrior*.

AWARD £6000.

Arvon Foundation International Poetry Competition
2nd Floor, 42a Buckingham Palace Road, London SW1W 0RE
☎020 7931 7611 Fax 020 7963 0961
✉ london@arvonfoundation.org
www.arvonfoundation.org
Contact *The London Office*

Established 1980. Biennial competition (next in 2008) for poems written in English and not previously broadcast or published. There are no restrictions on the number of lines, themes, age of entrants or nationality. No limit to the number of entries. Entry fee: £7 per poem. Previous winners: Paul Farley *Laws of Gravity*; Don Paterson *A Private Bottling*.

PRIZE (1st) £5000 and £5000 worth of other prizes.

Asham Award for Women
Asham Literary Endowment Trust, c/o Town Hall, High Street, Lewes BN7 2QS

☎01273 483159
www.ashamaward.com
Contact *Carole Buchan*

Founded in 1996, the Award (named after the house in Sussex where Virginia Woolf lived) is a biennial short story competition for women and is administered by the Asham Literary Endownment Trust which encourages new writing through competitions, mentoring, training and publication. Candidates must be female, over 18, resident in the UK and must not have had a novel or complete anthology of work previously published. See website for details. 2005 winner: Annie Kirby.

PRIZE £3600 cash; 12 winning writers are published by Bloomsbury to include specially commissioned stories by leading professional writers.

Authors' Club First Novel Award
Authors' Club, 40 Dover Street, London W1S 4NP
☎020 7499 8581 Fax 020 7409 0913
✉ stella@theauthorsclub.co.uk
Contact *Stella Kane*

Established 1954. This award is made for the most promising work published in Britain by a British author, and is presented at a dinner held at The Arts Club. Entries for the award are accepted from publishers from September of the year in question and must be full-length (short stories are not eligible). For further details/application form, contact *Lucy Jane Tetlow* or access the website. 2005 winner: Henry Shukman *Sandstorm*.

AWARD £1000.

Aventis Prizes for Science Books
c/o The Royal Society, 6–9 Carlton House Terrace, London SW1Y 5AG
☎020 7451 2576 Fax 020 7930 2170
✉ aventisprizes@royalsoc.ac.uk
www.aventisprizes.com
Contact *Aosaf Afzal*

Annual prizes established in 1988 to celebrate the best in popular science writing. Awarded to books that make science more accessible to readers of all ages and backgrounds. Owned and managed by the Royal Society and sponsored by the Aventis Foundation. All entries must be written in English and their first publication in the UK must have been between 1 January and 31 December; submission by publishers only. Educational textbooks published for professional or specialist audiences are not eligible. 2006 winners: David Bodanis *Electric Universe: How Electricity Switched on the Modern World* (General Prize); Kate Petty and Jenny Maizels *Global Garden* (Junior Prize).

PRIZES (total) £30,000: £10,000 to each winner; £1000 to each of the five shortlisted authors in each prize.

The BA/Nielson BookData Author of the Year Award

Booksellers Association Ltd, 272 Vauxhall Bridge Road, London SW1V 1BA
☎020 7802 0801   Fax 020 7802 0803
✉ anna.okane@booksellers.org.uk
www.booksellers.org.uk

Contact *Anna O'Kane*

Founded as part of the BA Annual Conference to involve authors more closely in the event. Authors must be British or Irish. Not an award open to entry but voted on by the BA's membership. 2005 winner: Michael Morpurgo.

AWARD £1000, plus trophy.

BAAL Book Prize

BAAL Publications Secretary, School of Education, University of Leeds, Leeds LS2 9JT
✉ a.g.white@education.leeds.ac.uk
www.baal.org.uk
Contact *Goodith White*

Annual award made by the British Association for Applied Linguistics to an outstanding book in the field of applied linguistics. Final entry at the end of October/November. Nominations from publishers only. 2005 winner: Viv Edwards *Multilingualism in the English Speaking World*.

Banipal Prize

See **The Translators Association Awards**

Verity Bargate Award

Soho Theatre Company, 21 Dean Street, London W1D 3NE
☎020 7287 5060   Fax 020 7287 5061
✉ rachel@sohotheatre.com
www.sohotheatre.com

Contact *Rachel Taylor*, Literary Assistant

The award was set up to commemorate the late Verity Bargate, co-founder and director of the **Soho Theatre Company**. This national award is presented biennially for a new and unperformed play (next in 2008). Access the mailing list on the website. Previous winners include: Matt Charman, Shan Khan, Fraser Grace, Lyndon Morgans, Adrian Pagan, Diane Samuels, Judy Upton and Toby Whithouse.

BBC Wildlife Magazine Poet of the Year Awards

BBC Wildlife Magazine, Origin Publishing, 14th Floor, Tower House, Fairfax Street, Bristol BS1 3BN
☎0117 927 9009   Fax 0117 933 8032
www.bbcwildlifemagazine.com

Annual award for a poem, the subject of which must be the natural world and/or our relationship with it. Entrants may submit one poem only of no more than 50 lines with the entry form which appears in the magazine. Closing date for entries varies from year to year. See website and the magazine for entry details.

PRIZES Poet of the Year: a wildlife break, publication in the magazine, plus the possibility of a reading of the poem on Radio 4's *Poetry Please*; runners-up: publication in the magazine; four young poets awards, categories: age 7 and under, 8–11, 12–14, 15–17.

BBC Wildlife Magazine Travel Writing Award

BBC Wildlife Magazine, Origin Publishing, 14th Floor, Tower House, Fairfax Street, Bristol BS1 3BN
☎0117 927 9009   Fax 0117 934 9008
✉ jamesfair@originpublishing.co.uk
www.bbcwildlifemagazine.com

Awarded to a travel essay that is a true account involving an intimate encounter with wildlife, either local or exotic. The essay should convey a strong impression of the environment and incorporate the idea of travel and discovery. Maximum 800 words. See website and the magazine for entry details.

PRIZE Publication in the magazine, plus 'holiday of a lifetime'.

BBC Wildlife Magazine Young Environmental Journalist of the Year

BBC Wildlife Magazine, Origin Publishing, 14th Floor, Tower House, Fairfax Street, Bristol BS1 3BN
☎0117 927 9009   Fax 0117 933 8032
www.bbcwildlifemagazine.com

Established to give young people a chance to get into environmental journalism. Entrants must be aged 16–25 and should submit an original 750-word profile, based on an interview with 'someone you regard as an environmental hero, not necessarily famous or renowned, who has contributed to conservation in some way'.

See website and the magazine for entry details.
PRIZE Publication in the magazine, plus a 12–14-day Earthwatch expedition.

The BBCFour Samuel Johnson Prize for Non-Fiction

Colman Getty PR, 28 Windmill Street, London W1T 2JJ
☎020 7631 2666 Fax 020 7631 2699
✉ lois@colmangettypr.co.uk
Contact *Lois Tucker*

Established 1998. Annual prize sponsored by BBCFour. Eligible categories include the arts, autobiography, biography, business, commerce, current affairs, history, natural history, popular science, religion, sport and travel. Entries submitted by publishers only. 2005 winner: Jonathan Coe *Like a Fiery Elephant: The Story of B. S. Johnson.*
PRIZE £30,000; £1000 to each shortlisted author.

David Berry Prize

Royal Historical Society, University College London, Gower Street, London WC1E 6BT
☎020 7387 7532 Fax 020 7387 7532
✉ rhs.info@sas.ac.uk
www.rhs.ac.uk/prizes
Contact *Executive Secretary*

Annual award for an essay of not more than 10,000 words on Scottish history. Closing date: 31 October.
PRIZE £250,

Besterman/McColvin Medal

c/o Information Services Group, CILIP, 7 Ridgmount Street, London WC1E 7AE
☎020 7255 0500 Fax 020 7255 0501
www.cilip.org.uk

Part of the ISG (CILIP)/BookData Reference Awards. Annual award for an outstanding reference work first published in the UK during the preceding year. Consists of two categories: printed and electronic. Works eligible for consideration include: encyclopedias, general and special dictionaries; annuals, yearbooks and directories; handbooks and compendia of data; atlases. Nominations are invited from members of **CILIP**, publishers and others. 2004 winners: *Oxford Dictionary of National Biography* ed. H.C.G. Matthew and Brian Harrison (electronic category); *The Design Encyclopaedia* Mel Byars (printed category).
AWARD Medal and cash prize for each category.

The Biographers' Club Prize

119A Fordwych Road, London NW2 3NJ
☎020 8452 4993
✉ anna@annaswan.co.uk
www.booktrust.org.uk
Contact *Anna Swan*

Established 1999 by literary agent, biographer and founder of the Biographers' Club, Andrew Lownie, to finance and encourage first-time writers researching a biography. Sponsored by the *Daily Mail.* Open to previously un-published writers, applicants should submit (preferably by e-mail) a proposal of 15–20 pages, including outline, sample chapter, a note on the market for the book, sources consulted, competing books and a c.v. 2004 winner: Linda Porter.
PRIZE £1000.

Birdwatch Bird Book of the Year

c/o Birdwatch Magazine, B403A The Chocolate Factory, 5 Clarendon Road, London N22 6XJ
☎020 8881 0550
✉ enquiries@birdwatch.co.uk
www.birdwatch.co.uk
Contact *Dominic Mitchell*

Established in 1992 to acknowledge excellence in ornithological publishing – an increasingly large market with a high turnover. Annual award. Entries, from publishers, must offer an original and comprehensive treatment of their particular ornithological subject matter and must have a broad appeal to British-based readers. 2005 winner: *Birds of England* Andy Brown and Phil Grice.

Biscuit International Short Fiction Prize

Biscuit Publishing, PO Box 123, Washington, Newcastle upon Tyne NE37 2YW
✉ info@biscuitpublishing.com
www.biscuitpublishing.com
Contacts *Brian Lister, Jacqui Lister*

Founded 2000. Annual award that aims to support new writers of short fiction. The 'Top Ten' winners are published in an anthology and recorded on audio CD. In addition, the winning author has separate publication. Closing date: 31 May. Previous winners: Tracey Fuller *The System Was Turned On*; Gillian Garnham *A Place Proper to Grow Wise In*; Sally Zigmond *Sailing to Byzantium.*
PRIZES Publication and cash awards.

Bisto Book of the Year Awards
See **CBI Bisto Book of the Year Awards**

James Tait Black Memorial Prizes
University of Edinburgh, David Hume Tower, George Square, Edinburgh EH8 9JX
☎0131 650 3619 Fax 0131 650 6898
www.englit.ed.ac.uk/jtbinf.htm
Contact *Department of English Literature*

Established 1918 in memory of a partner of the publishing firm of **A.&C. Black Ltd**. Two prizes, one for biography and one for fiction. Closing date for submissions: 31 January. Each prize is awarded for a book first published in Britain in the previous calendar year (1 January – 31 December. 2005 winners: Ian McEwan *Saturday* (fiction); Sue Prideaux *Edvard Munch: Behind the Scream* (biography).
PRIZES £10,000 each.

Blue Peter Book Awards
c/o Awards Administrator, Fraser Ross Associates, 6 Wellington Place, Edinburgh EH6 7EQ
☎0131 553 2759 Fax 0131 553 2759
✉ lindsey.fraser@tiscali.co.uk
www.bbc.co.uk/bluepeter
Contacts *Lindsey Fraser, Kathryn Ross*

Established in 1999 to highlight paperback fiction, illustrated books, poetry and non-fiction for young people. The initial shortlist is selected by a panel of adults and the final decisions are taken by a panel of Blue Peter judges. Final entry date: mid-June. Previous winners: Nicky Singer *Feather Boy*; William Nicholson *The Windsinger*; Philip Reeve *Mortal Engines*; Simon Bartram *Man on the Moon*; Michael Morpurgo *Private Peaceful*.
AWARD Trophy.

Boardman Tasker Award
Pound House, Llangennith, Swansea SA3 1JQ
☎01792 386215 Fax 01792 386215
✉ margaretbody@lineone.net
www.boardmantasker.com
Contact *Maggie Body*, Honorary Secretary

Established 1983, this award is given for a work of fiction, non-fiction or poetry, whose central theme is concerned with the mountain environment and which can be said to have made an outstanding contribution to mountain literature. Authors of any nationality are eligible, but the book must have been published or distributed in the UK for the first time between 1 November 2004 and 31 October 2005. Entries

from publishers only. 2005 joint winners: Andy Cave *Learning to Breathe*; Jim Perrin *The Villain*.
PRIZE £2000 (at Trustees' discretion).

Bollinger Everyman Wodehouse Prize
Everyman's Library, Northburgh House, 10 Northburgh Street, London EC1V 0AT
☎020 7566 6350 Fax 020 7490 3708
✉ dcampbell@randomhouse.co.uk *or* sarah@everyman.uk.com
www.everyman.uk.com
Contact *Sarah Peacock*

Established in 2000 by Everyman's Library, Bollinger and the Hay Festival to celebrate comic writing in memory of P.G. Wodehouse. Books are nominated by readers of the *Sunday Times* and visitors to www.bol.com. 2006 winner: Christopher Brookmyre *All Fun and Games Until Somebody Loses an Eye*.

The Booker Prize for Fiction
See **The Man Booker Prize for Fiction**

Booktrust Early Years Awards
Booktrust, Book House, 45 East Hill, London SW18 2QZ
☎020 8516 2972 Fax 020 8516 2978
✉ tarryn@booktrust.org.uk
www.booktrust.org.uk
Contact *Tarryn McKay*

Formerly the Sainsbury's Baby Book Award, established in 1999. Annual awards with three categories: the Baby Book Award, the Best Book for Pre-School Children (up to the age of 5), and an award for the Best New Illustrator. Books to be submitted by publishers only; authors and illustrators must be of British nationality or other nationals who have been resident in the UK for at least five years.
PRIZE £2000 for each category; in addition the Best New Illustrator receives a specially commissioned award.

Booktrust Teenage Prize
Book House, 45 East Hill, London SW18 2QZ
☎020 8516 2986 Fax 020 8516 2978
✉ hannah@booktrust.org.uk
www.bookheads.org.uk
Contact *Hannah Rutland*

Established 2003. Annual prize that recognises and celebrates the best in teenage fiction. Funded and administered by Booktrust. Open to works of fiction for young adults in the UK,

the books to be published between 1 July 2005 and 30 June 2006. Final entry date in March. 2005 winner: Sarah Singleton *Century*.
PRIZE £1500.

Harry Bowling Prize

c/o Coseley House, Munslow, Craven Arms SY7 9ET
✉ dana@mbalit.co.uk
www.harrybowlingprize.net
Contact *Dana Arnott*

Established 2000 in honour of Harry Bowling, 'the king of Cockney sagas' (died 1999). Biennial award (next in 2008), sponsored by **Headline Book Publishing**, to encourage writers of adult fiction set in London. Open to anyone who has not been published previously. Final entry date: 31 March. Entry fee charged; forms from address above (enclose s.a.e.) or via the website. 2004 winner: Clio Gray *London Spires*.
PRIZES Winner, £1000; two runners-up, £100 each.

The Branford Boase Award

8 Bolderwood Close, Bishopstoke, Eastleigh SO50 8PG
☎ 01962 826658 Fax 01962 856615
✉ anne.marley@tiscali.co.uk
www.branfordboaseaward.org.uk
Administrator *Anne Marley*

Established in 2000 in memory of children's novelist, Henrietta Branford and editor and publisher, Wendy Boase. To be awarded annually to encourage and celebrate the most promising novel by a new writer of children's books, while at the same time highlighting the importance of the editor in nurturing new talent. 2005 winner: Meg Rosoff *How We Live Now* (author); Rebecca McNally, **Puffin Books** (editor).
AWARD Specially commissioned box, carved and inlaid in silver with the Branford Boase Award logo; winning author receives £1000.

The Bridport Prize

Bridport Arts Centre, South Street, Bridport DT6 3NR
☎ 01308 485064 Fax 01308 485120
✉ frances@poorton.demon.co.uk
www.bridportprize.org.uk
Contact *Frances Everitt*, Administrator

Annual competition for poetry and short story writing. Unpublished work only, written in English. Winning stories are read by a literary agent, the winning poems are put forward to the **Forward Prize**, and an anthology of winning entries is published. Final entry date: 30 June. Send s.a.e. for entry forms.
PRIZES £5000, £1000 & £500 in each category, plus 10 supplementary prizes of £50 each. Winning stories are submitted to the National Short Story Prize.

Katharine Briggs Folklore Award

The Folklore Society, c/o The Warburg Institute, Woburn Square, London WC1H 0AB
☎ 020 7862 8564
✉ enquiries@folklore-society.com
www.folklore-society.com
Contact *The Convenor*

Established 1982. An annual award in November for the book, published in Britain and Ireland between 1 June in the previous calendar year and 30 May, which has made the most distinguished non-fiction contribution to folklore studies. Intended to encourage serious research in the field which Katharine Briggs did so much to establish. The term folklore studies is interpreted broadly to include all aspects of traditional and popular culture, narrative, belief, custom and folk arts. 2005 winner: Jeremy Harte *Explore Fairy Traditions*.
PRIZE £200, plus engraved goblet.

British Book Awards

Publishing News, 7 John Street, London WC1N 2ES
☎ 0870 870 2345 Fax 0870 870 0385
✉ mailbox@publishingnews.co.uk
www.britishbookawards.com

Established 1988. Viewed by the book trade as the one to win, 'The Nibbies' are presented annually. The awards are made in various categories. Each winner receives the prestigious Nibbie and the awards are presented to those who have made the most impact in the book trade during the previous year. 2006 winners included: Marina Lewycka, Alan Bennett, Anthony Horowitz, Martina Cole, Andrew Flintoff. For further information contact: Merric Davidson, PO Box 60, Cranbrook TN17 2ZR (☎/Fax 01580 212041; nibbies@mdla.co.uk).

British Czech & Slovak Association Prize

The BCSA Prize Administrator, 24 Ferndale, Tunbridge Wells TN2 3NS
☎ 01892 543206
✉ prize@bcsa.co.uk
www.bcsa.co.uk
Contact *Prize Administrator*

The British Czech & Slovak Association offers an annual prize for the best piece of original writing, in English, on the links between Britain and the Czech and Slovak Republics, or describing society in transition in those Republics since the Velvet Revolution in 1989. Entries can be fiction or factual, should not have been previously published and should be up to 2000 words in length. Submissions are invited from individuals of any age, nationality or educational background. Closing date: 30 June. Entry details for 2007 should be checked with the Prize Administrator. 2005 winners: Michal Sarapatka *The Czech Republic in the EUropean Context: What are the Problems of Freedom & Democracy?*; Deborah Richards *I'd Like to Get to Know You Better.*

PRIZE £300, presented at the BCSA's annual dinner in London. Second prize, £100. The winning entry is published in the *British Czech & Slovak Review.*

British Fantasy Awards

201 Reddish Road, South Reddish, Stockport SK5 7HR
☎0161 476 5368 (after 6.00 pm)
✉ faliol@yahoo.com
www.britishfantasysociety.org.uk
Secretary *Robert Parkinson*

Awarded by the **British Fantasy Society** by members at its annual conference for Best Novel and Best Short Story categories, among others. Not an open competition. Previous winners include: Ramsey Campbell, Dan Simmons, Michael Marshall Smith, Thomas Ligotti.

British Press Awards

Press Gazette, 10 Old Bailey, London EC4M 7NG
☎020 7038 1469 Fax 020 7038 1155
✉ franb@pressgazette.co.uk
www.pressgazette.co.uk

'The Oscars of British journalism.' Open to all British national newspapers and news agencies. March event. Run by *Press Gazette.*

British Science Fiction Association Awards

16 Napier Road, Oxford OX4 3JA
☎01865 749378
✉ bsfa.awards@gmail.com
www.bsfa.co.uk
Awards Administrator *Ian Snell*

Established 1970. Categories for novel, short fiction, non-fiction and artwork. The awards are announced and presented at the British

National Science Fiction Convention every Easter. 2005 winners: Geoff Ryman *Air* (novel); Kelly Link *Magic for Beginners* (short fiction); Gary K. Wolfe *Soundings: Reviews 1992–1996* (non-fiction); Pawel Lewandowski for the cover of *Interzone* (artwork).

British Sports Book Awards

National Sporting Club, Café Royal, 68 Regent Street, London W1B 5EL
☎020 7437 0144 Fax 020 7437 5441
✉ david@nationalsportingclub.co.uk
www.nationalsportingclub.co.uk
Chairman *David Willis*

Established 2003. Annual awards presented at a Café Royal lunch in London in March. Four categories: Best Autobiography, Best Biography, Best Illustrator , Best New Writer. Nominations received in November each year by e-mail (address above). Sponsors include Skysports, *The Times*, Stora Enso and Ladbrokes.

British Sports Journalism Awards

See **Sports Writers' Association of Great Britain** under *Professional Associations and Societies*

The Browning Society Poetry Prize

84 Addison Gardens, London W14 0DR
☎020 7602 3094 Fax 020 7602 3771
✉ pamela@tvdox.com
www.browningsociety.org
Contact *Pamela Neville-Sington*

Established in 2004 to encourage interest in the Brownings' poetry among young people. Held annually, the competition focuses on two different Browning poems – one by Elizabeth and one by Robert; visit the website for details. Open to students between the ages of 9 and 19 who are citizens of or resident in the UK. Final entry date: 15 March.

PRIZE £100 for students aged 9–13; £200 for students 14–19.

The Bruntwood Playwriting Competition for the Royal Exchange

See **Royal Exchange Theatre Company** under *Theatre Producers*

The Caine Prize for African Writing

51a Southwark Street, London SE1 1RU
☎020 7378 6234 Fax 020 7378 6235
✉ info@caineprize.com

www.caineprize.com
Administrator *Nick Elam*
Secretary *Jan Hart*

Annual award founded in 1999 in memory of Sir Michael Caine, former chairman of Booker plc, to recognise the worth of African writing in English. Awarded for a short story by an African writer, published in English anywhere in the world. 'An African writer' is someone who was born in Africa, or who is a national of an African country, or whose parents are African, and whose work has reflected African sensibilities. Final entry date: 31 January; submissions by publishers only. 2005 winner: S.A. Afolabi *Monday Morning*.
PRIZE $15,000.

The Calouste Gulbenkian Prize
See **The Translators Association Awards**

James Cameron Award
City University, Department of Journalism, Northampton Square, London EC1V 0HB
☎020 7040 8221 Fax 020 7040 8594
Contact *The Administrator*

Annual award for journalism to a reporter of any nationality, working for the British media, whose work is judged to have contributed most during the year to the continuance of the Cameron tradition. 2006 winner: Patrick Cockburn.

Canadian Poetry Association (Annual Poetry Contest)
Canadian Poetry Association, 331 Elmwood Dr., Suite 4-212, Moncton, New Brunswick E1A 1X6, Canada
✉ info@canadianpoetryassoc.com
www.canadianpoetryassoc.com

Annual contest open to members and non-members of the CPA worldwide. Submission fee: $5 per poem. See the website for entry details. All winning poems are published on the CPA website.
Three cash PRIZES and publication in *Poetmata*.

Cardiff International Poetry Competition
PO Box 438, Cardiff CF10 5YA
☎029 2047 2266 Fax 029 2049 2930
✉ post@academi.org
www.academi.org
Contact *Peter Finch*

Established 1986. An annual competition supported by Cardiff Council for unpublished poems in English of up to 50 lines. Closing date in January.
PRIZE £7000 (total).

Carey Award
Society of Indexers, Woodbourn Business Centre, 10 Jessell Street, Sheffield S9 3HY
☎0114 244 9561 Fax 0114 244 9563
✉ admin@indexers.org.uk
www.indexers.org.uk
Secretary *Ann Kingdom*

A private award made by the Society to a member who has given outstanding services to indexing. The recipient is selected by the Executive Board with no recommendations considered from elsewhere.

Carnegie Medal
See **CILIP: The Chartered Institute of Library and Information Professionals Carnegie Medal**

CBI Bisto Book of the Year Awards
17 North Great Georges Street, Dublin 1, Republic of Ireland
☎00 353 1 872 7475 Fax 00 353 1 872 8486
✉ info@childrensbooksireland.com
www.childrensbooksireland.com
Contact *Jenny Murray*

Founded 1990 as Bisto Book of the Decade Awards. This led to the establishment of an annual award made by the Irish Children's Book Trust, later to become Children's Books Ireland. Open to any author or illustrator of children's books born or resident in Ireland; open to English or Irish languages. Previous winners: Kate Thompson *The New Policeman* (Bisto Book of the Year); Siobhón Ní Shithigh *An Bhó Riabhach* (Eilís Dillon Award).
PRIZES €6000 (Bisto Book of the Year); €1000 (Eilís Dillon Award); three honour awards of €1000 each.

Sid Chaplin Short Story Competition
Shildon Town Council, Civic Hall Square, Shildon DL4 1AH
☎01388 772563 Fax 01388 775227
Contact *Mrs J.M. Stafford*

Established 1986. Annual short story competition. Maximum 3000 words; £2 entrance fee (juniors free). All stories must be unpublished and not broadcast and/or performed. Application forms available from March; closing date: May.

PRIZES £300 (1st); £150 (2nd); £75 (3rd); £50 (Junior).

Chapter One Promotions International Open Short Story Competition

PO Box 43667, London SE22 9XU
☎0845 456 5364   Fax 0845 456 5347
www.chapteronepromotions.com

Contact *Johanna Bertie*

Established in 2005, the competition is open to new and established writers to submit unpublished short stories of less than 2500 words. Author details on separate sheet. Submissions and payment accepted online. Closing date: 14 January. 2005 winner: Pablo Stewart.

PRIZES £2500, £1000, £500, plus top 13 entries published in anthology.

Chapter One Promotions Open Poetry Competition

PO Box 43667, London SE22 9XU
☎0845 456 5364   Fax 0845 456 5347
www.chapteronepromotions.com

Contact *Johanna Bertie*

Established 2005. Unpublished poems of no more than 30 lines. Judge decides on the best 20 poems which are displayed on the website and the public votes for their favourite poem. The three poems with most votes wins. Closing date: 1 June. Online voting period: 1–15 July. Winning poems appear on the website in August. Submissions and payment accepted online. 2005 winner: Graham Burchell.

PRIZES £1000, £500, £250.

Children's Book Circle Eleanor Farjeon Award

See **Eleanor Farjeon Award**

The Children's Laureate

Booktrust, Book House, 45 East Hill, London SW18 2QZ
☎020 8516 2976   Fax 020 8516 2978
✉ childrenslaureate@booktrust.org.uk
www.childrenslaureate.org

Contact *Nikki Marsh*

Established 1998. The Laureate is awarded biennially to an eminent British writer or illustrator of children's books both in celebration of a lifetime's achievement and to highlight the role of children's book creators in inspiring, informing and entertaining young readers. 2004 winner: Jacqueline Wilson.

AWARD Medal and £10,000.

CILIP: The Chartered Institute of Library and Information Professionals Carnegie Medal

7 Ridgmount Street, London WC1E 7AE
☎020 7255 0650   Fax 020 7255 0651
✉ ckg@cilip.org.uk
www.ckg.org.uk

Established 1936. Presented for an outstanding book for children written in English and first published in the UK during the preceding year. Fiction, non-fiction and poetry are all eligible. 2004 winner (presented in 2005): Frank Cottrell Boyce *Millions*.

AWARD Medal.

CILIP: The Chartered Institute of Library and Information Professionals Kate Greenaway Medal

7 Ridgmount Street, London WC1E 7AE
☎020 7255 0650   Fax 020 7255 0651
✉ ckg@cilip.org.uk
www.ckg.org.uk

Established 1955. Presented annually for the most distinguished work in the illustration of children's books first published in the UK during the preceding year. 2004 winner (presented in 2005): Chris Riddell *Jonathan Swift's 'Gulliver'*.

AWARD Medal. The Colin Mears Award (£5000 cash) is given annually to the winner of the Kate Greenaway Medal.

Arthur C. Clarke Award for Science Fiction

60 Bournemouth Road, Folkestone CT19 5AZ
☎01303 252939
✉ arthurcclarkeaward@yahoo.com
www.clarkeaward.com

Administrator *Paul Kincaid*

Established 1986. The Arthur C. Clarke Award is given annually to the best science fiction novel with first UK publication in the previous calendar year. Both hardcover and paperback books qualify. Made possible by a generous donation from Arthur C. Clarke, this award is selected by a rotating panel of judges nominated by the **British Science Fiction Association**, the **Science Fiction Foundation** and the Science Museum. 2005 winner: China Miéville *Iron Curtain*.

AWARD £2006 (award increases by £1 per year), plus trophy.

David Cohen Prize for Literature

Arts Council England, 14 Great Peter Street, London SW1P 3NQ
☎020 7973 5325   Fax 020 7973 6983
✉ info.literature@artscouncil.org.uk
www.artscouncil.org.uk

Literature Director *Gary McKeone*
Literature Administrator *Jessica Ryan*

Established 1993 by the Arts Council and awarded biennially, the David Cohen Prize for Literature is one of the most distinguished literary prizes in Britain. It recognises writers who use the English language and who are citizens of the UK and the Republic of Ireland, encompassing dramatists as well as novelists, poets and essayists. The prize is for a lifetime's achievement and is donated by the David Cohen Family Charitable Trust. Set up in 1980 by David Cohen, general practitioner and son of a property developer, the Trust has helped composers, choreographers, dancers, poets, playwrights and actors. The Council is providing a futher £12,500 (The Clarissa Luard Award) to enable the winner to commission new work, with the dual aim of encouraging young writers and readers. Previous winners: William Trevor, Dame Muriel Spark, Harold Pinter, V.S. Naipaul, Doris Lessing, Beryl Bainbridge and Thom Gunn. 2005 winner: Michael Holroyd.

AWARD £40,000, plus £12,500 towards new work.

The Commonwealth Writers Prize

Commonwealth Foundation, Marlborough House, Pall Mall, London SW1Y 5HY
☎020 7747 6576
✉ a.firmin@commonwealth.int
www.commonwealthwriters.com

Established 1987. An annual award to reward and encourage the upsurge of new Commonwealth fiction. Any work of prose or fiction is eligible, i.e. a novel or collection of short stories. No drama or poetry. The work must be first written in English by a citizen of the Commonwealth and be first published in the year before its entry for the prize. Entries must be submitted by the publisher to the region of the writer's Commonwealth citizenship. The four regions are: Africa, Eurasia, S.E. Asia and South Pacific, Caribbean and Canada. 2006 winner: Kate Grenville *The Secret River* (Best Book Award); Mark McWatt *Suspended Sentences: Fictions of Atonement* (Best First Book Award).

PRIZES £10,000 for Best Book; £3000 for Best First Book; 8 prizes of £1000 for each best and first best book in four regions.

The Duff Cooper Prize

54 St Maur Road, London SW6 4DP
☎020 7736 3729   Fax 020 7731 7638

Contact *Artemis Cooper*

An annual award for a literary work of biography, history, politics or poetry, published by a recognised publisher (member of the **Publishers Association**) during the previous 12 months. The book must be submitted by the publisher, not the author. Financed by the interest from a trust fund commemorating Duff Cooper, first Viscount Norwich (1890–1954). 2005 winner: Mark Mazower *Salonica: City of Ghosts*.

PRIZE £5000.

Costa Book Awards

The Booksellers Association, Minster House, 272 Vauxhall Bridge Road, London SW1V 1BA
☎020 7802 0802   Fax 020 7802 0803
✉ anna.okane@booksellers.org.uk
www.costabookawards.com

Contact *Anna O'Kane*

Established 1971. Formerly the Whitbread Book Awards. The awards celebrate and promote the best contemporary British writing. They are judged in two stages and offer a total of £50,000 prize money. The awards are open to novel, first novel, biography, poetry and children's book, each judged by a panel of three judges, with two young judges joining the panel for the Costa Children's Book Award. The winner of each award receives £5000. The Costa Book of the Year (£25,000) is chosen from the category winners. Writers must have lived in Britain and Ireland for three or more years. Submissions received from publishers only. Closing date: early July. Sponsored by Costa. 2005 winners: Ali Smith *The Accidental* (novel); Tash Aw *The Harmony Silk Factory* (first novel); Hilary Spurling *Matisse the Master* (biography & overall winner); Christopher Logue *Cold Calls* (poetry); Kate Thompson *The New Policeman* (children's).

Rose Mary Crawshay Prize

The British Academy, 10 Carlton House Terrace, London SW1Y 5AH
☎020 7969 5200   Fax 020 7969 5300
www.britac.ac.uk

Contact *British Academy Secretary*

Established 1888 by Rose Mary Crawshay, this prize is given for an historical or critical work by a woman of any nationality on English literature, with particular preference for a work on Keats, Byron or Shelley. The work must have been published in the preceding three years. PRIZES under review.

John Creasey Dagger
See **Crime Writers' Association (The New Blood Dagger for Best First Crime Novel)**

Crime Writers' Association (Cartier Diamond Dagger)
PO Box 273, Boreham Wood WD6 2XA
✉ secretary@thecwa.co.uk
www.thecwa.co.uk
Contact *The Secretary*
Established 1986. An annual award for a lifetime's outstanding contribution to the genre. 2006 winner: Elmore Leonard.

Crime Writers' Association (The Gold Dagger for Non-Fiction)
PO Box 273, Boreham Wood WD6 2XA
✉ secretary@thecwa.co.uk
www.thecwa.co.uk
Contact *The Secretary*
Biennial award for the best non-fiction crime book published during the year. Nominations from publishers only. 2005 winner: Gregg and Gina Hill *On the Run*.
AWARD Dagger, plus cheque (sum varies).

Crime Writers' Association (The Dagger in the Library)
PO Box 273, Boreham Wood WD6 2XA
✉ secretary@thecwa.co.uk
www.thecwa.co.uk
Contact *The Secretary*
Reinstated 2002. Annual award (sponsored by **Random House**) to the author whose work has given most pleasure to readers. Nominated and judged by librarians. 2005 winner: Jake Arnott.
AWARD Dagger, plus cheque.

Crime Writers' Association (The Debut Dagger)
New Writing Competition, P.O. Box 273, Boreham Wood WD6 2XA
✉ debut.dagger@thecwa.co.uk
www.thecwa.co.uk
Contact *The Secretary*

Annual competition (sponsored by **Orion**) for unpublished writers to submit the first 3000 words and 500 word outline of a crime novel (entry fee and form required). For full details see website or send s.a.e. to address above. 2005 winner: Ruth Dugdall *The Woman Before Me*.
AWARD Dagger, plus cheque.

Crime Writers' Association (The Ian Fleming Steel Dagger)
PO Box 273, Boreham Wood WD6 2XA
✉ secretary@thecwa.co.uk
www.thecwa.co.uk
Contact *The Secretary*
Founded 2002. Annual award for the best thriller, adventure or spy novel. Sponsored by Ian Fleming (Glidrose) Publications Ltd to celebrate the best of contemporary thriller writing. 2005 winner: Henry Porter *Brandenburg*.
AWARD Dagger, plus cheque.

Crime Writers' Association (The Gold and Silver Daggers for Fiction)
Contact *The Secretary*
These awards have now been superseded by the **Duncan Lawrie Dagger** (see entry).

Crime Writers' Association (The New Blood Dagger for Best First Crime Novel)
PO Box 273, Boreham Wood WD6 2XA
✉ secretary@thecwa.co.uk
www.thecwa.co.uk
Contact *The Secretary*
Established in 1973 following the death of crime writer John Creasey, founder of the **Crime Writers' Association**. This award, sponsored by **BBC Audio Books**, is given annually for the best crime novel by an author who has not previously published a full-length work of fiction. Fomerly known as the John Creasey Dagger. Nominations from publishers only. 2005 winner: Dreda Say Mitchell *Running Hot*.
AWARD Dagger, plus cheque.

Crime Writers' Association (The CWA Ellis Peters Award)
PO Box 273, Boreham Wood WD6 2XA
✉ secretary@thecwa.co.uk
www.thecwa.co.uk
Contact *The Secretary*
Sponsored by the Estate of Ellis Peters, Time Warner and **Headline**. Established 1999. Annual

award for the best historical crime novel. Nominations from publishers only. 2005 winner: C.J. Sansom *Dark Fire*.

AWARD plus cheque.

Crime Writers' Association (The Short Story Dagger)

Established 1993. This Award has been discontinued. 2005 winner: Danuta Reah *No Flies on Frank*.

Hunter Davies Prize

See **Lakeland Book of the Year Awards**

Felix Dennis Prize for Best First Collection

See **The Forward Prizes for Poetry**

George Devine Award

9 Lower Mall, Hammersmith, London W6 9DJ

Contact *Christine Smith*

Annual award for a promising new playwright writing for the stage in memory of George Devine, artistic director of the **Royal Court Theatre**, who died in 1965. The play, which can be of any length, does not need to have been produced. Send two copies of the script, plus outline of work, to *Christine Smith*. Closing Date: 1 March 2007. Send s.a.e. for the script to be returned if required. Information leaflet available from January on receipt of s.a.e.

PRIZE £10,000.

Dingle Prize

British Society for the History of Science, 5 Woodcote Green, Fleet GU51 4EY
☎01252 641135
✉ execsec@bshs.org.uk
www.bshs.org.uk

Biennial award made by the BSHS to the best book in the history of science (broadly construed) which is accessible to a wide audience of non-specialists. Next award: 2007. Previous winners: Ken Alder, *The Measure of All Things*; Deborah Cadbury *The Dinosaur Hunters*; Steven Shapin *The Scientific Revolution*.

PRIZE £300.

Dolman Best First Travel Book Award

Authors' Club, 40 Dover Street, London W1S 4NP
☎020 7408 5092 Fax 020 7409 0913
✉ stella@theauthorsclub.co.uk

Contact *Stella Kane*

William Dolman, a former chairman of the **Authors' Club**, instituted this new prize for the most promising first book of travel literature. Books published in Great Britain by British writers are eligible and submissions are accepted in January of each year.

AWARD £1000.

Drama Association of Wales Playwriting Competition

The Old Library, Singleton Road, Splott, Cardiff CF24 2ET
☎029 2045 2200 Fax 029 2045 2277
✉ aled.daw@virgin.net

Contact *Teresa Hennessy*

Annual competition held to promote the writing of one-act plays in English and Welsh of between 20 and 50 minutes' playing time. Application forms from the address above. Closing date: 31 January.

The John Dryden Competition

British Comparative Literature Association/British Centre for Literary Translation, School of Literature and Creative Writing , University of East Anglia, Norwich NR4 7TJ Fax 01603 250599
✉ transcomp@uea.ac.uk
www.bcla.org

Competition Organiser *Dr Jean Boase-Beier*

Established 1983. Annual competition open to unpublished literary translations from all languages. Maximum submission: 25 pages.

PRIZES £350 (1st); £200 (2nd); £100 (3rd); plus publication for all winning entries in the Association's annual journal. Other entries may receive commendations.

The Duke of Westminster's Medal for Military Literature

Royal United Services Institute for Defence and Security Studies, Whitehall, London SW1A 2ET
☎020 7930 2602 Fax 020 7321 0943
www.rusi.org

Established 1997 this annual award is sponsored by the Duke of Westminster and aims to mark a notable and original contribution to the study of international or national security, or the military profession. Work must be in English, by a living author, and have been published as a book, rather than an article, in the preceding or next six months of the closing date for entries. 2005 winner: *The Command of the Ocean: A*

Naval History of Britain 1649–1815 Professor Nicholas Rodger.

PRIZE Silver medal, £1000. Winning author is invited to give lecture at RUSI and collect medal from the Duke of Westminster.

T.S. Eliot Prize

Truman State University Press, 100 East Normal Street, Kirksville, MO 63501, USA
☎001 660 785 7336　Fax 001 660 785 4480
✉ tsup@truman.edu
tsup.truman.edu

Contact *Nancy Rediger*

An annual award, established in 1997 in honour of native Missourian, T.S. Eliot, to publish and promote contemporary English-language poetry regardless of a poet's nationality, reputation, stage in career or publication history. Entry requirements: 60–100 pages of original poetry with $25 fee. Final entry date: 31 October. 2006 winner: Carol Ann Duffy *Rapture*.

PRIZE $2000 plus publication.

The Encore Award

The Society of Authors, 84 Drayton Gardens, London SW10 9SB
☎020 7373 6642　Fax 020 7373 5768
✉ info@societyofauthors.org
www.societyofauthors.org

Established 1990. Awarded biennially for the best second published novel or novels of the year. Final entry date: 30 November 2008. Details from the **Society of Authors**. 2005 winner: Nadeem Aslam *Maps for Lost Lovers*.

PRIZE £10,000.

Envoi Poetry Competition

Envoi, 44 Rudyard Road, Biddulph Moor, Stoke on Trent ST8 7JN
☎01782 517892

Contact *Roger Elkin*

Run by *Envoi* poetry magazine. Competitions are featured regularly, with prizes of £300, plus three annual subscriptions to *Envoi*. Winning poems along with full adjudication report are published. Send s.a.e. to Competition Secretary at the address above.

Geoffrey Faber Memorial Prize

Faber & Faber Ltd, 3 Queen Square, London WC1N 3AU
☎020 7465 0045　Fax 020 7465 0034

Established 1963 as a memorial to the founder and first chairman of **Faber & Faber**, this prize is awarded in alternate years for the volume of verse and the volume of prose fiction published in the UK in the preceding two years, which is judged to be of greatest literary merit. Authors must be under 40 at the time of publication and citizens of the UK, Commonwealth, Republic of Ireland or South Africa. 2005 winner: David Mitchell *Cloud Atlas*.

PRIZE £1000.

The Alfred Fagon Award

The Royal Court Theatre, Sloane Square, London SW1W 8AS
www.talawa.com/afa/how.htm

First presented in 1997. An annual award, in memory of playwright Alfred Fagon, which is open to any playwright of Caribbean descent, resident in the UK, for the best new stage play in English (television and radio plays and film scripts not eligible). Two copies of the script (plus s.a.e. for return), together with a brief history of the play and c.v. (including author's Caribbean connection), should be sent the address above by 31 August. 2005 winner: Michael Bhim.

AWARD £5000.

Eleanor Farjeon Award

✉ childrensbookcircle@hotmail.co.uk
www.childrensbookcircle.org.uk

This award, named in memory of the much-loved children's writer, is for distinguished services to children's books either in this country or overseas, and may be given to a librarian, teacher, publisher, bookseller, author, artist, reviewer, television producer, etc. or occasionally to an organisation. Nominations from members of the **Children's Book Circle**. 2005 winner: Malorie Blackman.

AWARD £750.

Fish Fiction Prizes

Fish Publishing, Durrus, Bantry, Co. Cork, Republic of Ireland
☎00 353 27 55645
✉ info@fishpublishing.com
www.fishpublishing.com

Contact *Clem Cairns*

Offers several writing contests including the International Short Story Prize, an annual award, founded in 1994, which aims to discover, encourage and publish new literary talent. The best 15 stories are published in an anthology. Also the Historical Short Fiction Prize, run in conjunction with the Historical Novel Society. Details of these and other contests can be found on the website.

Sir Banister Fletcher Award

Authors' Club, 40 Dover Street, London
W1S 4NP
☎020 7408 5092 Fax 020 7409 0913
✉ stella@theauthorsclub.co.uk
Contact *Sarah Kane*

Founded in 1954, this award was created by the late Sir Banister Fletcher, former President of the **Authors' Club** and the Royal Institute of British Architects, and is presented for 'the most deserving book on architecture or the arts'. The Award is open to titles written by British authors or those resident in the UK and published under a British imprint. 2005 winner: Cecil Balmond *Informal*.

PRIZE £1000.

The John Florio Prize

See **The Translators Association Awards**

The Paul Foot Award

Private Eye, 6 Carlisle Street, London
W1D 3BN
www.private-eye.co.uk
Contact *Ben Tisdall* (Midas PR ☎020 7584 7474)

Annual award, established in 2005 by *The Guardian* and *Private Eye* for campaigning journalism in memory of former contributor Paul Foot. Submissions can be made by individual journalists, teams of journalists or publications for work appearing between October 2005 and August 2006. Single pieces or entire campaigns are eligible. Final entry date: 12 September 2006. No broadcast material. 'Please do not send original material as no correspondence can be entered into.' Inaugural winner: John Sweeney.

AWARD £10,000.

The Forward Prizes for Poetry

Administrator: Colman Getty PR, Middlesex House, 28 Windmill Street, London W1T 2JJ
☎020 7631 2666 Fax 020 7631 2699
✉ kate@colmangettypr.co.uk
www.forwardartsfoundation.co.uk
Contact *Kate Wright-Morris*

Established 1992. Three awards: the Forward Prize for Best Collection, the Felix Dennis Prize for Best First Collection and the Forward Prize for Best Single Poem in memory of Michael Donaghy, which is not already part of an anthology or collection. All entries must be published in the UK or Republic of Ireland and submitted by poetry publishers (collections) or newspaper and magazine editors (single

poems). Individual entries of poets' own work are not accepted. 2005 winners: David Harsent (best collection), Helen Farish (best first collection), Paul Farley (best single poem).

PRIZES £10,000 (best collection); £5000 (best first collection); £1000 (best single poem).

The Frogmore Poetry Prize

42 Morehall Avenue, Folkestone CT19 4EF
☎07751 251689
www.frogmorepress.co.uk
Contact *Jeremy Page*

Established 1987. Awarded annually and sponsored by the Frogmore Foundation. The winning poem, runners-up and short-listed entries are all published in the magazine. Previous winners: Bill Headdon, John Latham, Diane Brown, Tobias Hill, Mario Petrucci, Gina Wilson, Ross Cogan, Joan Benner, Ann Alexander, Gerald Watts, Katy Darby, David Angel, Howard Wright, Caroline Price, Julie-ann Rowell.

PRIZE The winner receives 200 guineas and a life subscription to the biannual literary magazine, *The Frogmore Papers*.

FT & Goldman Sachs Business Book of the Year Award

Financial Times, One Southwark Bridge, London SE1 9HL
☎020 7873 3000 Fax 020 7873 3072
✉ bookaward@ft.com
www.ft.com/bookaward
Contacts *Katy Hemmings, Stephanie Jones*

Established in 2005 to identify the book that provides the most compelling and enjoyable insight into modern business issues, including management, finance and economics. Titles must be published for the first time in the English language, or in English translation, between 31 October 2005 and 1 November 2006. Submissions by a publisher or *bona fide* imprint which holds English language rights in the book. Inaugural winner: Thomas Friedman *The World is Flat*.

AWARD £30,000 (winner); shortlisted authors receive £5000 each.

Martha Gellhorn Trust Prize

Rutherfords, Herbert Road, Salcombe
TQ8 8HN

Annual prize for journalism in honour of one of the twentieth century's greatest reporters. Open for journalism published in English, giving 'the view from the ground – a human story that penetrates the established version of events and illuminates an urgent issue buried by prevailing

fashions of what makes news'. The subject matter can involve the UK or abroad. Six copies of each entry should be sent to the address above by 30 March 2007. Previous winners include: Ghaith Abdul-Ahad, Patrick Cockburn, Robert Fisk, Jeremy Harding, Geoffrey Lean.
PRIZE £5000.

The Gladstone History Book Prize
Royal Historical Society, University College London, Gower Street, London WC1E 6BT
☎020 7387 7532   Fax 020 7387 7532
✉ rhs.info@sas.ac.uk
www.rhs.ac.uk/prizes
Contact *Executive Secretary*

Established 1998. Annual award for the best new work on any historical subject which is not primarily related to British history, published in the UK in the preceding calendar year. The book must be the author's first (solely written) history book and be an original and scholarly work of historical research. Closing date: 31 December. 2004 winner: Nikolaus Wachsmann *Hitler's Prisons: Legal Terror in Nazi Germany*.
PRIZE £1000.

Glenfiddich Food & Drink Awards
c/o Wild Card PR, 299 Oxford Street, London W1C 2DZ
www.glenfiddich.com/foodanddrink

Known as the 'Cooker Bookers' or the 'Oscars' of the gastronomic world, the awards aim to recognise excellence in writing, publishing and broadcasting on the subjects of food and drink. There were 13 category winners in 2006 from work published or broadcast in the UK and the Republic of Ireland. 2006 winners: Food Book: *Arabesque* Claudia Roden; Drink Book: *Wine Science* Jamie Goode; Food Writer: Alex Renton for work in *Observer Food Monthly*; Cookery Writer: Rowley Leigh for work in *FT Weekend*; Drink/Bar Writer: Dave Broom for work in *Whisky Magazine*; Wine Writer: Tim Atkin for work in *Observer Food Monthly* and *World of Fine Wine*; Restaurant Critic: no award given; Regional Writer: Ruth Wood for work in the *Western Daily Press*; Television Programme: *Ramsay's Kitchen Nightmare*, Optomen TV, Channel 4; Radio Programme: *First Taste: The Flavours of Childhood*, BBC Radio 4; Photography: Patrice de Villiers for work in *Style: The Sunday Times*; Glenfiddich Independent Spirit Award: Barny Haughton; GQ/Glenfiddich Food & Drink Personality of the Year: Gordon Ramsay; Glenfiddich Trophy: Alex Renton.

AWARD Overall winner (chosen from the category winners) £3000, plus the Glenfiddich Trophy (which is held for one year); category winners £1000 each, plus a case of Glenfiddich Single Malt Scotch Whisky.

Golden PEN Award for Lifetime Distinguished Service to Literature
English PEN, 6–8 Amwell Street, London EC1R 1UQ
☎020 7713 0023   Fax 020 7837 7838
✉ enquiries@englishpen.org
www.englishpen.org

Awarded to a senior writer, with a distinguished body of work over many years, who has made a significant and constructive impact on fellow writers, the reading public and the literary world. Nominations by members of English PEN only. Previous winners include: Harold Pinter, Doris Lessing, Michael Frayn, Nina Bawden. 2005 winner: Jan Morris.

The Phillip Good Memorial Prize
QWF Magazine, PO Box 1768, Rugby CV21 4ZA
✉ jo.good@ntlworld.com
www.qwfmagazine.co.uk
Contact *Competition Secretary*

Established in 1997, the competition is run by *QWF Magazine*. The prize commemorates the memory of Phillip Good (late husband of *QWF* editor, Jo Good) and is for short stories of less than 5000 words in any style or genre (except children's). Open entry. Entrants may request in-depth critique of their stories for an extra fee. For entry forms send s.a.e. to the address above. Closing date: 31 December.
PRIZES (total) at least £525, plus free subscription to *QWF Magazine*; also book prizes and publication for winning authors.

Goss First Novel Award (formerly Pendleton May First Novel Award)
Guildford Book Festival, c/o Tourist Information Centre, 14 Tunsgate, Guildford GU1 4QT
☎01483 444334
✉ deputy@guildfordbookfestival.co.uk
www.guildfordbookfestival.co.uk
Contacts *Glenis Pycraft, Pamela Thomas*

Established in 1998 and sponsored by Goss & Co, this annual award was originally to encourage local talent but now all writers in the UK are eligible. Submissions must be from agents or

publishers with accompanying letter (proofs accepted). Books to be published between one Guildford Book Festival and the next (October to October) and shortlisted authors must be prepared to attend the presentation. 2005 winner: Clare Clark *The Great Stink*.
PRIZE £2500 (presented during the Festival).

Gourmand World Cookbook Awards
Pintor Rosales 36, 28008 Madrid, Spain
☎00 34 91 541 6768 Fax 00 34 91 541 6821
✉ icr@virtualsw.es
www.cookbookfair.com
Contact *Edouard Cointreau*

Founded in 1995 by Edouard Cointreau to reward those who 'cook with words'. The only world competition for food and wine books in all languages. Annual event. In 2003 there were 53 local or regional competitions worldwide, with the winners competing for the 'Best Book in the World' award. Previous winner: *Family Food* Heston Blumenthal.

Kate Greenaway Medal
See **CILIP: The Chartered Institute of Library and Information Professionals Kate Greenaway Medal**

The Griffin Poetry Prize
6610 Edwards Boulevard, Mississauga, Ontario, Canada L5T 2V6
☎001 905 565 5993 Fax 001 905 564 3645
✉ info@griffinpoetryprize.com
www.griffinpoetryprize.com
Contact *Ruth Smith*, Manager

Annual award established in 2000 by Toronto-based entrepreneur, Scott Griffin, for books of poetry written in or translated into English. Trustees include Margaret Atwood and Michael Ondaatje. Submissions from publishers only.
PRIZES A total of C$100,000, divided into two categories: International and Canadian.

The Guardian Children's Fiction Award
The Guardian, 119 Farringdon Road, London EC1R 3ER
☎020 7239 9694 Fax 020 7239 9933
Children's Book Editor *Julia Eccleshare*

Established 1967. Annual award for an outstanding work of fiction for children aged seven and over by a British or Commonwealth author, first published in the UK in the year of the award, excluding picture books. Final entry date: 1 June.

No application form necessary. 2005 winner: Kate Thompson *The New Policeman*.
AWARD £1500.

The Guardian First Book Award
The Guardian, 119 Farringdon Road, London EC1R 3ER
☎020 7239 9694
Contact *Literary Editor*

Established 1999. Annual award for first time authors published in English in the UK. All genres of writing eligible, apart from academic, guidebooks, children's, educational, manuals, reprints and TV, radio and film tie-ins. 2005 winner: Alexander Masters *Stuart: A Life Backwards*. Submissions are only received direct from publishers, not from individual authors. Self-published work is not eligible.
AWARD £10,000, plus *Guardian/Observer* advertising package.

Guild of Food Writers Awards
9 Colman House, High Street, London SE20 7EX
☎020 8659 0422
✉ awards@gfw.co.uk
www.gfw.co.uk
Contact *Jonathan Woods*

Established 1985. Annual awards in recognition of outstanding achievement in all areas in which food writers work and have influence. Entry is not restricted to members of the Guild. Entry form available from the address above. 2005 winners: Derek Cooper Award for Campaigning or Investigative Food Journalism: Charles Clover *The End of the Line*; Michael Smith Award for Work on British Food: John Burnett *England Eats Out*; Jeremy Round Award for Best First Book: Felicity Lawrence *Not on the Label*; Evelyn Rose Award for Cookery Journalist of the Year: Mark Hix, for work in *The Independent Magazine*; Food Book of the Year: Matthew Fort *Eating Up Italy*; Cookery Book of the Year: Shaun Hill *How to Cook Better*; and Food Journalist of the Year: Caroline Stacey, for work in *The Independent*.

Gwobr Llyfr y Flwyddyn
See **Academi Book of the Year Awards**

The Anthony Hecht Poetry Prize
The Waywiser Press, 9 Woodstock Road, London N4 3ET
☎020 8374 5526 Fax 020 8374 5536
✉ waywiserpress@aol.com
www.waywiser-press.com/hechtprize.html

Contact *Philip Hoy*, Managing Editor
Established 2005. Annual prize awarded for an outstanding, unpublished, full collection of poems. Entrants must be at least 18 years of age and may not have published more than one previous collection. Postmark deadline for submissions is 1 December with the winner announced the following May. Detailed guidelines and entry forms available from July on the website or by sending an A4-sized s.a.e.
PRIZE £1750 and publication by Waywiser in the UK and USA.

Hellenic Foundation Prize
See **The Translators Association Awards**

Felicia Hemans Prize for Lyrical Poetry
University of Liverpool, PO Box 147, Liverpool L69 7WZ
☎0151 794 2458 Fax 0151 794 2454
✉ wilderc@liv.ac.uk
Contact *The Sub-Dean, Faculty of Arts*
Established 1899. Annual award for published or unpublished verse. Open to past or present members and students of the University of Liverpool. One poem per entrant only. Closing date 1 May.
PRIZE £30.

The Hessell-Tiltman Prize for History
English PEN, 6–8 Amwell Street, London EC1R 1UQ
☎020 7713 0023 Fax 020 7837 7838
✉ enquiries@englishpen.org
www.englishpen.org
Founded 2002. Awarded for a history book, written in English (including translations) and aimed at a wide audience. Submissions by publishers only. 2006 winner: Bryan Ward Perkins *The Fall of Rome and the End of Civilisation.*
PRIZE £3000.

Hidden Brook Press International Poetry Anthology Contests
109 Bayshore Road, RR#4, Brighton, Ontario, Canada K0K 1H0
☎001 613 475 2368
✉ writers@hiddenbrookpress.com
www.HiddenBrookPress.com
International poetry competitions: The Open Window Poetry Anthology Contest and Seeds International Poetry Chapbook Anthology

Contest. E-mail for details. (HBP is also a contract publisher and print broker.)

William Hill Sports Book of the Year
Greenside House, Station Road, Wood Green, London N22 7TP
☎020 8918 3731 Fax 020 8918 3728
✉ pressoffice@williamhill.co.uk
Contact *Graham Sharpe*
Established 1989. Annual award introduced by Graham Sharpe of bookmakers William Hill. Sponsored by William Hill and thus dubbed the 'Bookie' prize, it is the first, and only, Sports Book of the Year award. Final entry date: September. 2005 winner: Gary Imlach *My Father and Other Working Class Heroes.*
PRIZE (reviewed annually) £20,000 package including £16,000 cash, hand-bound copy, £2000 free bet. Runners-up prizes.

Calvin & Rose G. Hoffman Prize
King's School, Canterbury CT1 2ES
☎01227 595544
Contact *The Bursar*
Annual award for distinguished publication on Christopher Marlowe, established by the late Calvin Hoffman, author of *The Man Who was Shakespeare* (1955) as a memorial to himself and his wife. For unpublished works of at least 5000 words written in English for their scholarly contribution to the study of Christopher Marlowe and his relationship to William Shakespeare. Final entry date: 1 September each year.

L. Ron Hubbard's Writers of the Future Contest
PO Box 218, East Grinstead RH19 4GH
Contest Administrator *Andrea Grant-Webb*
Established 1984 by L. Ron Hubbard to encourage new and amateur writers of science fiction, fantasy and horror. Quarterly awards with an annual grand prize. Entrants must submit a short story of up to 10,000 words, or a novelette less than 17,000 words, which must not have been published previously. The contest is open only to those who have not been published professionally. Previous winners: Roge Gregory, Malcolm Twigg, Tom Brennan, Alan Smale, Janet Barron. Send s.a.e. for entry form.
PRIZES £640 (1st), £480 (2nd) and £320 (3rd) each quarter; Annual Grand Prize: £2500. All winners are awarded a trip to the annual L. Ron Hubbard Achievement Awards which

include a series of professional writers' workshops, and are published in the *L. Ron Hubbard Presents Writers of the Future* anthology.

The Richard Imison Memorial Award

The Society of Authors, 84 Drayton Gardens SW10 9SB
☎020 7373 6642 Fax 020 7373 5768
✉ info@societyofauthors.org
www.societyofauthors.org
Contact *The Secretary, The Broadcasting Committee*

Annual award established 'to perpetuate the memory of Richard Imison, to acknowledge the encouragement he gave to writers working in the medium of radio, and in memory of the support and friendship he invariably offered writers in general, and radio writers in particular'. Administered by the **Society of Authors** and generally sponsored by the **Peggy Ramsay Foundation**, the purpose is 'to encourage new talent and high standards in writing for radio by selecting the radio drama by a writer new to radio which, in the opinion of the judges, is the best of those submitted.' An adaptation for radio of a piece originally written for the stage, television or film is not eligible. Any radio drama first transmitted in the UK between 1 January and 31 December by a writer or writers new to radio, is eligible, provided the work is original piece for radio and it is the first dramatic work by the writer(s) that has been broadcast. Submission may be made by any party to the production in the form of two copies of an audio cassette (not-returnable) accompanied by a nomination form. 2005 winner: Steve Coombes *Mr Sex*.
PRIZE £1500.

The Independent Foreign Fiction Prize

c/o Literature Department, Arts Council England, 14 Great Peter Street, London SW1P 3NQ
☎020 7973 5204 Fax 020 7973 6983
✉ info.literature@artscouncil.org.uk
www.artscouncil.org.uk
Contact *Bethany King*

Awarded for translated fiction by living authors first published in Britain in the year preceding the award. 2006 winner: *Out Stealing Horses* by Per Petterson, translated by Anne Born.
Prize £10,000 shared equally between author and translator.

The International Dundee Book Prize

City of Discovery Campaign, 3 City Square, Dundee DD1 3BA
☎01382 434214 Fax 01382 434650
✉ karin.johnston@dundeecity.gov.uk
www.dundeebookprize.com
Contact *Karin Johnston*

Launched in 1996, this is a biennial award. Previous winners include Andrew Murray Scott for *Tumulus* and Claire-Marie Watson for *The Curewife*. Entry qualifications are detailed in the entry form. Launch date: April 2007. Final entry date: March 2008.
PRIZE £10,000, plus publication of novel.

The International IMPAC Dublin Literary Award

Dublin City Library & Archive, 138–144 Pearse Street, Dublin 2, Republic of Ireland
☎00 353 1 674 4802 Fax 00 353 1 674 4879
✉ literaryaward@dublincity.ie
www.impacdublinaward.ie

Established 1995. Sponsored by Dublin City Council and a US-based productivity improvement firm, IMPAC, this prize is awarded for a work of fiction written and published in the English language or written in a language other than English and published in English translation. Initial nominations are made by municipal public libraries in major and capital cities worldwide, each library putting forward up to three books to the international panel of judges in Dublin. 2006 winner: Colm Toibin *The Master*.
PRIZE €100,000 (if the winning book is in English translation, the prize is shared €75,000 to the author and €25,000 to the translator).

International Student Playscript Competition

See **University of Hull** under *UK and Irish Writers' Courses*

Jerwood Aldeburgh First Collection Prize

The Poetry Trust, The Cut, 9 New Cut, Halesworth IP19 8BY
☎01986 835950 Fax 01986 835949
✉ info@thepoetrytrust.org
www.thepoetrytrust.org
Contact *Naomi Jaffa*

Awarded to the author of what in the opinion of the panel of judges is the best first full collection of poetry published in Great Britain and

Eire in the preceding twelve months. The prize was relaunched in 2003 with substantial new funding from Jerwood Charity. The winner receives £2000 plus an invitation to read at the **Aldeburgh Poetry Festival** the following year. 2005/6 winner: Nick Laird *To A Fault*.

Jewish Quarterly Literary Prizes
PO Box 37645, London NW7 1WB
☎020 8343 4675
www.jewishquarterly.org
Administrator *Pam Lewis*

Formerly the H.H. Wingate Prize. Annual award (for fiction or non-fiction) for a work that best stimulates an interest in and awareness of themes of Jewish interest. Books must have been published in the UK in the year of the award (written in English originally or in translation) by an author resident in Britain, the Commonwealth, Israel, Republic of Ireland or South Africa. 2006 winner: Imre Kertesz *Fatelessness* (fiction).
PRIZES £5000.

Samuel Johnson Prize
for Non-Fiction
See **The BBCFour Samuel Johnson Prize for Non-Fiction**

Mary Vaughan Jones Award
Cyngor Llyfrau Cymru (Welsh Books Council), Castell Brychan, Aberystwyth SY23 2JB
☎01970 624151 Fax 01970 625385
✉ wbc.children@wbc.org.uk
www.wbc.org.uk
Contact *The Administrator*

Triennial award for distinguished services in the field of children's literature in Wales over a considerable period of time. 2003 winner: Elfyn Pritchard.
AWARD Silver trophy.

Keats–Shelley Prize
Keats–Shelley Memorial Association, 117 Cheyne Walk, London SW10 0ES
☎020 7352 2180 Fax 020 7352 6705
✉ harrietcullenuk@yahoo.com
www.keats-shelley.com
Contact *Harriet Cullen*

Established 1998. Annual award to promote the study and appreciation of Keats and Shelley, especially in the universities, and of creative writing inspired by the younger Romantic poets. Two categories: essay and poem; open to all ages and nationalities. 2005 winners: Edmund Cusick,

William Palmer, Siriol Troup (poems), David Taylor, Polly Robinson, Michaela Bronstein (essays).
PRIZE £3000 distributed between the winners of the two categories.

Kelpies Prize
Floris Books, 15 Harrison Gardens, Edinburgh EH11 1SH
☎0131 337 2372 Fax 0131 347 9919
✉ floris@florisbooks.co.uk
www.florisbooks.co.uk/kelpiesprize
Contact *Prize Administrator*

Established 2004. Annual prize to encourage and reward new Scottish writing for children. The prize is for an unpublished novel (40–60,000 words) for children aged 9–12, set wholly or mainly in Scotland. The author does not need to be Scottish. Application form, guidelines, terms and conditions are available on the website. 2005 winner: *Catscape* Mike Nicholson.
PRIZE £2000 and publication in Floris Books' Kelpies series.

The Petra Kenney Poetry Competition
PO Box 32, Filey YO14 9YG
✉ morgan@kenney.uk.net
www.petrapoetrycompetition.co.uk
Contact *Secretary*

Established 1995. Annual poetry award. Original, unpublished poems up to 80 lines on any theme. Closing date: 1 December. Entry fee: £3 per poem. Send s.a.e. for rules and entry form.
PRIZES £1000 (1st); £500 (2nd); £250 (3rd) plus inscribed Royal Brierley Crystal Vase; and three highly commended prizes of £125 each. New prizes for comic verse: £250 (1st) and Young Poets (14–18): £250 (1st); £125 (2nd).

Kent & Sussex Poetry Society Open Competition
13 Ruscombe Close, Southborough, Tunbridge Wells TN4 0SG
☎01892 543862
Chairman *Clive R. Eastwood*

Annual competition. Entry fee: £3 per poem, maximum 40 lines.
PRIZES £1000 (total).

Kiriyama Pacific Rim Book Prize
Kiriyama Institute, 650 Delancy St, Suite 101, San Francisco, CA 94107–2082, USA
☎001 415 777 1628 Fax 001 415 777 1646
✉ info@kiriyamaprize.org

www.kiriyamaprize.org
Contact *Jeannine Cuevas*, Prize Manager
Founded 1996 with the aim of promoting books that contribute to greater understanding and cooperation among the peoples and nations of the Pacific Rim and South Asia, this annual award takes its name from the Reverend Seiyu Kiriyama. Entry details may be obtained from the address above or from the website. 2006 winners: Luis Alberto Urrea *The Hummingbird's Daughter* (fiction); Piers Vitebsky *The Reindeer People: Living with Animals and Spirits in Siberia* (non-fiction).
PRIZES $30,000, divided between both winners.

Kraszna-Krausz Book Awards
122 Fawnbrake Avenue, London SE24 0BZ
☎020 7738 6701
✉ awards@k-k.org.uk
www.k-k.org.uk
Administrator *Andrea Livingstone*
Established 1985. Annual award to encourage and recognise ousanding achievements in the publishing and writing of books on the art, practice, history and technology of still photography and the moving image (film, television, video and related screen media). Books in any language, published worldwide, are eligible. Entries must be submitted by publishers only. 2004 winners: Antonio Biasiucci *Res: Lo Stato delle Cose*; Mitch Epstein *Family Business*. No awards given in 2005; restructured awards to be announced in 2006.

Lakeland Book of the Year Awards
Cumbria Tourist Board, Ashleigh, Holly Road, Windermere LA23 2AQ
☎01539 444444 Fax 01539 444041
✉ slindsay@gocumbria.org
www.golakes.co.uk
Contact *Sheila Lindsay*
Established in 1984 by local author and broadcaster Hunter Davies in conjunction with the Cumbria Tourist Board, the books entered can be about any aspect of life in the county of Cumbria, from local history books and walking guides to novels and poetry. The contest attracts entries from both new and established authors. Since the establishment of the awards they have grown in importance and are now attracting in the region of 60 entries annually, all competing for the Hunter Davies Prize for the Lakeland Book of the Year.
In addition to the Hunter Davies Prize there are currently five categories including Award for Guides, Walks and Places; Award for People and Social History; Award for Arts and Culture; Award for Heritage and Tradition; and the Best Illustrated Book. Closing date for entries is mid-March. The awards are presented at a charity luncheon in early June.
AWARDS £100 for each category together with a framed certificate. Overall winner of the Hunter Davies Prize for the Lakeland Book of the Year also receives a cheque for £100 and a framed certificate.

Lancashire County Library Children's Book of the Year Award
Lancashire County Library Headquarters, County Hall, PO Box 61, Preston PR1 8RJ
☎01772 534751 Fax 01772 534880
✉ jacob.hope@lcl.lancscc.gov.uk
Award Coordinator *Jake Hope*
Established 1986. Annual award, presented in June for a work of original fiction suitable for 12–14-year-olds. The winner is chosen by 13–14-year-old secondary school pupils in Lancashire. Books must have been published between 1 September and 31 August in the previous year of the award and authors must be UK and Republic of Ireland residents. Final entry date: 1 September each year. 2005 winner: Jonathan Stroud *The Amulet of Samarkand*.
PRIZE £1000, plus engraved glass decanter.

Lannan Literary Award
Lannan Foundation, 313 Read Street, Santa Fe, New Mexico 87501, USA
☎001 505 986 8160
www.lannan.org
Established 1989. Annual awards given to writers of exceptional poetry, fiction and non-fiction who have made a significant contribution to English-language literature, as well as emerging writers of distinctive literary merit who have demonstrated potential for outstanding future work. On occasion, the Foundation recognises a writer for lifetime achievement. Candidates for the awards are recommended to the Foundation by a network of writers, literary scholars, publishers and editors. Applications for the awards are not accepted.

The Duncan Lawrie Dagger (in association with Crime Writers' Association)
PO Box 273, Boreham Wood WD6 2XA
✉ secretary@thecwa.co.uk
www.thecwa.co.uk

Contact *The Secretary*

Established 2006. Sponsored by Duncan Lawrie Bank. An annual award for the best crime fiction published during the year. Nominations from publishers only.

AWARD Dagger, plus cheque for £20,000.

Legend Writing Award

39 Emmanuel Road, Hastings TN34 3LB
www.legendwritingaward.com

Contact *Legend Coordinator*

Established 2001. Annual award to encourage new fiction writers resident in the UK. The competition is for short stories of 2000 words maximum and there is no set theme. Closing date: 31 August. Entry fee: £5. Rules/entry form available from website or by sending s.a.e. to address above. The competition is organised by Hastings Writers' Group and prize-winning entries are selected by its patron, author, David Gemmell.

PRIZES £500 (1st); £250 (2nd); £100 (3rd); plus three runners-up prizes of £50.

The Bernard Levin Award

Society of Indexers, Woodbourn Business Centre, 10 Jessell Street, Sheffield S9 3HY
☎0114 244 9561 Fax 0114 244 9563
✉ admin@indexers.org.uk
www.indexers.org.uk

Secretary *Ann Kingdom*

Established in 2000 to celebrate the late Bernard Levin, a journalist and author whose writings showed untiring and eloquent support for indexers and indexing. Awarded for outstanding services to the Society of Indexers. 2005 winner: John Halliday.

The Library Association Awards

See **CILIP: The Chartered Institute of Library and Information Professionals** individual awards

The Astrid Lindgren Memorial Award for Literature (ALMA)

Swedish National Council for Cultural Affairs, PO Box 7843, SE-103 98 Stockholm, Sweden
☎00 46 8 519 264 00
Fax 00 46 8 519 264 99
✉ literatureaward@alma.se
www.alma.se

Director *Anna Cokorilo*

Established 2002 by the Swedish government in memory of the children's author Astrid Lindgren. Administered by the Swedish National Council for Cultural Affairs, it is an international award for children's and young people's literature given annually to one or more recipients, irrespective of language or nationality. Writing, illustrating and storytelling, as well as reading promotion activities may be awarded. Selected organisations worldwide are invited to submit nominations once a year; jury members may also contribute nominations. 2006 winners: Katherine Paterson (USA), Ryôji Arai (Japan).

AWARD SEK 5 million (approx. €500,000)

John Llewellyn Rhys Prize

Booktrust, Book House, 45 East Hill, London SW18 2QZ
☎020 8516 2972 Fax 020 8516 2978
✉ tarryn@booktrust.org.uk
www.booktrust.org.uk

Contact *Tarryn McKay*

Established 1942. An annual young writer's award for a memorable work of any kind. Entrants must be 35 or under at the time of publication; books must have been published in the UK in the year of the award (the award runs a year behind; the next prize will be 2005). The author must be a citizen of the UK or the Commonwealth, writing in English. 2004 winner: Jonathan Trigell *Boy A*.

PRIZE £5000 (1st); £500 for shortlisted entries.

The London Writers Competition

Wandsworth Council, Room 224a, The Town Hall, Wandsworth High Street, London SW18 2PU
☎020 8871 8711 Fax 020 8871 7630
✉ arts@wandsworth.gov.uk
www.wandsworth.gov.uk

Contact *Wandsworth Arts Office*

Arranged by Wandsworth Borough Council in association with Roehampton University. An annual competition, open to all writers who live, work or study in the Greater London area. Work must not have been published previously. There are four sections: poetry, short story, play and fiction for children.

PRIZES £1000 for each section, with a first prize of £600. All winning entries are published.

The Elizabeth Longford Prize for Historical Biography

The Society of Authors, 84 Drayton Gardens, London SW10 9SB
☎020 7373 6642 Fax 020 7373 5768
✉ info@societyofauthors.org
www.societyofauthors.org

Established in 2003 in memory of Elizabeth Longford and sponsored by Flora Fraser and Peter Soros. Awarded annually for a historical biography published in the year preceding the prize. No unsolicited submissions. 2005 winner: Ian Kershaw *Making Friends With Hitler*. PRIZE £3000.

Longman-History Today Book of the Year Award

c/o History Today, 20 Old Compton Street, London W1D 4TW
☎020 7534 8000
Contact *Peter Furtado*

Established 1993. Annual award set up as joint initiative between the magazine *History Today* and the publisher Longman (**Pearson Education**) to mark the past links between the two organisations, to encourage new writers, and to promote a wider public understanding of, and enthusiasm for, the study and publication of history. Submissions are made by publishers only.
PRIZE £1000 (see *History Today* from July 2006).

The Clarissa Luard Award
See **David Cohen Prize for Literature**

The Lulu Blooker Prize
✉ blookerprize@lulu.com
www.lulublookerprize.com

Established in 2006 by **Lulu.com**, the publish-on-demand website, the prize is the first to be devoted to 'blooks', bound and printed books based on either blogs or websites. Awarded in three categories: fiction, non-fiction and comic books. Entries are accepted from publishers or individual authors from any country but must be printed in English. E-books are not accepted. Full entry details on the website. 2006 winners: *Four and Twenty Blackbirds* Cherie Priest (fiction); *Julie & Julia. 365 days, 524 Recipes, 1 Tiny Apartment Kitchen* Julie Powell (non-fiction); *Totally Bones: A Joe and Monkey Collection* Zach Miller (comic book).
CASH PRIZES.

Sir William Lyons Award
The Guild of Motoring Writers, 39 Beswick Avenue, Ensbury Park, Bournemouth BH10 4EY
☎01202 518808 Fax 01202 518808
✉ chris@whizzco.freeserve.co.uk
www.guildofmotoringwriters.co.uk
Contact *Patricia Lodge*

An annual competitive award, sponsored by Jaguar, to encourage young people in automotive journalism and to foster interests into motoring and the motor industry. Entrance by two essays and interview with Awards Committee. Applicants must be British, aged 17–23 and resident in UK. Final entry date: 1 October.

McColvin Medal
See **Besterman/McColvin Medal**

W.J.M. Mackenzie Book Prize
Political Studies Association, Dept. of Politics, University of Newcastle, Newcastle upon Tyne NE1 7RU
☎0191 222 8021 Fax 0191 222 3499
✉ psa@ncl.ac.uk
www.psa.ac.uk
PSA Executive Director *Jack Arthurs*

Established 1987. Annual award to best work of political science published in the UK during the previous year. Submissions from publishers only. Final entry date: 31 October. Prizes are judged in the year following publication and awarded the year after that. 2004 winner: Andrew Vincent *The Nature of Political Theory*.

McKitterick Prize
Society of Authors, 84 Drayton Gardens, London SW10 9SB
☎020 7373 6642 Fax 020 7373 5768
✉ info@societyofauthors.org
www.societyofauthors.org
Contact *Awards Secretary*

Annual award for a full-length novel in the English language, first published in the UK or unpublished. Open to writers over 40 who have not had any novel published other than the one submitted (excluding works for children). Closing date: 20 December. 2005 winner: Lloyd Jones *Mr Vogel*.
PRIZE £4000.

Enid McLeod Prize
Franco-British Society, 2 Dovetail Studios, 465 Battersea Park Road, London SW11 4LR
☎020 7924 3511
www.francobritishsociety.org.uk
Executive Secretary *Kate Brayn*

Established 1982. Annual award to the author of the work of literature published in the UK which, in the opinion of the judges, has contributed most to Franco-British understanding. Any full-length work written in English by a citizen of the UK, Commonwealth, Republic of Ireland, Pakistan, Bangladesh and South Africa. No English translation of a book written originally in any other language will be considered. Nominations from publishers for books published between 1 January and 31 December of the year of the prize. Closing date: 31 December. 2004 winner: Antonia Fraser *Marie Antoinette*.

PRIZE Cheque.

Macmillan Prize for a Children's Picture Book Illustration

Macmillan Children's Books, 20 New Wharf Road, London N1 9RR
☎020 7014 6124 Fax 020 7014 6142
✉ d.pinner@macmillan.co.uk
www.panmacmillan.com

Contact *Dianne Pinner*, Macmillan Children's Books

Set up in order to stimulate new work from young illustrators in art schools, and to help them start their professional lives. Fiction or non-fiction. Macmillan have the option to publish any of the prize winners.

PRIZES £1000 (1st); £500 (2nd); £250 (3rd).

The Mail on Sunday Novel Competition

Postal box address may changes annually (see below)

Annual award established 1983. Judges look for a story/character that springs to life in the 'tantalising opening 50–150 words of a novel'. Details of the competition, including the postal box address, are published in *The Mail on Sunday* in July/August. 2005 winner: Julie Halford.

AWARDS £400 book tokens and a writing course at the **Arvon Foundation** (1st); £300 tokens (2nd); £200 tokens (3rd); three further prizes of £150 tokens each.

The Man Booker International Prize

Colman Getty PR, 28 Windmill Street, London W1T 2JJ
☎020 7631 2666 Fax 0207631 2699
✉ pr@colmangettypr.co.uk
www.manbookerinternational.com

Established in 2004 to complement **The Man Booker Prize for Fiction** by recognising one writer's achievement in literature and their significant influence on writers and readers worldwide. Sponsored by the Man Group, this biennial award is given to a living author who has pub-

lished fiction either originally in English or whose work is generally available in translation into the English language. Submissions for the prize are not invited. Where the winning author's work has been translated into English an additional prize of £15,000 is awarded to the translator. The winning author chooses who the translator's prize should go to and whether it is to be awarded to one translator or divided between several. Inaugural winner (2005): Ismail Kadare; David Bellos (translator's prize).

PRIZE £60,000.

The Man Booker Prize for Fiction

Colman Getty PR, 28 Windmill Street, London W1T 2JJ
☎020 7631 2666 Fax 020 7631 2699
✉ pr@colmangettypr.co.uk
www.themanbookerprize.com

Contact *Lois Tucker* (Submissions)

The Booker Prize for Fiction was originally set up by Booker plc in 1968 to reward merit, raise the stature of the author in the eyes of the public and encourage an interest in contemporary fiction. In April 2002 it was announced that the Man Group had been chosen by the Booker Prize Foundation as the new sponsor of the Booker Prize. The sponsorship is due to run until 2011 during which time the prize will be known as the Man Booker Prize for Fiction.

United Kingdom publishers may enter up to two full-length novels, with scheduled publication dates between 1 October 2006 and 30 September 2007. In addition, any title by an author who has previously won the Booker or Man Booker Prize and any title by an author who has been shortlisted in the last ten years may be submitted. 2005 winner: John Banville *The Sea*.

PRIZE The winner receives £50,000. The six shortlisted authors each receive £2500.

Marsh Award for Children's Literature in Translation

National Centre for Research in Children's Literature, Roehampton University, Froebel College, Roehampton Lane, London SW15 5PJ
☎020 8392 3008 Fax 020 8392 3819
✉ g.lathey@roehampton.ac.uk

Contact *Dr Gillian Lathey*

Established 1995 and sponsored by the Marsh Christian Trust, the award aims to encourage translation of foreign children's books into English. It is a biennial award (next award: 2007),

open to British translators of books for 4–16-year-olds, published in the UK by a British publisher. Any category will be considered with the exception of encyclopedias and reference books. No electronic books. 2005 winner: Sarah Adams for her translation of *Eye of the Wolf* by Daniel Pennac.
PRIZE £1000.

Marsh Biography Award

The English-Speaking Union, Dartmouth House, 37 Charles Street, London W1J 5ED
☎020 7529 1564   Fax 020 7495 6108
✉ katie_brock@esu.org
www.esu.org
Contact *Katie Brock*

A biennial award for the most significant biography published over a two-year period by a British publisher. Next award October 2007. 2005 winner: John Guy *My Heart is My Own: The Life of Mary Queen of Scots*.
AWARD Membership of the ESU and £4000, plus a silver trophy presented at a gala dinner.

MCA Management Writing Awards

49 Whitehall, London SW1A 1BX
☎020 7321 3990   Fax 020 7321 3991
✉ natalia.kay@mca.org.uk
www.mca.org.uk
Contact *Natalia Kay*

Annual awards, established in 2004 by the Management Consultancies Association in association with *Management Today* magazine in order to recognise and reward excellence in management writing. Books and articles submitted must have been first published in the UK in the previous 12 months. Entries can be accepted from journalists, authors or their publishers. Full entry details on the website. 2005 winners: 'The organic milk of human kindness overflows at Pret' Sathnam Sanghera, *Financial Times* (Best Management Article); *Growth Gamble* Andrew Campbell and Robert Park (Best Management Book); Stefan Stern (Best Management Interview); Lisa Miles (Best Young Writer).

Colin Mears Award

See **CILIP: The Chartered Institute of Library and Information Professionals Kate Greenaway Medal**

Medical Book Awards

The Society of Authors, 84 Drayton Gardens, London SW10 9SB
☎020 7373 6642   Fax 020 7373 5768

✉ info@society of authors.org
www.societyofauthors.org
Contact *Secretary, Medical Writers Group*

Annual awards sponsored by the Royal Society of Medicine. Nine categories for medical textbooks published in the twelve months preceding the deadline. Contact the **Society of Authors** for entry details. Closing date: 20 April.
PRIZES £6500 (total).

The Mercedes-Benz Award for the Montagu of Beaulieu Trophy

Guild of Motoring Writers, 39 Beswick Avenue, Ensbury Park, Bournemouth BH10 4EY
☎01202 518808   Fax 01202 518808
✉ chris@whizzco.freeserve.co.uk
www.guildofmotoringwriters.co.uk
Contact *Patricia Lodge*

First presented by Lord Montagu on the occasion of the opening of the National Motor Museum at Beaulieu in 1972. Awarded annually to a member of the **Guild of Motoring Writers** who, in the opinion of the nominated jury, has made the greatest contribution to recording in the English language the history of motoring or motor cycling in a published book or article, film, television or radio script, or research manuscript available to the public. Cash PRIZE sponsored by Mercedes-Benz UK.

Mere Literary Festival Open Competition

'Lawrences', Old Hollow, Mere BA12 6EG
☎01747 860475
www.merewilts.org.uk
Contact *Mrs Adrienne Howell* (Events Organiser)

Annual open competition which alternates between short stories and poetry. The winners are announced at the **Mere Literary Festival** during the second week of October. The 2007 competition is for poetry. Closing date for entries: July. For further details, including entry fees and form, access the website or contact the address above from 1 March with s.a.e.
Cash PRIZES.

Meyer-Whitworth Award

Arts Council England, 14 Great Peter Street, London SW1P 3NQ
☎020 7973 6480
✉ charles.hart@artscouncil.org.uk
www.artscouncil.org.uk
Contact *Theatre Writing, Theatre Department*

This annual award is intended to help further the careers of UK playwrights who are not yet established, and to draw contemporary theatre writers to the public's attention. Nominations are made by directors of professional theatre companies. Plays must have been written in the English language and produced professionally in the UK during the past 12 months. Candidates will have had no more than two of their plays professionally produced. No writer who has won the award previously may reapply and no play that has been submitted previously for the award is eligible. Apply for further details and application form.
AWARD £8000.

MIND Book of the Year
Granta House, 15–19 Broadway E15 4BQ
☎020 8215 2301   Fax 020 8215 2269
✉ j.bird@mind.org.uk
www.mind.org.uk

Established 1981. Annual award, in memory of Sir Allen Lane, for the author of a book published in the current year (fiction or non-fiction), which furthers public understanding of mental health problems. 2006 winner: Valerie Mason-John *Borrowed Body*.

The Mitchell Prize for Art History/The Eric Mitchell Prize
c/o The Burlington Magazine, 14–16 Duke's Road, London WC1H 9SZ
☎020 7388 8157   Fax 020 7388 1230
✉ annette.bradshaw@burlington.org.uk
Executive Director *Richard Shone*
Contact *Annette Bradshaw*

The Mitchell Prize is awarded for a book which has made an outstanding and original contribution to the understanding of the visual arts, and The Eric Mitchell Prize is awarded for the best exhibition catalogue. Both must be on western art, written in English and published in the previous two years. Nominations should be submitted by publishers before the end of April. 2004 winners: Colin Bailey *Patriotic Taste: Collecting Modern Art in Pre-Revolutionary Paris* (The Mitchell Prize); Thomas Kren and Scot McKendrick *The Triumph of Flemish Manuscript Painting in Europe*, The J. Paul Getty Museum, Los Angeles and the Royal Academy of Arts, London (The Eric Mitchell Prize).
PRIZES $10,000 each.

Momaya Press Short Story Writing Competition
Momaya Press, Flat 1, 189 Balham High Road, London SW12 9BE
☎020 8673 9616
✉ infouk@momayapress.com
www.momayapress.com
Contact *Monisha Saldanha*

Established 2004. Annual short story competition sponsored by Momaya Press. Open to writers in the English language worldwide. Entries, which should not have been published previously, can be in any style and format and on any subject, 2500 words maximum. Entry fee: £6; final entry date: 30 May 2007. Submissions via entry form on the website.
PRIZES cash; all winners are published in the *Momaya Annual Review*.

Scott Moncrieff Prize
See **The Translators Association Awards**

The Oscar Moore Screenwriting Prize
The Oscar Moore Foundation, c/o Screen International, 33–39 Bowling Green Lane, London EC1R 0DA
☎020 7505 8080   Fax 020 7505 8087
✉ sade.sharp@emap.com
www.screendaily.com
Coordinator *Sade Sharp*

Established 1997. Annual prize in honour of Oscar Moore, former *Guardian* columnist and editor-in-chief of *Screen International*, who died in 1996. The genre for the competition changes each year (comedy for 2005), as does the closing date. Contact the Foundation to obtain an entry form. 2004 winner: Marcus Shepherd *A Killing in the Woods*.
AWARD £10,000 cash, plus week-long script development course courtesy of Arista, and performance of the winning script by **The Script Factory**.

Nasen & TES Special Educational Needs Book Awards
Nasen House, 4–5 Amber Business Village, Amber Close, Amington, Tamworth B77 4RP
☎01827 311 500   Fax 01827 313 005
✉ welcome@nasen.org.uk
www.nasen.org.uk

Organised by the Nasen and the *Times Educational Supplement*. Three awards: The Children's Book Award, for the book that most successfully provides a positive image of children with special educational needs; The Academic Book Award celebrates the work of authors and editors who have made an out-

standing contribution to the theory and practice of special education; The Book for Teaching and Learning Award is presented for curriculum materials for pupils or teachers in early years, primary or secondary phases. Deadline: 21 June each year. Eligibility: books must have been published in the UK within the year preceding the awards.
PRIZE £500 each category.

National Poetry Anthology
United Press, Admail 3735, London EC1B 1JB
☎0870 240 6190 Fax 0870 240 6191
www.unitedpress.co.uk
Contact *Julie Embury*

Free-to-enter annual poetry competition. Organisers United Press allow up to three poems (20 lines and 160 words maximum each) by annual closing date of 30 June. They select around 250 regional winners in the UK. These receive a free copy of the annual book, *The National Poetry Anthology* and vote for the overall winner who receives £1000 and a trophy to keep for life.

National Poetry Competition
The Poetry Society, 22 Betterton Street, London WC2H 9BX
☎020 7420 9895 Fax 020 7240 4818
✉ marketing@poetrysociety.org.uk
www.poetrysociety.org.uk
Contact *Competition Organiser (WH)*

One of Britain's major open poetry competitions. Closing date: 31 October. Poems on any theme, up to 40 lines. For rules and entry form send s.a.e. to the competition organiser at the address above or enter the competition via the website.
PRIZES £5000 (1st); £1000 (2nd); £500 (3rd); plus 10 commendations of £50.

The National Short Story Prize
Room 316, BBC Henry Wood House, 3 – 6 Langham Place, London W1B 3DF
www.bbc.co.uk/radio4

Launched at the 2005 Edinburgh International Book Festival, this annual short story award – the largest for a single story – is funded by NESTA (the National Endowment for Science, Technology and the Arts) and supported by BBC Radio 4 and *Prospect* magazine. The award, which is open to UK nationals or residents, aged 18 or over, is for stories of no more than 8000 words. Entrants must have a prior record of publication in creative writing; only two stories

(written in English) will be accepted per author. Full entry details from the address above or via the website. Inaugural winners: James Lasdun *An Anxious Man* (overall winner); Michel Faber *The Safehouse* (runner up).
PRIZES £15,000 (overall); £3000 (runner up).

Bill Naughton Short Story Competition
Box No. 2006, Aghamore, Ballyhaunis, Co. Mayo, Republic of Ireland
✉ paulwdrogers@eircom.net
www.aghamoreireland.com/kennynaughton/shortstory.htm

Organised by the **Kenny/Naughton Society**. Stories may be on any topic and no more than 2500 words in length. All work must be unpublished; typed scripts only with no name or address appearing on the work. Entry fee: £5, e7 or US$8 per story; three stories may be submitted for the price of two. Closing date: 1 September each year. No entry form required.
PRIZES £150 (€200) (1st); £100 (€130) (2nd); £50 (€65) (3rd). Best stories published in a collection entitled *Splinters*.

Nestlé Children's Book Prize
Booktrust, Book House, 45 East Hill, London SW18 2QZ
☎020 8516 2986 Fax 020 8516 2978
✉ hannah@booktrust.org.uk
www.booktrusted.com
Contact *Hannah Rutland*

Established 1985 to encourage high standards and stimulate interest in books for children, this prize is given for a children's book (fiction or poetry), written in English by a citizen of the UK or an author resident in the UK, and published in the UK in the year ending 30 September. There are three age-group categories: 5 and under, 6–8 and 9–11. Uniquely, the shortlist for each age category is judged by classes of schoolchildren, who enter a competition to win a chance to be Young Judges. 50 classes from each age category judge the books, deciding who gets Gold, Silver and Bronze. The class projects entered for the judging process are then judged to see which classes will come to London for the prize presentation. 2005 Gold Award winners: Oliver Jeffers *Lost and Found* (5 and under); Nick Butterworth *The Whisperer* (6–8); Sally Gardner *I, Coriander* (9–11).
PRIZES in each category: £2500 (gold); £1500 (silver); £500 (bronze).

The New Writer Prose & Poetry Prizes

The New Writer, PO Box 60, Cranbrook TN17 2ZR
☎01580 212626 Fax 01580 212041
✉ admin@thenewwriter.com
www.thenewwriter.com

Contact *Merric Davidson*

Established 1997. Annual award. Open to all poets writing in the English language for an original, previously unpublished poem or collection of six to ten poems. Also open to writers of short stories and novellas/serials, features, articles, essays and interviews. Final entry date: 31 October. Full guidelines on the website. Previous winners: Mario Petrucci, Ros Barber, Celia de Fréine, Andrew McGuinness, Katy Darby, David Grubb.

PRIZES (total) £2000, plus publication in annual collection published by *The New Writer*.

New Writing Ventures

c/o Book Trust, Book House, 45 East Hill, London SW18 2QZ
☎020 8516 2972 Fax 020 8516 2978
✉ tarryn@booktrust.org.uk
www.booktrust.org.uk
www.newwritingpartnership.org.uk

Contact *Tarryn McKay*

Established in 2005 by The New Writing Partnership in association with Arts Council England, and administered by Booktrust, this annual award is aimed at emerging writers of adult fiction, non-fiction and poetry, written in English. Open only to unpublished writers who are resident in England. Final entry date to be confirmed.

PRIZES £5000 for each category

'The Nibbies'

See **British Book Awards**

Nielsen Gold & Platinum Book Awards

Nielsen BookScan, 3rd Floor, Midas House, 62 Goldsworth Road, Woking GU21 6LQ
☎01483 712222 Fax 01483 712220
✉ gold&platinumawards@nielsenbookscan.co.uk
www.nielsenbookscan.co.uk

Contact *Kim Crooke*

Established in 2000 to award actual consumer purchases of a title through UK bookshops. Awarded to any title, in all its editions, that sells more than 500,000 copies (Gold) or one million copies (Platinum) over a period of six consecutive years.

AWARDS Commemorative plaque issued by the publisher to the author.

Nobel Prize

The Nobel Foundation, PO Box 5232, 102 45 Stockholm, Sweden
☎00 46 8 663 0920 Fax 00 46 8 660 3847
www.nobel.se

Contact *Information Section*

Awarded yearly for outstanding achievement in physics, chemistry, physiology or medicine, literature and peace. Founded by Alfred Nobel, a chemist who proved his creative ability by inventing dynamite. In general, individuals cannot nominate someone for a Nobel Prize. The rules vary from prize to prize but the following are eligible to do so for Literature: members of the Swedish Academy and of other academies, institutions and societies similar to it in constitution and purpose; professors of literature and of linguistics at universities or colleges; Nobel Laureates in Literature; presidents of authors' organisations which are representative of the literary production in their respective countries. British winners of the literature prize, first granted in 1901, include Rudyard Kipling, John Galsworthy and Winston Churchill. Winners since 1996: Wislawa Szymborska (Poland); Dario Fo (Italy); José Saramago (Portugal); Günter Grass (Germany); Gao Xingjian (France); V.S. Naipaul (UK); Imre Kertész (Hungary); J.M. Coetzee (South Africa); Elfriede Jelinek (Austria). Nobel Laureate in Literature 2005: Harold Pinter (UK).

The Noma Award for Publishing Africa

PO Box 128, Witney OX8 5XU
☎01993 775235 Fax 01993 709265
✉ maryljay@aol.com
www.nomaaward.org

Contact *Mary Jay*, Secretary to the Managing Committee

Established 1979. Annual award, founded by the late Shoichi Noma, President of Kodansha Ltd, Tokyo. The award is for an outstanding book, published in Africa by an African writer, in three categories: scholarly and academic; literature and creative writing; children's books. Entries, by publishers only, by 31 March for a title published in the previous year. Maximum number of three entries. Previous winners: Abosede Emanuel *Odun Ifa/Ifa Festival*; Hamdi

Sakkut *The Arabic Novel: Bibliography and Critical Introduction 1865–1995*; Elinor Sisulu *Walter and Albertina Sisulu – In Our Lifetime*; Were Liking *La memoire amputee*.
PRIZE US$10,000 and presentation plaque.

C.B. Oldman Prize
Special Libraries & Archives, University of Aberdeen, King's College, Aberdeen
AB24 3SW
☎01224 274266   Fax 01224 273891
✉ r.turbet@abdn.ac.uk
Contact *Richard Turbet*

Established 1989 by the International Association of Music Libraries, UK & Ireland Branch. Annual award for best book of music bibliography, librarianship or reference published the year before last (i.e. books published in 2004 considered for the 2006 prize). Previous winners: Andrew Ashbee, Michael Talbot, Donald Clarke, John Parkinson, John Wagstaff, Stanley Sadie, William Waterhouse, Richard Turbet, John Gillaspie, David Fallows, Arthur Searle, Graham Johnson, Michael Twyman, David Wyn Jones.
PRIZE £200.

Ondaatje Prize
See **The Royal Society of Literature Ondaatje Prize**

Open Window Poetry Anthology Contest
See **Hidden Brook Press International Poetry Anthology Contests**

Orange Prize for Fiction/ Orange Award for New Writers
Booktrust, 45 East Hill, London SW18 2QZ
☎020 8516 2972   Fax 020 8516 2978
✉ tarryn@booktrust.org.uk
www.orangeprize.co.uk
Contact *Tarryn McKay*

Established 1996. Annual award founded by a group of senior women in publishing to 'create the opportunity for more women to be rewarded for their work and to be better known by the reading public'. Awarded for a full-length novel written in English by a woman of any nationality, and published in the UK between 1 April and 31 March of the following year. 2006 winner: Zadie Smith *On Beauty*.
PRIZE £30,000 and a work of art (a limited edition bronze figurine known as 'The Bessie' in acknowledgement of anonymous prize endowment).

A new prize, the **Orange Award for New Writers**, was awarded for the first time in 2005. All first works of fiction, written by women of any age or nationality, published in the UK between 1 April 2005 and 31 March 2006, will be eligible (short story collections and novellas also eligible). Inaugural winner: Diana Evans *26a*.

The Orwell Prize
Blackwell Publishing, 9600 Garsington Road, Oxford OX4 2DQ
☎01865 476255   Fax 01865 471255
✉ lucie.crowther@oxon.blackwellpublishing.com
Contact *Lucie Crowther*

Jointly established in 1993 by the George Orwell Memorial Fund and the *Political Quarterly* to encourage and reward writing in the spirit of Orwell's 'What I have most wanted to do ... is to make political writing into an art'. Two categories: book or pamphlet; newspaper and/or articles, features, columns, or sustained reportage on a theme in non-fiction or fiction. Submissions by editors, publishers or authors. 2005 winners (for work published in 2004): Delia Jarrett-Macauley *Moses, Citizen and Me* (book); Timothy Garton Ash (journalism).
PRIZES £1000 for each category.

Ottakar's and Faber National Poetry Competition
Ottakar's Plc, Brewery House, 36 Milford Street, Salisbury SP1 2AP
☎01722 428500   Fax 01722 428502
✉ enquiries@ottakars.co.uk
www.ottakars.co.uk
Contacts *Jon Howells, Jo James*

Established 1997. Annual competition in support of National Poetry Day and to promote poetry within Ottakar's bookshops and their local communities. Maximum 40 lines; only one poem per applicant. The poems, which must be previously unpublished, can be on any subject and in any style. 2004 winner: Jessika Hartleb.
PRIZE £500 (National winner) plus publication in a national newspaper.

Ottakar's Children's Book Prize
Ottakar's, Brewery House, 36 Milford Street, Salisbury SP1 2AP
☎01722 428500   Fax 01722 428535
✉ enquiries@ottakars.co.uk
www.ottakars.co.uk
Contact *Fiona Martin*

Founded 2004/5. Annual award to help support new and emerging writers of fiction for 7–14–year-olds. Eligibility: authors of any nationality with not more than three previously published children's books or published author new to children's books. Books submitted: can be unpublished; previously published in hardback or paperback original; parts of series or trilogies (but the title must make sense as a stand alone novel). Final entry date: May/June. Previous winners: Stuart Hill *The Cry of the Icemark*; Julia Golding *The Diamond of Drury Lane*.

The Wilfred Owen Award for Poetry
c/o 17 Belmont, Shrewsbury SY1 1TE
☎01743 460089
www.1914-18.co.uk/owen
Contact *Michael Grayer*

Established in 1988 by the **Wilfred Owen Association**. Given to a poet whose poetry reflects the spirit of Owen's work in its thinking, expression and inspiration. Applications are not sought; the decision is made by the Association's committee. Previous winners: Seamus Heaney, Christopher Logue, Michael Longley, Harold Pinter.
AWARD A silver and gunmetal work of art, suitably decorated and engraved.

OWG Awards for Excellence
Outdoor Writers' Guild, PO Box 118, Twickenham TW1 2XB
☎020 8538 9468 Fax 020 8538 9468
✉ sec@owg.org.uk
www.owg.org.uk
Contact *Hazelle Jackson*, Secretary

Established 1980. Annual awards by the **Outdoor Writers' Guild** to raise the standard of outdoor writing, journalism, broadcasting and photography. Categories include guidebook, outdoor book, feature (one-off), feature (regular), photography. Open to OWG members only. Final entry date: July.

The Oxford Weidenfeld Translation Prize
St Anne's College, Oxford OX2 6HS
☎01865 274820 Fax 01865 274899
✉ sandra.madley@st-annes.ox.ac.uk
Contact *The Fellows' Secretary*

Established in 1996 by publisher Lord Weidenfeld to encourage good translation into English. Annual award to the translator(s) of a work of fiction, poetry or drama written in any living European language. Translations must have been published in the previous calendar year. Submissions from publishers only.
PRIZE £1500.

PEN Awards
See **J.R. Ackerley Prize**; **Golden PEN Award for Lifetime Distinguished Service to Literature**; **The Hessell-Tiltman Prize for History**

Samuel Pepys Award
Samuel Pepys Award Trust, Montreal House, Winson, Cirencester GL7 5EL
☎01285 740331
Contact *Jolyon Dromgoole, MA (Oxon), FRSA*

Established 2003. Biennial award (next in 2007) given by the Samuel Pepys Award Trust for a book that makes the greatest contribution to the understanding of Samuel Pepys, his times or his contemporaries. 2005 winner: Frances Harris *The Transformations of Love*.
AWARD £2000, plus commemorative medal.

Peterloo Poets Open Poetry Competition
The Old Chapel, Sand Lane, Calstock PL18 9QX
☎01822 833473
✉ info@peterloopoets.com
www.peterloopoets.com
Contact *Harry Chambers*

Established 1986. Annual competition for unpublished English language poems of not more than 40 lines. Final entry date: 1 March. Send s.a.e. for rules and entry form. Previous winners: David Craig, Rodney Pybus, Debjani Chatterjee, Donald Atkinson, Romesh Gunesekera, Anna Crowe, Carol Ann Duffy, Mimi Khalvati, John Lyons, M.R. Peacocke, Alison Pryde, Carol Shergold, John Weston, Maureen Wilkinson, Chris Woods, Judy Gahagan, Carol Rumens, John Godfrey.
PRIZES £1500 (1st); £1000 (2nd); £500 (3rd); £100 (4th); plus 10 prizes of £50; 15–19 age group: 5 prizes of £100.

Ben Pimlott Prize for Political Writing
Fabian Society, 11 Dartmouth Street, London SW1H 9BN
☎020 7227 4900 Fax 020 7976 7153
www.fabians.org.uk
www.guardian.co.uk

Contact *Claire Willgress* (Office Manager)
Founded 2005. Annual award in memory of
Ben Pimlott, political writer, regular contributor to *Guardian Review*, and a major intellectual
force in the Fabian Society. The aim of the prize
is to encourage young/new writers and the
political essay as a literary form. The topic for
the award is announced each January. The 2006
theme was 'Who do you think you are? Can
history help us to define British identity today,
or is it part of the problem?' Open to all. Final
entry date: mid-March. Inaugural winner: Mark
Hayhurst on Aneurin Bevan.

AWARD £3000 plus publication in *Guardian
Review* and on the Fabian Society website.

Poetry Business Competition

The Studio, Byram Arcade, Westgate,
Huddersfield HD1 1ND
☎01484 434840 Fax 01484 426566
✉ edit@poetrybusiness.co.uk
www.poetrybusiness.co.uk

Contact *The Competition Administrator*

Established 1986. Annual award which aims to
discover and publish new writers. Entrants
should submit a short manuscript of poems.
Winners will have their work published by the
Poetry Business under the Smith/Doorstop
imprint. Final entry date: end of October.
Contact for conditions of entry. Previous win-
ners include: Pauline Stainer, Michael Laskey,
Mimi Khalvati, David Morley, Moniza Alvi,
Selima Hill, Catherine Smith, Daljit Nagra.

PRIZES Publication of full collection; runners-up have pamphlets; 20 complimentary
copies. Also cash prize (£1000) to be shared
equally between all winners.

The Poetry Society's National Poetry Competition

See **National Poetry Competition**

The Portico Prize

The Portico Library, 57 Mosley Street,
Manchester M2 3HY
☎0161 236 6785 Fax 0161 236 6803
✉ librarian@theportico.org.uk
www.theportico.org.uk

Contact *Miss Emma Marigliano*

Established 1985. Administered by the Portico
Library in Manchester. Biennial award for a
work of fiction or non-fiction published
between the two closing dates. Set wholly or
mainly in the North West of England, including
Cumbria and the High Peak District of

Derbyshire. Previous winners include: Anthony
Burgess *Any Old Iron*; Jenny Uglow *Elizabeth
Gaskell: A Habit of Stories*. 2004 winner: Terry
Wyke *Public Sculpture of Greater Manchester*.
PRIZE £3000.

The Dennis Potter Screenwriting Award

BBC Broadcasting House, Whiteladies Road,
Bristol BS8 2LR
☎0117 974 7586

Contact *Jeremy Howe*, Executive Producer,
Drama

Annual award established in 1995 in memory of
the late television playwright to 'nurture and
encourage the work of new writers of talent
and personal vision'. Submissions should be
made through a BBC TV drama producer or an
independent production company. 2006 winner: Russell T. Davies.

Practical Art Book of the Year

PO Box 3, Huntingdon PE28 0QX
☎01832 710201 Fax 01832 710488
✉ award@acaward.com
www.acaward.com

Contact *Henry Malt*

Jointly sponsored by Artists' Choice book club
and *Leisure Painter* and *The Artist* magazines. A
short list is drawn up by the editors and the
winner voted by readers. Shortlist will be
announced in June and the inner in November.

The Premio Valle Inclán

See **The Translators Association Awards**

V.S. Pritchett Memorial Prize

The Royal Society of Literature, Somerset
House, Strand, London WC2R 1LA
☎020 7845 4676 Fax 020 7845 4679
✉ paula@rslit.org
www.rslit.org

Established 1999. Awarded for a previously
unpublished short story of between 2000 and
5000 words. For entry forms, please contact the
Secretary from 15 November onwards. Closing
date: 31 January. Open to UK and Irish writers
and writers who have been resident in the UK
for at least three years.
PRIZE £1000.

Pulitzer Prizes

The Pulitzer Prize Board, 709 Journalism
Building, Columbia University, 2950
Broadway, New York, NY 10027, USA

☎001 212 854 3841 Fax 001 212 854 3342
✉ pulitzer@www.pulitzer.org
www.pulitzer.org
Awards for journalism in US newspapers, and for published literature, drama and music by American nationals. 2006 winners include: Geraldine Brooks *March* (fiction); Caroline Elkins *Imperial Reckoning: The Untold Story of Britain's Gulag in Kenya* (general non-fiction).

The Red House Children's Book Award
The Federation of Children's Book Groups, The Old Malt House, Aldbourne SN8 2DW
☎01672 540629 Fax 01672 541280
✉ marianneadey@aol.com
www.redhousechildrensbookaward.co.uk
Coordinator *Marianne Adey*

Established 1980. Awarded annually for best book of fiction suitable for children. Unique in that it is judged by the children themselves. 2006 winner: Rick Riordan *Percy Jackson and the Olympians: Lightning Thief.*

AWARD Portfolio of letters, drawings and comments from the children who took part in the judging. Silver bowls and trophy.

Trevor Reese Memorial Prize
Institute of Commonwealth Studies, School of Advanced Studies, University of London, 28 Russell Square, London WC1B 5DS
☎020 7862 8844 Fax 020 7862 8820

Established in 1979 with the proceeds of contributions to a memorial fund to Dr Trevor Reese, Reader in Commonwealth Studies at the Institute and a distinguished scholar of Imperial History (d.1976). Biennial award (next award 2007 for works published 2005–06) for a scholarly work, usually by a single author, in the field of Imperial and Commonwealth History published in the preceding two academic years. All correspondence relating to the prize should be marked 'Trevor Reese Memorial Prize'.
PRIZE £1000.

Regional Press Awards
Press Gazette, 10 Old Bailey, London EC4M 7NG
☎020 7038 1469 Fax 020 7038 1155
✉ franb@pressgazette.co.uk
www.pressgazette.co.uk

Open to all regional newspapers and regional journalists, whether freelance or staff. July event. Run by the *Press Gazette.*

Renault UK Journalist of the Year Award
Guild of Motoring Writers, 39 Beswick Avenue, Ensbury Park, Bournemouth BH10 4EY
☎01202 518808 Fax 01202 518808
✉ chris@whizzco.freeserve.co.uk
www.guildofmotoringwriters.co.uk
Contact *Patricia Lodge*

Originally the Pierre Dreyfus Award and established 1977. Awarded annually by Renault UK Ltd in honour of Pierre Dreyfus, president director general of Renault 1955–75, to the member of the **Guild of Motoring Writers** who is judged to have made the most outstanding journalistic effort in any medium during the year. Particular emphasis is placed on initiative and endeavour.

Romantic Novel of the Year
Flat C, 40 Lexham Gardens, London W8 5JE
www.rna-uk.org
Honorary Administrator *Mrs P. Fenton*

Established 1960. Annual award for the best romantic novel of the year, open to non-members as well as members of the **Romantic Novelists' Association**. Novels must be first published in the UK between specified dates. Full details on the RNA website. 2006 winner: Erica James *Gardens of Delight.* Send s.a.e. to the organiser for entry form.
AWARD £10,000.

Rooney Prize for Irish Literature
Rooney Prize, Strathin, Templecarrig, Delgany, Co. Wicklow, Republic of Ireland
☎00 353 1 287 4769/287 4376 Fax 00 353 1 287 2595
✉ rooneyprize@ireland.com
Contacts *Jim Sherwin, Thelma Cloake*

Established 1976. Annual award to encourage young Irish writing to develop and continue. Authors must be Irish, under 40 and published. A non-competitive award with no application procedure.
PRIZE €10,000.

Royal Economic Society Prize
The Economic Journal, Department of Economics, London Business School, Regent's Park, London NW1 4SA
☎020 7706 6777 Fax 020 7402 0718
✉ econjournal@london.edu
www.res.org.uk/society.resprize.asp
Contact *Heather Daly*

Annual award for the best article published in *The Economic Journal*. Open to members of the Royal Economic Society only. Previous winners: Professors Kip Viscusi, Mark Armstrong, Jim Heckman, Jeffrey Smith, Richard Dickens and Casey Mulligan.
PRIZE £3000.

Royal Mail Awards for Scottish Children's Books (Administrated by BRAW in partnership with the Scottish Arts Council)

Scottish Book Trust, Sandeman's House, Trunk's Close, 55 High Street, Edinburgh EH1 1SR
☎0131 524 0160 Fax 0131 524 0161
✉ anna.gibbons@scottishbooktrust.com
www.braw.org.uk

Manager, BRAW *Anna Gibbons*

Awards are given to new and established authors of published books in recognition of high standards of writing for children in three age groups categories: younger children (0–7 years); younger readers (8–12), older readers (13–16). A shortlist is drawn up by a panel of children's book experts and the winner in each category is selected by children and young people voting for their favourites in schools and libraries across Scotland. Authors should be Scottish or resident in Scotland, but books of particular Scottish interest by other authors are eligible. Final entry date: 31 January; guidelines available on request.
AWARDS £5250 in total; £1000 for winner in each category; £250 each runner-up.

Royal Society of Literature Awards

The Royal Society of Literature Ondaatje Prize, V.S. Pritchett Memorial Prize and (under *Bursaries, Fellowships and Grants*) The Royal Society of Literature/Jerwood Awards

The Royal Society of Literature Ondaatje Prize

The Royal Society of Literature, Somerset House, Strand, London WC2R 1LA
☎020 7845 4676 Fax 020 7845 4679
✉ paulaj@rslit.org
www.rslit.org

Submissions *Paula Johnson*

Administered by the **Royal Society of Literature** and endowed by Sir Christopher Ondaatje, the prize is awarded annually to a book of literary merit, fiction, non-fiction or poetry, best evoking the spirit of place. All entries must be published within the calendar year 2006 and should be submitted between 1 September and 1 December 2006. The writer must be a citizen of the UK, Commonwealth or Ireland. Further details available on the website. 2006 winner: James Meek *The People's Act of Love.*
PRIZE £10,000.

Runciman Award

The Anglo-Hellenic League, c/o The Hellenic Centre, 16–18 Paddington Street, London W1U 5AS
☎020 7486 9410 Fax 020 7486 4254 (c/o Hellenic Centre)

Contact *The Administrator*

Established 1985. Annual award, sponsored by the National Bank of Greece. Founded by the Anglo-Hellenic League to promote Anglo-Greek understanding and friendship, for a work wholly or mainly about some aspect of Greece or the world of Hellenism, published in English in any country of the world in its first edition during 2005. Books published anywhere in the world are eligible. It is a condition of the award that shortlisted books should be available for purchase to readers in the UK at the time of the award ceremony. Named after the late Sir Steven Runciman, former chairman of the Anglo-Hellenic League. No category of writing will be excluded from consideration. Works in translation, with the exception of translations from Greek literature, will not be considered. Final entry date in late January; award presented in May/June. 2005 winner: Mark Mazower *Salonica, City of Ghosts: Christians, Muslims and Jews.*
AWARD £9000.

Sagittarius Prize

Society of Authors, 84 Drayton Gardens, London SW10 9SB
☎020 7373 6642 Fax 020 7373 5768
✉ info@societyofauthors.org
www.societyofauthors.org

Established 1990. For first published novel by an author over the age of 60. Final entry date: 20 December. Full details available from the **Society of Authors**. 2005 winner: Lauro Martines *Loredana.*
PRIZE £4000.

Sainsbury's Baby Book Award

See **Booktrust Early Years Awards**

The David St John Thomas Charitable Trust & Awards

The David St John Thomas Charitable Trust.
PO Box 6055, Nairn IV12 4YB
☎01667 453351   Fax 01667 453351
✉ dsjtcharitynairn@fsmail.net

Competition & Awards Manager *Lorna Edwardson*

A large programme of writing competitions and awards including annual ghost story and love story competitions (each 1600–1800 words with £1000 first prize), and open poetry competition (poems up to 32 lines, total prize money £1000). Publication of winning entries is guaranteed, usually in *Writers' News/Writing Magazine*. The awards are led by the annual Self-Publishing Awards open to anyone who has self-published a book during the preceding calendar year. There are four categories each with a £250 prize; the overall winner is declared Self-Publisher of the Year with a total award of £1000. For full details of these and many others, including an annual writers' groups anthology and letter-writers of the year, send large s.a.e. to the address above.

The Saltire Literary Awards

Saltire Society, 9 Fountain Close, 22 High Street, Edinburgh EH1 1TF
☎0131 556 1836   Fax 0131 557 1675
✉ saltire@saltiresociety.org.uk
www.saltiresociety.org.uk

Administrator *Kathleen Munro*

Established 1982. Annual awards, one for Book of the Year and one for Best First Book by an author publishing for the first time. Open to any author of Scottish descent or living in Scotland, or to anyone who has written a book which deals with either the work and life of a Scot or with a Scottish problem, event or situation. Nominations are invited from editors of leading newspapers, magazines and periodicals. 2005 winners: The Faculty of Advocates/Saltire Society Scottish Book of the Year: Kate Atkinson *Case Histories*; Royal Mail/Saltire Society Scottish First Book of the Year: John Aberdein *Amande's Bed*.
   PRIZES £5000 (Scottish Book); £1500 (First Book).

Schlegel–Tieck Prize

See **The Translators Association Awards**

Science Writer Awards

The Daily Telegraph, 1 Canada Square, Canary Wharf, London E14 5DT
☎0845 634 6349 (Hotline: 10.00 am to 4.00 pm Mon–Fri)   Fax 020 7513 2512
✉ enquiries@science-writer.co.uk
www.science-writer.co.uk

Contact *Roger Highfield*

Established 1987, this award is designed to bridge the gap between science and writing, challenging the writer to come up with a piece of no more than 700 words that is friendly, informative and, above all, understandable. Sponsored by Bayer, the award is open to two age groups: 16–19 and 20–28.
   AWARD Winners and runners-up receive cash prizes and have the opportunity to have their pieces published on the science pages of *The Daily Telegraph*. The winner in each category also gets a cash prize and a chance to meet the judges, which include Bill Bryson, Sir David Attenborough and Adam Hart-Davis. There is also a prize for schools and a prize for teachers. To check launch date, visit the website, telephone the hotline number or e-mail for further information.

The Scotsman & Orange Short Story Award

c/o The Scotsman, 108 Holyrood Road, Edinburgh EH8 8AS
☎0131 620 8613
✉ drobinson@scotsman.com

Contact *David Robinson*, Books Editor

An annual award, established in 2004, to encourage, support and reward short story-writing in Scotland. Open to people who were born or are living in Scotland, the competition is themed each year.
   PRIZES £7500 (1st); £500 (five runners-up); 20 best entries selected for publication in annual book.

Scottish Arts Council Book Awards

Scottish Arts Council, 12 Manor Place, Edinburgh EH3 7DD
☎0131 226 6051   Fax 0131 225 9833
✉ gavin.wallace@scottisharts.org.uk
www.scottisharts.org.uk

Contact *Gavin Wallace*, Head of Literature

Awards are made annually and are given in recognition of high standards in fiction, poetry and literary non-fiction. Authors should be Scottish or resident in Scotland, but books of Scottish interest by other authors are eligible for consideration. Applications are made by publishers only and the closing date is 31 January for books published in the previous calendar year. 2005 winner: Kathleen Jamie *The Tree House* (Book of the Year).

AWARDS Three shortlisted adult writers each receive an award of £2000. The Scottish Arts Council Book of Year Award is worth a total of £10,000. (The Awards will be relaunched in a different format in 2007.)

Scottish Book of the Year
See **The Saltire Literary Awards**

Scottish History Book of the Year
The Saltire Society, 9 Fountain Close, 22 High Street, Edinburgh EH1 1TF
☎0131 556 1836 Fax 0131 557 1675
✉ saltire@saltiresociety.org.uk
www.saltiresociety.org.uk
Administrator *Kathleen Munro*

Established 1965. Annual award in memory of the late Dr Agnes Mure Mackenzie for a published work of distinguished Scottish historical research of scholarly importance (including intellectual history and the history of science). Editions of texts are not eligible. Nominations are invited and should be sent to the Administrator. Previous winner: Michael Penman *David II*.
PRIZE Bound and inscribed copy of the winning publication.

Seeds International Poetry Chapbook Anthology Contest
See **Hidden Brook Press International Poetry Anthology Contests**

SES Book Prizes
24 Ireton Grove, Attenborough, Nottingham NG9 6BJ
☎0115 925 5959 Fax 0115 925 5959
✉ grahamlittler@msn.com
Honorary Secretary *Professor Graham Littler*

Annual awards given by the Society for Educational Studies for the best books on education published in the UK during the preceding year. Nominations by publishers or by individual authors based in the UK.
PRIZES £2000 (1st); £1000 (2nd); £400 (highly commended).

Bernard Shaw Translation Prize
See **The Translators Association Awards**

André Simon Memorial Fund Book Awards
29a Great Pulteney Street, Bath BA2 4BU
☎01225 336305 Fax 01225 421862
✉ tessa@tantraweb.co.uk
Contact *Tessa Hayward*

Established 1978. Awards given annually for the best book on drink, best on food and special commendation in either. 2005 winners: Hugh Fearnley-Whittingstall *The River Cottage Meat Book*; Nicholas Faith *Cognac*.
AWARDS £2000 (best book); £1000 (special commendation); £200 to shortlisted books.

The Society for Theatre Research Annual Theatre Book Prize
c/o The Theatre Museum, 1e Tavistock Street, London WC2E 7PR
✉ e.cottis@btinternet.com
www.str.org.uk

Established 1997. Annual award for books, in English, of original research into any aspect of the history and technique of British or British related theatre. Not restricted to authors of British nationality nor books solely from British publishers. Books must be first published in English (no translations) during the calendar year. Play texts and those treating drama as literature are not eligible. Publishers submit books directly to the independent judges and should contact the Book Prize Administrator for further details. 2006 winner: James Shapiro *1599: A Year in the Life of William Shakespeare*.
AWARD £400.

Sony Radio Academy Awards
Alan Zafer & Associates, 47–48 Chagford Street, London NW1 6EB
☎020 7723 0106 Fax 020 7724 6163
✉ secretariat@radioawards.org
www.radioawards.org
Contact *The Secretariat*

Established 1982 in association with the **Society of Authors** and Sony UK. Presented in association with the **Radio Academy**. Annual awards to recognise excellence in radio broadcasting. Entries must have been broadcast in the UK between 1 January and 31 December in the year preceding the award. The categories for the awards are reviewed each year.

Southport Writers' Circle Poetry Competition
32 Dover Road, Southport PR8 4TB
Contact *Mrs Hilary Tinsley*

For previously unpublished work. Entry fee: £2 per poem. Any subject, any form; maximum 40 lines. Closing date: end April. Poems must be entered anonymously, accompanied by a sealed envelope marked with the title of poem, containing s.a.e. Entries must be typed on A4 paper and be accompanied by the appropriate fee payable to Southport Writers' Circle. No application form is

required. Envelopes should be marked 'Poetry Competition'. Postal enquiries only. No calls.
PRIZES £200 (1st); £100 (2nd); £50 (3rd); additional £25 Humour Prize.

The Spoken Word Awards

The Audiobook Publishing Association, c/o 18 Green Lanes, Hatfield AL10 9JT
☎07971 280788
✉ charlotte.mccandlish@ntlworld.com
www.theapa.net
Contact *Charlotte McCandlish*

Hosted by the **Audiobook Publishing Association**, the Awards are for excellence in the spoken word industry and recognise the valuable work of all those involved with the production of audiobooks. There are 23 categories of award, consisting of 16 Consumer Awards (including Drama, Biography, Original Audio, Poetry, Children's and Comedy), four Trade Awards (including Best Retailer and Best Media Coverage) and three Performance Awards (Male and Female Performer of the Year and Spoken Word Audio of the Year).
PRIZES Glass trophy for the 'Gold' awards; certificates for 'Silver' and 'Bronze.'

Bram Stoker Awards for Superior Achievement

Horror Writers Association, PO Box 50577, Palo Alto, CA 94303, USA
✉ hwa@horror.org
www.horror.org
Contact *Nancy Etchemendy*

Founded 1988 and named in honour of Bram Stoker, author of *Dracula*. Presented annually by the **Horror Writers Association** (HWA) for works of horror first published in the English language. Works are eligible during their first year of publication. HWA members recommend works for consideration in eight categories: Novel, First Novel, Short Fiction, Long Fiction, Fiction Collection, Poetry Collection, Anthology and Non-fiction. In addition, Lifetime Achievement Stokers are occasionally presented to individuals whose entire body of work has substantially influenced horror.

Strokestown International Poetry Prize

Strokestown International Poetry Festival, Strokestown, Co. Roscommon, Republic of Ireland
☎00 353 71 9638540
✉ slawe@eircom.net
www.strokestownpoetryprize.com

Administrator *Sheila Lawe*

Annual poetry festival and competition now in its eighth year. Established to reward excellence in poetry. The festival takes place the first weekend in May. Readings and competitions over three days. A centrepiece of the festival is the Strokestown International Poetry prize for unpublished poems not exceeding 70 lines. Entry forms available on the website or call the Festival Office.
PRIZES €4000, €2000 and €1000 for a poem in English; €4000, €2000 and €1000 for a poem in Irish, Scottish Gaelic or Manx.

Sunday Times Writer of the Year Award

The Sunday Times, 1 Pennington Street, London E1 9XW
☎020 7782 5770 Fax 020 7782 5798
www.societyofauthors.org

Established 1987. Annual award to fiction and non-fiction writers. The panel consists of *Sunday Times* journalists and critics. Previous winners: Anthony Burgess, Seamus Heaney, Stephen Hawking, Ruth Rendell, Muriel Spark, William Trevor, Martin Amis, Margaret Atwood, Ted Hughes, Harold Pinter, Tom Wolfe, Robert Hughes. No applications; prize at the discretion of the Literary Editor.

Sunday Times Young Writer of the Year Award

The Society of Authors, 84 Drayton Gardens, London SW10 9SB
☎020 7373 6642 Fax 020 7373 5768
✉ info@societyofauthors.org
Contact *Awards Secretary*

Established 1991. Annual award given on the strength of the promise shown by a full-length published work of fiction, non-fiction, poetry or drama. Entrants must be British citizens, resident in Britain and under the age of 35. The panel consists of *Sunday Times* journalists and critics. Closing date: 31 October. The work must be by one author, in the English language, and published in Britain. Applications by publishers via the **Society of Authors**. 2004 winner: Robert Macfarlane *Mountains of the Mind*.

Reginald Taylor and Lord Fletcher Essay Prize

Journal of the British Archaeological Association, Institute of Archaelogy, c/o 18 Stanley Road, Oxford OX4 1QZ |
Contact *Dr John McNeill*

A biennial prize, in memory of the late E.

Reginald Taylor and of Lord Fletcher, for the best unpublished scholarly essay, not exceeding 7500 words, on a subject of archaeological, art history or antiquarian interest within the period from the Roman era to AD 1830. The essay should show *original* research on its chosen subject, and the author will be invited to read the essay before the Association. The essay may be published in the journal of the Association if approved by the Editorial Committee. Closing date for entries is 30 April 2008. All enquiries by post, please. No phone calls. Send s.a.e. for details.

PRIZE £300 and a medal.

Theakston's Old Peculier Prize for the Crime Novel of the Year

1 Victoria Avenue, Harrogate HG1 1EQ
☎01423 562303 Fax 01423 521264
✉ crime@harrogatefestival.org.uk
www.harrogate-festival.org.uk/crime

Contact *Sharon Canavar*, Festival Manager

Established 2005. Sponsored by Theakston's Old Peculier in association with Ottakar's Bookshops, the award is open to full-length crime or mystery novels by British authors, published in the UK. It is the only crime fiction prize to be voted for by the general public following announcement of a long list in April. The inaugural winner – announced on the opening night of the **Theakston's Old Peculier Harrogate Crime Festival** (see entry under *Festivals*) – was *Lazybones* by Mark Billingham.

PRIZE £3000 cash.

The Dylan Thomas Prize

The Dylan Thomas Centre, Somerset Place, Swansea SA1 1RR
☎01792 474051
✉ tim@dylanthomasprize.com
www.dylanthomasprize.com

Contact *Tim J. Prosser*

Founded 2004. A major biennial prize which rewards writing in the English language by authors under the age of 30 from anywhere in the world. Final entry date: 30 April. The award will be presented at the Dylan Thomas Literary Festival in Swansea on 27 October, 2006. Further entry details can be found on the website.

PRIZE £60,000.

The Tir Na N-Og Award

Cyngor Llyfrau Cymru (Welsh Books Council), Castell Brychan, Aberystwyth SY23 2JB
☎01970 624151 Fax 01970 625385
✉ wbc.children@wbc.org.uk

www.wbc.org.uk

An annual award given to the best original book published for children in the year prior to the announcement. There are three categories: Best Welsh Fiction; Best Welsh Non-fiction; Best English Book with an authentic Welsh background.

AWARDS £1000 (each category).

The Translators Association Awards

The Translators Association, 84 Drayton Gardens, London SW10 9SB
☎020 7373 6642 Fax 020 7373 5768
✉ info@societyofauthors.org
www.societyofauthors.org

Contact *Awards Secretary*

Various awards for published translations into English from Arabic (Banipal Prize), Dutch and Flemish (The Vondel Translation Prize), French (Scott Moncrieff Prize), German (Schlegel-Tieck Prize), Modern Greek (Hellenic Foundation Prize), Italian (The John Florio Prize), Portuguese (The Calouste Gulbenkian Prize), Spanish (The Premio Valle Inclán) and Swedish (Bernard Shaw Translation Prize). Contact the **Translators Association** for full details.

The Betty Trask Awards

See entry under *Bursaries, Fellowships and Grants*

The Trollope Society Short Story Prize

Maritime House, Old Town, Clapham, London SW4 0JW
☎020 7720 6789
✉ pamela@tvdox.com
www.trollopestoryprize.org

Contacts *Pamela Neville-Sington, John Williams*

Established in 2001 to encourage interest in Trollope's novels among young people with the emphasis on reading – and writing – for fun. The competition, which is held annually, focuses on a different Trollope book each year; visit the website for details. Open to students (aged 21 and younger) of all countries. Final entry date: 15 January. The winning story will be published in the Society's quarterly journal, *Trollopiana*.

PRIZE £1000.

UNESCO International Reading Association Literacy Award

International Reading Association, 800 Barksdale Road, PO Box 8139, Newark, Delaware 19714–8139, USA

☎001 302 731 1600
✉ pubinfo@reading.org
www.reading.org
Executive Director *Alan E. Farstrup*

The International Reading Association is a non-profit education organisation devoted to improving reading instruction and promoting literacy worldwide. In addition to the US $20,000 award presented by UNESCO each year on International Literacy Day (8 September), the organisation gives more than 25 awards in recognition of achievement in reading research, writing for children, media coverage of literacy and literacy instruction.

Sir Peter Ustinov Television Scriptwriting Award

The International Academy of Television Arts & Science, 888 Seventh Avenue, 5th Floor, New York, NY 10019, USA
☎001 212 489 6969   Fax 001 212 489 6557
✉ info@iemmys.tv
www.iemmys.tv
Contact *Award Administrator*

Established 1998. The late Sir Peter Ustinov gave his name to the International TV Academy Foundation's Television Scriptwriting Award. This annual competition is designed to motivate novice writers worldwide. The scriptwriter cannot be a United States citizen nor resident and must be below 30 years of age. Further details and entry form available on the website. Final entry date: 1 September. 2005 winner: John Allison (UK).

PRIZE The award winner will receive US$2500 and the opportunity to work with an established writer as mentor.

Ver Poets Open Competition

181 Sandridge Road, St Albans AL1 4AH
☎01727 762601
✉ gillknibbs@yahoo.co.uk
Contact *Gillian Knibbs*

Various competitions are organised by **Ver Poets**, the main one being the annual Open for unpublished poems of no more than 30 lines written in English. Entry fee: £3 per poem. Entry form available from address above. Two copies of poems typed on A4 white paper. *Vision On*, the anthology of winning and selected poems, and the adjudicators' report are normally available from mid-June. Final entry date: 30 April. Back numbers of the anthology are available for £4, post-free; one copy each free to those included.

PRIZES £500 (1st); £300 (2nd); £100 (3rd). Also runs High Lights, an open competition for younger poets with an October 31 closing date. Details available from address above.

Vogue Talent Contest

Vogue, Vogue House, Hanover Square, London W1S 1JU
☎020 7152 3003   Fax 020 7408 0559
Contact *Frances Bentley*

Established 1951. Annual award for young writers and journalists (under 25 on 1 January in the year of the contest). Final entry date is in April. Entrants must write three pieces of journalism on given subjects.

PRIZES £1000, plus a month's paid work experience with *Vogue*; £500 (2nd).

The Vondel Translation Prize

See **The Translators Association Awards**

Wadsworth Prize for Business History

Dept. of Management, HumSS, University of Reading, PO Box 218, Whiteknights, Reading RG6 6AA
✉ p.m.scott@reading.ac.uk
Contact *Dr Peter Scott*

Now in its 30th year, the Wadsworth Prize is awarded annually by the Business Archives Council to an individual judged to have made an outstanding contribution to the study of British business history. Books are nominated by publishers. 2004 winner: Professor Robin Pearson *Insuring the Industrial Revolution. Fire Insurance in Great Britain, 1700–1850*.

Walford Award

42 Moors Lane, Winsford CW7 1JX
☎020 7255 0500   Fax 020 7255 0501
www.cilip.org.uk

Part of the ISG (CILIP)/Nielsen BookData Reference Awards. Awarded to an individual who has made a sustained and continual contribution to British bibliography over a period of years. The nominee need not be resident in the UK. The award is named after Dr A.J. Walford, a bibliographer of international repute. 2005 winner: Alan Day.

AWARD Cash prize and certificate.

The David Watt Prize

Rio Tinto plc, 6 St James's Square, London SW1Y 4LD
☎01985 844613   Fax 01985 844002
✉ davidwattprize@riotinto.com

Contact *The Administrator*

Initiated in 1988 to commemorate the life and work of David Watt. Annual award, open to writers currently engaged in writing for English language newspapers and journals, on international and national affairs. The winners are judged as having made 'an outstanding contributions towards the greater understanding of national, international or global issues'. Entries must have been published during the year preceding the award. Final entry date 31 March. 2006 winner: Hamish McRae for his article 'To tackle poverty look to China and India'.
    PRIZE £10,000.

The Harri Webb Prize
10 Heol Don, Whitchurch, Cardiff CF14 2AU
☎029 2062 3359
Contact *Professor Meic Stephens*

Established 1995. Annual award to commemorate the Welsh poet, Harri Webb (1920–94), for a single poem in any of the categories in which he wrote: ballad, satire, song, polemic or a first collection of poems. The poems are chosen by three adjudicators; no submissions. Previous winner: Grahame Davies.
    PRIZES £100/£200.

The Wheatley Medal
Society of Indexers, Woodbourn Business Centre, 10 Jessell Street, Sheffield S9 3HY
☎0114 244 9561 Fax 0114 244 9563
✉ admin@indexer.org.uk
www.indexers.org.uk
Secretary *Ann Kingdom*

The Wheatley Medal is awarded for an outstanding index and was established by the Society of Indexers and the Library Association to highlight the importance of good indexing and confer recognition on the most highly regarded practitioners and their publishers. First awarded in 1963, it has since been presented for indexes to a wide range of publications, from encyclopedias to journals.
    PRIZE Cash, plus medal and certificate.

Whitbread Book Awards
See **Costa Book Awards**

Whitfield Prize
Royal Historical Society, University College London, Gower Street, London WC1E 6BT
☎020 7387 7532 Fax 020 7387 7532
✉ rhs.info@sas.ac.uk
www.rhs.ac.uk/prizes
Contact *Executive Secretary*

Established 1977. An annual award for the best new work within a field of British history, published in the UK in the preceding calendar year. The book must be the author's first (solely written) history book and be an original and scholarly work of historical research. Final entry date: 31 December. Previous winners: Christine Peters *Patterns of Piety: Women, Gender and Religion in Late Medieval and Reformation England*; M.J.D. Roberts *Making English Morals: Voluntary Association and Moral Reform in England 1787–1886*.
    PRIZE £1000.

John Whiting Award
Arts Council England, 14 Great Peter Street, London SW1P 3NQ
☎020 7973 6480
✉ charles.hart@artscouncil.org.uk
www.artscouncil.org.uk
Contact *Theatre Writing, Theatre Department*

Founded 1965. Annual award to commemorate the life and work of the playwright John Whiting (*The Devils*, *A Penny for a Song*). Open to any writer who has received an award during the previous two years from **Arts Council England** or a commission or production by a theatre in receipt of Arts Council subsidy. Awarded to the writer whose play most nearly satisfies the following criteria: a play in which the writing is of special quality; a play of relevance and importance to contemporary life; a play of potential value to the British theatre. No writer who has won the award previously may reapply and no play that has been submitted for the award previously is eligible. Contact the theatre writing section for full details and application form.
    PRIZE £6000.

Wilkins Memorial Poetry Prize
Birmingham & Midland Institute, 9 Margaret Street, Birmingham B3 3BS
☎0121 236 3591 Fax 0121 212 4577
www.bmi.org.uk
Administrator *Mr P.A. Fisher*

The structure of the Wilkins Memorial Poetry Prize is currently under discussion. For further information, contact the Administrator.

H.H. Wingate Prize
See **Jewish Quarterly Literary Prize**

Wolfson History Prizes
Wolfson Foundation, 8 Queen Anne Street, London W1G 9LD
☎020 7323 5730 Fax 020 7323 3241
www.wolfson.org.uk

Contact *Prize Administrator*

The Wolfson History Prizes, established in 1972, are awarded annually to promote and encourage standards of excellence in the writing of history for the general reading public. Submissions are made through publishers. 2004 winners (awarded in 2005): Christopher A. Bayly for his distinguised contribution to the writing of history; David Reynolds *In Command of History: Churchill Fighting and Writing the Second World War,* Richard Overy *The Dictators: Hiler's Germany and Stalin's Russia.*

The David T.K. Wong Prize for Short Fiction

International PEN, 9/10 Charterhouse Buildings, Goswell Road, London EC1M 7AT
☎020 7253 4308   Fax 020 7253 5711
✉ gvincent@dircon.co.uk
www.internatpen.org

Contact *Gilly Vincent*

Established 2000, this international prize is presented every other year to promote literary excellence in the form of the short story written in English. Unpublished stories of between 2500 words to 6000 words are welcome from writers worldwide, but entries must incorporate one or more of International PEN's ideals as set out in its Charter. *Entries should not be sent direct to International PEN but should be submitted via the entrant's local PEN Centre.* Details of closing date should be obtained from individual Centres. In those few countries without a PEN Centre, entrants can be directed to the nearest appropriate centre by International PEN. Copies of PEN's Charter, in English, French and Spanish and addresses of PEN Centres can be found on the website. 2004/5 winner: Sefi Atta *Twilight Trek.*
PRIZE £7500 (1st).

The World Fantasy Awards

UK Administrator: 24 Pearl Road, London E17 4QZ
☎020 8521 3034
✉ fletcherove@hotmail.com
www.worldfantasy.org/awards

UK Administrator *Jo Fletcher*

Annual awards, founded in 1975 by Kirby McCauley and other professionals working in fantasy and horror to recognise and award excellence in the field. The shortlist is selected by popular vote by members of the World Fantasy Conventions and a panel of judges working in the field, with judges selecting the winners. Categories: Life Achievement, Novel, Novella,

Short Fiction, Anthology, Collection, Artist, Special Award – Professional, Special Award – Non-Professional. Unpublished work is not eligible. Final entry date: May.

The Writers Bureau Poetry and Short Story Competition

The Writers Bureau, Sevendale House, 7 Dale Street, Manchester M1 1JB
☎0161 228 2362   Fax 0161 228 3533
✉ studentservices@writersbureau.com
www.writersbureau.com/competition

Competition Secretary *Angela Cox*

Established 1994. Annual award. Poems should be no longer than 40 lines and short stories no more than 2000 words. £5 entry fee. Closing date: 30 June 2007.
PRIZES in each category: £1000 (1st); £400 (2nd); £200 (3rd); £100 (4th); £50 (x 6).

Writers' Forum Short Story & Poetry Competitions

See *Writers' Forum* under **Magazines**.

Yorkshire Post Book Awards

Yorkshire Post Newspapers Ltd, PO Box 168, Wellington Street, Leeds LS1 1RF
Contact *Duncan Hamilton,* Deputy Editor

Annual awards: **Yorkshire Post Novel of the Year Award**; **Yorkshire Post Non-Fiction Book of the Year Award**; **Best Title With a Yorkshire Theme**. Awarded to the book which, in the opinion of the judges, is the best work published in the preceding year.
PRIZE £1200 (Novel of the Year); £1200 (Non-Fiction Book of the Year); £500 (Best Title with a Yorkshire Theme) .

YoungMinds Book Award

Youngminds, 48–50 St John Street, London EC1M 4DG
☎020 7336 8445   Fax 020 7336 8446
✉ bookaward@youngminds.org.uk
www.youngminds.org.uk/bookaward

Contact *Jessica Peters*

Established 2003. This award is given to a published work of literature that throws fresh light on the ways a child takes in and makes sense of the world he or she is growing into – novels, memoirs, diaries, poetry collections which portray something of the unique subtlety of a child's experience. 2005 winner: Nick Warren *Thirty Years in a Turtleneck Sweater.*
PRIZE £3000.

The Price of Borrowing
Simon Tait assesses the future of Public Lending Right

It took a small but impassioned army of eminent writers three decades to get financial recognition of the fact that every time one of their books was borrowed from a public library, they lost out.

In 1951 the writer John Brophy called for borrowers to give a penny a time to the authors whose work they enjoyed free – 'less than the cost of half a cigarette,' he said in an interesting insight into the domestic priorities of the time. The fight for 'Brophy's Penny' was taken up by his daughter Brigid who, with Maureen Duffy, co-founded the Writers' Action Group to drive the campaign. A succession of iconic literary names became associated with the battle for lending rights: A.P. Herbert, Angus Wilson, Michael Holroyd, Frank Muir, Antonia Fraser, Ted Willis, Michael Foot, Francis King.

It was a tough mission. For libraries to ask borrowers to hand over cash, however small the amount, was seen as a negation of their very purpose which was to provide free access to literature and learning. For the government to fork out for something it had never had to pay for before and which would never bring any financial return for its investment was an equally difficult concept for which to get universal acceptance.

The chief argument in favour of lending rights was that it was fair – never a great swayer of government opinion – but it had the support of Hugh Jenkins, the arts minister in Harold Wilson's last government, and he drew up the legislation and battled hard for it, at first without success. Fortunately, the Leader of the House at the time was Michael Foot, an esteemed author and journalist, who got the Bill through parliament before the 1979 General Election. It was then ready for another sympathiser, Norman St John Stevas, who was Mrs Thatcher's first Arts Minister, to push through its operating rules.

What was galling to the campaigners was that other northern European countries had Public Lending Rights (PLR) firmly established well before John Brophy cast down his penny gauntlet – Denmark was the first as long ago as 1946 followed by Norway a year later and Sweden in 1954.

'For some of us old warhorses in the thirty years' campaign,' Michael Holroyd says, 'the dawn seemed so long in coming that we still feel a tremor of wonder and much secret rejoicing when our payments arrive.'

For triumph they did, and the Public Lending Right Act received the royal assent on 22 March 1979, going fully active three years later – and what a triumph it has turned out to be. Since 1982 the scheme has distributed close to £100 million to authors, and in 2006 the fund was worth over £7.5 million, so Brophy's penny has multiplied more than five fold. Though getting writers registered was slow at first, the money is now being shared among 18,000 writers, illustrators, and now editors and translators are included too.

For many authors what makes PLR important isn't just the money. Early each year the PLR organisation, run by its Registrar Dr Jim Parker from his eyrie in Stockton-on-Tees, also distributes information on which books have been borrowed. 'As a lonely writer at my desk,' says the creator of *Postman Pat*, John Cunliffe, 'I feel that there is really someone out there reading and enjoying my books when that PLR listing comes just at the time of year when my spirits are likely to be at their lowest.' Mary Stewart, the prolific historical fiction writer, feels the same. 'For me, the annual PLR statement acts as a sort of barometer – a sliding scale of reassurance, letting me know my work is still appreciated,' she says.

The question is, what now? Libraries are changing, with more and more of the reason why people go to them to do with the computers they house rather than their groaning bookshelves. Lending is falling with more people   buying books because they are less expensive now than they have ever been. European copyright laws are making the whole operation increasingly complicated to run because of conflicts in national and continental copyright laws, while globalisation is also bringing new and unforeseen technical problems with the increasingly widespread international use of the Internet.

The fact is, we are moving away from printed material, and although that is not a major problem yet because lending is still the biggest part of library business, the trend has the look of being immutable and PLR is restricted by law to the printed word.

So borrowing from libraries is on the wane, while use of libraries appears to be on the increase because of that extraordinary innovation of our age, the computer, and, more precisely, the Internet.

The information super-highway as it was known in its infancy increases a challenge to PLR that has always been there, but which has until now been manageable. It could be offering PLR a route to the future, too. Because reference books are not lent and do not leave the library premises, they have never been subject to PLR. Although they could have been included in PLR, it was thought to be too complicated and too much extra work for already busy library staff to make the primary legislation required.

Although reference books have always been a feature of public libraries which provide the only access to dictionaries and encyclopaedias for most of us for whom tomes like the *Oxford English Dictionary*, the *Encyclopaedia Britannica* or *Who's Who* are too expensive to buy, fewer libraries are currently adding to their physical reference sections. More and more reference books are being digitised and available to library users through the Internet which, increasingly, they can access at their local library.

Incidentally, there is an interesting north–south divide identified by the PLR research which shows that while libraries in the south of England are moving inexorably towards virtual reference sections, as they might be called, in the north. With its tradition of working-class autodidactism there is still a positive satisfaction in having to look things up in printed books that is dying hard.

The Internet has started a reference boom, in which almost any question can be answered by logging on to a service like Google. Access to digitalised reference books is not classed as lending in European copyright law so, unless the law changes, PLR will never be able to include this kind of service. It would need an Act of Parliament to do this, and because PLR's parent, the Department for Culture, Media and Sport, is the smallest government department, it is not so much a legislative department introducing new law to Parliament, as a regulatory one, managing the system as it is – albeit sometimes fairly radically adapting existing rules without having to make new ones. What Jim Parker and his small team need is some general legislative housekeeping to modernise the, now, rather dated legislation. This requires low-key parliamentary action, on the back of which PLR law could be modified to enable it and its authors to take some small advantage of the rush of Internet information-giving. PLR needs to move with the times, and there have already been important if, in parliamentary terms, minor changes to PLR that haven't required new statutes. For instance, the categories of people receiving PLR have been expanded from just authors of fiction and non-fiction to include editors and translators, contributors to the value and enjoyment of reading who are now, rightly, recognised as such.

The computer age has also been embraced, with registration now available via e-mail. This has brought an upsurge in the number of registered authors since its introduction in 2003 – now more than half of first-time applications are being received online. Legislation is needed to put registration fully online, because the law still requires a physical signature from those signing on for the first time.

In this past couple of years the PLR computer system has been in overdrive, coping with the worldwide book industry's International Standard Book Numbers, or ISBNs, which are unique to each book. It's a bit like changing the format for car registrations. We had been running out of ten-digit ISBNs and the solution arrived at was to change to a thirteen-digit number; this is due to happen for all new books published after 1 January 2007.

It seems simple enough: the new ISBN would be the same as the old one, but prefixed with 978. Even so, it has been a huge job for the PLR, a bit like coping with the terrifying (but in the end venomless) millennium bug. Two IT experts have been working flat out for eighteen months going through all the PLR's programmes – some publications were already using the numbers a year ago, and the system was not able to cope straight away – to make sure that no registered author lost out.

A continuing legislative challenge has been the European Copyright Directive which was issued as long ago as 1992 and is still causing problems in the UK. It says lending right for authors should cover not just books but CDs, tapes and videos on which copyright already exists, and that the rights holder is not only the author but also the publisher/producer and performer. British legislators dislike and distrust generalisations, which means that picking the bones out of the EC's directive has proved a nightmare of convolution and complication. It might have been all right, even so, except that the European Commission added to the complications by allowing countries to opt out of it, something the British Government has never been happy about.

Take talking books, the written word read by actors, presented by directors and produced by recording technicians for whom copyright licences have never been negotiated. Under the EU Lending Right Directive, who is entitled to PLR? The British Government eventually implemented the EU Directive into UK copyright law by making the borrowing of non-book materials in libraries a licensing rather than a copyright issue. This means libraries pay the licence holder a fee, rather than their being paid through PLR. If it could be reversed, PLR would be the natural vehicle for remunerating authors (and maybe performers of talking books and other eligible rights holders too) of all categories of media used and lent by libraries. Sadly, it may already be too late because government lawyers recently ruled that things must stay as they are, and payments for the lending of talking books must remain under licence.

Although PLR has been an apolitical issue which ministers of all party complexions have, and continue to support, Jim Parker has been encouraged to pare the costs of the operation to a working minimum. The Registrar and his team are in one of the least expensive parts of the country, and in the last few years staff numbers have been reduced from eighteen to just twelve.

PLR has also been encouraged by the department of culture to be supportive of libraries, an enjoinder which was not really necessary because the team has always worked in partnership with libraries. Dr Parker is a patron of the LASER Foundation, a charity which gives money to library good causes. This support can get PLR in the government's good books, too, by supporting its enthusiasms for access and literacy.

PLR provides the information it gleans for its membership about the lending of books, and it is from the PLR that we get an annual report via the national press of the most borrowed books. For years the queen of that list was Catherine Cookson, who only gave way in 2002 to the children's author Jacqueline Wilson who was still the most borrowed author in 2006.

So libraries' problems have been the PLR's as well. They need more money to meet their copyright responsibilities and to buy books so they can give the public the assurance that the latest Man Booker shortlisted novel will be available as well as GCSE guidance text books. Libraries should be convenient places for busy urbanites, next to the supermarket, say, rather than tidied away to an inaccessible suburb; and they should be attractive to visit, well maintained and with appropriately skilled staff.

Libraries have been hit by local authority spending cuts which have meant reduced book funds. There has also been curtailments of opening times, particularly in London boroughs.

Yet there are also successful library authorities whose commitment has been rewarded by a dramatic local growth in library use. Brighton, Glasgow, Croydon and Liverpool, for instance, have invested in new buildings in the heart of their communities to which the council tax payers have responded with enthusiasm.

The new £3.5 million library at Kirkwall, Orkney, which opened at the end of 2003, saw user numbers leap by 21 per cent in the following year.

PLR is taking that upbeat mood as it looks to its own future, with the Library Enquiry Web Information Service (LEWIS), an enterprise which makes even more use of the unique bibliographic tool it has – borrowing statistics – and the Internet. LEWIS can give information on trends no other source can, and when it is freely available to publishers, local authorities, the press, government, travel operators, investment-fund managers, even rail-timetable planners it will be a resource that might see its name enter the Web lexicon halfway between Amazon and Yahoo.

What is the most borrowed cookery book, for instance? *Happy Days with the Naked Chef* by Jamie Oliver, though borrowers in London and Wales prefer Delia Smith's *How to Cook*. When people move abroad permanently, where are they going? The top three destinations are Spain, Australia and France, but there are regional variations. Orcadians are particularly interested in Tuscany, while those in the Kingdom of Fife have a penchant for Canada; people in Pembrokeshire and Devon go to France, and Northumbrians nurse an affinity with Australia. What health advice do library book borrowers seek? Across the UK, they mostly want relief from back pain, but in the north they are concerned about high blood pressure and in Wales the most borrowed book was *The Vitamins and Minerals Handbook*.

Nice stories for a features writer to get his teeth into, but LEWIS has initial limitations: it cannot be made widely available at present because the PLR, saddled with having to make savings rather than be expansive, is concerned about costs, and is currently negotiating with potential partners to bring it into the public domain, such as the largest supplier of IT systems to libraries, Talis.

Meanwhile, PLR continues to grow at the rate of 1,200 to 1,300 authors a year, despite predictions by some commentators that there would be a falling off of registrations. Authors will not get rich from their PLR income, and there will never be another Catherine Cookson whose books were being borrowed at the rate of about six million a year, compared with Jacqueline Wilson's current two million. But they will, perhaps, be given an economic margin to continue writing by the simple enthusiasm of the library-using public for their work. 'I'm lucky enough to be relatively wealthy nowadays, but I had to struggle hard for many years to make ends meet,' Ms Wilson says, 'and that wonderful boost to the bank account just after Christmas was a real blessing.'

Simon Brett, the current chair of the PLR Advisory Committee, is as enthusiastic about the scheme as any of his predecessors. 'S.J. Perelman wrote "The dubious privilege of a freelance writer is he's given the freedom to starve anywhere." Long may PLR continue to ease those authorial starvation statistics,' he says.

Simon Tait is a freelance journalist, writer and editor. The former arts correspondent of The Times, *he is co-editor of the fortnightly cultural news magazine,* Arts Industry.

Library Services

Aberdeen Central Library

Rosemount Viaduct, Aberdeen AB25 1GW
☎01224 652500 Fax 01224 641985
✉ centrallibrary@aberdeencity.gov.uk
www.aberdeencity.gov.uk

OPEN 9.00 am to 8.00 pm Monday to
Thursday; 9.00 am to 5.00 pm Friday &
Saturday (Info Services & Local Studies/
Business & Technical: 9.00 am to 8.00 pm).
Branch library opening times vary

OPEN ACCESS
General reference and loans. Books, pamphlets, periodicals and newspapers; videos, CDs,
DVDs; arts equipment lending service; Internet
and Learning Centre for public access; photographs of the Aberdeen area; census records,
maps, newspapers; online databases, patents and
standards. The library offers special services to
housebound readers. Non-resident administrative fee.

Armitt Collection, Museum & Library

Rydal Road, Ambleside LA22 9BL
☎015394 31212 Fax 015394 31313
✉ info@armitt.com
www.armitt.com

OPEN 10.00 am to 5.00 pm Monday to Friday
(last admission 4.30 pm)

FREE ACCESS (To view original material please
give prior notice)
A small but unique reference library of rare
books, manuscripts, pictures, antiquarian prints,
maps and museum items, mainly about the Lake
District. It includes early guidebooks and topographical works, books and papers relating to
Ruskin, H. Martineau, Charlotte Mason and
others; fine art including work by W. Green, J.B.
Pyne, John Harden, K. Schwitters, and Victorian
photographs by Herbert Bell; also a major collection of Beatrix Potter's scientific watercolour
drawings and microscope studies. Museum and
Exhibition open seven days per week from 10.00
am to 5.00 pm. Entry charge for museum.

The Athenaeum, Liverpool

Church Alley, Liverpool L1 3DD
☎0151 709 7770 Fax 0151 709 0418
✉ info@theathenaeum.org.uk

www.theathenaeum.org.uk
OPEN 9.00 am to 4.00 pm Monday and
Tuesday; 9.00 am to 9.00 pm Wednesday to
Friday

ACCESS To club members; researchers by application only
General collection, with books dating from
the 15th century, now concentrated mainly on
local history with a long run of Liverpool
directories and guides. SPECIAL COLLECTIONS
Liverpool playbills; William Roscoe; Blanco
White; Robert Gladstone; 18th-century plays;
19th-century economic pamphlets; the Norris
books; Bibles; Yorkshire and other genealogy.
Some original drawings, portraits, topographical material and local maps.

Bank of England Information Centre

Threadneedle Street, London EC2R 8AH
☎020 7601 4715 Fax 020 7601 4356
✉ informationcentre@bankofengland.co.uk
www.bankofengland.co.uk

OPEN 9.00 am to 5.30 pm Monday to Friday
ACCESS For research workers by prior arrangement only, when material is not readily available elsewhere
50,000 volumes of books and periodicals.
2000 periodicals taken. UK and overseas coverage of banking, finance and economics. *Special
collections* Central bank reports; UK 17th–19th-
century economic tracts; government reports in
the field of banking.

Barbican Library

Barbican Centre, London EC2Y 8DS
☎020 7638 0569/7638 0568 (24-hr renewals)
Fax 020 7638 2249
✉ barbicanlib@cityoflondon.gov.uk
www.cityoflondon.gov.uk/libraries

Librarian *John Lake*

OPEN 9.30 am to 5.30 pm Monday and
Wednesday; 9.30 am to 7.30 pm Tuesday
and Thursday; 9.30 am to 2.00 pm Friday;
9.30 am to 4.00 pm Saturday

OPEN ACCESS
Situated on Level 2 of the Barbican Centre, this
is the Corporation of London's largest lending

library. Study facilities are available plus free Internet access. In addition to a large general lending department, the library seeks to reflect the Centre's emphasis on the arts and includes strong collections (including DVDs, videos and CD-ROMs), on painting, sculpture, theatre, cinema and ballet, as well as a large music library with books, scores and CDs (sound recording loans available at a small charge). Also houses the City's main children's library and has special collections on basic skills, materials for young adults, finance, natural resources, conservation, socialism and the history of London. Service available for housebound readers. A literature events programme is organised by the Library which supplements and provides cross-arts planning opportunities with the Barbican Centre artistic programme. Reading groups meet in the library on the first Tuesday and Thursday of every month and a weekly Basic Skills advice service is offered during term time.

Barnsley Public Library
Central Library, Shambles Street, Barnsley S70 2JF
☎01226 773930 Fax 01226 773955
✉ barnsleylibraryenquiries@barnsley.gov.uk
www.barnsley.gov.uk/service/libraries/index.asp
OPEN Lending & Reference: 9.30 am to 7.00 pm Monday and Wednesday; 9.30 am to 5.30 pm Tuesday and Friday; 9.30 am to 4.00 pm Saturday. Telephone to check hours of other departments and other branch libraries.

OPEN ACCESS
General library, lending and reference. Archive collection of family history and local firms; local studies: coal mining, local authors, Yorkshire and Barnsley; large junior library. (Specialist departments are closed on certain weekday evenings and Saturday afternoons.)

BBC Written Archives Centre
Caversham Park, Reading RG4 8TZ
☎0118 948 6281 Fax 0118 946 1145
✉ heritage@bbc.co.uk
www.bbc.co.uk/heritage
Contact *Jacqueline Kavanagh*
OPEN 9.30 am to 5.30 pm Monday to Friday
ACCESS For reference, by appointment only, Wednesday to Friday
Holds the written records of the BBC, including internal papers from 1922 to the 1980s and published material to date. 20th century biography, social history, popular culture and broadcasting. Charges for certain services.

Bedford Central Library
Harpur Street, Bedford MK40 1PG
☎01234 350931/270102 (Reference Library)
Fax 01234 342163
www.bedfordshire.gov.uk
OPEN 9.30 am to 6.00 pm Monday to Friday; 9.00 am to 5.00 pm Saturday
OPEN ACCESS
Lending library with a wide range of stock, including books, music, audiobooks, DVDs and videos; reference and information library, children's library, local history library and Internet facilities.

Belfast Public Libraries: Central Library
Royal Avenue, Belfast BT1 1EA
☎028 9050 9150 Fax 028 9033 2819
✉ info.belb@ni-libraries.net
www.belb.org.uk
www.ni-libraries.net
OPEN 9.00 am to 8.00 pm Monday and Thursday; 9.00 am to 5.30 pm Tuesday, Wednesday, Friday; 9.00 am to 1.00 pm Saturday
OPEN ACCESS To lending libraries; reference libraries by application only
Over two million volumes for lending and reference. SPECIAL COLLECTIONS United Nations depository; complete British Patent Collection; Northern Ireland Newspaper Library; British and Irish government publications. The Central Library provides the following Reference Departments: General Reference; Belfast, Ulster and Irish Studies; Music. A Learning Gateway includes public Internet facilities and a Learndirect Centre. The Lending Library is one of over 20 branches along with a range of outreach services to hospitals, care homes and housebound readers.

BFI National Library
21 Stephen Street, London W1T 1LN
☎020 7255 1444 Fax 020 7436 2338
✉ library@bfi.org.uk
www.bfi.org.uk
OPEN 10.30 am to 5.30 pm Monday and Friday; 10.30 am to 8.00 pm Tuesday and Thursday; 1.00 pm to 8.00 pm Wednesday; Telephone Enquiry Service operates from 10.00 am to 5.00 pm (closed 1.00 pm to 2.00 pm)
ACCESS For reference only; annual, 5-day and limited day membership available
The world's largest collection of information

on film and television including periodicals, cuttings, scripts, related documentation, personal papers. Main library catalogue available via website.

Birmingham and Midland Institute

9 Margaret Street, Birmingham B3 3BS
☎0121 236 3591 Fax 0121 212 4577
www.bmi.org.uk
Administrator & General Secretary *Philip Fisher*
ACCESS Members only
Established 1854. Later merged with the Birmingham Library which was founded in 1779. The Library specialises in the humanities, with approximately 100,000 volumes in stock. Founder member of the **Association of Independent Libraries**. Meeting-place of many affiliated societies devoted to poetry and literature.

Birmingham Library Services

Central Library, Chamberlain Square, Birmingham B3 3HQ
☎0121 303 4511
✉ central.library@birmingham.gov.uk
www.birmingham.gov.uk/libraries
OPEN 9.00 am to 8.00 pm Monday to Friday; 9.00 am to 5.00 pm Saturday

Over a million volumes. *Research collections* include the Shakespeare Library; War Poetry Collection; Parker Collection of Children's Books and Games; Johnson Collection; Milton Collection; Cervantes Collections; Early and Fine Printing Collection (including the William Ridler Collection of Fine Printing); Joseph Priestley Collection; Loudon Collection; Railway Collection; Wingate Bett Transport Ticket Collection; Labour, Trade Union and Co-operative Collections. *Photographic archives:* Sir John Benjamin Stone; Francis Bedford; Francis Frith; Warwickshire Photographic Survey; Boulton and Watt Archive. Also, Charles Parker Archive; Birmingham Repertory Theatre Archive and Sir Barry Jackson Library; Local Studies (Birmingham); Patents Collection; Song Sheets Collection; Oberammergau Festival Collection.

Bournemouth Library

22 The Triangle, Bournemouth BH2 5RQ
☎01202 454848 Fax 01202 454840
✉ bournemouth@bournemouthlibraries. org.uk
www.bournemouth.gov.uk/libraries
OPEN 10.00 am to 7.00 pm Monday; 9.30 am to 7.00 pm Tuesday, Thursday, Friday; 9.30

am to 5.00 pm Wednesday; 10.00 am to 2.00 pm Saturday
OPEN ACCESS
Main library for Bournemouth with lending, reference and music departments, plus the Heritage Zone – local and family history.

Bradford Central Library

Princes Way, Bradford BD1 1NN
☎01274 433600 Fax 01274 395108
✉ public.libraries@bradford.gov.uk
Wide range of books and media loan services. Comprehensive reference and information services, including major local history collections and specialised business information service.

Brighton Jubilee Library

Jubilee Street, Brighton BN1 1GE
☎01273 290800
www.citylibraries.info/libraries/jubilee.asp
OPEN 10.00 am to 7.00 pm Monday and Tuesday; 10.00 am to 5.00 pm Wednesday and Friday; 10.00 am to 8.00 pm Thursday; 10.00 am to 4.00 pm Saturday
ACCESS Stock on open access and in onsite store; material for reference use and lending
Specialisations include art and antiques, history of Brighton, local illustrations, Hebrew and Oriental literature, natural history, children's books, World War Two and large bequests of rare and historical books.

Bristol Central Library

College Green, Bristol BS1 5TL
☎0117 903 7200 Fax 0117 922 1081
www.bristol-city.gov.uk
OPEN 9.30 am to 7.30 pm Monday, Tuesday and Thursday; 10.00 am to 5.00 pm Wednesday; 9.30 am to 5.00 pm Friday and Saturday; 1.00 pm to 5.00 pm Sunday
OPEN ACCESS
Lending, reference, art, music, business and local studies are particularly strong. DVD, video and CD collections on site. Facilities available: PCs (large screen with Jaws and Zoomtext), Internet, printing; videophone on site; black & white and colour photocopiers.

British Architectural Library

Royal Institute of British Architects, 66 Portland Place, London W1B 1AD
☎020 7580 5533 Fax 020 7631 1802
✉ info@inst.riba.org
www.architecture.com
RIBA British Architectural Library Drawings &

Archives Collections: ☎020 7307 3708
Members' Information Line: ☎020 7307 3600
(membership number required); Public Information Line (50p per min.): ☎0906 302 0400
OPEN 10.00 am to 8.00 pm Tuesday; 10.00 am to 5.00 pm Wednesday to Friday; 10.00 am to 1.30 pm Saturday; Closed Sunday, Monday and any Saturday preceding a Bank Holiday; full details on the website
ACCESS Free to RIBA members; non-members must buy a day ticket (£10/£7 concessions, but on Tuesdays between 5.00 pm–8.00 pm and Saturdays £7/£3.50); subscriber membership available (write for details); loans available to RIBA and library members only
Collection of books, drawings, manuscripts, photographs and periodicals. All aspects of architecture, current and historical. Material both technical and aesthetic, covering related fields including: interior design, landscape architecture, topography, the construction industry and applied arts. Brochure available; queries by telephone, letter, e-mail or in person. Charge for research (min. charge £40 + VAT).

The British Library
Admission to St Pancras Reading Rooms – British Library Readers' Passes

Everyone is welcome to visit the British Library exhibition galleries or to tour the building. However, to use the reading rooms you will need to apply for a reader's pass, for which identification is required. The British Library issues passes to those who want to use its collections – researchers, innovators and entrepreneurs across all fields of study, and in academic, commerce or personal research – whether or not they are affiliated to a research institution. Two pieces of identification are required (original documents only). One proof of home address: e.g. a utility bill, bank statement or driving licence; and proof of signature, i.e. a bank or credit card, passport, driving licence or national identity card.

It would also be helpful to take with you anything to support your application (such as a student card, business card, professional membership card or details of the items you wish to see).

For further information, visit the website at www.bl.uk or contact the Reader Admissions Office, The British Library, 96 Euston Road, London NW1 2DB ☎020 7412 7676 Fax 020 7412 7794; reader-admissions@bl.uk

British Library Asia, Pacific and Africa Collections
96 Euston Road, London NW1 2DB

☎020 7412 7873 Fax 020 7412 7641
✉ iooc-enquiries@bl.uk
www.bl.uk
OPEN 10.00 am to 5.00 pm Monday; 9.30 am to 5.00 pm Tuesday to Saturday; closed for public holidays
ACCESS By British Library reader's pass
A comprehensive collection of printed volumes and manuscripts in the languages of North Africa, the Near and Middle East and all of Asia, plus records of the East India Company and British government in India until 1947. Also prints, drawings and paintings by British artists of India.

For information on British Library collections and services, visit the website.

British Library Business & IP Centre
96 Euston Road, London NW1 2DB
☎020 7412 7454 (free enquiry service)
Fax 020 7412 7453 (free enquiry service)
✉ business-information@bl.uk
www.bl.uk/bis
OPEN 10.00 am to 8.00 pm Monday; 9.30 am to 8.00 pm Tuesday to Thursday; 9.30 am to 5.00 pm Friday and Saturday; closed for public holidays
ACCESS By British Library reader's pass
The Business & IP Centre holds the most comprehensive collection of business information literature and patent specifications in the UK. Includes market research reports and journals, directories, company annual reports, trade and business journals, up-to-date literature on patents, trade marks, designs and copyright.

British Library Early Printed Collections/Rare Books and Music Reading Room
96 Euston Road, London NW1 2DB
☎020 7412 7676 Fax 020 7412 7577
✉ rare-books@bl.uk
www.bl.uk
General enquiries about reader services & advance reservations: ☎020 7412 7676
Fax 020 7412 7609
✉ reader-services-enquiries@bl.uk
OPEN 10.00 am to 8.00 pm Monday; 9.30 am to 8.00 pm Tuesday to Thursday; 9.30 am to 5.00 pm Friday and Saturday; closed for public holidays
ACCESS By British Library reader's pass
Early Printed Collections, which is an integral part of British Library Scholarship and

Collections, selects, acquires, researches and provides access to material printed in the British Isles to 1914 and in Western European languages before 1851. The collections are available in the Rare Books and Music Reading Room at St Pancras which also functions as the focus for the British Library's extensive collection of humanities microforms.

Further information about Early Printed Collections can be found at the British Library website.

British Library Humanities Reading Room

96 Euston Road, London NW1 2DB
☎020 7412 7676 Fax 020 7412 7789
✉ reader-services-enquiries@bl.uk
www.bl.uk/resources/humanities

OPEN 10.00 am to 8.00 pm Monday; 9.30 am to 8.00 pm Tuesday, Wednesday, Thursday; 9.30 am to 5.00 pm Friday and Saturday; closed for public holidays

ACCESS By British Library reader's pass

This reading room is the focus for the Library's modern collections service in the humanities. It is on two levels, Humanities 1 and Humanities 2 and provides access to the Library's comprehensive collections of books and periodicals in all subjects in the humanities and social sciences and in all languages apart from Oriental. These collections are not available for browsing at the shelf. Material is held in closed access storage and needs to be identified and ordered from store using an online catalogue. A selective open access collection on most humanities subjects can be found in Humanities 1 whilst in Humanities 2 there are open access reference works relating to periodicals and theses, to recorded sound and to librarianship and information science.

To access British Library catalogues, go to the website.

British Library Manuscript Collections

96 Euston Road, London NW1 2DB
☎020 7412 7513 Fax 020 7412 7745
✉ mss@bl.uk
www.bl.uk

OPEN 10.00 am to 5.00 pm Monday; 9.30 am to 5.00 pm Tuesday to Saturday; closed for public holidays

ACCESS Reading facilities only, by British Library reader's pass; a written letter of recommendation and advance notice is required for certain categories of material

Two useful publications, *Index of Manuscripts in the British Library,* Cambridge 1984–6, 10 vols, and *The British Library: Guide to the Catalogues and Indexes of the Department of Manuscripts* by M.A.E. Nickson, help to guide the researcher through this vast collection of manuscripts dating from Ancient Greece to the present day. Approximately 300,000 mss, charters, papyri and seals are housed here.

For information on British Library collections and services and to access British Library catalogues, including the Manuscripts online catalogue, visit the website.

British Library Map Collections

96 Euston Road, London NW1 2DB
☎020 7412 7702 Fax 020 7412 7780
✉ maps@bl.uk
www.bl.uk/collections/maps

OPEN 10.00 am to 5.00 pm Monday; 9.30 am to 5.00 pm Tuesday to Saturday; closed for public holidays

ACCESS By British Library reader's pass

A collection of about 4.5 million maps, charts and globes, manuscript, printed and, increasingly, digital, with particular reference to the history of British cartography. Maps for all parts of the world in a wide range of scales, formats and dates, including the most comprehensive collection of Ordnance Survey maps and plans. SPECIAL COLLECTIONS King George III Topographical Collection and Maritime Collection, the Crace Collection of maps and plans of London and the cartographic archive of the Ministry of Defence (i.e. GSGS).

For information on British Library collections and services, visit the website. To access main British Library catalogues, go to the website at catalogue.bl.uk

British Library Music Collections

96 Euston Road, London NW1 2DB
☎020 7412 7772 Fax 020 7412 7751
✉ music-collections@bl.uk
www.bl.uk

OPEN 10.00 am to 8.00 pm Monday; 9.30 am to 8.00 pm Tuesday to Thursday; 9.30 am to 5.00 pm Friday and Saturday; closed for public holidays

ACCESS By British Library reader's pass

SPECIAL COLLECTIONS The Royal Music Library (containing almost all Handel's surviving autograph scores), The Zweig Collection of Music & Literary Mss, The Royal Philharmonic Society Archive and the Paul Hirsch Music Library. Also a large collection (about one and a half million items) of printed music (UK via legal deposit) and about 100,000 items of manuscript music, both British and foreign.

The British Library website contains details of collections and services, and provides access to the catalogues.

British Library Newspapers

Colindale Avenue, London NW9 5HE

☎020 7412 7353 Fax 020 7412 7379

✉ newspaper@bl.uk

www.bl.uk/collections/newspapers.html

OPEN 10.00 am to 5.00 pm Monday to Saturday (last newspaper issue 4.15 pm); closed for public holidays

ACCESS By British Library reader's pass or Newspaper Library pass (available from and valid only for Colindale)

Major collections of English provincial, Scottish, Welsh, Irish, Commonwealth and selected overseas foreign newspapers from c.1700 are housed here. Some earlier holdings are also available. London newspapers from 1801 and many weekly and fortnightly periodicals are also in stock. (London newspapers pre-dating 1801 are housed at the new library building in St Pancras (96 Euston Road, NW1) though many are available at Colindale Avenue on microfilm.) Readers are advised to check availability of material in advance.

For information on British Library Newspapers collections and services, visit the website.

British Library Science, Technology and Business Collections

96 Euston Road, London NW1 2DB

☎020 7412 7676 (General Enquiries)

Fax 020 7412 7495

✉ scitech@bl.uk

www.bl.uk

Business enquiries: ☎020 7412 7454 (Free enquiry service)

OPEN 10.00 am to 8.00 pm Monday; 9.30 am to 8.00 pm Tuesday to Thursday; 9.30 am to 5.00 pm Friday and Saturday; closed for public holidays

Engineering, business information on companies, markets and products, physical science and technologies. See also **British Library Business & IP Centre**.

For information on British Library collections and services, visit the website.

To access British Library catalogues go to the website at catalogue.bl.uk

British Library Social Sciences & Official Publications

96 Euston Road, London NW1 2DB

☎020 7412 7676 Fax 020 7412 7761

✉ social-sciences@bl.uk

www.bl.uk/collections/social/social.html

OPEN Reading Room: 10.00 am to 8.00 pm Monday; 9.30 am to 8.00 pm Tuesday to Thursday; 9.30 am to 5.00 pm Friday and Saturday; closed for public holidays

ACCESS By British Library reader's pass

Provides an information service on the social sciences, law, public administration, and current and international affairs, and access to current and historical official publications from all countries and intergovernmental bodies. Maerial available in the reading room includes House of Commons sessional papers, UK legislation, UK electoral registers, up-to-date reference books on official publications and on the social sciences, a major collection of statistics and a browsing collection of recent social science books and periodicals; other collections are kept in closed stores and items have to be ordered for delivery to the reading room.

To access British Library catalogues, go to the website at catalogue.bl.uk

British Library Sound Archive

96 Euston Road, London NW1 2DB

☎020 7412 7676 Fax 020 7412 7441

✉ sound-archive@bl.uk

www.bl.uk/soundarchive

OPEN 10.00 am to 8.00 pm Monday; 9.30 am to 8.00 pm Tuesday to Thursday; 9.30 am to 5.00 pm Friday and Saturday; closed for public holidays

Listening service (by appointment)

Northern Listening Service British Library Document Supply Centre, Boston Spa: 9.15 am to 4.30 pm Monday to Friday

OPEN ACCESS

An archive of over 1,000,000 discs and more than 200,000 hours of tape recordings, including all types of music, oral history, drama, literature, poetry, wildlife, selected BBC broadcasts and BBC Sound Archive material. Produces a twice-yearly newsletter, *Playback*.

For information on British Library Sound Archive collections and services, visit the website.

British Psychological Society Library

c/o Psychology Library, Senate House Library, University of London, Senate House, Malet Street, London WC1E 7HU

☎020 7862 8451/8461   Fax 020 7862 8480
✉ enquiries@shl.lon.ac.uk
www.shl.lon.ac.uk
OPEN Term-time: 9.00 am to 9.00 pm
Monday to Thursday; 9.00 am to 6.30 pm
Friday; 9.30 am to 5.30 pm Saturday
(Holidays: 9.00 am to 6.00 pm Monday to
Friday; 9.30 am to 5.30 pm Saturday)
ACCESS Members only; Non-members £5 day
ticket
Reference library, containing the British
Psychological Society collection of periodicals
– over 140 current titles housed alongside the
University of London's collection of books and
journals. Largely for academic research. General
queries referred to **Swiss Cottage Library** in
London which has a good psychology collec-
tion.

Bromley Central Library
London Borough of Bromley – Directorate of
Education & Libraries, High Street, Bromley
BR1 1EX
☎020 8460 9955   Fax 020 8313 9975
✉ reference.library@bromley.gov.uk
www.bromley.gov.uk
OPEN 9.30 am to 6.00 pm Monday,
Wednesday, Friday; 9.30 am to 8.00 pm
Tuesday and Thursday; 9.30 am to 5.00 pm
Saturday
OPEN ACCESS
A large selection of fiction and non-fiction
books for loan, both adult and children's. Also
DVDs, videos, CDs, cassettes, language courses,
open learning packs, CD-ROM and Playstation
games for hire. Other facilities include CD-
ROMs, computer hire, People's Network
Internet, local studies library, 'Upfront' teenage
section, large reference library with photocopy-
ing, fax, microfiche and film facilities, 'Bromley
Knowledge' – online community information,
reading groups and Local Links (access to
council services). Library and Archives catalogues online, 'Bromley Training Truck' – free
computer and basic skills training. SPECIALIST
COLLECTIONS include: H.G. Wells, Walter de la
Mare, Crystal Palace, The Harlow Bequest, and
the history and geography of Asia, America,
Australasia and the Polar regions.

Bromley House Library
Angel Row, Nottingham NG1 6HL
☎0115 947 3134
✉ nfl@bromho.freeserve.co.uk
Librarian *Carol Allison*
OPEN 9.30 am to 5.00 pm Monday to Friday;

also first Saturday of each month from
10.00 am to 12.30 pm
ACCESS For members only
Founded 1816 as the Nottingham Subscription Library. Collection of 35,000 books
including local history, topography, biography,
travel and fiction.

CAA Library and Information Centre
Aviation House, Gatwick Airport South,
Gatwick RH6 0YR
☎01293 573725   Fax 01293 573181
✉ infoservices@caa.co.uk
www.caa.co.uk
OPEN 9.00 am to 5.00 pm Monday to Friday
OPEN ACCESS
A collection of books, reports, directories,
statistics and periodicals on most aspects of civil
aviation and related subjects.

Cambridge Central Library (Reference Library & Information Service)
7 Lion Yard, Cambridge CB2 3QD
☎0845 045 5225   Fax 01223 712011
✉ cambridge.central.library@
cambridgeshire.gov.uk
www.cambridgeshire.gov.uk/library
OPEN 9.00 am to 7.00 pm Monday to Friday;
9.00 am to 5.30 pm Saturday
OPEN ACCESS
Large stock of books, periodicals, newspapers,
maps, plus comprehensive collection of directories and annuals covering UK, Europe and the
world. Microfilm and fiche reading and printing
services. Online access to news and business
databases. News databases on CD-ROM;
Internet access. Monochrome photocopiers.

Camomile Street Library
12–20 Camomile Street, London EC3A 7EX
☎020 7247 8895
✉ camomile@cityoflondon.gov.uk
www.cityoflondon.gov.uk/camomilestlibrary
OPEN 9.30 am to 5.30 pm Monday to Friday
OPEN ACCESS
Corporation of London lending library. Wide
range of fiction and non-fiction books and language courses on cassette, foreign fiction, paperbacks, maps and guides for travel at home and
abroad, children's books, a selection of large print,
and collections of DVDs, videos and music CDs,
books in Bengali. Spoken word recordings on
cassette and CD. Free Internet access.

Cardiff Central Library

Frederick Street, St David's Link, Cardiff
CF10 2DU
☎029 2038 2116 Fax 029 2087 1599
✉ robboddy@hotmail.com
www.libraries.cardiff.gov.uk
OPEN 9.00 am to 6.00 pm Monday, Tuesday,
Wednesday, Friday; 9.00 am to 7.00 pm
Thursday; 9.00 am to 5.30 pm Saturday
General lending library with the following
departments: leisure, music, children's, local
studies, information, science and humanities.

Carmarthen Public Library

St Peter's Street, Carmarthen SA31 1LN
☎01267 224824 Fax 01267 221839
✉ wtphillips@carmarthenshire.gov.uk
www.carmarthenshire.gov.uk
OPEN 9.30 am to 7.00 pm Monday, Tuesday,
Wednesday, Friday; 9.30 am to 5.00 pm
Thursday and Saturday
OPEN ACCESS
Comprehensive range of fiction, non-fiction,
children's books and reference works in English
and in Welsh. Large local history library. Free
Internet access and CD-ROM facilities. Large
Print books, books on tape, CDs, CD-ROMs,
cassettes, DVDs and videos available for loan.

Catholic Central Library

St Michaels Abbey, Farnborough Road,
Farnborough GU14 7NQ
✉ librarian@catholic-library.org.uk
www.catholic-library.org.uk
OPEN ACCESS For reference (non-members
must sign in; loans restricted to members)
    Contains books, many not readily available
elsewhere, on theology, religions worldwide,
scripture and the history of churches of all
denominations.

The Centre for the Study of Cartoons and Caricature

See entry under *Picture Libraries*

City Business Library

1 Brewers' Hall Garden, off Aldermanbury
Square, London EC2V 5BX
☎020 7332 1812/(3803 textphone)
Fax 020 7332 1847
✉ cbl@cityoflondon.gov.uk
www.cityoflondon.gov.uk/libraries
OPEN 9.30 am to 5.00 pm Monday to Friday
(except public holidays)
OPEN ACCESS

Local authority free public reference library
run by the Corporation of London. Books,
directories, periodicals, newspapers and electronic databases of current business interest.
Provided for anyone with a business informatin
enquiry and is one of the leading public resource
centres in Britain in its field. Large directory collection for both the UK and overseas, plus companies information, market research reports,
management, banking, insurance, investment and
statistics. Free public Internet access. No academic journals or textbooks.

Commonwealth Secretariat Library

Marlborough House, Pall Mall, London
SW1Y 5HX
☎020 7747 6164 Fax 020 7747 6168
✉ library@commonwealth.int
www.thecommonwealth.org
Library Services Manager *David Blake*
OPEN 10.00 am to 4.45 pm Monday to Friday
ACCESS For reference only, by appointment
    Extensive reference source concerned with
economy, development, trade, production and
industry of Commonwealth countries; also
human resources including women, youth,
health, management and education. Includes
the archives of the Secretariat.

Corporation of London Libraries

See **Barbican Library**; Camomile Street
Library; **City Business Library**; **Guildhall
Library**

Coventry Central Library

Smithford Way, Coventry CV1 1FY
☎024 7683 2314/2395 (Minicom)
Fax 024 7683 2440
✉ central.library@coventry.gov.uk
www.coventry.gov.uk
OPEN 9.00 am to 8.00 pm Monday to Friday;
9.00 am to 4.30 pm Saturday; 12.00 am to
4.00 pm Sunday
OPEN ACCESS
    Located in the middle of the city's main
shopping centre. Approximately 120,000 items
(books, cassettes, CDs and DVDs) for loan; plus
reference collection of business information
and local history. SPECIAL COLLECTIONS
Cycling and motor industries; George Eliot;
Angela Brazil; Tom Mann Collection (trade
union and labour studies); local newspapers on
microfilm from 1740 onwards. Over 300 periodicals taken. 'Peoplelink' community information database available.

Department for Environment, Food and Rural Affairs

Nobel House, 17 Smith Square, London SW1P 3JR

☎020 7238 3000 Fax 020 7238 6591

DEFRA Helpline 08459 335577 (local call rate): general contact point which can provide information on the work of DEFRA, either directly or by referring callers to appropriate contacts. Available 9.00 am to 5.00 pm Monday to Friday (excluding Bank Holidays)

OPEN 9.30 am to 5.00 pm Monday to Friday

ACCESS For reference (but at least 24 hours notice must be given for intended visits)

Large stock of volumes on temperate agriculture.

Derby Central Library

Wardwick, Derby DE1 1HS

☎01332 255398 Fax 01332 369570

www.derby.gov.uk/libraries

OPEN 9.30 am to 7.00 pm Monday, Tuesday, Thursday, Friday; 9.30 am to 1.00 pm Wednesday; 9.30 am to 4.00 pm Saturday

Local Studies Library

25B Irongate, Derby DE1 3GL

☎01332 255393 Fax 01332 255381

OPEN 9.30 am to 7.00 pm Monday and Tuesday; 9.30 am to 5.00 pm Wednesday, Thursday, Friday; 9.30 am to 4.00 pm Saturday

OPEN ACCESS

General library for lending, information and Children's Services. The Central Library also houses specialist private libraries: Derbyshire Archaeological Society; Derby Philatelic Society. The Local Studies Library houses the largest multimedia collection of resources in existence relating to Derby and Derbyshire. The collection includes mss deeds, family papers, business records including the Derby Canal Company, Derby Board of Guardians and the Derby China Factory. Both libraries offer free Internet access.

Devon & Exeter Institution Library

7 Cathedral Close, Exeter EX1 1EZ

☎01392 251017

✉ J.P.Gardner@exeter.ac.uk

www.devonandexeterinstitution.org.uk

OPEN 9.30 am to 5.00 pm Monday to Friday

ACCESS Members only (temporary membership available)

Founded 1813. Under the administration of Exeter University Library. Contains over 36,000 volumes, including long runs of 19th-century journals, theology, history, topography, early science, biography and literature. A large and growing collection of books, journals, newspapers, prints and maps relating to the South West.

Doncaster Library and Information Services

Central Library, Waterdale, Doncaster DN1 3JE

☎01302 734305 Fax 01302 369749

✉ Reference.Library@doncaster.gov.uk

library.doncaster.gov.uk

OPEN 9.00 am to 6.00 pm Monday; 8.30 am to 6.00 pm Tuesday and Friday; 8.30 am to 8.00 pm Wednesday and Thursday; 9.00 am to 5.00 pm Saturday

OPEN ACCESS

Books, spoken word cassettes/CDs, DVDs, videos. Reading aids unit for people with visual impairment; activities for children during school holidays, including visits by authors, readers' groups, etc. Also reference library and Local Studies library.

Dorchester Library (part of Dorset County Library)

Colliton Park, Dorchester DT1 1XJ

☎01305 224440 (lending)/224448 (reference) Fax 01305 266120

✉ Dorchesterreflibrary@dorsetcc.gov.uk

www.dorsetforyou.com/libraries

OPEN 10.00 am to 7.00 pm Monday; 9.30 am to 7.00 pm Tuesday, Wednesday, Friday; 9.30 am to 5.00 pm Thursday; 9.00 am to 4.00 pm Saturday

OPEN ACCESS

General lending and reference library, including special collections on Thomas Hardy, the Powys Family and William Barnes. Periodicals, children's library, CD-ROMs, free Internet access. Video lending service.

Dundee Central Library

The Wellgate, Dundee DD1 1DB

☎01382 431500 Fax 01382 431558

✉ central.library@dundeecity.gov.uk

www.dundeecity.gov.uk

OPEN Lending & Local Studies Departments and General Reference: 9.30 am to 6.00 pm Monday, Tuesday, Friday; 10.00 am to 6.00 pm Wednesday; 9.30 am to 8.00 pm Thursday; 9.30 am to 5.00 pm Saturday.

Commerce & Technology: 9.30 am to 9.00 pm Monday, Tuesday, Thursday, Friday; 10.00 am to 9.00 pm Wednesday; 9.30 am to 5.00 pm Saturday.

ACCESS Reference services available to all; lending services to those who live, work, study or were educated within Dundee City

Adult lending, reference and children's services. Art, music, audio, video and DVD lending services. Internet access. Schools service (Agency). Housebound and mobile services. SPECIAL COLLECTIONS The Wighton Collection of National Music; The Wighton Heritage Centre; The Wilson Photographic Collection; The Lamb Collection.

Durning-Lawrence Library
See **Senate House Library**

English Nature
Northminster House, Peterborough PE1 1UA
☎01733 455000 Fax 01733 568834
✉ enquiries@english-nature.org.uk
www.english-nature.org.uk

OPEN 8.30 am to 5.00 pm Monday to Thursday; 8.30 am to 4.30 pm Friday

ACCESS *Bona fide* students only. Telephone library for appointment on 01733 455094

Information on nature conservation, nature reserves, SSSIs, planning, legislation, etc. English Nature is the government-funded body whose purpose is to promote the conservation of England's wildlife and natural features.

Equal Opportunities Commission
Arndale House, Arndale Centre, Manchester M4 3EQ
☎0845 601 5901 Fax 0161 838 8312
✉ info@eoc.org.uk
www.eoc.org.uk

The EOC is open to the public via the Helpline (0845 601 5901) 9.00 am to 5.00 pm Mondays to Fridays.

Essex County Council Libraries
Goldlay Gardens, Chelmsford CM2 0EW
☎01245 284981 Fax 01245 492780
✉ essexlib@essexcc.gov.uk
www.essexcc.gov.uk

Essex County Council Libraries has 73 static libraries throughout Essex as well as 13 mobile libraries and three special-needs mobiles. Services to the public include books, newspapers, periodicals, CDs, cassettes, videos, CD-ROMs and Internet access. Specialist subjects and collections are listed below at the relevant library.

Chelmsford Library
PO Box 882, Market Road, Chelmsford CM1 1LH
☎01245 492758 Fax 01245 492536
✉ chelmsford.library@essexcc.gov.uk

OPEN 8.30 am to 7.00 pm Monday to Friday; 8.30 am to 5.30 pm Saturday; 12.30 pm to 4.30 pm Sunday

Colchester Library
Trinity Square, Colchester CO1 1JB
☎01206 245900 Fax 01206 245901
✉ colchester.library@essexcc.gov.uk

OPEN 8.30 am to 7.30 pm Monday to Friday; 8.30 am to 5.00 pm Saturday; 12.30 pm to 4.30 pm Sunday

Local studies; Castle collection (18th-century subscription library); Cunnington collection; Margaret Lazell collection; Taylor collection.

Harlow Library
The High, Harlow CM20 1HA
☎01279 413772 Fax 01279 424612
✉ harlow.library@essexcc.gov.uk

OPEN 9.00 am to 7.00 pm Monday to Friday; 9.00 am to 5.00 pm Saturday; 1.00 pm to 4.00 pm Sunday

Sir John Newson Memorial collection; Maurice Hughes Memorial collection.

Loughton Library
Traps Hill, Loughton IG10 1HD
☎020 8502 0181 Fax 020 8508 5041
✉ loughton.library@essexcc.gov.uk

OPEN 9.00 am to 7.00 pm Monday to Friday; 9.30 am to 5.30 pm Saturday; 11.00 am to 3.00 pm Sunday

National Jazz Foundation Archive.

Saffron Walden Library
2 King Street, Saffron Walden CB10 1ES
☎01799 523178 Fax 01799 513642

OPEN 9.00 am to 7.00 pm Monday, Tuesday, Friday; 9.00 am to 8.00 pm Thursday; 9.00 am to 5.00 pm Saturday; 1.00 pm to 4.00 pm Sunday (closed Wednesday)

Victorian studies collection.

Witham Library
18 Newland Street, Witham CM8 2AQ
☎01376 519625 Fax 01376 501913

OPEN 9.00 am to 7.00 pm Monday, Tuesday, Thursday, Friday; 9.00 am to 1.00 pm Wednesday; 9.00 am to 5.00 pm Saturday; 1.00 pm to 4.00 pm Sunday

Dorothy L. Sayers and Maskell collections.

Family Records Centre
1 Myddleton Street, London EC1R 1UW
☎020 8392 5200 Fax 020 8487 9214
✉ frc@nationalarchives.gov.uk
www.familyrecords.gov.uk/frc

OPEN 9.00 am to 5.00 pm Monday,
Wednesday, Friday; 10.00 am to 7.00 pm
Tuesday; 9.00 am to 7.00 pm Thursday; 9.30
am to 5.00 pm Saturday (closed Sunday)

ACCESS for reference; no i.d. required
    The Centre provides a family history service
to visitors, advising on how to use the wealth of
genealogical records available, including births,
marriages and deaths and census returns. Part of
the **National Archives** (see entry).

The Fawcett Library
See **The Women's Library**

Foreign and Commonwealth Office Library
King Charles Street, London SW1A 2AH
☎020 7008 3925 Fax 020 7008 3270
✉ library.enquiries@fco.gov.uk
www.fco.gov.uk

ACCESS By appointment only
    An extensive stock of books, pamphlets and
other reference material on all aspects of historical, socio-economic and political subjects relating to countries covered by the Foreign and
Commonwealth Office. Particularly strong on
colonial history, early works on travel, and photograph collections, mainly of Commonwealth
countries and former colonies, c. 1850s–1960s.

Forestry Commission Library
Forest Research Station, Alice Holt Lodge,
Wrecclesham, Farnham GU10 4LH
☎01420 22255 Fax 01420 23653
✉ library@forestry.gsi.gov.uk
www.forestry.gov.uk
www.forestresearch.gov.uk

OPEN 9.00 am to 5.00 pm Monday to
Thursday; 9.00 am to 4.30 pm Friday

ACCESS By appointment for personal visits
    Approximately 20,000 books on forestry and
arboriculture, plus 500 current journals. CD-
ROMS include TREECD (1939 onwards).
Offers a Research Advisory Service for advice
and enquiries on forestry (☎01420 23000)
with a charge for consultations and diagnosis of
tree problems exceeding ten minutes.

French Institute Library
Institut français, 17 Queensberry Place,
London SW7 2DT

☎020 7073 1350 Fax 020 7073 1363
✉ library@ambafrance.org.uk
www.institut-francais.org.uk

OPEN 12 noon to 7.00 pm Tuesday to Friday;
12 noon to 6.00 pm Saturday; Children's
Library: 12 noon to 6.00 pm Tuesday to
Saturday; closed in August; closed for one
week at Christmas

OPEN ACCESS For reference and consultation
(loans restricted to members)
    A collection of over 55,000 volumes mainly
centred on French cultural interests with special
emphasis on language, literature and history.
Books in French and English. Collection of
videos, periodicals, CDs (French music), CD-
ROMs; special collections:'France Libre'. Denis
Saurat MSS, recordings of lectures, press-cut-
tings on French current affairs. Inter-library
loans; quick information service; Internet access
to members. Group visits on request. Children's
library (8000 documents).

Froebel Archive Digital Collection
See entry under *Useful Websites*

John Frost Newspapers
22b Rosemary Avenue, Enfield EN2 0SS
☎020 8366 1392/0946 Fax 020 8366 1379
✉ andrew@johnfrostnewspapers.com
www.johnfrostnewspapers.co.uk

Contacts *Andrew Frost, John Frost*
    A collection of 80,000 original newspapers
(1630 to the present day) and 200,000 press
cuttings available, on loan, for research and ros-
trum/stills work (TV documentaries, book and
magazine publishers and audiovisual presentations). Historic events, politics, sports, royalty,
crime, wars, personalities, etc., plus many in-
depth files.

Gloucestershire County Council Libraries & Information
Quayside House, Shire Hall, Gloucester
GL1 2HY
☎08452 305420 Fax 01452 425042
✉ libraryhelp@gloucestershire.gov.uk
www.gloucestershire.gov.uk

Head of Libraries & Information *David Paynter*
OPEN ACCESS
    The service includes 39 local libraries and six
mobile libraries. The website includes library
opening hours, mobile library route schedules;
the library catalogue; book renewal/reserva-
tions facility; and information about news and
events.

Goethe-Institut Library

50 Princes Gate, Exhibition Road, London
SW7 2PH
☎020 7596 4040   Fax 020 7594 0230
✉ library@london.goethe.org
www.goethe.de/london
Librarian *Gerlinde Buck*
OPEN 1.00 pm to 8.00 pm Monday to
Thursday; 1.00 pm to 5.00 pm Saturday

Library specialising in German literature and
books/audiovisual material on German culture
and history: 20,000 books (4000 of them in
English), 120 periodicals, 13 newspapers, 3700
audiovisual media (including 1200 videos/
DVDs), selected press clippings on German
affairs from the German and UK press, information service, photocopier, video facility. Also
German language teaching material for teachers and students of German. See website for
membership details.

Goldsmiths' Library

See **Senate House Library**

Greater London Record Office

See **London Metropolitan Archives
Library Services**

Guildford Institute of the University of Surrey Library

Ward Street, Guildford GU1 4LH
☎01483 562142   Fax 01483 451034
✉ c.miles@surrey.ac.uk
Librarian *Clare Miles*
OPEN 10.00 am to 3.00 pm Tuesday to Friday
OPEN ACCESS To members only but open to
enquirers for research purposes

Founded 1834. Some 14,000 volumes of
which 7500 were printed before the First World
War. The remaining stock consists of recently
published works of fiction and non-fiction.
Newspapers and periodicals also available.
SPECIAL COLLECTIONS include an almost complete run of the *Illustrated London News* from
1843–1906, a collection of Victorian and early
20th century local history ephemera albums, and
about 400 photos and other pictures relating to
the Institute's history and the town of Guildford.
Publishes Library newsletter twice-yearly.

Guildhall Library

Aldermanbury, London EC2V 7HH
☎See below   Fax 020 7600 3384
www.cityoflondon.gov.uk/guildhalllibrary
ACCESS For reference (but much of the material

is kept in storage areas and is supplied to
readers on request; proof of identity is required
for consultation of certain categories of stock).
Free, *limited* enquiry service available.
Also a fee-based service for in-depth research:
☎020 7332 1854   Fax 020 7600 3384
✉ search.guildhall@corpoflondon. gov.uk
Website www.cityoflondon.gov.uk/
search_guildhall

Part of the Corporation of London libraries.
Seeks to provide a basic general reference service
but its major strength, acknowledged worldwide,
is in its historical collections. The library is
divided into three sections, each with its own
catalogues and enquiry desks. These are: Printed
Books; Manuscripts; the Print & Maps Room.

PRINTED BOOKS
☎020 7332 1868/1870
✉ printed books.guildhall@cityoflondon.gov.uk
OPEN 9.30 am to 5 pm Monday to Saturday;
NB closes on Saturdays preceding Bank
Holidays; check for details

Strong on all aspects of London history, with
wide holdings of English history, topography
and genealogy, including local directories, poll
books and parish register transcripts. Also good
collections of English statutes, law reports, parliamentary debates and journals, and House of
Commons papers. Home of several important
collections deposited by London institutions:
the Marine collection of the Corporation of
Lloyd's, the Stock Exchange's historical files of
reports and prospectuses, the Clockmakers'
Company library and museum, the Gardeners'
Company, Fletchers' Company, the Institute of
Masters of Wine, International Wine and Food
Society and Gresham College.

MANUSCRIPTS
☎020 7332 1862/3
✉ manuscripts.guildhall@cityoflondon.
gov.uk
www.history.ac.uk/gh/
OPEN 9.30 am to 5.00 pm Monday to
Saturday (no requests for records after 4.30
pm; no manuscripts can be produced
between 12 noon and 2 pm on Saturdays);
NB closes on Saturdays preceding Bank
Holidays; check for details

The official repository for historical records
relating to the City of London (except those of
the City of London Corporation itself, which
are housed at the City of London Records
Office). Records date from the 11th century to
the present day. They include archives of most
of the City's parishes, wards and livery com-

panies, and of many individuals, families, estates, schools, societies and other institutions, notably the Diocese of London and St Paul's Cathedral, as well as the largest collection of business archives in any public repository in the UK. Although mainly of City interest, holdings include material for the London area as a whole and beyond.

PRINTS & MAPS ROOM
☎020 7332 1839
✉ prints&maps@cityoflondon.gov.uk
OPEN 9.30 am to 5.00 pm Monday to Friday

An unrivalled collection of prints and drawings relating to London and the adjacent counties. The emphasis is on topography, but there are strong collections of portraits and satirical prints. The map collection includes maps of the capital from the mid-16th century to the present day and various classes of Ordnance Survey maps. Other material includes photographs, theatre bills and programmes, trade cards, book plates and playing cards as well as a sizeable collection of Old Master prints. Over 30,000 items have been digitally imaged on the 'Collage' website, including topographical prints, some maps, a small number of photographs and all the Guildhall Art Gallery collection. 'Collage' website: collage.cityoflondon.gov.uk

Guille–Alles Library

Market Street, St Peter Port, Guernsey GY1 1HB
☎01481 720392 Fax 01481 712425
✉ ga@library.gg
www.library.gg

OPEN 9.00 am to 5.00 pm Monday, Thursday, Friday, Saturday; 10.00 am to 5.00 pm Tuesday; 9.00 am to 8.00 pm Wednesday

OPEN ACCESS For residents; payment of returnable deposit by visitors. Music CD collection: £10 for two-year subscription
Lending, reference and information services. Public Internet service.

Herefordshire Libraries

Shirehall, Hereford HR1 2HY
☎01432 261644 Fax 01432 260744
www.libraries.herefordshire.gov.uk

OPEN Opening hours vary in the libraries across the county

ACCESS Information and reference services open to anyone; loans to members only (membership criteria: resident, being educated, working, or an elector in the county or neighbouring authorities; temporary membership to visitors.

Proof of identity and address required)
Information service, reference and lending libraries. Non-fiction and fiction for all age groups, including normal and large print, spoken word cassettes, and CDs, music CDs, videos, DVDs, playstation2. Hereford Library houses the largest reference section and the county local history collection, although some reference material and local history is available at all libraries. Internet access at all libraries. *Special collections* Cidermaking; Beekeeping; Alfred Watkins; John Masefield; Pilley.

University of Hertfordshire Library

College Lane, Hatfield AL10 9AB
☎01707 284678 Fax 01707 284666
www.herts.ac.uk/lis

OPEN See website for term-time and vacation opening hours

ACCESS For reference use of printed collections. Appropriate ID required for Visitor's pass.
For further information please refer to the website.

Highgate Literary and Scientific Institution Library

11 South Grove, London N6 6BS
☎020 8340 3343 Fax 020 8340 5632
✉ librarian@hlsi.net

OPEN 10.00 am to 5.00 pm Tuesday to Friday; 10.00 am to 4.00 pm Saturday (closed Sunday and Monday)

ANNUAL MEMBERSHIP £55 (individual); £90 (household)

25,000 volumes of general fiction and non-fiction, with a children's section and extensive local archives. SPECIAL COLLECTIONS on local history, London, and local poets Samuel Taylor Coleridge and John Betjeman.

Highland Libraries, The Highland Council, Education, Culture and Sport Service

Library Support Unit, 31a Harbour Road, Inverness IV1 1UA
☎01463 235713 Fax 01463 236986
✉ libraries@highland.gov.uk
www.highland.gov.uk

OPEN Library opening hours vary to suit local needs. Contact administration and support services for details (8.00 am to 6.00 pm Monday to Friday)

OPEN ACCESS
Comprehensive range of lending and refer-

ence stock: books, pamphlets, periodicals, newspapers, compact discs, audio and video cassettes, maps, census records, genealogical records, photographs, educational materials, etc. Free access to the Internet in all libraries. Highland Libraries provides the public library service throughout the Highlands with a network of 43 static and 12 mobile libraries.

Holborn Library
32–38 Theobalds Road, London WC1X 8PA
☎020 7974 6345
OPEN 10.00 am to 7.00 pm Monday and Thursday; 10.00 am to 6.00 pm Tuesday, Wednesday and Friday; 10.00 am to 5.00 pm Saturday

OPEN ACCESS
London Borough of Camden public library. Includes the London Borough of Camden Local Studies and Archive Centre.

Sherlock Holmes Collection (Westminster)
Marylebone Library, Marylebone Road, London NW1 5PS
☎020 7641 1206   Fax 020 7641 1019
✉ ccooke@westminster.gov.uk
www.westminster.gov.uk/libraries/special/sherlock.cfm
OPEN 9.30 am to 8.00 pm Monday, Tuesday, Thursday, Friday; 10.00 am to 8.00 pm Wednesday; closed Saturday and Sunday (unless by prior arrangement)

ACCESS By appointment only
Located in Westminster's Marylebone Library. An extensive collection of material from all over the world, covering Sherlock Holmes and Sir Arthur Conan Doyle. Books, pamphlets, journals, newspaper cuttings and photos, much of which is otherwise unavailable in this country. Some background material.

IHR Library
See **The Institute of Historical Research Library**

Imperial College Central Library
See **Science Museum Library**

Imperial War Museum
Department of Printed Books, Lambeth Road, London SE1 6HZ
☎020 7416 5342   Fax 020 7416 5246
✉ books@iwm.org.uk
www.iwm.org.uk
OPEN 10.00 am to 5.00 pm Monday to

Saturday (restricted service Saturday; closed on Bank Holiday Saturdays and two weeks during the year for annual stock check)

ACCESS For reference (but at least 24 hours' notice must be given for intended visits)
A large collection of material on British and Commonwealth 20th-century life with detailed coverage of the two World Wars and other conflicts. This collection includes substantial holdings of European language material. Books, pamphlets and periodicals, including many produced for short periods in unlikely wartime settings; also maps, biographies and privately printed memoirs, and foreign language material. Additional research material available in the following departments: Art, Documents, Exhibits and Firearms, Film, Sound Records, Photographs. See www.iwmcollections.org.uk for their online catalogues. Active publishing programme based on reprints of rare books held in library. Catalogue available online.

The Institute of Historical Research
Senate House, Malet Street, London WC1E 7HU
☎020 7862 8760   Fax 020 7862 8762
✉ IHR.Library@sas.ac.uk
www.history.ac.uk/library
catalogue.ulrls.lon.ac.uk
OPEN 9.00 am to 8.45 pm Monday to Friday; 9.00 am to 4.45 pm Saturday

ACCESS For reference only. Non-members are advised to telephone to check availability of items before visiting.

Reference collection of printed primary sources, bibliographies, guides to archives, periodicals and works covering the history of Western Europe from the fall of the Roman Empire. Holds a substantial microform collection of mainly British material from repositories outside London.

Instituto Cervantes
102 Eaton Square, London SW1W 9AN
☎020 7201 0757   Fax 020 7235 0329
✉ biblon@cervantes.es
londres.cervantes.es
OPEN 12 noon to 7.30 pm Monday to Thursday; 12 noon to 6.30 pm Friday; 9.30 am to 2.00 pm Saturday

OPEN ACCESS For reference and lending
Spanish language and literature, history, art, philosophy. The library houses a collection of books, periodicals, videos, DVDs, slides, tapes,

CDs, cassettes, CD-ROMs specialising entirely in Spain and Latin America.

Italian Institute Library

39 Belgrave Square, London SW1X 8NX
☎020 7396 4425   Fax 020 7235 4618
www.italcultur.org.uk

OPEN 10.00 am to 1.30 pm and 2.30 pm to 5.00 pm Monday to Friday; 2.30 pm to 8.00 pm Wednesday (during term time only)

OPEN ACCESS For reference
A collection of over 25,000 volumes relating to all aspects of Italian culture, including DVDs and CDs relating to Italian cinema. Texts are mostly in Italian, with some in English.

Jersey Library

Halkett Place, St Helier, Jersey JE2 4WH
☎01534 759991 (lending)/759992 (reference)
Fax 01534 769444
✉ library@jsylib.gov.je
www.jsylib.gov.je

OPEN 9.30 am to 5.30 pm Monday, Wednesday, Thursday, Friday; 9.30 am to 7.30 pm Tuesday; 9.30 am to 4.00 pm Saturday

OPEN ACCESS
Books, periodicals, newspapers, CDs, DVDs and language packs, cassettes, videos, microfilm, specialised local studies collection, public Internet access. Branch Library at Les Quennevais School, St Brelade. Mobile library and homes services. Open Learning Centre.

Kent County Central Library

Kent Libraries and Archives, Springfield, Maidstone ME14 2LH
☎01622 696511   Fax 01622 696494
✉ countycentrallibrary@kent.gov.uk
www.kent.gov.uk/libs

OPEN 9.30 am to 5.30 pm Monday, Wednesday, Friday; 9.30 am to 6.00 pm Tuesday; 9.30 am to 7.00 pm Thursday; 10.00 am to 5.00 pm Saturday

OPEN ACCESS
50,000 volumes available on the floor of the library plus 250,000 volumes of non-fiction, mostly academic, available on request to staff. English literature, poetry, classical literature, drama (including play sets), music (including music sets). Strong, too, in sociology, art history, business information and government publications. Loans to all who live or work in Kent; those who do not may consult stock for reference or arrange loans via their own local library service.

Leeds Central Library

Calverley Street, Leeds LS1 3AB
☎0113 247 8911   Fax 0113 247 8426
www.leeds.gov.uk/libraries

OPEN 9.00 am to 8.00 pm Monday, Tuesday, Wednesday; 9.30 am to 5.30 pm Thursday; 9.00 pm to 5.00 pm Friday; 10.00 am to 5.00 pm Saturday; 12.00 noon to 4.00 pm Sunday

OPEN ACCESS to lending libraries; reference material on request. Free public Internet access.

Lending Library.
☎0113 247 8270
✉ centrallending@leedslearning.net

Music Library
☎0113 247 8273
✉ musiclibrary@leedslearning.net
Scores, books, video and audio.

Business & Research Library
☎0113 247 8282
✉ businessandresearch@leedslearning.net
Company information, market research, statistics, directories, journals and computer-based information. Extensive files of newspapers and periodicals plus all government publications since 1960. SPECIAL COLLECTIONS include military history, Judaic, early gardening books.

Art Library
☎0113 247 8247
✉ artlibrary@leedslearning.net
Major collection of material on fine and applied arts.

Local Studies Library
☎0113 247 8290
✉ localstudies@leedslearning.net
Extensive collection on Leeds and Yorkshire, including maps, books, pamphlets, local newspapers, illustrations and playbills. Census returns for the whole of Yorkshire also available. International Genealogical Index and parish registers.

Leeds City Libraries has an extensive network of 65 branch and mobile libraries.

Leeds Library

18 Commercial Street, Leeds LS1 6AL
☎0113 245 3071   Fax 0113 245 1191

OPEN 9.00 am to 5.00 pm Monday to Friday

ACCESS To members; research use upon application to the librarian
Founded 1768. Contains over 125,000 books and periodicals from the 15th century to the

present day. SPECIAL COLLECTIONS include Reformation pamphlets, Civil War tracts, Victorian and Edwardian children's books and fiction, European language material, spiritualism and psychical research, plus local material.

Library of the Religious Society of Friends

Friends House, 173 Euston Road, London NW1 2BJ
☎020 7663 1135 Fax 020 7663 1001
✉ library@quaker.org.uk
www.quaker.org.uk
OPEN 1.00 pm to 5.00 pm Monday, Tuesday, Thursday, Friday; 10.00 am to 5.00 pm Wednesday

OPEN ACCESS A letter of introduction from a college, employer, publisher or Friends meeting is required for researchers who are not members of the Society (it is advisable to make an appointment before visiting)

Quaker history, thought and activities from the 17th century onwards. Supporting collections on peace, anti-slavery and other subjects in which Quakers have maintained long-standing interest. Also archives and manuscripts relating to the Society of Friends.

Lincoln Central Library

Free School Lane, Lincoln LN2 1EZ
☎01522 510800 Fax 01522 535882
✉ lincoln.library@lincolnshire.gov.uk
www.lincolnshire.gov.uk
OPEN 9.30 am to 7.00 pm Monday to Friday; 9.30 am to 4.00 pm Saturday

OPEN ACCESS to the library; appointment required for the Tennyson Research Centre

Lending and reference library. Special collections include Lincolnshire local history (printed and published material, photographs, maps, directories and census data) and the Tennyson Research Centre (contact *Grace Timmins* grace.timmins@lincolnshire.gov.uk).

Linen Hall Library

17 Donegall Square North, Belfast BT1 5GB
☎028 9032 1707 Fax 028 9043 8586
✉ info@linenhall.com
www.linenhall.com
Librarian *John Gray*
OPEN 9.30 am to 5.30 pm Monday to Friday; 9.30 am to 1.00 pm Saturday

OPEN ACCESS For reference (loans restricted to members)

Founded 1788. Contains about 200,000 books. Major Irish and local studies collections, including the Northern Ireland Political Collection relating to the current troubles (c. 250,000 items).

Literary & Philosophical Society of Newcastle upon Tyne

23 Westgate Road, Newcastle upon Tyne NE1 1SE
☎0191 232 0192 Fax 0191 261 4494
✉ library@litandphil.org.uk
www.litandphil.org.uk
Librarian *Kay Easson*
OPEN 9.30 am to 7.00 pm Monday, Wednesday, Thursday; 9.30 am to 8.00 pm Tuesday; 9.30 am to 5.00 pm Friday; 9.30 am to 1.00 pm Saturday

ACCESS Members; research facilities for *bona fide* scholars on application to the Librarian

200-year-old library of 140,000 volumes, periodicals (including 130 current titles), classical music on vinyl recordings and CD, plus a collection of scores. Free public lectures, events and recitals. Recent publications include: *The Reverend William Turner: Dissent and Reform in Georgian Newcastle upon Tyne* Stephen Harbottle; *History of the Literary and Philosophical Society of Newcastle upon Tyne, Vol. 2 (1896–1989)* Charles Parish; *Bicentenary Lectures 1993* ed. John Philipson.

Liverpool Libraries and Information Services

William Brown Street, Liverpool L3 8EW
☎0151 233 5829 Fax 0151 233 5886
✉ refbt.central.library@liverpool.gov.uk
www.liverpool.gov.uk/libraries
OPEN 9.00 am to 6.00 pm Monday to Friday; 9.00 am to 5.00 pm Saturday; 12 noon to 4.00 pm Sunday

OPEN ACCESS

Humanities Reference Library
A total stock in excess of 120,000 volumes and 24,000 maps, plus book plates, prints and autographed letters. SPECIAL COLLECTIONS Walter Crane and Edward Lear illustrations, Kelmscott Press, Audubon.

Business and Technology Reference Library
Extensive stock dealing with all aspects of science, commerce and technology, including British and European standards and patents and trade directories.

Audio Visual Library Extensive stock relating to all aspects of music. Includes 128,000 volumes and music scores, over 3000 CDs, 2000 videos and 800 DVDs.

Record Office and Local History Department

Material relating to Liverpool, Merseyside, Lancashire and Cheshire, together with archive material mainly on Liverpool. Proof of name and address required to obtain reader's ticket.

University of the Arts London – London College of Communication

Library and Learning Resources, Elephant and Castle, London SE1 6SB

☎020 7514 6527 Fax 020 7514 6597

www.lcc.arts.ac.uk

ACCESS Appointment required

Library and Learning Resources provides books, periodicals, slides, CD-ROMs, videos and computer software on all aspects of the art of the book, printing, management, film/photography, graphic arts, plus retailing. SPECIAL COLLECTIONS history and development of published and unpublished scripts and the art of the western book.

The London Library

14 St James's Square, London SW1Y 4LG

☎020 7930 7705 Fax 020 7766 4766

✉ membership@londonlibrary.co.uk

www.londonlibrary.co.uk

Librarian *Miss Inez Lynn*

OPEN 9.30 am to 5.30 pm Monday, Friday, Saturday; 9.30 am to 7.30 pm Tuesday, Wednesday, Thursday

ACCESS For members only (£180 p.a., 2005)

With over a million books and 8000 members, The London Library 'is the most distinguished private library in the world; probably the largest, certainly the best loved'. Founded in 1841, it is a registered charity and wholly independent of public funding. Its permanent collection embraces most European languages as well as English. Its subject range is predominantly within the humanities, with emphasis on literature, history, fine and applied art, architecture, bibliography, philosophy, religion, and topography and travel. Some 8000–9000 titles are added yearly. Most of the stock is on open shelves to which members have free access. Members may take out up to 10 volumes; 15 if they live more than 20 miles from the Library. The comfortable Reading Room has an annexe for users of personal computers. There are photocopiers, CD-ROM workstations, free

access to the Internet, and the Library also offers a postal loans service.

Membership is open to all: prospective members are required to submit a refereed application form in advance of admission, but there is at present no waiting list for membership. The London Library Trust may make grants to those who are unable to afford the full annual fee; details on application.

London Metropolitan Archives Library Services

History Library: 40 Northampton Road, London EC1R 0HB

☎020 7332 3820/7278 8703 (Minicom)

Fax 020 7833 9136

✉ ask.lma@cityoflondon.gov.uk

www.cityoflondon.gov.uk/lma

Contact *The Enquiry Team*

ACCESS For reference only

This 100,000 volume library covers all aspects of the life and development of London, with strong holdings on the history and organisation of London local government. As the former Greater London Council History Library, the collection covers all subjects of London life, from architecture and biography to theatres and transport. The collection includes London directories from 1677 to the present, Acts of Parliament, statistical returns, several hundred periodical titles and public reports.

Lord Louis Library

Orchard Street, Newport, Isle of Wight PO30 1LL

☎01983 527655/823800 (Reference Library)

Fax 01983 825972

✉ reflib@postmaster.co.uk

OPEN 9.00 am to 5.30 pm Monday to Wednesday and Friday; 10.00 am to 8.00 pm Thursday; 9.00 am to 5.00 pm Saturday; 10.00 am to 1.00 pm Sunday

OPEN ACCESS

General adult and junior fiction and non-fiction collections; local history collection at Library HQ (Tel 01983 203880 for details). Internet access in all branches of the library on the Isle of Wight Also the county's main reference library.

Manchester Central Library

St Peters Square, Manchester M2 5PD

☎0161 234 1900 Fax 0161 234 1963

✉ mclib@libraries.manchester.gov.uk

www.manchester.gov.uk/libraries

OPEN 9.00 am to 8.00 pm Monday to Thursday; 9.00 am to 5.00 pm Friday and

Saturday. Commercial and European Units: 9.00 am to 6.00 pm Monday to Thursday; 9.00 am to 5.00 pm Friday and Saturday

OPEN ACCESS

One of the country's leading reference libraries with extensive collections covering all subjects. Departments include: Commercial, European, Technical, Social Sciences, Arts, Music, Local Studies, Chinese, General Readers, Language & Literature. Large lending stock and VIP (visually impaired) service available. Free Internet access.

Marylebone Library (Westminster)

See **Sherlock Holmes Collection**

The Mitchell Library

North Street, Glasgow G3 7DN
☎0141 287 2999 Fax 0141 287 2815
www.glasgowlibraries.org

OPEN 9.00 am to 8.00 pm Monday to Thursday; 9.00 am to 5.00 pm Friday and Saturday

OPEN ACCESS

One of Europe's largest public reference libraries with stock of over 1,200,000 volumes. It subscribes to 48 newspapers and more than 1200 periodicals. There are collections in microform, records, tapes and videos, as well as CD-ROMs, electronic databases, illustrations, photographs, postcards, etc.

The library contains a number of special collections, e.g. the Robert Burns Collection (5000 vols), the Scottish Poetry Collection (12,000 items) and the Scottish Drama Collection (1650 items).

Morrab Library

Morrab House, Morrab Gardens, Penzance TR18 4DA
☎01736 364474
Librarian *Annabelle Read*
OPEN 10.00 am to 4.00 pm Tuesday to Friday; 10.00 am to 1.00 pm Saturday

ACCESS Non-members may use the library for a small daily fee but may not borrow books

Formerly known as the Penzance Library. An independent subscription lending library of over 40,000 volumes covering virtually all subjects except modern science and technology, with large collections on history, literature and religion. There is a comprehensive Cornish collection of books, newspapers and manuscripts including the Borlase letters; a West Cornwall photographic archive; many runs of 18th and 19th-century periodicals; a collection of over 2000 books published before 1800.

The National Archives

Kew, Richmond TW9 4DU
☎020 8876 3444 Fax 020 8487 1974
www.nationalarchives.gov.uk

OPEN 9.00 am to 5.00 pm Monday, Wednesday, Friday; 10.00 am to 7.00 pm Tuesday; 9.00 am to 7.00 pm Thursday; 9.30 am to 5.00 pm Saturday (closed public holidays and 29 November to 4 December for annual stocktaking)

ACCESS for reference, by reader's ticket, available free of charge on production of proof of identity (UK citizens: banker's card or driving licence; non-UK: passport or national identity card. Telephone for further information)

Over 168 kilometres of shelving house the national repository of records of central government in the UK and law courts of England and Wales, which extend in time from the 11th to the 20th century. Medieval records and the records of the State Paper Office from the early 16th to late 18th century, plus the records of the Privy Council Office and the Lord Chamberlain's and Lord Steward's departments. Modern government department records, together with those of the Copyright Office dating mostly from the late 18th century. Under the Public Records Act, records are normally only open to inspection when they are 30 years old.

National Library of Ireland

Kildare Street, Dublin 2, Republic of Ireland
☎00 353 1 603 0200 Fax 00 353 1 676 6690
✉ info@nli.ie
www.nli.ie

OPEN 10.00 am to 9.00 pm Monday to Wednesday; 10.00 am to 5.00 pm Thursday and Friday; 10.00 am to 1.00 pm Saturday

ACCESS Passes are issued for genealogical research or to consult newspapers; Reader's Ticket required for access to other material.

Collections include books, manuscripts, prints and drawings, maps, photographs, newspapers, music, ephemera and genealogical materials.

National Library of Scotland

George IV Bridge, Edinburgh EH1 1EW
☎0131 623 3700 Fax 0131 623 3701
✉ enquiries@nls.uk
www.nls.uk

OPEN Main Reading Room: 9.30 am to 8.30 pm Monday, Tuesday, Thursday, Friday; 10.00 am to 8.30 pm Wednesday; 9.30 am to 1.00 pm Saturday. Map Library: 9.30 am to 5.00 pm Monday, Tuesday, Thursday,

Friday; 10.00 am to 5.00 pm Wednesday; 9.30 am to 1.00 pm Saturday

ACCESS to all reading rooms, for research not easily done elsewhere, by reader's ticket
Collection of over seven million volumes. The library receives all British and Irish publications. Large stock of newspapers and periodicals. Many special collections, including early Scottish books, theology, polar studies, baking, phrenology and liturgies. Also large collections of maps, music and manuscripts including personal archives of notable Scottish persons.

National Library of Wales

Aberystwyth SY23 3BU
☎01970 632800   Fax 01970 615709
www.llgc.org.uk
OPEN 9.30 am to 6.00 pm Monday to Friday; 9.30 am to 5.00 pm Saturday (closed Bank Holidays and the week after Christmas)

ACCESS to reading rooms by reader's ticket, available on application. Open access to a wide-ranging exhibition programme
Collection of over four million books and including large collections of periodicals, maps, manuscripts and audiovisual material. Particular emphasis on humanities in printed foreign material, and on Wales and other Celtic areas in all collections.

National Meteorological Library and Archive

FitzRoy Road, Exeter EX1 3PB
☎01392 884841   Fax 0870 900 5050
✉ metlib@metoffice.gov.uk
www.metoffice.gov.uk
OPEN Library: 8.30 am to 4.30 pm Monday to Friday. Archive: 10.00 am to 6.00 pm

ACCESS By Visitor's Pass available from the reception desk; advance notice of a planned visit is appreciated
The major repository of most of the important literature on the subjects of meteorology, climatology and related sciences from the 16th century to the present day. The Library houses a collection of books, journals, articles and scientific papers, plus published climatological data from many parts of the world. The Technical Archive (National Meteorological Archive, Great Moore House, Sowton Industrial Estate, Bittern Road, Exeter EX2 7NL ☎01392 360987, Fax 0870 900 5050; metarc@metoffice.gov.org.uk) holds the document collection of meteorological data and charts from England, Wales and British overseas bases, including ships' weather logs.

Records from Scotland are stored in Edinburgh and those from Northern Ireland in Belfast.

The Natural History Museum Library

Cromwell Road, London SW7 5BD
☎020 7942 5460   Fax 020 7942 5559
✉ library@nhm.ac.uk
www.nhm.ac.uk/library/index.html
OPEN 10.00 am to 4.30 pm Monday to Friday

ACCESS To bona fide researchers, by reader's ticket on presentation of identification (telephone first to make an appointment)
The library is in five sections: general; botany; zoology; entomology; earth sciences. The sub-department of ornithology is housed at the Zoological Museum, Akeman Street, Tring HP23 6AP (☎020 7942 6156). Resources available include books, journals, maps, manuscripts, drawings and photographs covering all aspects of natural history, including palaeontology and mineralogy, from the 14th century to the present day. Also archives and historical collection on the museum itself.

Newcastle upon Tyne City Library

Princess Square, Newcastle upon Tyne NE99 1DX
☎0191 277 4100   Fax 0191 277 4137
✉ city.information@newcastle.gov.uk or
local.studies@newcastle.gov.uk or
information@newcastle.gov.uk
www.newcastle.gov.uk/libraries
OPEN 9.00 am to 8.00 pm Monday to Thursday; 9.00 am to 5.00 pm Friday and Saturday; 12 noon to 4.00 pm Sunday
The City library has extensive reference collections, including a local collection comprising newspapers, illustrations and genealogical information

Norfolk Library & Information Service

Norfolk and Norwich Millennium Library, The Forum, Millennium Plain, Norwich NR2 1AW
www.norfolk.gov.uk/council/departments/lis/libhome.htm
OPEN Lending Library, Reference and Information Service and Norfolk Studies: 9.00 am to 8.00 pm Monday, Wednesday, Thursday, Friday; 10.00 am to 8.00 pm Tuesday; 9.00 am to 5.00 pm Saturday. EXPRESS: 9.00 am to 9.30 pm Monday to

Friday; 9.00 am to 8.30 pm Saturday; 10.30 am to 4.30 pm Sunday

OPEN ACCESS

Reference lending library (stock merged together) with wide range, including books, recorded music, music scores, plays and videos. Houses the 2nd Air Division Memorial Library and has a strong Norfolk Heritage Library. Extensive range of reference stock including business information. Online database and CD-ROM services. Public fax and colour photocopying, free access to the Internet. EXPRESS (fiction, sound & vision library within a library): selection of popular fiction, videos, CDs and DVDs available, with extended opening hours.

Northamptonshire Libraries & Information Service

Library HQ, PO Box 216, John Dryden House, 8–10 The Lakes, Northampton NN4 7DD
☎01604 237959 Fax 01604 237937
✉ nlis@northamptonshire.gov.uk

Since 1991, the Libraries and Information Service has offered its 'Wordworks' diary of literature events. The rolling programme now attracts exciting literary names as well as new and locally-based writers. Writers have an opportunity to read at a variety of venues around the country. Literature workshops, activities and other events are supported. Regular book displays and dedicated notice boards in libraries support the programme across the county.

Northumberland Central Library

The Willows, Morpeth NE61 1TA
☎01670 534518/534514 Fax 01670 534513
✉ libraries@northumberland.gov.uk
www.northumberlandlibraries.com

OPEN 10.00 am to 8.00 pm Monday, Tuesday, Wednesday, Friday; 9.30 am to 12.30 pm Saturday (closed Thursday)

OPEN ACCESS

Books, periodicals, newspapers, story cassettes, CD-ROMs, DVDs, CDs, videos, Free Internet access, word processing facilities, prints, microforms, vocal scores, playsets. SPECIAL COLLECTIONS Northern Poetry Library: 15,000 volumes of modern poetry (see entry under *Organisations of Interest to Poets*); Cinema: comprehensive collection of about 5000 volumes covering all aspects of the cinema; Family History.

Nottingham Central Library

Angel Row, Nottingham NG1 6HP
☎0115 915 2828 Fax 0115 915 2840
✉ enquiryline@nottinghamcity.gov.uk
www.nottinghamcity.gov.uk

OPEN 9.00 am to 7.00 pm Monday to Friday; 9.00 am to 1.00 pm Saturday

OPEN ACCESS

City Centre Library; includes wide range of stock. Strengths: Business collection; Sound and Vision collection; comprehensive Nottinghamshire Local Studies. Drama and music sets for loan to groups. Free Internet access for visitors. Contemporary Art Gallery.

Nottingham Subscription Library Ltd

See **Bromley House Library**

Office for National Statistics, National Statistics Information and Library Service

1 Drummond Gate, London SW1V 2QQ
☎0845 601 3034/01633 812399
Fax 01633 652747
✉ info@statistics.gov.uk
www.statistics.gov.uk

OPEN 9.00 am to 5.00 pm; appointment required; visitors must supply some form of identification

Also: National Statistics Information and Library Service, Government Buildings, Cardiff Road, Newport NP9 1XG

OPEN as above

Wide range of government statistical publications and access to government Internet-based data. Census statistical data from 1801; population and health data from 1837; government social survey reports from 1941; recent international statistical data (UN, Eurostat, etc.); monograph and periodical collections of statistical methodology. The library in south Wales holds a wide range of government economic and statistical publications.

Orkney Library and Archive

44 Junction Road, Kirkwall KW15 1AG
☎01856 873166 Fax 01856 875260
✉ general.enquiries@orkney.gov.uk *and* archives@orkneylibrary.org.uk
www.orkneylibrary.org.uk

Principal Archivist *Alison Fraser*
Principal Librarian *Karen Walker*

OPEN 9.00 am to 7.00 pm Monday to Thursday; 9.00 am to 5.00 pm Friday and

Saturday. Archives: 9.00 am to 5.00 pm Monday, Tuesday, Wednesday, Friday; 9.00 am to 7.00 pm Thursday; 9.00 am to 5.00 pm Saturday

OPEN ACCESS
Local studies collection. Archive includes sound and photographic departments.

Oxford Central Library
Westgate, Oxford OX1 1DJ
☎01865 815549   Fax 01865 721694
✉ oxfordcentral.library@oxfordshire.gov.uk
www.oxfordshire.gov.uk
OPEN 9.00 am to 7.00 pm Monday to Thursday; 9.00 am to 5.30 pm Friday and Saturday

General lending and reference library including Oxfordshire Studies. Also periodicals, audio visual materials, music library, children's library and Business Information Point.

PA News Centre
Central Park, New Lane, Leeds LS11 5DZ
☎0870 830 6824   Fax 0870 830 6825
✉ palibrary@pressassociation.co.uk
www.pa.press.net
OPEN 8.00 am to 6.00 pm Monday to Friday; 8.00 am to 4.00 pm Saturday (closed Sunday)

OPEN ACCESS
PA News, the 24-hour national news and information group, offers the PA Digital Library which holds Press Association stories. Personal callers welcome or research undertaken by in-house staff.

Penzance Library
See **Morrab Library**

City of Plymouth Library and Information Services
Central Library, Drake Circus, Plymouth PL4 8AL
☎01752 305923
✉ library@plymouth.gov.uk
www.plymouthlibraries.info
OPEN ACCESS

CENTRAL LIBRARY LENDING DEPARTMENTS:
Lending ☎01752 305912
✉ lendlib@plymouth.gov.uk

Children's Department ☎01752 305916
✉ childrens.library@plymouth.gov.uk

Music & Drama Department ☎01752 305914 ✉ music@plymouth.gov.uk
OPEN 9.00 am to 7.00 pm Monday and

Friday; 9.00 am to 5.30 pm Tuesday, Wednesday, Thursday; 9.00 am to 5.00 pm Saturday

The Lending departments offer books on all subjects; language courses on cassette and foreign language books; the Holcenberg Jewish Collection; books on music and musicians, drama and theatre; music parts and sets of music parts; play sets; DVDs, videos; song index; cassettes and CDs; public Internet access.

CENTRAL LIBRARY REFERENCE DEPARTMENTS:
Reference ☎01752 305907
✉ ref@plymouth.gov.uk

Business Information ☎ 01752 305908
✉ keyinfo@plymouth.gov.uk

Local Studies & Naval History Department ☎01752 305909
✉ localstudies@plymouth.gov.uk
OPEN 9.00 am to 7.00 pm Monday to Friday; 9.00 am to 5.00 pm Saturday

The Reference departments include an extensive collection of Ordnance Survey maps and town guides; community and census information; marketing and statistical information; Patents; books on every aspect of Plymouth; naval history; Mormon Index on microfilm; Baring Gould manuscript of 'Folk Songs of the West'; public Internet access, including some electronic subscriptions.

Plymouth Proprietary Library
Alton Terrace, 111 North Hill, Plymouth PL4 8JY
☎01752 660515
Librarian *John R. Smith*
OPEN Monday to Saturday from 9.30 am (closing time varies)
ACCESS To members; visitors by appointment only

Founded 1810. The library contains approximately 17,000 volumes of mainly 20th-century work. Member of the **Association of Independent Libraries**.

The Poetry Library
See entry under *Organisations of Interest to Poets*

Polish Library
238–246 King Street, London W6 0RF
☎020 8741 0474   Fax 020 8741 7724
✉ bibliotekapolska@posklibrary.fsnet.co.uk *or* polish.library@posk.org

Librarian *Mrs Jadwiga Szmidt*
OPEN 10.00 am to 8.00 pm Monday and Wednesday; 10.00 am to 5.00 pm Friday; 10.00 am to 1.00 pm Saturday (library closed Tuesday and Thursday)

ACCESS For reference to all interested in Polish affairs; limited loans to members and *bona fide* scholars only through inter-library loans
Books, pamphlets, periodicals, maps, music, photographs on all aspects of Polish history and culture. SPECIAL COLLECTIONS Emigré publications; Joseph Conrad and related works; Polish underground publications; bookplates.

Poole Central Library
Dolphin Centre, Poole BH15 1QE
☎01202 262424 Fax 01202 262442
✉ poolelibrary@poole.gov.uk
www.boroughofpoole.com/libraries
OPEN 9.00 am to 6.00 pm Monday to Thursday; 9.00 am to 7.00 pm Friday; 9.00 am to 3.00 pm Saturday

OPEN ACCESS
General lending and reference library, including Healthpoint health information centre, business information, children's library, periodicals and newspapers, cafe, IT suite and meeting room.

Press Association Library
See **PA News Centre**

Public Record Office
See **The National Archives**

Reading Central Library
Abbey Square, Reading RG1 3BQ
☎0118 901 5950 Fax 0118 901 5954
✉ info@readinglibraries.org.uk
www.readinglibraries.org.uk
OPEN 9.30 am to 5.30 pm Monday and Friday; 9.30 am to 7.00 pm Tuesday and Thursday; 9.30 am to 5.00 pm Wednesday and Saturday

OPEN ACCESS
Ground Floor: Fiction, audio-visual material, children's library; First Floor: Newspapers, non-fiction – biography, business, careers, cookery, DIY, engineering, gardening, health, languages, law, mind, body & spirit, pets, science, social studies, sport, transport, travel; Second Floor: LearnDirect, non-fiction – art, music, literature, plays, computing; Third floor: Non-fiction – world history, national history, local history. Magazines and periodicals and Internet access on all floors.

Richmond Central Reference Library
Old Town Hall, Whittaker Avenue, Richmond TW9 1TP
☎020 8940 5529 Fax 020 8940 6899
✉ reference.services@richmond.gov.uk
www.richmond.gov.uk
OPEN 9.30 am to 6.00 pm Monday, Thursday, Friday; 9.30 am to 5.00 pm Tuesday; Wednesday, 8.00 pm and Saturday, 5.00 pm)

OPEN ACCESS
General reference library serving the needs of local residents and organisations. Internet access and online databases for public use.

Royal Geographical Society (with the Institute of British Geographers)
1 Kensington Gore, London SW7 2AR
☎020 7591 3000 Fax 020 7591 3001
www.rgs.org
See website for details. For information on the Picture Library see entry under *Picture Libraries.*

Royal Institute of Philosophy
See **Senate House Library, University of London**

Royal Society Library
6–9 Carlton House Terrace, London SW1Y 5AG
☎020 7451 2606 Fax 020 7930 2170
✉ library@royalsoc.ac.uk
www.royalsoc.ac.uk
OPEN 10.00 am to 5.00 pm Monday to Friday

ACCESS Open to all researchers with an interest in the history of science, the Fellowship of the Royal Society and science policy. Researchers are advised to contact the Library in advance of their first visit.
History of science, scientists' biographies, science policy reports, and publications of international scientific unions and national academies from all over the world.

RSA (Royal Society for the Encouragement of Arts, Manufactures & Commerce)
8 John Adam Street, London WC2N 6EZ
☎020 7930 5115 Fax 020 7839 5805
www.theRSA.org
OPEN Library: 8.30 am to 8.00 pm every weekday. Archive material by appointment
ACCESS to Fellows of RSA; Archive: by appoint-

ment to all researchers (contact the Archivist,
☎020 7451 6874; archive@rsa.org.uk)
Archives of the Society since 1754. A collection of approximately 10,000 volumes; international exhibition material.

Royal Society of Medicine Library
1 Wimpole Street, London W1G 0AE
☎020 7290 2940   Fax 020 7290 2939
✉ library@rsm.ac.uk
www.rsm.ac.uk
Contact *Director of Information Services*
OPEN 9.00 am to 8.30 pm Monday to
Thursday; 9.00 am to 5.30 pm Friday

ACCESS For reference only, on introduction by
Fellow of the Society or temporary membership is available to non-members; £12 per day;
£35 per week; £90 per month. Identification
required.
Books, periodicals, databases on postgraduate
biomedical information. Extensive historical
collection dating from the fifteenth century and
medical portrait collection.

Eric Frank Russell Archive
See **Science Fiction Foundation Research
Library**

St Bride Library
Bride Lane, Fleet Street, London EC4Y 8EE
☎020 7353 4660   Fax 020 7583 7073
✉ library@stbrideinstitute.org
www.stbride.org
OPEN 12 noon to 5.30 pm Tuesday and
Thursday; 12 noon to 9.00 pm Wednesday
OPEN ACCESS
A public reference library maintained by the St
Bride Foundation. Appointments advisable for
consultation of special collections. Every aspect of
printing and related matters: publishing and
bookselling, newspapers and magazines, graphic
design, calligraphy and typography, papermaking
and bookbinding. One of the world's largest specialist collections in its field, with over 50,000
volumes, over 3000 periodicals (200 current
titles), and extensive collection of drawings, manuscripts, prospectuses, patents and materials for
printing and typefounding. Noted for its comprehensive holdings of historical and early technical literature.

Science Fiction Foundation
Research Library
Liverpool University Library, PO Box 123,
Liverpool L69 3DA
☎0151 794 3142   Fax 0151 794 2681

✉ asawyer@liverpool.ac.uk
www.sfhub.ac.uk
Contact *Andy Sawyer*
ACCESS For research, by appointment only
(telephone first)
This is the largest collection outside the US
of science fiction and related material – including autobiographies and critical works. SPECIAL
COLLECTION Runs of 'pulp' magazines dating
back to the 1920s. Foreign-language material
(including a large Russian collection), and the
papers of the Flat Earth Society. The collection
also features a growing range of archive and
manuscript material, including the Eric Frank
Russell archive. The University of Liverpool
also holds the Olaf Stapledon and John
Wyndham archives.

Science Museum Library
Imperial College Road, London SW7 5NH
☎020 7942 4242   Fax 020 7942 4243
✉ smlinfo@nmsi.ac.uk
www.sciencemuseum.org.uk/library
OPEN 8.30 am to 11.00 pm Monday to Friday
(closes 5.30 pm outside academic terms);
9.30 am to 5.30 pm Saturday
OPEN ACCESS Reference only; no loans
National reference library for the history and
public understanding of science and technology, with a large collection of source material.
Operates jointly with Imperial College Central
Library.

Scottish Poetry Library
See entry under *Organisations of Interest to
Poets*

Senate House Library, University
of London
Senate House, Malet Street, London
WC1E 7HU
☎020 7862 8461/62 (Information Centre)
Fax 020 7862 8480
✉ enquiries@shl.lon.ac.uk (Information Centre)
www.shl.lon.ac.uk
MEMBERSHIP DESK: ☎020 7862 8439/40
✉ userservices@shl.lon.ac.uk
OPEN Term-time: 9.00 am to 9.00 pm Monday
to Thursday; 9.00 am to 6.30 pm Friday; 9.30
am to 5.30 pm Saturday. Vacation: 9.00 am to
6.00 pm Monday to Friday; 9.30 am to 5.30
pm Saturday (closed on Sundays and at
certain periods during Bank Holidays)
The Senate House Library is a major academic

research library predominantly based across the Humanities and Social Sciences. Housed within its 16 floors are some two million titles including 5500 current periodicals and a wide range of electronic resources. It contains a number of outstanding research collections which, as well as supporting the scholarly activities of the University, attract researchers from throughout the UK and internationally. These include: English (e.g. the Durning-Lawrence Library and Sterling Collection of first editions); Economic and Social History (the Goldsmiths' Library, containing 70,000 items ranging from 15th to early 19th century); Modern Languages (primarily Romance and Germanic); Palaeography (acclaimed as being the best open access collection in its field in Europe); History (complementary to the Institute of Historical Research); Music, Philosophy (acts as the Library of the Royal Institute of Philosophy); Psychology (includes the BPS library); Major area studies collections (Latin-American, including Caribbean; United States and Commonwealth Studies, British Government Publications and maps). The Library has a wide range of Special Collections holdings. Check the website for full details of collections and current access arrangements.

Sheffield Libraries, Archives and Information

Central Library, Surrey Street, Sheffield
S1 1XZ
☎0114 273 4712 Fax 0114 273 5009
✉ libraries@sheffield.gov.uk
www.sheffield.gov.uk (click on 'In your area')

Central Lending Library
☎0114 273 4727 (enquiries)/
4729 (book renewals)
OPEN 10.00 am to 8.00 pm Monday; 9.30 am to 5.30 pm Tuesday, Thursday and Friday; 9.30 am to 8.00 pm Wednesday; 9.30 am to 5.30 pm Saturday
Books, talking books, large print, language courses, European fiction, books in cultural languages, play sets. Free Internet access. Writers' Resource Centre, Wednesday evenings, 5.00 pm to 7.00 pm. Proof of signature and a separate proof of address required to join.

Sheffield Archives
52 Shoreham Street, Sheffield S1 4SP
☎0114 203 9395 Fax 0114 203 9398
✉ archives@sheffield.gov.uk
OPEN 10.00 am to 5.30 pm Monday; 9.30 am to 5.30 pm Tuesday to Thursday; 9.30 am to 1.00 pm and 2.00 pm to 5.00 pm Saturday

(documents should be ordered by 5.00 pm Thursday for Saturday); closed Friday
ACCESS By reader's pass
Holds documents relating to Sheffield and South Yorkshire, dating from the 12th century to the present day, including records of the City Council, churches, businesses, landed estates, families and individuals, institutions and societies. Free Internet access.

Arts and Social Sciences and Sports Reference Service
☎0114 273 4747/8
OPEN 10.00 am to 8.00 pm Monday; 9.30 am to 5.30 pm Tuesday, Thursday, Friday, Saturday; 9.30 am to 8.00 pm Wednesday
ACCESS For reference only
A comprehensive collection of books, periodicals and newspapers covering all aspects of arts (excluding music), sports, social sciences and free Internet access.

Music and Video Service
☎0114 273 4733
✉ musicandav.library@sheffield.gov.uk
OPEN As for Central Lending Library above
ACCESS For reference and lending
An extensive range of books, CDs, cassettes, scores, etc. related to music. Also a video cassette and DVD loan service. Free Internet access.

Local Studies Service
☎0114 273 4753
✉ localstudies.library@sheffield.gov.uk
OPEN As for Arts & Social Sciences above (except Wednesday 9.30 am to 5.30 pm)
ACCESS For reference
Extensive material covering all aspects of Sheffield and its population, including maps, photos and videos. Free Internet access. Photograph collection available on www.picturesheffield.com

Business, Science and Technology Reference Services
☎0114 273 4736/7 or 273 4743
✉ businessand tech.library@sheffield.gov.uk
OPEN As for Arts & Social Sciences above
ACCESS For reference only
Extensive coverage of science and technology as well as commerce and commercial law. British patents and British and European standards with emphasis on metals. Hosts the World Metal Index. The business section holds a large stock of business and trade directories, and reference works with business emphasis. Free Internet access.

Sheffield Information Service
☎0114 273 4712 Fax 0114 275 7111
✉ sis@sheffield.gov.uk
OPEN 10.00 am to 5.30 pm Monday; 9.30 am
   to 5.30 pm Tuesday to Saturday
Full local information service covering all aspects
of the Sheffield community. Free Internet access.

Central Children's Library
☎0114 273 4734
✉ kidsandteens.library@sheffield.gov.uk
OPEN 10.30 am to 5.00 pm Monday and
   Friday; 1.00 pm to 5.00 pm Tuesday,
   Wednesday, Thursday; 9.30 am to 5.30 pm
   Saturday
Books, spoken word sets, videos; under-five
play area; teenage reference section; readings
and promotions; storytime sessions. Free
Internet access.

Shetland Library
Lower Hillhead, Lerwick ZE1 0EL
☎01595 743868 Fax 01595 694430
✉ shetlandlibrary@sic.shetland.gov.uk
www.shetland-library.gov.uk
OPEN 9.30 am to 8.00 pm Monday and
   Thursday; 9.30 am to 5.00 pm Tuesday,
   Wednesday, Friday, Saturday
   General lending and reference library; extensive local interest collection including complete
set of The Shetland Times, The Shetland News and
other local newspapers on microfilm and many
old and rare books; audio collection including
talking books/newspapers. Junior room for children. Disabled access and Housebound Readers
Service (delivery to reader's home). Mobile
library services to rural areas. Open Learning
Service. Same day photocopying service.
Publishing programme of books in dialect, history, literature. Learning centre providing access
to learning opportunities including Internet.

Shoe Lane Library
Hill House, Little New Street, London
EC4A 3JR
☎020 7583 7178 Fax 020 7353 0884
✉ shoelane@cityoflondon.gov.uk
www.cityoflondon.gov.uk
OPEN 9.00 am to 5.30 pm Monday,
   Wednesday, Thursday, Friday; 9.00 am to
   6.30 pm Tuesday
OPEN ACCESS
   Corporation of London general lending
library, with a comprehensive stock of 50,000
volumes, most of which are on display. Free
Internet access.

Shrewsbury Library and Reference & Information Service
Castlegates, Shrewsbury SY1 2AS
☎01743 255300 Fax 01743 255309
✉ shrewsbury.library@shropshire-cc.gov.uk
www.shropshire.gov.uk/library.nsf
OPEN 9.30 am to 5.00 pm Monday,
   Wednesday, Friday; 9.30 am to 8.00 pm
   Tuesday and Thursday; 9.00 am to 5.00 pm
   Saturday; 1.00 pm to 4.00 pm Sunday
OPEN ACCESS
   The largest public library in Shropshire.
Books, cassettes, CDs, talking books, DVDs,
videos, language courses. Open Learning and
study centre with public use computers for
word processing and Internet access. Music, lit-
erature and art book collection for lending and
reference. The West Midlands Literary Heritage
Collection is housed at Shrewsbury Library.

Spanish Institute Library
See **Instituto Cervantes**

Olaf Stapledon
See **Science Fiction Foundation Research Library**

Sterling Collection
See **Senate House Library**

Suffolk County Council – Suffolk Libraries
Endeavour House, Russell Road, Ipswich
IP1 2BX
☎01473 583727 Fax 01473 583700
✉ asksuffolk@libher.suffolkcc.gov.uk
www.suffolk.gov.uk/LeisureAndCulture/
   Libraries/SuffolkLibrariesDirect
OPEN See website for details of individual
   libraries or contact Endeavour House.
   Major libraries open seven days a week; all
   libraries open Sunday
ACCESS A single library card gives access to the
lending service of 43 libraries and resource centres across the county. Loans can be collected
and/or returned at any service point. Details on
website
   Full range of lending and reference services,
free public access to the Internet. Wide range of
online services for registered library users
through the Suffolk Libraries Direct pages, e.g.
self-service reservations, renewals, free access to
subscription services. Suffolk InfoLink Plus database gives details of local organisations throughout the county. SPECIAL COLLECTIONS include

Suffolk Archives and Local History Collection; Benjamin Britten Collection; Edward Fitzgerald Collection; Seckford Collection and Racing Collection (Newmarket). The Suffolk Infolink service gives details of local groups and societies and is available in libraries throughout the county and on the website.

Sunderland City Library and Arts Centre

28–30 Fawcett Street, Sunderland SR1 1RE
☎0191 514 1235   Fax 0191 514 8444
✉ enquiry.desk@sunderland.gov.uk
www.sunderland.gov.uk/libraries
OPEN 9.30 am to 7.30 pm Monday and Wednesday; 9.30 am to 5.00 pm Tuesday, Thursday, Friday; 9.30 am to 4.00 pm Saturday

The city's main library for lending and reference services. Local studies and children's sections, plus Sound and Vision department (CDs, DVDs, videos, CD-ROMs, talking books). The City of Sunderland also maintains community libraries of varying size, offering a range of services, plus mobile libraries. Free Internet access is available in all libraries across the city. A Books on Wheels service is available to housebound readers; the Schools Library Service serves teachers and schools. Two writers' groups meet at the City Library and Arts Centre: Janus Writers, every Wednesday, 1.30 pm to 3.30 pm. Foyle Street Writers Group, every Wednesday, 10.00 am to 12 noon.

Swansea Central Reference Library

Alexandra Road, Swansea SA1 5DX
☎01792 516753/516757   Fax 01792 516759
✉ central.library@swansea.gov.uk
www.swansea.gov.uk/libraries

OPEN 9.00 am to 6.00 pm Monday, Tuesday, Thursday; 9.00 am to 8.00 pm Wednesday and Friday; 9.00 am to 5.00 pm Saturday. The Library has a lending service open the same hours, including books, DVDs, videos, music CDs and talking books (☎01792 516750/1)

ACCESS For reference only (many local studies items now available on open access; other items must be requested on forms provided)
General reference material; also Welsh Assembly information, statutes, company information, maps, European Community information. Local studies: comprehensive collections on Wales; Swansea & Gower; Dylan Thomas. Local maps, periodicals, illustrations, local newspapers from 1804. B&w and colour photocopying and fax facilities, free computer and Internet access available (library membership required and pre-booking recommended) and microfilm/microfiche copying facility.

Swiss Cottage Central Library

88 Avenue Road, London NW3 3HA
☎020 7974 6522   Fax 020 7974 6532
OPEN 10.00 am to 7.00 pm Monday and Thursday; 10.00 am to 6.00 pm Tuesday, Wednesday, Friday; 10.00 am to 5.00 pm Saturday
OPEN ACCESS
Over 300,000 volumes in the lending and reference libraries. Home of the London Borough of Camden's Information and Reference Services.

Theatre Museum Library & Archive

1e Tavistock Street, London WC2E 7PR
☎020 7943 4727   Fax 020 7943 4777
✉ tmenquiries@vam.ac.uk
www.theatremuseum.org.uk
OPEN 10.30 am to 4.30 pm Wednesday to Friday
ACCESS By appointment only
The Theatre Museum was founded as a separate department of the Victoria & Albert Museum in 1974 and moved to its own building in Covent Garden in 1987. The museum (open Tuesday to Sunday 10.00 am to 6.00 pm) houses permanent displays, temporary exhibitions, a studio theatre, and organises a programme of special events, performances, lectures, guided visits and workshops. The Theatre Museum's Collections Centre in Kensington Olympia houses the UK's largest performing arts research collections, including books, photographs, designs, engravings, programmes, press cuttings, etc. All the performing arts are covered but strengths are in the areas of theatre, dance, musical theatre and stage design. The public reading room is located in the Olympia building.

Thurrock Communities, Libraries & Cultural Services

Grays Library, Orsett Road, Grays RM17 5DX
☎01375 383611   Fax 01375 370806
✉ grays.library@thurrock.gov.uk
www.thurrock.gov.uk/libraries
OPEN 10.00 am to 7.00 pm Monday; 9.00 am to 7.00 pm Tuesday, Thursday; 9.00 am to

5.00 pm Wednesday, Friday, Saturday; branch library opening times vary

OPEN ACCESS
General library lending and reference through ten libraries and a mobile library. Services include books, magazines, newspapers, audiocassettes, CDs, videos and language courses. Large collection of Thurrock materials. Internet and Microsoft Office.

Truro Library
Union Place, Truro TR1 1EP
☎01872 279205 (lending)/272702 (reference)
✉ truro.library@cornwall.gov.uk
www.cornwall.gov.uk/library
OPEN 8.30 am to 6.00 pm Monday, Tuesday, Thursday, Friday; 9.30 am to 6.00 pm Wednesday; 9.00 am to 4.00 pm Saturday
Books, cassettes, CDs, videos, DVDs and pc games for loan through branch or mobile networks. Internet access and IT support and training. Reference collection. SPECIAL COLLECTIONS on local studies.

Western Isles Libraries
Public Library, 19 Cromwell Street, Stornoway HS1 2DA
☎01851 708631   Fax 01851 708676
www.cne-siar.gov.uk
OPEN 10.00 am to 5.00 pm Monday to Wednesday; 10.00 am to 6.00 pm Thursday and Friday; 10.00 am to 5.00 pm Saturday
OPEN ACCESS
General public library stock, plus local history and Gaelic collections including maps, videos, printed music, cassettes and CDs; census records and Council minutes; music collection (CDs and cassettes). Branch libraries on the isles of Barra, Benbecula, Harris and Lewis.

City of Westminster Archives Centre
10 St Ann's Street, London SW1P 2DE
☎020 7641 5180/4879 (Minicom)
Fax 020 7641 5179
✉ archives@westminster.gov.uk
www.westminster.gov.uk/archives
OPEN 10.00 am to 7.00 pm Tuesday Wednesday, Thursday, 10.00 am to 5.00 pm Friday and Saturday (closed Monday)
ACCESS For reference
Comprehensive coverage of the history of Westminster and selective coverage of general London history. 22,000 books, together with a large stock of maps, prints, photographs, local newspapers, theatre programmes and archives.

Westminster Music Library
Victoria Library, 160 Buckingham Palace Road, London SW1W 9UD
☎020 7641 1300   Fax 020 7641 4281
✉ musiclibrary@westminster.gov.uk
www.westminster.gov.uk/libraries/special/music
OPEN 11.00 am to 7.00 pm Monday to Friday; 10 am to 5.00 pm Saturday
OPEN ACCESS
Located at Victoria Library, this is the largest public music library in the South of England, with extensive coverage of all aspects of music, including books, periodicals and printed scores. No recorded material, notated only. Lending library includes a small collection of CDs and videos.

Westminster Reference Library
35 St Martin's Street, London WC2H 7HP
☎020 7641 1300   Fax 020 7641 4606
✉ referencelibrarywc2@westminster.gov.uk
www.westminster.gov.uk/libraries
OPEN Main Library: 10.00 am to 8.00 pm Monday to Friday. Art & Design: 1.00 pm to 8.00 pm Monday to Friday; 10.00 am to 5.00 pm Saturday
ACCESS For reference only
A general reference library with emphasis on the following: Art & Design – fine and decorative arts, architecture, graphics and design; Performing Arts – theatre, cinema, radio, television and dance; Official Publications – major collection of HMSO publications from 1947, plus parliamentary papers dating back to 1906 (TSO subscription ceased April 2006); Business – UK directories, trade directories, company and market data; Periodicals – long files of many titles. One working day's notice is required for some government documents and most older periodicals. Extensive picture resource library.

The Wiener Library
4 Devonshire Street, London W1W 5BH
☎020 7636 7247   Fax 020 7436 6428
✉ info@wienerlibrary.co.uk
wienerlibrary.co.uk
Director *Ben Barkow*
Education and Outreach Coordinator *Katherine Klinger*
OPEN 10.00 am to 5.30 pm Monday to Friday

Access By letter of introduction (readers needing to use the Library for any length of time should become members)

Private library – one of the leading research centres on European history since the First World War, with special reference to the era of totalitarianism and to Jewish affairs. Founded by Dr Alfred Wiener in Amsterdam in 1933, it holds material that is not available elsewhere. Books, periodicals, press archives, documents, pamphlets, leaflets, photo archive, audiovisual material, brochures.

Vaughan Williams Memorial Library

English Folk Dance and Song Society, Cecil Sharp House, 2 Regent's Park Road, London NW1 7AY
☎020 7485 2206 ext. 33 Fax 020 7284 0523
✉ library@efdss.org
www.efdss.org

Contact *Malcolm Taylor*
Open 9.30 am to 5.30 pm Tuesday to Friday; 10.00 am to 4.00 pm 1st & 3rd Saturday (sometimes closed between 1.00 pm and 2.00 pm)

Access For reference to the general public, on payment of a daily fee; members may borrow books and use the library free of charge

A multimedia collection: books, periodicals, manuscripts, tapes, records, CDs, films, videos. Mostly British traditional culture and how this has developed around the world. Some foreign language material, and some books in English about foreign cultures. Also, the history of the English Folk Dance and Song Society.

Dr Williams's Library

14 Gordon Square, London WC1H 0AR
☎020 7387 3727
✉ enquiries@dwlib.co.uk
Open 10.00 am to 5.00 pm Monday, Wednesday, Friday; 10.00 am to 6.30 pm Tuesday and Thursday

Open access to reading room (loans restricted to subscribers). Visitors required to supply identification. Requests to see manuscripts and rare books must be made in advance; separate registration required. Annual subscription £10; ministers of religion and undergraduate students £5

Primarily a library of theology, religion and ecclesiastical history. Also philosophy, history (English and Byzantine). Particularly important for the study of English Nonconformity. Also

major manuscript collections. Trustees of Dr Williams's Library manage the Congregational Library on behalf of the Memorial Hall Trustees. The Dr Williams's Centre for Dissenting Studies is a collaboration with Queen Mary, University of London.

Wolverhampton Central Library

Snow Hill, Wolverhampton WV1 3AX
☎01902 552025 (lending)/552026 (reference)
Fax 01902 552024
✉ wolverhampton.libraries@dial.pipex.com
www.wolverhampton.gov.uk/libraries
Open 9.00 am to 7.00 pm Monday to Thursday; 9.00 am to 5.00 pm Friday and Saturday

Archives & Local Studies Collection

42–50 Snow Hill, Wolverhampton WV2 4AB
☎01902 552480
Open 10.00 am to 5.00 pm Monday, Tuesday, Friday, 1st and 3rd Saturday of each month; 10.00 am to 7.00 pm Wednesday; closed Thursday

General lending and reference libraries, plus children's library and audiovisual library holding cassettes, CDs, videos and music scores. Internet access.

The Women's Library

London Metropolitan University, Old Castle Street, London E1 7NT
☎020 7320 2222 Fax 020 7320 2333
✉ moreinfo@thewomenslibrary.ac.uk
www.thewomenslibrary.ac.uk
Director *Antonia Byatt*
Open Reading Room: 9.30 am to 5.00 pm Tuesday to Friday (8.00 pm Thursday); 10.00 am to 4.00 pm Saturday
Open access Exhibition: 9.30 am to 5.30 pm Monday to Friday (8.00 pm Thursday); 10.00 am to 4.00 pm Saturday

The Women's Library, national research library for women's history, is the UK's oldest and most comprehensive research library on all aspects of women in society, with both historical and contemporary coverage. The Library includes materials on feminism, work, education, health, the family, law, arts, sciences, technology, language, sexuality, fashion and the home. The main emphasis is on Britain but many other countries are represented, especially the Commonwealth and the developing countries. Established in 1926 as the library of the

London Society of Women's Service (formerly Suffrage), a non-militant organisation led by Millicent Fawcett. In 1953 the Society was renamed after her and the library became the Fawcett Library.

Collections include: women's suffrage, work, education, women and the church, the law, sport, art, music, abortion, prostitution. Mostly British materials but some American, Commonwealth and European works. Books, journals, pamphlets, archives, photographs, posters, postcards, audio-visual materials, artefacts, scrapbooks, albums and press cuttings dating mainly from the 19th century although some materials date from the 17th century.

The Library's new building, which opened in 2002, includes a reading room, exhibition space, café, education areas and a conference room, and is the cultural and research centre for anyone interested in women's lives and achievements.

Worcestershire Libraries and Information Service

Cultural Services, Worcestershire County Council, County Hall, Spetchley Road, Worcester WR5 2NP
☎01905 766231   Fax 01905 766244
✉ libraries@worcestershire.gov.uk
www.worcestershire.gov.uk/libraries

OPEN Opening hours vary in the 22 libraries, the History Centre and mobile libraries covering the county; all full-time libraries open at least one evening a week until 8.00 pm, and on Saturday until 5.30 pm; part-time libraries vary

ACCESS Information and reference services open to anyone; loans to members only (membership criteria: resident, being educated, working, or an elector in the county or neighbouring authorities; temporary membership to visitors. Proof of identity and address required. No charge for membership or for borrowing books.)

Information service, and reference and lending libraries. Non-fiction and fiction for all age groups, including normal and large print, spoken word cassettes, sound recordings (CD, cassette), videos, maps, local history, CD-ROMs for reference at main libraries, free public Internet access in all libraries. Joint Libraries Service/County Record Office History Centre with resources for local and family history. SPECIAL COLLECTIONS Carpets and Textiles; Needles & Needlemaking; Stuart Period; A.E. Housman.

John Wyndham Archive
See **Science Fiction Foundation Research Library**

York Central Library
Museum Street, York YO1 7DS
☎01904 655631   Fax 01904 611025
✉ reference.library@york.gov.uk

Lending Library
OPEN 9.30 am to 8.00 pm Monday, Tuesday, Friday; 9.30 am to 5.30 pm Wednesday and Thursday; 9.30 am to 4.00 pm Saturday

General lending library including videos, CDs, DVDs, CD-ROMs, music cassettes, audio books, children's storytapes language courses and printed music. Large print books. Photocopying, Internet and fax facilities.

Reference Library
OPEN 9.00 am to 8.00 pm Monday, Tuesday, Wednesday, Friday; 9.00 am to 5.30 pm Thursday; 9.00 am to 4.00 pm Saturday

General reference library; periodicals, newspapers, local newspaper index, EU information, organisations database; local studies library for York and surrounding area; business information service; microfilm/fiche readers for national and local newspapers; census returns and family history resource; general reference collection. Maintains strong links with other local history resource centres, namely the Borthwick Institute, York City Archive and York Minster Library. CD-ROM and Internet facilities. Room 18: IT resource centre available to the public. In addition, 14 branch libraries and one mobile, serving the City of York Council area.

Zoological Society Library
Regent's Park, London NW1 4RY
☎020 7449 6293   Fax 020 7586 5743
✉ library@zsl.org
www.zsl.org

OPEN 9.30 am to 5.30 pm Monday to Friday

ACCESS To members and staff; non-members by application

160,000 volumes on zoology including 5000 journals (1300 current) and a wide range of books on animals and particular habitats. Slide collection available and many historic zoological prints. Library catalogue available online (library.zsl.org).

Picture Libraries

Acme
See **Popperfoto.com**

actionplus sports images
54–58 Tanner Street, London SE1 3PH
☎020 7403 1558 Fax 020 7403 1526
✉ pictures@actionplus.co.uk
www.actionplus.co.uk

Founded 1986. Specialist sports and action library providing complete and creative international coverage of over 300 varieties of professional and amateur sport. Elite, junior, professional, amateur, extreme, disabled, minority, offbeat, major and minor events, adults, children, high and low, fast and slow. Millions of images covering over 30 years of sport.

Lesley & Roy Adkins Picture Library
Ten Acre Wood, Whitestone, Exeter EX4 2HW
☎01392 811357 Fax 01392 811435
✉ mail@adkinsarchaeology.com
www.adkinsarchaeology.com

Colour coverage of archaeology, antiquity, heritage and related subjects in the UK, Europe, Egypt and Turkey. Subjects include towns, villages, housing, landscape and countryside, churches, temples, castles, monasteries, art and architecture, gravestones and tombs, inscriptions, naval and nautical and antiquarian views. No service charge if pictures are used.

The Advertising Archive Limited
45 Lyndale Avenue, London NW2 2QB
☎020 7435 6540 Fax 020 7794 6584
✉ suzanne@advertisingarchives.co.uk
www.advertisingarchives.co.uk
Contacts *Suzanne Viner, Larry Viner*

With over one million images, the largest collection of British and American press ads, TV commercial stills and magazine cover illustrations in Europe. Material spans the period from 1850 to the present day. Expert in-house research; rapid service, competitive rates. On-line database and digital delivery available. Visitors by appointment.

akg-images Ltd, The Arts and History Picture Library
5 Melbray Mews, 158 Hurlingham Road, London SW6 3NS
☎020 7610 6103 Fax 020 7610 6125
✉ enquiries@akg-images.co.uk
www.akg-images.co.uk
Contact *Julia Engelhardt*

250,000 images online with direct access to ten million kept in the Berlin AKG Library. Specialises in art, archaeology, history, topography, music, personalities and film.

Bryan & Cherry Alexander Photography
Higher Cottage, Manston, Sturminster Newton DT10 1EZ
☎01258 473006 Fax 01258 473333
✉ alexander@arcticphoto.co.uk
www.arcticphoto.co.uk
Contact *Cherry Alexander*

Arctic and Antarctic specialists; indigenous peoples, wildlife and science in polar regions; Norway, Iceland, Siberia and Alaska.

Alpine Garden Society
AGS Centre, Avon Bank, Pershore WR10 3JP
☎01386 554790 Fax 01386 554801
✉ ags@alpinegardensociety.org
www.alpinegardensociety.org
Contact *Peter Sheasby*

Over 28,000 colour transparencies (35mm) covering plants in the wild from many parts of the world; particularly strong in plants from mountain and sub-alpine regions, and from Mediterranean climates; South Africa, Australia, Patagonia, California and the Mediterranean. Extensive coverage of show alpines in pots and in gardens and of European orchids. Full slide list available.

Alvey & Towers
The Springboard Centre, Mantle Lane, Coalville LE67 3DW
☎01530 450011 Fax 01530 450011
✉ office@alveyandtowers.com
www.alveyandtowers.com

Contact *Emma Rowen*

Houses one of the country's most comprehensive collections of transport images depicting not only actual transport systems but their surrounding industries as well. Also specialist modern railway image collection.

Andes Press Agency

26 Padbury Court, London E2 7EH
☎020 7613 5417 Fax 020 7739 3159
✉ apa@andespressagency.com
www.andespressagency.com

Contacts *Val Baker, Carlos Reyes*

80,000 colour transparencies and 300,000 b&w, specialising in social documentary, world religions, Latin America and Britain.

Heather Angel/Natural Visions

Highways, 6 Vicarage Hill, Farnham GU9 8HJ
☎01252 716700 Fax 01252 727464
✉ hangel@naturalvisions.co.uk
www.naturalvisions.co.uk

Contact *Heather Angel*

Constantly expanding worldwide natural history, wildlife and landscapes: polar regions, tropical rainforest flora and fauna, all species of plants and animals in natural habitats from Africa, Asia (notably China and Malaysia), Australasia, South America and USA, urban wildlife, pollution, biodiversity, global warming. Also worldwide gardens and cultivated flowers. Can send a digital lightbox to authors with an e-mail. The library then supplies high resolution digital files direct to the publisher.

Anova Books Images

151 Freston Road, London W10 6TH
☎020 7314 1400

One million photographs and illustrations, colour and b&w, on military, history, transport, cookery, crafts, natural history, space and travel.

Aquarius Library

PO Box 5, Hastings TN34 1HR
☎01424 721196 Fax 01424 717704
✉ aquarius.lib@clara.net
www.aquariuscollection.com

Contact *David Corkill*

A unique collection of film stills, star portraits and candids covering the entire history of the cinema to the present day. Available as high resolution downloads from the Aquarius Library website containing thousands of film and TV titles and over 100,000 high quality stills. Postal deliveries and free searches also available.

Architectural Association Photo Library

36 Bedford Square, London WC1B 3ES
☎020 7887 4066 Fax 020 7414 0782
✉ valerie@aaschool.ac.uk
www.aaschool.ac.uk/photlib

Contacts *Valerie Bennett, Sarah Franklin, Henderson Downing*

100,000 35mm transparencies on architecture, historical and contemporary. Archive of large-format b&w negatives from the 1920s and 1930s.

ArenaPAL

Lambert House, 55 Southwark Street, London SE1 1RU
☎020 7403 8542 Fax 020 7403 8561
✉ enquiries@arenapal.com
www.arenapal.com

'All the entertainment pictures you'll ever need.' Continually updated specialist performing arts image collection covering classical music, opera, theatre, musicals, film, pop, rock, jazz, instruments, festivals, venues, circus, ballet and contemporary dance, props and personalities. Over two million images from late 19th century onwards. Phone, fax or e-mail to make a selection.

ArkReligion.com

57 Burdon Lane, Cheam SM2 7BY
☎020 8642 3593 Fax 020 8395 7230
✉ images@artdirectors.co.uk
www.arkreligion.com

Contacts *Helene Rogers, Bob Turner*

Extensive coverage of all religions, including festivals.

The Art Archive

2 The Quadrant, 135 Salusbury Road, London NW6 6RJ
☎020 7624 3500 Fax 020 7624 3355
✉ info@picture-desk.com
www.picture-desk.com

Picture library holding over 80,000 high-resolution images covering fine art, history and ancient civilizations.

Art Directors & Trip Photo Library

57 Burdon Lane, Cheam SM2 7BY
☎020 8642 3593 Fax 020 8395 7230
✉ images@artdirectors.co.uk
www.artdirectors.co.uk

Contacts *Helene Rogers, Bob Turner*

Extensive coverage, with over 750,000 images, of all countries, lifestyles, peoples, etc. with detailed coverage of all religions. Backgrounds a speciality.

Aspect Picture Library Ltd

40 Rostrevor Road, London SW6 5AD
☎020 7736 1998/7731 7362
Fax 020 7731 7362
✉ Aspect.Ldn@btinternet.com
www.aspect-picture-library.co.uk

Colour and b&w worldwide coverage of countries, events, industry and travel, with large files on art, namely paintings, space, China, the Middle East, French villages, English villages and Ireland.

Australia Pictures

28 Sheen Common Drive, Richmond
TW10 5BN
☎020 7602 1989   Fax 020 7602 1989
✉ equilibrium.films@virgin.net

Contact *John Miles*

Collection of 4000 transparencies covering all aspects of Australia: Aboriginal people, paintings, Ayers Rock, Kakadu, Tasmania, underwater, reefs, Arnhem Land, Sydney. Also Africa, Middle East and Asia.

Aviation Picture Library

116 The Avenue, St Stephens, West Ealing, London W13 8JX
☎020 8566 7712/07860 670073 (mobile)
Fax 020 8566 7714
✉ avpix@aol.com
www.aviationpictures.com

Contact *Austin John Brown*

Specialists in the aviation field but also a general library which includes travel, architecture, transport, landscapes and skyscapes. SPECIAL COLLECTIONS aircraft and all aspects of the aviation industry, including the archival collection of John Stroud; aerial obliques of Europe, USA, Caribbean and West Africa; architectural and town planning. Photographers for *Flyer* magazine in the UK. Commissions undertaken on the ground and in the air.

aviation-images.com

42B Queens Road, London SW19 8LR
☎020 8944 5225   Fax 020 8944 5335
✉ pictures@aviation-images.com
www.aviation-images.com

Contacts *Mark Wagner, Steve Lake*

500,000+ aviation images, civil and military, archive and modern, from the world's best avi-

ation photographers. Member of **BAPLA** and RAeS.

Axel Poignant Archive

115 Bedford Court Mansions, Bedford Avenue, London WC1B 3AG
☎020 7636 2555   Fax 020 7636 2555
✉ Rpoignant@aol.com

Contact *Roslyn Poignant*

Anthropological and ethnographic subjects, especially Australia and the South Pacific. Also Scandinavia (early history and mythology), Sicily and England.

Barnaby's Photographic Library

See **Mary Evans Picture Library**

Barnardo's Photographic and Film Archive

Barnardo's House, Tanners Lane, Barkingside, Ilford IG6 1QG
☎020 8498 7345   Fax 020 8498 7090
✉ stephen.pover@barnardos.org.uk
www.barnardos.org.uk

Image Librarian *Stephen Pover*

The Barnardo's image archive is a unique resource of images of social history from 1872 to 1905. Images can be sent either by post, ISDN or e-mail. Office hours: Monday to Friday, 9.30 am to 4.30 pm.

Colin Baxter Photography Limited

Woodlands Industrial Estate, Grantown-on-Spey PH26 3NA
☎01479 873999   Fax 01479 873888
✉ sales@colinbaxter.co.uk
www.colinbaxter.co.uk

Contact *Mike Rensner* (Editorial)

Over 50,000 images specialising in Scotland. Also the Lake District, Yorkshire, France, Iceland and a special collection on Charles Rennie Mackintosh's work. Publishes guidebooks plus books, calendars, postcards and greetings cards on landscape, cityscape and natural history containing images which are primarily, but not exclusively, Colin Baxter's. Also publishers of the *Worldlife Library* of natural history books, and a range of books and stationery based on reproductons of the designs of Charles Rennie Mackintosh.

BBC Natural History Unit Picture Library

See **Nature Picture Library**

The Photographic Library Beamish, The North of England Open Air Museum

The North of England Open Air Museum, Beamish DH9 0RG
☎0191 370 4000 Fax 0191 370 4001
✉ museum@beamish.org.uk
www.beamish.org.uk

Comprehensive collection; images relate to the North East of England and cover agricultural, industrial, topography, advertising and shop scenes, people at work and play. On laser disk for rapid searching. Visitors by appointment weekdays.

Francis Bedford

See **Birmingham Library Services** under *Library Services*

Ivan J. Belcher Colour Picture Library

57 Gibson Close, Abingdon OX14 1XS
☎01235 521524 Fax 01235 521524
✉ ivan.belcher@tiscali.co.uk

Extensive colour picture library specialising in top-quality medium-format transparencies depicting the British scene. Particular emphasis on tourist, holiday and heritage locations, including famous cities, towns, picturesque harbours, rivers, canals, castles, cottages, rural scenes and traditions photographed throughout the seasons. Mainly of recent origin and constantly updated.

bfi Stills, Posters and Designs

British Film Institute, 21 Stephen Street, London W1T 1LN
☎020 7957 4797 Fax 020 7323 9260
✉ stills.films@bfi.org.uk
ww.bfi.org.uk/collections/stills/index.html

'*bfi* Stills, Posters and Designs is the world's most comprehensive collection of film and television images.' The collection captures on and off screen moments, portraits of the world's most famous stars – and those behind the camera who made them famous – as well as publicity posters, set designs, images of studios, cinemas, special events and early film and TV technologies. Rapid access to these images can be provided by photographic or digital reproduction. Visits by appointment only.

Anthony Blake Photo Library

20 Blades Court, Deodar Road, Putney, London SW15 2NU
☎020 8877 1123 Fax 020 8877 9787
✉ info@abpl.co.uk

www.abpl.co.uk

'Europe's premier source' of food and wine related images. From the farm and the vineyard to the plate and the bottle. Cooking and kitchens, top chefs and restaurants, country trades and markets, worldwide travel with an extensive Italian section. Many recipes available to accompany images.

Peter Boardman Collection

See **Chris Bonington Picture Library**

Chris Bonington Picture Library

Badger Hill, Hesket Newmarket, Wigton CA7 8LA
☎016974 78286 Fax 016974 78238
✉ frances@bonington.com
www.bonington.com

Contact *Frances Daltrey*

Based on the personal collection of climber and author Chris Bonington and his extensive travels and mountaineering achievements; also work by Doug Scott and other climbers, including the Peter Boardman and Joe Tasker Collections. Full coverage of the world's mountains, from British hills to Everest, depicting expedition planning and management stages, the approach march showing inhabitants of the area, flora and fauna, local architecture and climbing action shots on some of the world's highest mountains.

Boulton and Watt Archive

See **Birmingham Library Services** under *Library Services*

The Bridgeman Art Library

17–19 Garway Road, London W2 4PH
☎020 7727 4065 Fax 020 7792 8509
✉ london@bridgeman.co.uk
www.bridgemanart.co.uk

Head of Picture Research *Jenny Page*

Fine art photo archive acting as an agent to more than 1000 museums, galleries and picture owners around the world. Large-format colour transparencies of private collections, artists, paintings, sculptures, prints, manuscripts, antiquities and the decorative arts. The Library is currently expanding at the rate of 500 new images each week and has offices in Paris, New York and Berlin. Collections represented by the library include the British Library, the National Galleries of Scotland, the National Library of Australia, and the National Gallery of South Africa. Fully searchable catalogue online.

British Library Picture Library and Images Online/ Reproductions

British Library, 96 Euston Road, London NW1 2DB

Images Online

☎020 7412 7614 Fax 020 7412 7771

✉ imagesonline@bl.uk

www.bl.uk/imagesonline

Reproductions

☎01937 546060 Fax 01937 546333

✉ reproductions-customer-services@bl.uk

www.bl.uk/reproductions

The Picture Library holds a growing number of images from the British Library's collections of manuscripts, books, maps, music and philately. Transparencies and digital images are available for hire.

The fully searchable website, Images Online, includes images scanned from the Library's existing transparencies. High-resolution digital images are available on CD or delivered electronically.

Reproductions offers high quality paper copying, microfilming, photographic and digital services to customers who require copies from the following collection areas: Maps, Music, Printed Books, Manuscripts and the Asia, Pacific and Africa Collections. Copying service available; see Reproductions website for details.

Brooklands Museum Picture Library

Brooklands Museum, Brooklands Road, Weybridge KT13 0QN

☎01932 857381 Fax 01932 855465

✉ info@brooklandsmuseum.com

www.brooklandsmuseum.com

Contacts *John Pulford* (Curator of Collections), *Julian Temple* (Curator of Aviation)

About 40,000 b&w and colour prints and slides. Subjects include: Brooklands Motor Racing 1907–1939; British aviation and aerospace, 1908 to the present day, particularly BAC, Hawker, Sopwith and Vickers aircraft built at Brooklands.

Hamish Brown MBE, D.Litt, FRSGS Scottish Photographic

26 Kirkcaldy Road, Burntisland KY3 9HQ

☎01592 873546 Fax 01592 873546

Contact *Hamish Brown*

Coverage of most topics and areas of Scotland (sites, historic, buildings, landscape, mountains), also travel, mountains, general (50,000 items) and Morocco. Commissions undertaken.

Capital Pictures

85 Randolph Avenue, London W9 1DL

☎020 7286 2212 Fax 020 7286 1218

✉ sales@capitalpictures.com

www.capitalpictures.com

Contact *Phil Loftus*

Specialises in photographs of famous people from the worlds of showbusiness, rock and pop, television, politics, royalty and film stills.

The Centre for the Study of Cartoons and Caricature

The Templeman Library, University of Kent, Canterbury CT2 7NU

☎01227 823127 Fax 01227 823127

✉ N.P.Hiley@kent.ac.uk *or* J.M.Newton@kent.ac.uk

www.kent.ac.uk/cartoons

Contacts *Dr Nicholas Hiley, Jane Newton*

A national research archive of over 120,000 original cartoons and caricatures by 350 British cartoonists, supported by a library of books, papers, journals, catalogues, cuttings and assorted ephemera. A computer database of 120,000 cartoons provides quick and easy catalogued access via the Web. A source for exhibitions and displays as well as a picture library service. Specialises in historical, political and social cartoons from British newspapers.

Cephas Picture Library

A1 Kingsway Business Park, Oldfield Road, Hampton TW12 2HD

☎020 8979 8647 Fax 020 8941 4001

✉ pictures@cephas.com

www.cephas.com

The wine industry and vineyards of the world is the subject on which Cephas has made its reputation. 100,000 images make this one of the most comprehensive and up-to-date archive in Britain. Almost all wine-producing countries and all aspects of the industry are covered in depth. Spirits, beer and cider also included. A major food and drink collection now also exists, through preparation and cooking, to eating and drinking.

Giles Chapman Library

25 Homefield Road, Sevenoaks TN13 2DU

☎01732 452547

✉ chapman.media@virgin.net

www.gileschapman.com

Contact *Giles Chapman*

Some 150,000 colour and b&w images of cars

and motoring, from 1945 to the present day. No research fees.

Christian Aid Photo Section

PO Box 100, London SE1 7RT
☎020 7523 2232/5   Fax 020 7620 0719
✉ photos@christian-aid.org
www.christian-aid.org

Contacts *J. Cabon, B. Nicholson, C. Lands*

Pictures are mainly from Africa, Asia and Latin America, relating to small-scale, community-based programmes. Mostly development themes: health, agriculture, education, urban and rural life.

Christie's Images Ltd

1 Langley Lane, London SW8 1TJ
☎020 7582 1282   Fax 020 7582 5632
✉ imageslondon@christies.com
www.christiesimages.com

Contact *Mark Lynch*

The collection spans 80 categories representing every culture, from the distant past to the present day. An unrivalled collection from Old Masters to Impressionists and Twentieth Century master-pieces. Antiquities, Art Nouveau and Decorative Art, Books and Manuscripts, Contemporary Art and Furniture, Music and Movie Memorabilia, Textiles, Toys. Experienced researchers will search for specific requests.

The Cinema Museum

The Master's House, Old Lambeth Workhouse, 2 Dugard Way, off Renfrew Road, London SE11 4TH
☎020 7840 2200   Fax 020 7840 2299
✉ martin@cinemamuseum.org.uk *and* pixdesk@rgapix.com
www.ronaldgrantarchive.com

Colour and b&w coverage (including stills) of the motion picture industry throughout its history, including the Ronald Grant Archive. Smaller collections on theatre, variety, television and popular music.

John Cleare/Mountain Camera

Hill Cottage, Fonthill Gifford, Salisbury SP3 6QW
☎01747 820320   Fax 01747 820320
✉ cleare@btinternet.com
www.mountaincamera.com

Colour and b&w coverage of mountains and wild places, climbing, ski-touring, trekking, expeditions, wilderness travel, landscapes, people

and geographical features from all continents. Specialises in the Himalaya, Andes, Antarctic, Alps and the British countryside, and a range of topics from reindeer in Lapland to camels in Australia, from whitewater rafting in Utah to ski-mountaineering in China. Commissions and consultancy work undertaken. Researchers welcome by appointment. Member of **BAPLA** and the **OWG**.

Michael Cole Camerawork

The Coach House, 27 The Avenue, Beckenham BR3 5DP
☎020 8658 6120   Fax 020 8658 6120
✉ mikecole@dircon.co.uk

Contacts *Michael Cole, Derrick Bentley*

Probably the largest and most comprehensive collection of tennis pictures in the world. Over 50 years' coverage of the Wimbledon Championships. M.C.C. incorporates the tennis archives of Le Roye Productions, established in 1945. Picture requests and enquiries by e-mail.

Collections

13 Woodberry Crescent, London N10 1PJ
☎020 8883 0083   Fax 020 8883 9215
✉ collections@btinternet.com
www.collectionspicturelibrary.co.uk
www.collectionspicturelibrary.com

Contact *Simon Shuel*

Extensive coverage of the British Isles and Ireland, from the Shetlands to the Channel Islands and Connemara to East Anglia, including people, traditional customs, landscapes, buildings old and new – both well known and a bit obscure, 'plus a considerable collection of miscellaneous bits and pieces which defy logical filing'. Images supplied digitally or as original transparencies. Visitors welcome but please call first.

Corbis Images

111 Salusbury Road, London NW6 6RG
☎020 7644 7644   Fax 020 7644 7645
✉ sales.uk@corbis.com
www.corbis.com

A unique and comprehensive resource containing more than 65 million images, with over 2.1 million of them available online. The images come from professional photographers, museums, cultural institutions and public and private collections worldwide. Subjects include history, travel, celebrities, events, science, world art and cultures.

Sylvia Cordaiy Photo Library

45 Rotherstone, Devizes SN10 2DD
☎01380 728327 Fax 01380 728328
✉ info@sylvia-cordaiy.com
www.sylvia-cordaiy.com
www.alamy.com/sylviacordaiyphotolibrary

Over 170 countries on file from the obscure to main stock images – Africa, North, Central and South America, Asia, Atlantic, Indian and Pacific Ocean islands, Australasia, Europe, polar regions. Covers travel, architecture, ancient civilisations, world heritage sites, people worldwide, environment, wildlife, natural history, Antarctica, domestic pets, livestock, marine biology, veterinary treatment, equestrian, ornithology, flowers. UK files cover cities, towns villages, coastal and rural scenes, London collection. Transport, railways, shipping and aircraft (military and civilian). Aerial photography. Backgrounds and abstracts. Also the Paul Kaye B/W archive.

Country Images Picture Library

27 Camwood, Bamber Bridge, Preston
PR5 8LA
☎01772 321243 Fax 0870 137 8888
✉ terrymarsh@wpu.org.uk
www.countryimages.info

Contact *Terry Marsh*

35mm film and digital colour coverage of landscapes and countryside features generally throughout the UK (Cumbria, North Yorkshire, Lancashire, southern Scotland, Isle of Skye, St Kilda and Scottish islands, Wales, Cornwall), France (Alps, Pyrenees, Provence, Charente-Maritime, Hérault, Aube-en-Champagne, Loire valley, Somme), Madeira and Australia. Commissions undertaken.

Country Life Picture Library

King's Reach Tower, Stamford Street, London
SE1 9LS
☎020 7261 6337 Fax 020 7261 6216
✉ camilla_costello@ipcmedia.com
www.clpicturelibrary.co.uk

Contact *Camilla Costello*

Over 150,000 b&w negatives dating back to 1897, and 80,000 colour transparencies. Country houses, stately homes, churches and town houses in Britain and abroad, interiors of architectural interest (ceilings, fireplaces, furniture, paintings, sculpture), and exteriors showing many landscaped gardens, sporting and social events, crafts, people and animals. Visitors by appointment. Open Tuesday to Friday.

Philip Craven Worldwide Photo-Library

Surrey Studios, 21 Nork Way, Nork, Banstead
SM7 1PB
☎0870 220 2121
www.philipcraven.com

Contact *Philip Craven*

Extensive coverage of British scenes, cities, villages, English countryside, gardens, historic buildings and wildlife. Worldwide travel and wildlife subjects on medium and large-format transparencies.

Sue Cunningham Photographic

56 Chatham Road, Kingston upon Thames
KT1 3AA
☎020 8541 3024 Fax 020 8541 5388
✉ pictures@scphotographic.com
www.scphotographic.com

Contacts *Patrick Cunningham, Sue Cunningham*

Extensive coverage of many geographical areas: South America (especially Brazil), Eastern Europe from the Baltic to the Balkans, various African countries, Western Europe including the UK. Colour and b&w. Member of **BAPLA**.

Dale Concannon Collection

See **Phil Sheldon Golf Picture Library**

Dalton–Watson Collection

See **Ludvigsen Library**

The Defence Picture Library

14 Mary Seacole Road, The Millfields,
Plymouth PL1 3JY
☎01752 312061 Fax 01752 312063
✉ picdesk@defencepictures.com
www.defencepictures.com

Contacts *David Reynolds, Jessica Kelly, James Rowlands, Andrew Chittock*

Leading source of military photography covering all areas of the UK Armed Forces, supported by a research agency of facts and figures. More than one million images. Visitors welcome by appointment.

Douglas Dickins Photo Library

2 Wessex Gardens, Golders Green, London
NW11 9RT
☎020 8455 6221

Sole Proprietor *Douglas Dickins, FRPS*

Worldwide colour and b&w coverage, specialising in Asia, particularly India, Indonesia and Japan. *In Grandpa's Footsteps*, highly illustrated book of world travel published by The Book Guild in 2000.

Dominic Photography
4B Moore Park Road, London SW6 2JT
☎020 7381 0007   Fax 020 7381 0008
Contacts *Zoë Dominic, Catherine Ashmore*

Colour and b&w coverage of the entertainment world from 1957 onwards: dance, opera, theatre, ballet, musicals and personalities.

E&E Picture Library – Ecclesiastical and Eccentricities
Beggars Roost, Woolpack Hill, Brabourne Lees, Ashford TN25 6RR
☎01303 812608   Fax 01303 812608
✉ info@picture-library.freeserve.co.uk
www.eeimages.com
www.eeimages.co.uk
www.picture-library.freeserve.co.uk
Contact *Isobel Sinden*

World religion – the buildings, artefacts, clothes, festivals, clergy, arts, culture, history, pilgrimages – are the main subject areas of E&E, plus large collections of manuscripts, Bible lands, saints, stained glass, both religious and secular. Ancient images: buildings, stones, artefacts and also architecture worldwide. Death and commemorative, eccentricities such as symbols, carvings, follies, knights, signs, illustrations, anything unusual, festivals, heritage. Places from Guatemala to Japan. Nature, including wind, water, sunsets. Transport.

Patrick Eagar Photography
1 Queensberry Place, Richmond TW9 1NW
☎020 8940 9269   Fax 020 8332 1229
✉ patrick@patrickeagar.com
www.patrickeagar.com

The cricket library consists of Patrick Eagar's work over the last 30 years with coverage of over 290 Test matches worldwide, unique coverage of all eight World Cups, countless one-day internationals and player action portraits of over 2000 cricketers. The wine library consists of vineyards, grapes and festivals from Argentina to New Zealand. France and Australia are specialist areas. Photographs can be supplied by e-mail, on CD or DVD.

Ecoscene
Empire Farm, Throop Road, Templecombe BA8 0HR
☎01963 371700
✉ sally@ecoscene.com

www.ecoscene.com
Contact *Sally Morgan*

Expanding colour library of over 80,000 transparencies specialising in all aspects of the environment: pollution, conservation, recycling, restoration, wildlife (especially underwater), habitats, education, landscapes, industry and agriculture. All parts of the globe are covered with specialist collections covering Antarctica, Australia, North America. Sally Morgan, who runs the library, is a professional ecologist and expert source of information on all environmental topics. Photographic and writing commissions undertaken. Images delivered by e-mail or available for download.

Edifice
Cutterne Mill, Evercreech BA4 6LY
☎01749 831400
✉ info@edificephoto.com
www.edificephoto.com
Contacts *Philippa Lewis, Gillian Darley*

Colour material on exteriors of all possible types of building worldwide from grand landmarks to the small and simple. Specialists in domestic architecture, garden features, architectural detail, ornament, historical and period style, building materials and techniques. Website searchable online, but expert help and advice happily given over the phone or by e-mail.

Education Photos
April Cottage, Warners Lane, Albury Heath, Guildford GU5 9DE
☎01483 548031
✉ johnwalmsley@educationphotos.co.uk
www.educationphotos.co.uk

Formerly the John Walmsley Photo Library. Specialist library of learning/training/working subjects. Comprehensive coverage of learning environments such as playgroups, schools, colleges and universities. Images reflect a multiracial Britain. Commissions undertaken.

English Heritage Photo Library
Kemble Drive, Swindon SN2 2GZ
☎01793 414600   Fax 01793 414606
✉ photo.library@english-heritage.org.uk
www.english-heritage.org.uk
Contact *Celia Sterne*

Images of English castles, abbeys, houses, gardens, Roman remains, ancient monuments, battlefields, industrial and post-war buildings, interiors, paintings, artifacts, architectural details, conservation, archaeology, scenic views, landscapes.

Mary Evans Picture Library

59 Tranquil Vale, Blackheath, London SE3 0BS
☎020 8318 0034 Fax 020 8852 7211
✉ pictures@maryevans.com
www.maryevans.com

Historical archive of illustrations, photographs, prints and ephemera documenting all aspects of the past, from ancient times to the later decades of the 20th century. Subject areas: social and political history, portraits, events, transport, costume, trade and industry, places worldwide and natural history plus specialist material on folklore and paranormal phenomena. Notable collections include the Weimar Archive documenting the Third Reich and Barnaby's Photographic Library covering social scenes and events from the 1930s to the 1970s. MEPL's own material is complemented by many contributors such as Sigmund Freud Copyrights, the **Women's Library** (women's rights) and the Meledin Collection of 20th century Russian history. Over 150,000 images searchable online with 60,000 scanned in high-resolution for immediate download. Brochure on request. Founder member of **BAPLA**. Compilers of the *Picture Researcher's Handbook* by Pira International.

Exile Images

1 Mill Row, Brighton BN1 3SU
☎01273 208741 Fax 01273 382782
✉ pics@exileimages.co.uk
www.exileimages.co.uk

Contact *Howard Davies*

Online photo library with over 10,000 pictures of refugees, conflict, asylum seekers, UK protests and Third World issues. Picture editors can search and download high resolution photographs online.

Eye Ubiquitous

65 Brighton Road, Shoreham BN43 6RE
☎01273 440113 Fax 01273 440116
✉ library@eyeubiquitous.com
www.eyeubiquitous.com

General stock specialising in social documentary worldwide, and an extensive travel related collection.

Faces and Places

28 Sheen Common Drive, Richmond
TW10 5BN
☎020 7602 1989/07930 622964 (mobile)
✉ equilibrium.films@virgin.net *or*
john@facesandplacespix.com
www.facesandplacespix.com

Extensive worldwide library built up over 20 years which covers 40,000 photographs focusing mainly on travel, tourism, unusual locations, indigenous peoples, scenery and underwater photography; Australia, Tibet, Mali, Yemen and Iran.

Famous Pictures & Features Agency

13 Harwood Road, London SW6 4QP
☎020 7731 9333 Fax 020 7731 9330
✉ info@famous.uk.com
www.famous.uk.com

'Famous is a long-established celebrity features and pictures agency that has worked successfully for many years with writers who value our integrity and efficiency.' Represents top celebrity writers from the UK, LA, New York, Europe and Australia, syndicating their copy worldwide. 'We are always interested in new showbiz material, so please contact us if you are a journalist or freelancer looking to sell your celebrity interviews, features or gossip stories.'

ffotograff

10 Kyveilog Street, Pontcanna, Cardiff
CF11 9JA
☎029 2023 6879
✉ ffotograff@easynet.co.uk
www.ffotograff.com

Contact *Patricia Aithie*

Library and agency specialising in travel, exploration, the arts, architecture, traditional culture, archaeology and landscape. Based in Wales but specialising in the Middle and Far East; Africa, Central and South America; Yemen and Wales are strong aspects of the library. Churches and cathedrals of Britain and Crusader castles.

Financial Times Pictures

One Southwark Bridge, London SE1 9HL
☎020 7873 3671 Fax 020 7873 4606
✉ photosynd@ft.com

Contacts *Nicky Burr, Richard Pigden*

Photographs from around the world ranging from personalities in business, politics and the arts, people at work and other human interests and activities. '*FT* Graphics are outstanding in their ability to make complex issues comprehensible.' Delivery via ISDN or e-mail.

Fine Art Photographic Library Ltd

2A Milner Street, London SW3 2PU
☎020 7589 3127 Fax 020 7584 1944
✉ info@fineartphotolibrary.com
www.fineartphotolibrary.com

Over 30,000 large-format transparencies, with a specialist collection of 19th and 20th century paintings. CD-ROM available.

Firepix International

68 Arkles Lane, Anfield, Liverpool L4 2SP
☎0151 260 0111/0777 5930419 (mobile)
Fax 0151 260 0111
✉ info@firepix.com
www.firepix.com

Contact *Tony Myers*

The UK's only fire photo library. 23,000 images of fire-related subjects, firefighters, fire equipment manufacturers. Website contains 15 categories from industrial fire, domestic, digital images and abstract flame. Member of **BAPLA**.

Fogden Wildlife Photographs

16 Locheport, North Uist, Western Isles HS6 5EU
☎01876 580245   Fax 01876 580777
✉ susan.fogden@virgin.net
www.fogdenphotos.com

Contact *Susan Fogden*

Natural history collection, with special reference to rain forests and deserts. Emphasis on quality rather than quantity; growing collection of around 15,000 images.

Food Features

Stream House, West Flexford Lane, Wanborough, Guildford GU3 2JW
☎01483 810840   Fax 01483 811587
✉ frontdesk@foodpix.co.uk
www.foodpix.co.uk

Contacts *Steve Moss, Alex Barker*

Specialised high-quality food and drink photography, features and tested recipes. Clients' specific requirements can be incorporated into regular shooting schedules.

Forestry Commission Picture Library

231 Corstorphine Road, Edinburgh EH12 7AT
☎0131 314 6411
✉ neill.campbell@forestry.gsi.gov.uk
www.forestry.gov.uk/pictures

Contact *Neill Campbell*

The official image bank of the Forestry Commission, the library provides a single source for all aspects of forest and woodland management. The comprehensive subject list includes tree species, scenic landscapes, employment, wildlife, flora and fauna, conservation, sport and leisure.

Werner Forman Archive Ltd

36 Camden Square, London NW1 9XA
☎020 7267 1034   Fax 020 7267 6026
✉ wfa@btinternet.com
www.werner-forman-archive.com

Colour and b&w coverage of ancient civilisations, oriental and primitive societies around the world. A number of rare collections. Searchable website.

Formula One Pictures

2013 Pomaz, Buzavirag U.6. Hungary
☎00 36 26 322 826/07747 862606 (UK mobile)
✉ jt@f1pictures.com
www.f1pictures.com

Contact *John Townsend*

500,000 35mm colour slides, b&w and colour negatives and digital images of all aspects of Formula One Grand Prix racing including driver profiles and portraits.

Robert Forsythe Picture Library

16 Lime Grove, Prudhoe NE42 6PR
☎01661 834511   Fax 01661 834511
✉ robert@forsythe.demon.co.uk
www.forsythe.demon.co.uk

Contacts *Robert Forsythe, Fiona Forsythe*

30,000 transparencies of industrial and transport heritage; plus a unique collection of 100,000 items of related publicity ephemera from 1945. Image finding service available. Robert Forsythe is a transport/industrial heritage historian and consultant. Nationwide coverage, particularly strong on northern Britain. A bibliography of published material is available.

Fortean Picture Library

Henblas, Mwrog Street, Ruthin LL15 1LG
☎01824 707278   Fax 01824 705324
✉ janet.bord@forteanpix.demon.co.uk
www.forteanpix.demon.co.uk

Contact *Janet Bord*

30,000 colour and 45,000 b&w images: mysteries and strange phenomena worldwide, including ghosts, UFOs, witchcraft and monsters; also antiquities, folklore and mythology. Subject list available.

The Fotomas Index (UK)

12 Pickhurst Rise, West Wickham BR4 0AL
☎020 8776 2772   Fax 020 8776 2236
✉ fotomasindex@btconnect.com

Contact *John Freeman*

General historical collection, mostly pre-1900.

Subjects include London, topography, art, satirical, social and political history. Large portrait section.

The Francis Frith Collection
Frith's Barn, Teffont, Salisbury SP3 5QP
☎01722 716376 Fax 01722 716881
✉ julia_skinner@francisfrith.co.uk
www.francisfrith.co.uk
Contact *Julia Skinner*, Managing Editor

Publishers of *Frith's Photographic Memories* series of illustrated local books, all featuring nostalgic photographs from the archive, founded by Frith in 1860. The archive contains over 360,000 images of 7000 British towns.

John Frost Newspapers
See entry under *Library Services*

Andrew N. Gagg's Photo Flora
Town House Two, Fordbank Court, Henwick Road, Worcester WR2 5PF
☎01905 748515
✉ info@photoflora.co.uk
www.photoflora.co.uk
Contact *Andrew Gagg*

Specialist in British and European wild plants, flowers, ferns, grasses, trees, shrubs, etc. with colour coverage of most British and many European species (rare and common) and habitats; also travel in India, Sri Lanka, Nepal, Egypt and North Africa, China, Mexico, Thailand, Tibet, Vietnam and Cambodia.

Galaxy Picture Library
34 Fennels Way, Flackwell Heath, High Wycombe HP10 9BY
☎01628 521338 Fax 01628 520132
✉ robin@galaxypix.com
www.galaxypix.com
Contact *Robin Scagell*

Specialises in astronomy, space, telescopes, observatories, the sky, clouds and sunsets. Composites of foregrounds, stars, moon and planets prepared to commission. Editorial service available.

Garden and Wildlife Matters Photo Library
'Marlham', Henley's Down, Battle TN33 9BN
☎01424 830566 Fax 01424 830224
✉ gardens@gmpix.com
www.gardenmatters.uk.com
www.gmpix.com
Contact *Dr John Feltwell*

Collection of 110,000 6x4″ and 35mm images.

General gardening techniques and design; cottage gardens and USA designer gardens. 10,000 species of garden plants and over 1000 species of trees. Flowers, wild and house plants, trees and crops. Environmental, ecological and conservation pictures, including sea, air, noise and freshwater pollution, SE Asian and Central and South American rainforests; Eastern Europe, Mediterranean. Recycling, agriculture, forestry, horticulture and oblique aerial habitat shots from Europe and USA. Digital images supplied worldwide.

Garden Picture Library
Unit 12, Ransome's Dock, 35 Parkgate Road, London SW11 4NP
☎020 7228 4332 Fax 020 7924 3267
✉ info@gardenpicture.com
www.gardenpicture.com
Contact *Richard Keenan*

'Our inspirational images of gardens, plants and gardening lifestyle offer plenty of scope for writers looking for original ideas to write about.' The collection covers all garden related subjects; everything from plant portraits to floral graphics and garden design details to whole landscapes. Brings together the work of over 100 professional photographers from across the gardening globe. Holds approximately 400,000 fully captioned images of which around 35,000 are available digitally. In-house picture research can be undertaken on request or searches can be made online via keyword or subject category to create lightboxes which can be e-mailed or downloaded. Visitors to the library are welcome by appointment and copies of promotional literature are available on request.

Ed Geldard Photo Collection
9 Sunderland Bridge Village, Durham DH6 5HB
☎0191 378 2592
✉ ed@camera-one.freeserve.co.uk
Contact *Ed Geldard*

Approximately 25,000 colour transparencies and b&w negs, all by Ed Geldard, specialising in mountain landscapes: particularly the mountain regions of the Lake District, and the Yorkshire limestone areas, from valley to summit. Commissions undertaken. Books published: *Wainwright's Tour of the Lake District*; *Wainwright in the Limestone Dales*; *The Lake District*.

Genesis Space Photo Library
20 Goodwood Park Road, Bideford EX39 2RR
☎01237 477883

✉ tim@spaceport.co.uk
www.spaceport.co.uk
Contact *Tim Furniss*
Contemporary and historical colour and b&w spaceflight collection including rockets, spacecraft, spacemen, Earth, moon and planets. Catalogue of 775 images on website.

Geo Aerial Photography

4 Christian Fields, London SW16 3JZ
☎020 8764 6292/0115 981 9418 Fax 020 8764 6292/0115 981 9418
✉ geo.aerial@geo-group.co.uk
www.geo-group.co.uk
Contact *Kelly White*
Established 1990 and now a growing collection of aerial oblique photographs from the UK, Scandinavia, Asia and Africa – landscapes, buildings, industrial sites, etc. Commissions undertaken.

GeoScience Features

6 Orchard Drive, Wye TN25 5AU
☎01233 812707 Fax 01233 812707
✉ gsf@geoscience.demon.co.uk
www.geoscience.demon.co.uk
Fully computerised and comprehensive library containing the world's principal source of volcanic phenomena. Extensive collections, providing scientific detail with technical quality, of rocks, minerals, fossils, microsections of botanical and animal tissues, animals, biology, birds, botany, chemistry, earth science, ecology, environment, geology, geography, habitats, landscapes, macro/microbiology, peoples, sky, weather, wildlife and zoology. Over 450,000 original colour transparencies in medium and 35mm-format. Subject lists and CD-ROM catalogue available. Incorporates the RIDA photolibrary and Landform Slides.

Geoslides Photography

4 Christian Fields, London SW16 3JZ
☎020 8764 6292/0115 981 9418
Fax 020 8764 6292/0115 981 9418
✉ geoslides@geo-group.co.uk
www.geo-group.co.uk
Contact *John Douglas*
Established in 1968. Landscape and human interest subjects from the Arctic, Antarctica, Scandinavia, UK, Africa (south of Sahara), Middle East, Asia (south and southeast). Also specialist collections of images from British India (the Raj) and Boer War.

Getty Images

101 Bayham Street, London NW1 0AG
☎0800 376 7981 Fax 020 7544 3334
✉ sales@gettyimages.com
www.gettyimages.com
Contact *Sales Department*
'Getty Images is the world's leading imagery company, creating and providing the largest collection of still and moving images to communication professionals around the globe. From sports and news photography to archival and contemporary imagery, Getty Images' products are found each day in newspapers, magazines, advertising, films, television, books and websites.' For those who wish to commission photographers to fulfil specific needs, the company maintains a full-service department for custom-shot images.

Martin and Dorothy Grace

Boxwood Cottage, The Row, Lyth, Kendal LA8 8DD
☎01539 568569
✉ graces@lineone.net
Colour coverage of Britain's natural history, specialising in trees, shrubs and wild flowers. Also ferns, birds and butterflies, habitats, landscapes, ecology.

Ronald Grant Archive

See **The Cinema Museum**

Sally and Richard Greenhill

357 Liverpool Road, London N1 1NL
☎020 7607 8549 Fax 020 7607 7151
✉ sr.greenhill@virgin.net
www.srgreenhill.co.uk
Photo Librarian *Denise Lalonde*
Social documentary photography in colour and b&w of working lives: pregnancy and birth, child development, education, work, old people, medical, urban. Also Modern China, 1971 to the present; most London statues. Some material from Borneo, USA, India, Israel, Philippines and Sri Lanka.

V.K. Guy Ltd

Silver Birches, Troutbeck, Windermere LA23 1PN
☎015394 33519 Fax 015394 32971
✉ vic@vkguy.co.uk
www.vkguy.co.uk
Contacts *Vic Guy, Mike Guy, Paul Guy, Nicola Simon*

25,000 5x4″ UK and Ireland scenic transparencies from Shetland in the north to the Channel Isles in the south, suitable for tourism brochures, calendars, etc. Can be supplied digitally and browsed through via the online database. Colour catalogue also available.

Angela Hampton 'Family Life Picture Library'

Holly Tree House, The Street, Walberton, Arundel BN18 0PH
☎01243 555952 Fax 01243 555952
✉ aham@flpics.co.uk

Contact *Angela Hampton*

Specialist library of over 100,000 images on all aspects of contemporary lifestyle, including pregnancy, childbirth, babies, children, parenting, behaviour, education, medical, holidays, pets, family life, relationships, teenagers, women and men's health, over-50s and retirement. Also domestic and farm animal life. Environmental and travel. Commissions undertaken. Offers fully illustrated text packages on most subjects and welcomes ideas for collaboration from writers with proven, successful background.

Tom Hanley

41 Harefield, Esher KT10 9TG
☎020 8972 9165 Fax 020 8972 9164
✉ Tomhanley31@hotmail.com

Colour and b&w coverage of London, England, Europe, Canada, India, the Philippines, Brazil, China, Japan, Korea, Taiwan, the Seychelles, Cayman Islands, USA. Also pop artists of the 1960s, First World War trenches, removal of London Bridge to America, and much more. Current preoccupation with Greece, Turkey, Spain and Egypt, ancient and modern.

Robert Harding Picture Library

58–59 Great Marlborough Street, London W1F 7JY
☎020 7478 4000 Fax 020 7478 4161
✉ info@robertharding.com
www.robertharding.com

A leading source of stock photography with over two million colour images covering a wide range of subjects – worldwide travel and culture, geography and landscapes, people and lifestyle, architecture, business and industry, medicine, sports, food and drink. Rights protected and royalty-free images. Can supply images as transparencies, on CD or ISDN. Visitors welcome; telephone or visit the website.

Dennis Hardley Photography, Scottish Photo Library

Rosslynn, Benderloch, Oban PA37 1ST
☎01631 720434 Fax 01631 720434
✉ dennis.hardley@btinternet.com
www.scotphoto.com

Contacts *Dennis Hardley, Tony Hardley*

Established 1974. About 30,000 images (6x7″, 6x9″ format colour transparencies) of Scotland: castles, historic, scenic landscapes, islands, transport, etc. Also English views – Liverpool, Chester, Bath, Weston Super Mare, Sussex, Somerset and Cambridge.

Jim Henderson Photography

Crooktree, Kincardine O'Neil, Aboyne AB34 4JD
☎01339 882149 Fax 01339 882149
✉ JHende7868@aol.com
www.jimhendersonphotography.com

Contact *Jim Henderson*

Scenic and general activity coverage of north east Scotland (Aberdeenshire) and Highlands for tourist, holiday and activity illustration. Specialist collection of over 300 Aurora Borealis displays from 1989–2005 on Royal Deeside and co-author of *The Aurora* (pub. 1997). Author and photographer for *Aberdeen* and *Aberdeen & Royal Deeside* titles for Aberdeen Journals. Recent images of ancient Egyptian sites: Cairo through to Abu-Simbel. **BAPLA** and Alamy member. Commissions undertaken.

John Heseltine Archive

Mill Studio, Frogmarsh Mill, South Woodchester GL5 5ET
☎01453 873792
✉ john@heseltine.co.uk
www.heseltine.co.uk

Contact *John Heseltine*

Over 200,000 colour transparencies and digital files of landscapes, architecture, food and travel with particular emphasis on Italy and the UK.

Christopher Hill Photographic

17 Clarence Street, Belfast BT2 8DY
☎028 9024 5038 Fax 028 9023 1942
✉ sales@scenicireland.com
www.scenicireland.com

Contact *Christopher Hill*

A comprehensive collection of scenic landscapes of Ireland. Every aspect of Irish life is shown, concentrating on the positive. Also large miscellaneous section. The website contains over 7000 images available to buy online.

Hobbs Golf Collection

5 Winston Way, New Ridley, Stocksfield
NE43 7RF
☎01661 842933 Fax 01661 842933
✉ info@hobbsgolfcollection.com
www.hobbsgolfcollection.com

Contact *Margaret Hobbs*

Specialist golf collection: players, courses, art, memorabilia and historical topics (1300–present). 40,000+ images, mainly 35mm colour transparencies and b&w prints. Commissions undertaken. Author of 30 golf books.

David Hoffman Photo Library

c/o BAPLA, 18 Vine Hill, London
EC1R 5DZ
☎020 8981 5041
✉ info@hoffmanphotos.com
www.hoffmanphotos.com

Contact *David Hoffman*

Commissioned photography and stock library with a strong emphasis on social issues built up from 35mm journalistic and documentary work dating from the late 1970s. Files on drugs and drug use, policing, disorder, riots, youth, prostitution, protest, homelessness, housing, environmental demonstrations and events, waste disposal, alternative energy, industry and pollution. Wide range of images especially from UK and Europe but also USA, Canada, Venezuela, Mexico and Thailand. General files on topical issues and current affairs plus specialist files from leisure cycling to local authority services. Many photographs available for online delivery from www.alamy.com/davidhoffman

Holt Studios International Ltd

See **Frank Lane Picture Agency Ltd**

Houghton's Horses/ Kit Houghton Photography

Radlet Cottage, Spaxton, Bridgwater
TA5 1DE
☎01278 671362 Fax 01278 671739
✉ kit@enterprise.net
www.houghtonshorses.com

Contacts *Kit Houghton, Debbie Cook*

Specialist equestrian library of over 300,000 transparencies and digital images on all aspects of the horse world, with images ranging from the romantic to the practical, step-by-step instructional and competition pictures in all equestrian disciplines worldwide. Online picture delivery. Commissions undertaken.

Chris Howes/Wild Places Photography

PO Box 100, Abergavenny NP7 9WY
☎01873 737707 Fax 08717 505277
✉ photos@wildplaces.co.uk

Contacts *Chris Howes, Judith Calford*

Expanding collection of over 50,000 colour transparencies, b&w prints and digital photos covering travel, topography and natural history worldwide, plus action sports such as climbing. Supply now fully digital. SPECIALIST AREAS include caves, caving and mines (with historical coverage using engravings and early photographs), wildlife, landscapes and the environment, including pollution and conservation. Europe (including Britain), USA, Africa and Australia are all well represented within the collection. Commissions undertaken.

Huntley Film Archive

22 Islington Green, London N1 8DU
☎020 7226 9260 Fax 020 7359 9337
✉ films@huntleyarchives.com
www.huntleyarchives.com

Contact *Amanda Huntley*

Originally a private collection, the library is now a comprehensive archive of rare and vintage documentary film dating from 1895. 50,000 films on all subjects of a documentary nature. Online catalogue available.

Jacqui Hurst

66 Richford Street, Hammersmith, London
W6 7HP
☎020 8743 2315/07970 781336 (mobile)
✉ jacquih@dircon.co.uk
www.jacquihurstphotography.co.uk

Contact *Jacqui Hurst*

A specialist library of traditional and contemporary applied arts, regional food producers and markets. The photos form illustrated essays of how something is made and finish with a still life of the completed object. The collection is always being extended and a list is available on request. Commissions undertaken.

Hutchison Picture Library

65 Brighton Road, Shoreham-by-Sea
BN43 6RE
☎01273 440113
✉ library@hutchisonpictures.co.uk
www.hutchisonpictures.co.uk

Worldwide contemporary images from the straight-forward to the esoteric and quirky. Over half a million documentary colour photographs on file, covering people, places, customs and faiths, agriculture, industry and transport. SPECIAL COLLECTIONS include the environment and climate, family life (including pregnancy and birth), ethnic minorities worldwide (including Disappearing World archive), conventional and alternative medicine, and music around the world. Search service available.

Illustrated London News Picture Library
20 Upper Ground, London SE1 9PF
☎020 7805 5585 Fax 020 7805 5905
✉ research@ilnpictures.co.uk
www.ilnpictures.co.uk

Engravings, photographs and illustrations from 1842 to the present day, taken from magazines published by Illustrated Newspapers: *Illustrated London News*; *Graphic*; *Sphere*; *Tatler*; *Sketch*; *Illustrated Sporting and Dramatic News*; *Illustrated War News 1914–18*; *Bystander*, *Britannia & Eve*. Social history, London, Industrial Revolution, wars, travel. Visitors occasionally admitted by appointment. Research and scanning services available.

Images of Africa Photobank
11 The Windings, Lichfield WS13 7EX
☎01543 262898 Fax 01543 417154
✉ info@imagesofafrica.co.uk
www.imagesofafrica.co.uk
Contact *David Keith Jones, FRPS*

Over 135,000 images covering Botswana, Chad, Egypt, Ethiopia, Kenya, Lesotho, Madagascar, Malawi, Morocco, Namibia, Rwanda, South Africa, Swaziland, Tanzania, Uganda, Zaire, Zambia, Zanzibar and Zimbabwe. 'Probably the best collection of photographs of Kenya in Europe.' A wide range of topics covered. Strong on African wildlife with over 80 species of mammals including sequences showing action and behaviour. Popular animals like lions and elephants covered in encyclopædic detail. More than 100 species of birds and many reptiles included. Other strengths: National Parks and reserves, natural beauty, tourism facilities, traditional and modern people. Most work is by David Keith Jones, FRPS; several other photographers are represented. An attractive colour brochure is available. The Library offers next day delivery by post or same day by e-mail when requested.

Imperial War Museum Photograph Archive
All Saints Annexe, Austral Street, London SE11 4SJ

☎020 7416 5333 Fax 020 7416 5355
✉ photos@iwm.org.uk
www.iwm.org.uk

A national archive of ten million photographs illustrating all aspects of 20th and 21st century conflict. Emphasis on the two world wars but includes material from other conflicts involving Britain and the Commonwealth. Majority of material is b&w, although holdings of colour material increases with more recent conflicts. Visitors welcome by appointment, Monday to Friday, 10.00 am. to 5.00 pm.

International Photobank
Unit D1, Roman Hill Business Park, Broadmayne DT2 8LY
☎01305 854145 Fax 01305 853065
✉ peter@internationalphotobank.co.uk
www.internationalphotobank.co.uk
Contacts *Peter Baker, Gary Goodwin*

Over 450,000 transparencies, partly medium-format. Colour coverage of travel subjects: places, people, folklore, events. Digital broadband service available for newspapers, magazines and other users. Pictures can also be selected from the comprehensive website.

Robbie Jack Photography
45 Church Road, Hanwell, London W7 3BD
☎020 8567 9616 Fax 020 8567 9616
✉ robbie@robbiejack.com
www.robbiejack.com
Contact *Robbie Jack*

Built up over the last 23 years, the library contains over 400,000 colour images of the performing arts – theatre, dance, opera and music. Includes West End shows, the RSC and Royal National Theatre productions, English National Opera and Royal Opera. The dance section contains images of the Royal Ballet, English National Ballet, the Rambert Dance Company, plus many foreign companies. Also holds the largest selection of colour material from the Edinburgh International Festival. Researchers are welcome to visit by appointment. From 2001 began offering colour transparencies as digital images which are being added to on a daily basis.

Jayawardene Travel Photo Library
7A Napier Road, Wembley HA0 4UA
☎020 8795 3581 Fax 020 8795 4083
✉ jaytravelphotos@aol.com
www.jaytravelphotos.com
Contact *Rohith Jayawardene*

160,000 travel and travel-related images – digital and original transparencies. Many places photographed in depth, with more than 800 pictures per country. Over 7000 images available online.

David King Collection
90 St Pauls Road, London N1 2QP
☎020 7226 0149 Fax 020 7354 8264
✉ davidkingcollection@btopenworld.com
www.davidkingcollection.com
Contact *David King*

250,000 b&w original and copy photographs and colour transparencies of historical and present-day images. Russian history and the Soviet Union from 1900 to the fall of Khrushchev; the lives of Lenin, Trotsky and Stalin; the Tzars, Russo-Japanese War, 1917 Revolution, World War I, Red Army, the Great Purges, Great Patriotic War, etc. SPECIAL COLLECTIONS on China, Eastern Europe, the Weimar Republic, John Heartfield, American labour struggles, Spanish Civil War. Open to qualified researchers by appointment, Monday to Friday, 10.00 am to 6.00 pm. Staff will undertake research; negotiable fee for long projects. David King's latest photographic books: *The Commissar Vanishes*, documenting the falsification of photographs and art in Stalin's Russia, and *Ordinary Citizens*, mugshots of victims shot without trial from the archives of Stalin's secret police. Soviet posters from the David King Collection are on display throughout 2006 at Tate Modern, London.

The Kobal Collection
2 The Quadrant, 135 Salusbury Road, London NW6 6RJ
☎020 7624 3500 Fax 020 7624 3355
✉ info@picture-desk.com
www.picture-desk.com

Picture library holding colour and b&w coverage of Hollywood films, portraits, stills, publicity shots, posters and ephemera.

Kos Picture Source Ltd
7 Spice Court, Ivory Square, Plantation Wharf, London SW11 3UE
☎020 7801 0044 Fax 020 7801 0055
✉ images@kospictures.com
www.kospictures.com
Contact *Chris Savage*

Specialists in water-related images including international yacht racing and cruising, classic boats and superyachts, and extensive range of watersports. Also worldwide travel including seascapes, beach scenes, underwater photography and the weather.

Ed Lacey Collection
See **Phil Sheldon Golf Picture Library**

Landform Slides
See **GeoScience Features**

Frank Lane Picture Agency Ltd
Pages Green House, Wetheringsett, Stowmarket IP14 5QA
☎01728 860789 Fax 01728 860222
✉ pictures@flpa-images.co.uk
www.flpa-images.co.uk

Colour coverage of natural history, environment, pets and weather. Represents Sunset from France, Foto Natura from Holland, Minden Pictures from the US, Holt Studios and works closely with Eric and David Hosking, plus 270 freelance photographers. Website with 80,000 images.

Last Resort Picture Library
Manvers Studios, 12 Ollerton Road, Tuxford, Newark NG22 0LF
☎01777 870166 Fax 01777 871739
✉ LRPL@dmimaging.co.uk
www.dmimaging.co.uk
Contacts *Jo Makin, Dick Makin*

Subject areas include agriculture, architecture, IT, education, food, industry, landscapes, people at work, skiing, trees, flowers. Images cover a wide variety of topics, ranging from the everyday to the obscure. 'Bespoke service available through our linked photographic studio. Contact us for details.'

LAT Photographic
Teddington Studios, Broom Road, Teddington TW11 9BE
☎020 8251 3000 Fax 020 8251 3001
✉ lat.photo@haynet.com
www.latphoto.co.uk
Contact *Zoë Mayho*

Motor sport collection of over nine million images dating from 1895 to the present day.

Lebrecht Music and Arts
58b Carlton Hill, London NW8 0ES
☎020 7625 5341/7372 8233
Fax 020 7625 5341
✉ pictures@lebrecht.co.uk
www.lebrecht.co.uk
Contact *Elbie Lebrecht*

Classical music, opera, jazz, rock, musicians, instruments, performers, writers, artists, architects, sculptors, historical personalities, politicians, society and glamorous showbusiness personalities.

The Erich Lessing Archive of Fine Art & Culture

c/o ak-images Ltd, The Arts and History Picture Library, 5 Melbray Mews, 158 Hurlingham Road, London SW6 3NS
☎020 7610 6103   Fax 020 7610 6125
✉ enquiries@akg-images.co.uk
www.akg-images.co.uk

Top quality high resolution scans depicting the contents of many of the world's finest art galleries as well as ancient archaeological and biblical sites available in the UK via the akg-images website.

Lindley Library, Royal Horticultural Society

80 Vincent Square, London SW1P 2PE
☎020 7821 3051   Fax 020 7821 3022
Contact *Picture Librarian*

22,000 original drawings and approx. 8000 books with hand-coloured plates of botanical illustrations. Appointments are necessary to visit the collection; all photography is carried out by their own photographer.

Link Picture Library

41A The Downs, London SW20 8HG
☎07947 884517
✉ library@linkpicturelibrary.com
www.linkpicturelibrary.com
Contact *Orde Eliason*

100,000 images of South Africa, India, China, Vietnam and Israel. A more general collection of colour transparencies from 100 countries worldwide. Link Picture Library has an international network and can source material not in its file from Japan, Scandinavia, India and South Africa. Original photographic commissions undertaken.

London Aerial Photo Library

Studio D1, Fairoaks Airport, Chobham, Woking GU24 8HU
☎01276 855997/855344   Fax 01276 855455
✉ info@londonaerial.co.uk
www.londonaerial.co.uk
www.flightimages.com
Contact *Amanda Campbell*
Librarian *Glyn Tassell*

Extensive collections of aerial imagery. 450,000

images including continually updated photography of London plus excellent coverage of the UK in general. Covers landmarks, industrial/ retail properties, sporting venues football stadiums, conceptual shots. Library searches by expert staff, free of charge. Selection of digital images also available via website. Commissioned photography undertaken.

London Metropolitan Archives

40 Northampton Road, London EC1R 0HB
☎020 7332 3820   Fax 020 7833 9136
✉ ask.lma@cityoflondon.gov.uk
www.cityoflondon.gov.uk/lma
Contact *The Enquiry Team*

London Metropolitan Archives (LMA) is the largest local authority record office in the UK. Holds over 32 miles of archives – an enormous amount of information about the capital and its people. These include records of London government, hospitals, charities, businesses and parish churches. Types of record range from books and manuscript documents to photographs, maps and drawings. 'Nearly 900 years of London history can be brought to life at LMA.' There is also a 100,000 volume reference library specialising in London history. See entry under *Library Services*.

London's Transport Museum Photographic Library

39 Wellington Street, London WC2E 7BB
☎020 7379 6344   Fax 020 7565 7252
✉ photo@ltmuseum.co.uk
www.ltmuseum.co.uk
Contacts *Hugh Robertson, Simon Murphy*

Around 100,000 b&w images from the 1860s and 20,000 colour images from c.1975. SPECIALIST COLLECTIONS Poster archive, Underground construction, corporate design and architecture, street scenes, London Transport during the war. Collection available for viewing by appointment on Monday and Tuesday. No loans system but prints and transparences can be purchased. Digital images available on CD-ROM.

Ludvigsen Library

Scoles Gate, Hawkedon, Bury St Edmunds IP29 4AU
☎01284 789246   Fax 01284 789246
✉ library@ludvigsen.com
www.ludvigsen.com
Contact *Karl Ludvigsen*

Extensive information research facilities for writers and publishers. Approximately 400,000 images (both b&w and many colour transparencies) of automobiles and motorsport, from 1890s through 1980s. Glass plate negatives from the early 1900s; Formula One, Le Mans, motor car shows, vintage, antique and classic cars from all countries. Includes the Dalton-Watson Collection and the work of noted photographers such as John Dugdale, Edward Eves, Peter Keen, Max le Grand, Karl Ludvigsen, Rodolfo Mailander, Ove Nielsen, Stanley Rosenthall and others.

MacQuitty International Photographic Collection

7 Elm Lodge, River Gardens, Stevenage Road, London SW6 6NZ
☎020 7385 5606   Fax 020 7385 5606
✉ miranda.macquitty@btinternet.com
Contact *Dr Miranda MacQuitty*

Colour and b&w collection on aspects of life in over 70 countries: dancing, music, religion, death, archaeology, buildings, transport, food, drink, nature. Visitors by appointment.

Magnum Photos Ltd

Ground Floor, 63 Gee Street, London EC1V 3RS
☎020 7490 1771   Fax 020 7608 0020
✉ magnum@magnumphotos.co.uk
www.magnumphotos.com
Head of Library *Nick Galvin*

Founded 1947 by Cartier Bresson, George Rodger, Robert Capa and David 'Chim' Seymour. Represents over 70 of the world's leading photo-journalists. Coverage of all major world events from the Spanish Civil War to present day. Also a large collection of travel images and personalities.

The Raymond Mander & Joe Mitchenson Theatre Collection

Jerwood Library of the Performing Arts, Trinity College of Music, King Charles Court, Old Royal Naval College, London SE10 9JF
☎020 8305 4426   Fax 020 8305 9426
✉ rmangan@tcm.ac.uk
www.mander-and-mitchenson.co.uk
Contact *Richard Mangan*

Enormous collection covering all aspects of the theatre: plays, actors, dramatists, music hall, theatres, singers, composers, etc. Visitors welcome by appointment.

The Roger Mann Collection

Wensley Court, 48 Barton Road, Torquay TQ1 4DW
☎01803 323868   Fax 01803 616448
✉ rogermann48bart@aol.com
www.therogermanncollection.co.uk
Contact *R. F. Mann*

Comprehensive collection of cricket photographs covering the period 1750 to 1945. The photographs feature most of the first-class players, teams, Test match action and overseas tours of the period. This collection includes almost 2000 original match scorecards, cartoons, images, prints, postcards, cigarette cards, letters and the personal memorabilia of many of the best-known players of the time. Also some coverage of the period 1946 to 1970.

S&O Mathews Photography

Little Pitt Place, Brighstone, Isle of Wight PO30 4DZ
☎01983 741098
✉ oliver@mathews-photography.com
www.mathews-photography.com

Specialist stock library of fine photographs of botanical and horticultural subjects, plants, plant portraits and plant associations, as well as gardens, including views, details and features.

Institution of Mechanical Engineers

1 Birdcage Walk, London SW1H 9JJ
☎020 7973 1274   Fax 020 7222 8762
✉ library@imeche.org.uk
www.imeche.org.uk

Historical images and archives on mechanical engineering. Open 9.15am to 5.30pm, Monday to Friday. Telephone for appointment.

Meledin Collection

See **Mary Evans Picture Library**

The MerseySlides Collection

See **Tropix Photo Library**

Lee Miller Archives

Farley Farm House, Chiddingly, Near Lewes BN8 6HW
☎01825 872691   Fax 01825 872733
✉ archives@leemiller.co.uk
www.leemiller.co.uk

The work of Lee Miller (1907–77). As a photojournalist she covered the war in Europe from early in 1941 to VE Day with further reporting from the Balkans. Collection includes photographic portraits of prominent Surrealist artists: Ernst, Eluard, Miró, Picasso, Penrose, Carrington, Tanning, and others. Surrealist and contemporary art, poets and writers, fashion, the Middle East, Egypt, the Balkans in the 1930s, London during the Blitz, war in Europe and the liberation of Dachau and Buchenwald.

Mirrorpix
21 Bruton Street, London W1J 6QD
☎020 7293 3700 Fax 020 7293 0357
✉ desk@mirrorpix.com
www.mirrorpix.com
Commercial Director *John Churchill*
Account Manager *Lisa Rayman*

'For over 100 years the photographers and journalists of the *Daily Mirror* and its sister titles have recorded both the light and dark sides of British life in startling detail. The people, places, events and movements that have shaped modern Britain can be researched and located in our comprehensive editorial and pictorial archives.'

Monitor Picture Library
The Forge, Roydon, Harlow CM19 5HH
☎01279 792700 Fax 01279 792600
✉ info@monitorpicturelibrary.com
www.monitorpicturelibrary.com

Colour and b&w coverage of 1960s, '70s and '80s personalities and celebrities from: music, entertainment, sport, politics, royals, judicial, commerce etc. Specialist files on Lotus cars. Syndication to international, national and local media.

Moroccan Scapes
Seend Park, Seend SN12 6NZ
☎01380 828533 Fax 01380 828630
✉ chris@realmorocco.com
www.realmorocco.com
Contact *Chris Lawrence*

Specialist collection of Moroccan material: scenery, towns, people, markets and places, plus the Atlas Mountains. Over 18,000 images.

Motoring Picture Library
National Motor Museum, Beaulieu
SO42 7ZN
☎01590 614656 Fax 01590 612655
✉ motoring.pictures@beaulieu.co.uk
www.motoringpicturelibrary.com
www.alamy.com/mpl
Contacts *Jonathan Day, Tim Woodcock, Tom Wood*

Three-quarters of a million b&w images, plus over 100,000 colour images covering all forms

of motoring history from the 1880s to the present day. Commissions undertaken. Own studio.

Mountain Camera
See **John Cleare**

Moving Image Communications
The Maidstone Studios, Vinters Park, Maidstone ME14 5NZ
☎01622 684569 Fax 01622 687444
✉ mail@milibrary.com
www.milibrary.com
Contact *Nathalie Banaigs*

Over 16,000 hours of quality archive and contemporary footage, including: Channel X; TVAM Archive 1983–92; British Tourist Authority – BTA (1930 to present day); Drummer Films (travel classics, 1950–70); The Freud Archive (1930–39); Film Finders (early cinema); Adrian Brunel Films; Cuban Archives; Stockshots (time-lapse, cityscapes, land and seascapes, chroma-key); Space Exploration (NASA); Wild Islands; Flying Pictures; National Trust.

Museum of Antiquities Picture Library
University and Society of Antiquaries of Newcastle upon Tyne, Newcastle upon Tyne NE1 7RU
☎0191 222 7846 Fax 0191 222 8561
✉ m.o.antiquities@ncl.ac.uk
www.ncl.ac.uk/antiquities
Contact *Lindsay Allason-Jones*

25,000 images, mostly b&w, of special collections including: Hadrian's Wall Archive (b&ws taken over the last 100 years); Gertrude Bell Archive (during her travels in the Near East, 1900–26); and aerial photographs of archaeological sites in the North of England. Visitors welcome by appointment.

Museum of London Picture Library
150 London Wall, London EC2Y 5HN
☎020 7814 5604 Fax 020 7600 1058
✉ picturelib@museumoflondon.org.uk
www.museumoflondon.org.uk
Contacts *Julie Cochrane, Sarah Williams*

The Museum of London picture library holds over 35,000 images illustrating the history of London and the life of its people from prehistoric times to the present day. The images are drawn from the Museum's extensive and unique collections of oil paintings, historic photographs, drawings, prints maps and artefacts including costume, jewellery and ceramics..

The National Archives Image Library

Ruskin Avenue, Kew, Richmond TW9 4DU
☎020 8392 5225   Fax 020 8487 1974
✉ image-library@nationalarchives.gov.uk
www.nationalarchives.gov.uk/imagelibrary
Contacts *Paul Johnson, Hugh Alexander*

British and colonial history from the Domesday Book to the 1970s, shown in photography, maps, illuminations, posters, advertisements, textiles and original manuscripts. Approximately 30,000 5x4" and 35mm colour transparencies and b&w negatives. Open: 9.00 am to 5.00 pm, Monday to Friday.

National Galleries of Scotland Picture Library

The Dean Gallery, Belford Road, Edinburgh EH4 3DS
☎0131 624 6258/6260   Fax 0131 623 7135
✉ picture.library@nationalgalleries.org
www.nationalgalleries.org

Contact *Shona Corner*

Over 80,000 b&w and several thousand images in colour of works of art from the Renaissance to present day. SPECIALIST SUBJECTS cover fine art (painting, sculpture, drawing), portraits, Scottish, historical, still life, photography and landscape. Colour leaflet and CD-ROM guide available on request.

National Maritime Museum Picture Library

Greenwich, London SE10 9NF
☎020 8312 6631/6704   Fax 020 8312 6533
✉ picturelibrary@nmm.ac.uk
www.nmm.ac.uk/picturelibrary
Contacts *David Taylor, Doug McCarthy*

Over 400,000 images from the leading collection of maritime art and artefacts, including oil paintings from the 16th century to present day, prints and drawings, historic photographs, ships plans, models, rare maps and charts, globes, manuscripts and navigation and scientific instruments. Images are available as transparencies and high resolution digital files. Contact for further information or for picture research assistance.

National Monuments Record

National Monuments Record Centre, Kemble Drive, Great Western Village, Swindon SN2 2GZ
☎01793 414600   Fax 01793 414606
www.english-heritage.org.uk

The National Monuments Record is the first stop for photographs and information on England's heritage. Over 10 million photographs, documents and drawings are held. English architecture from the first days of photography to the present, air photographs covering every inch of England from the first days of flying to the present, and archaeological sites. The Record is the public archive of English Heritage (see **English Heritage Photo Library**).

National Museum of Photography, Film & Television

See **Science & Society Picture Library**

National Portrait Gallery Picture Library

St Martin's Place, London WC2H 0HE
☎020 7312 2474/5/6   Fax 020 7312 2464
✉ picturelibrary@npg.org.uk
www.npg.org.uk

Contact *Tom Morgan*

Pictures of brilliant, daring and influential characters who have made British history are available for publication. Images can be searched, viewed and ordered on the website. Copyright clearance is arranged for all images supplied.

National Railway Museum Research Centre

Leeman Road, York YO26 4XJ
☎01904 686235   Fax 01904 611112
✉ nrm.researchcentre@nmsi.ac.uk
www.nrm.org.uk

Part of the **Science & Society Picture Library**. 1.5 million images, mainly b&w, covering every aspect of railways from 1850s to the present day. The Research Centre is closed for refurbishment until October 2007 but is taking e-mail and postal enquiries.

The National Trust Photo Library

Heelis, Kemble Drive, Swindon SN2 2NA
☎01793 817700   Fax 01793 817401
✉ photo.library@nationaltrust.org.uk
www.ntpl.org.uk

Contact *Chris Lacey*

The National Trust Photo Library houses a unique collection of contemporary photography which vividly illustrates the rich diversity and historical range of properties in the National Trust's care, throughout England, Wales and Northern Ireland. The Library has an exceptional choice of images, created by commissioned specialist photographers, suitable for a broad range of creative applications. 30,000 images can be searched and ordered online.

Natural History Museum Picture Library

Cromwell Road, London SW7 5BD
☎020 7942 5401/5324 Fax 020 7942 5212
✉ nhmpl@nhm.ac.uk
www.nhm.ac.uk/piclib

Contacts *Rupert Calvocoressi, Jamie Owen*

Pictures from the Museum's collections, including dinosaurs, man's evolution, extinct species and fossil remains. Also pictures of gems, minerals, birds and animals, plants and insect specimens, plus historical artworks depicting the natural world.

Nature Photographers Ltd

West Wit, New Road, Little London, Tadley
RG26 5EU
☎01256 850661
✉ info@naturephotographers.co.uk
www.naturephotographers.co.uk

Contact *Dr Paul Sterry*

Over 150,000 images, digitised to order, on worldwide natural history and environmental subjects. The library is run by a trained biologist and experienced author on his subject.

Nature Picture Library

BBC Broadcasting House, Whiteladies Road,
Bristol BS8 2LR
☎0117 974 6720 Fax 0117 923 8166
✉ info@naturepl.com
www.naturepl.com

Contact *Helen Gilks*

A collection of 300,000 nature photos from around the world, including strong coverage of animal portraits and behaviour. Other subjects covered include plants, pets, landscapes and travel, environmental issues and wildlife filmmakers at work. Thousands of images can be viewed online and downloaded direct for reproduction.

Peter Newark's Picture Library

3 Barton Buildings, Queen Square, Bath
BA1 2JR
☎01225 334213 Fax 01225 480554

Over one million images covering world history from ancient times to the present day. Includes an extensive military collection of photographs, paintings and illustrations. Also a special collection on American history covering Colonial times, exploration, social, political and the Wild West and Native-Americans in particular. Subject list available. Telephone, fax or write for further information.

NHPA Ltd

Little Tye, 57 High Street, Ardingly
RH17 6TB
☎01444 892514 Fax 01444 892168
✉ nhpa@nhpa.co.uk
www.nhpa.co.uk

Library Manager *Tim Harris*

Extensive coverage on all aspects of natural history – animals, plants, landscapes, environmental issues, gardens and pets. Over 150 photographers worldwide provide a steady input of high-quality images. SPECIALIST FILES include the unique high-speed photography of Stephen Dalton, extensive coverage of African and American wildlife, also rainforests, marine life and the polar regions. UK agents for the ANT collection of Australasian material. Pictures are generally supplied direct to publishers; individual writers must request material via their publisher. See the website to view over 37,000 pictures available at high resolution.

Odhams Periodicals Library

See **Popperfoto.com**

Offshoot

See **Skishoot**

Only Horses Picture Agency

27 Greenway Gardens, Greenford UB6 9TU
☎020 8578 9047 Fax 020 8575 7244
✉ onlyhorsespics@aol.com
www.onlyhorsespictures.com

Colour and b&w coverage of all aspects of the horse. Foaling, retirement, racing, show jumping, eventing, veterinary, polo, breeds, personalities.

Oxford Picture Library

15 Curtis Yard, North Hinksey Lane, Oxford
OX2 0LX
☎01865 723404 Fax 01865 725294
✉ opl@cap-ox.com
www.cap-ox.co.uk

Contacts *Chris Andrews, Annabel Matthews*

Specialist collection on Oxford: the city, university and colleges, events, people, spires and shires. Also, the Cotswolds, architecture and landscape from Stratford-upon-Avon to Bath; the Thames and Chilterns, including Henley on Thames and Windsor; Channel Islands, especially Guernsey and Sark. Aerial views of all areas specified above. General collection includes wildlife, trees, plants, clouds, sun, sky, water and teddy bears. Commissions undertaken.

Oxford Scientific (OSF)

Ground Floor, Network House, Station Yard, Thame OX9 3UH
☎01844 262370   Fax 01844 262380
✉ enquiries@osf.co.uk
www.osf.co.uk

Account Executive – stills *Lucinda Coulton* (l.coulton@osf.co.uk)
Account Executive – footage *Vicky Turner* (v.turner@osf.co.uk)

Collection of 350,000 colour transparencies and digital files of wildlife and natural science images supplied by over 300 photographers worldwide, covering all aspects of wildlife plus landscapes, weather, seasons, plants, pets, environment, anthropology, habitats, science and industry, space, creative textures and backgrounds, and geology. Macro and micro photography. UK agents for Animals Animals, USA, Okapia, Germany and Dinodia, India. Research by experienced researchers for specialist and creative briefs. Visits welcome, by appointment.

Panos Pictures

1 Honduras Street, London EC1Y 0TH
☎020 7253 1424   Fax 020 7253 2752
✉ pics@panos.co.uk
www.panos.co.uk

Documentary colour and b&w library specialising in Third World and Eastern Europe, with emphasis on environment and development issues. Leaflet available. Fifty per cent of all profits from this library go to the Panos Institute to further its work in international sustainable development.

Charles Parker Archive

See **Birmingham Library Services** under *Library Services*

Ann & Bury Peerless Picture Library

St David's, 22 King's Avenue, Minnis Bay, Birchington-on-Sea CT7 9QL
☎01843 841428   Fax 01843 848321
www.peerlessimages.com

Contacts *Ann Peerless, Bury Peerless*

Specialist collection on world religions: Hinduism, Buddhism, Confucianism, Taoism, Jainism, Christianity, Islam, Sikhism, Zoroastrianism (Parsees of India). Geographical areas covered:

India, Afghanistan (Bamiyan Valley of the Buddhas), Pakistan, Bangladesh, Sri Lanka, Cambodia (Angkor), Java (Borobudur), Bali, Thailand, Taiwan, Russia, China, Spain, Poland, Uzbekistan (Samarkand and Bukhara), Vietnam. Basis of collection (35mm colour transparencies), historical, cultural, extensive coverage of art (sculpture and miniature paintings), architecture including Pharaonic Egypt.

Photofusion

17A Electric Lane, London SW9 8LA
☎020 7733 3500   Fax 020 7738 5509
✉ library@photofusion.org
www.photofusionpictures.org

Contact *Liz Somerville*

Colour and b&w coverage of contemporary social and environmental UK issues including babies and children, disability, education, the elderly, environment, family, health, housing, homelessness, people and work. Brochure available.

The Photolibrary Wales

2 Bro-nant, Church Road, Pentyrch, Cardiff CF15 9QG
☎029 2089 0311   Fax 029 2089 0311
✉ info@photolibrarywales.com
www.photolibrarywales.com

Contacts *Steve Benbow, Kate Benbow*

Over 100,000 colour transparences covering all areas and subjects of Wales. Represents the work of 140 photographers, living and working in Wales.

Photos Horticultural

PO Box 105, Ipswich IP1 4PR
☎01473 257329   Fax 01473 233974
✉ library@photos-horticultural.com
www.photos-horticultural.com

Pictures *Ashley Warren*
Editorial *Michael Warren*

Wide selection of horticultural subjects, gardens, practical, plants cultivated and wild from around the world. Now available online via their website. Commissions for photography and illustrated features undertaken.

PictureBank Photo Library Ltd

Parman House, 30–36 Fife Road, Kingston upon Thames KT1 1SY
☎020 8547 2344   Fax 020 8974 5652
✉ info@picturebank.co.uk
www.picturebank.co.uk

Over 400,000 colour transparencies covering people (girls, couples, families, children), travel and scenic (UK and world), moods (sunsets, seascapes, deserts, etc.), industry and technology, environments and general. Commissions undertaken. Visitors welcome. Member of **BAPLA**. New material on medium/large format welcome.

Pictures Colour Library
10 James Whatman Court, Turkey Mill, Ashford Road, Maidstone ME14 5SS
☎01622 609809 Fax 01622 609806
✉ enquiries@picturescolourlibrary.co.uk
www.picturescolourlibrary.co.uk

Travel and travel-related images depicting lifestyles and cultures, people and places, attitudes and environments from around the world, including a comprehensive section on Great Britain.

H.G. Ponting
See **Popperfoto.com**

Popperfoto.com
The Old Mill, Overstone Farm, Overstone, Northampton NN6 0AB
☎01604 670670 Fax 01604 670635
✉ inquiries@popperfoto.com
www.popperfoto.com

Home to over 14 million images, covering 150 years of photographic history. Renowned for its archival material, a world-famous sports library and stock photography. POPPERFOTO's credit line includes Bob Thomas Sports Photography, UPI, Acme, INP, Planet, Paul Popper, Exclusive News Agency, Victory Archive, Odhams Periodicals Library, Illustrated, Harris Picture Agency, and H.G. Ponting. Colour from 1940, b&w from 1870 to the present. Major subjects covered worldwide include events, personalities, wars, royalty, sport, politics, transport, crime, history and social conditions. Material available on the same day to clients throughout the world. Nearly 200,000 high-resolution images online available by direct download, e-mail, FTP and CD. Researchers welcome by appointment.

PPL (Photo Agency) Ltd
Bookers Yard, The Street, Walberton, Arundel BN18 0PF
☎01243 555561 Fax 01243 555562
✉ ppl@mistral.co.uk
www.pplmedia.com

Contacts *Barry Pickthall, Emma Brenton*

Two million pictures covering watersports, sub-aqua, business and commerce, travel and tourism; pictures of yesteryear and a fast grow-ing archive on Sussex and the home counties. Pictures available in high resolution directly from website.

Premaphotos Wildlife
Amberstone, 1 Kirland Road, Bodmin PL30 5JQ
☎01208 78258 Fax 01208 72302
✉ enquiries@premaphotos.com
www.premaphotos.com

Contact *Jean Preston-Mafham*, Library Manager

Natural history worldwide. Subjects include flowering and non-flowering plants, fungi, slime moulds, fruits and seeds, galls, leaf mines, seashore life, mammals, birds, reptiles, amphibians, insects, spiders, habitats, scenery and cultivated cacti. Commissions undertaken. Searchable website. Visitors welcome.

Professional Sport UK Ltd
18–19 Shaftesbury Quay, Hertford SG14 1SF
☎01992 505000 Fax 01992 505020
✉ pictures@prosport.co.uk
www.professionalsport.com

Photographic coverage of tennis, soccer, athletics, golf, cricket, rugby, winter sports and many minor sports. Major international events including the Olympic Games, World Cup soccer and all Grand Slam tennis events. Also news and feature material supplied worldwide. Online photo archive; photo transmission services available for editorial and advertising.

Public Record Office Image Library
See **The National Archives**

Punch Cartoon Library
87–135 Brompton Road, London SW1X 8XL
☎020 7225 6710 Fax 020 7225 6712
✉ punch.library@harrods.com
www.punch.co.uk

Owner *Punch Limited*

Gives access to the 500,000 cartoons published in *Punch* magazine between 1841–1992. The library has a 500+ subject listing and can search on any topic. Social history, politics, fashion, fads, famous people and more by the world's most famous cartoonists, including Tenniel, du Maurier, Pont, Fougasse, E.H. Shepard and Emmett.

PWA International Ltd
4 Brightfield Road, Lee, London SE12 8QF
☎020 8297 3434 Fax 020 8297 0617

✉ pwaint@dircon.co.uk
www.pwainternational.com
Contact *Terry Allen*
Leading comprehensive library of story illustrations comprising work by some of the UK's best-known illustrators, including book covers and magazines.

Railfotos
Millbrook House Ltd., Unit 1, Oldbury Business Centre, Pound Road, Oldbury B68 8NA
☎0121 544 2970
Fax 0121 253 6836 (quote Millbrook House)
One of the largest specialist libraries dealing with railway subjects worldwide. Colour and b&w dating from the turn of the century to present day. Up-to-date material on UK, South America and Far East. Visitors by appointment.

Redferns Music Picture Library
7 Bramley Road, London W10 6SZ
☎020 7792 9914   Fax 020 7792 0921
✉ info@redferns.com
www.redferns.com
Picture library covering every aspect of music, from 18th century classical to present day pop. Over one million archived artists and other subjects including musical instruments, recording studios, crowd scenes, festivals, etc. Brochure available. Over 150,000 images available on the website.

Retna Pictures Ltd
Stills Road, Pinewood Studios, Pinewood Road, Iver Heath SL0 0NH
☎01753 785450   Fax 01753 785 451
✉ info@retna.co.uk
www.retna.co.uk
Established 1978, Retna Pictures Ltd is a leading picture agency with two libraries: celebrity/music and lifestyle. The former specialises in images of international and national celebrities, music from the '60s to the current day, films and personalities. The lifestyle library specialises in people, family life, work, leisure and food. Both libraries are constantly receiving new material from established and up and coming photographers.

Rex Features Ltd
18 Vine Hill, London EC1R 5DZ
☎020 7278 7294   Fax 020 7696 0974
✉ library@rexfeatures.com
www.rexfeatures.com

Contact *Glen Marks*, Sales Manager
Extensive picture library established in the 1950s. Daily coverage of news, politics, personalities, showbusiness, glamour, humour, art, medicine, science, landscapes, royalty, etc.

RIDA Photolibrary
See **GeoScience Features**

Royal Air Force Museum
Grahame Park Way, Hendon, London NW9 5LL
☎020 8205 2266   Fax 020 8200 1751
✉ photographic@rafmuseum.org
www.rafmuseum.org
About a quarter of a million images, mostly b&w, with around 1500 colour in all formats, on the history of aviation. Particularly strong on the activities of the Royal Air Force from the 1870s to 1970s. Researchers are requested to enquire in writing only.

The Royal Collection, Photographic Services
St. James's Palace, London SW1A 1JR
☎020 7839 1377   Fax 020 7024 5643
✉ picturelibrary@royalcollection.org.uk
www.royalcollection.org.uk
www.royal.gov.uk
Contacts *Shruti Patel, Karen Lawson*
Photographic material of items in the Royal Collection, particularly oil paintings, drawings and watercolours, works of art, and interiors and exteriors of royal residences. Over 35,000 colour transparencies, plus 25,000 b&w negatives.

Royal Geographical Society Picture Library
1 Kensington Gore, London SW7 2AR
☎020 7591 3060   Fax 020 7591 3001
✉ images@rgs.org
www.rgs.org/images
Contact *Justin Hobson*
A strong source of geographical and historical images, both archival and modern, showing the world through the eyes of photographers and explorers dating from the 1830s to the present day. The RGS Contempory Collection provides up-to-date transparencies from around the world, highlighting aspects of cultural activity, environmental phenomena, anthropology, architectural design, travel, mountaineering and exploration. Offers a professional and comprehensive service for both commercial and academic use.

RSPB Images
PO Box 7515, Billericay CM11 1WR
☎01268 711471 Fax 01268 710353
✉ rspb@thatsgood.biz
www.rspb-images.com
Contact *Wendy Hollis*

RSPB Images represents some of the UK's leading wildlife photographers, and holds stunning images ranging from birds, butterflies, moths, mammals, reptiles and their habitats to most RSPB reserves, plants and abstract subjects. Online search facility of over 30,000 digitised images.

RSPCA Photolibrary
RSPCA Trading Limited, Wilberforce Way, Southwater, Horsham RH13 9RS
☎0870 754 0150 Fax 0870 753 0150
✉ pictures@rspcaphotolibrary.com
www.rspcaphotolibrary.com

Photolibrary Manager *Andrew Forsyth*

Over 100,000 colour transparencies and over 5000 b&w/colour prints. A comprehensive collection of natural history images whose subjects include mammals, birds, domestic and farm animals, amphibians, insects and the environment, as well as a unique photographic record of the RSPCA's work. Also includes the Wild Images collections. Catalogue available. No search fees.

Russia and Eastern Images
'Sonning', Cheapside Lane, Denham, Uxbridge UB9 5AE
☎01895 833508
✉ easteuropix@btinternet.com
www.easteuropix.com

Architecture, cities, landscapes, people and travel images of Russia and the former Soviet Union. Considerable background knowledge available and Russian language spoken.

Peter Sanders Photography Ltd
24 Meades Lane, Chesham HP5 1ND
☎01494 773674/771372 Fax 01494 773674
✉ photos@petersanders.com
www.petersanders.com

Contacts *Peter Sanders, Hafsa Garwatuk*

Specialises in the world of Islam in all its aspects from culture, arts, industry, lifestyles, celebrations, etc. Areas included are north, east and west Africa, the Middle East (including Saudi Arabia), China, Asia, Europe and USA. A continually expanding library.

ScenicIreland.com
See **Christopher Hill Photographic**

Science & Society Picture Library
Science Museum, Exhibition Road, London SW7 2DD
☎020 7942 4400 Fax 020 7942 4401
✉ piclib@nmsi.ac.uk
www.scienceandsociety.co.uk
Contact *David Thompson*

'The Science & Society Picture Library has one of the widest ranges of photographs, paintings, prints, posters and objects in the world.' The images come from the Science Museum, the **National Railway Museum** and the National Museum of Photography, Film & Television which now includes the Royal Photographic Society collection. Images are available as high or low resolution files via e-mail, FTP or direct from the website.

Science Museum
See **Science & Society Picture Library**

Science Photo Library
327–329 Harrow Road, London W9 3RB
☎020 7432 1100 Fax 020 7286 8668
✉ info@sciencephoto.com
www.sciencephoto.com

Subjects covered include the human body, health and medicine, research, genetics, technology and industry, space exploration and astronomy, earth science, satellite imagery, environment, flowers, plants and gardens, nature and wildlife and the history of science. The whole collection, more than 200,000 images, is available online.

Seaco Picture Library
Sea Containers House, 20 Upper Ground, London SE1 9PF
☎020 7805 5831 Fax 020 7805 5905
✉ seaco.pictures@seacontainers.com
Contact *Luci Gosling*

Approx. 250,000 images of containerisation, shipping, fast ferries, manufacturing, fruit farming, ports, hotels and leisure.

Mick Sharp Photography
Eithinog, Waun, Penisarwaun, Caernarfon LL55 3PW
☎01286 872425 Fax 01286 872425
✉ mick.jean@virgin.net
Contacts *Mick Sharp, Jean Williamson*

Archaeology, ancient monuments, buildings,

churches, countryside, environment, history, landscape, past cultures and topography. Emphasis on British Isles but material also from other countries. Features the photos of both Mick Sharp and Jean Williamson. Access to other specialist collections on related subjects. Commissions undertaken. Medium format and 35mm colour transparencies plus b&w prints from 5x4 negatives.

Phil Sheldon Golf Picture Library
40 Manor Road, Barnet EN5 2JQ
☎020 8440 1986 Fax 020 8440 9348
✉ gill@philsheldongolfpics.co.uk *or*
info@philsheldongolfpics.co.uk
www.philsheldongolfpics.co.uk

An expanding collection of over 600,000 quality images of the 'world of golf'. In-depth worldwide tournament coverage including every Major championship and Ryder Cup since 1976. Instruction, portraits, trophies and over 400 golf courses from around the world. Also the Dale Concannon collection covering the period 1870 to 1940, the classic 1960s collection by photographer Sidney Harris and the Ed Lacey Collection.

Skishoot–Offshoot
Hall Place, Upper Woodcott, Whitchurch RG28 7PY
☎01635 255527 Fax 01635 255528
✉ pictures@skishoot.co.uk
www.skishoot.co.uk

Contacts *Claire Randall, Judi Kitchin*

Skishoot ski and snowboarding picture library has 500,000 images. Offshoot travel library specialises in France.

The Skyscan Photolibrary
Oak House, Toddington, Cheltenham GL54 5BY
☎01242 621357 Fax 01242 621343
✉ info@skyscan.co.uk
www.skyscan.co.uk

As well as the Skyscan Photolibrary collection of unique balloon's-eye views of Britain, the library now includes the work of photographers from across the aviation spectrum; air to ground, aviation, aerial sports – 'in fact, anything aerial!' Links have been built with photographers across the world; photographs can be handled on an agency basis and held in house, or as a brokerage where the collection stays with the photographer; terms 50/50 for both. Commissioned photography arranged. Enquiries welcome.

Snookerimages (Eric Whitehead Photography)
10 Brow Close, Bowness on Windermere LA23 2HA
☎015394 48894
✉ snooker@snookerimages.co.uk
www.snookerimages.co.uk

Over 30,000 images of snooker from 1982 to the present day.

Solo Syndication Ltd
17–18 Haywards Place, Clerkenwell, London EC1R 0EQ
☎020 7566 0360 Fax 020 7566 0388
Syndication Director *Trevor York*
Sales *Danny Howell, Nick York*
Online transmissions *Geoff Malyon* (☎020 7566 0370)

Three million images from the archives of the *Daily Mail, Mail on Sunday, Evening Standard* and *Evening News*. Hard prints or Mac-to-Mac delivery. 24-hour service.

Sotheby's Picture Library
34–35 New Bond Street, London W1A 2AA
☎020 7293 5383 Fax 020 7293 5062
✉ piclib@sothebys.com
www.sothebys.com

Contacts *Joanna Ling, Sue Daly*

The library consists of over 300,000 selected transparencies of pictures sold at Sotheby's. Images from the 15th to the 20th century. Oils, drawings, watercolours, prints and decorative items. 'Happy to do searches or, alternatively, visitors are welcome by appointment.'

South American Pictures
48 Station Road, Woodbridge IP12 4AT
☎01394 383963 Fax 01394 380176
✉ morrison@southamericanpictures.com
www.southamericanpictures.com Specialist site: www.nonesuchinfo.info

Contact *Marion Morrison*

Colour and b&w images of South/Central America, Cuba, Mexico, New Mexico (USA), Dominican Republic and Haiti, including archaeology and the Amazon. There is an archival section, with pictures and documents from most countries. Now with 40 contributing photographers. All images are supplied digitally.

Still Digital
8 Saxe Coburg Place, Edinburgh EH3 5BR
☎0131 332 3874
✉ info@stilldigital.co.uk

www.stillmovingpictures.com

Contact *John Hutchinson*

Fully searchable and downloadable service for thousands of Scottish images.

Still Pictures' Whole Earth Photolibrary

199 Shooters Hill Road, London SE3 8UL
☎020 8858 8307   Fax 020 8858 2049
✉ info@stillpictures.com
www.stillpictures.com

Contacts *Kate Watson, Teresa Schiappi*

Founded 1970. High profile photo library specialising in environment, the Third World, social issues and nature. Represents 10 leading European and US agencies and over 400 photographers as well as the United Nations Environment Programme (UNEP) archive, the **Christian Aid** collection (see entry) and a growing selection of images from **Woodfall Wild Images** (see entry). The website has nearly 100,000 images online, ready for instant download.

Stockfile

5 High Street, Sunningdale SL5 0LX
☎01344 844428   Fax 01344 843513
✉ info@stockfile.co.uk
www.stockfile.co.uk

Contacts *Jill Behr, Steven Behr*

Specialist cycling collection with emphasis on mountain biking. Expanding adventure sports section covering snow, land, air and water activities.

Stockscotland.com

Croft Studio, Croft Roy, Crammond Brae, Tain IV19 1JG
☎01862 892298   Fax 01862 892298
✉ info@stockscotland.com
www.stockscotland.com

Contact *Hugh Webster*

150,000 Scottish images with 10,000 currently available online.

Sir John Benjamin Stone

See **Birmingham Library Services** under *Library Services*

Jessica Strang Photo Library

504 Brody House, Strype Street, London E1 7LQ
☎020 7247 8982   Fax 020 7247 8982
✉ jessica@jessicastrang.plus.com

Contact *Jessica Strang*

Approximately 60,000 transparencies covering architecture, interiors (contemporary), gardens, 'obsessive and not just small but tiny, or from almost no space at all', men, women, couples and animals in architecture, and vanishing London details. Recycled ideas for the home.

Joe Tasker Collection

See **Chris Bonington Picture Library**

Tate Enterprises Picture Library

Top Floor, The Lodge, Tate Britain, Millbank, London SW1P 4RG
☎020 7887 8871/8890/4933
Fax 020 7887 8805
✉ picture.library@tate.org.uk
www.tate.org.uk

Contact *Alison Fern*

Images of British art from the 16th century; international 20th century painting and sculpture. Artists include William Blake, William Hogarth, J.M.W. Turner, Dante Gabriel Rossetti, Barbara Hepworth, Henry Moore, Stanley Spencer, Pablo Picasso, Mark Rothko, Salvador Dali, Lucien Freud and David Hockney. Colour transparencies of more than half the works in the main collection are available for hire. For a fee, new photography is available depending on the location and condition of the art work. B&w prints of nearly all the works in the collection can be purchased. Colour slides and prints can be made on request providing a colour transparency exists. A digital service for picture buyers is under development and a specific site, accessible via the Tate homepage, will soon be available.

Bob Thomas Sports Photography

See **Popperfoto.com**

Thoroughbred Photography Ltd

The Hornbeams, 2 The Street, Worlington IP28 8RU
☎01638 713944
✉ mail@thoroughbredphoto.com
www.thoroughbredphoto.com

Contacts *Trevor Jones, Gill Jones, Laura Green*

Extensive library of high-quality colour images depicting all aspects of thoroughbred horseracing dating from 1987. Major group races, English Classics, studs, stallions, mares and foals, early morning scenes, personalities, jockeys, trainers and prominent owners. Also international work: USA Breeders' Cup, Arc de Triomphe, French Classics, Irish Derby, Dubai racing scenes, Japan Cup and Hokkaido stud farms; and more unusual scenes such as racing on the sands at low tide, Ireland, and on the frozen lake at St Moritz. Visitors by appointment.

Rick Tomlinson
Marine Photo Library
St George's Bay House, Bay View Road, Port St Mary, Isle of Man
☎01624 834272 Fax 01624 835363
✉ rick@rick-tomlinson.com
www.rick-tomlinson.com
Contacts *Rick Tomlinson*
Established 1985. Specialises in marine subjects. 100,000 35mm transparencies of yachting, racing, cruising, Whitbread Round the World Race, Volvo Ocean Race, Americas Cup, Tall Ships, RNLI Lifeboats, Antarctica, wildlife and locations.

TopFoto
PO Box 33, Edenbridge TN8 5PF
☎01732 863939 Fax 01732 860215
✉ admin@topfoto.co.uk
www.topfoto.co.uk
Contact *Alan Smith*
International editorial distributor with over one million pictures available online to download and 12 million in hard copy, representing 40 leading suppliers.

B.M. Totterdell photography
Constable Cottage, Burlings Lane, Knockholt TN14 7PE
☎01959 532001 Fax 01959 532001
✉ btrial@btinternet.com
whatvolleyball.co.uk
Contact *Barbara Totterdell*
Specialist volleyball library covering all aspects of the sport.

Tessa Traeger Picture Library
7 Rossetti Studios, 72 Flood Street, London SW3 5TF
☎020 7352 3641 Fax 020 7352 4846
✉ info@tessatraeger.com
www.tessatraeger.com
Food, gardens, travel and artists.

Travel Ink Photo & Feature Library
The Old Coach House, 14 High Street, Goring on Thames, Nr Reading RG8 9AR
☎01491 873011 Fax 01491 875558
✉ info@travel-ink.co.uk
www.travel-ink.co.uk

Contacts *Frances Honnor, Felicity Bazzell*
A collection of over 120,000 travel, tourism and lifestyle images, carefully edited and constantly updated, from countries worldwide. SPECIALIST COLLECTIONS from the UK, Greece, France, Far East and Caribbean. The website offers a fully captioned and searchable selection of over 28,000 images and is ideal for picture researchers.

Peter Trenchard's Image Store Ltd
The Studio, West Hill, St Helier, Jersey JE2 3HB
☎01534 769933 Fax 01534 789191
✉ peter-trenchard@jerseymail.co.uk
www.peter-trenchard.com
Contact *Peter Trenchard, FBIPP, AMPA, PPA*
Slide library of the Channel Islands – mainly tourist and financial-related. Commissions undertaken.

Tropix Photo Library
44 Woodbines Avenue, Kingston upon Thames KT1 2AY
☎020 8546 0823/0151 625 4576
Fax 0870 706 1317
✉ images@tropix.co.uk
www.tropix.co.uk
Contact *Veronica Birley*
Specialises in images of developing nations: travel and editorial pictures emphasising the attractive and progressive, not just the problems. Evocative photos concerning the economies, environment, culture and society of 100+ countries across Africa, Central and South America, Caribbean, Eastern Europe, Middle East, Indian sub-continent, South East Asia, CIS and Far East; also Antarctica. Also incorporating MerseySlides Collection. Assignment photography available worldwide. All photos supplied with detailed captions. Rapid response with one-hour digital delivery available. Established 1982. **BAPLA** member.

Ulster Museum Picture Library
Botanic Gardens, Belfast BT9 5AB
☎028 9038 3000 ext 3113
Fax 028 9038 3103
✉ patricia.mclean@magni.org.uk
www.ulstermuseum.org.uk
Contact *Mrs Pat McLean*
SPECIALIST SUBJECTS art (fine and decorative, late 17th–20th century), particularly Irish art, archaeology, ethnography, treasures from the Armada shipwrecks, geology, botany, zoology,

local history and industrial archaeology. Commissions welcome for objects not already photographed.

United Nations Environment Programme (UNEP)
See **Still Pictures' Whole Earth Photolibrary**

Universal Pictorial Press & Agency Ltd
29–31 Saffron Hill, London EC1N 8SW
☎020 7421 6000
✉ contact@uppa.co.uk
www.photoshot.com
News Editor *Peter Dare*

Photo archive dates back to 1944 and contains approximately four million pictures. Colour and b&w coverage of news, royalty, politics, sport, arts, and many other subjects. Commissions undertaken for press and public relations. Fully interactive digital photo archive accessible via ISDN or modem. Full digital scanning, retouching and transmission facilities.

UPI
See **Popperfoto.com**

V&A Images
Victoria and Albert Museum, Cromwell Road, South Kensington, London SW7 2RL
☎020 7942 2489 (commercial)/2479 (academic) Fax 020 7942 2482
✉ vanda.images@vam.ac.uk
www.vandaimages.com
A vast collection of photographs from the world's largest museum of decorative and applied arts, reflecting culture and lifestyle spanning over 1000 years of history to the present time. Digital delivery of contemporary and historical textiles, costumes and fashions, ceramics, furniture, metalwork, glass, sculpture, toys, and games, design and photographs from around the world. Unique photographs include 1960s fashion by John French, Harry Hammond's behind the scenes pop idols, Houston Rogers theatrical world of the 1930s to 1970s, images of royalty by Lafayette, Cecil Beaton, and the 19th century pioneer photographers. Images from the National Art Library and Library of Art & Design, and from the Theatre Museum and Museum of Childhood are readily available.

Victory Archive
See **Popperfoto.com**

Vin Mag Archive Ltd
84–90 Digby Road, London E9 6HX
☎020 8533 7588 Fax 020 8533 7283
✉ piclib@vinmag.com
www.vinmagarchive.com
Formerly the Vintage Magazine Company. A collection of half a million movie, TV, celebrity and sports images available online. Contact *Angela Maguire* for code and password.

John Walmsley Photo Library
See **Education Photos**

Warwickshire Photographic Survey
See **Birmingham Library Services** under *Library Services*

Waterways Photo Library
39 Manor Court Road, Hanwell, London W7 3EJ
☎020 8840 1659 Fax 020 8567 0605
✉ watphot39@aol.com
www.waterwaysphotolibrary.com
Contact *Derek Pratt*

A specialist photo library on all aspects of Britain's inland waterways. Top-quality 35mm and medium-format colour transparencies, plus a large collection of b&w. Rivers and canals, bridges, locks, aqueducts, tunnels and waterside buildings. Town and countryside scenes, canal art, waterway holidays, boating, fishing, windmills, watermills, watersports and wildlife.

Philip Way Photography
2 Green Moor Link, Winchmore Hill, London N21 2ND
☎020 8360 3034
✉ pwphotography1@btinternet.com
Contact *Philip Way*

Over 10,000 images of St Paul's Cathedral: historical exteriors, interiors and events (1686–2004).

Weimar Archive
See **Mary Evans Picture Library**

The Wellcome Trust Medical Photographic Library
210 Euston Road, London NW1 2BE
☎020 7611 8348 Fax 020 7611 8577
✉ medphoto@wellcome.ac.uk
medphoto.wellcome.ac.uk
Contact *Clive Coward*

Approximately 180,000 images on the history of medicine and human culture worldwide, including religion, astronomy, botany, genetics, landscape and cell biology.

Eric Whitehead Photography
20 Brow Close, Bowness on Windermere LA23 2HA
☎015394 48894
✉ snooker@snookerimages.co.uk
www.snookerimages.co.uk

The agency covers local news events, PR and commercial material, also leading library of snooker images (see **Snookerimages**).

Wild Images
See **RSPCA Photolibrary**

Wild Places Photography
See **Chris Howes**

David Williams Picture Library
50 Burlington Avenue, Glasgow G12 0LH
☎0141 339 7823 Fax 0141 337 3031
✉ david@scotland-guide.co.uk

Specialises in travel photography with wide coverage of Scotland, Iceland and Spain. Many other European countries also included plus smaller collections of Western USA and Canada. The main subjects in each country are: cities, towns, villages, 'tourist haunts', buildings of architectural or historical interest, landscapes and natural features. The Scotland and Iceland collections include many pictures depicting physical geography and geology. Photographic commissions and illustrated travel articles undertaken. Catalogue available.

The Neil Williams Classical Collection
22 Avon, Hockley, Tamworth B77 5QA
☎01827 286086 Fax 01827 286086
✉ neil@classicalcollection.co.uk
Contact *Neil Williams, MA(Hum), MA(Mus)*

Archive specialising in classical music ephemera, particularly portraits of composers, musicians, conductors and opera singers, comprising old and sometimes very rare photographs, postcards, antique prints, cigarette cards, stamps, First Day Covers, concert programmes, Victorian newspapers, etc. Also modern photos of composer references such as museums, statues, busts, paintings, monuments, memorials and graves. Other subjects covered include bal-

let, musical instruments, concert halls, opera houses, 'music in art', manuscripts, opera scenes, music-caricatures, bands, orchestras and other music groups. Also writer of concert programme notes and CD inserts for classical music, as well as being a commissionable composer.

Vaughan Williams Memorial Library
English Folk Dance and Song Society, Cecil Sharp House, 2 Regent's Park Road, London NW1 7AY
☎020 7485 2206 ext. 18/19
Fax 020 7284 0523
✉ library@efdss.org
www.efdss.org

Mainly b&w coverage of traditional/folk music, dance and customs worldwide, focusing on Britain and other English-speaking nations. Photographs date from the late 19th century to the present day.

The Wilson Photographic Collection
See **Dundee Central Library** under *Library Services*

Woodfall Wild Images
17 Bull Lane, Denbigh LL16 3SN
☎01745 815903 Fax 01745 814581
✉ wwimages@woodfall.com
www.woodfall.com
Contact *David Woodfall*

A comprehensive and specialist collection of wildlife, landscape and environmental photographs from both the UK and the rest of the world. Award winning photography by the world's more imaginative photographers. All formats, 35mm to panoramic. 'Personal and friendly service.' Subjects include: birds, animals, insects and marine life, trees and forests, wildflowers, all habitats worldwide and canals. Environmental issues such as pollution, conservation and habitat destruction, the weather and climate, landscapes and scenics. Suitable for advertising, editorial, calendars and design purposes.

World Pictures
43–44 Berners Street, London W1T 3ND
☎020 7580 1845/7436 0440
Fax 020 7580 4146
✉ worldpictures@btinternet.com
www.worldpictures.co.uk
Contact *David Brenes*

600,000 colour transparencies of travel and emotive material.

Yemen Pictures

28 Sheen Common Drive, Richmond
TW10 5BN
☎020 7602 1989 Fax 020 7602 1989
www.facesandplacespix.com

Large collection (4000 transparencies) covering all aspects of Yemen – culture, people, architecture, dance, qat, music. Also Africa, Australia, Middle East, and Asia.

York Archaeological Trust Picture Library

Cromwell House, 13 Ogleforth, York
YO1 7FG
☎01904 663051 Fax 01904 663024
✉ ckyriacou@yorkarchaeology.co.uk
www.yorkarchaeology.co.uk

Specialist library of rediscovered artifacts, historic buildings and excavations, presented by the creators of the highly acclaimed Jorvik Viking Centre. The main emphasis is on the Roman, Anglo-Saxon, Medieval and Viking periods.

Settling Accounts

Ian Spring takes an expert look at the latest budget and explains how writers can be tax-wise

When he was Chancellor of the Exchequer, Norman Lamont said:

'Tax should be
- Simple and certain
- Fair and reasonable
- Easy to collect'

Unfortunately over the years, tax law has become ever more complicated and it has become more and more difficult for the 'ordinary' person to understand it. Until recently it was inconceivable that tax changes would be passed which had retrospective effect but this is no longer the case and is happening. With the recent merger of the Inland Revenue and Customs and Excise, the former have taken on some of the powers and practices of the latter and have become more aggressive in enforcing the law, as they see it, in their never ending endeavour to increase the tax take.

Tax is not simple and a taxpayer cannot be certain that a tax planning action legally taken now will be legal in years to come. Tax and its ramifications such as tax credits are ever increasingly viewed by the general public as being unfair and unreasonable and whilst tax collection is regarded by the Revenue as being easier this is only because taxpayers are now responsible for paying rather than the Revenue being responsible for collecting.

It is against this background that authors have to comply with the law and complete and submit a tax return each year.

Income Tax

What is a professional writer for tax purposes?

Writers are professionals while they are writing regularly with the intention of making a profit; or while they are gathering material, researching or otherwise preparing a publication.

A professional freelance writer is taxed under section 5 Income Tax (Trading and Other Income) Act 2005. The taxable income is the amount receivable, either directly or by an agent, on his behalf, less expenses wholly and exclusively laid out for the purpose of the profession. If expenses exceed income, the loss can either be set against other income of the same or preceding years or carried forward and set against future income from writing. If tax has been paid on that other income, a repayment can be obtained, or the sum can be offset against other tax liabilities. Special loss relief can apply in the opening years of the profession. Losses made in the first four years can be set against income of up to three earlier years.

Where a writer receives very occasional payments for isolated articles, it may not be possible to establish that these are profits arising from carrying on a continuing profession. In such circumstances these 'isolated transactions' may be assessed under section 687 Income Tax (Trading and Other Income) Act 2005. Again, expenses may be deducted in arriving at the taxable income but, if expenses exceed income, the loss can only be set against the profits from future isolated transactions or other income assessable under section 687.

In the tax year 1996/97 a new tax system came into effect called Self Assessment. Under Self Assessment the onus is on the individual to declare income and expenses correctly. Each writer therefore has to decide whether profits arise from a professional or occasional activity. The consequences of getting it wrong can be expensive by way of interest, penalties and surcharges on additional tax subsequently found to be due. If in any doubt the writer should seek professional advice.

Income

A writer's income includes fees, advances, royalties, commissions, sale of copyrights, reimbursed expenses, etc., from any source anywhere in the world whether or not brought to the UK (non UK resident or domiciled writers should seek professional advice).

Agents

It should be borne in mind that the agent stands in the shoes of the principal. It is not always realised that when the agent receives royalties, fees, advances, etc. on behalf of the author those receipts became the property of the author on the date of their receipt by the agent. This applies for Income Tax and Value Added Tax purposes.

Expenses

A writer can normally claim the following expenses:

(a) Secretarial, typing, proof-reading, research. Where payment for these is made to the author's wife or husband they should be recorded and entered in the spouse's tax return as earned income which is subject to the usual personal allowances. If payments reach relevant levels, PAYE should be operated.

(b) Telephone, faxes, Internet costs, computer software, postage, stationery, printing, equipment maintenance, insurance, dictation tapes, batteries, any equipment or office requisites used for the profession.

(c) Periodicals, books (including presentation copies and reference books) and other publications necessary for the profession, but amounts received from the sale of books should be deducted.

(d) Hotels, fares, car running expenses (including repairs, petrol, oil, garaging, parking, cleaning, insurance, road fund tax, depreciation), hire of cars or taxis in connection with:

    (i) business discussions with agents, publishers, co-authors, collaborators, researchers, illustrators, etc.

    (ii) travel at home and abroad to collect background material.

As an alternative to keeping details of full car running costs, a mileage rate can be claimed for business use. This rate depends on the engine size and varies from year to year. This is known as the Fixed Profit Car Scheme and is available to writers whose turnover does not exceed the VAT registration limit, currently £ 61,000.

(e) Publishing and advertising expenses, including costs of proof corrections, indexing, photographs, etc.

(f) Subscriptions to societies and associations, press cutting agencies, libraries, etc., incurred wholly for the purpose of the profession.

(g) Rent, council tax and water rates, etc., the proportion being determined by the ratio of the number of rooms used exclusively for the profession, to the total number of rooms in the residence. But see note on Capital Gains Tax below.

(h) Lighting, heating and cleaning. A carefully calculated figure of the business use of these costs can be claimed as a proportion of the total.

(i) Agent's commission, accountancy charges and legal charges incurred wholly in the course of the profession including cost of defending libel actions, damages in so far as they are not covered by insurance, and libel insurance premiums. However, where in a libel case damages are awarded to punish the author for having acted maliciously the action becomes quasi-criminal and costs and damages may not be allowed.

(j) TV and video rental (which may be apportioned for private use), and cinema or theatre tickets, if wholly for the purpose of the profession.

(k) Capital allowances

(i) On motor cars the allowance is 25% in the first year and 25% of the reducing balance in each successive year limited to £3000 each year.

(ii) For all other business equipment, e.g. TV, radio, hi-fi sets, tape and video recorders, Dictaphones, office furniture, photographic equipment, etc. for small businesses (which most authors will be), there is a First Year Allowance of 50%. After the first year there is an annual Writing Down Allowance of 25% of the reducing balance.

The allowances for both categories mentioned above will be reduced to exclude personal (non-professional) use where necessary.

(l) Lease rent. The cost of lease rent of equipment is allowable; also on cars, subject to restrictions for private use, and for expensive cars.

(m) Other expenses incurred wholly and exclusively for professional purposes. (Entertaining expenses are not allowable in any circumstances.)

NB It essential to keep detailed records. Diary entries of appointments, notes of fares and receipted bills are much more convincing to the Inland Revenue who are very reluctant to accept estimates.

The Self Assessment regime makes it a legal requirement for proper accounting records to be kept. These records must be sufficient to support the figures declared in the tax return.

In addition to the above, tax relief is available on:

(a) Premiums to pension schemes or personal pension plans. Prior to 6th April 2006, depending on age, up to 40% of net earned income can be paid into a personal pension plan. New rules for allowing pension premiums came into effect on 6th April 2006 and premiums up to £215,000 a year can be paid.

(b) Gift Aid payments to charities. Any amount.

Capital Gains Tax

The exemption from Capital Gains Tax which applies to an individual's main residence does not apply to any part of that residence which is used exclusively for business purposes. The appropriate proportion of any increase in value of the residence, since purchase or 31 March 1982 if later, can be taxed when the residence is sold, subject to adjustment for inflation to March 1998 and subsequent length of ownership, at the individual's highest rate of tax.

Writers who own their houses should bear this in mind before claiming expenses for the use of a room for writing purposes. Arguments in favour of making such claims are that they afford some relief now, while Capital Gains Tax in its present form may not stay for ever. Also, where a new house is bought in place of an old one, the gain made on the sale of the first study may be set off against the cost of the study in the new house, thus postponing the tax payment until the final sale. For this relief to apply, each house must have a study and the author must continue his profession throughout. On death there is an exemption of the total Capital Gains of the estate.

Alternatively, writers can claim that their use is non-exclusive and restrict their claim to the cost of extra lighting, heating and cleaning to avoid any Capital Gains Tax liability.

Can a writer average out his income over a number of years for tax purposes?
The Budget in March 2001 introduced measures which enable writers to average their profits (made wholly or mainly from creative works) over two or more consecutive years. If the profits of the lower year are less than 70% of the profits of the higher year or the profits of one year (but not both) are nil, the author will be able to claim to have the profits averaged. Where the profits of the lower year are more than 70% but less than 75% of the profits of the higher year a pro-rata adjustment is made to both years to reduce the difference between them.

It is also possible to average out income within the terms of publishers' contracts, but professional advice should be taken before signature. Where a husband and wife collaborate as writers, advice should be taken as to whether a formal partnership agreement should be made or whether the publishing agreement should be in joint names.

Is a lump sum paid for an outright sale of the copyright or part of the copyright exempt from tax?
No. All the money received from the marketing of literary work, by whatever means, is taxable. Some writers, in spite of clear judicial decisions to the contrary, still seem to think that an outright sale of, for instance, the film rights in a book is not subject to tax. The averaging relief described above should be considered.

Remaindering
To avoid remaindering authors can usually purchase copies of their own books from the publishers. Monies received from sales are subject to income tax but the cost of books sold should be deducted because tax is only payable on the profit made.

Is there any relief where old copyrights are sold?
No. There was relief available until April 2001 but was then withdrawn. The averaging relief described above should be considered.

Are royalties payable on publication of a book abroad subject to both foreign tax as well as UK tax?
Where there is a Double Taxation Agreement between the country concerned and the UK, then on the completion of certain formalities no tax is deductible at source by the

foreign payer, but such income is taxable in the UK in the ordinary way. When there is no Double Taxation Agreement, credit will be given against UK tax for overseas tax paid. A complete list of countries with which the UK has conventions for the avoidance of double taxation may be obtained from the Centre for Non-Residents, Inland Revenue, St John's House, Merton Road, Bootle, Merseyside L69 9BB, or a local tax office.

Residence abroad

Writers residing abroad will, of course, be subject to the tax laws ruling in their country of residence, and as a general rule royalty income paid from the United Kingdom can be exempted from deduction of UK tax at source, providing the author is carrying on his profession abroad. A writer who is intending to go and live abroad should make early application for future royalties to be paid without deduction of tax to the Centre for Non-Residents, address as above. In certain circumstances writers resident in the Irish Republic are exempt from Irish Income Tax on their authorship earnings.

Are grants or prizes taxable?

The law is uncertain. Some Arts Council grants are now deemed to be taxable, whereas most prizes and awards are not, though it depends on the conditions in each case. When submitting the Self Assessment annual returns, such items should be excluded, but reference made to them in the 'Additional Information' box on the self-employment (or partnership) pages.

What is the item 'Class 4 N.I.C.' which appears on my Self Assessment return?

All taxpayers who are self-employed pay an additional national insurance contribution if their earned income exceeds a figure which varies each year. This contribution is described as Class 4 and is calculated when preparing the return. It is additional to the self-employed Class 2 contribution but confers no additional benefits and is a form of levy. It applies to men aged under 65 and women under 60.

Should an author use a limited company?

Changes in the tax regime has made the incorporation of businesses more and more attractive and there are advantages in so doing for businesses with relatively low levels of profit although these advantages were reduced in the 2004 and 2005 Budgets. However, there are disadvantages in all cases and particular considerations for authors. The advice of an accountant, knowledgeable about the affairs of authors, should be sought if incorporation is contemplated.

Value Added Tax

Value Added Tax (VAT) is a tax currently levied at 17.5% on:
(a) the total value of taxable goods and services supplied to consumers,
(b) the importation of goods into the UK,
(c) certain services or goods from abroad if a taxable person receives them in the UK for the purpose of their business.

Who is taxable?

A writer resident in the UK whose turnover from writing and any other business, craft or art on a self-employed basis is greater than £61,000 annually, before deducting agent's commission, must register with HM Revenue & Customs as a taxable person. Turnover includes fees, royalties, advances, commissions, sale of copyright, reimbursed expenses, etc. A business is required to register:

- at the end of any month if the value of taxable supplies in the past twelve months has exceeded the annual threshold; or
- if there are reasonable grounds for believing that the value of taxable supplies in the next twelve months will exceed the annual threshold.

Penalties will be claimed in the case of late registration. A writer whose turnover is below these limits is exempt from the requirements to register for VAT but may apply for voluntary registration and this will be allowed at the discretion of HM Revenue & Customs.

A taxable person collects VAT on outputs (turnover) and deducts VAT paid on inputs (taxable expenses) and where VAT collected exceeds VAT paid, must remit the difference

Inputs (Expenses)

Taxable at the standard rate if supplier is registered	Taxable at the zero or special rate	Not liable to VAT
Rent of certain commercial premises	Books (zero)	Rent of non-commercial premises
Advertisements in newspapers, magazines, journals and periodicals	Coach, rail and air travel (zero)	Postage
Agent's commission (unless it relates to monies from overseas)	Agent's commission (on monies from overseas)	Services supplied by unregistered persons
Accountant's and solicitor's fees for business matters	Domestic gas and electricity (5%)	Subscriptions to the Society of Authors, PEN, NUJ, etc.
Agency services (typing, copying, etc.)		Insurance
Word processors, type-writers and stationery		
Artists' materials		
Photographic equipment		
Tape recorders and tapes		
Hotel accommodation		Outside the scope of VAT
Taxi fares		
Motorcar expenses		PLR (Public Lending Right)
Telephone		Profit shares
Theatres and concerts		Investment income
NB This list is not exhaustive		

to HM Revenue & Customs. In the event that input exceeds output, the difference will be refunded by HM Revenue & Customs

Outputs (Turnover)

A writer's outputs are taxable services supplied to publishers, broadcasting organisations, theatre managements, film companies, educational institutions, etc. A taxable writer must invoice, i.e. collect from, all the persons (either individuals or organisations) in the UK for whom supplies have been made, for fees, royalties or other considerations plus VAT. An unregistered writer cannot and must not invoice for VAT. A taxable writer is not obliged to collect VAT on royalties or other fees paid by publishers or others overseas. In practice, agents usually collect VAT for the registered author.

Remit to Customs

The taxable writer adds up the VAT which has been paid on taxable inputs, deducts it from the VAT received and remits the balance to Customs. Business with HM Customs is conducted through the local VAT offices of HM Revenue & Customs which are listed in local telephone directories, except for VAT returns which are sent direct to the HM Revenue & Customs VAT Central Unit, Alexander House, 21 Victoria Avenue, Southend on Sea, Essex SS99 1AA.

Accounting

A taxable writer is obliged to account to HM Revenue & Customs at quarterly intervals. Returns must be completed and sent to VAT Central Unit by the dates shown on the return. Penalties can be charged if the returns are late.

It is possible to account for the VAT liability under the Cash Accounting Scheme (leaflet 731), whereby the author accounts for the output tax when the invoice is paid or royalties, etc., are received. The same applies to the input tax, but as most purchases are probably on a 'cash basis', this will not make a considerable difference to the author's input tax. This scheme is only applicable to those with a taxable turnover of less than £660,000 and, therefore, is available to the majority of authors. The advantage of this scheme is that the author does not have to account for VAT before receiving payments, thereby relieving the author of a cash flow problem.

If turnover is less than £1,350,000 and the taxable writer has been registered for at least 12 months it is also possible to pay VAT by monthly instalments, with a final balance at the end of the year (see leaflet 732). This annual accounting method also means that only one VAT return is submitted. If turnover is expected to be £150,000 or less, the taxable writer can apply to start at any time.

Flat Rate Scheme

Small businesses can elect to pay VAT under a flat rate scheme (FRS). This is open to businesses with business income up to £150,000 a year. Under the normal VAT accounting rules, each item of turnover and every claimed expense must be recorded and supported by evidence, e.g. invoices, receipts, etc. Under the FRS, detailed records of sales and purchases do not have to be kept. A record of gross income (including zero rated and excepted income) is maintained and a flat rate percentage is applied to the total. This percentage is then paid over to HM Revenue & Customs. The percentage varies from one profession or business to another but for authors is 11%. In the first year of registration this percent is reduced by 1%.

The aim of the scheme is to reduce the amount of time and money spent in complying with VAT regulations and this is to be welcomed. However, there are disadvantages:

- The detailed records of income and expenses are still going to be required for taxation purposes.
- Invoices on sales are issued in the normal way.
- The percentage is applied to all business income. So 11% VAT will effectively be paid on income from abroad, zero rated under the normal basis, and PLR, otherwise exempt.

For many authors, normal VAT accounting has imposed a good, timely discipline for dealing with accounting and taxation matters.

Registration
A writer will be given a VAT registration number which must be quoted on all VAT correspondence. It is the responsibility of those registered to inform those to whom they make supplies of their registration number. The taxable turnover limit which determines whether a person who is registered for VAT may apply for cancellation of registration is £59,000.

Voluntary registration
A writer whose turnover is below the limits may apply to register. If the writer is paying a relatively large amount of VAT on taxable inputs – agent's commission, accountant's fees, equipment, materials, or agency services, etc. – it may make a significant improvement in the net income to be able to offset the VAT on these inputs. A writer who pays relatively little VAT may find it easier, and no more expensive, to remain unregistered.

Fees and royalties
A taxable writer must notify those to whom he makes supplies of the VAT Registration Number at the first opportunity. One method of accounting for and paying VAT on fees and royalties is the use of multiple stationery for 'self-billing', one copy of the royalty statement being used by the author as the VAT invoice. A second method is for the recipient of taxable outputs to pay fees, including authors' royalties, without VAT. The taxable writer then renders a tax invoice for the VAT element and a second payment, of the VAT element, will be made. This scheme is cumbersome but will involve only taxable authors. Fees and royalties from abroad will count as payments for exported services and will accordingly be zero-rated.

Agents and accountants
A writer is responsible to HM Revenue & Customs for making VAT returns and payments. Neither an agent nor an accountant nor a solicitor can remove the responsibility, although they can be helpful in preparing and keeping VAT returns and accounts. Their professional fees or commission will, except in rare cases where the adviser or agent is himself unregistered, be taxable at the standard rate and will represent some of a writer's taxable inputs.

Income Tax
An unregistered writer can claim some of the VAT paid on taxable inputs as a business expense allowable against income tax. However, certain taxable inputs fall into categories

which cannot be claimed under the income tax regulations. A taxable writer, who has already claimed VAT on inputs, cannot charge it as a business expense for the purposes of income tax.

Certain services from abroad

A taxable author who resides in the United Kingdom and who receives certain services from abroad must account for VAT on those services at the appropriate tax rate on the sum paid for them. Examples of the type of services concerned include: services of lawyers, accountants, consultants, provision of information and copyright permissions.

Inheritance Tax

Inheritance Tax was introduced in 1984 to replace Capital Transfer Tax, which had in turn replaced Estate Duty, the first of the death taxes of recent times. Paradoxically, Inheritance Tax has reintroduced a number of principles present under the old Estate Duty.

The general principle now is that all assets owned at death are chargeable to tax (currently 40%) except for the first £285,000 of the estate and any assets passed to a surviving spouse or a charity. Gifts made more than seven years before death are exempt, but those made within this period may be taxed on a sliding scale. No tax is payable at the time of making the gift.

In addition, each individual may currently make gifts of up to £3000 in any year and these will be considered to be exempt. A further exemption covers any number of annual gifts not exceeding £250 to any one person.

If the £3000 is not fully utilised in one year, any unused balance can be carried forward to the following year (but no later). Gifts out of income, which do not reduce one's living standards, are also exempt if they are part of normal expenditure.

At death all assets are valued; they will include any property, investments, life policies, furniture and personal possessions, bank balances and, in the case of authors, the value of copyrights. All, with the sole exception of copyrights, are capable (as assets) of accurate valuation and, if necessary, can be turned into cash. The valuation of copyright is, of course, complicated and frequently gives rise to difficulty. Except where they are bequeathed to the owner's husband or wife, very real problems can be left behind by the author.

Experience has shown that a figure based on two to three years' past royalties may be proposed by the Inland Revenue in their valuation of copyright. However, this may not be reasonable and may require negotiation. If a book is running out of print or if, as in the case of educational books, it may need revision at the next reprint, these factors must be taken into account. In many cases the fact that the author is no longer alive and able to make personal appearances, or provide publicity, or write further works, will result in lower or slower sales. Obviously, this is an area in which help can be given by the publishers, and in particular one needs to know what their future intentions are, what stocks of the books remain, and what likelihood there will be of reprinting.

There is a further relief available to authors who have established that they have been carrying on a business for at least two years prior to death. It has been possible to establish that copyrights are treated as business property and in these circumstances. Inheritance Tax 'business property relief' is available. This relief at present is 100% so that the tax saving can be quite substantial. The Inland Revenue may wish to be assured that the business is continuing and consideration should therefore be given to the appointment, in the author's will, of a literary executor who should be a qualified business person or, in certain circumstances, the formation of partnership between the author and spouse, or other relative, to ensure that it is established the business is continuing after the author's death.

If the author has sufficient income, consideration should be given to building up a fund to cover future Inheritance Tax liabilities. One of a number of ways would be to take out a whole life assurance policy which is assigned to the children, or other beneficiaries, the premiums on which are within the annual exemption of £3000. The capital sum payable on the death of the assured is exempt from inheritance tax.

Tax Credits

Working authors may also be eligible to claim Child Tax Credit and Working Tax Credit.

Child tax credit is the main way that families receive money for their younger children and for 16 - 18 year olds in education. A claim is based on your income and you can claim whether or not you are working. All families (with children) with an income up to £58,000 a year (or up to £66,000 a year if your child is under one year old) can claim. To qualify, you must be aged 16 or over, usually live in the UK and if single, (or separated) claim based on your individual circumstances. If you are married or a man and woman living together (or a same sex couple from December 2005) you must claim together based on joint circumstances and income.

Working tax credit is a payment to top up earnings of the lower paid (whether employed or self employed including those who do not have children). To qualify, you must be aged 16 or over and you or your partner responsible for a child and you must work at least 16 hours a week. If you are part of a couple with children, greater amounts may be claimed if you jointly work at least 30 hours a week provided one of you works for at least 16 hours. Childless couples cannot add their hours together to qualify for the 30 hour element. If you do not have children and you do not have a disability, you must be aged 25 or over and work at least 30 hours a week. It is also possible that your working tax credit will be increased to assist with the cost of registered or approved childcare

Anyone wondering how best to order his affairs for tax purposes should consult an accountant with specialised knowledge in this field. Experience shows that a good accountant is well worth his fee which, incidentally, so far as it relates to professional matters, is an allowable expense.

The information contained in this section has been prepared by Ian Spring of Moore Stephens, Chartered Accountants, who will be pleased to answer questions on tax problems. Please write to Ian Spring, c/o The Writer's Handbook, 34 Ufton Road, London N1 5BX.

Index of Companies

Subject Index

Children: Publishers (US)

Children: Small Presses

Children: TV and Radio

Children: Writers' Circles & Workshops

Children: Writers' Courses (UK)

Children: Writers' Courses (US)

China: Library Services

China: Literary Agents (UK)

Literature: Literary Agents (Irish)

Literature: Literary Agents (UK)

Literature: Literary Agents (US)